STONEHENGE
FOR THE ANCESTORS

STONEHENGE
FOR THE ANCESTORS

PART 1: LANDSCAPE AND MONUMENTS

Mike Parker Pearson,
Joshua Pollard, Colin Richards,
Julian Thomas, Chris Tilley
and Kate Welham

Published by Sidestone Press, Leiden
www.sidestone.com

Lay-out & cover design: Sidestone Press

Photograph front cover: Stonehenge from the northeast; © Aerial-Cam Ltd.
Photograph back cover: Stonehenge Stone 10 from the south, © Aerial-Cam Ltd.

ISBN 978-90-8890-702-9 (softcover)
ISBN 978-90-8890-703-6 (hardcover)
ISBN 978-90-8890-704-3 (PDF e-book)

Contents

Preface

This is the first of the four volumes in which we present the full results of archaeological investigations carried out at and around Stonehenge in 2003–2009 by the Stonehenge Riverside Project. This volume addresses those sites and areas of the landscape around Stonehenge, including the stone circle itself, that date to the Neolithic and Chalcolithic. Volume 2 provides a synthesis of various bodies of artefactual and environmental evidence, along with an overview of changes in the Stonehenge landscape from the Mesolithic to the Early Bronze Age. Volume 3 covers the Neolithic and Chalcolithic sites of Durrington Walls, Woodhenge and monuments south of Woodhenge. Volume 4 includes all investigations of sites and assemblages dating to periods after the *floruit* of Stonehenge (*i.e.* from the Early Bronze Age onwards). The work of the Stonehenge Riverside Project and its successor, the Feeding Stonehenge Project (during which most of the post-excavation analyses were carried out) has already produced over 80 academic and popular articles, including three books.

The Stonehenge Riverside Project was conceived as a large-scale investigation by a group of researchers leading teams from several British universities. Its inspiration was a hypothesis developed from the observation by a Malagasy archaeologist, Ramilisonina, that Stonehenge might have been built for the ancestors – hence the title of this volume. Since then, a great deal of new information has been accumulated by the SRP and other projects focused on Stonehenge. Certain established 'facts' about Stonehenge itself have been found to be wanting or even erroneous as a result of our investigations. The chronology of Stonehenge has been modified as a result of reassessment of earlier excavations, new excavations and new radiocarbon dates.

During the lifetime of the project, the Stonehenge Riverside Project (SRP) was not the only field research conducted within the Stonehenge World Heritage Site. In 2008, the SPACES project (Strumble–Preseli Ancient Communities and Environment Study), led by Tim Darvill and Geoff Wainwright, carried out an excavation at Stonehenge, in the same year as our own investigation of Aubrey Hole 7; their results are published separately but their main conclusions are discussed in this volume and, where pertinent, are incorporated into our analysis of Stonehenge and its chronology.

Since the fieldwork component of the SRP ended, Tim Darvill and a team from the Deutsches Archäologisches Institut, Berlin and Vince Gaffney and a team from the Ludwig Boltzmann Institut, Vienna have conducted extensive geophysical surveys of the Stonehenge environs. Some of these projects' geophysical results have already been ground-truthed by excavation, but much remains to be done to understand their results. David Jacques and a team from the University of Buckingham have investigated an area of dense and long-lasting Mesolithic activity at Blick Mead, east of Vespasian's Camp. Wessex Archaeology have continued to excavate and publish on an impressive range and number of prehistoric sites threatened by development.

Also dating to after the fieldwork years of the SRP is English Heritage's Stonehenge WHS Landscape Project. The outstanding work of Dave Field, Mark Bowden and their colleagues in carrying out new topographic surveys and pulling together archival material is a gift to future researchers. Another of the excellent EH reports covers the laser-scanning of the stones of Stonehenge. I look at these reports with a certain wistfulness – if the English Heritage project had taken place before the SRP, rather than after, it would have made our lives much easier!

While completing this volume, it has become ever more obvious that great credit should go to some rather unsung heroines – Ros Cleal, Karen Walker and Rebecca Montague. They and the team who worked on the 1995 volume on Stonehenge's earlier excavations, under the guiding hand of Andrew Lawson, produced an indispensable source, fundamental to our understanding of Stonehenge. My own copy of their book is falling apart through overuse, and I thank them.

Similarly battered is my copy of Julian Richard's 1990 report on the Stonehenge Environs Project. Julian's work was the baseline for some of the excavations and analyses in this volume and his hard-won findings are central to our understanding of the Stonehenge landscape.

At the time of writing, the future of the Stonehenge World Heritage Site is uncertain. A planned road tunnel, to deal with traffic problems on the A303 which passes close to the monument, threatens the integrity of the WHS and the archaeology within it. A final decision on whether the tunnel scheme goes ahead has not yet been made. I am amongst those archaeologists who oppose vehemently the scheme as it stands – the proposed tunnel is simply too short, and the proposed archaeological mitigation strategy is simply inadequate. For the record, however much I have disagreed with the decisions of Historic England and other bodies, my relationships – indeed friendships – with the staff involved remain unchanged. The Highways Agency, on the other hand, probably think I'm deliberately obstructive. I have every confidence in the professionalism and expertise of the archaeological contractors working on the tunnel scheme thus far – but they can only deliver what they have been instructed to do, and what they have been instructed to do is simply not good enough for this iconic and fragile site.

Mike Parker Pearson
1 May 2020

Acknowledgements

We are grateful to the landowners – Stan and Henry Rawlins, Sir Edward and Lady Antrobus, the National Trust, English Heritage, the Royal School of Artillery, the Rowlands family – and the tenants – Stuart Crook, Robert Turner, Richard Bawden, Phil Sawkill, Billy King and Hugh Morrison – for allowing us to survey and excavate on their land. We also thank Jason Lewis, land agent for the Antrobus family. Thanks also go to Mike Clarke and other local residents for their interest and support. Permissions for survey and excavation were granted by DCMS, as advised by English Heritage (though, since then, this statutory function has passed to Historic England).

Chris Gingell, Martin Papworth and Lucy Evershed of the National Trust guided and helped us at every step. We also thank the National Trust's archaeology panel for their interest and advice. Particular thanks go to Amanda Chadburn of Historic England (formerly English Heritage) for advising on each year's fieldwork from its earliest stages of planning. We also thank her colleagues who were then at English Heritage, particularly David Batchelor, Isabelle Bedu, Peter Carson, Rachel Foster, Kath Graham and Harriet Attwood. MoD archaeologists Richard Osgood and Martin Brown are thanked for making arrangements on Defence land. Mike Pitts and Julian Richards were a source of information and support throughout.

We also thank the various contractors – Steve Dodds and Norman of Wernicks, Messrs Kite & Sons, Paul Hams, Abfab loos – and several local farmers who found accommodation for finds and vehicles during the wet weather of 2008 in particular. Reg Jury organised the plant hire and Richard Bawden kindly helped with reinstatement. We also thank the Massey family for loan of their marquee and Rushall Village Hall for loan of tables and chairs. Paul and Margot Adams were marvellous hosts at the Woodbridge Inn. They used our fairly hefty campsite fees to build a shower block on the campsite – after our final season there, unfortunately! – which is an otherwise uncredited outcome of the project. The grant-giving bodies do like outcomes that involve the public, but they would probably be rather taken aback by new toilets ...

The research officer on site was Mark Dover who compiled and maintained the project's enormous digital database. The site supervisors were Hugo Anderson-Whymark, Ben Chan, Fiona Eaglesham, Ian Heath, Bob Nunn, Phil Powers, Becca Pullen, Dave Robinson, Jim Rylatt, Lawrence Shaw, Ellen Simmons and Charlene Steele, and the site assistants were Olaf Bayer, Lizzie Carleton, Chris Casswell, Ralph Collard, Jolene Debert, Irene Garcia Rovira, Ellie Hunt, CJ Hyde, Dave Shaw, Anne Teather and Neil Morris. Many of these younger archaeologists changed role during the lifetime of the project: indeed, some first dug for the SRP as undergraduate students, of whom there were hundreds over the years, too many to mention by name. By 2008 several supervisors, site assistants and former student diggers were directing work in their own trenches. This is an opportunity to say how intensely proud I am of all of them: they are now in their glory years, and archaeology is safe in their hands.

The considerable job of processing and cataloguing finds was enabled by many hands but in particular by Lesley Chapman, Jane Ford and, most especially, by Eileen Parker. We owe a profound debt to Karen Godden who kept us organised in the field and on the campsite, managing the logistics before, during and after excavation with seemingly effortless efficiency. Karen also edited every report by every author and proof-read the text, and even took the whole field team to Tongeren for a project reunion – we are enormously grateful, and that's putting it mildly!

Pat Shelley, Megan and David Price, James Thomson and Susan Stratton ran the outreach and were joined by Phil Harding and Edwin Deady on Open Weekends. With over 10,000 visitors to the excavations in 2008 alone, we would never have coped without Pat Shelley's skills in organising the large team of National Trust volunteers and student guides to show visitors around the excavations.

Adam Stanford took exceptional aerial photos. Helen Wickstead co-ordinated the artists in residence who are thanked for bringing a new dimension to the project. Alastair Pike added all sorts of other dimensions. Snail samples were processed for Mike Allen at Bournemouth University; thanks to Dr Iain Green and Damian Evans for their support. Louise Martin was involved with producing the magnetometer surveys.

Illustrations were drawn by Irene de Luis (Figures 1.4, 2.5, 3.5–3.9, 3.14–3.20, 3.23–3.28, 3.30, 3.36–3.37, 3.43–3.44, 3.47, 3.50, 3.58–3.59, 3.61–3.62, 3.64, 3.66, 3.68–3.70, 3.72, 3.77, 4.4, 4.6–4.10, 4.16, 4.21, 4.25–4.26, 5.13–5.14, 5.17, 5.19, 5.21, 5.24, 5.26, 5.29–5.30, 5.32, 5.34–5.36, 5.39–5.43, 5.45–5.46, 5.50, 5.52–5.54, 5.56, 5.58–5.61, 5.71–5.80, 6.12, 6.14, 6.27, 7.8, 7.11, 7.13–7.14, 7.16, 7.21–7.22, 7.29, 7.32, 7.34, 7.38, 8.4–8.6, 8.8, 8.10–8.13, 8.15–8.16, 8.18, 8.26, 8.28–8.30, 8.32, 8.34, 8.36–8.37, 8.39–8.40, 8.42, 8.44, 8.46), Umberto Albarella (Figures 7.27–7.28), Mike Allen (Figures 3.53–3.54), Ben Chan (Figures 3.63, 3.78–3.79, 6.15–6.19, 6.26, 6.28, 7.20, 10.5–10.8), Ros Cleal (Figure 3.76), Roger Doonan (Figure 4.44), Mark Dover (Figures 2.1, 2.3, 4.13, 4.31–4.40, 5.5–5.6, 6.8, 7.4, 9.1), Abby George (Figures 3.75, 5.70), Barney Harris (Figures 6.20–6.25), Peter Marshall (Figures 3.55–3.57, 5.66–5.69, 7.18–7.19, 8.47–8.49, 11.1–11.17), Doug Mitcham (Figure 5.8), Mike Parker Pearson (Figures 1.1, 4.5, 4.17, 5.9, 8.51), Josh Pollard (Figures 1.2, 1.3, 3.65, 8.1), Colin Richards (Figure 6.10), Rob Scaife (Figures 9.7–9.9), Charlene Steele (Figures 1.7–1.11, 2.6–2.8, 3.1–3.2, 5.3–5.4, 6.7, 7.5–7.6, 7.31, 8.2–8.3), Julian Thomas (Figures 3.3, 3.12, 3.21, 3.31–3.32, 3.34, 3.41, 3.48, 4.1), Katy Whitaker (Figures 6.30–6.41) and Christie Willis (Figures 10.18, 10.23–10.24).

Photographs were taken by Adam Stanford (copyright of Aerial-Cam Ltd.; Figures 1.6, 4.3, 4.11, 4.18–4.20, 4.22, 4.24, 5.7, 5.11, 5.15–5.16, 5.51, 6.4, 6.9, 6.11, 6.13, 7.7, 7.9–7.10, 7.12, 8.7, 8.9, 8.14, 8.24, 8.27, 8.31, 8.45, 8.55), Umberto Albarella (Figures 7.23–7.26), Mike Allen (Figures 3.49, 3.51, 5.31, 5.33, 5.37), Chris Casswell (Figure 5.55), Tim Daw (Figure 7.41), David Field (Figures 2.2, 2.4), Charles French (Figures 3.39, 3.52, 3.74, 4.27–4.28, 5.12, 8.22, 9.3–9.6), Ian Heath (Figure 5.57), Mike Parker Pearson (Figures 4.30, 5.38, 6.42, 8.17, 8.19–8.21, 9.2), Mike Pitts (Figure 4.23), Josh Pollard (Figures 3.67, 3.71, 3.73), Colin Richards (Figures 7.3, 7.15, 7.17, 7.30, 7.33, 7.35–7.37, 7.39–7.40), Dave Robinson (Figures 8.33, 8.35), James Rylatt (Figures 5.10, 5.18, 5.20, 5.22–5.23, 5.25, 5.27–5.28, 5.44, 5.47–5.49, 5.62–5.65), Dave Shaw (Figures 8.38, 8.41), David Sugden (Figures 10.21–10.22, 10.31), Anne Teather (Figures 3.60, 8.50), Julian Thomas (Figures 3.4, 3.10–3.11, 3.13, 3.22, 3.29, 3.33, 3.35, 3.38, 3.42, 3.45–3.46, 6.1–6.2), Katy Whitaker (Figure 6.29) and Christie Willis (Figures 10.9–10.14, 10.16–10.17, 10.19–10.20, 10.25–10.30, 10.32–10.37).

Christie Willis's sincere gratitude goes to David Sugden, Superintendent Radiographer CT, Royal Hallamshire Hospital, for scanning the petrous bones from Stonehenge, and also to Dr. Charles Romanowski, consultant neuroradiologist, Royal Hallamshire Hospital, for identifying and measuring the lateral angle of the petrous canal from the scanned images. Her thanks also go to Professor Charlotte Roberts, Dr. Tina Jakob, Dr. Becky Gowland and Dr. Anwen Caffell from the University of Durham and to Professor Tony Waldron of UCL for taking the time to examine the pathological lesion on the distal femoral fragment. You were all a great help! She thanks also Ben Chan for digitising the plans and spit layers of AH7.

Charles French thanks Julie Boreham of Earthslides and Tonko Rajkovaca of the McBurney Laboratory, Department of Archaeology, University of Cambridge, for making the thin-section slides, and Boriana Boneva and Alejandra Diaz who assisted with some of the descriptions.

We thank everyone at Sidestone Press for their hard work, especially Karsten Wentink and Corné van Woerdekom, Sasja van der Vaart-Verschoof, Kayleigh Hines and Eric van den Bandt who rose to the challenge of typesetting this enormous volume and Nicola King prepared the index. Any reader who is puzzled by the cost of archaeological monographs these days should bear in mind that some project reports are grant-funded by national agencies but Sidestone has taken on the task of publishing the Stonehenge Riverside Project monograph series with no grant funding at all. We thank them.

Funding for the project was provided from a variety of sources, notably the Arts and Humanities Research Council with two large grants for the Stonehenge Riverside Project (2006–2009) and the Feeding Stonehenge Project (2010–2013), the latter covering the post-excavation analysis and reporting. Other grants were received from the following bodies, in order of their scale of contribution: the National Geographic Society, Google, the Society of Antiquaries of London, the Royal Archaeological Institute, the British Academy, Andante Travel, the Robert Kiln Charitable Trust, the Royal Society of Northern Antiquaries (Copenhagen), and the Prehistoric Society. English Heritage and University of Sheffield Enterprise provided funds for visitor outreach.

Chapter 1

Introduction

M. Parker Pearson, J. Pollard, C. Richards,
J. Thomas, C. Tilley, K. Welham and P.D. Marshall

Stonehenge and its immediate environs, within the Stonehenge and Avebury World Heritage Site and beyond (Figure 1.1), form one of the most significant archaeological landscapes of the third millennium BC in the world. Located on the chalklands of Salisbury Plain, the Stonehenge area contains just one of a number of Neolithic monument complexes situated along the chalk plateau that extends northwards and southwards from Salisbury Plain (Figure 1.2).

There are many hundreds of books and academic articles on Stonehenge and its landscape, as well as numerous forums and blogs on the web. The monument itself generates an enormous level of public interest and attracts over 1.5 million visitors annually from around the world. In 2013 the visitor centre was moved from its location immediately northwest of Stonehenge and rebuilt over a mile away to the northwest. As part of these changes, a stretch of road alongside Stonehenge (the A344) was closed. Many of the Stonehenge Riverside Project's results recorded here have been incorporated into the visitor centre within its indoor and outdoor displays.

This is the first of four volumes presenting the detailed results of the Stonehenge Riverside Project (SRP). Three books (Aronson 2010; Parker Pearson 2012; Parker Pearson *et al.* 2015) and over 80 academic papers have already been written about the project and its results, but these monographs bring together the full details of the project's surveys, excavations and analyses.

This volume (Volume 1) is organised thematically, starting with an examination of the Neolithic period in this locality before Stonehenge was built (Chapters 2 and 3), then examining the stones of which Stonehenge is composed, first the Welsh bluestones (Chapters 4 and 5) and then the sarsen stones (Chapters 6 and 7). The features which articulate Stonehenge within its wider landscape – the Stonehenge Avenue and the River Avon – are the subject of Chapters 8 and 9. The last two chapters are devoted to Stonehenge itself: the human remains from Stonehenge (Chapter 10) and the radiocarbon-dated chronology of Stonehenge's sequence of construction and use (Chapter 11).

Volume 2 is a synthesis of thematic analyses. Its first half comprises the detailed analysis of the lithics and land mollusca recovered during all the excavations carried out by the Stonehenge Riverside Project (SRP) and full reports on petrography and soil micromorphology. The second half of Volume 2 provides an account of the chronological sequence of the Stonehenge landscape, starting in the Mesolithic and Early Neolithic, before Stonehenge was built, and then examining the changing landscape alongside specific constructional episodes at Stonehenge itself. It presents the fruits of our understanding to date about the people who built Stonehenge and lived in this landscape over many millennia in prehistory.

Figure 1.1. Location of Stonehenge and other formative henges, major cremation enclosures and cemeteries of the Middle Neolithic (*c.* 3400–3000 BC) and early Late Neolithic (*c.* 3000–2800 BC) in Britain

Volume 3 addresses the site of Durrington Walls and its smaller neighbour, Woodhenge. This documents the SRP discoveries of Neolithic houses at Durrington Walls, alongside the remains of a ceremonial avenue and monumental timber architecture such as the Southern Circle, the outer post circle at Woodhenge, and monuments south of Woodhenge. It also examines the construction of a henge on top of the Neolithic settlement at Durrington Walls, and explores the large assemblages of ceramics, lithics and faunal remains from this impressive complex.

Volume 4 is devoted to the development of the landscape after Stonehenge, from the Early Bronze Age cemeteries of round barrows to the construction of ditched field systems later in the Bronze Age. It also pulls together the evidence for activity nearby on Salisbury Plain in the Iron Age, Roman period and later. Much of this later material was uncovered whilst pursuing the SRP's research objectives, which focused on questions relating to the Neolithic period.

1.1. The Stonehenge Riverside Project

The Stonehenge Riverside Project (SRP) was initiated in 2003, with an overarching aim of investigating the purpose of Stonehenge and understanding its context in terms of its chronological and topographical relationships with other monuments and natural features within its surrounding landscape (Figure 1.3). With publication of the Stonehenge World Heritage Site[1] (WHS) archaeological research framework (Darvill 2005), a set of research priorities were identified for Stonehenge and its environs. The Stonehenge Riverside Project was initiated during the same period as that framework document was being compiled and it addressed many of the research objectives published in the WHS framework document.

The Stonehenge Riverside Project was conceived as a 'stand-alone' project but it also had links with the Beaker People Project (Parker Pearson *et al.* 2019) and an

1 Stonehenge is part of a larger World Heritage Site, the Stonehenge and Avebury WHS, designated in 1986.

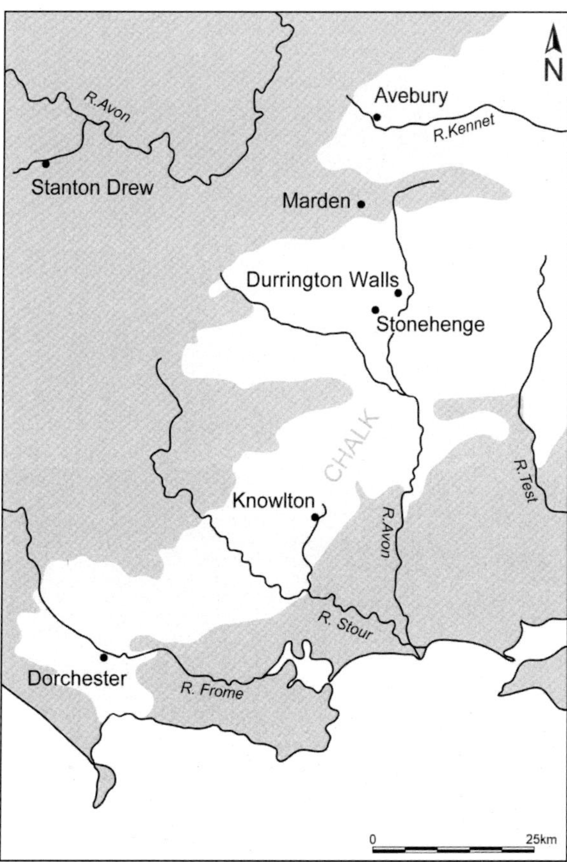

Figure 1.2. Stonehenge and the other major henge complexes of the Late Neolithic (*c.* 3000–2450 BC) in Wessex

international project into cultural diversity and change in the third millennium BC in Britain and Scandinavia (Larsson and Parker Pearson 2007). It also liaised with the Strumble–Preseli Ancient Communities and Environment Study (SPACES) in southwest Wales (Darvill and Wainwright 2009), with Wessex Archaeology's relevant development-led research in the Stonehenge area, and with English Heritage's Stonehenge Archaeological Advisory Panel.

Within the decade prior to 2003, the Stonehenge landscape benefited from a concerted attempt to improve its management: archaeological research formed a fundamental element of existing and future management plans (Batchelor 1997). Several research frameworks were published for the monument and its landscape before and at the time our research started (Wainwright 1997; English Heritage 2000; Darvill 2005). A fourth was published in 2016 (Leivers and Powell 2016), articulating a perceived need for continuing research. The major works of synthesis published in the 1990s (Cleal *et al.* 1995; Cunliffe and Renfrew 1997; Richards 1990) provided a platform for launching new theories, new research projects and new management initiatives. Among ideas being explored immediately prior to the inception of the SRP were Darvill's (1997) conceptions of sacred geography, Ruggles' (1997) minimalist reinterpretation of Stonehenge's astronomical orientations, Darvill and Wainwright's healing hypothesis (Darvill and Wainwright 2009), theories addressing the material meanings of the stones and their environs (Bender 1998; Whittle 1997) and how to decide between glacial or human transport of the bluestones from Wales (Green 1997; Scourse 1997; Williams-Thorpe *et al.* 1997; Burl 2000; 2006).

In the decade prior to the Stonehenge Riverside Project, a considerable amount was learned about Stonehenge and its environs from non-invasive methods such as geophysical survey (David and Payne 1997), archival research (Cleal *et al.* 1995; Pollard 1995a & b), viewshed analysis (Cleal *et al.* 1995; Exon *et al.* 2000), finds research (Albarella and Serjeantson 2002; Muhkerjee *et al.* 2008) and experimental archaeology (Richards and Whitby 1997).

However, apart from the archaeological works and watching briefs required by the road and visitor centre proposals, there had been virtually no plans for archaeological research excavations since the Stonehenge Environs Project (SEP) of the early 1980s (Richards 1990), almost twenty years before. Of course, the decision to excavate deposits which are otherwise unthreatened cannot be taken lightly and requires strong justification in terms of theoretical basis, methodological advance, research gain and public benefit.

More broadly, the study of the British Neolithic had gone through a transformation as a result of the flourishing of new theoretical approaches by leading academics in the previous two decades (*e.g.* Barrett 1994; Bender 1998; Bradley 1993; 1998; 2002; Edmonds 1999; Edmonds and Richards 1998; Thomas 1999; Tilley 1994; Whittle 1988; 1996). Interpretations of the meaning of the great henge monuments now focused on the beliefs, cosmology, agency and practices of their builders and users: prehistorians were now attempting to explore not only how the people of Neolithic Britain lived in their world but how they experienced it and made sense of it. Research interests included the understanding of monuments not as intended, finished items but as projects in the making, and the integration of practical activities and spiritual beliefs within the Stonehenge landscape. Many of these ideas were not restricted to circulation within a closed group of prehistorians but were being communicated to a wider public audience through television documentaries and popular books (*e.g.* Burl 2000; Pitts 2000; Pryor 2001; 2003). The main theory that motivated our own project (SRP) was that Stonehenge was built for the community's ancestors (Parker Pearson and Ramilisonina 1998a) but we also drew on a much wider range of approaches, and revised hypotheses as the project developed.

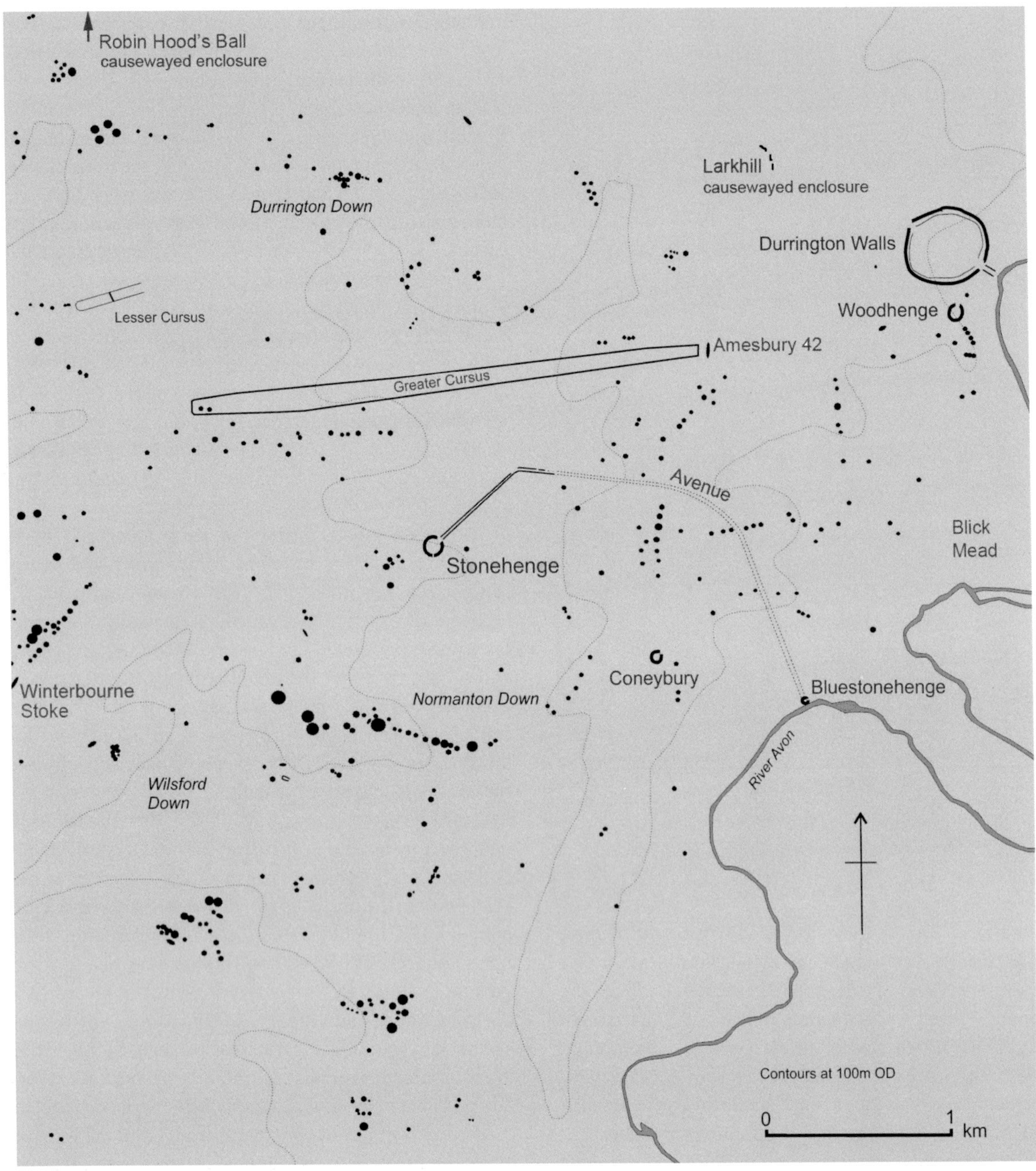

Figure 1.3. The Stonehenge Neolithic and Early Bronze Age landscape, showing the Early Neolithic causewayed enclosures (Larkhill and Robin Hood's Ball) and long barrows (black oblongs *e.g.* Winterbourne Stoke Crossroads), Middle Neolithic cursuses, Late Neolithic Stonehenge, Coneybury, Bluestonehenge, Durrington Walls and Woodhenge, and Early Bronze Age round barrows (black circles). The Mesolithic site at Blick Mead is also marked

In the twenty years leading up to the SRP, considerable advances had been made in archaeological method, not only in the improvement of excavation methods and recording techniques (computerised data recording, high-precision geographical positioning systems *etc.*; Roskams 2000) but also in interpretation (*e.g.* Hodder 1999; Lucas 2001).

There were also major developments in the range and effectiveness of the analytical techniques used (see Brothwell and Pollard 2001). The more widely adopted of these included soil micromorphology (French 2003), systematic flotation of soil samples to retrieve carbonised plant remains and other small materials from the heavy residues, integrated with phosphate and magnetic

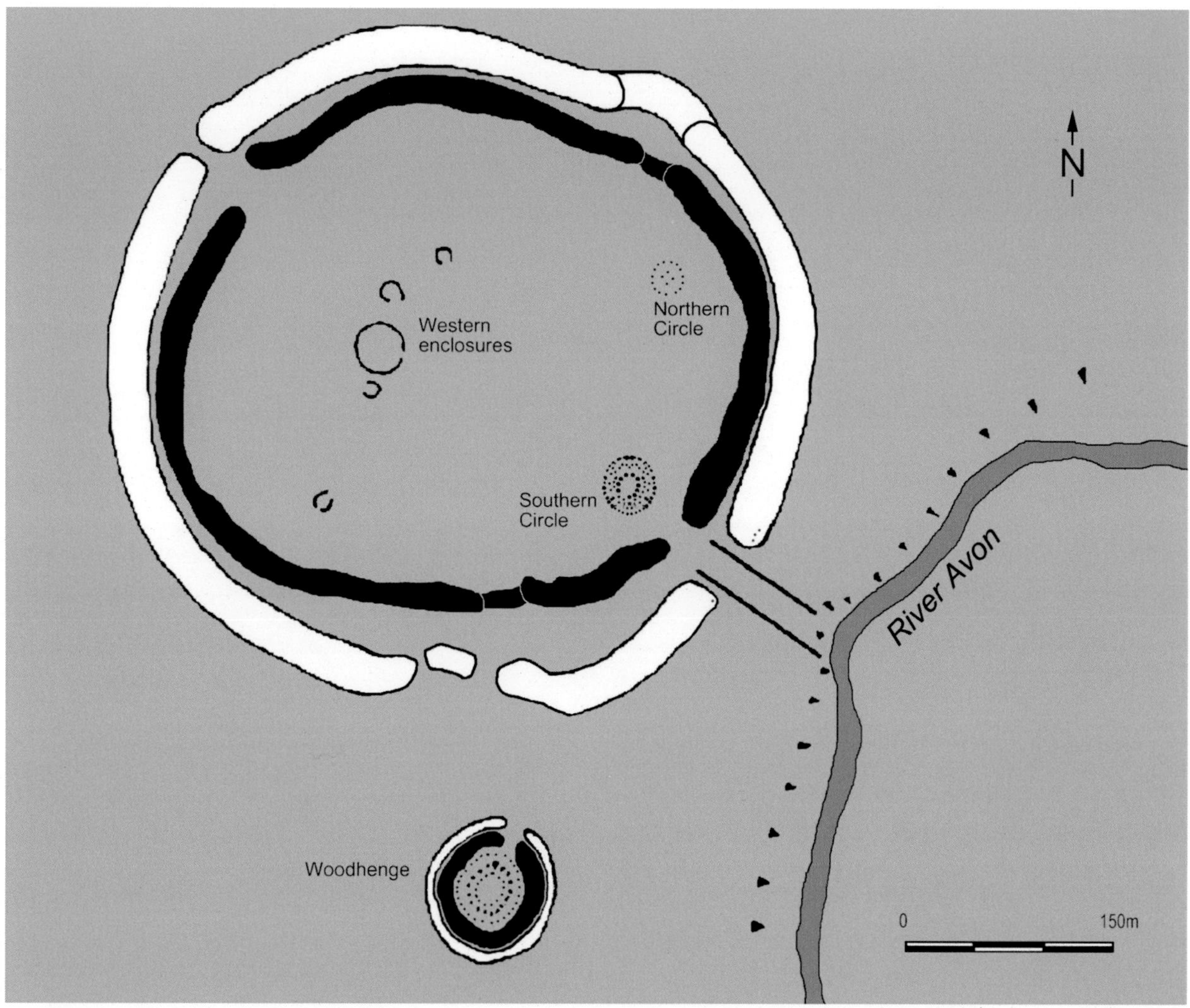

Figure 1.4. Durrington Walls henge and Woodhenge. The ditches are shaded black and the banks are white. An avenue leads to the river

susceptibility measurement (Smith *et al.* 2001), and a whole host of environmental recovery techniques for molluscs, pollen, insects, human remains and animal bones (*e.g.* Allen 1997; Scaife 1995; Buckland and Sadler 1998; Chamberlain 1994; Mays 1998; Payne 1973; Hillam *et al.* 1987).

Advances in absolute dating include greater precision in radiocarbon determination and optically stimulated luminescence dating (OSL), together with the use of Bayesian statistical approaches (Buck *et al.* 1996). The advent of Accelerator Mass Spectrometry (AMS) has allowed archaeologists to choose from a far greater range of small materials for dating (Taylor and Aitken 1997). This has led to an increased emphasis on taphonomy, minimising the age difference between the sample dated and the context from which it came. It has also made it possible to date single-entity, rather than bulked, samples (Ashmore 1999), meaning fewer assumptions about the source of material in a context. The routine identification of wood charcoal to species/genus before submission for dating has made it possible to select short-life samples, thus minimising the possibility of an 'old wood offset' (Bowman 1990: 15). All these factors combine to increase the reliability of dated archaeological samples and their capacity to answer the chronological questions posed of them.

Scientific developments have also improved the accuracy and precision of the radiocarbon measurements themselves. Firstly, formal approaches to quality assurance have been adopted, including a series of international laboratory inter-comparison exercises with published results (*e.g.* Scott 2003; Scott *et al.* 2010). Secondly, technical developments in sample processing and measurement have also enabled high-precision dating to be developed (Pearson 1986). The advent of internationally agreed high-precision calibration datasets (*e.g.* Reimer *et al.* 2009), based on independently

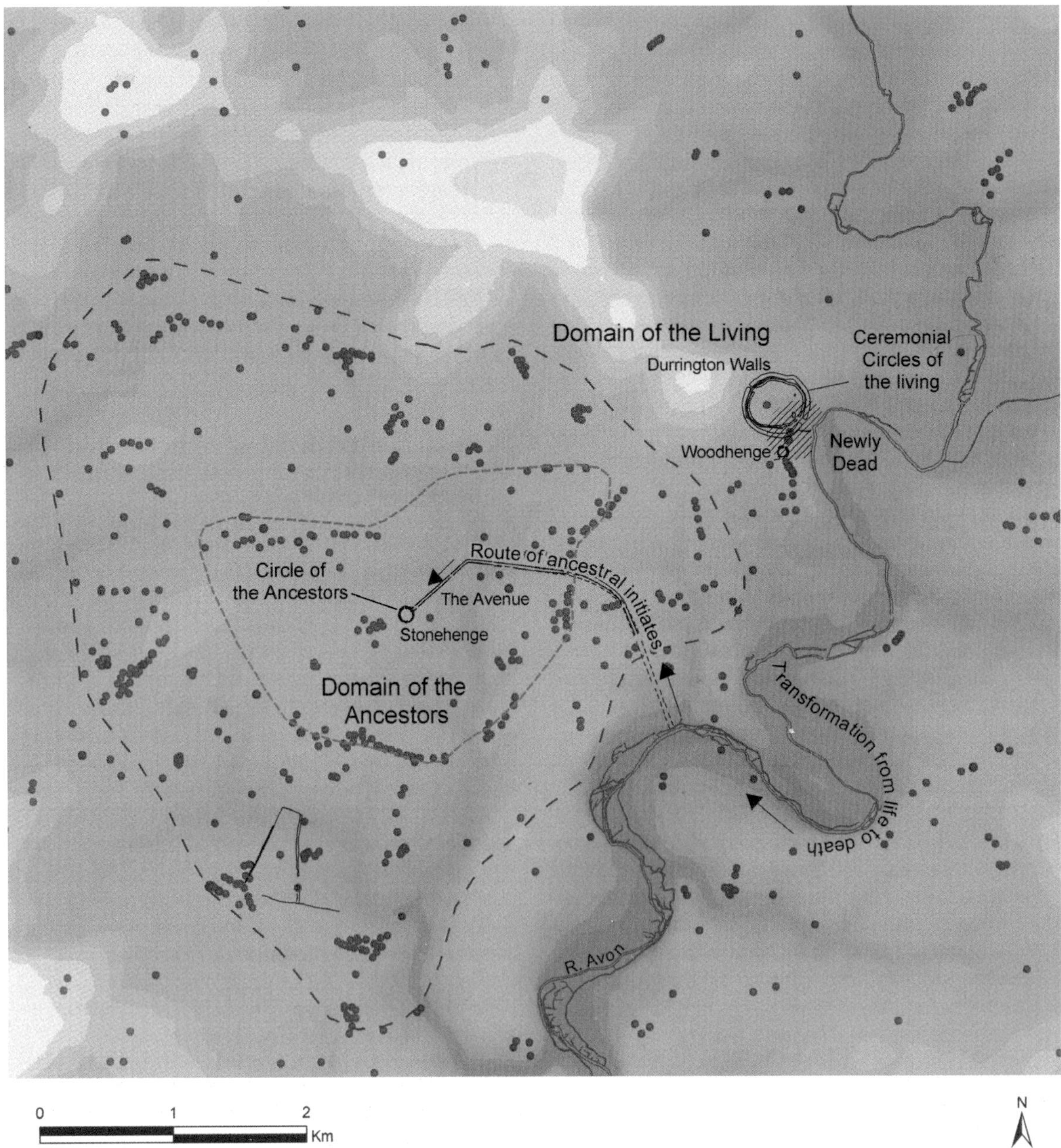

Figure 1.5. The 'Stonehenge for the ancestors' hypothesis developed by Parker Pearson and Ramilisonina in 1998, showing the proposed relationship between Stonehenge, its Avenue, the River Avon, and Durrington Walls and Woodhenge in the Late Neolithic. Early Bronze Age round barrows are marked in red, with a dashed black line marking the envelope of visibility around Stonehenge and the dashed red line indicating the outer edge of the densest concentration of Stonehenge's round barrows. The trapezoidal feature in the bottom left is North Kite, an Early Bronze Age enclosure (after Darvill 2005: 113); © English Heritage

dated tree-ring samples, has also increased the accuracy and precision of calibrated dates and is fundamental to the applications and analyses presented here.

Immediately prior to the inception of the SRP, new methods became available for identifying lipid and protein residues within ceramics (Dudd *et al.* 1999; Craig *et al.* 2000), for DNA extraction from plant, animal and human remains (Jones 2001), and for measuring stable isotopes from human and animal bones and teeth to infer diet and mobility (*e.g.* Lidén 1995; Budd *et al.* 2003). Increased expertise in experimental archaeology in modelling archaeological formation processes on chalk (*e.g.* Bell *et al.* 1996) was also a valuable advance by this point.

Figure 1.6. Ramilisonina digging at West Amesbury in 2009

Background to the project

For readers unfamiliar with all the Neolithic monuments in and around the Stonehenge WHS, the main sites and monuments are shown in Figure 1.3 and a concise summary of these sites is provided as an appendix to this chapter.

Situated just 3km northeast of Stonehenge, the sites of Durrington Walls and Woodhenge (Figure 1.4) form part of an extensive and dense distribution of archaeological remains on the west bank of the River Avon. Excavation during the twentieth century revealed that these remarkable henge monuments were constructed as banks and ditches enclosing concentric circles of wooden posts (Cunnington 1929; Wainwright with Longworth 1971).

The landscape context of these monuments and the records of the excavations carried out here had been re-examined (Wainwright 1971; Richards and Thomas 1984; Pollard 1995; Albarella and Serjeantson 2002) and extensive surveys undertaken (David and Payne 1997). Yet, until 2003, there had been little excavation in this area since Wainwright's work 35 years earlier.

In the wake of recent re-analyses of the Durrington Walls ceramic and bone assemblages (Albarella and Serjeantson 2002; Muhkerjee *et al.* 2008), the moment had come for a new fieldwork initiative, with the Stonehenge Riverside Project's excavations starting in 2004, guided by research questions formulated since 1998 (Parker Pearson and Ramilisonina 1998a and b; Parker Pearson *et al.* 2004).

In 1998 a new interpretation was proposed for Stonehenge, explaining the construction of its stone circle as a monument to the ancestors (Parker Pearson and Ramilisonina 1998a) and suggesting a direct relationship between Stonehenge and the timber circle complex at Durrington during the third millennium BC, articulated primarily along the River Avon (Figure 1.5).

The relationship between Durrington Walls (with its evidence of great gatherings and ceremonies) and Stonehenge (with its lack of any significant activity within the henge, other than construction) was proposed by the 'PP&R' hypothesis to concern the treatment of the dead and the process by which they were transformed into ancestors. It was further proposed that here along the River Avon, the rites of passage by which the dead left the physical world entailed entering the river at Durrington Walls, the beginning of a physical and incorporeal journey down the river to the circle of the ancestors at Stonehenge (Parker Pearson 2000; 2002; Parker Pearson and Ramilisonina 1998a and b).

Most of the inhabitants of Neolithic–Early Bronze Age Wessex (*c.* 4000–1500 BC) were evidently not buried in barrows or dryland sites (Parker Pearson 2016a), and it has long been suspected that the bodies of many of the dead within southern Britain were disposed of in rivers such as the Thames (Bradley and Gordon 1988; Schulting and Bradley 2013; Lamdin-Whymark 2008), the Trent (Garton *et al.* 1997), the Ribble (Turner *et al.* 2002) and the Nene (Harding and Healy 2007: 227), where human bones from this period have been recovered from dredged or excavated river channels.

For the Avon, there has been relatively little disturbance of its palaeochannels, and no Neolithic human remains have ever been recovered. We hypothesised that this stretch of the River Avon between Durrington Walls and Stonehenge might, however, have been one such place of deposition. Unfortunately the Site of Special Scientific Interest (SSSI) status of the river and its banks prevented the SRP from conducting any invasive investigations to test this proposition. We were, however, able to excavate at the point where the River Avon met the beginning of the Stonehenge Avenue, and Ramilisonina was able to join us for our excavations there in 2009 (Figure 1.6).

Implications of the hypothesis

The close relationship between henges and rivers within Britain (Richards 1996) and more specifically between Durrington Walls and the River Avon (Parker Pearson 2000: fig. 17.3; Parker Pearson *et al.* 2004; 2006) was highlighted in the years before the project began. More

Figure 1.7. Locations of trenches excavated by the Stonehenge Riverside Project

specifically, the impetus for the SRP's research developed out of the theory that Stonehenge and Durrington Walls were built as a single complex, in which the transition from the wooden circles at Durrington and Woodhenge to the stone circle at Stonehenge was integral to the religious purpose of these monuments. The stone–timber hypothesis, formulated in 1998 to explore this possibility, provided predictive expectations to be met if the theory were to be supportable. The first of these was that Stonehenge (in its sarsen phase) should be contemporary with Durrington Walls. The second was the requirement for complementarity between the two monuments, particularly the provision of an avenue at Durrington that should, the hypothesis required, lead from the henge to the River Avon, comparable to the Stonehenge Avenue.

The date of Stonehenge itself required reconsideration; Cleal *et al.*'s (1995) chronological scheme of three main phases (with three sub-phases within its Phase 3) was eventually replaced by a new scheme of five stages of construction based on the SRP's and SPACES' results (Darvill *et al.* 2012; Marshall *et al.* 2012). Minor refinements to the 2012 revised chronology are published in this volume. The dates of the five stages of the construction of Stonehenge can be found in the appendix to this chapter; they are detailed in Chapter 11.

Particular problems with the 1995 chronology were:

- The dates of bluestone and sarsen erection at Stonehenge in Cleal *et al.*'s (1995) Phases 3i and 3ii remained uncertain.
- Phase 3i (construction of the bluestone setting in the Q and R Holes, now Stage 2 in the new chronology) was entirely undated by radiocarbon measurements.
- Phase 3ii (the sarsen trilithons and sarsen circle, now Stage 2) was dated by four radiocarbon measurements, the two pairs of which were not statistically consistent. Research by SRP resolved the dating problem. The two later determinations came from within a large pit interpreted by Richard Atkinson as a chalk ramp used in the erection of the great trilithon, but it is in fact evident that stratigraphically the pit postdates the trilithon. The pit, and the dates derived from it, therefore belong to Stage 3. This meant that only the earliest two dates for Phase 3ii are acceptable, placing erection of the sarsen trilithons and circle in Stage 2 (Parker Pearson *et al.* 2007; Darvill *et al.* 2012; Marshall *et al.* 2012).

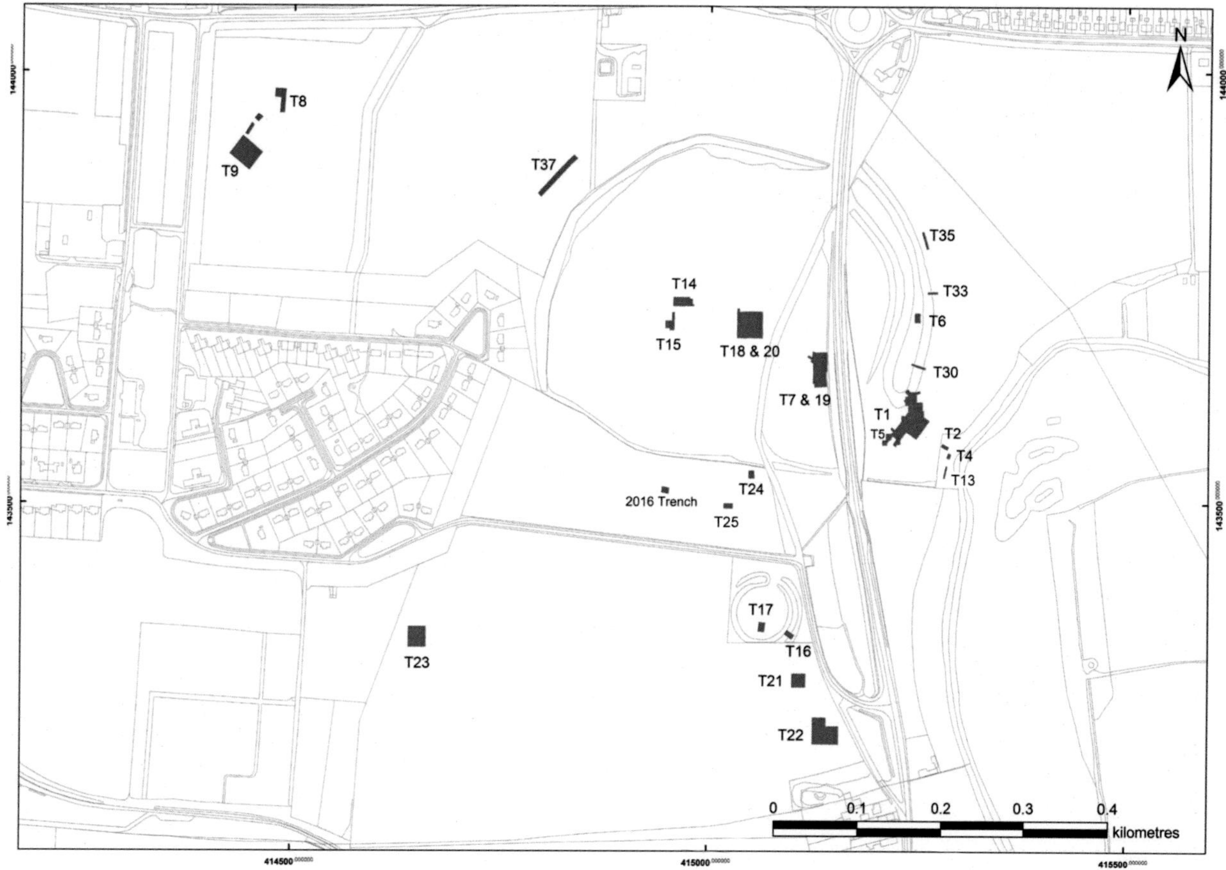

Figure 1.8. Detailed map of locations of Stonehenge Riverside Project trenches at and around Durrington Walls

Similarly, the SRP's reassessment of the Stonehenge Avenue's date of construction now indicates that all but one of its radiocarbon-dated samples are likely to have come from re-cuts or from upper fills of its ditches. An antler pick from the floor of the Avenue ditch at its Stonehenge terminal was dated to 2580–2280 cal BC but this too could have come from the bottom of a re-cut. Consequently, we hoped to establish whether the digging of the Avenue's ditches was contemporary with Stonehenge's period of sarsen stone construction in Stage 2/Phase 3ii (Cleal *et al.* 1995; Parker Pearson *et al.* 2007).

Geophysical survey and coring were successfully carried out from 2003 at Durrington Walls, followed by excavation from 2004 onwards, to begin the process of establishing whether the predictions of contemporaneity and complementarity with Stonehenge had any basis in reality. The project also addressed research questions about the wider landscape, its human population and the timing and purpose of other monuments in the vicinity, notably the Greater Cursus, the Stonehenge palisade, the Early Mesolithic postholes found just northwest of Stonehenge, the round barrows of the 'Wessex culture', and Stonehenge itself (Figures 1.7–1.11; see appendix).

Phenomenological studies of monuments and terrain by Chris Tilley, David Field and Wayne Bennett further contributed to the project.

The project was intended not only to shed light on the relationship between the various monuments and the River Avon, and on the environmental context and history of the Avon valley, but also to yield useful information for the improved interpretation and management of Stonehenge's wider landscape.

Research aims and objectives

A set of five overarching aims were laid out by the SRP team:

- To better understand social change in third millennium BC Britain, including the rise and decline of the great henges, the adoption of metal and transformations in funerary practice.
- To explore alternative explanations for Stonehenge and its surrounding monuments, including investigation of theories concerning materiality and permanence.
- To reassess and re-date Stonehenge's landscape history from the fourth to the second millennium BC.

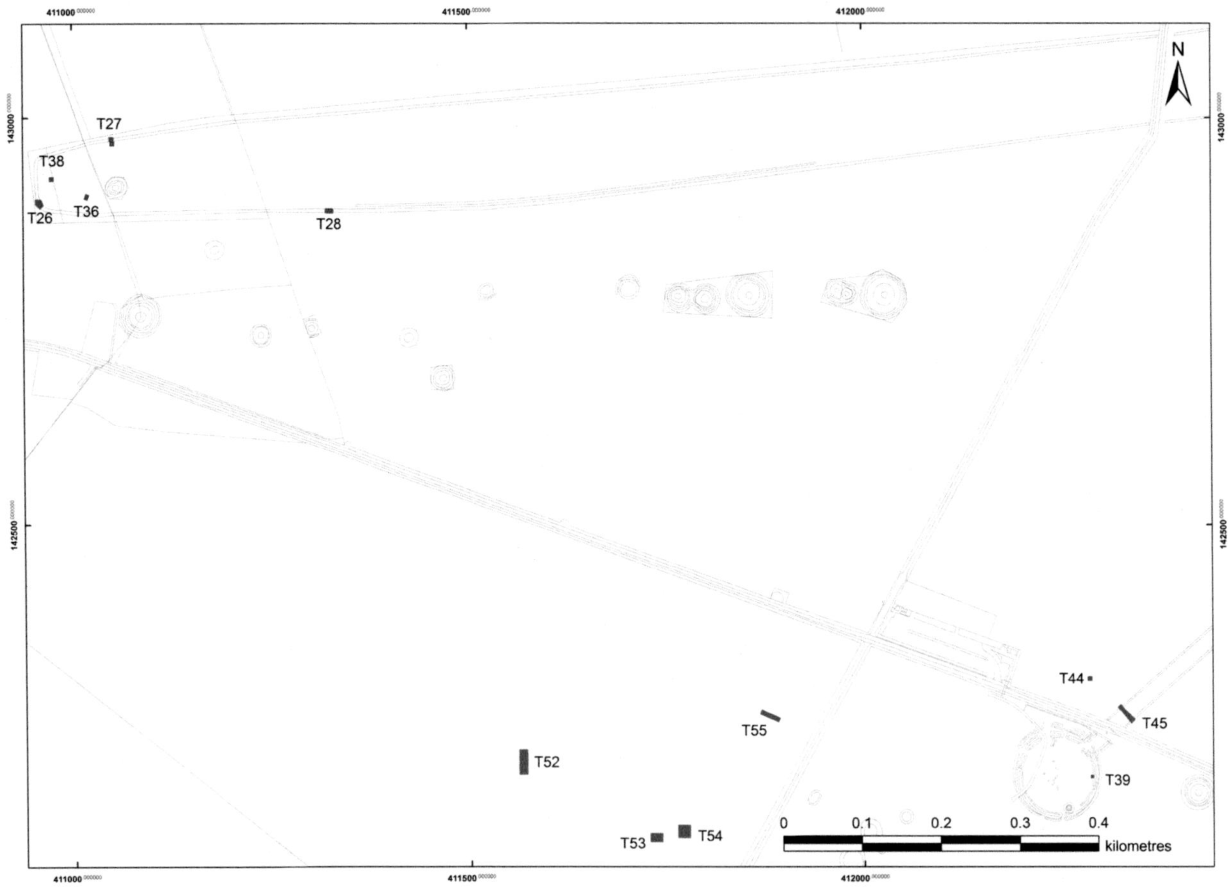

Figure 1.9. Detailed map of locations of Stonehenge Riverside Project trenches at and around the west end of the Greater Cursus, west of Stonehenge and at Stonehenge itself

- To contribute to public enjoyment of, and improved management of, the wider Stonehenge landscape through close co-operation with English Heritage, the National Trust and other stakeholders.
- To train students and volunteers within a scheme that integrated university researchers with professional archaeological contractors.

The project addressed many of the research issues and objectives listed in the archaeological research framework for the Stonehenge WHS (Darvill 2005: 107–36, specifically issues 1–19, 21–26 and 28, and objectives 1, 2, 3, 4, 5, 6, 8, 14, 15, 16 and 24).

The convention that aims and objectives should be recorded quite separately from a project's results proves hard for the authors to follow in this section. On many of the sites investigated, the results of each year's work informed the objectives of subsequent years, so of necessity the following account of the aims and objectives also includes 'spoilers' about what we found.

Research objectives for 2004 onwards

Research objectives for the beginning years of the project were published in the *Journal of Nordic Archaeological Science* (Parker Pearson *et al.* 2004). They are summarised here; background information on each monument appears in the appendix.

Durrington Walls riverside

We aimed to characterise, date and determine the extent of the archaeological depositional sequence on that part of the west bank of the River Avon nearest the entrance to Durrington Walls. We hoped to find out if there was an avenue leading from the entrance of Durrington Walls to the water's edge. This was achieved by a trench outside the east entrance of the henge (Trench 1; Figures 1.7–1.8). Another three smaller trenches (Trenches 2, 4 and 13) were dug at the riverside but, given the extent of riverbank erosion, failed to locate any surviving sections of the avenue where it might have met the water's edge (see Volume 3).

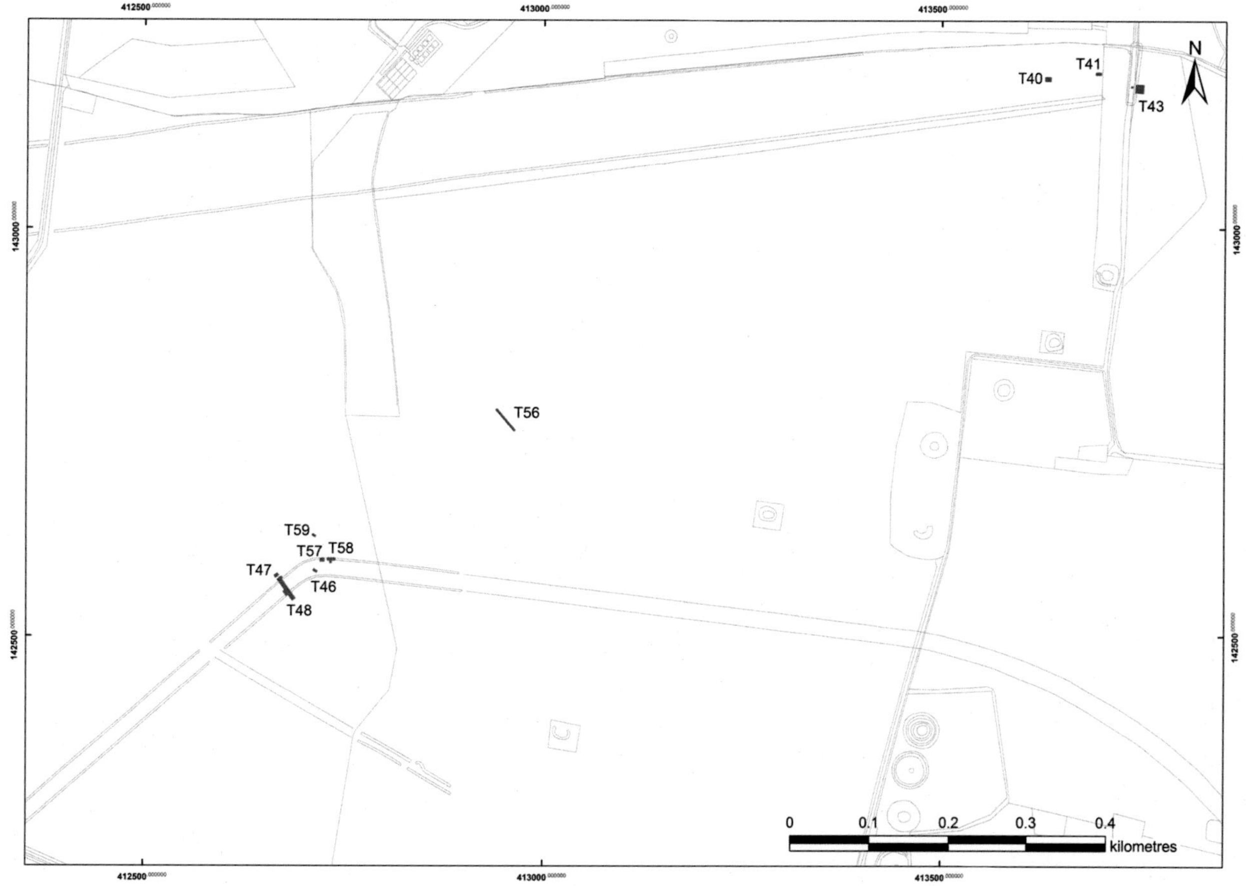

Figure 1.10. Detailed map of locations of Stonehenge Riverside Project trenches at and around the Stonehenge Avenue elbow and the east end of the Greater Cursus

Durrington Walls henge

Before our research, it had always been assumed that this henge enclosure had no more than two entrances, one in the east and one in the west (Wainwright with Longworth 1971). We examined geophysical anomalies in the south and north parts of the henge ditch and bank and were able to recognise two additional former entrances, both of them later cut through and blocked off (see Figure 1.4). Blocking appears to have involved digging through the two causeways at the north and south, and throwing up the spoil to create banks which joined the circuit of the henge bank. This later digging across the entrance causeway explains the unusually late dates (in the late third–early second millennium cal BC) obtained by Wainwright from two charcoal samples taken from a lower fill of the north ditch of the henge (3560±120 BP, BM-285; 3630±110 BP, BM-286), dating to half a millennium after the henge's construction (see Volume 3).

Magnetometry survey revealed anomalies on the west side of the southern entrance which we thought might be the remains of a row of timber posts running towards Woodhenge. Excavations (Trenches 24 and 25) were carried out in 2007 but were inconclusive. Only in 2016 was it possible to reveal elements of the blocked southern entrance, through the Stonehenge Hidden Landscapes Project's ground-penetrating radar (GPR) survey of this area. A joint excavation by the SRP and the SHLP was carried out that year into the southern bank of the henge to confirm that anomalies forming a circuit around Durrington Walls were large postholes for wooden posts (and not fallen sarsen stones) erected and taken down before the henge bank was built (see Volume 3).

The Southern Circle within Durrington Walls

Apparent structured deposition of sherds, bones and artefacts within what had been described as the 'weathering cones' of the Southern Circle's postholes (Richards and Thomas 1984) raised unresolved questions about the association of this debris with the rotting of the huge timber posts *in situ*. We considered that these artefacts might not have been residual, supposedly left against the sides of rotting posts (Wainwright with Longworth 1971), but instead were deposited much later, in pits cut into the postholes once the posts had rotted.

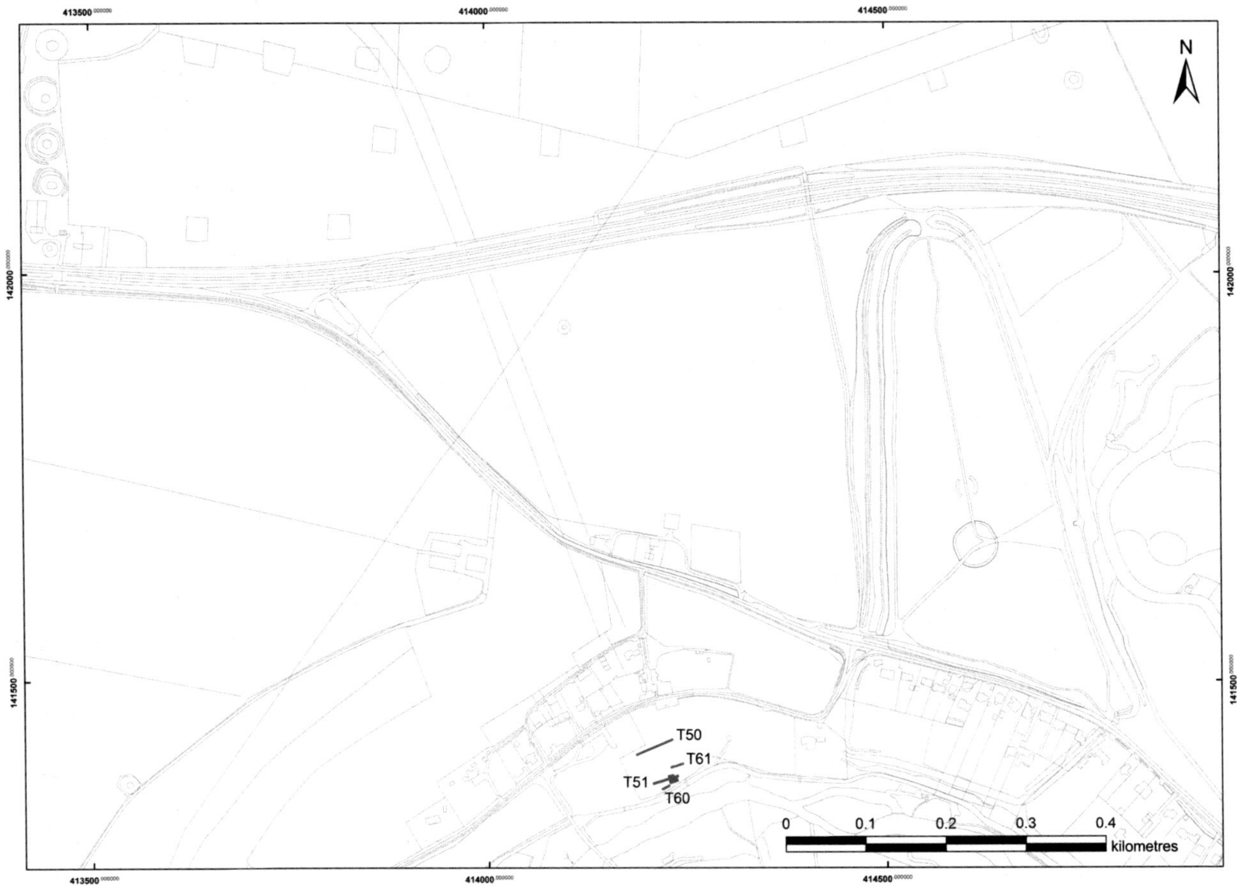

Figure 1.11. Detailed map of locations of Stonehenge Riverside Project trenches at the east end of the Stonehenge Avenue in West Amesbury

One of our preliminary interpretations was that the rotting of the posts, possibly metaphorical of the decay of human flesh and the end of memory, was the culmination of acts of commemoration of the dead. Another was that, in depositing material into the rotted-out timber 'pipes' in the postholes, the circle was being treated in a similar way to contemporary Neolithic houses.

Although most of the Southern Circle's plan had been recorded during the 1967 excavations (Wainwright with Longworth 1971), geophysical survey and further excavation was required to recover its full plan. Our research questions were investigated by the excavation of Trenches 7 and 19, reported in Volume 3.

Larkhill

The southeast end of this hill appears to be a pivotal location within the Stonehenge landscape, probably being the only place from which all the major monuments would have been visible. The large, flat summit – which we named 'the Larkhill panopticon' – would have provided dramatic views of Bronze Age round barrow cemeteries as well as the major Neolithic monuments, including a midwinter sunset solstice vista along the Avenue and into Stonehenge. We hypothesised that this was the point at which ceremonials might have begun, before moving downhill into Durrington Walls and thence to the river. We suspected that, like the dry valley in which Durrington Walls sits, this hilltop location had significance in the fourth as well as the third millennium BC. Although the SRP excavations here (Trenches 8 and 9) found little prehistoric material (see Volume 4), excavations 500m to the northwest in 2016 by Wessex Archaeology uncovered part of an Early Neolithic causewayed enclosure dating to *c.* 3750–3650 cal BC (Thompson *et al.* 2017).

The Avenue riverside and environmental study of the Avon valley floor

We aimed to characterise, date and determine the extent of any archaeological depositional sequences on the west bank of the Avon associated with the suspected terminal of the Stonehenge Avenue (Trenches 50, 51, 60 and 61; Figure 1.11). We intended to clarify the character of the Avenue's terminal and its relationship to the riverbank in the third millennium BC. Environmental analysis was to be carried out along the valley floor of the Avon to sample ancient sediment sequences, to characterise and date the traces of geomorphological processes of deposition and erosion within the valley, and to provide a geomorphological and environmental context for archaeological activity within the valley. Whilst this proved successful (French *et al.* 2012), environmental legislative constraints prevented us from searching in appropriate locations for human remains in riverine sediments downstream of Durrington Walls (see Chapter 9). The findings of the excavations at the end of the Avenue in 2008 and 2009 (including West Amesbury henge and 'Bluestonehenge' within it) are reported in Chapter 6.

Fargo Plantation

A small henge in Fargo Plantation, excavated by J.F.S. Stone (1938), produced a bluestone chip, one of ten in this locality (Stone 1947; Castleden 1993: fig. 69). Although these chips have been interpreted as debris from a stone-dressing area or originating from a later monument secondary to Stonehenge (Castleden 1993: 172), we wondered if they might derive from a bluestone monument constructed in Fargo Plantation or its environs as early as the late fourth millennium BC (Parker Pearson and Ramilisonina 1998b). Geophysical surveys and archaeological test-pitting were carried out in this area in 2006 and 2008, revealing the chippings' association with a spread of artefacts dating to the Beaker period (see Chapter 4).

Phenomenological analysis of the Stonehenge landscape

Three seasons of landscape study were undertaken in 2004–2006, carried out by Tilley, Bennett and Field. The first season concentrated on the landscape and river from Durrington Walls to Stonehenge (see Chapter 9), as well as the Greater Cursus, Lesser Cursus, henges and long barrows (see Chapter 2). In 2005 and 2006 Bronze Age barrows were analysed (see Volume 4), together with study of the wider landscape and follow-up work on results from 2004.

Research objectives added for 2005–2006

Discoveries in 2004 of Late Neolithic pits outside the east entrance of Durrington Walls and in 2005 of preserved house floors and of an avenue leading from the entrance to the river led to the revision of the research objectives focused on this henge and new objectives for its outlier, Woodhenge.

Durrington Walls riverside

We aimed to determine the date, size and direction of the flint-surfaced avenue leading from the riverside to the henge's east entrance and to excavate the remains of Late Neolithic houses on both sides of the avenue (in Trench 1 which also incorporated Trench 5 at its south end). These houses were associated with midden deposits and an old ground surface protected beneath the henge bank. This remarkable preservation permitted the recovery of stratigraphic relationships between the henge bank, the houses, their middens and the avenue. Overall, the excellent stratification and large number of suitable radiocarbon samples in this area on the east side of the henge offered scope for devising a radiocarbon-dating programme incorporating statistical modelling to closely date the entire sequence to within a couple of generations (see Volume 3).

Durrington Walls henge bank

A small trench (Trench 6) was excavated within the henge bank (*c.* 150m north of the east entrance) to fully investigate a geophysically identified pre-henge anomaly and to establish the mode of bank and ditch construction. Geophysical survey indicated that the bank and ditch might have been built in segments, and Trench 6 was positioned at the intersection of two of these segments of bank (see Volume 3).

Durrington Walls interior: the western enclosures

A large circular anomaly in the western half of the henge interior was one of five small enclosures previously detected by geophysical survey (David and Payne 1997). We excavated part of this large enclosure and one of the smaller ones, to establish their date and character (Trenches 14 and 15; the results are reported in Volume 3). We also wondered what might have stood in the centre of the henge, within the natural amphitheatre enhanced by the ditch and bank circuit. Removal of the top metre of sterile colluvium across the centre of the henge interior allowed geophysical survey to establish whether there is a large prehistoric structure in this focal location. However, results were negative, indicating no large monument in this location (see Volume 3).

Woodhenge

Several research issues were identified here in the light of Pollard's reassessment of the monument (1995a). Recent work on the Sanctuary at Avebury (Pitts 2001) indicated that much could be learned from re-excavating some of the postholes dug out by Maud Cunnington at Woodhenge in 1926 (Cunnington 1929). Her report on Woodhenge reveals that several posts (mostly in the middle and outer rings) were replaced in antiquity (indicated by mixed fills, oval plans and stepped profiles). It was thought possible that localised deposits of fill might still remain *in situ*, and that re-excavation of a small group of postholes could reveal construction sequences. Cunnington's identification of stone sockets within Woodhenge also raised questions about the sequence of wood and stone construction within the monument. There was also a case for excavating a section of the bank with regard to characterising pre-henge activity. The results of the excavation of Trenches 16 and 17 are reported primarily in Volume 3, but Early Neolithic features in those trenches appear in Chapter 3 of this volume.

Research objectives added for 2007–2009

In the project's later years of fieldwork, new questions emerged about the wider landscape, notably around Woodhenge, at the Greater Cursus, and at and around Stonehenge.

South of Woodhenge

The area south of Woodhenge contains ploughed-out ring ditches, one of which was known to be associated with a Grooved Ware-period timber structure (*i.e.* Late Neolithic) similar to Durrington Walls' Northern Circle (Pollard 1995b). Further excavations around these ring ditches (Durrington 67, 68 and 70) in 2007 were designed to reveal other traces of timber structures, two of which were found (Trenches 21 and 22; see Volume 3).

Woodhenge environs

We hoped to clarify the relationship between Woodhenge and Durrington Walls by exploring a possible route between Durrington Walls' putative south entrance and Woodhenge but found no evidence of a formal avenue, even though there had been a south entrance through Durrington Walls' henge bank, facing towards Woodhenge (see *Durrington Walls henge* [2004 objectives], above). To the west of Woodhenge we investigated the Cuckoo Stone, a recumbent sarsen stone. Although moved in relatively modern times, it sits close to an unusual arrangement of pits detected by geophysical survey. These were evaluated in 2007 to establish their date, character and extent, to provide evidence of prehistoric activity on this significant axis between the Cursus and Woodhenge (Trench 23; the results are reported in Chapter 5).

The Greater Cursus

Prior to 2007, there was only one radiocarbon date for this monument, and this was unusually late (2900–2460 cal BC [95% confidence; OxA-1403; 4100±90 BP]; Richards 1990: 260). This date was from an antler recovered in 1947 by J.F.S. Stone; it was thought to have been deposited in a later pit cut into the Cursus ditch and therefore post-dating it. Yet Stone himself did not really entertain this possibility, describing the feature as a 'recess' rather than a re-cut (1947: 12–14). Following geophysical survey, new excavations were carried out in 2007 to gain dateable material from primary contexts, and to resolve the context of Stone's antler pick (Trenches 26–28, 36, 38).

The long barrow at the monument's east end was still undated, despite excavation of its eastern ditch in the 1980s (Richards 1990: 96–109), so excavations were carried out within this ditch in 2008 to obtain suitable dating material (Trench 43). Two trenches (40 and 41) investigated the east end of the Cursus. Results of all these excavations are reported in Chapter 3.

Geophysical survey was carried out along stretches of the Cursus to establish whether there were gaps within the ditch and bank (on both north and south sides) to indicate entrances. Magnetometry results revealed one such entrance into the Cursus (see Chapter 2) and others have been located since (see Darvill *et al.* 2013).

The Stonehenge palisade and Later Neolithic settlement on Stonehenge Down

Previous excavation had failed to provide a date for the construction and use of this long and curving ditch west and northwest of Stonehenge. Together with the Gate Ditch (see Chapter 8), it appeared to form a large, interrupted enclosure (Pollard *et al.* 2017). Surface scatters of lithics and Peterborough Ware indicated the presence of Later Neolithic activity which could have derived from a large third millennium BC settlement, potentially contemporary with the earlier phases of Stonehenge. Four trenches (Trenches 52–55) were excavated in the palisade field in 2008 (see Volume 4).

Early Mesolithic postholes

Three pits thought to be large postholes were excavated in 1967 beneath the now grassed-over, pre-2013 Stonehenge visitors' car park (which is marked on Figure 8.2; Vatcher and Vatcher 1973; Cleal *et al.* 1995: 42–55). These may have originally been part of a long east–west arrangement of posts. It was hoped that geophysical survey might identify further such features, which could then be investigated through selective excavation. This could resolve whether this unusually early monument formed a major landscape arrangement (Allen and Gardiner 2002). No postholes were found during the SRP's surveys. Despite several geophysical surveys with different methods by different teams in later years (*e.g.* Darvill *et al.* 2013; Gaffney *et al.* 2012), no further Mesolithic postholes have so far been identified in this area.

The Stonehenge Avenue

'Periglacial stripes' identified by Mike Allen from records of Atkinson's 1956 trench across the Avenue, close to its terminal at Stonehenge (Cleal *et al.* 1995: fig. 178), appeared to be aligned on the midsummer sunrise. We aimed to clarify whether these really were natural features, given their apparent solstitial orientation. In addition, we aimed to establish whether the Avenue was surfaced, in line with William Hawley's neglected observation of a flint gravel surface on the Avenue south of the Heel Stone. The excavation of Trench 45 in 2008 addressed these questions (see Chapter 8). Thirdly, if a large enough area could be excavated, we hoped to check Stukeley's observation of lines of hollows for former standing stones either side of the Avenue (Burl 2006: 193, fig. 28). However, the size of the SRP trench in this area (Trench 45) was severely restricted by English Heritage and the National Trust, so we were unable to test Stukeley's hypothesis.

Investigation at the Avenue's 'elbow' (where it turns eastwards from its solstice axis) was planned to see if the Avenue was built in one or more phases. Re-opening of Atkinson and Evans' poorly recorded trenches (C62/C40, C96 and C97), together with small extensions to these, could establish whether the Avenue ditch originally terminated here. We would also be able to observe whether the parallel lines of geophysical anomalies running within the Avenue (possibly 'periglacial stripes'; see above) extended as far as the elbow. The Gate Ditch, which runs parallel to the Avenue at this point, also remained undated; it appears to have formed part of the same linear feature as the Stonehenge palisade (Pollard *et al.* 2017; and see Volume 4). Trenches 46–48, 56–59 were excavated at the Avenue elbow in 2008, and are reported in Chapter 8.

Stonehenge – the stone-dressing area

During our strolls in 2004–2007 in the field immediately north of Stonehenge, we noticed that moles were turning up many sarsen chips in their molehills. Results of geophysical survey and augering confirmed that the zone immediately north of Stonehenge and west of the Avenue (adjacent to the former visitors' centre) was an area where Stonehenge's sarsens were dressed before erection. A trench here (Trench 44) revealed that this was a major stone-working area, casting new light on how the stone-dressing was carried out (see Chapter 4).

Stonehenge

Excavation of Aubrey Hole 7 was planned to recover almost 60 human cremations excavated within Stonehenge in 1919–1926. Excavated by William Hawley from the eastern half of Stonehenge, they were subsequently buried in this pit by his assistant, R.S. Newall, in 1935. Aubrey Hole 7, previously dug out by Hawley in 1920, was used by Newall and his colleague, William Young, as a storage place for these cremated human bones because at the time no museum was prepared to curate them. Trench 39, excavated in 2008, retrieved the reburied remains and examined the form and fills of the Aubrey Hole (see Chapter 4). Analysis of the human remains has provided valuable insights into the dating, demography, palaeopathology, and the origins and mobility of the prehistoric people who were buried at Stonehenge (see Chapters 10 and 11, and also Snoeck *et al.* 2018).

Two other excavations – of 'Hawley's Graves' and of Aubrey Hole 34 – were planned but never implemented because of constraints of time, money and 'red tape'. Hawley's Graves, located about 80m south of Stonehenge, are the six large pits containing stone debris excavated by William Hawley from Stonehenge; he decided to discard into them most of the stone fragments that he excavated at Stonehenge during 1919–1926 because of the sheer quantity of such material. Hawley's excavated debris would have provided information about stone types and stone-working methods. It would have been useful to compare, for example, the proportions of various types of Welsh bluestones represented in the lithic assemblage with those still in place at Stonehenge. Excavation of Aubrey Hole 34, its immediate environs and a contiguous stretch of bank and ditch could have helped to clarify further whether the Aubrey Holes were indeed stone sockets, and whether there may be an outer circle of postholes or 'cavities' (Cleal *et al.* 1995: 107–8).

1.2. Appendix

Principal sites and monuments of the Early–Middle Neolithic (*c.* 4000–3000 BC) in the vicinity of Stonehenge

The Stonehenge landscape is well known for its long barrows, causewayed enclosures, cursuses, mortuary enclosure and other sites of the Early Neolithic (*c.* 4000–3400 BC) and Middle Neolithic (*c.* 3400–3000 BC). Long barrows in Britain generally date to *c.* 3800–3400 BC, although the few from the Stonehenge landscape that have been dated were constructed towards the end of this range. Causewayed enclosures in Britain fall within a similar chronological range to long barrows. Cursuses are dated to *c.* 3600–3200 BC and appear to have been built after causewayed enclosures on both chronological and stratigraphic grounds. Long mortuary enclosures are not well dated but the example from Normanton Down (see below) is, like Stonehenge's two cursuses, dated to the Early/Middle Neolithic.

Figure 1.3 shows the majority of these sites and monuments.

Coneybury Anomaly

An Early Neolithic pit on Coneybury Hill, 1.4km east-southeast of Stonehenge. It was filled with broken ceramics and freshly butchered bones of cattle, deer and pigs, indicative of a major feasting event in 3760–3700 cal BC. Excavated by Julian Richards for the Stonehenge Environs Project (Richards 1990: 40–61; Barclay 2014).

Larkhill causewayed enclosure

An Early Neolithic causewayed enclosure, 3.3km northeast of Stonehenge, of unknown dimensions. Interrupted ditches forming its northeastern arc were excavated in 2016 in advance of development. Preliminary dating places it *c.* 3750–3650 cal BC. Excavated by Wessex Archaeology (Thompson *et al.* 2017).

Robin Hood's Ball causewayed enclosure

An Early Neolithic causewayed enclosure, 4.2km northwest of Stonehenge, consisting of two concentric circuits of interrupted ditches and banks measuring 250m southwest–northeast × 200m southeast–northwest. Its construction has recently been dated to 3640–3500 cal BC (Whittle *et al.* 2011: 197). Excavated by Nicholas Thomas (Thomas 1964).

Woodhenge pit

An Early Neolithic pit beneath the bank of Woodhenge on its southwest side. It contained broken ceramics of a style similar to those from Coneybury Anomaly. Although no radiocarbon date could be obtained for the digging of the pit, the ceramic style indicates a likely date in the second quarter of the fourth millennium cal BC. Excavated by Josh Pollard and Dave Robinson as part of the Stonehenge Riverside Project. Site code: WOE06.

Winterbourne Stoke Crossroads long barrow

An Early/Middle Neolithic long barrow, 2.4km west-southwest of Stonehenge. With its mound *c.* 73m long × *c.* 23m wide × 2.5m high, it is the largest long barrow in the environs of Stonehenge. A primary burial of an adult male beneath the mound is dated to 3630–3360 cal BC. Excavated by John Thurnam (Thurnam 1869).

Amesbury 42 long barrow

An Early/Middle Neolithic long barrow, 1.8km northeast of Stonehenge and positioned at the east end of the Greater Cursus. Although flattened, the long barrow is one of the largest in the Stonehenge environs, *c.* 60m long × *c.* 40m wide (including flanking ditches). A broken antler pick from the primary fill of its eastern ditch dates its construction to 3520–3350 cal BC. Excavated by John Thurnam (Thurnam 1869), Julian Richards (1990: 96–109) and then in 2008 by Julian Thomas as part of the Stonehenge Riverside Project. Site code: GCE08.

The Greater Cursus

An Early/Middle Neolithic rectangular ditched enclosure, 700m north of Stonehenge. Oriented east–west, this monument is 2.8km long × 150m wide. A broken antler pick from the primary fill of its western terminal is dated to 3630–3370 cal BC. Excavated by Percy Farrer (Farrer 1917), J.F.S. Stone (Stone 1947), Patricia Christie (Christie 1963), Julian Richards (Richards 1990: 93–109) and then in 2007 and 2008 by Julian Thomas as part of the Stonehenge Riverside Project. Site codes: GC07 and GCE08.

The Lesser Cursus

An Early/Middle Neolithic rectangular ditched enclosure, 2km west-northwest of Stonehenge. Oriented west-southwest–east-northeast, this monument is 400m long × 60m wide. Initially just 220m long, its eastern half was later extended yet leaving its east end open. An antler from the first phase has a wide-ranging date of 3640–2900 cal BC whilst one from its second phase has been confirmed by the SRP to date to 3500–3340 cal BC. Excavated by Julian Richards as part of the Stonehenge Environs Project (Richards 1990: 72–93).

Normanton Down long mortuary enclosure

An Early/Middle Neolithic rectangular ditched enclosure, 1.3km southwest of Stonehenge. At 36m long (east-southeast–west-northwest) by 21m wide, it is much smaller than a cursus and is similar in plan to a long barrow. Its causewayed ditch and internal bank were interrupted by an entrance at its east-southeast end which was defined by two opposing bedding trenches, each containing three postholes. One of the antler picks from the ditch is dated to 3520–2910 cal BC. Although long mortuary enclosures are not always associated with human remains, their name is derived from their similarity in plan to long barrows. Excavated by Faith Vatcher in 1959 (Vatcher 1961).

Principal sites and monuments of the Late Neolithic (*c.* 3000–2450 BC) to Chalcolithic (*c.* 2450–2200 BC): Stonehenge and sites in its vicinity

The most significant monuments of the Late Neolithic in the Stonehenge landscape are Stonehenge and Durrington Walls. Stonehenge is connected by its Avenue to West Amesbury henge, inside which is Bluestonehenge, beside the River Avon. Durrington Walls also has an avenue connecting it to the River Avon. Woodhenge lies just south of Durrington Walls, and Coneybury henge is located between Durrington Walls and Stonehenge. Other monuments of this period in the Stonehenge area include pit circles, standing stones, pits, ditched enclosures and post-built structures.

Stage	95% probability (cal BC)
Stage 1 start	*3080–2950*
Stage 1 end	*2865–2755*
Stage 2 start	*2740–2505*
Stage 2 end	*2470–2300*
Stage 3 start	*2400–2220*
Stage 3 end	*2300–2100*
Stage 4 start	*2210–2030*
Stage 4 end	*2155–1920*
Stage 5 start	*1980–1745 (94%)*
Stage 5 end	*1620–1465*

Table 1.1. Estimates for the beginnings and endings of the five Stages of construction at Stonehenge

Figure 1.3 shows the majority of these sites and monuments.

Stonehenge

For plans and photographs of Stonehenge showing its various components, and the sequence of its construction, the reader should refer to the figures in the subsequent chapters, particularly Chapter 4.

Stonehenge's principal features are a horseshoe of five sarsen trilithons (pairs of uprights with a lintel), open to the northeast (towards midsummer solstice sunrise) and encircled by a sarsen circle of originally 30 uprights with conjoining lintels (of which only six remain in place). The largest trilithon, now fallen and broken, originally framed the midwinter solstice sunset to the southwest. Whilst one of its uprights stands vertical, the great trilithon's other two fallen stones lie on top of the Altar Stone, a sandstone monolith sourced to the Brecon region of south Wales. This is one of the bluestones, a variety of dolerite, rhyolite, volcanic and sandstone pillars that (with the exception of the Altar Stone) originate in the Preseli region of west Wales. In contrast, sarsens are a sedimentary silcrete found locally in central-southern and southeast England.

The bluestones – much smaller than the sarsens – are arranged today in two formations: a horseshoe nested within the sarsen trilithon horseshoe, and a circle between the trilithons and the outer sarsen circle. Two of the pillars of the bluestone circle are actually former lintels, demonstrating that some of the bluestones had previously been set up as trilithons.

Outside Stonehenge's sarsen circle, two sarsen stones survive from the rectangular setting of four Station Stones. These lie close to the inside edge of the circular bank and ditch that enclose the monument, with entrances through this earthwork at the northeast and south. Within the northeast entrance the sarsen Slaughter Stone is one of originally three sarsens that formed a façade across this main entrance. Beyond the Slaughter Stone, within the start of Stonehenge's Avenue, stands the Heel Stone, the only sarsen at Stonehenge which shows no signs of stone-dressing. The Heel Stone provides a sightline from the centre of Stonehenge towards the midsummer sun which rises immediately to the north of this stone.

Stonehenge's stones are individually numbered in a system devised by Flinders Petrie (1880), with numbers below 100 for uprights and above it for lintels. Additional identifiers have been given to separate fragments of the same stone (*e.g.* 160a, 160b, 160c for broken lintel 160) or to stones not visible in Petrie's day but later revealed through excavation (*e.g.* 32c, 32d, 32e for stumps of three separate bluestones).

The circle of pits known as the Aubrey Holes inside the enclosure bank has its own numbering system (1–56), as do the two concentric circles of pits known as the Y Holes (1–30) and Z Holes (1–30) outside the sarsen circle. Four stoneholes within the enclosure's entrance (two of them beside the Slaughter Stone) and leading out of it are lettered 'B–E' but a fifth stonehole just north of the Heel Stone is numbered '97'.

Stonehenge has five constructional stages. The chronology of these stages was published in 2012 (Darvill *et al.* 2012; Marshall *et al.* 2012), superseding the phases of construction proposed in Cleal *et al.* (1995). A number of new radiocarbon dates of material from Stonehenge have been obtained since 2012. These are reported in Chapter 11 of this volume. As a result of the additional dating, the chronology of the stages has some minor modifications. The revised chronology for the beginnings and endings of the five stages is shown in Table 1.1 Further relevant figures and tables in Chapter 11 show, for example, the modelled timespan of each Stage, and modelled intervals between them.

Stage 1 starts *3080–2950 cal BC* at 95% probability. Circular earthwork enclosure and Aubrey Holes, associated with cremation burials. Postholes within the enclosure's interior may have formed five or more rectangular structures as well as a pathway leading from the south entrance through a timber façade. Six lines of posts across the northeast entrance, and another line further out (lettered 'A') towards the Heel Stone (96) may also have been erected at this time. Stoneholes B, C and 97, on an alignment northeast from the entrance, are thought to date to this stage and to have held sarsens. Four features within the enclosure's interior may also have held sarsens. In contrast, the Aubrey Holes are thought to have held bluestones.

Stage 2 starts *2740–2505 cal BC* at 95% probability. The sarsen trilithon horseshoe and sarsen circle were erected, with a bluestone double circle or arc (the Q and R Holes) constructed in between them (and possibly employing bluestone lintels). The small size of Stone 11 in the sarsen circle suggests that its full circuit of 30 sarsen lintels could never have been completed. The Altar Stone (80) may have been set up in Stage 2 in front (northeast) of the great trilithon (55a, 55b, 56, 156), either as a standing stone or recumbent in the position in which it lies today. The four Station Stones (91–94) were erected, one of them (92) set within a South Barrow (a chalk-plaster floored building beside the south entrance, later covered by a mound) and another (94) within a North Barrow. The Slaughter Stone (95) and two accompanying sarsen stones (D and E) were set up across the north entrance. The Heel Stone (96), encircled by a small ditch (which could have been dug in Stage 3), is likely to have been in position at this time but could have been erected in Stage 1. Either the Heel Stone stood as one of a pair with a sarsen in Stonehole 97, or it was the stone that stood originally in that hole (97) and was subsequently moved in Stage 2 to its current and final position.

Stage 3 starts *2400–2220 cal BC* at 95% probability. A *c.* 10m-diameter circle of *c.* 25 bluestones (possibly those from Bluestonehenge beside the River Avon) is thought to have been erected within the centre of Stonehenge, followed by the digging-out of a large pit at the foot of the great trilithon, which disturbed some of the Q and R Holes as well as the central bluestone circle. The two sarsen stones (D and E) accompanying the Slaughter Stone were taken down, and the enclosure ditch was re-cut. The earliest dates for the Avenue indicate that it was in place by this stage (though it could have been constructed in Stage 2). A Beaker-style inhumation in the enclosure ditch is the last of Stonehenge's Late Neolithic–Copper Age burials (which included cremations and disarticulated unburnt human remains as well as this one inhumation).

Stage 4 starts *2210–2030 cal BC* at 95% probability. The bluestones were taken down and rebuilt as an inner bluestone oval of *c.* 25 stones (inside the sarsen trilithon horseshoe) and an outer circle (inside the sarsen circle). At some stage, possibly in either Stage 4 or 5 or later, the bluestone oval was turned into a horseshoe (by removal of pillars at its northeast end), mimicking the plan of the sarsen trilithon horseshoe. It is possible that the putative oval is a misinterpretation of the stone sockets and that the bluestones were arranged as a horseshoe throughout Stage 4 (see Volume 2). The Avenue's ditch was re-cut during this stage.

Stage 5 starts *1980–1745 cal BC* at 94% probability. Some of the bluestone pillars were likely used in this stage to make Early Bronze Age ground-stone tools. Two concentric circles of pits, the Y and Z Holes, were dug outside the sarsen circle but were left to silt up (1635–1520 cal BC). Carvings of three daggers and over 100 axe-heads (of Early Bronze Age Arreton style, *c.* 1650–1500 BC) were made on five sarsen uprights. The area around Stonehenge, used for mound burials since Stage 3, continued to fill with numerous and large round barrow cemeteries.

Stonehenge Avenue

A Late Neolithic/Chalcolithic avenue formed of two parallel ditches with internal banks, running 2.8km from Stonehenge's northeast entrance to Bluestonehenge beside the River Avon. The ditches were re-cut at least once, so a date of 2580–2280 cal BC on an antler pick from its base may not necessarily indicate its initial construction. The Avenue is aligned on the midwinter sunset/midsummer sunrise axis for its first 500m from Stonehenge before turning eastwards at its elbow to cross Stonehenge Bottom, climb King Barrow Ridge and then descend to West Amesbury. Excavated by O.G.S. Crawford and A.D. Passmore (Crawford 1923), William Hawley (Hawley 1924; 1925), R.C.C. Clay (Clay 1927), Faith and Lance Vatcher (Cleal *et al.* 1995: 296), Richard Atkinson and John Evans (Evans 1984; Cleal *et al.* 1995: 295–6), George Smith (Smith 1973), Mike Pitts (Pitts 1982), Wessex Archaeology (2013) and by the Stonehenge Riverside Project in 2008. Site codes: SAV08, SAB08 and NAE08.

West Amesbury henge and Bluestonehenge stone circle

A Late Neolithic former stone circle enclosed within a Copper Age henge beside the River Avon at the riverside end of the Stonehenge Avenue, 2km southeast of Stonehenge. The first structure was a 10m-diameter circle of *c.* 25 standing stones placed in intercutting sockets; imprints left by the stones in the soft riverside chalk are consistent with their having been bluestones originating in Wales. Although the date of the bluestone circle's erection cannot be established precisely, it was dismantled in 2470–2210 cal BC, around the same time that a 30m-diameter henge ditch with external bank was constructed around it. Excavated by Jim Rylatt as part of the Stonehenge Riverside Project. Site codes: ARS08 and ARS09.

Coneybury Henge

A Late Neolithic henge on Coneybury Hill, 1.4km east-southeast of Stonehenge. Its ditch and former outer bank enclosed a deliberately levelled area (*c.* 38m in diameter) in which likely timber structures were erected. An arc of postholes around the inner edge of the ditch may have been part of a timber circle. In the centre of the henge, a setting of pits is likely to have held timber posts, possibly forming a four-post structure and its approach. A single animal bone from the primary fill of the henge ditch dates to 2920–2610 cal BC. Excavated by Julian Richards as part of the Stonehenge Environs Project (Richards 1990: 123–58).

Durrington Walls

A Late Neolithic settlement and henge within a tributary dry valley of the River Avon, 2.8km northeast of Stonehenge. The henge's external bank, 440m in diameter, was built on top of the remains of houses and associated occupation deposits which indicate a settlement covering potentially 17ha, inhabited in *c.* 2515–2470 cal BC. The centre of the settlement was relatively empty except for two large timber circles, the Southern and Northern Circles, and five small henges, at least two of which were built around single houses. A 180m-long avenue, aligned on midsummer sunset, connected the midwinter sunrise-oriented Southern Circle to the River Avon. Towards the end of the settlement's use, its perimeter was first encircled by wooden posts and then by a large henge ditch and external bank, completed by 2480–2450 cal BC. Erroneous interpretations of geophysical survey data by the Stonehenge Hidden Landscapes Project suggested the presence of stone sockets near the henge's southern entrance. Excavation in 2016 showed that the geophysical anomalies recorded by the SHLP are postholes, not stone sockets. All references to stone sockets at Durrington Walls (*e.g.* reports on the web about the work of the SHLP) are entirely wrong. The SHLP survey also located a 2km-diameter penannular ring of massive pits, each c. 20m in diameter and 5m or more deep, encircling Durrington Walls (Gaffney et al. 2020). Excavated by Percy Farrer (Farrer 1918), J.F.S. Stone (Stone *et al.* 1954), Geoffrey Wainwright (Wainwright with Longworth 1971) and by the Stonehenge Riverside Project. Site codes: DW04, DW05, DW06, DW07, DSE07, DWE07, SC05, SC06, WE06, DSE16 (with SHLP).

Woodhenge

A Late Neolithic timber circle and henge, 100m south of the southern entrance of Durrington Walls. This oval setting of concentric rings of postholes is dated to 2580–2450 cal BC, earlier than the date of 2480–2030 cal BC for the encircling henge ditch and external bank. Excavated by Maud Cunnington (Cunnington 1929), Geoffrey Wainwright and John Evans (Evans in Wainwright 1971) and by Josh Pollard and Dave Robinson as part of the Stonehenge Riverside Project. Site code: WOE06.

Three timber monuments south of Woodhenge

A group of three Late Neolithic square, four-post settings preserved under Early Bronze Age round barrows (Durrington 67, 68 and 70) within 300m south of Woodhenge on a ridge overlooking the River Avon. The two larger ones are surrounded by incomplete stake settings; one of these (under Durrington 70) went out of use before 2480–2290 cal BC. Larger than the Durrington Walls houses, these are thought to be small timber monuments. Excavated by Maud Cunnington (Cunnington 1929) and by Josh Pollard and Dave Robinson as part of the Stonehenge Riverside Project. Site code: WHS07.

Airman's Corner pit circle

A 30m-diameter circle of *c.* 22 pits, 3km west-northwest of Stonehenge. This monument is undated but is likely to date to the Late Neolithic on the basis of its form. Whether it was a timber circle, a stone circle or a pit circle is unknown. Discovered by Wessex Archaeology (Wessex Archaeology 2008) and topsoil-sampled by the Stonehenge Riverside Project. Site code: FEC09.

Fargo Plantation lithic concentration and henge

A scatter of bluestone fragments, Beaker ceramics and lithics south of the Greater Cursus and east of the wooded area of Fargo Plantation. This is part of a much larger scatter of Beaker-period artefacts which extends 3km north–south (from north of the Greater Cursus to southwest of Stonehenge) and 0.5km east–west, with an outlier area, about 1km across, south of the Longbarrow Crossroads round barrow cemetery (Richards 1990: figs 154, 159; Pollard *et al.* 2017: fig. 8). Its unusually large extent makes it potentially one of the largest known Bell Beaker settlements in Europe. Discovered by William Young and J.F.S. Stone (Stone 1947) and by the Stonehenge Environs Project (Richards 1990). Stone also excavated a small henge within Fargo Plantation (Stone 1938). Topsoil-sampled by the Stonehenge Riverside Project. Site codes: FP06 and FP08.

Cuckoo Stone

A recumbent sarsen stone, 400m southwest of Durrington Walls. This former standing stone was originally erected in the natural hollow in which it had lain, close to two Late Neolithic pits dating to *c.* 2910–2870 cal BC. Excavated by Colin Richards as part of the Stonehenge Riverside Project. Site code: CUS06.

Tor Stone, Bulford

A recumbent sarsen stone, 2.2km east-southeast of Durrington Walls. This former standing stone was originally erected beside the natural hollow in which it had lain. Likely to date to the Late Neolithic, it was enclosed within an Early Bronze Age round barrow at the centre of which was a well-equipped Food Vessel Urn cremation grave. Excavated by Colin Richards as part of the Stonehenge Riverside Project. Site code: TS05.

Stonehenge chalk plaque pit

A small pit on King Barrow Ridge, 1km east of Stonehenge and 250m northwest of Coneybury henge. This pit, dating to 2920–2630 cal BC, contained two carved chalk plaques as well as lithics, animal bones and ceramic sherds. Excavated by Faith Vatcher (Vatcher 1969; Harding 1988).

Woodlands and Ratfyn pits

Three pits containing lithics, ceramic sherds and animal bones, excavated on the ridges above the River Avon between Woodhenge and Amesbury. The presence of flint axes and chisel arrowheads suggests that they were filled in the early part of the Late Neolithic. Excavated by J.F.S. Stone (Stone 1935; 1949; Stone and Young 1948).

Boscombe Down pit circle

A Late Neolithic pit circle, on the east bank of the River Avon 5km east of Stonehenge. Some of the pits in this oval setting, 65m northeast–southwest × 45m southeast–northwest, apparently held posts. Other Late Neolithic pits were found in its vicinity. Excavated by Wessex Archaeology (Fitzpatrick 2004).

Bulford double henge

A conjoined pair of Late Neolithic henges, 3km east of Durrington Walls. In their vicinity were many Late Neolithic pits, some of them containing crude flint axeheads among their assemblages of lithics, animal bone and ceramic sherds. Excavated by Wessex Archaeology (Pitts 2018).

Wilsford penannular enclosure

A small Late Neolithic penannular enclosure, 600m south of Winterbourne Stoke Crossroads. Two cremation burials, recovered during archaeological evaluation and dating to 2890–2620 cal BC and 2930–2870 cal BC, may be part of a small cemetery within this feature. Excavated by Wessex Archaeology (Arup Atkins Joint Venture 2017b: 19–21).

Durrington post alignments

Lines of Late Neolithic postholes, 1km north-northeast of Durrington Walls, which may have formed fences for rectilinear enclosures. A Late Neolithic cremation burial was placed in a large hollow close by. Excavated by Wessex Archaeology (Thompson and Powell 2018).

Principal sites and monuments of the Early Bronze Age (*c.* 2200–1600 BC) in the vicinity of Stonehenge and mentioned in this volume

Stonehenge Palisade

A long and curving pre-Iron Age ditch containing closely-set postholes along its base. Positioned to the west and northwest of Stonehenge, this palisade would have had a significant impact on movement and visibility within the environs of the monument. Prior to 2008, the palisade was thought to date to the Late Neolithic (Cleal *et al.* 1995: 161). Together with the Gate Ditch (Cleal *et al.* 1995: 292), it appears to form a large, interrupted enclosure dating to the Early Bronze Age (Pollard *et al.* 2017). Within and immediately west of the suspected palisade enclosure, surface scatters of lithics and Peterborough Ware (Richards 1990: fig. 158) indicate the presence of Later Neolithic activity which could derive from a large third millennium BC settlement, potentially contemporary with the earlier phases of Stonehenge. Excavated by Faith and Lance Vatcher in 1967 and by Josh Pollard and Paul Garwood as part of the Stonehenge Riverside Project in 2008. Site code: PAL08.

North Kite

A three-sided trapezoidal bank and external ditch, 2km southwest of Stonehenge, enclosing an area of *c.* 8ha. The enclosure has Beaker pottery beneath its bank and is later than two Early Bronze Age round barrows which it slights. Curiously, three pieces of spotted dolerite were found in the buried soil beneath the bank. Excavated by Ernest Greenfield in 1958 and by Julian Richards in 1983.

Chapter 2

Fourth millennium BC beginnings: monuments in the landscape

C. Tilley and K. Welham*

* **With contributions by:**
W. Bennett, D. Field, L. Martin, A. Payne and C. Steele

2.1. The landscape of the fourth millennium BC

C. Tilley, W. Bennett and D. Field

The study area (180 sq km) was designed to include all the major Neolithic and Bronze Age barrow cemeteries around Stonehenge but it extends considerably beyond the landscape area studied by the RCHME (1979), Richards (1990) and Cleal *et al.* (1995) and the 'core' area of Exon *et al.* (2000). It also differs from previous studies by deliberately decentring Stonehenge and placing the Avon valley and Durrington Walls at the heart of the study area (Figures 2.1, 2.3).

The area comprises a 10km (north–south) by 18km (east–west) block of land (180 sq km) with the Avon valley and Durrington Walls at its centre. This study area extends from Shrewton and Winterbourne Stoke in the west to South Tidworth and Cholderton in the east, and from Boscombe Down in the south to Figheldean in the north. This area was chosen so as to include the valleys of the River Till to the west and parts of the Bourne valley and Nine Mile River to the east, and to include the most striking topographic feature of the area (apart from the Avon valley itself), the Beacon Hill Ridge.

This is a rolling chalk downland landscape in which topographic distinctions are subtle. It has been, and still is, primarily shaped by the agency of water. Across the study area seven main topographic elements may be distinguished:

1. The Avon river valley, the only perennial water source;
2. The winterbourne river valleys of the Till and the Bourne and Nine Mile rivers to the west and east;
3. The coombes or dry valley systems which run into these perennial or seasonal watercourses;
4. Well-defined and smoothly sloping ridges and spurs of various forms running between these valleys and coombes;
5. More rounded localised high points such as Rox Hill, Oatlands Hill and Robin Hood's Ball;
6. More amorphous and ambiguously defined sloping areas of slightly higher ground dissected by coombes;
7. The Beacon Hill Ridge with a pronounced northern scarp slope and a much gentler and more irregular and dissected southern dip slope.

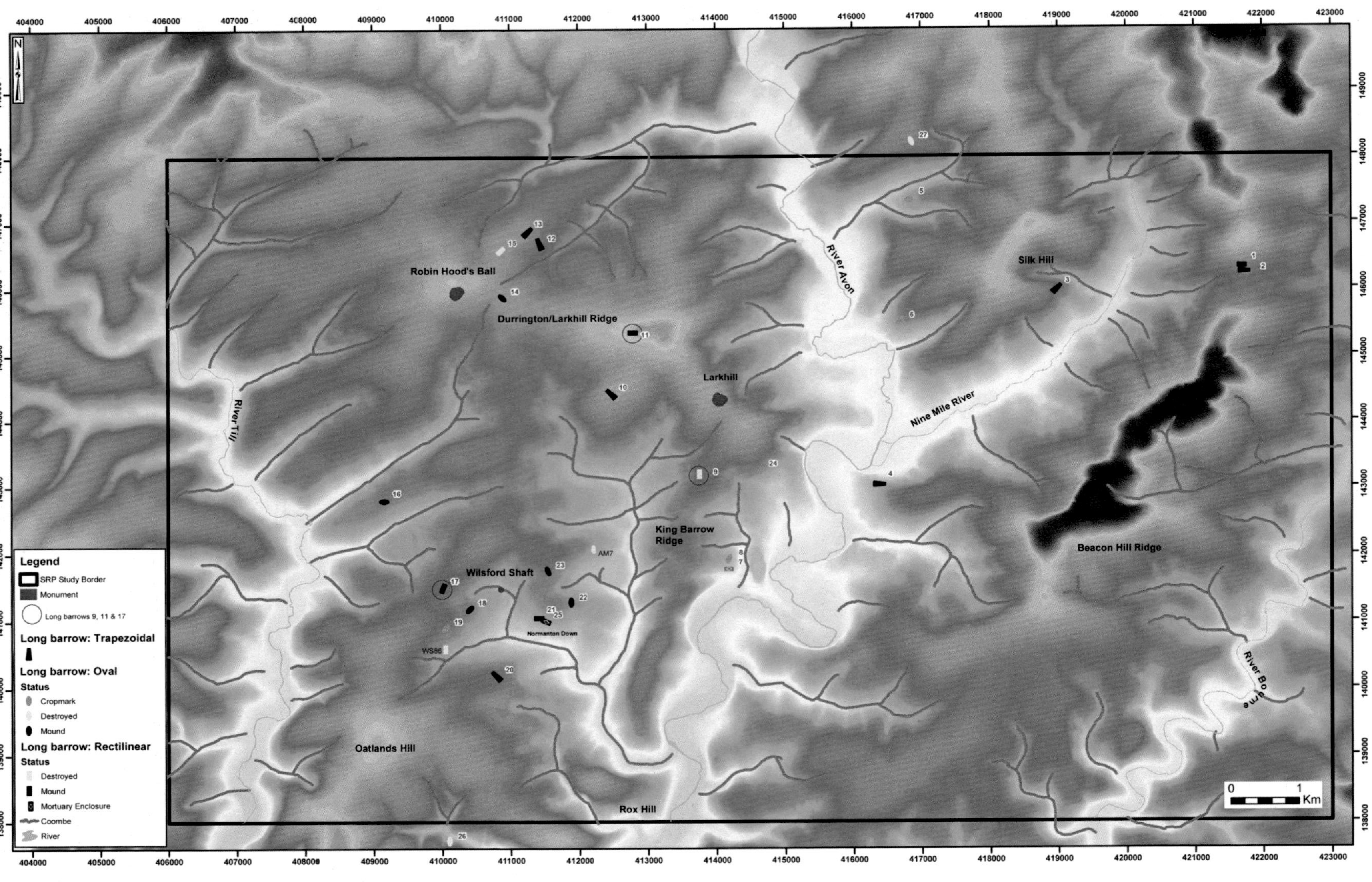

Figure 2.1. The distribution of long barrows and other earlier Neolithic monuments in the Stonehenge landscape

The River Avon is directly or indirectly linked to all the winterbournes and coombes in the study area or beyond it to the south. The Till is linked to the Avon via the Wylye to the west, and the Bourne joins it to the east, as does the Nine Mile River. All the coombe systems link into the same overall dendritic system. Thus the Avon effectively articulates and joins together the entire landscape, defined by water, the source of all life.

The river valleys and coombe systems both define and divide this landscape. Their courses delimit areas of higher ground and provide well-defined routes of movement through it. They can be conceptualised in terms of boundaries, transition points from the lowest to the highest ground, providing pathways to follow through the landscape. The association of coombes with water in various ways, periodically filling in wet weather, would have been noticed by prehistoric populations, as would their resemblance to river valleys with water such as the Avon. A problem that might have required a mythological explanation could have been: why did these rivers of the past run dry?

Both Beacon Hill Ridge to the east and Sidbury Hill, beyond the study area to the northeast, punctuate the skyline in a distinctive manner in this landscape. They are, relatively speaking, 'jagged' compared with the rest of the landscape where the coombe systems wind their way through the chalk downland in a localised topography of rises and ridges. These features are either slight and indistinct or, if higher, rounded and smoothly rolling. By contrast, Beacon Hill Ridge (maximum height 204m OD) and Sidbury Hill (223m OD) are by far the highest hills in the area and, indeed, among the highest in Wiltshire.

Beacon Hill Ridge (Figure 2.4) is by far the most dramatic hill in the study area. At the end of their landscape study, Exon *et al.* state that 'we became overpowered by the influence of Beacon Hill. Lying towards the eastern margin of our study area its high and jagged profile forms a visual focus for many monuments' (Exon *et al.* 2000: 108). This is indeed the case. The ridge extends for about 4km on an approximately southwest-to-northeast alignment. It is comprised of five distinctive summit areas with lower ground in-between and, because of its orientation, most of this ridge can be seen from Stonehenge.

Three of these summit areas of Beacon Hill Ridge (Jukes Brown [1905] only notes two), and Sidbury Hill, have a thin but nevertheless distinctive capping of flint and quartz pebbles in a clayey soil overlying the chalk, known geologically as the Reading Beds (Jukes Brown 1905: 40). These pebbles are round or oval in form, the largest being 5–6cm in diameter, the smallest 2cm. They are water-worn and perfectly smooth and rounded. They vary considerably in colour from white to black, to red, yellow and brown. Their presence explains the unusual stepped form of Beacon Hill Ridge, contrasting with all other chalk ridges in the Stonehenge area which have much more rounded and even contours, lacking distinctive and discrete summit areas.

Beacon Hill Ridge may have been significant to people long before the construction of any Neolithic monuments in this landscape. It is intriguing to note that the line of Early Mesolithic pine timber posts discovered *c.* 300m northwest of Stonehenge (Cleal *et al.* 1995: 43–7) is orientated toward it.

A particular feature of the landscape survey that needs to be stressed is that as much time and effort was spent recording and describing 'natural' (*i.e.* non-humanly modified) aspects of the landscape such as the Avon valley, ridges and coombe systems as the prehistoric monuments within it. So we visited not just the monuments themselves but also places without monuments, to try to build up, by this method, a holistic interpretative understanding of the significance of landscape and place from a human and somatic experiential perspective.

2.1.1. Long barrows in the Early Neolithic landscape *c.* 3800–3400 BC

Within the SRP landscape study area there are 23 certain, or probable, long barrows, one long mortuary enclosure and a further possible mortuary enclosure (see Chapter 1; Table 2.1 gives the site numbering of the barrows in the study set). Two further long barrows fall just outside the study area but nevertheless are included in this analysis (Figure 2.1: nos 26 and 27).

Two further long barrows were recently discovered. One was found during exploratory excavations in advance of the proposed Stonehenge tunnel route in the southwest area of the study zone (Winterbourne Stoke 86, 300m south of long barrow 19; Arup Atkins Joint Venture 2017a: 18; 2017b: 18–19; Roberts *et al.* 2018). The other is Amesbury 7, a supposed round barrow near Stonehenge that may be an oval long barrow (Bowden *et al.* 2015: 26). Neither of these recently discovered sites has been included in the analysis below.

All of the sites in this landscape study, and the recent discoveries, were identified by other fieldworkers. Of these sites only 16 (59%) survive in the landscape as visible mounds today.

The rest have been totally destroyed and are indicated only by the presence of soil- and cropmarks on aerial photographs and, in a few cases, as slight undulations on the land surface. Their overall distribution is markedly uneven:

- None occur in the southeast of the study area, south of Beacon Hill Ridge and east of the Avon.
- They are completely absent along the course of the Bourne river valley (both inside and outside the study area).

Map no.	Grid reference	Name	Status
1	SU21694663	Milston 40	Mound
2	SU21714625	Milston 39	Mound
3	SU18974587	Milston 1	Mound
4	SU16364304	Bulford 1	Mound
5	SU16834734	Figheldean	Cropmark
6	SU166644561	Brigmerston	Cropmark
7	SU14164174	Vespasian's Camp	Mortuary enclosure?
8	SU14184194	Vespasian's Camp (Amesbury 140)	Cropmark
9	SU13744318	Amesbury 42	Destroyed
10	SU12474437	Larkhill (Durrington 24)	Mound
11	SU12784535	Knighton (Figheldean 27)	Mound
12	SU11434667	Netheravon 6	Mound
13	SU11234687	Netheravon 8	Mound
14	SU10884588	Figheldean 31	Mound
15	SU10874663	Netheravon Bake (excavated by Julian Richards)	Cropmark
16	SU09154279	Winterbourne Stoke 53	Mound
17	SU10004151	Winterbourne Stoke Crossroads (Winterbourne Stoke 1)	Mound
18	SU10404118	Wilsford 34	Mound
19	SU10054090	Winterbourne Stoke 71	Cropmark
20	SU10794019	Lake (Wilsford 41)	Mound
21	SU11414106	Wilsford 30	Mound
22	SU11884129	Normanton Down (Wilsford 13)	Mound
23	SU11544175	Amesbury 14 by A303	Mound
24	SU14644324	Woodhenge (Durrington 76)	Cropmark
25	SU11424100	Normanton Down	Mortuary enclosure
26	SU10103760	Woodford G2	Cropmark
27	SU16864822	Sheer Barrow	Destroyed
AM7*	SU12034208	Amesbury 7	Destroyed
WS86*	SU10094059	Winterbourne Stoke 86	Destroyed

Table 2.1. Long barrows and mortuary enclosures in the SRP study area. Names with numbers are after Goddard's and Grinsell's lists. Barrows marked with * were not included in this study but are shown in Figure 2.1

Map no.	Orientation	Length	Max. width	Max. height	Shape
1	E-W	25	14	1.2	Rectilinear
2	E-W	28	18	2.5	Trapezoidal
3	NE-SW	43	23	2	Trapezoidal
4	E-W	41	20	2.5	Trapezoidal
5	E-W	*c.* 40			Oval
6	NE-SW	*c.* 40			Oval
7	E-W	*c.* 30			Rectilinear
8	NNE-SSW	*c.* 20			Oval
9	N-S	55	15	0.9	Rectilinear
10	NW-SE	45	16	1	Trapezoidal
11	E-W	55	21	3	Rectilinear
12	NNW-SSE	33	18	0.4	Trapezoidal
13	NE-SW	57	27	0.8	Trapezoidal
14	NW-SE	50			Oval
15	NE-SW	30			Rectilinear
16	E-W	32	18	1.7	Oval
17	NE-SW	73	23	2.5	Rectilinear
18	NE-SW	50	18	1.8	Oval
19	NE-SW	*c.* 50			Oval
20	NW-SE	43	24	3.5	Trapezoidal
21	E-W	38	16	2.2	Rectilinear
22	N-S	20	10	1	Oval
23	NNW-SSE	31	16	1.8	Oval
24	NE-SW	*c.* 40			Oval
25	WNW-ESE	36	21		Rectilinear
26	N-S	22	14	1.2	Oval
27	NNW-SSE	36	18		Oval
AM7	SSE-NNW	20	12		Oval
WS86	NNW-SSE	45	15		Rectilinear

Table 2.2. The orientations and dimensions of the certain or probable barrows and long mortuary enclosures in the SRP area

- Seven occur to the east of the Avon, to the north and west of Beacon Hill Ridge (26%).
- The remainder occur to the west of the Avon.

Three of the long barrows to the east of the Avon occur in the catchment area of the Nine Mile River (Figure 2.1: nos 1–3). At least seven are closely associated with the course of the River Avon (Figure 2.1: nos 4–8, 24 and 27), being located on spurs running down to it from the east and west. Only one is located on a spur running down to the Till valley, in the western part of the study area (Figure 2.1: no. 16), although there are others further north around the Till's source.

Sixteen (59%) occur in a broad 4km-wide north–south band of land, broken up with coombes and ridges, between the Avon and the Till valleys. Ten of these are closely associated with the long and reticulated Stonehenge Bottom/Lake Bottom coombe system (Figure 2.1: nos 9–10, 17–23 and 25), being located near to and in-between the coombe branches that make it up. The remaining five barrows are located on higher ground between coombes that eventually join the Avon to the east (Figure 2.1: nos 11–15). One further barrow, Woodford G2, is associated with a coombe system running down to join the Avon just to the south of the study area (Figure 2.1: no. 26).

Figure 2.2. Winterbourne Stoke Crossroads long barrow, viewed from the north

Length and morphology

Table 2.2 lists the dimensions and orientations of the barrows. The majority are 'short' long barrows of rectilinear, oval or trapezoidal form. There are at least eight rectilinear barrows, seven trapezoidal barrows and the rest are either oval-shaped or intermediate between trapezoidal and oval.

There are only four barrows greater than 50m in length (Figure 2.1: nos 9, 11, 13 and 17). These all occur to the west of the Avon.

- One of these is Amesbury 42 (no. 9), *c.* 55m long, at the eastern end of the Greater Cursus. Its mound is now reduced to less than 0.30m high (see Chapter 3) but the ground plan indicates that it was rectangular (Richards 1990: fig. 64).
- The original form of the Amesbury 42 mound may have been similar to that of the Knighton barrow (no. 11; Figheldean 27) and that at Winterbourne Stoke Crossroads (no. 17; Winterbourne Stoke 1). These are very long rectangular mounds with virtually flat tops which are 2.50m to over 3m above ground level and rise significantly higher above their broad, flanking side-ditches.
- The fourth particularly long barrow in the study area is Netheravon 8 (Figure 2.1: no. 13), to the east of Robin Hood's Ball causewayed enclosure (see below). However, the mound of this barrow is trapezoidal in form and, were it not for plough damage, it would in all probability have resembled the shorter but well-preserved examples at Bulford and Lake (Figure 2.1: nos 4 and 20).

Table 2.3. Some comparative notes on the locations of the long barrows and mortuary enclosures in the SRP area

Map no.	General description of landscape location
1	Low down in the landscape with higher ground to north and south
2	Low down in the landscape with higher ground to north and south
3	Aligned across the end of a spur on gentle SW–NE slope
4	On flat shelf of land on spur running down to River Avon
5	On gentle NE–SW slope dropping down to coombe to north
6	On gentle NE–SW slope of spur running down to River Avon
7	Gently sloping land running down to coombe to east and River Avon to south
8	Gently sloping land running down to coombe to east and River Avon to south
9	On King Barrow Ridge top. Axis runs along the ridge
10	On ridge top towards south end of spur. Long axis diagonal across spur
11	Long axis aligned along ridge top
12	Halfway up a gentle north–south slope running down to coombe to south
13	Almost at summit of ridge top and aligned along it
14	On flat ground near to rising ground up to Robin Hood's Ball to west
15	Middle of flat ridge top
16	On flat ridge top which runs down to a spur of the Till valley
17	On flat ground which then rises up to northwest and southeast
18	Almost flat land, low point in landscape
19	Almost flat land, low point in landscape
20	On localised high point
21	Halfway up a gentle northeast to southwest slope
22	In middle of ridge top. Long axis runs across the ridge
23	On low rise in flat landscape
24	On gentle north–south and west–east slope
25	Halfway up a gentle northeast to southwest slope
26	Long axis orientated down top of steep slope to coombe bottom
27	Near to flat ridge top to north on gentle north–south slope

Three of these very long barrows are orientated along ridge-tops, and their long axis follows or duplicates the orientation of the ridge, providing an explanation for the very different mound alignments. By contrast, the barrow at Winterbourne Stoke Crossroads is located at a flat point in the landscape, with the land rising up beyond it to the northeast and southwest (Figure 2.2).

The majority of the long barrows cannot be described as monumental landscape markers. Most of these mounds, even when taking plough damage into account, were not only comparatively short but were rather low and flat and would not have been prominent or visible over very long distances. The four barrows mentioned above are exceptional in this respect, as are the 'short' but high trapezoidal mounds at Bulford and Lake (Figure 2.1: nos 4 and 20).

This point is also underlined by the choices made for the barrows' locations in the landscape. Only a minority are in prominent positions on ridge-tops (Table 2.3); the rest are on gently sloping or undulating ground and their visible presence as a monument had only a localised significance. Almost all are aligned along the contours and they were, of course, most prominent when seen from the side and invariably from the coombe or valley floor. However, there are exceptions: the direction from which they would best be seen in the landscape may have been an important factor for at least some of them. The long barrow at Bulford (Figure 2.1: no. 4) is most prominent when seen from the west looking down onto it and along the long axis of the mound from the end of the Larkhill/Durrington ridge.

The length and maximum width of these mounds differ considerably (Table 2.2), as do the details of the overall morphology or characteristics of the mounds. Detailed field surveys (McOmish *et al.* 2002) have shown that the well-preserved Knighton barrow (no. 11) has a ledge at the western end of the mound that can be traced along its sides, perhaps indicating that the barrow construction was multi-phase and that the mound was raised up on a pre-existing berm or raised platform. The same is true of the southern barrow of the pair at Milston (Figure 2.1: nos 1 and 2; Field 2006: fig. 26). Profile surveys undertaken along the long axis and horizontally across the mounds of selected barrows show that these all differ quite significantly (McOmish *et al.* 2002).

What this suggests is that the individual shapes and dimensions of these barrows were not at all standardised. Each barrow, whether it was basically rectilinear, oval or trapezoidal in form, had its own idiosyncratic and recognisable characteristics, which is why it is often very difficult to distinguish between oval-shaped and trapezoidal-shaped mounds in the field today or on the basis of plans.

So not only was the location of each – marking a specific place in the landscape – unique but so were the dimensions and morphological characteristics of the barrows that were constructed in these places. One barrow on Alton Down (Figure 2.1: no. 14) has three sarsen stones in its northern ditch. While these stones were almost certainly brought here and dumped, they indicate the presence of sarsens in the vicinity of the monument which might have been an important factor in its location.

Landscape locations

Three generalised landscape locations (Table 2.3) can be distinguished as follows:

- Barrows found on flat or only gently undulating land (*n* = 7; 26%). These are all situated in lower areas of the landscape between river valleys and coombes.
- Barrows which occur on sloping ground on the ends of spurs or on the upper or lower slopes of ridges or land dropping down to coombes (*n* = 12; 44%)
- Barrows found on ridge-tops or on localised high points in the landscape (*n* = 8; 30%)

It is interesting to note that no barrows are located at the lowest points in the landscape (*i.e.* along or near to the coombe bottoms). Only one long barrow, that at Woodford (Figure 2.1: no. 26), is situated on the lip of a steep coombe, with the mound located on the slope to the coombe bottom. The majority of the barrows occur more or less in the centre of blocks of land broken up or defined by coombes, which means that the outlines of the coombes are visible from them but not the coombe bottoms.

These barrows are conspicuously absent from the very highest land in the study area, the Beacon Hill Ridge. However, this ridge would have been visible from all but one of the long barrows (that at Woodford, just to the south of the project study area [Figure 2.1: no. 26]) and a possible long mortuary enclosure to the west of Amesbury (Figure 2.1: no. 25; Table 2.4). Today the Beacon Hill Ridge is not visible from two other barrows – Netheravon 6 (Figure 2.1: no. 12) and Figheldean 31 (Figure 2.1: no. 14) – but this appears to be a product of nearby modern tree lines to their east. GIS analysis conducted by Mark Dover has shown that the highest summit areas of the Beacon Hill Ridge would probably have been visible from both these barrows in the absence of the recent plantations.

Barrow groups

Three loose sub-regional barrow groups based on distribution clusters may be tentatively defined as follows:

1. A group of four barrows lies in close proximity to the Greater Cursus (Figure 2.3). These are:

    - the large barrow (Amesbury 42) on the King Barrow Ridge at its eastern terminal, which effectively dictated the eastern limit of the Greater Cursus;
    - the Bulford long barrow (Bulford 1) to the east of the Avon, which is orientated on the Cursus's eastern terminal;
    - the Larkhill barrow (Durrington 24), also orientated on the Cursus's eastern terminal;
    - Winterbourne Stoke 53, orientated on the Cursus's western terminal.

The orientations of three of these barrows on the terminals of the Greater Cursus suggest that they are later in date or contemporary with it. Since the Greater Cursus runs up and ends beside Amesbury 42, this suggests that this barrow may be earlier (although its radiocarbon date for construction is statistically consistent with that for the Cursus; see Chapter 3). By contrast, there is little evidence for any close relationship between the Lesser Cursus and long barrows. All but one long barrow (no. 16; Winterbourne Stoke 53) are more than 2km from it, and neither the Winterbourne Stoke barrow nor any others are orientated towards it (Figure 2.3).

2. A group of seven barrows and one mortuary enclosure (all with distances of 1km or considerably less between neighbouring barrows) to the south of the Greater Cursus includes the monumental Lake and Winterbourne Stoke Crossroads long barrows that define the southern and western limits of the overall barrow distribution in this study area. Approximately midway between no. 19 (Winterbourne Stoke 71) and no. 20 (Lake; Wilsford 41), the ploughed-out remains of an eighth long barrow (Winterbourne Stoke 86) were found within this zone of the study area during archaeological evaluations in 2016 for the proposed Stonehenge A303 tunnel (Arup Atkins Joint Venture 2017a; 2017b; Roberts *et al.* 2018).

    These barrows all occur around the head of a bifurcating coombe system that joins Stonehenge Bottom/Lake Bottom, towards the end of which the Wilsford Shaft is located (see below). In an interesting fashion they are clustered around the site of the shaft itself: all but the Lake long barrow (no. 20; Wilsford 41), and the 2016 discovery, are 1km (or less) distant from it. From Lake long barrow, situated 1.25km distant, there is a splendid view directly up the dry valley to the site of the shaft itself.

Map no.	BHB	RHB	Greater Cursus	Lesser Cursus	Stonehenge location
1	Yes	No	No	No	No
2	Yes	No	No	No	No
3	Yes	No	No	No	No
4	Yes	No	Yes	No	No
5	Yes	No	No	No	No
6	Yes	No	No	No	No
7	No	No	No	No	No
8	Yes	No	No	No	No
9	Yes	Yes	Yes	Yes	Yes
10	Yes	Yes	Yes	Yes	Yes
11	Yes	Yes	Yes	Yes	Yes
12	Yes*	No	No	No	No
13	Yes	No	No	No	No
14	Yes*	No	No	No	No
15	Yes	No	No	No	No
16	Yes	Yes	Yes	No	No
17	Yes	No	Yes	No	No
18	Yes	No	No	No	No
19	Yes	No	No	No	No
20	Yes	Yes	Yes	Yes	Yes
21	Yes	No	No	No	No
22	Yes	No	Yes	Yes	Yes
23	Yes	No	Yes	Yes	Yes
24	Yes	No	No	No	No
25	Yes	No	No	No	No
26	No	No	No	No	No
27	Yes	No	No	No	No

Table 2.4. The visibility of the Beacon Hill Ridge (BHR), Robin Hood's Ball causewayed enclosure (RHB), Greater and Lesser Cursus, and the Stonehenge location from the mounds of the long barrows in the SRP area (*=extrapolated)

3. A group of five barrows, including the monumental barrow at Knighton, lies to the north of the Greater Cursus and to the east of Robin Hood's Ball causewayed enclosure.

The other 11 barrows are relatively isolated from each other in the landscape and do not form coherent groups. These include a unique pair of barrows with their mounds running parallel to each other, at Milston in the far east of the study area (Figure 2.1: nos 1 and 2).

Map no.	Visible barrows (by map number)	Frequency of visible barrows n	Coombes visible	Coombe bottoms visible
1	2	1	No	No
2	1	1	No	No
3	0	0	Yes	No
4	6 9	2	Avon	Yes
5	0	0	Yes	No
6	4	1	Yes	Yes
7	8	1	Yes	No
8	7 9 10	3	Yes	No
9	10 11 16 17	4	Yes	No
10	9 11 13 14 15	5	No	No
11	9 10 12 13 14 15	6	Yes	No
12	11 13	2	Yes	Yes
13	10 11 14 15	4	Yes	Yes
14	10 11 13 15	4	Yes	Yes
15	11 12 13 14	4	Yes	No
16	9 17	2	Yes	No
17	16 18 19 20 21 23	6	Yes	Yes
18	17 19 20 21 23 25	6	Yes	Yes
19	17 18 20 21 23 25	6	Yes	Yes
20	17 18 19 21 23 25	6	Yes	Yes
21	9 17 18 19 20 23 25	7	Yes	Yes
22	9 17 18 19 20 23	6	Yes	No
23	9 10 11 17 18 19 20	7	Yes	No
24	4 9	2	Yes	No
25	9 17 18 19 20 23	6	Yes	Yes
26	0	0	Yes	Yes
27	0	0	Yes	Yes

Table 2.5. Visibility from each barrow site in the SRP study area of other barrows or barrow locations (field data representing minimum numbers; some are extrapolations), the frequency of barrows visible, and the visibility of coombe lines and coombe bottoms

Barrow inter-visibility

In attempts to obtain data on how the Neolithic landscape and the monuments within it were perceived and experienced, studies of the inter-visibility of monuments have become widespread during recent decades, and the investigation here sought to determine the degree to which this might be useful (Table 2.5).

The undulating, high, level plateau of Salisbury Plain means that panoramic vistas are obtained from almost any point not tucked away in the river valleys or in the crevice-like coombes. Constructions made in such topography are inevitably visible from large parts of the landscape and whether inter-visibility between them is therefore a relevant aspect of their construction is not always clear. It would often have been difficult to place monuments so that they were *not* inter-visible.

Study of the barrows' aspect may help with this; that is, where they are partly masked by natural undulations and so visible only from a certain direction. However, even then it can be difficult to narrow things down to inter-visibility between monuments as opposed to general landscape features. It is more often easier to explain the relevance of barrows that do the opposite. The Fussell's Lodge long barrow (Ashbee 1966) to the south of Salisbury is one that achieves this by being placed on the floor of an enclosed valley, thereby ensuring that it is visible only from within the valley. It is integrally tied in to its valley location with no hint of expression to an outside body.

Some mounds in the study area, tucked away on valley slopes, such the Wilsford 30 barrow (no. 21) to the south of the round barrow cemetery on Normanton Down, provide similar indications that the coombe itself was the focus, and that inter-visibility within was incidental. Moving the mound 100m or so up the slope would have expressed a greater intention in terms of inter-visibility. Perhaps the classic local example of deliberate inter-visibility is the spire of Salisbury Cathedral, at 123m the tallest in the country and said to have been constructed to that height as part of an agreement whereby tithes could be obtained from all land that could be seen from its summit. It is difficult to be certain of similar observations here.

The barrows fall neatly into two groups in relation to how many other barrows are visible from them (Table 2.5):

- From 13 sites (48%), up to three other barrows are visible in the landscape. From four of these sites (five if we include the pair of barrows at Milston), no other barrows are visible. The mounds from which no other, or only a few other, barrows are visible are all located to the east of the Avon, in the vicinity of Robin Hood's Ball in the north of the study area, and immediately to the west of the Avon.
- From 14 barrows (52%), between four and seven other barrows are visible, seven being the maximum number recorded. Apart from the ridge-top barrows at Larkhill and Knighton, these are located to the south of the Greater Cursus and include the massive Winterbourne Stoke long barrow.

Aside from the recently discovered, levelled example within the Stonehenge Triangle (Field *et al.* 2014), the smallest barrow in the study region (no. 22) is located on the summit of Normanton Down. This example is only 20m long, has a maximum width of 10m and is about 1m high. It has well-preserved flanking ditches, and there is no evidence that the mound has been reduced by ploughing. From here, at least six other long barrows are visible to the west and north but not the nearby long barrow and mortuary enclosure along the southern slopes of Normanton Down, only about 500m distant. Since the mound of this barrow is so low and situated right in the centre of the ridge-top, with its mound aligned unusually across the ridge, it is doubtful whether it would ever have been visible from other long barrows.

This pattern of nearby barrows not being inter-visible while more distant barrows can be seen is apparent from the GIS studies conducted by Exon *et al.* (2000: figs 4.11–4.12) of 'short' and 'long' inter-visibility patterns. The pattern occurs among the group of barrows to the east of Robin Hood's Ball, where barrows Netheravon 6 and Figheldean 31 (Figure 2.1: nos 12 and 14) are not inter-visible (Exon *et al.* 2000: fig. 4.11 incorrectly plots these as being visible) while, from both, the Knighton barrow (Figure 2.1: no. 11) is prominently sky-lined on the Larkhill/Durrington ridge-top a much greater distance away. By far the most prominent barrow in terms of distant visibility is the Knighton barrow, which is visible right across Salisbury Plain to the north and, theoretically at least, to 13 other long barrows (Exon *et al.* 2000: 37).

This suggests that, in some cases, smaller barrows in lower locations in the landscape were sited in relationship to larger barrows in more prominent locations some distance away, rather than with reference to each other. This has probable chronological implications: the more massive and prominent barrows being earlier, as has long been suggested, and the smaller oval barrows somewhat later (Thurnham 1869: 41; Drewett 1975; Darvill 2006: 84). However, caution should be expressed here, as a short 'oval' long barrow beneath the trapezoidal mound at Wayland's Smithy was undoubtedly earlier (see Whittle *et al.* 2007 for Bayesian analysis of radiocarbon dates). That said, both of the Wayland's Smithy mounds fall late within the overall sequence, so oval mounds could still be a relatively late phenomenon. It might be more useful to consider that long barrows became more diverse over time, with some of the smallest *and* largest built later on, and some of the latter being enlarged through rebuilding or addition.

Often the barrows' landscape relationship is subtle at a local scale. Thus the rectangular Winterbourne Stoke Crossroads long barrow is situated on a flat area of land rising up to the southwest and northeast. So the location chosen does not appear to be the most prominent in the immediate landscape. However, when seen from the southeast, where the majority of other nearby inter-visible and smaller oval and trapezoidal long barrows are found, the location of this barrow is much more prominent.

The mound of the Winterbourne Stoke Crossroads barrow is orientated southwest–northeast and all the other smaller and inter-visible long barrows occur to the southeast of it and only one to the northwest. In other words, they are positioned in the landscape at various places from which the long axis of the Winterbourne Stoke mound is most prominent and visible. There are no long barrows on the higher ground to the southwest and northeast of the mound, from which only the short ends might be visible.

Similarly, the full east–west long axis of the Knighton barrow (no. 11) is visible from the four barrows to the east of Robin Hood's Ball, situated about 2km to the northwest of it. The trapezoidal barrow at Bulford (no. 4), situated on a low spur above the Avon, is orientated east–west and, from it, the full north–south long axis of the originally prominent long barrow (Amesbury 42) at the eastern end of the Cursus on the top of the King Barrow Ridge would have been a striking landmark. In turn, from this barrow the full east–west long axis of the Knighton long barrow on the top of the Larkhill/Durrington ridge would have been prominent.

In this manner we can begin to understand aspects of the siting, orientation and morphologies of the mounds in relation to each other. Specifically the argument is that the earliest barrows to the west of the Avon were the Knighton barrow, the Winterbourne Stoke Crossroads barrow and Amesbury 42 (the barrow at the eastern end of the Greater Cursus), all of which have (or might have had, in the latter case) long, high and rectangular-shaped mounds with flat tops. No barrows of this kind occur to the east of the Avon. In this area, the barrows are much more widely dispersed, with limited or no inter-visibility with other barrows.

Other factors are also no doubt at work in relation to barrow orientation. The higher and broader end of the mounds, where any wooden mortuary chamber might have been located, is invariably to the east. Eight barrows are orientated northeast–southwest, in the direction of the rising of the midsummer sun and the setting of the midwinter sun, and a further seven west–east, which may be related to the equinoctial sunrise and sunset. Thus at least 56% may be orientated in relation to major solar events. Only two are orientated north–south. Others are orientated southeast–northwest and south-southeast–north-northwest.

Another important feature of barrow location is their relationship to other major topographic features of the landscape: the ridges, spurs and coombes (Table 2.5). In relation to the barrows located on ridges and spurs, the norm is that the long axis of the mound follows the long axis of the ridge or spur. Thus the long axis of the Knighton long barrow is aligned east–west along the ridge-top on which it is situated, whilst Amesbury 42 at the eastern end of the Greater Cursus is aligned north–south along the line of the King Barrow Ridge. The ridge-top barrows at Netheravon Bake (Figure 2.1: nos 13 and 15) similarly follow the line of the ridge, as does the long barrow on Winterbourne Stoke Down (Figure 2.1: no. 16), and so on. However, there are some interesting exceptions:

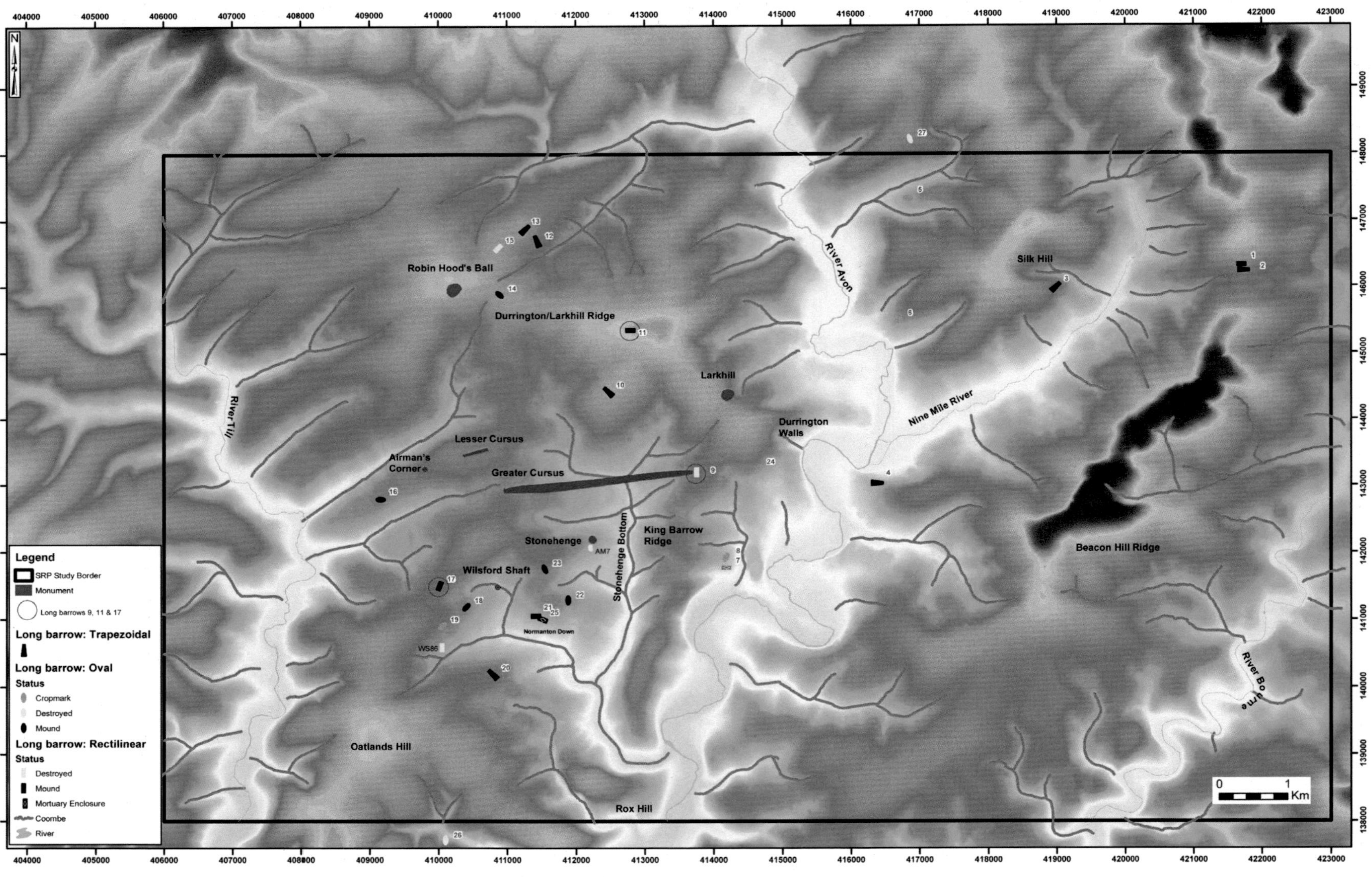

Figure 2.3. The Early/Middle Neolithic Cursuses in relation to earlier monuments in the Stonehenge landscape. The locations of Late Neolithic Stonehenge and Durrington Walls and the undated circle at Airman's Corner are also shown

- The small, and as suggested above, probably 'invisible' barrow on the top of Normanton Down is orientated north–south across the ridge-top rather than respecting its natural axis.
- The long axis of the Larkhill long barrow is orientated diagonally across a spur of the Larkhill/Durrington ridge.
- The barrow at Milston Firs is situated across the end of a spur leading down to the Nine Mile River.

Why do these barrows not conform to the norm? The overriding factor in the case of the Larkhill long barrow (no. 10) might have been that its orientation was intended to point towards the eastern end of the Greater Cursus (Figure 2.3) and/or the midwinter sunrise. It is one of only three barrows in the dataset orientated southeast–northwest, although this alignment is commonly found elsewhere on Salisbury Plain (Ashbee 1970: fig. 20; Kinnes 1992: figs 2.2.8–2.2.11). The orientation of the barrow at Milston Firs may be related to the rising and setting of the sun at the solstices and that of Normanton Down to these events at the equinoxes.

There are only three barrows (the unique pair at Milston and probably that at Larkhill) from which the outlines of coombes cutting across the landscape are not visible. Coombe bottoms are only visible from 13 barrows (48%) because almost all are situated some distance away (between 200m and 500m) from the lines of the coombes closest to them. In most cases, those parts of the coombe bottoms that are visible are seen by looking along the lines of the coombes rather than looking directly down into the coombe from the barrow location itself, *i.e.* towards the point of the coombe bottom(s) closest to the barrow site. Thus, for example, from the Lake long barrow (Figure 2.1: no. 20), a branch of the Stonehenge Bottom/Lake system is prominent from the barrow, running north with a view along the coombe bottom to its head. The barrow is 500m distant from the nearest point of the coombe.

There are two interesting exceptions to these 'distant' views of coombe bottoms from long barrow locations. One of the Netheravon Bake long barrows (Figure 2.1: no. 12) is on a gentle slope leading down to the coombe bottom only 200m distant, and the long axis of this barrow points down towards the coombe. As a consequence, most of the northeast–southwest line of the coombe is not visible from the barrow. The site of the destroyed Woodford barrow (no. 26) is particularly interesting. This barrow is one of only two in the study region orientated north–south and is even more unusual in that, unlike the other north–south barrow (Amesbury 42), it has been built across the contours.

The Woodford barrow is furthermore located on a steep south–north slope running down into the coombe. It is the only long barrow from which the Beacon Hill Ridge is *not* visible. The view from the barrow location itself is very restricted in all directions except to the east, looking down onto the coombe bottom. The barrow is located at the point at which a whole series of coombe branches converge from the northeast, northwest and west, with the main coombe running east to join the Avon. The coombes here, compared with many of those found elsewhere in the central and northern parts of the study area, are deeply incised in the landscape. This seems to be a clear instance of a common pattern where the barrow is located within the coombe system at the point where it dissects and branches. This barrow is peculiarly isolated (2.50km from the nearest barrow at Lake): no other barrows are inter-visible with it, nor is the Beacon Hill Ridge in sight.

Considering a more generalised relationship between long barrows and the coombe systems, the sight-lines along coombes running down to the Avon are visible from 11 barrows (41%). Coombes draining towards the River Till are visible from only three barrows (11%) while parts of the Stonehenge Bottom/Lake system, which eventually joins the Avon, are visible from a further eight (30%). By contrast, the watery course of the River Avon itself is only visible from the Bulford long barrow, which is not only the closest to it but the only long barrow currently visible from the Avon itself.

Sometimes the long barrows appear sky-lined in the landscape when seen from the perspective of moving along the coombes. Thus the barrow to the south of Stonehenge (no. 23) appears very prominent when seen from the point at which a western-running coombe branches off from Stonehenge Bottom. In relation to distant views of the coombe systems from the majority of the barrows, the most significant factor might have been not any specific or individualised relationship between barrow and coombe (except in a few cases discussed above) but where the coombe branches went. Additionally, almost all connect up with the River Avon.

Relationships with other Early and Middle Neolithic monuments

The lack of any close relationship between any of the long barrows and the Lesser Cursus has already been noted. This monument would have been visible from only six barrows (Figure 2.3: nos 9, 10, 11, 20, 22 and 23), all of which are 1km–3km or more distant from it (Table 2.4). This contrasts with the visibility of four barrows from the western and eastern terminals of the Greater Cursus, with the location of a fifth at its eastern terminal. The Greater Cursus itself would have been visible from at least nine barrows (Figure 2.3: nos 4, 9–11, 16–17, 20, 22 and 23). Although four barrows lie to the east of Robin Hood's Ball causewayed enclosure, none of these are orientated towards the causewayed enclosure and it is visible from only the nearest one of these (Figure 2.1: no. 14).

However, Robin Hood's Ball is (or would have been) visible from more distant barrows, including that at

Larkhill, Amesbury 42 at the eastern terminal of the Greater Cursus, that at Lake and one on Winterbourne Stoke Down (Figure 2.1: nos 9–11, 16 and 20). So, whilst Robin Hood's Ball is not visible from most of the barrows in its immediate vicinity, it could be seen from other barrows located up to 4km–5km distant from it to the south and the east. This is exactly the same kind of relationship that is found among the long barrows themselves: more distant barrows may be inter-visible while barrows located quite close to each other may not be.

There is an enormous difference between the degree of visibility of the Greater Cursus in the landscape when seen from the long barrows and that of Robin Hood's Ball and the Lesser Cursus (Table 2.4). This is, of course, in part because, in comparison with both, the Greater Cursus extends over such a great distance through the middle of the landscape. However, while the Lesser Cursus runs along a ridge-top, only the western and eastern terminals of the Greater Cursus lie on high points, of which only the eastern terminal on King Barrow Ridge is prominent. The location and orientation of the Lesser Cursus, running along the axis of a ridge-top, is typical for that of the mounds of some long barrows, whereas the size, scale and landscape location of the Greater Cursus is utterly different and far more complex.

Aside from the recently discovered example beneath Amesbury 7 round barrow (Bowden *et al.* 2015: 26), only two long barrows occur within 1km of the site of Stonehenge (Figure 2.3: nos 22 and 23) which is visible from both of these, as well as from four more distant barrows (nos 9–11 and 20). It is of interest to note the presence of one probable long barrow and a possible long mortuary enclosure near to the Avon, very close to the later course of the Avenue (Figure 2.1: nos 7 and 8). The site of the Durrington Walls henge would have been visible from only two barrows (nos 4 and 24).

Mortuary practices

The overriding preservational ethos in current heritage management practices is such that virtually our only knowledge of the use of these barrows is based on antiquarian investigations well over a hundred years old. There have only been five modern investigations of long barrows within the study area, all of destroyed barrows and structures: of part of the ditch of Amesbury 42 long barrow at the eastern end of the Greater Cursus (see Chapter 3; Richards 1990: 96–109), of ditch sections of Winterbourne Stoke 71 and 86 (Roberts *et al.* 2018), of destroyed barrows at Netheravon Bake (Richards 1990: 265) and Woodford (Harding and Gingell 1986; Carton *et al.* 2016), and of a long mortuary enclosure on Normanton Down (Vatcher 1961).

The evidence that we have indicates an extraordinarily wide range of mortuary practices. At Amesbury 42, excavations by Thurnam in 1866 found the skeletons of two infants and a crouched adult inhumation, and animal bones including an ox skull (Thurnam 1869). Excavations in 1983 across the eastern ditch and mound edge found evidence of flint-knapping debris in the ditch, and sherds of Beakers, Collared Urns and Late Bronze Age vessels (Richards 1990: 96–109). Further excavations by the SRP in 2008 recovered Neolithic human remains and ditch deposits including part of an antler pick dating construction to 3520–3350 cal BC (see Chapter 3).

Excavations of a destroyed barrow at Netheravon Bake demonstrated at least two constructional phases, the first of them dating to 3780–3350 cal BC (Richards 1990: 259, 265). Thurnam reported finding a primary deposit of two skeletons, one with a cleft skull, at ground level at the south-southeast end of Netheravon 6 (Figure 2.1: no. 12).

Figheldean 31 (no. 14) was also excavated by Thurnam, who reports a stratum of black earth near ground level, a primary single skeleton and a secondary crouched skeleton with a Beaker from the southeast end. The primary burial comprised the disarticulated bones of a single individual deposited in a small pile, which had been carefully arranged so that two tibiae were placed side by side but in opposing directions (Thurnam 1869: 184; Cunnington 1914: 39; Thomas 1999: 170).

Winterbourne Stoke 53 (no. 16) was opened by Sir Richard Colt Hoare who reported a primary cremation mixed with chalky marl, covered with a large pile of flints at the eastern end. Further east there were two cists containing large quantities of wood ash (Cunnington 1914: 207).

The long barrow at Winterbourne Stoke Crossroads (no. 17; Winterbourne Stoke 1) was dug into by Thurnam in 1863, who reported a primary male flexed inhumation with a flint implement at the eastern end, and six 'secondary' burials (Thurnam 1869). The primary burial has been dated to 3630–3360 cal BC (Susan Greaney pers. comm.).

Multiple inhumations are recorded elsewhere at monuments in the study area. Excavations at Wilsford 34 (Figure 2.1: no. 18) by Thurnam found five secondary burials and a Beaker. Cunnington and Colt Hoare's excavations at Wilsford 30 (Figure 2.1: no. 21) discovered a 'primary deposit' of four skeletons deposited together at the eastern end (Hoare 1812: 206). Three skeletons were discovered by Thurnam within Amesbury 14 (no. 23), two of which had cleft skulls, and there were two further secondary burials (Cunnington 1914: 382).

Excavations by Vatcher and Vatcher of the destroyed Woodford long barrow (no. 26) suggest that a timber mortuary house was probably situated at the lower northern end of the mound. This was possibly associated with human remains covered with a pile of flints. These bones derive from a minimum of three adults and a juvenile (Carton *et al.* 2016). Prior to the construction of the mound a group of six large pits had been dug on the site (Harding and Gingell 1986: 15*ff*).

Faith Vatcher (1961) also excavated a so-called long mortuary enclosure – assumed by some such as Atkinson to be an excarnation site for bodies whose bones were later to be deposited in long barrows (Atkinson 1951) – on the southern slopes of Normanton Down (Figure 2.1: no. 25), 100m to the south of the Wilsford 30 long barrow (no. 21). This enclosure was defined by a discontinuous ditch with an internal bank. There was an entrance through the structure at the southeast end. Eleven antler picks (one of them dated to 3520–2910 cal BC; BM-505; 4510±103 BP; Richards 1990: 259) were found in the ditch but no human remains. Another such possible long 'mortuary enclosure' (no. 7) is visible on aerial photographs a short distance to the south of another probable destroyed long barrow, Amesbury 140 (no. 8), to the west of Amesbury.

Discussion: barrow zones and groups

Previous accounts of the long barrows in the Stonehenge landscape have attempted to consider them in terms of 'zones of activity'. Richards (1990) suggests a zone of strong 'domestic' activity characterised by the presence of many flint scatters, concentrations of ground flint axes, and pits with animal bones and Early Neolithic pottery on high ground to the east of his study area (in our study area, this is immediately to the west of the Avon and to the east of Stonehenge Bottom). These include the Coneybury Anomaly on Coneybury Hill (Richards 1990: 40–61) and pit groups on King Barrow Ridge and on the Vespasian's Camp spur (*ibid.*: 65; see Figure 1.3), in contrast to a concentration of funerary monuments to the west. This distinction between an eastern domestic and a western funerary zone is followed by Bradley (1993). By contrast, Thomas has suggested a northern zone and a southern zone, marked out by the presence of the Greater Cursus that would 'inhibit the movement of people and livestock between north and south' (Thomas 1999: 171).

North of the Cursus, Thomas regards the landscape as being dominated by Robin Hood's Ball, associated with the 'exotic, distant and marginal', together with the long barrows near to it. The group of long barrows to the south of the Greater Cursus are regarded by him as more closely associated with localised 'domestic' activities. He suggests that this group may be earlier in date, with those around Robin Hood's Ball being constructed later.

Exon *et al.* (2000: 39) suggest three distinct groups of barrows in the Stonehenge landscape: a northern group of four barrows in the vicinity of Robin Hood's Ball 'linked visually' to the Knighton and Larkhill long barrows, a southern group around the head of Wilsford Bottom, and finally a group of three barrows to the north of Amesbury on either side of the Avon. In our analysis we agree with their first two groups but would define a third group of six barrows, intermediate between the two and associated with the Greater Cursus. Their third group can be questioned as it includes a supposed long barrow to the south of Woodhenge, now better interpreted as conjoined round barrows (RCHME 1979: 1), but excludes Durington 76, to the west of Woodhenge, found by the RCHME when recording parchmarks (Figure 2.1: no. 24; Field 2008: fig. 5.2; Bowden *et al.* 2015: fig. 4.14). These fall into a riverine distribution alongside the River Avon.

The long barrows are unevenly scattered across the landscape, and occur in a very wide variety of different locations. Three coherent groupings or closely structured clusters of barrows are, however, possible to define in terms of a fine-grained analysis of their relationship to each other, the Greater Cursus and the landscape. These comprise 18 of the monuments (67%). As regards the rest, our analysis suggests very strongly that the choices of their specific locations were contingent on, and heavily improvised in relation to, a wide variety of different factors including their localised relationships to coombe systems, ridges and spurs, and the movements of the sun at important points in the year; such factors also relate to the locations of the barrows found in the three groups that we have defined.

The variability apparent from what little we know about the mortuary practices that were taking place in these barrows is similarly apparent in relation to the sizes and individual morphologies of the mounds themselves and the choice of specific barrow locations in the landscape. The only truly unifying factor appears to have been the great significance of the Beacon Hill Ridge, visible from all but one of the long barrows in the study area.

Quite clearly, there was no overall Early Neolithic 'plan' or 'template' at work with regard to where best one might locate a barrow in this landscape and, while the regular spacing along the River Avon may point to discrete social territories (as with those along the River Wylye to the west; Field 2008: 43, fig. 4.6), those situated within the Stonehenge environs are more difficult to explain in this respect. Concomitantly, the notion that a single barrow or groups of barrows might have defined discrete social territories is not possible to maintain.

The orientation and positioning of some barrows do seem to have been specifically related to the presence of others and, in particular, to the three massive rectilinear mounds at Knighton, Winterbourne Stoke Crossroads and at the eastern end of the Greater Cursus (Figure 2.1: nos 9, 11 and 17). It is also the case that where some barrows could best be seen from in the landscape was as significant as what might, or might not, be visible from them. Others were related to the Greater Cursus itself.

Surprisingly, no very close relationship seems to have existed between the barrows and the Lesser Cursus or Robin Hood's Ball causewayed enclosure. In terms of topography, however, the over-riding factor in the drainage pattern is that here the Rivers Avon and Till momentarily move closer together, so that social groups and monument construction set along their flanks were inevitably forced to inhabit and coexist in the restricted interfluve between them.

2.1.2. Causewayed enclosures in the Early Neolithic landscape *c.* 3800–3400 BC

Two causewayed enclosures occupy the northern part of the Stonehenge landscape (Figure 2.1). They are set almost 4km apart and the northwesterly example, Robin Hood's Ball, is located some 60m higher than its recently discovered partner at Larkhill (see below). The former is set on the upper levels of the Till drainage while the Larkhill enclosure is set above a coombe leading northeastwards towards the River Avon: only part of the latter has currently been excavated (Thompson *et al.* 2017).

Robin Hood's Ball

Robin Hood's Ball comprises two circuits of interrupted banks with outer ditches, enclosing an area of 3 ha. Both banks and ditches have been much denuded by ploughing. Roughly 15 causeways are visible across the inner ditch circuit and 22 across the outer ditch circuit. There are no corresponding gaps in the banks (McOmish *et al.* 2002: 32) and there is an external bank around at least the northwestern sector of the outer enclosure. The inner enclosure is roughly ovoid in shape, the outer being much more irregular in form, more of a slack D-shape, with a pronounced curve and change in direction in the outer bank on the western side, perhaps indicating an entrance here. While the long axis of each enclosure is slightly different, both are broadly oriented to the northeast, that is, the direction of midsummer sunrise.

This causewayed enclosure is located on a gentle north–south slope, just below a local high point. If it had been sited immediately to the north, the enclosure would have embraced the flat summit of the hill. Instead, it is deliberately tilted to face towards the south and the landscape around Stonehenge, as if to exclude the northern part of Salisbury Plain and any communities, animals, or supernatural elements that dwelt there; the northern part of the Plain is invisible from the interior of the causewayed enclosure. As if to emphasise this, the major earthworks, including that part of the monument with an external bank, are those in the north.

Looking east from the centre of the inner circuit of ditches and banks, the Beacon Hill Ridge appears on the distant horizon. Battery Hill and Porton Down are visible to the far southeast, and the sites of Stonehenge and Coneybury are visible. Looking south, Newton Barrow Hill, some 10km distant, marks the horizon line, with Yarnbury hill marking the limit of the view to the southwest. To the west-northwest the distant horizon disappears just beyond the perimeter of the outer circuit. The northern horizon is limited to the northern section of the outer circuit. Views out from the monument are roughly equidistant in all directions, giving a strong sense of circularity in the landscape, except to the north and northwest where they are dramatically curtailed by the hill summit beyond.

It is conceivable that some of the gaps in the ditch are aligned on solar/lunar events. The RCHME survey (McOmish *et al.* 2002: 34) depicts a number of causeways at points around the circuit and they are particularly clear on a recent geophysical survey plot (Bayer and Griffiths 2016). There is a small gap facing due southeast in the inner circuit and two slightly off due southeast in the outer circuit. There are also two aligned gaps in the inner and outer circuits facing northwest (midsummer sunset), and gaps in both the inner and outer circuit facing northeast (midsummer sunrise). All of this could indicate that the enclosure preceded Stonehenge in terms of providing an assembly point that incorporated references to astronomical orientations.

There are, however, some problems with such assumptions because both the inner and outer banks are near-continuous in the northern half of each enclosure (south of the parish boundary they are almost levelled by cultivation) and they may originally, therefore, have restricted visibility including across the causeways between ditches. Nevertheless, the earthworks represent the final stage of development of each enclosure and, given that the excavated sections revealed that the ditch had been recut (Thomas 1964), original gaps in the bank could have existed and been subsequently blocked.

It is worth noting that the long axis of the monument is aligned on the contours, much as are the axes of most long barrows. If deliberate, as is thought to be the case for long barrows, of which the majority face the rising sun (Burl 2006: 76), then the implication is that the topography was carefully selected; had Robin Hood's Ball been positioned a little further in either direction, then its contour would have changed. This is quite significant because, on the one hand, the positioning of the monument reflects a desire for harmony within the landscape, with built structures blending in with natural forms and, on the other, it satisfies a dual purpose of providing celestial orientations as well as showing the monument's long profile when seen from the valleys below.

In midsummer the location of the monument would have afforded a view of the sun rising on the distant northeastern horizon, but the setting sun would have disappeared below the outer bank of the northern circuit to the northwest. The broken nature of the causeways means that this monument is permeable in relationship to the landscape beyond, except to the north where the bank circuits appear to have been larger and higher. Robin Hood's Ball would only have been visible and prominent in the surrounding landscape when seen from the south and the east. Set below the hill summit, it is invisible from the north.

From the northern centre of the inner circuit bank, the distant horizon expands dramatically so that it now embraces the Plain to the north. Once inside this bank, this northern horizon disappears. The northern ditch of the outer circuit is positioned precisely at the top of the slope and, beyond it to the north, the land is completely flat with extensive panoramic views. The tilted nature of the position of the enclosure in relation to the hilltop means that it affords a distant view of long barrows such as those at Knighton, Larkhill and Winterbourne Stoke Crossroads. Yet three out of the four long barrows (Figure 2.1: nos 12–13 and 15) in its immediate vicinity cannot be seen.

Robin Hood's Ball is at the approximate centre of a series of six coombe branches, which radiate out from it in almost all directions: to the north, northeast, south, southeast, west and southwest. This is a unique feature of the location of this hill, paralleled only by the relationship of coombe systems to the nearby Knighton/Larkhill ridge. However, in the latter case, all the coombes run so as to join up with the Avon either to the south, north or east. The coombes running down from Robin Hood's Ball are linked both to the Till valley to the west and the Avon to the east. It is a locale that transcends a local sense of place.

Views into the enclosure are very different as you approach it from different directions in the surrounding landscape. From the north, the entire enclosure is only visible when you reach the outer circuit. Before this point, virtually the entire interior is concealed. From the western side, the whole of the interior is only visible from just 60m away. From the southern point of the outer circuit, the whole enclosure is visible. The whole of the outer circuit from the northeast to the north across to the southwest appears sky-lined from here, excluding the world beyond. The northern section of the outer circuit banks disappears from sight when viewed from just 30m downslope to the south.

During our investigation, the banks of the enclosure were marked out with 1m-high flags, the assumption being that this was about their original height, *i.e.* about 1m higher than at present. Looking at the enclosure from the northwest and the east, the outer bank would have effectively prevented any views of both the interior and the inner bank. Approached from the north, the outer bank of Robin Hood's Ball would have only been visible from 100m or less distant. The inner bank would have only been visible from the outer bank. From downslope to the south, as from the west and east, it would not have been possible to see much or any of the interior because of the blocking effect of the outer bank in relation to the character of the hill slope. This contrasts with the internal visibility of Durrington Walls whose entire interior is visible from the southwest (see discussion below).

To the west of Robin Hood's Ball the land at first rises very gently for 75m or so before then dipping down to the west, severely restricting visibility into the interior from this direction. The outer enclosure banks can be seen only from about 200m away from this direction and nothing of the interior. Here there is a row of six gnarled sarsen stones, possibly moved from nearby, but nevertheless indicating that the Robin Hood's Ball area was a local source of this stone. Possibly the three sarsens now found in the northern ditch of the Figheldean 31 long barrow (no. 14) originated from here (McOmish *et al.* 2002: 151–2). The presence of sarsens links together Robin Hood's Ball with the nearest and only inter-visible long barrow, only some 250m distant to the southwest. From the east, the outer enclosure bank is first visible from about 500m away, and from a similar distance to the south.

The enclosure is thus peculiarly discrete and hidden when approached from the immediate landscape surrounding it. It therefore appears to be a place from which one looked out, rather than into, even though it can be seen on the horizon from long distances away elsewhere. It is a monument whose form and meanings could be appreciated only from the inside.

There may have been a particularly close relationship between Robin Hood's Ball and the Lesser Cursus. The Lesser Cursus is situated along the top of a ridge some 2.50km due south of Robin Hood's Ball (Figure 2.3). Looking out from Robin Hood's Ball, the Lesser Cursus would have been prominently sky-lined on the mid-horizon and would undoubtedly have been the dominant monument visible in the landscape. We have already noted that, from the Lesser Cursus looking north, the Robin Hood's Ball enclosure would have been prominent immediately before the northern horizon formed by the top of the hill above it. When freshly constructed, Robin Hood's Ball would have appeared quite dramatic from here and the whole of the interior would have been visible. But this view would have been far too distant to be able to observe in any detail the activities taking place within it. What is interesting is that the Lesser Cursus marks the only point in the surrounding landscape affording a view into the entire enclosure. Equally important is that this is a distant view and, when much closer to the monument, all or much of the interior is completely hidden from view until approaching either the outer bank or the immediate area to the south of the monument.

Limited excavations by Nicholas Thomas (1964) showed evidence for periodic re-cutting of the ditches and that the monument was constructed in an area of open grassland in *3640–3500 cal BC (91% probability; build Robin Hood's Ball*; Whittle *et al.* 2011: 197, fig. 4.51) or *3430–3400 cal BC (4% probability)*. Material found in the ditch fills included pottery with flint temper, probably local, pots tempered with oolitic limestone or shell, probably from 50km to the northwest (Cornwall and Hodges 1964), and one or two bowls tempered with gabbro from Lizard Head in western Cornwall (Peacock 1969). These pots and some of the flintwork are indicative of long-distance contacts and links that are quite typical for causewayed enclosures (Edmonds 1999).

Larkhill causewayed enclosure

This causewayed enclosure was only discovered in 2016 during developer-funded excavations by Wessex Archaeology (Thompson *et al.* 2017). Although only the northeastern part of its circuit has been revealed, we can assume that most of the enclosure lies beneath modern-day woodland that slopes gently to the east and northeast, overlooking coombes that feed into the River Avon north of Durrington. This enclosure faces away from the Stonehenge landscape to its south, from which it would have been completely obscured. It would have dominated the Avon valley on approaches southwards towards the Stonehenge area (Thompson *et al.* 2017: 33) and several long barrows set along the valley's flanks would have been within view. A line of five postholes, one of them cut into a causewayed ditch, points northeast towards one of them, an Early Neolithic long barrow (Figure 2.1: no. 5) near Barrow Clump at Figheldean (*ibid.*: 33–4), while beyond Sidbury Hill provides a prominent backstop. A radiocarbon date places the Larkhill causewayed enclosure's construction around 3750–3650 cal BC (Thompson *et al.* 2017).

2.1.3. The Wilsford Shaft

Just over a kilometre to the southwest of the site of Stonehenge, an extraordinary shaft was discovered during the excavation of a shallow depression about 13m in diameter and surrounded by a bank, thought to be the site of a pond barrow (Ashbee *et al.* 1989). Excavations revealed that at the centre of the depression is a shaft, 2m wide and 30m deep, cut into the chalk. The lowest 2m are permanently waterlogged but the water levels have fluctuated up and down the shaft up to 20m below ground level. The shaft only finally silted up to the top and became invisible by early Roman times and most of the fill seems to have accumulated during the later second and first millennia BC.

The lowest 2m of the shaft is narrower than the rest and was cut with antler picks. This bottom part of the shaft contained remains of a wooden container, radiocarbon-dated to 3640–3120 cal BC (Ashbee *et al.* 1989: 69; Bayliss *et al.* 2012: 313), indicating that the shaft was probably cut initially during the Early–Middle Neolithic and is therefore contemporary with the construction of some of the first monuments in this landscape, earthen long barrows. The shaft was cut in the bottom of a coombe, a western branch of Stonehenge Bottom/Lake Bottom, just to the south of the point at which the coombe bifurcates before terminating to the southwest and northeast of the shaft (Figure 2.1).

What might the significance of this shaft have been? Two main arguments have been proposed: that it was simply a well, on the one hand, or that it had 'ritual' significance with no functional use (see Ashbee *et al.* 1989). However, these two interpretations are not necessarily opposed. A 'ritual' shaft into the ground might, in principle, have been dug anywhere in this landscape, for example on a ridge-top, but this shaft is located in the bottom of a coombe, or dry valley, closest to the water table in that locality. The shaft terminates at the point at which the bottom is permanently waterlogged so its purpose does seem to have been to find and collect water.

It does not take a great leap of the imagination to suggest that this water must have had sacred significance and may have been used in ceremonies conducted at the nearby long barrows (see below) and later at Stonehenge itself. So this may well have been a holy well, the only one known in this landscape. Others might be expected in Stonehenge Bottom, where more recent wells are present (Bowden *et al.* 2015; Field *et al.* 2012) and in the main part of Wilsford Bottom, south of Normanton Down, where ancient fields focus. Square, wood-lined Early Neolithic wells have been found in northern Germany (Tegel *et al.* 2012; Rengert Elburg pers. comm.) but within Britain, aside from flint mine shafts, no other certain shafts have been encountered that reach the water table. The nature of shafts at Eaton Heath in Norfolk (Wainwright 1973) remains disputed.

Yet the immense effort involved in cutting the Wilsford Shaft indicates something further. Like the flint mines, this was a Neolithic voyage of discovery into the earth. Cutting it would have answered a very basic question: what is underneath my feet, the ground on which I stand? It would have answered another question that might have been significant to Neolithic populations: why are the streams in this landscape, the winterbournes, periodically dead? The Neolithic inhabitants, like us, would have been highly likely to recognise the similarity between dry-valley or coombe systems and those valleys in which the water flowed such as the Avon and the Till. Did they once contain permanent water? What happened to it? On the basis of their discovery of water at the base of the Wilsford Shaft and the manner in which the water level could be observed to fluctuate up and down it at different seasons of the year, the shaft's builders might have concluded that the coombe systems crossing this landscape marked the courses of invisible underground rivers that had previously flowed across the land, rivers perhaps associated with the people who had come before, the ancestral dead who might now reside in a watery underworld.

2.1.4. The Early/Middle Neolithic cursus monuments *c.* 3500–3300 BC

The Lesser Cursus

Excavations at the Lesser Cursus have revealed that it was constructed in two phases (Richards 1990: 72–93). In its first phase, it comprised a rectilinear enclosure 220m long and 60m wide, with an internal bank and external ditch. It has a curving west end and a more irregular and open eastern end (see Figure 1.3). Geophysical surveys have indicated the presence of two narrow entrances, about 2m wide, into this enclosure in the approximate centre of the long sides, and the presence of pits scattered inside the Cursus and to the north of its western end (David and Payne 1997: 87–9). In the second phase, it was elongated to the east by a further 200m. The eastern end was left open and not enclosed by banks or ditches. It has a small irregular oval enclosure within it, of uncertain date. Re-dating of an antler rake by the SRP places the construction of the Lesser Cursus's second phase during 3500–3340 cal BC (at 95% confidence; see Table 3.4 and Chapter 3).

Sadly this monument's earthworks have been completely destroyed by ploughing. When built, it was a huge monument. Its rectilinear plan resembles that of the more massive rectilinear long barrows with flanking, external ditches but the western part was more than twice as long, and the eastern extension made it more than four times the size of any long barrow. How might this monument have originally appeared in the landscape?

Like some of the long barrows, it is orientated east-northeast–west-southwest and, similarly, it is also situated on flat ground in the very centre of a ridge-top at the very highest point (115m OD), its linear ditches and banks following the line of the ridge itself through the landscape. Parallel coombes draining into the River Till in the west bound and define this ridge both to the north and the south, with the Till itself curving round and cutting through and terminating the ridge at its western end (Figure 2.3). There is no clearly defined eastern end to this ridge, bounded to the east by coombes. In other words, the ridge is 'open' at the eastern end, just as the Lesser Cursus remains open. The ridge is defined by the 'ditches' of the coombes and the Till on three sides just as the enclosure is formed by its own three ditches.

There thus appears to be a strong and localised mimetic relationship between the monument and the landscape.

From the site of the Lesser Cursus, there are panoramic views: east as far as the Beacon Hill Ridge some 8km distant, west as far as Yarnbury about the same distance away, with similarly extensive views to the south. To the north the view is far more restricted, extending just over 2km to the much higher ground on which Robin Hood's Ball causewayed enclosure is situated (141m OD). From the Lesser Cursus one looks *up* to Robin Hood's Ball and down or across the landscape in other directions. The long axis of the Cursus is best seen from the surrounding landscape from Robin Hood's Ball to the north and from higher points in it to the south such as Oatlands Hill, the higher ground on which the Lake long barrow is situated (Figure 2.3: no. 20), and from Normanton Down. Looking from these directions the linear banks of the monument running along the ridge-top would have appeared quite dramatic and, at these distances of 2km or more, any view of the open interior of the Cursus would have been blocked by its banks.

From a distance, the Lesser Cursus would thus have appeared to resemble a huge rectilinear long barrow of the same form as the Knighton or Winterbourne Stoke Crossroads long barrows. The absence of a mound covering the interior would have become apparent only when visiting it. Unlike the rectilinear long barrows found in this landscape, the Lesser Cursus had a ditch running around the western end. In some respects, the design is similar to that of the Normanton Down long mortuary enclosure, with a ditch and a bank running around the western end and an entrance with some form of portal structure at the east. Like the Lesser Cursus, the Normanton Down enclosure had no internal mound and was open inside. However, the location of the Normanton Down enclosure in the landscape is very different (Figure 2.3: no. 25): a far more discreet and less visible structure, situated on sloping ground along the side of a ridge, that would only have been prominent when seen from the south, and it is, of course, tiny in comparison: a mere 36m long.

The open character of the Normanton Down structure, and the lack of any actual mortuary remains, suggest that it was a place for ceremonies for the living, perhaps closely associated with long barrows in its immediate vicinity to the north and perhaps further afield to the west and south. As has already been noted, the nearest long barrow to the Lesser Cursus is Winterbourne Stoke 53 (no. 16), situated over 1km away to the southwest.

The Lesser Cursus was an impressive enclosure possibly connected with ceremonies for the living rather than for the dead. The open eastern end of the second phase of the monument suggests ceremonial movement along it from the east and towards the western, completely enclosed end of the monument. This contrast between the western enclosure with narrow side-entrances and the open character of the eastern end indicates perhaps both differential access (restricted and unrestricted) into the interiors and a different character to the ceremonial activities taking place inside both. The landscape location of the Lesser Cursus indicates that the character of these activities may be much more strongly linked to activities taking place at Robin Hood's Ball causewayed enclosure to the north than to those associated with the construction and use of the long barrows.

Figure 2.4. Beacon Hill Ridge, looking west from King Barrow ridge

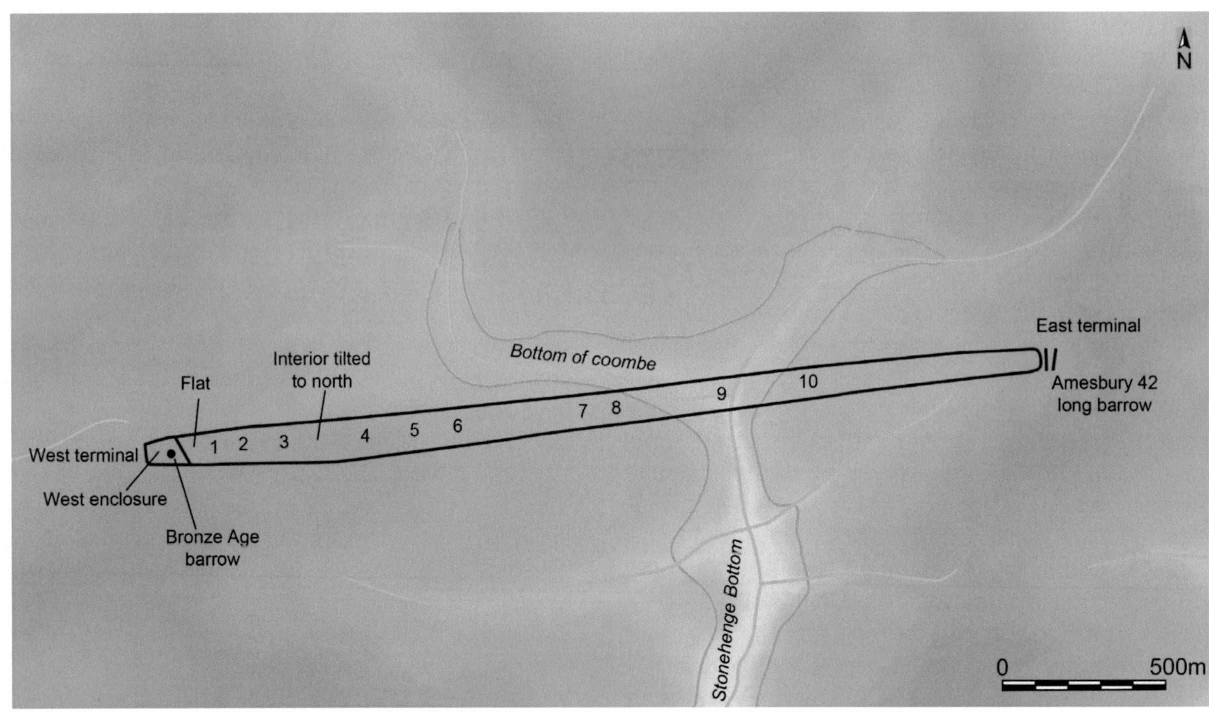

Figure 2.5. The Greater Cursus: points on the west-to-east walk

The Greater Cursus

The Greater Cursus dwarfs the Lesser Cursus. It runs approximately east–west across the western part of centre of the survey area for nearly 3km and is between 100m and 150m wide. The banks are built of chalk rubble derived from external ditches. The northern bank is comparatively straight while the southern bank is slightly more irregular (see figures in Chapter 3).

The far eastern terminal of the Cursus butts against the Amesbury 42 long barrow. This east end narrows so that its width matches the terminals of the Amesbury 42 ditches, strongly suggesting that the long barrow is earlier and that the Greater Cursus was constructed so as to run up to and terminate at it (even though their radiocarbon dates for construction cannot be distinguished: see Marshall *et al.* in Chapter 3). It should be noted, though, that the western terminal of the Cursus also narrows dramatically to a similar length (Pearson and Field 2011). Nevertheless, the barrow would once have been an impressive feature on the skyline, perhaps rising up just beyond the terminal at the Cursus' eastern end.

The general east–west orientation of the Cursus has long been held to suggest a relationship to equinoctial sunrise and sunset, albeit astronomically inaccurate (Burl 2006: 84–5), and perhaps what is more significant is that it is aligned directly towards the highest summit areas of the Beacon Hill Ridge, 6km distant from its eastern end (Figure 2.4). Significantly, the Lesser Cursus is not aligned on this ridge. It rather follows the general alignment of the ridge-top on which it is located. The form of the Lesser Cursus suggests an east–west axis of movement along it. The presence of the long barrow and Beacon Hill Ridge to the east of the Greater Cursus both suggest that ceremonial movement along this monument was probably, instead, from the west to the east.

Unlike the Lesser Cursus, the Greater Cursus is aligned eastwards towards Beacon Hill Ridge, which must have had great significance in relation to the monument. If one walked from west to east along the eastern part of the Cursus, both the long barrow and the Cursus terminal (both destroyed) would have created a blocking effect in relation to Beacon Hill Ridge which would only have been visible (or prominent) on passing up and over or beyond them. The eastern end of the Cursus is on a localised high point at the northern end of King Barrow Ridge, with the land sloping away to the north to a shallow coombe – the far northern and eastern arm of Stonehenge Bottom. The Cursus thus terminates here where the most prominent coombe in this entire landscape rises. Beyond the eastern terminal, the land dips down very gently towards Durrington 76 (beside Woodhenge) and then to the River Avon, neither of which are visible. In terms of the river course, the Cursus itself is 'aligned' on a significant, huge meander or loop (Figure 2.3).

Inside the eastern terminal, looking west, the interior of the Cursus is level across its width but slopes gently to the west and towards Stonehenge Bottom, which is invisible from here. The interior length can be seen continuously for about 750m before it dips out of sight and rises again to the western terminal, beyond which the High Down Ridge is visible in the distance. This is indistinct compared with the dramatic profile of Beacon Hill and suggests, as Exon *et al.* (2000) point out, that the Cursus may have been primarily meant to be encountered and experienced from the western end (where no long barrows or other Neolithic monuments occur) to the eastern end. Neolithic monuments visible in the far distance from the eastern end include both Winterbourne Stoke long barrows (nos 16 and 17), the long barrow at Lake (no. 20) and the Normanton Down long barrow (no. 22).

Like the Dorset Cursus (Green 2000), the Greater Cursus at Stonehenge may have been constructed in two stages: an earlier eastern section extending down to Stonehenge Bottom and a later western extension terminating at Fargo Plantation (see Figure 3.1). Here it is interesting to note the bipartite division of the Lesser Cursus and its short length. It is also of interest to note that the western terminal of the Greater Cursus was built on the ridge-top at precisely the same point longitudinally, where the Lesser Cursus 'begins', 500m to the north.

Walking down the centre of the Cursus: from east to west

(i) The eastern section of the Cursus

The slope to the west is very gentle and, after a few hundred metres, levels out entirely so that the interior of the monument is completely flat (north–south and west–east). Outside the Cursus, the land rises gently to the south but falls to the north towards the northeastern arm of Stonehenge Bottom. This section of the Cursus parallels the directionality of the coombe to the north (Figure 2.5) that is itself invisible from the centre of the monument. After 700m, the interior is still virtually level and the base of Stonehenge Bottom is not visible. Ahead, the visual 'end' of the Cursus appears circular, dipping away without any perceived defining cross-bank. To the south there is another slight coombe so the Cursus itself now parallels two coombes, one on either side of it. The base of Stonehenge Bottom first comes into view about 200m distant, but only on its northern side, the southern part still being concealed from view.

The great width of the Cursus, *c.* 120m, means that despite the original height of the banks you would still have been able to see over them from the centre of the monument to parts of the wider landscape beyond. They would only have restricted the view to the immediate vicinity beyond them and not to the rising ground some distance away to either the north or the south. What the banks would definitely have concealed and shut out would be any view to the coombes paralleling this part of the Cursus to the north and south, and the only coombe visible would be Stonehenge Bottom across which one would cross. This 'shutting out' and 'slighting' of the coombe systems has direct parallels with the relationship of the Avenue to the coombes (see Chapter 9).

Moving along this stretch of the Cursus, all the distant long barrows to the south and west rapidly slip out of sight, one by one, but Robin Hood's Ball remains in view as does Stonehenge. All of the flat base of Stonehenge Bottom ahead only becomes evident 100m before reaching it. By the eastern edge of the coombe bottom, Stonehenge becomes sky-lined and is most impressive. Both Cursus terminals are out of view but the round barrow of later date near to the western terminal is sky-lined (Figure 2.5).

In the middle of Stonehenge Bottom, the tips of the trilithons remain just visible. All other monuments have disappeared and one's entire view of the landscape is restricted except looking northwards up Stonehenge Bottom itself. The coombe here, however, is relatively wide and one does not feel the sense of confinement that occurs in other coombe systems. Nevertheless, the low elevation means that the eastern part of the Cursus is almost invisible from here, one's view extending to no more than 50m up the slope. The Cursus appears far wider than it is long, and the linear character of the monument is not apparent at all, only hinted at by the presence of the banks. The view westwards is considerably more extensive.

At the point at which the Cursus crosses Stonehenge Bottom, the coombe is peculiarly wide because it is here that the branches running from the northwest and northeast merge into a single coombe. The orientation of the Cursus to the west now follows the line of the coombe bottom of the northwestern branch. Proceeding across the coombe bottom, the western horizon becomes more and more curtailed. The military sewage works placed in the Bottom have partly obscured the Cursus earthworks, although a bulbous portion of the southern bank provides hints of an entrance and there are several interrupted portions of bank a little further west. Whether these gaps are original is uncertain. Some may relate to recent agricultural or military activity, others potentially to natural drainage. There is a gap of *c.* 50m in the northern bank in the Bottom, evidently original (Pearson and Field 2011; Bowden *et al.* 2015: 21), the only place where, with any certainty, entry could be obtained. Geophysical surveys (*e.g.* Darvill *et al.* 2013) also indicate that the banks and ditches continue here despite the potentially boggy nature of the ground, prone to seasonal flooding.

(ii) The western section of the Cursus

As noted above, the eastern end of the western section occupies the base of a coombe, the northwestern branch of Stonehenge Bottom. Here the land rises to the north and the south on either side of the coombe, and the Cursus banks for the first couple of hundred metres follow the line of the coombe. The visual field is totally restricted because of this, and effectively the cultural monument and the coombe are one and the same. The northern Cursus bank is here almost superfluous in defining the monument except on the south side. The southern bank was constructed along the bottom of the coombe whereas the northern counterpart follows the natural topography of the side of the coombe. The coombe then extends to the northwest, while both banks and ditches continue westwards, effectively cutting diagonally across it.

After *c.* 350m, the western terminal ahead remains invisible but, just to its east, the later round barrow (Amesbury G56) within the Cursus can be seen. Views to the south and north are constricted by the rising land. The interior of the Cursus has changed enormously and is now on a south–north slope with the coombe bottom beyond to the north. Robin Hood's Ball appears again on the northern horizon, and the Cursus has a distinct incline across the interior and is markedly different from the eastern half. The coombe opens up to the north, allowing for more extensive views in this direction, contrasting with the south side where the view is restricted to the southern bank.

The Cursus now climbs steadily up a shallow east-to-west slope. In the middle of the open corridor through Fargo Plantation (trees still stand here to the north and south of the Cursus), glimpses of a wider landscape start to come into view. The relict boundaries of Fargo Plantation within the Cursus corridor are R1 and M2 on Figures 2.6–2.7. Up to this point, the visual field west along the course of the Cursus has become successively shorter and shorter and is always limited, extending only as far as the round barrow, with the terminal remaining out of sight and nothing indicating its presence. The slope levels out 50m to the east of the barrow. The western terminal itself becomes visible *c.* 200m distant from it, and the landscape opens up to the west beyond it. Views to the north are limited to the ridge across which the Lesser Cursus runs, and to the south by rising ground. Immediately beyond the western terminal, the land begins to drop away and the Lesser Cursus becomes sky-lined to the north. The only long barrow visible is the northern of the Winterbourne Stoke pair (no. 16).

Walking down the centre of the Cursus: from west to east

From the western terminal looking east, the entire length of the Cursus is visible except where it crosses Stonehenge Bottom. Beyond the eastern terminal, part of the profile of the long barrow (Amesbury 42) might have been seen, with the Beacon Hill Ridge beyond (Figure 2.4). The Cursus itself appears to be aligned on the third summit area of the ridge. From both terminals, the monument appears divided into two parts by Stonehenge Bottom.

The land drops away gradually from the western terminal to the east along the course of the Cursus. It gradually rises to the north towards the Lesser Cursus and to the south. At the western terminal, both Stonehenge and Coneybury, both later sites, are in the field of view. The whole length of the Lesser Cursus would have been sky-lined to the north and northwest. Robin Hood's Ball is also visible on the skyline to the north. A number of other long barrows can (or could) be visible from here: Winterbourne Stoke 53 (behind the walker, to the west) and Knighton and Larkhill to the east (nos 16, 11 and 10).

The flat ground of the terminal area breaks to a gentle slope 50m to the west of Fargo Plantation's current edge. Walking down the Cursus, the ground surface of the site of Stonehenge disappears and, shortly afterwards, the stone monument goes out of sight (Figure 2.5: point 1) and then Coneybury disappears about 150m further to the east (Figure 2.5: 2; Coneybury is marked on Figure 1.3). After passing Fargo Plantation the character of the Cursus interior changes from a simple west-to-east slope to a more complex ground surface where the land also dips to the north, running down to a shallow coombe head, just to the north of the northern Cursus bank and ditch, a western branch of Stonehenge Bottom.

Robin Hood's Ball soon slips out of sight as one walks east down the slope (Figure 2.5: 3). Gradually the southern bank of the Cursus becomes sky-lined from the centre of the monument, blocking out any view beyond it to the south, and the eastern slope flattens off, with the ground tilting only in a northerly direction. Views out of and beyond the Cursus are only to the north.

Robin Hood's Ball comes into view again (Figure 2.5: 4). The western terminal is now well out of sight. Looking east, there is the near horizon of King Barrow Ridge and the distant horizon beyond is the Beacon Hill Ridge. Further along (Figure 2.5: 5), the Coneybury ridge reappears for about 70m, together with the tips of the Stonehenge trilithons, and then slips out of sight again (Figure 2.5: 6). Now the Cursus runs parallel to the coombe to the north, and the slope of the interior downwards from south to north becomes more pronounced. The northern Cursus bank effectively excludes the coombe as it runs east, and any view to the south beyond the Cursus would have been effectively blocked out by the original height of the earthen bank.

There is a distinct northern bias to the Cursus along this stretch, in the manner in which the interior tilts down to the north, affording views of the landscape beyond and along the adjacent coombe. The full extent of Stonehenge Bottom comes into view (Figure 2.5: 7). The only visible Neolithic monuments are all to the north: Robin Hood's Ball, the Lesser Cursus and (probably) the Knighton and Larkhill long barrows. Robin Hood's Ball slips out of sight again (Figure 2.5: 8) and the line of the coombe to the north becomes more pronounced and starts to swing into the path of the Cursus.

There is now a distinct change in the character of the Cursus as it approaches Stonehenge Bottom. As this happens, the wider landscape and all the other Neolithic monuments in it disappear from view. Stonehenge Bottom itself becomes the major orientation and reference point as one enters the enclosed world of the coombe. The sight to the east, of the Cursus banks climbing the slope beyond the coombe, effectively asserts the significance of the monument over the power of the natural line of the coombe. It incorporates part of it but goes beyond it.

After point 8, the centre of the Cursus runs along and incorporates the coombe branch running into Stonehenge Bottom. Its banks envelop the coombe itself and the coombe and the monument become one. Walking along the coombe bottom, the banks maintain their direction but the overall effect of bank crossing coombe is disorientating because of the difference between the ceremonial architecture of the monument and the natural 'architecture' of the flow of the line of the coombe. On reaching Stonehenge Bottom itself, this tension is resolved with the banks rising up ahead west–east and the main coombe system now running north–south.

The Cursus crosses Stonehenge Bottom at the highly significant point where two coombe branches merge into Stonehenge Bottom. Here the entire landscape is excluded. Neolithic passage across Stonehenge Bottom may have involved crossing a seasonally flooding winterbourne stream. The eastern terminal, King Barrow Ridge and Beacon Hill Ridge are all out of view. Only the Cursus banks are seen to the sides and ahead to the east, rising up out of the coombe and towards the sky. Walking into Stonehenge Bottom, the eastern horizon becomes shorter and shorter, and the slope ahead more and more dominant, rising like a great rampart.

Crossing Stonehenge Bottom (Figure 2.5: 9), there is only one distant reference point visible in the landscape: Rox Hill which is situated next to the point at which the coombe system itself joins the Avon (Figure 2.3). On reaching the eastern side of Stonehenge Bottom, a vista of the Cursus behind to the west opens up as far as the Bronze Age barrow a short distance to the east of the western terminal, which remains out of sight. The view to the east is limited to about 20m. Gradually climbing the slope, the eastern terminal comes into view (Figure 2.5: 10).

The course of the Cursus gradually flattens off to a gentle east–west slope which continues to the terminal, and Robin Hood's Ball comes into view again. There is no south–north dip of the interior at this eastern end which is similar in this respect to the initial stretch to the east of the western terminal. Walking up the slope, the eastern terminal reappears after *c.* 200m but Beacon Hill Ridge remains obscured until the terminal itself is reached.

Although this is now impossible to verify in the field, there may have been an important visual contrast between the asymmetry of the Amesbury 42 long barrow profile (long axis orientated north–south with perhaps a higher southern end) and the formal squared-off symmetry of the terminal bank itself. In turn, the long barrow when seen in profile from the west (high-south : low-north) reverses the profile of Beacon Hill beyond to the east (high-north: low-south). Such a dramatic reversal or inversion in relationships between long barrow profiles and Beacon Hill occurs nowhere else and, indeed, the north–south orientation of Amesbury 42 long barrow is almost unique in the study area. The social and symbolic significance of the eastern terminal of the Cursus is further underlined by the orientation of the Bulford and Larkhill long barrows towards it (Figure 2.3: nos 4 and 10).

Summary

The most significant points to be made from these descriptions of walking the Greater Cursus in both directions are:

1. The basic symmetry of the Cursus, beginning and ending on inter-visible ridges, descending from either end and crossing a watery coombe – Stonehenge Bottom – roughly at its centre.
2. That it may be conceived in terms of a bipartite division and could have been constructed in two phases, like the Lesser Cursus. If the sequence of construction was the same, the western section would have been earlier, ending at Stonehenge Bottom, with the eastern section added later. If movement along it was part of the purpose, this might originally have been north–south along the coombe, and then east–west along the line of the Cursus slighting and blocking out the western branch of the coombe end.
3. Later movement along the entire, completed Cursus may have been from west to east, ending at the unusually orientated long barrow Amesbury 42 with a dramatic panorama of Beacon Hill Ridge, in which the profiles of ridge and long barrow are inverted.
4. In terms of the wider landscape, the Cursus is: a) centrally positioned in relation to Beacon Hill Ridge, and: b) centrally positioned in relation to the overall distribution of long barrows, a point which has not been sufficiently appreciated in the literature.
5. It seems highly significant that the Cursus crosses Stonehenge Bottom at its far northern end and at a point where this coombe bifurcates to the west and east. Part of the western section of the Cursus follows and then crosses the line of the coombe. As is the case with Durrington Walls, this reinforces the significance of coombes both as important and recognised topographic features of the landscape and as passages of movement.
6. The Greater Cursus may well be later in date than the Lesser Cursus (although their radiocarbon dates are indistinguishable; see Chapter 3) and might have superseded the use of that monument, which was possibly abandoned without ever being finished. The Lesser Cursus, running along an undifferentiated ridge-top, was in the 'wrong' place in terms of the overall symbolic and social significance of the landscape. It could not be extended to cut across or connect with coombe systems that were of the utmost importance. In an alternative scenario, the two cursus monuments might have formed a contemporary pairing to mirror the pair of causewayed enclosures of Robin Hood's Ball and Larkhill. It may be significant that where the Greater Cursus crosses Stonehenge Bottom, the coombe bifurcates with arms leading northwest and northeast towards the respective causewayed enclosures. It is worth recording that the northwestern arm no longer appears continuous on the ground as a vast amount of military paraphernalia from the nearby camp was buried here when the camp was bulldozed and landscaped over. Contours that appear on modern maps are not original.
7. It is evident that the Cursus earthworks formed a formidable barrier to north–south movement and stock in particular would have needed to be escorted via the respective river valley slopes.

Comparing the Lesser and the Greater Cursus

If we contrast, in a general way, these two cursus monuments, we find that there are enormous differences between them in their relationship to the landscape and to other monuments, with only a few basic similarities. The Lesser Cursus runs along a ridge-top bounded by coombes to the north and south. It follows or has a mimetic relationship to the landscape. By contrast, the Greater Cursus runs between high points, incorporating and then crossing a coombe system. Rather than following the lie of the land, it deliberately slights or crosses it as, quite literally, a monumental imposition. The Lesser Cursus is a 'dry' monument associated with the sky. The Greater Cursus is a 'wet' monument at its approximate centre. The experience of walking the

Lesser Cursus is rather static and unchanging, with panoramic views from the centre. The experience of walking the Greater Cursus is constantly changing and, for most of its course, its chosen position effectively excludes the landscape to the south.

The most significant monument in the landscape beyond the Lesser Cursus is Robin Hood's Ball causewayed enclosure, a monument with which it might have been intimately linked. There is a similarly close relationship between the Greater Cursus and Larkhill, although this causewayed enclosure's positioning on an east-facing slope might well have obscured it from any part of the Greater Cursus. The orientational focus of long barrows, in relation to the terminal ends of the Greater Cursus, has no counterpart in relation to the Lesser Cursus, which itself might suggest an earlier date for the lesser monument. While the propitious direction to walk the Lesser Cursus was in all probability from east to west, the Greater Cursus reverses this. Passage was from west to east and towards Beacon Hill Ridge.

The utterly different experiential effects of these monuments may be held to suggest a very different relationship to the landscape. The Lesser Cursus has a strong mimetic relationship to the landscape, in a similar fashion to some of the long barrows aligned along ridges and high points. By contrast, the Greater Cursus is an imposition of cultural form, a massive monument that slights the topography and imposes itself on what is there; in so doing, it produces a series of contrasting experiential bodily effects in relation to ridges, coombes and monuments beyond it. It thus directs attention towards different component parts of the topography and monuments within the landscape in a manner in which the Lesser Cursus does not, enacting a way of thinking and a way of remembering.

Although the site of the future Stonehenge is visible from Robin Hood's Ball, from the Lesser Cursus, and from the western and eastern ends of the Greater Cursus, it does not appear to be significant at all, and the pathway of the Greater Cursus seems designed to deliberately exclude the landscape to the south and to emphasise the importance of that to the north, where both causewayed enclosures are located.

2.1.5. The first Stonehenge

Stonehenge was first constructed in *3080–2950 cal BC (95% probability; first_stage_1*; see Table 11.7), anything up to 700 years later than the construction of the long barrows, cursus monuments and the Wilsford Shaft. It consisted of a bank with external ditch forming a circular enclosure about 90m across. The ditch was up to 1.60m deep and 4m wide and the bank perhaps up to 2m high: a fairly modest circular enclosure, far smaller in scale and simpler in design than the two causewayed enclosures situated 3km–4km distant to the northeast and northwest. The ditch was, however, dug using the same technique of interconnecting separate pits along its circumference to create a continuous cutting.

Unlike Robin Hood's Ball, this monument was an almost perfect circle, which contrasted utterly with the long linear cursus monuments and the long barrows and long mortuary enclosures. If the former were connected with east–west or west–east processions across the landscape, the architectural form of Stonehenge encouraged circular movement within and around it. This monument had two, probably three, entrances. The widest faced to the northeast; there was a smaller south-facing entrance and, in the south-southwest, a causeway through the ditch, coupled with a stretch of lower bank, may indicate the original position of a third (Cleal *et al.* 1995: 501, fig. 260).

The locations of Robin Hood's Ball and Larkhill causewayed enclosures contrast significantly with that of Stonehenge. Both are situated almost on the top of hills, with commanding views to the south and the northeast respectively. By comparison, views out from Stonehenge are very limited and the visual field out from the monument is very irregular. Robin Hood's Ball could be seen on the distant skyline from here, as could the eastern part of the Greater Cursus and the eastern end of the Lesser Cursus (but possibly not Larkhill causewayed enclosure). Four long barrows were also visible from Stonehenge, the closest (Amesbury 14) to the southwest and, further afield, the Larkhill, Knighton and Amesbury 42 long barrows to the north and northeast (Figure 2.3). A fifth – a small Cranborne Chase-style monument – lay 200m to the southwest, but was later subsumed by a round barrow.

While Robin Hood's Ball and Larkhill are situated on the northwestern and northeastern peripheries of the overall long barrow distribution to the west of the Avon, Stonehenge is more or less at its geographical centre. But most of these barrows were out of sight of the monument, as were most of the Greater and the Lesser Cursus. Robin Hood's Ball and Larkhill seem to have been deliberately located some distance away from the long barrows, occupying spaces that were empty of other earlier monuments. Both occupy significant topographical positions though, at either end of a northwest–southeast ridge. Aside from Beacon Hill, this is the highest hill in the locality, with the huge Knighton barrow located on its highest point. Located in the centre of a landscape associated with ancient ceremony and with the ancestral dead, as marked by the presence of the long barrows, the Stonehenge enclosure itself was used as a cremation cemetery after *3080–2950 cal BC (95% probability; first_stage_1*; see Table 11.7 and Chapters 4, 10 and 11).

2.1.6. Conclusions

The locations chosen for the long barrows within the Stonehenge 'pinchpoint', where the Till and Avon briefly move closer together, were both highly individualised and improvised. Those on the river flanks – the Winterbourne Stoke pair, Bulford, and the levelled example west of Woodhenge – mirrored the riverine arrangement encountered elsewhere (*e.g.* in the Wylye valley to the west; Field 2008: 43, fig. 4.6). Within the Stonehenge environs, however, no overall 'template' can be identified. These were venerated places chosen by individual communities for the collective burial of the ancestral dead. The variability found in terms of the landscape locations chosen is replicated in the orientations, morphology and construction of the mounds themselves. Many are clearly multi-phase monuments used repeatedly, and added to and altered over the course of time. Some will have become, in the course of these events, much more significant landscape markers than initially. Today, where mounds survive, we see the final and last phase of a long period of use and reuse of the same locations.

An important link between all these monuments is the ritually significant Beacon Hill Ridge to the east with its 'jagged' profile, a hill that was itself an inappropriate site for long barrow construction. This ridge must have assumed enormous cosmological significance because of its pebble summits. Pebbles normally associated with the beach and the sea were here, instead, brushing against the sky.

Another connecting link between the barrows is their very close relationship to the course of the coombe systems crossing the landscape and the symbolism and significance of water. This is confirmed by a clustering of some of the barrows in the vicinity of the Wilsford Shaft, which we have suggested might have been a symbolic investigation of a watery underworld.

The ancestral dead buried in the barrows were presenced in dry land intersected by, and with a view to, the coombe lines and, in some cases, down into the coombe bottoms themselves. In terms of the 'conceptualised landscape' (Ashmore and Knapp 1999), we can then envisage three cosmological worlds:

- first, a world of ancestral beings associated with the highest points in the landscape, people who had come before and first inhabited it;
- second, there was an intermediate world populated by the living who presenced their dead in the barrows in a landscape defined by the River Avon, the river of all life, along with a series of occasional watercourses dissecting the landscape around it;
- thirdly, flowing underneath the coombes or dead rivers there was the underworld river system, the domain to which the people buried in the barrows returned.

The long barrows were places where a community's rites took place. By contrast, the cursus monuments were collectively used by all the kin groups, each associated with a barrow. Hence they were huge in comparison and very different in their character and landscape setting. They might have been conceptualised as gigantic versions of the long barrows. They were not sealed but open, and do not appear to have been associated with mortuary rites. Interpretations differ: some focus around longitudinal movement involving games or processions, perhaps even of spirits or animals, during the course of which the cosmological system of domains structuring the world could be reinforced. In contrast, the earthworks would certainly have created barriers and ensured that movement north and south had to detour via the valley slopes on either side. The control of animal access to the interior might have been important, the small entrances perhaps even preventing their entry inside.

The Lesser Cursus was in the wrong place to perform the ritual processions envisaged above; consequently it might have been superseded by the much larger Greater Cursus in which processions could proceed from west to east, crossing the 'dead river' of Stonehenge Bottom and rising up to the top of the King Barrow Ridge, the culminating point being a view towards the Beacon Hill Ridge that would have been dramatically highlighted at equinoctial sunrise.

These activities took place in a linear fashion in a monument that cut across the landscape and did not respect its contours and coombe systems, in contrast to the long barrows that did. In the day-to-day world of the living, people may have walked along the ridge-tops, one of which was monumentalised by the construction of the Lesser Cursus. They could also have followed the sinuous lines of the coombes guiding them through the landscape, between and past the barrows. The cosmological significance of the River Avon and the coombe systems and the structuring of experiential encounters with the Stonehenge landscape was to take on a radically different form later in the Neolithic, with a riverine route to Stonehenge down the River Avon and up the Avenue to the monument (see Chapter 9).

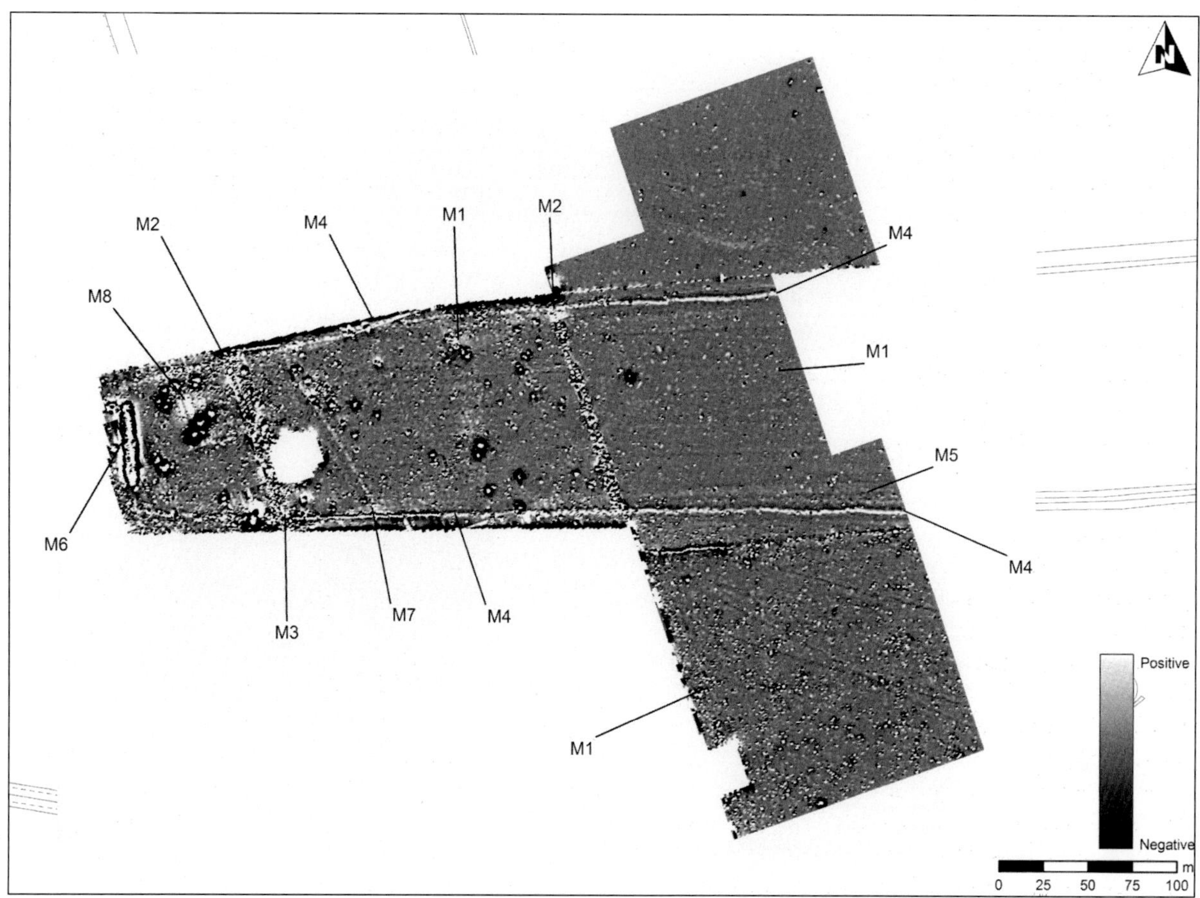

Figure 2.6. Enhanced magnetometer plot (de-striped, de-spiked, clipped and interpolated) of the west end of the Greater Cursus; the area not surveyed is extant round barrow Amesbury G56 (see Figure 3.1)

2.2. Geophysical surveys of the Greater Cursus and Amesbury 42 long barrow

K. Welham, C. Steele, L. Martin and A. Payne

Geophysical surveys of the Stonehenge Greater Cursus were undertaken as part of the SRP in 2006 and 2007 (see also Payne 2006). Earth resistance and magnetometer surveys covered the area between the western terminal of the monument and the east of the current boundary of Fargo Plantation. The eastern terminal of the Cursus and the eastern extent of Amesbury 42 long barrow were surveyed using earth resistance only. These surveys were conducted in order to explore the northern and eastern environs of the small henge monument in Fargo Plantation excavated by Stone (1938; Figure 2.7), to determine the presence of any geophysical anomalies that could be related to the bluestone scatter reported by Stone (1947; see Chapter 4; see also Howard in Pitts 1982; Stone 1938; Thorpe *et al.* 1991) and in order to explore the possible existence of pre-Cursus features such as pits, postholes and tree-throw holes similar to those discovered at other cursus monuments such as Dorchester-on-Thames, Oxfordshire (Whittle *et al.* 1992: 153) and Maxey, Cambridgeshire (Loveday 2006: 128).

The earth resistance surveys were carried out using Geoscan RM15-D earth resistance meters in the twin electrode 0.50m configuration. Readings were taken at 1m intervals along north–south traverses spaced 1m apart over 20m and 30m. The magnetometer survey was undertaken with Bartington Grad601 fluxgate gradiometers. Readings were recorded at 0.25m intervals along north–south traverses spaced 1m apart using the 200 nTm^{-1} range setting of the magnetometer over 30m grids. Numbers in parentheses refer to those on Figures 2.6, 2.7 and 2.8.

A band of Icknield soils crossing the landscape to the south of the Cursus has caused earth resistance anomalies in the data from the eastern end of the monument to become reversed. It is also possible this change in response could have been produced by the ground drying out in the hot weather, but this reversal is not present in the data taken during the same field season from the west of the monument.

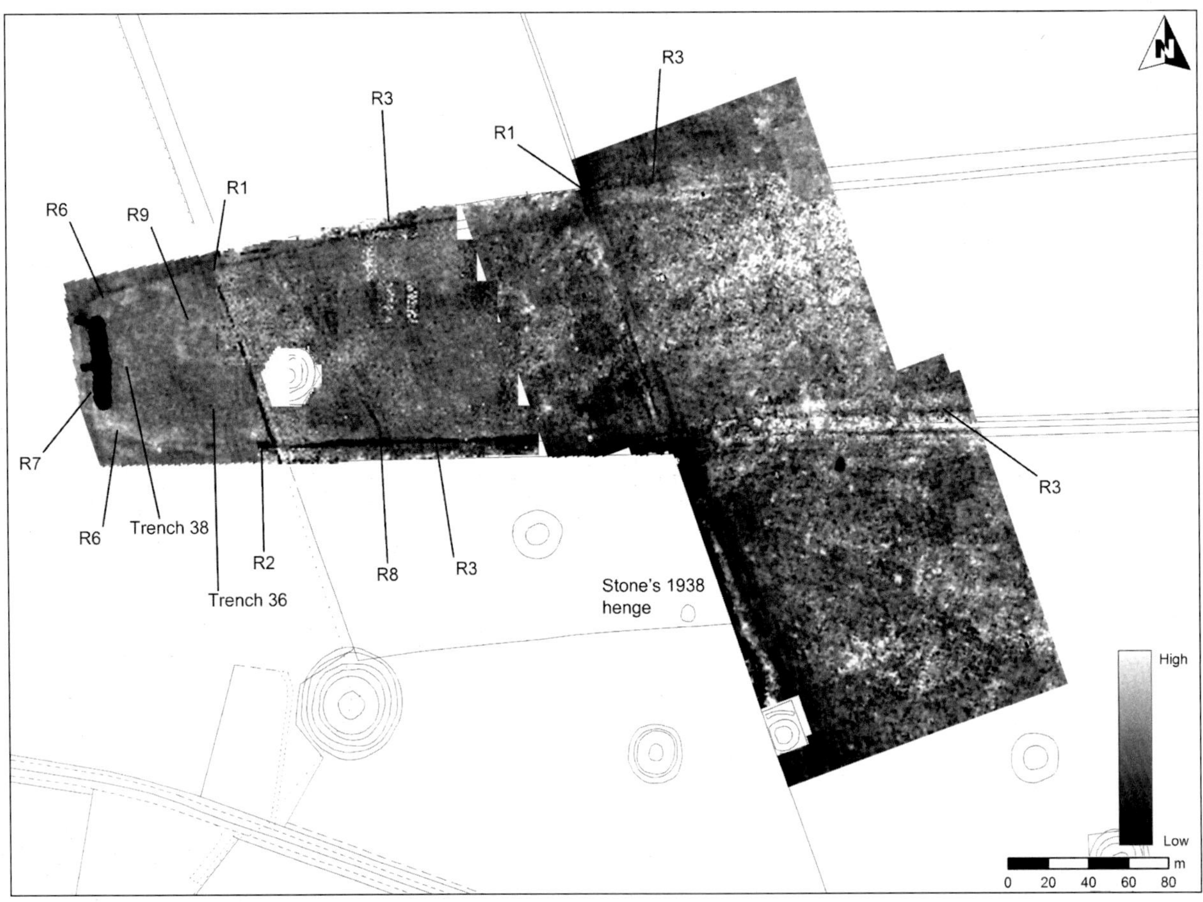

Figure 2.7. Enhanced earth resistance plot (de-striped, de-spiked, clipped and interpolated) of the west end of the Greater Cursus; the area not surveyed is extant round barrow Amesbury G56 (see Figure 3.1)

There has been a substantial amount of modern disturbance in and around the Greater Cursus. In the magnetometer data there are many small, intense dipole responses (M1) south of the Cursus, which are typical of ferrous litter. It is possible this material is connected to previous widespread military activity on Salisbury Plain or to the use of the area as a campsite during some of the Stonehenge Free Festivals (see Chapter 4). The intense dipole responses are larger and more widely spaced where the monument extends through the cleared corridor within Fargo Plantation and it is possible that here they are representative of the former positions of cleared trees and ferrous contamination linked to their removal.

The relict boundaries of the plantation where it crossed the Cursus are also present (R1/M2). Southwest of the western relict boundary is the response to a previous archaeological intervention (R2/M3), probably by Christie, to examine the Cursus bank and ditch (see Chapter 3; Christie 1963; Richards 1990). In both datasets the Cursus boundary shows differential survival and it can be seen that the western end of the monument is highly degraded.

The Greater Cursus ditches (R3/M4) exhibit a stronger response where they were previously covered by Fargo Plantation, suggesting better preservation in this area. It is also of note that the southern ditch appears to exhibit a better state of preservation than the north. Approximately 100m west of the eastern terminal of the Cursus is a gap in the course of the ditch (R4; Figure 2.8) and the terminals either side of the gap appear enlarged. This may be indicative of an original entrance into the monument. A ditch oriented northeast–southwest (R5) crosses the Cursus boundary immediately east of this entrance gap and is likely to represent later activity not associated with the monument. The gap and linear feature are also present in the magnetometry surveys undertaken by Darvill *et al.* (2013) and Gaffney *et al.* (2012), both of which show the enlarged ditch terminals.

The Cursus banks are visible as very ephemeral, intermittent anomalies (R6/M5) that are reflective of their poor state of preservation. The section of reinstated bank at the western terminal of the Cursus (R7/M6) presents a strong response caused by the highly conductive wire mesh that forms a protective covering over the reconstructed

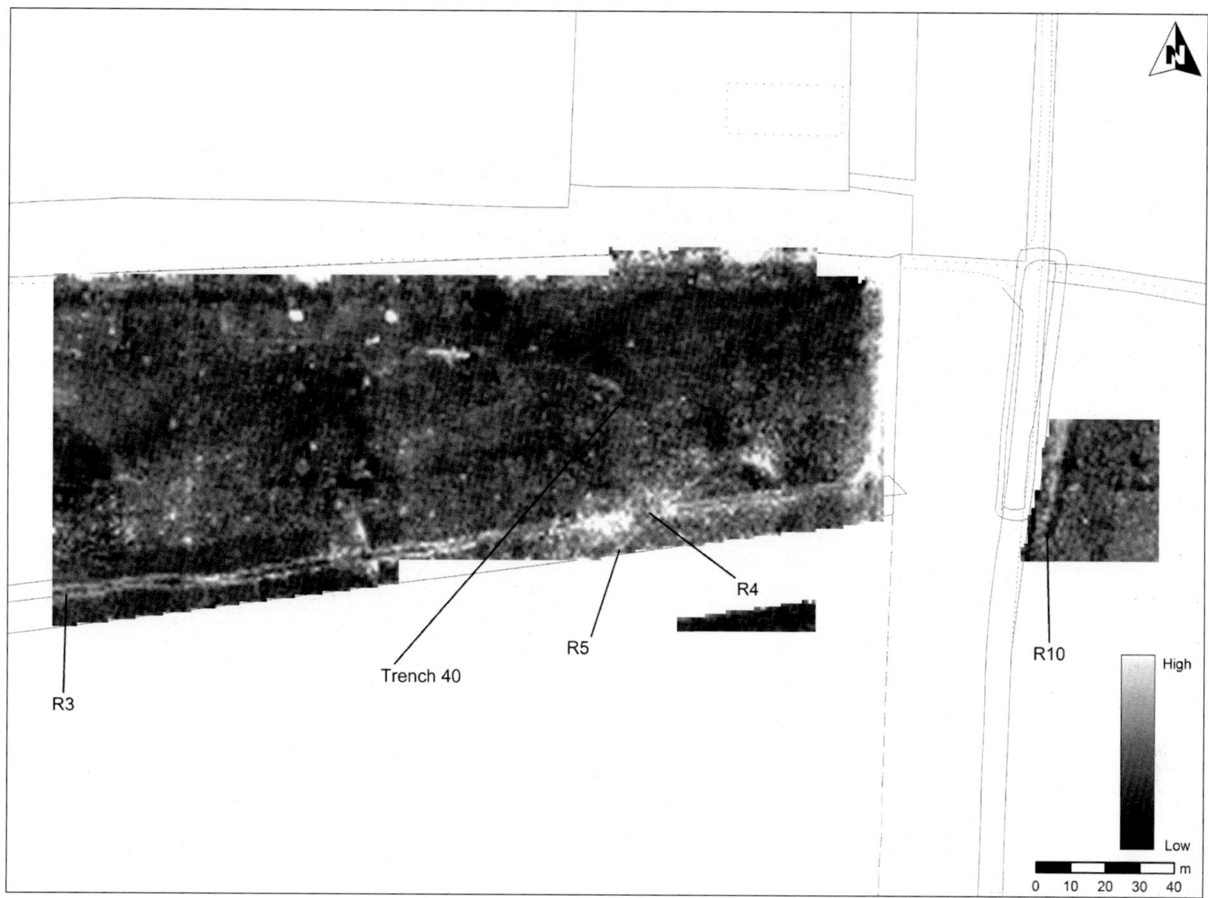

Figure 2.8. Enhanced earth resistance plot (de-striped, de-spiked, clipped and interpolated) of the east end of the Greater Cursus and the southeast corner of Amesbury 42 long barrow

earthwork. East of Amesbury G56 round barrow is the cross-ditch (R8/M7) first identified in Stukeley's 1740 drawing of the Greater Cursus. This feature was also recognised by Richard Colt Hoare (1812: 159) and was detected by Bewley *et al.* (2005) in their LiDAR survey of the area. Upon excavation, the ditch was shown to contain a palisade slot. Traces of the destroyed Winterbourne Stoke G30 round barrow (R9) were detected to the west of the cross-ditch and it is unclear if several intense magnetic responses in this area (M8) are related to the excavation of the barrow or to demolished military buildings.

The ditch and possibly the mound of the degraded Amesbury 42 long barrow (R10; Figure 2.8) at the eastern terminal of the Cursus were detected and confirmed the location of these features in advance of excavation. Potential geophysical anomalies identified by the survey within the Greater Cursus were also selected for excavation in 2007 and 2008 (see Chapter 3). These consisted of a small area of high resistance within the western end (Trench 38; Figure 2.7), a group of low-resistance features in the southwest of the interior (Trench 36; Figure 2.7) and an arc of low-resistance features within the eastern end (Trench 40; Figure 2.8).

Chapter 3

Fourth millennium BC beginnings: the Greater Stonehenge Cursus, Amesbury 42 long barrow and Early Neolithic activity at Woodhenge

J. Thomas and J. Pollard*

*** With contributions by:**
U. Albarella, M. Allen, C. Bronk Ramsey, A. Chamberlain, B. Chan, R. Cleal, G. Cook, G. Davies, C.A.I. French, P.D. Marshall, C. Minniti, D. Mitcham, E. Simmons, A. Teather, S. Viner-Daniels and C. Willis

3.1. The Greater Stonehenge Cursus

J. Thomas

The Greater Stonehenge Cursus was first identified by William Stukeley in 1723. After the Dorset and Heathrow cursuses, it represents the third longest such structure in the British Isles, at nearly three kilometres in extent. Cursus monuments defined by a bank and ditch are distributed throughout much of Britain and Ireland, and are generally later in date than pit and post cursuses, which are concentrated in the Scottish lowlands (Thomas 2006). Broadly speaking, bank-and-ditch cursuses date to a horizon between 3600 and 3200 cal BC (Thomas *et al.* 2009).

The Greater Cursus is unusual in that its side ditches do not run parallel with each other, for the southern ditch has a pronounced 'kink' outwards in its western portion (see Figure 2.5), so that the width of the enclosure varies between 100m and 150m along its length (Darvill 2006: 89). The northern ditch is generally straighter, but aerial photographs reveal that, at a smaller scale, it follows a comparatively uneven and meandering course. The banks lay inside the ditches; very little trace of these banks survives today.

The Cursus runs roughly east–west, linking two areas of higher ground, at Fargo Plantation and King Barrow Ridge (see Figure 1.3), and dips into Stonehenge Bottom between them (see Chapter 2). In this respect it conforms to the common pattern amongst cursus monuments of incorporating seasonally wet ground, or even watercourses, into their fabric (Brophy 2000).

At the western end, it is notable that the Greater Cursus encloses the crest of the Fargo ridge, while the terminal faces westward towards Airman's Corner (see Chapter 4) and Winterbourne Stoke Down. From the terminal, much of the rest of the Cursus is invisible, and Beacon Hill rises up above the near eastern horizon. The Lesser Cursus crests the northern skyline, with Robin Hood's Ball causewayed enclosure beyond it. Lying northwest of the Greater Cursus' west end, the Lesser Cursus was found by Julian Richards to have been constructed in two phases, both within the second half of the third millennium BC (Richards 1990: 72–93; see Marshall *et al.*, below, for its re-dating).

Perhaps intentionally, then, the western end of the Greater Cursus seems to relate to a quite different set of landscape referents than the rest of the monument (see Chapter 2). At the eastern end of the Greater Cursus, the situation is quite different, for the terminal ditch runs parallel with the long barrow Amesbury 42, which occupies the crest of King Barrow Ridge. The excellent recent survey by Dave Field and others for English Heritage (now Historic England), which took place after the SRP excavations on the Cursus, contains a full overview of the history, the landscape and the earthworks (Pearson and Field 2011). The even more recent extensive geophysical surveys by Darvill *et al.* (2013) and Gaffney *et al.* (2012) have contributed further information about the Cursus, with findings that will need be investigated by future excavation.

This long mound of Amesbury 42 was excavated by Thurnam, who describes encountering an ox skull in a primary position, but only secondary human burials (Thurnam 1869: 180). Further investigations by Julian Richards (1990: 98) concluded that the mound had been flanked by two successive sets of side ditches, the assumed later and outermost of which were considerably wider and deeper. However, the 2008 excavation by the SRP showed that this interpretation is incorrect, and that the features identified by Richards as an inner side ditch are later than the outer ditch (see *Amesbury 42 long barrow*, below).

Eastwards from the King Barrow Ridge, the axis of the Cursus leads through Woodhenge and the Cuckoo Stone (see Figures 1.3 and 7.3). Burl (2006: 85) argues that the latter was originally a massive monolith, standing 5.50m high, and that the Cursus was oriented upon it. Excavations conducted by Colin Richards in 2007 (see Chapter 7) indicate that this is unlikely, for the Cuckoo Stone appears to have always been relatively diminutive, and to have been erected after the Cursus was built, having been quarried from a pit adjacent to its present resting place.

3.1.1. History of investigation of the Greater Cursus

Stukeley's 1740 drawing of the Cursus shows a further ditch and bank cutting off the western end of the enclosure, and this feature was also recognised by Colt Hoare (1812: 159). This cross-ditch is still recognisable today, running at an angle roughly north-northwest–south-southeast between the northern and southern ditches (see Figures 2.6–2.7, 3.12). A bank originally stood to the west of the cross-ditch, so that the western end of the Cursus effectively represented a distinct D-shaped enclosure. In this respect, it bears comparison with the southeastern end of the Dorchester-on-Thames cursus, where such an enclosure was evidently a primary feature onto which the cursus was appended (Bradley and Chambers 1988; Whittle *et al.* 1992). However, the suspicion that the cross-ditch of the Greater Cursus was a later feature has now been confirmed (see *Trench 27*, below).

The Cursus has suffered from various depredations in recent history. Much of the monument was ploughed during the Napoleonic and Crimean Wars and, in the nineteenth century, Fargo Plantation was planted across its western end. Military buildings were constructed within the western terminal during the First World War, and the presence of a pig farm resulted in the bulldozing of the western terminal bank during the 1950s, and its complete eradication as an earthwork. The progressive acquisition of the land north of Stonehenge by the National Trust introduced a more enlightened regime and, in 1983, the portion of Fargo Plantation between the Cursus ditches was felled, enabling the course of the monument to be properly appreciated.

The first archaeological investigation of the Cursus was undertaken by Farrer (1917), who dug a cutting across the northern bank and ditch toward the eastern end. He described a flat-bottomed ditch, and a bank composed of turf with little chalk content. Interestingly, he pointed to the comparatively limited quantity of chalk rubble in the ditch, and argued that it might have been deliberately kept clean until it was backfilled in a single episode.

Further excavations on the southern ditch, a little to the east of Fargo Plantation, were conducted by Stone (1947). His small cutting revealed a causeway, too narrow to represent an entrance, and constituted by one rounded and one square ditch terminal. These circumstances strongly suggest that the causeway represented the meeting between sections of the Cursus ditch that had been dug by separate work gangs (Richards 1990: 93). Stone's ditch section is puzzling, for it portrays only a very little chalk silt on either side of the base, and a homogeneous reddish soil containing little or no chalk filling much of the rest of the profile (Stone 1947: 14). He conjectured that the chalk of the bank might not have been returned quickly into the ditch as it had been contained within a turf revetment. Following Farrar, Stone also pointed to the lack of any turf-line within the ditch fill, implying that a deliberate backfilling had taken place.

Stone's excavations were especially notable for recovery of flakes of both sarsen and Stonehenge bluestone from the Cursus ditch. The latter (1947/142.18; Ixer *et al.* 2017: 9–10) has been identified as a fragment of Lower Palaeozoic Sandstone, originating north of the Preseli hills, a coherent lithological group of Stonehenge's bluestone debitage that probably includes Stones 40g and 42c[2] on the west side of the bluestone circle (Ixer and Turner 2006; Ixer *et al.* 2017). The upper part of the ditch in Stone's trench also produced fragments of Late Bronze Age pottery.

2 For the arrangement and numbering of Stonehenge's stones, see the appendix to Chapter 1 and Figure 4.2.

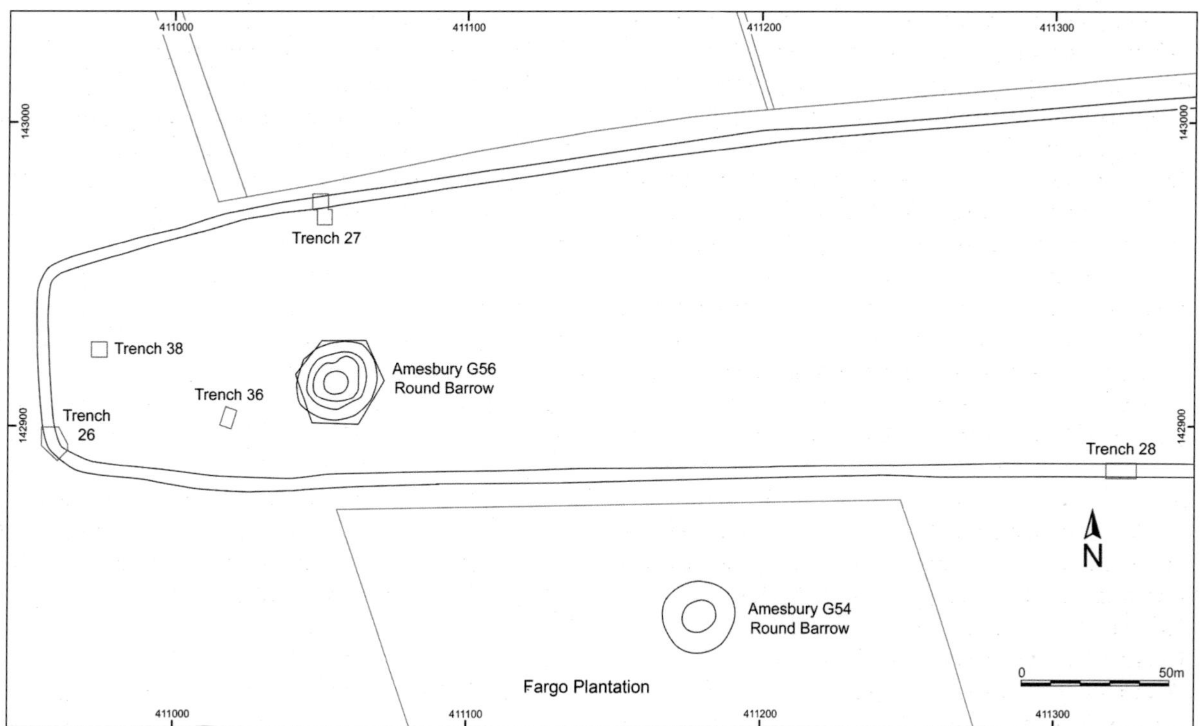

Figure 3.1. Plan of trench locations at the west end of the Greater Cursus (the boundaries of Fargo Plantation are marked in blue)

On the southern side of the ditch, Stone identified an 'embayment' or recess, cut back into the ditch edge, which contained an antler crown with two tines. This later provided a radiocarbon date of 2890–2460 cal BC (OxA-1403; 4100±90 BP; Richards 1990: 259). Julian Richards (1990: 96) pointed out that this feature was probably intrusive, and that the date of the antler is likely to be considerably later than the construction of the Cursus. However, the Late Neolithic attribution continued to exercise some influence in the literature. Finally, Stone identified two small flint-knapping clusters on the ditch base.

More extensive excavations at the western end of the cursus were carried out by Patricia Christie in 1959 (Christie 1963). At the terminal, Christie observed that the ditch was considerably deeper than it was along the sides of the Cursus, providing quarried material for a much more substantial bank (*ibid.*: 370). As she noted, the massive terminal bank would have resembled a long barrow, a point that is echoed by the Thickthorn Terminal of the Dorset Cursus, where the cursus bank has two long barrows aligned upon it, forming a continuous line of mounds (Barrett *et al.* 1991: 50). Passing beside these structures, it is difficult to tell which is bank and which is barrow. Furthermore, when Canon Greenwell excavated the terminal of Rudston Cursus A (Yorkshire), he fully believed himself to be digging a long barrow (with his discovery of Neolithic pottery serving to confirm this belief; Greenwell 1877: 253–7), so the affinity between the two kinds of monuments might have been quite intentional.

Christie (1963: 374) noted the marked differences in the character of the filling of the Cursus's terminal and side ditches. Her explanation was that they had probably been dug as entirely separate episodes. In the terminal ditch, Christie found a primary filling of coarse chalk rubble and fine rain-washed silt, with dark grey bands which she identified as collapses of turf from the bank. Above this was a fine grey silt, which she considered to have been a wind-blown deposit (Christie 1963: 372). The primary rubble at the terminal contained a well-defined flint-flaking deposit, but similar deposits were absent from the side ditches. The technology of this material has been the subject of some debate: the removals do not suggest parallel blades struck from a prepared core, but they appear rather fine for a Later Neolithic flake-based assemblage (Richards 1990: 96; Darvill 2006: 87).

Following the felling of a portion of Fargo Plantation in 1983, Julian Richards was able to excavate two small trenches in the side ditches of the Cursus. The first of these (W56A) was on the southern ditch, immediately inside the eastern part of Fargo Plantation (Richards 1990: 93). This was less than 100m west of Stone's cutting, and the results were very similar. The basal chalky fill (context 17) was very limited in extent, and was succeeded by a red-brown decalcified fill (context 16), similar to that described by Stone. The interstice between the two layers on Richards' section appears to be marked by a V-shaped arrangement of stones, which may represent a cut, truncating context 17 (Richards 1990: fig. 62). A run of stones across the ditch (context 13) suggests that a stabilisation might have occurred between the deposition of context 16 and the similar material above it (context 11).

Richards' second trench (W56B) cut the southern ditch adjacent to the Larkhill byway (roughly in the middle of the Cursus; see Figure 2.5: near point 7). Here, the ditch fills were less decalcified, and the section lacked any indication of a V-shaped re-cut (Richards 1990: 95), as was found during the SRP excavation (see *Trench 28*, below). Evidently some significant change overcame the ditch deposits as the Cursus descended into Stonehenge Bottom, but it was not clear from the 1983 excavations whether this was gradual or abrupt in character.

Two round barrows of Early Bronze Age date are contained within the western terminal of the Greater Cursus. The easternmost of the two, Amesbury G56 (Figure 3.1), contained a Beaker inhumation and a child burial, as well as a cist enclosing a further inhumation with a knife-dagger (Stone 1947: 9). The other mound, Winterbourne Stoke G30 (R9 in Figure 2.7), was excavated by Colt Hoare and contained a cremation deposit with a central cremation pit, which had been discoloured by heat. Re-excavation by Christie of this destroyed barrow revealed another small pit, which pre-dated the barrow and produced a quantity of pine charcoal (Christie 1963: 377). This suggests (but does not prove) a Mesolithic date for the pit and, together with the Early Mesolithic postholes northwest of Stonehenge (Cleal *et al.* 1995: 43–7; Allen and Gardiner 2002), raises the possibility that the Cursus was constructed in an area with a long history of use and significance.

3.1.2. Excavations of the Greater Cursus in 2007 and 2008

Fieldwork conducted in August and September 2007 by the SRP was designed to address a series of outstanding questions that had been raised by the investigations of Farrar, Stone, Christie and Richards:

- Since the antler in Stone's 'embayment' was probably secondary, the construction of the Cursus was effectively undated. Both clarifying the nature of the 'embayment' and recovering new dating material from primary stratigraphic positions were therefore major objectives.
- Stone's description of the position of the bluestone fragment in the southern Cursus ditch lacked precision, and it was desirable to attempt to replicate his discovery, clarifying the position of bluestone debitage within this ditch's stratigraphic sequence.
- The variation in the filling of the Cursus ditches demanded clarification, and it was considered important to examine sections in different parts of the structure simultaneously as a basis for comparison.
- The presence of a potentially early pit in association with Winterbourne Stoke G30 and the discovery of cut features immediately inside the terminals of other cursus monuments (Thomas 2007: 166–97) indicated the importance of investigating areas of the Cursus interior.
- Similarly, the long-standing question of whether some kind of megalithic bluestone structure (see Chapter 4; Castleden 1993: 172, fig. 69) had existed in or around the Cursus raised the possibility that features which *post-dated* as well as *pre-dated* the monument might be encountered. To this end, geophysical surveys conducted by Andrew Payne and Neil Linford for English Heritage and by Kate Welham under the aegis of the project (see Chapter 2) were used as a basis for the identification of suitable anomalies that might be tested by excavation.
- Finally, the investigation of the structural sequence within the Cursus was defined as a priority and, in particular, the relationship between the cross-ditch (which had never previously been excavated) and the main perimeter ditch was a pressing question.

In order to address these issues, five trenches were laid out in 2007, all at the western end of the Cursus (Figure 3.1; see Figures 2.6–2.7 for the geophysical survey results). Trench 26 was set at the southern end of the terminal ditch, where the geophysical survey suggested that it entered a gentle curve to meet the side ditch. The unusual shape of the trench was designed to accommodate this apparent curve, and to provide perpendicular sections at either end of the cutting. In practice, the ditch ran straight across the trench, indicating that the western terminal is much more rectilinear than was anticipated. Trench 27 was opened over the northern side ditch of the Cursus, at the point where geophysical survey suggested that it intersected with the cross-ditch. In reality the cross-ditch terminated about two metres short of the side ditch, and the 5m square of Trench 27 needed to be extended to the south in order to reveal the butt end of the cross-ditch.

Trench 28 was designed to test the results of Stone's 1947 cutting, sampling the ditch sequence in this area and attempting to recover further bluestone flakes from the ditch. Stone described his trench as having been '76 yards east of Fargo Wood', but there was little indication on the surface of where the excavation might have been located. The procedure followed was to open a 5m square in the area where published sources indicated that Stone's cutting had been, and extend this to a 10m ×

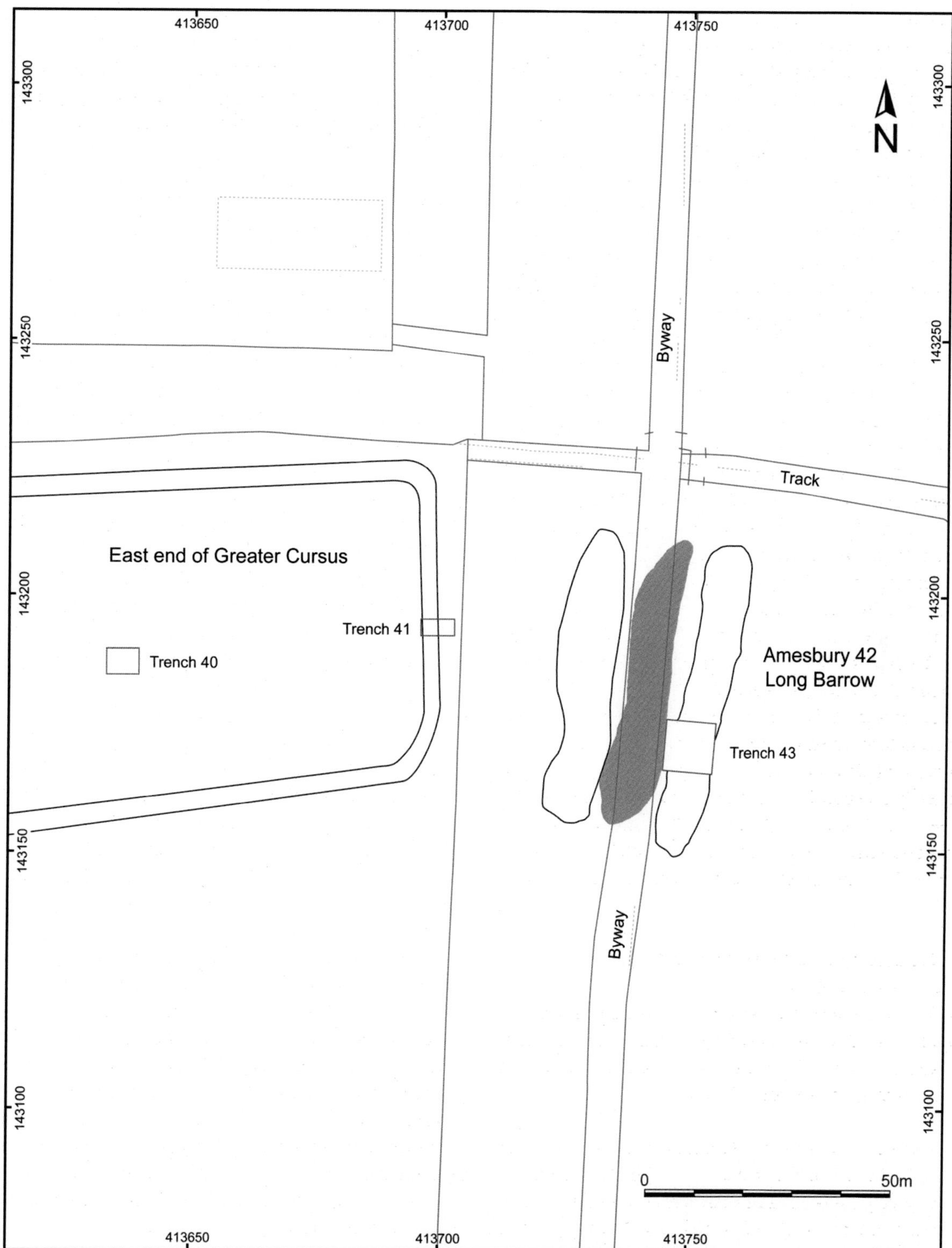

Figure 3.2. Plan of trench locations at the east end of the Greater Cursus and Amesbury 42 long barrow; the mound of Amesbury 42 is shaded grey (present-day field boundaries are marked in blue)

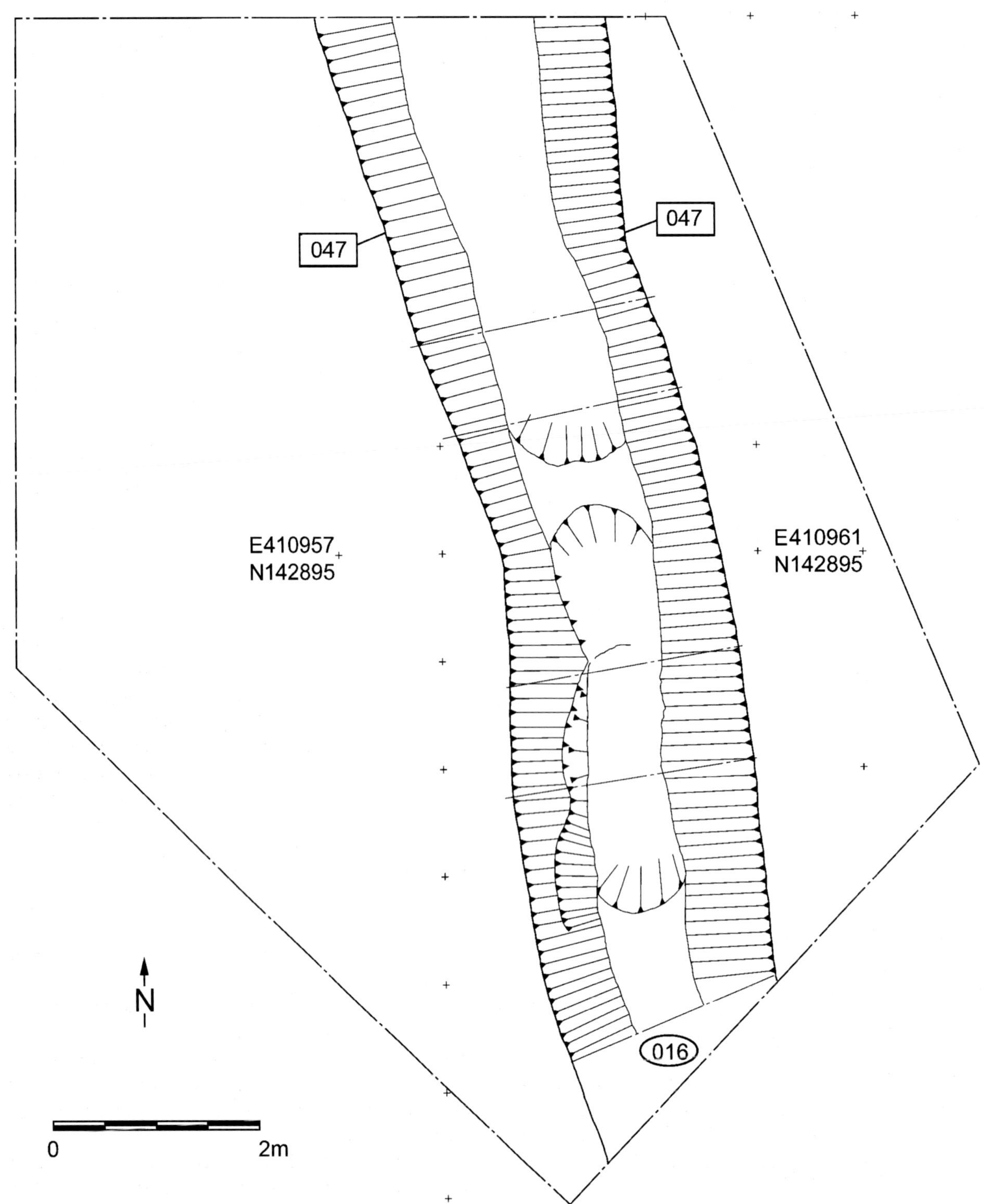

Figure 3.3. Plan of Trench 26 at the west end of the Greater Cursus

Figure 3.4. Excavation of the western terminal ditch of the Greater Cursus in Trench 26, viewed from the southeast

5m area when the position of the 1947 trench had been established. The object of this method was to avoid re-opening a large proportion of Stone's backfill. Happily, the strategy proved very effective, and the initial trench revealed the easternmost 1m or so of Stone's cutting. The trench was then extended 5m to the east.

Trenches 36 and 38 were positioned in relation to promising geophysical anomalies: the former a portion of an arc of putative features in the southern interior west of the round barrows, and the latter immediately inside the western terminal, north of the median line.

Prior to excavation of each trench, the area to be excavated was test-pitted. The test pits were arranged in a systematic grid (see Volume 2 for the full report). All the trenches were then de-turfed by hand, and the topsoil was also removed manually. In each trench a 20% sample of the topsoil was sieved through 10mm mesh, in units of 1m squares. Finds recovered from this procedure were retained, and were identified according to grid square as well as context.

The test-pitting prior to full excavation provided the opportunity to compare topsoil and subsoil assemblages, and to place the results of the excavations into the context of earlier fieldwalking and shovel-testing surveys. The lithics from the test pits and the full excavation are reported separately below. All deposits from closed contexts were sieved on site using a number of 10mm-mesh swing-sieves, and flotation samples and magnetic susceptibility/phosphate samples were taken from all cut features and ditch layers. All trenches were backfilled and returfed at the end of the excavation.

Three trenches were laid out for excavation in 2008, all located at the eastern end of the Greater Cursus, and all designed to address issues left unresolved by previous investigations (Figure 3.2). All trenches were dug by hand from turf level; all of the topsoil was removed in metre squares and this 100% sample of topsoil was sieved through 10mm mesh, in order to collect all artefacts from the overburden, recorded by metre grid square. The trenches were backfilled and returfed at the end of excavation.

Inside the eastern end of the Cursus, a trench 7m × 5m in extent was opened to explore a possible enclosure revealed by resistivity survey (Trench 40). The geophysical anomalies apparently showed the northern half of a sub-circular pit circle, the southern part of which might conceivably have been present but less visible in the survey data (see Figure 2.8). The trench was designed to sample 50% of the features visible in the survey data. Any cut features would be half-sectioned, and 50% of the deposit left *in situ*. The anomaly was potentially similar to pit- and post-circles identified within and surrounding the cursus monuments at Dorchester-on-Thames, Oxfordshire (Atkinson *et al.* 1951), and Springfield, Essex (Hedges and Buckley 1981; Brown 1997), and consequently the possibility that features might contain secondary deposits of cremation burials needed to be considered.

At the eastern terminal of the Cursus, west of the byway that runs north–south past the terminal between Strangways and the Old King Barrows, a trench 7m × 3m in extent was opened, in order to test the character of the Cursus ditch and its filling at this point (Trench 41). While the possibility of identifying dating material for the cutting of the ditch was acknowledged, the principal aim of the cutting was to compare the eastern and western terminal ditches, in terms of their extent and the presence of distinctive deposits such as knapping clusters.

Finally, immediately to the east of the byway, a trench 10m × 10m in extent was excavated (Trench 43), with the intention of investigating the eastern flanking ditch of the Amesbury 42 long barrow, in an area immediately to the north of Julian Richards' 1983 excavation. Here it was hoped that material might be recovered to provide a date for the tumulus in relation to the Cursus, while further clarifying the relationship between the long barrow's two phases of construction (the outer ditch and the inner 'ditch' recorded by Richards [1990]).

3.1.3. The western terminal ditch of the Cursus

As noted above, Trench 26 was laid out in order to investigate a possible curve in the Cursus ditch where the deep terminal ditch meets the shallower side ditch (Figures 3.1, 3.3–3.4). In practice, the terminal ditch ran north–south across the trench, and showed little appreciable variation in depth over the 10m of its length that were exposed (Figures 3.5–3.9). No features other than the Cursus ditch were revealed in the trench, although the chalk surface showed signs of disturbance by ploughing and bulldozing. The western terminal ditch had been weathered back to 2.70m wide at the top, but was only 1.00m wide at the base.

In the top of the ditch, context 016 consisted of heterogeneous disturbed material: broadly a loose, dark red-brown silty clay loam immediately below the topsoil (001) and extending outward from the ditch itself in places, notably toward the northeast. Here, modern demolition deposits spread toward the reconstructed Cursus bank, which was rebuilt by Julian Richards in 1983 using bulldozed material scooped up from the terminal ditch. Layer 016 contained bricks, roofing material, the lower part of a military incinerator, and a series of concrete post-bases, which remained *in situ* from the First World War buildings. Layers 001 and 016 produced large numbers of .303 bullet cases, many of them dating to 1940 and 1942, indicating that military activity here continued into the Second World War.

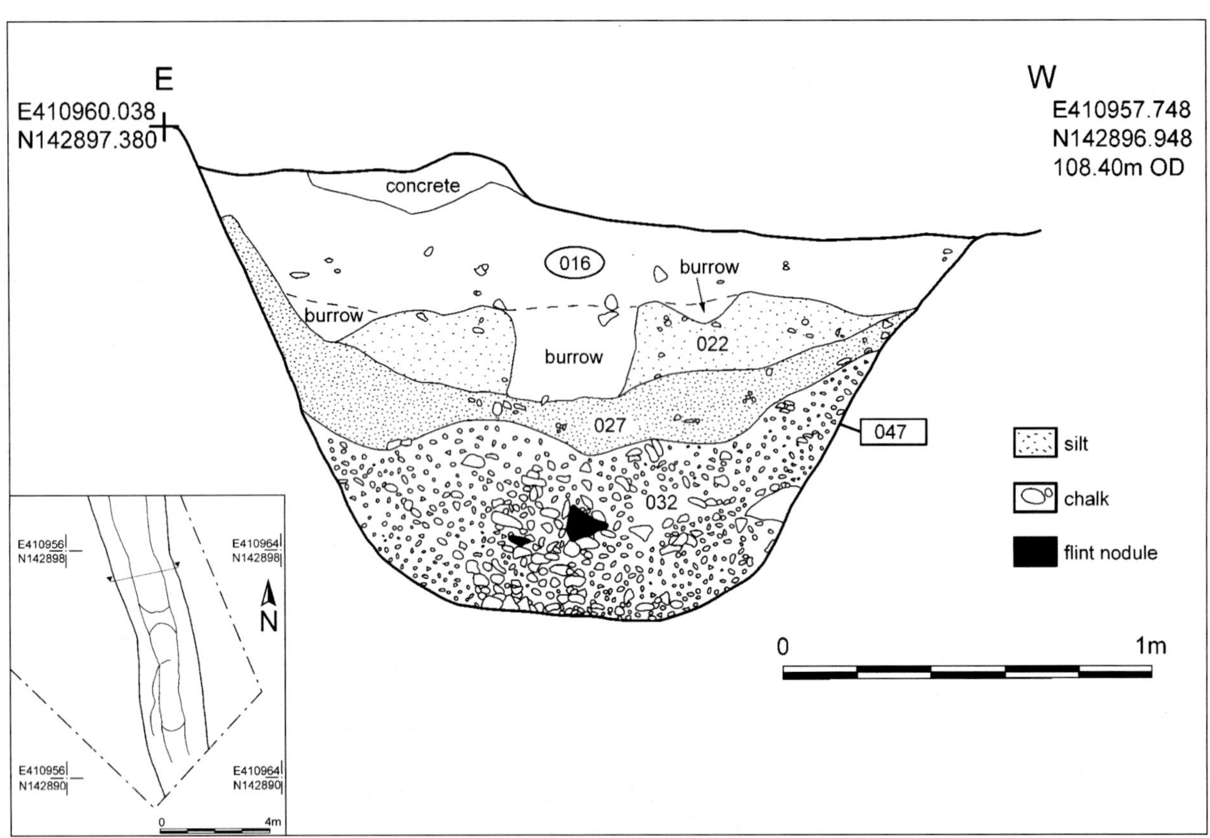

Figure 3.5. Section 5 (the most northerly) of the Greater Cursus ditch in Trench 26

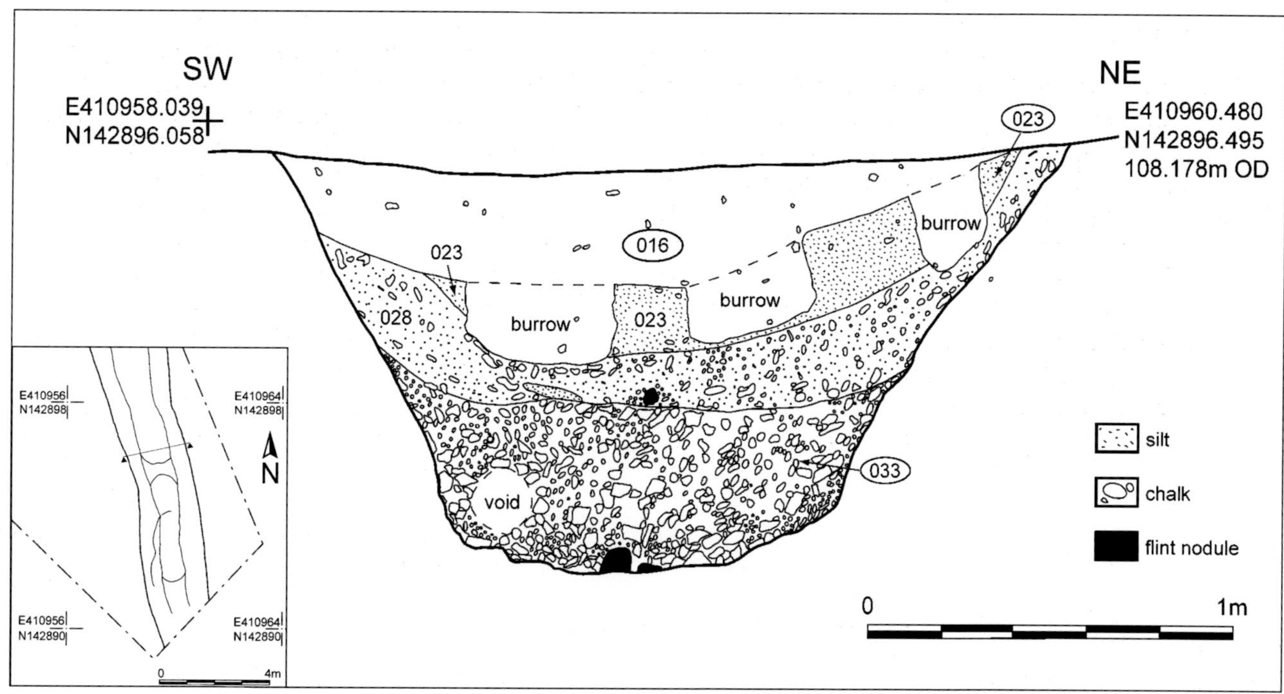

Figure 3.6. Section 1 of the Greater Cursus ditch in Trench 26

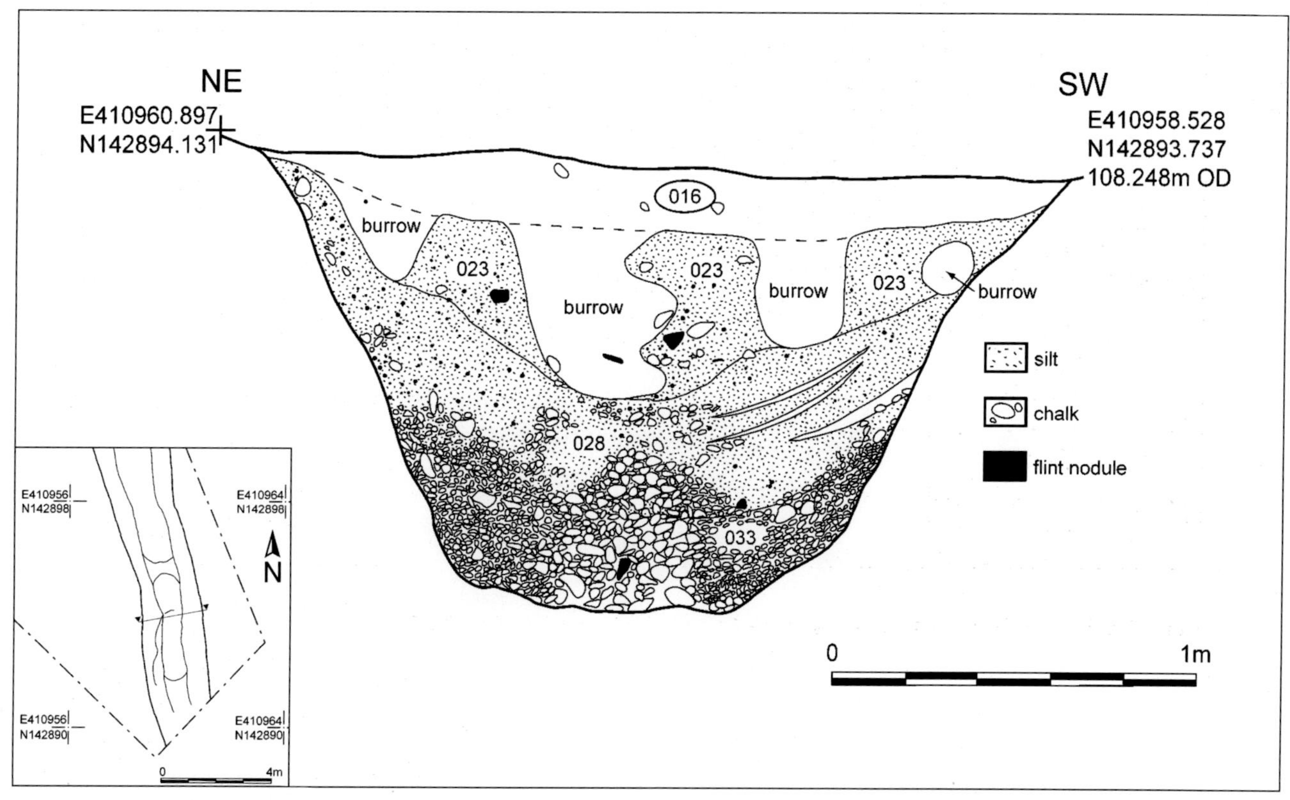

Figure 3.7. Section 2 of the Greater Cursus ditch in Trench 26

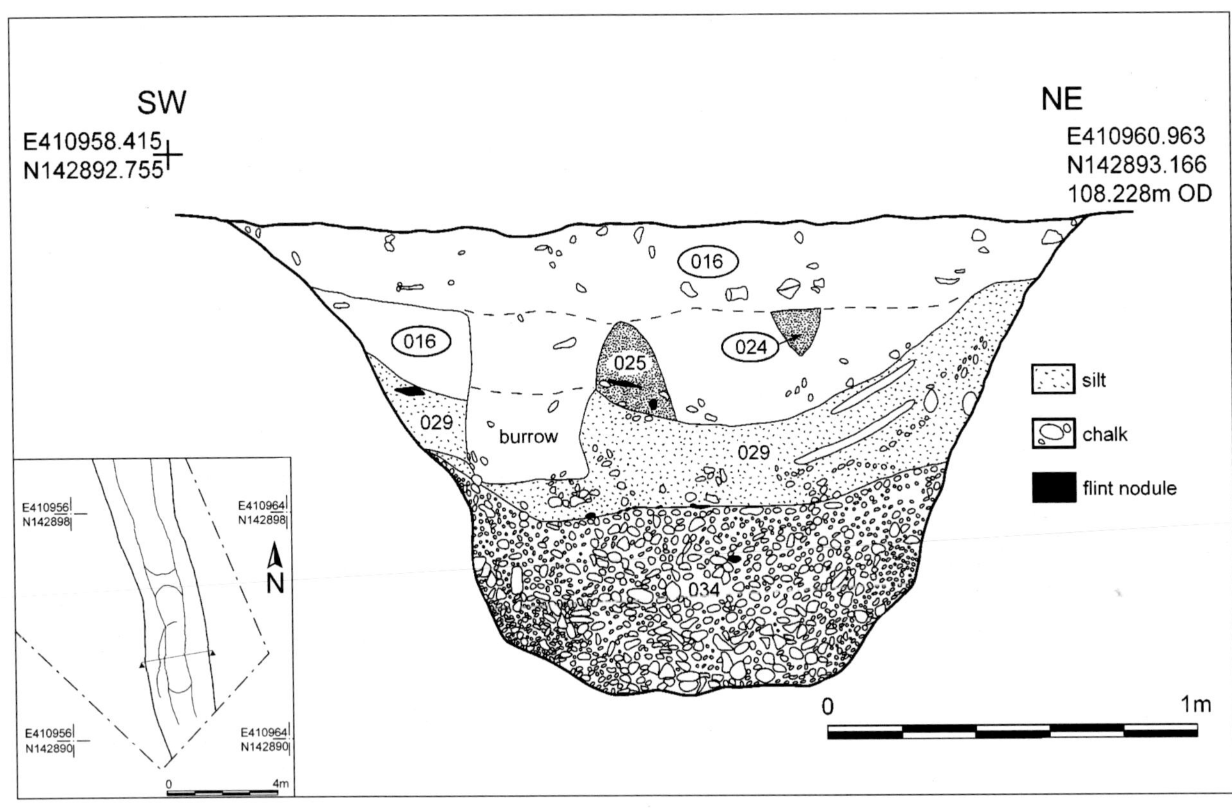

Figure 3.8. Section 3 of the Greater Cursus ditch in Trench 26

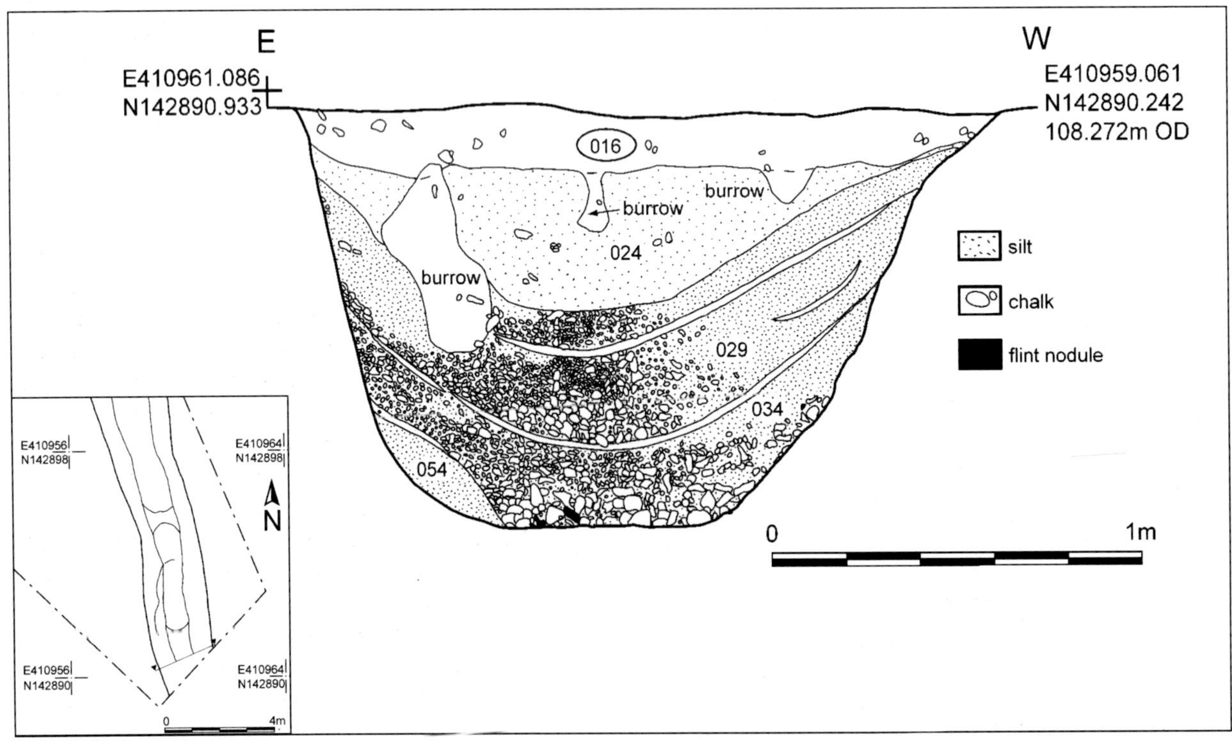

Figure 3.9. Section 4 (the most southerly) of the Greater Cursus ditch in Trench 26

Figure 3.10. Discovery of an antler tine (SF 17) at the bottom of the Greater Cursus ditch, viewed from the east

Figure 3.11. The antler tine (SF 17), viewed from the north

A Late Neolithic oblique arrowhead (SF 20393; see Figure 3.62) came from the topsoil (001) and in one of the test pits this topsoil produced a human bone of Late Neolithic date (2890–2670 cal BC at 95% confidence (SUERC-75196; 4187±30 BP; see Willis, below). Both are residual. Layer 016 contained large numbers of flint flakes, probably comparatively late in date, which appeared to have been washed in from the area surrounding the Cursus rather than representing activity that had taken place in the silted ditch-top. The entire deposit had been heavily disturbed by rabbit burrowing and, as excavation progressed downwards, the other forms of disturbance gave way to rabbit holes, which occasionally penetrated as far as the primary chalk rubble.

Below 016, and still heavily eroded by rabbit activity, was a friable, dark grey-brown, slightly clayey silt containing small rolled chalk fragments, numbered 022, 023, 024 and 025 in the different sections excavated. This was equivalent to the fine grey silt in Christie's Cutting V, which she considered to have been of aeolian origin (Christie 1963). In the southern part of the excavated area, a localised area of this material was rather darker, and was given the number 025. It was striking that 022/023/024 and 025 contained much less struck flint than 016, underlining the fact that the lithics in the latter were of external origin.

Beneath the relatively homogeneous grey silt was a coarser and more compact chalky silt (027/028/029). This was a light yellowish-beige in colour, and contained frequent inclusions of small angular chalk fragments. This was a characteristic secondary silting, and was rather coarser on the inner side of the ditch, presumably reflecting the erosion of the Cursus bank. Within this material were a number of darker lenses. These were probably what Christie identified as turf slips, but it is equally probable that they represent episodes of winter silting.

Layer 027/028/029 lay above a thick deposit of primary chalk rubble, numbered 033, 034 and 032, evidently derived from the ditch edges. This material was angular and varied in size, and was contained within a loose matrix of light yellow-brown silt. Dispersed within this material were a group of flint cores and a series of discrete knapping clusters, each no more than 0.70m in diameter.

These knapping deposits were each given their own context number, and lifted in their entirety by bagging the lithics and surrounding sediment, so as to make sure that any micro-debitage was retained. It is notable that these clusters were found throughout the primary chalk rubble, from top to bottom. Knapping deposits 099 and 042 were on the base of the ditch, sealed by the rubble; 041 was toward the base of 034, and 040 was in the lowest 0.08m of 033; 037 was contained within 032, and 036 was on the top of rubble 034.

This suggests that the knapping clusters were not all precisely contemporary, but that they were being generated throughout the period during which the initial weathering-back of the ditch edge was taking place. Indeed, as this process of weathering-back would have resulted in the periodic exposure of flint nodules in the ditch edge, it is possible that knapping took place as this material came to the surface. Flint was visible in the side of the ditch at the close of excavation, and samples of this were taken to compare with the knapping clusters.

At the base of rubble 033, on the floor of the ditch, the most significant find of the excavation was discovered; a battered frontal tine from a red deer antler pick (SF 17) provided an ideally placed radiocarbon sample to date the digging of the Cursus ditch to 3630–3370 cal BC at 95% confidence (OxA-17953 and OxA-17954; 4716±34 BP and 4695±34 BP; Figures 3.10–3.11, 3.58; see Table 3.5).

On the inner side of the ditch, a small pocket of light brownish-yellow silt (054; Figure 3.9) pre-dated the rubble, representing an initial weathering wash of fine

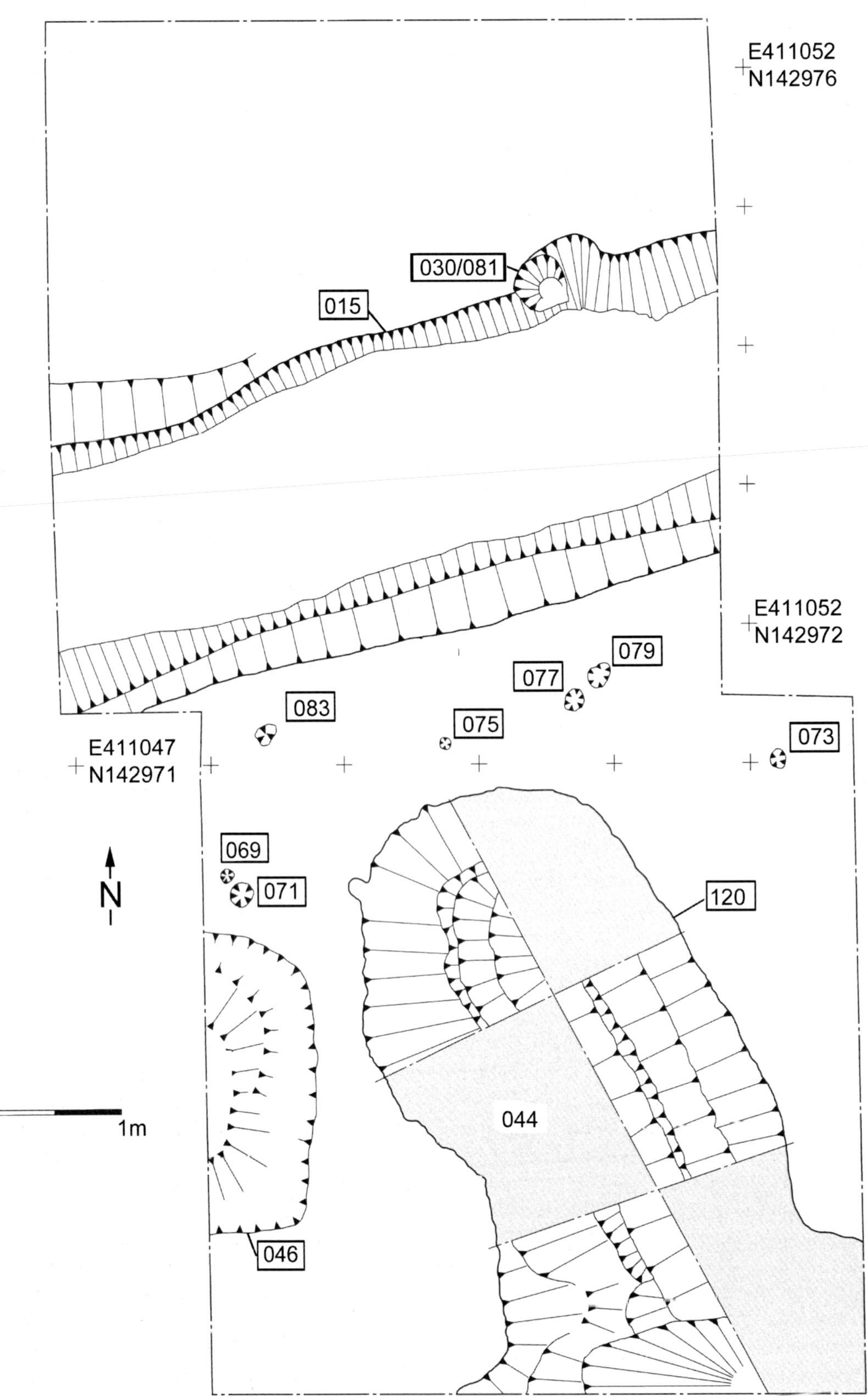

Figure 3.12. Plan of Trench 27 near the west end of the Greater Cursus

Figure 3.13. The northern terminal of the cross-ditch in Trench 27 under excavation, viewed from the northwest

sediment from the ditch edge, prior to the first frost to affect the exposed chalk.

The cut of the ditch (047) was linear in plan but somewhat sinuous, particularly on the outer, westward side. The break of slope at the upper edge was abrupt, and the ditch sides were steep. At its deepest point, the ditch was 1.50m deep from the modern turf-level, or 1.20m from the subsoil surface. Allowing for weathering, the sides may originally have approached the vertical. The base of the ditch was relatively flat, but there were indications of segmented scoops, visible in Figure 3.3, which suggests that the ditch was originally dug as a series of distinct lengths separated by causeways. As with the causeway revealed by Stone (1947), this is evidence that the Cursus ditch as a whole was gang-dug.

3.1.4. The northern Cursus ditch and the cross-ditch

Trench 27 was a 5m × 5m square cutting opened over the northern side ditch of the Cursus, at the point where geophysical survey results indicated a junction with the cross-ditch (M7/R8 in Figures 2.6–2.7). In the event, the cross-ditch came to a butt end roughly 2m short of the side ditch, and it proved necessary to extend the cutting 5m to the south in order to investigate this ditch terminal (Figures 3.1, 3.12–3.13). The location of the cross-ditch terminal implies that it would theoretically have impinged upon the Cursus bank, but this does not in itself provide a strong indication that it was substantially later than the main Cursus ditch.

It was noted that, within Trench 27, the Cursus ditch did not run precisely east–west, as might have been supposed from the overall morphology of the monument. Instead, the line of the ditch was displaced southwards at the westward end of the trench, confirming the somewhat erratic course of the northern side ditch, as mentioned above.

The ditch in Trench 27 (cut 015) was much shallower than at the western terminal, but its filling was broadly comparable (Figures 3.14–3.15). The uppermost fill (014) was a loose, dark humic loam, barely distinguishable from the ploughsoil. Below this was a grey, slightly clayey silt (021) with small rolled chalk fragments, comparable with 022/023/024 in Trench 26. Both of these layers had been extensively damaged by rabbit burrowing (identified as contexts 056/057, 142/143 and 144/145). In the eastern part of the trench, a lens of dark

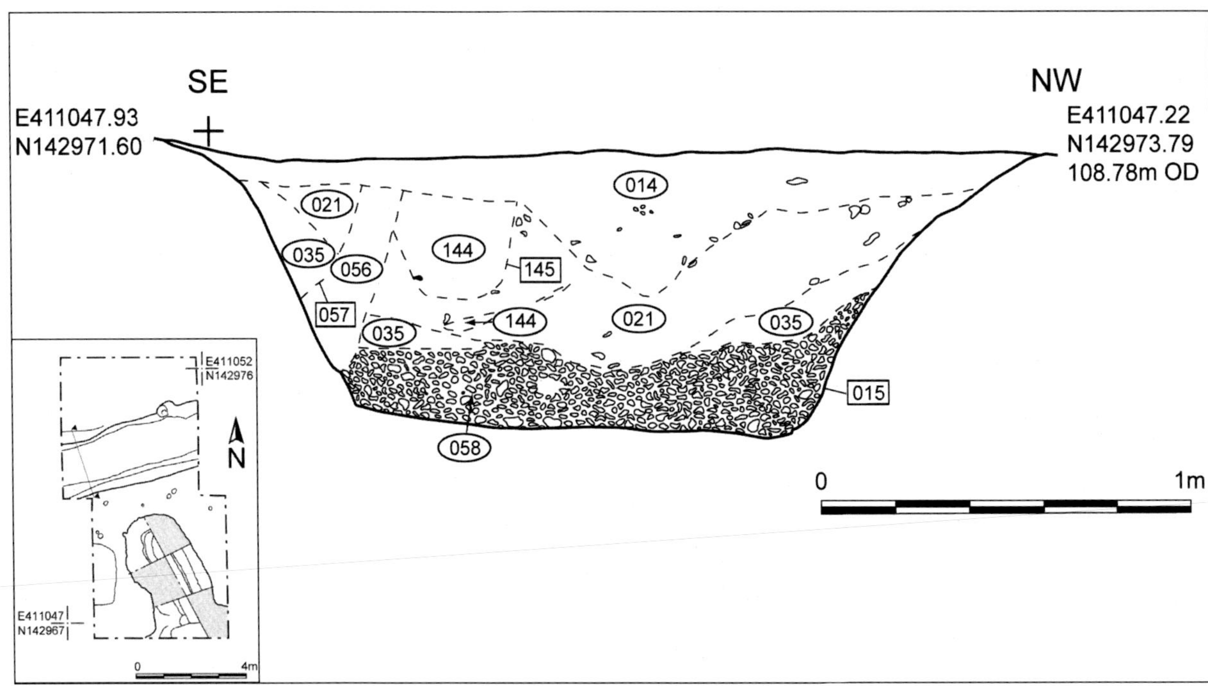

Figure 3.14. Section 2 through the Greater Cursus ditch in Trench 27

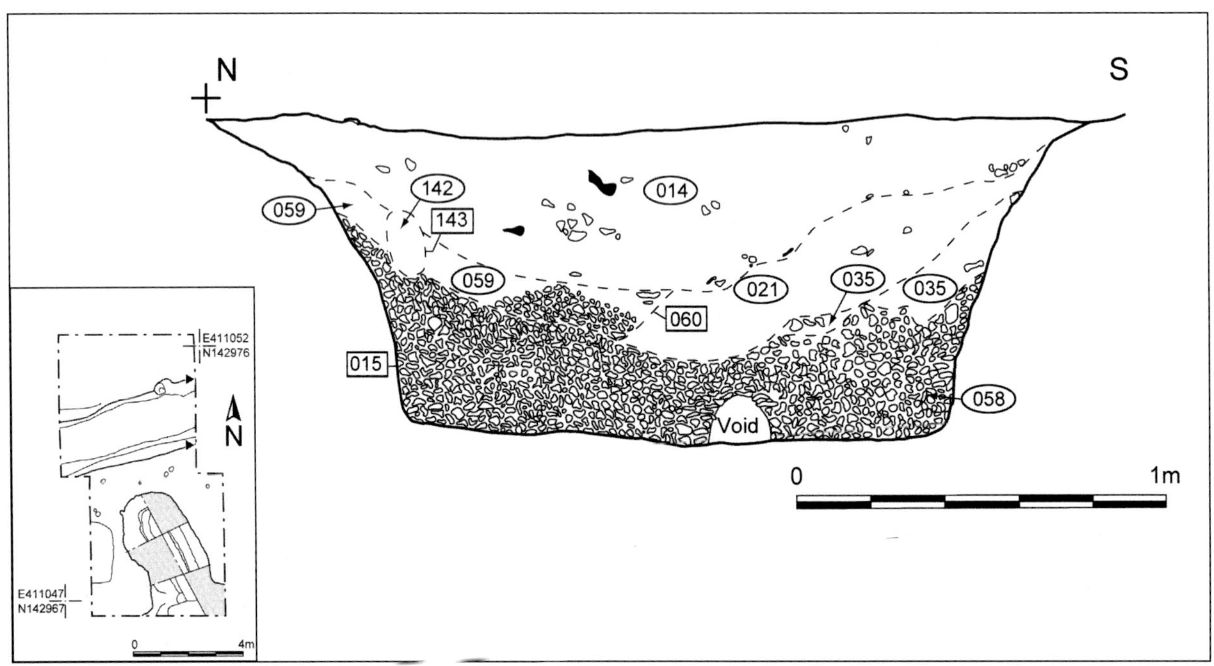

Figure 3.15. Section 1 through the Greater Cursus ditch in Trench 27

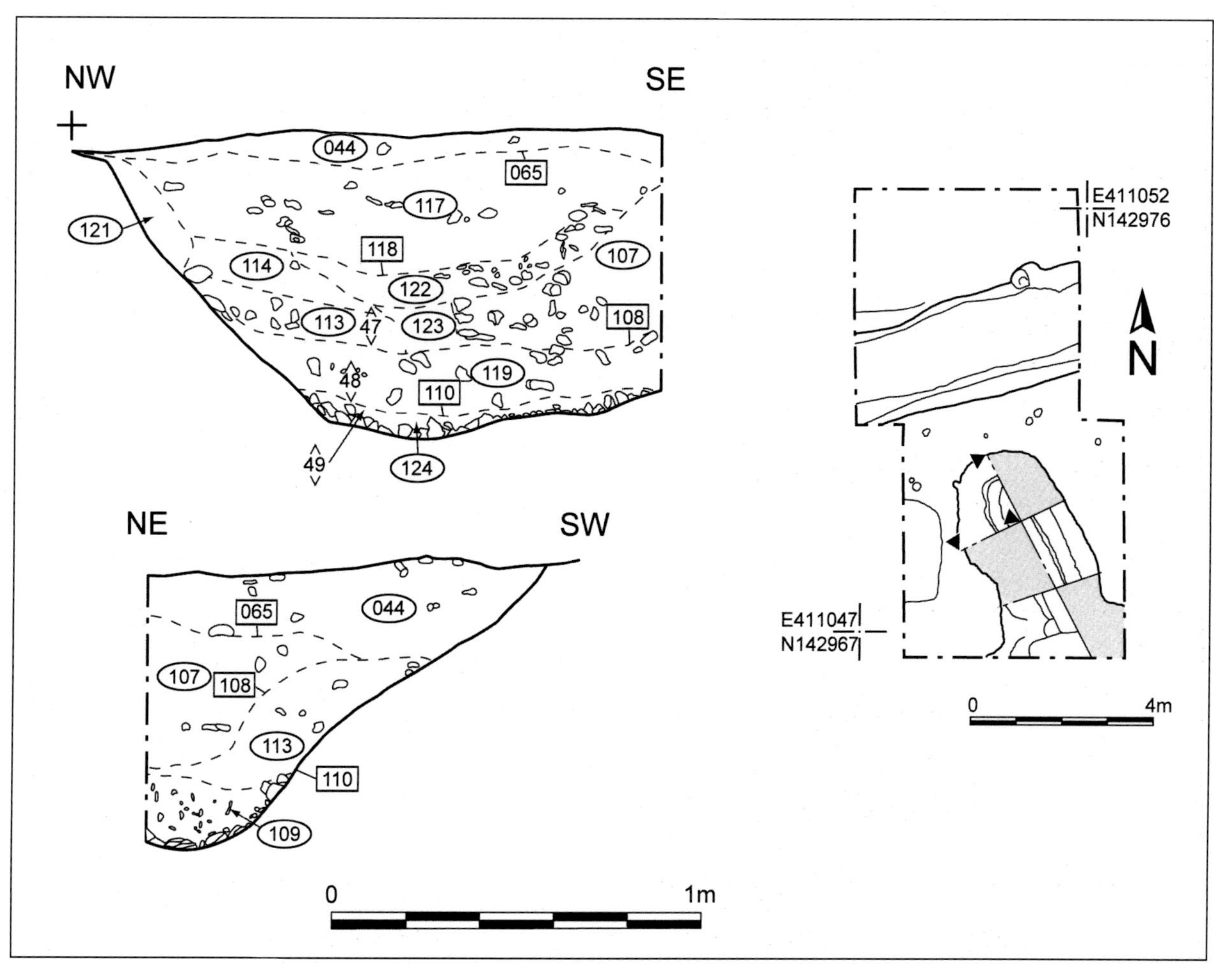

Figure 3.16. Longitudinal and cross-sections through the cross-ditch in Trench 27

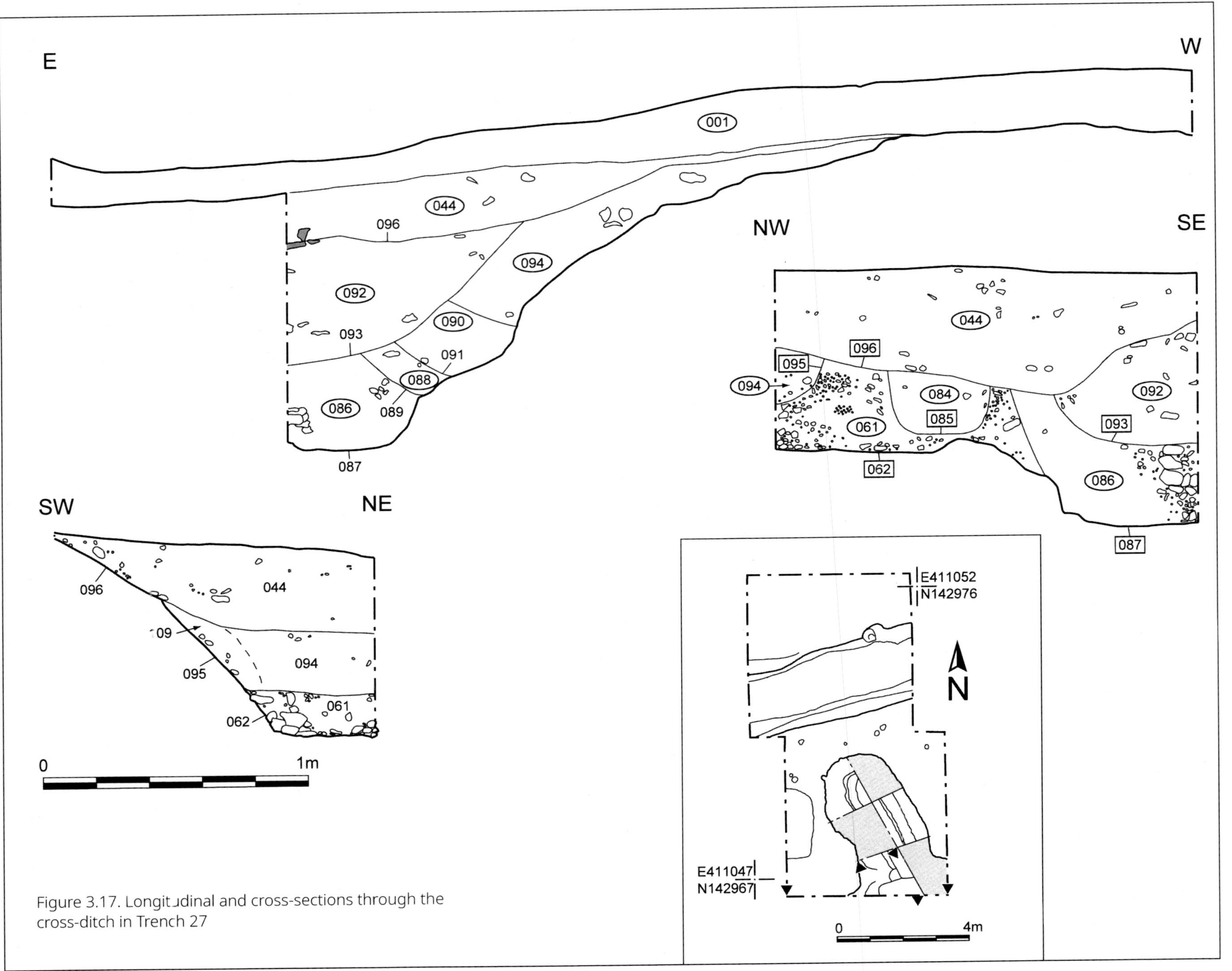

Figure 3.17. Longitudinal and cross-sections through the cross-ditch in Trench 27

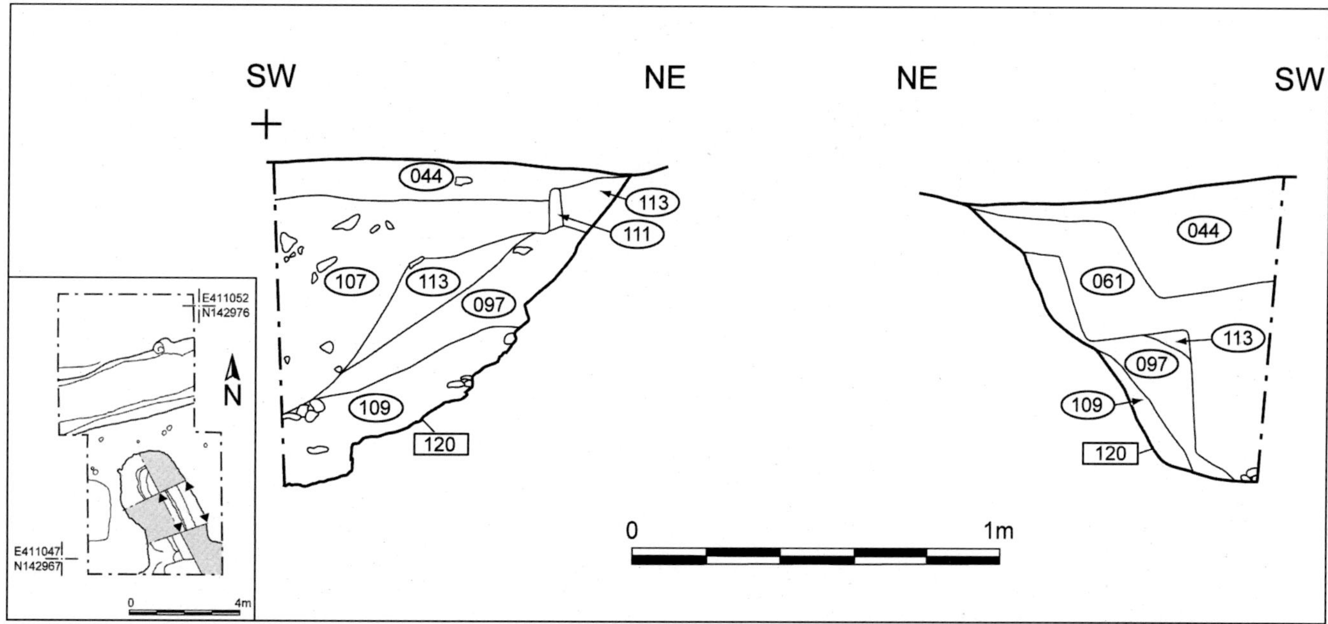

Figure 3.18. Cross-sections through the cross-ditch in Trench 27

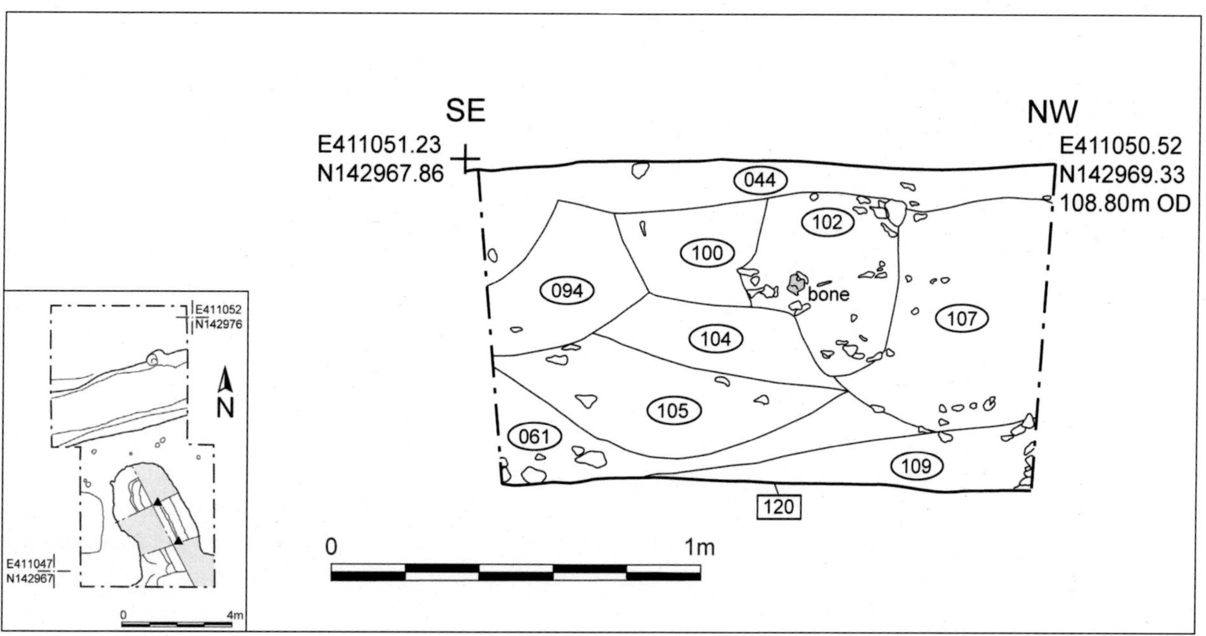

Figure 3.19. Longitudinal section through the cross-ditch in Trench 27

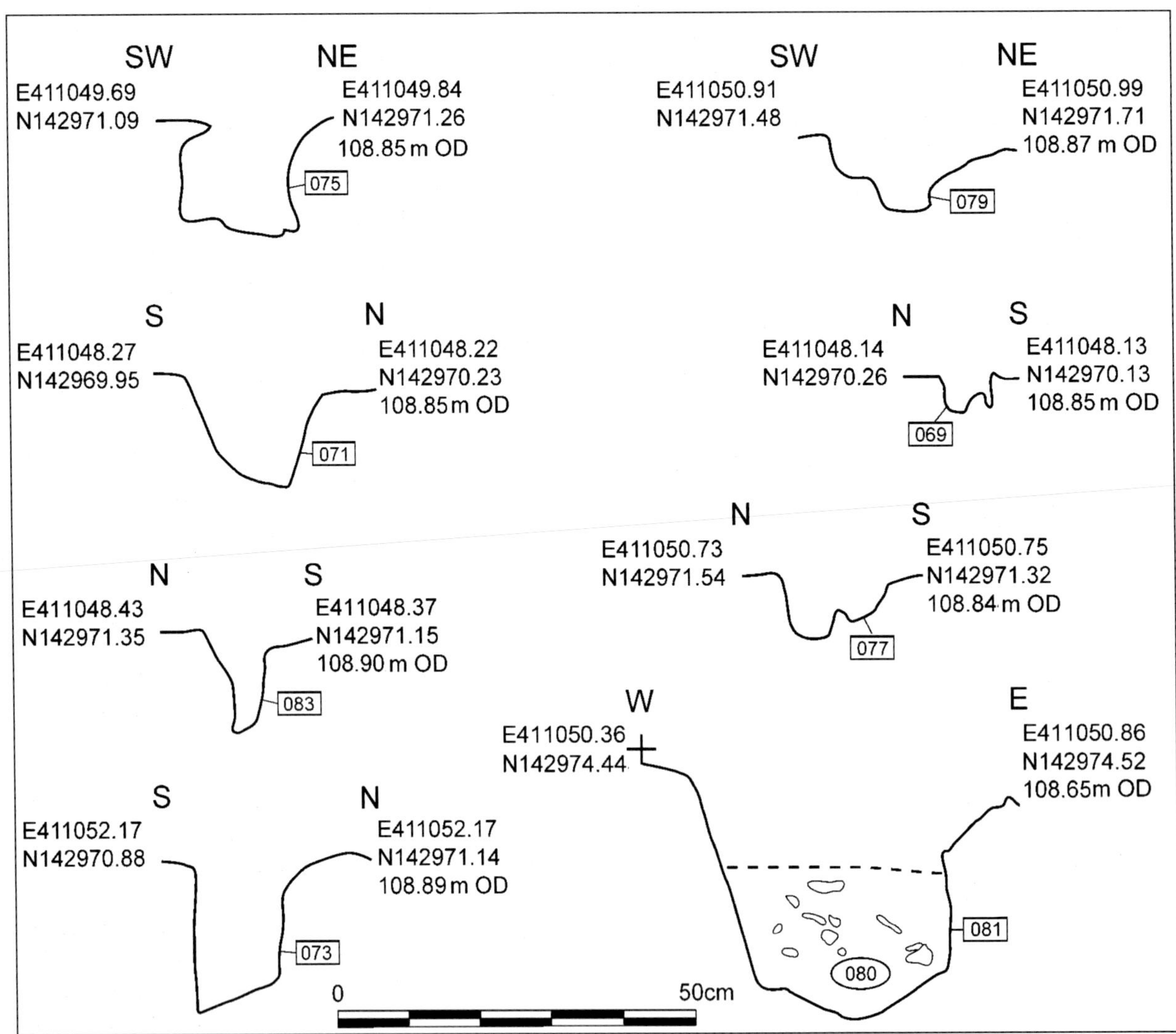

Figure 3.20. Sections through the small features in Trench 27

brown silty loam (059) lay between 014 and 021, and it is possible that this represented the fill of a cut (060) which locally truncated 021. By contrast with Trench 28 (across the southern ditch; see below), all of the layers in Trench 27 appeared to be bedded naturally, forming U-shaped angles of rest. There was little to suggest re-cutting or similar human disturbance in these layers, and their composition was in line with conventional expectations of chalkland ditch erosion.

Layer 035, below 021, was a secondary silting of compact mid-grey/buff chalky silt with small rolled chalk fragments. In the course of investigating this material, a friable, dark brownish-grey loam with angular chalk fragments (031/080) was encountered on the northern side of the ditch. At first it was considered to be the fill of a badger or rabbit burrow, similar to several others in the ditch. However, its further investigation revealed that it was contained within cut 030/081 (Figures 3.12, 3.20), a flat-based and straight-sided cylindrical feature which suggested a posthole, although no indication of a post-pipe was present. Its position in the side of the ditch, cut through the ditch silts and thus post-dating the digging of the ditch by some while, together with the character of its fill, identified 030/081 as comparable with the 'embayments' in Trench 28 (see below).

The primary chalk rubble (058) in the ditch was composed of blocky fragments with compacted powdered chalk. There was considerably less of this material here than at the terminal, and it is conceivable that the ditch had been cleaned out on one or more occasions. However, the rubble covered the base of the ditch, and its lesser quantity may simply be a function of the relative shallowness of the ditch at this point. The ditch cut (015) was again flat-based and straight-sided, and the depth of the ditch was 1.10m from the modern ground surface or 0.80m from the subsoil surface.

The butt-end of the cross-ditch was somewhat irregular in plan (Figure 3.12). It was excavated using the quadrant method in order to preserve 50% of the deposit contained within. This had the advantage of providing both lateral and axial sections (Figures 3.16–3.19). Its uppermost fill, which extended across the entire feature, was a compact to friable mid-brown silty clay loam (044) containing small rounded chalk fragments. In the southernmost part of the trench this sealed a dark grey-brown silty humic loam (092) with poorly sorted angular flint inclusions, filling a steep recut (093), which cut across an earlier intrusive feature (087) that cut into the ditch (Figure 3.17). A lower fill (086) was a soft friable silty loam.

The central part of the ditch was occupied by a distinct slot (cut 062), which appeared to be cut through the primary fill (109). This primary fill (109) of the cross-ditch was a friable, light beige chalk rubble with chalky silt; it contained no finds.

The principal fill of the slot cutting fill 109 was a compact to friable mid-grey silty humic loam (061). Within this material, a great number of smaller fills (084, 094, 100, 102, 104, 105 and 107; Figure 3.19) appeared to inter-cut one another in complicated ways. The best way to rationalise this is to suggest that these fills represent the traces of a series of posts set within a palisade slot, and that their elaborate stratigraphic relationships resulted from the process of the posts' collapse and/or removal. Of these, 084 was set within a clear cut (085), indicating that not all of the posts had been disturbed. Cut 087 itself may represent the digging-out of a post, although the cut extended westward into the chalk natural, indicating that it represented a more formal and substantial feature. Several of these contexts produced animal bones and sherds of Late Bronze Age pottery.

The excavation showed that the cross-ditch stops short of northern Cursus ditch, and the work of Dave Field and his colleagues for the Stonehenge WHS Landscape Project (Pearson and Field 2011) has subsequently clarified the dating of the cross-ditch:

'The field evidence clearly shows that the cross-ditch stops short of the Cursus ditch on the north but cuts across the Cursus ditch on the south. The 2007 excavation (Trench 27) established that the cross-ditch ends some 2m short of the north ditch of the Cursus but this is so close that it must have cut into the north bank of the Cursus... The cross-ditch is therefore stratigraphically later' (Pearson and Field 2011: 29)

As mentioned in the preface, in a perfect world Dave Field's survey would have occurred before our excavation rather than after it, so that we could have drawn on his findings, but such is life. We can now say that the cross-ditch was not an original structural element of the Cursus, and is at least Late Bronze Age and probably earlier, given the presence of the pottery in the upper fills of the palisade slot. Furthermore, the cross-ditch's cut (120) gave the impression that a deeper and narrower slot had been cut through an originally shallow linear feature.

A series of stakeholes (069, 071, 073, 075, 077, 079 and 083) surrounded the terminal of the cross-ditch (Figures 3.12, 3.20). Their fills were broadly similar, but they varied in depth and morphology (although none was wider than 0.20m or deeper than 0.20m). The only other feature in the trench was a tree-throw hole (046) containing a chalky deposit (043/045) which presumably represented the material torn up by the tree roots. The position of this chalky mass immediately below the modern turf indicates that it was comparatively recent in date.

3.1.5. The southern Cursus ditch beside the 1947 excavation

As noted above, the position of Trench 28 (Figure 3.1) was decided in relation to that of J.F.S. Stone's 1947 cutting and, in the event, overlapped by about 1m, within which the cut of the so-called 'embayment' was identified (Figures 3.21–3.22). The removal of turf and topsoil from the 10m × 5m trench revealed a surface that was heavily scored by plough-ruts running approximately north–south, many of which had obviously cut into the upper lip of the Cursus ditch. There was no trace of the shallow linear scoops less than 100m to the west described by Julian Richards (his cuts 22 and 23) as running outside of and parallel with the ditch, in the cleared part of Fargo Plantation (Richards 1990: 93). Richards rejected these as evidence for any form of counterscarp structure on the sides of the Cursus, and their absence from the area of Trench 28 would support his view.

In the extreme west of the trench, the backfill of Stone's cutting was immediately visible as a mottled mixture of topsoil, chalk and sediment (004). The cut of the 1947 trench (SRP cut 005) formed a distinct, straight-sided feature, which had evidently been dug down below the weathered surface of the natural chalk. A corroded halfpenny was discovered on the base of the ditch at the extreme eastern end of Stone's cutting, presumably deliberately deposited by the excavator. The full extent of Stone's original 1947 trench (not all re-excavated by the SRP) is shown in plan in Figures 3.23–3.27, where it is added to the western end of SRP Trench 28.

The uppermost filling (003) of the Cursus ditch (cut 052) was also revealed by the removal of the topsoil (001). This was a striking orange-brown, fine silty clay with no trace of chalk content, and was very friable in texture (Figures 3.23–3.27). This material contained

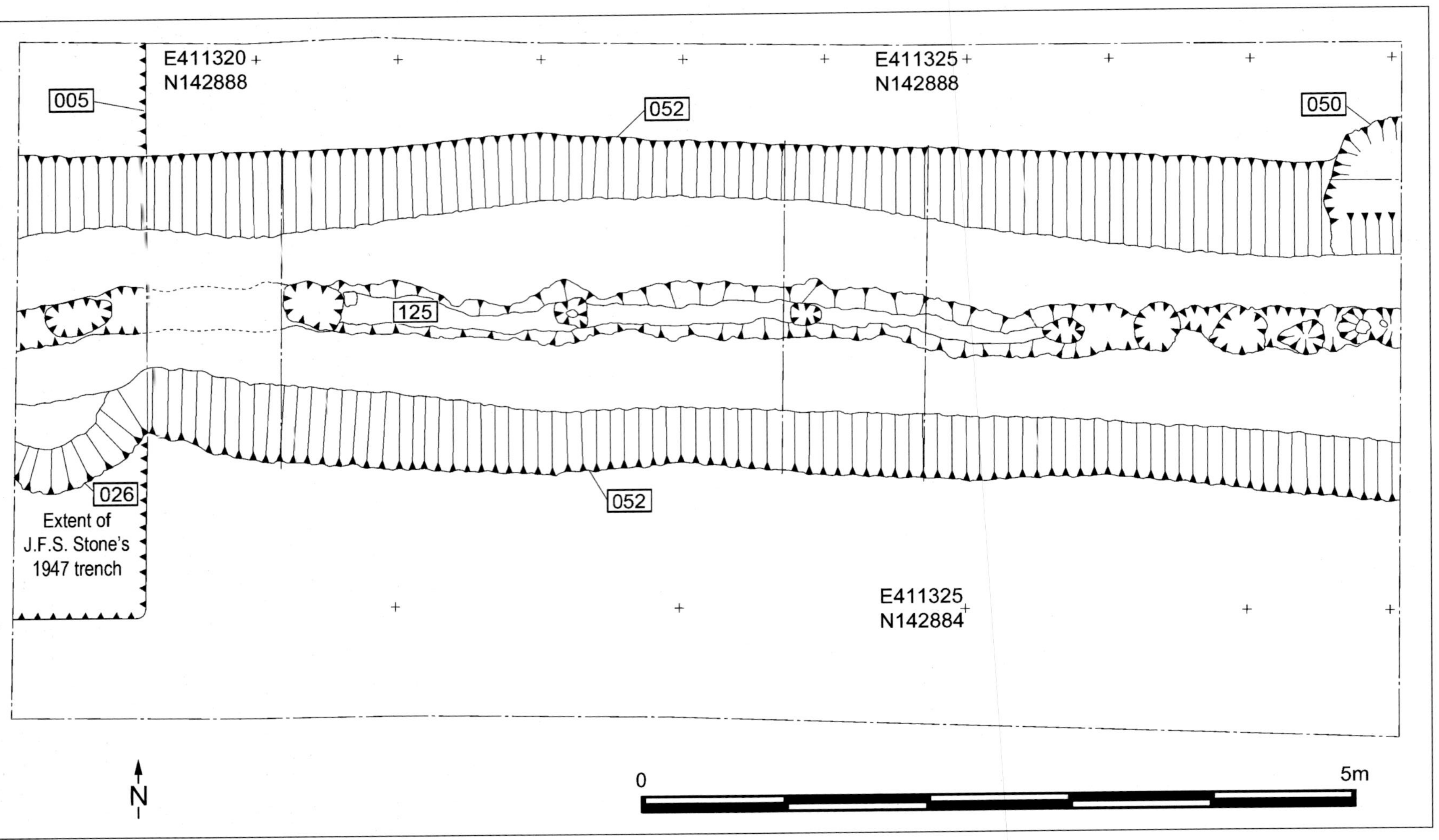

Figure 3.21. Plan of Trench 28 on the south side of the Greater Cursus

Figure 3.22. Trench 28 at close of excavation, viewed from the west. The bottom of recut 125 can be seen along the base of the ditch

a Beaker sherd and a barbed-and-tanged arrowhead (SF 12; see Figure 3.62).

Layer 003 was contained within a V-shaped cut (125) which descended through the earlier ditch fills to form a furrow in the ditch bottom, strongly signalling its intrusive character. Layer 003 was thus clearly the fill of a ditch re-cut, but the character of this infilling is uncertain. The fine silty fill had a loessic character, and may be a wind-blown deposit. It is surprising, then, that it is relatively constrained spatially, occurring in SRP Trench 28, in Richards' trench W56A and in Stone's cutting, but absent elsewhere. This may suggest that the deposit was a deliberate backfill, but again this interpretation presents difficulties. A sloping band of stones (065/067/126/128/129) ran through layer 003 in each of the sections drawn in Trench 28, and this was obviously the equivalent of Richards' context 13. The presence of this material strongly suggests that the accumulation of layer 003 halted temporarily, only to be followed by the resumption of a similar depositional environment. Such a sequence is more likely to be the result of natural rather than human agencies. A small amount of silty chalk wash (051) was deposited within cut 125 before layer 003 began to accumulate.

The removal of layer 003 revealed a cut feature (050) on the northern side of the ditch, at the eastern end of the trench (Figures 3.21, 3.27). This shallow, semi-circular, bowl-shaped cut extended into the edge of the ditch as well as cutting into the ditch silts. It was therefore securely stratified between the cutting and silting of the Cursus ditch and the re-cut 125. The fill of cut 050 was composed of densely-packed angular chalk fragments in a matrix of friable buff chalky silt (048/119). Cut 050 was similar in location and morphology to cut 026, the 'embayment' described by Stone (Figure 3.21), from which Stone recovered an antler pick subsequently dated to 2900–2460 cal BC at 95% confidence (OxA-1403; 4100±90 BP; see Marshall *et al.*, below). It is extremely likely that cut 050 and cut 026 (Stone's embayment) form elements of a group of contemporary features, also including cut 030/081 in Trench 27.

Re-cut 125 truncated silty deposits (038 and 039) on the northern and southern side of the ditch respectively. These deposits were composed of compact, mottled grey-buff chalk silt containing small rolled chalk fragments. A small patch of chalk rubble (066) lay on top of layer 038, and presumably represented a localised collapse of fresh chalk from the ditch edge. Its presence served to emphasise the complete absence of chalk rubble in the ditch bottom beneath 038 and 039. Strictly

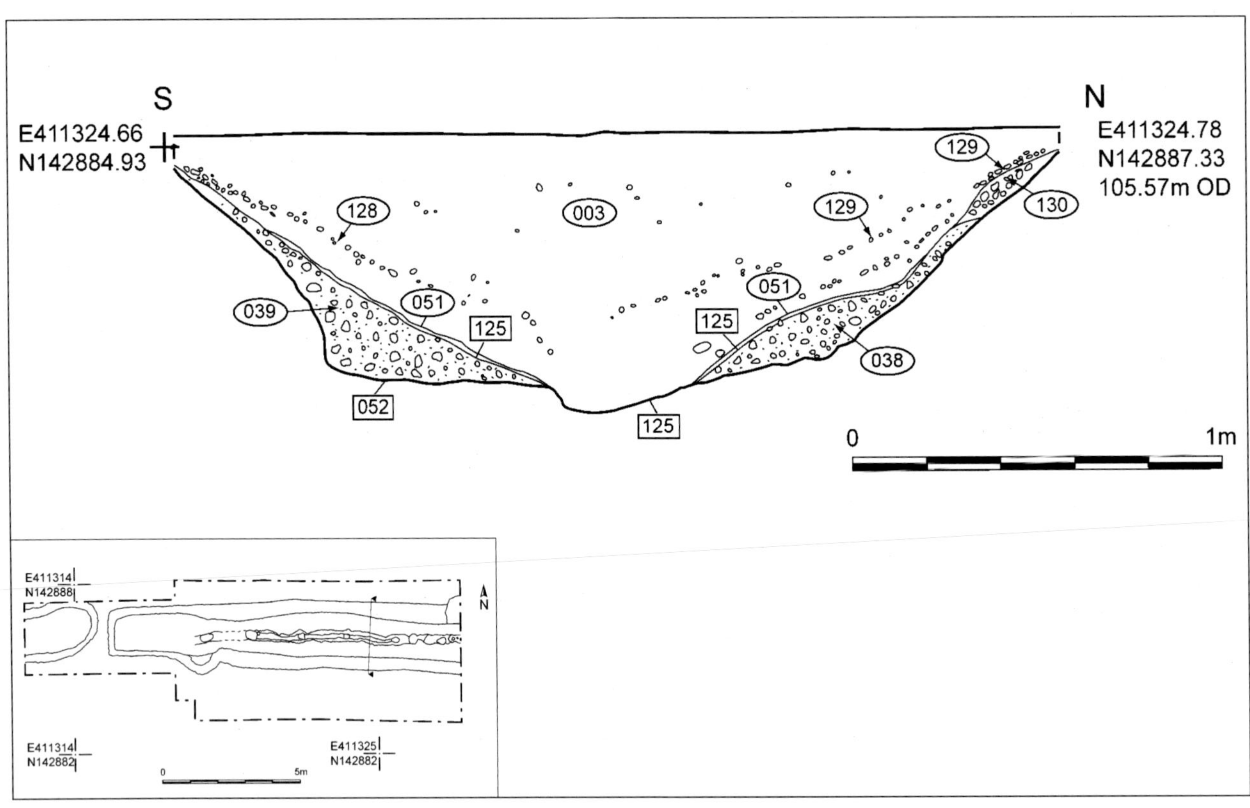

Figure 3.23. Section 1 of the Greater Cursus ditch in Trench 28

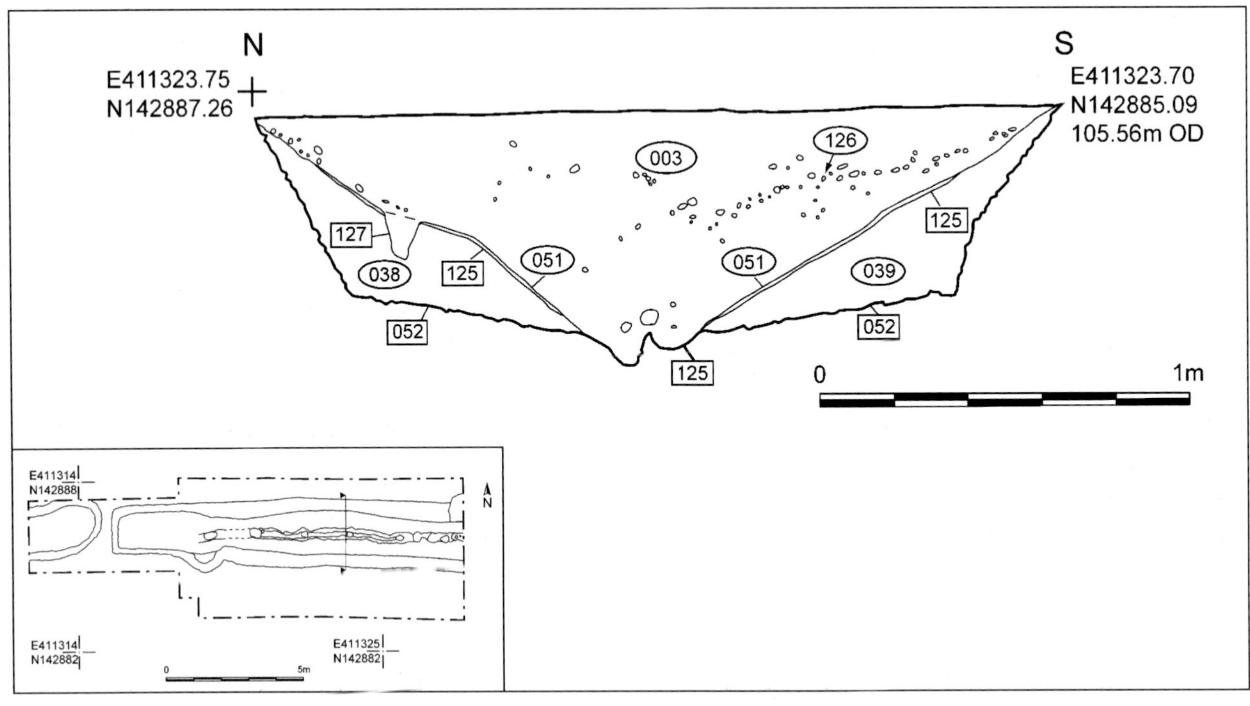

Figure 3.24. Section 2 of the Greater Cursus ditch in Trench 28

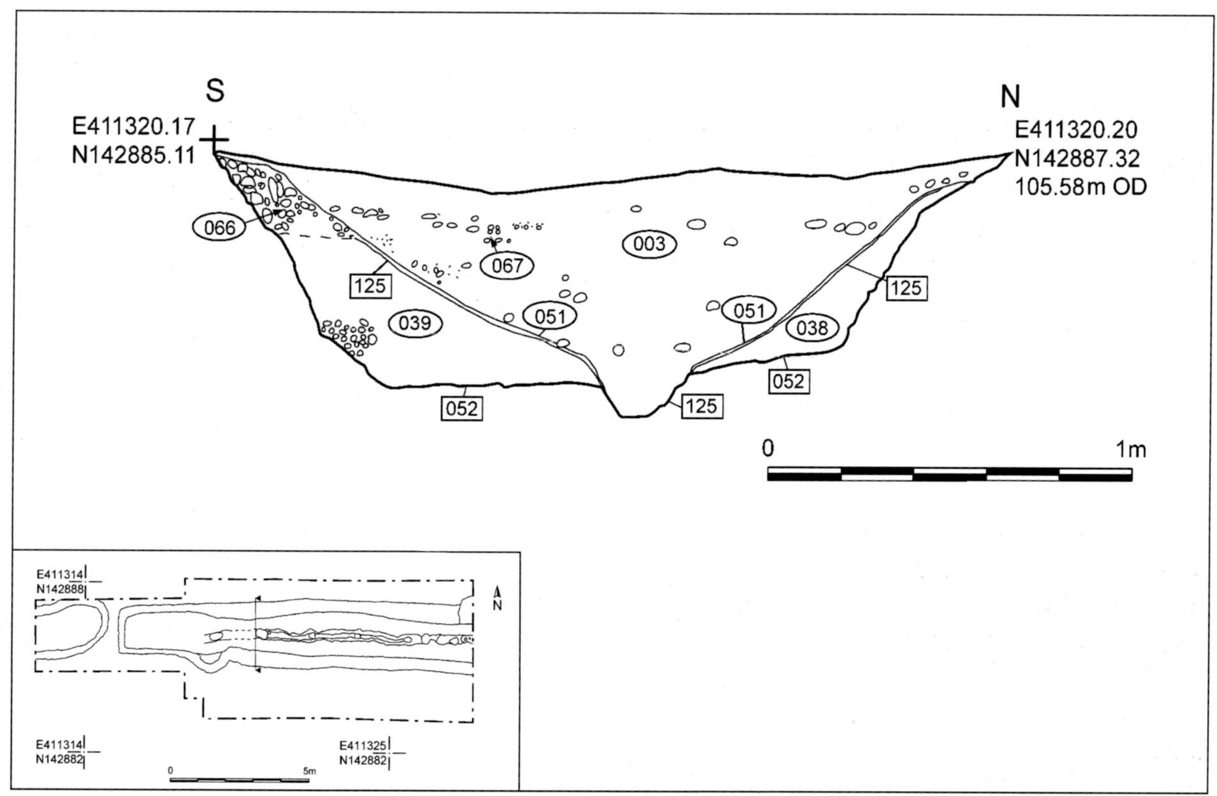

Figure 3.25. Section 3 of the Greater Cursus ditch in Trench 28

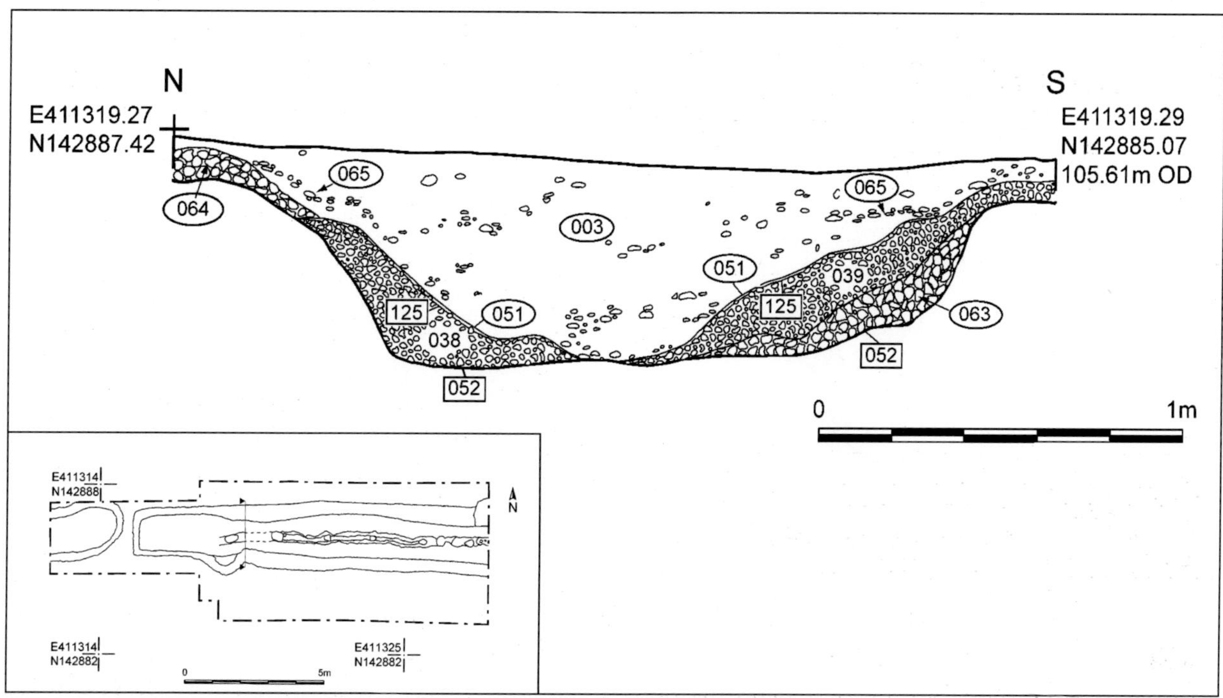

Figure 3.26. Section 4 (the most westerly) of the Greater Cursus ditch in Trench 28

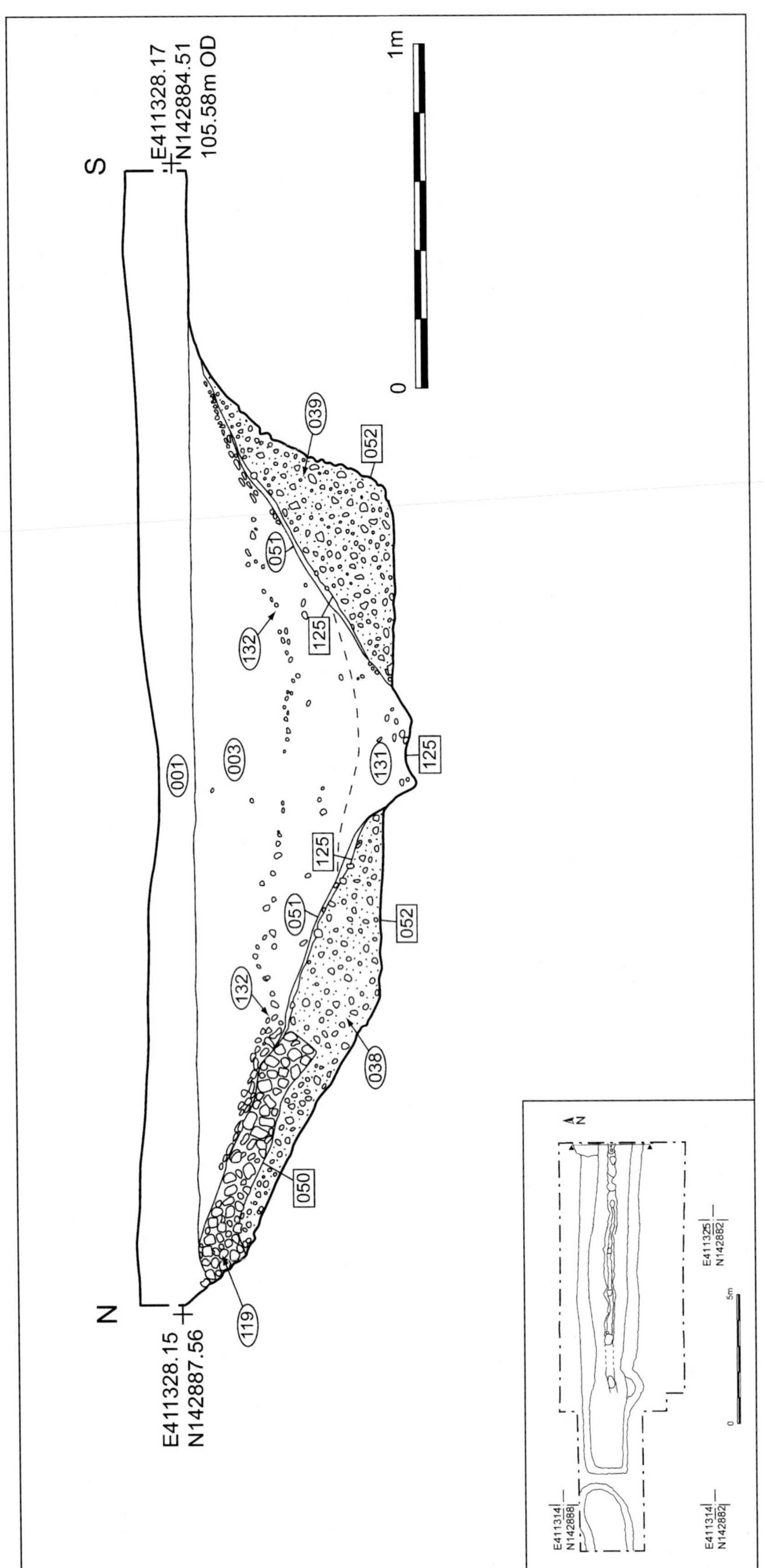

Figure 3.27. Section 5 (the most easterly) of the Greater Cursus ditch in Trench 28

speaking, these layers were 'secondary silts', and the absence of primary rubble can only be satisfactorily explained by the cleaning-out of the ditch prior to the accumulation of the chalky silting of the Cursus ditch (038 and 039).

It should be emphasised that the sequence of events documented in the ditch in Trench 28 contrasts entirely with that in Trench 26 at the western end of the Cursus and Trench 27 on the north side. While some cleaning-out may have taken place in Trench 27, the absence of chalk rubble in much of Trench 28 is striking, while the V-shaped re-cut digging into the ditch bottom, and the colour, texture and decalcified character of fill 003 were quite unlike anything encountered in the other ditch sections.

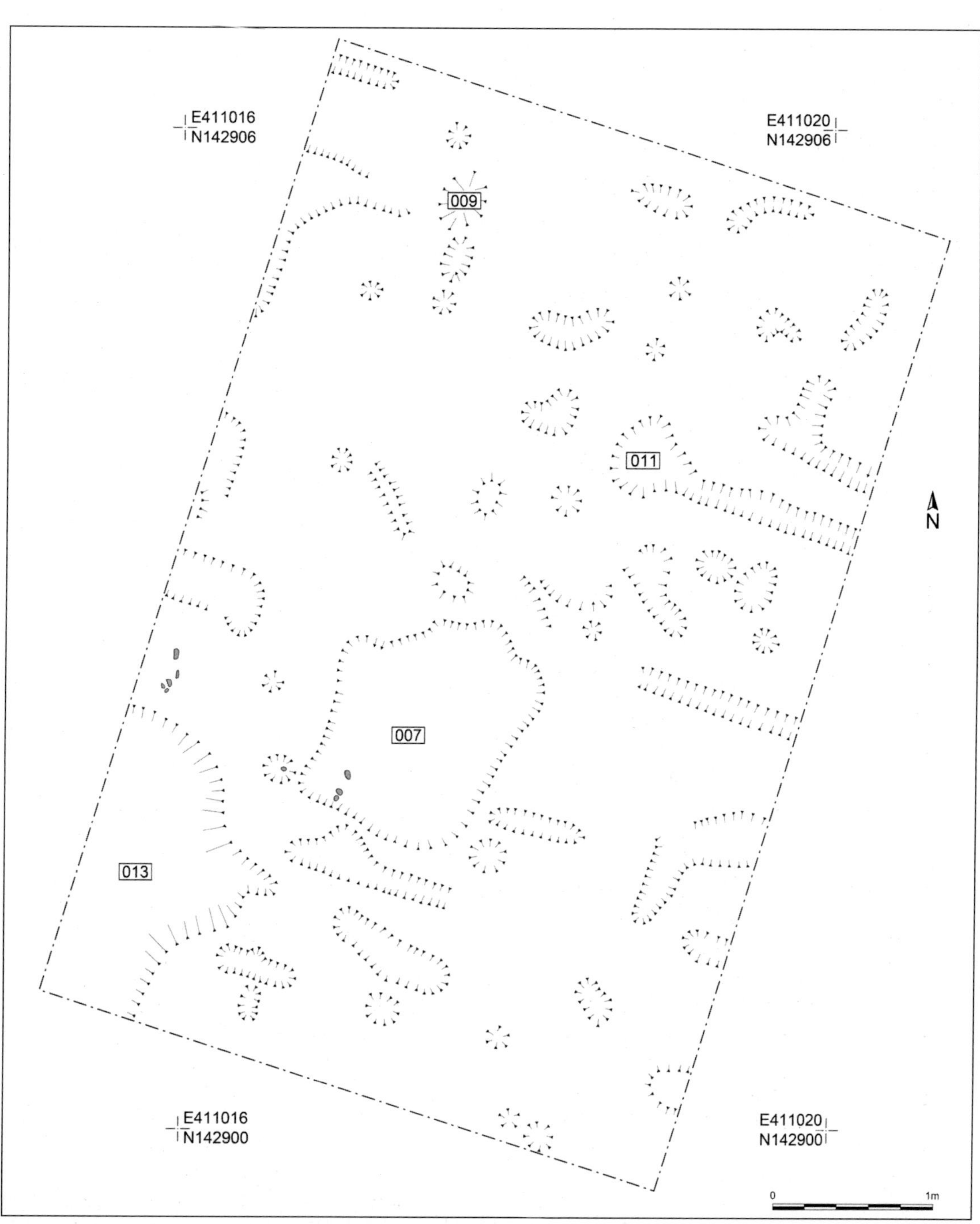

Figure 3.28. Plan of Trench 36 near the west end of the Greater Cursus

Figure 3.29. Trench 36, viewed from the north

3.1.6. Cuttings inside the Cursus

Trench 36 was a cutting measuring 6m × 4m (Figures 3.1, 3.28–3.29), laid out in order to investigate a series of geophysical anomalies forming a semi-circle of roughly 10m diameter, a little to the southwest of the two round barrows within the western terminal of the Cursus (visible on the geophysics plot in Figure 2.7). The well-sorted ploughsoil (001) was removed to reveal a thin layer of chalky pea-gravel (002), which overlay a series of features cut into the parent chalk (Figure 3.30). Unfortunately, none of these proved to be unambiguously of human origin. Feature 006/007 was probably a mass of root disturbance caused by a plant such as a hawthorn bush. Features 008/009 and 010/011 were further root disturbance. Feature 012/013, in the southwestern corner of the trench, was a pit with clearer edges than the other features, but was nonetheless very irregular in shape, and certainly did not relate to the pattern of geophysical anomalies.

Trench 38, a 5m × 5m cutting immediately inside the western terminal of the Cursus, north of the axial line (Figure 3.1), was also opened to test a promising geophysical anomaly (see Figure 2.7). As in Trench 36, the subsoil was covered by a thin layer of pea-gravel. The trench contained no features other than a series of modern postholes, with the bases of wooden posts *in situ* (Figure 3.31).

Trench 40 was located within the eastern terminal of the Cursus (Figure 3.2), where it was hoped that it would reveal the northwest quadrant of a circle of discontinuous geophysical anomalies, possibly part of an enclosure roughly 12m in diameter (visible on the geophysics plot in Figure 2.8). Upon the removal of a thin topsoil (101), it was immediately apparent that the chalk in this area was uneven and fragmented, so that the identification of any cut features would depend upon the laborious cleaning of the subsoil surface. Nonetheless, a series of linear features could readily be identified running east-northeast–west-southwest across the trench (cuts 125, 126, 127, 128; Figures 3.32–3.33). These had fills of light red-brown silty loam (102, 103, 105, 107, 109, 112, 113).

Although it was initially conjectured that these linear features might have been the result of chisel-ploughing, it seems more probable that they are cart-ruts, since they follow the line of the natural defile that leads from the Stonehenge Avenue out of Stonehenge Bottom, and up toward the modern gateway at the northeastern corner of the Cursus. This is presumably a long-established routeway.

Aside from a series of minor root disturbances and rodent holes, only three major features were revealed in the repeated trowel cleaning of the trench. These features (130, 131 and 132) correspond to the principal anomalies identified on the geophysical survey. These did indeed form an arc, although it was clear from the outset that they did not have clearly defined cut edges.

- Feature 130 was a ragged linear feature in the centre of the trench, aligned roughly north–south and around 2.00m long, and cut by cart-rut 126. It was shallow, with an uneven base, and was filled by light grey silt (124) beneath mid-brown loose silty loam (104). Everything about the morphology and filling of this feature suggests that it is a root-hole from a tree or large bush.
- In the southwestern corner of the trench, feature 131 was a broadly linear feature that ran south-south-west–north-northeast, intersecting with cart-rut 127.

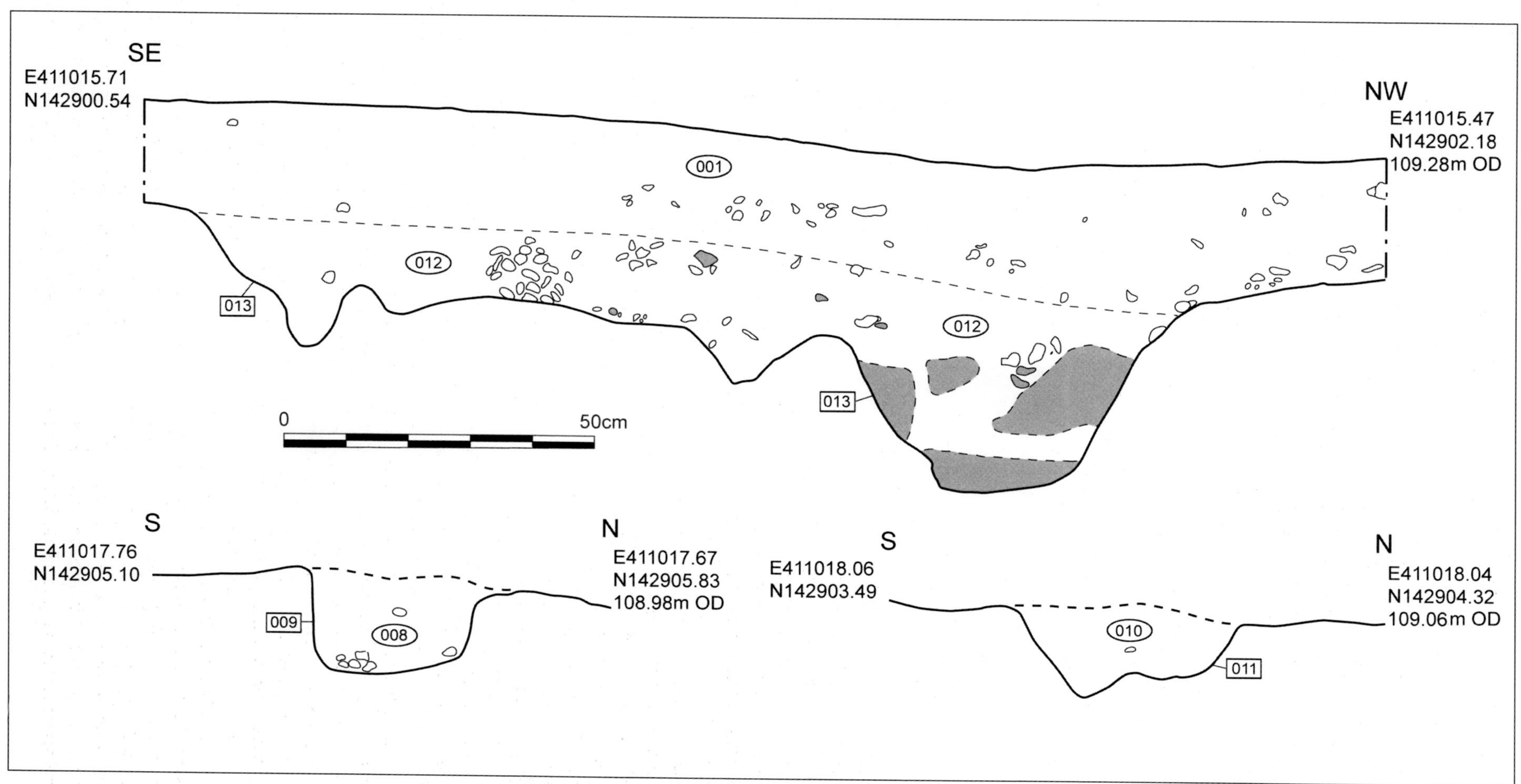

Figure 3.30. Sections through natural features in Trench 36

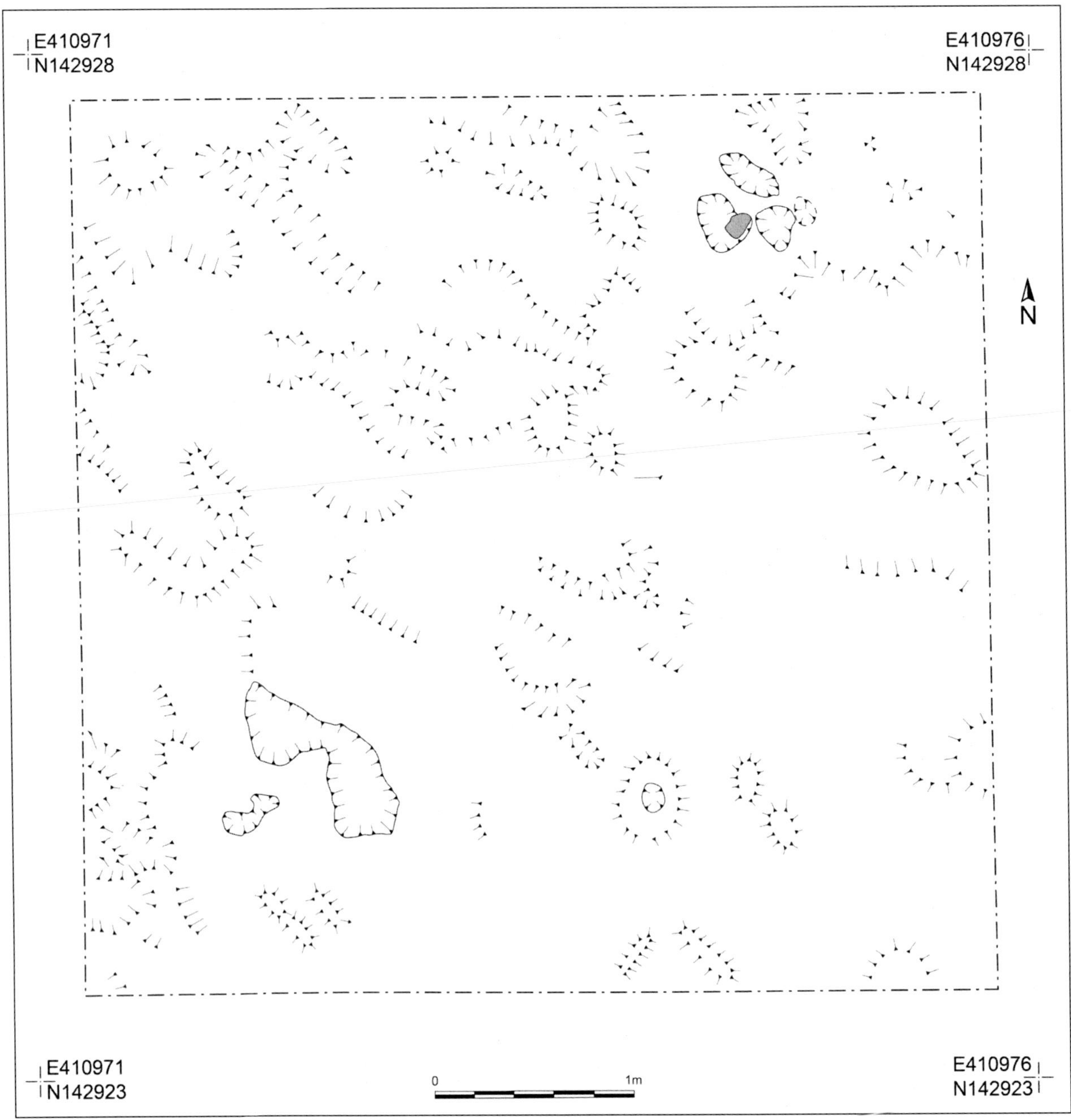

Figure 3.31. Plan of Trench 38 near the west end of the Greater Cursus

It proved to have poorly defined edges and an undulating base, and was filled by mid-brown silty loam (110).

- Finally, feature 132 lay in the northeastern corner of Trench 40, intersecting with cart-rut 126. This was still more diffuse and amorphous than the other two features, and contained a single fill of brown silty loam (108).

It is likely, then, that features 130, 131 and 132 are all tree-root bases, and that the semi-circular anomaly observed in the results of the geophysical survey was a small setting or grove of trees. This outcome is reminiscent of the Victorian plantation excavated at Barrow Hills, Radley, Oxfordshire (Barclay and Halpin 1998: 168). This was also excavated on the expectation that it might represent a Neolithic pit- or post-circle. In the case of the features revealed in Trench 40, it is worth considering whether a semi-circular plantation of trees established in the immediate vicinity of Stonehenge during the eighteenth or nineteenth centuries might have originally had some antiquarian significance, as a 'Druid grove', for instance.

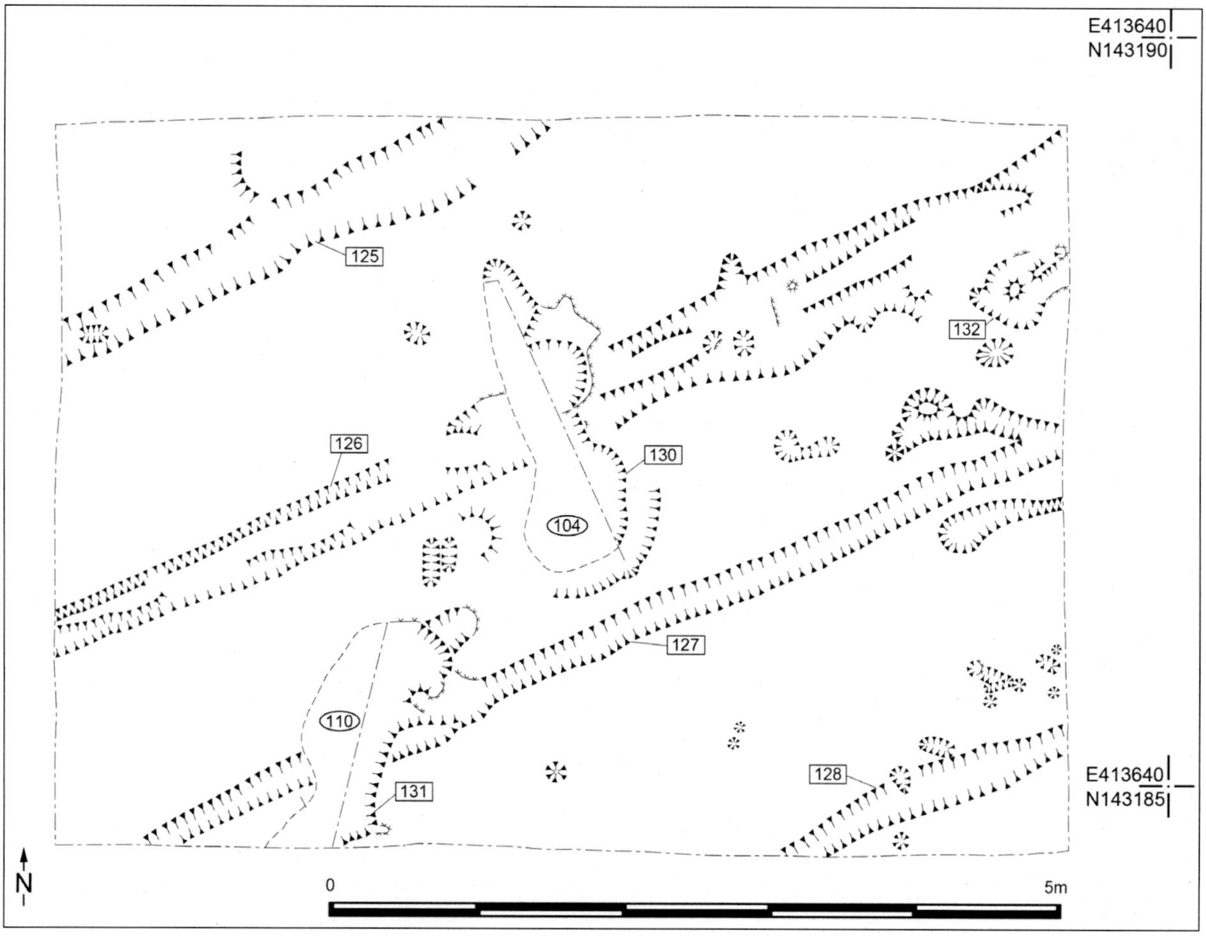

Figure 3.32. Plan of Trench 40 near the east end of the Greater Cursus

Figure 3.33. Trench 40, viewed from the south

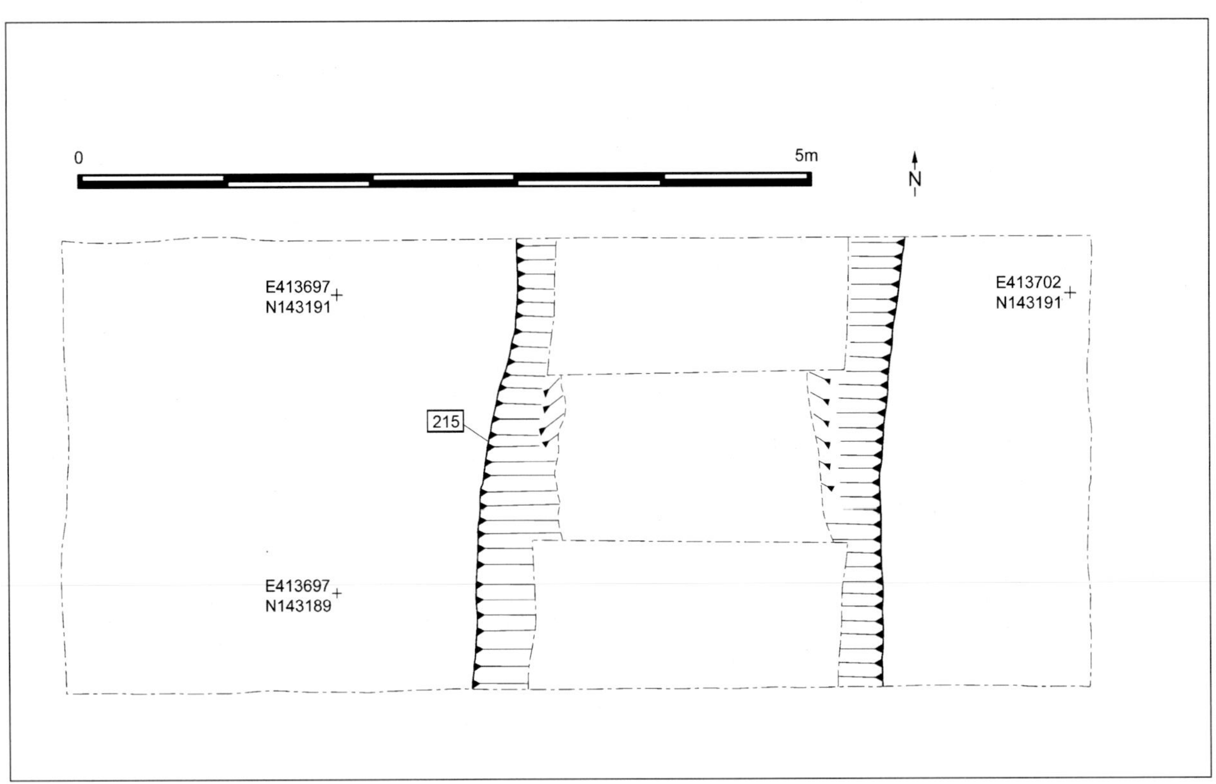

Figure 3.34. Plan of Trench 41 at the east end of the Greater Cursus

Figure 3.35. Trench 41, viewed from the west

3.1.7. The eastern terminal ditch of the Cursus

Prior to our excavations during the SRP, only Christie (1963) had excavated at the western terminal of the Cursus, and there had been no investigation of the eastern terminal ditch. Trench 41, measuring 7m by 3m (Figure 3.2), was designed to provide a basis for comparison, so that it could be judged whether the expanded terminal bank at the western end had been mirrored at the eastern end (Figures 3.34–3.35).

The results were somewhat unexpected. The Cursus ditch was shallower yet broader at the eastern terminal than at the western. The ditch was 1.40m deep from the modern turf surface, or 1.05m deep from the subsoil surface. This compares with depths of 1.50m from turf level and 1.20m from subsoil level at the western end. However, the eastern terminal ditch was 2.60m wide at the top, and 1.80m wide at the base (in contrast to the western terminal ditch, 2.70m wide at the top but only 1.00m wide at the base). In places, the inner edge of the ditch had been subject to root and other disturbance (214).

The sequence of filling in the eastern terminal ditch is broadly comparable with the western terminal (Figures 3.36–3.37). In the bottom corners of the ditch cut (215) were pockets of fine, compact, buff-yellow chalk silt (211 and 213). These would have formed very soon after the cutting of the ditch. Locally, a mass of material probably representing a collapse of turf (208) lay above these layers. Above these was the principal coarse chalk rubble fill (212). This material, derived from the sides of the ditch, was notably gravity-sorted, with large angular chalk fragments at the centre, shading into more compact, buff coarse silt with rolled chalk flecks toward the sides.

The quantity of coarse chalk fill seemed much less than at the western terminal. This may have been a result of the broader, shallower cut of the ditch, but it also seems likely that cleaning-out of the initial coarse silting, noted elsewhere in the Cursus ditch, took place at the eastern terminal. There was, however, no sign of either the circular re-cuts (the 'embayments') or the V-shaped slot recognised in the Cursus side ditches in 2007.

Above the coarse chalk fill was a coarse secondary silting (206). This was moderately compact, grey-brown in colour, and contained many small rolled chalk fragments. This was the most substantial fill of the ditch, and was followed by two layers of friable brown clayey silt (203 and 205). These were fairly similar materials, representing the tertiary, slow silting of the ditch, but they were separated by a patch of coarse chalky material (204) which may represent the collapse of the Cursus bank. Above these fills were a reddish-brown silty loam (202), presumably a ploughsoil, which extended beyond the ditch, and the topsoil (201).

3.1.8. Discussion

The 2007–2008 excavations served to clarify the history and character of the Greater Stonehenge Cursus in a variety of ways. Most importantly, they provided a date for construction. From the Cursus ditch, a broken antler pick was dated to 3630–3370 cal BC (OxA-17953; 4716±34 BP; and OxA-17954; 4695±34 BP; weighted mean 4706±25 BP; T'=0.2; T'(5%)=3.8; ν=1; Ward and Wilson 1978).

As concluded in Chapter 2, it is conceivable that the western end of the Cursus was laid out in relation to Beacon Hill, with Amesbury 42 long barrow providing the referent for the eastern portion (Figure 3.38). This implies that the southern side of the Cursus was laid out first, with the northern ditch added by a series of offsets, which may explain its more sinuous course. A further implication of this argument is that Amesbury 42 must pre-date the Cursus.

The opening of a 10m length of the Cursus ditch at the western terminal had significant benefits. For the first time, it was possible to recognise that the terminal ditch had been dug in a series of short segments, presumably by distinct working groups. Stone's work in 1947 indicated that the same might be the case in the side ditches, but here the segments were appreciably longer. This distinction can be interpreted in either ergonomic or social terms: either a work party of a particular size could dig a (short) length of terminal ditch or a (longer) length of side ditch in the same period, or it was important for each group of people engaged in the construction of the Cursus to 'own' a segment of the more significant terminal ditch.

The distinction between terminal ditch and side ditches was also evident in the comparative density of knapping clusters in Trench 26 by contrast with Trenches 27 and 28. These deposits were seemingly generated over a period during which the ditch edge was weathering back and nodules were being freshly exposed. The presence of debitage knapped *in situ* in the ditches of long barrows and cursus monuments has been remarked upon before (Thomas 1999: 78; Whittle *et al.* 1993: 210), and it has been conjectured that the manufacture of any artefact might have been less important than the practice of flintworking in itself. This seems to be supported by the material from the western terminal ditch which, technologically, appears atypical in a fourth millennium cal BC context, although not lacking in skill (see Chan, below and Volume 2).

While the contrast between terminal and side ditches is suggestive, that between Trench 28 (on the south side of the Cursus) and the other cuttings is startling. The orange-brown fine silty clay fill (003) is perplexing, as neither its explanation as a deliberate backfill nor as a wind-blown deposit derived from the ploughing of an area of clay-with-flints appears entirely satisfactory. Undoubtedly, this part of the Cursus ditch was treated in an entirely

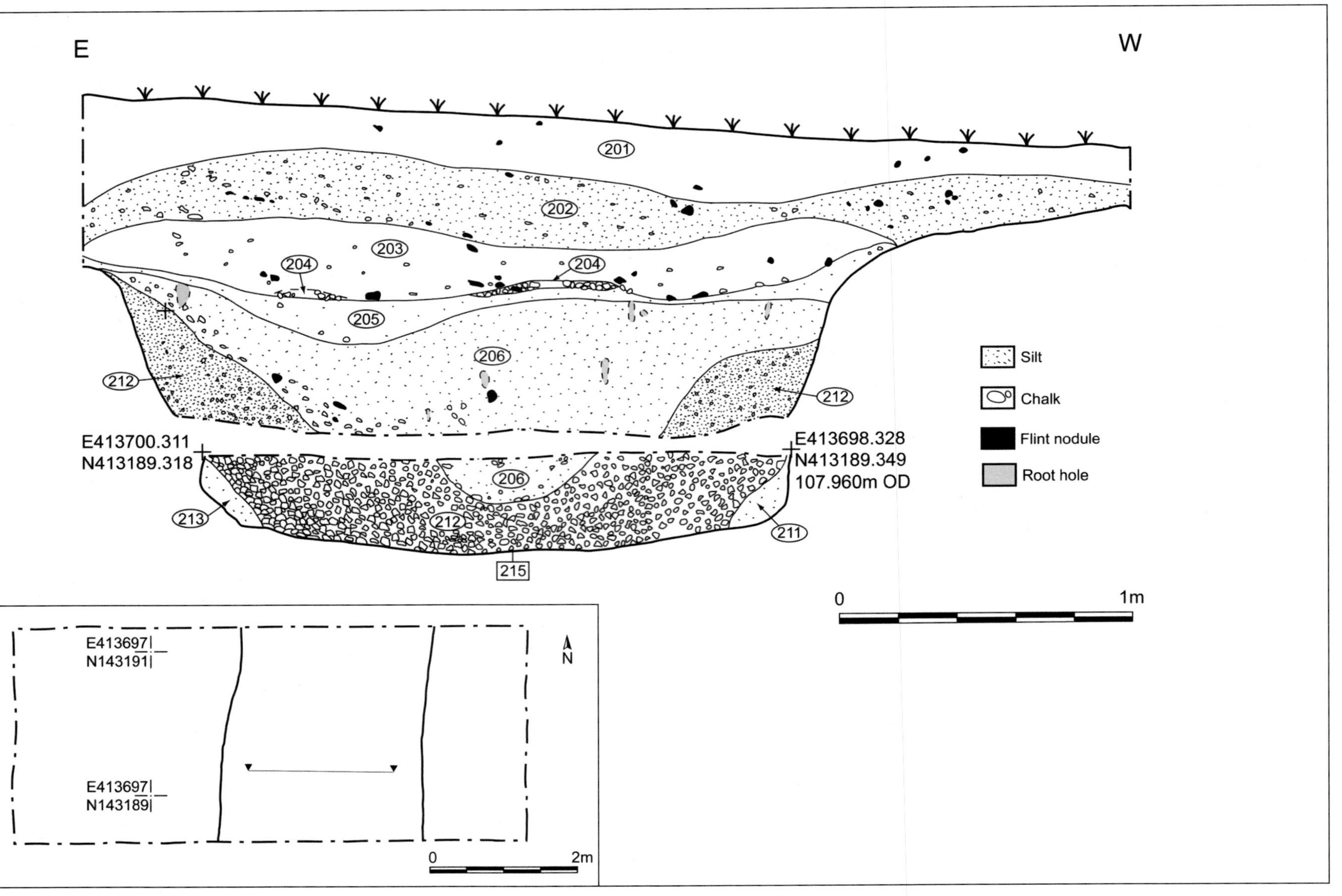

Figure 3.36. Section 1 through the Greater Cursus ditch in Trench 41

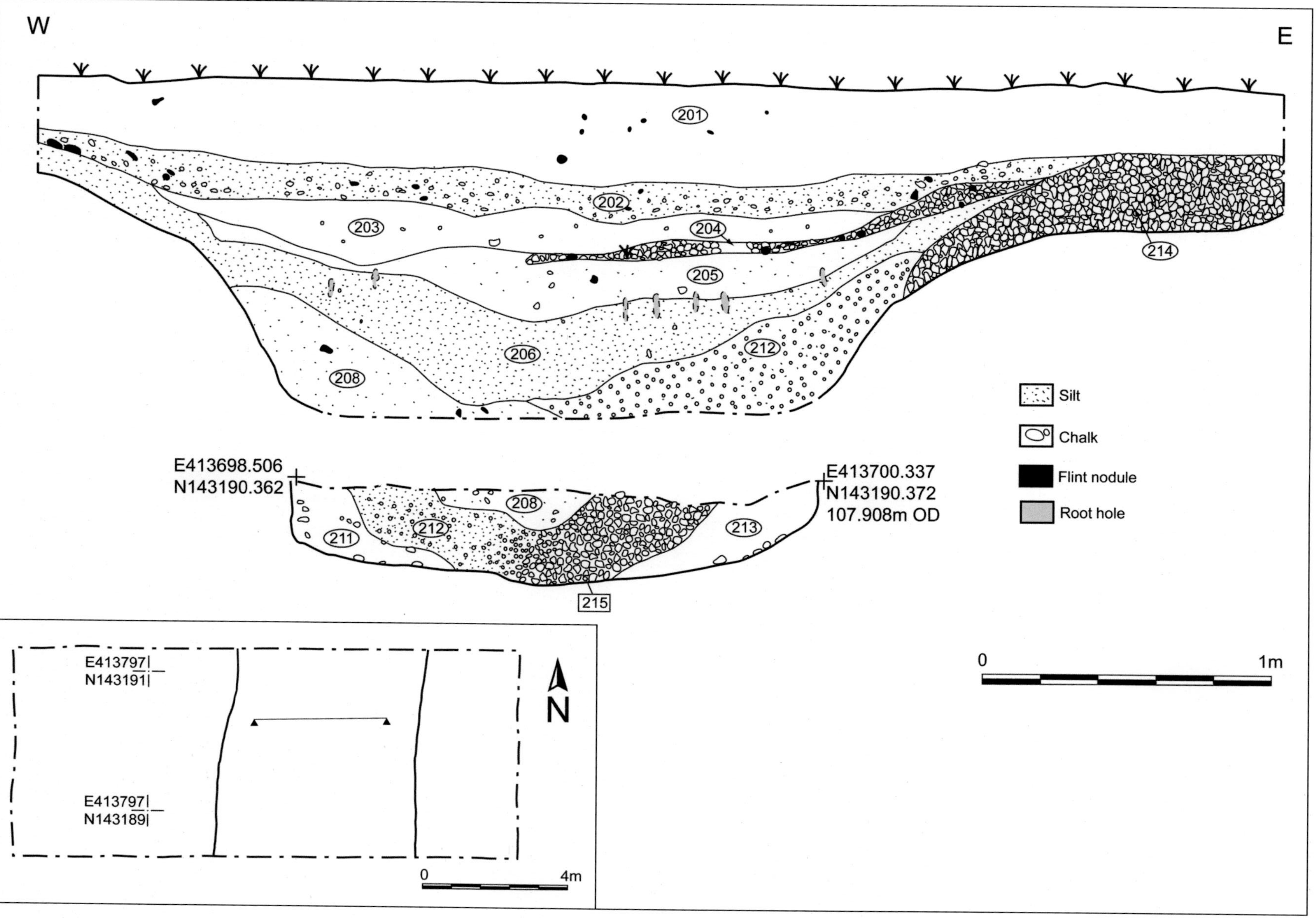

Figure 3.37. Section 2 through the Greater Cursus ditch in Trench 41

Figure 3.38. Trench 28, viewed from the west with Beacon Hill in the background; Amesbury 42 long barrow is behind the trees in the middle distance on the left of the picture

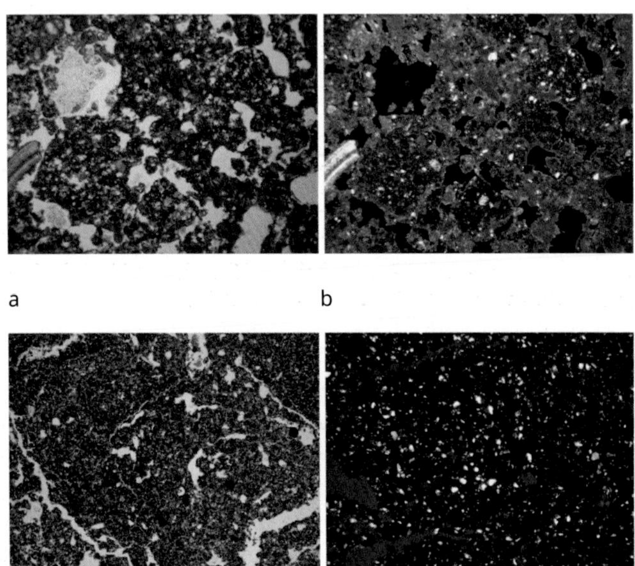

Figure 3.39. Photomicrographs (a and b) of chalk rubble and a micritic fine sandy loam fabric in the secondary fill of the west terminal ditch of the Stonehenge Cursus (frame width = 4.5mm) [a) plane-polarised light, b) cross-polarised light]; photomicrographs (c and d) of small blocky structured, very fine sandy clay loam with much humified organic and amorphous iron staining in the secondary fill of the southern ditch of the Stonehenge Cursus [c) frame width = 2cm; plane-polarised light; d) frame width = 4.5mm; cross-polarised light]

different way from the rest of the monument, first having its chalk rubble fill cleaned out, and later being re-cut, the re-cut then filling, probably naturally, during a time in which Beaker pottery was in use (at the earliest).

Despite the line of stones indicating a standstill horizon during its deposition, fill 003 of the southern side ditch was remarkably homogeneous, and this argues for a shorter rather than longer time over which it was laid down. We have noted that a very similar sequence was present in Julian Richards' W56A cutting, as well as in Stone's trench, but not in any other excavation that has been conducted on the Cursus ditches. It may not be coincidental that the evidence for ditch-cleaning, re-cutting and the deposition of orange-brown decalcified deposits is restricted to the westernmost part of the southern side ditch, precisely the portion of the ditch that is aligned on Beacon Hill, and which we have suggested may have been the first part of the Cursus to have been laid out. Is it possible, then, that this part of the monument possessed a certain primacy, which was recognised and remembered over a very long period, resulting in its refurbishment or re-creation on a number of separate occasions?

On the other hand, there is other evidence for the Cursus having been re-instantiated at other times. One of the most important pieces of evidence from the 2007 excavations is the recognition that Stone's 'embayment' was not an isolated feature, but part of a series of intrusive pits which may extend along the entire length of the monument. Embayment 026 was matched within Trench 28 by cut 050 and, in Trench 27, by cut 030/081. Cut 050, in particular, was tightly positioned stratigraphically, between the silting of the (Early Neolithic) Cursus ditch and the V-shaped (Beaker-period/Bronze Age) re-cut. This means that the Late Neolithic date from the antler that Stone recovered from his embayment is entirely comprehensible, but all the more intriguing. For it indicates that the architecture of the Greater Cursus was reinstated in the form of a discontinuous series of pits at much the same time as the construction of the sarsen settings at Stonehenge (Stage 2) and the Southern Circle at Durrington Walls. In other words, this was a time when the greater Stonehenge landscape as a whole was being extensively reconfigured.

The lack of evidence for internal features in the Cursus is disappointing. Although the geophysical surveys by Darvill *et al.* (2013) and Gaffney *et al.* (2012) revealed a number of geophysical anomalies within the Cursus that need to be investigated, the small number of such features does confirm the contrast between this massive enclosed space and monuments such as Durrington Walls, with their extensive evidence for occupation and deposition. The Cursus was a conspicuously 'clean' place, and this may reflect its status as an area that was important, and yet had been set aside as either sanctified or cursed (see Johnston 1999).

Given this comparative cleanness, the recovery of the antler from the base of the ditch in Trench 26 is particularly fortuitous. Its date in the late 37th–early 34th centuries BC is consistent with dates for large, ditched cursus monuments elsewhere in southern Britain (Barclay and Bayliss 1999; Thomas 2006; Thomas *et al.* 2009) and helps in untangling the development of an important (and early) portion of the Stonehenge landscape.

It had been anticipated prior to digging Trench 41 that the ditch at the eastern terminal of the Greater Cursus would be either of similar dimensions to that at the western terminal, or more akin to the shallower ditches along the sides of the Cursus. In practice, neither was the case. The eastern terminal ditch was shallower than the western, but rather broader. The quantity of upcast that would have been produced from this ditch must have been considerable, and might have formed a terminal bank comparable with that at the western end. However, this eastern terminal bank would have been diminutive by comparison to the massive mound of Amesbury 42, lying 30m to the east, and formed of the subsoil quarried from two ditches, each of the order of 3m deep. The fill of the eastern terminal ditch was relatively unremarkable, containing no re-cuts or other peculiarities. However, the quantity of chalk rubble within the ditch appeared rather limited, raising the possibility that, as elsewhere, this part of the Cursus ditch was cleaned out at some point.

3.1.9. Soil micromorphology of Greater Cursus ditch deposits

C.A.I. French

Two ditch deposits, from the southern side ditch of the Greater Cursus and from its western terminal, were selectively sampled for thin section micromorphology. The detailed soil micromorphology descriptions of these and other samples mentioned in this volume are given in full in Volume 2, and we provide here an overview of the findings. Analysis followed the methodology of Murphy (1986) and uses the descriptive terminology of Bullock *et al.* (1985) and Stoops (2003).

Western terminal: Trench 26

This ditch profile is composed of a primary fill of chalk rubble (layers 032/033/034 and 027/028/029; 1.05m–0.60m) with organic/humified calcareous silt loam lenses or 'standstill horizons' at 0.84m–0.80m and 0.60m–0.57m, with the remainder of the profile made up of fine chalk rubble (layer 022/023/024/025) and calcareous silt loam (layer 016). The upper standstill horizon (at the top of layer 029) was sampled for micromorphological analysis.

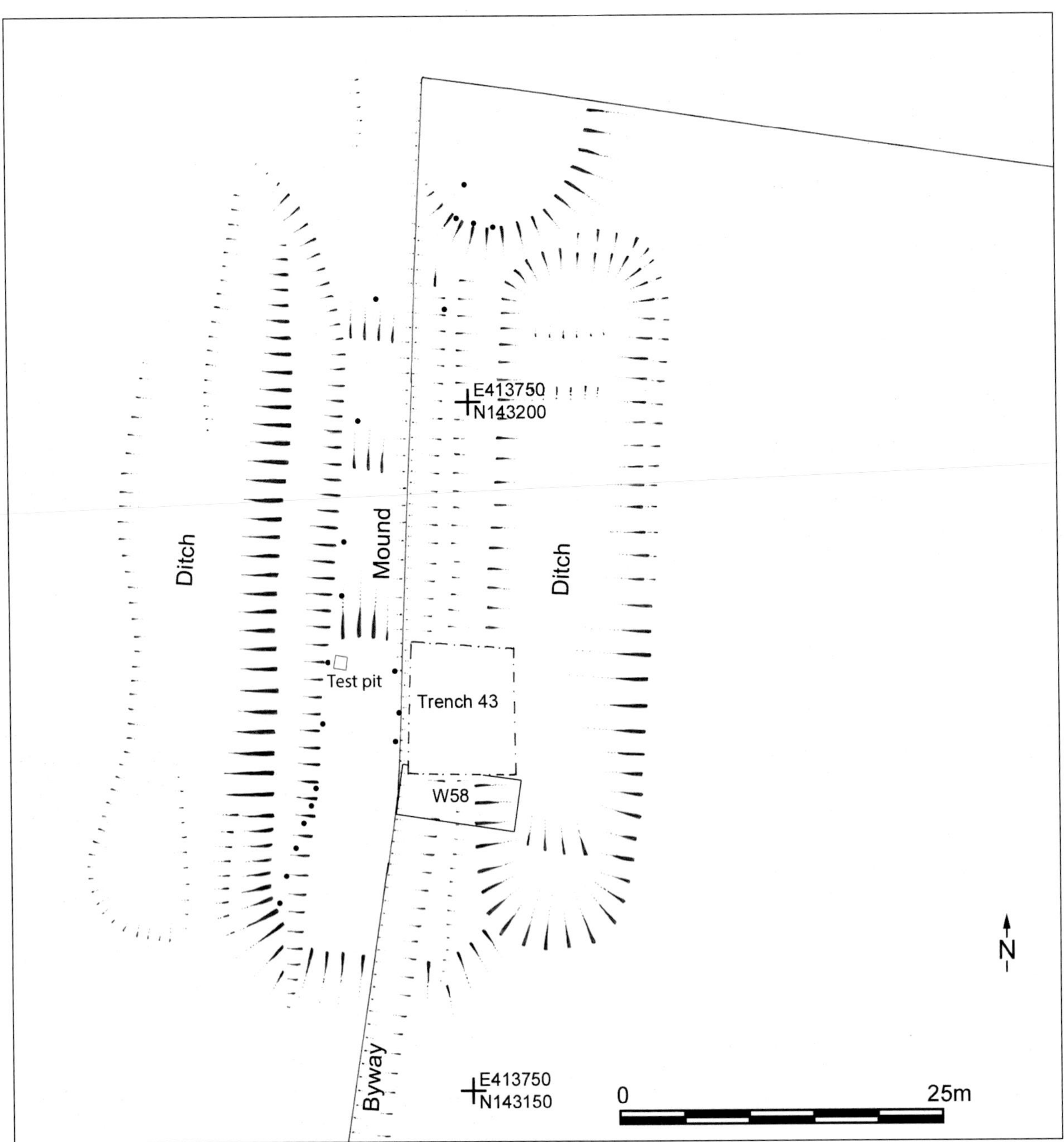

Figure 3.40. Plan of Amesbury 42 long barrow, showing positions of Trench 43, the 1983 trench (W58), the 2009 test pit, and auger hole locations (black dots)

This sample was composed of chalk rubble and a micritic fine sandy loam fabric (Figure 3.39a–b) similar to the ubiquitous rendzina soil fabric observed elsewhere in the SRP study area (see Volume 2). Interestingly, this sample also contained a fine dust of charcoal and humified organic matter, perhaps testifying to many fires in the immediate landscape in the Middle/Late Neolithic, and also a very minor amount of impure clay, possibly derived from disturbance of bare soils on either edge of the ditch.

Southern side ditch: Trench 28

About 350m from the western terminal of the Greater Cursus, the southern ditch exhibited a pale orangey-brown upper secondary fill deposit (layer 003). This was sampled for micromorphological analysis to check this fabric type and possible derivation. The results could contribute to the debate about the presence of late glacial loessic silts being once much more widespread in the chalklands of Wessex as Catt (1978) has postulated, and these being subsequently reworked because of prehistoric clearance and arable activities.

This sample exhibited a stone-free, small, moderately well-developed blocky structure of very fine sandy clay loam. It is unlike any other soil or deposit sampled in the project in terms of its strong reddish-brown colour (resulting from much impregnation with amorphous iron), its small blocky structure, and the very fine quartz sand and silty clay dominated fabric (Figure 3.39c–d). The well-sorted and ubiquitous very fine sand and silt fine fractions is what one could expect in a loessic soil (Catt 1978; Goldberg and Macphail 2006: 143).

Unfortunately, it was not feasible to excavate a section through the adjacent Cursus bank and associated old land surface, so it is not possible to say whether the pre-monument buried soil was also characterised by similar loessic components. Nonetheless, this material must be derived from the immediate vicinity of the open Cursus ditch in the Chalcolithic/Early Bronze Age, and implies the exposure of bare loessic-like soils adjacent.

This loessic-like fill has occasionally been noted elsewhere on the chalklands of Wessex, such as nearby along the route of the A303 to the north of Amesbury (Macphail and Crowther 2008) and as the tertiary fill of Early Bronze Age round barrow ring-ditches of the Wyke Down group and Iron Age linear ditches on Gussage Cow Down, both on Cranborne Chase (French *et al.* 2007: 75 and 101). Whether reworked from the adjacent soil through weathering or accumulating as an aeolian deposit, it certainly implies that loessic deposits were not far away and were open as bare ground surfaces to enable transport and then redeposition through washing out of the atmosphere through precipitation (Goldberg and Macphail 2006: 143).

3.2. Amesbury 42 long barrow

J. Thomas

In 2008, the eastern flanking ditch of Amesbury 42 long barrow was investigated with a 10m × 10m cutting (Trench 43; Figures 3.2, 3.40), located immediately to the north of Julian Richards' 1983 excavation of the long barrow ditch (W58; Richards 1990: 96–109). In practice, the two cuttings overlapped by around 0.10m, so that the southern section of Trench 43 was composed of Richards' backfill. At an early stage it was recognised that it would be impractical to shore up the sections of the long barrow ditch, and a decision was made to step the ditch section. Since the ditch was over 2.80m deep, this meant that two steps were required at each end of the cutting. In consequence, a length of only 6m of the ditch bottom was eventually revealed (Figures 3.41–3.42).

3.2.1. The ditch

As in the cases of Trenches 40 and 41, all of the topsoil was removed in metre squares and sieved; each of these test-pit squares had its own number. This proved extremely laborious, as in the area over the ditch the topsoil (001) and the underlying ploughsoil (002) were upwards of 0.70m thick (Figure 3.43). The topsoil produced lithics (see Mitcham, and Chan, below) and a fragment of human bone, which produced a Late Bronze Age date of 920–800 cal BC at 95% confidence (SUERC-75197; 2712±30 BP; Table 3.6). All the material from the topsoil is residual/redeposited.

Layer 002 was a dark grey silty clay loam containing small rolled chalk pebbles, which produced appreciable numbers of Roman and medieval finds. This lay above a mixed horizon of friable, reddish-brown silty clay (003) which contrasted markedly with the underlying layer (006), a moderately compact mid-brown silty clay containing considerable quantities of small to medium-sized rolled chalk fragments. It is highly likely that this chalk was derived from the barrow mound, and that layer 006 represented the destruction of the tumulus.

Significantly, layer 006 overlay a layer of eroded and fragmented chalk (035) on the inner berm of the ditch, and a chalk interface (044), the erosion surface surrounding the ditch. Contexts 035 and 044 ran up from the edge of the ditch to an area of protected chalk in the western part of Trench 43, which probably reflected the original extent of the barrow mound (see *Features west of the causewayed pits*, below). It is probable that the erosion surrounding the ditch was caused by ploughing, which would have repeatedly clipped the ditch edge, progressively forming the shallow surface of 044. The survival of the protected chalk immediately to the east of the byway suggests that, for some period, the long barrow served as a headland. The implication is that the destruction of the long barrow took place long after the establishment of a post-medieval plough agricultural regime in the area, possibly as late as the nineteenth century.

Beneath the destruction deposit (006) was a friable, reddish-brown silty clay with lenses of grey weathered chalk (007). This was again a ploughsoil, although it also represents the stabilisation of the deposits in the ditch. Layer 007 did not extend beyond the ditch cut (037), although it was contiguous with 010, 011 and 012, the uppermost deposits in three causewayed pits on the inner side of the ditch (Figures 3.43–3.44; see below). Layer 007 was notable for containing relatively large quantities of struck flint, later prehistoric pottery and a few pieces of butchered animal bone. Beneath it lay a friable, mid-brown clayey silt loam containing quantities of small rolled chalk pebbles and much pea grit (017). This is likely to have been the result of the erosion of mound material into the ditch, at a time in the post-medieval period after the commencement of arable farming locally. Layer 017 contained a fragment of Peterborough Ware (the only Neolithic pottery from Amesbury 42) and a human

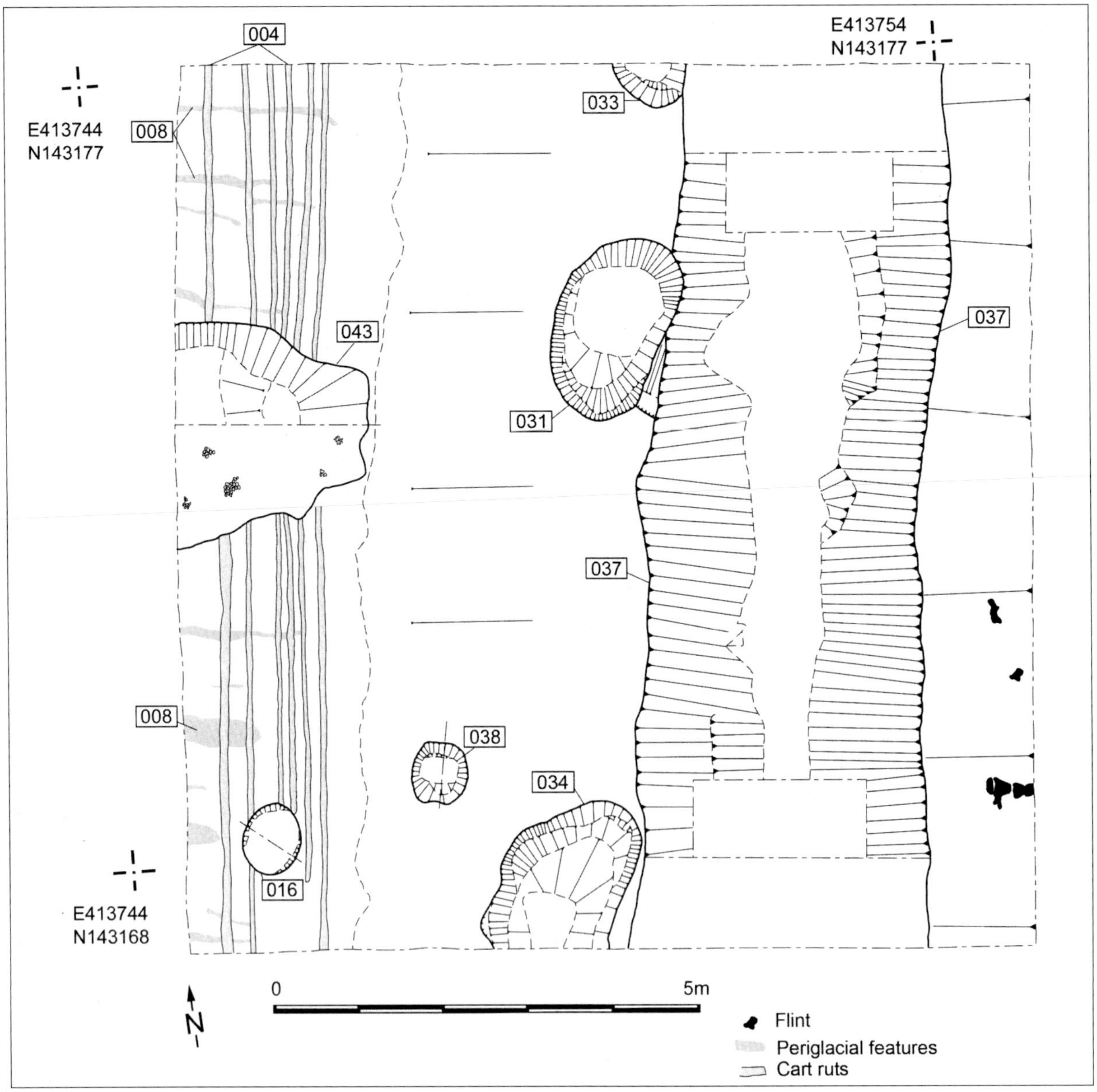

Figure 3.41. Plan of Trench 43 dug into the east ditch of Amesbury 42 long barrow

Figure 3.42. Trench 43 at Amesbury 42 long barrow showing the east ditch cut on its west side by pit 031, viewed from the north

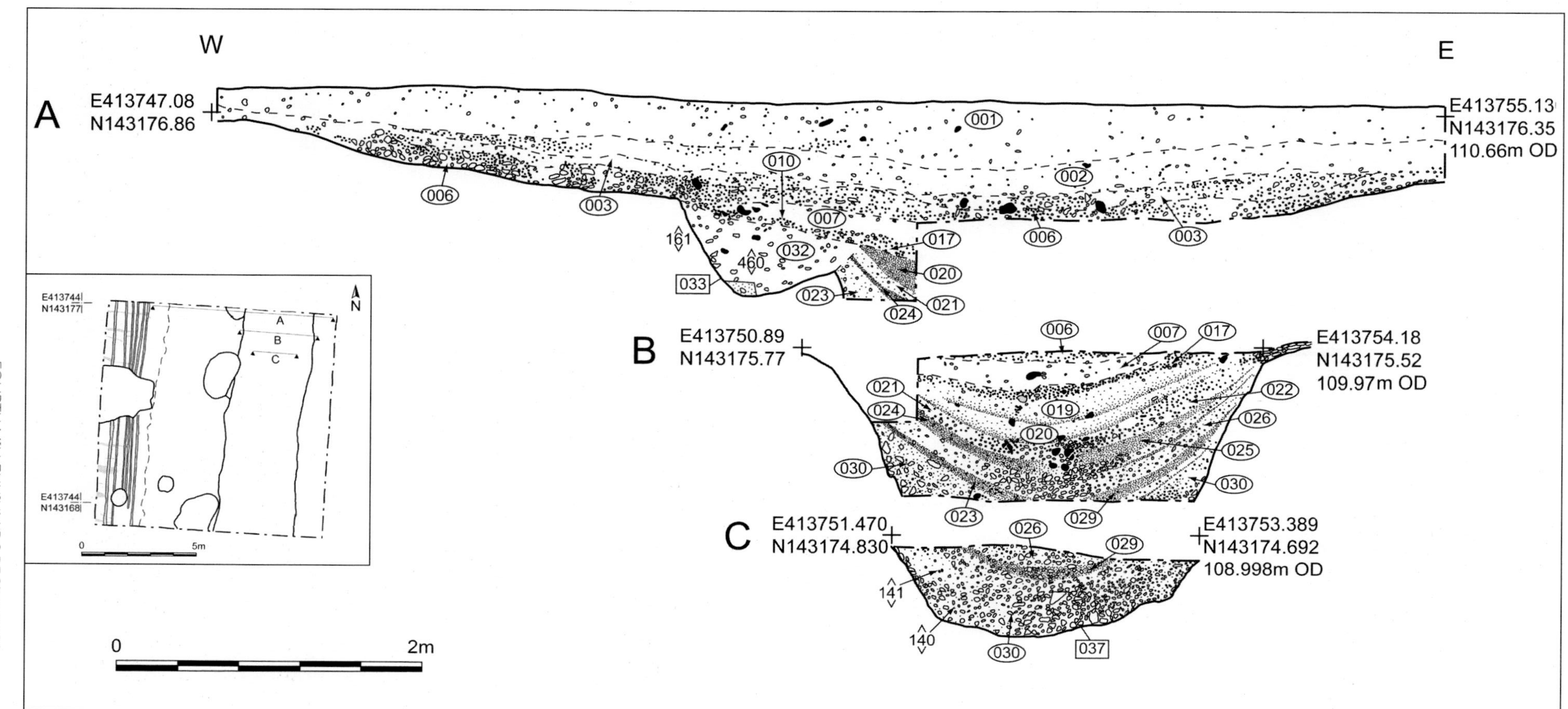

Figure 3.43. Section 2 of the east ditch of Amesbury 42 long barrow in Trench 43

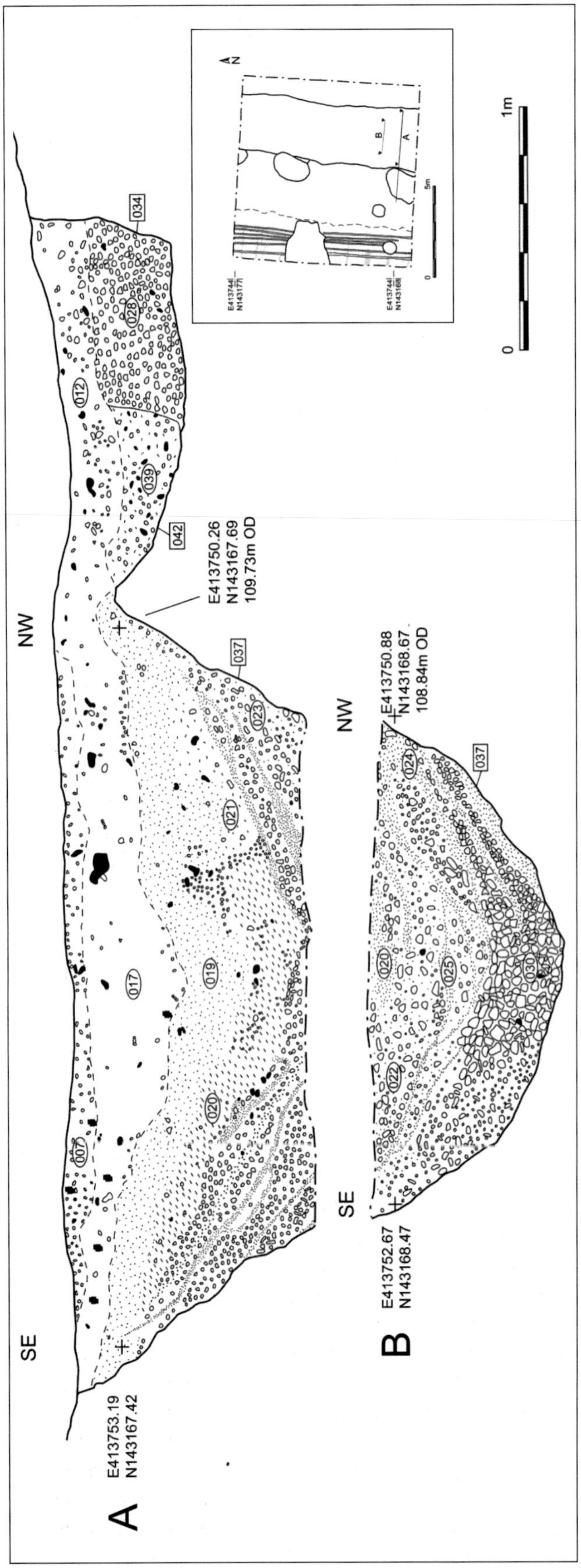

Figure 3.45. The antler pick fragment (SF 1407) in the bottom of the long barrow ditch, viewed from the east

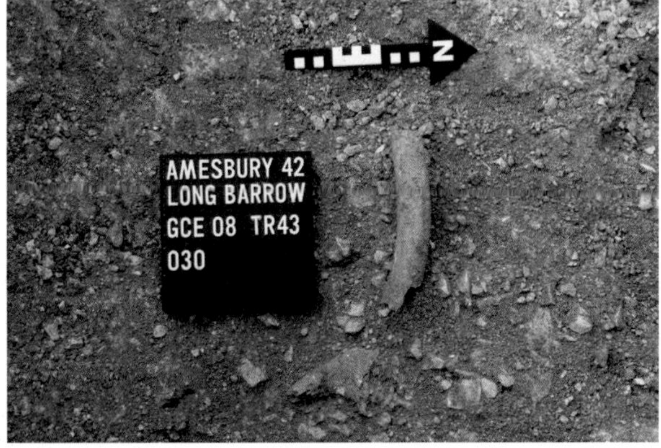

Figure 3.46. The antler pick fragment (SF 1407), viewed from the east

Figure 3.44 (left). Section 1 of the east ditch of Amesbury 42 long barrow in Trench 43

femur shaft of Middle Neolithic date of 3360–3100 cal BC at 95% confidence (OxA-21961; 4520±32 BP; see Table 3.6). Both have been redeposited.

Below layer 017 was a friable, mid-grey/brown silty clay loam with a few small rolled chalk fragments (019). This relatively fine, dark tertiary silt also presumably accumulated after the development of an arable regime in the vicinity. It lay above a quite different deposit, composed of friable, buff-grey silty clay loam containing an appreciably greater quantity of small rolled chalk fragments (020). Beneath this, contexts 021 and 022 were actually the same layer, initially identified separately on the inner and outer sides of the ditch respectively: layer 021/022 was a friable to compact mid-grey silty clay loam with around 40% small to medium rolled chalk inclusions.

Beneath 021/022 was 024/025, a friable, fine, mid- to dark-grey clayey silt. When this material was first revealed, we speculated that it might represent a layer of burning, but on excavation it contained no obvious traces of charcoal at all. It is more likely that it represented a collapse of turf (from the mound or sides of the ditch), or a formation of vegetation within the ditch. Beneath this was a compact mass of light grey chalky secondary silt (023/026) with *c.* 50% small to medium rolled chalk fragments. These became larger toward the centre of the ditch, indicating that they had tumbled in from the sides. This material had been cut by two of the causewayed pits (031 and 033; Figure 3.44), providing a very important stratigraphic relationship (see below).

Layer 029, the layer below 026, was similar to 024/025: a fine, friable dark grey-brown silt with a few small rolled chalk fragments. Like 024/025, it contained no charcoal and it probably represents a collapse of turf into the ditch. Finally, below layer 029 lay the primary chalk rubble fill (030) of the ditch. The chalk fragments within 030 were large and angular, and, at the centre of the ditch, there were voids between the individual lumps. Toward the sides of the ditch, layer 030 contained a series of distinct lenses of compact, coarse, buff to light grey silt.

In all of the layers below 007, the relative sparseness of cultural material was notable. At most, a few flint flakes were present in each context. This was also true of the primary fill (030), although a single fragment of antler beam was found on the base of the ditch, near to the southern standing section (SF 1407; Figures 3.45–3.46, 3.59). Although this was a fragment of beam rather than tine, the presence of burning to detach the proximal end of the antler indicates its manufacture as an antler tool or an off-cut from a short-handled pick. It dates to 3520–3350 cal BC at 95.5% probability (SUERC-24308; 4645±30 BP; see Marshall *et al.*, below).

Layer 030 was the basal fill within ditch cut 037, which had originally been cut with a comparatively flat base and straight sides (Figures 3.43–3.44). The tabular character of the chalk bedrock was very clear, and it was evident that the ditch had been dug by levering out blocks of chalk. The ditch was deepest toward the south of Trench 43, where it was over 2.80m below turf level. The base of the ditch rose slightly toward the centre of the excavation trench, before falling again further north. The highest point coincided with a slight narrowing in the width of the ditch, and this gave the impression of a slight causeway. It is highly likely that this marks the point where two separate work gangs met in the course of ditch-digging.

3.2.2. The causewayed pits

In Julian Richards' excavation of 1983, a smaller ditch appeared to run parallel with the main long barrow ditch, along its inner (western) side (Richards 1990: 98). This ditch (his cut 111) was interrupted by a causeway, but there was no reason to suspect that it did not represent an otherwise continuous linear feature. In Richards' section (1990: fig. 65) it is evident that ditches 111 and 133 (the main long barrow ditch) do not intersect, and that his layer 88 (the equivalent of our 007) runs unbroken across the two features. Nonetheless, in the circumstances, Richards' argument that cut feature 111 was an earlier ditch, possibly relating to an earlier and relatively diminutive stage in the development of the long barrow, was wholly reasonable (1990: 99). In this scenario, the larger ditch (his cut 133) would represent the elaboration of the mound into a much larger structure, and this might acceptably be conjectured to have taken place at the same time as the construction of the Greater Cursus.

However, the opening of Trench 43 provided an unexpected refutation of Richards' evidence. Rather than a continuous ditch running parallel with the eastern ditch (cut 037), three separate and discrete features were revealed: causewayed pits 033, 031 and 034. Pit 034 was the northern half of Richards' context 111, but it is noteworthy that this was separated from pit 031 by a considerable distance. Pit 033 was only a little to the north of pit 031 (see Figure 3.41).

The line of causewayed pits runs at a slight angle to ditch 037 so that, although pit 034 does not intersect with the long barrow ditch, pits 031 and 033 do. Thus, while Richards was not able to observe the stratigraphic relationship between the two sets of features, this was possible in Trench 43. It is quite clear that pits 031 and 033 both cut the fills of ditch 037, reversing the sequence that Richards suggested. Most significantly, pits 031 and 033 both cut ditch fill 023/026 (Figure 3.43), demonstrating that the causewayed pits were dug at a time when the secondary silts were forming in the long barrow ditch. It was noticeable, however, that the causewayed pits had not been dug into the long barrow ditch as such, but into the inner lip of the ditch, so that the material quarried from the pits would have been clean chalk rather than ditch silt. This point may be significant (see *Discussion*, below).

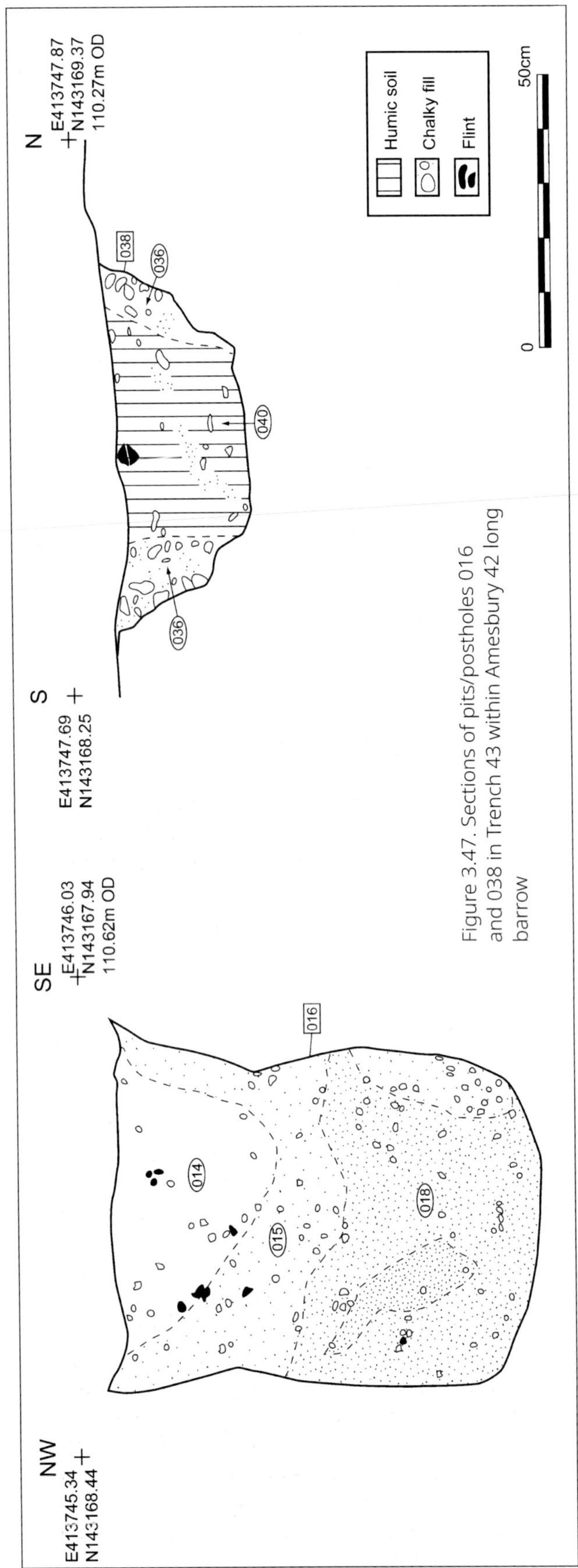

Figure 3.47. Sections of pits/postholes 016 and 038 in Trench 43 within Amesbury 42 long barrow

The principal fills of pits 031, 033 and 034 were indistinguishable from each other. Pit fills 027, 032 and 028 respectively were compact, light grey-buff chalky silts with a large proportion of medium-sized angular and rolled chalk fragments. In each case, the equivalents of ploughsoil 007 washed across and sealed the surfaces of the causewayed pits (contexts 010, 011 and 012).

The southernmost pit (034) departed from this pattern, however, in that its fill (028) had been cut by feature 042, an oval re-cut oriented north–south, slightly stepped and with a rounded base. This re-cut contained a light brown, clayey silt loam of moderate compaction (039). Within layer 039 was a concentrated scatter of flint chips and flakes, including large chunks, evidently representing working *in situ*. This material was block-lifted under the context number 041, to allow fine sieving and the recovery of microdebitage. Apparently, the knapping deposit within pit 034 was the same material as that discovered by Richards within the southern part of the same feature (Richards 1990: 99).

3.2.3. Features west of the causewayed pits

As noted above, the area to the west of the long barrow ditch had been subject to extensive weathering (surface 044), and this had clearly truncated both the ditch edge and the causewayed pits. Westward from surface 044 lay a strip of preserved chalk surface roughly 2m wide and it is conjectured that this area had originally been protected by the long barrow mound. Two sets of linear features created a criss-cross pattern on this surface. Running roughly east–west was a series of periglacial stripes, given the collective context number 008, with tenacious, light brown clayey silt fills (009). Cutting across these on a north–south axis was a series of cart-ruts, collectively numbered 004, and filled with friable, light brown clayey silts (005). The presence of these ruts running parallel with the modern byway suggests that at some point the track must have been appreciably wider than it is now. Moreover, for the ruts to have penetrated into the subsoil at this point, this must have been at a time subsequent to the slighting of the long barrow mound.

In the middle of the western side of Trench 43 was a large tree-throw hole (043). This was filled by 013, a compact, coarse, buff sandy chalk silt with many chalk fragments. Layer 013 contained several pieces of worked flint.

In the southwestern corner of Trench 43, a large pit or posthole (016) was located, with straight, slightly undercut sides and a flat base (0.42m deep). It contained three fills: 018 at the base was a loose, light grey chalky silt; 015 above this was a compact, light pinkish-grey sandy silt; 014 at the top was a friable, dark greyish-brown clayey silt loam (Figure 3.47). During excavation, layer 014 appeared to form the fill of a post-pipe but,

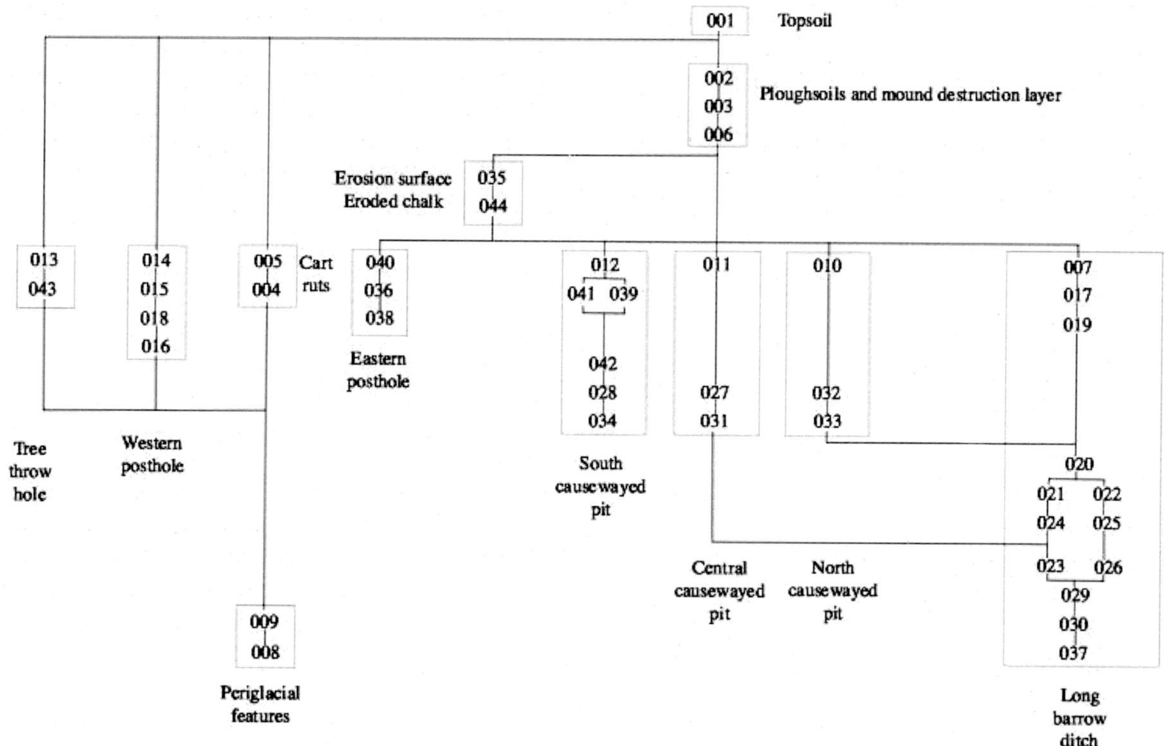

Figure 3.48. Stratigraphic matrix for contexts in Trench 43

once a section had been cut, the fill of the feature seemed to be horizontally bedded. One possibility is that the feature originally contained a post that was subsequently withdrawn. Although the shape and fill of pit 016 do not appear typical for a Neolithic feature, the only finds recovered from it were flint flakes.

Cut 038 was another sub-circular feature of similar diameter to pit/posthole 016, located a little further east. This was initially masked by the eroded chalk layer 035, and was only revealed after a vigorous cleaning of the erosion surface late in the excavation. Like pit 016 it had a flat base, and while it was considerably shallower at 0.24m, much of this could be attributed to its truncation by erosion surface 044. It is therefore not unreasonable to argue that it may have been associated with pit 016. Cut 038 contained a post-pipe (040) of loose, light to mid brownish-grey silt, and a packing layer (036) of friable, buff-grey coarse chalky silt.

3.2.4. Discussion

The excavation of the ditch of Amesbury 42 long barrow (Figure 3.48) was highly successful. The principal objective was the acquisition of good-quality dating material, and this was achieved in the form of an antler pick fragment from the base of the ditch. The date acquired falls relatively late within the long mound tradition in southern Britain (Whittle *et al.* 2007: 125) but its place in the mid-fourth millennium BC is very similar to the new date for the Greater Cursus. Rather than representing a multi-phase construction, it now seems that the Amesbury 42 long barrow was built in a single episode, at much the same time as the adjacent Cursus. This would imply that the two structures represent intentional elements of an integrated complex, rather than separate steps in a landscape building up through a process of accretion.

In addition to this, new information has been provided concerning the structural history of Amesbury 42. Strikingly, the lesser features running parallel with the long barrow ditch have been demonstrated to be a series of pits rather than an earlier ditch. Indeed, they have been shown to be later than the ditch. This invites the suggestion that they were re-cuts of some kind, a means of redefining the long mound at a time when the ditch had begun to silt up. We have noted that, as well as simply forming a discontinuous boundary around the long mound, the causewayed pits appear to have been deliberately cut into the chalk on the inner lip of the original ditch. This would suggest that the acquisition of fresh chalk was itself of significance. It is conceivable that this chalk was used to re-surface the mound, restoring it to its pristine condition and enhancing its visibility.

Figure 3.49. The Amesbury 42 test pit, viewed from the south; the surviving chalk mound is on the left (west)

This may be comparable with the series of sub-circular re-cuts dug into the Greater Cursus ditches in the mid-third millennium BC, of which J.F.S. Stone's 'embayment' or recess was one. These too might be understood as a means of quarrying fresh chalk to visually re-establish the Cursus bank as a landscape feature. An antler pick from Stone's 'embayment' has been dated to 2900–2460 cal BC (OxA-1403; 4100±90 BP). If we suggest that the causewayed pits of Amesbury 42 and the re-cuts within the Greater Cursus represent similar phenomena, and that they may indeed be of similar date, then the refurbishment of the Cursus 'complex' as a conspicuous aspect of the landscape may have taken place at some time between the first (bluestone) and second (sarsen) stages of construction at Stonehenge itself (see appendix to Chapter 1 for the dates of the stages).

The final point that demands consideration concerns the two possible postholes, 016 and 038. Although it is by no means clear that 016 was a posthole at all, the similarity of the two features gives the impression that they are in some way related. The possibility is that they represent two elements of a timber façade, itself associated with more extensive timber structures (such as a linear chamber), which may survive as traces beneath the present byway. Only further excavation, either beneath the byway or in the verge further west, can resolve this matter.

3.2.5. Investigations of the buried soil beneath the mound of Amesbury 42

M.J. Allen and C.A.I. French

The interpretation and reconstruction of the land-use history of the chalkland landscape of the Stonehenge area are predicated on the fact that ancient woodland dominated this landscape by the later Mesolithic and Neolithic (Boreal and Atlantic) periods. Disturbance, clearance and removal of the woodland were piecemeal and progressive, primarily to clear land for corralling cattle, monument-building (long barrows and enclosures) and occupation, and latterly for farming and tillage (*cf* Evans 1971a; 1971b; 1975; Bell and Walker 2005). It was on this basis that graphical reconstructions of the landscapes and land-use of Avebury (Smith 1984) and Stonehenge (Allen *et al.* 1990; Allen 1997a) have been made. However, with the suggestion of more open post-glacial landscapes on the chalklands of Cranborne Chase (Allen 2002; French *et al.* 2003; 2005; 2007), the Dorchester environs (Allen 1997b), and the southern chalkland (Allen and Scaife 2007; Allen and Gardiner 2009; Allen 2017), these preconceptions need challenging.

In addition, prior to the work of the SRP, previous work (*c.* 1980–2003) in the Stonehenge landscape had largely not investigated buried soils, either because they have not survived or because previous research was specifically designed to avoid these potentially preserved contexts (Richards 1990; Allen 1997a). Consequently, palaeo-environmental studies have largely been restricted to proxy records derived from ditch sequences or infilled features (*cf* Entwistle in Richards 1990; Allen 1995b; 1997a). Clear exceptions are the early work at Durrington Walls (Evans 1971c), Woodhenge (Evans and Jones 1979) and Stonehenge itself (Evans 1984; Allen 1995b).

In previous environmental analysis at Amesbury 42 long barrow for the Stonehenge Environs Project, the buried soil contained too few land mollusc shells for detailed palaeo-environmental reconstruction (Entwistle 1990) whilst soil micromorphological analysis was not a component of that study. The buried soil was not encountered in the 2008 excavation by the SRP of the long barrow ditch (see above).

This author [Allen] needed to re-examine the presence, extent and specific nature of the post-glacial woodland on the chalk downs of Salisbury Plain. No longer could the existence of total woodland cover be assumed in the post-glacial period before the construction of Amesbury 42 and other Neolithic monuments. Among the earliest buried soils likely to survive in the Stonehenge environs are those under long barrows of the Early–Middle Neolithic. They provide the best opportunity to examine the nature of the earlier prehistoric woodland cover, and its impact on later human activities (Allen and Gardiner 2009; French *et al.* 2005; 2007).

Amesbury 42: augering of the long barrow mound and buried soil

A contour survey in 1983 (Richards 1990: fig. 64) indicated the survival of a slight barrow mound only about 0.40m–0.50m high; this 'suggested that the mound within the cultivated area had been totally destroyed with the consequent loss of the buried soil' (*ibid.*: 97–8). The buried soil's limited survival as 'sporadic traces' was recorded in 1983 (Richards 1990: 98) and sampled, but very few land snail shells were recorded (Entwistle 1990: 108).

An auger survey was conducted through the extant mound in 2009 to establish the presence, preservation, thickness and character of the mound and buried soil under the byway that runs north–south along the top of the barrow (Figure 3.2). The auger survey, consisting of hand-augering at 20 points (Figure 3.40), was conducted along the byway and in the verges adjacent to this gravel trackway. Augering was carried out with a 4cm-diameter Dutch auger at 10m intervals, and closer where further clarification was required.

Results

The chalk mound was encountered in eight of the auger holes and varied in thickness between 0.17m and 0.27m (averaging 0.18m) except on the margins (0.10m) and where it lay directly under the byway (0.03m). The buried soil was well-preserved and present in nine auger holes, varying in thickness from 0.16m to 0.37m and averaging 0.23m.

The mound

The long barrow's mound is comprised largely of chalk pieces, including a number of medium-sized flints (not recovered in the auger) and clear patches of re-deposited periglacial marl. At its upper surface, there is clear weathering of the present soil into the top of the mound material, especially under light woodland to the west of the track (between the byway and the eastern terminal of the Cursus).

The buried soil

This was a dark brown silty to silty clay soil, varying from slightly calcareous to weakly calcareous rendzina with the possible presence of a shallow brown earth. In one location (adjacent to a test pit excavated in 2009; see below) there is a hint of a preserved turf-line.

Extent of the preserved long barrow

Augering clearly showed the presence of the chalk mound, up to 0.27m thick, extending for about 22.50m north–south. Beneath the mound was a buried soil up to 0.37m thick, extending for a distance of about 55.50m and surviving beyond the extent of the mound. Limited deposits of buried soil and mound survive in the formerly ploughed field to the east, and buried soil and mound are absent against the edge of the western ditch.

The byway crosses the barrow obliquely so that more of the southern (higher) end survives outside the formerly ploughed field, whereas a larger portion of the northern end of the mound has been depleted by ploughing. Much of the southern end of the barrow above 111.10m OD contains extant mound material, while much of the northern end, west of the formerly arable field, still retains an intact buried soil, albeit truncated in the northern part by the current byway. This leaves an area of preserved and upstanding mound and buried soil *c.* 55.50m long and possibly as much as 10m wide.

Depth	Soils
0–22cm	Dark yellowish-brown silty loam, weak-medium crumb structure, stone-free, many roots, rare-medium woody roots, abrupt to sharp boundary. *Worm-worked Ah horizon; modern rendzina, trampled grass soil*
22–36/41cm	Compacted medium chalk in a chalk matrix, the lower 50mm (*i.e.* 36–41cm) in patches has more discrete subrounded chalk pieces and Ah horizon from below, abrupt boundary. *Chalk mound*
41–43cm	Dark yellowish-brown compact silt loam (almost 'greasy'), stone-free, no obvious structure, intermittently present along section profile, sharp to boundary. *Turf and Ah horizon, worm-worked*
43–48cm	Dark yellowish-brown silt loam, rare small chalk pieces and chalk flecking, large, weak crumb structure (especially noticed on excavation), abrupt to clear boundary. *A horizon ('topsoil')*
48–55cm	Dark to very dark silty clay loam, massive, with some reddish-brown (relict clay) inclusions, common small and rare-medium chalk pieces, becoming more common at the base. Abrupt to sharp boundary with the chalk. *A to A/C horizon, rendzina*
55cm+	Chalk. *C horizon*

Table 3.1. The soils in the 2009 test pit adjacent to Amesbury 42 long barrow

Soil stratigraphy in snail sequence 2	Mollusc assemblages
0–2cm: mixed Ah and bank	
2–4cm: Ah stone-free turf	3. 2–6cm: Ah turf, low snail numbers and top (turf) rising below; *P. muscorum* dominant
4–6cm: Ah stone-free	
6–16cm: worm-worked A – topsoil	2. 6–10cm: A upper, stone-free: *V. excentrica* and *P. muscorum*
	1b. 10–18/20cm: A lower, stone-free; *V. costata* and *H. itala*
16–26cm: A/C	1a. 18/20–26cm A/C few shells

Table 3.2. Comparison of soil horizon and mollusc assemblages from the buried soil beneath Amesbury 42 long barrow

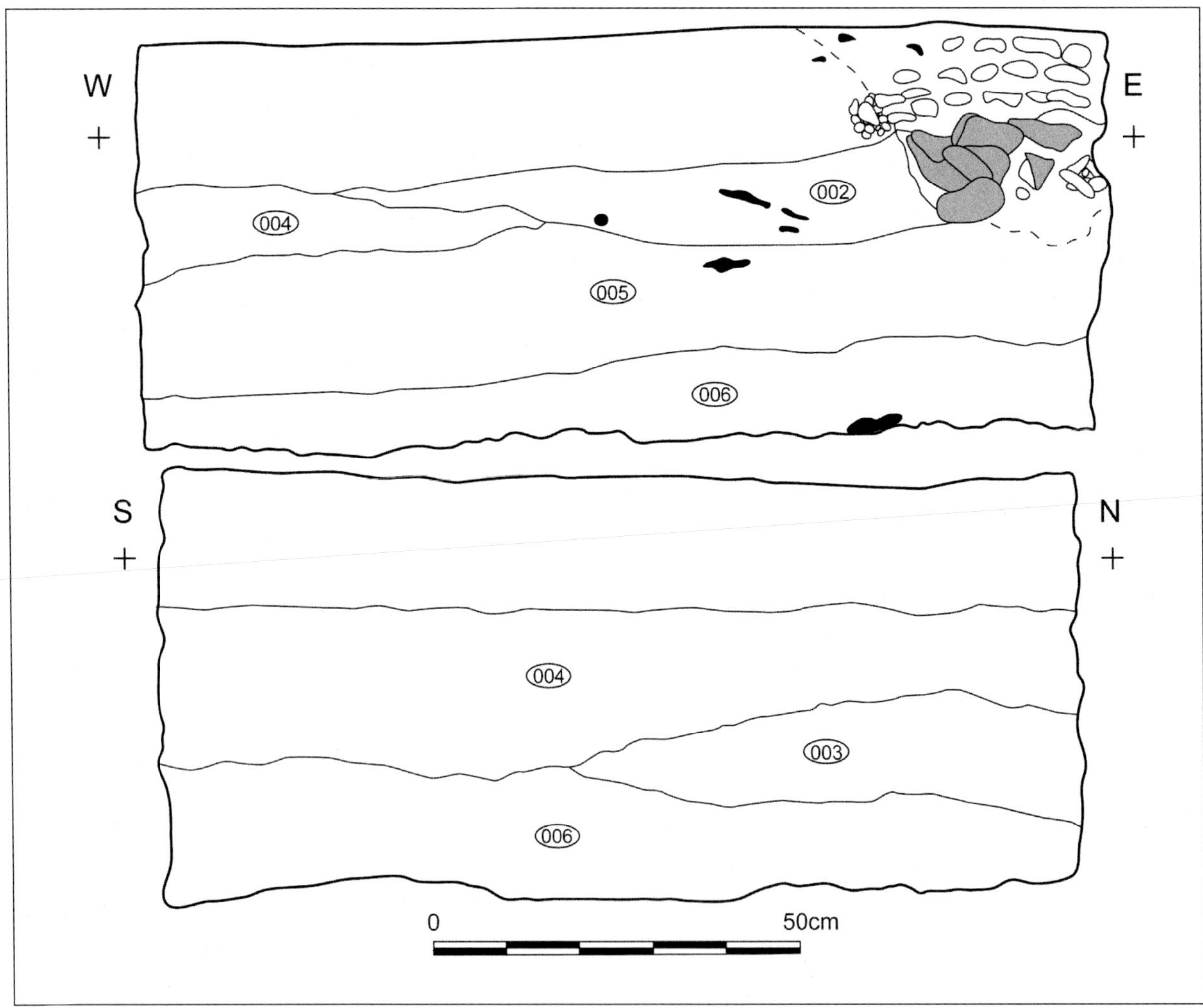

Figure 3.50 (below). Section through Amesbury 42's surviving mound and buried soil in the test pit

This buried soil covers an area of *c.* 480 sq m, of which just over 50 sq m is capped by the surviving chalk mound.

2009 test pit into Amesbury 42 mound and buried soil

In 2009, a 1.50m × 1.50m test pit was hand-excavated west of Trench 43 and west of the byway (Figures 3.40, 3.49–3.51). Its purpose was to evaluate the preservation and character of the buried soils, assess the presence of pre-barrow activity and any features, and obtain well-stratified palaeo-environmental data.

The mound survived in the western edge of the test pit, whilst on its eastern side most of the mound had been removed and the chalk was rutted by vehicular traffic. Under a thin (0.22m), compacted, worm-worked and essentially stone-free modern rendzina soil (supporting short-trampled grass) was a shallow chalk mound, surviving to 0.19m thick and comprised of compacted cemented chalk and crushed chalk with medium chalk pieces, lying with a sharp contact on the buried soil (Table 3.1). This chalk layer had soil (Ah horizon; topsoil) admixed with it in places (Figure 3.51). The buried soil was a shallow (0.19m), compacted, worm-worked rendzina, mirroring the modern soil. At its surface it had a well-developed, worm-worked, stone-free, weakly structured horizon up to 50mm thick (Ah horizon).

Sampling

Two columns of land snails were taken through the buried soil. The first was more disturbed and 10 samples were taken at contiguous intervals between 20mm and 30mm; the second, where the soil was more intact, contained 11 samples taken at 20mm contiguous intervals (see *Land snails*, below; Figure 3.51; Table 3.2). Sub-samples from column 2 were taken for soil magnetic susceptibility. Adjacent to these two columns, soil samples were taken for soil micromorphology. Sub-samples were removed in the field from column 2 for pollen analysis, but results were not promising.

Figure 3.51. Amesbury 42's remnant chalk mound and the Neolithic buried soil beneath the modern trackway

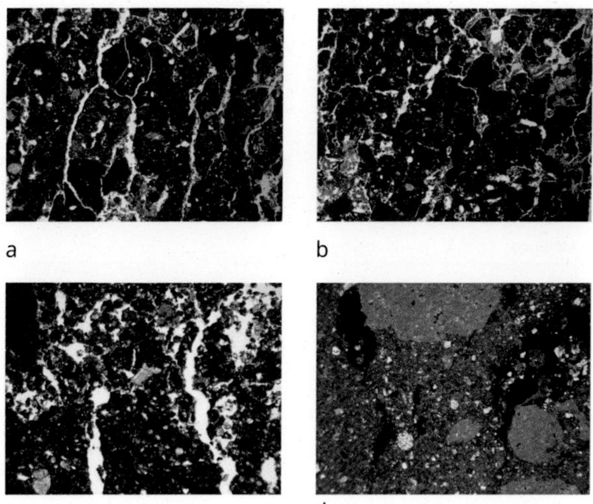

Figure 3.52. Photomicrographs of sediments beneath Amesbury 42 long barrow: a) turf with fine columnar blocky ped structure, column 2, sample 1 (frame width = 2cm; plane-polarised light); b) pea-grit zone, calcitic fine sandy loam and sparite beneath turf, column 2, sample 1 (frame width = 2cm; plane-polarised light); c) small columnar blocky and pellety micritic sandy loam fabric, column 1, sample 1 (frame width = 4.5mm; plane-polarised light); d) mixture of amorphous sesquioxide impregnated, bioturbated, micritic sandy loam and sparite, column 1, samples 1 and 2 (frame width = 4.5mm; cross-polarised light)

Soil micromorphology: the pre-mound soil beneath Amesbury 42

C.A.I. French

Analysis followed the methodology of Murphy (1986) and uses the descriptive terminology of Bullock *et al.* (1985) and Stoops (2003). Detailed descriptions are presented in Volume 2.

The buried soil in column 2 revealed four horizons. The uppermost horizon was a mixture of fine chalk rubble and pellety to small, irregular blocky micritic sandy loam. This distinctly overlay a 20mm-thick dark brown micritic sandy loam with a well-developed fine columnar blocky ped structure and much humified organic matter (Figure 3.52a). Beneath was a similar fabric over a *c.* 30mm zone, but less well organised and with an even mixture of at least 50% very fine chalk gravel (2mm–5mm; Figure 3.52b). At the base of the profile was a *c.* 60mm zone of chalk gravel and micritic fine sand overlying the solid chalk substrate.

This sequence appears to suggest that there is a well preserved but thin *in situ* turf horizon present beneath the mixed soil and chalk rubble deposits of the barrow mound, overlying a well-sorted pea-grit zone typical of a long-established turf grassland (Evans 1972), all on the weathered chalky A/C horizon above the chalk substrate. This is a textbook example of a turf grassland rendzina soil (Limbrey 1975: 128–30), *c.* 0.12m thick.

The buried soil in column 1 revealed three horizons. The upper horizon was a similarly mixed calcitic sandy loam and chalk gravel but, in this case, overlying a mixture of strongly and not amorphous iron-stained and bioturbated calcitic sandy loam (Figure 3.52c). This overlay a mixture of chalk gravel, micrite and micritic sandy loam material typical of the weathering A/C zone found on the chalk (Figure 3.52d). Unlike column 2, there was no *in situ* turf and pea-grit zone; rather, there was mixed mound material situated directly on the organic-stained and bioturbated lower organic A horizon of a rendzina. This suggests that, on the very margin of the mound, the turf was removed prior to burial and/or through subsequent land use 'nibbling' at the margin of the mound. However, where there is a greater thickness of mound, the whole rendzina soil profile survives, albeit with the turf probably somewhat compressed.

Land snails: pre-barrow land-use history

M.J. Allen and J. Sugrue

A set of twelve samples from the edge of the buried soil beneath Amesbury 42 long barrow was taken for the Stonehenge Environs Project, prior to the SRP, by Entwistle (1990: 108). These samples were taken at close (20mm–40mm)

Context	Old land surface										
	A/C		*Lower A*					*Upper A*		*Turf Ah*	
Sample number	194	193	192	191	190	189	188	187	186	185	184
Depth (cm)	24-26	22-24	20-22	18-20	14-18	12-14	10-12	8-10	6-8	4-6	2-4
Weight (g)	1300	1465	1500	1500	1429	1500	1500	1500	1460	1500	1500
Mollusca						*n*					
Pomatias elegans (Müller)	+	4	6	10	13	17	9	10	6	9	5
Carychium tridentatum (Risso)	-	-	-	-	-	1	-	-	1	-	1
Cochlicopa cf *lubrica* (Müller)	-	-	-	-	-	-	3	-	-	-	1
Cochlicopa cf *lubricella* (Porro)	-	-	-	-	-	1	24	+	-	-	1
Cochlicopa spp	3	5	6	12	26	33	4	28	19	10	5
Truncatellina cylindrica (Férussac)	-	2	1	9	13	16	8	2	5	2	-
Vertigo pygmaea (Draparnaud)	-	-	-	-	3	4	4	8	3	1	1
Pupilla muscorum (Linnaeus)	3	4	4	18	19	40	40	37	22	98	4
Vallonia costata (Müller)	5	6	14	23	56	97	73	43	23	4	7
Vallonia cf *excentrica* Sterki	2	-	2	8	16	38	21	52	23	15	12
Vallonia spp	-	-	-	5	7	12	7	11	3	3	1
Punctum pygmaeum (Draparnaud)	-	-	-	-	1	-	1	-	3	-	-
Discus rotundatus (Müller)	-	-	1	-	-	-	-	-	-	-	-
Vitrina pellucida (Müller)	-	-	1	-	-	-	-	-	1	-	-
Aegopinella nitidula (Draparnaud)	-	-	1	-	-	-	-	-	-	-	-
Cecilioides acicula (Müller)	-	(1)	-	-	-	-	-	(1)	-	-	-
Helicella itala (Linnaeus)	1	4	19	17	30	47	19	17	16	6	6
Trochulus hispidus (Linnaeus)	-	-	1	-	5	3	1	8	1	1	2
Cepaea spp	-	-	-	-	1	-	-	-	-	-	-
Cepaea/Arianta spp	1	-	-	4	-	2	2	2	6	1	1
Number of taxa	*6*	*6*	*11*	*8*	*11*	*11*	*12*	*10*	*12*	*10*	*11*
Total	15	25	56	106	190	311	216	219	132	150	47

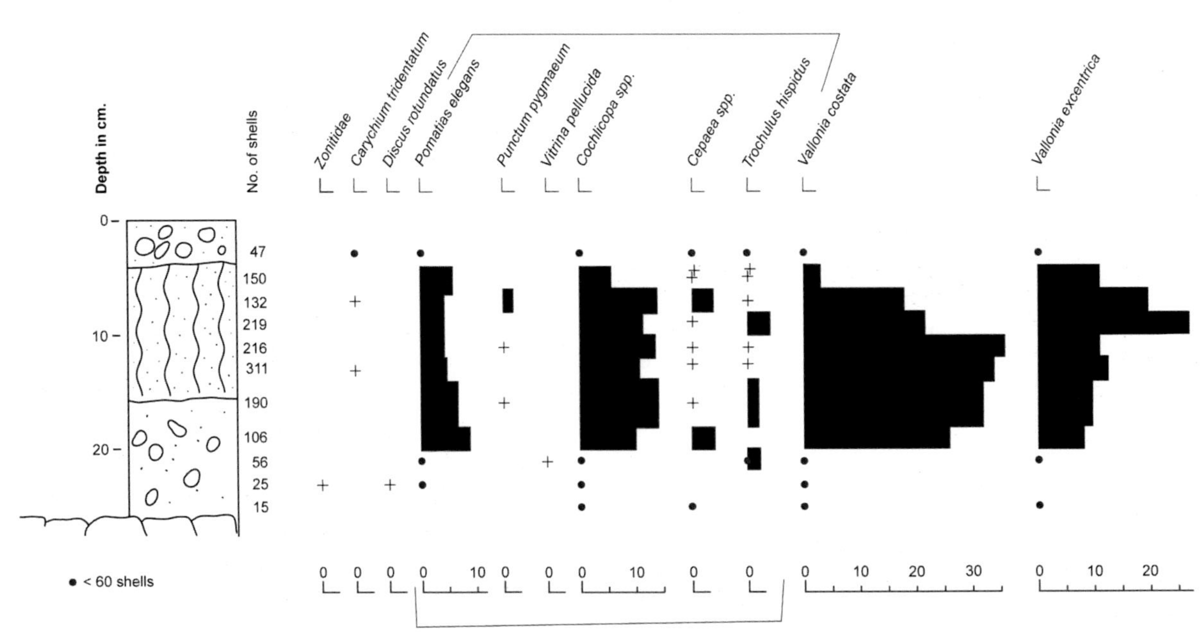

intervals but only between 2 and 77 land mollusc shells were recovered per sample. Although Entwistle admitted that little could be said about the pre-barrow environment, he did report that those shells from the upper part of the buried soil were of species indicating open country, which reinforced the pedological evidence for a stable grassland environment. The lack of shells, and the lack of soil micromorphological evidence, were the two key spurs to the work here immediately after the SRP excavation.

In the 2009 test pit, two columns of land snail samples were taken at contiguous, close 20mm intervals through the soil. Samples of up to 1,500g were processed following standard methods (Allen 2017b: 35–6) adapted from Evans (1972: 44–5). Both sequences contained similar assemblages of shells, but column 2 produced more shells throughout and is discussed here. The results are presented in Table 3.3 and Figure 3.53, with full analysis (sequence 1, Entwistle's buried soil data, and ditch profile) presented in Volume 2. The variation in shell preservation between the two sequences is also discussed there.

The assemblages throughout are overwhelming dominated by open-country species (the *Vallonia* spp, *Helicella itala* and *Pupilla muscorum*), with the two most prominent catholic species being *Cochliopa* sp. and *Pomatias elegans*. There is an almost total absence of shade-loving species, with only two species present at all.

Four main soil and snail assemblage zones have been identified and are characterised in Table 3.2; interpretation provides a land-use history for the setting of the Amesbury 42 long barrow prior to its construction in 3630–3370 cal BC. These are summarised in chronological succession from the base upwards.

Mollusc zone 1a) 18/20–26cm (A to A/C horizon): stony and calcareous, few molluscs, over chalk. The basal portion of the profile was stony A material and contained few shells (less than 37 p/kg). Nevertheless, of the 96 shells in the three samples from this basal portion of the column, only two are shade-loving species. The limited assemblage is overwhelmingly of open-country species and includes *H. itala, P. muscorum, Vallonia costata, V. excentrica and Truncatellina cylindrica,* which suggests long well-established open-country conditions of either dry short grassland or, more tentatively, disturbed ground and arable (*P. elegans* and *H. itala*).

Mollusc zone 1b) 10–18/20cm (A horizon): lower stone-free A horizon, characterised by *V. costata, H. itala* and *P. elegans*. The assemblage from the base of the developed stone-free rendzina is characteristic of very open dry grassland and disturbed contexts. Shell numbers rise in the samples from this zone (from *n*=106 to 311), and open-country species predominate. The presence of *P. elegans* and initially moderately high levels of *P. muscorum* may suggest disturbed and bare soil, but in a very open, dry, short-grazed grassland (*T. cylindrica*). The occurrence of *H. itala* at about 15–16% is very high (Evans 1972: 152), confirming very xerophilic calcareous conditions, probably indicating an ancient short-turfed grassland

Table 3.3. (left) Mollusc species from column 2 within the buried soil beneath Amesbury 42 long barrow (see Volume 3 for data from column 1 and from Entwistle 1990)

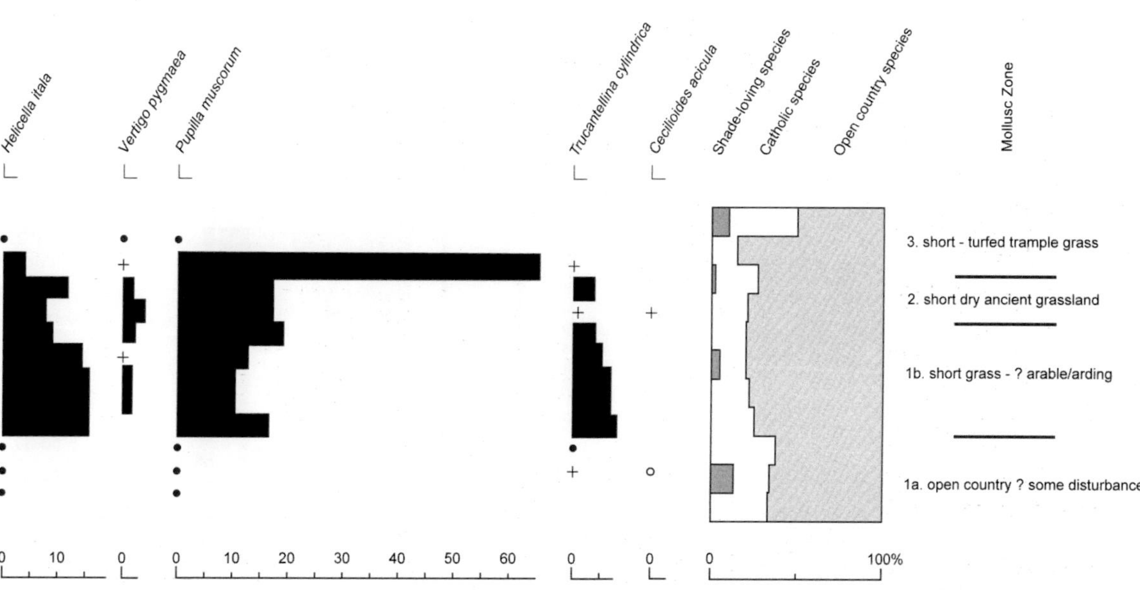

Figure 3.53. (below) Land snail histogram from the buried soils beneath Amesbury 42 long barrow

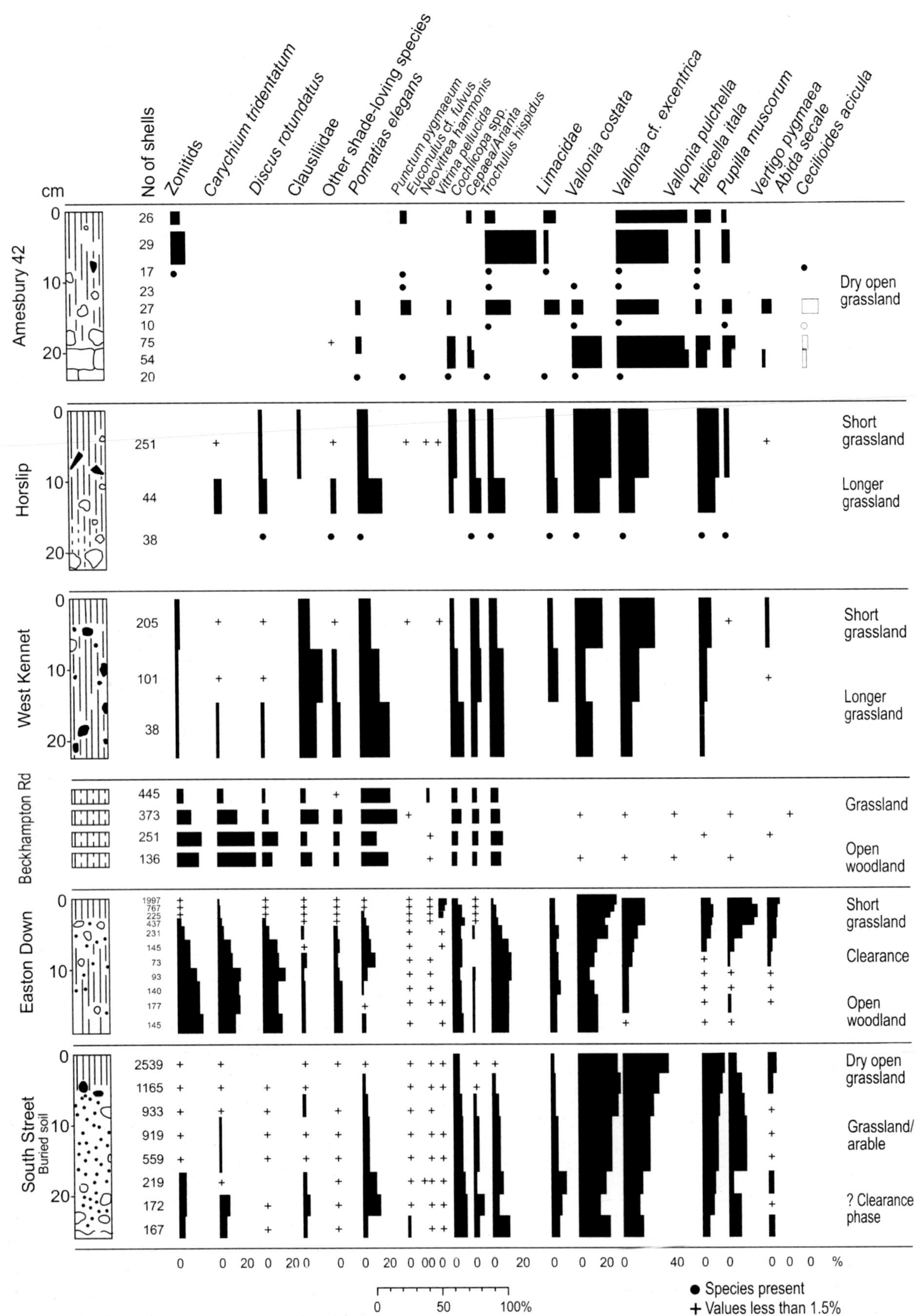

cm
No of shells
Zonitids
Carychium tridentatum
Discus rotundatus
Clausiliidae
Other shade-loving species
Pomatias elegans
Punctum pygmaeum
Euconulus cf. fulvus
Neovitrea hammonis
Vitrina pellucida
Cochlicopa spp.
Cepaea/Arianta
Trochulus hispidus
Limacidae
Vallonia costata
Vallonia cf. excentrica
Vallonia pulchella
Helicella itala
Pupilla muscorum
Vertigo pygmaea
Abida secale
Cecilioides acicula
Amesbury 42
Dry open grassland
Horslip
Short grassland
Longer grassland
West Kennet
Short grassland
Longer grassland
Beckhampton Rd
Grassland
Open woodland
Easton Down
Short grassland
Clearance
Open woodland
South Street
Buried soil
Dry open grassland
Grassland/ arable
? Clearance phase
%
0 50 100%
● Species present
+ Values less than 1.5%

(Kerney 1992: 182) with bare soil patches, and possibly animal disturbance, trampling *etc.*

Mollusc zone 2) 6–10cm upper (A horizon): upper, stone-free; *V. excentrica* and *P. muscorum.* The upper portion of the stone-free rendzina shows stable shell numbers (*n*=132–219) and continued high levels of open-country species and taxa (Table 3.3). Subtle changes can be detected, in particular a decrease in the proportions of *P. elegans, V. costata,* and *H. itala,* a small but consistent decrease in *T. cylindrica,* and a concomitant rise in *V. excentrica* and *P. muscorum.* This is taken to indicate the establishment of a firm, grazed, short-grassland sward.

Mollusc zone 3) 2–6cm (Ah horizon): worm-worked turf, entirely stone-free; *P. muscorum*-dominated. The upper samples show a rise in shells and a dramatic drop-off in numbers at the contact with the chalk mound. The assemblage that can be examined (4–6cm) contained 150 shells with a super-abundance of *P. muscorum,* and a proportional and numerical decline in most other species. This superabundance may be taken to indicate effects of worm-working of the turf (Carter 1990), and possibly pre- or post-depositional mixing and taphonomic effects, but suggests a well-established, short-grassland sward and worm-worked, possibly trampled, turf.

The nature of the assemblages suggests very short, dry grassland. *P. muscorum,* which enjoys very short grassland and is often recorded in areas of soil bare of vegetation (Evans 1972: 146), was similarly common in the buried soils under the Early Bronze Age barrows on King Barrow ridge (Allen and Wyles in Cleal and Allen 1994), only 1.50km to the west. Among the Amesbury 42 assemblages is *T. cylindrica,* a rare species now extinct in Wiltshire but once common in the Stonehenge area, being present in Neolithic contexts at Durrington Walls (Evans 1971c), Woodhenge (Evans and Jones 1979) and in a few Early Bronze Age deposits on King Barrow Ridge (Allen and Wyles in Cleal and Allen 1994). It is indicative of dry sunny slopes, but its absence today probably suggests subtle but significant differences between the nature of the Neolithic grassland sward and that which survives today.

Interpretation

Despite the almost wholly open-country assemblages through the buried soil beneath Amesbury 42 long barrow in the study for the Stonehenge Environs project (Richards' trench W58), Entwistle continued to assume a transition from woodland to more open-county conditions, following a similar chronology to that published by Evans for Durrington Walls (1971c: 329–37). However, from the most recent mollusc evidence we can see a wholly open landscape, with little shade and no evidence of trees or leaf-litter locally, contrary to other Neolithic long barrows in Wessex (Evans 1972).

The almost total lack of shade-loving species and the restricted taxa of intermediate or catholic species confirm the early and pre-Neolithic post-glacial sequence not as one of vegetation succession and woodland but, locally, as largely open downland. There was little shade, few trees, and no long grassland refugia in the barrow's locality for decades, centuries or even millennia before the long barrow was constructed.

Evans indicated that the slightly more shade-loving assemblages at the bases of the buried soils in the long barrows of South Street, West Kennet and Horslip (all in Wiltshire) and Waylands Smithy (Oxfordshire), for instance, were relict refugia after clearance of the former post-glacial woodland. We now suggest that many of these represent long grassland, and there is, in fact, an *absence* of heavy post-glacial woodland on the chalk (Figure 3.54; Allen 2017a).

We can summarise a history of events beneath Amesbury 42 long barrow:

- Mollusc zone 1a. Open country, possibly some disturbance;
- Mollusc zone 1b. Open short grassland, some disturbance, possible arable/ard ploughing;
- Mollusc zone 2. Short-turfed, dry ancient grassland;
- Mollusc zone 3. Turf: short-turfed, trampled grass;
- Mound. Long barrow construction.

In some ways, this mirrors in part the land-use history seen at, for instance, South Street long barrow (Evans 1971a; 1972), showing a history of human activity prior to barrow construction.

Discussion

M.J. Allen and C.A.I. French

The buried soil, even within the 1.50m square test pit, was variable and the two columns revealed different preservation of molluscs and soil. Column 1 had lower snail numbers throughout and the soil included some mixed rubble mound material over a rubbly lower A horizon with the turf/organic Ah horizon missing – possibly indicating disturbance, digging or bioturbation at that locality. In contrast, column 2 had a skim of mixed soil and chalk rubble mound material over an *in situ,* well-structured, organic Ah horizon (turf), over a mixed/disorganised soil/chalk lower A horizon with a pea-grit zone towards its base, over a weathered, chalky C horizon. This marries with the snail data in many respects: turf over a variable and more disturbed lower A horizon. However, from the evidence of soil micromorphology, we cannot say much about how the soil has been disturbed,

Figure 3.54 (left). Land snail histograms from buried soils under other key long barrows

Lab number	Sample ID	Material and context	Radiocarbon age (BP)	δ¹³C (‰)	Calibrated date range (95% confidence)	Posterior density estimate (95% probability)
OxA-1404		Red deer. Heavily eroded antler fragment from Area A, ditch 44, context 51. Primary chalk rubble fill of ditch subsequently cut by ditch which extended monument to east. Phase 1 (Richards 1990: 72–93, fig. 45)	4550±120	-21	3640–2900 cal BC	*3640–3330 (91%)* or *3295–3195 (4%) cal BC*
OxA-1405	SF 217	Red deer. Antler rake used for groove-and-splinter (Richards 1990: fig. 55) from Area A, ditch 10, context 21. With other antlers on floor of ditch cutting ditch 44. Phase 2 (Richards 1990: 72–93, figs 45, 47)	4640±100	-21		
OxA-22238	LC SF 217	As OxA-1405	4611±32	-22.0		
		Weighted mean (T'=0.1; T' (5%)=3.8; v=1; Ward and Wilson 1978)	4614±31		3500–3340 cal BC	*3500–3335 (84%)* or *3215–3185 (5%)* or *3160–3125 (6%} cal BC*
OxA-1406		Red deer. Antler fragments from Area C, ditch 304, context 320. In cemented chalk rubble in secondary fills, possibly derived from slighting of bank (Richards 1990: 72–93, fig. 51)	4000±120	-21	2890–2140 cal BC	*2900–2275 cal BC*

Table 3.4. Stonehenge Lesser Cursus radiocarbon results

Lab number	Sample ID	Material and context	Radiocarbon age (BP)	δ¹³C (‰)	Calibrated date range (95% confidence)
OxA-17953	32	Red deer. Battered frontal tine of antler from context 033 (within cut 032, used as the sample ID), Trench 26, at base of western ditch terminal, below primary chalk rubble	4716±34	-21.7	
OxA-17954	32	As OxA-17953	4695±34	-21.6	
		Weighted mean (T'=0.2; T' (5%)=3.8; v=1; Ward and Wilson 1978)	4706±25		3630–3370 cal BC
OxA-1403		Red deer. Antler from 'recess' or 'embayment' cut into the ditch edge (Stone 1947; Richards 1990: 259)	4100±90	-21	2900-2460 cal BC
SUERC-75196	GC 001 TP 33	Human femur fragment from topsoil above ditch at west end of Cursus (Trench 26)	4187±30	-21.8	2890–2670 cal BC

Table 3.5. Stonehenge Greater Cursus radiocarbon results

Lab number	Sample ID	Material and context	Radiocarbon age (BP)	δ¹³C (‰)	Calibrated date range (95% confidence)
SUERC-24308	GCE 030 SF 1407	Red deer. Antler from context 030, the primary chalk fill of the ditch. The beam fragment had evidence of burning	4645±30	-22.1	3520–3350 cal BC
OxA-21961	GCE 017 SF 1349	Human femur fragment from context 017, eroded mound material in tertiary fill of ditch	4520±32	-21.75	3360–3100 cal BC
SUERC-75197	GCE 001 TP 104	Human humerus fragment from topsoil above long barrow ditch (Trench 43)	2712±30	-20.4	920–800 cal BC

Table 3.6. Amesbury 42 long barrow radiocarbon results

other than that it does not have the structure expected for well-established grassland.

Two major conclusions can be drawn from this:

1. Although the post-glacial woodland was clearly a component of the chalk downland (Evans 1972), it was not a completely uniform blanket of woodland. As we have seen, studies of areas such as Dorchester (Allen 1997c) and Cranborne Chase (French *et al.* 2003; 2007), where full post-glacial woodland succession did not occur in early prehistory, led to speculation that this lighter vegetation cover encouraged the range and intensity of Early Neolithic activity in these areas (Allen and Scaife 2007; Allen and Gardiner 2009; Allen 2017a; see Chapter 9). Such an open landscape and its human potential has also been argued for the Stonehenge area (*op. cit.*) and might also have existed in parts of the Avebury landscape (current research by Allen and French). For the Stonehenge area, this landscape hypothesis seems also to be borne out by recent research on riverside and waterlogged deposits at Blick Mead (Tony Brown pers. comm.; Jacques *et al.* 2018: 35–66).
2. There is clear evidence on the chalk downland of human activity at some time prior to the construction of the earliest-dated monuments (long barrows

of the Early–Middle Neolithic) in this landscape. There is tentative evidence of former soil disturbance, and possibly tillage (ard-ploughing), prior to re-establishment of a short-grassland sward. The time duration after the episode of destruction was great enough to allow the establishment of such ancient short-turfed (grazed) downland grass, before the construction of the mound of Amesbury 42 long barrow – a land-use history similar to that postulated by Evans (1971a) for South Street long barrow. Clearly the long barrows are the first monumental architecture on the chalk, but not the first human activity in the area.

3.3. Scientific and artefactual analyses

3.3.1. Stonehenge Lesser Cursus, Stonehenge Greater Cursus and the Amesbury 42 long barrow: radiocarbon dating

P.D. Marshall, C. Bronk Ramsey and G. Cook

Previous dating

Three radiocarbon dates were obtained on samples from antlers excavated by Julian Richards in the 1980s from the western terminal of the Lesser Cursus (Richards 1990; Table 3.4) and one antler from J.F.S. Stone's excavation of the Greater Cursus in 1947 (Table 3.5).

New dating

Lesser Cursus

A red deer antler rake (SF 217) was excavated by Julian Richards in the 1980s from the floor of ditch 10, the last of two phases of the Lesser Cursus's construction (phase 2, cutting ditch 44 [phase 1]; Richards 1990: 76–7). A sample from this antler artefact was dated at the Oxford Radiocarbon Accelerator Unit before 1990 (ORAU; OxA-1405; Table 3.4). Re-sampling and dating of this antler rake were undertaken for the SRP to take advantage of the improvements in the errors achieved on AMS measurements since the initial analysis was undertaken. This sample was again dated at ORAU (OxA-22238).

Greater Cursus

Replicate samples on a tine fragment from an antler pick (SF 17, context 033) excavated from the base of the western terminal ditch of the Greater Cursus in 2007 (Table 3.5) were dated at ORAU in that year (Thomas *et al.* 2009)

Amesbury 42 long barrow

A single sample from a fragment of an antler pick (SF 1407; Table 3.6) deposited in the primary chalk fill (context 030) of the long barrow ditch, excavated in 2008, was dated at Scottish Universities Environmental Research Centre (SUERC) in 2009.

Two fragments of human femur and a fragment of human humerus from the Greater Cursus and Amesbury 42 were radiocarbon-dated but have not been included in the modelling because they came from residual contexts in topsoil and tertiary ditch fill.

Radiocarbon analysis

The sample from the antler from the Greater Cursus ditch submitted to ORAU was processed using the gelatinisation and ultrafiltration protocols described by Bronk Ramsey *et al.* (2004a). It was then combusted, graphitised, and dated by Accelerator Mass Spectrometry (AMS) as described by Bronk Ramsey *et al.* (2004b). The sample was measured twice (OxA-17953 and OxA-17594), the second result forming part of internal laboratory quality assurance procedures.

At SUERC the antler from the ditch of Amesbury 42 was pre-treated following a modified version of the method outlined in Longin (1971). The sample was then converted to carbon dioxide in a pre-cleaned sealed quartz tube (Vandeputte *et al.* 1996), graphitised as described by Slota *et al.* (1987), and measured by AMS (Xu *et al.* 2004; Freeman *et al.* 2010).

Both laboratories maintain continual programmes of quality assurance procedures, in addition to participation in international inter-comparisons (Scott 2003; Scott *et al.* 2010a), which indicate no laboratory offsets and demonstrate the validity of the precision quoted.

Radiocarbon results

The results are conventional radiocarbon ages (Stuiver and Polach 1977), and are quoted in accordance with the international standard known as the Trondheim convention (Stuiver and Kra 1986).

Radiocarbon calibration

The calibrations of these results, which relate the radiocarbon measurements directly to the calendrical time scale, are given in Tables 3.4–3.6 and in Figures 3.55–3.56. All have been calculated using the datasets published by Reimer *et al.* (2009) and the computer program OxCal v4.1 (Bronk Ramsey 1995; 1998; 2001; 2009a and b). The calibrated date ranges cited are quoted in the form recommended by Mook (1986), with the end points rounded outward to 10 years if the error term is greater than or equal to 25 radiocarbon years, or to 5 years if it is less.

The ranges quoted in italics are *posterior density estimates* derived from mathematical modelling of archaeological problems (see below). The ranges in plain

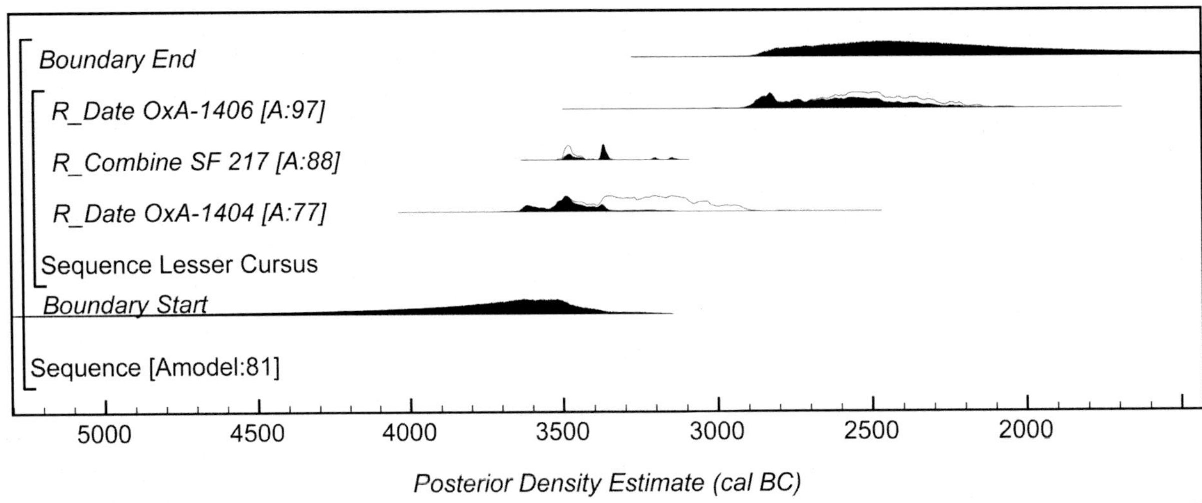

Figure 3.55. Probability distributions of dates from the Stonehenge Lesser Cursus: each distribution represents the relative probability that an event occurs at a particular time. For each of the radiocarbon dates two distributions have been plotted, one in outline, which is the result of simple calibration, and a solid one, which is based on the chronological model used. Figures in brackets after the laboratory numbers are the individual indices of agreement which provide an indication of the consistency of the radiocarbon dates with the prior information included in the model (Bronk Ramsey 1995). The large square brackets down the left-hand side along with the OxCal keywords define the model exactly

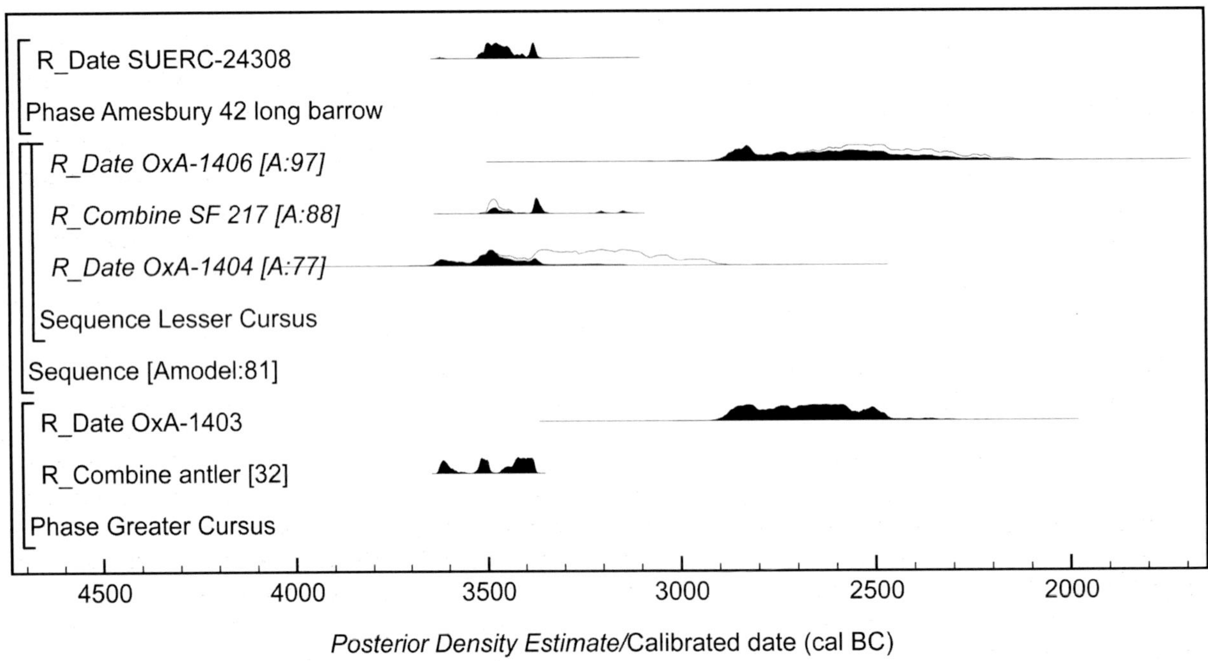

Figure 3.56. Probability distributions of dates from the Stonehenge Lesser Cursus (derived from the model shown in Figure 3.55), Stonehenge Greater Cursus and the Amesbury 42 long barrow

type in Tables 3.4–3.6 have been calculated according to the maximum intercept method (Stuiver and Reimer 1986). All other ranges are derived from the probability method (Stuiver and Reimer 1993).

Methodological approach

A Bayesian approach has been adopted for the interpretation of the chronology from the Lesser Cursus (Buck *et al.* 1996; Bayliss *et al.* 2007a). Although the simple calibrated dates are accurate estimates of the dates of the samples, this is usually not what archaeologists really wish to know. It is the dates of the archaeological events, which are represented by those samples, which are of interest. In the case of the Lesser Cursus, it is the date of the digging of the ditches that is under consideration, not the dates of individual samples. The dates of this activity can be estimated not only using the scientific dating information from the radiocarbon measurements, but also by using the stratigraphic relationships between samples.

Fortunately, methodology is now available which allows the combination of these different types of information explicitly, to produce realistic estimates of the dates of interest. It should be emphasised that the posterior density estimates produced by this modelling are not absolute. They are interpretative estimates, which can and will change as further data become available and as other researchers choose to model the existing data from different perspectives.

The technique used is a form of Markov Chain Monte Carlo sampling, and has been applied using the program OxCal v4.1 (http://c14.arch.ox.ac.uk/). Details of the algorithms employed by this program are available from the on-line manual or in Bronk Ramsey (1995; 1998; 2001; 2009a and b). The algorithm used in the models described below can be derived from the structures shown in Figure 3.55–3.56.

Lesser Cursus samples and sequence

The replicate measurement (OxA-22238) on the antler rake (SF 217) is statistically consistent (T'=0.1; T' (5%)=3.8; ν=1; Ward and Wilson 1978) with that previously obtained (OxA-1405) and a weighted mean has therefore been calculated prior to calibration (SF 217; 4614±31 BP).

The antler rake (SF 217) was found with other antlers on the floor of the secondary ditch (Lesser Cursus phase 2) cutting primary ditch 44 (Lesser Cursus phase 1). It is therefore later than a red deer antler fragment from the primary chalk fill of this phase 1 ditch (OxA-1404). An antler from the secondary fill of the ditch, possibly derived from slighting of the bank (OxA-1406), was also dated; that antler is therefore later than SF 217 but had no stratigraphic relationship with phase 2 of the Cursus.

The model shows good overall agreement between the radiocarbon dates and stratigraphy (Amodel: 81; Figure 3.55) and estimates that the Lesser Stonehenge Cursus was probably constructed in the 36th or 35th centuries cal BC.

The Greater Cursus, the Lesser Cursus and Amesbury 42 long barrow

The samples associated with the construction of the three monuments (*antler* [32] – Greater Cursus; OxA-1404 – Lesser Cursus; and SUERC-24308 – Amesbury 42 long barrow) are statistically consistent (T'=3.6; T' (5%)=6.0; ν=2; Ward and Wilson 1978) and could therefore be of the same actual age. The calibration curve for this period has some pronounced wiggles (Figure 3.57) and thus, in order to demonstrate the contemporaneity of the three monuments' construction, the dating of further samples would provide more precise date estimates.

3.3.2. Antler artefacts from the Greater Cursus and Amesbury 42 long barrow

G. Davies

A single piece of broken antler tine of red deer (SF 17; Figure 3.58) was found in context 033 in Trench 26, at the base of the terminal ditch at the western end of the Greater Cursus (Figure 3.10). The poor surface condition of this piece of antler tine makes identification of working or wear difficult but the tip is broken off, with the end now blunt and rounded off. There are a few faint scratches around the tip. Length (incomplete) 240mm.

A piece of broken antler beam (SF 1407; Figure 3.59) was found in context 030 in Trench 43 at the base of the eastern ditch of Amesbury 42 long barrow at the eastern end of the Greater Cursus (Figure 3.45). Its poor surface condition is similar to that of SF 17 but the distal end is scorched; burning may have facilitated removal of the burr and bez tine at this end of the antler but it is in too poor condition to identify any cut-marks or signs of deliberate breakage. At the other end, the antler is broken at the junction of the trez tine and beam. Length (incomplete) 246mm.

3.3.3. Pottery from the Greater Cursus and Amesbury 42 long barrow

R. Cleal

Only one sherd of Neolithic and one sherd of Beaker pottery were recovered from excavations of the Greater Cursus and Amesbury 42 long barrow. The remaining handful of sherds of Late Bronze Age and later date from these trenches will be reported in Volume 4.

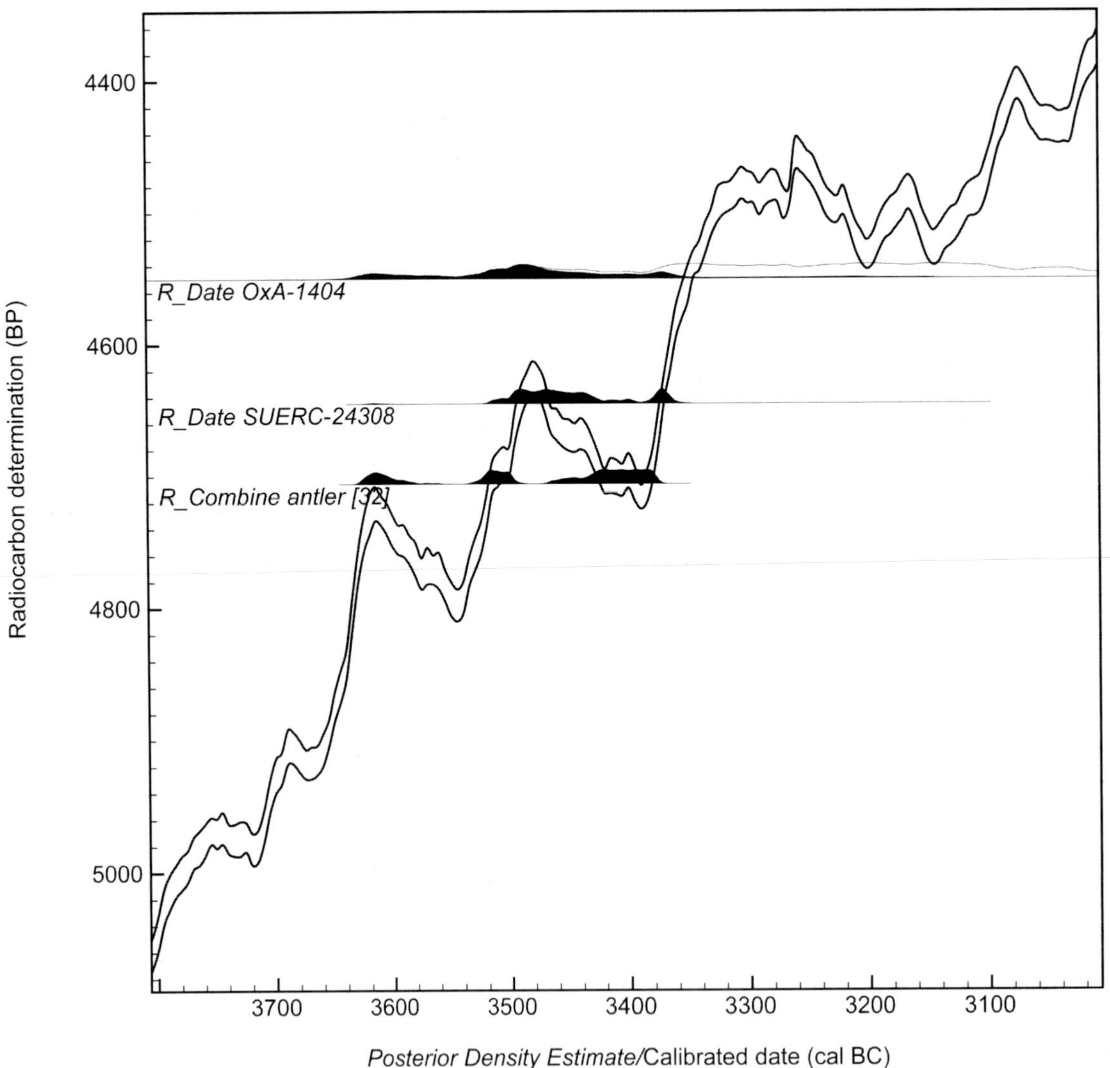

Figure 3.57. Probability distributions of dates from the construction of the Stonehenge Lesser Cursus (derived from the model shown in Figure 3.55), the Stonehenge Greater Cursus and the Amesbury 42 long barrow plotted on the radiocarbon calibration curve (Reimer *et al.* 2009)

Greater Cursus southern ditch, Trench 28, context 003, SF 009 (2007)

One decorated body sherd (3g) of a Beaker in a fine, very hard, smooth fabric with very fine sand (quartz), mica flakes, dark opaque grains and reddish soft inclusions (probably iron oxides). Almost all the inclusions are less than 0.25mm maximum dimension. The exterior is dark orange-brown, the core dark grey and the interior surface mid-grey. The sherd is weathered, with edges very worn, and on the exterior a concave patch of damage may have been caused by spalling during firing and has subsequently become weathered.

The decoration is of very fine-tooth comb, the teeth measuring around 1.25mm × 0.75mm (*i.e.* they are rectangular but not markedly so). At least three horizontal lines of continuous comb-impression bound an area that shows two lines of similar impression, which cross. So little of the sherd survives undamaged (only *c.* 2 sq cm of surface) that it is not possible to interpret the decorative motif, but it is likely that it is a horizontal zone of crosshatching. Unfortunately, this is very common, and occurs in Beakers of different styles and dates, so it is not helpful in terms of placing the Beaker within that tradition.

Amesbury 42 long barrow eastern ditch, Trench 43, context 017, SF 1341 (2008)

One small decorated body sherd (2g) of a Peterborough Ware vessel in a fabric with frequent small flint inclusions (<3mm max. dimension, most >1mm);

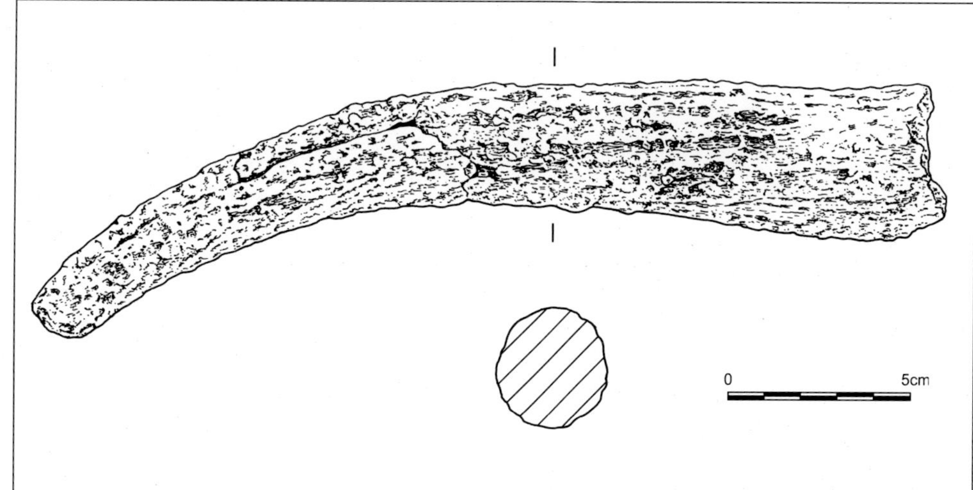

Figure 3.58. An antler tine (SF 17) at the bottom of the ditch at the west end of the Greater Cursus

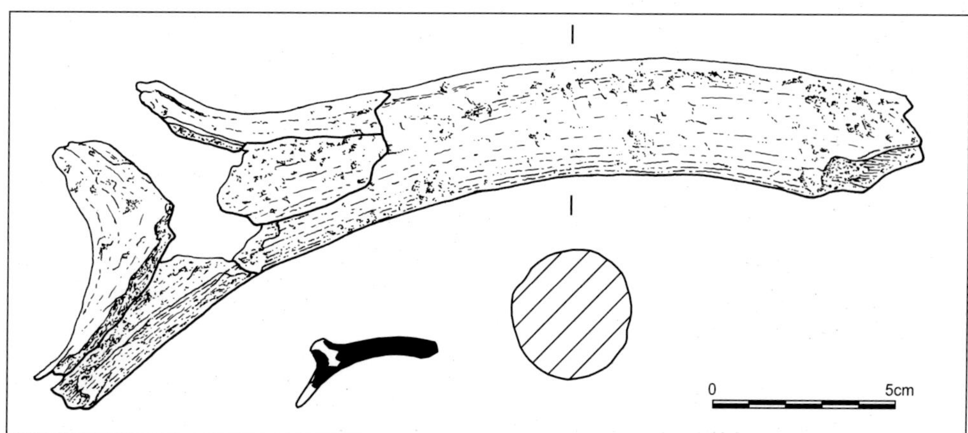

Figure 3.59. An antler pick handle (SF 1407) from the bottom of the long barrow ditch

although the sherd is very small (under 2 sq cm), it is clear that the flint is likely to be moderate (say up to about 15% by surface area). Quartz sand, some angular quartz fragments (<2mm max. dimension, most <1mm) and reddish-brown soft fragments, probably iron oxides, are also present. The surfaces are pale grey-brown, the core is black and the condition is fair, with only a little weathering on the interior surface. The exterior carries four well-defined impressions which are probably from bird or small mammal bones and are probably arranged in rows. The fabric and decoration clearly indicate that the sherd is Peterborough Ware and belongs either to the Ebbsfleet or Mortlake sub-styles (and probably the latter, in which bird-bone impressions are more common).

3.3.4. A chalk artefact from the Greater Cursus

A. Teather

A perforated chalk artefact (C27 in the worked chalk catalogue; see Volume 3 for the catalogue) was found in a topsoil context in Test Pit 20 in Trench 28 along the southern side of the Cursus. Broadly triangular in form, it has two full perforations and one incomplete perforation (Figure 3.60). The larger of the full perforations exhibits a spall fracture on one side, whilst the smaller full perforation only just breaks through. There is another hole that is not a full perforation: two sides appear finished whereas the third is angular. The whole surface, apart from the interior of the holes, is slightly abraded. Its sides are 26mm × 22mm × 26mm with depths varying between 11mm and 13.5mm (larger full perforation 4mm wide each side; smaller full perforation 4mm across on one side, and only 1mm on the other; incomplete perforation, 4mm wide by 4mm deep).

Figure 3.60. A perforated chalk artefact (C27) from topsoil within the Greater Cursus

Trench number	Location	Frequency	Percent
26	Western ditch	2910	82.2
27	Northern ditch	160	4.5
28	Southern ditch	217	6.1
36	Interior	19	0.5
38	Interior	4	0.1
40	Interior	36	1.0
41	Eastern ditch	192	5.4
	Total	3538	100.0

Table 3.7. The worked flint assemblages from trenches at the Greater Cursus

Conclusion

This artefact appears to be a preparatory bead. Since it comes from an unstratified context, it is difficult to date but is likely to be Neolithic rather than Bronze Age. Its repeated perforation is similar to examples excavated by the SRP at Durrington Walls that were probably used as trial pieces for practising boring. Despite indications that this is a bead, it appears never to have been strung, a finding reflected also in other pieces (see *A chalk artefact* in Chapter 8 and chalk artefacts from Durrington Walls in Volume 3).

Chalk artefacts were excavated from earlier excavations in the Stonehenge area and are summarised by Montague (in Cleal *et al.* 1995: 399–406). While perforated objects are noted, these are largely perforated discs; none are beads. Until the excavations by the SRP, chalk beads were an uncommon artefact type, being rarely recorded, with forms that vary considerably. A possible bead was noted from Windmill Hill (Smith 1965: 133), with a rounded rectangular shape and a perforation on one of the shorter sides. At West Kennet long barrow, a perforated piece of chalk, re-bored diagonally, was excavated in association with Peterborough Ware (Piggott 1962: 48). At the Arreton Down barrow on the Isle of Wight, beads were excavated from the probable primary burial (Alexander *et al.* 1960: 275–6). A full typology and categorisation of chalk artefacts has recently been offered (Teather 2016), together with an updated revision (Teather 2017), which include data from the SRP excavations.

3.3.5. Worked flint from stratified contexts of the Greater Cursus

B. Chan

The lithic assemblage from the excavations of the Greater Cursus consists of 3,538 pieces of worked flint derived from seven trenches, three of which were located within the interior of the monument, with the remaining four being placed to investigate the northern, eastern, southern and western ditches. The trenches in the interior produced less than 2% of the assemblage as a whole. The remaining assemblage is unevenly distributed between the different ditch areas, with 82%, 6%, 5%, and 5% of the assemblage coming from the western, southern, eastern and northern ditches respectively (Table 3.7). Worked flint from the topsoil test-pitting carried out before full excavation commenced is reported separately below.

Raw material and condition

The flint from the Greater Cursus excavations is chalk-derived flint from the local area. The flint has grey cherty inclusions and a light beige cortex, which varies in thickness from 2mm–10mm. The majority of the flint is heavily patinated to white, with some pieces being less patinated and blue-grey in colour. The material has a variable condition which correlates with its depositional context. The flint from the primary fills of the Cursus ditch is in mint condition, material from secondary fills is generally in fresh condition, and material from the tertiary fills and ploughsoil is of mixed condition and includes some heavily abraded, plough-rolled artefacts.

Assemblage composition, technology and chronology

The technology within the assemblage is generally homogeneous and reflects the working of single- and multi-platform cores for the production of flakes and occasionally blades (Table 3.8). A crude, crested blade is present in the assemblage from Trench 26 (the western terminal ditch), but otherwise the production of blades appears to have been slightly *ad hoc*, with none of the cores from the primary fills showing evidence of prolonged or systematic removal of blades; many of them clearly only ever produced flakes. The lack of specialised techniques for initiating blade removals

Table 3.8 (right). The composition of worked flint assemblages from all Cursus trenches

	Artefact type		Trench number							Total
			26	*27*	*28*	*36*	*38*	*40*	*41*	
Debitage and cores	Blade	Count	82	1	8	0	0	0	8	99
		% within trench no.	2.8%	0.6%	3.7%	0%	0%	0%	4.2%	2.8%
	Blade-like flake	Count	30	0	0	0	0	0	2	32
		% within trench no.	1.0%	0%	0%	0%	0%	0%	1.0%	0.9%
	Bladelet	Count	54	0	2	0	0	0	0	56
		% within trench no.	1.9%	0%	0.9%	0%	0%	0%	0%	1.6%
	Core on a flake	Count	3	2	0	0	0	0	0	5
		% within trench no.	0.1%	1.3%	0%	0%	0%	0%	0%	0.1%
	Crested blade	Count	1	0	0	0	0	0	0	1
		% within trench no.	<0.1%	0%	0%	0%	0%	0%	0%	<0.1%
	Flake	Count	2629	156	197	16	4	34	175	3211
		% within trench no.	90.3%	97.5%	90.8%	84.2%	100.0%	94.4%	91.1%	90.8%
	Irregular waste	Count	49	0	0	0	0	0	3	52
		% within trench no.	1.7%	0%	0%	0%	0%	0%	1.6%	1.5%
	Keeled non-discoidal flake-core	Count	2	0	1	0	0	0	0	3
		% within trench no.	0.1%	0%	0.5%	0%	0%	0%	0%	0.1%
	Multi-platform flake-core	Count	18	0	0	0	0	0	0	18
		% within trench no.	0.6%	0%	0%	0%	0%	0%	0%	0.5%
	Rejuvenation flake tablet	Count	0	0	0	0	0	0	1	1
		% within trench no.	0%	0%	0%	0%	0%	0%	0.5%	<0.1%
	Single-platform blade-core	Count	2	0	0	0	0	0	0	2
		% within trench no.	0.1%	0%	0%	0%	0%	0%	0%	0.1%
	Single-platform flake-core	Count	14	1	1	0	0	0	0	16
		% within trench no.	0.5%	0.6%	0.5%	0%	0%	0%	0%	0.5%
	Tested nodule/bashed lump	Count	13	0	1	0	0	0	0	14
		% within trench no.	0.4%	0%	0.5%	0%	0%	0%	0%	0.4%
	Unclassifiable/fragmentary core	Count	1	0	0	0	0	0	0	1
		% within trench no.	<0.1%	0%	0%	0%	0%	0%	0%	<0.1%
Retouched flakes and tools	Barbed and tanged arrowhead	Count	0	0	1	0	0	0	0	1
		% within trench no.	0%	0%	0.5%	0%	0%	0%	0%	<0.1%
	End-scraper	Count	1	0	0	0	0	0	0	1
		% within trench no.	<0.1%	0%	0%	0%	0%	0%	0%	<0.1%
	Misc. retouched flake	Count	1	0	2	0	0	0	0	3
		% within trench no.	<0.1%	0%	0.9%	0%	0%	0%	0%	0.1%
	Notch	Count	3	0	0	0	0	0	0	3
		% within trench no.	0.1%	0%	0%	0%	0%	0%	0%	0.1%
	Oblique arrowhead	Count	1	0	0	0	0	0	0	1
		% within trench no.	<0.1%	0%	0%	0%	0%	0%	0%	<0.1%
	Other scraper	Count	3	0	0	0	0	0	0	3
		% within trench no.	0.1%	0%	0%	0%	0%	0%	0%	0.1%
	Utilised/edge-damaged flake/blade	Count	3	0	4	3	0	2	3	15
		% within trench no.	0.1%	0%	1.8%	15.8%	0%	5.6%	1.6%	0.4%
Total		Count	2910	160	217	19	4	36	192	3538
		% within trench no.	100.0%	100.0%	100.0%	100.0%	100.0%	100.0%	100.0%	100.0%

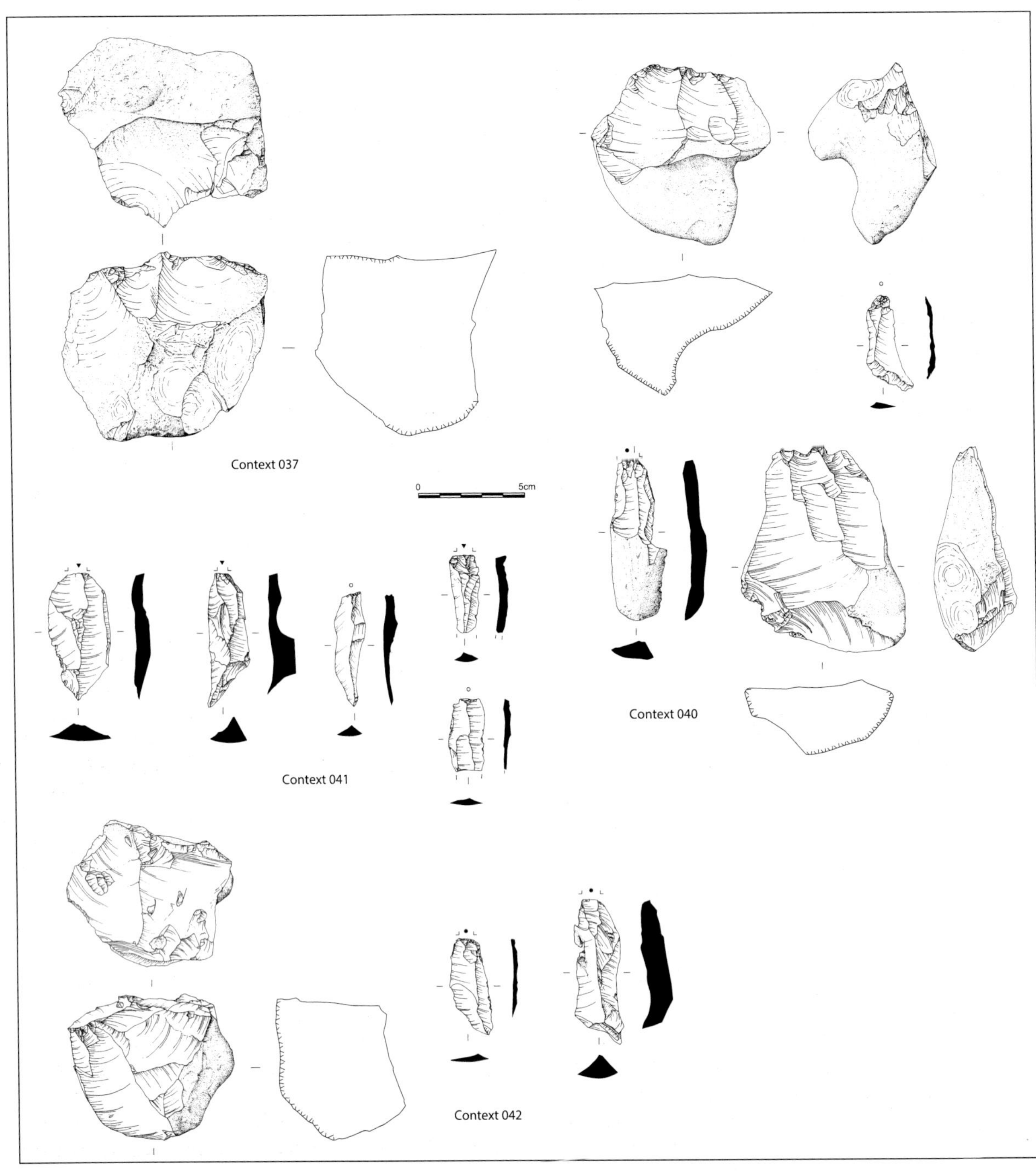

Figure 3.61. Lithics from the knapping cluster at the base of the west ditch of the Greater Cursus in Trench 26

is in keeping with other assemblages of the period within the Stonehenge landscape (Harding 1990: 99–104).

The composition of the assemblage is notable for the low frequency of retouched tools, with none being found within the primary fills. In this respect, the assemblage seems to largely represent the working-down of nodules and the production of flakes and blades, rather than the production and use of tools. In the case of the knapping clusters from Trench 26, it is likely that this flintworking took place within the vicinity of the terminal ditch, or within the ditch itself.

The scarcity of chronologically diagnostic artefacts limits the potential for defining a chronology for the majority of the Cursus lithic assemblage, and it is likely that material from the tertiary fills is mixed chronologically. Despite this, the production of flakes and occasional blades, both of which are present within the assemblage from the primary fills, fits broadly within our understanding of flintworking within the broader Stonehenge environs around the time when the western terminal ditch was constructed (*i.e.* 3630–3370 cal BC [Thomas *et al.* 2009]). Some of the lithic material also makes it clear that there was sporadic later activity in the area, as represented by a crude Late Neolithic oblique arrowhead (SF 20393) from the topsoil of Trench 26 and a well-worked Early Bronze Age barbed-and-tanged arrowhead (SF 12) from the uppermost fill (003) of a re-cut of the southern Cursus ditch in Trench 28 (Figure 3.62).

Trench 26: the western terminal ditch of the Cursus

The assemblage from Trench 26 consists of 2,910 worked flint artefacts (Table 3.8), 39 of which came from ploughsoil 001, with the remainder coming from within the Cursus ditch. Further material recovered during topsoil test-pitting at the western end of the Cursus is reported separately (see *Worked flint from the ploughsoil*, below).

Excluding chips, 90% of the assemblage from the ditch consists of flakes, and 6% are blades, bladelets and blade-like flakes. Blade production is also indicated by the presence of a crude, crested blade from knapping cluster 041 (Figure 3.61). Cores make up *c.* 2% of the assemblage, and retouched flakes and formal tools are also a minor component. In total, there are 52 cores of different types from the ditch fills, including single- and multi-platform flake-cores, keeled cores, bashed lumps and two blade-cores. Retouched tools from the ditch fills are represented by a miscellaneous retouched flake, two notched flakes and three scrapers. As noted above, a crude oblique arrowhead (SF 20393; Figure 3.62) was also recovered from the topsoil.

The assemblage was differentially distributed between the ditch fills, with the greatest quantity of artefacts coming from tertiary fills, followed closely by primary and then secondary fills (Table 3.9). The assemblage composition from different fills is also variable, with high proportions of cores and miscellaneous waste in the primary fills and all of the formal tools and retouched flakes coming from the tertiary fills. The size of the assemblage from the primary fills is also notable as these deposits derived from the rapid initial weathering and collapse of the chalk sides of the ditch; Christie (1963: 374) suggests these deposits would have accumulated in less than five years.

When taken together, the variability in assemblage composition and size indicates some clear differences in both the nature and frequency of flint use in the area between the time of the primary infilling and slower tertiary filling of the ditch. Specifically, it appears that there was a greater focus on the working and/or deposition of flint during the initial stages of ditch-infilling than at any time in its subsequent history. This suggestion is further strengthened by the character and condition of the flint from the primary fills, which is universally in mint condition, indicating that the material was deposited into the ditch shortly after it was worked.

The primary fills contained a series of knapping clusters dotted at different levels throughout the deposits, including on the floor of the ditch, within the chalk rubble and on the interface between the primary and secondary fills. This clearly indicates that a number of different knapping episodes took place throughout the period of the initial erosion of the chalk ditch. A refitting exercise revealed multiple short series of refits, with the longest identified sequence consisting of six refitting flakes. In several cases, flakes could be refitted on to rough cores from which only a few flakes had been removed. This assessment does not, therefore, suggest the presence of complete, extended reduction sequences. However, a more thorough refitting exercise would aid in understanding the exact character of the reduction sequence. What can be said is that technologically the assemblage from the primary ditch fills of Trench 26 is mixed and includes primary, secondary and tertiary flakes, as well as a significant number of cores.

Within the primary fills, blades, bladelets and blade-like flakes make up 7.5% of the assemblage. One notable feature of the assemblage is the number of nodule-trimming and core-preparation flakes (Figure 3.61). This is reflected in the character of flakes, the areas of nodules that the flakes removed, and the proportion of more heavily cortical flakes in the assemblage. This pattern is most clear when a sample of flakes from the primary fills of Trench 26 is compared with a random sample of flakes from the midden (593) at Durrington Walls (Figure 3.63; Parker Pearson 2007). Although Durrington Walls is of a later date, it provides an important contrast to the Cursus material because: a) it is a settlement site and context 593 includes a full spectrum of the *chaîne opératoire* including core preparation, blank production and tool manufacture and use, and b) because it is in the same landscape and therefore provides similarities in availability and type of flint raw materials.

A comparison of the cortex remaining on flakes from the two sites confirms that, at Durrington Walls, there are higher proportions of flakes from established reduction sequences where most cortex has already been removed from cores (Figure 3.63). This confirms the task-specific nature of the Cursus material and suggests that it either represents the result of shorter and less productive reduction sequences, or that a significant number of flakes/blades or prepared cores were removed for use elsewhere. On the basis of the condition of the material and refits within the primary fills, it is likely that the

	Artefact type		Ditch fill type				Total
			Ploughsoil	*Primary*	*Secondary*	*Tertiary*	
Debitage and cores	Blade	Count	3	33	20	26	82
		% within ditch fill type	7.7%	3.2%	3.5%	2.1%	2.8%
	Blade-like flake	Count	0	15	7	8	30
		% within ditch fill type	0%	1.4%	1.2%	0.6%	1.0%
	Bladelet	Count	0	30	9	15	54
		% within ditch fill type	0%	2.9%	1.6%	1.2%	1.9%
	Core on a flake	Count	0	0	2	1	3
		% within ditch fill type	0%	0%	0.4%	0.1%	0.1%
	Crested blade	Count	0	1	0	0	1
		% within ditch fill type	0%	0.1%	0%	0%	<0.1%
	Flake	Count	32	900	520	1177	2629
		% within ditch fill type	82.1%	86.0%	91.9%	93.6%	90.3%
	Irregular waste	Count	0	38	7	4	49
		% within ditch fill type	0%	3.6%	1.2%	0.3%	1.7%
	Keeled non-discoidal flake-core	Count	0	0	0	2	2
		% within ditch fill type	0%	0%	0%	0.2%	0.1%
	Multi-platform flake-core	Count	1	11	0	6	18
		% within ditch fill type	2.6%	1.1%	0%	0.5%	0.6%
	Single-platform blade-core	Count	0	0	1	1	2
		% within ditch fill type	0%	0%	0.2%	0.1%	0.1%
	Single-platform flake-core	Count	0	9	0	5	14
		% within ditch fill type	0%	0.9%	0%	0.4%	0.5%
	Tested nodule/bashed lump	Count	0	9	0	4	13
		% within ditch fill type	0%	0.9%	0%	0.3%	0.4%
	Unclassifiable/fragmentary core	Count	0	1	0	0	1
		% within ditch fill type	0%	0.1%	0%	0%	<0.1%
Retouched flakes and tools	End-scraper	Count	1	0	0	0	1
		% within ditch fill type	2.6%	0%	0%	0%	<0.1%
	Misc. retouched flake	Count	0	0	0	1	1
		% within ditch fill type	0%	0%	0%	0.1%	<0.1%
	Notch	Count	1	0	0	2	3
		% within ditch fill type	2.6%	0%	0%	0.2%	0.1%
	Oblique arrowhead	Count	1	0	0	0	1
		% within ditch fill type	2.6%	0%	0%	0%	<0.1%
	Other scraper	Count	0	0	0	3	3
		% within ditch fill type	0%	0%	0%	0.2%	0.1%
	Utilised/edge-damaged flake/blade	Count	0	0	0	3	3
		% within ditch fill type	0%	0%	0%	0.2%	0.1%
Total		Count	39	1047	566	1258	2910
		% within ditch fill type	100.0%	100.0%	100.0%	100.0%	100.0%

Table 3.9. The composition of the worked flint assemblage by context type from from the western terminal ditch (Trench 26) of the Greater Cursus

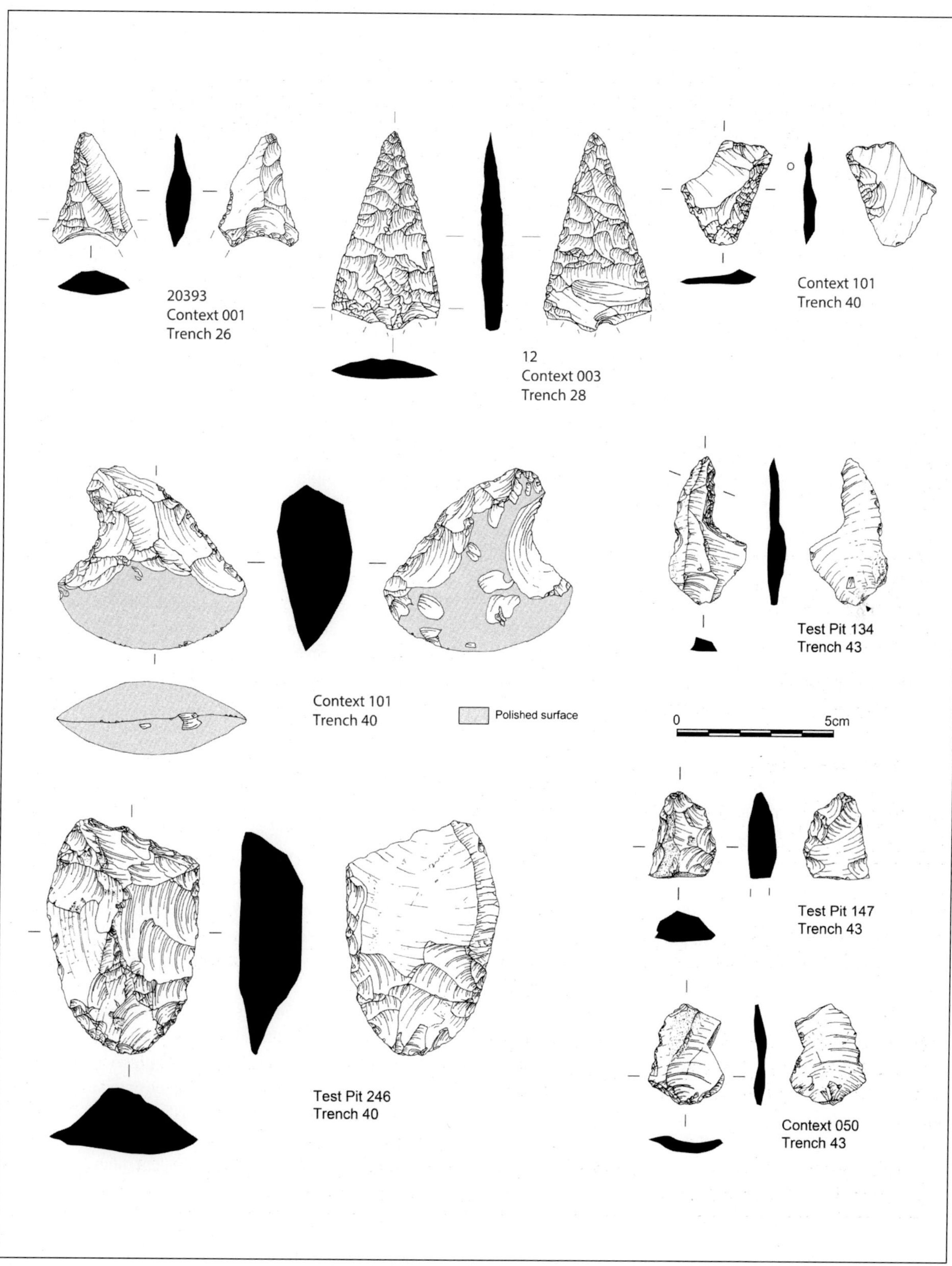

Figure 3.62. Lithics from the topsoil and other upper layers of the Greater Cursus

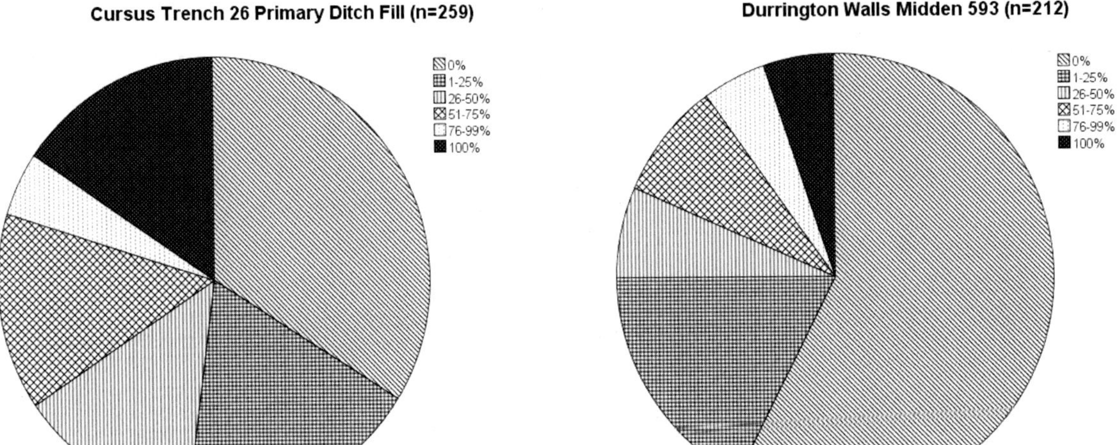

Figure 3.63. The percentage of cortex remaining on the dorsal surface of a sample of flakes from the primary fill of the western terminal ditch of the Greater Cursus (Trench 26) and midden 593 from Durrington Walls

material was knapped within the western terminal ditch, or entered it almost immediately after it was worked.

Trench 27: the northern Cursus ditch and the cross-ditch

Trench 27 yielded an assemblage of 160 pieces of worked flint derived from nine different contexts (Table 3.8). Overall, the assemblage is characterised by having a high proportion of flakes (98%) and a lack of any retouched flakes or tools. In terms of its distribution, the material is spread between a series of different contexts associated with the Cursus ditch and the adjacent cross-ditch.

Unlike the western terminal ditch, the primary fills of the northern Cursus ditch in Trench 27 did not contain any worked flint. The earliest fill that produced worked flint was the secondary ditch fill (035), above which lay fill 021. Between them, these fills produced a relatively small assemblage of 36 artefacts, consisting of 35 flakes and a blade. A larger assemblage of 57 flakes was found within the uppermost fill (014) of the ditch, which is described as being similar to the surrounding ploughsoil. The only other context within the northern Cursus ditch that contained worked flint was fill 080 of posthole/embayment 081, which produced a single flake.

The remaining assemblage came from the fills of the adjacent cross-ditch and the stakeholes that surrounded it. This material comprises 47 flakes and a core from the uppermost fill (044) of the cross-ditch, and six flakes from fill 061 of the slot (062) cut into the primary fill of the ditch. Lastly, four flakes in total were found within fills 070 and 082 of stakeholes 071 and 083 respectively, which lay to the west and northwest of the terminus of the cross-ditch.

Overall, the assemblage from Trench 27 is unremarkable, except for its overall assemblage composition. Moreover, it is possible that all of the material is essentially residual within later ditch fills. Therefore, the most interesting aspects of the assemblage are that it demonstrates the character of general activities in the immediate vicinity of the northern ditch, and the contrasting nature of this assemblage compared to that from the western terminal ditch.

Trench 28: the southern Cursus ditch

The worked flint from Trench 28 was derived from ploughsoil 001, fill 004 (the backfill of Stone's excavation trench; Stone 1947), fill 003 of Cursus ditch re-cut 125, and secondary silts 038 and 039 at the bottom of the southern Cursus ditch. In total, these contexts produced a total of 217 pieces of worked flint, which were unevenly distributed between the fills. The majority of the assemblage (63%) came from the fill of re-cut 125; 18% of the assemblage came from ploughsoil 001, and 9% from backfill 004. The secondary silts at the bottom of the ditch (038 and 039) produced only 22 pieces of worked flint (10% of the assemblage) but it should be noted that the ditch's re-cut presumably disturbed the primary fills of the ditch, so it is possible that material from these contexts has been lost or incorporated into the fills of the re-cut ditch.

In terms of its composition, the assemblage is heavily dominated by flakes, alongside which are 10 blades/bladelets, two cores, a tested nodule, two miscellaneous retouched flakes, four utilised/edge-damaged flakes, and a single barbed-and-tanged arrowhead (Table 3.8). The barbed-and-tanged arrowhead (SF 12) was found within fill 003, the top layer of re-cut 125 within the Cursus ditch (Figure 3.62). It is the only chronologically

Artefact type		Ditch fill type			Total
		Primary	Secondary	Tertiary	
Blade	Count	0	5	0	5
	% within ditch fill type	0%	4.5%	0%	2.9%
Blade-like flake	Count	0	0	1	1
	% within ditch fill type	0%	0%	1.7%	0.6%
Flake	Count	5	101	57	163
	% within ditch fill type	100.0%	91.8%	96.6%	93.7%
Irregular waste	Count	0	3	0	3
	% within ditch fill type	0%	2.7%	0%	1.7%
Rejuvenation flake tablet	Count	0	1	0	1
	% within ditch fill type	0%	0.9%	0%	0.6%
Utilised/edge-damaged flake/blade	Count	0	0	1	1
	% within ditch fill type	0%	0%	1.7%	0.6%
Total	Count	5	110	59	174
	% within ditch fill type	100.0%	100.0%	100.0%	100.0%

Table 3.10. The composition of the worked flint assemblage by context type from from the eastern terminal ditch (Trench 41) of the Greater Cursus

diagnostic artefact within the lithic assemblage from this trench and its presence fits with the ceramic evidence for a Beaker-period date for the re-cutting of the Cursus ditch. As with the eastern terminal ditch (see below), the absence of tools – except for the arrowhead – is notable and seems to reflect the lack of tool production, use or discard within the general area of the Cursus.

Trenches 36, 38, 40: the interior of the Cursus

A total of 54 flakes and five utilised/edge-damaged flakes were recovered during the excavation of the three trenches within the interior of the Cursus (Table 3.8). Within Trenches 36 and 38, towards the western end of the Cursus, 23 struck flints were recovered, all of which came from the ploughsoil. The remaining material was from Trench 40, at the Cursus's eastern end, and came from ploughsoil, a tree-throw and a series of linear features thought to be cart-ruts. Except for a Middle Neolithic petit tranchet (PT) arrowhead (context 101, Trench 40), a flint axe rough-out, and the worked-down blade of a polished Neolithic flint axe, both from the topsoil (Figure 3.62), the material is undiagnostic. This assemblage from Trenches 36, 38 and 40 has less archaeological value than lithics from secure contexts.

The only aspect worthy of mention is that the distribution of the material between the trenches points towards a slightly higher density within the eastern end of the interior of the Cursus compared to the western end. Despite this, the overall density of material within the Cursus is low.

Trench 41: the eastern terminal ditch of the Cursus

The excavation of the eastern terminal ditch of the Greater Cursus produced an assemblage of 192 pieces of worked flint. Further material from the topsoil test pits dug prior to excavation of the trench is described below.

A total of 174 of the artefacts from the full excavation came from within the ditch, whilst the remaining 18 artefacts came from context 202, a ploughsoil that was washed into the top of the ditch and spread either side of it. The assemblage consists predominantly of flakes, with a small number of blades, blade-like flakes, pieces of irregular waste, utilised/edge-damaged flakes, and a possible core rejuvenation tablet (Table 3.10). The blades are not particularly well-worked, but appear to have come off single-platform cores producing elongate flakes/blades and, technologically, can broadly be considered to be Early Neolithic. The waste flakes, which make up over 90% of the assemblage, are chronologically and technologically undiagnostic. Perhaps the most significant feature of the assemblage is that it lacks any cores or tools.

Within the ditch fills, the worked flint was unevenly distributed and contrasts with the western terminal ditch (see above). This is because there were no *in situ* knapping clusters (and only five flakes in total) within the primary fills of the eastern terminal ditch. The majority of the assemblage came from the secondary fills of the ditch, and it is notable that only a small amount of material was washed into the ditch during the slow accumulation of the tertiary fills (Table 3.10).

Discussion

From the seven SRP trenches excavated on the Greater Cursus, 82% of the worked flint was found within the area of the western terminal ditch (Table 3.7). The lower proportions of flint from the other ditches are broadly comparable with each other. The high proportion of the overall assemblage from the western ditch is even more marked if only the primary ditch fills are considered. To some extent the large quantity of flint in the western terminal ditch can be explained by the trench's larger size but, beyond this, it is clear that there was a concentration of flintworking activities in the area of the ditch. These activities produced a flint assemblage defined by high proportions of debitage and the absence of retouched tools.

The character of the assemblages from the SRP excavations along the Greater Cursus is in keeping with the results of previous excavations of the monument. The greater relative quantities of flint within the western terminal ditch of the Greater Cursus were noted by Christie (1963; *cf* Saville 1980). Moreover, the flint within the primary fills in Christie's excavation is described as lying on the floor of the ditch, being comprised of only flakes and cores, and had several series of refitting flakes (Saville 1980: 17). Richards (1990: 96) also makes reference to the retrieval of an *in situ* knapping cluster from the western terminal ditch associated with the production of blades. Both these assemblages appear to be exactly the same as that encountered during the SRP excavation of the western terminal ditch. In this respect, it seems likely that the pattern witnessed within Trench 26 may continue along much of the length of the western ditch.

Previous excavations into the southern and northern Cursus ditches also produced assemblages in keeping with the current findings. Christie (1963: 372) noted the lack of tools, and stated that the bulk of the flint from her excavations of the northern and southern ditches came from the 'upper brownearth filling'. Two trenches dug into the southern ditch by the Stonehenge Environs Project (Richards 1990: 92–6) produced an assemblage of 294 pieces of struck flint, dominated by flakes alongside six retouched flakes and three scrapers. It is unclear whether the retouched implements came from primary or subsequent fills.

The only potential variation in the general scarcity of flint from the primary fills of the northern and southern ditches comes from Stone's trench into the southern ditch. Details of the flint assemblage are scarce but, interestingly, two knapping clusters were found on the base of the ditch, consisting of 550 flakes, a scraper and several cores (Stone 1947: 14). This assemblage is clearly reminiscent of that from the western terminal ditch and is notable for representing the only *in situ* clusters from the primary fills of any of the Cursus ditches apart from the western ditch.

Some caution is warranted, however, as the SRP excavations show that the southern ditch was reworked in the Late Neolithic period (through the cutting of embayments and cleaning out the ditch) and again in or before the Beaker period (through re-cutting by a V-profiled ditch; see *Trench 28*, above). The results of the Stonehenge Environs Project suggest that there was some refitting potential amongst the assemblage from their excavations of the secondary ditch fills of the southern Cursus ditch (Richards 1990: 96). Therefore, it is possible that the knapping clusters mentioned by Stone are related to one of the periods of remodelling of the southern ditch, rather than its initial infilling. Whilst inconclusive, Stone's plan of the location of the clusters (Stone 1947: fig. 3) does, however, suggest that at least one of them was spread over a sufficient area of the ditch for it to be unlikely that it was entirely within the area of the ditch's V-shaped re-cut. Hence, there is a strong possibility that Stone's clusters date to the initial use of the monument.

In terms of the overall quantities of flint from the ditches of the Cursus, it is important to note that the generally low density of flint within most of its ditches is also represented at a landscape level in the density of lithic scatters in the area. Extensive fieldwalking by the Stonehenge Environs Project (Richards 1990) showed that the ploughsoil at the eastern and western ends of the Greater Cursus has a low density of lithics in relation to most other surveyed areas in the landscape. In contrast, for example, the fields immediately to the north of the Cursus contain the most extensive and dense lithic scatter in the Stonehenge environs. This scatter represents a density of flint on the surface of the ploughsoil over ten times greater than that found at the eastern and western ends of the Cursus (Richards 1990; Chan 2010). The generally low density of flint within the ploughsoil and ditch fills excavated by the SRP (see also the ploughsoil worked flint report, below) confirms this pattern and suggests that it also continues across the large area of the interior of the monument.

In this respect, during some periods in prehistory, the Cursus can be argued to have been an area that was avoided in terms of activities involving the large-scale production and use of flint tools. These types of activities may not have been limited to, but should certainly be taken to include, settlement and residential occupation. The fact that tools appear more frequently by the time of the secondary, and especially the tertiary, filling of the ditches, suggests that, during the Beaker period and perhaps starting in the Late Neolithic, this pattern began to change, albeit on a small scale.

In general, these patterns make the scale of nodule trimming and core preparation in the area of the western terminal ditch all the more remarkable. More widely, the presence of knapping clusters in the ditches of Early Neolithic monuments, such as long barrows, is a recognised phenomenon, occurring at sites such as the Alfriston oval barrow, East Sussex (Drewett 1975) and Thickthorn Down long barrow, Dorset (Drew and Piggott 1936).

Artefact type	Frequency	Percent
Blade	1	0.6
Blade-like flake	2	1.2
Bladelet	1	0.6
Core on a flake	5	3.0
Flake	141	86.0
Irregular waste	8	4.9
Misc. retouched flake	1	0.6
Multi-platform flake-core	2	1.2
Rejuvenation flake-core face/edge	1	0.6
Single-platform flake-core	1	0.6
Utilised/edge-damaged flake	1	0.6
Total	164	100.0

Table 3.11. The lithic assemblage from the test pits at the western end of the Greater Cursus

The principal debate concerning these deposits is whether they represent the opportunistic knapping of nodules exposed in the sides of ditches, or some form of structured deposition (Thomas 1999: 77–80). In the case of the Cursus material, I see no reason why these possibilities need be mutually exclusive. It seems likely that the flint-knapping within the western ditch did produce products that were taken away for use elsewhere. In this sense, the knapping fulfilled a practical purpose. However, the location of the knapping clusters within the western ditch and not in the other ditches of the Cursus suggests that there was some degree of structuring in the activities involved in the working of flint. The lack of settlement evidence from the surface lithic scatters at the western end of the Cursus suggests that this patterning does not simply reflect the presence of an adjacent settlement whose inhabitants were looking for workable flint.

It should also be noted that the shorter east and west ends of the Cursus were constructed more massively than the long north and south sides, to make them stand out. The western end of the Cursus had an exaggerated bank and was also a focus for flint-knapping. The eastern end was marked by the Amesbury 42 long barrow, with the primary fills of its ditch containing very little worked flint (see Chan, below).

In the case of the western terminal ditch, the presence of knapping clusters throughout the depth of the primary fills suggests that flintworking did not just signal the initial opening of the ditch. People returned to the site periodically over the first few years that the ditch was open and repeatedly worked down nodules of flint, leaving the remains lying in the ditch as it gradually filled with chalk rubble. Even though the primary infilling might have taken as little as five years, once the chalk sides of the ditch stabilised and the secondary fills started to accumulate, this practice abruptly stopped. The wider significance of this practice is discussed further in Volume 2.

3.3.6. Worked flint from the ploughsoil of the Greater Cursus

D. Mitcham

Part of the SRP fieldwork strategy was to use test-pit survey to examine artefact distributions within the ploughsoil. This involved hand-excavation of the topsoil in 1m × 1m squares (termed test pits) to recover a sample of artefacts present. The full research context, aims, methods and site plans are reported in Volume 2. This report describes the unstratified lithic assemblages from the ploughsoil within test pits excavated in 2007 and 2008 in advance of the SRP trenches dug to investigate the Greater Cursus.

Western end of the Greater Cursus

The test pits were arranged in a systematic grid, and a 20% sample of the topsoil was sieved through a 10mm mesh. This produced a small assemblage of mostly local chalkland flint, of 164 worked pieces. The material is predominantly debitage – flakes comprise 86% of the assemblage – with a heavy white patina, although some mixing of patination is evident. A few pieces demonstrate only a light patina, on flint that is blue or brown in colour. A few flakes are on a grey flint with a high proportion of chert inclusions and a heavy patina. There is, therefore, a very small amount of material which could be from a different source of raw materials than the local, chalk-derived flint.

The assemblage from these test pits derives predominantly from a flake-based technology which is typical of later prehistoric flintworking in general, is *ad hoc* in character, and is not particularly diagnostic of a specific period. The test pits did not produce any formal tools, or pieces that are chronologically diagnostic (Table 3.11). There is one miscellaneous retouched piece, on a thick flake with a predominantly cortical surface, from Test Pit 13 (TP; Trench 27). The retouch is irregular and, whilst this could have been intended as a crude scraper, it is not convincing as such. It is worth noting that two of the test pits (TP 15 and TP 38 in Trench 27 on the north side of the Cursus) produced a mixture of primary, secondary and tertiary flakes. This suggests that most stages of the reduction sequence took place in the area, and that any finished tools, if produced, were then potentially taken elsewhere.

A tiny number of pieces (four in total) belong to a blade technology but this is best interpreted as a very slight background signature. One fragment of the medial

Artefact type	Frequency	Percent
Blade	12	0.8
Blade-like flake	39	2.7
Bladelet	8	0.6
Chip	1	0.1
Core on a flake	6	0.4
Crested blade	2	0.1
Denticulate	1	0.1
Edge-damaged/utilised blade	1	0.1
End-scraper	2	0.1
Fabricator	1	0.1
Flake	1274	89.1
Flake from ground implement	1	0.1
Flint axe/axe roughout	1	0.1
Hammerstone	1	0.1
Irregular waste	46	3.2
Misc. retouched flake	2	0.1
Multi-platform flake-core	6	0.4
Notch	1	0.1
Oblique arrowhead	1	0.1
Other blade-core	2	0.1
Other/unclassifiable (general)	3	0.2
Piercer	1	0.1
Rejuvenation flake-core face/edge	5	0.3
Retouched blade	1	0.1
Single-platform flake-core	1	0.1
Spurred implement	1	0.1
Tested nodule/bashed lump	1	0.1
Unclassifiable/fragmentary core	6	0.4
Utilised/edge-damaged flake	3	0.2
Total	1430	100.0

Table 3.12. The lithic assemblage from the test pits at the eastern end of the Greater Cursus

portion of a blade from TP 5 (Trench 28) does not show any signs of being deliberately broken by truncation of the edge or by direct percussion, and one bladelet is also present. However, both of these pieces look deliberately produced and cannot be explained as accidental. They could be Mesolithic or Neolithic in date, but are not sufficiently diagnostic on their own.

The cores present are all flake-cores, several of which are heavily exhausted with, for example, four or five platforms. The working is fairly *ad hoc* in character, with a poor level of knapping control evident. There are also several cores on natural flakes which are extremely irregular and poorly worked, with only a few removals present.

Artefact type	Frequency	Percent
Blade	27	3.2
Blade-like flake	9	1.1
Bladelet	4	0.5
Core on a flake	1	0.1
Crested blade	1	0.1
Flake	773	90.2
Flake from ground implement	1	0.1
Irregular waste	14	1.6
Keeled non-discoidal flake-core	1	0.1
Misc. retouched flake	7	0.8
Multi-platform flake-core	6	0.7
Notch	1	0.1
Other knife	1	0.1
Rejuvenation flake-core face/edge	1	0.1
Single-platform flake-core	3	0.4
Utilised blade	1	0.1
Utilised/edge-damaged flake/ blade	6	0.7
Total	857	100.0

Table 3.13. The worked flint assemblage from Trench 43

This Greater Cursus test-pit assemblage is generally unremarkable, and typical of the background ploughsoil assemblages within the wider Stonehenge landscape. However, whatever the activities and post-depositional processes that led to the creation of the ploughsoil assemblage, the test-pit assemblage's character is similar to the *in situ* knapping deposits recovered from the Cursus ditch in Trench 26 (see above).

Eastern end of the Greater Cursus

The SRP's investigations here aimed to clarify the chronology of and relationships between Amesbury 42 long barrow and the Greater Cursus. Prior to the full excavation of Trenches 40, 41 and 43, a 100% sample of topsoil was sieved from 1m × 1m test pits. The test pits here produced a total worked flint assemblage of 1,430 pieces, and a noticeably wider range of artefact types (Table 3.12) than were found in many of the smaller test-pit assemblages recovered by the SRP. Note that the report on the excavated lithics from Trenches 40 and 41 (the eastern end of the Cursus) are reported above, whereas the excavated lithics from the eastern ditch of Amesbury 42 long barrow are reported below.

The raw material is predominantly local chalk-derived flint, with most pieces having a heavy white patina. A few fresher pieces were noted, with light blue/grey patina, and light brown raw material. The overall composition of the test-pit assemblage is worthy of note: while flakes comprise the majority of the assemblage at

89.1%, high proportions of miscellaneous waste (3.2%) and blade-like flakes (2.7%) are present.

A number of interesting tools and diagnostic pieces were present in the test pits at the eastern end of the Cursus, and merit detailed description here. One of these is a flake from a ground implement, from TP 123 in Trench 43, above the ditch of Amesbury 42 long barrow. Trench 40, within the eastern half of the Cursus, produced an axe rough-out (in TP 246) and a worked-down polished flint axe (topsoil context 101; Figure 3.62).

The axe rough-out is fairly flat on one side, with some removals and part of a natural surface evident. The piece has been worked bifacially in places, with a triangular cross-section and well-defined edge, and appears unfinished. Some removals have taken place from the flat side, and this could be evidence of its secondary use as a single-platform core, or an attempt at blunting this edge. However, it is not possible to tell whether it broke and was deliberately worked into this shape because the latter sequence has potentially removed any trace of a break, if once present. It is best interpreted as an attempted axe rough-out and is therefore broadly Neolithic in date. It could also be interpreted as an attempt at bifacial working or an apprentice piece.

Also worthy of note here are a piercer from TP 134 and a denticulate from TP 50 (both Trench 43). The former is on a flake, with a 20mm protrusion created by retouch on the dorsal side (Figure 3.62). The bulb and platform are still in place and show crushing and clumsy working. The most likely interpretation of this is that it was intended to create a long spur or piercer (see similar examples from Durrington Walls; Wainwright with Longworth 1971: 174). The denticulate is a fragment with two surviving notches defined by small removals, the rest of the retouched edge being destroyed by later damage. The piece has a heavy white patina, with crushing on the flake butt, and may date to the Early Neolithic (*cf* Clark *et al.* 1960: 217 and Gardiner 1984: 19).

Only two end-scrapers were identified from the test-pitting in this area; one example from TP 226 (Trench 40 within the eastern end of the Cursus) is on a broad, squat flake blank, with a slightly dipping profile. The piece is retouched around the distal end, but is heavily damaged and partly re-corticated. In addition, a spurred implement and a second crude notched-and-spurred implement came from TP 37 (Trench 27) and TP 134 (Trench 43). Although neither is particularly chronologically diagnostic, the latter is a combination tool of a type found in Late Neolithic assemblages (Butler 2005: 168).

The broken end of a quite damaged fabricator from TP 147 (Trench 43) exhibits crushing and wear on a flattened end. This piece appears to have been made on a blade blank with a triangular cross-section, with flake removals on the edges and on both surfaces. This wear pattern suggests use as a strike-a-light or perhaps as a knapping tool. Although fabricators occur in various periods of prehistory, the blade blank's form would be consistent with a Mesolithic or Early Neolithic date (Butler 2005: 110, 132, 174).

Whilst the technology present here is predominantly flake-based, a number of blades and blade-like flakes are present. Of the latter, several appear to have been struck from blade-cores, and at least one comes from a bipolar (opposed platform) blade-core. Of the blades and bladelets, a few have been very carefully produced, and are potentially Mesolithic or Early Neolithic. A few pieces are either broken or medial fragments, but no evidence of deliberate breaking by truncation is evident. However, the majority of this material does not show any evidence of edge-preparation techniques, or any evidence of soft-hammer percussion. There is enough evidence here to suggest the presence of a small blade industry in the area, which has a light footprint and may be Neolithic in date.

At least two crested blades are present, from TP 213 (Trench 40) and TP 39 (Trench 27). The piece from TP 213 is a fragment of the proximal end, with a triangular cross-section around 30mm thick. This could have been quite a long blade, and has two parallel ridges on its dorsal surface, one of which has been partially flaked to create the ridge. This is interpreted as evidence of cresting, creating parallel ridges on the core face by a series of small flake removals, to prepare the core in order to subsequently remove a blade.

The core technology exhibited in the assemblage from the Cursus's eastern end is predominantly flake-based. A number of cores on flakes are present, some of which are on thermal flakes, and were often unproductive with only a small number of removals. A number of single- and multiple-platform flake-cores are also present, typically *ad hoc* with poor knapping control evident. Several unclassifiable core fragments are present and several of the cores are small and exhausted.

Two other blade-cores were found, in TP 212 and TP 235 (Trench 40). The example from TP 212 is a heavily worked-out small piece, with at least three platforms. It possesses a mixture of blade-like linear removals along with a few flake scars, with noticeable crushing and step fractures, suggesting a lack of knapping control. Whilst this is difficult to date, it is most likely to be Neolithic given the *ad hoc* character and lack of control evident, although it could be an earlier (Mesolithic) apprentice piece. The second example, from TP 235, is a broken fragment of a single-platform blade-core, of a small size (30mm wide × 20mm long). A few blade-removal scars are present on one face, whilst the second face is rather irregular. Again, this is difficult to date given its fragmentary state and is not particularly diagnostic, but it is most likely to be Neolithic rather than Mesolithic.

Artefact type		Ditch fill type			Total
		Primary	*Secondary*	*Tertiary*	
Blade	Count	1	3	18	22
	% within ditch fill type	7.1%	8.8%	4.8%	5.2%
Blade-like flake	Count	0	2	4	6
	% within ditch fill type	0%	5.9%	1.1%	1.4%
Bladelet	Count	0	0	3	3
	% within ditch fill type	0%	0%	0.8%	0.7%
Core on a flake	Count	0	0	1	1
	% within ditch fill type	0%	0%	0.3%	0.2%
Crested blade	Count	1	0	0	1
	% within ditch fill type	7.1%	0%	0%	0.2%
Flake	Count	12	27	326	365
	% within ditch fill type	85.7%	79.4%	86.9%	86.3%
Flake from ground implement	Count	0	0	1	1
	% within ditch fill type	0%	0%	0.3%	0.2%
Irregular waste	Count	0	2	1	3
	% within ditch fill type	0%	5.9%	0.3%	0.7%
Keeled non-discoidal flake core	Count	0	0	1	1
	% within ditch fill type	0%	0%	0.3%	0.2%
Misc. retouched flake	Count	0	0	5	5
	% within ditch fill type	0%	0%	1.3%	1.2%
Multi-platform flake core	Count	0	0	5	5
	% within ditch fill type	0%	0%	1.3%	1.2%
Notch	Count	0	0	1	1
	% within ditch fill type	0%	0%	0.3%	0.2%
Single platform flake core	Count	0	0	3	3
	% within ditch fill type	0%	0%	0.8%	0.7%
Utilised blade	Count	0	0	1	1
	% within ditch fill type	0%	0%	0.3%	0.2%
Utilised/edge-damaged flake/blade	Count	0	0	5	5
	% within ditch fill type	0%	0%	1.3%	1.2%
Total	Count	14	34	375	423
	% within ditch fill type	100.0%	100.0%	100.0%	100.0%

Table 3.14. The composition of the worked flint assemblage by context type from the Amesbury 42 long barrow ditch

3.3.7. Worked flint from stratified contexts of Amesbury 42 long barrow

B. Chan

The excavation of Trench 43, exploring the eastern ditch of the Amesbury 42 long barrow, produced an assemblage of 857 pieces of worked flint (Table 3.13). The assemblage is derived from a number of features as well as a series of later deposits connected with the destruction of the barrow and the development of a thick ploughsoil. Some of the features, such as the long barrow ditch and causewayed pits, are of secure Neolithic date whilst others, such as tree-throw 043 and possible postholes 016 and 038, are of less certain date.

Raw material and condition

The raw material within the assemblage and the condition of the artefacts is the same as that of the Cursus assemblages described above.

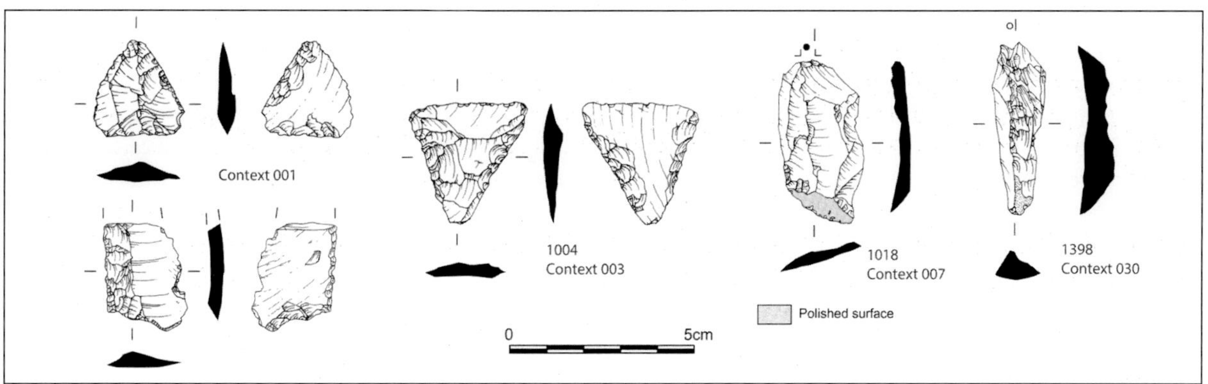

Figure 3.64. Lithics from Amesbury 42 long barrow (Trench 43)

Amesbury 42 long barrow eastern ditch

The long barrow ditch yielded an assemblage of 423 flint artefacts. This material was unevenly distributed, with very few artefacts coming from the primary fill and nearly 90% of the assemblage coming from the tertiary fills (Table 3.14). The primary chalk rubble fill (030) contained 12 flakes, a blade and a possible crested blade (Figure 3.64). Although the assemblage from the primary fill is small and does not contain any *in situ* knapping clusters, the material is generally in mint condition. A large nodule trimming flake was also found within context 030, a slight indication that some flintworking might have taken place in the ditch around the time that it was first dug.

The vast majority of the assemblage from the long barrow ditch comes from the tertiary fills, which mainly relate to the destruction of the barrow mound by ploughing and the subsequent infilling of the ditch by plough-wash. The worked flint from these contexts is undoubtedly residual, but it is generally in good condition and does not appear plough-rolled. This perhaps reflects the rapid accumulation of ploughsoil in the deep barrow ditch.

The material itself is largely derived from a broad flake technology that fits within Neolithic flintworking traditions, but is otherwise undiagnostic. The exception to this is the relatively large proportion of blades, bladelets and blade-like flakes, which make up nearly 7% of the material from the tertiary fills, and a single flake from a ground flint axe (SF 1018; Figure 3.64) from context 007. Only a small portion of the distal part of the dorsal surface of the flake is polished, with the rest of the surface being covered in multiple flake scars. The flake itself was clearly struck from a prepared and faceted platform, which was located within what would have been the body of the axe. The flake, therefore, has clearly not been removed accidentally during the use of the axe, but rather has resulted from the extensive use of the axe as a core for the removal of flakes.

Artefact type	Pit number 031	Pit number 034	Total
Blade	0	1	1
Flake	4	77	81
Irregular waste	0	10	10
Misc. retouch flake	0	1	1
Rejuvenation flake core face/ edge	0	1	1
Total	4	90	94

Table 3.15. The worked flint assemblage from the causewayed pits in Trench 43

The causewayed pits

Causewayed pit 034 contained 90 pieces of worked flint, predominantly consisting of flakes and irregular waste (Table 3.15). The material was principally derived from 012, a plough-wash deposit in the top of the pit, and 039=041, the fill of pit re-cut 042. Fill 039=041 contained 65 pieces of worked flint, which appear to represent an *in situ* knapping cluster probably related to the extensively refitted sequence from Richards' excavation of the other half of pit 034 (Richards 1990: 96–9). The flint from 039=041 is in fresh condition and refitting has revealed three sets of two conjoining flakes.

All of the conjoining flakes appear to relate to nodule trimming/core preparation. Compared to the sequences identified by Phil Harding in the assemblage from Julian Richards' excavation (Harding 1990: 99–104), the material from contexts 039=041 has limited refitting potential and, given that it contains no cores, it does not appear to be as complete a reduction sequence. This may suggest that much of the knapped flint was taken elsewhere. It should also be considered whether the flint from the deposit is not re-fittable because it is only part of a reduction sequence, with the remainder being contained within the part of the pit excavated by Richards (1990: 96–9).

Causewayed pit 031 contained four flakes, and causewayed pit 033 contained no worked flint. The difference between these two pits and pit 034 is that they did not contain a re-cut feature. Given that the majority of the material within pit 034 was contained within the re-cut of the pit, it is clear that the assemblages from the original fills of all three pits would have been comparably small and undistinguished.

The postholes, tree-throw hole and later deposits

The remaining features within Trench 43 contained very little worked flint. Tree-throw 043 contained two flakes, pit/posthole 016 contained four flakes and pit/posthole 038 contained no worked flint. In addition, a series of deposits sealing the prehistoric features within the trench also contained worked flint. These deposits (001, 002, 003, 005, 006, and 035) produced an assemblage of 334 pieces of worked flint. These contexts relate principally to the post-medieval destruction of the mound by ploughing, and the subsequent development of a ploughsoil. The vast majority of this assemblage derives from contexts 002, 003 and 006, which represent the uppermost layers under the topsoil.

The assemblage is dominated by flakes and also contains a small number of blades, a single retouched flake, a core and a broken flake with invasive retouch along one lateral margin that is either a knife or part of a scraper. The only notable feature of the assemblage is its unusually high proportion of flakes (96%) and correspondingly low proportion of cores and tools. Given that the assemblage is entirely residual, this pattern is of limited value archaeologically.

Discussion

Although the assemblage from Trench 43 amounts to nearly 900 flint artefacts, nearly 85% of the assemblage is residual within deposits most likely dating to the post-medieval period. These deposits include not only the ploughsoil itself, but also plough-wash deposits that infilled the top of the ditch and the other prehistoric features. The part of the assemblage that can be securely attributed to Neolithic contexts amounts to just 96 artefacts (Table 3.16). This material is dominated by flakes and, other than a possible crested blade, it does not contain any diagnostic artefacts.

The proportion of blades within the tertiary fills of the long barrow ditch is very close to that from the primary fills of the Greater Cursus western terminal ditch (see above). This perhaps indicates that this part of the assemblage was originally derived from an Early or Middle Neolithic assemblage in the vicinity of the ditch, perhaps originally contained within the barrow mound. However, the assemblage from secure Neolithic contexts in Trench 43 has a much lower proportion of blades than the assemblage from the western terminal primary fills, and also contains no cores.

This is significant in that, in many ways, if Amesbury 42 was built at the same time as the Cursus, it can be seen as a direct counterpart to the large ditch and bank that marked the opposite, western end of the Cursus. It is clear from the SRP excavation that, at least in terms of flintworking, there were distinct differences in the activities associated with either end of the monument. Whilst the knapping cluster excavated from causewayed pit 034, together with the other half of this cluster excavated by Richards (1990) from the southern part of the same pit, is much more in keeping with the findings in the western terminal ditch, it is clear that at the barrow these activities were much more localised, and they did not occur at all during the primary infilling of the long barrow ditch itself. In contrast, knapping clusters appear to be ubiquitous along the length of the primary fills of the western terminal ditch of the Cursus.

3.3.8. Human remains from the Greater Cursus and Amesbury 42 long barrow

A. Chamberlain and C. Willis

Femoral shaft, context 001 (topsoil) in Test Pit 33, Trench 26, western terminal of the Greater Cursus [C. Willis]

An adult right mid-femoral shaft was recovered from topsoil in a test pit dug before full excavation at the south end of Trench 26, above the inside edge of the western ditch of the Greater Cursus. The bone measures 96.5mm long × 26.9mm wide, with a cortical thickness of 7.6mm. The cortical surface of the bone has been badly damaged by root action and is graded at Stage 5 on the scale devised by Brickley and McKinley (2004: 16), which is indicative of 'heavy erosion... across whole surface, completely masking normal surface morphology, with some modification to profile'. The medio-lateral diameter of the shaft taken at the level of the nutrient foramen is 26.9mm while the antero-posterior diameter is 26.3mm. The diameter of the bone has been reduced by *c.* 2mm as a result of loss of surface bone layers from erosion.

The proximal end of the femoral shaft had been transversely broken sometime after death. The break is consistent in appearance with a break on a dry bone, and has been slightly stained by the minerals in the surrounding soil. The colouration of the break itself is lighter than the colouration on the surface of the shaft, suggesting that the two bone surfaces were exposed to the soil for different lengths of time. There are also grains of sediment embedded in the break, indicating that the bone was reburied after it was broken. There is no evidence of any root-etching on the break; thus the breakage occurred quite a while after death.

Artefact type	Frequency	Percent
Blade	2	2.1
Crested blade	1	1.0
Flake	82	85.4
Irregular waste	10	10.4
Rejuvenation flake core face/edge	1	1.0
Total	96	100.0

Table 3.16. The worked flint assemblage from secure Neolithic contexts in Trench 43

The distal extremity of the femoral shaft has been broken off either at the time of excavation or soon afterwards: this is a clean break with no sediment adhering to the breakage. The colour of the break is an off-white, again indicating that the bone has been broken recently.

A radiocarbon determination on this femur provides a Late Neolithic date of 2890–2670 cal BC at 95% confidence (SUERC-75196; 4187±30 BP). Its isotopic values are –21.8‰ for $\delta^{13}C$ and 12.2‰ for $\delta^{15}N$.

Distal humerus, context 001 (topsoil) in Test Pit 104, Trench 43, Amesbury 42 long barrow [C. Willis]

A broken adult right distal humeral shaft was recovered from the topsoil of a test pit dug before the full excavation of Trench 43 into the ditch of Amesbury 42 long barrow. Only the shaft containing the deltoid tuberosity down to the medial supracondylar ridge was recovered. Thus the distal end containing the olecranon fossa, trochlea, and capitulum is missing, as is the proximal portion of the shaft and humeral head. The shaft has been transversely broken at approximately the mid-point sometime after death; the proximal and distal breaks similarly occurred after death. All three breaks have been stained by minerals in the surrounding soil in which they were buried, but none show any evidence for root erosion. This suggests that the breaks occurred a long time after death. In addition, a small fragment of the upper shaft (anterior side) has been broken at some point after excavation. The break is clean, with no signs of staining or erosion.

The humeral shaft measures 16.2mm × 19.2mm, with a cortical thickness of 5.9mm. As with the other bones recovered from this area, the cortical surface of the bone has been badly damaged by root erosion and is graded between Stages 4 and 5 (Brickley and McKinley 2004: 16) which is indicative of 'erosive action...masking normal surface morphology'. The diameter of the bone has been reduced by *c.* 1mm–2mm as a result of the loss of surface bone layers from erosion. The medio-lateral diameter of the shaft taken at the level of the nutrient foramen is 19.3mm while the antero-posterior diameter is 15.8mm.

A radiocarbon determination on this humerus provides a Late Bronze Age date of 920–800 cal BC at 95% confidence (SUERC-75197; 2712±30 BP). Its isotopic values are –20.4‰ for $\delta^{13}C$ and 9.6‰ for $\delta^{15}N$.

Femur shaft, context 017 in Trench 43, Amesbury 42 long barrow [A. Chamberlain]

A single human bone (SF 1349) was found in the ditch of Amesbury 42 long barrow (Trench 43) in context 017. The specimen consists of a fragment of the shaft of a human femur. At its proximal extremity, it shows an irregular, ancient transverse break that is located roughly 10mm to 20mm above the mid-shaft point. This break is consistent in appearance with damage to dry bone, though the surface preservation of the specimen (see below) is too poor to enable the broken surface to be studied in detail – the surface of the break is root-etched and the break is therefore attributable to ancient damage.

At its distal extremity, the fragment shows an ancient, jagged pattern of spiral breakage that is located at about three-quarters of the way down the femoral shaft, between 40mm and 60mm below the location of the nutrient foramen. These distal breaks are more consistent with patterns of damage to fresh bone but, as with the case of the proximal break, the state of preservation of the bone surfaces prevents a confident statement being made concerning the lapse of time between death and post-mortem modification.

The external (periosteal) cortical surfaces show extensive penetrative chemical dissolution, most likely caused by root-etching. The grade of erosion is at Stage 4 on the scale devised by Brickley and McKinley (2004), which is assigned for '[a]ll of bone surface affected by erosive action ... general profile maintained and depth of modification not uniform across whole surface'. The internal (endosteal) surfaces are much better preserved since the medullary cavity offers some protection from root action. The poor preservation of the external surfaces prevents the detection of any potential bone surface modifications such as periosteal new bone formation or cut-marks.

The specimen is from a right femur, as indicated by the position of the opening of the nutrient foramen, which is discernible medial to the *linea aspera*, as well as by the medial inclination of the posterior face of the femoral shaft between the supracondylar lines. The absence of epiphyses prevents an accurate estimation of age at death, but the dimensions of the bone are consistent with those of a small adult, with a maximum femur length estimated at (very approximately) 380mm. The antero-posterior and medio-lateral diameters of the bone shaft at the level of the nutrient foramen are 24.8mm and 24.2mm respectively; these dimensions have probably been reduced by up to 2mm from ante-mortem values as a result of the erosive loss of surface bone layers.

A radiocarbon determination on this femur provides a Middle Neolithic date of 3360–3100 cal BC at 95% confidence (OxA-21961; 4520±32 BP). Its isotopic value for $\delta^{13}C$ is –21.75‰.

3.3.9. Charred plant remains and wood charcoal from the Greater Cursus and Amesbury 42 long barrow

E. Simmons

Bulk sieving samples were systematically taken from all the excavations carried out as part of the SRP. Thirty-four bulk sieving samples, comprising over 700 litres of sediment, were taken during the excavations at the Greater Cursus and the Amesbury 42 long barrow.

Recovery, processing and laboratory methods

Samples were processed by flotation for charred plant remains and wood charcoal using a Siraf-type water separation machine. Floating material was collected in sieves of 1mm and 300μm meshes, and the heavy residue was retained in a 1mm mesh. The flots were initially scanned using a low-power binocular microscope (x7–x45), in order to assess the concentration, diversity and state of preservation of any archaeobotanical material present. Identification of charred plant material was carried out using modern reference material in the Department of Archaeology, University of Sheffield and various reference works (Berggren 1981; Anderberg 1994; Cappers *et al.* 2006). Cereal identifications follow Jacomet (2006). Other plant nomenclature follows Stace (2010). Quantification of cereal grains is based on the presence of embryo ends and quantification of chaff is by glume base or rachis node (Jones 1990).

Species represented

The uppermost fill (014) of the northern Cursus ditch (Trench 27) produced an indeterminate cereal grain, an indeterminate barley grain (*Hordeum* sp. indet.) and a fragment of onion couch grass tuber (*Arrhenatherum elatius* ssp. *bulbosum*). The fill (061) of the slot 062, which was cut into the cross-ditch adjacent to the northern ditch, produced an indeterminate cereal grain and an indeterminate wheat grain (*Triticum* sp. indet.). The upper fill (092) of intrusive feature 087, which also cut into the cross-ditch, produced an indeterminate cereal grain, an indeterminate barley grain, a fragment of onion couch grass tuber and a fragment of hazel nutshell (*Corylus avellana*). Fill 080 of posthole/embayment 081 produced an indeterminate cereal grain and a fragment of onion couch grass tuber. Onion couch grass is frequently associated with ungrazed or irregularly grazed grassland (Rodwell 1992: 34) and is common in cultivated fields on the chalk (Grose 1979: 620)

Single tubers of onion couch grass were found to be present in the plough-wash deposits 011 and 012 at the top of causewayed pits 033 and 034 adjacent to the Amesbury 42 long barrow ditch.

The nature of some of the contexts from which charred plant remains were recovered, along with the low concentration and poor preservation of the material, indicates a high probability that the charred plant remains are intrusive. No further analysis of the charred plant remains was therefore undertaken. Wood charcoal fragments are occasionally present, but no wood charcoal analysis was undertaken given the small quantities of fragments >2mm in cross-section.

3.4. Early Neolithic activity at Woodhenge

J. Pollard

Woodhenge is situated immediately south of Durrington Walls, on the western escarpment bounding the River Avon (SU 1506 4337). From here, there are commanding views to the east and northeast, and to the valley of the Nine Mile River. The site's archaeological fame relates to the discovery – through aerial photography and excavation during the 1920s – of a penannular earthwork enclosing a multiple timber circle of prehistoric date recognised at the time as analogous to the stone settings of Stonehenge (Cunnington 1929). Previously, the site was considered to be a massive plough-reduced disc barrow (Colt Hoare 1810: 170). Its Late Neolithic date was firmly established by the time of the discovery of the analogous Southern Circle at Durrington Walls in 1967 (Wainwright and Longworth 1971). The surrounding bank and ditch may, however, have been constructed as late as the last quarter of the third millennium cal BC (dated by an antler pick in the base of the henge ditch to 2480–2030 cal BC; Pollard 1995a).

Following soon after its discovery from the air, the monument was extensively excavated over two seasons in 1926–1927 by Maud and Benjamin Cunnington (Cunnington 1929: 18–20). The whole of the interior was investigated and sections dug through the bank and ditch on the north, east, south and west sides. Part of its enclosure on the southeastern side was further examined by Evans and Wainwright in 1970 in order to obtain dating and environmental evidence (Evans and Wainwright 1979).

The work by the SRP in 2006 was undertaken in order to address a series of questions relating to the chronology of the various components of the monument, constructional processes, and the character of the pre-henge activity (mirroring, though not directly informed by, points raised in the Stonehenge landscape research framework; Darvill 2005: 112–13). Refining the date of the timber circles and establishing their sequential relationship both with the enclosure and with developments at Durrington Walls and Stonehenge were key concerns. This could only be achieved by recovering suitable samples for radiocarbon-dating. Although the interior of the monument and all the postholes were subject to 'total excavation' in 1926–1927, re-excavations at the Sanctuary (Pitts 2001) had shown that the Cunningtons did on occasion miss pockets of feature fill in which antler or freshly-deposited bone might occur. Published photographs of the 1920s excavation make it quite clear that an open-area technique was not employed at Woodhenge, and that the work was messy by modern standards (Cunnington 1929: plate 17).

The primary focus of the SRP excavations was on the Late Neolithic–Chalcolithic monument itself, and on attempting to identify surviving *in situ* deposits within its postholes from which samples might be retrieved for radiocarbon dating, and on evaluating whether features in the southern part of the timber rings related to a megalithic phase that followed the decay of the timber rings. Another issue that required attention related to the unusual character of the pre-bank deposits, which, from previous investigations, included un-weathered Grooved Ware sherds, plentiful animal bone and ash-filled pits. The possibility existed that these deposits derived from episodes of feasting and midden deposition contemporary with the (pre-henge) timber circles.

Two trenches were excavated in 2006: a 10m × 5m area (Trench 16) through the bank on the southeast of the monument; and a 10m × 7m area (Trench 17) in the southern part of the monument's interior around postholes A15–A17, B8–B9 and C5 (Figure 3.65). Deposits and features belonging to the timber circle and its later stone components will be described in Volume 3. Here, unanticipated features and deposits of Early Neolithic date are reported on.

Trench 16 was set adjacent and to the south of the trench excavated in 1970 by John G. Evans (Evans and Wainwright 1979). It comprised the investigation of *c.* 5% of the likely remaining bank deposits and underlying buried soil (though it is difficult to know with certainty the extent of Cunnington's 1920s excavations through the bank, or the general survival of bank-sealed material).

3.4.1. The bank, buried soil and a tree-throw pit

It became clear after removal of the topsoil that Trench 16 inadvertently intersected, at a slightly oblique angle, the southern edge of the 1970 excavation (Figure 3.66). Furthermore, the 1970 trench had, in turn, cut into the edge of an even earlier excavation along the same axis (this is not commented upon in the published report: Evans and Jones 1979)! The earlier excavation, which must belong to Cunnington's 1926 season, comprised a shallow linear cut (054) >1.50m wide (as measured from the edge of the old cut into that of the 1970 trench) through the bank and buried soil. It was filled with a backfill deposit of brown silty clay with chalk rubble and flint (025 and 055), containing glass and tile. As a result of these twentieth-century archaeological interventions and of truncation of the rear of the bank by Roman to post-medieval ploughing, an area of buried soil only 5.40m × 3.20m survived for investigation in the southern and western part of Trench 16.

Here, the buried soil (051) comprised a grey-brown, silty clay loam up to 0.17m deep, with variable quantities of small chalk and flint; more flint, including small rounded nodules, was present in the base of the profile. Upon exposure, quantities of animal bone, Early Neolithic pottery and worked flint were immediately evident *within* this, especially on the southern side of the excavated area (Figures 3.66, 3.68). Among the worked flint were two Late Neolithic oblique arrowheads. A sherd of Late Neolithic Grooved Ware also came from the buried soil.

Time prevented full excavation of the buried soil, which was sampled in alternate 0.50m × 0.50m squares dug across a 1m-wide strip along the middle of the trench, while a second 1m-wide strip of buried soil was totally excavated in 0.50m × 0.50m squares against the southwestern baulk of the trench (comprising 6.50 sq m in total; see Figure 3.78). The whole of the buried soil was sampled on the 0.50m grid for magnetic susceptibility and phosphorous, and bulk flotation samples for plant macrofossils were taken from five of the 26 0.50m × 0.50m squares that were fully excavated. Molluscan and soil micromorphology samples were also taken from the southwestern baulk. Finds from the interface of the buried soil (051) and the henge bank (026) above it were recorded as coming from context 050.

The full profile of the buried soil was not present. Comparison with the northern section of the 1970 excavation, only 2m to the north, shows that the top of the buried soil in Trench 16 (051) was truncated by *c.* 0.05m–0.10m; it lacked the dark brown, stone-free turf-line and sorted line of flints visible in the 1970 section (Evans and Wainwright 1979: fig. 41). The obvious interpretation is that the turf and top of the buried soil were stripped in this area prior to the construction of the bank, and

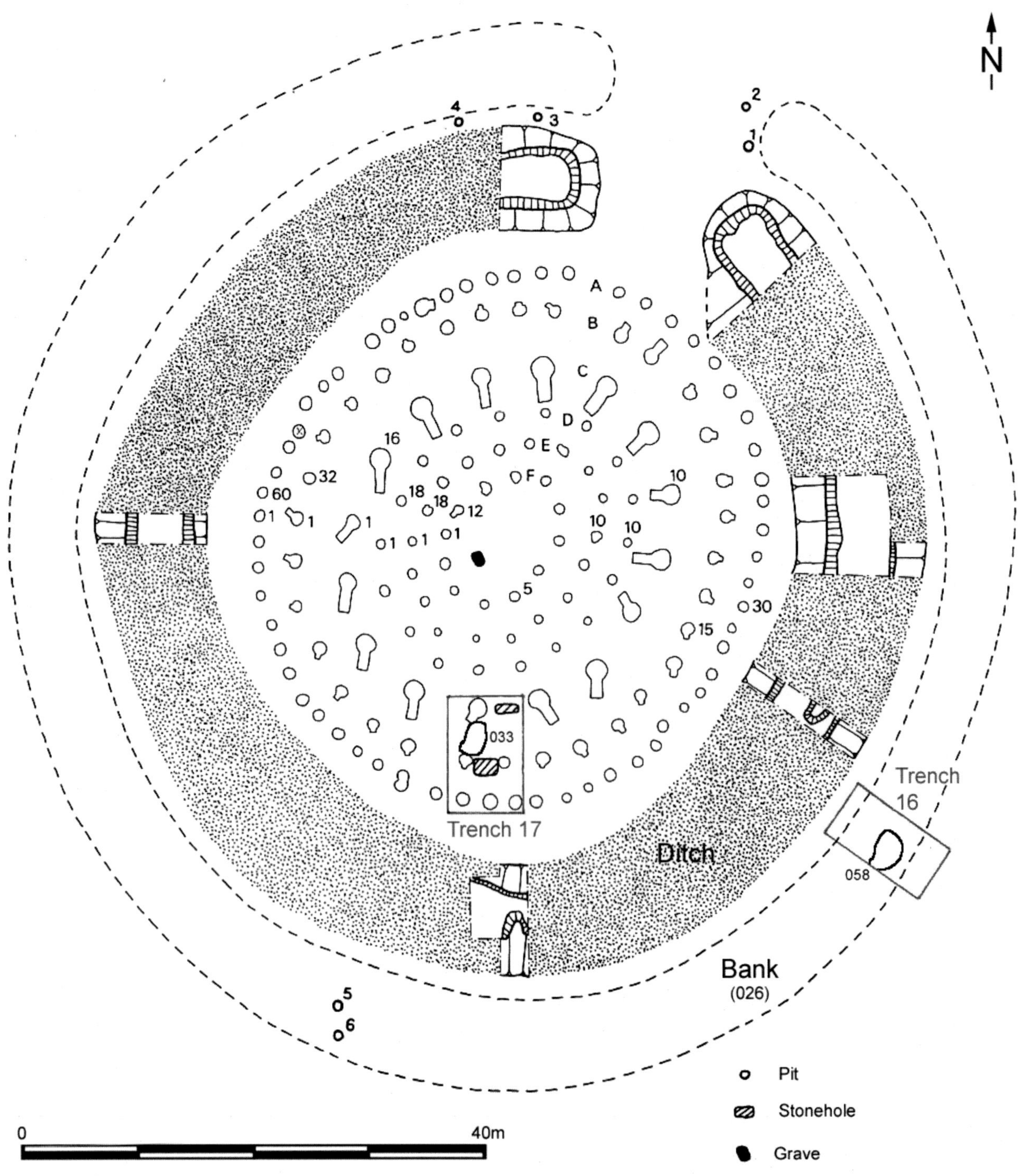

Figure 3.65. Plan of Woodhenge showing positions of Trenches 16 and 17. Cunnington's numbering system of post-rings A–F is indicated by the first, middle and last numbers in each ring, as well as individual postholes beyond the ditch

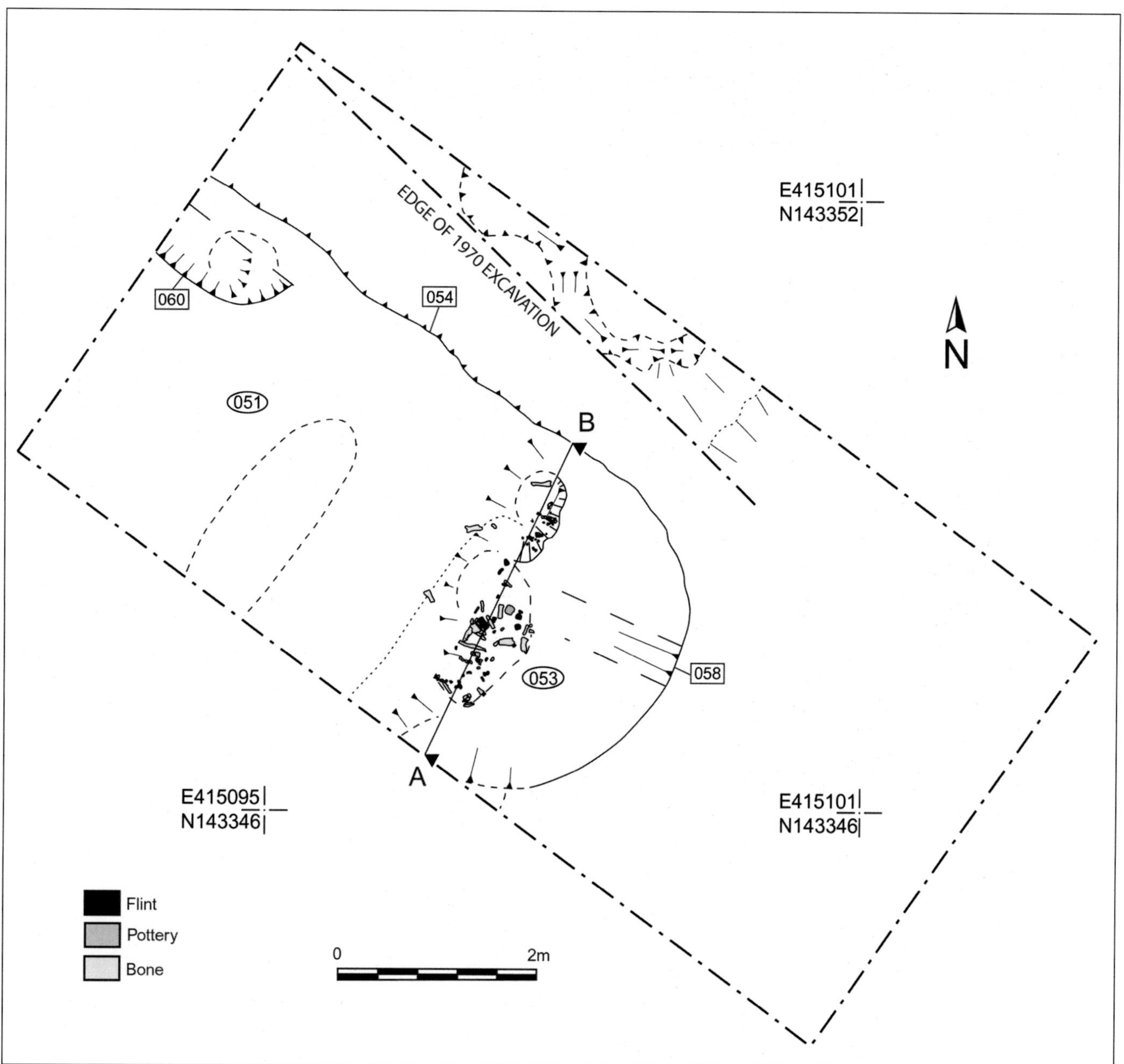

Figure 3.66. Plan of Trench 16 at Woodhenge

probably very soon before since a new turf-line did not have time to develop (see French, below).

The buried soil and artefact spread ran into the top of a substantial hollow under the tail of the bank (Figure 3.65). This proved to be a large, oval tree-throw pit (058), 3.50m × 2.50m and 0.50m deep (Figure 3.66). Subjected to *c.* 50% excavation by removing its east side, the truncated 'back' of the feature had shallow to moderately sloping sides merging with a slightly dished base, the chalk natural here being quite loosely structured (Figure 3.67). The fills were asymmetric, beginning with a primary fill (057) of chalk rubble within a friable beige silty clay, from which a small quantity of unweathered animal bone, 11 flakes and two bladelets were recovered. Sealing this was a mid-brown, silty clay loam with moderate chalk pea-grit, occasional small flint and burnt flint (056), and then an upper fill (053) which looked to be a continuation of the buried soil, again lacking its full profile.

Figure 3.67. Trench 16, viewed from the east, showing tree-throw pit 058 in half-section and, beyond it, gridded excavation squares in the buried soil

Figure 3.68 (below). Distribution of finds within the top of fill 053 of tree-throw 058

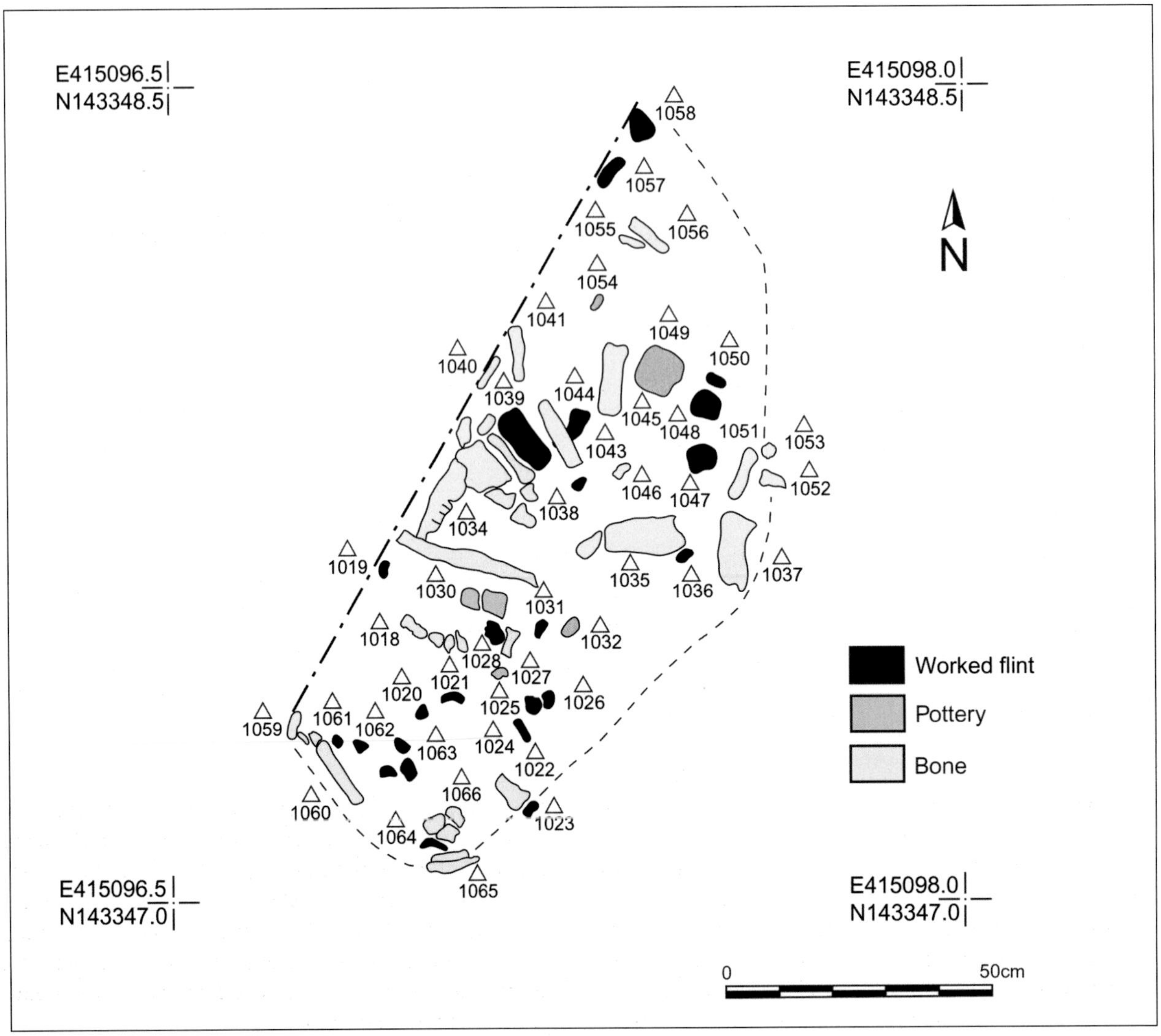

E415096.5
N143348.5

E415098.0
N143348.5

N

Worked flint
Pottery
Bone

E415096.5
N143347.0

E415098.0
N143347.0

0 50cm

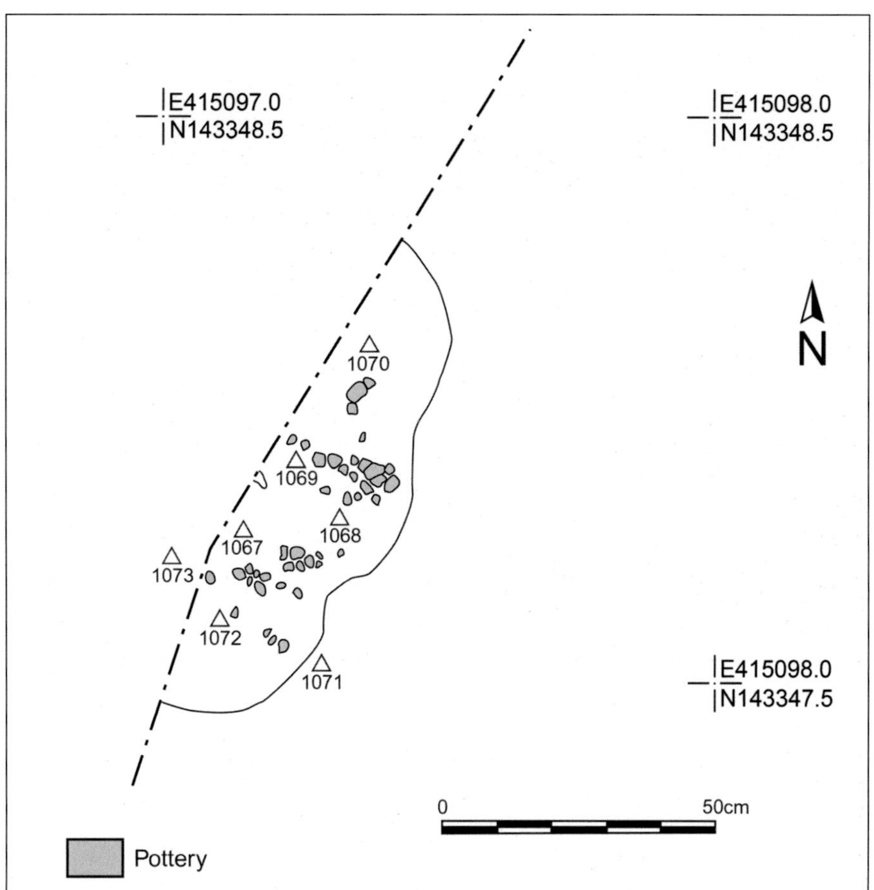

Figure 3.69. Distribution of pottery at the base of fill 053 of tree-throw 058

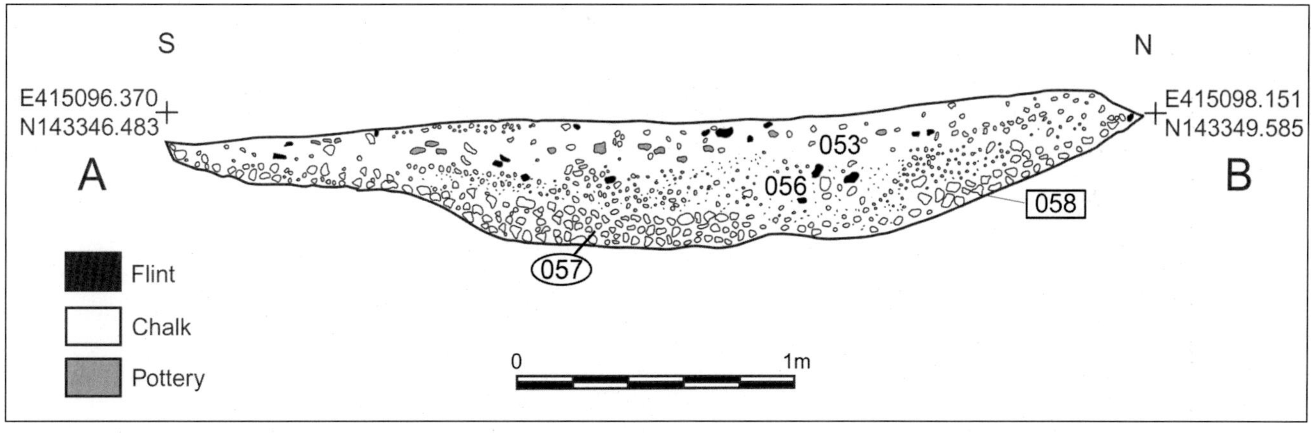

Figure 3.70. Section through tree-throw hole 058 in Trench 16

Layer 053 was a very dark, humic, grey-brown clay loam with rare small chalk. Quantities of bone (including mandible, rib and long-bone fragments) from large mammals (mainly cattle and pigs) were present in a loose concentration in the middle of the feature in the top of this context, while below this was a concentrated spread of Early Neolithic pottery, with most of the sherds lying horizontal (Figures 3.68–3.69). The fill was much more ashy towards the base of the layer (Figures 3.70–3.71). A cattle bone from the top of layer 053 provided a radiocarbon date of 2580–2450 cal BC at 95% confidence (SUERC-32161; 3980±30 BP). This Late Neolithic date is at odds with the presence of earlier Neolithic pottery in the lower part of layer 053 (but consistent with finds of Grooved Ware from the upper part of 053).

Figure 3.71. The deposit of animal bone and pottery in fill 053 of tree-throw 058, viewed from the east

Figure 3.72 (right). Plan of Trench 17 at Woodhenge, showing tree-throw pit 033. Late Neolithic features are in grey

Both the bone and pottery, along with a reasonable amount of worked flint and unworked small nodules, had evidently been dumped, in at least two separate events widely spaced in time, into the top of the partially filled tree-throw pit. The lithics from 056 and 053 include a high proportion of blades, bladelets and blade-like pieces (21 out of 136), along with an awl, four scrapers and retouched pieces. While the blade elements are early, some of the material from 053, such as an unfinished oblique arrowhead, belongs to the Late Neolithic (see Chan, below). All but three of the sherds derive from plain carinated bowls of the early fourth millennium BC (see Cleal, below). Representing an Early Neolithic presence, the assemblage is comparable to that from the Coneybury Anomaly, 2km to the southwest (Richards 1990; Barclay 2014).

Covering the area of the tree-throw pit – which had evidently survived as a discernible hollow into the Late Neolithic – was a 1m-wide band of extremely compacted chalk (052), made up of large angular blocks set two courses thick in places. Rather than forming a revetment to the rear of the bank (not otherwise attested), this deposit appears to have resulted from a deliberate act to 'seal' the tree-throw before, or at the time that, the bank was created.

At the western end of the trench, a small oval pit (060; 1.30m × >1.00m across, and 0.40m deep) was cut through the buried soil, extending into the northwestern baulk of the trench. It possessed a stepped profile on its east side; otherwise the sides were steep, merging with a rounded base. The fill (059) was a friable and largely stone-free dark brown silty clay loam (originally turf?), more chalky towards the sides and base, and including a little burnt flint. An oblique arrowhead came from the top of this and is reported in Volume 3.

The bank itself (026) has been heavily truncated by later ploughing, surviving as a thin spread of chalk rubble (up to 0.10m thick) within a grey-brown silty clay. The upper part of the profile comprised small to medium-sized chalk blocks, slightly weathered. Below this, the basal blocks were more angular and larger (up to 0.30m), especially towards the east side of the bank. At the rear of the bank (its western edge) were substantial deposits of grey-brown ploughsoil (009), from which came a little Roman, medieval and post-medieval pottery, and a fragment of a Roman blue-glass melon bead (reported on in Volume 4).

3.4.2. A tree-throw pit in the interior of Woodhenge

Because the 1926–1927 excavations involved trenching around the circuits of the post-rings, rather than the stripping of open areas, features between the rings could easily be missed. This was found to be the case in 2006 in the 3m-wide gap between posthole rings B and C. Within this area of Trench 17 were four features – a large hollow (033), surrounded by two pits (036 and 045) and a small posthole (014) – that had not been encountered by the Cunningtons (Figure 3.65). Since the two pits and posthole are considered to be broadly contemporary with the Woodhenge post structure, they are reported on in Volume 3.

The hollow (context 033) was irregular, roughly sub-oval (2.35m × 1.70m and 0.32m deep), and constricted slightly on the northwest, giving it an almost 'jelly bean' plan (Figure 3.72). Its sides were moderate to shallow, steeper on the west, merging with an undulating dished base. In places (*e.g.* on the north and east) there were slight depressions in the sides where flint nodules appear to

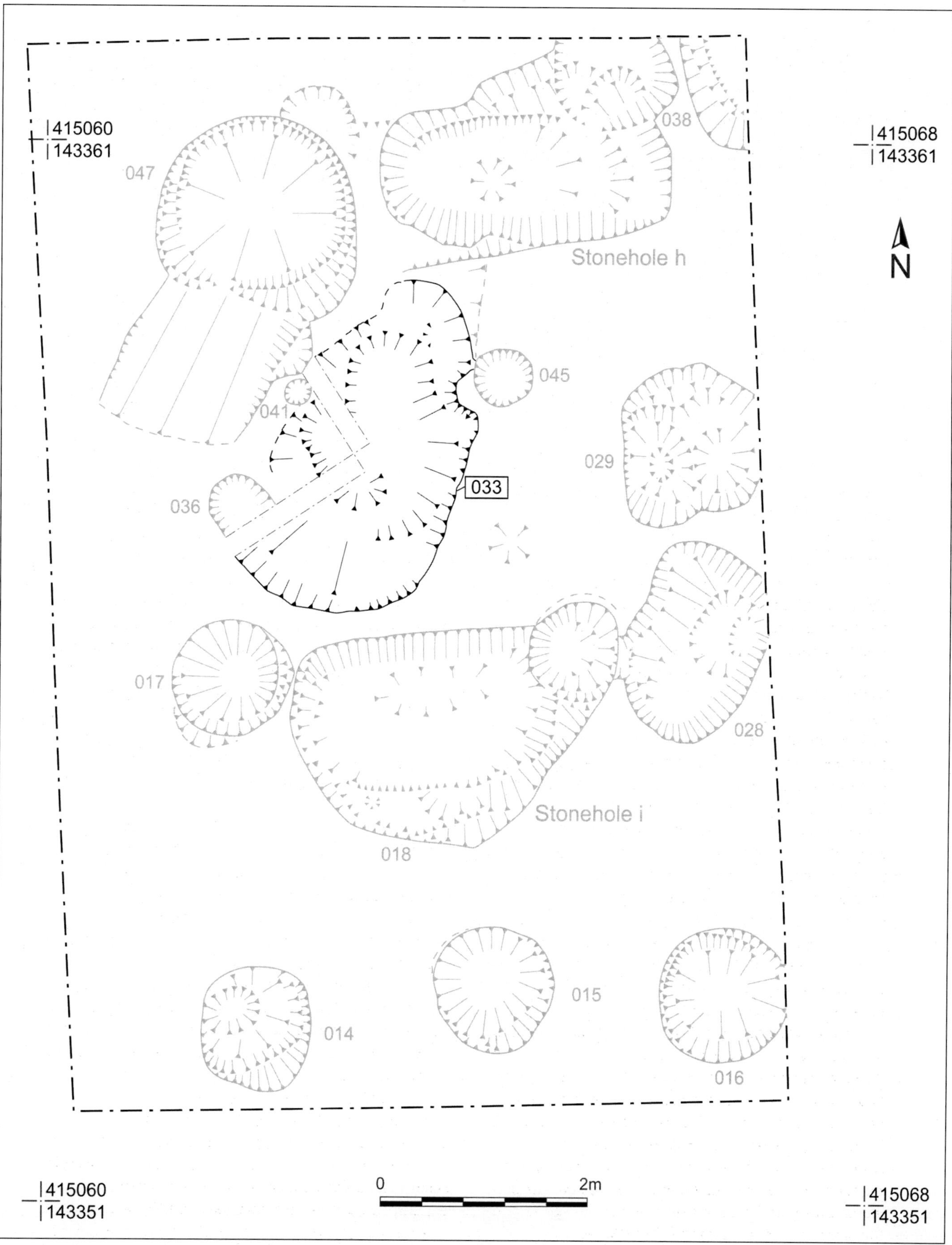
415060
143361
415068
143361
047
038
Stonehole h
N
045
041
029
033
036
017
028
Stonehole i
018
015
014
016
415060
143351
0
2m
415068
143351

Figure 3.73. Trench 17, viewed from the east, showing tree-throw pit 033 excavated except for its west quadrant

have been removed. Cut through a seam of irregular chalk containing flint nodules and pockets of poorly structured parent rock, the hollow is best interpreted as a tree-throw pit that saw limited reworking in order to extract flint. The upper fill (023) was a brown silty clay loam from which came three sherds of Early Neolithic pottery and several pieces of worked flint, including two bladelets and two blade-like flakes. This sealed a compact, silty clay (030) with more flint and chalk (Figure 3.73). Nine flakes were recovered from this.

3.4.3. Discussion

Previous excavations at Woodhenge, by the Cunningtons and Evans, produced evidence of Early Neolithic activity, represented by ceramics (see Cleal, below) and lithics (including at least one leaf-shaped arrowhead; Cunnington 1929: plate 23.11). This material was restricted to the eastern and southern part of the area occupied by the later monument, corresponding to the location of the two tree-throws with associated material of early fourth millennium BC date excavated in 2006 and reported here. Use of the tree-throws can be seen as responding to landscape affordances – naturally-created hollows that provided structure and shelter, and opportunity to prospect for workable flint – a pattern repeated elsewhere in the Early Neolithic of lowland Britain (*cf* Evans *et al.* 1999). The signature of activity was quite different in each case, with ceramic deposition in layer 058, and the extraction of flint nodules and limited flint-working in 033. Whether human engagement linked to these features was strictly contemporary or in any way connected remains uncertain.

Activity associated with 058 need not have been short-lived or 'event-like', as has been argued for the similar carinated bowl-associated pit deposition at the Coneybury Anomaly (Gron *et al.* 2018). Sherds from between five and ten medium-sized vessels were present, along with a respectable lithic assemblage (and perhaps some of the animal bone); enough material to have been generated over several months, if not slightly longer. We might envisage this as resulting from semi-sedentary settlement within an open, or opening, woodland environment. Its significance resides in this being one of the earliest Neolithic presences within the Stonehenge landscape, perhaps pre-dating that of the Coneybury Anomaly, now dated to the later 38th century cal BC (Barclay 2014: 12), though Cleal (see below) is rightly cautious about reliance on typo-chronological sequences for carinated bowls. Both sites reflect a preference for the riverside zone, and for higher ground on the west side of the Avon.

Tree-throw 058 had evidently survived as a discernible hollow into the later Neolithic. Curiously, at the time the later monument was created, it was capped by the rammed chalk deposit 052. This capping was not simply a revetment to the rear of the bank, but looks very much a deliberate act to 'seal' the tree-throw and its artefactual contents once chanced upon during stripping of the turf. The result was an almost 'archaeological' encounter in which the Late Neolithic monument-builders came face to face with the residues of human presence that had occurred at least a millennium and a quarter earlier. Whether an auspicious or inauspicious event, it is tempting to read the chalk capping as an exercise in controlling or containing an ancestral presence.

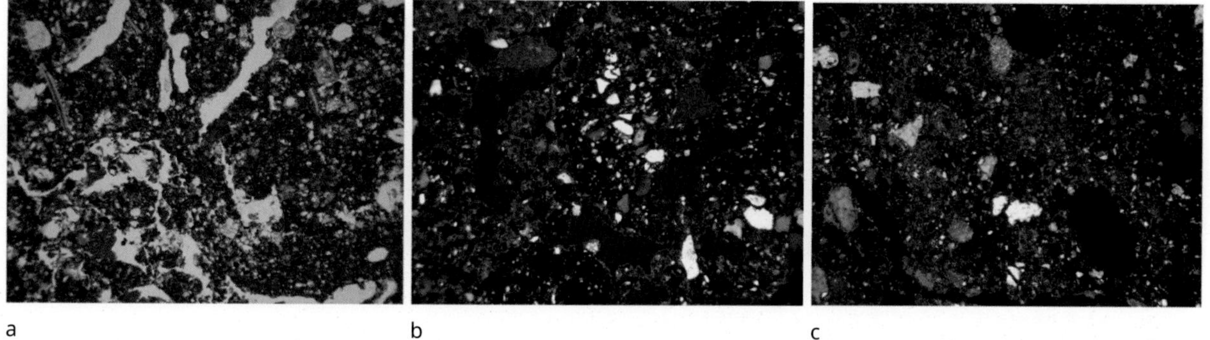

a b c

Figure 3.74. Photomicrographs of sediments within the pre-bank buried soil at Woodhenge: a) chalky, micritic fine sandy loam, profile 23/1 (frame width = 4.5mm; plane-polarised light); b) mixed fabrics of organic sandy loam, micrite and fine sandy loam, profile 23/2 (frame width = 4.5mm; cross-polarised light); c) micritic fine sandy clay loam fabric with reticulate striations, profile 23/2 (frame width = 4.5mm; cross-polarised light)

3.4.4. Soil micromorphology of the buried soil profile beneath the Woodhenge bank

C.A.I. French

Despite the very shallow nature of the modern topsoil at Woodhenge, the excavations investigated the old ground surface beneath the external bank, just to the south of John Evans' 1970 trench (Evans and Wainwright 1979).

The old land surface surviving beneath the chalk rubble bank (context 026) was composed of a brown silt loam with common chalk fragments of about 10–12cm in thickness (context 051) and is developed directly on a *c.* 6cm-thick horizon of weathered chalk, or the A/C horizon, above the solid chalk. It appears that this buried soil is largely missing its turf horizon, although it occasionally survives in slight undulations such as in grid square 15. This palaeosol sequence was sampled in two blocks as Profile 23.

The pre-bank buried soil

The uppermost sample is an even mixture of small to fine chalk rubble, with a fine sandy calcitic loam that is rich in humified organic matter (Figure 3.74a). Although not preserved everywhere beneath the Beaker-period bank, this is indicative of a turf fabric with much included chalk rubble, probably representing the organic A horizon just beneath the turf root matt. But the absence of a well-sorted stone-line may suggest that this turf horizon has suffered much disturbance associated with the construction of the overlying bank. Moreover, there are a few aggregates which contain poorly sorted admixtures of micrite, a micritic sandy (clay) loam with a hint of reticulate striations to the micritic dusty clay groundmass, and amorphous organic matter-stained micritic fine sandy clay loam similar to the fabric of the lower sample. This indicates that there is some disturbance and intermixing of soil material derived from all three horizons of the contemporary soil profile, and is undoubtedly indicative of redeposited soil material in the bank.

The lower sample is composed of a bioturbated, calcitic fine sandy loam with abundant chalk fragments (<10mm) and pebble-size pieces of chalk (1–4cm) which become much more abundant in the lower half of the profile (Figure 3.74b). In its upper one-third there are a few anthropogenic inclusions such as pottery, bone and charred wood fragments. In addition, there is a very minor amount of illuvial silty clay down-profile (Figure 3.74c), which is possibly suggestive of a once much greater clay component to this soil, and some ground disturbance.

This rubbly calcitic sandy loam soil which is missing its actual turf matt exhibits some weak development of an illuvial B (or Bw) horizon prior to the construction of the bank. Thus, although ostensibly a simple A over weathered A/C rendzina type of soil, the minor B horizon material presence suggests that there has been some soil development indicative of brown-earth development in the past, prior to burial by the bank. In addition, the intermixed fabric aggregates and the minor illuvial dusty clay component both suggest that there has been physical disturbance of the whole soil profile. There has also been some addition of anthropogenic debris to the soil profile and its incorporation down-profile through worm action. This need not imply anything more than some pre-monument human activity and disturbance created by building the earth and chalk bank.

Conclusion

Although there was not great preservation of the old land surface associated with Woodhenge, there was sufficient survival under the surviving henge bank to indicate the

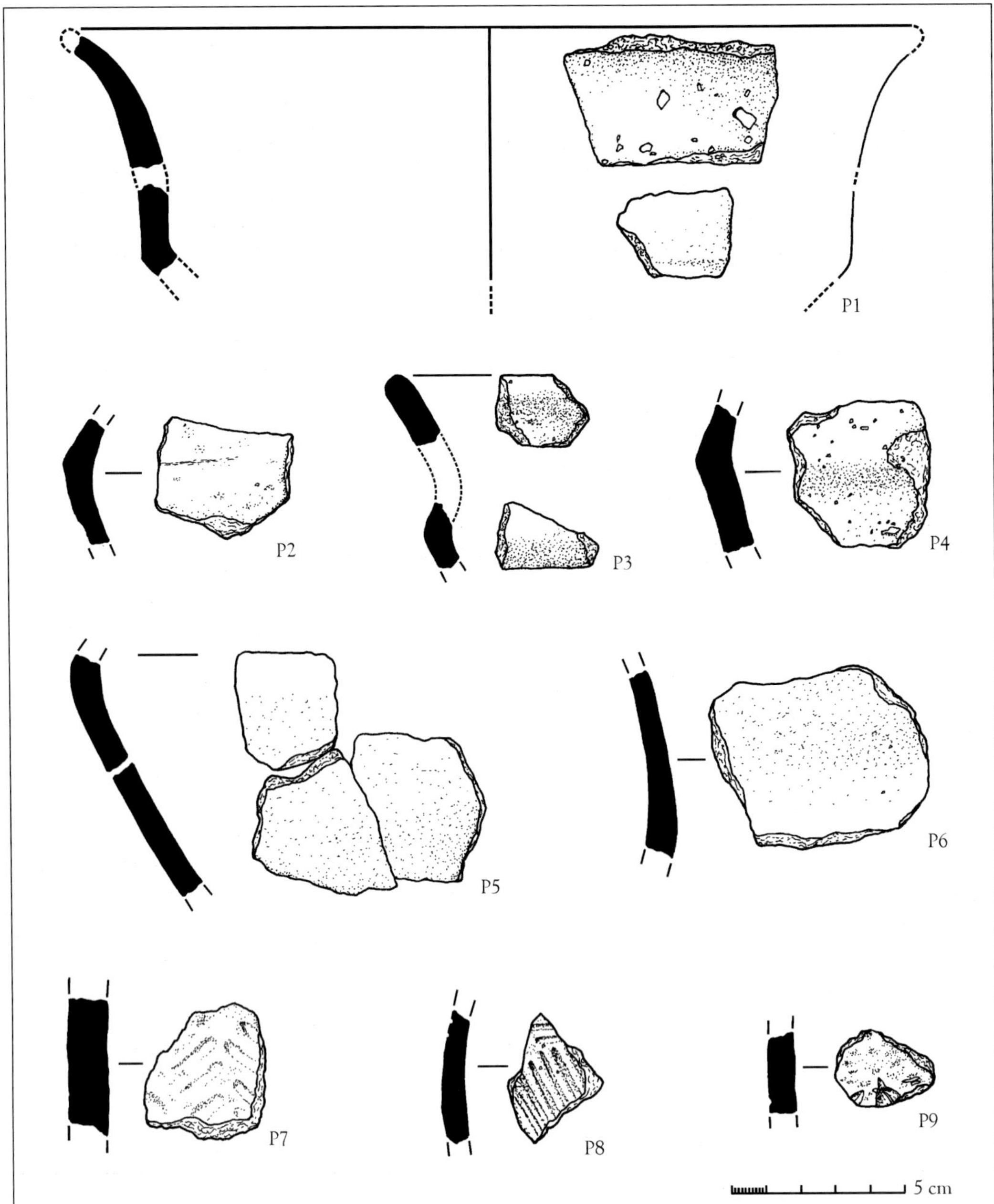

Figure 3.75. Early Neolithic, Late Neolithic and possible Beaker pottery from Woodhenge

presence of a pre-Late Neolithic, disturbed rendzina soil profile which exhibits indications of having previously been a weakly developed brown earth.

3.4.5. Pottery from the Woodhenge tree-throw pits and buried soil

R. Cleal

More than 500 sherds of Neolithic pottery (and one possible Beaker sherd), weighing over 3kg, were found during the excavations at Woodhenge (Figure 3.75). The majority of these belong to plain earlier Neolithic bowls with shoulder carinations and were found in spreads of sherds within the buried soil beneath the bank and in the top of a tree-throw pit. The excavators noted that there seemed to be some structure to the deposit, with large sherds in concentrated spreads. Three more earlier Neolithic sherds were recovered from the fill (023) of a second tree-throw pit (033) within Woodhenge. The very small assemblage of later material – Grooved Ware and Beaker sherds – from the tree-throw contexts is also reported here.

The sherds were examined macroscopically and at x20 magnification under a binocular microscope.

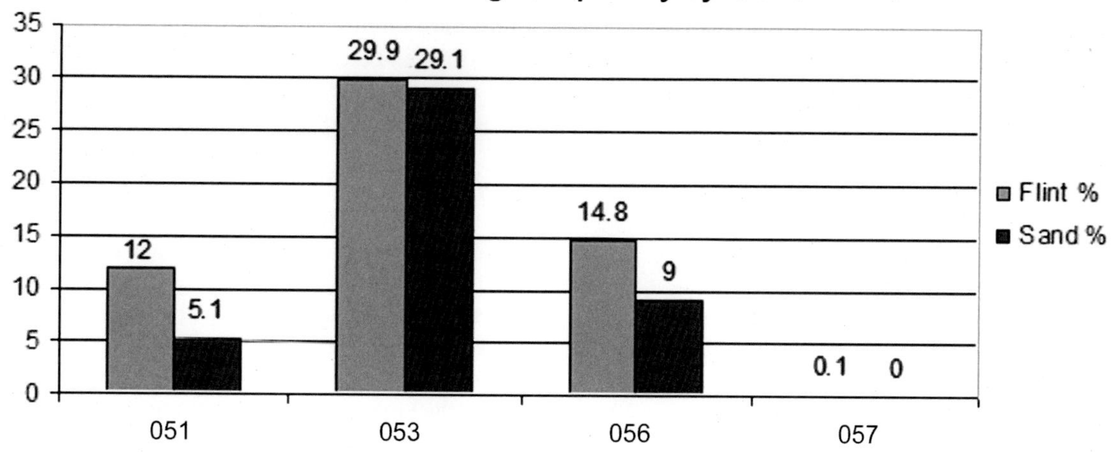

Figure 3.76. Early Neolithic pottery by fabric group for contexts 051, 053, 056 and 057 at Woodhenge

a) Early Neolithic

Context	FS1	FS2	FS3	FS-	S1	S2	FQS	S-
003	-	-	-	2/6g	-	-	-	2/6g
004	1/8g	-	-	-	-	-	-	-
011	-	-	-	4/14g	-	-	-	-
023	1/5g	-	-	1/2g	1/6g	-	-	-
035	-	-	-	1/1g	-	-	-	-
051 (buried soil)	34/196g	-	1/26g	34/133g	6/15g	5/38g	1/5g	34/96g
053 (upper fill tree-throw pit – continuation of buried soil)	72/547g	4/67g	1/19g	78/250g	112/ 651g	1/13g	-	57/194g
055 (backfill of 1926 trench)	-	1/7g	-	-	-	-	-	-
056 (fill of tree-throw pit)	33/218g	28/207g	-	2/12g	26/138g	26/124g	-	1/3g
057 (primary fill tree-throw pit)	-	-	-	1/2g	-	-	-	-
058	-	-	-	1/1g	-	-	-	-
Total	141/ 974g	33/ 281g	2/ 45g	124/ 421g	145/ 810g	32/ 175g	1/ 5g	94g/ 299g

b) Grooved Ware and ?Beaker

Context	FS-	GSSh	S-	SSh	Sh	S2	FQS
004	-	-	1/1g (Grooved Ware)	-	-	-	-
051	-	-	-	1/1g (Grooved Ware)	-	-	-
053	-	2/26g (Grooved Ware)	-	-	1/5g (Grooved Ware; from top of 053)	-	-
059	1/5g (?Grooved Ware/ Beaker)	-	-	-	-	-	-

Table 3.17. Ceramics from Woodhenge by context and fabric type: a) Early Neolithic; b) Grooved Ware and ?Beaker (shown as number/weight in gms)

Earlier Neolithic bowls

A total of 572 sherds weighing 3.01kg can be identified as belonging to earlier Neolithic plain bowls. These were found in both the buried soil and in a tree-throw pit (058). Only one sherd came from the primary fill of this tree-throw pit (057), and there was more pottery in the upper fill of that pit (053) than in the other contexts. Contexts 053, 056 and 057 together constitute the 50% excavation of tree-throw pit 058.

Fabric

Two fabric groups were identified, one including flint as the principal non-plastic inclusion and one quartz sand (Figure 3.76). Defining fabrics was difficult, as control by the makers over the distribution of non-plastics, particularly within the fabrics containing flint, seems to have been fairly poor and it is possible that sherds identified as belonging to different fabrics are in fact of the same vessel. In both the fabrics containing flint and those with sand there may be only one, rather variable fabric represented over more than one vessel. Table 3.17 shows the breakdown into the fabrics within the fabric groups.

Fabrics with flint inclusions

All the sherds are reasonably hard and sandy, with poorly sorted flint inclusions. The sand varies in frequency from moderate to very common or abundant (based on visual estimation using comparative charts); it is mainly of quartz, but with some opaque dark grains also present; the quartz sand grains are mainly fine (<0.5mm) but with a minority of around 1mm. The flint inclusions are varied in size, up to 10mm max. dimension, with most <5mm and are moderately frequent (around 15%–20% by surface area) but very patchily distributed. The individually identified fabrics in Table 3.17 are:

FS1: a hard sandy fabric with moderate to common sand (*c.* 15%–20% by surface area estimated by eye), and sparse to moderate flint (*c.* 5%–15%), most of which is <3mm, with some <8mm.

FS2: a hard fabric, sandier than FS1, with abundant sand (40%–50%) and moderate to common flint (15%–20%), most of which is <5mm but with some pieces <10mm.

FS3: a hard fabric, less sandy than either FS1 or FS2, with sparse sand and sparse small flint (<5%; <3mm).

Fabrics with only sand inclusions (or occasional rare flint, not present in every sherd

FS-, S-: these are all reasonably hard fabrics with a sandy feel, containing unevenly distributed grains varying from sparse to moderate (as above); the grains are mainly of quartz but include some dark grains and very occasional flint; the flint inclusions have a maximum dimension of 2mm, with most <1mm.

S1: a hard sandy fabric with sparse to moderate sand (5%–10%) and occasional flint.

S2: a hard sandy fabric with generally slightly more sand than in S1 (<15%).

Other fabric

FQS: a single small sherd (5g) from the buried soil (051) includes, among flint, quartz sand and dark grains, a single large piece apparently of sandstone (5mm max. dimension) which could be sarsen. The fabric is hard and compact and is unlike the other material from this context. As context 051 produced Grooved Ware (see below), and is sealed by the Beaker-period bank, it is clear that this sherd is likely to be Neolithic, but it is not possible to establish whether it is earlier or later in date.

Catalogue

Because of the apparent variability of the flint and sand fabrics within the vessels, and the fact that most are featureless body sherds, it did not prove possible to assign every sherd to a vessel. The catalogue below includes illustrated material (Figure 3.75) and some groups that seem to constitute at least part-vessels which may have been placed together.

Tree-throw pit 058

P1 At least eight featured sherds of a vessel with a moderately well-defined carination and concave neck. None of the rim top survives but the profile, which extends almost to the rim, suggests that it was of simple out-turned form. The diameter at the rim is *c.* 240mm. The fabric is FS1 and the exterior reddish-brown, the core dark brown, the interior surface mid-grey/brown. The interior is often well-smoothed, particularly on sherds from the concave neck. Condition: weathered on exterior surfaces and edges, but interior surfaces often in better condition than exterior.

Featured sherds archive Pot Record Numbers 16001, 16002, 16004, 16007, 16011–16013 and 16017. If all FS1 sherds were assigned to this vessel, this would give a total of 141 sherds weighing 974g but it is unlikely that all FS1 sherds belong to a single vessel. Illustrated sherds are PRN 16001 (context 056) and 16011 (context 056).

P2 Single shoulder sherd from a vessel in a hard, sandy fabric (S1). There are some occasional flint inclusions (*i.e.* not present in every sherd) and they are sparse and small when they do occur (<2mm max. dimension – most <1mm). The carination is irregular – sharper in some places than others – and generally not well-defined. Surfaces orange and moderately weathered, as are the edges. PRN 16009, context 056.

At least one other carinated sherd (PRN 16014 from context 053, not illustrated) may also belong to this vessel.

The sherds appear to belong to a small to medium-sized bowl, perhaps in the region of 200–240mm diameter at the shoulder (and likely to be of similar or slightly greater diameter at the rim as forms are likely to have been neutral or slightly open).

P3 At least one simple rim sherd and one carinated sherd probably from a single vessel, in the sandy fabric S1. The surfaces are orange and both surfaces and edges are moderately worn. PRN 16015 (rim) and 16016 (carinated sherd), context 053.

P4 A single sherd showing a well-defined, almost 'pinched-out' carination, in a hard fabric (FS3) with sparse (<*c.* 5%) flint, <3mm max. dimension, irregular pieces, some blocky; and sparse sand, including dark grains. This was recorded as part of SF 1070 in context 053 but is a different vessel from the other sherds in this small finds group. Surfaces and core orange, condition fair with exterior and edges slightly worn. PRN 16028, context 053, SF group 1070.

P5 Ten body sherds and two sherds from just below the angle of a carination (not all illustrated), in fabric S1, recorded on excavation as a group (SF 1070). Surfaces orange, condition fair. PRN 16029 and 16030 illustrated, context 053, SF group 1070.

Buried soil

P6 Single sherd from the neck of a vessel with a long concave neck, in a hard, sandy fabric with unevenly distributed quartz and dark grains (*c.* 5%–15%); the fabric appears similar to, but generally sandier than S1 although it is possible that the sherd is from the same vessel as some of the S1 sherds. There is occasional flint in this sherd. It is possible that it belongs to the same vessel as P5. Surfaces orange and moderately weathered. PRN 16008, context 051, SF 1015.

Form, number of vessels, finish and condition

The presence of moderately sharp carinations (P1, P4 and perhaps P2) and concave necks (P1 and P6) clearly indicates that most, and perhaps all, the vessels represented are carinated to some degree, although some of the sherds show shoulders which are not sharply defined.

Although the excavators noted spreads of pottery, fairly few large portions of vessels are identifiable among the sherd material. Only five rims survive, and 11 sherds with sharp carinations; a further nine have rounded shoulders rather than a sharp change in angle, but, as with the fabrics, the carination and shoulders may have varied on a single vessel. In the case of both sharp carinations and more rounded shoulders, the mean sherd size is small, only 11g in the case of carinations and 6g for the rounded shoulders.

The number and size of rim sherds are both very low, given the size and nature of the assemblage. Apart from the rim sherd of P3, and the near-rim of P1, the remaining three small rims weigh a total of only 28g. This highlights how little of the vessels is represented. In most cases it is impossible even to estimate rim or shoulder diameter, so it has not been possible to calculate the percentage of the surviving vessel circumference.

The six earlier Neolithic sherds and sherd groups illustrated (P1–P6) probably represent four separate vessels (P1, P3, P4 as certainly separate vessels and P5 and P6 probably belonging to another single vessel, with P2 only possibly representing another pot). It is also likely that some other vessels are represented among plain body sherds which have not been illustrated.

To enable an estimation of whether one or more vessels might be represented by the fabric FS1, which is the commonest in the assemblage, a medium carinated bowl made by the author in a recipe similar to FS1 was weighed. This vessel had an external rim diameter of 210mm, a height of around 130mm, and a wall thickness around the rim and neck of about 5mm (with a slightly thicker lower body, as is common in Neolithic pots); it weighed 0.95kg. This experimental vessel is likely to be only slightly smaller than the vessel P1. So, although all the sherds in fabric FS1 could belong to vessel P1 on the grounds of similarity of fabric, in fact it seems highly unlikely, as there are so few rim sherds and carinated sherds among the 0.97kg of fabric FS1. A more reasonable interpretation of the material, therefore, is that there is more than one vessel represented by the sherds in fabric FS1.

Finish and condition

Most of the sherds are in fair rather than fresh condition, and many are slightly weathered, with one or more surfaces showing some wear and the hackly edges of the breaks slightly blunted. Overall, the impression is of material which was exposed for some time, but not trampled. Exposure on a midden which was not a walking surface might well have caused this degree of weathering, with deposition in tree-throw pit 058 having taken place sometime after the initial discard of the pottery (as it had had time to weather). P1 shows a fairly well-finished, smoothed surface on the interior of the neck sherds, presumably the result of those surfaces having been protected from weathering before deposition.

None of the material in the assemblage is burnished and this absence does not appear to be the result of weathering as it would be expected that some traces would survive. A few conjoins were identified, but fewer than might be expected from the description of the conditions in which the sherds were found.

Other featured sherds

A single plain body sherd in fabric FS2 from context 056 has what appears to be a grain impression on the exterior surface.

Early Neolithic pottery: summary and discussion

The assemblage from Woodhenge tree-throw pit 058 is small and comprises a limited range of fabric and form; it seems likely to derive from a deposit of broken pots somewhere in the vicinity, probably a small midden. Most of the sherds do not have fresh surfaces or breaks. The excavators noted some evidence for sherds having been placed, and it is possible that there was some selection for deposition, with featureless sherds being preferred over rims and carinations; it is also possible, however, that most of the rims and carinated sherds lie in the unexcavated part of tree-throw pit 058, perhaps as the result of the deliberate placing which the excavators felt was represented by the deposit.

The composition of the assemblage appears to have been a small number of medium-sized bowls, with almost certainly no very large vessels present and no evidence for cups or small bowls. The total number of vessels represented is probably less than 10 and possibly not more than five or six, some of which may be represented only by plain, featureless sherds.

In terms of form, the few surviving featured sherds all suggest that the vessels were carinated and the few rim sherds are simple, that is, with no added clay and not manipulated into rolled-over forms. A few of the carinated sherds show a sharp change in wall angle, but others are more rounded. There is no indication that the vessels were ever well-finished and there are no traces of burnishing. Although some allowance must be made for the fact that most surfaces and edges show some effects of weathering, these vessels do not appear to have been 'fine' in the way that some carinated vessels clearly are.

The occurrence of these vessels under the bank surrounding Woodhenge is consistent with the results of the excavations in the 1920s. Plain Neolithic pottery was found under the eastern bank, close to the SRP's Trench 16, one sherd of which was illustrated by Mrs Cunnington (1929: plate 32, no. 43), who noted the presence of other small sherds (*op. cit.*: 132). The vessel illustrated as no. 43 is in a fine flint-gritted fabric with small flint inclusions and has at least been very well smoothed and might have been burnished; the angle of the rim is more upright than shown in the illustration (author's observation).

Other sherds recorded as from 'E.R.' (presumably 'Eastern Rampart') in the unpublished collection all have simple rims and appear to be from upright or slightly open-necked bowls with concave necks (and therefore probably carinated, as sinuous vessels with no carination of any sort would be unusual). This would seem to suggest that a possibly quite short-lived episode of activity was associated with plain carinated vessels in the area later covered by the bank or in its vicinity. As there are no radiocarbon dates from the deposit, the pottery is key to dating this activity.

Although there are a considerable number of findspots for earlier Neolithic pottery in the local area, it is likely that not all are contemporary; the possibility of refining the dating of the Neolithic pottery in tree-throw pit 058 is thus worth pursuing. Apart from the material from under the eastern bank from excavations by Mrs Cunnington in 1926 and by John G. Evans in 1970 (in which only two plain sherds were found; Longworth 1979: 91, table 4), the nearest earlier Neolithic ceramics are from postholes in the B and F rings of the monument (Figure 3.65), in which they must have been redeposited. These include one simple rim with slashes, one slightly rolled-over and one enlarged rim with slashes across the top (Cunnington 1929: plate 34, nos 56, 57, 58).

Only just over 500m to the north of Woodhenge, beneath the northern bank of Durrington Walls henge, there were 370 sherds, representing around 21 vessels, with rolled, everted and thickened rims (Wainwright with Longworth 1971: 14). Although some of the rims (*e.g. op. cit.*: fig. 30, P14) could belong to vessels similar to those from tree-throw pit 058, the collection beneath the northern bank of Durrington Walls appears to relate to one episode and is dominated by vessels which have heavier or more elaborated rims, and at least two with fingertip fluting on the interior (*ibid.*: P1, P3).

Further afield, there are simple hemispherical bowls from a pit pre-dating Amesbury barrow G132 (Gingell 1988: fig. 18), and decorated bowls and bowls with elaborated rims from King Barrow Ridge ('Feature B', SEB Trench and Amesbury G39 [Cleal 1994: figs 7–8]) and from Stonehenge (a single rim with a perforation as decoration; Cleal 1995a: fig. 193). All these locations are 2km–3km to the southwest of Woodhenge. Another find – a small collection from a single pit on King Barrow Ridge – contained pottery which, although the rims are simple, also includes two lugs (Cleal 1990b: fig. 35). In all these cases, the pottery appears to belong to types which are present in causewayed enclosures such as Windmill Hill, in the north of the county, and Robin Hood's Ball (Thomas 1964) 6km to the northwest, and which can be characterised as within the South-Western and Decorated traditions (Whittle 1977).

More recently, Bayliss *et al.* have sought to distinguish the currency for Carinated, Plain Bowl and Decorated Bowl (2011: 756–78), although southern Britain does not have quite sufficient well-associated radiocarbon dates to discriminate as finely as Sheridan has been able to do for Scotland and parts of northern Britain (Sheridan 2007). Whittle, Healy and Bayliss' work on causewayed enclosures has now established that many were constructed during a relatively limited time period of the Early Neolithic, and within the south Wessex area (including Robin Hood's Ball) not before the 37th century cal BC (Healy *et al.* 2011: 203–4). Robin Hood's Ball causewayed enclosure, northwest of Woodhenge, is not well dated but is suggested as having been constructed not before the mid-37th century cal BC, and probably not before the last third, although Healy *et al.* urge caution because of the paucity of dates available (*op. cit.*: 197).

It would seem reasonable to infer, therefore, that all of these occurrences of heavier-rimmed, elaborated-rimmed and decorated pottery, although not themselves associated with radiocarbon determinations, are probably at least 37th century cal BC in date or later, and perhaps late in that century at the earliest. In contrast, there is only one clearly comparable local group which includes carinated bowls with simple rims similar to those from the Woodhenge tree-throw: the large assemblage from the Coneybury Anomaly, on Coneybury Hill, at the southern end of King Barrow Ridge, 2.50km to the southwest of Woodhenge (Richards 1990).

The Coneybury Anomaly was a large, deep pit on the summit of Coneybury Hill, with a rich assemblage of earlier Neolithic pottery and other Neolithic material, excavated in 1980–1981 (Richards 1990: 40–61). Until recently it was dated only by a single radiocarbon date and it appeared possible that it was of very early fourth millennium cal BC date. As the result of a recent dating programme, however, it can now 'be confidently placed in the later part of the thirty-eighth century [cal BC]' (Barclay 2014: 12), that is, perhaps up to a century before the causewayed enclosures were established at Larkhill (Thompson *et al.* 2017) and Robin Hood's Ball.

The ceramic assemblage from the Coneybury Anomaly certainly includes several vessels comparable to those at Woodhenge, in that they are carinated, but with thick walls and lacking fine fabrics or finish. As well as these, however, there are other forms, including one necked jar, one closed-mouthed globular form and several small simple bowls (Cleal 1990a), all of which distinguish the Coneybury assemblage from the Woodhenge tree-throw assemblage, which shows a more limited range of forms.

It remains the case, however, that the Coneybury Anomaly pottery is the closest local parallel for the Woodhenge tree-throw pottery and, although it is possible that the lack of the other forms could indicate an earlier date for the Woodhenge material, this would, in the present understanding of pottery in the early to middle centuries of the fourth millennium cal BC, be stretching the evidence too far. Whether or not the Woodhenge tree-throw assemblage is contemporary with the Coneybury Anomaly or earlier than it, this review of the ceramic evidence in the area clearly indicates that the users of the pottery excavated from tree-throw pit 058 were probably familiar with a landscape which was not yet as fully inhabited or used, as it seems to have become only perhaps a century or so later, when findspots of pottery appear widely and Robin Hood's Ball and Larkhill causewayed enclosure were constructed and used.

Grooved Ware

Three sherds of Grooved Ware were found in the upper fill (053) of tree-throw pit 058 under the bank, and one came from the buried soil (051). The only other Neolithic pottery from the SRP excavations at Woodhenge was a sherd possibly of Grooved Ware, although in an atypical fabric, recovered from Cunnington's backfill of stonehole B8 (context 004, a later Neolithic feature and therefore reported in Volume 3). These four sherds are derived from three or possibly four vessels.

Catalogue

Not illustrated. One very small body sherd (1g) in a hard oxidised fabric with some sand. It has two deeply grooved lines on the exterior, one of which stops. Orange throughout. Condition: exterior surface good, edges and interior have some weathering. Trench 17, context 004.

P7 Two body sherds, almost certainly belonging to a single vessel. The fabric contains sparse shell (*c.* 5% by area, and <2mm max. dimension), with both fine and coarse sand grains, the latter including dark grains; there is almost certainly some small grog (<2mm) present, possibly as much as 10%–15% by area, but it is difficult to distinguish from the matrix. One sherd is markedly worn, with worn surfaces and edges, while the other is slightly less weathered. Both sherds have pale brown exterior surfaces, dark grey to black cores where visible, and grey-brown interior surfaces. The illustrated sherd has at least two rows of short broad grooves forming chevrons, and there is a trace of another row, suggesting that it was part of an area of grooved herringbone. Although these two sherds appear to belong to a single vessel, the other sherd has irregular impressions rather than herringbone, although it is very weathered. It is likely therefore that the sherds come from a vessel with zones of contrasting decoration. PRN 16026 and 16027, both context 053 (only the latter illustrated).

P8 A single body sherd with one fragment of shell visible; some grog may be present but is impossible to distinguish it with confidence from the matrix. The condition of the sherd is generally good, with some wear to the external surface. The sherd is black throughout. The decoration is of grooved lines. PRN 16031, context 053 (noted as the top of 053).

	Artefact type		Context type and number						Total
			Tree-throw 033		*Buried soil*		*Tree-throw 058*		
			023	*030*	*051*	*053*	*056*	*057*	
Debitage and cores	Blade	Count	0	0	28	7	3	0	38
		% within context	0%	0%	6.6%	10.3%	4.4%	0%	6.3%
	Blade-like flake	Count	2	0	17	2	2	0	23
		% within context	10.0%	0%	4.0%	2.9%	2.9%	0%	3.8%
	Bladelet	Count	2	0	16	5	2	2	27
		% within context	10.0%	0%	3.8%	7.4%	2.9%	14.3%	4.5%
	Core on a flake	Count	0	0	0	1	0	0	1
		% within context	0%	0%	0%	1.5%	0%	0%	0.2%
	Flake	Count	16	9	343	45	56	11	480
		% within context	80.0%	100.0%	80.5%	66.2%	82.4%	78.6%	79.3%
	Irregular waste	Count	0	0	3	1	0	0	4
		% within context	0%	0%	0.7%	1.5%	0%	0%	0.7%
	Multi-platform flake-core	Count	0	0	0	1	1	0	2
		% within context	0%	0%	0%	1.5%	1.5%	0%	0.3%
	Rejuvenation flake-core face/edge	Count	0	0	1	0	0	0	1
		% within context	0%	0%	0.2%	0%	0%	0%	0.2%
	Single-platform flake-core	Count	0	0	1	0	0	0	1
		% within context	0%	0%	0.2%	0%	0%	0%	0.2%
	Thinning flake	Count	0	0	1	0	0	0	1
		% within context	0%	0%	0.2%	0%	0%	0%	0.2%
Retouched flakes and tools	Awl	Count	0	0	1	1	0	0	2
		% within context	0%	0%	0.2%	1.5%	0%	0%	0.3%
	End-and-side scraper	Count	0	0	0	0	2	0	2
		% within context	0%	0%	0%	0%	2.9%	0%	0.3%
	End-scraper	Count	0	0	0	1	1	0	2
		% within context	0%	0%	0%	1.5%	1.5%	0%	0.3%
	Hammerstone	Count	0	0	0	1	0	0	1
		% within context	0%	0%	0%	1.5%	0%	0%	0.2%
	Misc. retouched flake	Count	0	0	3	2	1	1	7
		% within context	0%	0%	0.7%	2.9%	1.5%	7.1%	1.2%
	Oblique arrowhead	Count	0	0	2	0	0	0	2
		% within context	0%	0%	0.5%	0%	0%	0%	0.3%
	Unfinished arrowhead/blank	Count	0	0	0	1	0	0	1
		% within context	0%	0%	0%	1.5%	0%	0%	0.2%
	Utilised/edge-damaged flake/blade	Count	0	0	10	0	0	0	10
		% within context	0%	0%	2.3%	0%	0%	0%	1,7%
Total		Count	20	9	426	68	68	14	605
		% within context	100.0%	100.0%	100.0%	100.0%	100.0%	100.0%	100.0%

Table 3.18. The composition of the worked flint assemblage by context type from Early Neolithic contexts at Woodhenge

General artefact category		Tree-throw 033		Buried soil		Tree-throw 058		Total
		023	*030*	*051*	*053*	*056*	*057*	
Cores	Count	0	0	1	2	1	0	4
	% within context	0%	0%	0.2%	2.9%	1.5%	0%	0.7%
Flakes and blades	Count	20	9	406	59	63	13	570
	% within context	100.0%	100.0%	95.3%	86.8%	92.6%	92.9%	94.2%
Formal tools	Count	0	0	3	3	3	0	9
	% within context	0%	0%	0.7%	4.4%	4.4%	0%	1.5%
Misc. waste	Count	0	0	3	1	0	0	4
	% within context	0%	0%	0.7%	1.5%	0%	0%	0.7%
Other	Count	0	0	0	1	0	0	1
	% within context	0%	0%	0%	1.5%	0%	0%	0.2%
Retouched flakes and utilised flakes	Count	0	0	13	2	1	1	17
	% within context	0%	0%	3.1%	2.9%	1.5%	7.1%	2.8%
Total	Count	20	9	426	68	68	14	605
	% within context	100.0%	100.0%	100.0%	100.0%	100.0%	100.0%	100.0%

(Column group heading: Context type and number)

Table 3.19. The worked flint assemblage by artefact category and context type from Early Neolithic contexts at Woodhenge

Grooved Ware or Beaker sherd

P9 A single body sherd, weighing only 5g, with only the tip of a pair of non-plastic fingernail impressions surviving. The sherd is in a hard fabric containing some flint, sand and possibly grog and is dark brown throughout. The sherd was found within the fill (059) of a small pit (060), which was cut through the buried soil beneath the bank in Trench 16; a Late Neolithic oblique arrowhead was found in the top of the fill. (The excavation of the pit and the Late Neolithic arrowhead are reported in Volume 3.) As noted above, the construction of the bank may be as late as the last quarter of the third millennium cal BC , so it is possible that this is an early Beaker sherd, although it is not possible to be definitive because of its size. PRN 16032, context 059.

Non-plastic paired fingernail decoration does occur on Grooved Ware but it is rare. In the local area there is none in the assemblage excavated by Mrs Cunnington from Woodhenge, where only paired *plastic* fingernail impressions occur on Grooved Ware (Cunnington 1929), nor were any non-plastic impressions recorded by Longworth (1971) on Grooved Ware from Durrington Walls. Fingernail impression is also a not-uncommon feature of relatively early Beakers, as was noted by David Clarke (1970: 57–9, 286).

There must be some doubt as to the correct attribution of this sherd although, as the construction of the bank appears to be after 2480 cal BC, it is possible that it could be Beaker; around 3km to the southeast, at Boscombe Down, the end of Grooved Ware activity and early Beaker activity are well-dated within the 24th century cal BC (Barclay *et al.* 2011: 181).

3.4.6. Worked flint from the Woodhenge tree-throw pits and buried soil

B. Chan

The assemblage of worked flint from all the SRP excavations at Woodhenge consists of 1,390 artefacts. This report details the assemblage of flint from Early Neolithic contexts only, consisting of 605 artefacts (Tables 3.18–3.19). The remainder of the assemblage from the Woodhenge excavations is from Late Neolithic and post-medieval contexts. The Early Neolithic assemblage comes from two tree-throws and a buried soil horizon and provides insight into use of the area before Woodhenge was constructed.

Raw material and condition

All but one of the worked flints from the excavation, from Early Neolithic and later contexts, is chalk-derived flint typical of the local area. The majority of this material was worked down from nodular flint with a thin light brown to beige cortex. It is likely that this material could have been found on the surface or near to the surface, as indicated by the flint nodules in the side of tree-throw 033. The only exception to chalk-derived flint is a single piece of gravel flint, part of the later assemblage reported in Volume 3. It was found within the backfill of Cunnington's posthole B9 (Cunnington 1929) and so cannot be relied upon to indicate the use of different sources of raw material on the site.

All of the flint is heavily patinated, ranging in colour from light blue-grey to white. The material from beneath

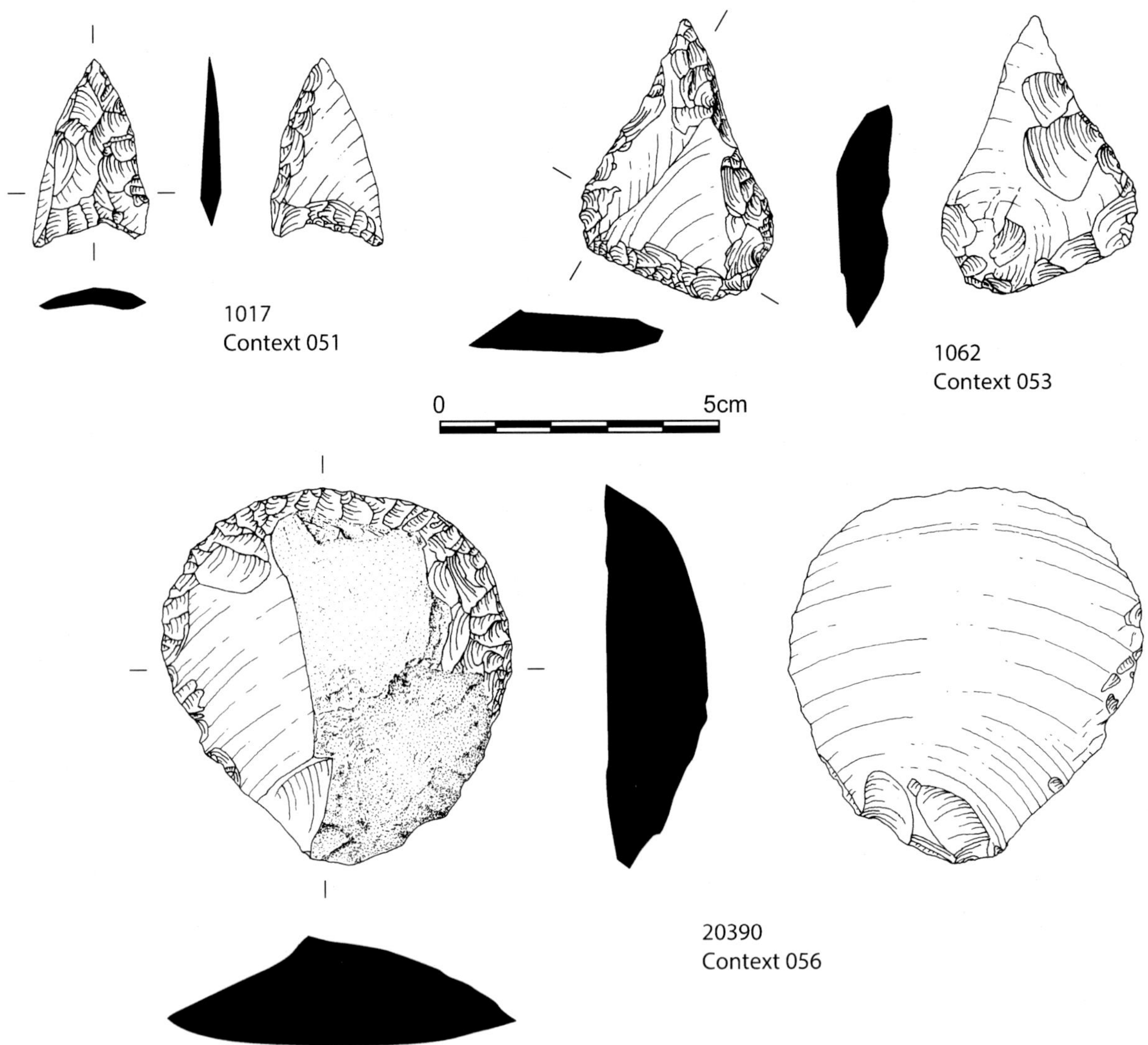

Figure 3.77. Lithics from Trench 16 at Woodhenge

the henge bank is generally more heavily patinated to white, though some of the material from later contexts is also approaching this degree of patination.

Contextual and spatial distribution of the assemblage

The Early Neolithic finds from Woodhenge come from two distinct areas. The first and largest in extent and assemblage size is a buried soil (051) and an associated tree-throw pit (058) and its fills (053, 056, 057), all of which were sealed beneath the bank of the henge in Trench 16. The second series of deposits was found within Woodhenge in Trench 17, between rings B and C, and comes from another tree-throw (033) and its fills (023, 030).

It was suggested during excavation that tree-throw 033 was used for the opportunistic extraction of flint nodules which were exposed in its sides. Although the assemblage from this tree-throw pit may be partially derived from material washed into the hollow, its composition – 25 flakes, two bladelets and two blade-like flakes – fits with the suggestion that flint nodules were worked here. Amongst this small assemblage are four primary flakes, three secondary core-trimming flakes and no cores or tools. It is therefore possible that the assemblage represents the extraction and initial trimming of a group of nodules. If this were the case, the small size of the assemblage suggests that only a limited amount of working took place within the hollow, with the majority of the material being removed for use elsewhere. The upper fill (023) of tree-throw pit 033 contained three

Context number	Burnt worked flint		Burnt unworked flint	
	Frequency	Weight (g)	Frequency	Weight (g)
023	1	1	0	0
030	1	35	0	0
035	2	9	3	83
044	0	0	1	14
051	24	60	121	1116
053	9	218	48	504
056	0	0	21	338
059	0	0	11	222
Total	37	323	205	2277

Table 3.20. The frequency of burnt worked and unworked flint from Early Neolithic contexts at Woodhenge

terms. It should be noted, however, that the primary fill has a similar proportion of blades to buried soil 051 and is similarly lacking in tools and cores. In contrast, a higher proportion of tools came from the secondary and uppermost fills. The secondary fill (056) contained a blade with extensive retouch along one lateral margin, a well-worked end-scraper made on an elongated flake (SF 20347), another circular scraper (SF 20390; Figure 3.77) with extensive retouch around its distal and lateral margins, and an unusual scraper (SF 20348) also with retouch along the distal and both lateral margins. This latter scraper was also notched on both lateral margins towards the distal end, suggesting that both the retouch and notching on its lateral margins were to facilitate hafting.

The material from the uppermost fill (053) of tree-throw 058 includes two cores, a hammerstone (SF 1063) made on a thermally fractured tabular nodule, a large cortical preparation flake, a retouched flake (SF 1064), a broken or snapped retouched blade, an end-scraper (SF 1048), a probable awl (SF 1062; Figure 3.77) and an oblique arrowhead rough-out (SF 20349). Compared to the material from the surrounding buried soil, the assemblages from the two upper fills of tree-throw 058 represent a wider range of activities, in the sense that they contain a number of cores, tools and core-preparation flakes, and thus a more extended *chaîne opératoire* is represented.

Whilst the assemblage in the tree-throw's uppermost fill (053) can be dated at least partly to the Late Neolithic (on the basis of its Grooved Ware pottery, oblique arrowhead type, and a radiocarbon date on animal bone), the lithics in the lower part of 053 and the fills beneath it are likely to date to the Early Neolithic on the basis of both their technology and associated pottery.

It should also be noted that the peak in density of worked flint in buried soil 051 – occurring in an area of 1m × 2m about a metre west of tree-throw 058 (Figure 3.78) – consists of 271 artefacts, which far

outweighs th
the tree-thro
deposition wa
and took plac

Burnt flint

Burnt worked
worked flint f
Given that fill
towards the b
dumped into t
burnt worked f
is backed up b
limited to the s
the northern t

A total of
weighing 2.277
correlation betw
presence of bu
worked flint, th
within buried s
throw 058. The s
within buried so
distribution of w

Discussion

The most striki
Early Neolithic
under-represen
throw pit 033 an
of tree-throw 0
may reflect the e
exposed areas o
tools for use else
is a little more
over an area of
to the northwes
the material sug
the area of exca
be spread over a

Moreover, as
soil, it represents
occurring during
the one hand, the
arrowheads in b
earlier and later N
the high proporti
does much to sug
Early Neolithic, a
practices or even
of this Woodhen
material from the
the ascription of a
assemblage. The

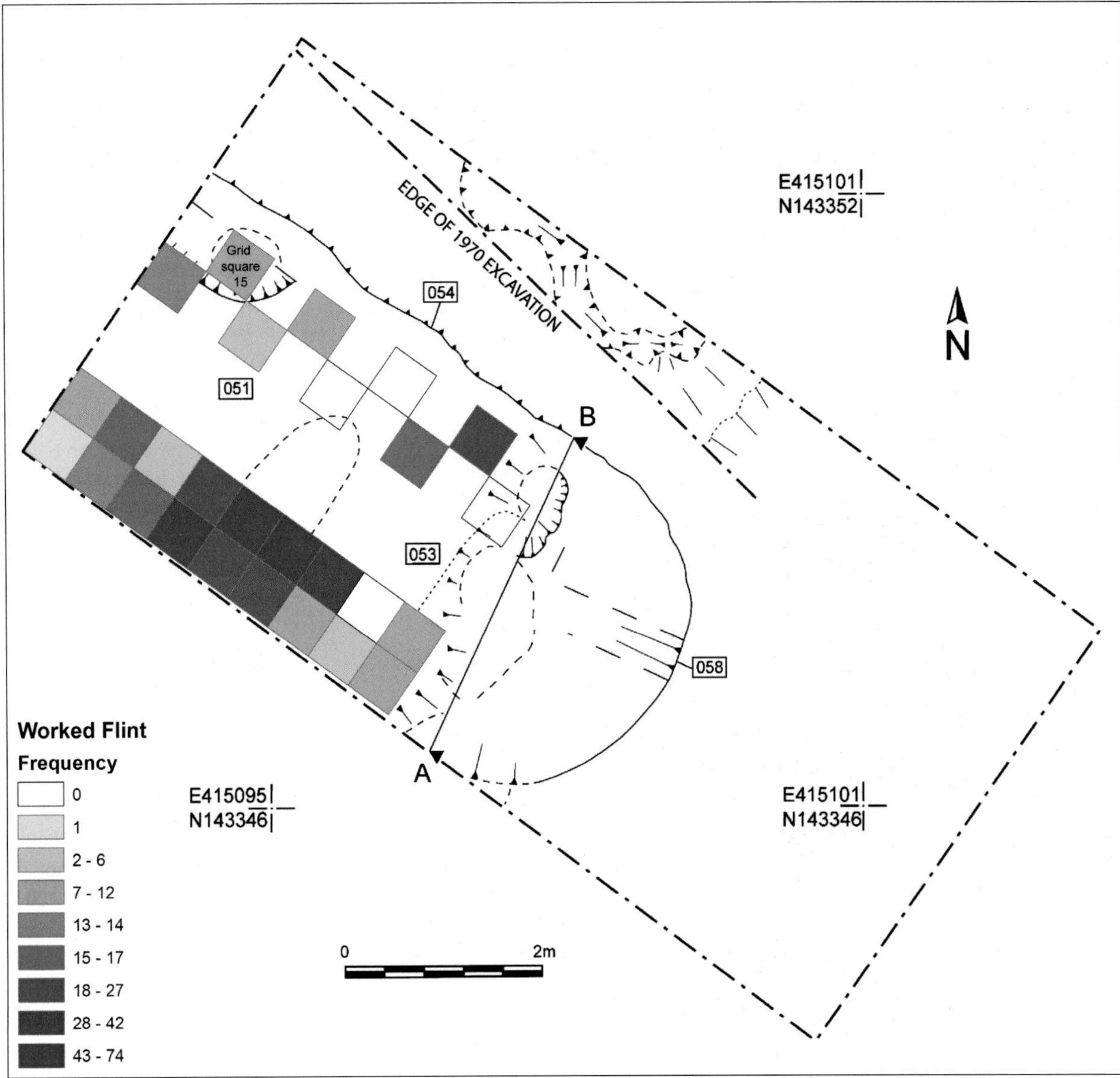

Figure 3.78. The frequency of worked flint from sample squares within buried soil 051 at Woodhenge

sherds of Early Neolithic pottery and the element of bladelets and blade-like flakes within the assemblage similarly suggests an Early Neolithic date for the deposit.

In comparison to the material from tree-throw pit 033, the Early Neolithic assemblage sealed beneath the bank of the henge is much larger (576 artefacts). The majority of the assemblage (426 artefacts) comes from the buried soil (051). Given the size of the assemblage, it is notable that formal tools and cores are under-represented, with only three retouched flakes, the tip of a broken probable awl, two oblique arrowheads (*e.g.* SF 1017; Figure 3.77) and a single flake-core present (Tables 3.18–3.19). The core, which is chronologically undiagnostic, has a single platform but is poorly worked and heavy edge-recession made the platform unworkable. There are also 10 edge-damaged/utilised flakes within the assemblage which appear to have been damaged by trampling rather than through utilisation.

The two oblique arrowheads indicate that the material within buried soil 051 derived from pre-bank activity stretching from the earlier to the later Neolithic. This is consistent with a find of a Grooved Ware sherd in 051, and of three further such sherds and a Late Neolithic date of 2580–2450 cal BC (95% confidence; SUERC-32161; 3980±30 BP) on cattle bone from layer 053. Despite this, almost all the ceramics from the buried soil and the fills of tree-throw 058 are from earlier Neolithic plain bowls, and the majority of the diagnostic elements within the lithic assemblage are characteristic of earlier Neolithic blade technology, with blades, bladelets and blade-like flakes making up 14% of

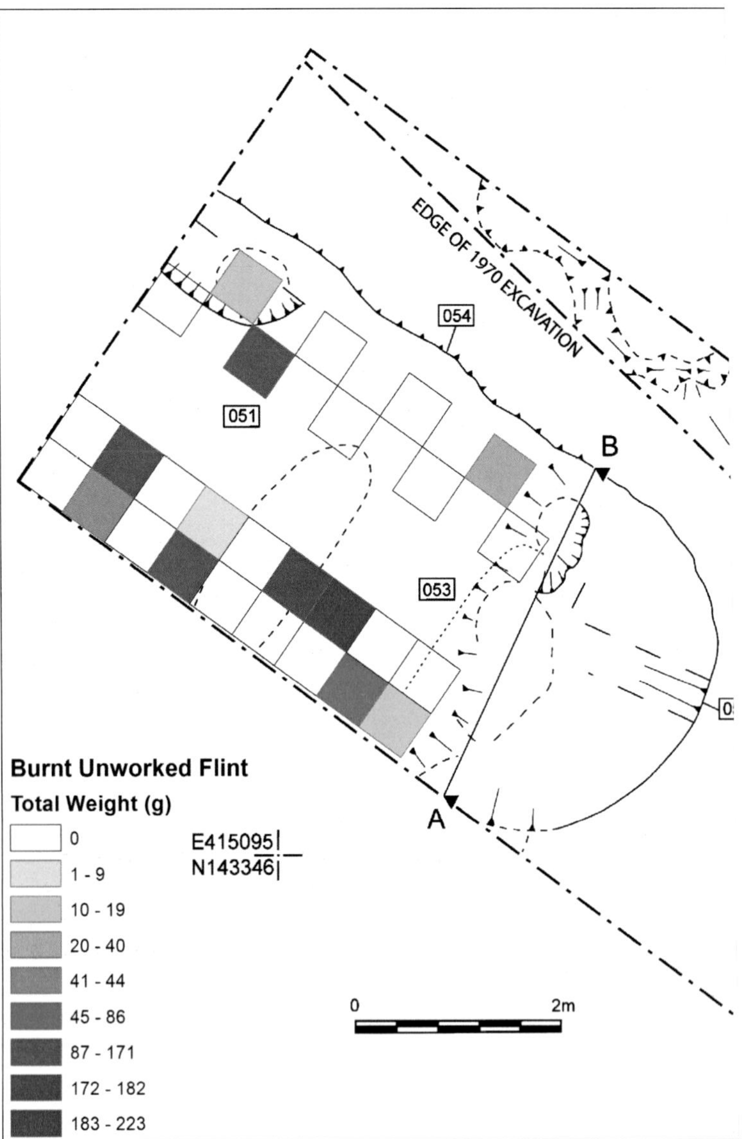

Figure 3.79. The weight of unworked burnt flint from sample squares withi

the assemblage. A number of these show signs of platform maintenance in the form of trimming, abrasion and faceting. A Level-2 metrical and techno-typological analysis of a sample of flakes and blades from 051 and 053 was conducted and is reported in detail in Volume 2.

In addition to the blades from buried soil 051, there is also a single thinning flake from the manufacture of a bifacial implement such as a flint axe. Only the medial section of the flake remains, making identification difficult. However, the remaining portion is thin, with a slightly curved profile and dorsal flake scars emanating from different directions, all of which are common attributes of thinning flakes (Newcomer 1971).

The material from buried soil 051 was excavated in a series of 0.50m sample squares forming two transects

across the a
was unever
the main co
the souther
tree-throw (

The mat
primary fill
(053). In ge
fills of tree-t
that from th
from contex
10% and 14

The prin
amount of m
it is difficult

Mesolithic has, in this case, been discounted because of the overall quality of the blades and the lack of any diagnostic elements such as Mesolithic blade-cores or microliths.

Given the lack of tools within the assemblage, it is tempting to suggest that the flintwork within buried soil 051, like the material from tree-throw 033, represents the residues of nodule extraction and trimming associated with tree-throw 058. However, there are key differences between these two assemblages. Firstly, the material from 051 is spread across a sizeable area around the tree-throw, rather than being confined to it. Secondly, the assemblage from 051 is large and contains a high proportion of blades: it therefore contains products of extended reduction sequences rather than just nodule testing and trimming.

Therefore, unlike the smaller assemblage from tree-throw pit 033, it is likely that the assemblage from buried soil 051 represents an episode of flintworking in which nodules were fully worked down into usable products in the form of cores, blades, flakes and tool blanks, which were then taken away for use elsewhere. The location of this activity close to tree-throw pit 058 may suggest that the tree-throw was the source of the raw material used for the flintworking, but this cannot be stated conclusively.

The other element that needs to be addressed is why the composition of the assemblage from tree-throw 058 is different to that from the surrounding buried soil (051). Whereas 051 contained almost no tools, the much smaller assemblage from the deposits filling 058 contains four scrapers, an awl and an unfinished arrowhead. Moreover, upper fill 053 also contained ashy material and a dump of Early Neolithic pottery sherds (given the radiocarbon date on a cattle bone, the animal bone was deposited much later). Like the flint assemblage, this ceramic material is more reminiscent of a settlement or a camp than an opportunistic extraction site.

The deposition of large assemblages of pottery and flint into tree-throws is a practice that has been noted in both Britain (Evans *et al.* 1999) and Ireland (Smyth 2014: 115–16). At Hinxton and Barleycroft Farm in Cambridgeshire, for example, the quantity of material within the tree-throws contrasted with the paucity of Early Neolithic material in the surface scatters in their environs (Evans *et al.* 1999: 248–9). This, combined with the character of the Early Neolithic pottery and diverse flint assemblage from the tree-throws, led the excavators to suggest that the material represented midden that had been buried as part of a structured process of 'tidying up' occupation debris at the closure of a settlement. It is argued that this occurred during the earliest Neolithic episodes of woodland clearance and was a practice born out of the particular perception that Early Neolithic people had of ancient woodland and its gradual clearance.

The case of tree-throw 058 seems parallel, to some extent, to these comparative examples. Certainly the mixed flint assemblage, which also contained burnt flint, might well have originally derived from a midden. One way in which the situation at Woodhenge is, however, quite different to that described at Hinxton and Barleycroft Farm is that the density of artefacts around tree-throw 058 is greater than that within it. Moreover, the assemblage composition is significantly different between the tree-throw pit and the surrounding buried soil, which suggests that the two assemblages originally derived from different sources. In this respect, it would appear that the material from within the tree-throw was brought from outside of the immediate surroundings of the tree-throw itself.

It should also be noted that, although small, the assemblage from the primary fill of the tree-throw lacks tools and cores and therefore has more in common with the material from the surrounding buried soil than with the upper fills of the tree-throw. These are probably two distinct phases of activity, with the primary fill and surrounding buried soil representing initial activity involving the working-down of blade-cores, and the upper fills representing the dumping of midden-like material derived from a much wider range of activities associated with more established settlement.

Having discussed the character of activities that produced the Early Neolithic flint assemblage from the buried soil (051), it is also necessary to consider its scale, or more accurately its density. The density of worked flint within buried soil 051 is 65.4 flints per sq m, retrieved from an area of 6.50 sq m. This suggests that the flint scatter is quite dense, though the significance of this figure is hard to grasp without a meaningful comparison. The easiest means of providing one is to compare the figure with the density of worked flint across the midden at Durrington Walls, which lies close by to the north (see Volume 3 for a full description of the Durrington Walls assemblage excavated by the SRP). Although the deposits are separated by over a millennium, the artefact recovery strategies at the two sites were the same; the east entrance of Durrington Walls offers rare data on artefact assemblages from undisturbed occupation surfaces of a Neolithic settlement site in Wessex. Selecting just the dry-sieved sample fraction, to compare with the dry-sieved assemblage from buried soil 051 at Woodhenge, the density of worked flint from midden 593 at Durrington Walls was 67.4 flints per sq m retrieved from an area of 132.75 sq m.

Although Durrington Walls midden 593 was spread over a much larger area than Woodhenge buried soil 051, the similarity in density is striking. Moreover, the soil profile of 051 suggests that, prior to the laying-down of the bank of Woodhenge in the Beaker period, the turf was stripped from the buried soil (see French, above). It is possible that this process would have removed a significant number of artefacts from the buried soil and that therefore its original artefact density was higher than it is now. In either case, the

Context	050	051	053	056	Total
Mammal	CS	CS	CS	CS	
	NISP	NISP	NISP	NISP	NISP
Cattle		6	3	2	11
?Cattle				1	1
Sheep/Goat		3			3
Pig	2	2	5	1	10
Total	2	11	8	4	25

Table 3.21. Numbers of animal bones and teeth (NISP) from the Early Neolithic layers of the buried soil and the tree-throw pit (058) Woodhenge

point is not that the two sites are the same as each other, but that the density of worked flint within the buried soil at Woodhenge is as high as that from a midden from an intensively occupied settlement site.

It must be remembered, however, that an essential element in comparing scales of activity through artefact densities is an appreciation of time depth. The issue here is that it is known that the settlement at the east entrance of Durrington Walls was remarkably short-lived, with a chronology spanning as little as a few decades. In contrast, the time depth represented in the assemblage from buried soil 051 at Woodhenge is unknown, further complicated by the fact that at least some of its lithics – such as the two Late Neolithic oblique arrowheads – were deposited over a thousand years later. Potentially, the density of likely Early Neolithic material within 051 represents more than a background scatter of generalised Neolithic activity. Rather, it suggests that something altogether more purposeful took place at this particular locale.

Conclusion

The assemblage of worked flint from the Early Neolithic contexts at Woodhenge provides some important insights into the potential significance of this locale more than a millennium before the construction of the timber circle. Although the nature of the stratigraphy and the coarseness of the chronology does not allow for precise dating or phasing of events, it is argued that a likely sequence is that initial activity involved the extraction and preliminary working of nodules exposed in the sides of one or both tree-throws. A more extensive episode of flake and blade production might have taken place around the same time, located close to tree-throw pit 058. This flintworking might have involved the reduction of nodules retrieved from the tree-throw itself but this is hard to establish definitively. It is tentatively suggested here that these activities were part of woodland clearance.

Sometime after this initial activity, people returned to the tree-throw and deposited an assemblage of flint that was, in part, burnt and contained a range of different types of tools. This material was found alongside pottery and could represent midden material that was dumped into the top of the tree-throw. By analogy with other examples of Early Neolithic deposits in both tree-throws and pits, it is likely that this activity indicates the presence of a settlement nearby and that this deposit may relate to its closing-down. Finally, in the Late Neolithic, the uppermost parts of the tree-throw depression were filled with animal bones, a few sherds of Grooved Ware and lithics, around the same time that Woodhenge's timber structure was erected.

3.4.7. Faunal remains from Woodhenge tree-throw pit 058 and buried soil

C. Minniti, U. Albarella and S. Viner-Daniels

A small assemblage of animal teeth and bones was recovered from different layers of tree-throw pit 058 and the buried soil under the bank, together with Early Neolithic pottery and worked flint. Materials and methods of faunal analysis are described in Chapter 7. The faunal remains mainly belong to cattle and pigs, whilst sheep/goats are less well represented (Table 3.21). Canid gnawing-marks were observed on a few pig bones. A large perforation, perhaps resulting from marrow extraction, was noted on a cattle first phalanx from buried soil 051. A radiocarbon date of 2580–2450 cal BC at 95% confidence (SUERC-32161; 3980±30 BP) was obtained on a cattle bone from tree-throw fill 053. This Late Neolithic date indicates that the faunal assemblage from under the henge bank cannot be assumed to have been deposited any earlier; there is no evidence that any of the animal bones date to the Early Neolithic.

3.4.8. Charred plant remains and wood charcoal from Woodhenge tree-throw pit 058 and buried soil

E. Simmons

Fourteen flotation samples, comprising over 100 litres of soil, were processed and assessed using the methods outlined above in the report on the material from the Greater Cursus and Amesbury 42 long barrow. No charred plant remains were found to be present in the sampled contexts. Buried soil 051 produced a moderate assemblage of just under 80 wood charcoal fragments >2mm in size in cross-section. The wood charcoal assemblage from buried soil 051 was therefore selected for full identification (see Table 7.13). Buried soil 051 was well sealed beneath the bank of Woodhenge, although given the problem of intrusive charred material in chalk soils (see above and Chapter 7), there remains the strong possibility that many of the charcoal fragments are intrusive.

Methods

A minimum charcoal fragment size of 2mm in cross-section was chosen for identification, as smaller fragments are difficult to fracture in all three planes and therefore difficult to identify. This may, however, result in a bias against the representation of species such as lime (*Tilia* sp.) which tend to be fragile and fracture easily into small fragments. All of the wood charcoal fragments >2mm in size were identified. The fragments were fractured manually, and the resultant anatomical features observed in transverse, radial and tangential planes using high-power binocular reflected-light (episcopic) microscopy (x50, x100 and x400). Identification of each fragment was carried out to as high a taxonomic level as possible by comparison with material in the reference collections at the Department of Archaeology, University of Sheffield and various reference works (*e.g.* Schweingruber 1990; Hather 2000).

A record was also made, where possible, of the ring curvature of the wood and aspects of the ligneous structure, in order to determine which part of the woody plant had been burnt, as well as the state of the wood before charring (*cf* Marguerie and Hunot 2007). The ring curvature of charcoal fragments was designated as weak, intermediate or strong, indicating larger branches or trunk material, intermediate-sized branches and smaller branches or twigs, based on the classification in Marguerie and Hunot (*ibid.*: 1421). The presence of thick-walled tyloses in vessel cavities, which indicate the presence of heartwood and therefore mature wood, was recorded (*ibid.*: 1419). The presence of fungal hyphae, which indicate the use of dead or rotting wood, was also recorded (*ibid.*: 1419). The degree of vitrification of the charcoal fragments was recorded as a measure of preservation, with levels of vitrification classified as either low brilliance refractiveness (degree 1), strong brilliance (degree 2) or total fusion (degree 3) (*ibid.*: 1421).

The taxa present in the charcoal assemblage and observations of the ligneous structure of the charcoal fragments are recorded in Table 7.13 alongside the data from the Late Neolithic Cuckoo Stone. Nomenclature follows Stace (2010). The abbreviation *cf* means 'compares with' and denotes that a specimen most closely resembles that particular taxon more than any other. Identified charcoal fragments were grouped by taxa and stored in sealable plastic bags.

Species represented

The taxa present in buried soil 051 are yew (*Taxus baccata*), blackthorn (*Prunus* cf *spinosa*), blackthorn/cherry (*Prunus* sp.), hawthorn/apple/pear/whitebeams (Pomoideae), buckthorn (*Rhamnus cathartica*), oak (*Quercus* sp.), alder (*Alnus glutinosa*) and hazel (*Corylus avellana*).

It is often not possible to identify charcoal beyond a certain taxonomic level given the similarities between related genera. Pomoideae is a large sub-family of the Rosaceae (rose family), containing many species that cannot be differentiated using morphological characteristics, although the native woody plant species most likely represented would be *Pyrus communis* L. (wild pear), *Malus sylvestris* (L.) Mill. (crab apple), *Sorbus domestica* L. (service tree), *Sorbus aucuparia* L. (rowan), *Sorbus aria* (L.) Crantz (common whitebeam), *Crataegus monogyna* Jacq. (hawthorn) or *Crataegus laevigata* (Poir.) DC. (Midland hawthorn). Oak charcoal cannot be identified to species using morphological characteristics so either *Quercus petraea* (Matt.) Leibl. (sessile oak) or *Quercus robur* L. (pendunculate oak) is represented. The species of oak most likely to be present is *Quercus robur* L., which is generally dominant on the heavy basic soils of southern and eastern England (Godwin 1975: 279) and is the dominant oak species in present-day woodland communities in Wiltshire (Grose 1979: 504).

The size of the wood charcoal fragments was generally too small for a reliable assessment to be made of growth-ring curvature. It was, however, possible to determine growth-ring curvatures on four fragments, of which one yew, one cherry/blackthorn and one hazel fragment have strong curvature and one hazel has intermediate curvature. Tyloses were not observed as present in the vessel cavities of any of the charcoal fragments. Fungal hyphae were also not observed as present in the vessel cavities of any of the charcoal fragments.

Preservation of the wood charcoal fragments was relatively good, with only 11 fragments exhibiting some form of vitrification, whereby charcoal takes on a glassy appearance with anatomical features becoming fused and unidentifiable.

Discussion

A relatively diverse range of taxa is represented in the charcoal assemblage from buried soil 051, indicating the utilisation of a mix of woody taxa as fuel. The reader may note in Table 7.13 the greater range of taxa present in the Early Neolithic Woodhenge assemblage than in the Late Neolithic material from the Cuckoo Stone.

It was not generally possible to determine the diameter of the wood used, given the small size of the majority of the charcoal fragments, although intermediate and strong ring curvatures were noted as present, suggesting the likely use of a mix of small and larger diameter wood. No evidence for the use of dead or rotting wood was observed to be present in the assemblage.

The composition of the charcoal assemblage is likely to have been influenced by a number of taphonomic factors, including anthropogenic wood-collection strategies, combustion factors, and depositional and post-depositional processes (Théry-Parisot *et al.* 2010). It is unlikely, therefore, that the dominance of a particular taxon within the charcoal assemblage directly reflects a dominance of that taxon in the surrounding environment. It is also likely that woodland and the uses of wood had ceremonial and symbolic associations (Austin 2000: 64).

Hazel is the most abundant taxon present in the charcoal assemblage from buried soil 051, which is likely to be due in part to the use of hazel wood for utilitarian purposes such as wattle fencing (Rackham 2003: 203) and to the excellent properties of hazel as a fuel wood (Webster 1919: 45; Porter 1990: 93). Yew, oak and Pomoideae are also relatively frequently occurring taxa in this assemblage. Oak can be readily coppiced and pollarded, is an excellent structural timber (Rackham 2003: 284) and is an excellent fuel wood which burns hot and slowly once it has been well-seasoned (Webster 1919: 45; Porter 1990: 93). Yew is one of the best fuel woods, burning slowly but with a fierce heat (Webster 1919) although, unless seasoned for at least two years, can be explosive on an open fire (Porter 1990: 93). Yew is also a dense strong wood which is particularly useful for carving (Rodwell 1991: 237) and is resistant to decay (Porter 1990: 19). Taxa potentially represented by Pomoideae, such as hawthorn, apple and pear, are also good fuel woods, producing good heat and burning slowly (Webster 1919: 45; Porter 1990: 93).

Hazel is a common underwood shrub in open woodland but can also grow to canopy height (Rackham 2003: 203). Yew grows in association with other woodland trees such as oak, as well as forming pure yew woodland, particularly on base-rich soils (Tansley 1968: 128). Cherry, blackthorn and buckthorn, along with hawthorn, wild apple, wild pear and most of the members of the whitebeam genus, which are potentially represented by Pomoideae, are all underwood shrubs or trees of open woodland (Rackham 2003: 349).

Many of the taxa present in the charcoal assemblage are also components of chalk scrub which colonises open grassland on chalk soils in areas where grazing pressure is reduced (Tansley 1968: 127–8; Rodwell 1991: 339; Vera 2000: 343–4). Hawthorn is one of the main shrubs which becomes established in thorny scrub, along with other shrubs such as buckthorn (which is characteristic of chalk soils) and blackthorn (which is a more general scrub species). Hazel can also be present but is less common than other shrubs. Saplings of trees such as whitebeam and yew are also characteristic components of thorny scrub on chalk soils (Rodwell 1991: 339), although other trees such as oak may also be present. The thorny scrub acts as a nursery for the tree saplings, protecting them from grazing until the trees eventually grow to form a grove (Vera 2000).

The composition of buried soil 051's charcoal assemblage is therefore consistent with open woodland, woodland clearings and woodland fringes as well as with chalk scrub colonising areas of open grassland. Palaeo-environmental evidence from the Stonehenge and Durrington Walls environs indicates that a mosaic of established grazed grassland and areas of woodland most likely characterised the landscape in the Early Neolithic (French *et al.* 2012). Pollen data from the palaeo-channel of the River Avon adjacent to Durrington Walls indicate that the Early Neolithic woodland was dominated by hazel but included oak, elm, lime and pine with alder present along the river floodplain (French *et al.* 2012; see also *Palynology* in Chapter 9).

The absence of elm, lime and pine in the charcoal assemblage from buried soil 051 demonstrates that charcoal is often only a partial indication of available woodland. Elm is a somewhat poor fuel wood (apart from where heartwood has been well-seasoned) and pine produces lots of flames but little heat, although it is useful as a fire-lighter (Webster 1919: 45; Porter 1990: 93). Lime is a poor fuel wood but can also be under-represented in charcoal assemblages since lime charcoal is susceptible to fragmentation. Some of the taxa that are present in the charcoal assemblage, such as blackthorn, buckthorn and the species potentially represented by Pomoideae, are entomophilous and are therefore likely to be under-represented in pollen data.

A similar assemblage of wood charcoal, consisting of oak, hazel, Pomoideae, blackthorn/cherry and yew, was recovered from the fill of the Early Neolithic Coneybury Anomaly (Gale 1990: table 136). The association of hazel, oak and Pomoideae is also evident in the relatively small charcoal assemblages from Early Neolithic deposits at Fussell's Lodge long barrow near Salisbury (Dimbleby 1966: 73), South Street long barrow near Avebury, where blackthorn was also present (Sheldon 1979: 288), and within the mound core of Easton Down long barrow, also near Avebury, where blackthorn was present as well as ash (*Fraxinus* sp.; Cartwright 1993: 222). At Windmill Hill causewayed enclosure, sampling of the ditch circuits and the old land surface for charcoal produced an assemblage that is dominated by oak and hazel but also includes Pomoideae, cherry/blackthorn, ash, birch and yew (Cartwright 1999: 160).

Chapter 4

The Stonehenge bluestones

M. Parker Pearson and C. Richards*

4.1. The bluestones at Stonehenge – a reappraisal

M. Parker Pearson and C. Richards

The bluestones are a key element of Stonehenge, consisting of some 43 surviving monoliths and many thousands of fragments of debris, apparently all that remains of approximately 80 original bluestone monoliths. Compared to Stonehenge's sarsen standing stones (estimated as originally totalling 83), the bluestones are comparatively small: the 4.70m-long Altar Stone (Stone 80) of Devonian Sandstone is the largest and the remainder are no greater than *c.* 4m long (Figure 4.1).

Bluestones are the 'foreign' rock at Stonehenge, consisting of a variety of lithologies including spotted dolerite, dolerite, rhyolite, volcanics and sandstone (Figure 4.2). In total, Stonehenge's bluestones can be divided into 15 geological groups. Their geological origin is not Salisbury Plain but west Wales, with most deriving from the Preseli hills in Pembrokeshire, some 140 miles away (220 km; Figure 4.3; see *Bluestones and Stonehenge*, below for information on the Welsh origins of these stones). The geological and petrological analysis of the bluestone fragments recovered during the SRP excavations is reported fully in Volume 2.

The presence of the bluestones at Stonehenge has been a focus of interest for over a century. Some major questions are:

- Were they were transported largely by sea or largely by land?
- Do they signify prehistoric beliefs about healing or ancestry?
- Were any bluestones erected elsewhere as one or more stone circles prior to (or along with) their emplacement at Stonehenge?
- When exactly did they arrive at Stonehenge?

Excavations during the twentieth century revealed that the bluestones were arranged and re-arranged in a number of settings within Stonehenge as the monument was built and re-built (Cleal *et al.* 1995). The chronology of these phases of construction has been recently reassessed, to provide a sequence of five stages – Stage 1 to Stage 5 (Darvill *et al.* 2012; Marshall *et al.* 2012; Parker Pearson 2012: 309–13). Subsequent to further radiocarbon dating of material from Stonehenge since the publication of the new chronology in 2012, some minor revisions can now be made to the dates of the five stages of construction. These revisions are published in Chapter 11 of this volume.

In this chapter, we examine the possibility that the first setting of Welsh bluestones at Stonehenge was in a stone circle inside Stonehenge's circular enclosure, where the bluestones stood in the circle of 56 pits known as Aubrey Holes, during Stonehenge's initial stage of

*** With contributions by:**
C. Casswell, B. Chan, R. Cleal, R. Ixer, D. Mitcham, M. Pitts, J. Pollard and J. Richards

Figure 4.1. A bluestone of spotted dolerite (Stone 68) at Stonehenge, viewed from the north

construction, beginning in *3080–2950 cal BC* (*95% probability*; see Table 11.7). In the next chapter, we present the results of the excavation of a henge at West Amesbury, at the east end of the Stonehenge Avenue, with evidence that approximately 25 bluestones were also installed there, perhaps around 3000 BC, as a stone circle – 'Bluestonehenge' – where the Avenue meets the River Avon.

This chapter also investigates the possibility that Welsh bluestones may have been erected within other parts of the Stonehenge landscape, notably at or around Fargo Plantation in the vicinity of the western end of the Greater Cursus. It is in this context that we discuss a pit circle at Airman's Corner which lies *c.* 1000m west of a scatter of bluestone chips at Fargo Plantation, and raise the possibility of this circle of pits being the remains of a small circle of bluestones.

This chapter concludes with a general discussion of the bluestones at Stonehenge, their biographies and origins, including our further investigations of the sources of the bluestones in west Wales, and the possibility that the Stonehenge bluestones derive from a bluestone monument first erected near the quarry sources in the Preseli hills.

4.1.1. The Aubrey Holes

Fifty-six pits form an 87m-diameter circle inside the line of the bank of Stonehenge's circular ditched enclosure (Figure 4.4). Thirty-two of them were excavated between 1920 and 1924 by William Hawley who named them the X Holes but also the Aubrey Holes since the seventeenth-century antiquarian John Aubrey had identified a number of cavities around the interior (published in *Monumenta Britannica*, 1665–1697; Fowles and Legg 1980–1982). Despite the fact that the features noticed by Aubrey may not in fact have been these pits identified and excavated by Hawley (Pitts 1981: 47), the name has stuck.

The Aubrey Holes (AH1–AH56) are, on average, 1.10m diameter and 0.88m deep (minimum 0.74m diameter × 0.56m deep; maximum 1.82m diameter × 1.14m deep) and are spaced every 4.5m–4.9m (Cleal *et al.* 1995: 96). Apart from the 32 opened during Hawley's extensive excavation of the eastern half of the Stonehenge enclosure in 1919–1926, only two others have been excavated – AH31 and AH32 (Atkinson *et al.* 1952) – although Colt Hoare (1812) may have dug into AH46 when

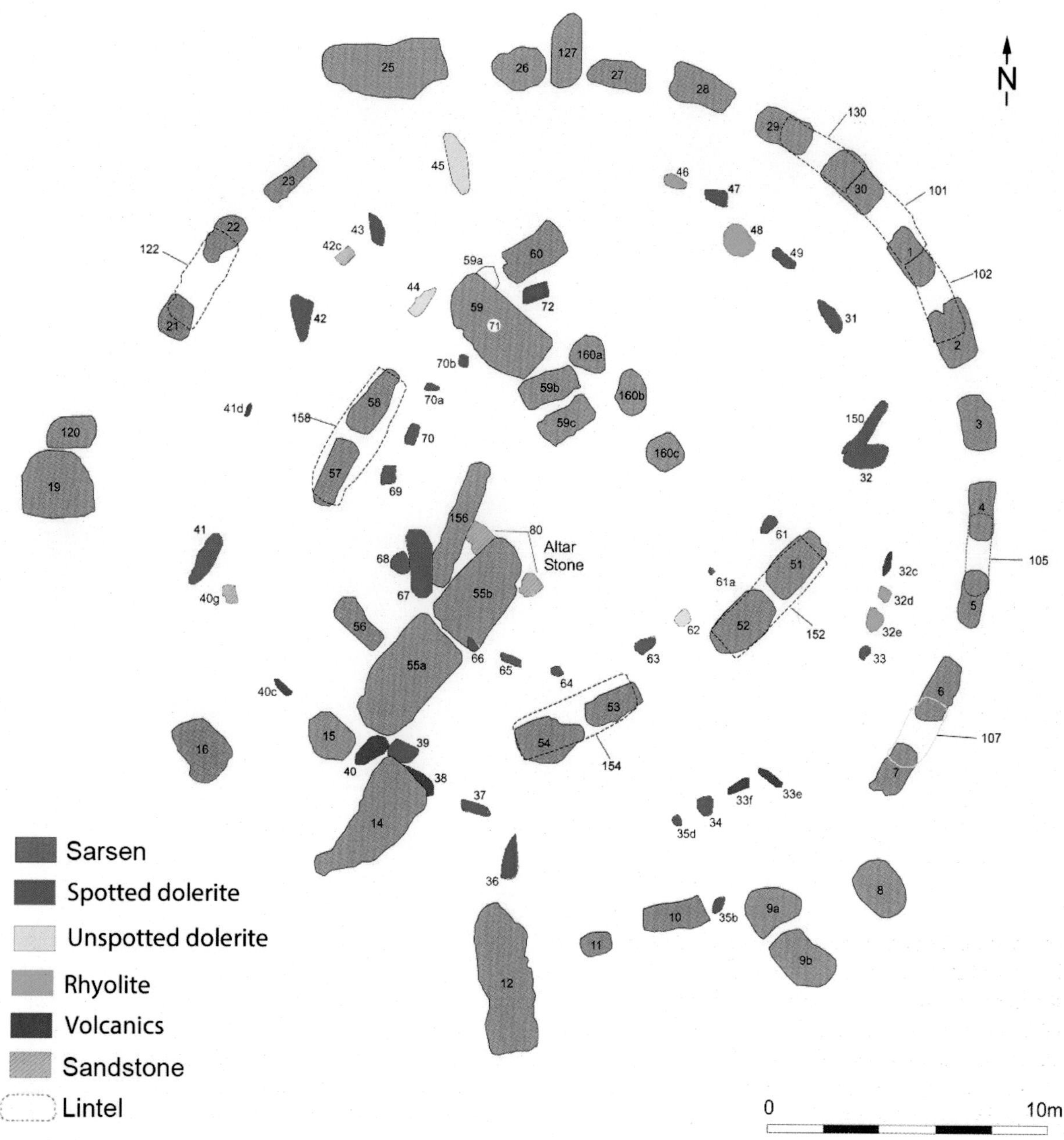

Figure 4.2. Plan of Stonehenge, identifying the different types of bluestones (after Richards 2017); © Julian Richards

Figure 4.3. Carn Goedog, a source of Stonehenge's spotted dolerite bluestones where monoliths were quarried in *c.* 3400–3000 BC, viewed from the south

excavating the North Barrow (a small circular mound inside and adjacent to the encircling bank; Newall 1929: 82; Cleal *et al.* 1995: 96). Cremated human bone from AH32 is radiocarbon-dated to 3080–2890 cal BC at 95% confidence (OxA-18036; 4332±35 BP; see Table 11.4).

Ever since their first investigations in the early twentieth century, the Aubrey Holes have caused interpretive problems concerning their purpose and filling. Within the last 100 years, archaeologists' opinions have wavered from their holding standing stones, to being pits that once held wooden posts, to being merely pits (Hawley 1921; 1928; Atkinson 1956; Cleal *et al.* 1995; Pollard and Ruggles 2001).

The idea that the Aubrey Holes originally held wooden posts stems from an uncertainty in William Hawley's interpretation of his own excavations. In 1921 Hawley was convinced the Aubrey Holes were stoneholes but changed his mind by 1923 on advice from the Cunningtons (Hawley 1921; 1923). Some years later, when Hawley visited Maud Cunnington's excavations at Woodhenge (see Chapter 3), he wrote that the postholes there 'correspond exactly to the original conditions of the Aubrey holes' (Hawley 1928: 156). Unfortunately, this is an incorrect comparison: the profiles of the Woodhenge postholes of equivalent diameter to the Aubrey Holes are consistently deeper (*c.* 1m–2m deep), in relation to their diameters (*c.* 0.70m–1.20m), than the Aubrey Holes. When comparing the detail of Hawley's observations of the Aubrey Holes (1921) with those of Cunnington at Woodhenge (1929), it is also evident that the fills of these features at the two monuments are also quite different.

This error by Hawley has led to lengthy discussion on whether the Aubrey Holes, severally or universally, did indeed hold timber posts, or even wooden stakes, inserted into their fills (Atkinson 1956: 13; Pitts 1982: 127; 2000: 108–9; Cleal *et al.* 1995: 102–7; Pollard and Ruggles 2001: 75; Burl 2006: 119–20). Our own experience of excavating postholes at Durrington Walls and Woodhenge highlights how unlikely it is that the Aubrey Holes ever held posts. A quantitative comparison of the Aubrey Holes' dimensions with equivalent-diameter postholes at Woodhenge and the Southern Circle at Durrington Walls (Cunnington 1929: 33–5; Wainwright with Longworth 1971: 380–1) illustrates this difference, with the Aubrey Holes' dimensions equivalent to those

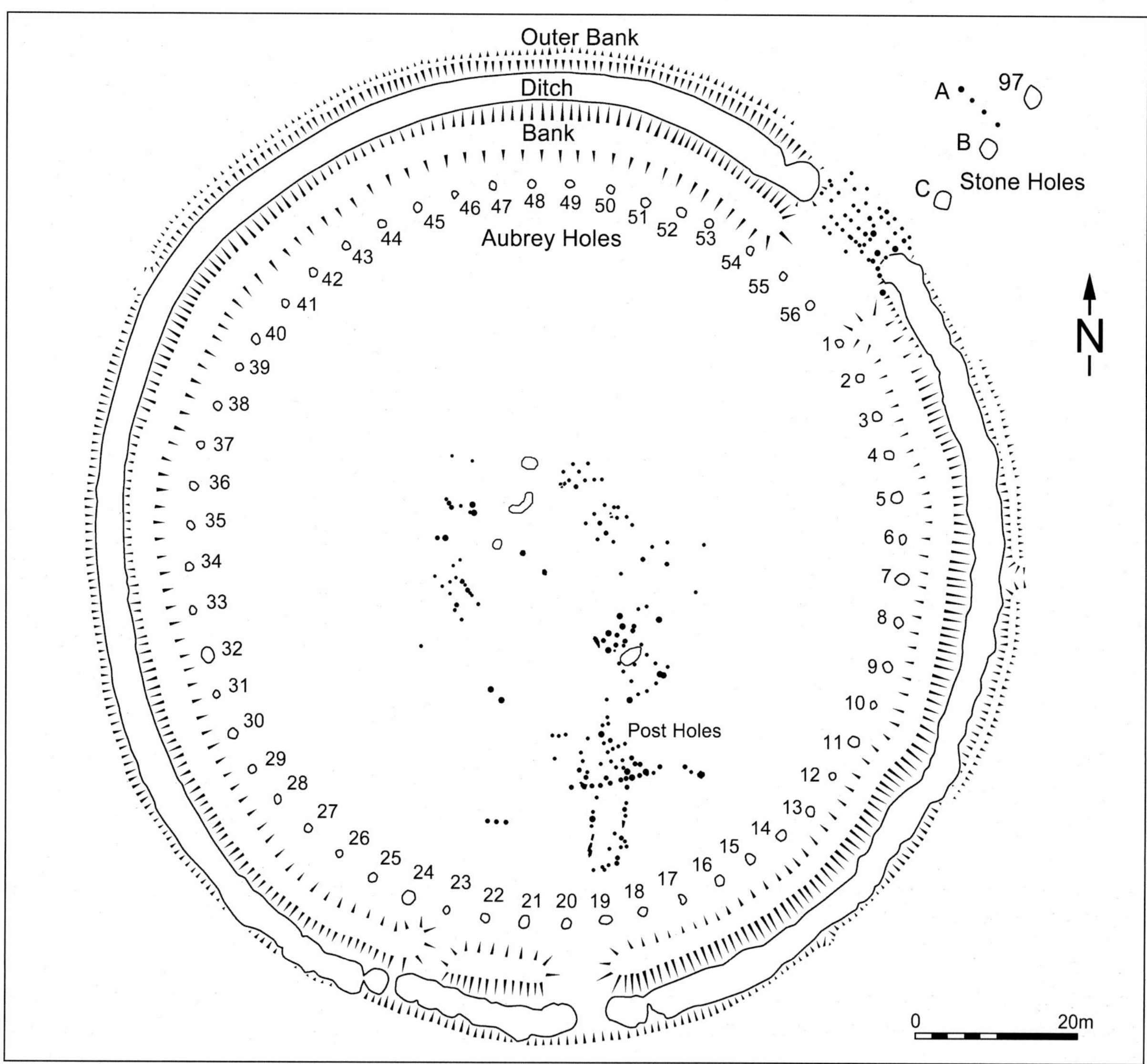

Figure 4.4. Plan of Stonehenge Stage 1 showing the Aubrey Holes

of Stage 2–Stage 4 bluestone sockets at Stonehenge but shallower than the vast majority of postholes (Figure 4.5; Parker Pearson *et al.* 2009: fig. 8).

Atkinson excavated two Aubrey Holes in 1950 and considered that these (and therefore all the others) were simply pits (1979: 172). He, like many others, discounted their interpretation as stoneholes even though the hard, compact primary fills (layers 6, 7 and 4; Cleal *et al.* 1995: fig. 55) that he encountered within Aubrey Hole 32 are consistent with its use as a stonehole.

Indeed, Hawley stated in his first report, having just excavated 25 Aubrey Holes, that 'there can be little doubt that they once held small upright stones', noting the compaction and crushing of basal chalk rubble in three of the Aubrey Holes (AH3, AH5 and AH24; Hawley 1921: 30–1). In this respect, it is important to note that the profiles, depths and diameters of the Aubrey Holes (averaging 1.10m in maximum diameter and 0.88m deep; Cleal *et al.* 1995: table 10, figs 51–55) are *indistinguishable* from those of known bluestone sockets of later phases (averaging 1.10m in maximum diameter and 0.96m deep; *ibid.*: figs 118, 120, 122, 131; Figure 4.5). Within this interpretive perspective, a cremation burial in Aubrey Hole 32, excavated by Atkinson, was located within what can now be interpreted as the chalk packing for a standing stone, thus being part of the primary fill of the pit (Atkinson *et al.* 1952; Cleal *et al.* 1995: fig. 55).

There is a strong case to be made for the Aubrey Holes having held stones, an argument that is reinforced by the findings of our re-excavation of Aubrey Hole 7 in 2008

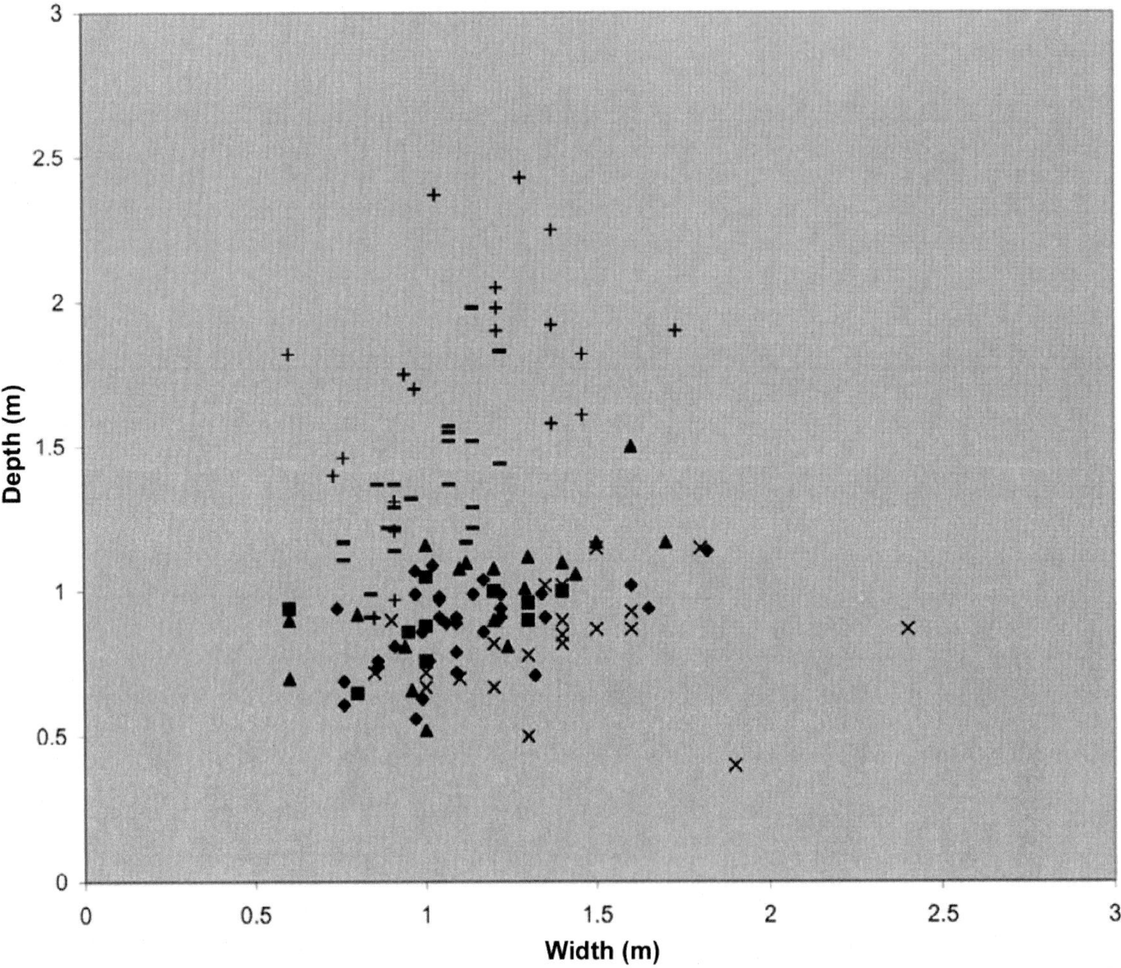

Figure 4.5. Pit sizes of excavated Aubrey Holes and other bluestone sockets at Stonehenge (Stages 2/3 and 4), postholes of similar diameter from Woodhenge (ring B) and Durrington Walls Southern Circle (ring 2B) and Late Neolithic pits from Dorchester-on-Thames Sites I and XI (Atkinson *et al.* 1951). All depths are measured from recorded ground level except for Durrington Walls (measured as depth from the top of natural chalk). Widths are maximum diameters

◆ Aubrey Holes
■ Stages 2 and 3 bluestone stoneholes at Stonehenge
▲ Stage 4 bluestone stoneholes at Stonehenge
× Dorchester-on-Thames Sites I and XI pits
+ Durrington Southern Circle 2B postholes
– Woodhenge ring B postholes

(see below), which revealed basal fills consistent with this pit having held a standing stone. The implications are considerable. These stones must have been bluestones because all the Stonehenge sarsens are too large to have sat in these holes. This re-interpretation of the Aubrey Holes as being sockets that once held bluestones puts the arrival of at least 56 bluestones at Stonehenge at the beginning of the third millennium BC (on the basis of the radiocarbon date from AH32), rather than in the mid-third millennium BC. This would place them at Stonehenge in Stage 1 (beginning in *3080–2950 cal BC* and ending in *2865–2755 cal BC*; see Table 11.7), as early as (or even slightly earlier than) the construction of the circular enclosure's ditch and bank in *2995–2900 cal BC* (*95% probability; ditch construction*; see Figure 11.2) or *2970–2915 cal BC* (*68% probability*). Note that the chronology of the ditch is slightly remodelled and supersedes the estimate in Marshall *et al.* (2012) and Darvill *et al.* (2012); the revisions are explained in Chapter 11.

We can presume that bluestones were first erected in the Aubrey Holes in an undressed state since no bluestone chippings from this earliest phase can be identified in material excavated from the enclosing ditch's primary or secondary fills (Cleal *et al.* 1995: 469). The large quantities of bluestone chippings from later contexts at Stonehenge

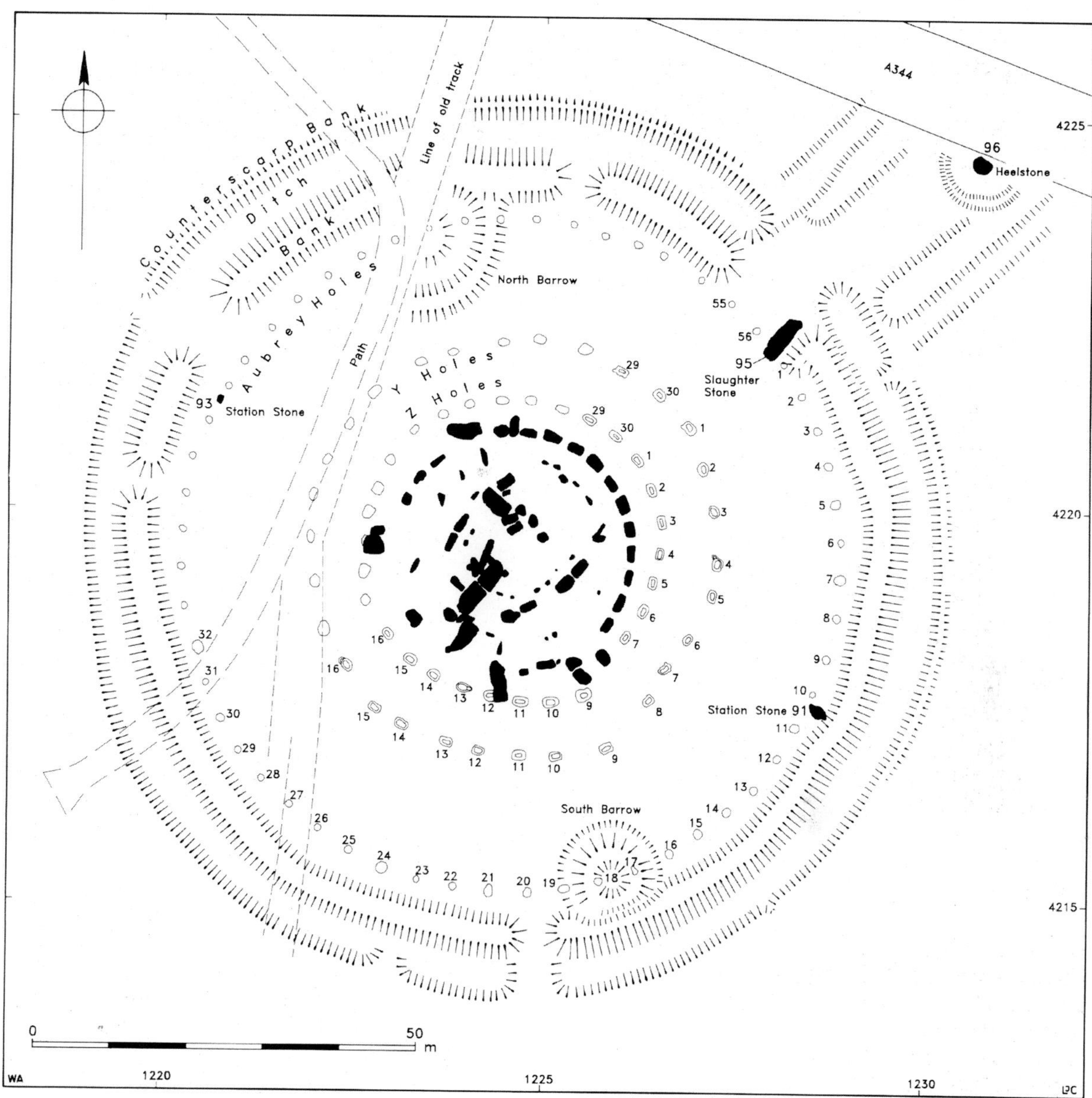

Figure 4.6. Plan of Stonehenge showing numbered Aubrey Holes in relation to standing stones (of different stages) visible today

indicate either that some bluestones were later dressed on site, or that these chippings derive from the monoliths' post-Neolithic destruction, or both.

No stones stand in the Aubrey Holes today. When were the bluestones removed from the Aubrey Holes, and where did they go after their removal? The known bluestone sockets elsewhere at Stonehenge – where they may have been re-erected – are those of the bluestone double arc (known as the Q and R Holes; Figures 4.6–4.7). This re-location of bluestones from the circle of Aubrey Holes to the double arc is dated in the new chronological framework to Stage 2 (beginning in *2740–2505 cal BC* and ending in *2470–2300 cal BC*; see Table 11.7).

4.1.2. Positions of bluestones within Stonehenge's Stages 2–5

Stage 2 represents the moment when Stonehenge changed from a *c.* 87m-wide circle of small standing bluestones to a more compact but much taller circle *c.* 30m in diameter, composed of bluestones and sarsens. A few sarsen standing stones had probably been erected during Stage 1, notably beyond the northeast entrance to the enclosure, including the Heel Stone and the three stones that once stood in Stoneholes B, C and 97 (Figure 4.4; see Chapter 7), and probably another two within the enclosure's interior (features WA 2321 and possibly WA 3433; Cleal *et al.* 1995: 181–2, figs 80, 82, 97).

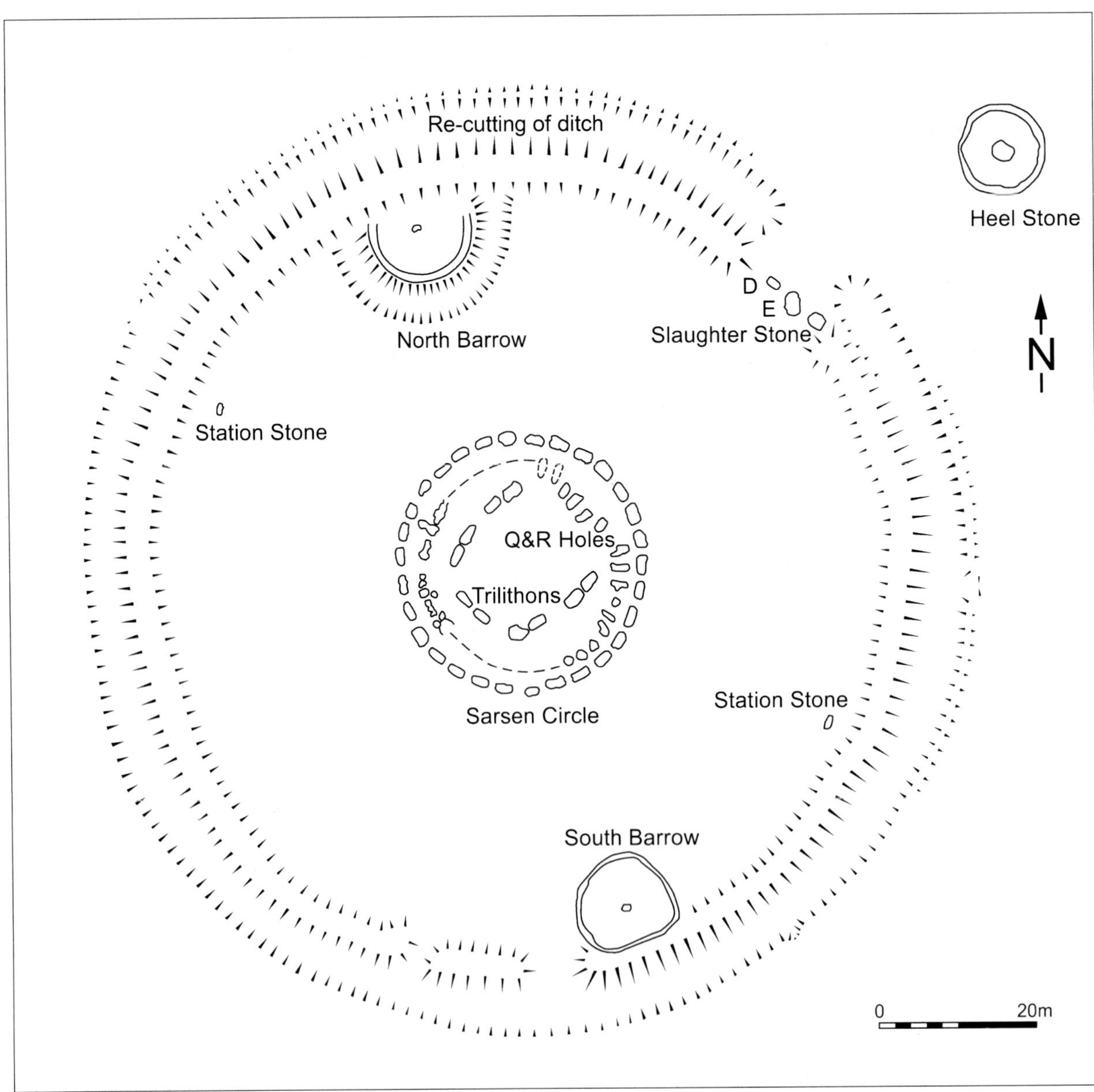

Figure 4.7. Plan of Stonehenge Stage 2 showing the Q and R Holes

However, in Stage 2, Stonehenge was transformed into a predominantly sarsen monument with its inner horseshoe of five trilithons and outer circle of lintelled uprights. Within this new sarsen monument, the bluestones were arranged in the Q and R Holes, in a formation that is still not well understood. In the northern and eastern sectors (see Cleal *et al.* 1995: fig. 80) the Q and R Holes form a double arc with a likely 1m-wide entrance in the northeast, marked by an indented pair of stoneholes (Q/R Hole 1 and Q/R Hole 38; *ibid.*: fig. 82).

Despite extensive excavation of the western sector of Stonehenge, little sense can be made of the Q and R Holes here (Figure 4.7), with only six likely features being assigned to the bluestone setting in this area (Cleal *et al.*: fig. 86). An argument has been made that the double arc of stoneholes originally continued here in the western sector (and in the largely unexcavated southern sector) to form a complete double circle of bluestones, but this entails a double circle in these sectors having been subsequently largely destroyed by the circle of single bluestones that replaced the Q and R Hole arrangement in Stage 4 (Darvill *et al.* 2012: 1030). This explanation is unsatisfactory because of the necessarily greater area occupied by a double circle of stone socket pairs as opposed to a circle of single stones: Stage 2 double stone sockets are unlikely to have been entirely obliterated by Stage 4 single sockets. Furthermore, the degree of below-

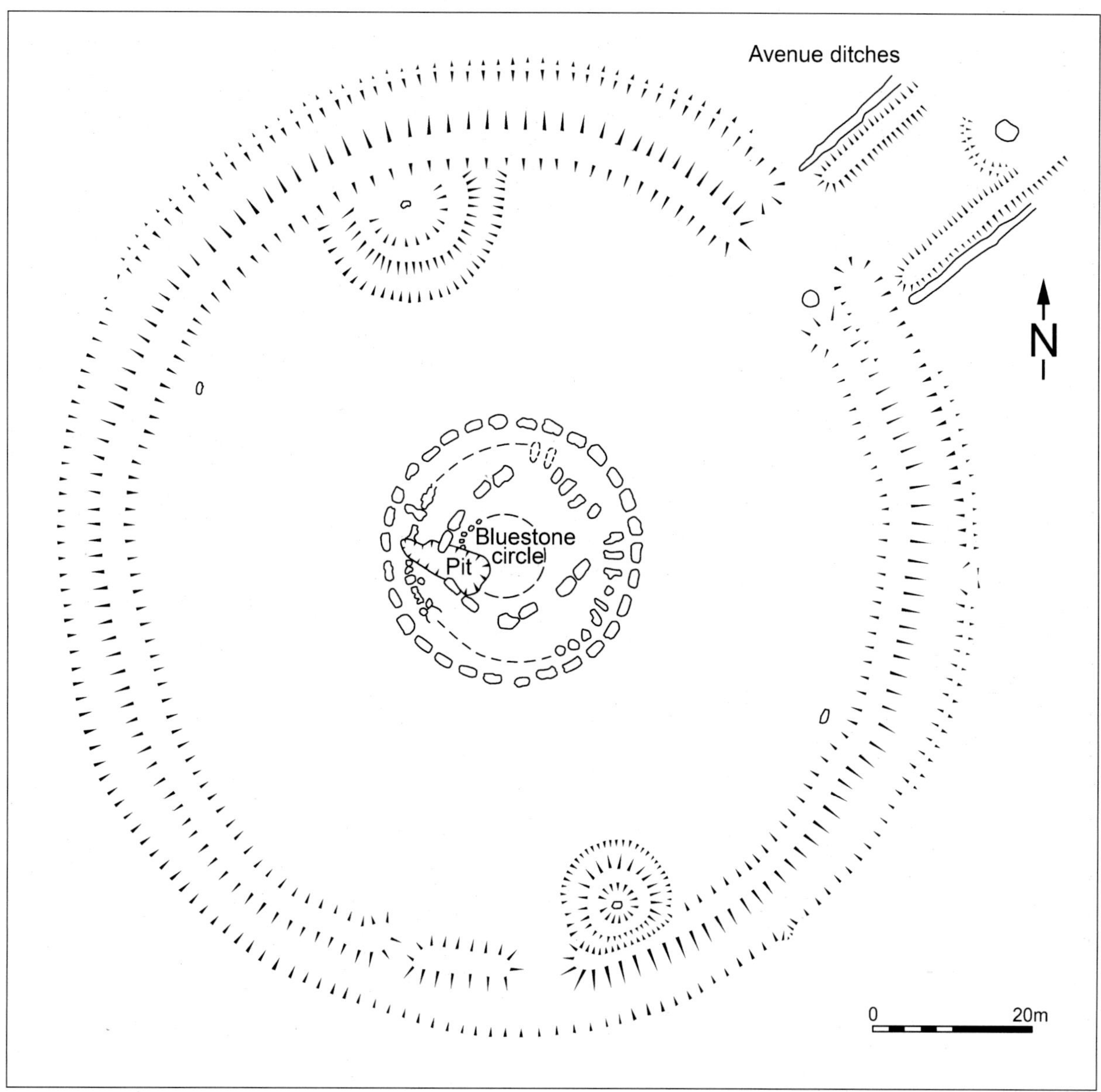

Figure 4.8. Plan of Stonehenge Stage 3 showing the suspected inner bluestone circle

ground disturbance, potentially obliterating any earlier cut features, is no greater in the western sector than in the eastern and northern sectors.

The most likely plan for the structure formed by the Q and R Holes is therefore not a complete double circle but a double arc incomplete around its southwestern half, where it either formed a single circle of standing stones (some of them in sockets later re-used in Stage 4), or remained largely open (Parker Pearson 2012: 169). Such a setting, in either form, would have been most prominent in its northeast quadrant, emphasising the northeast entrance of both the bluestone and sarsen structures, especially when viewed and approached from the northeast.

In Stage 3 (beginning in *2400–2220 cal BC* and ending in *2300–2105 cal BC*; see Table 11.7), the sarsen uprights remained in place as did the Q and R Hole bluestones, but the great trilithon and a few bluestones just beyond it were disturbed by the digging-out of a large, ramped pit (*c.* 8m northwest–southeast × 3m southwest–northeast) to a depth of 2.40m at the inside foot of the great trilithon (Parker Pearson *et al.* 2007: 623–6; Parker Pearson 2012: 128–32, 310). Another setting of bluestones might well have been introduced at this time, as indicated by an arc of five bluestone-sized sockets (Figure 4.8; Cleal *et al.* 1995: 207–9, fig. 109: WA 3402, WA 3702, WA 3700, WA 3286 and WA 3285). It is possible that this arc of small

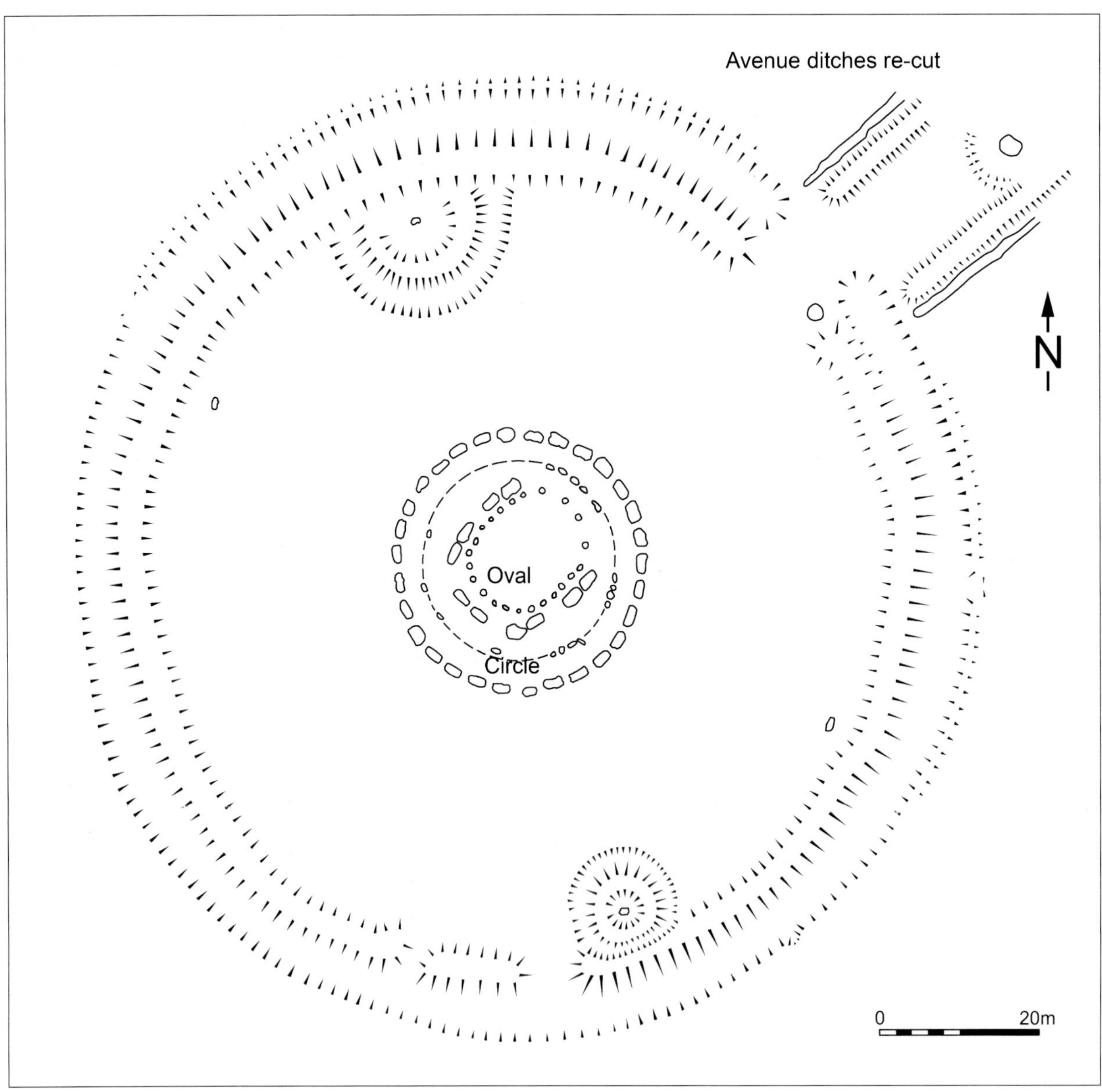

Figure 4.9. Plan of Stonehenge Stage 4 showing the circle of bluestones encircling the sarsen trilithons, and an oval of bluestones within the trilithon horseshoe

stones formed part of a *c.* 10m-diameter circle of standing bluestones within the centre of Stonehenge, positioned with the mid-points of the stones *c.* 1.30m apart.

In Stage 4 (beginning in *2210–2030 cal BC* and ending in *2155–1920 cal BC*), the bluestones in the Q and R Holes and in the central circle were taken down and rearranged as a ring of bluestones encircling the sarsen trilithons, and an oval of bluestones within the trilithon horseshoe, settings in which many of the bluestones still stand today (Figure 4.9). The inner oval is likely to have consisted of 23 standing stones (Cleal *et al.* 1995: fig. 116). Six of these in the northeast sector of the oval setting were subsequently taken down at some unknown period, to leave an arrangement of a 'horseshoe' of bluestones that mimics the plan and orientation of the much earlier sarsen trilithon horseshoe (Figure 4.2).

An oval is the currently accepted interpretation for the central arrangement of bluestones in Stage 4. However, there has to be some doubt as to whether the four empty sockets in the northeast are indeed the remnants of an oval formation. Whilst the stones of the bluestone horseshoe form a symmetrical and regular setting, the four sockets forming the oval's putative northeast end are more irregular in their positioning. A fifth stonehole is not in line with the curve of the four.

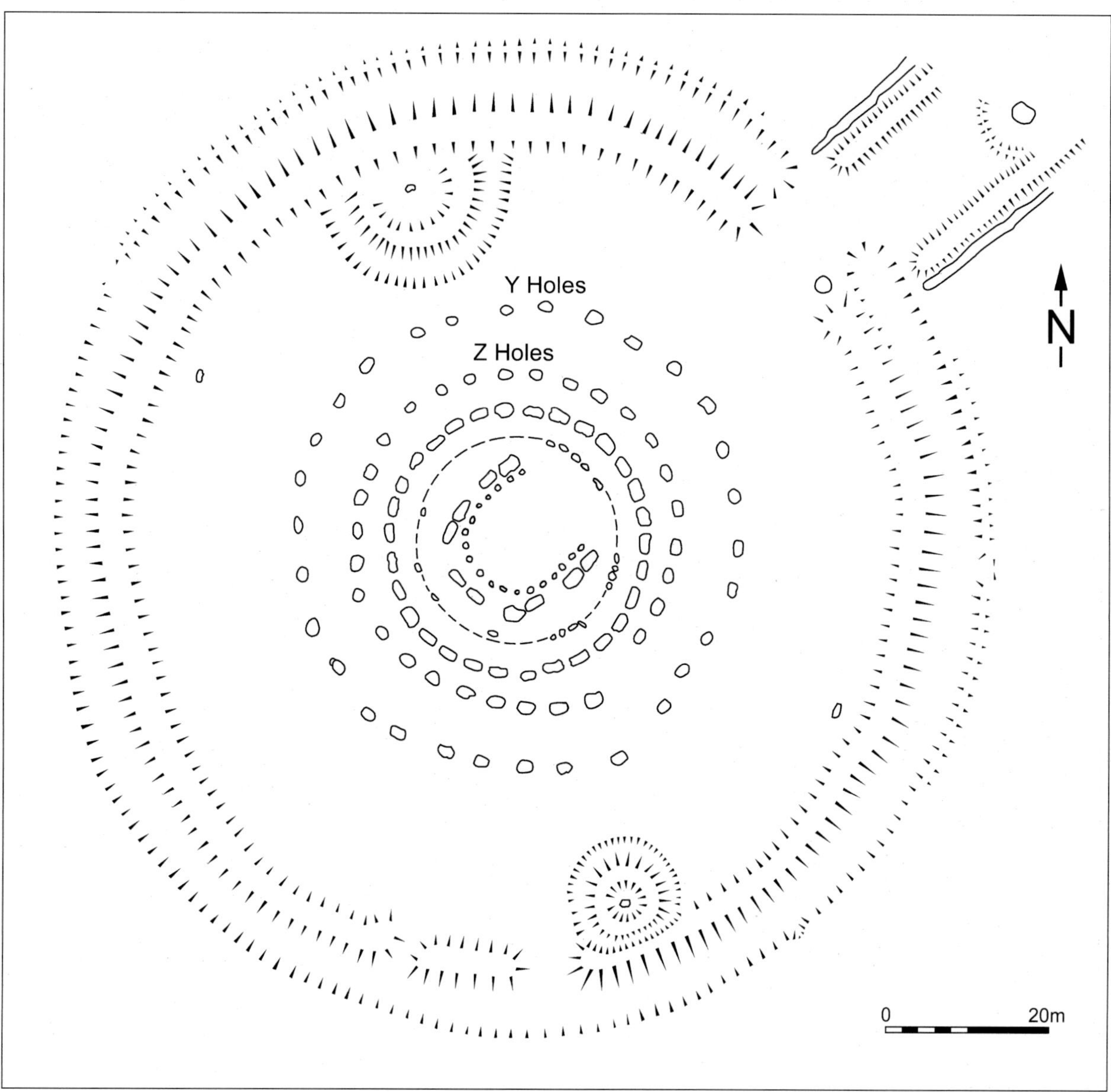

Figure 4.10. Plan of Stonehenge Stage 5 showing the Y and Z Holes and the horseshoe of bluestones within the trilithon horseshoe

Some of the surviving bluestones of the inner horseshoe and the outer ring have been carefully dressed, showing evidence of mortise and tenon joints (see *Dressing of the bluestones*, below).

In Stage 5 (beginning in *1980–1745 cal BC* and ending in *1620–1465 cal BC*), there is no evidence of any alterations to the stone settings. Instead, structural changes consisted of the digging-out of two concentric circles of sub-rectangular pits (the Y Holes and Z Holes, numbering 30 each), positioned outside the sarsen circle (Figure 4.10). Thirty-three of these were excavated by Hawley in 1923 and 1924 and one Y Hole and one Z Hole were excavated by Atkinson, Piggott and Stone in 1953. These pits' relatively small sizes make them appropriate as sockets for bluestones rather than for sarsens but they never held monoliths (however, for the argument that they did contain standing stones, see Richards 2013: 20–2). Atkinson noted that nine of the 18 excavated Y Holes and 14 of the 17 excavated Z Holes contained 'a fragment or two of bluestone (almost always rhyolite) on the very bottom' and thought that these may have been 'propitiatory token offerings, made as symbolic substitutes for the bluestones themselves' (1979: 84).

After Stage 5, the monument endured millennia of disrepair, dereliction and dismantling; many bluestones were pulled down, broken up and taken away. One of

Figure 4.11. Photogrammetric images of the bluestone erroneously attributed to Boles Barrow

those removed from the site, presumably in the post-medieval period, is the spotted dolerite bluestone stump now in Salisbury Museum, hitherto wrongly identified as having come from Boles Barrow, an Early Neolithic long barrow nine miles west of Stonehenge excavated by William Cunnington in 1801.

Part of this Salisbury Museum bluestone has been extensively worked down with metal tools (Figure 4.11), in the manner common at Stonehenge in the early modern period when visitors took away chippings as souvenirs. Furthermore, the 'Blue hard Stone' reported from Boles Barrow by Cunnington is in any case described as having been a much smaller stone (under 200lbs or 90kg) than the Salisbury Museum bluestone, estimated to weigh 611kg (Pitts 2000: 200). The Museum bluestone thus cannot be the Boles Barrow stone: it is not only too big but has been systematically worked by metal tools. Just what has happened to Cunnington's 'Blue hard Stone' is unknown. Whether it really was a piece of Preseli dolerite or rhyolite has to remain uncertain, although Cunnington seems to have known what he was talking about. As Pitts observes, Cunnington's report 'need refer to nothing more than a fragment of stone axe' (*ibid.*: 201). Just possibly the Boles Barrow stone survives buried in Cunnington's garden at Heytesbury, awaiting rediscovery.

4.1.3. Dressing of the bluestones

Whereas all of Stonehenge's sarsen stones reveal evidence of stone-dressing except for the Heel Stone (Stone 96) and a Station Stone (Stone 91), most of the 44 surviving bluestones are not dressed. Those that are dressed are the Altar Stone (Stone 80), Stones 36, 45 and 150 in the outer circle and the 14 surviving stones of the bluestone horseshoe at the centre of the monument: Stones 61–72, 61a, 70a and 70b. Stone 71, which is hidden beneath Stone 59 (a collapsed trilithon upright), and Stone 72 are apparently fragments from the same pillar (Atkinson 1956: 42).

These 14 include the majority of Stonehenge's taller and more elegant bluestones. All are of spotted dolerite except for Stone 62 which is of unspotted dolerite (Figure 4.2). In contrast, only three of 29 surviving stones in the outer bluestone circle are dressed: two lintels which had been reused as uprights, but now collapsed (Stones 36 and 150, both of which are of spotted dolerite), and Stone 45 (of unspotted dolerite; Abbott and Anderson-Whymark 2012: 24–5).

Four dressed bluestones from the bluestone horseshoe – Stones 67, 69, 70 and 72 – were formerly topped by tenons which have been removed by later pick dressing. Together with Stones 66 and 68, which have finely dressed tongue-and-groove joints down one side (Figure 4.1), these four uprights and the two bluestone lintels (36 and 150) may be remnants of a series of carefully dressed trilithon settings, possibly erected in Stage 2 or even within another monument altogether.

Since the method of fine transverse tooling found on the bluestones is also a feature of the sarsen trilithons (but not the sarsen circle except for Stone 122; Abbott and Anderson-Whymark 2012: 20), these bluestones may well have been dressed at the same time as the sarsen trilithons, presumably when these were erected in Stage 2.

The spacings of the mortise holes in Stones 36 and 150 indicate that the distances between the mid-points of the tenon-topped uprights on which they were once positioned as lintels would have been about 1m and 1.20m respectively. This raises some interesting points about where the dressed bluestones might originally have been located:

- These lintels are too short to have spanned Stonehenge's northeast-facing entrance through the Q and R Holes in Stage 2.
- Intriguingly, the span of Stone 150's mortise holes would have suited the 1.16m average mid-point of the uprights of the 10m-diameter stone circle of Bluestonehenge at West Amesbury (see Chapter 5). However, the total absence of bluestone debris from that monument beside the River Avon counts against such an interpretation unless these bluestones had already been dressed somewhere else entirely.
- Alternatively, the stones of the bluestone horseshoe were dressed when arranged into the 10m-diameter circle, with appropriately spaced mid-points, thought to have been erected within the centre of Stonehenge in Stage 3 (Figure 4.8). As suggested in Chapter 5, this circle could have been constructed using the stones of Bluestonehenge, dismantled from their original setting beside the Avon and transported into Stonehenge for re-erection there.

4.1.4. Bluestones elsewhere in the Stonehenge landscape

There is no doubt that the greatest concentration of bluestone fragments in England is at Stonehenge, mostly from inside the monument. Four small fragments of bluestone have been found in the Avebury area but all are from unstratified contexts (Ros Cleal pers. comm.). There is therefore no certainty that bluestones were ever taken to this area, 18 miles north of Stonehenge, in prehistory.

There is a handful of preselite (spotted dolerite) ground-stone artefacts from various locations in southern England (Williams-Thorpe *et al.* 2006); a good case can be made for many or even all of the latter being made of rough-outs hewn at some time in the Bronze Age from the bluestones standing at Stonehenge, during Stonehenge's Stage 5 when the monument was used as a stone quarry (Darvill and Wainwright 2009; Darvill *et al.* 2012).

Within the environs of Stonehenge, bluestone fragments have a scattered distribution (Figure 4.12). For example, few were found during excavations for the old visitors' car park in 1935 or 1967 (Vatcher and Vatcher 1973), although as many as 89 were found about 100m north of Stonehenge during the SRP's 2008 excavations (counting only those from stratified contexts, these number 18 from Trench 44 north of Stonehenge and 43 from Trench 45 on the Avenue; see Chapters 6 and 8 and Volume 2).

Beyond the immediate vicinity of Stonehenge (see Figure 1.3), there are minor concentrations and occasional finds of bluestone fragments:

- flakes and fragments of Group C rhyolite (Ixer and Bevins 2011) from within and around Fargo Plantation (south of the western end of the Greater Cursus; Stone 1947) and a fragment of Lower Palaeozoic sandstone (Ixer *et al.* 2017) from the southern ditch of the Greater Cursus (*ibid.*);
- two flakes and a fragment of spotted dolerite from beneath the Beaker-period earthwork of North Kite (Richards 1990: 185);
- a fragment of spotted dolerite from a flint scatter on Wilsford Down (Richards 1990: table 131);
- a flake of spotted dolerite from the surface in the Stonehenge Triangle (Richards 1990: table 131);
- a fragment of rhyolite from Fargo henge, south of the Greater Cursus (Stone 1938);
- multiple 'bluestones' from the fills of three round barrows: Winterbourne Stoke G28 (42 pieces), Amesbury G4 (16 pieces) and Amesbury G45 (30 pieces; Stone 1947);
- a rhyolite flake from the henge on Coneybury Hill (Richards 1990: table 131);
- three rhyolite artefacts from the lithic scatter north of the Greater Cursus (Richards 1990: 230–1, table 131);

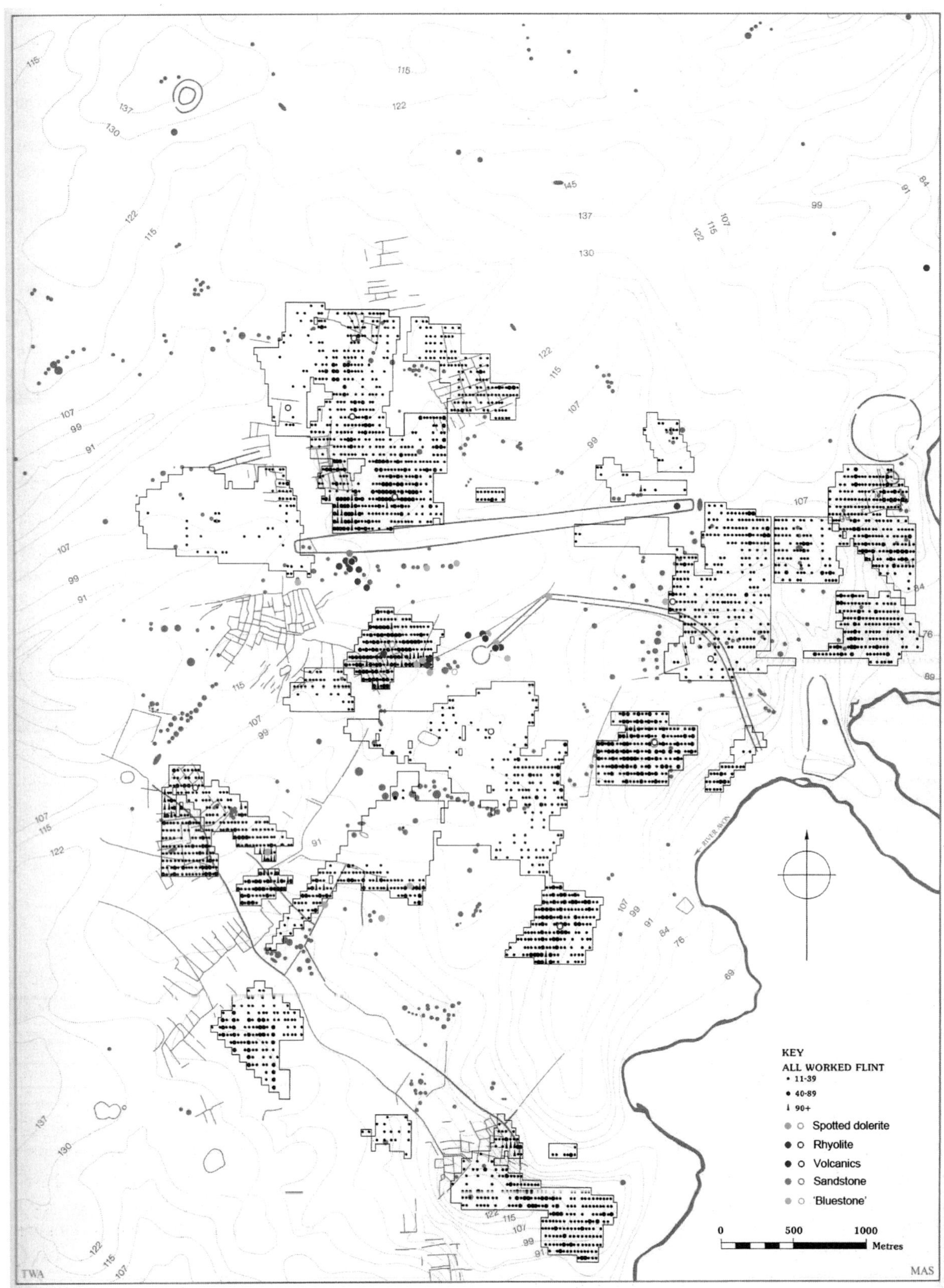

Figure 4.12. Map of bluestone fragments in the Stonehenge landscape; open circles indicate approximate locations (after Richards 1990); © Historic England

- a flake and a chip of rhyolite from a Neolithic flint scatter on King Barrow Ridge (Richards 1990: table 131);
- single flakes and tools of rhyolite from surface collection at a variety of locations within *c.* 2km of Stonehenge: The Diamond, Fargo Road, Horse Hospital, Spring Bottom, New King and Wood End (Richards 1990: table 131);
- a discoidal tool of Group C rhyolite from a Romano-British ditch northwest of Durrington village, *c.* 4km northeast of Stonehenge (Thompson and Powell 2018: 53–6).

In recent years, the identification by geophysical survey of a pit circle at Airman's Corner (west of the Greater Cursus; Wessex Archaeology 2009 and see below) and a pit circle beneath a round barrow south of the Greater Cursus (Gaffney *et al.* 2012) hints at the possibility that one or both of these could be dismantled bluestone circles.

4.2. Aubrey Hole 7 at Stonehenge

By M. Parker Pearson, C. Casswell, M. Pitts and J. Richards

4.2.1. Previous excavations

Aubrey Hole 7 (AH7; Figure 4.13) was excavated by Col. William Hawley on 5 March 1920. It contained a few cremated remains and a small quantity of wood ash within a fill of earthy chalk rubble and clean chalk rubble (Figure 4.14). Amongst the finds were a stone axe fragment, 29 mauls, sarsen flakes and bluestone chips, and prehistoric and Roman pottery. The pit is one of the larger Aubrey Holes; Hawley recorded its dimensions as a diameter of 1.35m and a depth of 0.91m (converted from feet and inches; Cleal *et al.* 1995: table 10)

It is highly likely that AH7 was backfilled by Hawley with its original pit fill. It was re-excavated in 1935 (see below), at which time a 'finely worked flint point, missed in the previous excavation' was found (Young 1935: 20). Young also tells us (*ibid.*: 21) that Hawley's assistant Robert Newall took the flint artefact 'in order to place it in the museum along with the other finds from this hole', presumably referring to Hawley's earlier discoveries from AH7 now in Salisbury Museum. Young's description of the object fits the 'unfinished arrowhead or knife' recorded by Phil Harding in that assemblage (in Cleal *et al.* 1995: 371, 375, fig. 202.18).

During his excavations at Stonehenge from 1919 to 1926, Hawley discovered many deposits of cremated human remains. Most of the Aubrey Holes excavated by Hawley contained cremated bone and there are also records of cremated bone from at least 11 separate locations within the Stonehenge ditch. On the basis of Hawley's excavation diary, these are estimated to total 58 cremation deposits (this differs from a slightly lower number of 52 estimated by McKinley in Cleal *et al.* 1995: 451). Unfortunately, the archaeological potential of human cremation burials was not appreciated at the time of excavation and nearly all the cremated bones from Stonehenge were re-buried in AH7 in 1935.

In 1935 William Young, curator of the Alexander Keiller Museum at Avebury, was excavating at Stonehenge during the building of a car park immediately north of the monument (Cleal *et al.* 1995: figs 21, 24) and Robert Newall, who had been Hawley's assistant, was looking for somewhere to dispose of the cremated remains. Newall had been storing them and other Stonehenge finds at his home. Whilst most of these other finds were sent to Salisbury Museum (with small sets donated to the Ashmolean Museum, the British Museum, the National Museum of Wales and the Museum of Archaeology and Anthropology in Cambridge), no museum was interested in curating the cremated bones. As Newall wrote in 1934, 'at present I have the bones in my loft as the museum had no room for them' (1934, unpublished letter, Public Record Office WORK 14/2463; see also Chippindale 1994: 194). Newall attempted to interest Sir Arthur Keith, the leading anatomist of his day, in analysing the bones but there is no record in Keith's diaries that he ever saw them (Chippindale 1994: 285, n. 41). In any case, there was little appreciation at this time of the value of studying cremated remains for investigating past populations and their lifestyles.

On 28 January 1935, according to Young's diary, he and Newall buried four sandbags filled with Hawley's excavated material in the bottom of AH7. These were accompanied by 'a stout leaden plate, which bore an inscription recording at length all the circumstances which led to their being deposited here, and the date' (Young 1935: 21). Just why they chose to re-open this Aubrey Hole rather than any other is not known, although its large size and proximity to the road might have been factors. There is a photograph of Young in the pit (Figure 4.15) but Young and Newall unfortunately made no record of how the cremated bones were placed in the pit.

Although Chippindale concluded from Young's diary and Ministry of Works documents in the Public Record Office that it was the animal bones that had been re-buried in Aubrey Hole 7 and that the cremated bones were disposed of elsewhere (1994: 194, 285, n. 41), more recent appraisal correctly rejected this interpretation (Gardiner in Cleal *et al.* 1995: 348; Serjeantson in Cleal *et al.* 1995: 438).

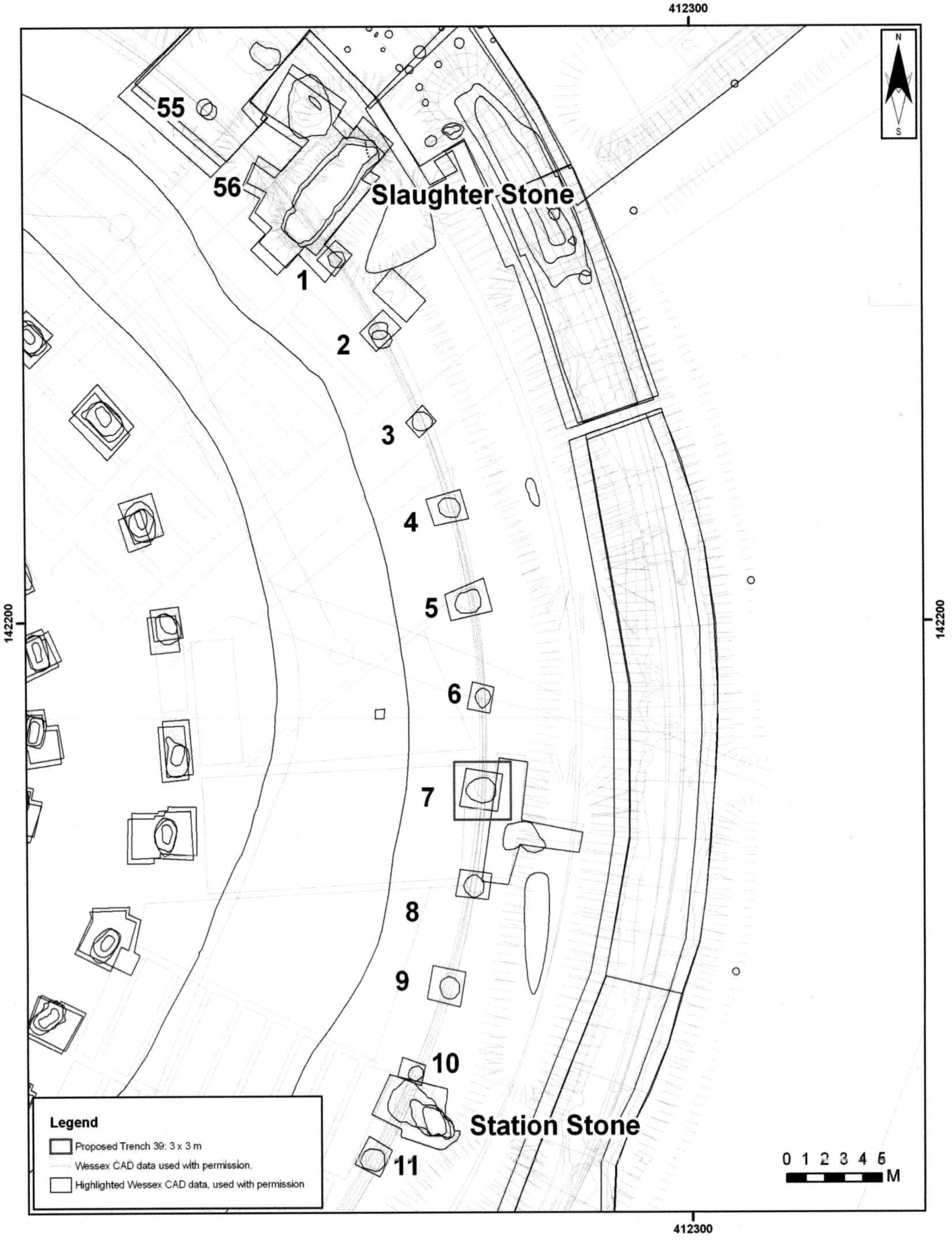

Figure 4.13. Location plan of Trench 39 over Aubrey Hole 7 within Stonehenge

4.2.2. Research background and objectives

There are relatively few human remains in Britain dated to the Late Neolithic (*c.* 3000–2450 BC), a period when the rite of inhumation burial seems, by and large, not to have been practised (Healy 2012: 148–52). Among rare exceptions of inhumations from within the period 3000–2450 BC are a child from Flagstones, Dorchester, Dorset (Healy 1997), an adult from Winterborne Monkton, Dorset (Parker Pearson *et al.* 2018), an adult male from North End Pot, North Yorkshire (Leech 2015: 29–38), and an adult female from Imperial College Sports Ground, Harlington (Powell *et al.* 2015).

In contrast to the very scarce inhumation burials, cremation burials are known from a small but growing number of sites of Middle Neolithic (*c.* 3400–3000 BC) and Late Neolithic date. Stonehenge is the largest known single

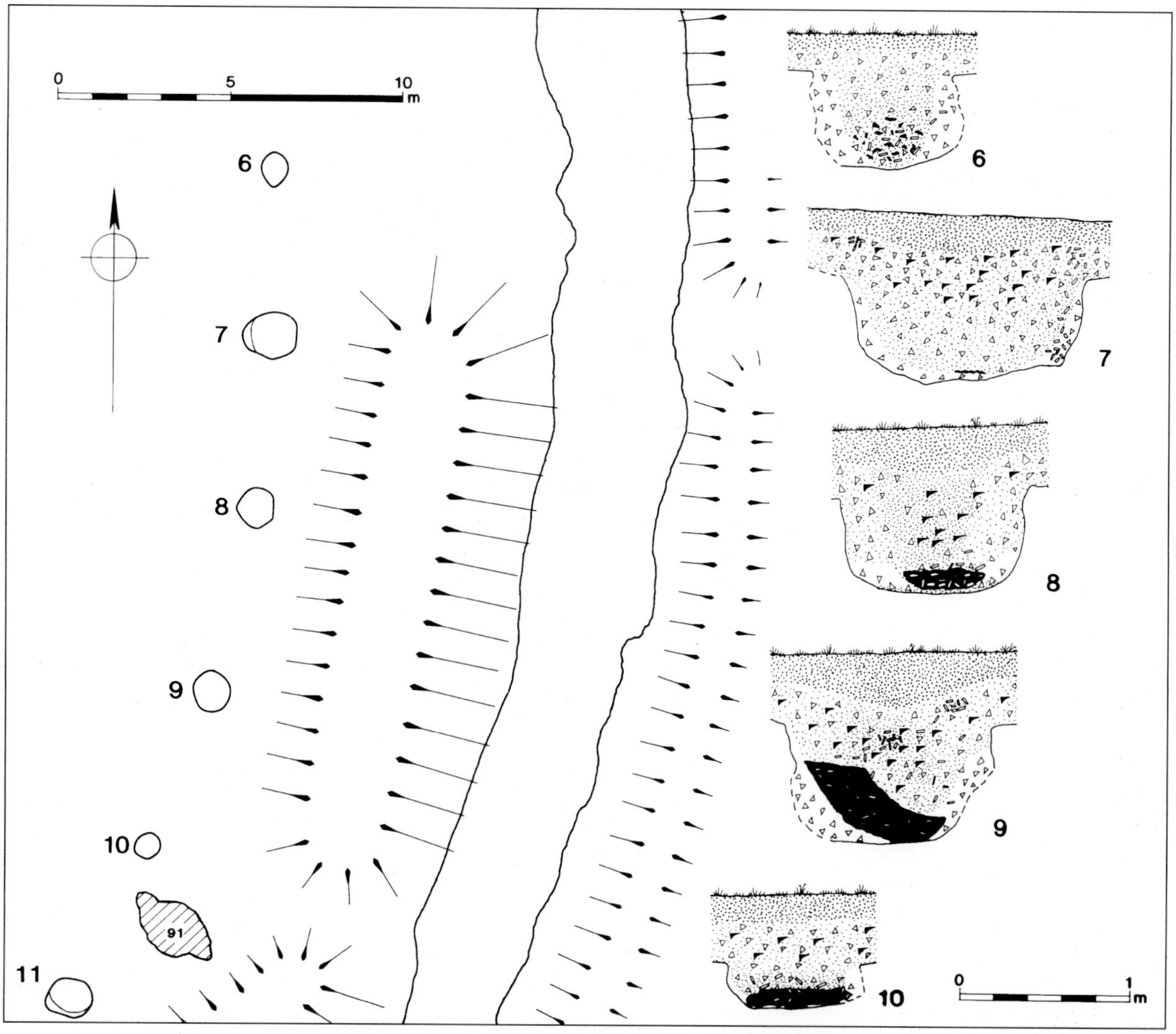

Figure 4.14. Hawley's section of Aubrey Hole 7 and adjacent Aubrey Holes (from Cleal *et al*. 1995); © Historic England

Figure 4.15. William Young re-excavating Aubrey Hole 7 on 28 January 1935. Although his excavation outfit is very different from the sartorial conventions of today's archaeologists, Young digs with a pointing trowel of a form that remains unchanged

cemetery enclosure from this period. Extrapolating from the numbers of cremation burials found during all excavations to date – and remembering that half of the Stonehenge enclosure has never been excavated – it has been estimated that a possible total for all cremation burials within Stonehenge is about 240 (Pitts 2000: 121). The re-buried *c.* 58 cremation deposits from Hawley's excavations thus form less than a quarter of the estimated total expected to lie within the unexcavated parts of the monument.

Cremation burials from eight small enclosures within the Middle–Late Neolithic monument complex at Dorchester-on-Thames, Oxfordshire, collectively number over 100 (Atkinson *et al.* 1951; Noble *et al.* 2017: 235), although no single enclosure produced as many as the 58 from Stonehenge. The total estimate for Stonehenge's cremation burials is more than all of those combined from this group of small Dorchester-on-Thames cemeteries.

As summarised by Noble *et al.* (2017) and Willis (2020), Middle–Late Neolithic cremation burials have also been found at Llandegai (Houlder 1968; Lynch and Musson 2004; Willis 2020), Forteviot (Noble *et al.* 2017), Balbirnie (Gibson 2010a), Cairnpapple (Piggott 1948a; Noble *et al.* 2017: 234), Sarn-y-bryn-caled (Gibson 2010b), Duggleby Howe (Mortimer 1905; Gibson and Bayliss 2009; Gibson *et al.* 2011) and West Stow (West 1990; Willis 2020) (see Figure 1.1).

Within the Stonehenge World Heritage Site, human remains dating to the Late Neolithic (3000–2450 BC) are known from several sites other than Stonehenge (see Figure 1.3):

- Two cremation burials from a small penannular enclosure at Wilsford, 600m south of Winterbourne Stoke long barrow (see Figures 1.3 and 2.1), may be part of a small cemetery (Arup Atkins Joint Venture 2017b: 19–21). Cremated human bones from the two deposits have been dated to 2890–2620 cal BC at 95% probability (SUERC-70556; 4167±33 BP) and 2930–2870 cal BC at 95% probability (SUERC-70557; 4280±33 BP).
- Human bone from a cremation burial within posthole C14 at Woodhenge (Cunnington 1929: 29) is dated to 2580–2450 cal BC at 95% probability (OxA-19047; 3997±30 BP).
- As mentioned in Chapter 3, an unburnt human femur fragment dating to 2890–2670 cal BC at 95% probability (SUERC-75196; 4187±30 BP) was recovered from the western end of the Greater Cursus during the SRP excavations.
- An undated cremation from the secondary fill of the ditch of Coneybury henge (Richards 1990: 158) may be Late Neolithic on the basis of its stratigraphic position.
- A cremation burial dating to 2590–2460 cal BC at 95% probability (SUERC-49176; 4000±34 BP), lying on the bottom of a hollow and covered by flint-knapping waste, was excavated in advance of development on the northwest side of Durrington village, 1km northeast of Durrington Walls (Thompson and Powell 2018: 17–18).
- It is possible that two round mounds immediately south of Stonehenge (Amesbury G6 and Amesbury G7) and a third some 800m to the northwest (Amesbury G50) could lie on top of Dorchester-on-Thames-style enclosures that may be expected to contain small cremation cemeteries (Bowden *et al.* 2015: 35–6).

Dating of the burial sequence from the largest Late Neolithic cemetery in Britain

With so few cremation burials adequately dated from the Late Neolithic, the Stonehenge assemblage is the most important in Britain, regardless of the significance of the site itself. By 2008 – *i.e.* towards the end of the fieldwork phase of the Stonehenge Riverside Project – advances in radiocarbon dating of cremated bone (Lanting and Brindley 1998; Lanting *et al.* 2001) had made possible the dating of cremation burials. We obtained new radiocarbon determinations on three sets of Late Neolithic cremated remains from Stonehenge excavated by Richard Atkinson, one from AH32 and two from the fills of the enclosure ditch west of the northeast entrance (contexts 3893 and 3898 from Cuttings 41 and 42 respectively; Parker Pearson *et al.* 2009; see Chapter 11 and Table 11.4).

Prior to the radiocarbon dating, these cremation burials had been conventionally ascribed to Phase 2 (within the former Stonehenge chronology) by Cleal *et al.* (1995) but their range of dates across the first half of the third millennium BC has revealed that burials at Stonehenge began in Stage 1 of the new chronology and probably continued into Stage 2.

The SRP research design for 2008 argued that if the assemblage buried in AH7 in 1935 could be recovered, it would provide an important opportunity to examine a large group of Late Neolithic individuals from a period when funerary rites by and large left no traces in the archaeological record. Permission to open AH7 and retrieve the cremated remains was granted by English Heritage and the Ministry of Justice; the full circumstances of this excavation, including pagan objections to it, are recounted in Parker Pearson (2012).

Age, sex and physical aspects of the people buried at Stonehenge

At the time of writing the research design for the 2008 excavations, the only complete cremation burial available for study from Stonehenge was that of a woman aged about 25 from context 3898 in the Stonehenge ditch (McKinley 1995: 456). Some further small fragments of cremated remains from twentieth-century excavations at Stonehenge were curated by Salisbury Museum (including those from AH32). As described above, the recovery and analysis of the assemblage of cremated remains reburied in AH7 would be an important step for advancing our knowledge of age and sex differences among the people buried at Stonehenge. The osteological analysis of the AH7 cremated remains appears in Chapter 10.

Possible evidence for trauma and pathology

Although evidence of trauma and pathology is harder to identify on cremated bones as opposed to unburnt bones, the research design proposed that the Stonehenge cremated remains might produce significant results (see Chapter 10). Recent surveys of the evidence for violence in the British Neolithic indicate that incidences of injury are common (Mercer 1999; Parker Pearson and Thorpe 2005; Schulting and Wysocki 2005; Schulting 2012). At Stonehenge, for example, an adult male buried in the ditch in Beaker style during the late third millennium cal BC had been shot at least three times (Evans 1984; Pitts 2000: 112), whilst a Late Neolithic human femur found by the Stonehenge Riverside Project in 2004 at Durrington Walls has two projectile impact marks (Parker Pearson *et al.* 2007; see Volume 3).

The Aubrey Holes as settings for the first bluestones at Stonehenge

As discussed at the beginning of this chapter, there has been disagreement and confusion about whether the Aubrey Holes were postholes, sockets for standing stones, or merely open pits. An important research objective was, therefore, to examine and record Aubrey Hole 7 and its fills to modern standards.

4.2.3. The 2008 excavation

A 3m × 3m trench was excavated around Aubrey Hole 7 between 26 August–1 September 2008 (Figure 4.16).[3] A sequence of layers filled the pit (Figure 4.17). Beneath the topsoil (001), a circular concrete slab[4] sat on top of a circular rubble spread (002) at the centre of which was a vertically-set 6” nail, presumably placed to mark the centre of the Aubrey Hole. Three shards of modern glass were recovered from layer 002.

Layer 002 was laid within a larger circular deposit of brown loam (003) which constituted the turf-mixed upper part of the backfill of the 1935 re-excavation. This deposit lay within the upper part of the pit (024) dug in 1935 into a mixed matrix of brown loam and eroded chalk (004), a layer formed from the weathered surface of the chalk bedrock. Layer 004 contained a sherd of blue-on-white porcelain. Beneath layer 004 was a more solid layer of brown loam, chalk lumps and pea grit (013; this is equated with 009, a limited spread east of the Aubrey Hole) that lay over the solid chalk bedrock (025).

The upper backfill layer (003) was artificially divided for recording purposes into layer 005 for its top 0.15m and layer 006 for the lower 0.60m. At the base of layer 006 a lead plaque was revealed, positioned horizontally and centrally within the pit with its upper edge to the northeast (Figure 4.18). The plate is, of course, that described by Young (1935: 21) and its text reads:

> MOST OF THESE BONES WERE DUG UP IN THE YEARS 1921 1922 1923 FROM THOSE HOLES JUST INSIDE THE BANK OF THIS MONUMENT AND CALLED AUBREY HOLES BY THE SOCIETY OF ANTIQUARIES OF LONDON IN CONNECTION WITH HIS MAJESTYS OFFICE OF WORKS SOME BONES WERE FOUND IN THE DITCH THE HOLES WERE CALLED AFTER AUBREY BECAUSE HE SUGGESTED THEIR EXISTANCE [*sic*] IN THE YEAR 1666 REBURIED 1935

Among the finds from this backfill (006) were an oblique flint arrowhead (SF 1003), a few flint flakes, a rim sherd of Roman pottery, two conjoining sherds of medieval green-glazed pottery, a clay pipe stem and three shards of modern glass.

Layer 003 (divided into 005 and 006) lay over the main layer of brown chalk–loam backfill within the 1935 cut (024) into the Aubrey Hole. The top layer of cremated bones lay below layer 006 within a mixed deposit of chalk, soil and cremated bone fragments (layer 100), less than 0.05m thick (Figure 4.19). Where the plaque had lain, the bones underneath had been kept clean of soil, thereby leaving a small rectangular area 0.21m × 0.12m devoid of this mixed horizon.

There was no trace of any of the four sandbags in which the bones were supposed to have been deposited. We expected these hessian sandbags (woven from jute or possibly sisal) to have decayed after 70 years, but it was thought possible that the AH7 bone deposit might exhibit sandbag-shaped outlines either in plan or in section. No such outlines were, however, identifiable. Despite Young’s diary reference to placing the sandbags in the pit, the empirical evidence of the bones themselves indicates that they were poured into the pit, creating a single undifferentiated mass, with the deepest part towards the northeast side of the pit.

---

3 Note that the Aubrey Hole was one of several sites excavated by the SRP during the 2008 field season: the site code for the excavation is AH08, used in the paper archive, on finds bags and on samples submitted for radiocarbon dating. Throughout this monograph, however, the Aubrey Hole is described by its number (AH7). AH08 and AH7 therefore refer to the same site; AH08 occurs in the radiocarbon-dating models in Chapter 11.

4 The locations of all the Aubrey Holes are marked by such 20th-century slabs.

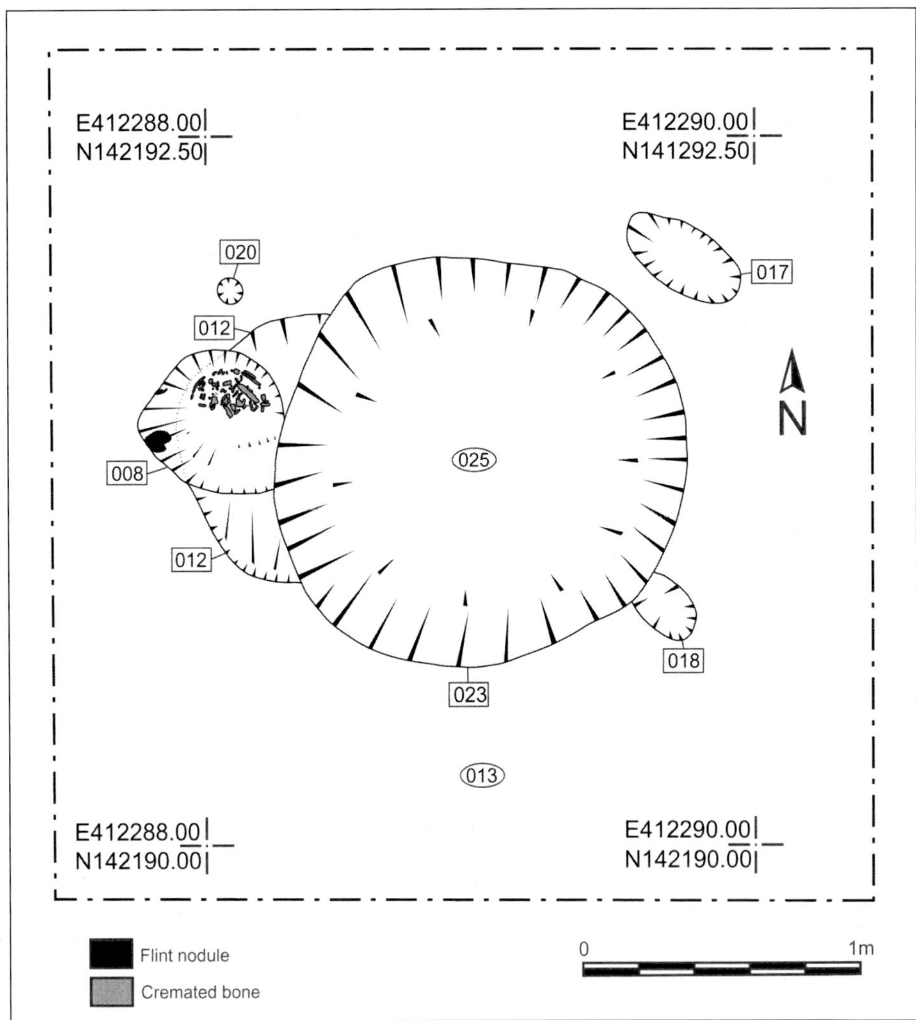

Figure 4.16. Plan of Trench 39 over Aubrey Hole 7

The mass of cremated bone could not, therefore, be excavated as distinct deposits or features. To ensure close spatial mapping of the bones within the undifferentiated deposit, the bone layer was excavated horizontally in 0.10m grid squares and vertically in a series of 50mm-deep spits (first spit, contexts 098–099 and 101–199; second spit, contexts 201–299 and 495–499; third spit, contexts 301–399 and 595–596; see Figures 10.6–10.8).

On reaching the bottom of the bone layer, it was clear that the previous excavations – Hawley in 1920 and Young and Newall in 1935 – had not succeeded in cleaning out the basal fills of the Aubrey Hole, and that the excavators' cut and/or re-cut (024) did not fully correspond with the original cut (023) of AH7. Two deposits remained unexcavated in the base of the pit: a thin layer of crushed chalk (022) and a deposit of hard-packed chalk lumps (021; see below; Figures 4.20–4.21).

Three features were found on the pit's edge (pit 008 cut by scoop 012 on the pit's west side, and scoop 018 on its southeast side) and two more (scoop 017 and stakehole 020) just beyond the limits of the AH7 pit on its northeast and northwest sides respectively.

The deposits remaining within the base of Aubrey Hole 7

The previous excavators failed to fully bottom AH7: within its base, there remained a thin patch of crushed chalk (022), extending 0.35m north–south × 0.40m east–west and up to 40mm thick (Figures 4.20–4.21). This was located within the southern and southwestern part of the pit. The chalk had clearly lost its structure here, due perhaps to the pressure of a stone having been set upright within this part of the pit. Alternatively, and perhaps more likely, the crushing might have resulted from Hawley or his colleagues standing in this location as they dug out the pit.

Most of the remainder of the Aubrey Hole's base was covered by a thin layer (021) of compacted chalk lumps, still *in situ* despite the two previous excavations. Layer 021 was up to 0.10m thick and extended in an arc 1.10m east–west and 0.55m north–south around layer 022. This

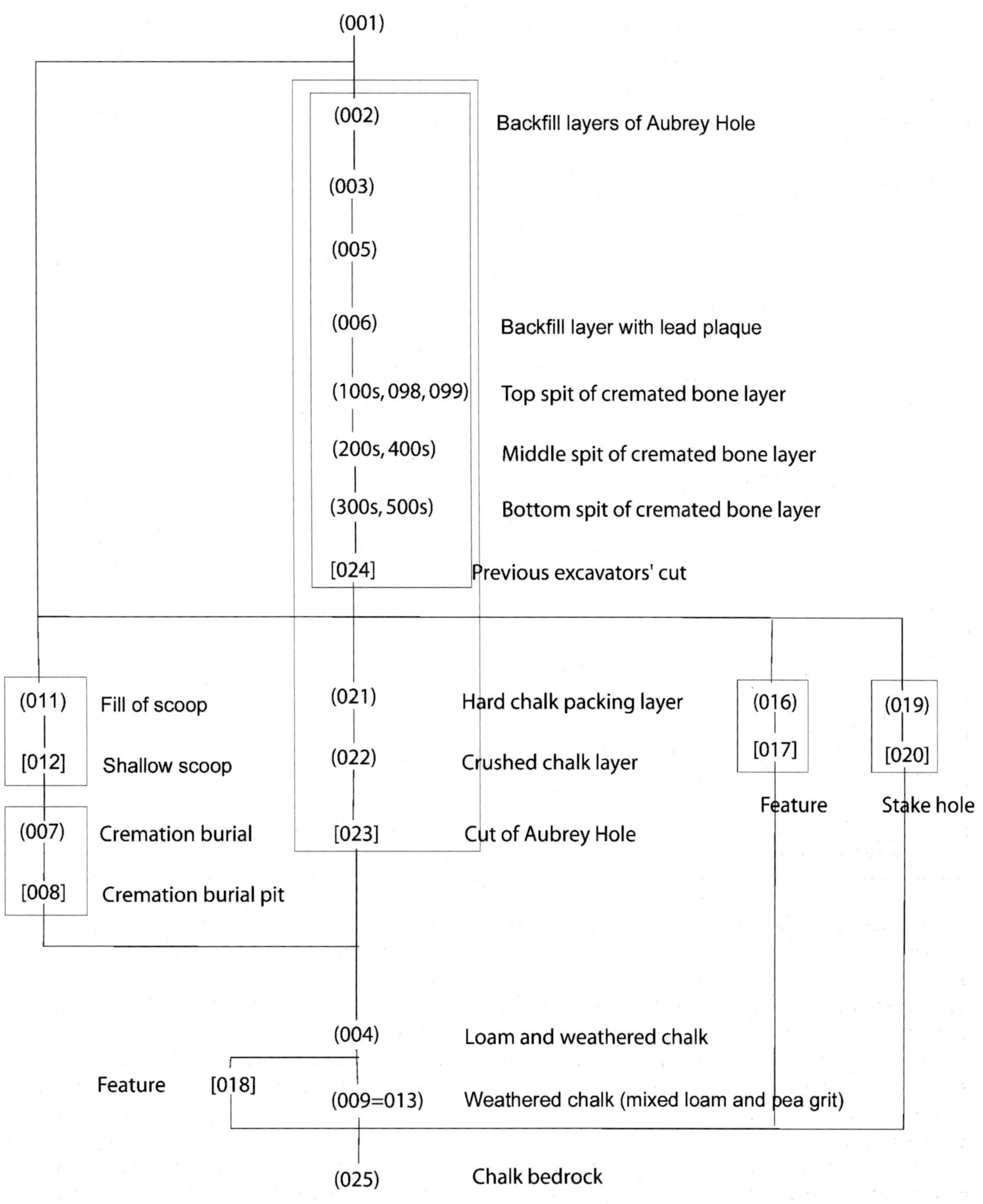

Figure 4.17. Stratigraphic matrix for Trench 39

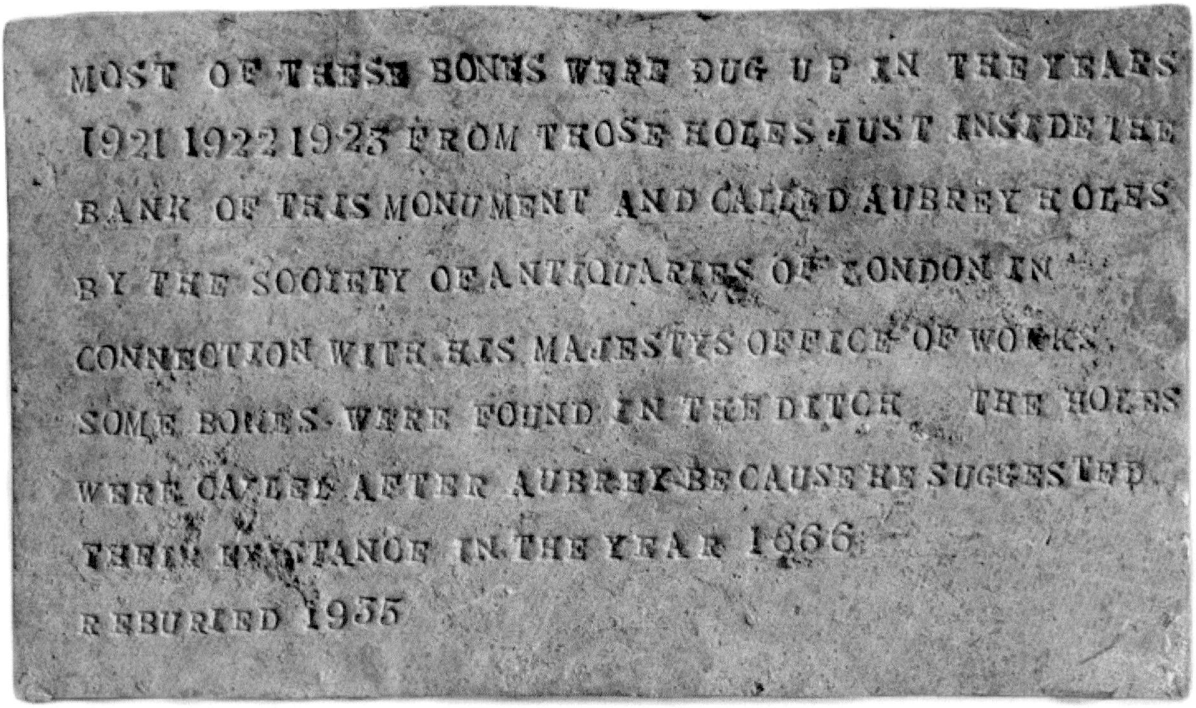

MOST OF THESE BONES WERE DUG UP IN THE YEARS
1921 1922 1923 FROM THOSE HOLES JUST INSIDE THE
BANK OF THIS MONUMENT AND CALLED AUBREY HOLES
BY THE SOCIETY OF ANTIQUARIES OF LONDON IN
CONNECTION WITH HIS MAJESTYS OFFICE OF WORKS.
SOME BONES WERE FOUND IN THE DITCH. THE HOLES
WERE CALLED AFTER AUBREY BECAUSE HE SUGGESTED
THEIR EXISTANCE IN THE YEAR 1666.
REBURIED 1935

Figure 4.18. The lead plaque deposited by William Young and Robert Newall

Figure 4.19. Cremated bones in Aubrey Hole 7, viewed from the northwest. The rectangular patch of clean bone fragments at the lower left is where the lead plaque lay

Figure 4.20. Aubrey Hole 7 emptied of bones, viewed from the south, with unexcavated deposits *in situ* in the base of the pit on the lower left (022) and upper right (021)

layer of chalk lumps was deepest on the northern side of the pit and is interpreted as a basal layer of chalk packing that held a standing stone in place. It was sampled for soil micromorphological analysis (see below).

Fully excavated, AH7 was 0.52m deep on its south and west sides and 0.56m deep on its east and north sides (Figure 4.22).[5] Its diameter was 1.51m east–west × 1.42m north–south at the top of the pit and 1.07m east–west × 0.95m north–south at the bottom (Figure 4.21). The gentler angle of slope (*c.* 65°) on the west side (as opposed to *c.* 75° on the other sides) is consistent with Hawley's (1921: 30–1) observation that the Aubrey Holes once held standing stones which had been extracted via the sides of the pits that face the centre of Stonehenge, their removal causing that side to be slightly broken down.

The interpretation of Aubrey Hole 7 as a socket that once held a standing stone, previously suspected from Hawley's description of his excavations of the Aubrey Holes in general, is supported by our excavation. The limited width and thickness of any stone that once sat in AH7 rule out its having been a Stonehenge sarsen. Instead, the dimensions of this and other Aubrey Holes conform to those of known bluestone holes within the monument (notably the Q and R Holes of Stage 2, the stone sockets belonging to the final bluestone circle of Stage 4 and the sockets of the bluestone oval/horseshoe, also Stage 4). It is thus likely that the Aubrey Holes contained bluestones, arranged in an 87m-diameter circle within the encircling bank and ditch. This first stone setting at Stonehenge dates to Stage 1, broadly within the 30th century BC (Parker Pearson *et al.* 2009; Willis *et al.* 2016).

The cremation burial and other features on and around the edge of the Aubrey Hole

On the northwestern edge of AH7, a bowl-shaped pit (008; 0.50m north–south × >0.50m east–west × 0.20m deep) had been dug and filled with a mid-brown loam (007) containing an undisturbed cremation burial (Figure 4.23; see also Figures 10.32–10.33). It was covered by topsoil (001) and was cut through natural deposits (layers 004, 013 and 025). Its relationship with Aubrey Hole 7 (023) could not be established because of truncation by previous excavations. However, it is likely that the cremation pit post-dates the Aubrey Hole; in other words, the cremation burial was most likely placed here when the Aubrey Hole stone was already in place to form a focus for the deposition.

The cremated bones formed a circular deposit about 0.30m in diameter, with this circular edge being clearest on its north side where it stopped within about 20mm of the pit edge. This circular shape is most likely due to the bones having been deposited within an organic container, since decayed, presumably a leather bag or perhaps a cylindrical birchbark box.

5 Note that these measurements differ from Hawley's (Cleal *et al.* 1995: table 10). There are several possible explanations. Hawley measured from the ground surface (in 2008 just *c.* 0.10m above the top of the chalk bedrock). Hawley's section (Figure 4.14) shows a much greater depth of topsoil (*c.* 0.32m). One must also bear in mind that his measuring is unlikely to have been as accurate as in 2008. In addition, he may have measured the diameter from further down in the pit rather than at the top of the bedrock.

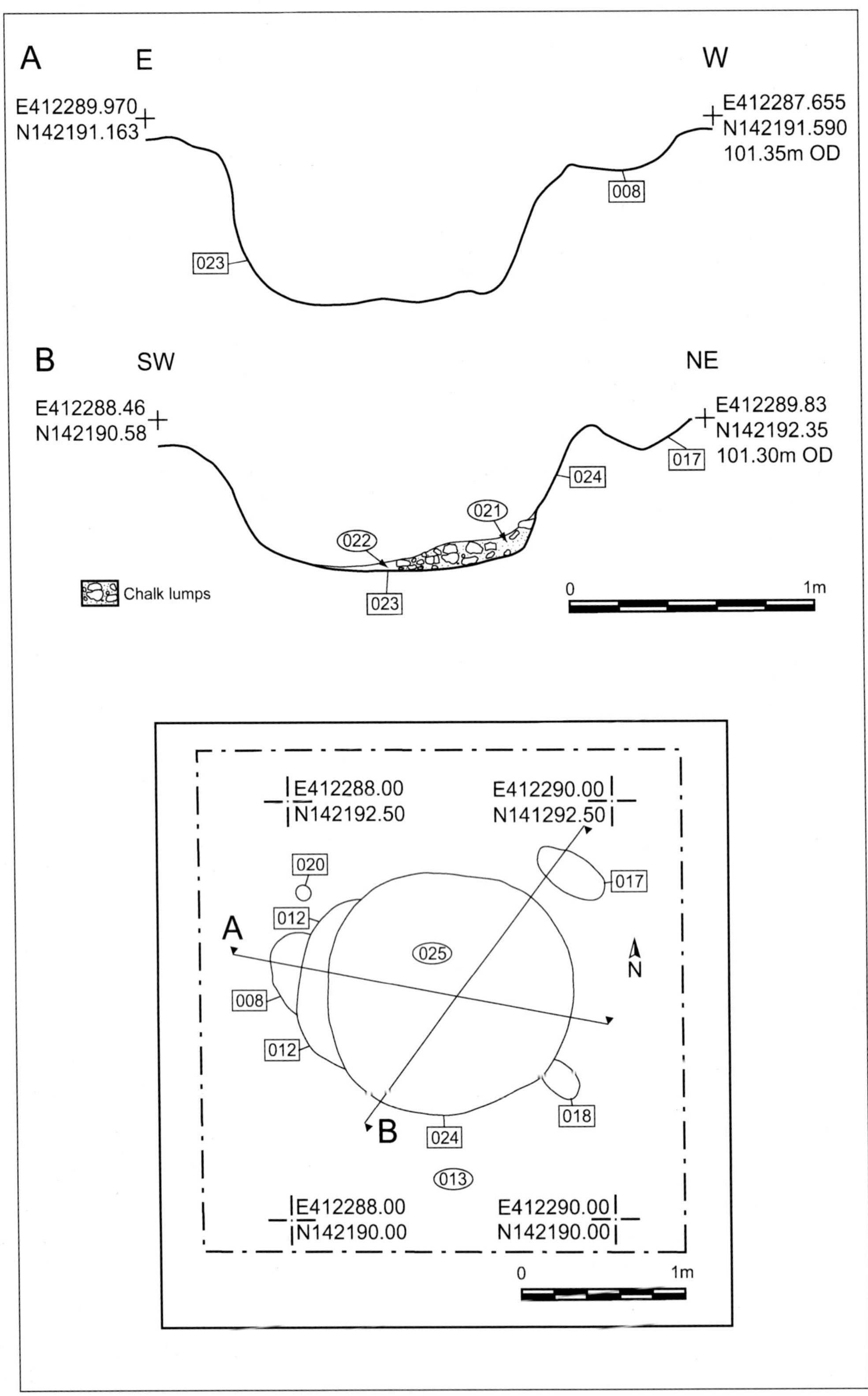

Figure 4.21. Profile of Aubrey Hole 7

Figure 4.22. Aubrey Hole 7 emptied, viewed from the south

Figure 4.23. Cremation burial 007 in half-section, viewed from the south

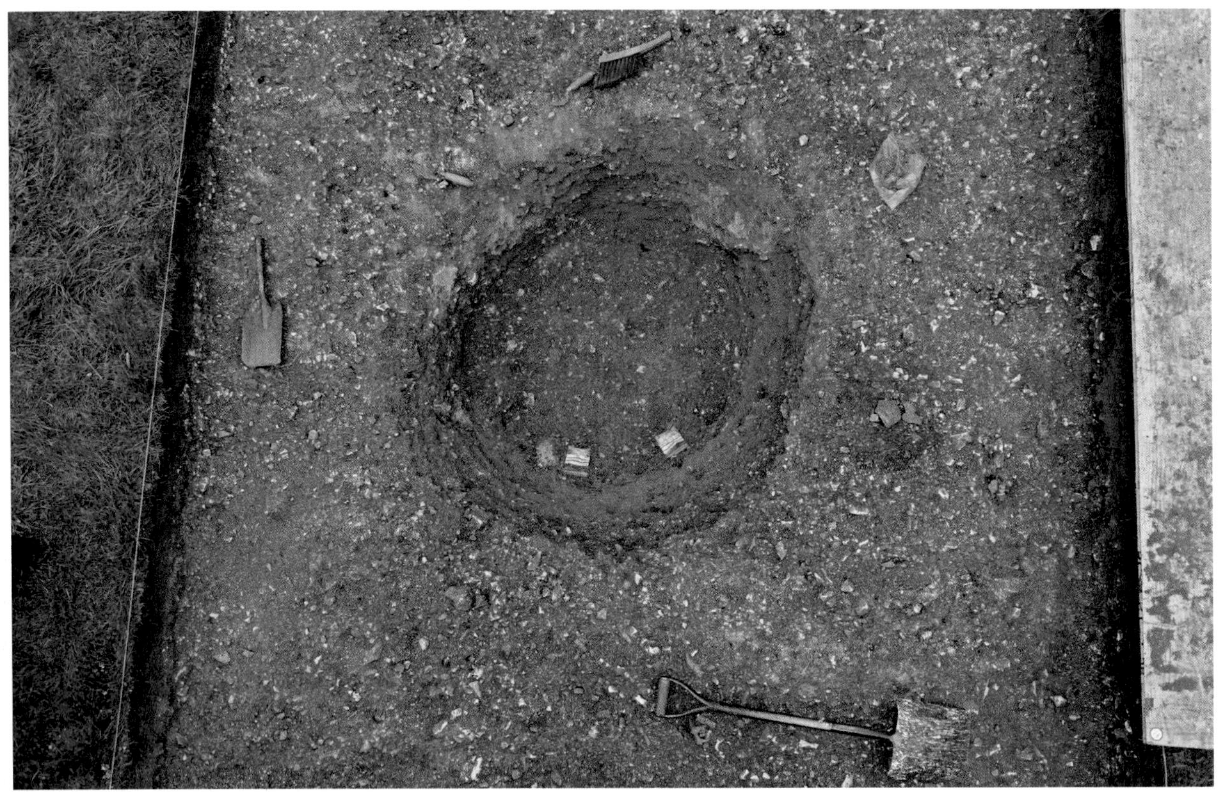

Figure 4.24. Aubrey Hole 7 under excavation, with north at the bottom of the picture. The sarsen flake on top of burial 007 lies immediately right of a frost-fractured flint nodule just beyond the lower right (northwest) side of Aubrey Hole 7

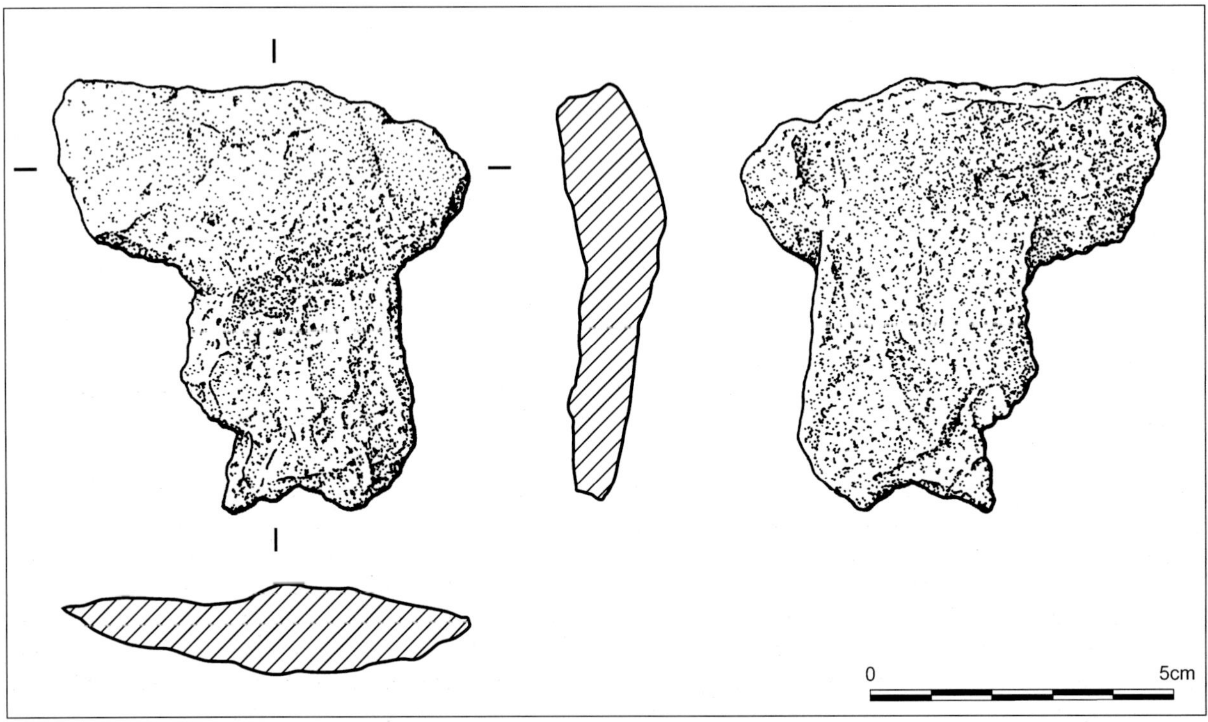

Figure 4.25. A sarsen flake from on top of cremation burial 007, beside Aubrey Hole 7

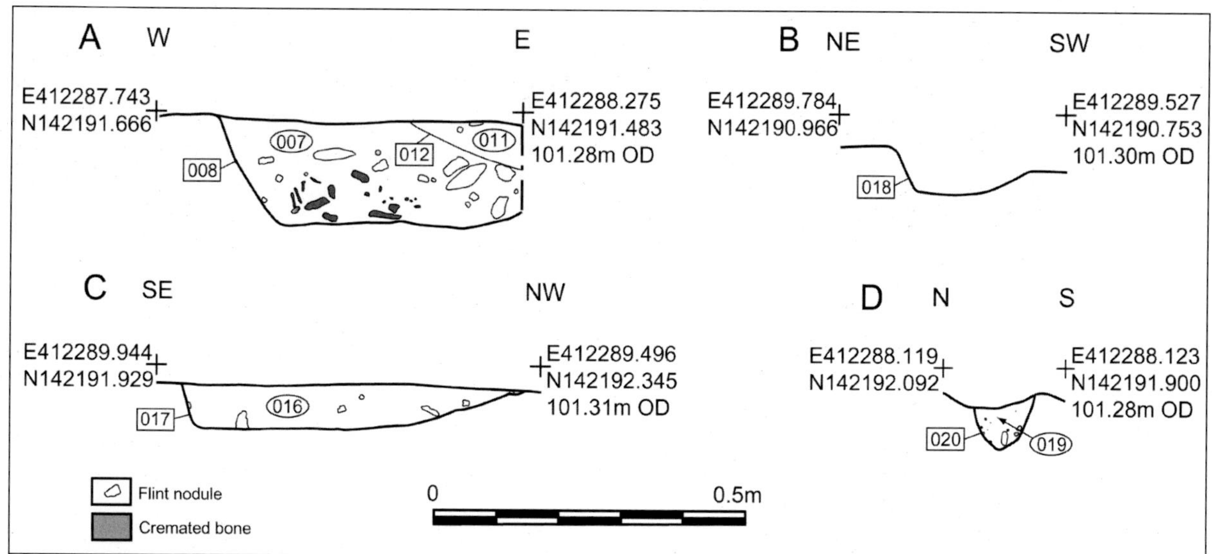

Figure 4.26. Section drawings of cremation burial 007 and other features in Trench 39

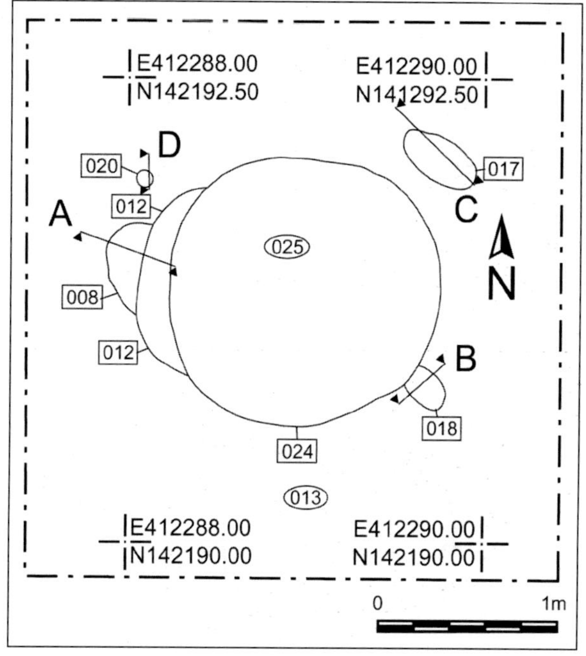

The bones were excavated within a grid of 0.10m × 0.10m squares in three 0.05m spits. On top of the bone deposit, there was a fist-sized sarsen flake beside a large frost-fractured but otherwise unmodified flint nodule (Figures 4.24–4.25). Whilst the size of this sarsen flake and its central location on top of the cremation deposit make it a likely accompaniment to the burial, three flint flakes from fill 007 (see below) are more likely to be accidental additions to this fill rather than grave goods or pyre goods.

Pit 008 was truncated on its east side by a shallow scoop (012), 1.00m north–south and 0.80m deep, filled with light to mid-brown loam (011). This shallow depression may be a product of Hawley's excavation but it could also have been created by the roots of a shrub. A single piece of cremated bone was found in layer 011 but this might have been displaced from layer 007.

On the southeast side of Aubrey Hole 7, there was a small depression (018; at least 0.22m northwest–southeast and 0.20m southwest–northeast, and 0.07m deep) filled with loam and chalk lumps (recorded as layer 004, the weathered chalk and loam above the bedrock). There was no cultural material within its fill but it might have been a feature connected with Hawley's diary observation that cremated remains were found within the southeast side of the pit from top to bottom.

Two other features were found beyond the edges of the AH7 pit (Figure 4.26). On the northeast side, a shallow feature (017; 0.46m northwest–southeast × 0.24m northeast–southwest by 0.07m deep) contained a light brown silt (016) without any cultural material. On the northwest side, there was a small, pointed stakehole (020), 0.10m in diameter and 0.10m deep, filled with brown loam (019). Neither of these features was spotted until layer 004 was removed.

A note on the soil micromorphology of the primary filling of Aubrey Hole 7

C.A.I. French

A soil block for micromorphological analysis was taken across the contact zone between the basal chalk rubble fill in Aubrey Hole 7 and the undisturbed chalk geology to ascertain whether the chalk had been subject to any compaction after it was dug/used in the past. Soil micromorphology methods are described briefly in Chapter 3 and in full in Volume 2.

The slide is completely comprised of pale greyish-white chalk rubble fragments over an *in situ* chalk substrate (Figure 4.27). The latter is characterised by a fine, 'wavy' crack structure (Figure 4.28), which is more frequent in the uppermost *c.* 20mm of the substrate. In both horizons and in the fine cracks, there is no intrusive soil material or organic matter present, rather only fine fragments of chalk in the voids towards the base of the primary fill.

The very 'clean' character of the primary fill and underlying chalk may suggest fast filling of the Aubrey Hole, almost immediately after its excavation. The zone of frequent fine cracking most probably reflects the zone of shear influence from the digging implement used and greater post-depositional weathering just below the cut surface of the chalk. Any association with compaction caused by use in the life of the Aubrey Hole cannot be substantiated by the micromorphological analysis.

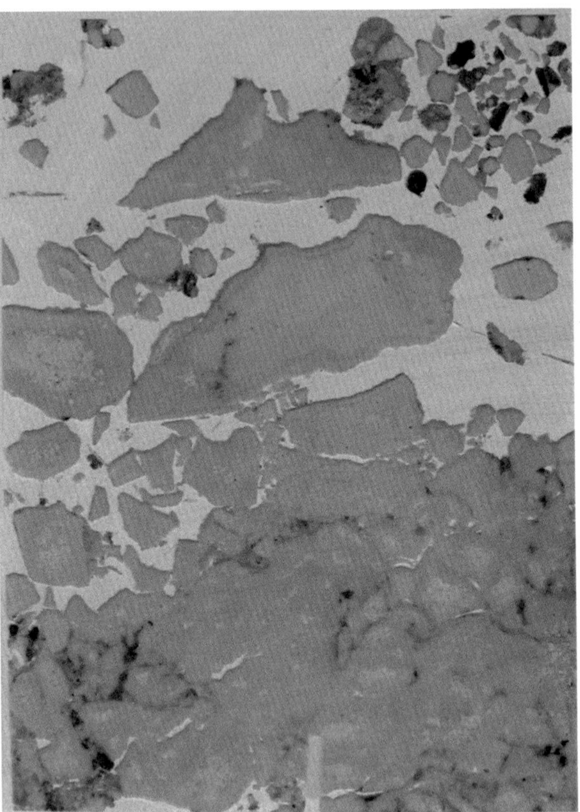

Figure 4.27. Full-size scan of the primary fill and underlying chalk substrate, Aubrey Hole 7 (*c.* 6 × 8.5cm slide dimensions; reflected light)

4.2.4. Conclusion

The absence of any clear contextual separation of the cremated bones deposited by Young and Newall in 1935 was disappointing but not disastrous. It has been possible to recover a reasonable MNI (minimum number of individuals) during the osteological analysis (see Chapter 10). Many of the bones are in excellent condition, despite having been in rather temporary storage for a lengthy period between the 1920s and 1935.

The discovery during the 2008 excavation of an undisturbed cremation burial on the lip of Aubrey Hole 7, clearly visible as soon as the topsoil was removed, was wholly unexpected since this area was supposedly fully excavated by William Hawley. Whilst this discovery provides a very important intact cremation burial to add to the three excavated by Atkinson, it also highlights the unexpectedly poor standards of excavation employed by twentieth-century excavators at Stonehenge.

On the positive side, the failure of Hawley (and later Young and Newall) to identify this feature bodes well for there being many more cremation burials surviving untouched within the extensive area excavated by Hawley. It is unlikely to have been the only one that he and his workmen did not spot. Consequently, the number of cremation burials known to have been excavated by Hawley is probably not the full total of cremation burials actually present in his excavated area. Since the total number of cremation burials present at Stonehenge in the entire monument is extrapolated from Hawley's sub-total, we should therefore regard such estimates for the total numbers of cremation burials (Pitts 2000: 121; Parker Pearson *et al.* 2009) as conservative estimates only.

Figure 4.28. Planar voids/cracks in the chalk substrate beneath Aubrey Hole 7 (frame width = 2cm; plane-polarised light)

Undoubtedly the most important conclusion from the re-excavation of Aubrey Hole 7 is the evidence of chalk packing, resulting from its use as a stonehole for holding a bluestone-sized stone. Since Aubrey Hole 32, excavated by Atkinson, has now been dated by the cremation burial in its primary fill to 3080–2890 cal BC (Parker Pearson *et al.* 2009), it is most likely that some or all of the bluestones were initially set up at Stonehenge in the Aubrey Holes between the end of the 31st and beginning of the 29th centuries cal BC (see Chapter 11).

4.2.5. Worked flint from Aubrey Hole 7

B. Chan

The assemblage from the excavation of Aubrey Hole 7 consists of 394 pieces of struck flint (Table 4.1). Nearly the entire assemblage was retrieved from modern backfill of the Aubrey Hole, with a small amount of worked flint also being found within the undisturbed fill of the small pit (008) containing a cremation burial adjacent to AH7.

Raw material and condition

All of the flint is chalk-derived and of local origin. The flint is patinated to varying degrees and is generally in good condition with a few individual artefacts being more heavily abraded.

Assemblage composition and contextual distribution

The AH7 worked flint assemblage is comparable to others from the area around Stonehenge. It is dominated by broad flakes, with the assemblage of cores all being flake cores (Table 4.1). In addition, it also includes a small number of blades and a few hammerstones, with the only tool being a poorly-worked oblique arrowhead found within context 006 (the lower part of the main backfill layer). The assemblage is relatively unremarkable but is technologically consistent with other Middle–Late Neolithic assemblages in the region.

Over 92% of the assemblage of worked flint was found within the backfilled layers of AH7. The material was found throughout all of the excavated spits and seems to have been randomly mixed in with the cremated bones. A small assemblage consisting of three flakes was found within fill 007 of the small cremation pit (008). The remaining artefacts were spread within the topsoil and the weathered layers of the chalk bedrock.

In addition to the worked flint, there are 44 pieces of unworked burnt flint, weighing 345g. All of the burnt flint was found within backfill deposits.

Discussion

The assemblage from Aubrey Hole 7 is relatively small and nearly entirely derived from backfill deposits. The presence of an oblique arrowhead within the assemblage is of some interest as there are only three other such arrowheads recorded in the Stonehenge excavation archive (Harding 1995: table 31). It is also of interest given the general lack of tools from other monuments in the wider landscape around Stonehenge (see Volume 2). However, the lack of an original finds location for this artefact lessens its potential archaeological significance. We should also remember that an unfinished arrowhead or knife (Harding 1995: 375) is also recorded as coming from Aubrey Hole 7, probably that found during its re-excavation in 1935.

Artefact type	Frequency	Percent
Blade	6	1.5
Core on a flake	1	0.3
Flake	348	88.3
Hammerstone	3	0.8
Irregular waste	22	5.6
Keeled non-discoidal flake-core	1	0.3
Multi-platform flake-core	9	2.3
Single-platform flake-core	3	0.8
Oblique arrowhead	1	0.3
Total	394	100.0

Table 4.1. The worked flint assemblage from Aubrey Hole 7

4.2.6. Sarsen and bluestone from Aubrey Hole 7

M. Parker Pearson with B. Chan and R. Ixer

Sarsen

The non-flint stone assemblage from the excavation of Aubrey Hole 7 includes 445 flakes and chunks of sarsen weighing 3.49kg (Table 4.2). Most of these are of quartzite sarsen, with 37% (114 fragments) being saccaroid sarsen. The majority of the quartzite sarsen pieces are flakes whereas most of the saccaroid sarsen pieces are generally smaller fragments (Table 4.3). Five quartzite sarsen hammerstones were found in AH7.

The findings from the sarsen-dressing floor in Trench 44, 100m north of Stonehenge (see Chapter 6), suggest that quartzite sarsen flakes and other pieces most likely represent fragments of hammerstones, whilst the saccaroid sarsen represents waste from sarsen-dressing.

The only piece of sarsen in the AH7 assemblage from within a likely prehistoric context is the fist-sized flake of quartzite sarsen found lying directly on top of the undisturbed cremation deposit (007) beside the Aubrey Hole. There is no indication that it was originally part of a hammerstone although this is likely, given the predominant use of quartzite sarsen on the site (see Chapter 6). It might well have been deliberately placed on top of the cremation burial and thus could constitute a grave good, placed there in the early third millennium BC; the cremation is dated to 3090–2900 cal BC at 95% confidence (weighted mean of OxA-27086 and SUERC-30410; see Chapter 11).

Bluestone

Of the 15 geological groups identified amongst Stonehenge's bluestones, at least six are represented among the finds from Aubrey Hole 7. A total of 63 bluestone chippings weighing 1.4084kg were recovered

Context	Frequency	Weight (g)
002	51	995
004	20	472
005	26	401
006	328	1456
007	1	71
013	2	16
103	1	2
108	1	3
128	1	1
157	1	2
215	1	10
259	1	4
303	1	3
307	2	4
308	4	9
320	1	7
327	1	3
347	1	23
354	1	3
Total	445	3485

Table 4.2. The frequency and weight of sarsen from Aubrey Hole 7 by context

Artefact type	Raw material type		Total
	Quartzite sarsen	*Saccaroid sarsen*	
	n	*n*	*n*
Hammerstone	5	0	5
Indeterminate	2	1	3
Waste flake (<1cm)	14	0	14
Waste flake (1-5cm)	228	0	228
Waste flake (>5cm)	59	3	62
Waste fragment (<1cm)	1	46	47
Waste fragment (1-5cm)	20	50	70
Waste fragment (>5cm)	2	14	16
Total	331	114	445

Table 4.3. The frequency of sarsen artefact types by raw material type from Aubrey Hole 7

from AH7, all of them from disturbed and redeposited contexts (fully reported on in Volume 2).

- The most numerous are rhyolite Group C (26 pieces weighing 467.1g; 'rhyolite with fabric' from Craig Rhos-y-felin; Ixer and Bevins 2011), followed by spotted dolerite (13 pieces weighing 689.9g; Bevins *et al.* 2013).
- Others are unspotted dolerite (two pieces weighing 39.2g; Bevins *et al.* 2013), rhyolite Group E (two pieces weighing 51.7g; Ixer and Bevins 2011) and one piece of rhyolite that could not be assigned to either Group C or E (1.9g).
- Eighteen pieces of tuff and argillaceous tuff (106.9g) derive from Volcanic Group A (Ixer and Bevins 2016) and a single tuff (51.7g) derives from Volcanic Group B (Ixer *et al.* 2015).

All of these types of bluestone can be sourced to the Preseli hills or their margins in west Wales. Rhyolite Group C ('rhyolite with fabric') can be sourced to the outcrop of Craig Rhos-y-felin in the Brynberian valley (Ixer and Bevins 2011) where the recess revealing the original position of a single monolith on the rock face has been identified (Parker Pearson *et al.* 2015). Spotted dolerites have been sourced to Carn Goedog and surrounding outcrops on the northern slope of the Preseli hills (Bevins *et al.* 2013). Unspotted dolerite is sourced to Cerrigmarchogion on the crest of the hills (*ibid.*). No sources of rhyolite Groups D or E or Volcanics Groups A or B have yet been located but they are considered to lie within the Preseli area (Ixer and Bevins 2016; Ixer *et al.* 2015).

Our work exploring the sources of the Stonehenge bluestones in the Preseli hills is described briefly in the conclusion to this chapter. The AH7 assemblage and all other bluestone recovered from all the SRP excavations is reported in full in Volume 2.

4.3. Fargo bluestone scatter

C. Richards, J. Pollard, D. Robinson and M. Parker Pearson

During excavations of the Stonehenge Greater Cursus in 1947, J.F.S. Stone recovered a fragment of bluestone from the southern ditch at a depth of '1 foot below the present surface' (1947: 14; see Chapter 3). This fragment was identified by F.S. Wallis and K.C. Dunham as similar to the Altar Stone at Stonehenge, in being a 'greyish-green sandstone' (*ibid.*: 14–15). Recently Stone's Cursus ditch fragment has been re-identified as Lower Palaeozooic sandstone, likely to derive from north of the Preseli hills (Ixer *et al.* 2017).

Stone made further surface finds of bluestone:

> 'By a fortunate chance the large field bounded by Fargo Plantation, the Cursus, and Stonehenge was under plough during 1948, and this was carefully searched for evidence of bluestone scatter. Contrary to all expectations and normal scatter-diagrams, fragments were found concentrated in the northwestern corner of the field, and only one near Stonehenge itself. With Mr Newall's assistance ten fragments were so obtained, and these have been plotted on the accompanying map (Fig. 4) together with other known pieces. The result suggests very intensive activity around the western end of the Cursus, and coinciding exactly with the scatter of flint implements' (Stone 1947: 16).

Additionally, a stratified piece of rhyolite was recovered from the ditch of the small 'hengiform' enclosure in Fargo Plantation (Stone 1938: 366; see Figures 2.7, 3.1), and multiple pieces of bluestone were recorded from early excavations within nearby round barrows Winterbourne Stoke G28 (42 pieces) and Amesbury G45 (30 pieces; Stone 1947: 16).

Moreover, Stone also recounts collecting by Young in December 1934, 'flinting' in the same field:

> 'Here he found nothing until he approached the Cursus near Fargo Plantation... and found several bluestone chips and a small piece of micaceous sandstone' (Stone 1947: 17).

In the implement petrology report for the region, six pieces of rhyolite are noted as coming from the Cursus (Evens *et al.* 1962, cited in Howard 1982: 126). While a clear preponderance of rhyolite is recognised among the fragments of bluestones recovered from the area adjacent to Fargo Plantation and the western end of the Greater Cursus (see also Thorpe *et al.* 1991: table 2), Stone (1947: 17–18) is quite specific in noting the variability of the assemblage. Indeed, he concluded that it contained 'five types of rock similar if not identical with those of Stonehenge' (*ibid.*: 18).

Given the revised bluestone architectural sequence at Stonehenge (see above), it was decided during the research design phase of the SRP that the scatter of bluestone chippings at the western end of the Cursus (Figure 4.29) was of sufficient quantity and variety to warrant further enquiry. The discrete situation of this material had spurred Stone to identify 'the existence of a bluestone structure of Late Neolithic or Grooved Ware age in the vicinity, possibly within the Cursus itself, which was subsequently dismantled' (Stone 1947: 18).

In rethinking the presence of dressed bluestones at Stonehenge, and the problems associated with situating them within the monumental process of construction, it seemed prudent to take notice of Stone's remark 'that we may have here a clue to the whereabouts of the original blue Stonehenge postulated by the presence of the mortised bluestones' (*ibid.*: 18). As part of the SRP, it was decided that research should include a re-evaluation of the observations of Stone and Young.

4.3.1. Research aims and objectives

A central question regarding the bluestones at Stonehenge revolves around their constructional and architectural history. In particular, the SRP research was designed to investigate whether the bluestones were restricted to the Stonehenge site or whether they underwent a process of movement from one megalithic site to another within its environs. The project research questions addressed the possibility of a 'blue Stonehenge' having been constructed in close proximity to Stonehenge:

- Do the bluestone fragments at Fargo maintain a discrete spatial distribution?
- Do the fragments represent the working of many bluestones or of a single stone?
- To what activities are the bluestone fragments attributable, *e.g.* stone-dressing, breakage, *etc.*?
- Are the fragments indicative of an original bluestone setting within this area?

The following objectives were addressed:

1. To record the distribution of bluestone fragments in the topsoil to the south of the Cursus.
2. To characterise the variability of types of bluestone present.
3. To characterise the range and nature of bluestone flaking.
4. To recognise any sub-surface features within the scatter of bluestones.
5. To record (but not collect) other archaeological material within the topsoil.

4.3.2. Fieldwork

The area identified by Stone (1947) was examined by gradiometer and resistivity survey in 2006 (see Chapter 2; Figures 2.6–2.7). Potential features were identified by the geophysical survey, but many were considered to be either modern, since the area was part of the campsite of solstice festivals in the late 1970s, or non-archaeological.

Fieldwork began in August 2006, directed by Colin Richards and consisting of test-pitting of the ploughsoil in 1m squares in the field south of the Greater Cursus and east of Fargo Plantation. A second season of test-pitting was carried out during June 2008, directed by

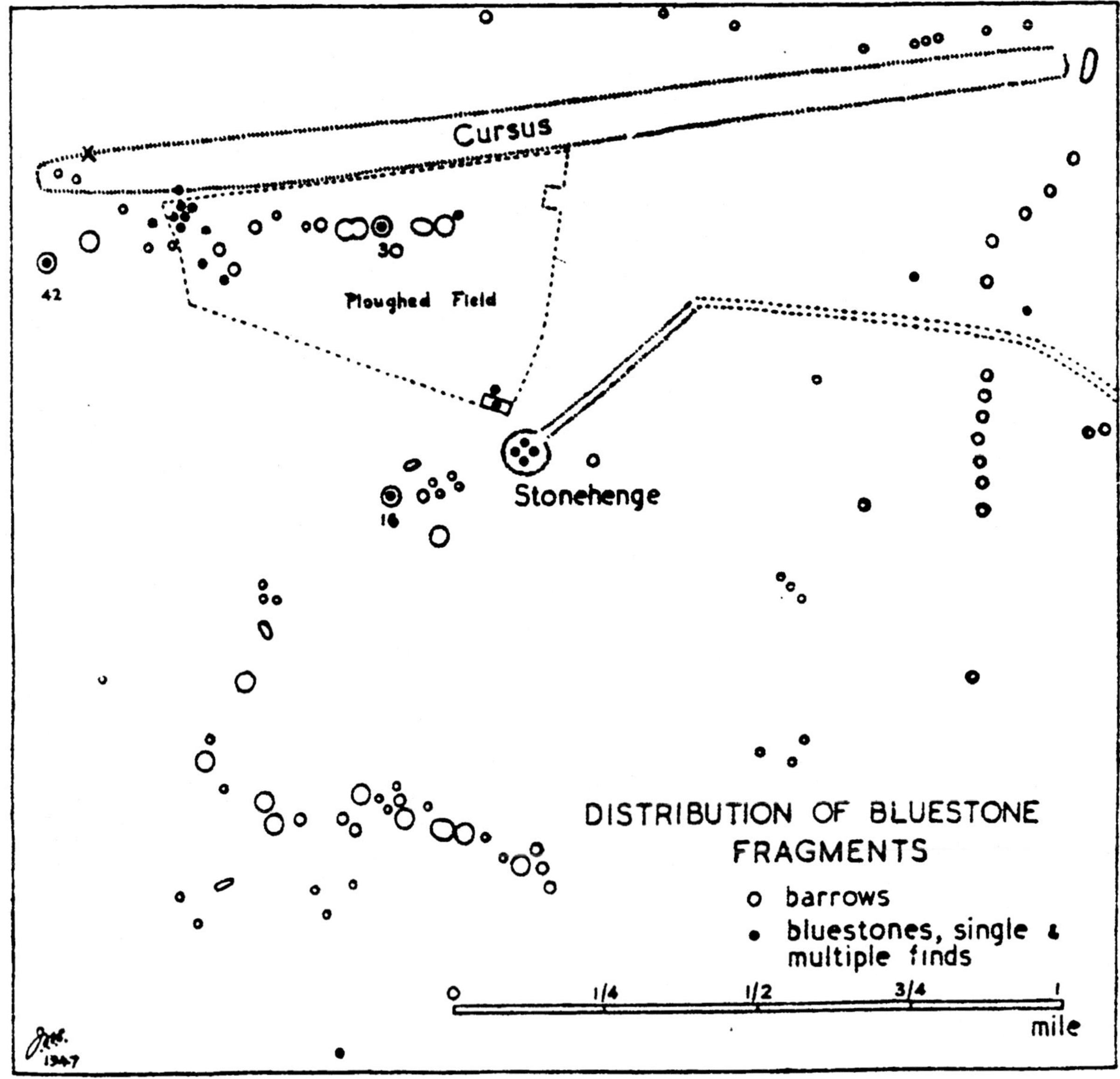

Figure 4.29. J.F.S. Stone's 1947 map of bluestone finds around Stonehenge (from Stone 1947: fig. 4); © Royal Archaeological Institute

Josh Pollard, Dave Robinson and Mike Parker Pearson (Figure 4.30).

To actually identify the area of the 'bluestone' scatter, a 4% sampling strategy of 1m-square test-pitting (supplemented with a 10% sample in areas of interest) was implemented (Figure 4.31). This was undertaken in 2006 in the area identified by Stone (1947), immediately south of the Cursus, although a 9m strip was left untouched between the Cursus ditch and the northernmost test pits. All the ploughsoil from these test pits was sieved through 10mm mesh to recover flints, pottery and other artefacts, and the pits were backfilled.

In 2008, ploughsoil within the area marked by Stone as the location of five bluestone chips was sampled within a systematic frame of four 1m squares within each 10m × 10m square, providing a 4% sample of the ploughsoil. Soil was sieved through a 10mm mesh. In all, 104 test pits were dug and backfilled in 2008.

Figure 4.30. Test-pit digging at Fargo in 2008, being supervised by Josh Pollard, looking northeast towards the Greater Cursus (beyond the cows)

4.3.3. Lithics and other artefacts

D. Mitcham and C. Richards

Artefact quantities from the test pits are generally low (330 worked flints and 202 burnt flints in the 2008 assemblage) and quantities of worked flints are mostly around 3–5 per square metre, and no higher than 11 per square metre. The majority of the lithic assemblage was recorded on site and not retained, whilst a small sample was examined subsequently. The results of this post-excavation analysis have been combined with the lithic data that was recorded during the fieldwork.

The Fargo test pits produced a total worked flint assemblage of 1,627 pieces (Tables 4.4–4.5). This assemblage is characterised by a low proportion of flakes and blades at 70.7%, with formal tools representing 1.9% of the assemblage. The debitage here is predominantly indicative of a flake-based technology with only a single blade present, although the nature of the core technology cannot be examined in detail as cores were not identified to specific types in the on-site recording system. These cores recorded in the field (Figure 4.32) have been assigned to the 'unclassifiable or fragmentary core' category here to allow the site data to be combined

Artefact type	Frequency	Percent
Barbed and tanged arrowhead	3	0.2
Blade	1	0.1
Blade-like flake	2	0.1
End-and-side scraper	1	0.1
End-scraper	3	0.2
Flake	1144	70.3
Flint axe/axe roughout	1	0.1
Irregular waste	279	17.1
Leaf arrowhead	1	0.1
Misc. retouched flake	8	0.5
Multi-platform flake-core	1	0.1
Oblique arrowhead	3	0.2
Other knife	7	0.4
Other scraper	10	0.6
Other/unclassifiable (general)	89	5.5
Plano-convex knife	2	0.1
Rejuvenation flake (other)	1	0.1
Serrated flake	3	0.2
Single-platform blade-core	1	0.1
Single-platform flake-core	1	0.1
Unclassifiable/fragmentary core	66	4.1
Total	1627	100.0

Table 4.4. The lithic assemblage composition from the Fargo Plantation test pits

General artefact category	Frequency	Percent
Cores	69	4.2
Flakes and blades	1151	70.7
Formal tools	31	1.9
Irregular waste	279	17.2
Misc. waste	89	5.5
Retouched flakes and utilised flakes	8	0.5
Total	1627	100.0

Table 4.5. The lithic assemblage from the Fargo Plantation test pits according to general artefact categories

with the synthesis of ploughsoil lithic analysis presented in Volume 2.

Seven arrowheads were found (Figure 4.33), consisting of a broken leaf-shaped arrowhead (earlier Neolithic), three oblique arrowheads (Late Neolithic) and three barbed-and-tanged arrowheads (Chalcolithic/ Early Bronze Age). The remaining tools are mostly scrapers or knives (Figure 4.34); although most are not chronologically diagnostic, a plano-convex knife is likely to date to the Late Neolithic–Early Bronze Age.

The Fargo Plantation test pits produced the greatest number of arrowheads compared to other SRP test pit locations. Along with the presence of scrapers and knives, this suggests an area of Late Neolithic and Chalcolithic/ Early Bronze Age activity, either settlement-related or funerary. The presence of a flint axe blade – a diagnostic Neolithic piece – may be related to this Late Neolithic–Early Bronze Age activity, but more likely represents limited activity taking place in the Early Neolithic. The possibility of Early Neolithic activity is also indicated by the presence of the leaf-shaped arrowhead, a few blade cores and some serrated flakes, although the lack of detail for the majority of the core types makes the extent of any activity of this period difficult to assess further. Possible Peterborough Ware sherds hint at Middle Neolithic activity as well (Figure 4.35).

Other finds include seven bluestone rhyolite chips (Group B from Test pit [TP] 50, Group C from 247, and Group D from 72, 74, 152, 157 and 173; see petrological synthesis in Volume 2), ceramic sherds from numerous test pits (see Cleal, below), a spherical fired clay bead (from TP 274), and a fragment of a burnt bone cylindrical artefact (from TP 212), possibly a medieval or later knife handle.

Finds of more recent date include a clay pipe stem and a variety of modern debris – bottle glass, tin cans, tent pegs – that is likely to derive from the 1977 Stonehenge festival campsite which was located here. Amongst those finds is a group of eight halfpennies (all from TP 270 except for one from TP 37) that could have been used as weights for dealing cannabis.

Spatial distributions

Although there was a background scatter of 1–2 flints or more per square metre across the entire area, worked flints were concentrated in the northwest (Figure 4.36). This concentration, which produced the Chalcolithic/ Early Bronze Age barbed-and-tanged arrowheads (Figure 4.33), also produced some of the Beaker sherds and is likely to relate to Beaker-period activities along the southern side of the Greater Cursus.

Worked flint in the southwest included a fragment of a leaf-shaped arrowhead (TP 232), a core rejuvenation flake and a number of blades, which all suggest activity here in the fourth millennium BC. A fragment of an oblique arrowhead was recovered from the northern limit of this concentration. Cores and scrapers, together with a small number of knives and retouched pieces, were found distributed across the whole area.

Burnt flint was found throughout the area of test-pitting. It occurred in moderate quantities throughout (Figure 4.37) but a greater concentration was identified in the east of the test-pitting area, where worked flints were few. This latter concentration could represent activity of post-Beaker date, perhaps as late as the modern solstice festivals. The burnt flints were not heavily burned and exhibited light cracking and crazing as opposed to the grey-coloured, severe fragmentation of heavily burnt flint from Durrington Walls, for example (reported in Volume 3).

Sarsen fragments were distributed across the test-pitted area (Figure 4.38) but five of the seven bluestone fragments were concentrated in the northwest (Figure 4.39); although slightly further north and west than Stone's indicated five pieces from this corner of the Cursus field, the relatively larger scale of his plan could mean that these were from the same broad location as ours. This relative concurrence between the SRP finds and Stone's finds suggests that bluestone chips were distributed mostly in the northwest part of the field.

4.3.4. Ceramics

R. Cleal

A total of 52 sherds, weighing 140g, was recovered from the Fargo test pits; all the sherds are small (mean weight 2.7g) and worn to a greater or lesser degree, as would be expected from such contexts. The majority (46) are identifiable as prehistoric, and of these, 42 are definitely or probably assignable to a style and/or date (Table 4.6). It has not been possible to create full fabric descriptions because the sherds are small and the largely prehistoric fabrics are likely to be so variable within each vessel that descriptions based on these sherds would not give an accurate representation of the overall vessel fabric.

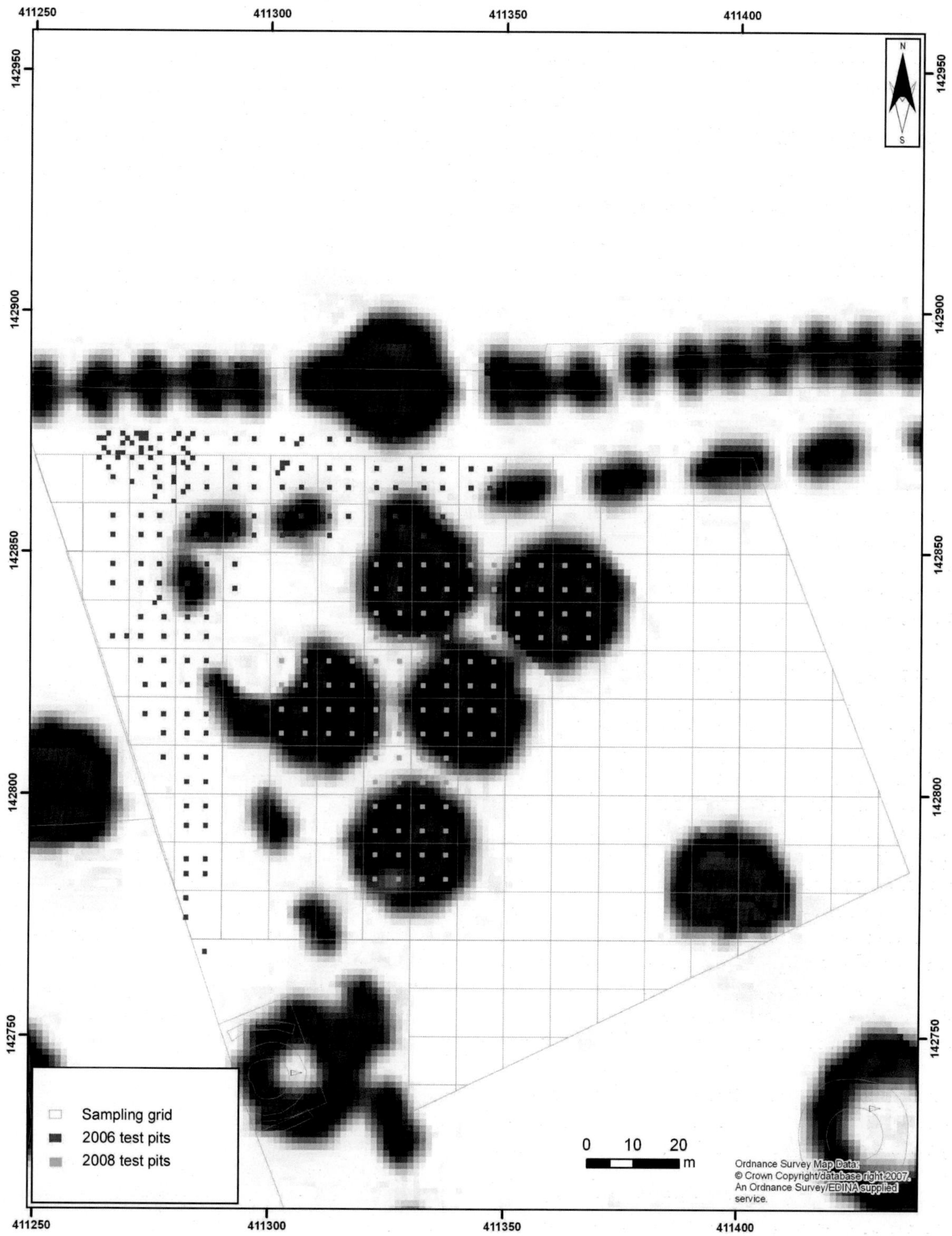

Figure 4.31. Test pits from 2006 and 2008 overlaid onto J.F.S. Stone's distribution map of bluestone rhyolite fragments recovered in 1947 (marked as large black circles)

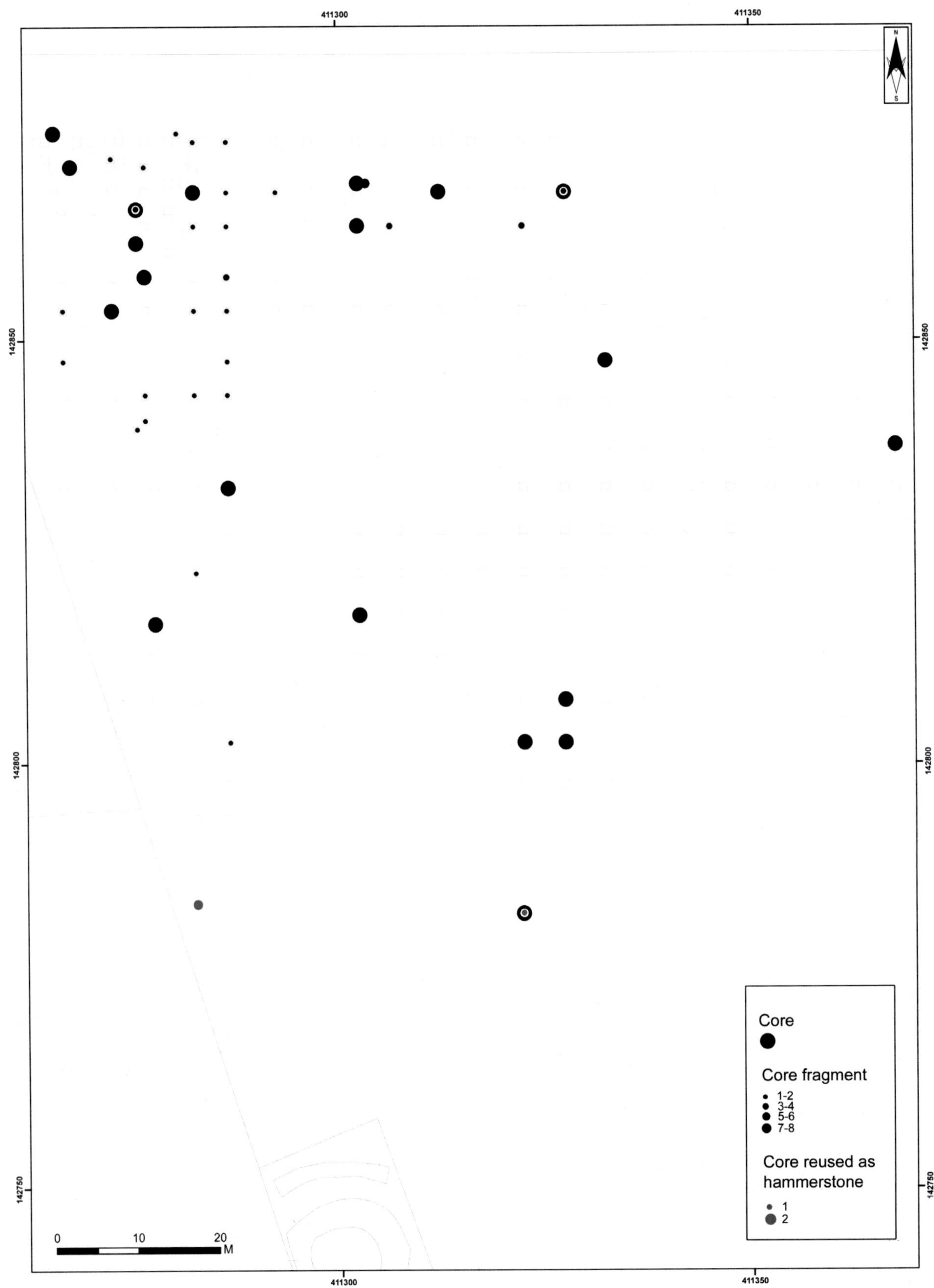

Figure 4.32. The distribution of flint cores from the test pits at Fargo Plantation

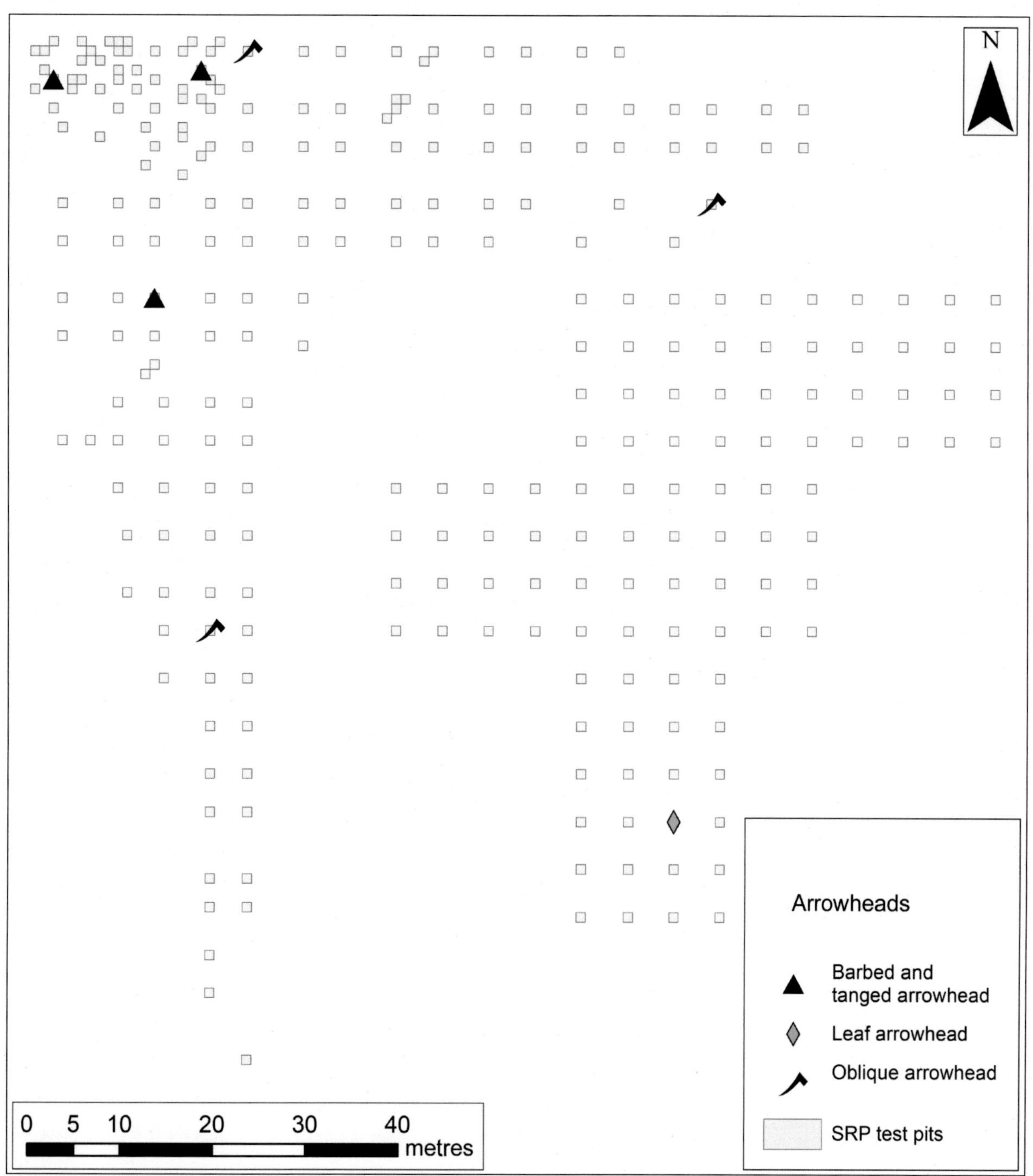

Figure 4.33. The distribution of arrowheads from the test pits at Fargo Plantation

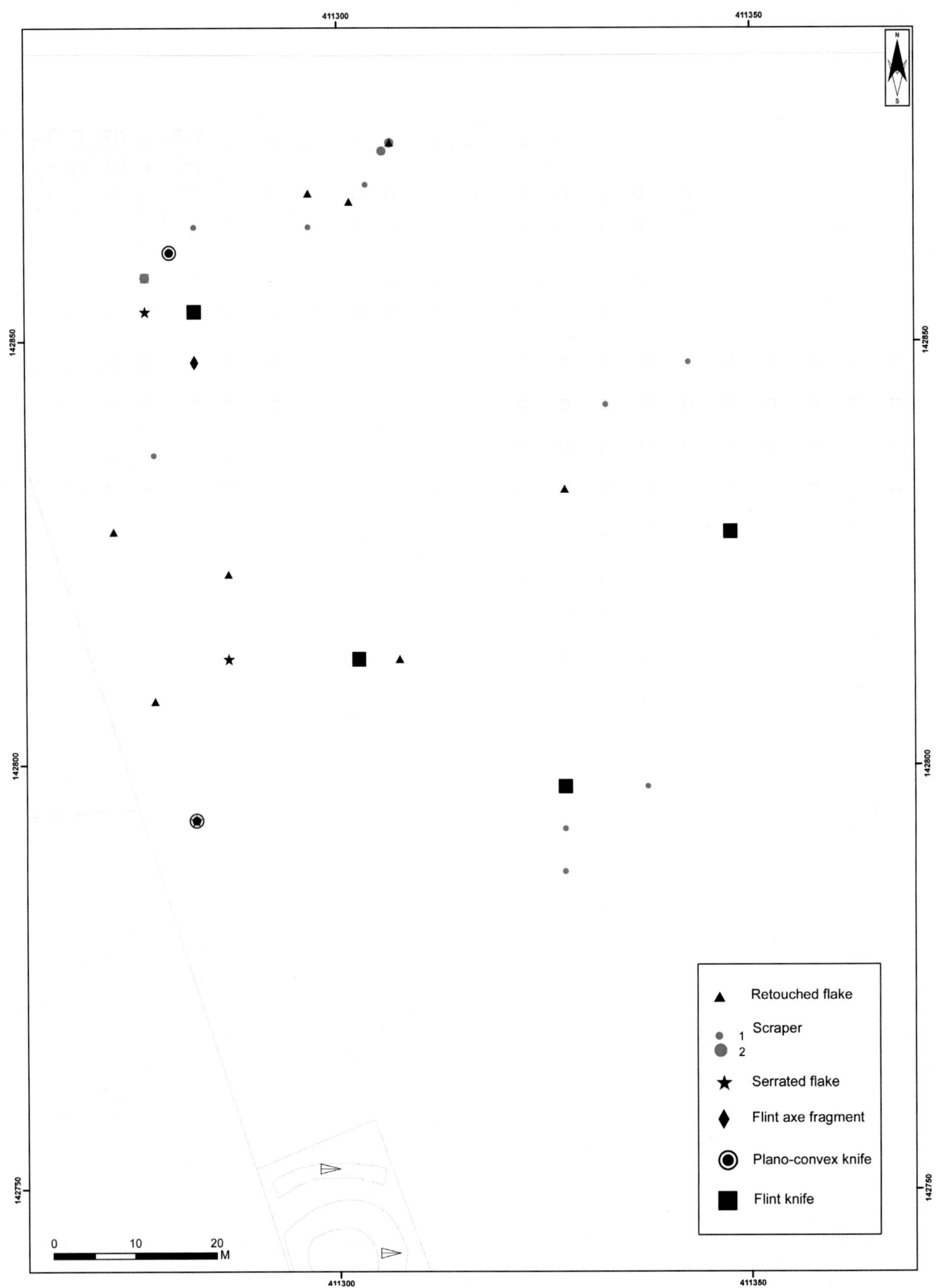

Figure 4.34. The distribution of flint tools from the test pits at Fargo Plantation

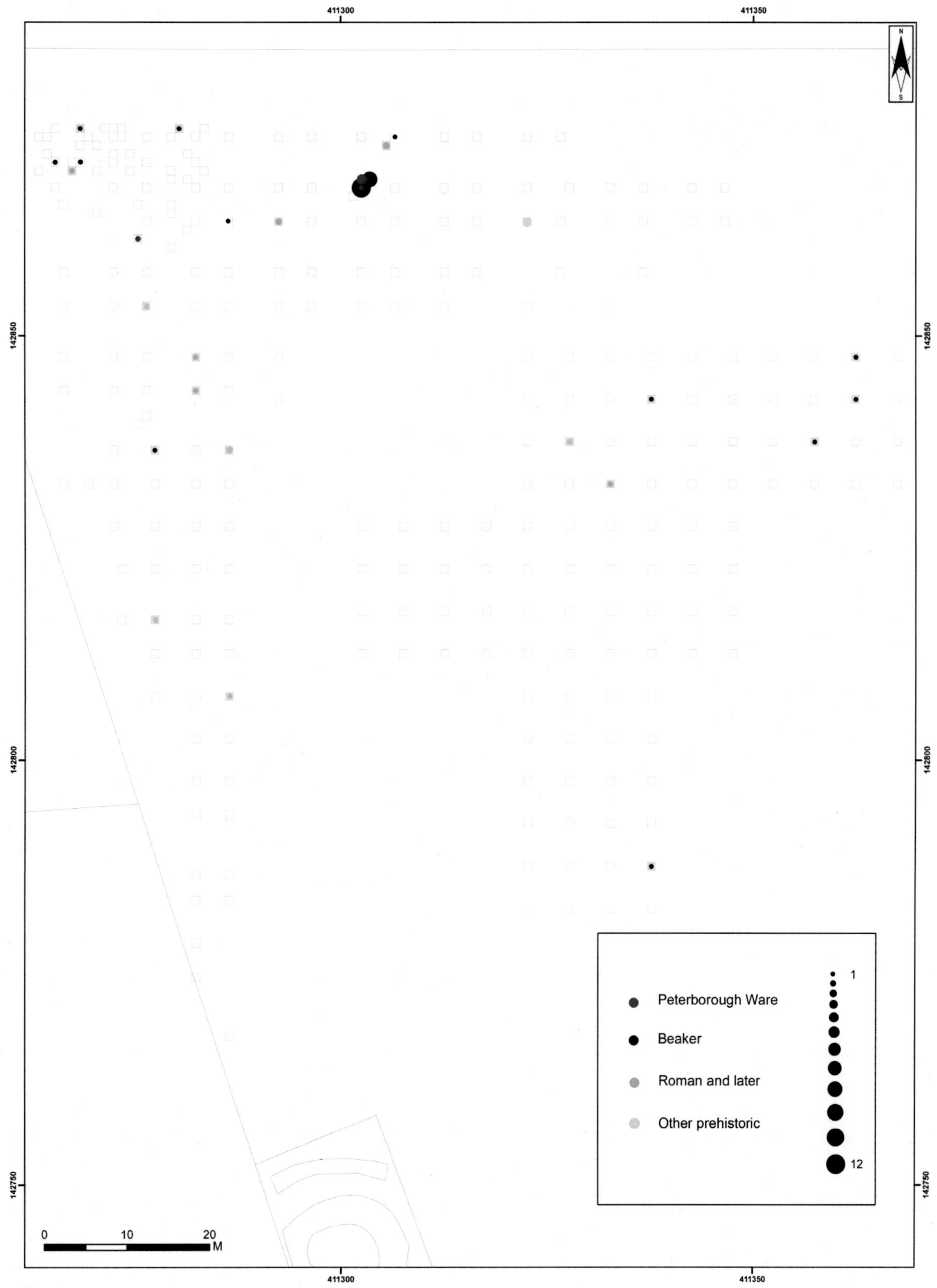

Figure 4.35. The distribution of pottery, including Beaker sherds and Peterborough Ware, from the test pits at Fargo Plantation

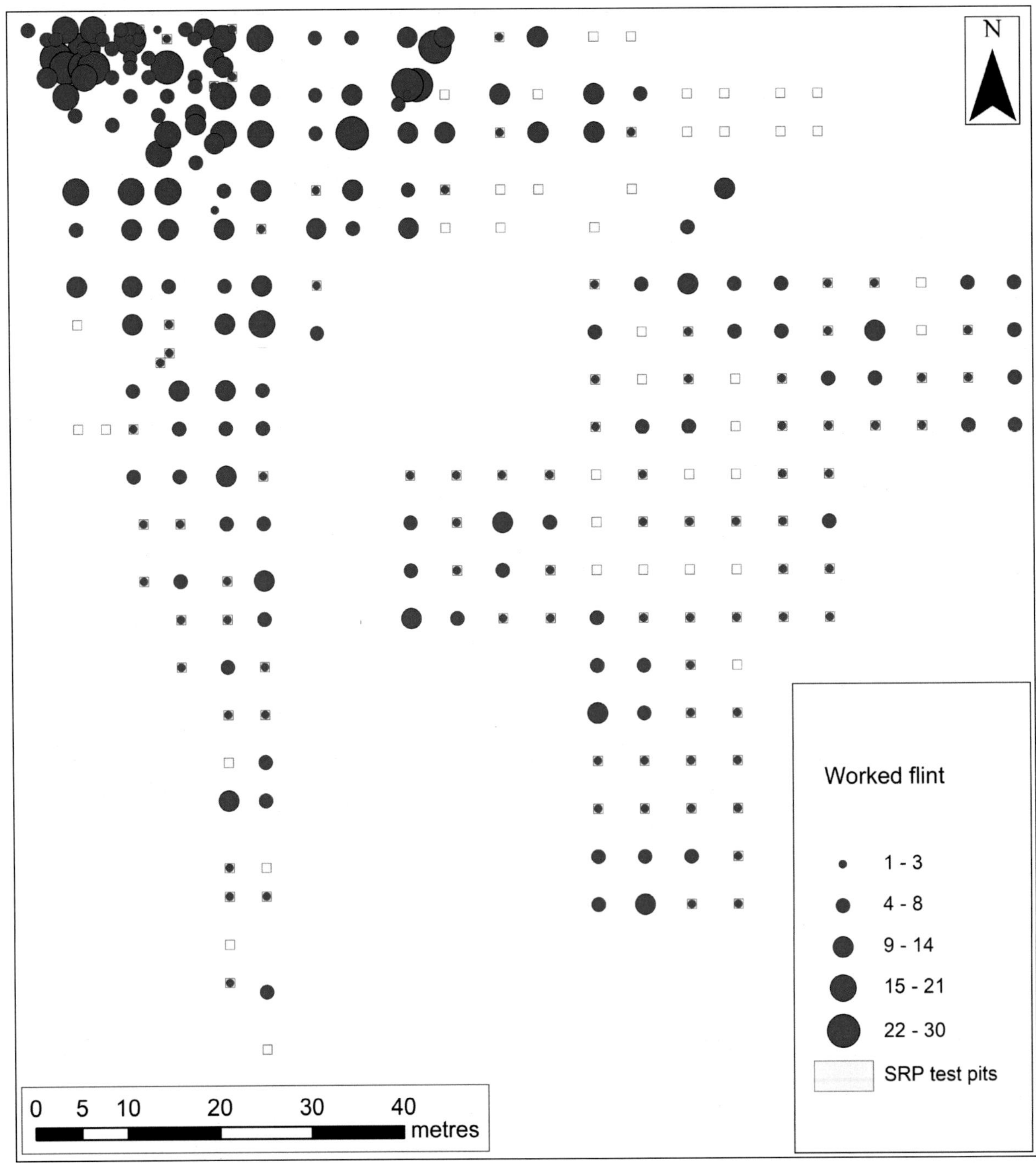

Figure 4.36. The total frequency of worked flint from the test pits at Fargo Plantation

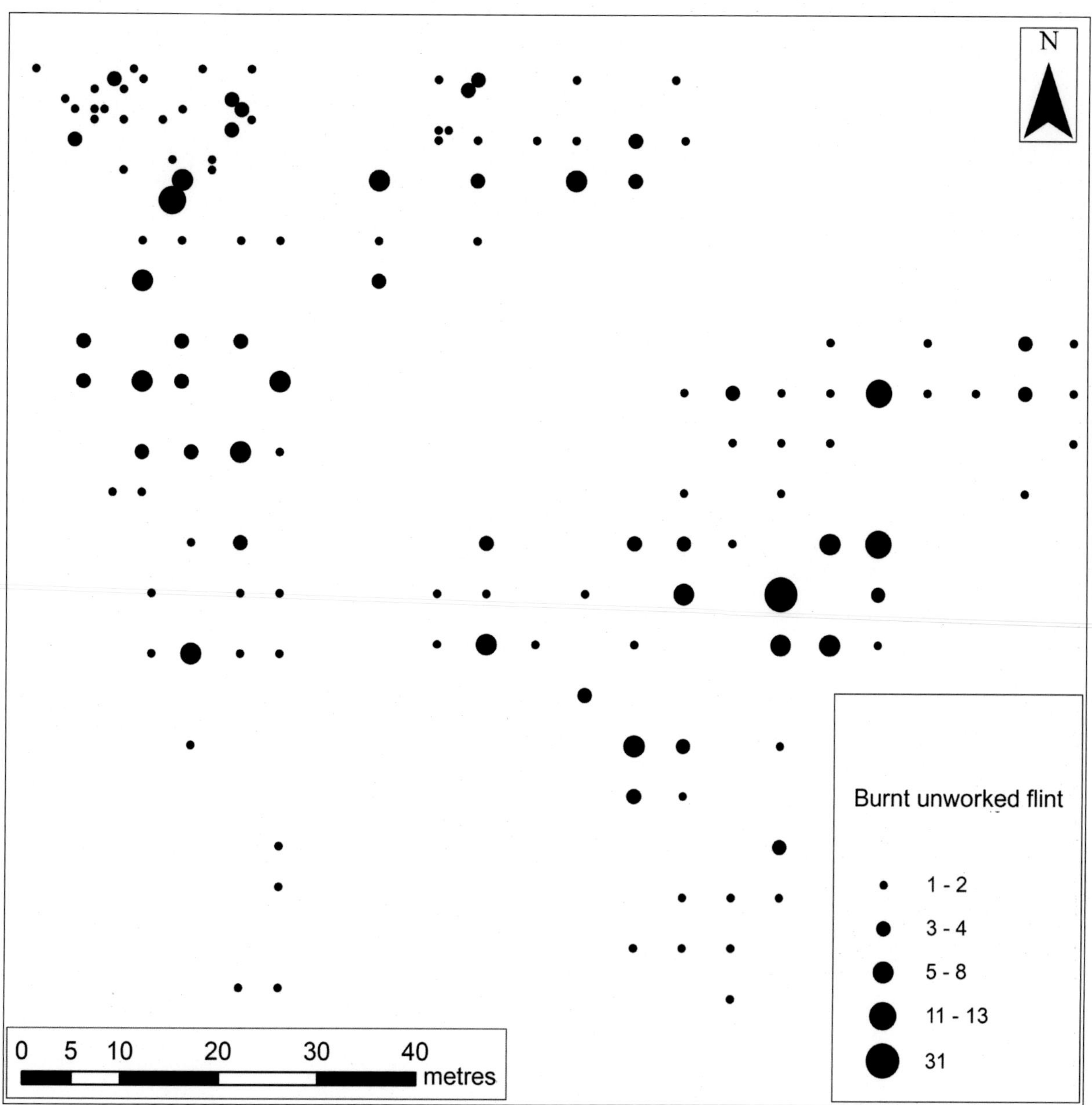

Figure 4.37. The total frequency of burnt unworked flint from the test pits at Fargo Plantation

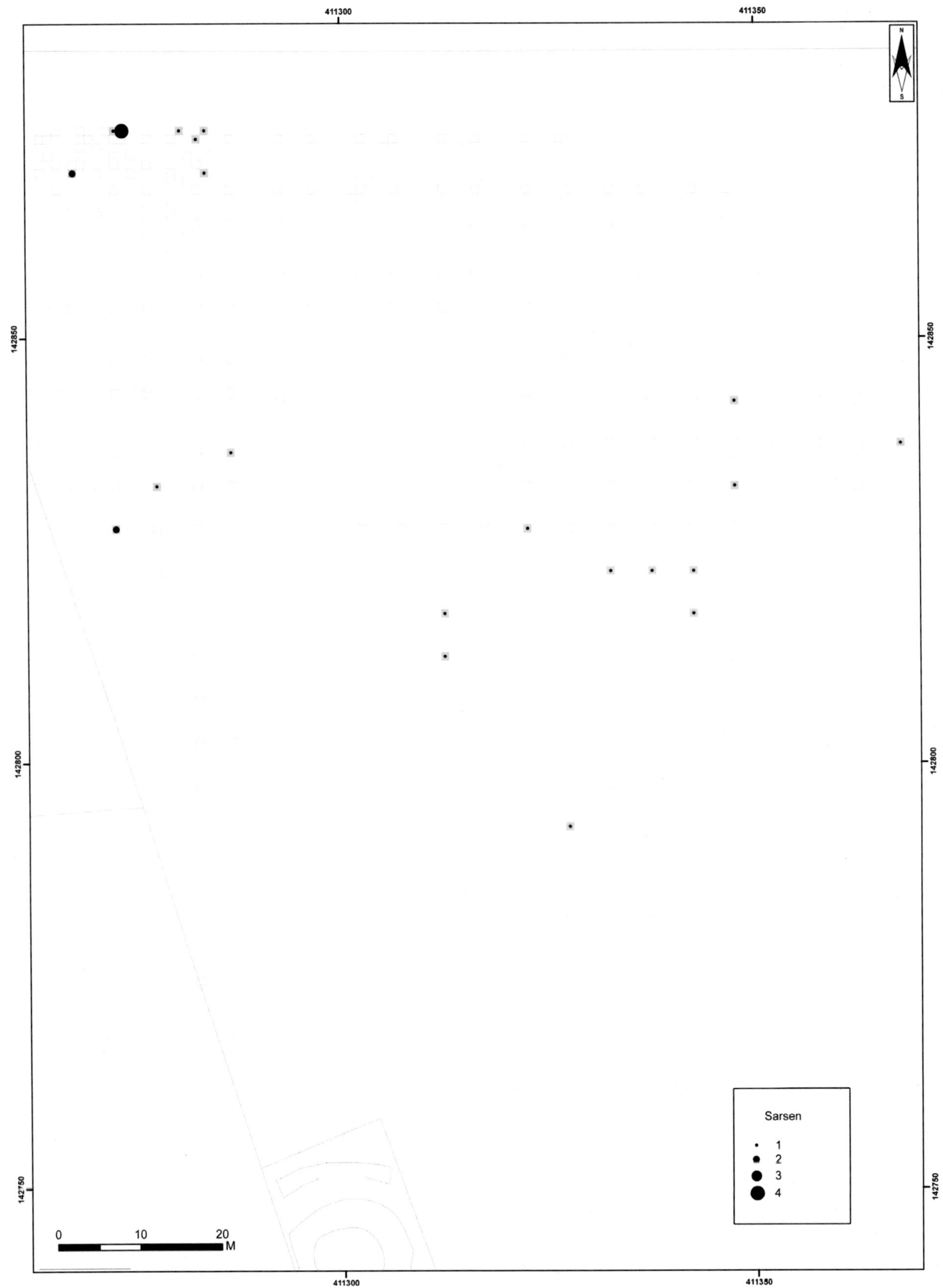

Figure 4.38. The distribution of sarsen pieces from the test pits at Fargo Plantation

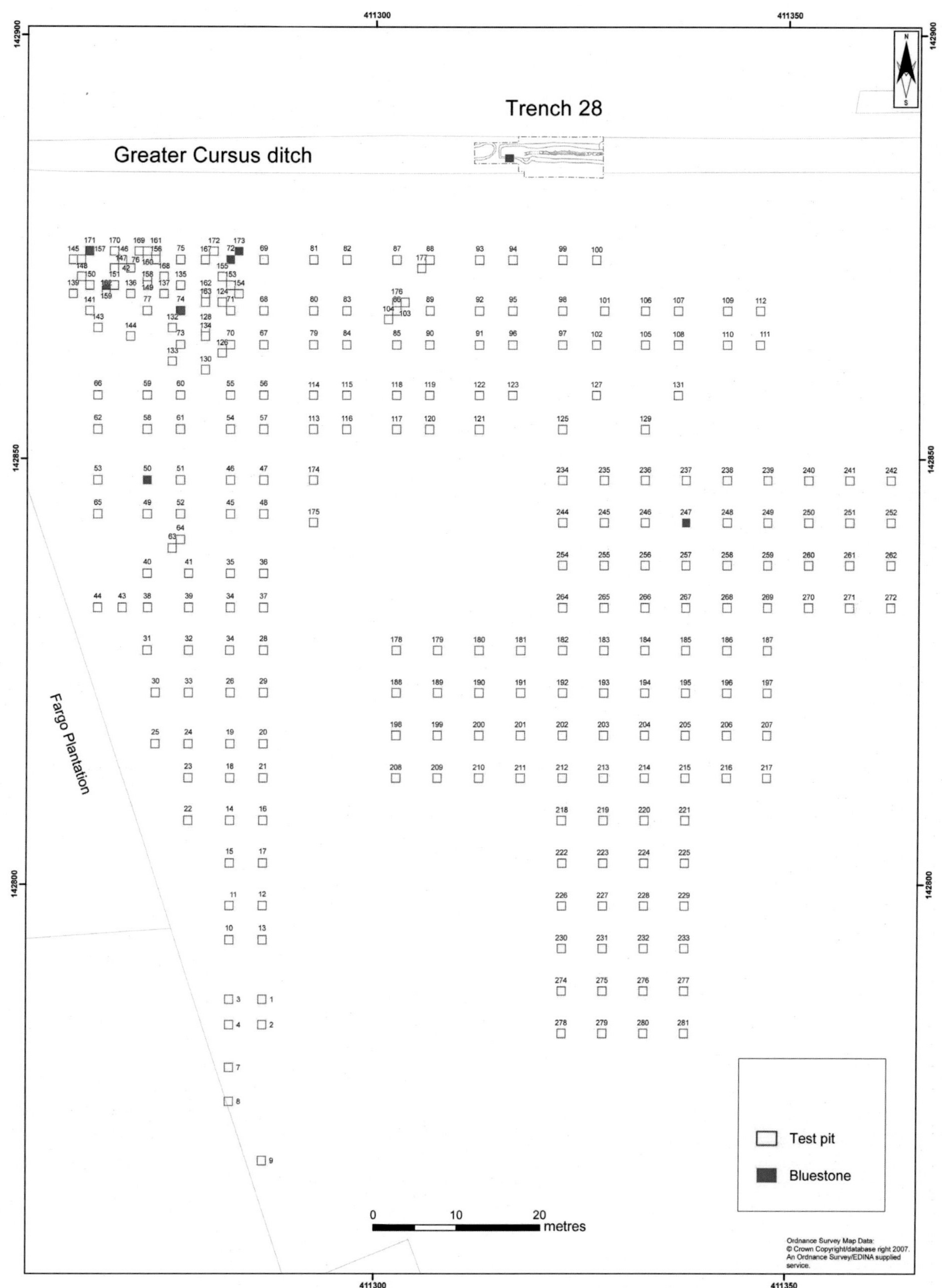

Figure 4.39. The distribution of bluestone pieces (in blue) from the test pits at Fargo Plantation. All are of rhyolite except for the sandstone piece from Stone's 1947 trench (on the west end of Trench 28)

Test Pit	? Peterborough Ware		Beaker		Neolithic or Early Bronze Age		?Middle Bronze Age or later		Prehistoric – not further identifiable		? Romano-British		Not prehistoric, not identifiable	
	n	weight	*n*	weight	*n*	weight	*n*	weight	*n*	weight	*n*	weight	*n*	weight
16									1	1g				
24									1	3g				
36									2	7g				
41			1	2g										
45													1	4g
46													1	3g
61					1	6g								
67			1	4g										
79											1	1g	1	1g
86			10	30g			2	6g						
88			1	1g										
97					4	7g								
103	1	11g	4	6g										
133	3	10g												
140			1	1g										
164			1	1g										
170			1	3g										
176	4	16g												
177			1	4g							1	1g		
242			1	1g										
247			1	4g										
252			1	1g										
255					1	1g								
261			1	2g										
266													1	1g
277			1	1g										
Total	8	37g	26	61g	6	14g	2	6g	4	11g	2	2g	4	9g

Table 4.6. Ceramics from the Fargo Plantation test pits

Peterborough Ware

There are no clearly identifiable Peterborough Ware sherds in the collection, but on the grounds of fabric, general appearance and some slight impressions, eight are identifiable as probably belonging to this tradition. All contain flint as an additive, and at least two vessels are represented.

Beaker

Twenty-six sherds are clearly identifiable as Beaker, of which 10 carry comb impressions (mainly rectangular-toothed comb) and six twisted-cord impressions (Z-twist impressions – *i.e.* impressions of S-twisted cords, from TP 86, 103 and 242). One has plastic fingernail impressions (*i.e.* 'rusticated') and one may also be rusticated but is less clear. It is impossible to identify the decorative schemes of the comb-impressed sherds, although there seems to be at least one with a ladder motif. The cord-impressed sherds presumably come from a vessel or vessels with all-over-cord impressed horizontal lines. It is not possible to determine how many vessels are represented, but the cord-impressed sherds are likely to represent no more than two at most.

Neolithic/Early Bronze Age

These six plain sherds are not assignable to a style, but are unlikely to be later in date than the Early Bronze Age, on the grounds of fabric and general appearance.

Possible Middle Bronze Age

Two sherds may be Middle Bronze Age or later Bronze Age, the tentative identification being on the grounds of fabric and general appearance.

Other

Eight sherds are not assignable to style or date at all, although four of these are probably prehistoric rather than later in date. Two sherds are probably Romano-British.

Discussion

Although this is a very small group of material, on the whole it reflects a pattern already identified from the Stonehenge Environs Project of the 1980s (Richards 1990). Finds from that project included Peterborough Ware from north of the Greater Cursus and east of Fargo Wood, although not in any considerable quantity (Cleal with Raymond 1990: fig. 154B) and Beaker pottery in a low frequency spread across the same area (*ibid.*: fig. 154C); there was also a considerable amount of Middle and later Bronze Age pottery in the same SEP collection areas (*ibid.*: fig. 154D).

In terms of use of the area by people using Beaker pottery, the collection from the test pits does have at least one novel feature. Among the material recovered from the whole of the Stonehenge Environs Project study area there were very few Beaker sherds with cord impressions; although some were found, they were few in number and largely confined to the Wilsford Down area (Cleal with Raymond 1990: 237). The Fargo test pits, however, produced six sherds with cord-impressions, although four probably belong to one vessel.

Although much more is now known about the early period of Beaker use, and it is now clear that comb-impressed Beakers exist alongside cord-impressed vessels in the earliest assemblages, it is not possible on the evidence of the small sherds from the test pits to establish whether the comb-decorated sherds here are also likely to be as early as the cord-impressed Beaker sherds. On present understanding of Beaker use, however, it is at least clear that cord-impressed sherds are more likely than not to date to the period before 2200 cal BC, and this assemblage is a new, albeit minor, addition to our understanding of the use of the Stonehenge landscape in the third millennium cal BC.

4.3.5. Results

The results from the test-pitting exercise are both interesting and perplexing. Just as Stone and Young suggested, the number of worked flints within test pits increased as the Greater Cursus was approached. Significantly, the proportion of 'foreign' stone also increased within *c.* 25m of the junction between Fargo Plantation and the Cursus (Figure 4.39). Here we identified a definite concentration of bluestone rhyolite within or close to the area described by Stone and Young (centred on SU 411275 142870). Sherds of Beaker pottery were also present within this area.

While several test pits were placed over geophysical anomalies, these proved to be either solution hollows or modern features. Geophysical surveys have failed to reveal any indication of a likely setting of dismantled, formerly standing bluestones in this part of the Stonehenge landscape.

Features were recorded beneath the ploughsoil in 14 test pits (Figure 4.40). While six of these were likely to be tree holes, the others were categorised as three pits, four postholes/stakeholes and, over to the west, a possible hearth. These features were mostly distributed to the south and east of the denser lithic scatters and the Beaker pottery. They coincide with the southern concentration of burnt flint. None of these features was dug out; some could date to the modern solstice festivals or other post-prehistoric episodes of activity but the characteristic orange-brown loam in many of the pits and postholes/stakeholes (as opposed to more recent organic-rich dark brown soils), filled with unworked, broken flint in their upper fills, makes a prehistoric origin likely.

Roughly located at 57m due east of Fargo Plantation (SU 411314 142883), Stone's excavation cut across the Cursus ditch, *c.* 35m east-northeast of the rhyolite concentration identified by the test pits (see Figures 3.21, 3.23, 4.39). It was at this point that a stratified bluestone fragment of Lower Palaeozoic metasandstone – of slightly different composition to the Altar Stone at Stonehenge (Ixer and Turner 2006; Ixer *et al.* 2017) – was discovered by Stone (1947: 14). Many Beaker pottery sherds, associated with a probable Peterborough ware sherd, were recovered from test pits situated *c.* 20m southwest of Stone's cutting. The Beaker pottery also coincided with a concentration of flint tools and barbed-and-tanged arrowheads.

Overall, the test-pitting exercise was useful in characterising Late Neolithic and Chalcolithic/Early Bronze Age activity south of the Greater Cursus. The presence of Beaker pottery within the test pits indicates some form of activity close to the Cursus. The coincidence of Beaker pottery, flint tools and barbed-and-tanged arrowheads supports this conviction.

The slight quantities of lithics and ceramics in this field south of the Greater Cursus indicate considerably less activity and deposition here than to the north of the Cursus, where fieldwalking by the Stonehenge Environs Project retrieved large quantities of both materials from a long span of occupation from the Early Neolithic to the Bronze Age (Richards 1990: figs 10, 16 and 154). Nonetheless, these small quantities of artefactual material south of the Greater Cursus allow clear recognition of discrete activity scatters – a Beaker-period spread immediately south of the Cursus and a hint of a more dispersed Early Neolithic scatter across the area (Figures 4.33–4.35).

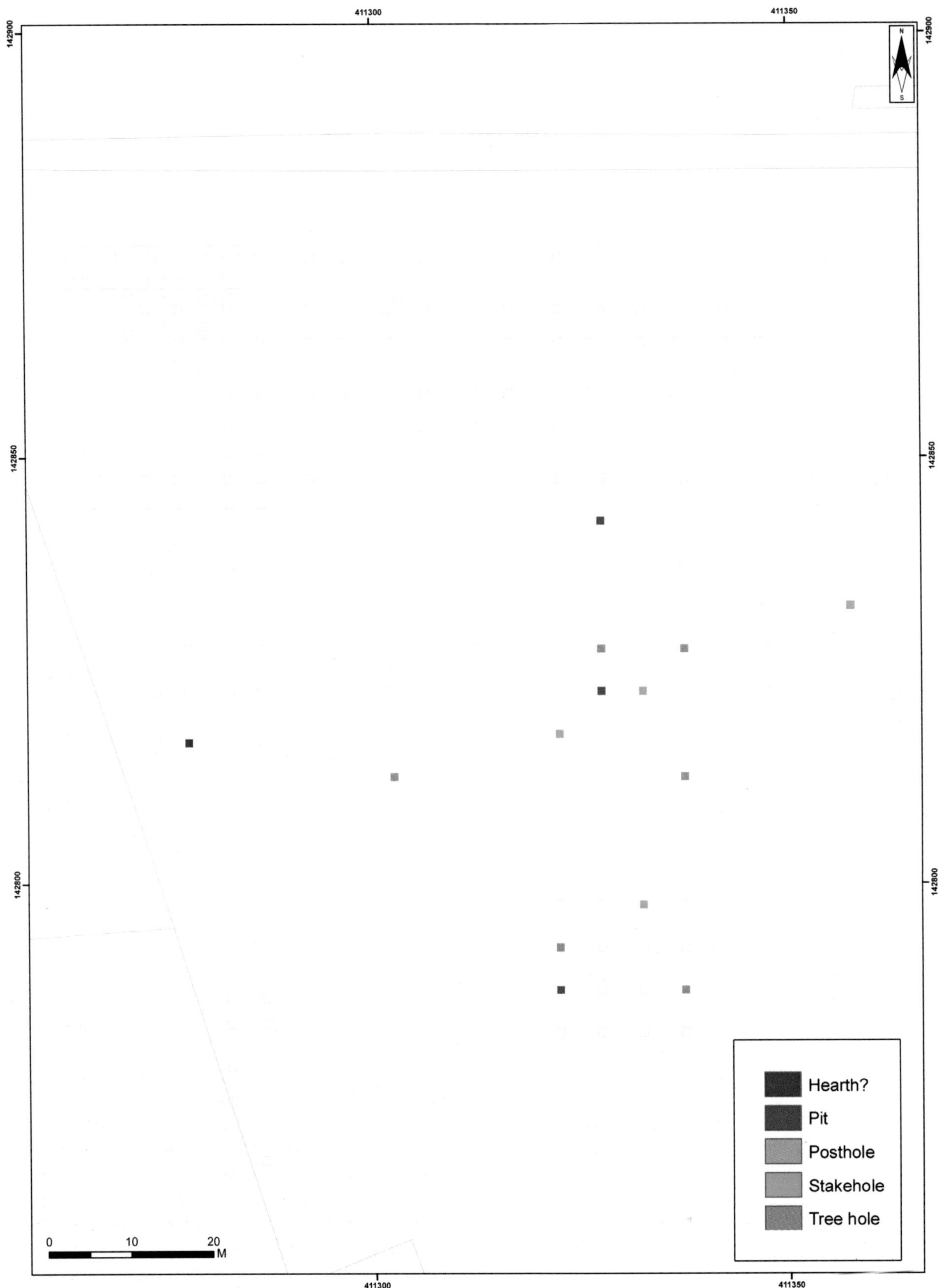

Figure 4.40. The distribution of sub-ploughsoil features within the test pits at Fargo Plantation

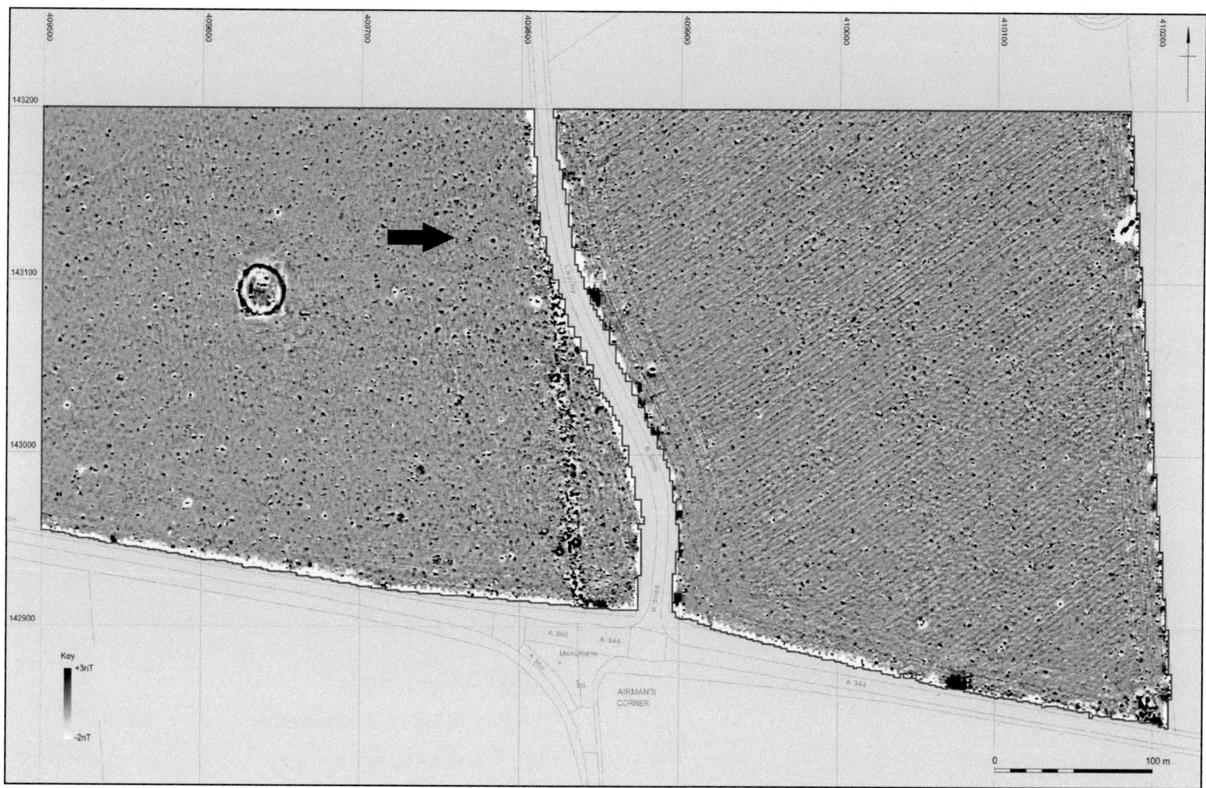

Figure 4.41. Location of the Airman's Corner pit circle, as revealed by gradiometer survey (from Wessex Archaeology 2009); © Wessex Archaeology reproduced courtesy of English Heritage

As foreshadowed by Stone's surface collection, bluestone chips forming a loose cluster were recovered from the test pits (Figure 4.39). However, given the low density of bluestone fragments revealed by the test-pit sampling, such fragments are unlikely to number more than 75 pieces within the ploughsoil of the test-pitted area. This low density is unlikely to indicate the presence of a debris zone resulting from the dressing or destruction of one or more monoliths.

However, the inability to extend the test pits into the wooded area of Fargo Plantation leaves in abeyance the possibility of denser and more discrete concentrations of bluestone chips and flakes in the area to the west. In this context, the piece of rhyolite recovered by Stone (1938) at the 'hengiform enclosure' in Fargo Plantation (marked on Figure 2.7) provides the tantalising possibility of a rhyolite bluestone monument in its vicinity. Nonetheless, the spatial coincidence to the east of Fargo Plantation of bluestone chippings with Beaker artefacts makes it possible that the bluestone chips relate to later activities coinciding with Stonehenge Stage 3 (between *2400–2220 cal BC* and *2300–2100 cal BC*; see Table 11.7) or thereafter. The inclusion of crushed bluestone in the fabric of Beaker-related ceramics in the secondary fills of the Lesser Cursus (Raymond in Richards 1990: 82) may provide one indication of bluestone fragments at nearby Fargo Plantation. Overall, the cluster of bluestone chips and flakes retrieved during the SRP test-pitting is difficult to understand, especially in being dominated by rhyolite Groups C and D, rhyolite types that are represented by possibly just two monoliths (Stones 32d and 32e) at Stonehenge (Rob Ixer pers. comm.).

4.4. Airman's Corner pit circle

M. Parker Pearson

In 2009, Wessex Archaeology discovered a probable pit circle north of Airman's Corner just outside the western edge of the World Heritage Site, while conducting a gradiometer survey as part of an archaeological evaluation for English Heritage in advance of construction of the Stonehenge visitor centre (Figure 4.41). Since this feature lay outside the footprint of the development, no further archaeological work was envisaged so the SRP team planned an evaluation excavation in September 2009 to date and characterise it. Although permission was kindly given by the landowner, Mr Rob Turner, Wessex Archaeology were concerned that their discovery should remain subject to client-confidentiality and requested that their client (English

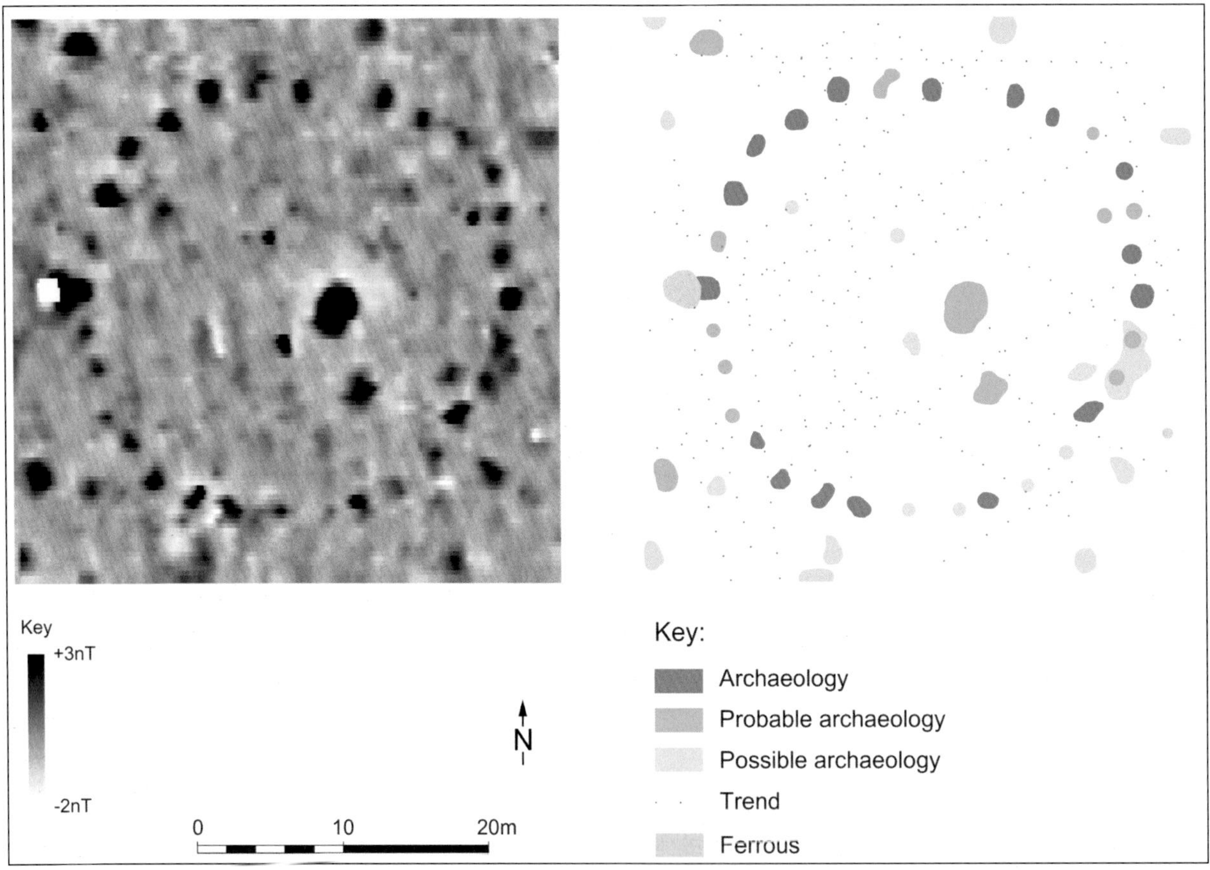

Figure 4.42. The gradiometer plot of Airman's Corner pit circle (left) and its interpretation (right) (from Wessex Archaeology 2009); © Wessex Archaeology reproduced courtesy of English Heritage

Heritage) prevent our excavation. Having completed test-pitting and magnetic susceptibility analysis of topsoil at the probable pit circle prior to excavation, we were asked by English Heritage not to carry out the excavation that we planned within the circle's northeast quadrant. If we failed to comply, English Heritage would immediately schedule the site as an ancient monument to prevent our excavation going ahead. Not wishing to jeopardise our good working relationship with Wessex Archaeology and English Heritage, we did not carry out the excavation.

In later years, English Heritage planned their own archaeological excavation of the pit circle but their project was aborted as a result of budgetary and resource constraints. The pit circle has not been scheduled. Today this enigmatic pit circle remains undated and uncharacterised as well as statutorily unprotected within a field that remains under cultivation.

4.4.1. Research background

Wessex Archaeology (2009) describe this feature (4001 at SU 0977 4313) as a complex of probable pits forming a near-perfect circle, about 24m in diameter, with a slightly oblate form in the north and east (Figure 4.42). Their gradiometer plot and interpretive plan (*ibid.*: fig. 10) reveal that the circle is formed of up to 30 pits, with their centres approximately 2.50m apart. The sizes of the anomalies indicate that these pits are likely to be mostly between 1m and 2m in diameter. Wessex Archaeology's report suggests that a possible gap between pits on the east side may be an entrance but concede that this gap may result from pits not being detected as clearly in this area. More likely as an entrance is a *c.* 4m-wide gap between pits on the north side. A large anomaly just east of the centre of the circle, and another to the south of it, may also be archaeological features.

Since this probable pit circle lies just 1500m west of the scatter of bluestone chips south of the Greater Cursus (see above), we wondered whether its pits might be the emptied sockets of a dismantled stone circle, to form Stone's 'blue Stonehenge' (1947).

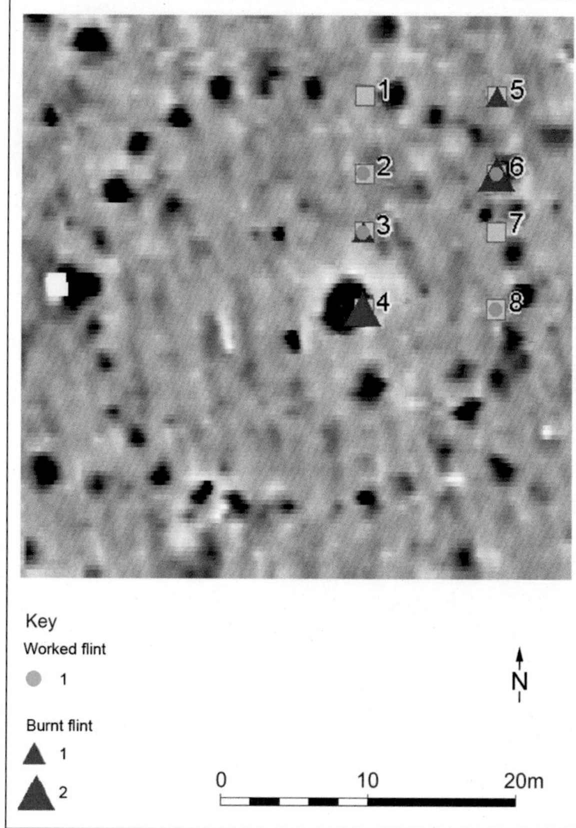

Figure 4.43. The positions of test pits and their finds within the Airman's Corner pit circle, overlaid on Wessex Archaeology's gradiometer survey

The only other such candidate for being a dismantled stone circle identified in the vicinity, just 100m southeast of the bluestone scatter, is a *c.* 20m-diameter oval ring of pit-like anomalies detected by the Stonehenge Hidden Landscape Project beneath Amesbury G50 round barrow (Stonehenge Hidden Landscape Project 2012: 15, fig. 34; Bowden *et al.* 2015: 35, fig. 3.7). These pits are likely to have diameters similar to those of the Airman's Corner pit circle but SHLP's GPR survey suggests that they are much deeper than bluestone sockets and are consistent with having held wooden posts (Gaffney *et al.* 2012; Paul Garwood pers. comm.).

Also within Stonehenge's environs, a Late Neolithic pit circle has been excavated on Boscombe Down to the east of the River Avon (Fitzpatrick 2004; Darvill 2006: 161, fig. 58). Most or all of these pits probably never held uprights.

A second research theme relates to the location of the Airman's Corner circle. It lies 600m and 1100m beyond the western ends of the Lesser and Greater Cursuses respectively (see Figure 2.3). Although not perfectly aligned on the cursuses' long axes, the circle's position beyond their terminals raises the possibility that it might have been associated with these monuments and may thus belong to the mid/later fourth millennium BC. However, the pit circle lies on an approximately northeast–southwest line of Bronze Age round barrows that extends from the west end of the Lesser Cursus so it could equally have been constructed in the Early Bronze Age as part of this linear cemetery, most likely as a circle of timber posts similar to that identified under Amesbury G50 by the SHLP survey.

4.4.2. Fieldwork

Eight 1m × 1m test pits were dug in two north–south rows within the northeast quadrant of the Airman's Corner pit circle, to constitute an 8% sample of that quadrant. Each test pit was excavated to the base of the *c.* 0.20m-deep ploughsoil (onto bare chalk) and the soil was sieved through a 10mm mesh.

Only four pieces of worked flint and six pieces of burnt flint were recovered (Figure 4.43). These unusually low densities contrast with those from many of the test pits at Fargo just south of the Greater Cursus (see above) but correspond with the very low numbers found during fieldwalking by the Stonehenge Environs Project west of the cursuses and immediately east of the location of the pit circle (Richards 1990: fig. 8 area 62, table 8). No bluestone fragments were recovered from the test pits, from the surface of the ploughsoil or from nearby fieldwalking by the Stonehenge Environs Project.

Low values of magnetic susceptibility, measured with a Bartington field probe by Dr Roger Doonan, similarly reveal little evidence of anthropogenic activity in the topsoil within the circle, though values tend to be higher just outside it (Figure 4.44).

4.4.3. Conclusion

The date and character of this probable pit circle remain unknown. It is almost certainly prehistoric on the basis of its plan and location but it could date to any point between the Middle Neolithic and the Middle Bronze Age. Its 30 likely pits have diameters suitable for having held timber or bluestone uprights but it might equally have been no more than a pit circle similar to that on Boscombe Down. The low densities of worked flint recovered by test-pitting reflect that of the surrounding area immediately to the east. This accords with low magnetic susceptibility within the circle, although higher values around its edges could conceivably indicate that the interior was kept free of human-related activities such as burning which might have occurred just beyond its perimeter where values are higher.

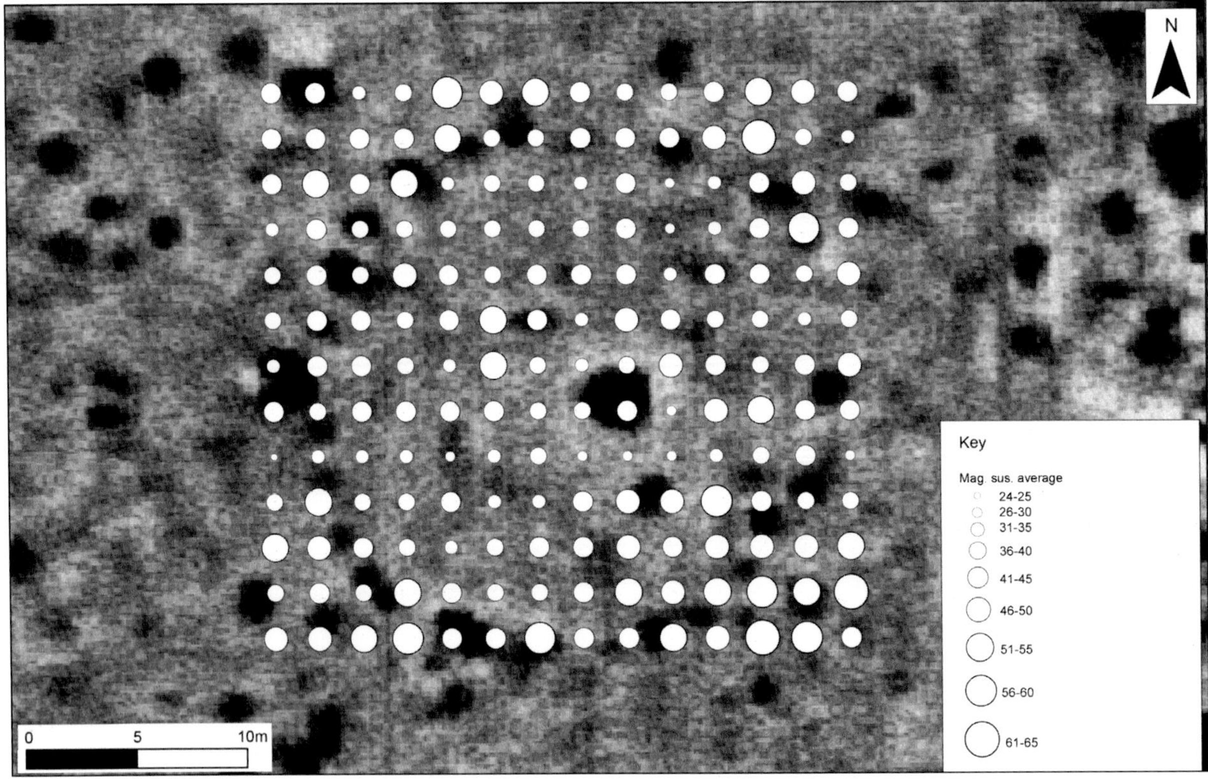

Figure 4.44. Magnetic susceptibility within the Airman's Corner pit circle, overlaid on Wessex Archaeology's gradiometer survey

4.5. Bluestones and Stonehenge

M. Parker Pearson and C. Richards

In taking an overview of the stones of Stonehenge, it is clear that, of the two different geological constituents – bluestones and sarsens – it is the former that have attracted far more attention as being 'exotic' elements of the monument (for discussion of the sarsens, see Chapter 6). Perhaps the only scheme to treat both stone types as a single material category is that proposed by Parker Pearson and Ramilisonina (1998a), where the material qualities of stone are contrasted with those of wood. Yet, in terms of appearance, size, texture and source, there is considerable variation between the bluestones and the sarsens. In this discussion, we will focus on the bluestones as distinct material entities; given their varied morphology and geology, a potentially complex and rather ambiguous picture emerges. This picture is framed by four converging strands of evidence.

4.5.1. Dressed and undressed bluestones

As described earlier, the presence of dressed bluestones of spotted dolerite and dolerite lithology within the inner horseshoe setting (arranged as an oval in Stage 4 and subsequently turned into a horseshoe by removing the monoliths at its northeastern end) has been interpreted since the last century as demonstrating the existence of an earlier bluestone monument.

In considering the dismantled monument represented by the dressed bluestones, Atkinson stated that 'the nature of this structure is even more uncertain than its position' (1979: 82). Because the dressed bluestones are of a unitary lithology (dolerite/spotted dolerite), there has been an assumption that they represent a single earlier monument that included at least two bluestone trilithons, potentially forming a component of an earlier phase of Stonehenge (*ibid.*: 177–8).

However, for many years, others have posited a location further afield – even Pembrokeshire, 180 miles away – for an earlier monument of bluestones (*e.g.* Thomas 1923: 258; Bradley 2000: 94; Parker Pearson 2012). The presence of disassembled and re-dressed bluestone trilithons in the inner bluestone horseshoe is curious, and begs the question of not only why bluestone trilithons were no longer deemed appropriate architecture, especially given that they were surrounded by sarsen trilithons, but also why some of the bluestones were re-dressed and transformed to the extent of the upper tenons being obliterated. Clearly there is a contradiction embedded in the architecture of the bluestone horseshoe because, in constitution, it refers to an earlier monument but, in composition, 'the specific architecture of this earlier manifestation is transformed and rendered unrecognisable' (Richards 2013: 19).

In contrast, there is no direct evidence that the undressed bluestones, mainly comprising the outer bluestone circle of Stage 4, ever formed part of an earlier monument, let alone a monument involving dressed stones. While the empty Q and R Holes, together with the Aubrey Holes, most likely held bluestones, there is no direct evidence that these were the same stones that were later re-arranged to form the outer bluestone circle, although it is a fair likelihood.

Appearances can often be deceptive and the 26 undressed constituents of Stage 4's outer bluestone circle, being unimpressively small and squat, contrast with the elegant, shaped, inner horseshoe bluestones. Consequently, a combination of morphology and lack of any sign of previous modification has, by default, had the effect of diverting archaeological interest away from the outer bluestone circle, certainly in terms of considering whether its stones might once have been components of a previous monument.

However, these undressed bluestones of the outer circle actually have more in common with third millennium BC stone circles than with the bluestones of the inner horseshoe because, throughout Britain and Ireland, one of the main features of stone circles is the use of undressed monoliths (Burl 2000; Richards 2013). If this line of reasoning is followed, then the mixed lithologies and shapes of the outer bluestone circle at Stonehenge may testify to longer and more complex biographies than those of the more remarked-upon inner horseshoe bluestones. Moreover, of all the bluestones present at Stonehenge, it actually may be the constituents of the outer circle that can trace their ancestry back to one or more stone circles originally erected in south Wales, rather than having been brought more directly from their geological source to be shaped at Stonehenge alongside the sarsen trilithons; this possibility is the focus of our current research in the Preseli hills. These dolerites of the inner horseshoe might well have been those erected at Bluestonehenge, at the riverside end of the Avenue (see Chapter 5), before being moved and re-erected firstly as an inner bluestone circle at Stonehenge in Stage 3.

4.5.2. From Aubrey Holes (Stage 1) to Q and R Holes (Stage 2) to the outer bluestone circle (Stage 4)

A second strand of evidence is the relationship between the bluestones and the Q and R stoneholes and, as we have argued earlier, the Aubrey Holes. As mentioned above, there is no direct evidence linking the bluestones comprising the final monument with these earlier empty stoneholes. For the Q and R Holes, the sizes of the sockets, and stone fragments recovered, indicate that they originally held bluestones. Judging from our reassessment of the Aubrey Holes, these too once held bluestones. The aim here is not to assess the evidence for this sequence of bluestone use, but to raise the possibility that, once the stones arrived in the Stonehenge landscape, such a sequence of deployment and redeployment might not have been restricted to the confines of Stonehenge (see Chapter 5 on the use of bluestones at Bluestonehenge).

For example, despite claims for a formal structure to the positioning of bluestones within Stonehenge's outer bluestone circle of Stage 4 (*e.g.* Bradley 2000: 92–5), in our analysis the impression given is one of near-disorder. In this final form, the arrangement of the Stonehenge bluestones, particularly the outer circle, appears more as a collection of stones with little regard to the creation of a megalithic architecture predicated on lithology, biography or source.

4.5.3. The distribution of bluestone fragments in the Stonehenge landscape

Following on from the above is the significant number and petrological range of fragments of bluestone present in the wider environs of Stonehenge (Figure 4.12). This distribution is a product of a number of different archaeological investigations, including excavation, test-pitting, casual surface prospection and systematic fieldwalking.

Most types of bluestone lithology found at Stonehenge itself are also present in the wider landscape, but one of the interesting features of this material is a tendency towards specific stone types occurring in different places. For example, rhyolite fragments predominate in the vicinity of Fargo Plantation, coming from a range of contexts including the Greater Cursus ditch (Stone 1947), Fargo hengiform enclosure (Stone 1938) and adjacent ploughed fields (Stone 1947; Richards 1990: 230–1) as well as the SRP test pits (see above). Equally, from a small 2m-wide cutting through the old land surface beneath the North Kite earthwork (see Figure 1.5), three pieces of bluestone were recovered, all of spotted dolerite (Richards 1990: 185). Given the small area excavated, this is likely to constitute a small proportion of a concentration of spotted dolerite in the vicinity.

4.5.4. Stone sockets of bluestone size in the Stonehenge landscape

The presence of empty stone sockets of bluestone size discovered by survey and excavation at different sites beyond Stonehenge is further potential evidence of settings of bluestones having been erected and dismantled in prehistory. As well as the stone sockets excavated within Bluestonehenge (described in Chapter 5), possible bluestone-sized sockets have been recognised at Coneybury henge (features 1848 and 1844; Richards 1990: 137–8, figs 98, 103), where a fragment of rhyolite was also recovered (*ibid.*: 124), and Woodhenge (posthole C14, which was packed with chalk rubble to raise the base for its upright to be set more shallowly than surrounding postholes; Cunnington 1929).

To these examples can be added at least two further candidates for early bluestone circles or settings. Just 130m west-southwest of Stonehenge, geophysical survey of Amesbury G9 round barrow revealed a ditch enclosing a *c.* 17m-diameter circle of *c.* 25 features that could potentially be stone sockets (Field *et al.* 2014: 13–14). The uncertainty surrounding the architecture and date of the Airman's Corner circle (see above) is particularly frustrating given its relatively close proximity to the bluestone scatter adjacent to the Greater Cursus.

When the dominance of rhyolite flakes and fragments around Fargo Plantation is considered in conjunction with the rhyolite tools collected during fieldwalking by the Stonehenge Environs Project on the north side of the Greater Cursus (Richards 1990: 230–1), the presence in the Cursus' vicinity of a rhyolite stone setting remains a possibility. However, the spatial association of rhyolite fragments and tools with Beaker-period ceramics and lithics on both sides of the Cursus may well indicate that these items were quarried and brought from one or more rhyolite monoliths within Stonehenge in its later stages.

From the above discussion we can certainly agree with Atkinson (1979: 82) that questions concerning the nature and composition of a pre-existing bluestone monument or monuments are both complicated and unresolved. Given the range and distribution of bluestone lithologies present within Stonehenge (Thorpe *et al.* 1991; see petrological synthesis in Volume 2), and bearing in mind their dressed and undressed morphology, could a similar assortment of lithologies and dressing be a feature of any pre-existing monuments? Alternatively, the presence of previous monuments comprising discrete bluestone lithologies – for instance, exclusively spotted dolerite or rhyolite – also remains a strong possibility.

If, as is suggested above, the Aubrey Holes once held bluestones, could a far more complex sequence of monumental construction and reconstruction have taken place than has hitherto been recognised? The moving of bluestones at Stonehenge could have entailed not simply the repositioning of stones that had arrived at the great monument in a single event, but a merging into Stonehenge of further bluestones brought from smaller early settings, situated either within the Stonehenge environs or further afield. Overall, the bluestone flakes and fragments that have been recovered from a range of external contexts beyond Stonehenge clearly represent a minor sample that, at the very least, testifies to a complicated narrative of bluestone deployment and redeployment through the third millennium BC.

The possibility that the dressed bluestones were derived from dismantled stone settings nearer the Welsh sources has long been considered (*e.g.* Thomas 1923: 258; Bradley 2000: 94; Parker Pearson *et al.* 2016). The recent discoveries of the quarries for one of the Stonehenge rhyolites at Craig Rhos-y-felin, and for the spotted dolerite Stonehenge stones at Carn Goedog (Parker Pearson *et al.* 2015; 2017; 2019) has served to not only emphasise the Preseli hills in Pembrokeshire as a major source, but also to highlight these outcrops' dramatic, almost monumental visual aspect (Figure 4.3). That these outcrops served as quarries for bluestone monoliths which were deployed in third millennium cal BC monumental architecture is of little surprise. Whilst the stones were extracted from these outcrops, they were not dressed at the quarries. What is surprising, however, is that once quarried and separated from the parent rock, these stones were destined to become part of the architecture of Stonehenge, a monument constructed over 150 miles away. Of the monuments in Wales that these may have been incorporated into before being dismantled for the journey, one may well be a large stone circle at Waun Mawn in Preseli and another an as yet unidentified monument in the eastern part of the Senni Formation around Crickhowell and Brecon where the Altar Stone appears to have derived from (Parker Pearson *et al.* 2019). The mystery of Stonehenge is inextricably tied up in these extraordinary bluestones even though the sarsens have dominated the monument since Stage 2.

Chapter 5

Bluestonehenge at West Amesbury: where the Stonehenge Avenue meets the River Avon

M. Parker Pearson, J. Pollard, J. Rylatt, J. Thomas and K. Welham*

5.1. Research background and objectives

M. Parker Pearson, J. Pollard, J. Thomas and K. Welham

As discussed at the end of the last chapter, there is a distinct possibility that the dressed bluestones (of spotted and unspotted dolerite) arranged as the inner horseshoe at Stonehenge have a different history of use and location to those undressed bluestones occupying the outer circle. We suspect that these undressed bluestones (of a variety of lithologies from Preseli – rhyolites, volcanics and sandstones as well as occasional spotted and unspotted dolerite) formed the original stone circle at Stonehenge, placed in the Aubrey Holes in Stage 1 and then moved to the Q and R Holes in Stage 2 before ending up in the outer bluestone circle in Stage 4. We further consider that the inner bluestone oval/horseshoe of Stage 4 was constructed out of a 10m-diameter circle of bluestones erected in the centre of Stonehenge in Stage 3. Yet where might these dressed dolerite pillars in this Stage 3 bluestone circle have stood before arriving at Stonehenge after *2400–2220 cal BC* but before *2300–2100 cal BC*.

Our hypothesis is that the bluestones of Stage 3's central circle and Stage 4's oval/horseshoe were first set up as a stone circle beside the River Avon and were then moved to Stonehenge. If so, were they dressed before they arrived at the riverside, while they were being put up there, or afterwards when they were erected at Stonehenge in Stage 3?

In August–September 2009, the Stonehenge Riverside Project discovered the dismantled remains of an entirely unknown bluestone circle at the end of the Stonehenge Avenue, beside the River Avon (SU 1421 4141; see Figure 9.4). The stones had been removed in prehistory but the sizes and shapes of the empty stone sockets are consistent with their once having held Welsh bluestones, brought 140 miles from the Preseli hills of southwest Wales. Nine stoneholes were excavated, part of a circle of *c.* 25 stone sockets. (Most of the circle remains unexcavated, preserved for future researchers, and the 2009 excavation [Figure 5.1] was backfilled immediately after the excavation was completed).

The stone circle was just under 10m in diameter and was surrounded by a henge – a circular ditch with an external bank – with a probable entrance to the east. The henge ditch is 23.40m in diameter and sits at the end of the 1¾-mile (2.8km) avenue that runs between Stonehenge and the River Avon (see Chapter 8 for SRP excavations along the course of the Avenue). Little trace of the henge bank remains other than as fill lying within the outer

*** With contributions by:**
U. Albarella, C. Bronk Ramsey, C. Casswell, B. Chan, G. Cook, R. Cleal, G. Davies, C.A.I. French, I. Heath, R. Ixer, P.D. Marshall, L. Martin, C. Minniti, D. Mitcham, R. Nunn, A. Payne, P. Pettitt, E. Simmons, C. Steele and S. Viner-Daniels

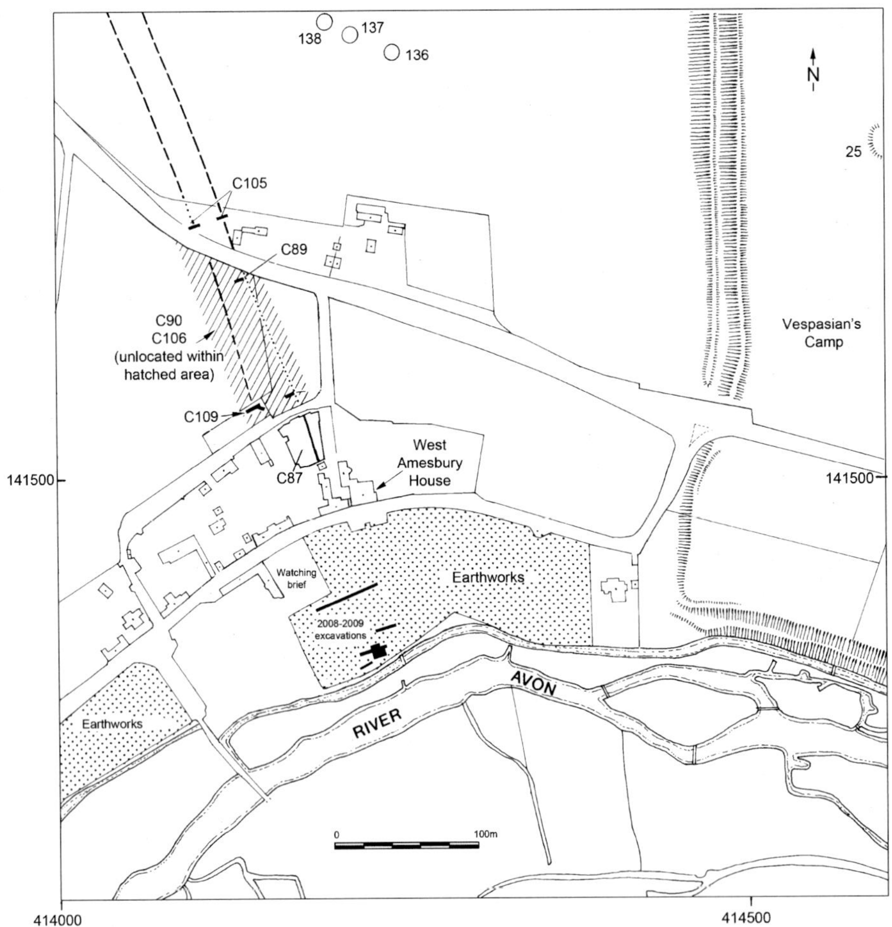

Figure 5.1. The riverside end of the Stonehenge Avenue, showing previous and recent excavation trenches in black (C numbers indicate excavations or cuttings undertaken before the SRP; other numbered features are round barrows). The Avenue is marked as parallel dashed lines. The River Avon is not a single course but has leats, notably on its north bank (after Cleal *et al.* 1995); © Historic England

side of the ditch. Excavations here at West Amesbury in 2008 established that this outer henge was built in the Chalcolithic: a date from the tip of a broken antler pick in the basal fill of the ditch places its construction within the period 2470–2200 cal BC, possibly contemporary with Stage 3 at Stonehenge (from *2400–2220 cal BC* until *2300–2100 cal BC*; see Table 11.7). The styles of arrowheads recovered from the stone sockets indicate that the stone circle is likely to have been much earlier than the surrounding henge, potentially dating to the Middle or Late Neolithic.

Activity within the area around the dismantled bluestone circle dates back to the Early Mesolithic (*c.* 8000–6000 BC) and Late Mesolithic (*c.* 6000–4000 BC), with a series of deposits of worked flint from these periods lying within former brown forest soils (preserved under the henge bank) on the east side of the chalk spur on which the circle is located. There is no flintwork diagnostic of activity here during the Early Neolithic period.

The SRP excavations also located the riverside end of the Stonehenge Avenue within this field on the bank of the Avon. It consists of two parallel ditches, 18.10m apart. These once held small upright posts, forming a palisade on either side of the Avenue itself. The eastern ditch was traced to within a few metres of the henge ditch and presumably terminated at or close to the outer bank of the henge[6]. It and the henge may have been built at the same time, given their proximity and symmetrical positioning. The Avenue ended within about 100m of the prehistoric river bank, separated from it by the 30m-diameter henge. Since prehistoric times, the River Avon has encroached northwards, removing 5m of the henge's southern ditch and interior.

The henge's ditch silted up gradually during the Bronze Age, with silts along its western side interspersed with flint cobble surfaces in the ditch bottom. After the ditch had fully silted up, it was re-cut along its northeastern circuit. The henge's interior was also re-used in the Late Bronze Age, with the digging of a small penannular ditch that terminated at its northeast in a large timber post. This and two other posts formed a façade or structure within the centre of the henge.

6 Note that here this Avenue ditch is referred to by its geographical position as the 'eastern' ditch, but that elsewhere along the course of the Avenue, this is the northern ditch; in the 500m-length of the Avenue from Stonehenge itself to the Avenue bend, this ditch is geographically the western ditch (see Chapter 8, especially Figure 8.1, for the changing orientation of the ditches).

Previous excavations

The position of the riverside end of the Stonehenge Avenue had not been established before the SRP work in 2009. To the south of West Amesbury House, the ground levels out onto a floodplain between the Woodford valley road and the river. In 1921 O.G.S. Crawford identified here what he considered to be a possible extension of the Avenue, about 30m wide and immediately adjacent to the river (Cleal *et al.* 1995: 292, fig. 169, plan 3). However, the alignment of the eastern edge of Crawford's putative Avenue earthwork diverges significantly from the line of the eastern ditch identified to the north of West Amesbury House by George Smith in 1973 (Smith 1973; Cleal *et al.* 1995: 295). The orientation of Crawford's putative extension is not only off-line but is now known to be part of a series of more recent earthworks (see *Topographical survey* below).

The excavations by Smith in 1973 north of West Amesbury House (C87; Figure 5.1) located only the eastern ditch of the Avenue. There was no clear evidence of an associated bank from the silting within the ditch. Nor was there any trace of the western ditch within a smaller trench (C109) excavated across its likely course. The eastern ditch was shallow and uneven, suggesting that it might have been petering out as it approached the river. Before the SRP's second season of excavation at West Amesbury in 2009, there was no clear indication of the Avenue's existence for a distance of *c.* 167m between Smith's excavations and the River Avon. We now know that it extends to within 20m of the present river course.

Smith (1973: 49) considered that the parallel, flanking banks might have been the significant elements of the Avenue (as is the case with the 180m-long Durrington avenue, reported in Volume 3; Parker Pearson *et al.* 2007) and that the ditches served only as quarries to provide bank material. Whilst that might have been the case for stretches of the Avenue further away from the river, the presence of the postholes found in the ditches in 2009 suggests that the line of the ditches was as or more important than the banks.

Topographical survey

Well before the start of the SRP, topographical survey of the earthworks within the water meadow south of West Amesbury House, between the Woodford valley road and the river, was carried out by Desmond Bonney and later Carenza Lewis for the former RCHME. They identified a complex distribution

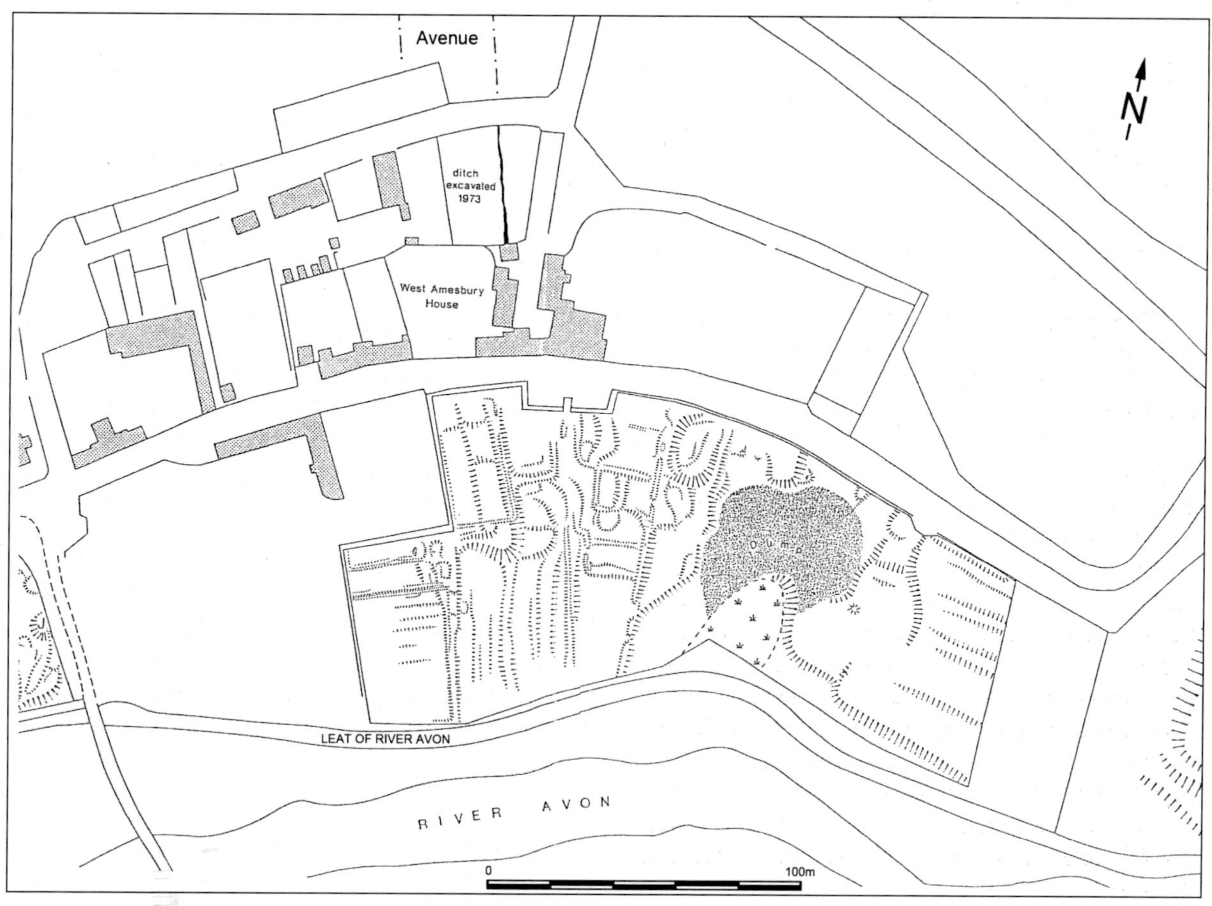

Figure 5.2. Topographic survey of West Amesbury earthworks by Desmond Bonney and Carenza Lewis for the RCHME; © Historic England

Figure 5.3. Magnetometer survey of West Amesbury showing linear features (M1) and the northwestern edge of the henge ditch (M2)

of largely rectilinear features which are interpreted as most likely being garden earthworks and other remains of a shrunken medieval village (Figure 5.2). None appear to be prehistoric features (Bowden 2011).

Watching brief

A watching brief was carried out by Kate Brayne of Rudyard Archaeology during the digging of a swimming pool in The Hatcheries in 2008 (Figure 5.1). This work revealed an east–west aligned feature at the south end of the house's garden, located west of the line of the north–south cob wall (the boundary between The Hatcheries' garden and the water meadow; see Figure 5.51). The feature was initially thought to be the northern edge of an east–west ditch but excavation in 2009 of SRP Trench 50 (Figure 5.5) confirmed that its clean fill (with a total absence of charcoal) and uneven bottom were due to its geomorphological origin (see below). This 'ditch' can now be interpreted as a natural terrace in the chalk, in which the lower component has filled with periglacial clay with flints; it is illustrated in plan, with its various context numbers, in Figure 5.50.

The watching brief also identified a 0.60m-deep posthole, dug through red clay with flints into bedrock, but there were no associated finds.

5.2. Investigations before excavation

Geophysical survey

K. Welham, C. Steele, A. Payne and L. Martin

Magnetometer and earth resistance surveys were carried out at West Amesbury in 2006 with the aim of detecting the riverside terminal of the Stonehenge Avenue.

Earth resistance survey utilised two Geoscan RM15-D earth resistance meters in the 0.50m twin electrode configuration. Readings were taken at 1m intervals along traverses spaced 1m apart over 20m by 20m grids. Magnetometer survey was undertaken using Bartington Grad601 fluxgate gradiometers over a series of 30m grid squares, with readings recorded at 0.25m intervals along north–south-orientated traverses spaced 1m apart at 200 nTm^{-1}. Numbers in parentheses refer to those in Figures 5.3 and 5.4.

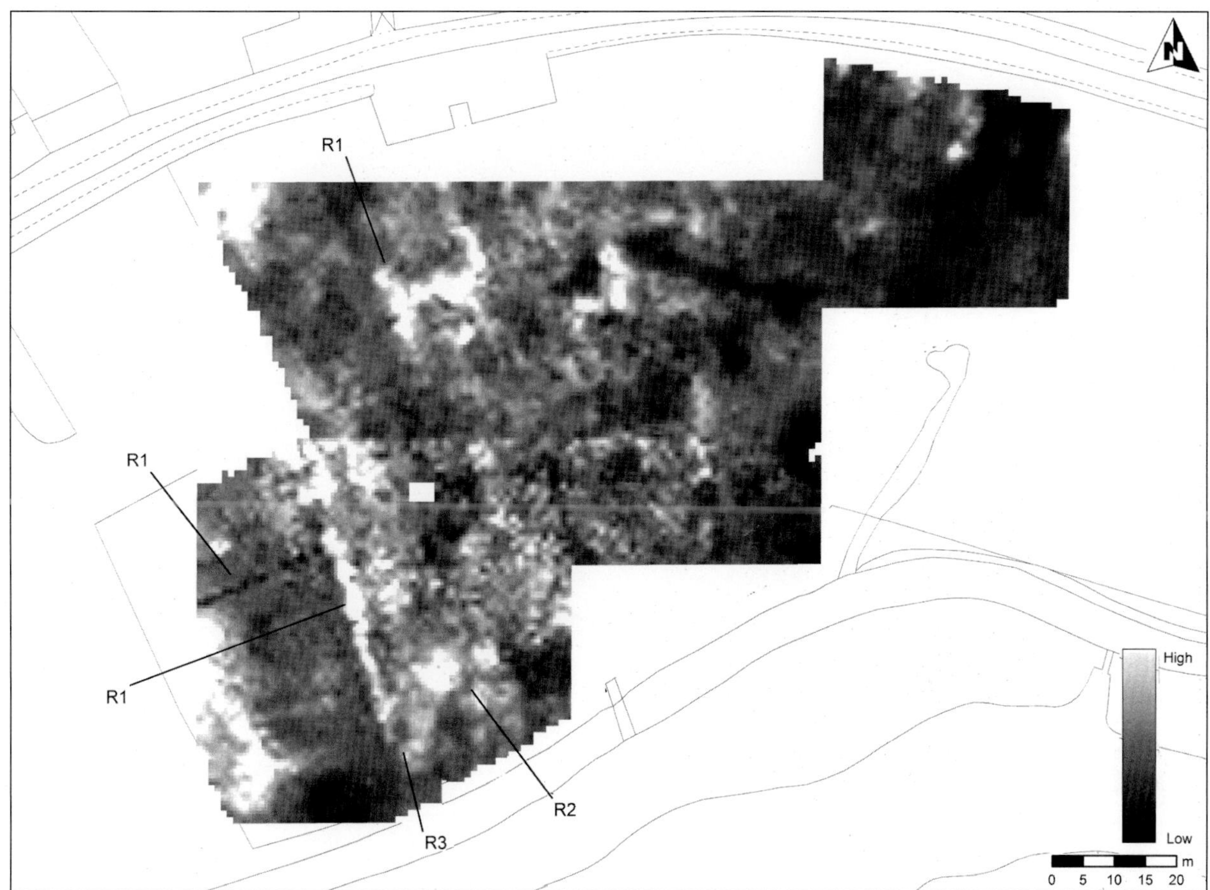

Figure 5.4. Earth resistance survey of West Amesbury showing linear features (R1), the henge ditch (R2) and a circular/curvilinear feature (R3) west of the henge

The area surveyed has been greatly disturbed by post-medieval and later activities, making it difficult to obtain a clear understanding of any potential prehistoric remains detected in these data. In both datasets, the majority of the linear anomalies (R1/M1) are representative of this disturbance and many correspond with the RCHME earthwork plan of the area (*cf.* Figure 5.2; Payne 2006: fig. 7). The Avenue was not detected in these data, although it was later identified in the survey area during excavation.

The northern half of the henge ditch is visible in these data (R2/M2) but was not identified prior to excavation. There is an ephemeral anomaly in the earth resistance data that may be indicative of a ring ditch (R3), and which correlates with a curving ditch identified during excavation, the fill of which contained charcoal flecks and worked flints.

Auger survey

M. Parker Pearson

Augering was carried out on the river bank along the axis of the future Trench 51 by Mike Allen, Mike Parker Pearson, Julie Gardiner and Josh Pollard in April 2008. This east–west auger transect identified flint gravel spreads and flanking ditches close to the edge of the present riverbank; the hypothesis prior to excavation was that these might be the Avenue's banks and ditches. Excavation of SRP Trench 51 in 2008 (Figure 5.5) demonstrated that these were medieval features together with the northern edge of the henge ditch. The flint gravel surface was further recorded within a north–south auger transect. A northern east–west transect (along the line of the future Trench 50) was not completed, except on its east side where it located a shallow feature which was thought to be possibly the Avenue ditch but, after excavation of Trench 50, was found to be one of many medieval features (see Figure 5.50 for the medieval and later features encountered in this trench, in relation to the Avenue ditches).

Test pits

M. Parker Pearson

In 2008, an east–west line of five test pits, each 1m × 1m in size, was dug at 6m intervals, parallel to the riverbank, in advance of Trench 51 (Figure 5.6). In 2009, a further 15 test pits were dug; the areas test-pitted were then excavated as Trenches 50, 60, 61 and the extensions of Trench 51. Twenty-seven further test pits were also dug on a systematic 20m grid across the

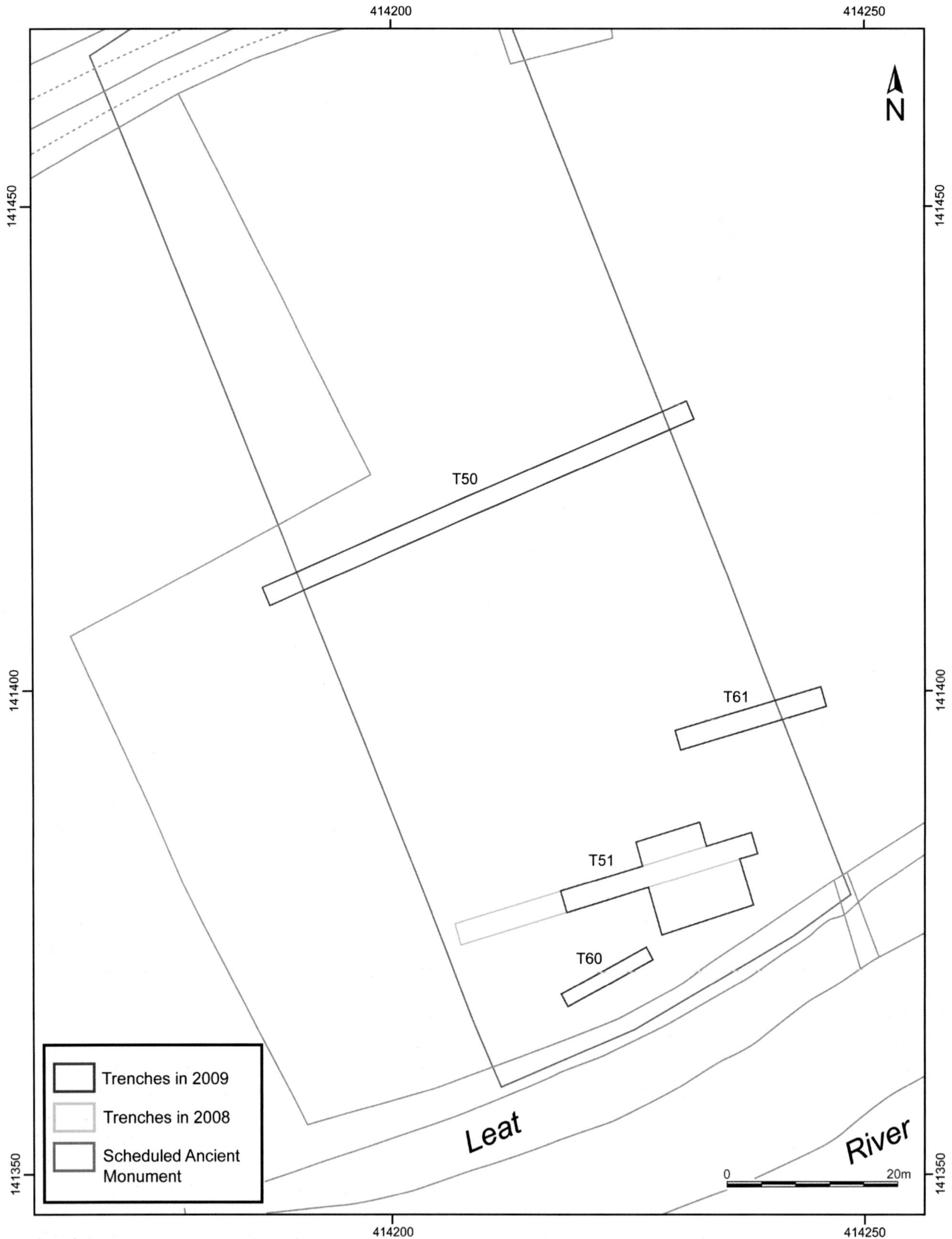

Figure 5.5. Plan of excavation trenches at West Amesbury, 2008–2009. The brown tram-lines indicate the extent of the statutorily protected scheduled ancient monument

Figure 5.6. Distribution of topsoil test pits (black squares) and excavation trenches (red lines) at West Amesbury. The area in green (woodland) is the low-lying ground around the spring and along the riverside

entire field outside the scheduled (statutorily protected) area (Figure 5.5), three to its west and 24 to its east.

The test pits were dug to the base of the topsoil (on average 0.30m deep), and the soil was sieved through a 10mm mesh (Figure 5.7). Finds included worked flint, burnt flint and a range of pottery sherds from the Iron Age to the post-medieval period.

Recovery of worked flints was particularly high within the scheduled area. In 2009, the 15 test pits in this location produced over 800 pieces of worked flint, although most of this was undiagnostic (Figure 5.8).

Lithics from the test pits

D. Mitcham

The West Amesbury riverside test pits produced an assemblage of 1,582 pieces of worked flint from 47 test pits (Table 5.1). The raw material is predominantly chalk-derived flint, and the degree of patination is quite mixed throughout the assemblage as a whole. Some of the material has only a light patina and bluish colour, whilst other pieces are heavily patinated. Some of the probably Mesolithic blades are very fresh with only slight patination, and it is clear that the test pits produced mixed assemblages from different periods. This is not surprising given the depth of the ploughsoil, and the degree of its medieval disturbance.

Outside the narrow corridor of the scheduled area, the density of lithics falls sharply on its west side, coinciding with the junction of sub-surface chalk bedrock under the Avenue and periglacial clay west of it. On the east side, high densities of lithics continue until the break of slope above a spring. This defines a concentration extending *c.* 80m east–west and over 100m north–south, on the high ground provided by the north–south chalk spur that extends from under West Amesbury House to the riverbank (the lithic assemblage is further discussed in the synthesis in Volume 2).

Assemblage character

Flakes and blades make up 85.7% of the total West Amesbury test-pit assemblage. Flakes comprise 83% of the overall assemblage whilst blades account for 3.7%. Flakes therefore dominate the assemblage; when unmodified flakes are removed, blades and bladelets form 20.6% of the rest of the assemblage, which then comprises 286 pieces of worked flint (Table 5.2).

The total blade industry element of the assemblage (*i.e.* blade-cores, blades, bladelets and blade-like flakes) represents 6.1% of the overall ploughsoil assemblage, with the caveat that some blade-like flakes could have been produced accidentally. Given the plough-zone

Figure 5.7. Test Pit 110 at West Amesbury under excavation

context of the material, this industry is potentially a palimpsest of Earlier and Later Mesolithic activity.

Blade production is evident at the site, with five single-platform blade-cores, one of which is a tiny microlithic core (6.3g), probably of Later Mesolithic date (Butler 2005: 86). The others are larger pieces ranging in weight from 25.5g to 62.6g. A blade-core from Test Pit [TP] 6 is very heavily patinated and damaged. Another blade-core (67.1g) is of bipolar (opposed platform) type. All these blade-cores are Mesolithic in character, and no diagnostic Earlier Neolithic flint was found on this site. Whilst blades and blade-cores are present, no microliths were recovered from the test pits, in contrast to those microliths found during the project's open-area excavations at the riverside (see Chan and Rylatt, below). This is not surprising given the mesh size of 10mm used to sieve the test pits' topsoil; the microliths from within the henge were recovered by flotation of environmental samples, using a 1mm mesh.

Retouched or utilised flakes account for 2.3% of the overall assemblage, whilst the retouched or utilised flake or blade category makes up 0.9%. TP 83 produced a retouched blade with a notch. A second retouched blade, also from TP 83, has been struck from an opposed platform blade-core. A relatively high percentage of miscellaneous waste (6.5%) is present in the assemblage.

The assemblage has few formal tools (a small percentage of 1.3%), which is a slightly greater proportion than the 0.9% present in the assemblages from the Stonehenge Palisade field that include Late Neolithic material (presented in Volume 2). Most of the tools are forms of scraper. A spurred implement on a blade is an unusual but not diagnostic piece. Given the lack of any diagnostically Early Neolithic artefacts at the site, the latter is most likely to be Mesolithic.

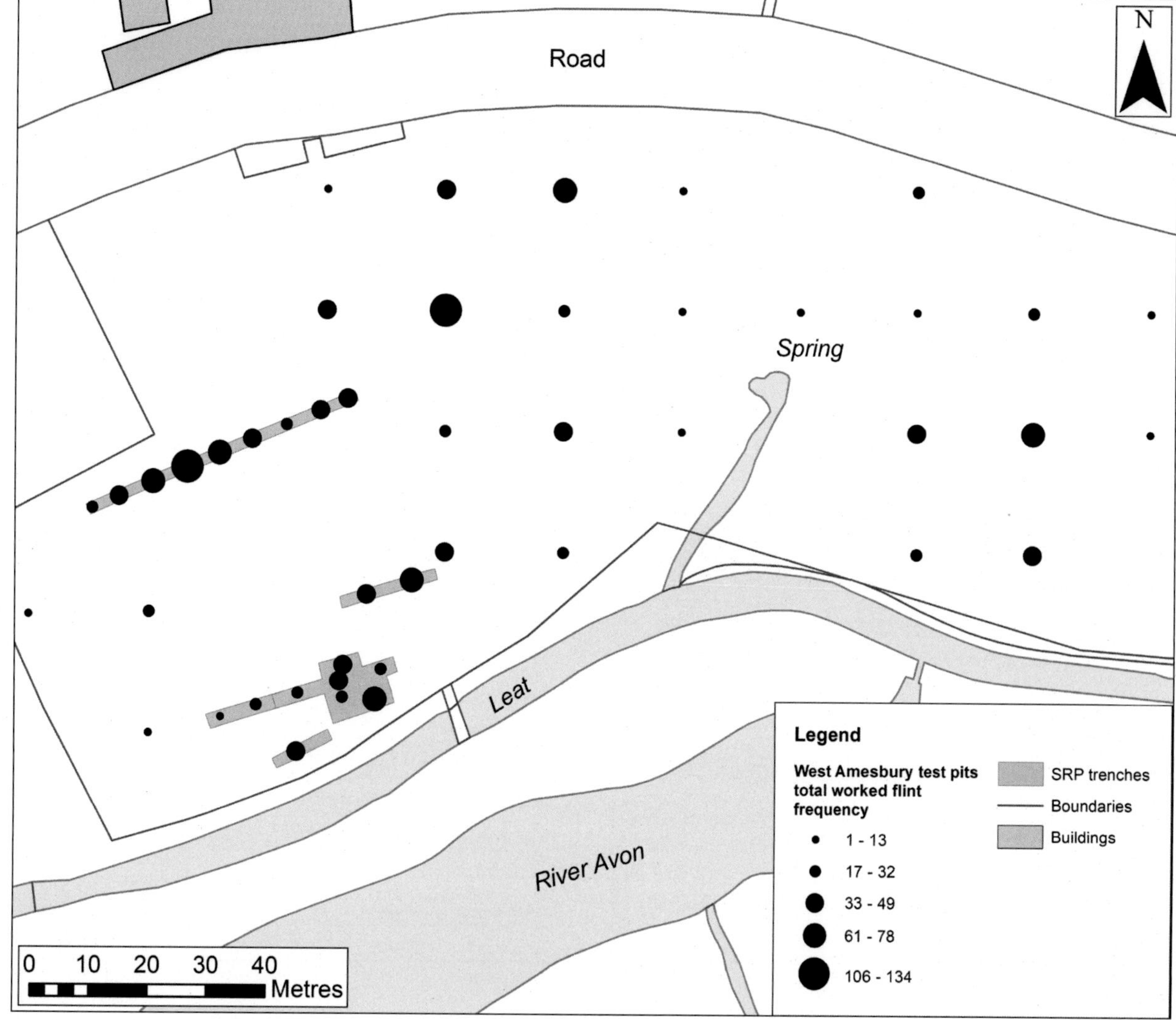

Figure 5.8. Distribution of prehistoric lithics from topsoil layers in the test pits

Only one chronologically diagnostic flint tool dating certainly to the Late Neolithic was recovered from the test pits. This oblique arrowhead was recovered from TP 122. A fragment of gabbro from TP 15 could possibly be derived from a Neolithic polished stone axe but Ixer's petrographic analysis reveals that it is not one of the recognised gabbros (Groups I–IV) presently defined as implement petrology groups (see the petrography report in Volume 2).

The core technology present within the ploughsoil is potentially more informative. The majority of cores (22 in total) are multiple-platform or single-platform flake-cores (Table 5.3). These are typical of later prehistoric flint working in general. One multiple-platform flake-core from TP 112 shows signs of re-use as a hammerstone. The presence of keeled, non-discoidal cores may relate to Late Neolithic activity in the area. These are known to occur in Late Neolithic assemblages (Butler 2005: 157). The two examples present here do not appear intended for Levallois-style flake production (*ibid.*: 2005: 157; Ballin 2011).

Finally, evidence of post-medieval knapping in TP 25 consists of a number of large and fresh, unpatinated flakes with very large and pronounced bulbs of percussion, with prominent points of impact. They derive from the finishing of the face of a flint nodule-composed post-medieval wall (its foundations discovered in the same test pit), the nodules having been struck with a metal hammer. A probably Mesolithic blade was also found in this test pit.

Artefact type	Frequency	Percent
Bipolar opposed-platform blade-core	1	0.1
Blade	45	2.8
Blade-like flake	18	1.1
Bladelet	14	0.9
Chip	9	0.6
Double-ended scraper	2	0.1
Edge-damaged/utilised blade	11	0.7
End-and-side scraper	1	0.1
End-scraper	1	0.1
Flake	1296	81.9
Ground stone axe or fragment	1	0.1
Hammerstone	2	0.1
Irregular waste	103	6.5
Keeled non-discoidal flake-core	2	0.1
Misc. retouched flake	19	1.2
Multi-platform flake-core	8	0.5
Notch	2	0.1
Oblique arrowhead	1	0.1
Other scraper	8	0.5
Other/unclassifiable (general)	6	0.4
Retouched blade	3	0.2
Single-platform blade-core	5	0.3
Spurred implement	1	0.1
Tested nodule/bashed lump	1	0.1
Unclassifiable/fragmentary core	5	0.3
Utilised/edge-damaged flake	17	1.1
Total	**1582**	**100.0**

Table 5.1. The lithic assemblage composition for the West Amesbury test pits

Artefact type	Frequency	Percent
Bipolar opposed-platform blade-core	1	0.3
Blade	45	15.7
Blade-like flake	18	6.3
Bladelet	14	4.9
Chip	9	3.1
Double-ended scraper	2	0.7
Edge-damaged/utilised blade	11	3.8
End-and-side scraper	1	0.3
End-scraper	1	0.3
Ground stone axe or fragment	1	0.3
Hammerstone	2	0.7
Irregular waste	103	36.0
Keeled non-discoidal flake-core	2	0.7
Misc. retouched flake	19	6.6
Multi-platform flake-core	8	2.8
Notch	2	0.7
Oblique arrowhead	1	0.3
Other scraper	8	2.8
Other/unclassifiable (general)	6	2.1
Retouched blade	3	1.0
Single-platform blade-core	5	1.7
Spurred implement	1	0.3
Tested nodule/bashed lump	1	0.3
Unclassifiable/fragmentary core	5	1.7
Utilised/edge-damaged flake	17	5.9
Total	**286**	**100.0**

Table 5.2. The lithic assemblage composition for the West Amesbury test pits with flakes excluded

5.3. Excavation of Bluestonehenge stone circle within West Amesbury henge, and of the Stonehenge Avenue ditches

M. Parker Pearson, J. Rylatt, J. Pollard and J. Thomas with C. Casswell, I. Heath and R. Nunn

Four trenches were excavated at West Amesbury (Figure 5.5):

Trench 51. In 2008 Trench 51 was 32m east–west × 2m north–south. In 2009, the eastern part of the trench was reopened and it was extended on its north and south sides. The southern extension was 10m east–west × 5m north–south. The northern extension was 7m east–west × 2.50m north–south. These extensions provided good coverage of the henge ditch's northern circuit, a portion of the area formerly covered by the henge's external bank, and the northeast quadrant of the henge's interior. Classically, henges have external earthen banks although Stonehenge and other 'formative' henges (Burrow (2010) have their bank on the inside of the ditch.

Trench 51 was initially located so as to cause little interference to medieval and later archaeological deposits (as indicated by the presence of earthworks). It was designed in 2008 to cut across a 30m-wide, high-resistance anomaly which was thought to be possibly the buried Avenue. This turned out to be a layer of natural coombe rock; thus the discovery of the henge's northern ditch – not readily identifiable on the geophysical plots prior to excavation (Figure 5.3) – was somewhat unexpected.

Artefact type	Frequency	Percent
Bipolar opposed-platform blade-core	1	4.5
Keeled non-discoidal flake-core	2	9.1
Multi-platform flake-core	8	36.4
Single-platform blade-core	5	22.7
Tested nodule/bashed lump	1	4.5
Unclassifiable/fragmentary core	5	22.7
Total	**22**	**100.0**

Table 5.3. Cores from the West Amesbury test pits

Trench 50. This was excavated in 2009, positioned so that its west end was close to the corner of the boundary between the water meadow and the adjacent property, The Hatcheries (see Figure 5.51). The trench was 50m × 2m, in order to cut across the likely lines of both Avenue ditches and to intersect with an undated east–west feature (found to be natural) identified during a watching brief on the construction of The Hatcheries' swimming pool (see above; Figure 5.50).

Trench 60. This small trench was excavated in 2009 on the southwest side of the henge, to establish the monument's size and shape in this area, and to provide a cross-section east–west through the henge (in conjunction with Trench 51's southern extension). It was 10m east–west × 1.50m wide.

Trench 61. This small trench was excavated in 2009 10m northeast of the henge ditch, to establish whether the eastern ditch of the Avenue extended this close to the river and to the henge. It was 15m east–west × 2m wide.

Turf and topsoil were stripped by machine. The archaeological layers (Figure 5.9) were dug by hand, with sieving of all fills through a 10mm mesh. A buried soil (050) in Trench 51 was sampled at 100% on a 0.50m × 0.50m grid for flotation through a 1mm mesh. All stratified prehistoric deposits were also sampled for flotation. The trenches were backfilled and returfed at the end of the excavation.

Natural landforms

The natural subsoil and bedrock at West Amesbury were extremely heterogeneous in all trenches, consisting of:

- a basal layer of decayed chalk (049 and 111=171 in Trench 51 and 517=551 in Trench 50) covered by various layers of periglacial orange clay (082, 221 and 233 in Trench 51 and 590 in Trench 50; see Figure 5.39);
- yellow periglacial silt (528 in Trench 50);
- coombe rock in the form of spreads of flint nodules (068);
- upper periglacial clay (088, 063 and 076) which was occasionally mixed with organic material (in the case of 076).

In the middle of Trench 51, north of the henge ditch and previously beneath its now-vanished outer bank, there was a weathered deposit of clay silt and flint nodules (161) over chalk bedrock (see Figure 5.39). East of this, the chalk bedrock (049) lay beneath a thick deposit of yellow-orange clay-loam (050, a post-glacial forest soil; 050=135; see *Mesolithic activity*, below).

In the west end of Trench 51, the coombe rock (068) and other periglacial deposits lay beneath spreads of broken flint (004, 006) and clay (009, 063) which were probably mixed deposits on the interface between culturally deposited layers and natural landforms.

The areas of coombe rock within Trench 51 corresponded with zones of high resistance as detected by earth resistivity. Therefore other zones of high resistance on the geophysics are probably also coombe rock, indicating that it forms a narrow tongue of high ground, about 30m across and at least 80m long, leading from the area of the present road to the riverside. This would have created a natural causeway towards which the Stonehenge Avenue appears to have been heading. It effectively predetermined the alignment of the Avenue between the riverside and the high ground.

Mesolithic activity

A concentration of Mesolithic flintwork was found in the upper 0.10m of yellow-orange buried soil (050) within the easternmost 3m of Trench 51 (Figures 5.10–5.11, 5.39–5.40). Most worked flints were recovered from flotation of twenty-one 0.50m × 0.50m squares, each divided into three 0.05m-deep spits in 2008. In 2009, a further twelve 0.50m × 0.50m squares were excavated in single 0.15m-deep blocks (since analysis of the previous year's results revealed no significant differences by depth).

In the southeast corner of the trench, a deposit of flint nodules (090), 0.75m north–south × 0.60m east–west, was discovered after removal of two 0.05m spits of layer 050. This was a natural deposit of coombe rock.

Most of the lithic assemblage from layer 050 consists of Late Mesolithic worked flints but a large crested blade hints at the presence of Upper Palaeolithic activity as well (see Chan and Rylatt, below).

A few flint blades were also recovered from a mottled orange-brown to mid-grey/brown clay (076) near the west end of Trench 51. This is probably a mixed layer at the top of a periglacial deposit of decalcified clay associated with the deposition of coombe rock. Layer 076 is probably the same as 063, slightly further west and separated from 076 by a medieval ditch.

In Trench 61, a brown silt layer (172) similar to layer 050 was encountered at the trench's east end (see Figure 5.56). The upper 0.10m–0.15m of layer 172 contained lithics (flakes, blades and micro-debitage) and burnt flint. It was excavated for flotation by 0.50m × 0.50m squares.

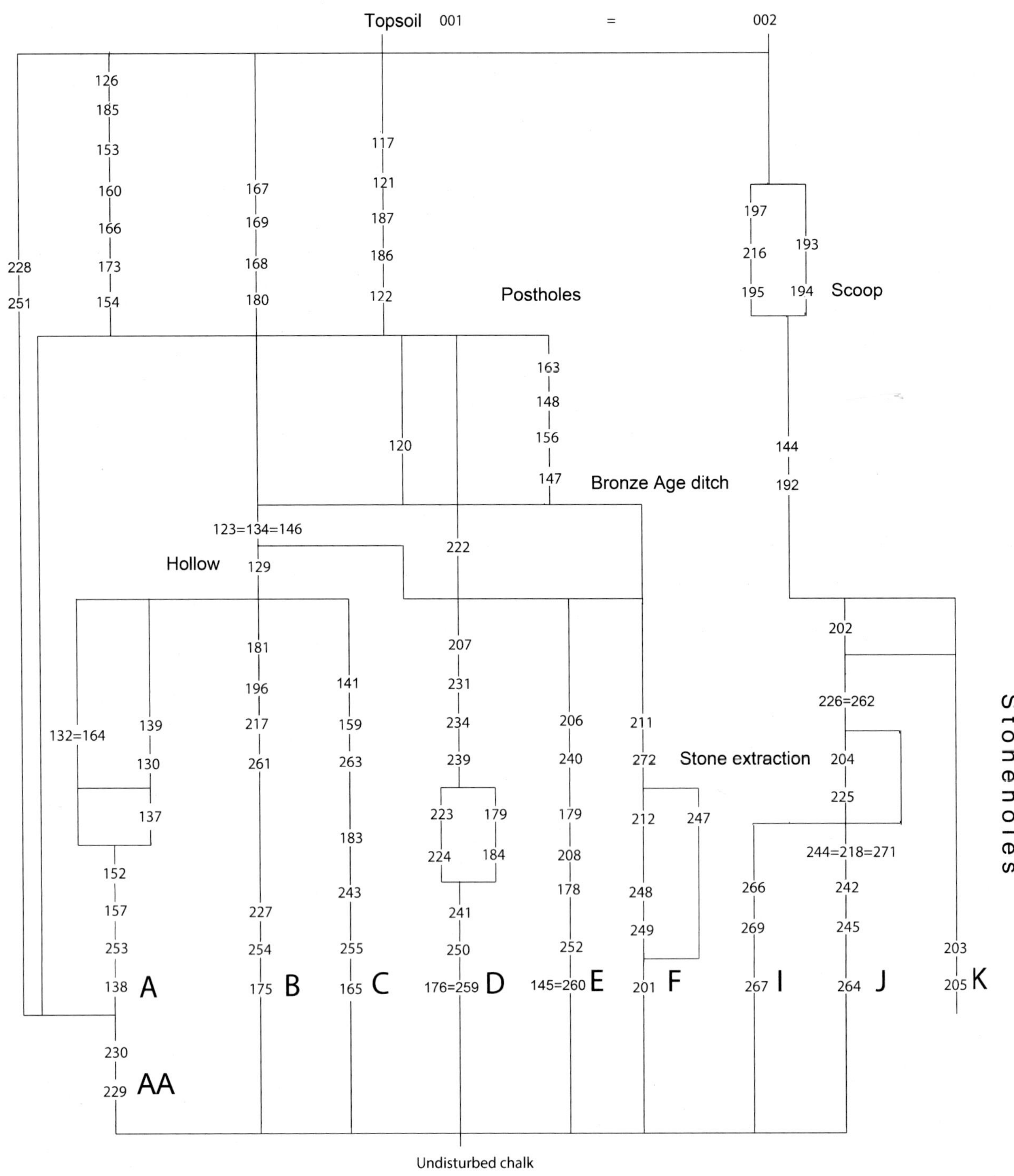

Figure 5.9. Stratigraphic matrix of contexts for the stone circle's Stoneholes A–F and I–K in Trenches 51 and 60

Soil micromorphology

C.A.I. French

Analysis follows the methodology of Murphy (1986) and uses the descriptive terminology of Bullock *et al.* (1985) and Stoops (2003). Trench 51 revealed a thick, silty, clay-loam modern topsoil, overlying a variety of deposits including possible garden soil, flint gravel, chalk rubble, coombe rock, archaeological features and a buried land surface with abundant Mesolithic flint artefacts. The latter (context 050) was best exposed in the northeastern end of the trench (see Figure 5.40), and was sampled as Profile 53. In addition, the fill (206) of Stonehole E was also sampled for micromorphology.

Profile 53: the buried soil (050)

This was a *c.* 0.20–0.25m-thick horizon of yellowish-brown to brown-mottled silty clay loam. The

Figure 5.10. Excavation of layer 050 containing Mesolithic flints, viewed from the west

Figure 5.11. Trench 51 in 2008, viewed from the north, with layer 050 excavated at its east end

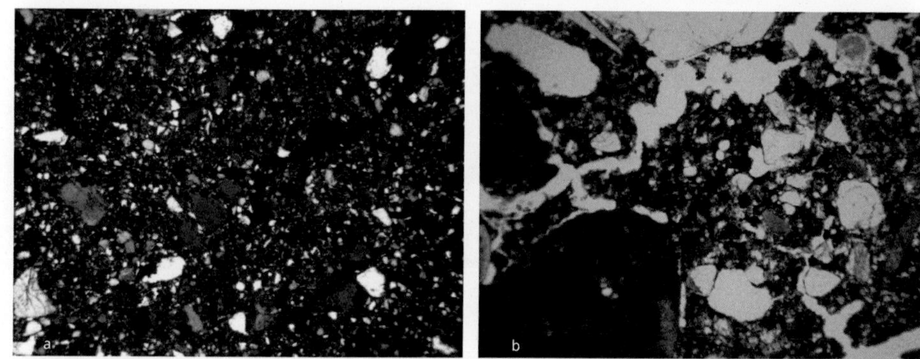

Figure 5.12. Photomicrographs of sediments at West Amesbury: a) weakly reticulate dusty clay striated fabric in sample 1, Profile 53 through the buried soil (050) under the former henge bank (frame width = 4.5mm; cross-polarised light); b) amorphous iron-stained micritic sandy clay loam and fine chalk from context 206 of Stonehole E (frame width = 4.5mm; plane-polarised light)

concentration of flint artefacts in this soil horizon suggests that it was a stable and earthworm-sorted soil profile prior to burial by later deposits (chalk and flint gravel), but it has suffered substantial truncation.

This demonstrably very early Holocene horizon's soil features can give us an idea of early Holocene soil formation in this important river-edge location, and enable comparisons with contemporary soil development trajectories derived from the associated soil and molluscan studies in the downland hinterland around Stonehenge and Durrington Walls.

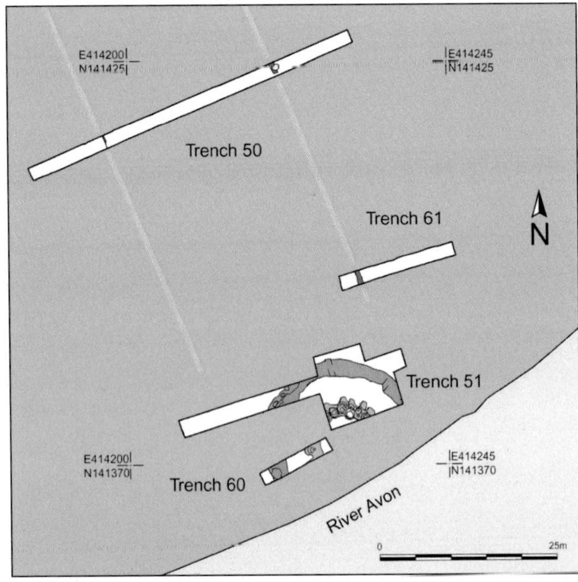

Figure 5.13. Plan of Trenches 50, 51, 60 and 61, showing outlines of the Neolithic/Chalcolithic features; the orange tram-lines indicate the likely positions of the Avenue ditches

The soil fabric of the palaeosol (050) preserved beneath the modern topsoil and alluvial deposits in the riverside trench, and formerly buried beneath the since-eroded henge bank, was a relatively chalk-free, dense, sandy (clay) loam (Figure 5.12a). Importantly, the dusty clay in the groundmass is weakly reticulate with moderate to strong birefringence. This is indicative of some stability and organisation to this soil. Moreover, up to about one-third of the fine fabric is depleted of clay. This would indicate that this soil was once a sandy clay loam soil with a clay-enriched or argillic aspect. Moreover, the 25%–30% of very fine quartz sand in the groundmass is suggestive of some loessic-like input in the past.

Although this buried soil profile has been affected subsequently by additions of alluvial material associated with seasonal wetting and drying, its surviving features point to this once having been a brown forest soil or an argillic brown earth (Avery 1980; Bullock and Murphy 1979; Fedoroff 1968; Fisher 1982) with a considerable loessic component (*cf* Catt 1978).

Fill 206 of Stonehole E

The large stoneholes within the henge (see *The bluestone circle*, below) contained what appears to be an organic standstill horizon at the top of their secondary fill. One of these (context 206; see Figure 5.29) was sampled for micromorphology as a possible proxy for post-monument soil development. In this case, the sample

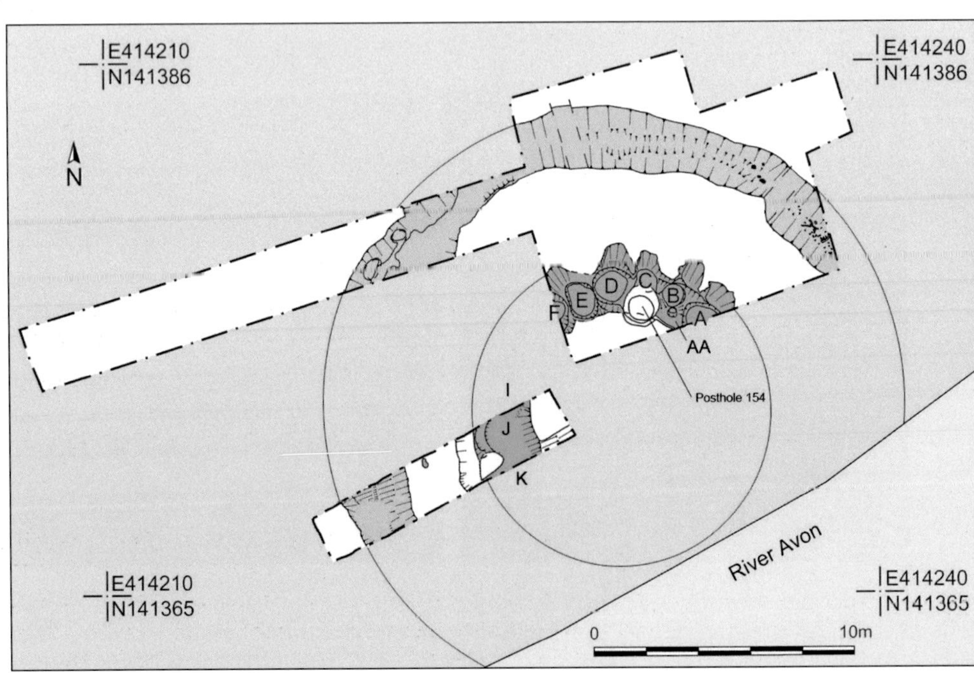

Figure 5.14. Plan of Trenches 51 and 60, showing the Neolithic stoneholes, the henge ditch and a Bronze Age posthole

Figure 5.15. 3-D laser scan of the stoneholes; from left to right, Stonehole F, Stonehole E, Stonehole D (marked by '1'), Stonehole C (together with Bronze Age posthole154), Stonehole B (cutting pit AA on its south side) and Stonehole A. North is at the top of the image

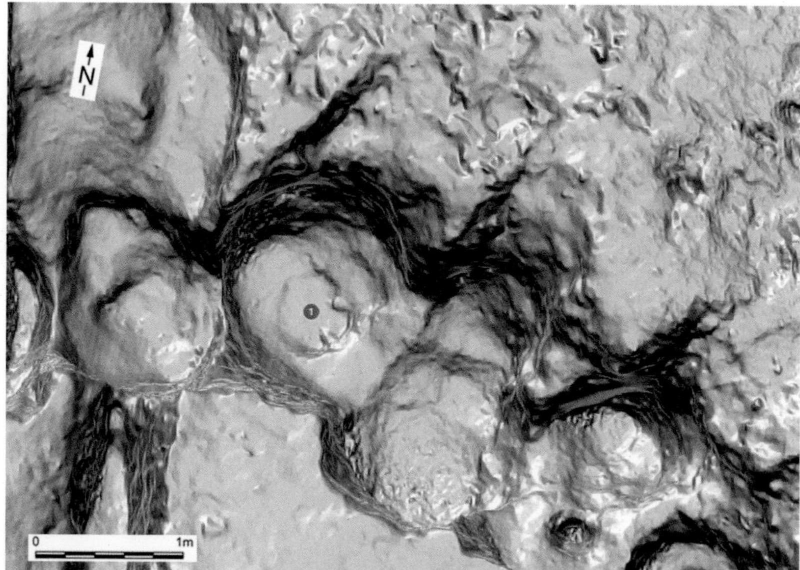

Figure 5.16. Team members stand in the excavated stoneholes, viewed from the northwest. The henge ditch is also visible

exhibited a very amorphous iron- and humic organic matter-stained, micritic sandy clay loam with abundant fine chalk rubble and micro-charcoal (Figure 5.12b). Although poorly sorted and with a high stone content, this backfill material is probably derived from the disturbed organic topsoil adjacent.

Discussion

Importantly, the palaeosol in the West Amesbury riverside trench that is associated with the Mesolithic flint scatter and overlying Neolithic henge bank is an argillic brown earth, and once most probably associated with woodland (*cf* Fedoroff 1968). Unfortunately,

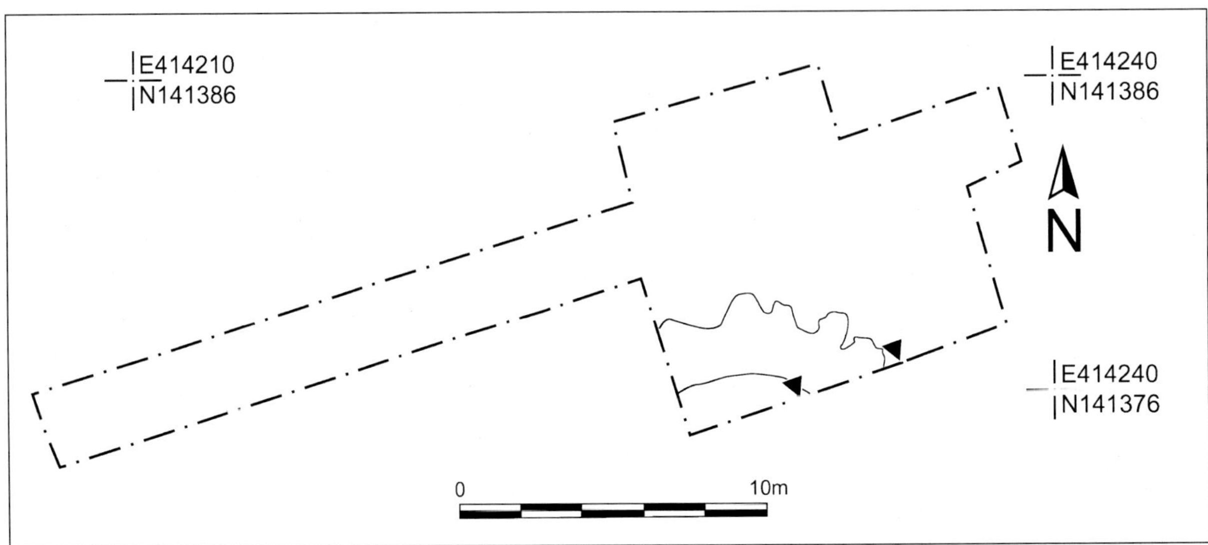

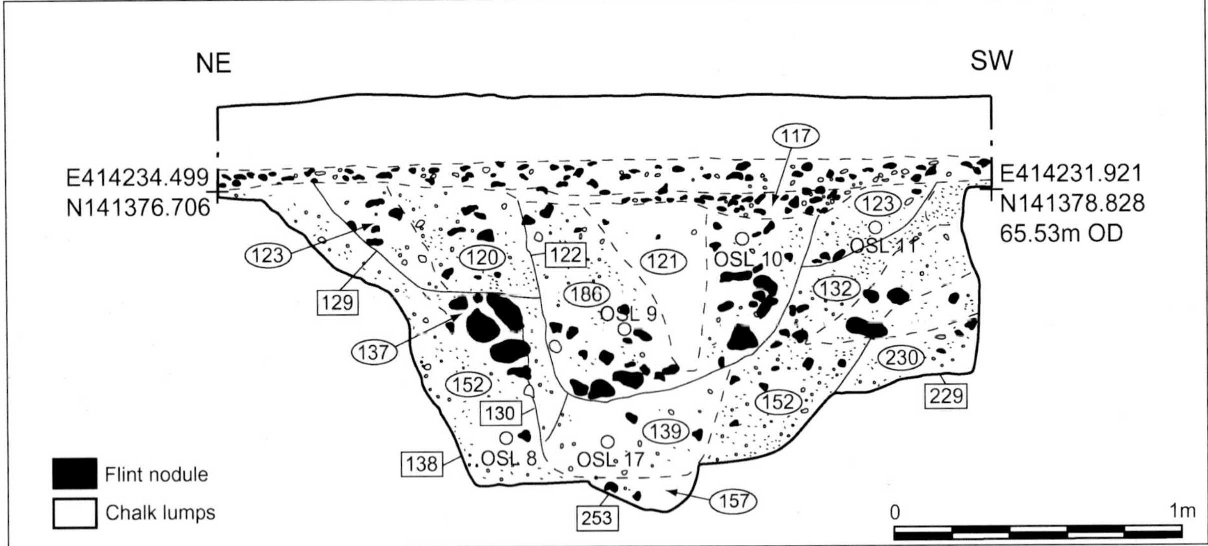

Figure 5.17. Section drawing of Stonehole A, showing pit AA, re-cut ditch 129 and Bronze Age posthole 122

the pollen data from palaeochannels in the adjacent floodplain of the River Avon probably fall in the later prehistoric and historic date range (Scaife 2004), and therefore cannot be equated with this soil record.

The only other such palaeosols that have been identified in this region are located at two loci along the proposed new route of the A303 on the northern side of Amesbury (Macphail and Crowther 2008). In contrast, almost all other buried soil exposures observed during the Stonehenge Riverside Project (such as under the Avenue at Stonehenge [see Chapter 8] and other pre-Early Bronze Age soils) are ubiquitously thin rendzina soils, or just occasionally brown earths (as under the Durrington Walls henge bank; French *et al.* 2012 and see the full soil micromorphology report in Volume 2).

The bluestone circle

Nine stoneholes (A–F, I–K) were identified in Trenches 51 and 60 (Figures 5.13–5.14). Five of them lay entirely within the trenches (B–E and J) and four lay partially or largely within the baulks of the trenches (A, F, I and K).

All the stoneholes have ramps which were probably used for removing rather than erecting the standing stones. These ramps are all on the outside of the circle, perpendicular to its circumference. They give the arc of Stoneholes A–F a scalloped fringe, in which the western edge of each ramp is steep whereas the eastern edge is shallow (Figures 5.15–5.16). These steep western edges of the ramps can be seen in the laser scan (Figure 5.15) running northeast–southwest from the northern edges of the stoneholes. The scan also shows the imprints in the

Figure 5.18. Pit AA (cut 229; southwest of the north arrow), the basal fill 227 of Stonehole B (north of the north arrow) and the bottom of Stonehole A (southeast of the north arrow)

bases of Stonehole D (marked as '1') and Stonehole E (to its left) left by the stones that originally stood in them.

During excavation Stoneholes I, J and K in Trench 60 were initially labelled as H, I and J. The circle of stoneholes is presumed to continue through the unexcavated area west of Trench 51 and north of Trench 60, and label G was assigned in the field to a hypothetical stonehole in this area. Early in the post-excavation analysis, however, it became clear that the spacing of the known stoneholes in relation to this unexcavated area indicates that not one but two stoneholes are likely to be positioned here beneath the baulk between Trenches 51 and 60 (putative Stoneholes G and H). To accommodate the two putative stoneholes in the analysis of the architecture of the stone circle, Stonehole H in the field records consequently became Stonehole I, field label I became Stonehole J, and field label J became Stonehole K.

While the stoneholes appear to have been contemporary, there was one feature (229 or pit AA), cut by Stoneholes A and B (Figures 5.17–5.18), which pre-dated the stonehole setting.

Pit AA

A large pit (229) was cut into on its east side by Stonehole A (138), on its northeast side by Stonehole B (175) and on its northwest side by a probably Bronze Age posthole (154; Figures 5.14, 5.18). Despite these substantial intrusions, enough remained of it to establish that it had been at least 1.10m northwest–southeast by at least 0.95m northeast–southwest and 0.75m–0.85m deep. Its full profile (from the top of the decayed chalk bedrock) survived on its southwest side to show that its upper 0.40m was vertical with a very slight overhang, above near-vertical sides leading to a flat base sloping slightly northeastwards (Figure 5.17). On its opposing northeast side, the wall of this pit sloped more gently from its base. At a depth of 0.85m below the top of bedrock (or 1.15m BGS [below current ground surface]), it was about 0.20m–0.40m shallower than the surrounding stoneholes.

Pit 229 was filled with cream-brown silty clay with few small flint inclusions (230). This basal layer survived to a depth of only 0.10m; all successive fills had been removed by later cuts. This primary fill is interpreted as re-deposited natural subsoil. It was wholly unlike the stony, clay fills introduced into Stoneholes A–K as packing material. Layer 230 was cut by a small posthole (251), 0.32m north–south by 0.30m east–west and 0.35m deep (Figure 5.19). It was vertical on all sides except its south, and was filled with grey-brown clay (228). Whilst this posthole may pre-date the stone circle, it is more likely to belong to the period of Bronze Age re-use.

The purpose of Pit AA is difficult to gauge. Perhaps it was a prehistoric sondage or proving pit, designed to establish the nature, depth and firmness of the decayed chalk bedrock before digging the circle of stoneholes.

Stonehole A

Stonehole A (138) was partially within the southern baulk of Trench 51 but sufficient of it lay within the trench for its dimensions to be established as 1.40m southwest–northeast by at least 0.75m southeast–northwest and 1m deep (Figures 5.17, 5.20–5.21). The baulk thus provided a section northeast–southwest, diagonally across the centre of the stonehole (Figure 5.20). On the stonehole's northeast side, its ramp was 1.20m wide (northwest–southeast) and 0.80m long (northeast–southwest). The ramp sloped gently

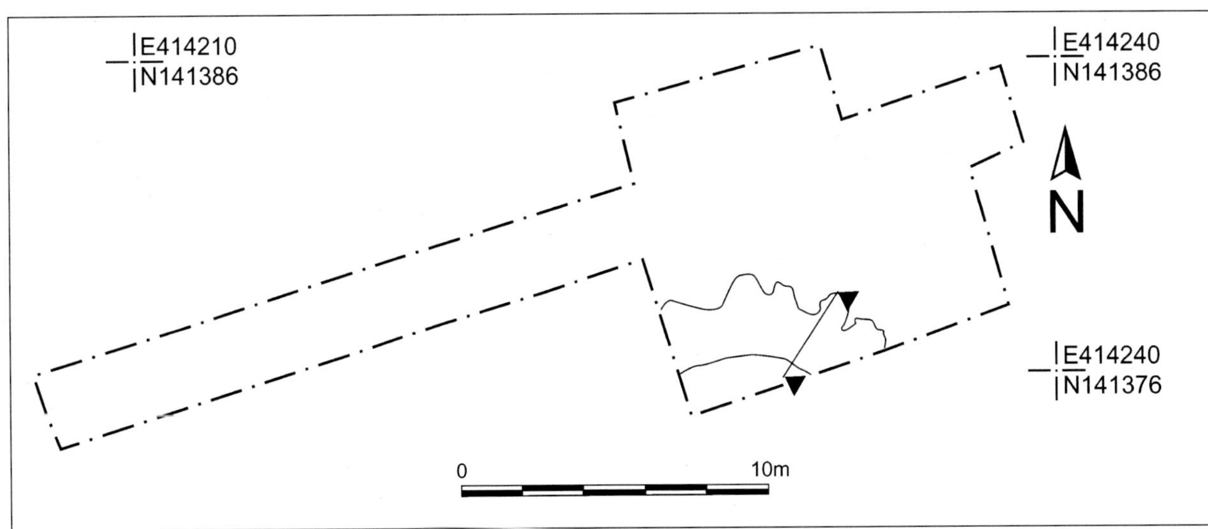

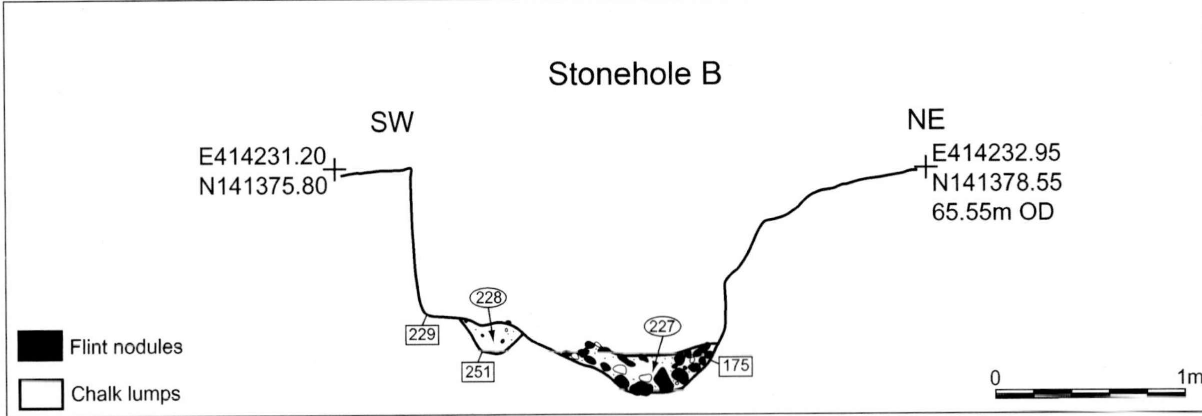

Figure 5.19. Profile of Stonehole B showing the basal layer 227 in section as well as the bottom of posthole 251

Figure 5.20. Stonehole A in section, viewed from the north

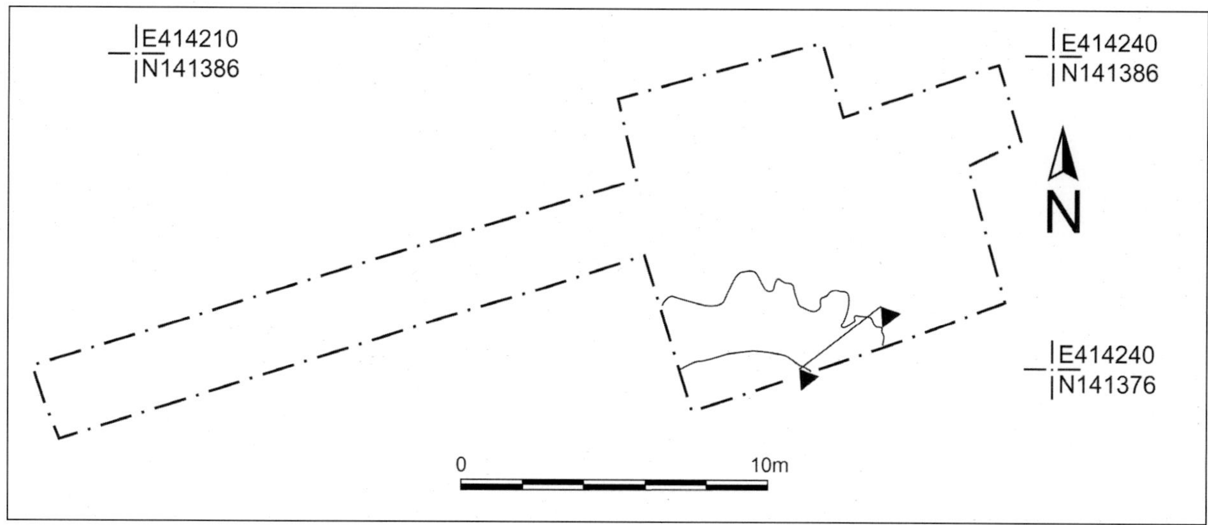

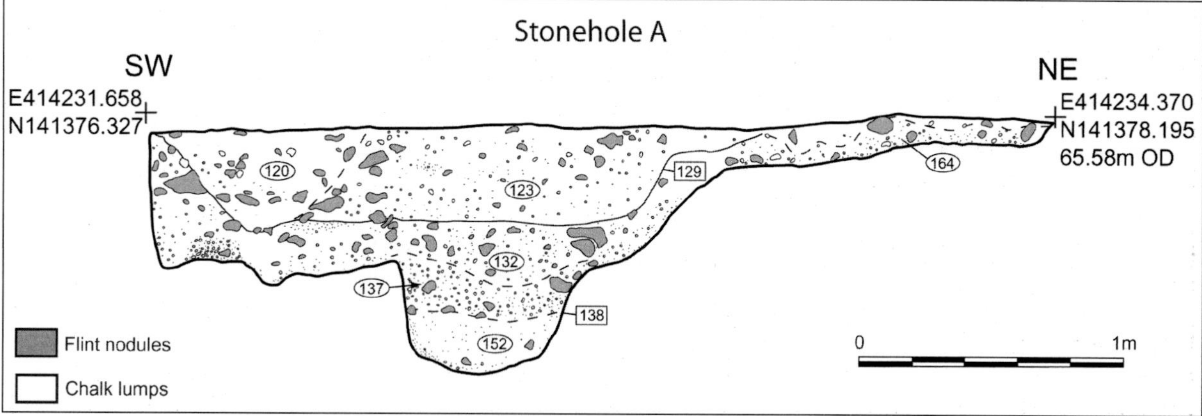

Figure 5.21. Section drawing of Stonehole A, showing the ramp on the right and re-cut hollow 129

at about 10°. Its northwestern edge, as mentioned above, was much steeper than its southeastern edge.

In the base of the stonehole at its centre (its southern part beside the baulk), there was a small, square depression with rounded corners (253), 0.30m east–west by at least 0.32m north–south and up to 0.10m deep (Figure 5.17). This was either a positioning hollow over which the standing stone and its packing were placed, or it was caused by indirect compression: the standing stone compressing the intermediate packing layer directly above the base of the pit, thereby creating an indirect imprint of the stone's base into the soft, decayed chalk bedrock.

The basal fill of Stonehole A was a tenacious pale grey-brown clay (157), containing about 20% small broken flints. It sat within the depression (253) to a depth of 0.10m and, in the stonehole's eastern side, to a depth of 0.18m. Unlike the basal fill (230) of pit AA, this was alluvial material introduced to the site, presumably from the river's margin. It is interpreted as the 'cushion' on which the standing stone stood.

Above layer 157, a pale brown silty clay (152) of similarly introduced alluvial origin, containing charcoal flecks and small flints in similarly low density, formed a doughnut-shaped layer of packing (up to 0.40m thick) around a filled-in void (cut 130) left by the removal of a standing stone. Layer 152 was covered by two deposits. One was a layer of re-deposited chalk marl (137), tinged green by incorporation of greensand which formed a banded layer within the decayed chalk here at about 1.00m BGS. Layer 137 contained large flint nodules (0.05m–0.30m in size; 60% by volume), a possibly Late Mesolithic microburin and two small sherds, one of Grooved Ware (sherd P2; see Cleal, below) and the other unassignable (SF 505; see below). The other deposit covering layer 152 was a layer of mixed grey-brown silty clay (132), which produced fewer large flint nodules (30%) and a chisel arrowhead (SF 587). Both layers are interpreted as packing around the former standing stone.

Within the 'doughnut' formed by these packing layers, there was a rectangular cut (130), visible in the section (which cut through it diagonally) as 0.55m wide at the base

Figure 5.22. The antler pick (SF 503) on the floor of the ramp (164=132) of Stonehole A, viewed from the south

and 0.70m wide higher up in its 0.65m-deep profile. In plan, it was 0.70m northeast–southwest and at least 0.60m northwest–southeast. This is the void left by the removal of the standing stone. It was filled with loose grey-brown silty clay (139), containing charcoal flecks and few, small broken flints (less than 20%). The base of the standing stone is likely to have been buried to a depth of 1.10m BGS, settling to 1.25m BGS.

The ramp on Stonehole A's northeast side was filled with dark grey-brown clay loam (164=132; Figure 5.21) which appears to have been compacted and contained patches of chalk marl, a high density of broken flint (up to 80%) and occasional lumps of imported chalk. An antler pick (SF 503, made from the left antler of a red deer), complete except for the end of its tine, lay within the upper part of this fill, with part of it within a centimetre of the floor of the ramp (Figure 5.22). Its top half was visible as soon as the topsoil (001 and 002) was removed.

Since the pick was not crushed, it has to have been deposited after the standing stone was withdrawn from the hole. There is no means of establishing whether the pick was used in the stone's removal or whether it was added later, as the ramp began to silt up. The antler pick (SF 503) dates to 2470–2210 cal BC (95% confidence; OxA-21278; 3884±30 BP; Table 5.4). This date is statistically consistent with radiocarbon determinations for an antler pick in Stonehole C as well as the broken-off tip of an antler pick from the henge ditch (see *The henge*, below), raising the possibility that SF 503 and the antler tip could derive from the same antler. If so, SF 503 was deposited after the Chalcolithic henge ditch was dug.

If the pick was deposited immediately after stone extraction, then why was it placed here and what exactly was it used for? Although the stone in Stonehole J in Trench 60 was undermined to remove it from its socket there is no evidence that the standing stones in Trench 51 were undermined in such a manner, so the placement of a pick here is odd. Since the ramps do appear to be related to extraction of the stones, then the positioning of the antler pick within the fill of the ramp may relate to activities sometime after extraction of the stones.

Hollow 129

As sediments settled within Stonehole A and the other stoneholes, a 0.50m-deep doughnut-shaped hollow (129) formed above the conjoining stoneholes. Hollow 129 had unusually steep sides at its northeastern end over Stonehole A (Figures 5.17, 5.21), suggesting that this feature was artificially deepened rather than being entirely the result of natural settling. It extended across Stoneholes A–E, bottoming out over Stonehole F. An equivalent hollow was detected in Trench 60, over Stoneholes I–J, where it was filled by layer 202. If hollow 129's depth was accentuated by digging-out, particularly towards its eastern end, this explains why the tops of the packing deposits and those deposits relating to stone removal were truncated in Stoneholes A–C.

Layers 123 and 120, the uppermost layers within Stonehole A, were sitting in hollow 129 (Figures 5.17, 5.21). Layer 123 was mixed yellow-brown clay-silt, the same as layers 134 and 146 in Stoneholes C and D and equivalent to layer 202 in Stonehole J. Layer 120 was grey-brown clay, above layer 123 in the fill of the hollow (129) cutting through the uppermost part of Stonehole A.

Layer 120 is probably the fill of a Bronze Age ditch (147=192) running along the filled hollow from Stoneholes

Figure 5.23. The deposit of flint nodules (227) in the base of Stonehole B in half-section (on the left) and the bottom of posthole 251 (on the right), viewed from the west

I–K through B–F (see *Bronze Age re-use*, below). If so, then it was cut by Bronze Age posthole 154. The curvilinear hollow (129) was cut into by a Bronze Age posthole (122) above Stonehole A (Figure 5.17). Other Bronze Age postholes were cut through these fills of hollow 129, so it must have filled before the Late Bronze Age.

Stonehole B

Stonehole B (175) was located entirely within Trench 51 and was therefore completely excavated (Figures 5.14, 5.19, 5.23). It cut into pit AA (229) and was cut by posthole 180 and, together with Stonehole C, posthole 154. It was an oval pit (175), >1.10m northeast–southwest by >0.95m northwest–southeast and 1.15m deep (1.45m BGS), with a vertical to near-vertical north side, an irregular, truncated south side, and an initially vertical then angled east side, sloping to a dished bottom. On its northeast, its ramp (0.95m wide northwest–southeast and 0.90m long northeast–southwest) was angled at about 10°, with a steep western edge and a shallow eastern one.

In the base of Stonehole B was a small depression (254) at its centre, similar to the basal depression (253) in Stonehole A. This formed a squashed oval in plan, 0.43m northeast–southwest by 0.34m northwest–southeast and up to 0.06m deep. Its form was more clearly that of a feature formed by compression rather than an actual cut, and it is presumably the imprint left indirectly from a standing stone set into a 'cushion' layer above. Thus the stone is likely to have been set 1m deep (1.30m BGS), settling perhaps a further 0.10m in depth.

The basal fill of Stonehole B (filling both 254 and the base of 175) was brown-grey clay (227), filled to 80% with flint nodules (0.05m–0.20m), some of them cracked, and occasional pieces of imported hard chalk. This deposit was oval in plan, 0.95m east–west by 0.80m north–south and 0.18m thick, and is interpreted as a pad on which a standing stone stood (Figures 5.19 and 5.23).

Layer 227 was cut through by a pit (261) filled with three layers (217, 196 and 181). The pit occupied the entire space of the stonehole and is interpreted as the robbing pit for removal of the standing stone. Layer 217 was mixed beige-cream chalk marl with patches of chalk and occasional flints, forming a compacted lower fill, pressed against the south side of the stonehole. This may have become compacted under pressure from the weight of the stone when it was removed. Above it, layer 196 was a grey-brown silty loam, 0.20m deep. The uppermost layer was a compact beige-pale brown clay (181) containing a single sherd of pottery (probably Late Bronze Age) and large flint nodules (0.10m–0.30m), especially tightly packed against the stonehole's northeast side.

Stonehole C

Stonehole C (165) had been destroyed on its south side by a Bronze Age posthole (154; Figures 5.14, 5.65) but enough of the stonehole survived to be able to gain information on its dimensions and fills, including the likely size of the standing stone which once stood within it. It was an oval pit (165), 1.00m east–west by >1.00m north–south cut by posthole 154 and 1.20m deep (Figure 5.24). Its west, north and east sides were near-vertical, with the north side's slope becoming less steep with depth. Even allowing for the extent of damage by posthole 154, this was a smaller and steeper hole than any of the other excavated stoneholes. Its ramp was also small (0.65m–1.00m wide northwest–southeast and 0.85m long northeast–southwest) and steep (35°).

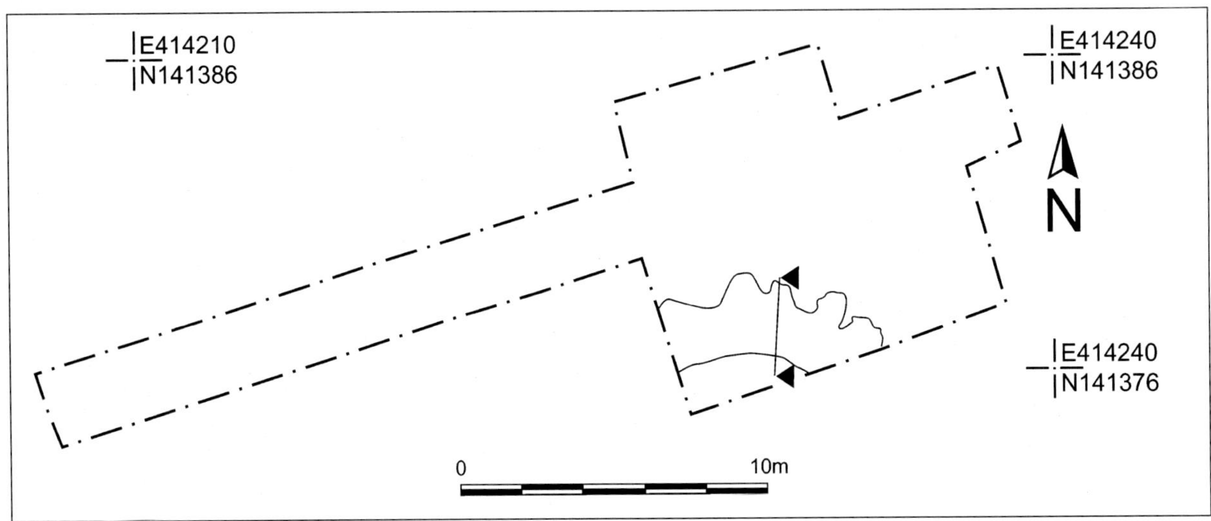

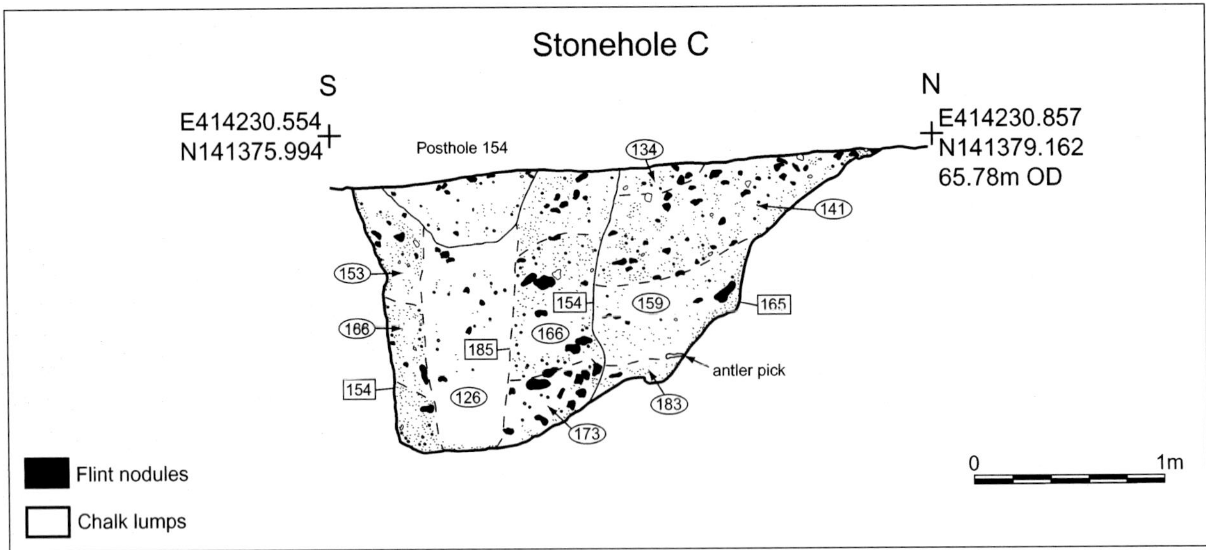

Figure 5.24. Section drawing of Stonehole C, cut by Bronze Age posthole 154

At the base of Stonehole C, there was a central depression (255) similar to those in Stoneholes A and B. Its plan was a squared oval, 0.55m east–west by at least 0.40m north–south and 0.18m deep (its southern edge was destroyed by posthole 154). This depression (255) was filled with pale grey-brown silty clay (243), 0.10m deep, containing 50% broken flints (0.05m–0.20m), many of which were compressed into the decayed chalk bedrock. Depression 255 is interpreted as the basal imprint of the stone that once stood in this hole.

The next layer of fill above layer 243 was mixed pale blue-grey-brown silty clay (183), 0.15m deep with occasional pieces of flint. It survived only on the north side of the stonehole and presumably formed a 'cushion' layer on which the stone originally sat. If this were so, then the stone would have been set about 1m deep (1.30m BGS), perhaps settling to about 1.20m deep (1.50m BGS).

In the northwest corner of the stonehole, an antler pick (SF 529/SF 571) lay with its tine embedded beneath the surface of this layer (183) and its handle higher up against the side of the pit, where it was covered with material from layer 159 above (Figure 5.25). It was initially thought to have been deposited with the final components of layer 183, before layer 159 was added. After dating, it was reconsidered to have been deposited with layer 159, and pushed into the top of layer 183. Its radiocarbon date is 2470–2200 cal BC (95% confidence; SUERC-27051; 3855±30 BP; Table 5.4), statistically consistent with the date of the antler pick left on the ramp of Stonehole A and with the antler tine tip from the henge ditch.

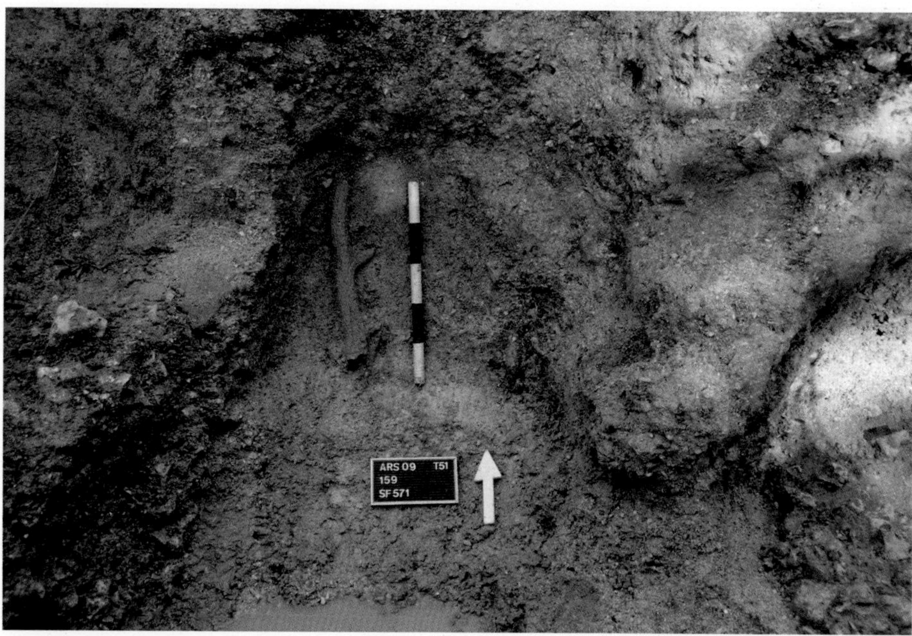

Figure 5.25. The antler pick (SF 529/SF 571) in Stonehole C, viewed from the south

Layer 159 was a yellow-brown clay with occasional flints and re-deposited chalk marl, 0.30m thick. It is interpreted as original packing material for the stone, subsequently disturbed during the stone's removal. It thus sits within a robbing pit (263), 0.90m northwest–southeast and 1.00m deep. A small sherd of medieval pottery, presumably a contaminant from above, was found in layer 159.

After deposition of layer 159 within it, Stonehole C's robbing pit (263) was filled within its base by a layer of soft, dark grey-brown loam (141), interpreted as topsoil fallen into the robbing pit. A fissured and pitted fragment of pig humerus from layer 141 was radiocarbon-dated to 2840–2470 cal BC (SUERC-26460; 4040±35 BP; Table 5.4). This bone fragment was initially identified as human but its unusually low $\delta^{15}N$ isotope value of 7.3‰ makes it most likely to derive from a pig (Mandy Jay pers. comm.; see the isotopic analysis in Volume 3). As a loose, weathered bone, it does not date the deposition of layer 141, and is likely to be earlier by decades or even centuries.

Stonehole D

Stonehole D (176) was excavated in its entirety and was largely undamaged by Bronze Age activity (Figures 5.26–5.28). It was an oval pit (176), 1.50m east–west by 1.80m north–south and 1.30m deep. The stonehole's ramp, angled at 15°, was 0.90m long (northeast–southwest) and widened towards the hole (from 0.80m at its terminal to over 1.20m near the lip of the hole). At the centre of Stonehole D's base, there was a circular depression (259), 0.14m deep and 0.60m in diameter, with a distinctive indentation (0.14m deep) on its northeast side (labelled as '1' in Figure 5.15). This is a particularly convincing product of compression by a standing stone (Figure 5.26); a close comparison can be drawn with the cross-section of Bluestone 68 at Stonehenge (*cf* Gowland 1902; Cleal *et al.* 1995: fig. 150).

The basal fill of Stonehole D was a thin layer of dark grey clay with charcoal fragments (250) within the base of the stonehole (259). Above layer 250 was a stiff grey clay (241), largely flint-free but containing a serrated flake (SF 20111). Layer 241 covered the entire bottom of the stonehole and was compressed into depression 259 where it was only 0.06m thick. It survived to its greatest depth on the south side of the stonehole, immediately south of depression 259, to a depth of 0.30m above the bedrock. Thus the stone that once stood in Stonehole D had settled to a depth of 1.24m (or 1.54m BGS), perhaps having been initially set on its clay 'cushion' layer (241) at a depth of 1.00m (or 1.30m BGS).

The clay layer (241) was covered by yellow-brown clay (184), containing a few large flint nodules forming a packing deposit (Figure 5.29). This in turn lay beneath a 0.45m-thick deposit of similar yellow-brown clay (179, identical to fill 159 in Stonehole C; layer 179 contained a small, unassignable sherd). On the south side of the stonehole, brown clay silt (223), with occasional pieces of angular flint and imported chalk lumps, lay on top of grey-brown clay (224) with inclusions of angular flint.

The void (239) left by the withdrawn stone was 0.20m wide at its base, widening to 0.90m at 0.90m above the base. Its lowest layer was yellow-grey-brown clay (234), containing decayed chalk, occasional flints and charcoal. This is interpreted as a mix of topsoil and subsoil collapsed in from the rim of the robbing hole.

Above layer 234, layer 231 was composed of brown-black silty clay, most likely topsoil and turf

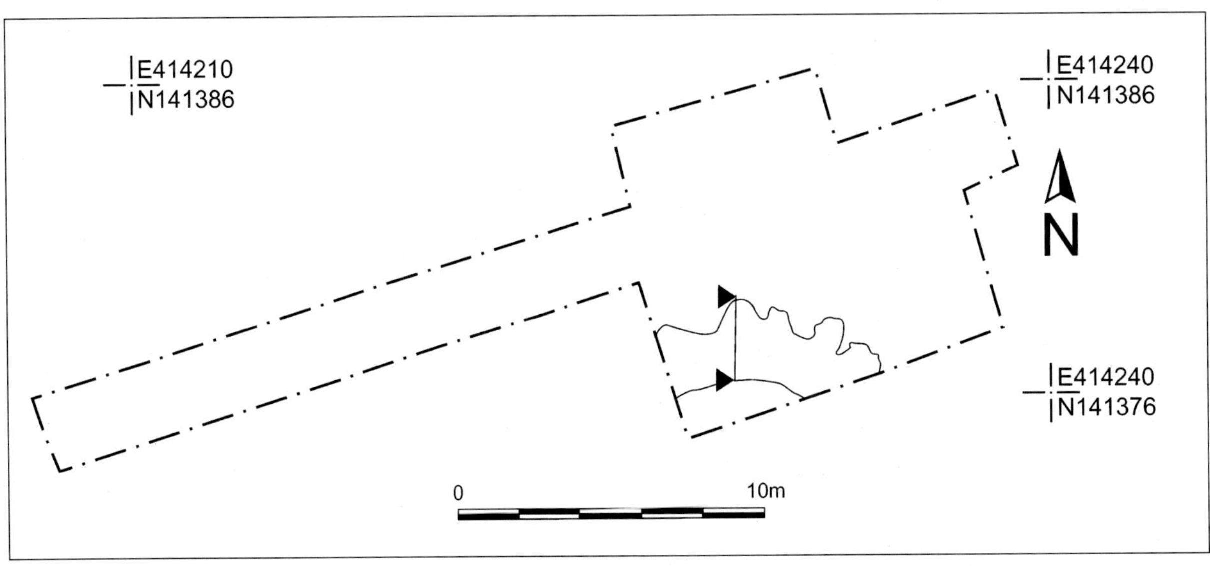

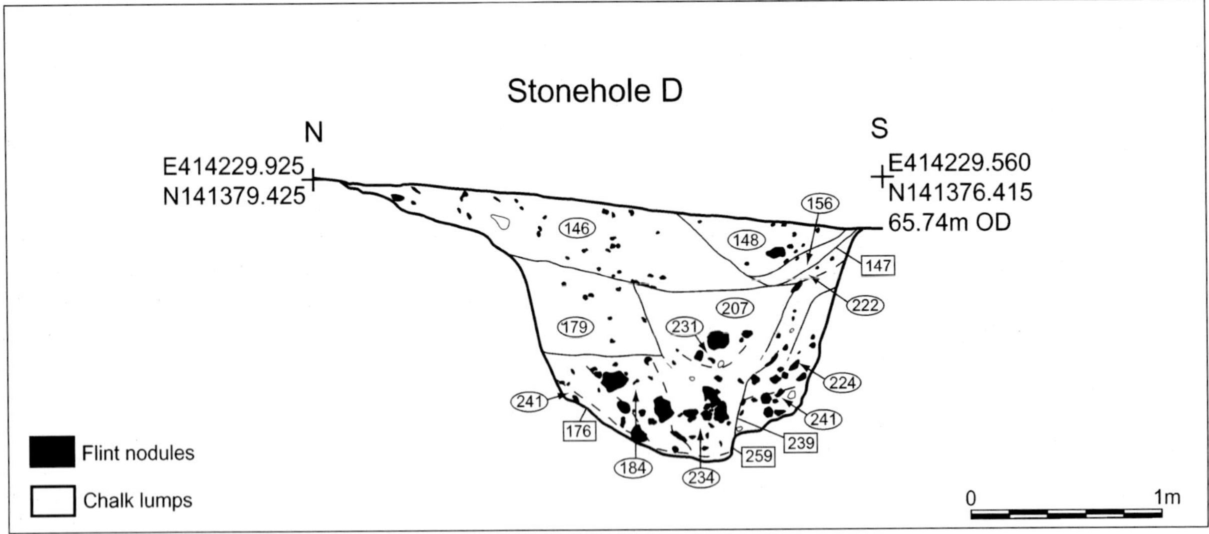

Figure 5.26. Section drawing of Stonehole D, cut by Bronze Age ditch 147

Figure 5.27. Grey clay (250) filling the impression (259) left by Stone D in the base of the stonehole. It is cut by removal pit 239 (dark brown fill in section), viewed from the west

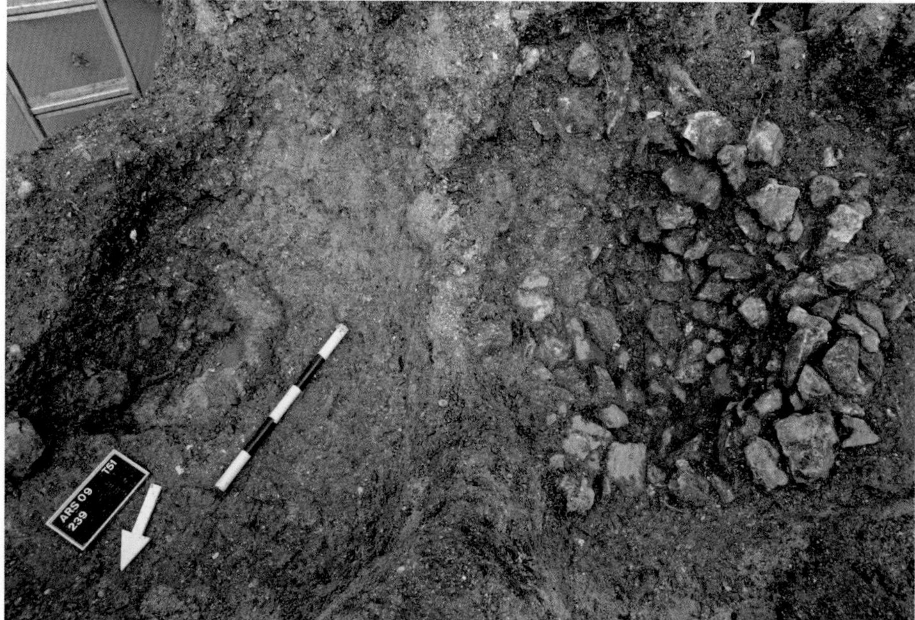

Figure 5.28. The bases of Stoneholes D and E, viewed from the north; the empty socket (239) of Stonehole D is on the left and the 'nest' of flints (208) on the right lies in the bottom of Stonehole E

fallen into the empty stonehole. The layer above it, of grey-brown clay silt (207) with charcoal inclusions, may also be collapsed topsoil. It contained a fist-sized flake of micaceous Mesozoic sandstone (of southern English provenance and thus not a bluestone of Lower Palaeozoic sandstone) and a piece of fired clay. Finally, a layer of orange-brown silt (222), 0.20m deep, was deposited on top of layer 207.

There are two possible interpretations of this sequence:

- In the more likely interpretation, the layers 184, 179 and 223 constitute undisturbed packing layers, with the stone having been removed northwards from its hole within the V-shaped cut (239), initially raised at an angle of 70°. Once the stone was raised 0.40m off the base of the stonehole, it was pulled down towards the north, its butt-end kicking back into the southern side of its socket to displace parts of layer 224. It could then be dragged out northwards along the ramp at a shallow angle of 15°.

- Alternatively, the stone within Stonehole D was removed by digging a substantial robbing pit (239) which left only a thin skim (0.05m thick) of the basal clay deposit (241) untouched on the north side of the stonehole (whilst it was 0.30m thick on the south side). In this scenario, the robbing pit extended to the northern edge of the stonehole and was subsequently filled with layers 184 (north), 179=159 and perhaps even 223 on its south side. However, this alternative fails to explain the steep 70° edge on the north side of layers 234, 231 and 207 (Figure 5.26).

For this reason, the first interpretation is preferred, even though it required the stone's removal initially at a steep angle of 70°, presumably by using a large A-frame.

The hollow (129) over Stonehole D and its ramp was finally filled in with a layer of yellow-brown clay-silt (146) containing a sherd of possible Grooved Ware, a sherd of probable Beaker and a piece of fired clay. Layer 146 was cut into by a Bronze Age ditch (Figure 5.26; see *Bronze Age re-use*, below).

Stonehole E

Stonehole E (145) was excavated in its entirety but its upper layers were cut through by both the Bronze Age penannular ditch (147) and a medieval or later ditch (014; Figure 5.29). Stonehole E was an oval pit (145), 1.20m east–west by 1.45m north–south and 0.95m deep. The stonehole's ramp was angled to the northwest, with an angle of slope of 32°, 1.20m long (northwest–southeast) and 1.10m wide (northeast–southwest). At the centre of Stonehole E's base, there was a trapezoidal depression (260), 0.70m northeast–southwest by 0.50m northwest–southeast and 0.10m deep. This is similar to the cross-section through the base of Bluestone 63 at Stonehenge (Cleal *et al.* 1995: figs 116 and 121).

The basal layer within depression 260 and the southern half of Stonehole E was light grey clay (252) covered by yellow-brown clay silt (178) with decayed chalk and occasional pieces of angular flint. Overlying and partially pressed into this deposit was a well-constructed circular nest of flint nodules within a matrix of mid-brown silt (208). A sarsen cobble is recorded as coming from Stonehole E, presumably from this deposit of flint nodules.

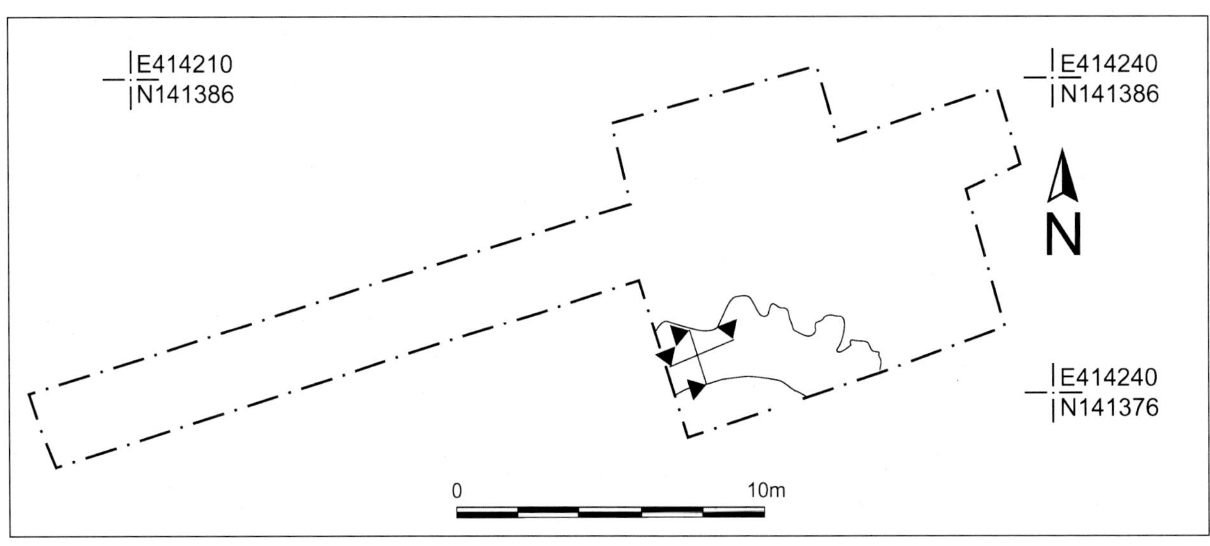

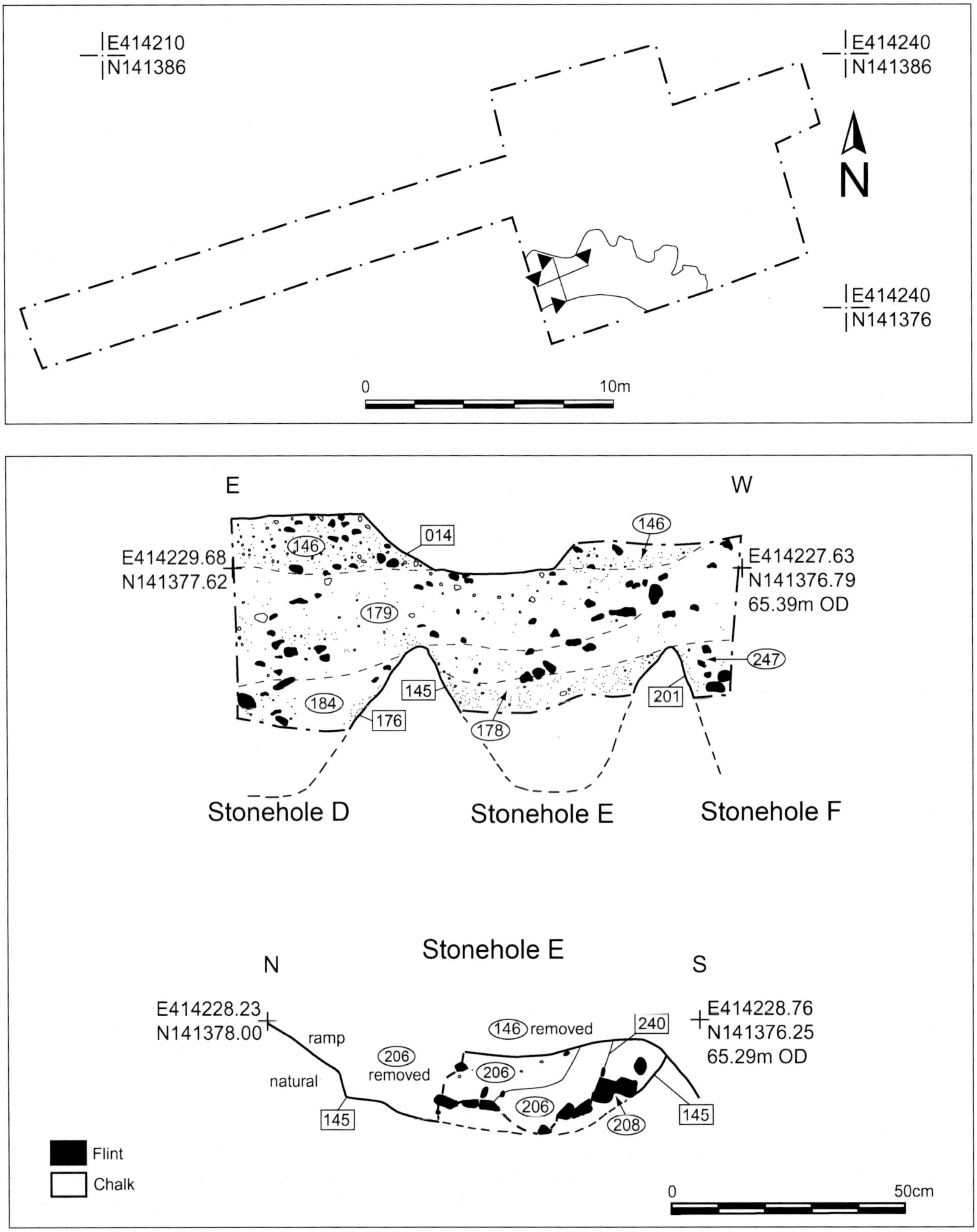

Figure 5.29. Section drawing of Stoneholes D, E and F, cut by medieval ditch 014

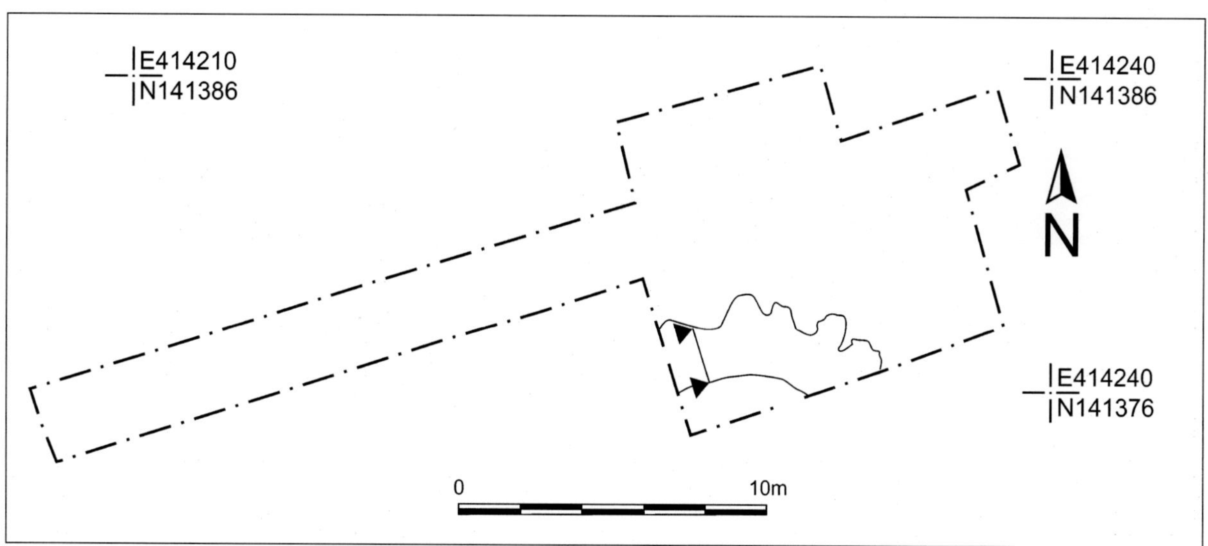

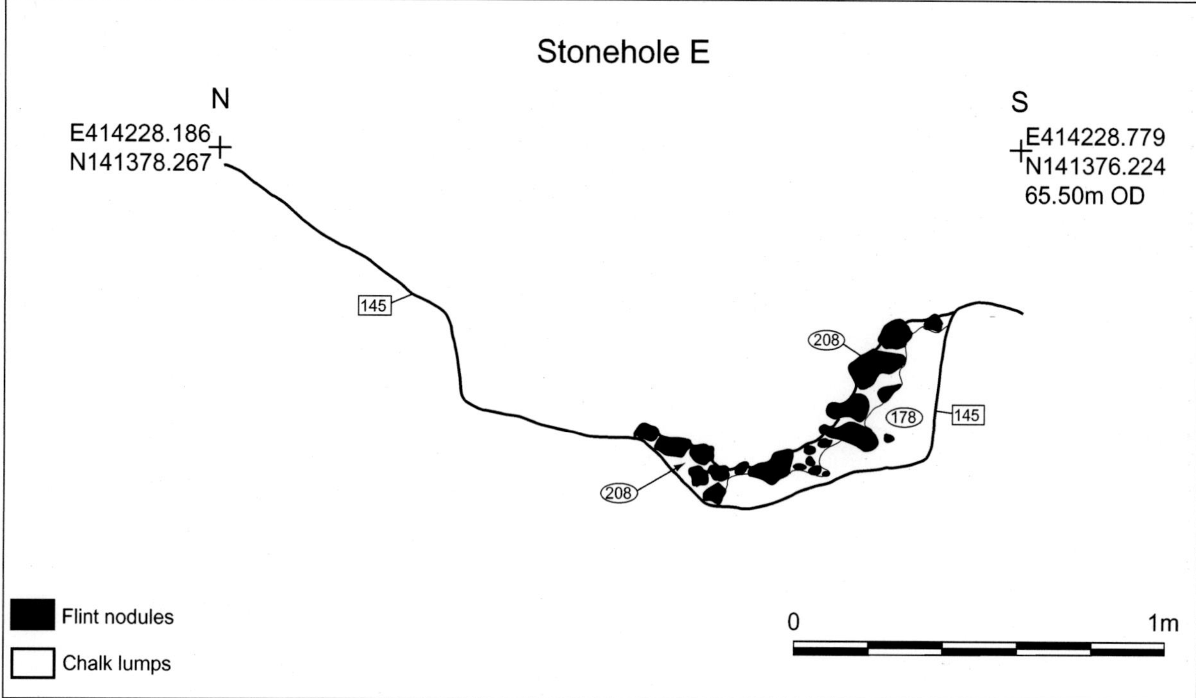

Figure 5.30. Profile of Stonehole E with all fills removed except the flint nodule 'nest' (208) and the basal fill (178)

The bowl-shaped nest of flint nodules had been carefully built, and seems not to have acquired its bowl shape from compression of a flat pad of stones, since the flint nodules formed a tightly packed structure rather than a stretched and splayed pattern.

The bowl-shaped feature measured at its maximum 0.80m in diameter and 0.50m deep at its highest side on the south (Figure 5.30). The bowl's internal diameter was 0.55m and its internal depth was 0.40m–0.50m. The nodules varied in size from 0.08m to 0.15m, and were tightly packed together to form a rigid structure.

The flint bowl's circular wall was present on its south and west sides but was missing its top two-thirds on its east and north sides (Figure 5.31). That these latter sides had once stood to a greater height is suggested by collapsed areas of flint on the bowl's northeast side, where nodules were lying in their original formation but had slumped inwards, coming to rest partly on the sides of the bowl-shaped feature and partly on its fill (206), which contained a Beaker sherd (see Cleal, below) and three pieces of sandstone, one of them worked (SF 186; see below; Figure 5.78).

Figure 5.31. The flint 'nest' (208) in Stonehole E, viewed from the north; to the right is the base of Stonehole F

Figure 5.32 (below). Section drawing of Stonehole F, with Bronze Age ditch fills

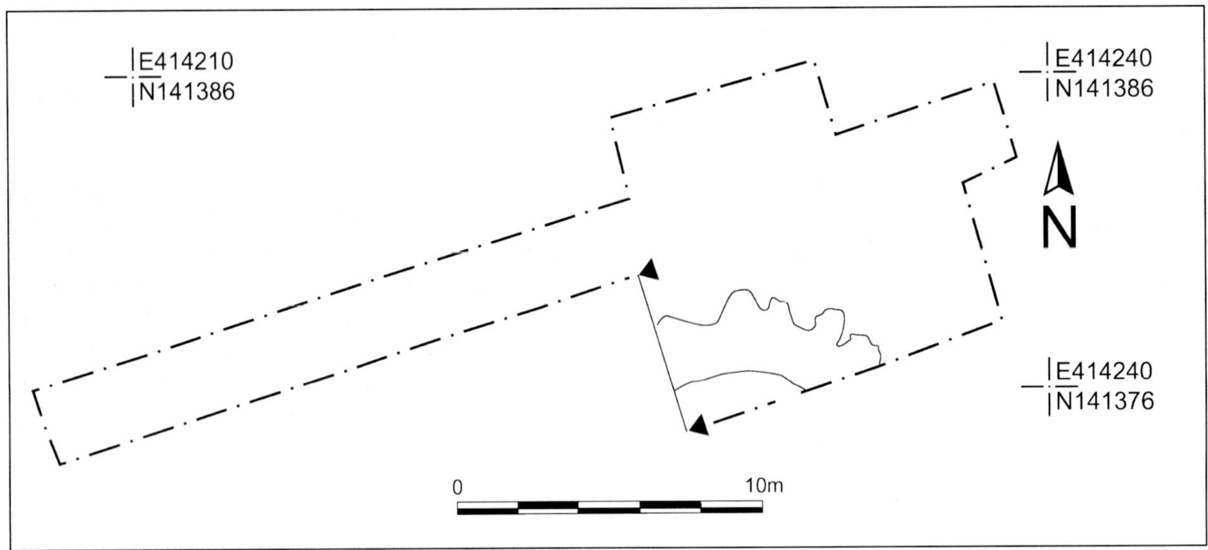

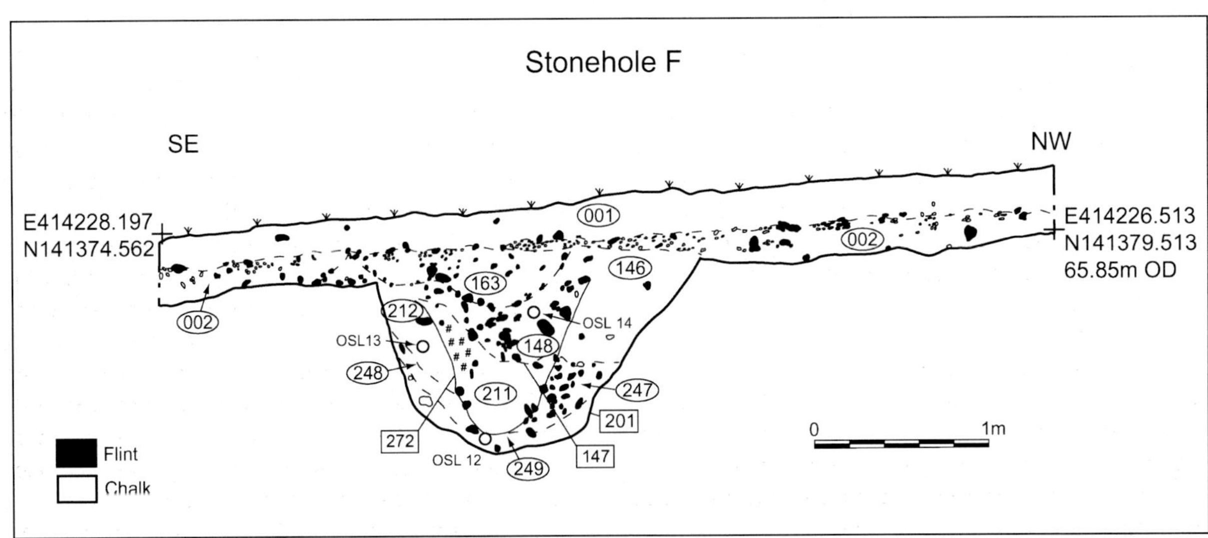

Figure 5.33. Stonehole E, viewed from the northeast; to its right is Stonehole F and to its left are Stoneholes D and C (partially excavated) whilst beyond it is a medieval ditch (014)

This pattern of partial collapse on the bowl's north and east sides is best explained as resulting from the removal of the standing stone. Presumably the standing stone was withdrawn from the northwest, up the external ramp (visible on Figures 5.14–5.15).

If the stone sat within this specially prepared flint nest, its depth was 0.85m (or 1.05m BGS). Thus it had the shallowest foundations of any of the standing stones at Bluestonehenge for which stoneholes have been excavated.

The flint bowl-shaped structure (208) was filled with dark brown clay mottled with yellow-brown clay silt (206; Figure 5.29), full of charcoal including a large piece (0.10m by 0.12m) of burnt wood. Layer 206 extended southwards, rising above the southern wall of the flint bowl. This deposit was sampled for soil micromorphology (see above). It is interpreted as collapsed turf and topsoil, mixed with upper fill from the edges of the robbing hole for the standing stone (240, 1.10m north–south by 1.10m east–west).

The uppermost layer of fill within Stonehole E was the same light yellow-brown clay-silt that similarly filled the tops of Stoneholes D and F, which shared this context number (146), and was the same as layer 134 in Stonehole C and layer 123 in Stoneholes A and B. The southern part of Stonehole E's upper fill was cut by the Bronze Age ditch (147).

Stonehole F

The greater part of Stonehole F (201), on its west side, lay beneath the western baulk of Trench 51 (Figure 5.14), so only 0.45m of its east–west width was excavated and then not to the base of the stonehole. Its upper fill on its south side was cut into by the Bronze Age ditch (147) but otherwise it was undisturbed by later features (Figure 5.32).

Its pit (201) was presumably oval (like the others), 1.75m long (north–south) and over 1.00m deep. Its ramp was not visible; it presumably lies to the northwest in the unexcavated area under the baulk, although Stonehole F could conceivably have shared Stonehole E's ramp.

The lowest layer excavated within Stonehole F was light yellow-brown silt (249), 0.15m deep and 0.90m north–south, sloping down from the pit's southern edge into its centre. This may have been the clay 'cushion' on which the standing stone formerly sat. Above it, there were two layers: layer 247 on the north side of the pit and layer 248 on the south (Figure 5.32). Layer 247 was mid-yellow/brown silty clay, 0.35m thick with 50% by volume of angular flints. It appears to have had a horizontal upper surface when deposited, suggestive of packing that was rammed into place around a standing stone.

On the south side, layer 248 was mid-dark brown silty clay, with little flint and only 0.15m thick. It is interpreted as packing, introduced from the south side of the stonehole and forming a steep, tipped layer down the side of the hole. Above it, layer 212 was mid–light brown clay silt, with few flints, 0.35m thick and similarly with a steep angle of tip. It is also interpreted as a layer of packing around the standing stone.

Layers 248, 212 and 247 were cut by a V-shaped feature (272) with a rounded bottom, 0.30m wide (north–south) at its base and probably 0.80m wide at its top (though its southern edge was cut into by ditch 147). It was 0.90m deep and was presumably the void in which the standing stone formerly stood at a depth of 1.25m BGS. Whilst the southern edge of cut 272 was compromised by Bronze Age ditch 147 (it might originally have been near-vertical), its northern edge had an angle of slope of 70°. This feature was filled with black-brown clay silt (211),

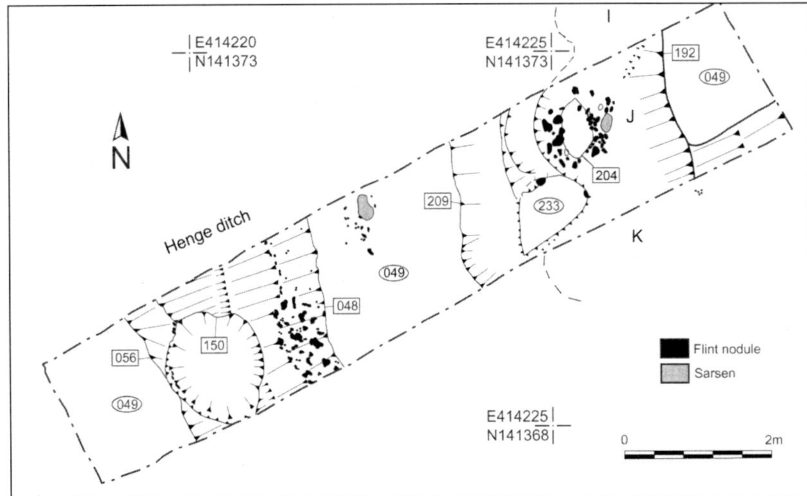

Figure 5.34. Plan of Trench 60, showing the henge ditch (048=056) cut by a medieval pit (150), and ditch (209), the Bronze Age ditch (147=192) and a pediment of natural clay (233)

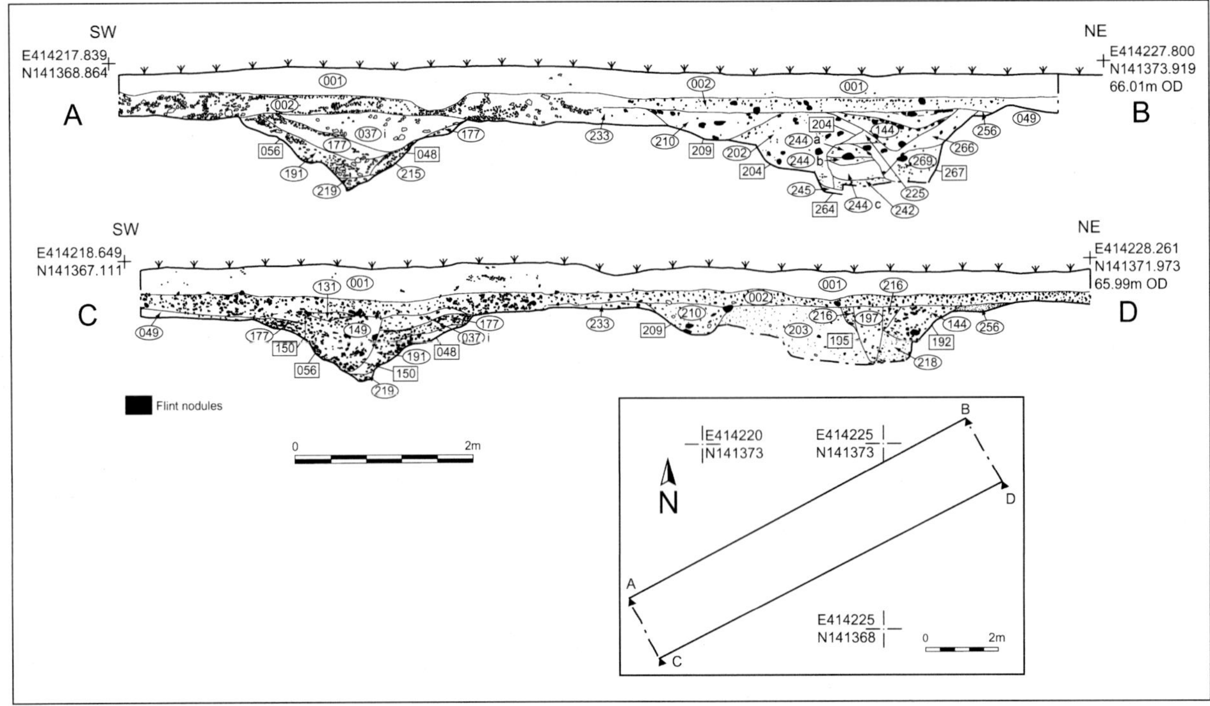

Figure 5.35. Section drawings of the long sides of Trench 60, showing the henge ditch and Stoneholes I, J and K, as well as Bronze Age and medieval features; section C–D has been flipped horizontally

0.30m thick and significantly darker on its south side than on its north. This is interpreted as a dump of topsoil and turf, fallen into the emptied stonehole from its rim.

The uppermost fill of the stonehole was light yellow-brown clay-silt (146), the same as the upper fill of the other stoneholes A–E (146=134=123).

Stonehole I

Only the southeastern edge of Stonehole I extended into Trench 60 by 0.35m, most of it lying beneath the trench's northern baulk (Figures 5.34, 5.38). Consequently, no dimensions can be given for this stonehole (267), other than that it was excavated to a depth of 0.75m and was probably 0.90m deep at its southwestern edge (Figure 5.35).

Stonehole I's sequence of packing layers could be identified only in the stonehole's southeast corner (towards the northernmost end of Trench 60). These consisted of orange-brown silty clay (269) beneath brown-orange clay silt (266). Since these two layers were observed only in the northeast–southwest section which hit Stonehole I at a glancing angle, little can be said about their formation or significance.

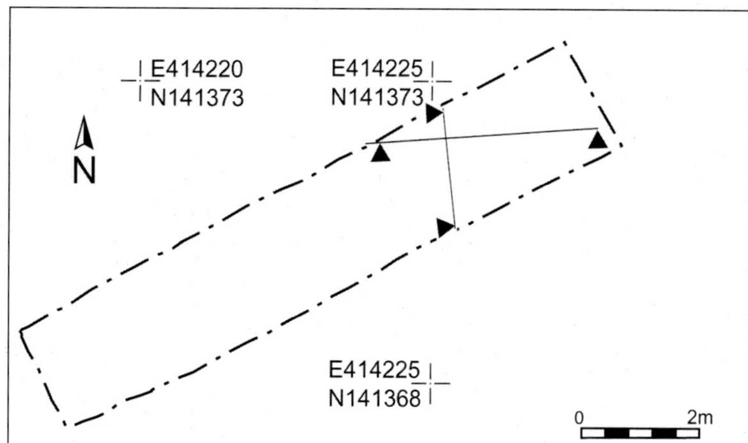

Figure 5.36. Section and profile of Stonehole J (with only the basal fill remaining), showing cuts of the Bronze Age ditch (147=192) and the medieval ditch (209)

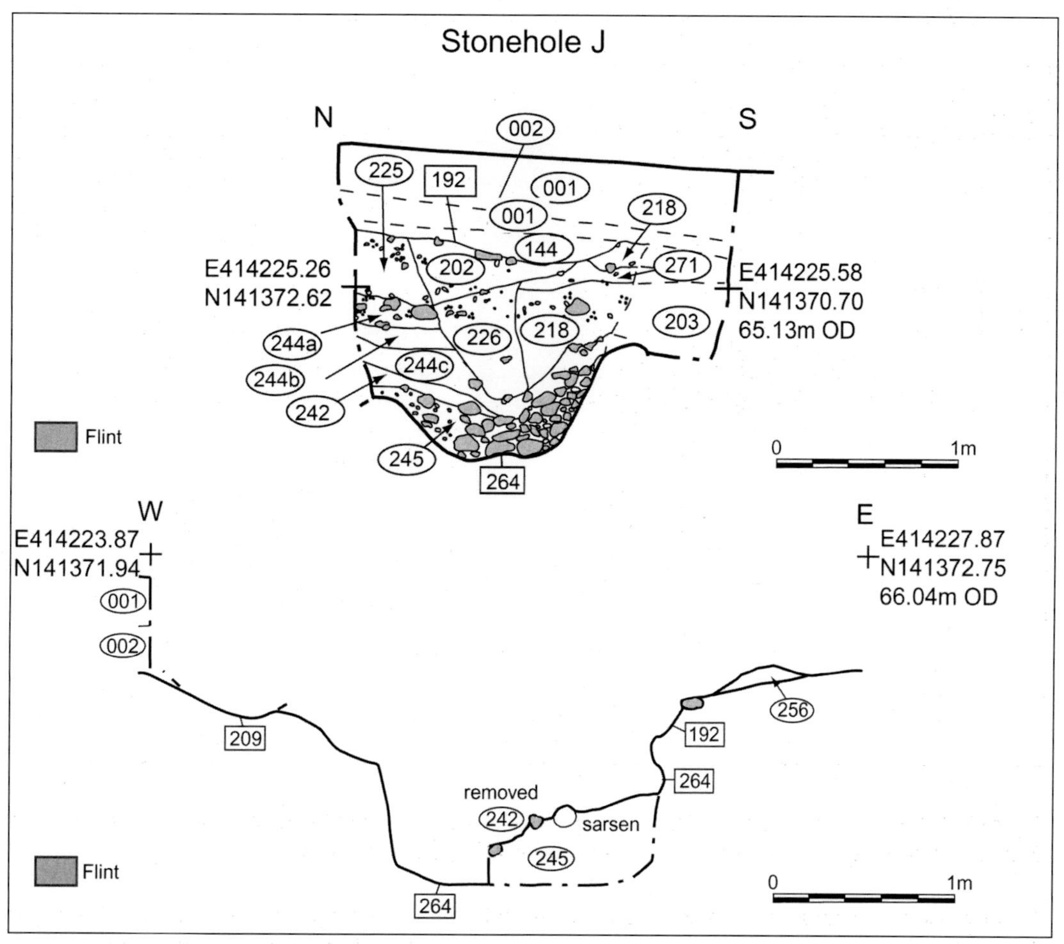

Stonehole J

Stonehole J (264) was 1.50m east–west by 1.50m north–south and 1.10m deep, with a ramp 1.25m long and at least 1.20m wide on its west side (Figures 5.35–5.38). Its eastern edge was slightly undercut but otherwise its sides were steep, descending to a flat bottom. On its southern side, its scalloped edge, demarcating it from Stonehole K, could be identified but not on its northern side towards Stonehole I. On its southwest side, a large pediment of periglacial orange-red clay (233; Figures 5.34–5.35) separated its ramp and the eastern part of its pit from the northern part of the ramp and pit of Stonehole K. Stonehole J's ramp had a lip, 0.35m from the edge of the hole, but the ramp's profile was interrupted by the cut of a medieval ditch (209, filled by 210; Figures 5.34–5.35). The angle of the ramp was about 20° from horizontal.

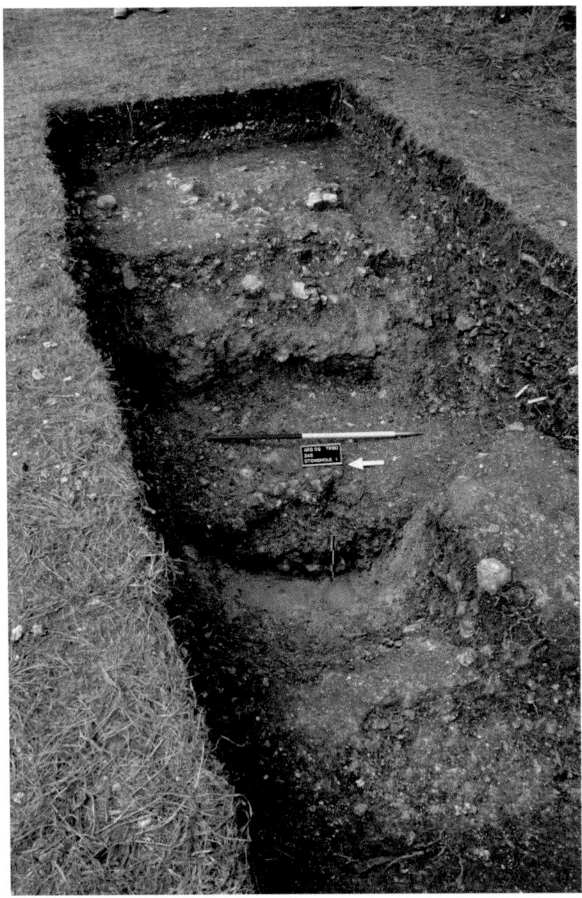

Figure 5.37. Stonehole J with its basal deposits in half section, viewed from the west. Although the photo board identifies this as Stonehole I, it was reassigned as Stonehole J after excavation

The bottom 0.30m–0.45m of Stonehole J was filled with a mixture of heavy grey clay (245), containing large flint nodules and occasional lumps of imported hard chalk, within a hard-packed matrix. These flint nodules, up to 0.16m across, constituted up to 80% of the matrix, especially on the south side of the pit. Since the stonehole was dug into predominantly decayed chalk (with a capping of undisturbed periglacial orange-red clay [233] on its west side), layer 245 was clearly composed of entirely imported material.

On the surface of layer 245, the flint nodules (together with a large waterworn sarsen cobble) were concentrated in the centre of the deposit, perhaps to provide a firm base on which the standing stone could sit. An indentation up to 0.10m deep into the top of layer 245 may have been caused by the weight of the stone or alternatively was deliberately created before the stone was erected to form a slight socket for the stone to sit in. Finds were few within layer 245, mostly consisting of worked flints. However, they did include a serrated flake (SF 588), a red deer tooth and the tip of a robust

Figure 5.38. Stonehole J in the centre of Trench 60 and Stonehole I in section in the baulk, viewed from the southeast; Stoneholes I, J and K during excavation were originally labelled on photo boards as H, I and J but were reassigned after excavation

bone point (see Figure 5.80). The red deer tooth has a radiocarbon date of 2480–2230 cal BC at 95% confidence (SUERC-32162; 3890±30 BP).

The north–south variation in the density of flint nodules (increasing in density southwards) within layer 245 may have been of no great consequence but it may also relate to the sequence of stone erection. If Stone K were erected prior to Stone J, then the denser stone packing on the south side of Stonehole J, together with the stones being packed against this edge to a height of 0.45m above the stonehole's base, may have ensured that Stone J did not encroach towards Stone K so that regular spacing between stones could be achieved.

Above the packing layer (245) was a sequence of clay layers (Figure 5.36). The lowest of these were orange-brown-grey clay (242) and, above it, orange-red-brown clay (244c). Both of these would have extended beneath the base of the stone and presumably acted as a cushion into which it settled to a depth of 0.25m below the top of layer 244c. Above this layer on the north side of the stonehole, there was a layer of brown clay (244b) beneath a layer of orange-brown-grey clay (244a), topped by a thicker layer of brown-grey clay and flint nodules (225).

The sequence on the south side of the stonehole above basal layer 245 was simpler, consisting of a thick deposit of grey-brown clay (218; a mix of imported grey clay and chalk fragments with backfill of decayed chalk and orange-red clay; equated with 244b). Towards the top of layer 218 (beneath its uppermost component), there was a band of orange clay (271). All four layers (218, 244a, 244b and 271) can be broadly equated and interpreted as packing fills for a standing stone within Stonehole J.

Whilst the base of Stonehole J's pit was packed with flint nodules, the standing stone actually sat on a relatively stone-free (10% by volume) orange-red clay (244c), the surface of which has preserved the partial imprint of the stone (distorted by its removal). After stone removal, layer 218 on the stonehole's southwest side may have slumped into the void left by the stone. Although the stone's basal imprint was oval in plan (0.70m east–west by 0.65m north–south), the stone may have been triangular in cross-section higher up, with its three corners in the southwest, east and north. The base of Stone J would have been 0.30m above the bottom of the stonehole and 1.25m BGS. Its slightly pointed base measured about 0.20m north–south, widening at a height of 0.30m above its base to 0.65m north–south and 0.70m east–west.

The void between the packing layers created by the removal of Stone J formed a lopsided V-shaped feature (204), 0.55m north–south by *c.* 0.70m east–west and 0.80m deep, filled with an organic mid-dark grey-brown silty clay (226=262) containing charcoal flecks. This may have been a mix of topsoil and clay from the upper edges of the stonehole, falling into the void after the stone was removed, but it is also possibly a deliberate backfilling of the hole. Either way, it preserved the basal imprint of the stone which had stood in this hole. The top of the void was filled with grey-brown clay silt (202).

The standing stone was removed from the northwest rather than from its west side. This might have been because its triangular cross-section made it easier to pivot it in that direction. A large, waterworn sarsen boulder, 0.35m × 0.20m, on the edge of the robber pit (Figures 5.34, 5.36), may have been one of the packing stones within layer 245 displaced during the robbing.

Stonehole K

Only the northernmost 0.45m of Stonehole K lay within Trench 60, forming a narrow, teardrop-shaped feature; most of this stonehole lay in the unexcavated area beneath the trench's southern baulk. The hole (205) was 1.60m east–west with a western ramp at least 0.60m long (truncated at its west end by a medieval ditch [209]).

Only the uppermost fill of the stonehole and ramp was excavated, to a depth of up to 0.60m. This upper part of the hole was filled with mid-dark grey-brown silty clay (203) which formed the upper layer of packing for the stone. It contained a chisel arrowhead (SF 20100).

The bluestone monoliths: discussion

There are good reasons for identifying the holes A–F and I–K as stoneholes and not as pits or postholes. Firstly, they are more than just pits, containing fills indicative of uprights having been placed in them. Secondly, they cannot be postholes in which the posts were left to rot since post-pipes leave clear traces (as is the case with Bronze Age postholes 122, 154, 180 and 195; see *Bronze Age re-use*, below). Thirdly, they cannot be postholes from which posts were removed because of the non-circular outlines and flat profiles of their basal imprints (wooden Neolithic posts being circular with pointed bases where cut from the tree trunk with a stone axe).

There are six strands of evidence as to why they are stoneholes:

- The holes are shallow in relation to the evident widths of the uprights that stood in them. The depth of each upright, recordable in seven instances, was between 0.85m and 1.24m below the top of the bedrock, and yet the diameters of each pit were 1m–1.80m. The minimum basal diameters of the uprights that stood in them can be calculated as between 0.30m and 0.70m. In comparison, postholes with similar diameters to the Bluestonehenge pits – such as Circle 2D of the Southern Circle at Durrington Walls – have much greater depths of 1.58m–2.49m below the top of bedrock chalk (Wainwright with Longworth 1971: 381–2). The depths of the stone sockets of the West Amesbury circle are most closely comparable with the deeper of the bluestoneholes at Stonehenge (see Figure 4.5). In particular, the two deepest at West Amesbury are the same depth as Bluestone 68, standing in the bluestone horseshoe at Stonehenge, which is set not into solid chalk bedrock but into a similarly soft matrix of re-deposited chalk rubble (Gowland 1902; Cleal *et al.* 1995: fig. 150.Sc64.3).

- A direct comparison between posthole and stonehole was possible within the Bluestonehenge circle itself. Bronze Age posthole 154 (see below) was of comparable diameter (1.40m–1.50m) to the stone sockets, but it was as deep (1.40m below top of bedrock) as it was wide (a ratio of 1:1), whereas the stoneholes are shallower than they are wide, at a ratio of 2:3. Thus posts were sunk deeper than standing stones of the same diameter.

- There was no evidence for any hourglass-shaped disturbance in the pits' cross-sections such as would have been caused by levering wooden uprights back and forth to loosen them. Stone extraction is different from post extraction in that the stone is pulled in one direction only (rather than being levered back and forth) to be lifted out, causing the butt to kick back against the packing on the opposite side to the extraction ramp.

- The careful preparation of pit bases with pad and cushion layers is found neither in the Bronze Age postholes at West Amesbury nor within any of the Neolithic postholes cut into solid chalk at Durrington Walls (Wainwright with Longworth 1971) or Woodhenge (Cunnington 1929).

- The considerable weight of the uprights that once stood in the West Amesbury sockets was enough to cause compression through the cushion layers and into the soft, decayed chalk bedrock beneath. Such compression is more likely to have resulted from stone rather than timber uprights.

- The imprints left by such compression reveal a variety of basal cross-sections, from oval to rectangular to triangular and indented, in contrast to the usual circular cross-sections and pointed bases of Neolithic timber posts.

We can argue confidently that these holes held stones, and there are cogent reasons why these stones were not local sarsens but bluestones from west Wales:

The dimensions of the stones' imprints and the voids created by their removal are directly comparable to Stonehenge's bluestones: the Stonehenge bluestone pillars are much narrower and thinner than any of the sarsens found at either Stonehenge (see Appendix 7 of Cleal *et al.* 1995: 566–71) or Avebury (Marshall 2016).

The basal imprints within each stonehole exhibited characteristics shared with Stonehenge's bluestones, namely rectangular, oval and triangular cross-sections. In particular, the imprints of Stones D and E are so similar to the distinctively indented and trapezoidal cross-sections of, respectively, Bluestones 68 and 63 at Stonehenge (Cleal *et al.* 1995: figs 116, 121, 124) that these could even be the very holes in which Bluestones 68 and 63 were initially erected.

The very limited presence of sarsen as a packing material (confined to just three water-worn cobbles among hundreds of flint nodules from within the excavated stoneholes; see *Raw materials*, below) makes it likely that there was virtually no sarsen available locally. None of the handful of sarsen pieces from the henge (within its ditch or beneath its bank, described below) are chippings from large stones. The lack of sarsen stone-working debris is not surprising: it is practically unfeasible for the Neolithic builders of Bluestonehenge to have worked the extremely hard sarsen into thin, narrow pillars like bluestones. Sarsen is a remarkably hard stone (see Chapter 6); with prehistoric technology, it would be extremely difficult to reduce a sarsen block to a pillar-like form.

The argument that standing bluestones could not have been erected here because there is no bluestone debris does not stand up to scrutiny. Since the stones were removed from their sockets without breakage, there was no smashed stone debitage, or broken-off stumps or detached stone chips. The cheese-like consistency of the soft chalk bedrock is a further factor in allowing monoliths to be erected and dismantled without damage to them.

Raw materials

Other than the bluestones themselves, which originated in west Wales, a variety of raw materials were imported to the site for use in constructing the stone circle. The construction site was a low spur of decayed chalk close to the River Avon. This decayed chalk or chalk marl formed a narrow tongue of soft, granular deposit flanked on its east and west sides by subsoil layers of red clay and coombe rock. Weathering and erosion of this soft, decayed chalk led to the accumulation of a skin of broken flint nodules on the top of this chalk peninsula. Stoneholes were dug through this top layer of flints and into the soft, gritty, sand-like chalk bedrock beneath.

Grey alluvial clay, large flint nodules and occasional lumps of unweathered chalk were among the items imported for the erection of the stones. Undoubtedly these were required because of the bedrock's inherent softness and unsuitability for supporting standing stones. The alluvial grey clay differs in colour and texture from the local red clay although both were used in cushioning and packing the stones. Without doubt, this alluvial clay derives from one or more locations along the edges of the river's channels.

The flint nodules from the stoneholes were appreciably larger than those excavated from the henge interior and had clearly been selected for their size. Their cortex varied from fresh to heavily weathered and it is most likely that they were obtained from the bases of chalk river cliffs such as those upstream along the Avon at Ratfyn and North Countess Road, from the river cliff of the tributary stream on the northeast side of Vespasian's Camp (see Figure 9.4), or even from the riverbed. The lumps of hard chalk might also have been picked up from the river cliffs. Two sarsen cobbles were found in and adjacent to Stonehole J and a smaller one was found in Stonehole E. All three were water-worn and were presumably found along the river's edge.

Sequences of erection and dismantling

One of the curious features of the stoneholes' construction is the diversity of methods used for preparing the hole to take the stone. Of seven instances where the construction sequence could be recovered, three differ markedly from the others.

- In Stoneholes A, C, D and F, the preparation for the stone involved the laying of a relatively flint-free cushion of clay. Even then, there were differences in the type of clay selected, with grey alluvial clay in Stoneholes A, C and D and yellow-brown clay in F.
- In Stoneholes B and J, a pad of compacted clay and flint nodules was laid down first, followed by a flint-free clay cushion (of grey-brown clay and chalk marl in Stonehole B and orange-red clay in Stonehole J).

- In Stonehole E, an elaborate nest of flint nodules was constructed but there was no clay cushion between it and the base of the standing stone.

Packing layers and methods also varied from stonehole to stonehole, with some multiple layering of horizontally-laid clay deposits, and other deposits being tipped in at an angle. There was also no regularity in the inclusion of flint nodules in the packing deposits. This variation in stonehole preparation suggests that different people might have been involved in erecting each of the stones, making different construction choices. Perhaps separate groups had the responsibility of transporting and erecting each stone.

The use of a cushion layer in most of the stoneholes is particularly interesting. The stone sank into this layer, crushing the decayed chalk beneath and leaving in that natural chalk an impression of the stone's base. The effect was something like pressing a thin layer of Plasticine into a bed of wet sand with the base of a pencil, squeezing the clay sideways and creating a ghost imprint of the pencil in the sand beneath. This cushion layer might have been useful in the two cases (Stoneholes B and J) where it sat on top of a hard pad layer, to prevent the stone cracking when it hit large flint nodules. Yet no such cushion layer was laid over the flint nest in Stonehole E. Perhaps pads and cushions were considered necessary to secure the base of the stone in position and to stop it from sliding or sinking deep into the sand-like natural chalk.

The sequence of stone removal involved loosening the stone, with varying degrees of disturbance of the packing, and then hauling out the stone – the full-sized bluestones present in the inner horseshoe at Stonehenge today are estimated to weigh around 3–4 tons (Abbott and Anderson-Whymark 2012; Field *et al.* 2015). The stoneholes' ramps indicate that the stones were extracted at a steep angle, in some cases at an angle of around 70° to the horizontal. This is considerably steeper than the angles of 65° or less for withdrawal of stones from the Aubrey Holes (see Chapter 4 and Cleal *et al.* 1995: figs 51–55) and would have required heavy lifting gear, presumably in the form of a simple large, timber A-frame, which could have been used to raise the stones out of their holes at such a steep angle. They could then have been pulled forwards to be lowered to rest at much gentler angles of 10°–35° on their extraction ramps before being dragged away.

The size and shape of the bluestone circle

If today's ground surface is close to that in the Neolithic (*i.e.* about 0.30m above subsoil and bedrock), then the standing stones were set between 1.05m and 1.54m into the ground. In Stoneholes A, B, C, D and J, there is evidence that the stones were set onto the top of a 'cushion' layer into which they then slowly settled, to a further depth of up to 0.20m.

As hypothesised at the beginning of this chapter, we propose that the West Amesbury stones were re-erected at Stonehenge after their removal from Bluestonehenge. If the stone that once stood in Stonehole D was indeed Stonehenge's Bluestone 68 (see above), then it would have stood 2.50m high, only 0.04m lower than it does today at Stonehenge. On average, however, the known depth of the sockets of Stonehenge's bluestone oval and circle is 0.98m–0.99m BGS (see Figure 4.5 and Cleal *et al.* 1995: figs 135–6, 141, 143–4), so at West Amesbury the stones were generally sunk to a greater average depth, of 1.32m BGS. For smaller stones of the Stonehenge bluestone circle, this would have made a substantial difference to their height above ground if they were sunk so deep at West Amesbury. It seems more likely that it was the taller pillars of the Stonehenge bluestone oval, each measuring up to 4.00m high, that were once set within the deep sockets of the West Amesbury circle. Thus at Bluestonehenge they would have stood to 2m–2.50m, well above head height.

The difference in the mean depth of the stone settings at Bluestonehenge, compared to other stone circles where the stones rest directly on bedrock (such as on the Isle of Lewis; Richards 2013), reflects the fact that the circle's builders had to come up with an unusual engineering solution to compensate for the relatively plastic nature of the substrate. In contrast to setting sockets directly into bedrock, the Bluestonehenge builders needed to construct their stoneholes more carefully.

With such a small portion of the ring of stone sockets excavated, it is impossible to be sure of its plan. Was it a circle? Or was it an oval? Or was it even an arc or façade? The lines of the interior and exterior edges of the stoneholes (4.10m radius and 5.50m radius respectively; see Figure 5.14) fit well with their having been laid out and dug as a circle, the diameter of which was 9.70m (measured from stone centre to stone centre). Yet the placing of stones within the holes – particularly the positions of Stones B and C – does not fit this circular plan particularly well. This may indicate that the stone ring was, in fact, an oval with a northeast–southwest axis, the long diameter of which would have measured 9.90m and its shorter diameter 7.80m (from stone centre to stone centre). Without further excavation or high-quality geophysical results, it is impossible to decide with certainty. However, the fact that the stoneholes conform best to a circle suggests that this is what was intended, with variations in the precise locations of particular stones due simply to minor inaccuracies in their erection. Thus we subscribe to the likelihood that this was a stone circle and not an oval, although this cannot be confirmed with certainty on the present evidence.

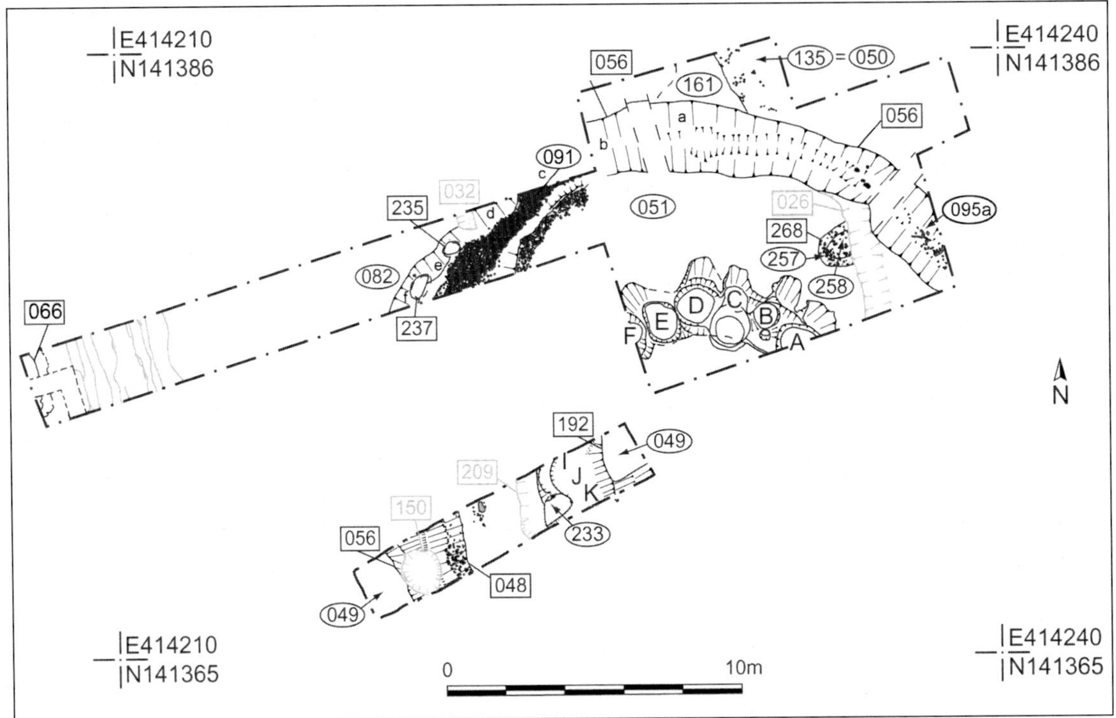

Figure 5.39. Plan of the henge ditch (048=056) and stoneholes, with later features in Trenches 51 and 60 also shown; medieval features are marked in grey

Distances between centres of stones in Stoneholes A–F average 1.16m. If it is assumed that this spacing was continuous around the circle then an estimate of the maximum number of stones can be obtained; however, this depends on whether the stones formed a true circle, an oval or some other arrangement.

- If we assume a perfect circle formed by the centre line of the stoneholes, then the circle's radius was about 4.85m and its circumference was 30.45m, providing spaces for 26 standing stones.
- If we assume an oval plan, 9.90m northeast–southwest by 7.80m northwest–southeast, with regular spacing, then there would have been spaces for 24 standing stones.

Yet the spacing between Stoneholes J and K – at least 1.40m – is much wider than among Stoneholes A–F (Figures 5.14, 5.34). Either a stone was left out of the ring on this west side or stones were spaced more widely on this side, either to form a western entrance into the ring or to provide a less tightly spaced western façade.

The henge

The northern half of the henge ditch (Figure 5.39) is, in retrospect, visible in the twin-electrode earth resistance survey of September 2006 and in the square-array earth resistance survey carried out in July 2006, whilst the henge ditch's northern tip is just about identifiable in the fluxgate magnetometer survey of July 2006 (Figures 5.3–5.4).

The interior of the henge had a natural surface formed by a deflated layer of flint cobbles (051; Figure 5.40). Layer 053 (=256) can be considered to have formed from earthworm-sorting of the finer component of layer 051, which it lies on top of. Layer 051 is interpreted as the weathered remains of a natural, flint-capped platform across the henge interior and also evident outside the henge in the northeast. It is visible on the earth resistivity plot of September 2006 as a zone of high resistance. These layers contained a tiny sherd of Beaker pottery, an undateable sherd, and a variety of flintwork; an end-and-side scraper (SF 141) was found in layer 053.

The interface between layer 051 and the base of the post-medieval B horizon (002) was a mixed deposit of cobbles, clay and black soil (099; Figure 5.40). There was no evidence that the flint cobble layer (051) had ever been covered by a mound; the only traces of the relict henge bank (270) were visible outside the northern edge of the henge ditch, and bank material was probably re-deposited as ditch fill (073) in much of the henge ditch along its northern side.

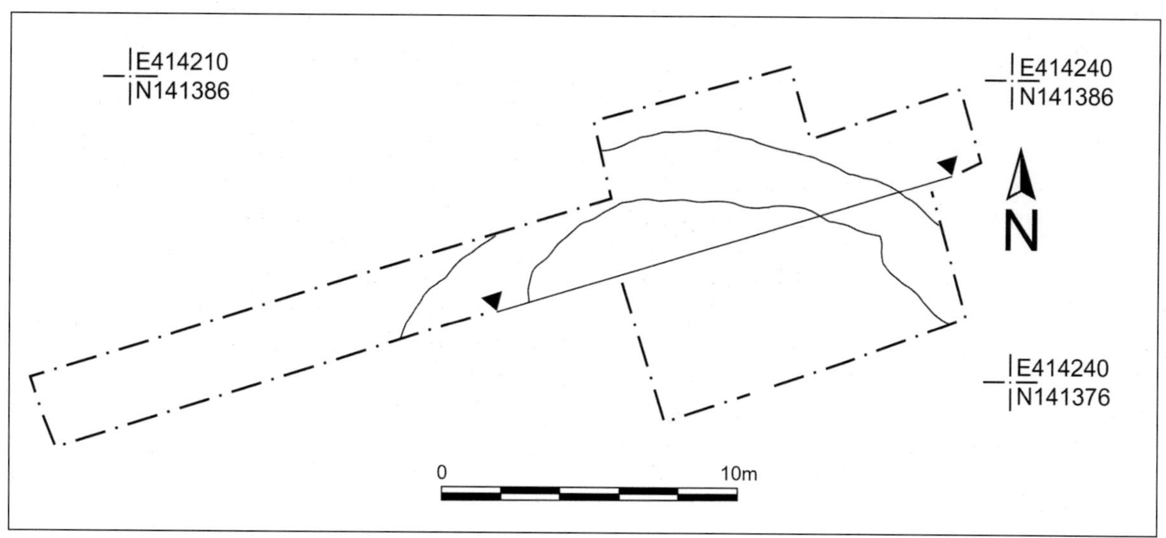

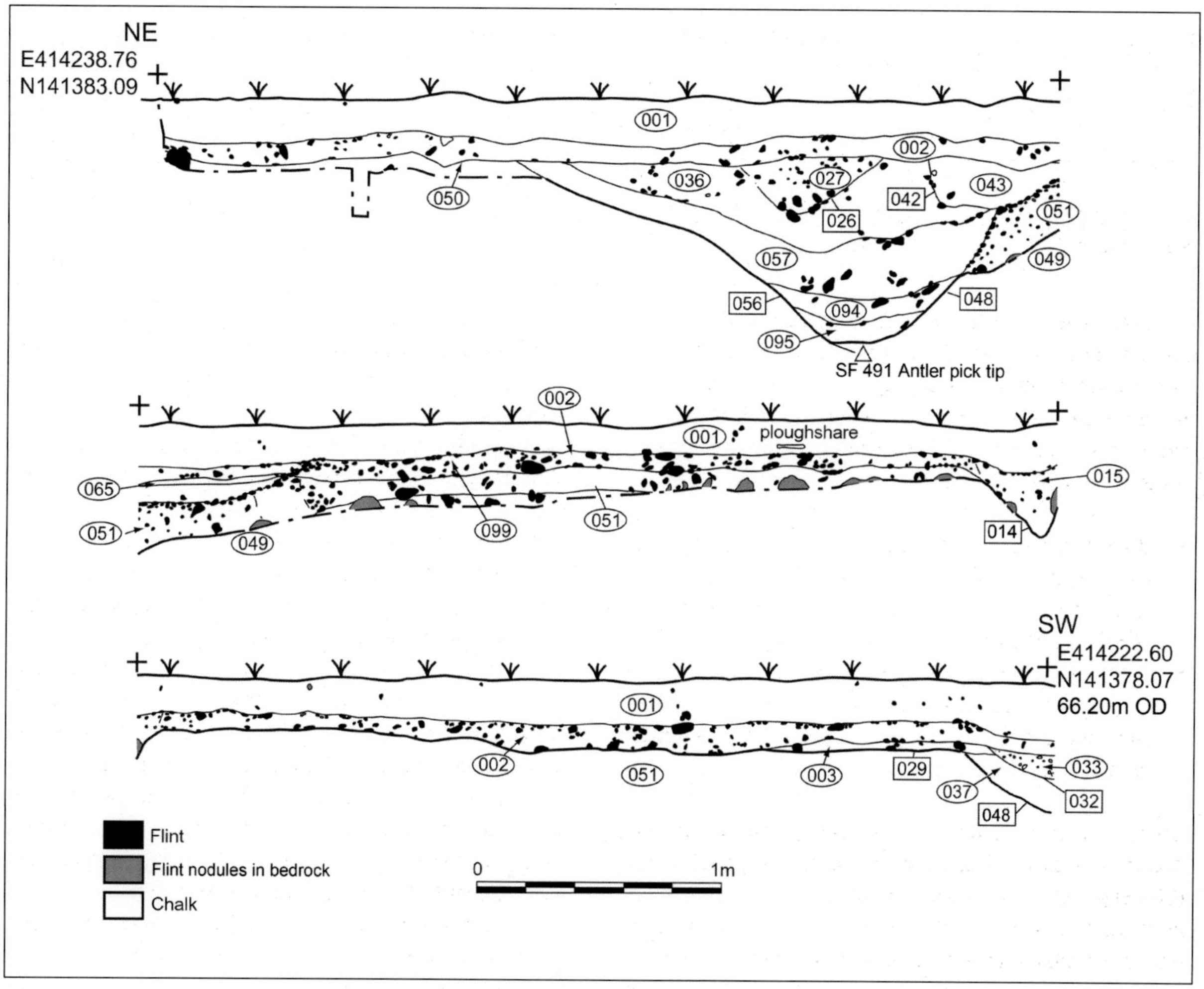

Figure 5.40. Section of the henge ditch and later features in Trench 51

The henge ditch was 2.60m wide and 1.20m deep, with a V-shaped profile (Figures 5.40–5.43). In the northwest quadrant, the ditch widened to at least 3.00m, although it was not excavated to its bottom in this quadrant. In 2008 the ditch was excavated in six segments, separated by wide baulks (a, b, c, d, e, f, marked in Figure 5.39). In 2009, two baulks were retained and a third was added within the area on the east side exposed within the extension to Trench 51 (Figure 5.16). The ditch was excavated to its base in the northeast quadrant and excavated to the lowest cobble surface within the secondary fill in the northwest quadrant.

The ditch was probably circular, with an east–west diameter of 23.40m between external ditch edges (cut 056), 20.80m between ditch centre lines, and 18.20m between internal ditch edges (cut 048). On its north side, the bottom of the ditch is relatively even and slopes southwards. In the northeast sector of the ditch, this bottom is uneven and strewn with flint nodules embedded in the solifluction deposit of chalk.

On its east side, the ditch narrows, perhaps to form a terminal on the north side of either an east-facing causeway or an entranceway into the henge. On the north side of the henge, two opposite, protruding ditch sides (where the ditch becomes narrow, immediately west of the baulk across the ditch) suggest two possibilities:

a. the former presence of a north-facing entrance, 2.00m wide, which was cut through by the ditch before silts began to accumulate in the ditch bottom;
b. the meeting of two gang-dug lengths, the one to the east of this narrow point being 10m long where it meets another narrowing at our baulk in the northeast. This is the more likely explanation for these changes in ditch width.

Almost a third of the henge ditch's circumference on its south side has been eroded by the encroaching River Avon. The bank around the outside of the henge is almost entirely missing (and there is no evidence that it was ever on the inside of the ditch). A small pocket of degraded chalk (270), 0.80m north–south and 0.17m thick, was noticed in section on the lip of the henge ditch on its northern edge; it is considered to be the remains of the otherwise vanished external bank of the henge. Along the fully excavated northeastern circuit of the henge ditch, the chalk-derived backfill of much of the ditch is most probably derived from this eroded henge bank. The former bank of the henge can be estimated as having been about 3.00m wide, giving the henge an original outer diameter of about 30m. The lack of redeposited bank material in the northwest sector of the henge ditch suggests that bank may have been positioned at some distance from the ditch, providing a wide berm.

Only in the northeast quadrant was the henge ditch excavated to its base. The primary fill of the ring ditch was a light grey to white-grey chalky clay (095), about 0.12m deep and formed from almost entirely re-deposited subsoil weathered and eroded off the ditch sides. In the northeast sector of the ditch, a broken-off tip of an antler pick (SF 491) was found in two pieces, embedded in a pocket into the bedrock (049), at the base of layer 095 (Figures 5.40, 5.44). This can be interpreted as having broken off from the pick, perhaps having been wedged between natural flint nodules in the ditch's bottom during digging of the ditch. The pick's tip is dated to 2460-2210 cal BC (95% confidence) as the weighted mean of three measurements (OxA-20351, OxA-20357 and SUERC-23207; see Table 5.4).

A broken and worn cattle scapula shovel (SF 485; see Figure 5.80) was found at the base of the henge ditch's primary fill (095). Worked flints were also found in this layer. Southeast of the northeastern baulk across the henge ditch, layer 095 was designated 095a as far as the southeastern corner of the trench. Within this 3m-long sector of the ditch lay a deposit consisting of an antler pick (SF 586) covered by two large pieces of antler (SF 557 and SF 573), a cattle sacrum, a cattle rib (SF 558), a small quartzite hammerstone, small unassignable sherds (likely to be either Grooved Ware or Beaker), and a small assemblage of worked flints (SFs 549–550, 555–560, 563, 565–579, 582–585; Figures 5.45–5.49, 5.73, 5.79–5.80). This constitutes a structured deposit within the henge ditch terminal. It is possible that the cattle rib was used for pressure flaking and that it and the hammerstone were flint-workers' tools. Struck flint flakes covered the antler pick, possibly as a deliberate capping for this artefact nearest the suspected ditch terminal.

Layer 095 was covered by a secondary fill (094) of brown-grey clay silt with chalky grit and broken flint. It was about 0.16m deep and contained a few worked flints and a Beaker rim sherd (SF 543). Two heavily weathered cattle ribs were found on the base of 094, both in the ditch's northwest segment. The eastern portion of the ditch southeast of the baulk was designated 094a. At its base there was a fragment of cattle pelvis, possibly constituting the top of the structured deposit found in 095a.

Layers 094 and 094a were covered by a layer of red-brown silty clay (numbered 213 and 213a respectively). This was truncated by a re-cut ditch (214; Figures 5.42–5.43) which had removed the upper fills (except for two thin strips against the chalk sides of the ditch) in the northeast and east sectors of the henge ditch for a distance of over 9.00m from the southern terminal. This re-cutting is associated with the Bronze Age re-use of the henge (see below).

In Trench 60, the henge ditch (048=056; Figures 5.34, 5.39) was largely destroyed by a medieval pit (150) but its primary fill was grey-brown clay (219) containing flint nodules, hard

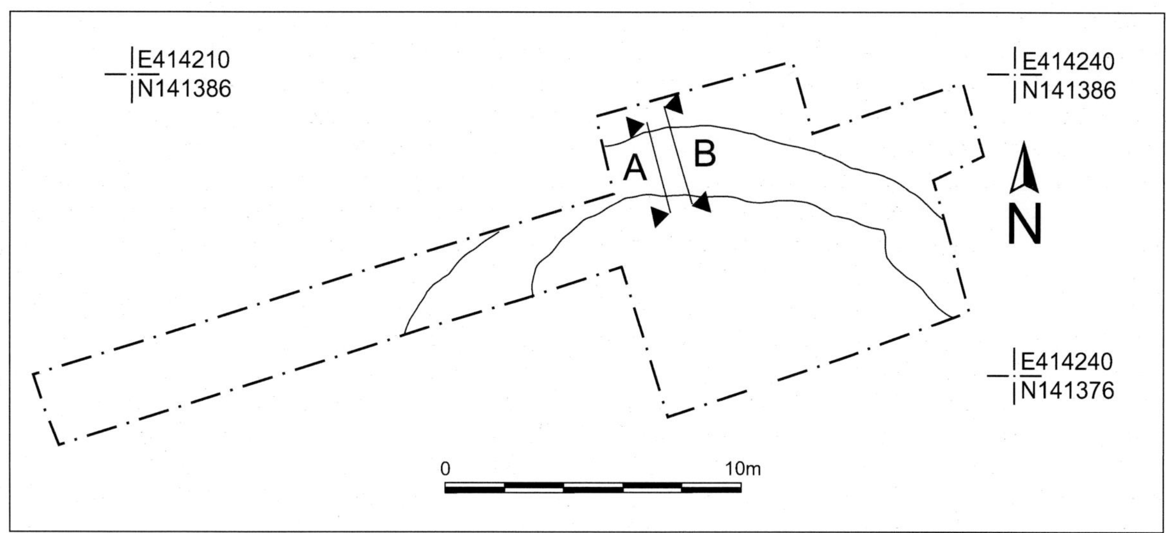

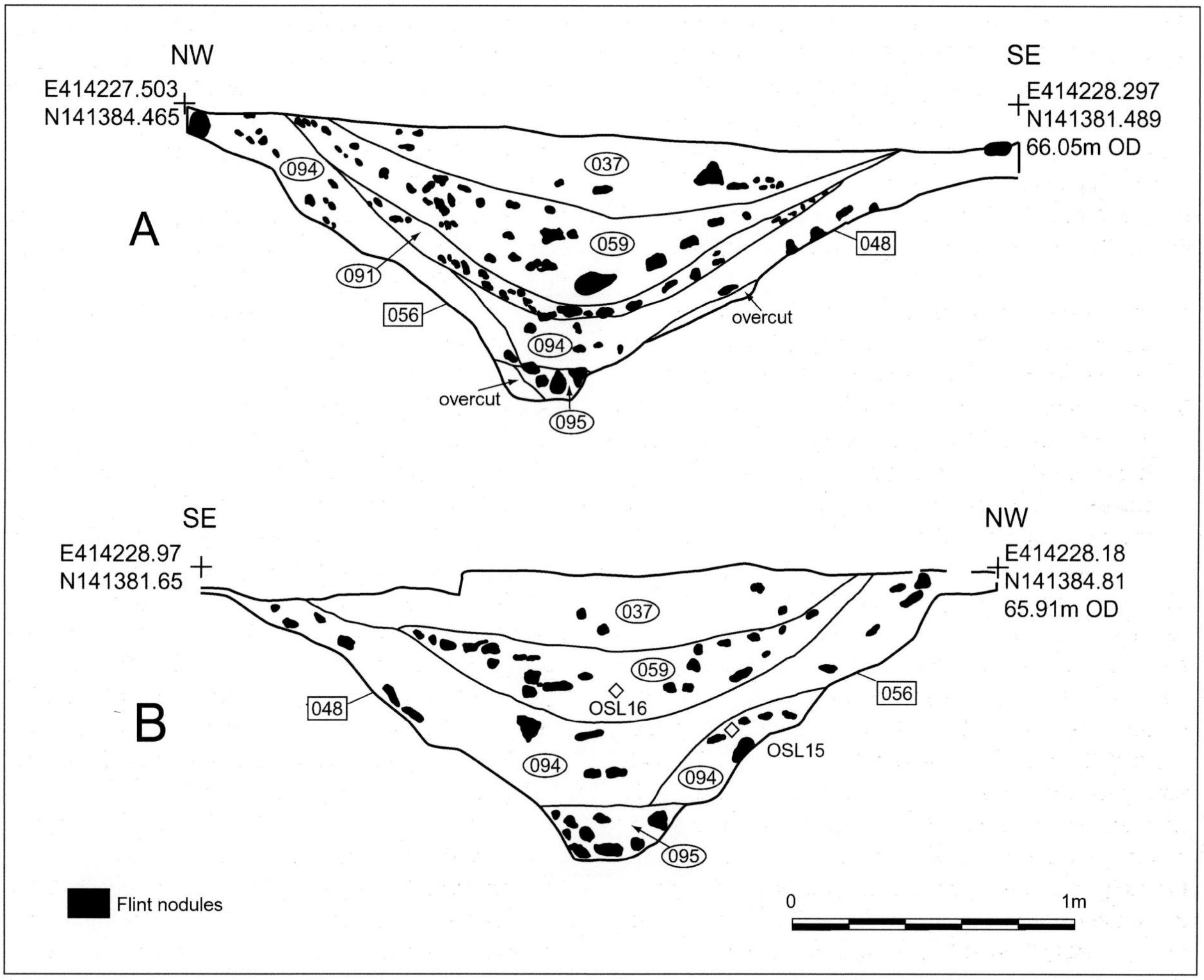

Figure 5.41. Sections of the henge ditch at the northern baulk in Trench 51; the section lines on the location plan mark the position of a baulk across the henge ditch

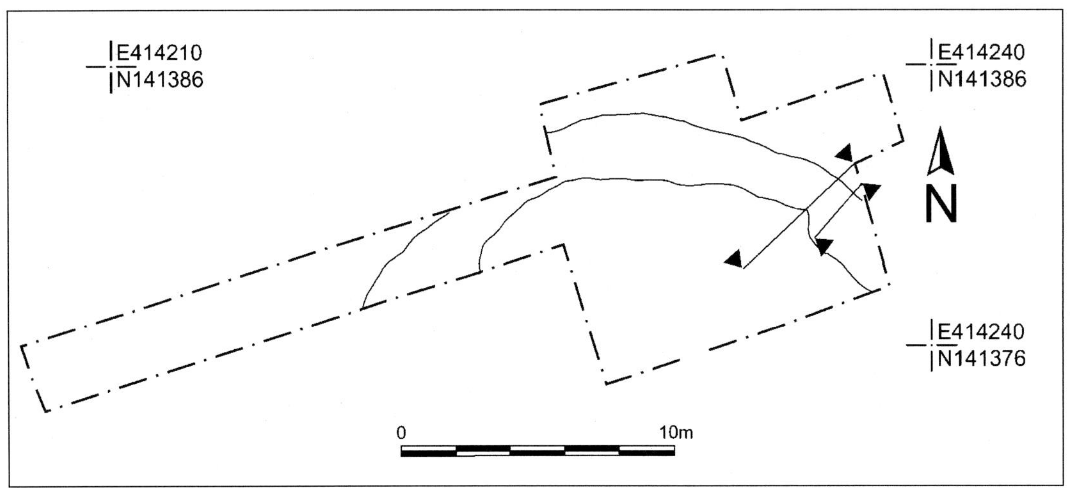

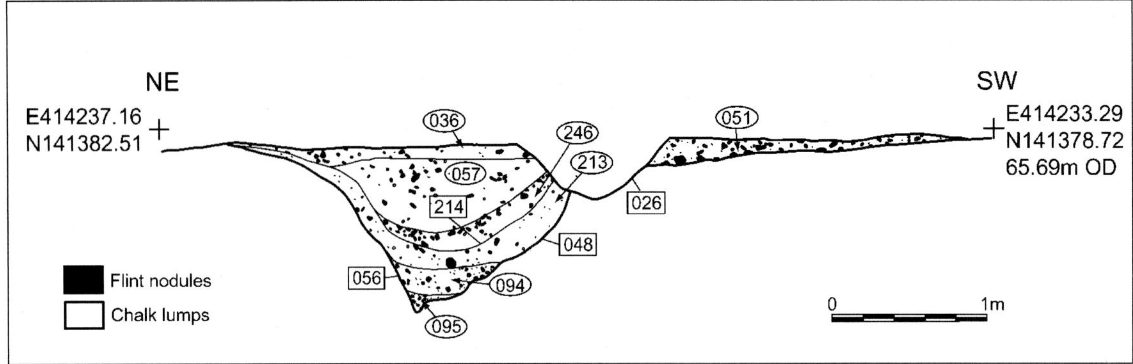

Figure 5.42. Southeast-facing section of the eastern baulk across the henge ditch, showing re-cut ditch (214). The section lines on the location plan mark the position of a baulk across the henge ditch

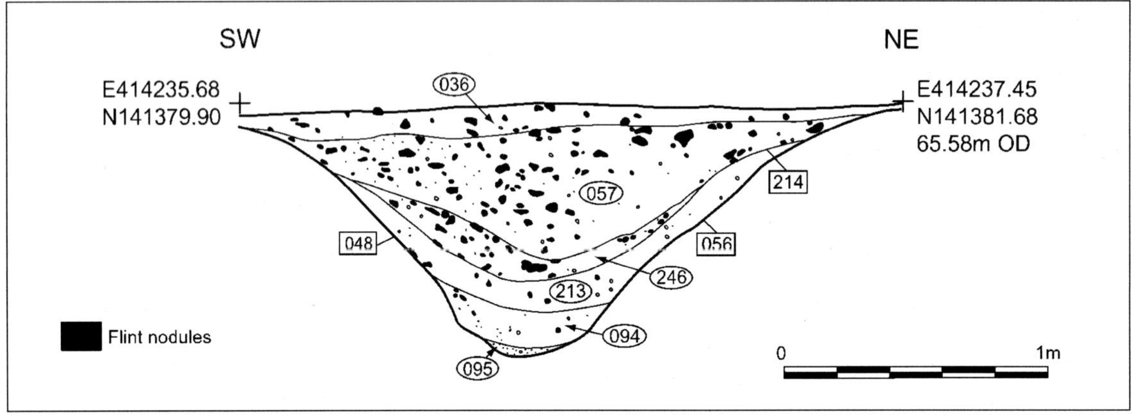

Figure 5.43. Northwest-facing section of the eastern baulk across the henge ditch, showing re-cut ditch (214). The section lines on the location plan in Figure 5.42 mark the position of a baulk across the henge ditch

Figure 5.44. The antler pick tip (SF 491) in the base of the henge ditch, just below the right-hand side of the photographic scale, viewed from the northwest

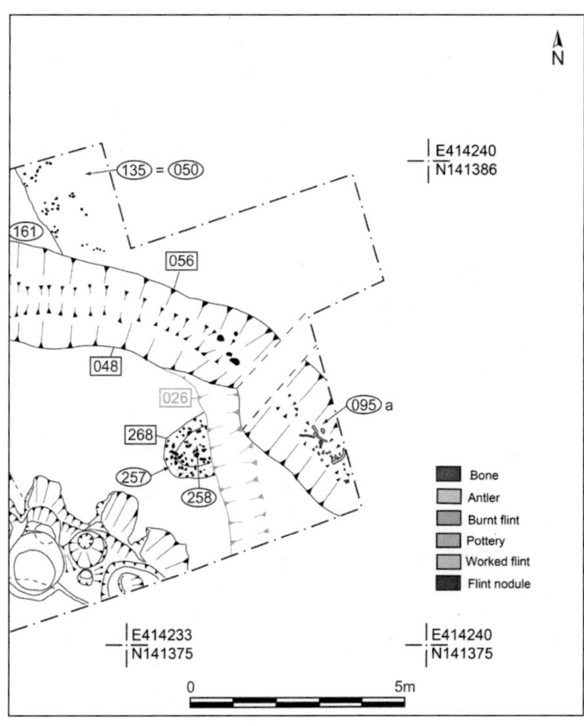

Figure 5.45. Plan of artefacts and deposits in the eastern part of the henge ditch

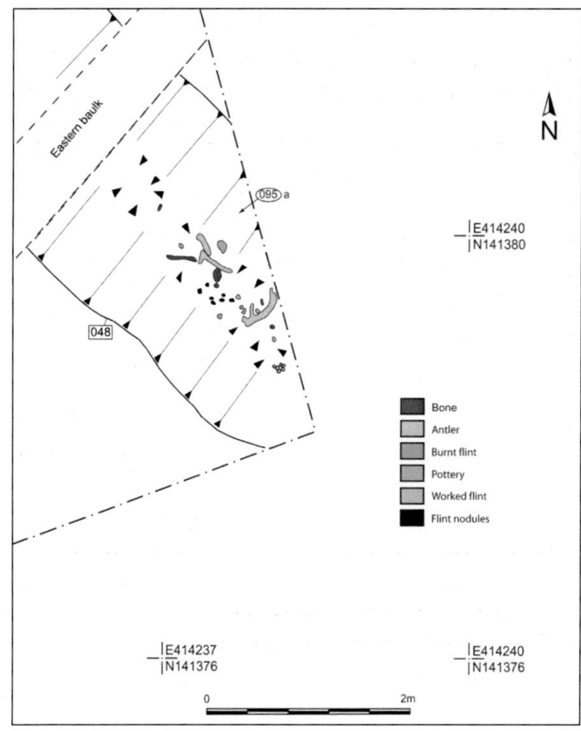

Figure 5.46. Close-up plan of the structured deposit of artefacts in the probable henge ditch terminal in the eastern part of the henge ditch

Figure 5.47. The deposit of artefacts in layer 095a in the probable henge ditch terminal, viewed from the south

Figure 5.48. The antler pick (SF 586) in layer 095a after removal of the surrounding special deposit, viewed from the west

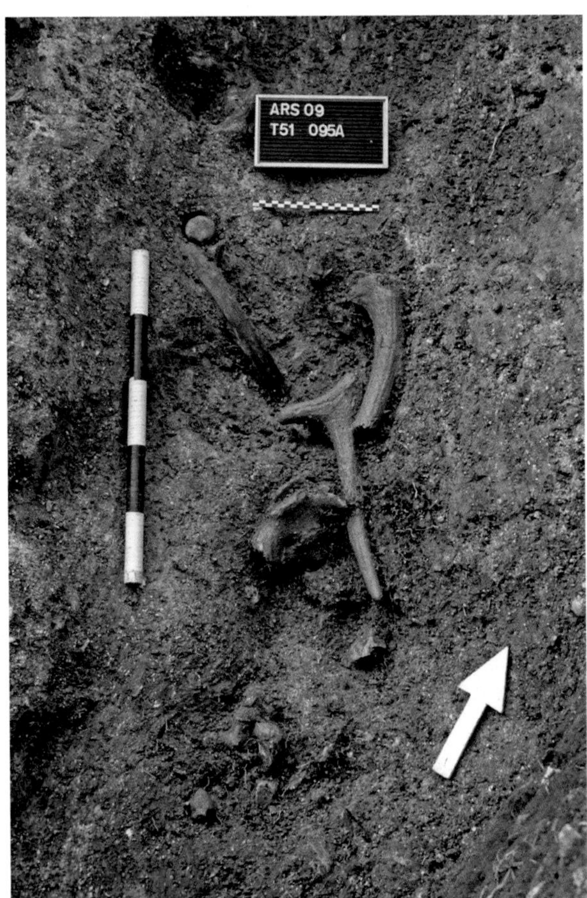

Figure 5.49. Two fragments of antler (SF 557 and SF 573) and other artefacts in the special deposit in layer 095, viewed from the southeast (see key to Figure 5.46)

chalk lumps (that have to have been imported to the site since the bedrock here is so soft) and a few worked flints. This deposit is probably equivalent to layers 095 and 095a in the northeast quadrant of the henge ditch. Thereafter in this area of the ditch, a series of layers were deposited (215, 191, 177 and 037i; Figure 5.35) which are described below as part of the Bronze Age silting of the ditch. Layers 191 and 177 derived, in part, from the erosion of the henge's outer bank.

The Stonehenge Avenue ditches

As described in the research background, above, the location and full extent of the Stonehenge Avenue at its eastern end – the north bank of the River Avon – were unknown prior to the SRP excavations in 2009. Excavations by the SRP elsewhere along the course of the Avenue ditches are reported in Chapter 8. As noted above, the geographically *eastern* ditch at this end of the Avenue is elsewhere the northern or western ditch. The geographically *western* ditch at West Amesbury is, conversely, elsewhere the southern or eastern ditch (see Figure 8.1).

The eastern Avenue ditch was identified within Trenches 50 and 61 (cuts 579 and 143), whilst the western ditch was found within Trench 50 (cut 593) (see Figure 5.13). The width of the Avenue here is 18.10m between internal edges of the ditches, 19.30m between ditch centre lines, and 20.60m between external sides of the ditches (Figures 5.50–5.51). This is slightly narrower than the widths between ditch centre lines of 22m at the Stonehenge end of the Avenue, 22.40m at the Avenue elbow (where the Avenue bends eastwards departing from its solstice axis before heading through Stonehenge Bottom and up onto King Barrow Ridge), and 25m where it is cut by the A303 (see Figures 8.2, 9.4; Cleal *et al.* 1995: 296–301).

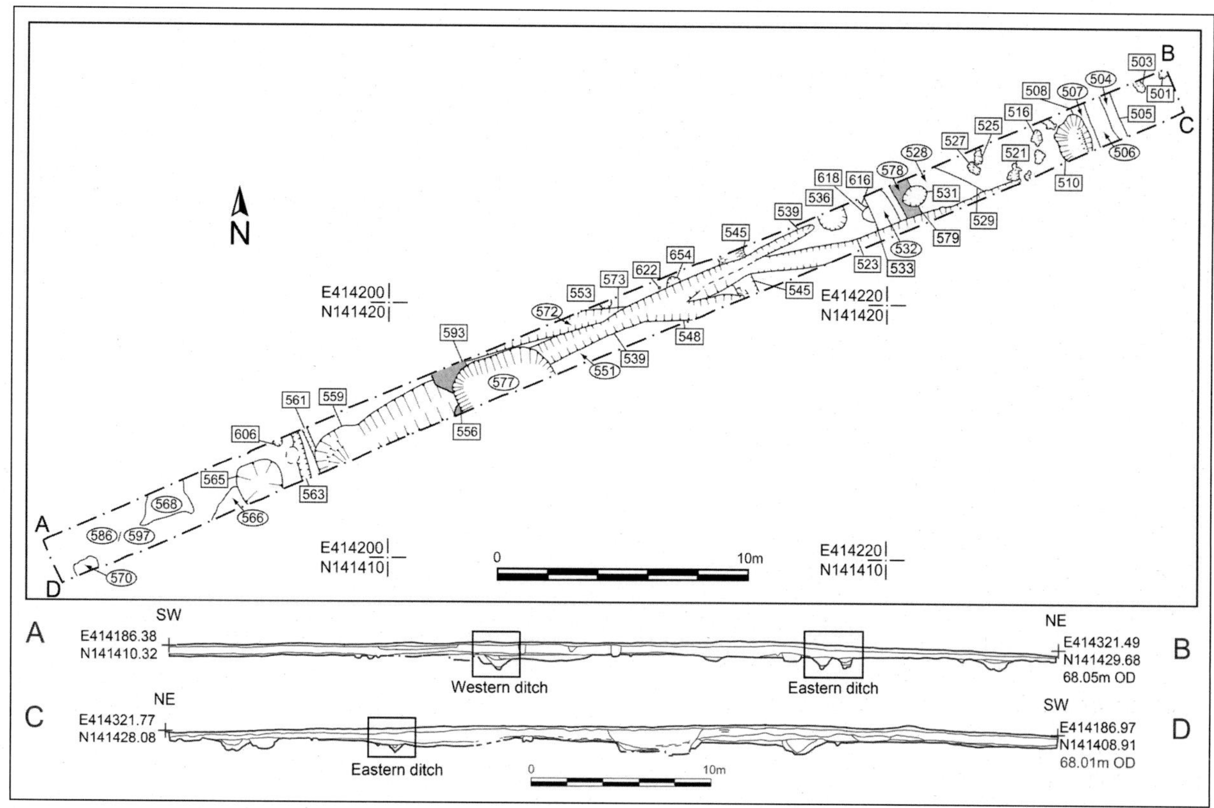

Figure 5.50. Plan of Trench 50 showing the two Stonehenge Avenue ditches (593 and 579, shown in grey), a prehistoric feature (533), basal chalk (551) and periglacial silt (528); the remaining features are all medieval or post-medieval. The two Avenue ditches are marked by boxes in the schematic long sections beneath the plan

Figure 5.51. Trench 50, viewed from the south, showing the two Stonehenge Avenue ditches (marked by horizontal ranging rods)

E414200
N141420
E414220
N141420
N
E414200
N141410
E414220
N141410
0
15m

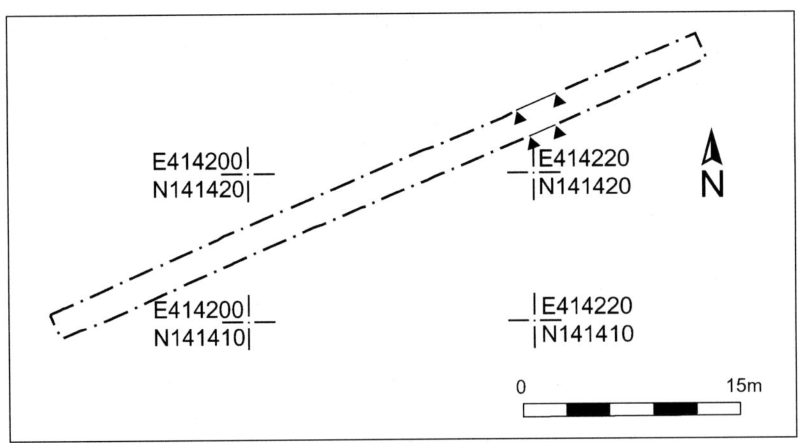

Figure 5.52. Sections of the eastern Avenue ditch and feature 533 in Trench 50

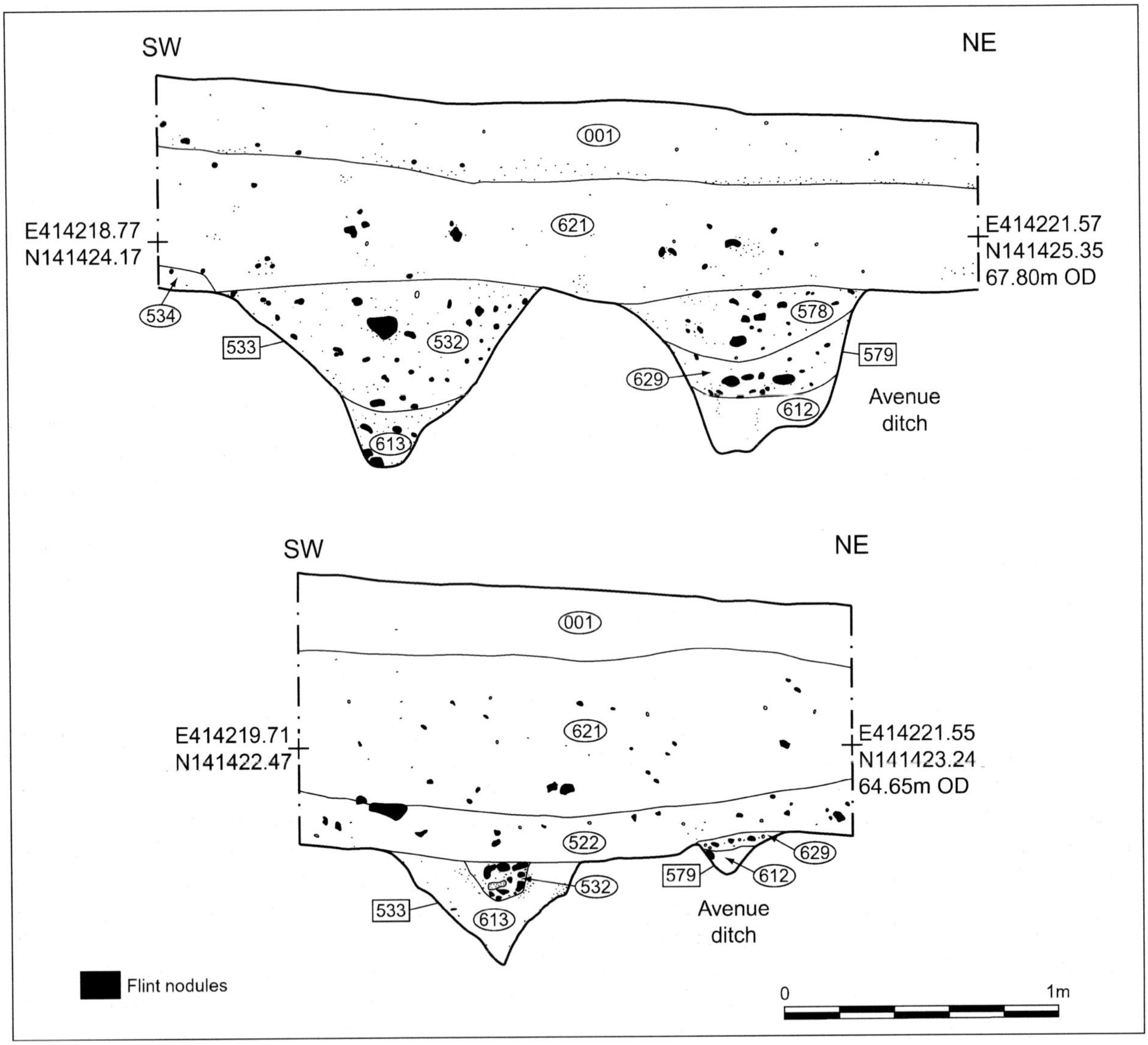

SW
NE
001
621
E414218.77
N141424.17
E414221.57
N141425.35
67.80m OD
534
533
532
613
578
579
629
612
Avenue ditch
SW
NE
001
621
E414219.71
N141422.47
E414221.55
N141423.24
64.65m OD
522
532
533
613
579
612
629
Avenue ditch
Flint nodules
0
1m

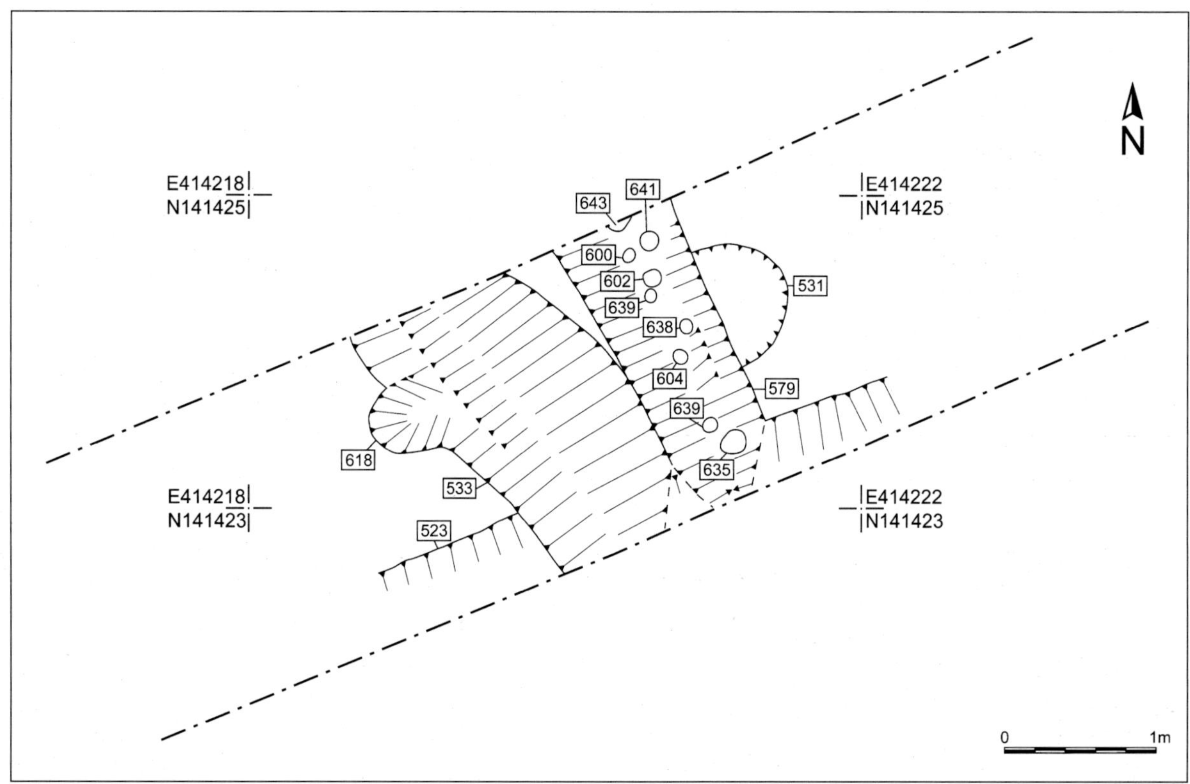

Figure 5.53. Postholes in the bottom of the eastern Avenue ditch in Trench 50

The eastern Avenue ditch in Trench 50 consisted of a north–south cut (579), 1m wide and 0.60m deep, sloping at 45° and steepening to 60° and near-vertical towards its base (Figure 5.52). Its primary fill was orange-brown silt (612), beneath brown silt (629), beneath a tertiary fill of brown clay (578). In the upper part of 578 there was an iron nail (SF 2006) lying vertically, point-down, within the fill. Layer 578 produced a large quantity of worked flints, including a flint core (SF 2003) and a ripple-flaked oblique arrowhead (SF 2007; see Figure 5.74) which lay flat with its point to the north.

A curvilinear ditch (533) ran close to the west side of the eastern Avenue ditch (579), intersecting with it at a point where the stratigraphic relationship between the two features was destroyed by a medieval ditch (523). The V-profiled curvilinear ditch, 1.20m wide and 0.65m deep, was filled with a primary deposit of dark grey-brown silt (613) and a secondary fill of mid grey-brown silt (532). Layer 532 contained worked flints including a chisel arrowhead, some bone fragments and, in its uppermost fills, small sherds of medieval pottery and a piece of metalworking slag. If this ditch is prehistoric (since the medieval sherds and slag are likely to be contaminants), it could have formed a circular feature such as an eaves-drip gully for a Bronze Age/Iron Age roundhouse or a Bronze Age ring ditch around a small round barrow. The presence of a chisel arrowhead raises the possibility – if the arrowhead was not residual – that this ditch was a Middle–Late Neolithic feature broadly contemporary with or even earlier than the Avenue.

The curvilinear ditch (533) cut through two small irregular features (616 filled with 615 and 618 filled with 617) on its west side but these are most likely irregular variations in the subsoil.

A series of nine small postholes or stakeholes (600 filled by 599, 602 filled by 601, 604 filled by 603, 635, 636, 638, 639, 641, 643) were cut into the bottom of ditch 579 (Figures 5.53–5.55). Postholes 600, 602 and 604 were each visible within the primary fill (612) as post-pipes. The postholes varied in diameter from 0.08m to 0.18m.

In Trench 61, the eastern Avenue ditch consisted of a similarly steep and narrow ditch (143), 1.50m wide and 0.33m deep (Figures 5.56–5.57). Although heavily truncated by a medieval ditch (125) on its west side, its upper edge sloped at 60° from the horizontal, steepening to near-vertical just above its base. It would originally have been about 1.80m wide. Its primary fill (140) was grey-brown silt, packed with broken flint, pockets of redeposited yellow chalk grit and a few charcoal flecks. A few worked flints were found in this layer, and a chisel arrowhead (SF 501; see Figure 5.74) was recovered from the upper fill (124) of the adjacent, inter-cutting medieval ditch (125).

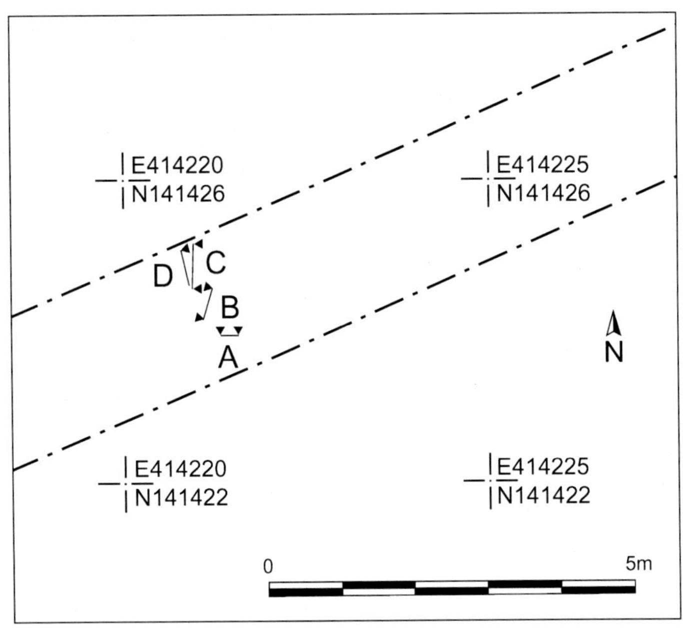

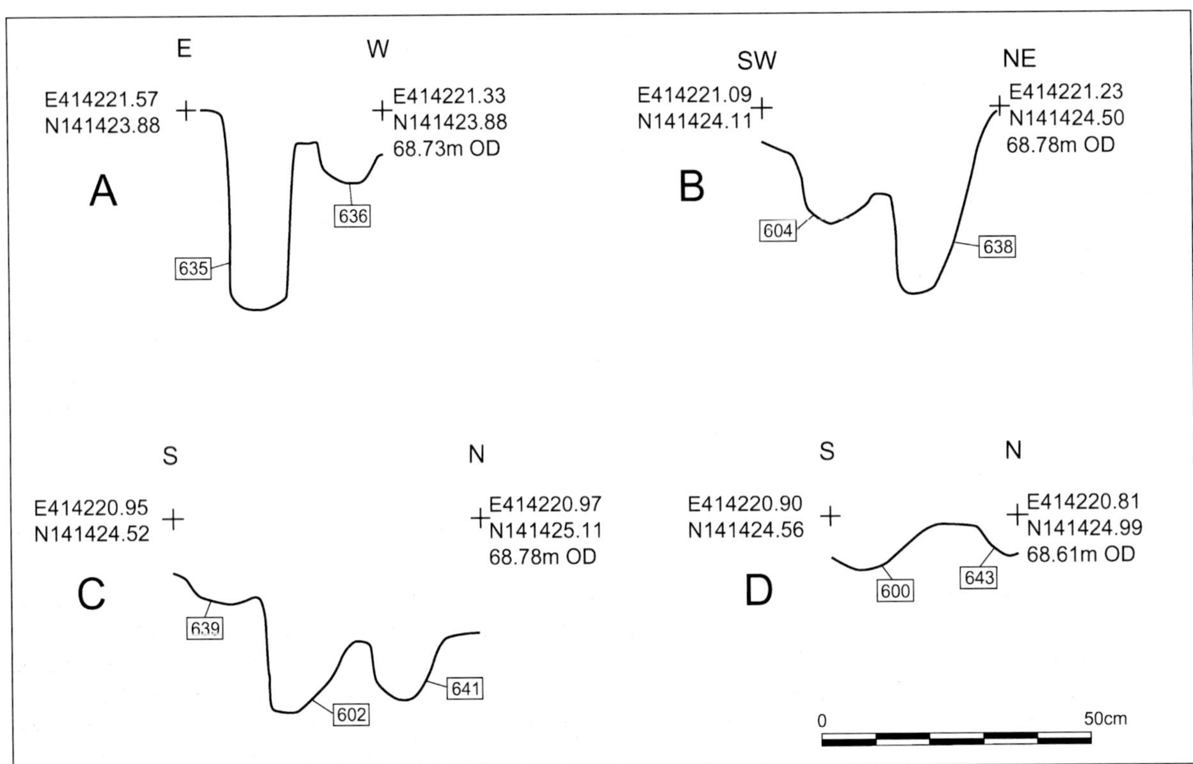

Figure 5.54. Profiles of the postholes in the bottom of the eastern Avenue ditch in Trench 50

Figure 5.55. The eastern Avenue ditch in Trench 50, viewed from the south and showing its postholes

The very bottom of the secondary fill of the eastern Avenue ditch in Trench 61 survived as a thin layer of grey-yellow-brown silt (220) which was recognised in section only after excavation of upper fill 124 of the medieval ditch (Figure 5.56). Unlike its continuation (579 in Trench 50), this southern part of the eastern Avenue ditch had no stakeholes cut into its base; nonetheless, its steep profile and the packed flints in its primary fill (140) support its interpretation as a ditch that contained a line of small posts or stakes.

The western Avenue ditch (593) was identified within Trench 50, about 18m west of the eastern Avenue ditch (579), also running north–south (Figure 5.50). Most of its extent within the trench had been destroyed by a post-medieval pit (556) but 0.60m of its length survived unscathed to the north of this pit (Figure 5.58). Its V-shaped profile sloped at 45° from the horizontal, steepening to 60° nearer its base (Figure 5.59). Although surviving in truncated form with a depth of *c.* 0.20m and a width of *c.* 0.50m within most of the trench, it was better preserved on the trench's north side where it reached 1.40m wide and 0.75m deep. Its primary fill was brown clay (620). Above this lay red-brown clay (619) and, above that, a tertiary fill of red-brown-grey clay (594) containing a sherd of Late Neolithic/Early Bronze Age pottery. A single posthole, about 0.15m in diameter, was cut into the base of the ditch and filled with primary fill (620; Figure 5.60). Finds from the ditch fills consisted only of a few worked flints.

The unexpected evidence for palisades in the Avenue ditches raises questions about the likely length of such post rows, which have not been recorded anywhere else along the Avenue. Did they extend from this end of the Avenue only as far as, or nearly to, the area excavated by George Smith in 1973? Might they have been built in alternate lengths of palisade and open ditch? Or might a palisade line have been partially or wholly re-cut by one or more re-diggings of the Avenue ditches? Certainly, several sections of the eastern ditch excavated in 1973 (see Cleal *et al.* 1995: fig. 172) bear a close resemblance to the bottoms of the 2009 West Amesbury Avenue ditches with their near-vertical profiles.

The riverside terminal of the Stonehenge Avenue remains as yet unlocated but, given its location in Trench 50 and Trench 61, and its absence from Trench 51 (see Figure 5.13), it has to have ended within the five metres or so between Trench 61 and Trench 51. The Avenue never reached as far as the West Amesbury henge ditch. Perhaps

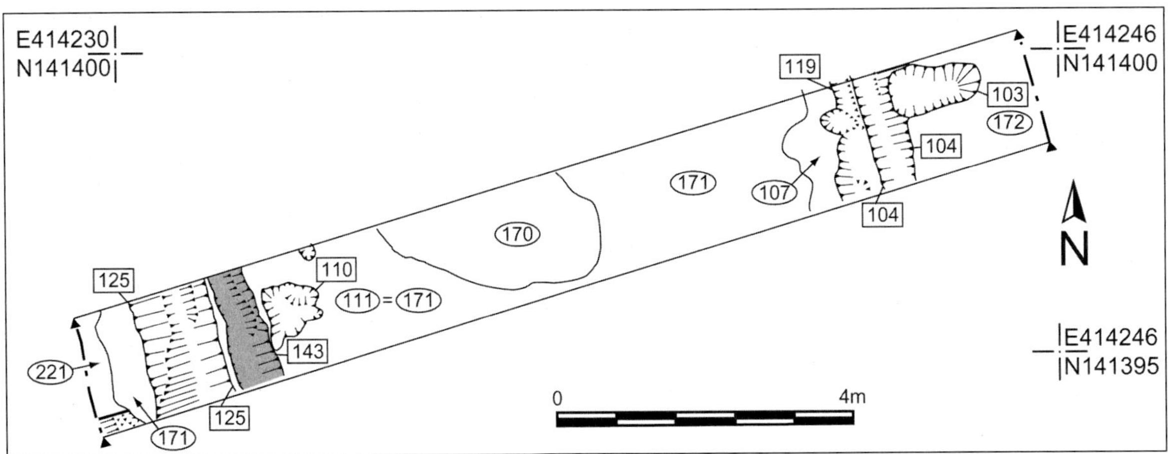

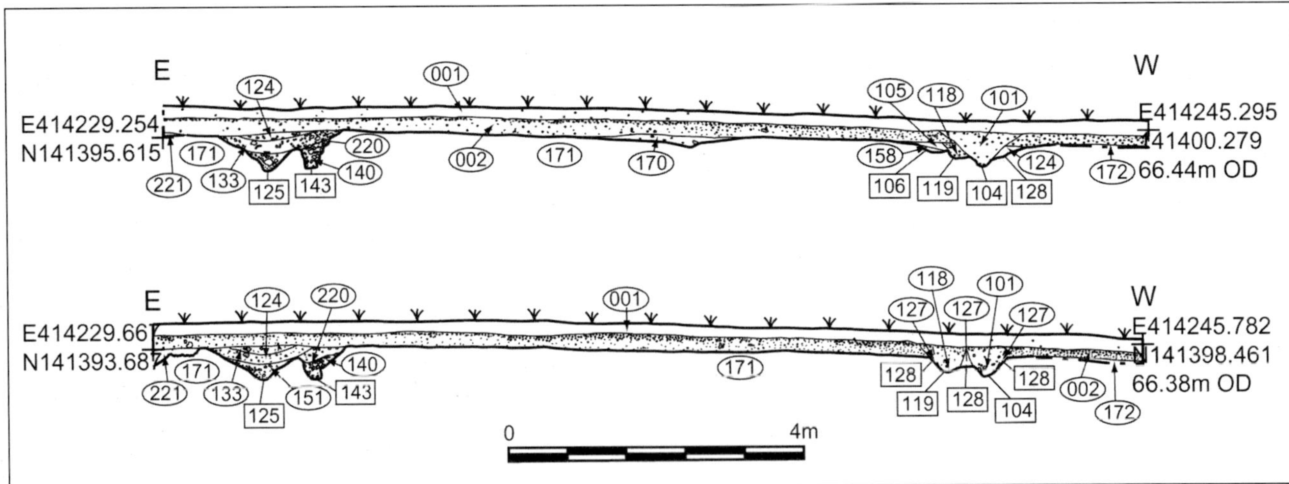

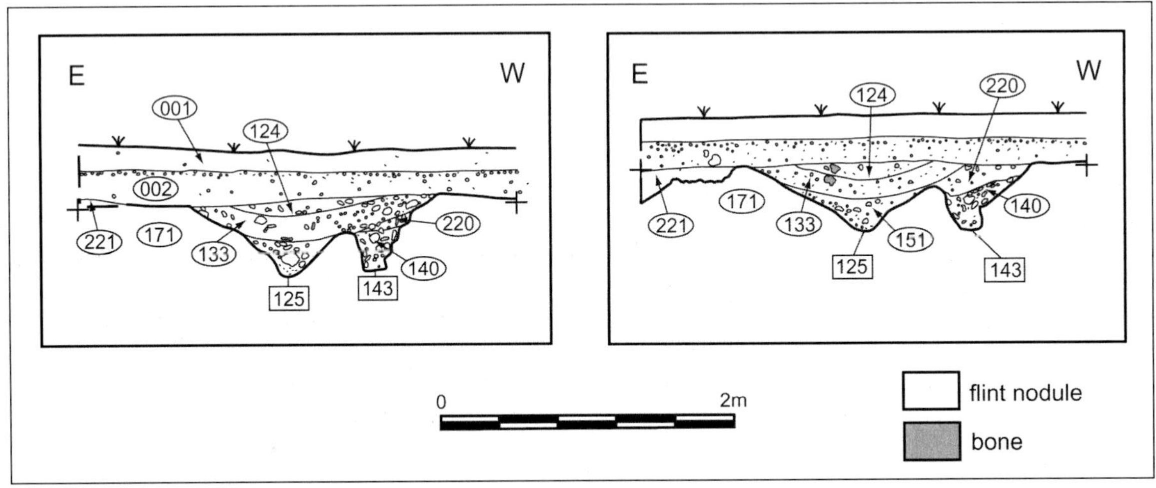

Figure 5.56. Plan and sections through the eastern Avenue ditch (shaded grey) and medieval and later features in Trench 61. The two lower sections are close-up views of the Avenue ditch

Figure 5.57. The eastern Avenue ditch in Trench 61, viewed from the west

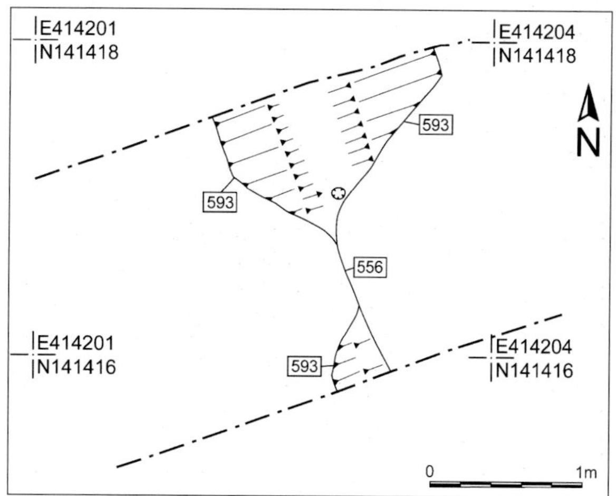

Figure 5.58. Plan of the western Avenue ditch in Trench 50

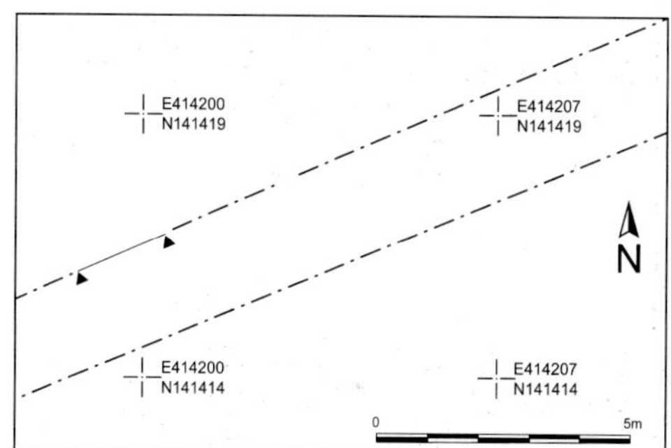

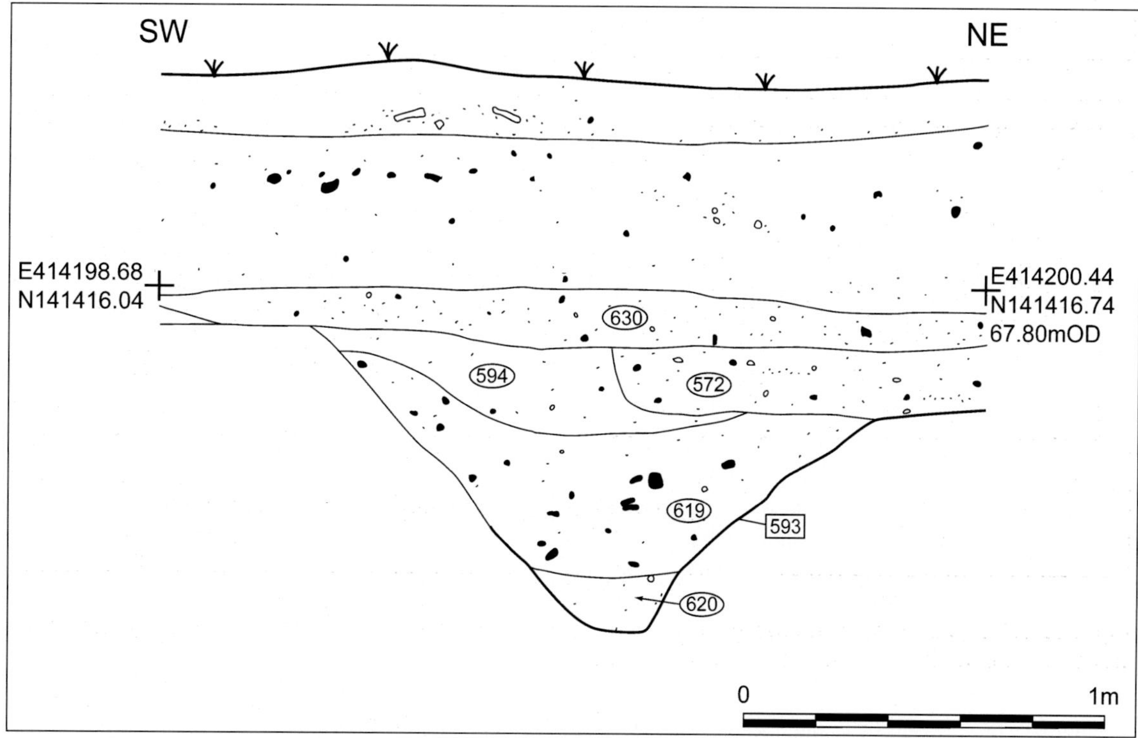

Figure 5.59. Section across the western Avenue ditch in Trench 50

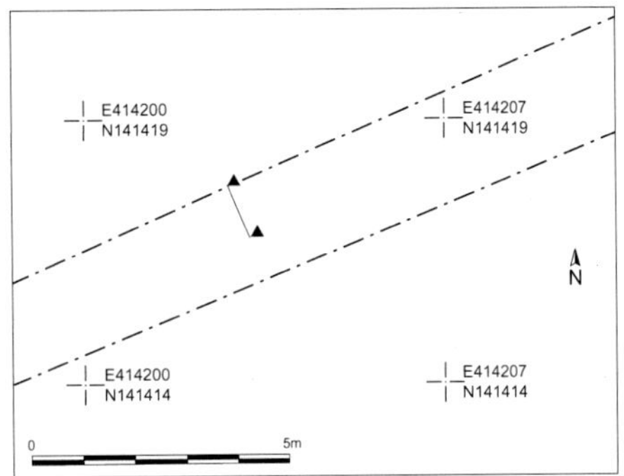

Figure 5.60. Section along the axis of the western Avenue ditch in Trench 50

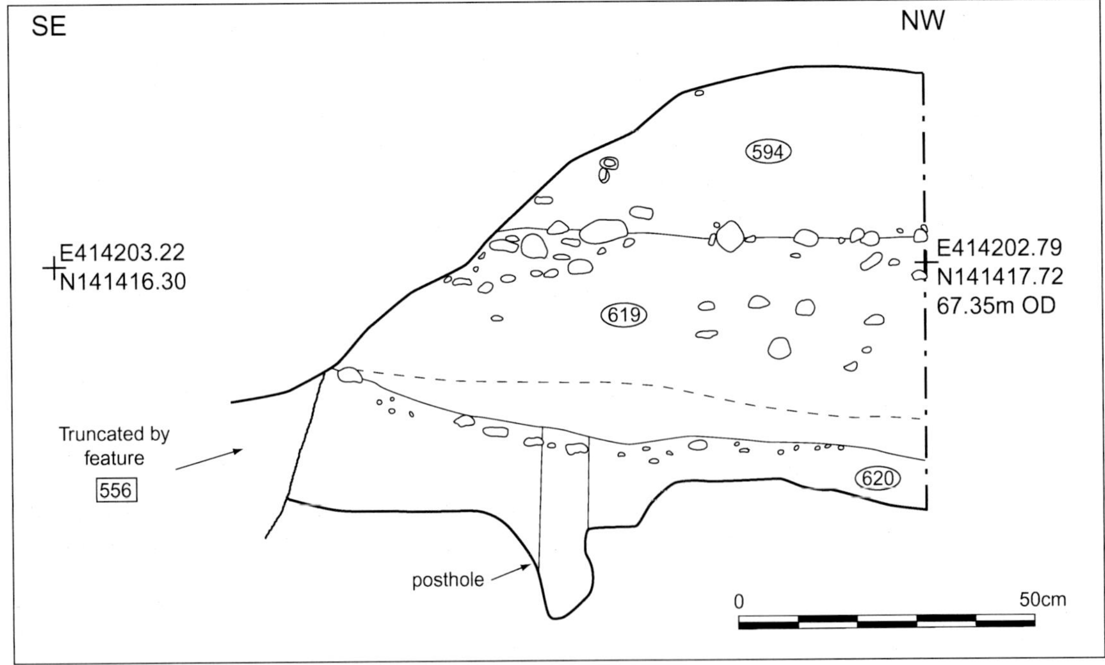

it terminated at the outer bank of the henge, in a fashion similar to that seen at its other end, where the Avenue terminates at the counterscarp bank of Stonehenge (Cleal *et al.* 1995: fig. 156; see Figure 4.8).

In summary, the Avenue is 20.60m wide here beside the River Avon, enclosing a width of 18.10m between the parallel ditches. Although heavily truncated by medieval pits and ditches, parts of it survive to a depth of 0.75m with evidence that the ditches had been up to 1.50m wide, equivalent to their widths elsewhere between the river and Stonehenge. It terminated within 30m of the (eroded-away) southern edge of West Amesbury henge which itself is likely during the Late Neolithic–Chalcolithic to have lain 50m or more north of the northern bank of the River Avon (see Figure 9.4).

The Bronze Age sequence in the henge ditch

The entirety of the prehistoric and pre-medieval sequence at West Amesbury is presented here as a coherent report. The features and deposits described in this section date to after the construction of the Bluestonehenge stone circle and the henge bank and ditch. These deposits are firmly dated to the Bronze Age on the basis of their material culture which is reported in full in the Bronze Age chapter of Volume 4 (*After Stonehenge*), but to provide clarity to the reader, the later stratigraphy of the henge ditch and details of other Bronze Age features and deposits are reported here, along with residual Mesolithic, Neolithic and Beaker-period artefacts in Bronze Age and later contexts.

Sequences of deposition within the henge ditch were very different in its eastern and western circuits. In the western circuit, the ditch was left undisturbed after it silted up, whilst in the eastern circuit it was re-cut after silting up.

The western circuit

In 2008, the northwestern circuit of the henge ditch was excavated as a series of artificially imposed segments (a–e), with (a) in the north and (e) in the west (Figure 5.61). In 2009, the baulks between ditch segments were removed (except for two baulks in the north, one of them at the

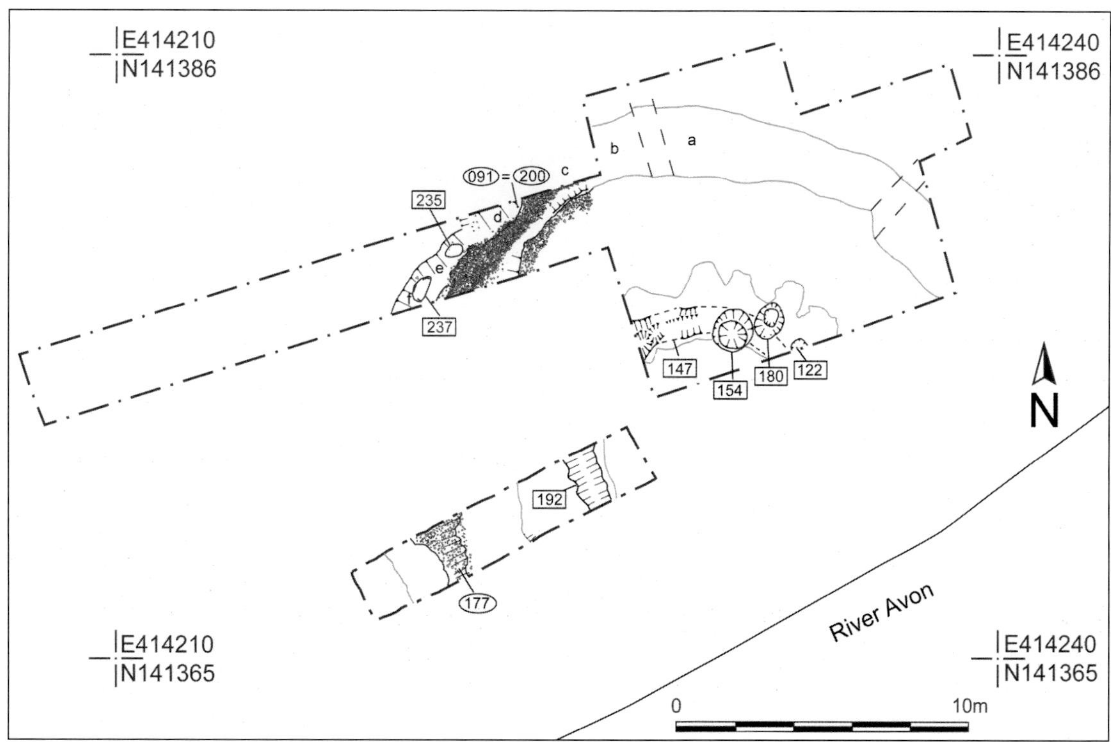

Figure 5.61. Plan of Bronze Age features in the henge ditch and henge interior

right-angle where the long narrow western arm of Trench 51 meets the open area) and this northwestern area of the ditch was excavated in plan to reveal a sequence of flint-cobbled surfaces. The excavation reached the lower of these surfaces (091) but did not continue to the ditch's bottom in this area.

The earliest features encountered in the northwestern circuit were a pair of small pits or postholes (235 filled by 236, and 237 filled by 238), 0.64m east–west by 0.40m north–south and 0.88m east–west by 0.46m north–south, cut into the outer wall of the ditch on its northwest side. Neither was excavated in its entirety since both pre-date the lowest cobble surface (091), where excavation ceased, although they appear not to pre-date the henge ditch. Their fills of grey-brown clay could conceivably have held posts since they darkened towards the centres but no firm conclusion on this can be drawn.

The lowest layer reached in this circuit of the ditch was a mass of flint cobbles (091=200) forming a cobbled surface sloping southwestwards along the ditch bottom (Figures 5.39, 5.41, 5.62). This surface extended for at least 10.60m from where it narrowed and fizzled out in the northeast (under layer 073; see below) to the western limit of the ditch as exposed within Trench 51. This cobble layer was mostly 0.60–0.80m wide, except at its west end where, as the ditch itself widened, so the cobbled surface widened to 1.10m. An antler tine (SF 580) and the end of a cattle long bone hollowed-out for use as a handle (SF 581) possibly constitute a placed deposit in layer 091, on the east side of the north baulk (Figure 5.63).

The cobble layer (091=200) was covered at its east end by a layer of mid-yellow/brown chalky silt (073), 0.20m thick, which had slumped into the ditch from its north side. This re-deposited chalk (073) presumably derived from the henge's outer bank which must have been constructed prior to the initial filling of the ditch. It formed a high point or saddle, 1.10m east–west and 1.50m north–south, 0.50m west of the end of a localised re-cut (214) of this ditch's northeast sector (this re-cut ditch post-dates layer 073's deposition; Figure 5.42). Here, layer 073 lay against the northern edge of the henge ditch, indicating that this bank material was tipped or pushed into the ditch, possibly to provide a narrow and informal access point into the henge from the north.

Layer 073 was covered by a grey-brown clay silt (071; neither 071 nor 073 are shown on the ditch sections) with flint gravel and nodules that had periodically eroded in from beyond the ditch's northern edge (ditch segment a). Layer 071 was contemporary with a light to mid-brown clay silt (174) in the northern part of the ditch. Layers 071, 174 and further layers of clay silt (069=072=198) were covered by a 0.10m-thick layer of mid-grey/brown clay silt with flints (058=059=064) tipped in from the northern edge of the henge ditch. Layer 064, on the north part of the

Figure 5.62. The cobbled surface 091=200 within the upper fill of the northwest quadrant of the henge ditch, viewed from the southwest

Figure 5.63. A deposit of an antler tine (SF 580) and a bone handle (SF 581) in the north sector of the henge ditch, viewed from the east

henge ditch, equates with layer 059 in ditch segment (a) and 058 in segment (d), and all were covered by layer 037. Within layer 064's flint spread lay the butt of a Neolithic ground-stone axe (SF 502; see Figure 5.78).

Layer 059 (ditch segment a) was covered by layer 037a, a light brown-orange clay (Figure 5.41). Layers 071 and 174 are probably secondary fills whilst 059 and 037 can be considered tertiary fills of the ditch; they are assigned a broadly Bronze Age date.

In the northwestern and western parts of the ditch, along its outer western edge, the cobble layer (091=200) was covered by a deposit of mid-brown/grey clay silt with flints (089=096). Within the middle of the ditch, layer 091=200 was covered by red-brown silt (199).

Layers 089 and 199 were both covered by a second layer of cobbles (074=078=079). This cobble layer was 4.80m long and up to 0.80m wide. It was more restricted in size within the ditch than the earlier cobble layer 091=200, fading out at its east end in the northern sector of the ditch, and fading out at its west end *c.* 1.00m from the southern baulk. Like layer 091=200, this cobble layer was laid in such an even fashion that it had the appearance of a well-worn pathway or walked-upon surface.

Cobble surface 074=078=079 lay not only within the fill of the ditch but also continued up the ditch's outer edge; it stopped in an irregular line against the base of the inner edge of the ditch. Here there was a small gap between surface 074=078=079 and the more irregular cobbles covering the inner edge of the henge ditch that had slumped into the ditch from the interior (053; see above). There was no sign of any fence line, stakeholes, postholes or beam slots that could account for this gap between the two cobble surfaces. On the inner edge of the gap, the cobbles (053) lining this section of the sloping inner face of the henge ditch were compacted and worn in a comparable way to the adjacent component of surface 074=079=078, possibly indicating that people were traversing the ditch and entering the interior of the henge at this point.

Above the second cobbled surface within the ditch (074=078=079), a layer of mid-brown clay silt with flint gravel and nodules (080), *c.* 0.35m wide and 0.13m deep, had slumped in from the henge interior within excavation segment (c) as a localised deposit of the weathered flint capping (051) covering the interior of the henge (Figure 5.40). At the western end of the ditch, the cobbled surface (074=078=079) was covered on its southeast side by a mid-brown clay silt (077) which similarly appears to have eroded into the ditch from the henge platform.

Layers 080 and 074=078=079 were covered by a surface of small flint cobbles set in a mid-brown clay silt (069=072=198), 0.10m–0.15m thick. This layer probably equates with a mid to dark orange-brown clay silt (098) in segment (e) and with layer 071 in ditch segment (a), described above.

The uppermost fill in the western part of the henge ditch was also layer 037, a light brown-orange clay. It was divided during excavation into segments (a) – (e) within Trench 51 and segment (i) in Trench 60. Although this layer contained a mix of Neolithic, Beaker and Late Bronze Age/Iron Age sherds, it may have been deposited as late as the medieval period since it also contained a dozen small sherds of medieval pottery, although these are small enough to have been worked in by bioturbation as contaminants into an earlier deposit.

Ditch segment (i)

Within Trench 60, this segment of the ditch had been largely destroyed by a medieval pit (150) but enough remained for the sequence of fills to be established (Figures 5.34–5.35). Above the primary fill (219; see *The henge*, above), a thin layer of dark grey-brown clay (215), containing worked and burnt flints, had slumped from the inside of the henge. This was either caused by bioturbation or was deliberately dumped; it is potentially equivalent to layer 053, a layer on the north side of the henge. The remaining ditch fills were deposited from the west, indicating that these derived from the henge's external bank. The secondary fill consisted of dark grey-brown clay (191) with shattered flint gravel, charcoal flecks, worked flint and Beaker (SF 530 and SF 532) and Bronze Age (SF 531) sherds. Above it, layer 177, an orange-brown clay capped with a layer of flint cobbles, formed the lower part of the tertiary fill; the upper ditch component was layer 037i.

The surviving fills in this western area of the henge ditch excavated within Trench 60 suggest that the sequence within segment (i) is very similar to that in the northwest quadrant of the henge ditch, where a series of fills, introduced mostly from the exterior (no doubt from the eroding henge bank), were capped with surfaces of flint cobbles. This suggests that the entire western half of the henge ditch was treated very differently to the northeastern quadrant (and possibly to the eastern half as a whole), where the ditch was re-cut (ditch 214), perhaps to enhance the presumed east entrance into the former henge.

The eastern circuit

Above fills 213 and 213a (see *The henge*, above; Figure 5.42), the henge ditch was cut by a new ditch (214), the edges of which did not extend quite to those of the original ditch (048=056). Its primary fill was a thin layer (0.12m thick) of brown silty clay (246 and 246a), containing knapping debris, a cattle bone (SF 547) and two prehistoric sherds, one of them a plain carinated sherd (P5; see Cleal, below). Tip lines indicate that this fill entered the ditch from inside the henge.

Layers 246 and 246a were covered by a secondary fill of orange-brown silty clay (057) with flint gravel (0.45m deep) containing significant numbers of artefacts (Figure 5.40). These consist of worked flints, burnt sarsen fragments, animal bone (SF 539), three comb-decorated Beaker sherds (SF 535) and pieces of charcoal (SFs 537–538). The knapping debris was localised into distinct clusters (E414237.36 N141379.62 to E414237.76 N141379.16 at 65.12m–65.15m OD), suggestive of individual acts of flint-knapping *in situ* within or adjacent to the open ditch. The deposit (057) closely resembles the buried soil (050) to its northeast (see Figure 5.40) and probably derives largely from this or similar material, incorporating cultural material from activities around and within the henge ditch. Unlike the western circuit of the henge ditch, there were no observable tip lines to indicate whether the ditch had filled from inside or outside the henge. This suggests rapid accumulation and possible deliberate backfilling, very different formation processes to those in the western circuit.

On top of layer 057 lay a thin and localised layer of flint gravel and nodules in a grey-brown clay silt (190), 0.55m north–south × 1.40m east–west. This was tipped in from the northeast side of the ditch, and may have resulted from a single act of slumping from a cobbled or stony outer edge of the ditch.

Layers 057 and 190 were covered by layer 036, the tertiary fill of the ditch (Figures 5.40, 5.42), a grey-brown clay silt which filled the entire length of this segment, also being recorded as 036a and 036b. Layer 036 contained small quantities of animal bone, a few tiny, undiagnostic crumbs of prehistoric pottery, and large quantities of struck flint, although flint tools were entirely absent. Within the base of layer 036b there was an *in situ* knapping cluster (087), with several hundred struck flakes lying within an area *c.* 1.00m in diameter.

A prehistoric feature northwest of the henge?

At the extreme west end of Trench 51, a deposit of red-orange-brown clay silt (067) filled a steep-sided, curving feature at least 1.95m long (066), to a depth of 0.34m where its base began to flatten out. The fill (067) contained charcoal flecks and worked flint. The diameter of this feature may have been at least 4.00m across, although it could have formed part of a larger ring ditch. There is the possibility that the faint outlines of such a ring ditch, up to 15m across, are interpretable from the earth resistance plot (R3 in Figure 5.4).

Bronze Age re-use of the henge interior

The circle of emptied stoneholes was used as the setting for a series of Bronze Age features (Figure 5.61). Although the primary fills (134=146=123=202) of the hollow (129) over the tops of the stoneholes had silted to at least the top of the decayed chalk bedrock, the inner edges of the holes were re-used as the inside edge of another ditch, a small penannular feature (ditch 147=192; Figures 5.26, 5.34–5.35). At its northeast, it was cut by a large and deep posthole (154, cutting Stoneholes B and C; Figures 5.14, 5.24) which, together with postholes 180 and 122, may have formed part of a setting of posts originally standing perhaps 4m–6m high.

Penannular ditch 147=192

Ditch 147 ran for 2.00m in Trench 60 and at least 2.60m within Trench 51, although layer 120 (Figures 5.9, 5.21) is probably its continuation into the edge of the excavation trench above Stonehole A. This circular/penannular feature was thus at least 7.60m long, potentially double that if it originally had a southern half symmetrical with this northern circuit, enclosing an area about 8.20m in diameter. Its profile varied from an open U-shape to a rounded V-shape, 0.30m deep and up to 0.90m wide. It had steep sides, about 45° from horizontal, with a steeper angle of slope on its inside edge.

Ditch 147's primary fill was red-brown clay (156), 0.10m thick with few flint inclusions and a piece of probable Middle Bronze Age pottery. Concentrated on the south side of the ditch, it must have entered from inside the enclosure, suggestive of an internal bank to ditch 147. Layer 156 was covered by mid grey-brown silty clay (148; Figure 5.32), 0.25m thick, with moderate amounts (25%) of rounded and angular flint and very occasional pieces of sarsen quartzite. The jumbled distribution of flints suggests that this layer (148) was deliberately backfilled rather than being the result of gradual silting. Slightly red-brown silty loam (163), 0.15m thick, formed a tertiary layer within the top of the ditch. Its junction with layer 148 was visible in section as a line of stones (Figure 5.32).

In Trench 60, the penannular ditch (147) continued as cut 192 (Figures 5.34–5.35). Its inner, eastern edge, curved but not scalloped, followed the inner edge of the filled-in stoneholes. The penannular ditch in this trench was filled with grey-brown clay (144) containing four sherds of prehistoric pottery and small fragments of fired clay (47g).

Since this ditch (147) cut into the uppermost fills of probably all the stoneholes and the fills of the silted-up hollow (129) above them, it is clear that the re-digging of the ditch along this line indicates that this circular hollow was probably still visible at that point in time.

Posthole 122

Posthole 122 cut into Stonehole A; it was bisected by the trench edge and about half the posthole lay beneath the southern baulk of Trench 51 (Figure 5.17). It was 1.00m in diameter and 0.65m deep, containing a packing deposit (186) and a post-pipe (187 filled by 121). Layer 186 was a mixed dark grey-brown silty clay loam, 0.65m

Figure 5.64. Post-pipe 169 in posthole 180, viewed from the northeast

thick, with frequent (40%) angular flint, which packed three sides (east, north and west) of the posthole. Layer 121 was dark grey-brown loam with some flint (20%) and charcoal fragments, filling the pipe (187) which was up to 0.40m in diameter and 0.65m deep. Only the very northern edge of the post-pipe protruded beyond the baulk. The western part of posthole 122 was covered by a thin layer of grey-brown loam with flints (117), interpreted as a patch of topsoil settled in the slight hollow left by the posthole.

Posthole 180

Posthole 180 was cut into the upper fill of Stonehole B (Figure 5.64). It was 0.60m in diameter and 1.00m deep, with near-vertical sides. It was filled with pale brown silty clay (168) packed with 60% flints and contained a sherd of probable later prehistoric pottery. Layer 168 formed a packing layer around a post-pipe (169) 0.50m in diameter and 1.00m deep. The post-pipe (169) was filled with grey-brown silty clay loam (167). There were no other finds from any of the posthole's fills.

Posthole 154

Posthole 154, cut into Stonehole C, was the largest of the postholes within the henge (Figures 5.24, 5.65). It cut ditch 147 and was 1.40m north–south by 1.50m east–west and 1.40m deep. It had held a flat-bottomed post within a post-pipe (185) 0.35m in diameter at its base and widening to 0.50m higher up. Around the post, a series of packing layers filled the posthole (Figure 5.24). The lowest of these was grey-brown clay (173), 0.30m thick. Above this was a 0.40m–0.70m thick deposit of grey-brown silty clay (166). On the east side only of the posthole, at a depth of about 0.40m–0.60m, layer 166 was covered by a localised spread of yellow-brown soft clay (160) containing up to 50% flint nodules, a few lumps of imported chalk and a chisel arrowhead (see Figure 5.74). Finally, layers 160 and 166 were covered by a 0.35m–0.60m thick deposit of yellow-brown silty clay (153) with occasional, large flint nodules.

Layers 173, 166, 160 and 153 were packed around post-pipe 185 which was filled with dark grey-brown loam (126), 1.40m deep and up to 0.50m in diameter. It was largely flint-free and contained large lumps of charcoal in the lower 0.50m. At 0.25m below the surface, post-pipe 185 widened to form a 0.80m-diameter weathering cone. A sherd and a fragment of pottery not identifiable to a ceramic tradition were recovered from the top 0.10m of this feature. Otherwise, there were no artefacts to indicate a date for this posthole. It can, however, be dated by its cutting of ditch 147 to the Bronze Age or later.

Tree-root and animal burrow disturbances

Features resulting from tree-root and animal burrow disturbances were present within all four trenches at West Amesbury.

In Trench 50, there were 12 features whose irregularity of form identified them as root or animal disturbances; some are shown in plan in Figure 5.50. These were 501 (filled with 500), 503 (filled with 502), 512 (filled with 511), 514 (filled with 513), 516 (filled with 515), 519 (filled with 518), 521 (filled with 520), 525 (filled with 524), 527 (filled with 526), 583 (filled with 584), 595 (filled with 596), and 624 (filled with 625).

In Trench 51, five areas of tree-root disturbance were detected in the western end of the trench, all of

Figure 5.65. Posthole 154 in half section cutting Stonehole C (to the right), viewed from the east

them beneath the topsoil layers (001 and 002) but only one of them beneath earlier archaeological layers. This was layer 062, beneath a mixed subsoil layer (063), located below a layer of flint nodules (004) which pre-dated a sequence of medieval and later ditches. The other tree-root disturbances, in the western end of the trench, were numbered 060/061, 028, 044/045 and 054/055. In the eastern part of the trench, a tree hole (268; Figures 5.39, 5.45), 1.40m across, inside the henge and cut by a medieval ditch (026), was filled by an outer and lower layer of red-brown-grey silt (257), beneath a layer of orange-brown silt (258). Layer 258 was excavated in half-section, yielding a handful of undiagnostic worked flints.

In Trench 60, there were many tree roots (from the adjacent hedge line of trees growing to the south of the trench), as well as patches of fills and subsoil disturbed by former tree roots. Although these disturbances were noted, they were not assigned context numbers in this trench.

In Trench 61, there was a tree hole (110 filled by 109) towards the west end of the trench, just east of the Avenue ditch (Figure 5.56).

Medieval and later features

As the earthwork survey demonstrated (Figure 5.2), this part of the riverside was extensively used in the medieval and post-medieval periods. In Trenches 51 and 60, the henge was cut by ditches 014, 026 and 032=209 running north–south and spaced approximately 7m apart (Figure 5.39). Similar ditches 104 and 125 were identified in Trench 61 (in which 125 is the continuation of 026; Figure 5.56). In Trench 50, apart from the Avenue ditches and curvilinear ditch (533), all of the other ditches and features are medieval or later (Figure 5.50).

Among the medieval and later artefacts were disarticulated human remains of early medieval date, a tibia fragment from ditch 014 in Trench 51 and a femur fragment from pit 556 in Trench 50. A shallow pit (042), cut into the top of the henge ditch in Trench 51 (Figure 5.40), contained over 500 worked flints redeposited in a layer (043) beneath a deposit (065) of charcoal and carbonised cereal grains. Another shallow pit (029=030 filled by 003) cut the inner edge of the henge ditch but was earlier than ditch 032=209. All of these contexts and their finds are reported in Volume 4.

5.4. Radiocarbon dating of Bluestonehenge and West Amesbury henge

P.D. Marshall, C. Bronk Ramsey and G. Cook

Introduction

Twenty-one samples from Bluestonehenge at West Amesbury were submitted to the Oxford Radiocarbon Accelerator Unit (ORAU) and Scottish Universities Environmental Research Centre (SUERC) for radiocarbon dating (Table 5.4). Four of these samples failed (GU-22729, GU-18391 [replicated by P-24259, which also failed], and P-25924). Of the remaining 17 radiocarbon dates obtained for the site, an antler pick (SF 491) from the primary fill of the henge ditch (095) was dated three times to produce a weighted mean, so the dates for the site derive from 15 different samples.

Lab number	Sample ID	Material and context	Radiocarbon age (BP)	δ13C (‰)	Calibrated date range (95% confidence)
SUERC-32175	168 no.1	Carbonised wheat grain from the fill (168) of posthole 180 cut into the filled-in Stonehole B	995±30	-22.7	cal AD 990–1160
SUERC-32176	168 no.2	Carbonised wheat grain from the fill (168) of posthole 180 cut into the filled-in Stonehole B	1050±30	-24.2	cal AD 890–1030
SUERC-32180	245 no.1	Carbonised wheat grain from the fill (245) of Stonehole J	890±30	-23.8	cal AD 1030–1220
SUERC-32181	245 no.2	Carbonised wheat grain from the fill (245) of Stonehole J	1145±30	-23.0	cal AD 770–990
SUERC-32182	245 no.3	Carbonised wheat grain from the fill (245) of Stonehole J	915±30	-24.7	cal AD 1020–1220
SUERC-32183	208 no.1	Carbonised wheat grain from the primary fill (208) of Stonehole E	1135±30	-23.6	cal AD 780–990
SUERC-32184	208 no.2	Carbonised wheat grain from the primary fill (208) of Stonehole E	870±30	-22.9	cal AD 1040–1230
SUERC-32185	208 no.3	Carbonised wheat grain from the primary fill (208) of Stonehole E	1140±30	-23.7	cal AD 780–890
SUERC-32162	245	*Cervus elaphus* tooth from the primary fill (245) of Stonehole J	3890±30	-23.4	2480–2230 cal BC
GU-22729	242	Animal bone from (242) in layer above (245) in the fill of Stonehole J	Sample failed; insufficient carbon		
SUERC-27051	ARS 159 571	Antler pick SF 529/571 with its tine embedded into the top of (183) was deposited in (159) and pushed into (183). (159) is interpreted as original packing material for the stone (Stonehole C) subsequently disturbed during the stone's removal.	3855±30	-23.3	2470–2200 cal BC
P-25924	ARS 183 529	As SUERC-27051	Failed due to no yield		
GU-18391	ARS 095 485	*Bos taurus* broken and worn scapula shovel from the centre ditch segment at the base of (095)	Sample failed		
P-24259	ARS 095 485	As GU-18391	Sample failed		
OxA-21278	ARS 132 503	*Cervus elaphus* pick from the upper part of fill 164, within 1cm of the base of the ramp for Stonehole A. Since the pick was not crushed, it was deposited after the standing stone was withdrawn from the hole. There is no means of establishing whether the pick was used in the stone's removal or whether it was added later, perhaps when hollow (129) was being dug.	3884±30	-23.1	2470–2210 cal BC
OxA-20351	ARS 095 491	*Cervus elaphus* pick from (095), the primary fill of the henge ditch. SF 491, from the northeast sector of the ditch, was found in two pieces, embedded in a pocket into bedrock (049).	3891±29	-21.6	
OxA-20357	ARS 095 491	As OxA-20351	3858±27	-21.3	
SUERC-23207	ARS 095 491	As OxA-20351	3825±30	-21.7	
		Weighted mean (T'=2.5; T' (5%)=6.0; ν=2; Ward and Wilson 1978)	3859±17		2460–2210 cal BC
SUERC-26460	ARS09 Trench 51 [141] SF514	Pig humerus, fissured and pitted fragment from the fill (141) of pit 263 in Stonehole C.	4040±35	-21.2	2840–2470 cal BC
SUERC-26458	ARS09 Trench 50 [555]	Human femur broken shaft from the fill (555) of pit (556) [Trench 50]	1280±35	-20.0	cal AD 660–810
SUERC-26459	ARS09 Trench 51 [015] SF497	Human right proximal tibia from the base of ditch (014) [Trench 51]	1250±35	-19.5	cal AD 660–880

Table 5.4. Bluestonehenge at West Amesbury: radiocarbon dates

Radiocarbon analysis and calibration

The samples were processed and calibrated as described in Chapter 3. The calibrations of these results, which relate the radiocarbon measurements directly to the calendrical time scale, are given in Table 5.4 and in Figure 5.66.

Interpretation

The henge ditch

The three measurements on the tip of an antler pick (SF 491) from the primary fill of the henge ditch (context 095), found in two pieces embedded in a pocket into bedrock (049) at the base of context 095, are statistically consistent (T'=2.5; T' (5%)=6.0; ν=2; Ward and Wilson 1978) and a weighted mean has been taken before calibration (SF 491; 3859±17 BP). The antler tip can be interpreted as having broken off from a pick during digging of the henge ditch and therefore provides an estimate for its construction of 2460–2210 cal BC (R_Combine [095] in Figure 5.66).

The bluestone circle

Four animal bone or antler samples were dated from contexts associated with the nine stoneholes (A–F, I–K) identified in Trenches 51 and 60 of the 'bluestone' circle.

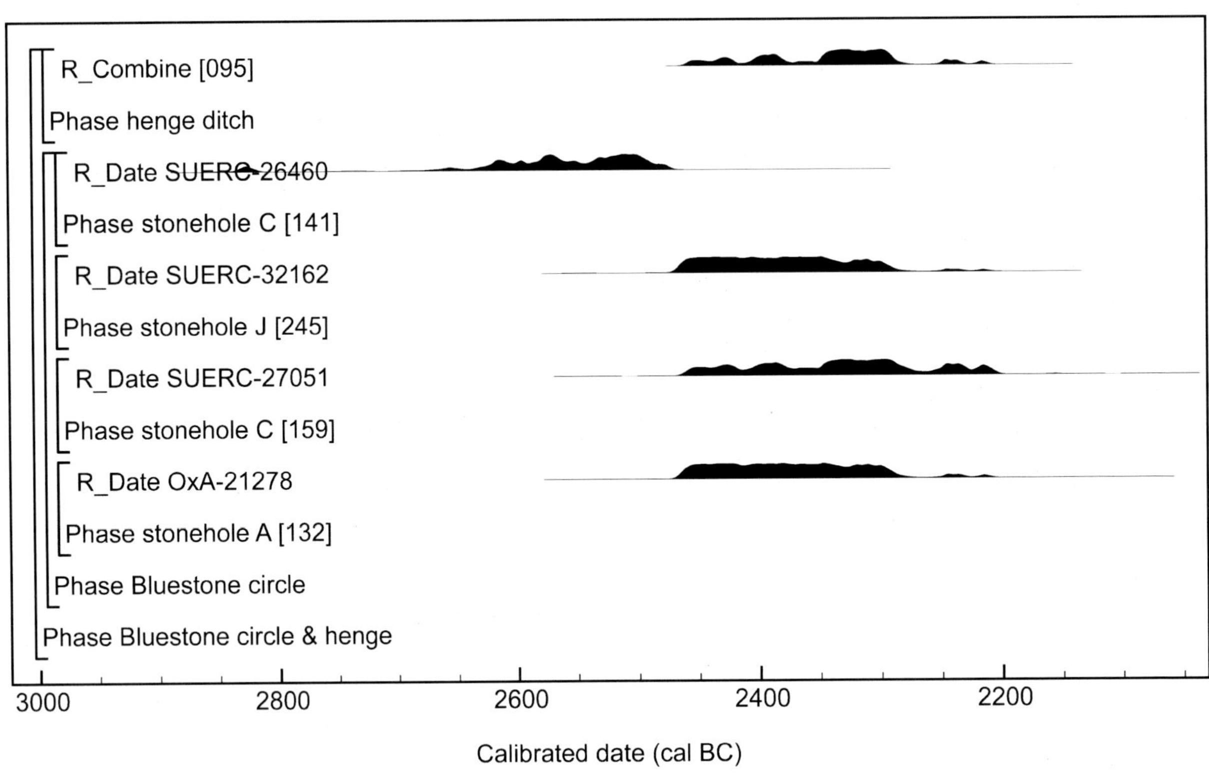

Figure 5.66. Probability distributions of dates from the bluestone circle and henge ditch at West Amesbury

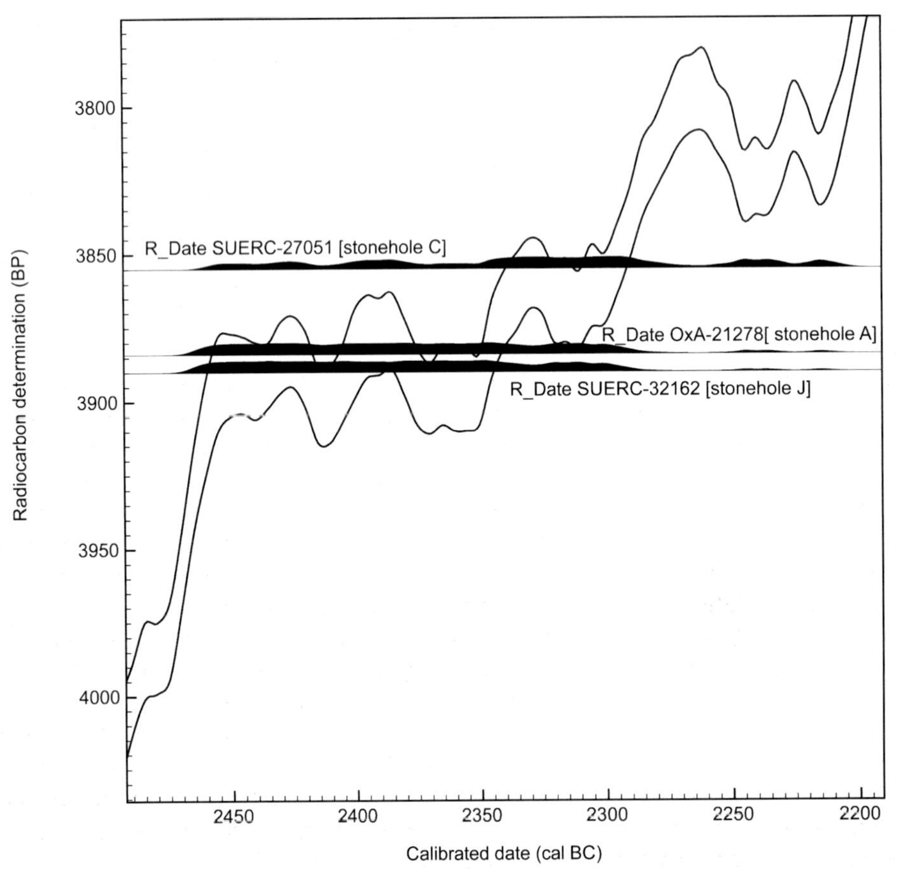

Figure 5.67. Probability distributions of dates from the bluestone circle stoneholes at West Amesbury plotted on the radiocarbon calibration curve

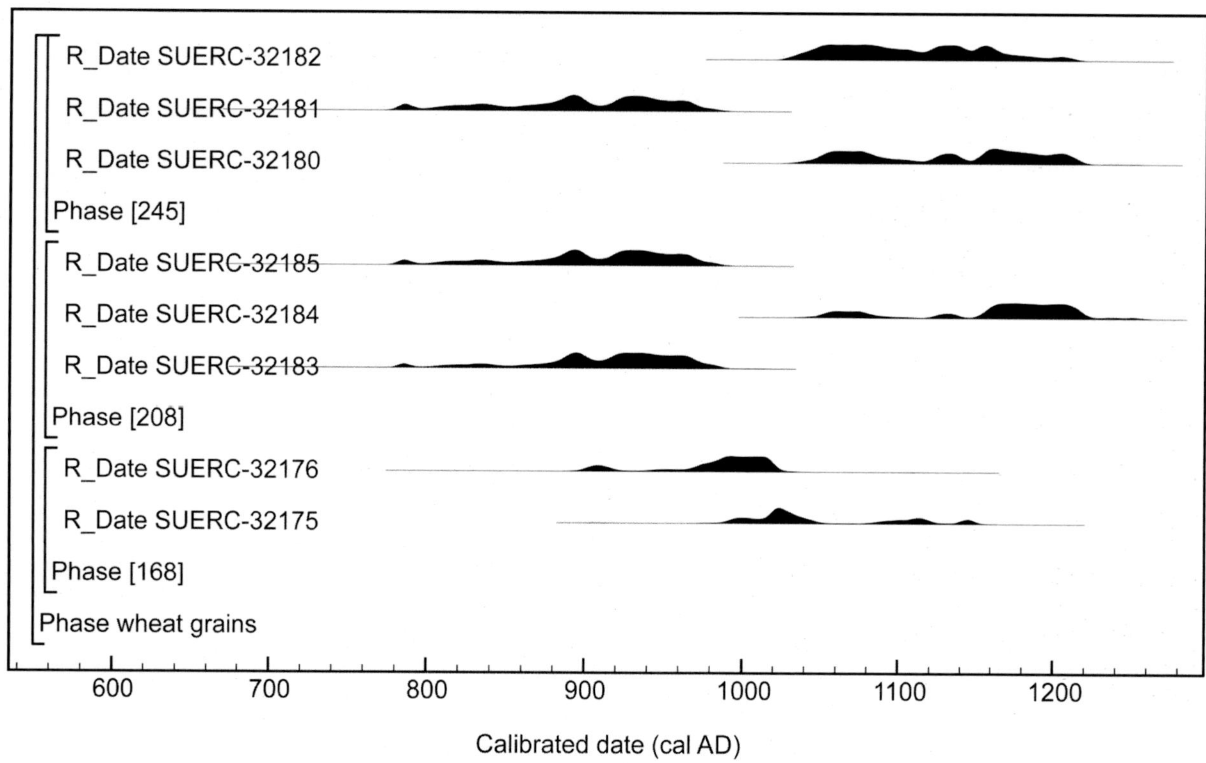

Figure 5.68. Probability distributions of dates from the wheat grains in stoneholes at West Amesbury

The antler from the ramp of Stonehole A was not crushed and must therefore have been deposited after the standing stone was withdrawn from its hole. The antler dates to 2470–2210 cal BC (OxA-21278; Figure 5.66) and it could conceivably have been used to remove the stone or was perhaps added at a later date, possibly if and when hollow 129 was artificially enhanced.

The fissured and pitted fragment of pig humerus from the fill (141) of Stonehole C provides a *terminus post quem* for the standing stone's removal of 2840–2470 cal BC (SUERC-26460; Figure 5.66).

The red deer tooth from the primary fill (245) of Stonehole J provides a *TPQ* of 2480–2230 cal BC (SUERC-32162; Figure 5.66) for the standing stone it once held as it could potentially be residual. Because of its small size, it could also be a contaminant from a higher stratigraphic level.

An antler pick (SF 529/SF 571) lay with its tine embedded beneath the surface of layer 183, interpreted as a 'cushion' on which the stone (Stonehole C) would have originally sat, with its handle higher up and covered by a later context (159, packing material for the stone, disturbed during stone removal). The antler was originally thought to have been deposited with layer 183 before packing material 159 was added, but this has been revised so it is now thought that the antler was deposited with fill 159, its tine pushed down into layer 183. The antler therefore provides a date for context 159 of 2470–2200 cal BC (SUERC-27051; Figure 5.66).

Understanding the chronology of the bluestone circle is not straightforward, not least because of where the dated samples fall on the radiocarbon calibration curve which is unhelpfully flat during this period (Figure 5.67). It therefore remains problematic at present to say precisely where the monument fits into the development of the Stonehenge landscape.

Later activity

A rich assemblage of charred plant remains was recovered from the site during the intensive programme of flotation (see Simmons, below). Given the lack of animal bone at West Amesbury, it was considered worth attempting a dating programme using charred grain as samples for radiocarbon dating, although the difficulties of such material being probably intrusive were known. Eight charred wheat grains from Stoneholes B, E, and J were therefore submitted for dating. All are early medieval in date (Table 5.4; Figure 5.68) and clearly intrusive, relating to later activity on the site (*cf* Pelling *et al.* 2015). The eight measurements are not statistically consistent (T'=105.6; T' (5%)=14.1; ν=7; Ward and Wilson 1978) and evidently derive from activity taking place at various times in the late first millennium AD.

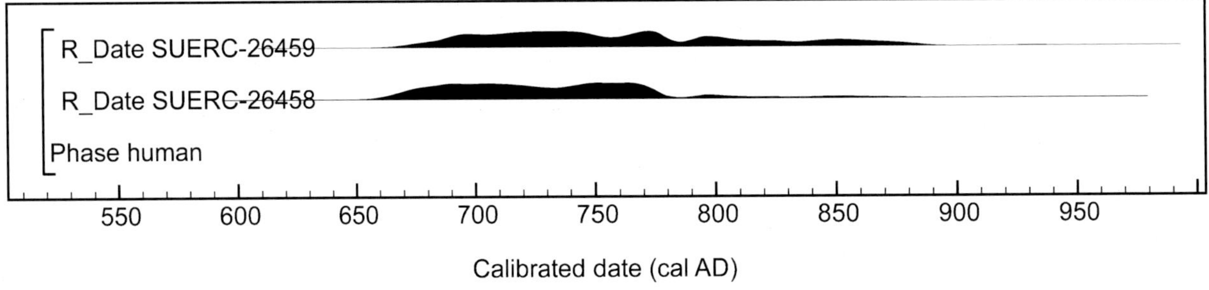

Figure 5.69. Probability distributions of dates from the isolated early medieval human remains from West Amesbury

The two isolated human bones from Trench 50 (SUERC-26458) and Trench 51 (SUERC-26459) were also submitted for radiocarbon dating (see *Medieval and later features*, above). Their dates are statistically consistent (T'=0.4; T' (5%)=3.8; ν=1; Ward and Wilson 1978) and the two samples could be of the same age (Table 5.4; Figure 5.69). Although they were isolated finds, these two bone fragments could conceivably be from the same individual.

5.5. Neolithic and Beaker pottery from West Amesbury

R. Cleal

For the excavations at West Amesbury, all the early prehistoric pottery is reported together in this report. Pottery of later periods is reported in Volume 4. Approximately 50 pieces of prehistoric pottery, weighing 140g, were found during the excavation of West Amesbury henge and stone circle but many pieces were broken into crumbs: the mean sherd weight, even with crumbs excluded, is just under 3g. Because of the fragmentary nature of the assemblage, attribution to ceramic style is difficult in many cases. All the ceramic material examined, including a small amount of what appears to be fired clay, is described in the catalogue by context and sherds which are identifiable to style are also discussed by style, below.

Peterborough Ware

Figure 5.70

P1. One body sherd (5g), probably from the neck of a Peterborough Ware bowl, in a hard fabric with sparse flint (most <3mm; less than about 5% by surface area, including the broken edges) and a few pieces of angular quartz (<2mm), with some fine sand. The external surface and edges are abraded, and the interior surface is in fair condition. Exterior: black and pinky buff; core: black; interior: dark grey-brown. The decoration was clearly not well-impressed originally and is now worn; there is one clear linear impression and one less distinct. It is possible that the decoration was made with a coarse twisted cord but this is uncertain given the condition of the surface. The sherd is not assignable to sub-style but is likely to be Ebbsfleet Ware or Mortlake Ware (Pot Record Number [PRN] 10004; context 037d).

The identification of P1 as Peterborough Ware is necessarily uncertain because of the condition of the sherd; both the poor condition of the sherd and the identification suggest that the sherd was redeposited in the context in which it was found (the Bronze Age upper fill of the henge ditch). The fabric is unlike any of the other fabrics among the excavated pottery, and angular quartz inclusions are a minor feature of Peterborough Ware in southern England generally and unusual in other ceramic traditions in the local area (Cleal 1995b: 189–90).

Middle Neolithic finds, including Peterborough Ware and chisel arrowheads, are found widely but thinly spread across the Stonehenge landscape. There is, however, a notable concentration around 1.50km to the northwest of West Amesbury, on King Barrow Ridge, and at Coneybury henge just under 1km to the west (Cleal with Raymond 1990: 234–5, fig. 154; Pitts 2017). To the east and northeast, however, there are few finds of Peterborough Ware: in particular, the river valley zone, which has seen substantial excavations including those at Durrington Walls, has produced virtually no Peterborough Ware, despite there being a notable spread of earlier Neolithic Bowl pottery beneath the banks of Durrington Walls and Woodhenge (Wainwright with Longworth 1971: 14, 53–4, 73–6, 192). It would seem that the Avon valley area, having been exploited in, probably, the middle centuries of the fourth millennium cal BC, was not a focus of activity again until perhaps nearly a thousand years later. Although the identification of this sherd as Peterborough Ware at West Amesbury has to be tentative because of its condition, the finding of chisel arrowheads strengthens the likelihood that there was some Middle Neolithic activity in this area.

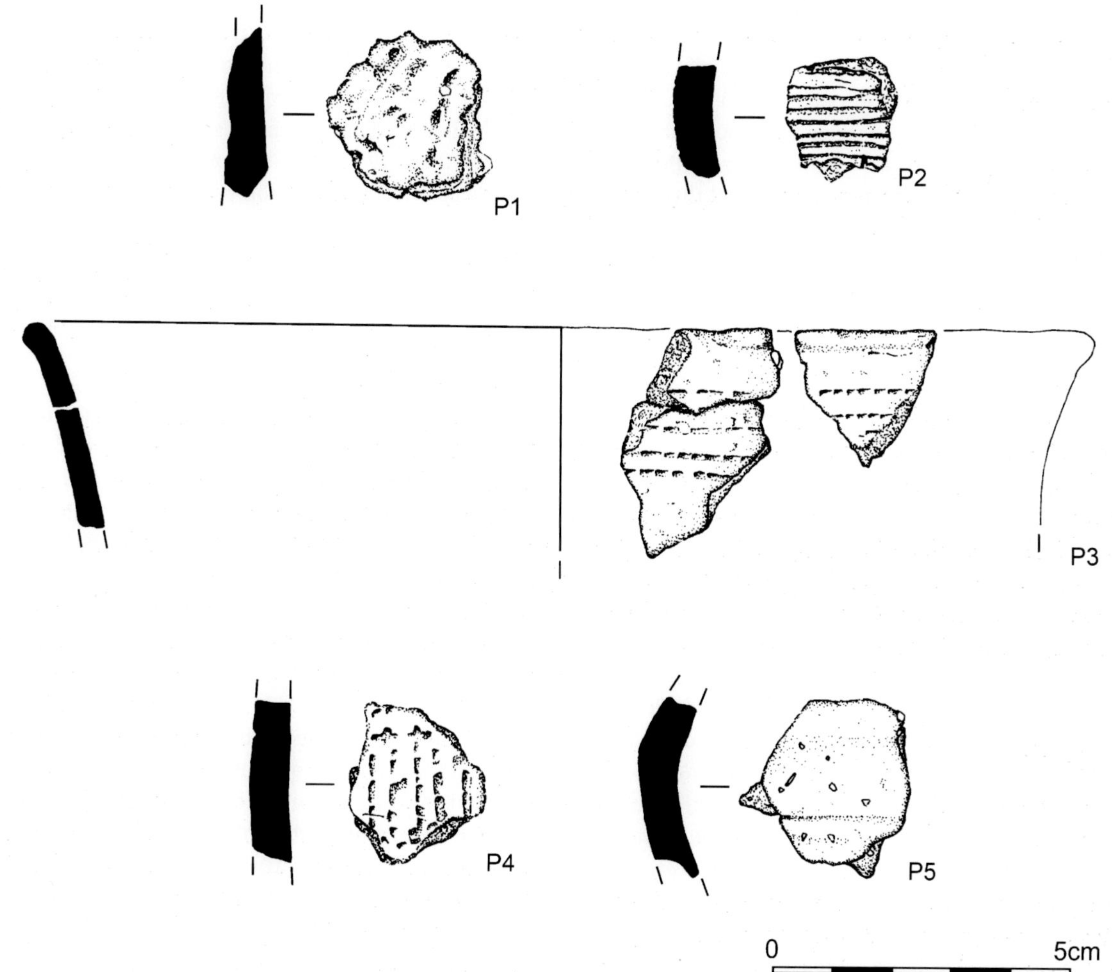

Figure 5.70. Prehistoric pottery from West Amesbury

Grooved Ware

Figure 5.70

P2. Single sherd (3g), probably of Grooved Ware, in a fairly hard but coarse fabric with some sand (including dark grains) and grog (max. dimension 3mm). The decoration is of fine incised lines, apparently scored individually (*i.e.* not a comb dragged across the surface). Exterior: orange; core and interior: black. Condition: slightly worn on edges and exterior, less so on interior where there is some residue (PRN 10016; context 137).

Only this one sherd (P2) can be identified with any confidence as Grooved Ware and, even in this case, the identification cannot be entirely certain. Some other fragments may also belong to this tradition; in particular, the very tiny sherds found in the primary fill (095) of the henge ditch are probably Grooved Ware: at least one contains what appears to be a tiny fragment of shell (a common non-plastic inclusion in Grooved Ware in the area). P2 was found in a non-primary context in Stonehole A.

The decoration of P2 is not absolutely typical of Grooved Ware from the area but falls within the range, and the existence of residue – presumably from cooking – is very characteristic of Grooved Ware generally (residues occur on just under 7% of *c.* 8,000 sherds from the SRP excavations at Durrington Walls; see Volume 3 for the ceramic report on that assemblage). In terms of directly comparable material, an atypical vessel from Durrington Walls (Longworth 1971: fig. 49, P222) has similar closely spaced lines of horizontal incision, in this case beneath the rim on the exterior. The occurrence of Grooved Ware at West Amesbury is very minor but the site lies within a zone in which Grooved Ware has commonly been found in pits as well as in the henges at Coneybury and Durrington Walls.

Beaker

Figure 5.70

P3. Two rim sherds (not conjoining) with one joining body sherd (rim PRN 10011 with body sherd PRN 10012), probably deriving from one Beaker with four horizontal rows of rectangular-toothed comb beneath the rim, probably around 160mm–200mm diameter at the mouth. There is insufficient of the vessel to give a definitive fabric description, but there is probably around 10% sand (by surface appearance) including dark grains and some grog (difficult to distinguish from the matrix). There is one small inclusion which may be flint. Exterior: orange-red, orange-brown; core: dark grey where visible; interior: pale brown, orange-brown. Condition: fair, edges and surfaces slightly weathered (PRN 10011 [3g], PRN 10012 [1g], context 057, secondary fill of ditch 214 cut into henge ditch, both SF 535; PRN 10013 (2g), context 094, secondary fill of henge ditch, SF 543).

P4. Single sherd from a Beaker, with rectangular-toothed-comb impressions. There is insufficient to give a definitive fabric description but the non-plastic inclusions are predominantly sand, of which about 10% are dark grains. There is some grog present but it is difficult to distinguish from the matrix. Exterior and interior: orange; core not visible. Condition: interior fair, edges and exterior some loss of detail. It is not clear what the motif is on this sherd: it could be from a vessel with floating geometric motifs such as lozenges or hexagons, or it may be that the motif is a running, filled chevron; in either case there is the trace of a line of comb-impression from an adjacent motif just visible (PRN 10010, context 057, secondary fill of ditch 214 cut into henge ditch).

A total of 18 sherds and crumbs, weighing in total only just over 23g, can be identified as Beaker with some confidence, and there are more pieces which cannot be assigned to this tradition with any certainty. At least six different vessels are represented but the mean sherd size of only just over 1g, and the highest weight of only 4g, clearly demonstrates how difficult it is to make any comments on style or date among this material.

There are no diagnostically early Beaker vessels certainly represented among the West Amesbury material: that is, there are no cord-decorated sherds or potentially early comb-impressed vessels such as those from the 'Amesbury Archer' or Boscombe Down burials (Cleal 2011; Barclay 2011), although it is possible that the vessel represented by P3 was such an early vessel. While most of the dated early Beakers from Amesbury have continuous coverage of multiple lines of comb impression, *i.e.* not arranged in zones, there are two from the Amesbury Archer's grave which do have multiple-line zones separated by empty zones (Cleal 2011: vessels 6590 and 6597). In one case (*op. cit.*: 6590) the zones are not well-defined, and in the other some of the zones have hanging triangle fringing, but the possibility of blank areas between multiple-line zones at a very early date in the local area is established by these vessels. The context of the sherds at West Amesbury is not helpful as they are from the secondary fill of the henge ditch and from a Bronze Age context, so that, if early, they must have been re-deposited.

One sherd (P4) is clearly not early and may belong to a Beaker from late in the period of Beaker use. It is possible that this sherd is from a vessel with reversed chevrons running around areas filled with vertical comb-impressed lines. This sort of decoration is fairly common on Long-Necked Beakers such as David Clarke's Southern Series (Clarke 1970). Considered late by Clarke, Long-Necked Beakers in Stuart Needham's 2005 scheme are suggested, on the basis of radiocarbon dates, to have been in use from the last two centuries of the third millennium cal BC, with some potentially later than this (Needham 2005: 195–6). The context of this sherd is the same as two of P3, that is, from the secondary fill of ditch 214 which re-cut the henge ditch. One other sherd of P3 was found in the secondary fill of the henge ditch.

There is, in addition, one small crumb which may be Beaker, from the fill (206) of the 'nest' of flints apparently prepared for the reception of Stone E, but it was thought possible during excavation that material might have been introduced into this context during removal of the stone; such a tiny crumb (0.7g) might also easily travel through the soil, meaning that its context must be viewed with caution. Several small crumbs of prehistoric pottery which were found in the primary fill of the henge ditch have been mentioned above; they are not diagnostic as either Grooved Ware or Beaker but seem slightly more likely to be the former, and there is no certain Beaker pottery from low in the henge ditch.

As indicated above, some of the Beaker sherds (P3) could derive from early Beakers, but there is nothing definitively early in their decoration, and too little survives to be sure of the form. One sherd (P4), at least, could have belonged to a vessel current towards the end of the third millennium cal BC. The location of the sherds is not incompatible with their having been associated with the dismantling of the stone setting, and the later stages of the henge.

Plain carinated

Figure 5.70

P5. A single plain body sherd (7g) with a fairly well-defined carination. The fabric is hard and contains sparse, small angular flint (<3mm, most <1mm) and sparse sand, including dark grains. There is a single shallow, scored line around 12mm below the shoulder but this may be from manufacture rather than decoration. Exterior: varied firing of pale grey-brown to buff; core: grey brown; interior: dark grey. Condition: fair. Context 246 (primary fill of ditch 214).

This is a particularly difficult sherd to assign to a ceramic tradition. Well-defined carinations in hard fabrics with flint and sand occur in traditions widely separated in time, and the likeliest possibilities in this case are the earlier Neolithic Bowl traditions and the late second/early first millennium BC plain wares in which angular forms with sharp shoulders occur. With so little of the vessel surviving, the difference in base form between these two traditions (*i.e.* round in one and flat in the other) is of no assistance, and, unlikely as it may seem, this sherd may have to be accepted as assignable to either.

West Amesbury henge: pottery by context

Northeast of henge ditch, Trench 51

Two tiny fragments (0.6g) belonging originally to one piece, possibly Neolithic or Bronze Age but too small to be certainly identified; the fragments appear to have been burnt. Context 050; found in environmental sample 188.

Surface across henge interior

One small Beaker body sherd (1g) decorated with rectangular-toothed-comb impressions in two parallel lines; the comb is large-toothed with the largest tooth 3.5mm × 1.5mm. The fabric is hard and smooth with frequent mainly fine quartz sand, with some dark grains and one flint fragment. The sherd may have been burnt after firing or leached by groundwater, as it has an unusual pale colouring. The sherd is abraded and does not appear to belong to any of the other Beakers from the site. PRN 10009, context 051b.

One plain sherd (3g) and crumbs (2g) from this context, from a single vessel. The fabric is laminated and friable, with frequent sand and some flint, including fragments up to 3mm maximum dimensions. One of the crumbs shows traces of what may be an applied or worked-up ridge on the exterior. They are likely to be either coarse Beaker or Grooved Ware but are too small for a certain identification. Context 051b.

Bluestone circle

Stonehole A

One decorated sherd (3g), possibly Grooved Ware (illustrated as P2; see above), and an unassignable sherd (8g; SF 505) in a hard fabric with approximately 5% flint by surface area (max. dimension 5mm, most <2mm). The exterior surface shows some irregularity which does not appear to be decoration, and the sherd is slightly abraded. It is not possible to identify this sherd to a ceramic tradition although there is some similarity in fabric to the possible Peterborough Ware sherd illustrated as P1. Context 137 *(in situ* packing around former stone).

Stonehole B

One plain, thick body sherd (3g) in a very hard fabric with flint and sand; likely to be later Bronze Age or later in date. Context 181 (uppermost layer of stone-robbing pit 261).

Stonehole D

One small plain body sherd (1g) in a very hard fabric containing flint, sand and some chalk; it is not assignable to a ceramic tradition. Context 179 (either packing of Stonehole D or fill of robbing pit).

One small fragment (1g) in a sandy, hard fabric. This could be fired clay rather than an abraded sherd. Context 207, sample 210 (fill of Stonehole D, possibly collapsed topsoil).

One small (1g) plain, slightly everted rim sherd (SF 525), probably from a Beaker, and possibly from one not otherwise represented on the site; the fabric is sandy, with quartz sand, some grog and flint, and at least one fragment of chalk. The sherd is abraded. Context 146 (primary fill of hollow 129 above Stonehole D, cut by the Bronze Age penannular ditch).

One small dark fragment (0.9g), broken in two, which may be Grooved Ware but cannot be identified with certainty. There is also a small lump of fired clay (1g) from this context. Context 146 (primary fill of hollow 129 above Stonehole D).

Stonehole E

One small probable Beaker sherd (0.7g) in a soft, crumbly fabric with some sand. There is an abraded line on the exterior which appears likely to be incision or possibly comb impressions. The sherd is abraded. Context 206, sample 192 (fill of the 'nest' of flints prepared for stone; may contain material which was introduced when the stone was removed).

Henge ditch

Henge ditch primary fill

Eight undecorated fragments (total weight 4.8g) from context 095a. They are likely to be either Grooved Ware or Beaker, but are not certainly identifiable. They comprise:

SF 555: two small crumbs (total weight 1g). The fabric is very sandy and the crumbs are oxidised to a bright orange colour. They appear to be fired clay rather than sherds.

SF 556: two small sherds (total weight 3g) in a hard slightly sandy fabric, the sand comprising largely quartz grains with some dark and rusty brown grains; there are occasional fragments of chalk, shell and grog. One sherd shows slight curvature; the other has an area of *c.* 8mm × 15mm with a curved edge which appears likely to be the scar from where an applied piece of clay has come off after firing. This small sherd also has very slight traces of a black residue in the interior. Although the fabric could be Grooved Ware or coarse Beaker, the former existence of applied clay, and the residue, would be more consistent with Grooved Ware.

SF 569: a very hard, partially oxidised fragment (less than 0.1g) which cannot be assigned to a ceramic tradition. From the postulated terminal of the ditch.

SF 570: one small sherd and two crumbs from the same vessel (total weight 0.8g). The fabric is laminated and friable and contains sand, probably some grog and a few small white fragments; one appears to be chalk and one may be shell. Shell is very rare in Beaker fabrics but not wholly unknown. Chalk is, by contrast, entirely unknown in Beaker fabrics yet is frequently found in Grooved Ware. On balance, it is more likely that the fragments are from a Grooved Ware vessel, but they cannot be certainly identified as either Grooved Ware or Beaker.

Henge ditch secondary fill

One decorated Beaker rim sherd (2g), illustrated as P3. One crumb (0.2g) may belong to the same vessel (PRN 10013). Context 094.

One small fragment (2g) of fired clay in a Beaker-like fabric. Context 213a.

Henge ditch uppermost fill

One decorated body sherd (5g), probably Peterborough Ware, illustrated as P1. Context 037d.

One plain body sherd (3g) in a very hard, very sandy black fabric; probably first millennium BC or later. Context 037e.

Two sherds (4g and 3g) possibly from the same vessel. Both sherds are in fabrics containing grog and sand, including dark grains, but one has more visible grog and fewer dark grains than the other, although this could be variation within a vessel. One sherd is concave on the exterior and the other appears to come from a slightly protruding foot; protruding feet are very rare on British Beakers, however, and, in this case, the foot 'turns under' quite markedly (*i.e.* it is not just a squeezed-out foot with an essentially flat base) and an alternative interpretation is that it is a cordon or ridge. Both cordons and ridges occur on 'coarse' Beakers, and a concave section of profile would also fit with this. In either case the attribution to the Beaker tradition seems fairly secure. PRN 10007, SF 510; PRN 10006, SF 516. Context 037f.

One sherd (0.6g) and one crumb (0.4g) in a soft fabric with some sand and probably some grog, apparently from a single vessel. The small sherd has a line of incision or fingernail impression. The fabric and decoration suggest that the vessel was a coarse Beaker. The sherds are only slightly worn. PRN 10005. Context 037f.

One small, featureless fragment (0.6g), probably from a Beaker, although the fabric is harder than is usual. SF 511. Context 037f.

One tiny Beaker fragment (0.5g) from either a rim or an applied cordon; the fragment is too small to describe the fabric but the appearance of the fragment is consistent with finer Beakers; the interior surface is entirely missing. The fragment has broken off in a way which does not seem consistent with its being part of a rim but, if from a cordon (which in finer Beakers is usually just below the rim in the concave neck area), more concavity would be expected; here the profile is virtually straight. PRN 10008, SF 512. Context 037f.

Two small fragments (2g) of fired clay. Context 037f.

Henge ditch Bronze Age fill partly derived from henge bank (Trench 60)

One small plain rim sherd from a fine Beaker, in a hard fabric with no visible inclusions (PRN 10017) and one Beaker body sherd decorated with rectangular-toothed-comb impressions, probably in a filled horizontal or chevron zone (total weight 1.4g). Both could be derived from vessels represented elsewhere on the site. Both SF 532. Context 191.

One small plain sherd (3g) from this context may be from a Beaker, but it is unusually hard for that ceramic tradition. It has lost some surface and may have had a line of incisions on the exterior. The sherd is abraded. SF 530. Context 191.

One thick, plain sherd (10g) with fine, well-sorted flint inclusions; it may be Middle Bronze Age in date. SF 531. Context 191.

Henge ditch western circuit (silts covering cobble surfaces in ditch)

A single plain, black, body sherd (2g) in a sandy fabric is unlikely to be Neolithic or Early Bronze Age in date, and is possibly first millennium BC or later. Context 199 (silt covering lower cobble layer).

Two very small unidentifiable fragments (weighing 0.5g). Context 077 (silt covering upper cobble layer).

Ditch 214 cut into the henge ditch

Primary fill

One carinated sherd (7g), illustrated as P5. Not certainly assignable to a ceramic tradition, it is possibly earlier Neolithic, but could alternatively belong to later prehistoric angular forms. Context 246.

One small, plain, very abraded body sherd (3g) in a very hard fabric containing small (<2mm) flint. It is not assignable to a ceramic tradition but is likely to be later prehistoric. Context 246.

Secondary fill

One Beaker rim sherd and two body sherds decorated with rectangular-toothed-comb impressions, probably from two vessels (illustrated as P3–P4); with one crumb from either of the vessels (total weight 8g; includes SF 535). Context 057.

Postholes

Posthole 154

Two small fragments, one a crumb (total weight 1.6g). The larger fragment, which appears highly abraded, is exceptionally hard but brittle; both could have been re-burnt. They are not identifiable to a ceramic tradition. Context 126 (fill of post-pipe 185 within posthole cut into Stonehole C).

Posthole 180

One small, very abraded sherd (4g), probably later prehistoric in date. Context 168 (fill of posthole cut into Stonehole B).

Penannular ditch 147

One plain body sherd (14g) in a fabric with well-sorted flint inclusions (*c.* 10%–15% by surface area) and quartz sand. It is likely to be Middle Bronze Age or later. Context 156 (primary fill).

Four plain sherds (33g), two of which are certainly later prehistoric and conjoin (SF 526). The remaining two (SF 518 and SF 520), both thick sherds (8mm) in a fabric with moderate flint inclusions, could be Neolithic (including Peterborough Ware) but are more likely to be later than Early Bronze Age. Context 144 (fill in Trench 60).

Twenty-one small fragments of fired clay (47g). Context 144.

Avenue ditch

Tertiary fill

One plain sherd (4g) in a silty fabric with some sand and one flint inclusion. On fabric and appearance, it could be later Neolithic or Early Bronze Age; the sherd is abraded. SF 2008. Context 594 (western ditch, Trench 50).

5.6. Worked flint dating to the Chalcolithic, Neolithic and earlier from stratified contexts at West Amesbury

B. Chan and J. Rylatt with a contribution by P. Pettitt

Introduction

Compared to the other assemblages from excavations undertaken by the SRP, the assemblage from West Amesbury is one of the most complex due to its size and chronological diversity. The assemblage totals 21,390 artefacts (Table 5.5) and comes from deposits thought to date to the Mesolithic, Neolithic, Chalcolithic, Bronze Age, medieval and post-medieval periods. Whilst the material in some of these deposits is residual, the assemblage contains diagnostic artefacts that span in date from the Upper Palaeolithic to the post-medieval period. This report concerns the assemblage from Chalcolithic and earlier deposits, which comprises 2,823 artefacts, representing 15% of the assemblage as a whole (Table 5.6).

There is evidence for at least some residual material in nearly all substantial contexts. Hence there is Mesolithic flintwork in Neolithic features, there are demonstrably Mesolithic and Neolithic artefacts in Bronze Age features, and there is prehistoric flintwork in most medieval and post-medieval deposits. Therefore, whilst the assemblage reported in this volume is from pre-Bronze Age features, there is much pre-Bronze Age flintwork in later features. This material is detailed in Volume 4, but will be discussed here where relevant, and some of this residual material is illustrated in Figures 5.72–5.77. Note that Table 5.5 lists all the lithic material, from contexts of all periods, and can be compared to the accompanying tables which list the material from the pre-Bronze Age deposits only.

Raw material and condition

Compared to other assemblages from the Stonehenge landscape, the assemblage from the West Amesbury excavations shows diversity in raw material usage. Despite this, local chalk flint still makes up 99% of the assemblage as a whole (Table 5.7). Whilst this material is undoubtedly locally derived, the cortex on the flint is often abraded and, given the riverside location of the site, it is likely that a significant portion of it had been eroded out of its primary context in the chalk and was procured from the river.

In addition to the local flint, a number of other types of flint were used in limited quantities, with each type typically representing 0.1% of the assemblage. Some of the non-local flint, such as the small quantities of Bullhead flint, might have been carried into the area by human transport, whilst others might have been washed down the river from other sources.

Alongside the flint two forms of chert are present in the assemblage, one being a fine-grained grey-black chert and the other a heavily patinated chert, thought to be Greensand chert. Chert is known to occur in a number of geological strata in the wider Salisbury area, including within both Upper and Lower Greensand formations (Hopson *et al.* 2007). Richards (1990: 231) notes that chert from the Tisbury area was used in the Stonehenge environs.

The variability in raw material usage reflects the proximity of the River Avon and the surface geology of the site, which consists of a series of periglacial clays and silts derived from a complex sequence of alluvial and colluvial deposition overlying the basal decayed chalk deposits.

Apart from abraded material from the topsoil, the material in the assemblage is generally in good to mint condition. This includes artefacts that are clearly residual in later features, suggesting that this

	Artefact type	Frequency	Percent
Debitage and cores	Bipolar opposed-platform blade-core	3	<0.1
	Blade	467	2.2
	Blade-like flake	128	0.6
	Bladelet	71	0.3
	Core on a flake	13	0.1
	Crested blade	6	<0.1
	Flake	18209	85.1
	Irregular waste	1441	6.7
	Keeled non-discoidal flake-core	6	<0.1
	Levallois/other discoidal flake-core	3	<0.1
	Microburin	3	<0.1
	Multi-platform flake-core	118	0.6
	Other blade-core	8	<0.1
	Rejuvenation flake-core face/edge	13	0.1
	Rejuvenation flake tablet	5	<0.1
	Single-platform blade-core	8	<0.1
	Single-platform flake-core	81	0.4
	Tested nodule/bashed lump	41	0.2
	Unclassifiable/fragmentary core	28	0.1
Retouched flakes and tools	Awl	4	<0.1
	Backed blade	2	<0.1
	Burin	1	<0.1
	Chisel	8	<0.1
	Chisel arrowhead	11	0.1
	Denticulate	1	<0.1
	Double-ended scraper	1	<0.1
	Edge-ground flake/blade	1	<0.1
	End-and-side scraper	7	<0.1
	End-scraper	22	0.1
	Fabricator	4	<0.1
	Fragmentary/unclassifiable/other arrowhead	2	<0.1
	Hammerstone	9	<0.1
	Janus flake	2	<0.1
	Levallois flake	1	<0.1
	Microlith	13	0.1
	Misc. blank	1	<0.1
	Misc. retouched flake	116	0.5
	Notch	14	0.1
	Oblique arrowhead	5	<0.1
	Other knife	5	<0.1
	Other scraper	13	0.1
	Petit tranchet arrowhead	2	<0.1
	Piercer	4	<0.1
	Retouched blade	1	<0.1
	Scraper on a non-flake blank	4	<0.1
	Serrated flake	5	<0.1
	Side-scraper	3	<0.1
	Spurred implement	2	<0.1
	Unfinished arrowhead/blank	1	<0.1
	Utilised blade	13	0.1
	Utilised/edge-damaged flake/blade	460	2.2
	Total	21390	100.0

	Artefact type	Frequency	Percent
Debitage and cores	Bipolar opposed-platform blade-core	3	0.1
	Blade	96	3.4
	Blade-like flake	34	1.2
	Bladelet	12	0.4
	Core on a flake	1	<0.1
	Crested blade	1	<0.1
	Flake	2355	83.4
	Irregular waste	162	5.7
	Microburin	1	<0.1
	Multi-platform flake-core	16	0.6
	Other blade-core	1	<0.1
	Rejuvenation flake-core face/edge	4	0.1
	Rejuvenation flake tablet	1	<0.1
	Single-platform blade-core	1	<0.1
	Single-platform flake-core	8	0.3
	Tested nodule/bashed lump	2	0.1
	Unclassifiable/fragmentary core	6	0.2
Retouched flakes and tools	Awl	1	<0.1
	Backed blade	1	<0.1
	Chisel arrowhead	3	0.1
	Edge-ground flake/blade	1	<0.1
	End-and-side scraper	1	<0.1
	End-scraper	4	0.1
	Fabricator	1	<0.1
	Fragmentary/unclassifiable/other arrowhead	2	0.1
	Hammerstone	1	<0.1
	Janus flake	1	<0.1
	Microlith	3	0.1
	Misc. retouched flake	23	0.8
	Notch	2	0.1
	Oblique arrowhead	1	<0.1
	Other knife	1	<0.1
	Other scraper	2	0.1
	Piercer	2	0.1
	Serrated flake	2	0.1
	Side scraper	1	<0.1
	Utilised blade	4	0.1
	Utilised/edge-damaged flake/blade	62	2.2
	Total	2823	100.0

Table 5.6 (above). The lithic assemblage from all pre-Bronze Age contexts from West Amesbury

Table 5.5 (left). The assemblage of worked flint and chert from all excavated contexts, of all periods, at Bluestonehenge, West Amesbury (excluding test pits)

Raw material description	Frequency	Percent
1 Local chalk flint	21561	99.2
2 Bullhead flint	21	0.1
3 Opaque grey-black flint with light orange-brown cherty inclusions	14	0.1
4 Dark grey-black chert	13	0.1
5 Opaque creamy grey flint with white cherty inclusions	11	0.1
6 Opaque yellow-brown to yellow-grey flint	25	0.1
7 Grey-black flint with a reddish-brown band beneath a light brown cortex	84	0.4
8 Yellowish-brown translucent flint	10	<0.1
9 Patinated light grey to white chert – Greensand chert	1	<0.1
Total	21740	100.0

Table 5.7. The frequency of lithic raw material types from West Amesbury (total includes chips)

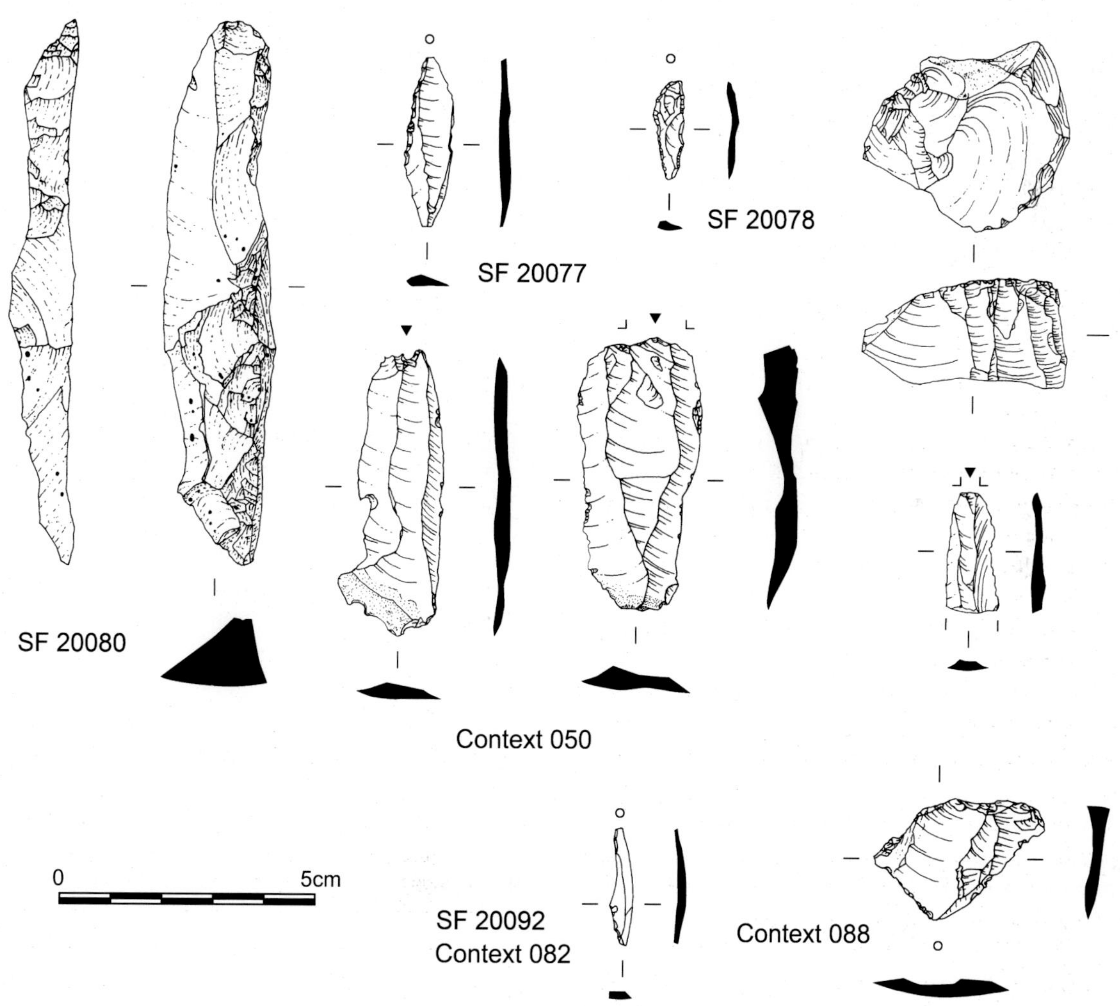

Figure 5.71. Lithics from the buried soils and periglacial clays at West Amesbury

Artefact type			Context number 050	135	172	Total
Debitage and cores	Blade	Count	21	0	4	25
		% within context no	11.2%	0%	8.0%	9.4%
	Blade-like flake	Count	5	0	1	6
		% within context no	2.7%	0%	2.0%	2.3%
	Crested blade	Count	1	0	0	1
		% within context no	0.5%	0%	0%	0.4%
	Flake	Count	122	28	39	189
		% within context no	64.9%	100.0%	78.0%	71.1%
	Irregular waste	Count	28	0	4	32
		% within context no	14.9%	0%	8.0%	12.0%
	Janus flake	Count	1	0	0	1
		% within context no	0.5%	0%	0%	0.4%
	Multi-platform flake-core	Count	1	0	0	1
		% within context no	0.5%	0%	0%	0.4%
	Rejuvenation flake-core face/edge	Count	1	0	1	2
		% within context no	0.5%	0%	2.0%	0.8%
	Rejuvenation flake tablet	Count	1	0	0	1
		% within context no	0.5%	0%	0%	0.4%
Retouched flakes and tools	Microlith	Count	2	0	0	2
		% within context no	1.1%	0%	0%	0.8%
	Misc. retouched flake	Count	1	0	0	1
		% within context no	0.5%	0%	0%	0.4%
	Notch	Count	1	0	0	1
		% within context no	0.5%	0%	0%	0.4%
	Utilised/edge-damaged flake/blade	Count	3	0	1	4
		% within context no	1.6%	0%	2.0%	1.5%
Total		Count	188	28	50	266
		% within context no	100.0%	100.0%	100.0%	100.0%

Table 5.8. The worked flint assemblage from the buried soils at West Amesbury

material probably entered the later features soon after it was disturbed from its original context. The varied surface geology of the site means that, in comparison to the more ubiquitous chalkland assemblages in the area, the flint from West Amesbury is significantly less patinated, with most material being unpatinated or lightly patinated.

Contextual distribution

The assemblage is split between material from the fills of cut features and material from layers. The layers primarily consist of the interface between geological and cultural deposits, a buried soil (050=135) thought to date to the Mesolithic to Early Neolithic, an alluvial layer (172) of similar date, and a number of deflated layers that pre-date the stoneholes and henge ditch. The material from cut features dating before the Bronze Age comes from the fills of the Bluestonehenge stoneholes, the ditches of the West Amesbury henge and the Stonehenge Avenue ditches. The remainder of the assemblage comes from curvilinear ditches 066 and 533 (both likely prehistoric features).

Buried soils and deflated surfaces

The series of deposits that pre-date the Neolithic features on the site are split into buried soils (050, 135 and 172) and deflated surfaces (051, 053 and 161). The deflated surfaces yielded an assemblage of 614 artefacts, whilst the buried soils produced an assemblage of 266 artefacts. The buried soils, which include a forest soil, are understood to be post-glacial in origin and, as they date to before the construction of the henge ditch, they are broadly dateable to the Mesolithic–Early Neolithic.

The assemblages from the three buried soil contexts are variable in terms of size (Table 5.8; Figure 5.71). There are differences also in terms of assemblage composition, but these probably relate to the lower frequency of artefacts from contexts 135 and 172. The most notable thing about the assemblage from these deposits is its proportion of blades and blade-like flakes (12%), which is significantly higher than that from all pre-Bronze Age contexts combined (5%). The presence of a blade technology is also indicated by a core rejuvenation tablet and two microliths from layer 050. The microliths are an obliquely truncated point and a small scalene triangle.

The production of blades is also indicated by the presence of a well-worked crested blade (SF 20080; Figure 5.71) from layer 050. This crested blade, probably made from Greensand chert, is 104mm long and is clearly longer than the other blades in the assemblage. Its surface is speckled with small spots of a black residue which may potentially be a hafting residue such as birch-bark pitch. The size and form of the crested blade suggest that it is likely to be Upper Palaeolithic in date (see below).

Whilst many of the blades from the buried soil have diffuse bulbs and show signs of platform maintenance, the flakes are of a more varied character. Many have plain butts and clearly pronounced bulbs, suggesting that they have been struck with a hard hammer. Some of these flakes are thick and cortical and are clearly core-preparation flakes. Others are more ambiguous, although most appear to have been struck from single-platform cores. Given the potentially broad chronological span of the buried soil, it is hard to interpret this part of the assemblage. With the exception of the lone Upper Palaeolithic artefact, it is possible that the whole assemblage represents Mesolithic blade production, with productive blade-cores and blades being removed for use elsewhere. It is equally possible that the assemblage is mixed chronologically and represents both Mesolithic and Early Neolithic flintworking.

In comparison to the assemblage from the buried soil, that from the deflated surfaces is notably different (Table 5.9). The proportion of blades, blade-like flakes and bladelets is significantly lower (2.4%), and the assemblage from the deflated surfaces contains more tools in the form of an end-scraper, a side-scraper and an end-and-side scraper as well as a microlith in the form of a straight-backed bladelet. The end-and-side scraper (SF 141) has two-phased cortication and was originally worked as an end-scraper and then, after a degree of patination had built up, it was reworked with retouch applied to its distal and lateral margins.

The stoneholes

The assemblage of worked stone from the stonehole fills consists of 1,281 artefacts retrieved from Stoneholes A, B, C, D, E, F, J and K (Table 5.10). The raw material in this part of the assemblage consists of various types of flint, except for four pieces of dark grey chert irregular waste. The quantity of material from the individual stoneholes varies from 17 to 459 artefacts (Table 5.11). These quantities are heavily affected by the fact that Stoneholes A, F, and K lay substantially within the baulks of the trenches and were not fully excavated, whilst Stoneholes B, C, E and F were substantially disturbed by later features. Therefore, only Stoneholes D and J were both completely excavated and not heavily disturbed by later features, which partly explains why these two stoneholes have amongst the largest individual stonehole assemblages.

The assemblage can be broken down into material coming from the basal fills (mostly described as pad deposits), the packing fills and the fills of the robber holes. During the excavation, 198 artefacts from Stonehole D were assigned to the cut number, rather than a fill, so have been listed under the column 'other'. All fill assemblages have the potential to contain residual artefacts, but the potential is greater for the fills of the robber holes as they accumulated during and after the pulling-out of the standing stones and contained both disturbed turf (presumably fallen in from the surface around the edges of the extraction hole) and the reworked fills of the original stonehole.

The distribution of artefacts throughout the fills is uneven. The basal fills, which were generally lower-volume deposits, produced the smallest proportion of the assemblage. There is considerable variation in the proportion of the assemblage from the packing and robber deposits (Table 5.11). This relates primarily to the extent of the stonehole fills available for excavation and the extent of disturbance of the original fills caused by the stone removals.

Compared to other assemblages in the Stonehenge landscape, the stoneholes contained a relatively low proportion of flakes (83%) and a significant proportion of blades, blade-like flakes and bladelets (5%), alongside two opposed-platform blade-cores (Figure 5.72). The blade component of the assemblage is likely to be residual and Later Mesolithic in date. This is backed up by the presence of a single possible proximal microburin from packing deposit 137 in Stonehole A.

The remaining assemblage of cores consists of a core on a flake, five multi-platform cores, five single-platform cores, two bashed lumps and two fragmentary cores. The majority of these cores fit within a Middle to Late Neolithic multi-platform technology. However, several exhibit greater core control than is common in the period and are likely to be earlier in date. Despite having only flake scars remaining on them, two of these

Group	Artefact type		051	053	161	Total
			Context number			
Debitage and cores	Blade	Count	8	1	0	9
		% within context no	1.4%	10.0%	0%	1.5%
	Blade-like flake	Count	2	0	0	2
		% within context no	0.3%	0%	0%	0.3%
	Bladelet	Count	4	0	0	4
		% within context no	0.7%	0%	0%	0.7%
	Flake	Count	527	8	18	553
		% within context no	90.2%	80.0%	90.0%	90.1%
	Irregular waste	Count	19	0	2	21
		% within context no	3.3%	0%	10.0%	3.4%
	Multi-platform flake-core	Count	1	0	0	1
		% within context no	0.2%	0%	0%	0.2%
	Other blade-core	Count	1	0	0	1
		% within context no	0.2%	0%	0%	0.2%
	Rejuvenation flake-core face/edge	Count	1	0	0	1
		% within context no	0.2%	0%	0%	0.2%
	Single-platform flake-core	Count	1	0	0	1
		% within context no	0.2%	0%	0%	0.2%
Retouched flakes and tools	End-and-side scraper	Count	0	1	0	1
		% within context no	0%	10.0%	0%	0.2%
	End-scraper	Count	1	0	0	1
		% within context no	0.2%	0%	0%	0.2%
	Microlith	Count	1	0	0	1
		% within context no	0.2%	0%	0%	0.2%
	Misc. retouched flake	Count	2	0	0	2
		% within context no	0.3%	0%	0%	0.3%
	Side-scraper	Count	1	0	0	1
		% within context no	0.2%	0%	0%	0.2%
	Utilised/edge-damaged flake/blade	Count	15	0	0	15
		% within context no	2.6%	0%	0%	2.4%
Total		Count	584	10	20	614
		% within context no	100.0%	100.0%	100.0%	100.0%

Table 5.9. The worked flint assemblage from deflated surfaces at West Amesbury

latter cores look as if they may well have produced blades during an earlier stage of their reduction.

In terms of tools, the stoneholes contained two chisel arrowheads, a fragmentary arrowhead, two serrated flakes, two end-scrapers, two miscellaneous scrapers, two piercers, a broken roughout for a fabricator and a notched flake. End-scraper SF 20014, from the robber fill of Stonehole J, was made on a well-worked blade and is likely to be a residual Early Neolithic artefact. The fragmentary arrowhead was found within the robber fill of Stonehole D. Given its incomplete state, it is unclear what type it is, but it is most likely a broken leaf-shaped arrowhead and, if so, it is also probably residual. The chisel arrowheads (SF 587 and SF 20100) date to the Middle Neolithic or earlier part of the Late Neolithic and were found within packing fills 132 and 203 of Stoneholes A and K respectively. They are the latest chronologically diagnostic artefacts within the stoneholes and therefore provide a *terminus post quem* for the construction of Bluestonehenge. Two other chisel arrowheads were residual finds in later contexts (124 and 160; Figure 5.74).

Serrated flakes were found within packing fill 245 of Stonehole J (SF 588) and basal fill 241 of Stonehole D (SF 20111). It is unlikely that serrated flake SF 588 is a residual artefact as it is in a fresh condition and has suffered no post-depositional damage to its finely serrated edge. The artefact is unpatinated and has no sign of polish, suggesting that it was not heavily used. By contrast, SF 20111 has some broken denticulations, which may have been lost through use rather than post-depositional damage, because under high-power microscopy the denticulations exhibit several areas of polish of the type typically found on serrated flakes (Juel Jensen 1994).

The West Amesbury henge ditch and the Stonehenge Avenue ditches

The assemblage from the Chalcolithic fills of the henge ditch consists of 348 artefacts split more or less evenly between the primary and secondary fills. The assemblage is dominated by flakes (85%), but also contains blades (5%, including blade-like flakes and bladelets), three miscellaneous retouched flakes, six cores and an assortment of other debitage (Table 5.12; Figure 5.73). The primary fills also contained an awl (SF 20011), whilst the secondary fills contained an end-scraper (SF 20064) and a knife with retouch along one lateral margin associated with a band of diffuse polish (SF 20065). The blades are presumably residual and derive from the buried soil deposits which the henge ditch is partly cut through. Several of the cores are poorly worked, multi-platform types typical of the Late Neolithic/Chalcolithic.

The short segments of the eastern and western Avenue ditches located in Trenches 50 and 61 produced a combined assemblage of 251 artefacts (Table 5.12), with 206 artefacts coming from the eastern ditch (cuts 143 and 579) and 45 from the western ditch (cut 593). The material was spread unevenly between the ditch fills, with primary fill 620 of the western ditch producing only a single flake, whereas primary fill 140 of the eastern ditch produced 63 flakes, a miscellaneous retouched flake, two multi-platform cores, a chip and a piece of irregular waste. The cores are poorly worked, one of them made on a thermally-flawed surface nodule, and are in keeping with the Late Neolithic technology in the area. Secondary fill 619 of the western ditch contained 31 flakes, three miscellaneous retouched flakes, four edge-damaged flakes and a fragmentary arrowhead (SF 20022). The arrowhead has bifacial retouch along its margins, but is too fragmentary to be identified to type.

In general, the assemblage from the Avenue ditches is broadly in keeping with the date of the Avenue (before the mid-23rd century cal BC; see Chapter 8) and the wider assemblage from the Chalcolithic contexts of the henge. The part of the assemblage that is most remarkable is that from tertiary fill 578 of the eastern ditch. This fill

Artefact type	Frequency	Percent
Bipolar opposed-platform blade-core	2	0.2
Blade	47	3.7
Blade-like flake	17	1.3
Bladelet	1	0.1
Chisel arrowhead	2	0.2
Core on a flake	1	0.1
Edge-ground flake/blade	1	0.1
End-scraper	2	0.2
Fabricator	1	0.1
Flake	1061	82.8
Fragmentary/unclassifiable/other arrowhead	1	0.1
Irregular waste	81	6.3
Microburin	1	0.1
Misc. retouched flake	13	1.0
Multi-platform flake-core	5	0.4
Notch	1	0.1
Other scraper	2	0.2
Piercer	2	0.2
Serrated flake	2	0.2
Single-platform flake-core	5	0.4
Tested nodule/bashed lump	2	0.2
Unclassifiable/fragmentary core	2	0.2
Utilised blade	4	0.3
Utilised/edge-damaged flake/blade	25	2.0
Total	1281	100.0

Table 5.10. The worked flint assemblage from the Bluestonehenge stoneholes

	Stonehole fill type				
Stonehole	*Basal*	*Packing*	*Robbing*	*Other*	**Total**
	Frequency				
A	22	120	104	0	246
B	4	19	73	0	96
C	1	0	116	0	117
D	37	149	75	198	459
E	13	15	37	0	65
F	0	17	0	0	17
J	60	90	87	0	237
K	0	44	0	0	44
Total	137	454	492	198	1281

Table 5.11. The worked flint assemblage by fill type from the stoneholes of Bluestonehenge

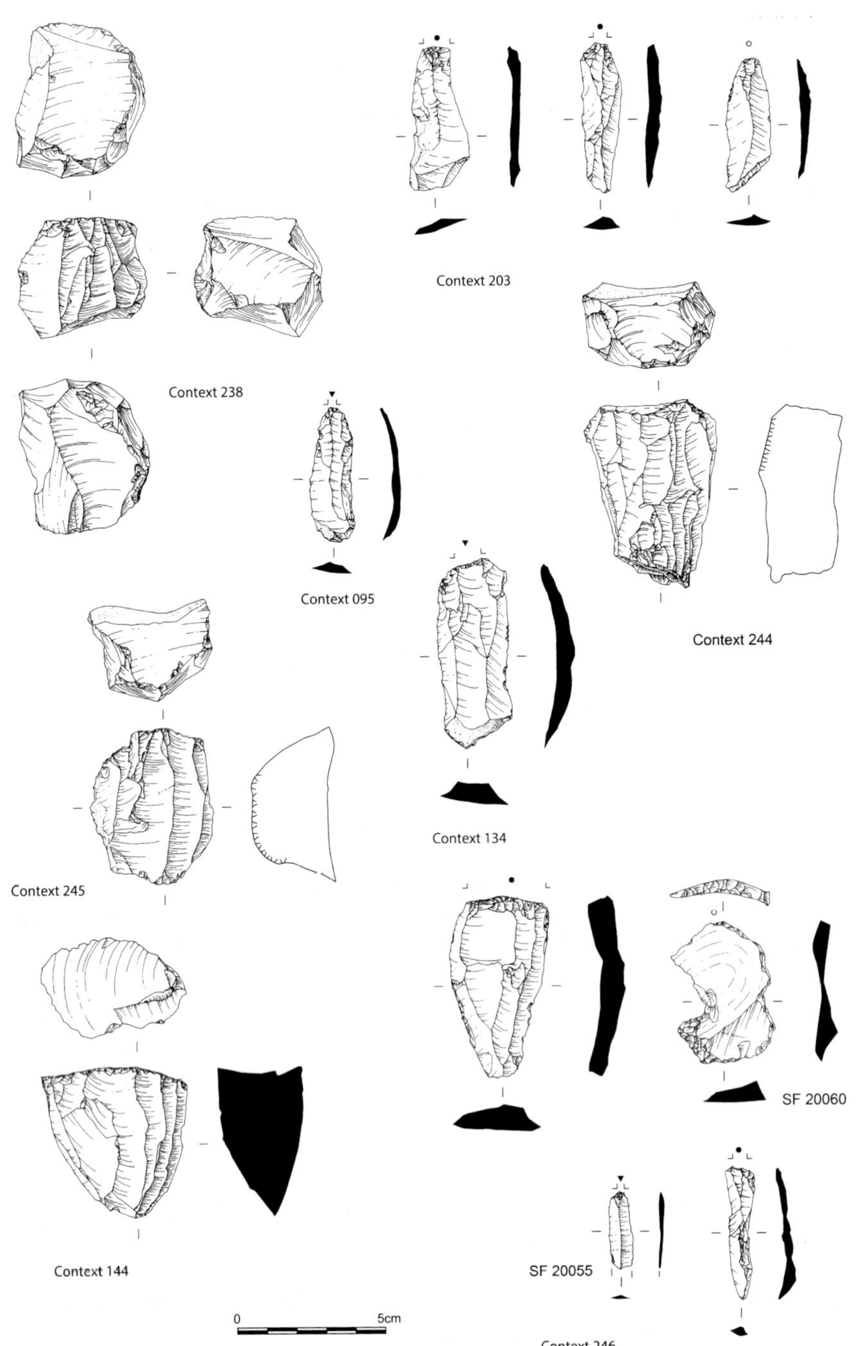

Figure 5.72. Lithics from the stoneholes and later fills at West Amesbury, those from contexts 144 and 246 at the bottom of the figure are residual finds in Bronze Age deposits

contained predominantly flakes, but also a range of blades and bladelets, an opposed-platform blade-core, a single-platform blade-core, two multi-platform flake-cores, several other pieces of debitage and an oblique arrowhead.

The arrowhead (SF 2007) is an outstandingly well-worked ripple-flaked oblique with fine, parallel-ripple flaking extending the entire length of one lateral margin (Figure 5.74). The basal concavity of the arrowhead is finely retouched and is flanked on either side by short square-butted barbs. One barb is slightly longer than the other and it is unclear whether a longer barb has snapped off, or whether the arrowhead is effectively complete. The tip of the arrowhead is retouched to a fine point that is still intact.

The delicate nature of the tip of the arrowhead suggests that the arrowhead was not used and, combined with the fact that the artefact is only lightly patinated and in mint condition, it is unlikely that it was disturbed from its original context of deposition, or otherwise left exposed for any length of time. This in itself is something

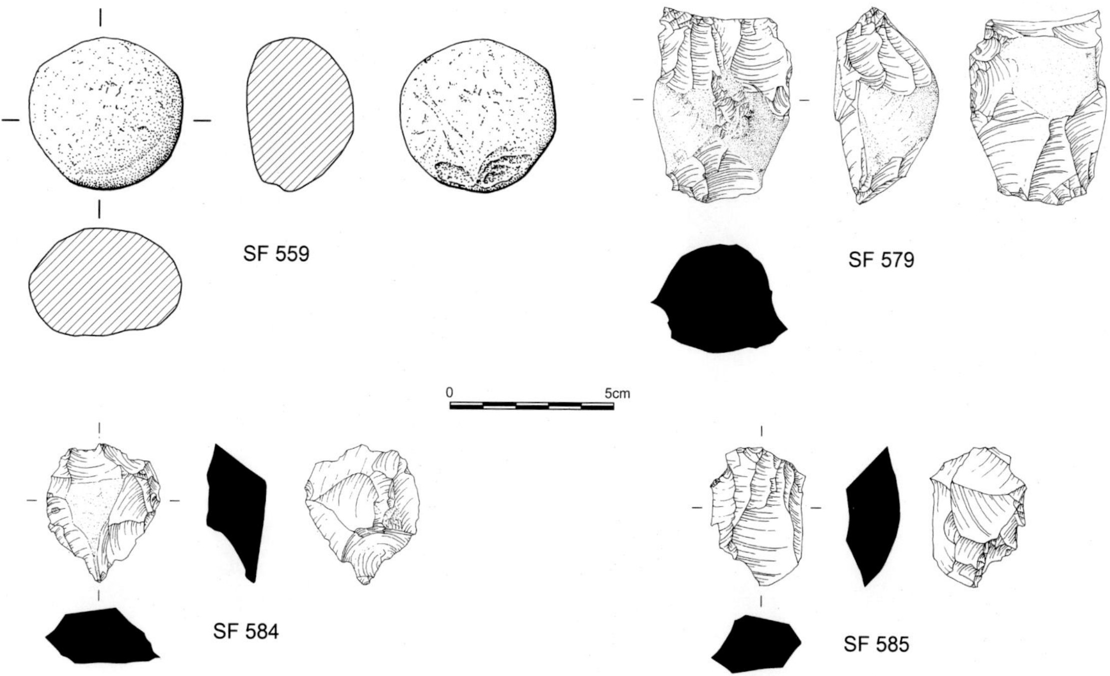

Figure 5.73. Lithics from the special deposit in layer 095a in the henge ditch at West Amesbury

of a conundrum as the upper part of fill 578 contained an iron nail. It is also notable that the blades and blade-cores from this context are clearly residual and yet no blades were present in any of the primary or secondary fills.

Hence, there is potentially both residual and intrusive material in the context. This unfortunately makes it difficult to be sure whether the oblique arrowhead was carefully placed into ditch fill 578, or was unintentionally incorporated after the disturbance of an adjacent context. What can be said though is that the level of skill displayed in the making of the arrowhead is exceptional and is certainly on a par with the finest examples found at Durrington Walls (see lithics report in Volume 3).

Given that the arrowhead from the eastern Avenue ditch is complete and unused, it seems unlikely that it was lost accidentally. Its condition certainly suggests that it was buried relatively rapidly. Therefore, it seems reasonable to suggest that it was intentionally placed either within context 578, or within an adjacent feature that was disturbed by the time of the tertiary infilling of the Avenue ditch.

Other prehistoric features

Besides the stoneholes, the henge ditch and the Avenue ditches, the only other potentially pre-Bronze Age features are two curvilinear ditches (066 and 533). Ditch 066 produced only three flakes, two pieces of irregular waste and two edge-damaged flakes but ditch 533, beside the eastern ditch of the Avenue in Trench 50, contained 58 flint artefacts, six of which came from its primary fills, with the remainder being retrieved from the secondary fills. The secondary fill (532), from which a piece of smithing slag was recovered, produced a blade-like flake with parallel blade-proportioned flake scars on its dorsal surface and a finely worked bladelet, both of which are likely to be Later Mesolithic in date. The same fill also contained a chisel arrowhead (SF 20018).

Technology and chronology

When considering the chronology of the assemblage, it is important to realise that the West Amesbury excavation produced evidence of persistent use of the area in the Mesolithic, Neolithic, Bronze Age, medieval and post-medieval periods.

Flake- and blade-working

The assemblage reported here is clearly chronologically diverse, as it comes from deposits that are known stratigraphically to date to the Mesolithic–Early Neolithic, the Late Neolithic and the Chalcolithic. The chronological range is mirrored in the technological variability within the assemblage. Specifically, both blades (typical of Mesolithic and Early Neolithic flint-working) and broad flakes (which dominate Late Neolithic and Chalcolithic assemblages) are present in significant numbers, with flakes being by far the most common.

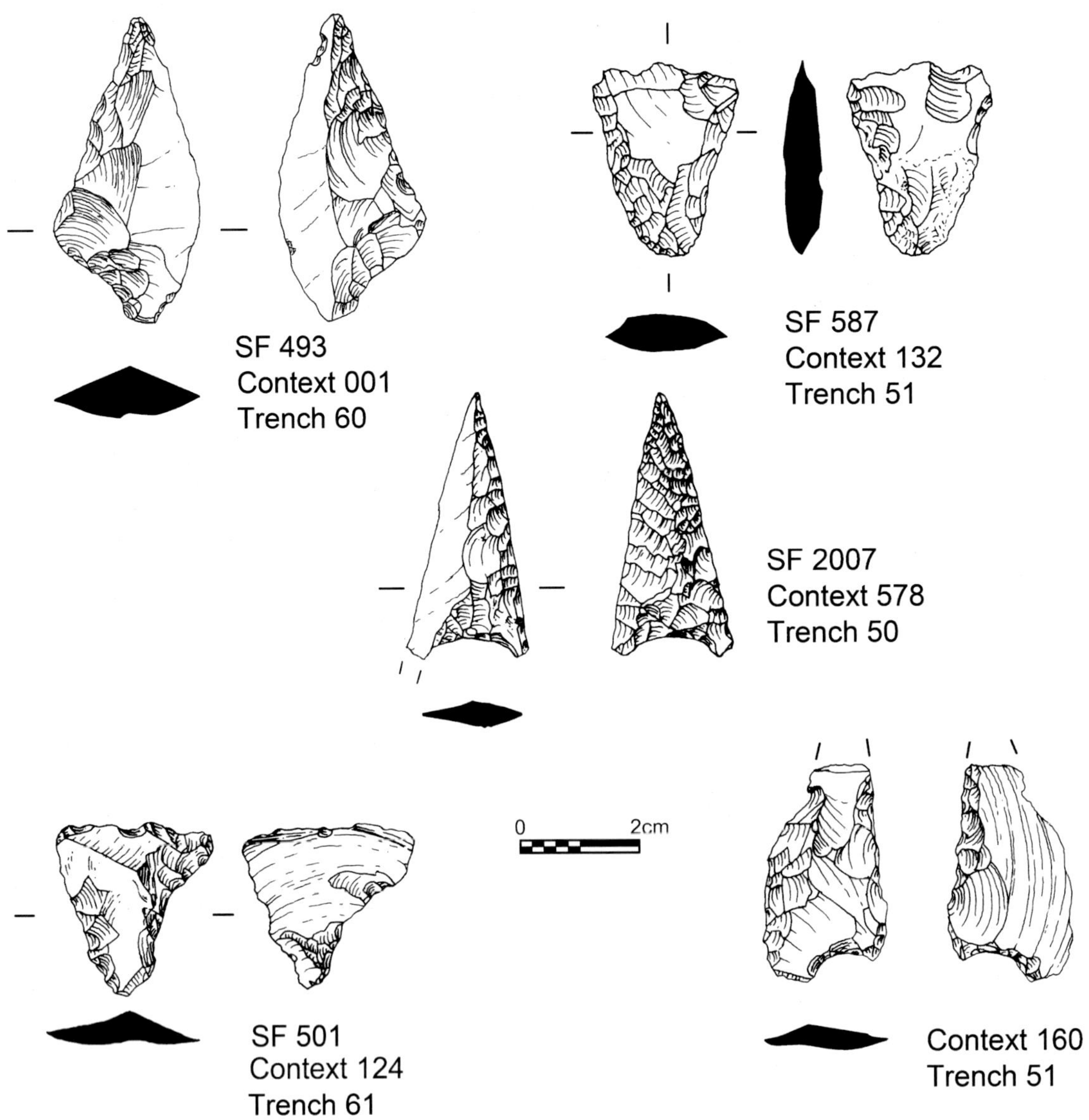

Figure 5.74. Arrowheads from various contexts at West Amesbury

The quality of blade production and the morphology of the resultant blades are variable. Morphology varies from thin bladelets to longer and broader blades (Figures 5.71–5.72, 5.75–5.77). The longest blade is the Upper Palaeolithic crested blade (SF 20080), which is 104mm in length, but there are also blades in the range of 70mm–90mm in length. Blades show frequent signs of abrasion, trimming and, less commonly, faceting used to strengthen the platform edge and to isolate the point of percussion. Bulb type is predominantly diffuse, making it likely that, most commonly, soft hammers and, in some cases, potentially indirect percussion were used to produce blades. A small number of larger blades or blade-like flakes were struck using hard hammers. Some of these examples represent the initial shaping of a blade-core, whilst others have a point of percussion deep into a platform and represent attempts to rejuvenate a failing flaking surface.

The degree of variability within the blade assemblage is also apparent in the assemblage of blade-cores, which vary from conical bladelet-cores to more *ad hoc* examples where blades have been removed with minimal effort expended in setting up the core. Several of the latter examples were made on thermally-fractured pieces of flint, which would have carried an inherent risk of failing due to thermal faults in the nodule. Other blade-cores were made on large thick flakes, with the margins of the flake probably being used as a natural

	Artefact type		Feature group				Total
			Henge ditch 048	*Avenue ditch 143*	*Avenue ditch 579*	*Avenue ditch 593*	
Debitage and cores	Bipolar opposed-platform blade-core	Count	0	0	1	0	1
		% within feature group	0%	0%	0.7%	0%	0.2%
	Blade	Count	9	0	5	0	14
		% within feature group	2.6%	0%	3.6%	0%	2.3%
	Blade-like flake	Count	6	0	2	0	8
		% within feature group	1.7%	0%	1.4%	0%	1.3%
	Bladelet	Count	4	0	2	0	6
		% within feature group	1.1%	0%	1.4%	0%	1.0%
	Flake	Count	294	63	112	36	505
		% within feature group	84.5%	94.0%	80.6%	80.0%	84.3%
	Irregular waste	Count	20	1	5	0	26
		% within feature group	5.7%	1.5%	3.6%	0%	4.3%
	Multi-platform flake-core	Count	4	2	2	0	8
		% within feature group	1.1%	3.0%	1.4%	0%	1.3%
	Fragmentary/unclass./other arrowhead	Count	0	0	0	1	1
		% within feature group	0%	0%	0%	2.2%	0.2%
	Hammerstone	Count	0	0	1	0	1
		% within feature group	0%	0%	0.7%	0%	0.2%
	Rejuvenation flake-core face/edge	Count	0	0	1	0	1
		% within feature group	0%	0%	0.7%	0%	0.2%
	Single-platform blade-core	Count	0	0	1	0	1
		% within feature group	0%	0%	0.7%	0%	0.2%
	Single-platform flake-core	Count	2	0	0	0	2
		% within feature group	0.6%	0%	0%	0%	0.3%
	Unclassifiable/ fragmentary core	Count	1	0	3	0	4
		% within feature group	0.3%	0%	2.2%	0%	0.7%
Retouched flakes and tools	Awl	Count	1	0	0	0	1
		% within feature group	0.3%	0%	0%	0%	0.2%
	End-scraper	Count	1	0	0	0	1
		% within feature group	0.3%	0%	0%	0%	0.2%
	Microlith	Count	0	0	1	0	1
		% within feature group	0%	0%	0.7%	0%	0.2%
	Misc. retouched flake	Count	3	1	0	3	7
		% within feature group	0.9%	1.5%	0%	6.7%	1.2%
	Oblique arrowhead	Count	0	0	1	0	1
		% within feature group	0%	0%	0.7%	0%	0.2%
	Other knife	Count	1	0	0	0	1
		% within feature group	0.3%	0%	0%	0%	0.2%
	Utilised/edge-damaged flake/blade	Count	2	0	2	5	9
		% within feature group	0.6%	0%	1.4%	11.1%	1.5%
Total		Count	348	67	139	45	599
		% within feature group	100.0%	100.0%	100.0%	100.0%	100.0%

Table 5.12. The worked flint assemblage from Chalcolithic features at West Amesbury

Artefact type	Frequency	Percentage of assemblage
Blades	467	2.18
Bladelets	71	0.33
Blade-like flakes	128	0.60
Crested blades	6	0.02
Utilised blades	21	0.10
Retouched blades	1	<0.01
Microliths	14	0.07
Microburins	3	0.01
Blade-cores	19	0.09
Total	730	3.40

Table 5.13. The blade-related lithic artefacts from the entire West Amesbury assemblage

crest to initiate the first blade removals. Butler (2005: 86) suggests that the latter is a feature of Early Mesolithic blade-core working. The formalised nature of blade production is indicated by the presence of both crested blades and core-rejuvenation tablets, which indicate defined strategies for initiating blade removals and for extending the life of carefully prepared blade-cores.

Alongside the production of blades, the vast majority of the debitage relates to the removal of flakes, which make up 83% of the assemblage from pre-Bronze Age features. Some of these flake removals may relate to the preparation and maintenance of blade-cores, but the frequency of flakes and the presence of single- and multi-platform flake-cores indicate that much of it relates to intentional flake production. A broad indication of the relative frequency of blade compared to flake technology in the pre-Bronze Age contexts is provided by the fact that there are 25 flake-cores in the assemblage compared to five blade-cores.

Given the degree of residuality on the site, the overall frequency of blade production is best viewed by looking at blade-related artefacts from features of *all* periods (Table 5.13; Figures 5.71–5.72, 5.75–5.77), which, in general, outnumber the quantity of blade-associated artefacts in the pre-Bronze Age contexts by about four times. Hence, it is clear that the vast majority of the artefacts produced during the long currency of blade-working (likely to include flakes and other undiagnostic artefacts) that are represented on the site are residual finds within later contexts.

Bearing this in mind, the different chronological phases of flintworking at West Amesbury can be summarised as follows:

Upper Palaeolithic: the crested blade

P. Pettitt with B. Chan

Activity in the Upper Palaeolithic is represented by a single crested blade (SF 20080; Figure 5.71), most probably made from Greensand chert.

This crested blade, entirely patinated to a grey white, is 104mm length, 22mm maximum width and 12mm maximum thickness, with a slight distal curvature in section. The piece is in fresh condition with sharp arêtes, and no obvious signs of use. The piece displays a plain, punctiform striking platform consistent with marginal flaking and diffuse flaking scars. It displays unidirectional (*i.e.* unilateral) cresting and has a thick, asymmetrical triangular section.

Crested blades are known in Britain from Late and Final Upper Palaeolithic Creswellian/Final Magdalenian, Hengistbury-type and Long Blade assemblages spanning the period from ~14670–~11650 cal BP (from the earlier part of the Greenland Interstadial 1e / the Lateglacial Interstadial to the end of Greenland Stadial 1 / the Younger Dryas), and represent the opening or rejuvenation of blade-cores. In this case, the presence of a long blade scar down much of one lateral extent of the piece's dorsal side shows that it relates to the rejuvenation of a unipolar core. More specifically, parallels can be found in lithic assemblages from:

- Gough's Cave (Cheddar, Somerset) of which the majority are unilaterally crested (Jacobi 2004);
- the assemblage with Hamburgian affiliation from Hengistbury Head (Dorset) in which small platforms indicative of marginal flaking and unidirectional scar patterns are evident (Barton and Bergman 1992);
- the Terminal Pleistocene 'Long Blade' assemblages (probably of Ahrensburgian affiliation) of the Kennet Valley such as Avington VI (Froom and Cook 2005), and of similar affiliation, Three Ways Wharf, Uxbridge, Greater London (Lewis and Rackham 2011).

It is somewhat curious that the crested blade, which was found in buried soil 050, is the only certain Upper Palaeolithic artefact on the site, given that the blade was removed to rejuvenate an already productive core. Hence, it is likely that further blades were removed both before and after the crested blade was struck from the core. Even if these removals were not as chronologically diagnostic, the distinctive character of the raw material is such that they would have been easily spotted within the wider assemblage.

Mesolithic–Early Neolithic

Activity dating to this broad period is represented primarily by blades, blade-cores and core-rejuvenation flakes. Much of this material can only be broadly

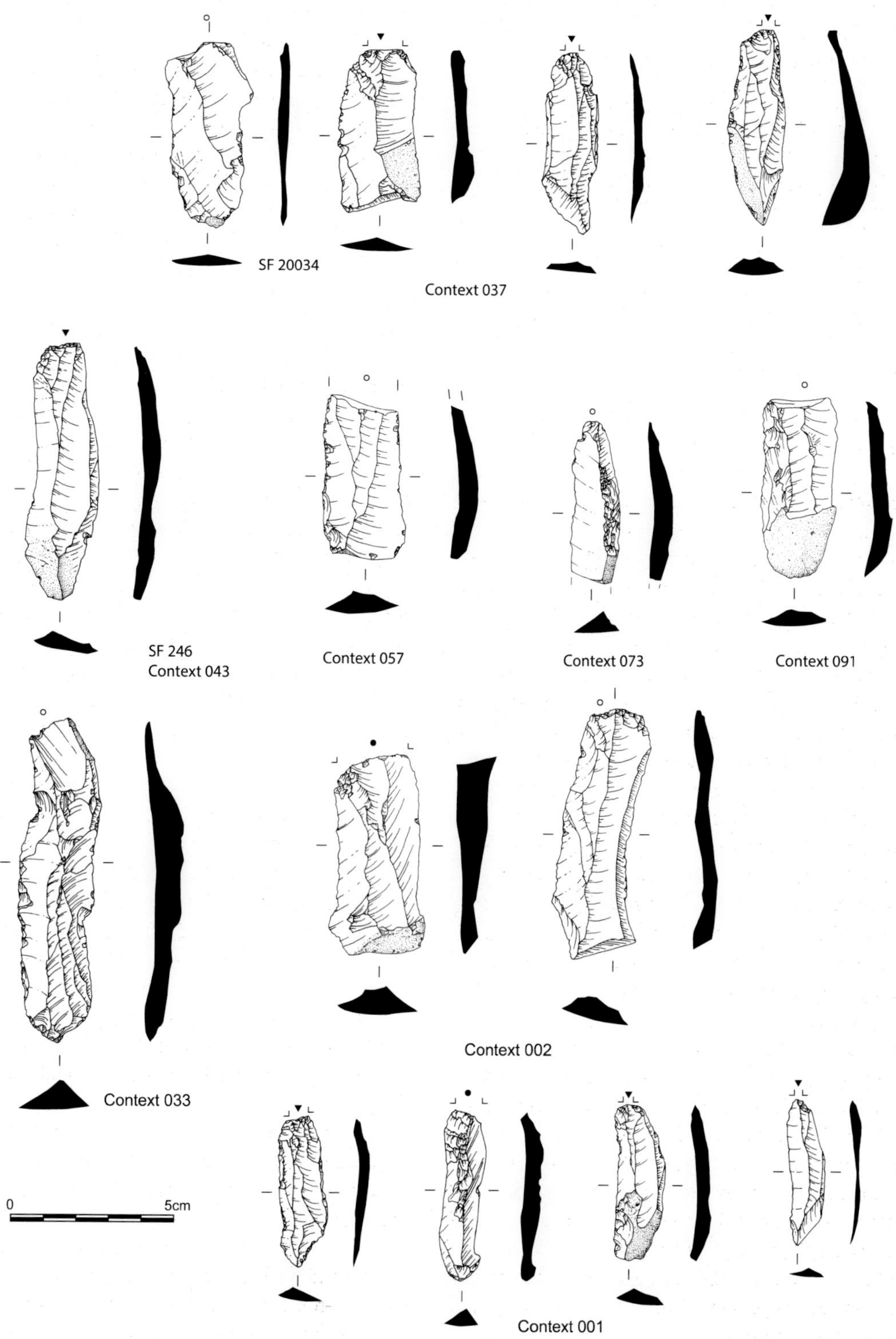

Figure 5.75. Residual blades from later contexts at West Amesbury

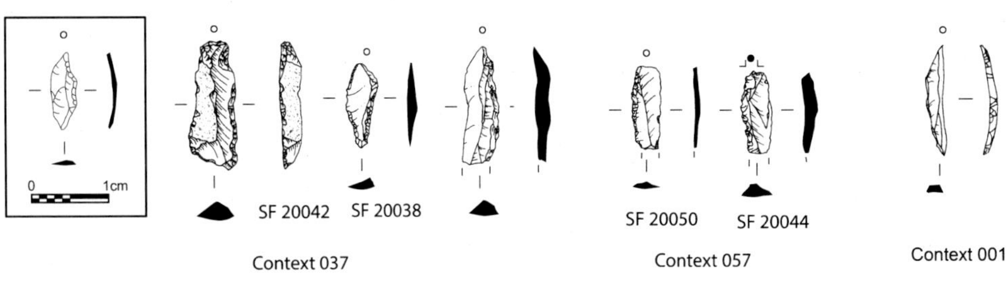

Figure 5.76. Residual microliths from later contexts at West Amesbury

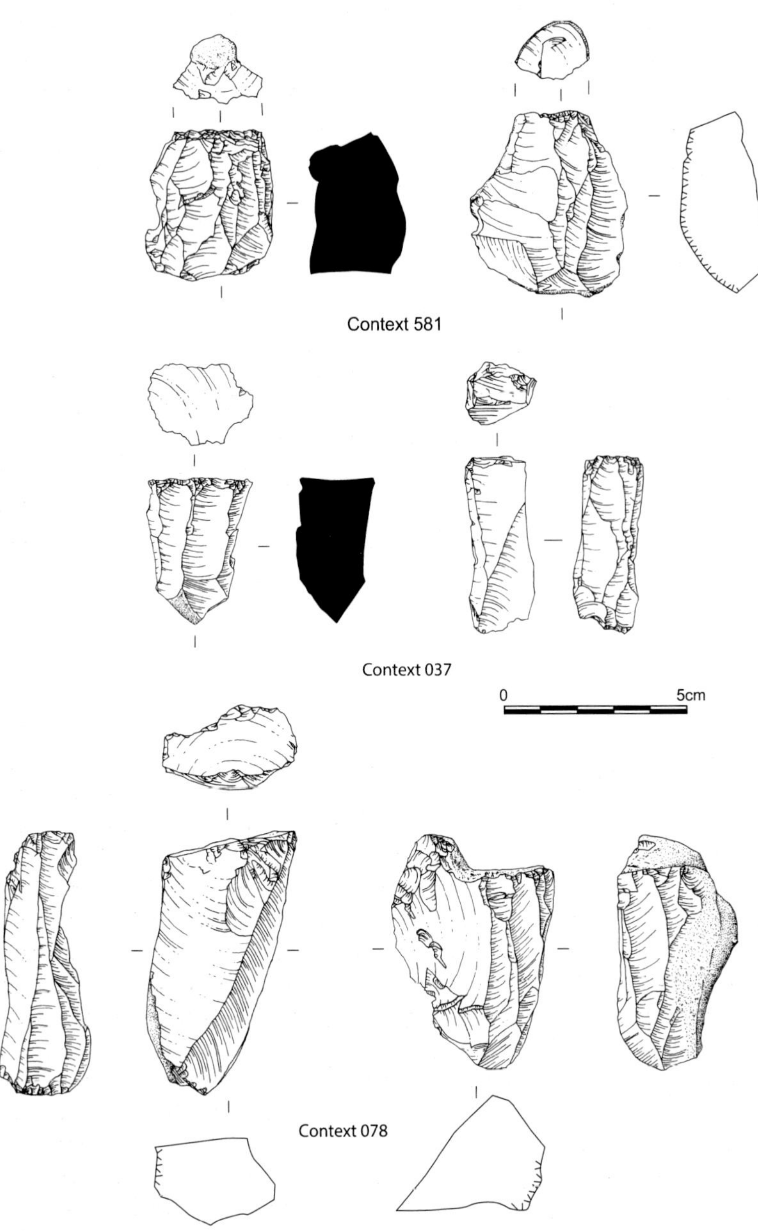

Figure 5.77. Residual blade cores from later contexts at West Amesbury

attributed to Late Mesolithic–Early Neolithic blade technology and hence the periods have been grouped together here. The main issue in this respect is recognising the difference between Early Mesolithic, Late Mesolithic and Early Neolithic blade industries. At a regional level, this problem is exacerbated by the almost complete lack of well-dated blade assemblages from these periods anywhere in the Stonehenge landscape (though see Bishop 2018 for Blick Mead). Reference to other assemblages across Britain suggests a basic pattern of broad blades in the Early Mesolithic, short narrow blades in the Late Mesolithic and short, less uniformly shaped blades in the Early Neolithic.

Associated with these shifts in blade morphology are associated changes in core-rejuvenation strategies and the degree of platform maintenance and general core control exhibited in each period. These technological shifts generate a continuous spectrum of different types of blades and it is therefore often difficult to assign an individual artefact confidently to a particular period. In the current assemblage (the material from pre-Bronze Age contexts only), it is certainly the case that many blades fall in the spaces between each idealised blade type. Hence, it is impossible to give an accurate proportion of Early Mesolithic, Late Mesolithic and Early Neolithic flint in the assemblage.

What can be said is that blades that likely relate to each of these periods are present and, on balance, it is likely that the larger proportion of them are closer to the types of blades expected of the Late Mesolithic than either of the other two periods. The reason for this is the general predominance of narrow blades with trimmed and abraded butts that have been struck from carefully prepared and maintained cores.

Whilst blades are a rather rough chronological indicator, the microliths and microburins in the assemblage more definitively suggest a Mesolithic date. Within the assemblage from pre-Bronze Age contexts there are four microliths and one microburin, whilst from deposits of all periods, there are 14 microliths and three microburins (Tables 5.5, 5.14). This indicates the relative proportion of Mesolithic material residual in later contexts. The microliths are of varied types, but most are small scalene triangles and straight-backed blades. The preference for small geometric forms suggests that this component of the assemblage is Late Mesolithic in date (Tolan-Smith 2008: 147), which confirms the assessment of the blade assemblage.

In terms of Early Neolithic activity, there are certainly some blades, blade-cores and scrapers that are relatively characteristic of flintworking of that period. Beyond this, there are no tools that are definitively Early Neolithic in date although the fragmentary arrowhead from Stonehole D could potentially be a leaf-shaped form. Whilst the low frequency of diagnostic Early Neolithic artefacts by no means excludes the possibility of Early Neolithic activity in the area, it does suggest that it was relatively limited.

Context	SF number	Type	Jacobi type
001	n/a	Small scalene triangle	7a
037b	37	Small scalene triangle	7a
037b	20042	Possible unfinished scalene triangle	7b
037c	203	Straight-backed blade	5a
037c	20038	Drill bit (mèche de forêt)	n/a
050	20077	Obliquely truncated point	1a
050	20078	Small scalene triangle	7b
051b	93	Straight-backed bladelet	5a
057	20050	Straight-backed blade	5a
057a	20044	Straight-backed blade	5a
082	20092	Miscellaneous type	n/a
547	20108	Rod	6a
578	20020	Small scalene triangle	7a
581	20021	Straight-backed blade	5a

Table 5.14. The assemblage of microliths from all contexts from the West Amesbury excavations (microlith types relate to Jacobi 1978)

Middle to Late Neolithic–Chalcolithic

Flintworking in the Late Neolithic in southern Britain generally revolves around the working of single- or multi-platform flake-cores in a manner that reflects a general decline in core control. In the Stonehenge environs during this period platform maintenance is rare and the failure of platforms is dealt with by either rotating the core or discarding it (Harding 1990: 217–18). In general, the debitage from the Late Neolithic contexts at West Amesbury fits within the character of flintworking in the period.

In terms of more diagnostic artefacts, the assemblage from pre-Bronze Age contexts is limited to two chisel arrowheads, from Stoneholes A and K, and the finely worked oblique arrowhead from the eastern Avenue ditch. The chisel arrowhead from ditch 533 comes from a secondary fill containing a lump of slag, whilst the oblique arrowhead from the Avenue ditch comes from a tertiary fill. Both of the chisel arrowheads from the stoneholes are from packing deposits associated with erecting the stones.

Within the total assemblage from deposits of all periods there are 11 chisel arrowheads, two petit tranchet derivative arrowheads and five oblique arrowheads. The arrowheads reported here from the stoneholes and the Avenue ditch are the only ones within the assemblage that have the potential to be contemporary with their deposits.

The chronology of transverse arrowheads is understood to broadly span the Middle to Late Neolithic. Chisel and petit tranchet (PT) arrowheads are most commonly found on sites with Peterborough Ware (Wainwright with Longworth 1971: 259; Edmonds 1995: 100), but have also been found with Grooved

Ware pottery. Oblique arrowheads are only found with Grooved Ware pottery associations (Wainwright with Longworth 1971: 257–9; Green 1980: 108; Butler 2005: 158). Therefore it appears that all three transverse types overlap chronologically, but PT and chisel arrowheads started earlier and only oblique arrowheads persisted in use after the first few centuries of the Late Neolithic.

In the context of the Stonehenge landscape, the connection between the different types of transverse arrowheads and Grooved Ware is best indicated by the contrast between the Grooved Ware pits at Woodlands (Stone 1949; Stone and Young 1948) and at Ratfyn (Stone 1935), which are associated with chisel and PT arrowheads, and the later assemblage from Durrington Walls, which is dominated by oblique arrowheads (Wainwright with Longworth 1971; Chan 2010; see synthesis in Volume 2).

The chronological implication of the West Amesbury arrowhead assemblage is that there was an increase in activity on the site during the currency of chisel and PT arrowheads (*i.e.* the Middle Neolithic and/or the earlier part of the Late Neolithic), rather than during the period of use of oblique arrowheads (*i.e.* the Late Neolithic). It was during this period of chisel and PT arrowhead use that the stone circle was constructed. Activity on the site then continued into the later part of the Late Neolithic, as indicated by the presence of the oblique arrowheads, which probably relate to the period of construction of the henge ditch and the Stonehenge Avenue before the mid-23rd century cal BC. Arrowheads of this type have frequent associations with henges in the area, such as at Durrington Walls (see Volume 3) and Coneybury (Richards 1990: 141).

Discussion

The assemblage from West Amesbury indicates the use of flint and chert on the site from the Upper Palaeolithic to the post-medieval period. The specifically pre-Bronze Age contexts on the site contain artefacts that can be dated to the Upper Palaeolithic, Early Mesolithic, Late Mesolithic, Early Neolithic and Late Neolithic. The only period represented stratigraphically that has produced no diagnostic artefacts is the Chalcolithic (*c.* 2450–2200 cal BC), although oblique arrowheads may have continued to its transition. It is evident, therefore, that the site bore witness to an extremely long trajectory of human activity prior to the construction of Bluestonehenge. At least in terms of lithics, the evidence for pre-monument activity is greater than for any of the other monuments excavated by the SRP.

What makes the site stand out in this respect is the evidence for Mesolithic activity which – barring stray artefacts and the postholes in the Stonehenge car park – has historically been conspicuously absent across the Stonehenge environs. It is perhaps unsurprising that, if Mesolithic activity is to be found, it should be discovered adjacent to the River Avon rather than on the chalk plateau where the majority of Stonehenge research has been focused. Indeed, the identification of Mesolithic activity at West Amesbury has coincided with the discovery of a much larger Mesolithic assemblage at the site of Blick Mead, situated around a spring approximately 900m northeast of Bluestonehenge near Vespasian's Camp (see Figure 9.4; Jacques *et al.* 2010; 2012; 2018; Jacques and Phillips 2014).

An evaluation in 2003 also identified a Mesolithic flint scatter associated with a buried forest soil 1.10km to the northeast of West Amesbury and about 150m from the present course of the River Avon (Wiltshire SMR No. SU14SE054). The well-known Late Mesolithic site of Downton (Higgs 1959) also lies close to the Avon, roughly 20km south of West Amesbury.

It seems then that there was a regular pattern of activity along the course of the River Avon in the Mesolithic. This fits with a picture of hunter-gatherers utilising an ecologically diverse area of the landscape that provided access to water (both rivers and springs), terrestrial and freshwater flora and fauna, and easily accessible flint. Perhaps the important question is where West Amesbury fitted within this pattern of occupation.

The assemblage suggests that Mesolithic activity at West Amesbury was at its height during the Late Mesolithic. The character of these activities might have differed from both Downton and Blick Mead because the microlith assemblage at West Amesbury consists mainly of small scalene triangles and straight-backed blades, whereas Downton (Higgs 1959: 220) and Blick Mead have many obliquely truncated points (Bishop pers. comm.). The microlith assemblage at West Amesbury is also considerably smaller in number than the other two sites, although it is difficult to assess whether this is due to the extent of post-Mesolithic disturbance of the site.

Whilst the size of the blade assemblage does point to the active working of blade-cores at West Amesbury, the small number of microburins may be taken to suggest that the production of microliths was not a primary activity. This is another point of contrast with Blick Mead, where microburins are numerous (Bishop in Jacques and Phillips 2014: 16). Hence, whilst it is difficult to assess, it is possible that the Mesolithic flintworking at West Amesbury was concerned mainly with the preparation of blade-cores and perhaps the production of blades for use elsewhere. In each case, the production and/or use of tools and microliths was not the primary concern.

Understanding the character of Mesolithic activity at West Amesbury is made difficult because much of the material was residual in later features. This makes it impossible to assess the time-depth represented by this part of the assemblage. Hence the Mesolithic assemblage could represent a single task-specific episode, or sporadic activity spread over a thousand years or more. On current evidence it seems more likely that the situation was closer to the latter than the former. Certainly, within the excavated area, there was no evidence of focused activity associated with a camp in the form of either burnt flint or burnt bone, as has been found at Blick Mead (Jacques *et al.* 2012; Jacques and Phillips 2014), or hearths and stakeholes as was found at Downton (Higgs 1959). The Mesolithic assemblage from Blick Mead is considerably larger than that from West Amesbury. There are also indications that the Mesolithic flintwork may be spread over an area of hundreds of square metres (Bishop in Jacques and Phillips 2014: 17).

With Blick Mead's timespan covering nearly four millennia from the eighth millennium BC until *c.* 4000 cal BC, its relative proximity to West Amesbury raises the possibility that the two sites might have been connected, with West Amesbury perhaps acting as an area for retrieving flint and producing blades for use at Blick Mead. Alternatively, the Mesolithic occupation at West Amesbury covers a much larger area than that excavated, with the flintwork found within the trenches and test pits (reported earlier in this chapter) representing only part of a much denser and larger scatter, the majority of which is located outside the riverside field in which the henge and stone circle are situated.

Despite uncertainties about the character of the Mesolithic activity, what can be said is that, unlike many other Neolithic monuments in the Stonehenge landscape, Bluestonehenge was constructed in a locale that had a demonstrably long history of use stretching well back into the Mesolithic. In this respect, perhaps its closest parallel lies at the other end of the Avenue, with Stonehenge itself and the Early Mesolithic postholes in the former Stonehenge car park (Vatcher and Vatcher 1973; see *The Avenue's construction and purpose* in Chapter 8).

If anything the evidence for activity at Bluestonehenge diminishes rather than increases after the Mesolithic. It seems that this part of the riverside was subject to little more than sporadic visits during the Early Neolithic. It was not until the Middle–Late Neolithic that the site became a focus for activity again. This activity evidently involved the construction of Bluestonehenge. The chisel arrowheads found in the packing of the stoneholes may date to this phase of activity, or may potentially pre-date it. Given that there are 11 chisel and two petit tranchet arrowheads in the assemblage from all contexts of all periods, it seems a little unlikely that such a concentration of arrowheads is unconnected with the stone circle. The arrowheads and other lithic material tell us that this part of the riverside was a focus of activity in this period, and there is no indication of any reason other than the stone circle for the presence here of this Middle–Late Neolithic assemblage.

More widely, the connection between the River Avon and chisel and PTD arrowheads is suggested by the Ratfyn and Woodlands Grooved Ware pits (Stone 1935; Stone 1949; Stone and Young 1948; see Figure 9.4). Another similarity between the finds from West Amesbury and the lithic material from the Ratfyn and Woodlands pits is the presence of serrated flakes. At West Amesbury, within the assemblages from all phases, five serrated flakes were found in total, two of which were in the fills of stoneholes. Although the number is small, it is of potential significance as it recalls the presence of serrated flakes in a series of pits along the course of the Avon including the Woodlands and Ratfyn pits, the Cuckoo Stone pit 180 (excavated by Colin Richards; see Chapter 7), pit 265 beneath Durrington 67 round barrow and pit 008 under Durrington 70 round barrow (excavated by Josh Pollard and Dave Robinson; see Volume 3).

Following the erection of Bluestonehenge, the construction and initial use of the West Amesbury henge and the east end of the Stonehenge Avenue do not appear to have been associated with an increase in the use of worked flint and chert. Indeed, the assemblage associated with these monuments is relatively unremarkable except for the oblique arrowhead deposited in the tertiary fill of the Avenue ditch. In this respect, apart from a few individual artefacts, there is little in the assemblage to suggest that unusual activities took place in and around this riverside end of the Avenue or the henge. This is a pattern repeated in the primary fills of many monuments across the Stonehenge landscape, such as the Greater Cursus and Amesbury 42 long barrow (see Chapter 3) as well as Coneybury henge (Richards 1990: 144), all of which produced few tools (see synthesis in Volume 2). In the case of the Cursus and Coneybury henge, knapping clusters in their ditches appear to relate to the working of flint nodules exposed in the ditch sides. This is not the case at West Amesbury, although this may relate either to the differing character and use of Bluestonehenge or to the fact that, unlike the other monuments mentioned, the West Amesbury henge was not cut into unweathered chalk.

5.7. Other artefacts of stone, antler and bone from West Amesbury

M. Parker Pearson with G. Davies and R. Ixer

Stone

SF 502 context 064. An incomplete polished stone axe, of which only the butt survives (Figure 5.78). It is 65mm long, 43mm wide and at least 25mm thick. Most of one flat side has been lost, and the butt end is damaged. According to Rob Ixer, this is a fine-grained tuff with such pronounced foliation that it would have made the axe-head unsuitable for use. It is not from any of the Implement Petrology Group's recognised axe groups, and its geological provenance is unknown. It was found not in a Neolithic

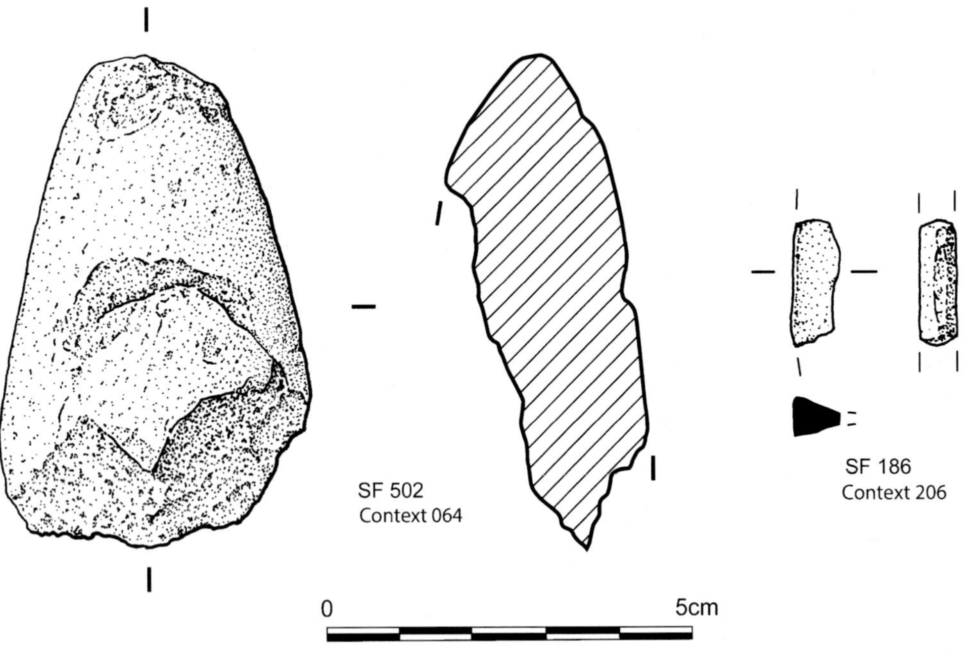

Figure 5.78. Stone artefacts from West Amesbury; a fragment of ground stone axe and a piece of ground sandstone

context but in Bronze Age tertiary fill (059=058=064) of the henge ditch.

SF 186 context 206. A thin sliver of sandstone (18mm × 5mm wide × 7mm thick). It may originally have had a V-shaped section; one of its sides is ground flat (Figure 5.78). This is the only worked example of three pieces of Mesozoic arkosic sandstone recovered from this context (see petrographic synthesis in Volume 2); they can probably be provenanced to a locality in southern England.

Antler

SF 491 context 095. The tip of a tine, most likely a brow tine (in two fragments, total length 106mm). It is likely to be the end of a red deer antler pick, broken-off and embedded in the chalk base of the henge ditch. Its tip is slightly worn (Figure 5.79).

SF 503 context 132. An antler pick (535mm long) made from a shed red deer antler. The brow tine which formed the point of the pick has been battered and broken. The bez tine survives only as a small, 40mm-long bud-like projection, which appears to be a developmental condition and not the result of bone-working (this can also be seen on a red deer antler from the Cuckoo Stone; see Chapter 7). The trez tine has been removed, and that part of the handle which continues beyond it appears to be heavily worn. The pick is in a very fragmentary condition (Figure 5.22).

SF 529/SF 571 context 159. An incomplete antler pick (460mm long) made from a red deer antler. The burr and brow tine at the base of the antler are missing, having been removed prior to deposition. The bez and trez tines survive as small protuberances but preservation is too poor to establish whether these were broken-off or not, or otherwise deliberately shortened. The pick is in a very fragmentary condition (Figure 5.25).

SF 580 context 091. The tip of a tine, most likely a brow tine (133mm long). It is likely to be the pick-end of a pick made from red deer antler. Its tip is slightly worn (Figures 5.63, 5.79).

SF 557 and SF 573 context 095a. Pieces of the beam (245mm long) and crown (360mm long) removed from a red deer antler. These appear not to have been fashioned into artefacts, but may have been removed in the manufacture of an antler pick (Figures 5.47, 5.49).

SF 586 context 095a. An antler pick (543mm long) made from a shed red deer antler. The brow tine which formed the point of the pick has been broken. Both the bez and trez tines have been removed, the latter less tidily. The beam ends in an irregular break (Figures 5.48, 5.79).

Bone

SF 485 context 095. A cattle scapula (175mm long and at least 50mm wide), heavily worn and broken. Wear-marks along its surviving blade are consistent with its having been used as a shovel (Figure 5.80).

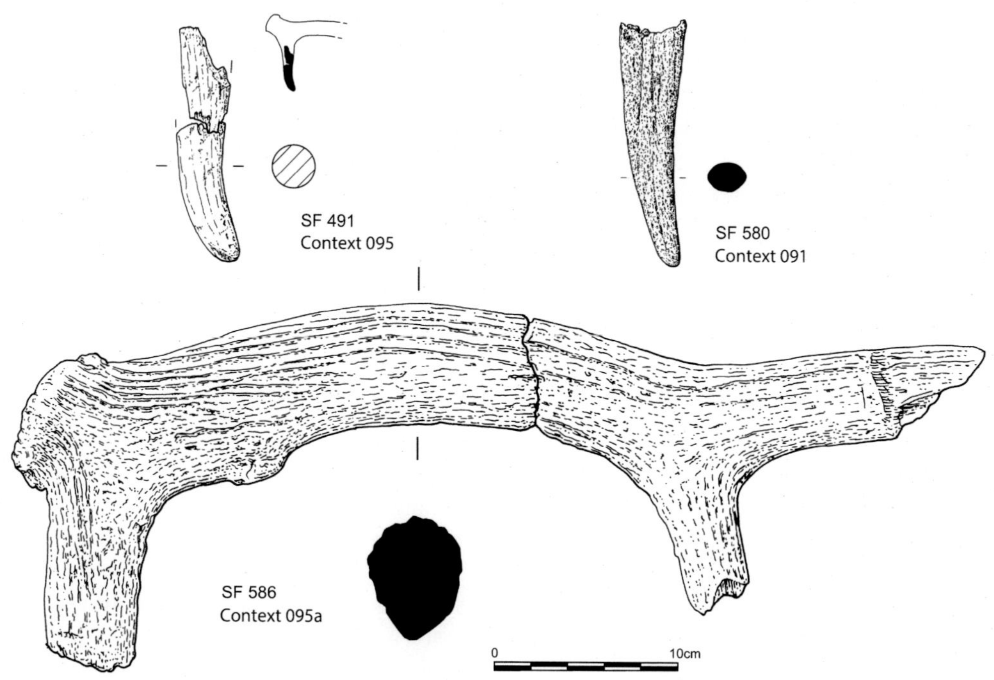

Figure 5.79. Antler artefacts from West Amesbury

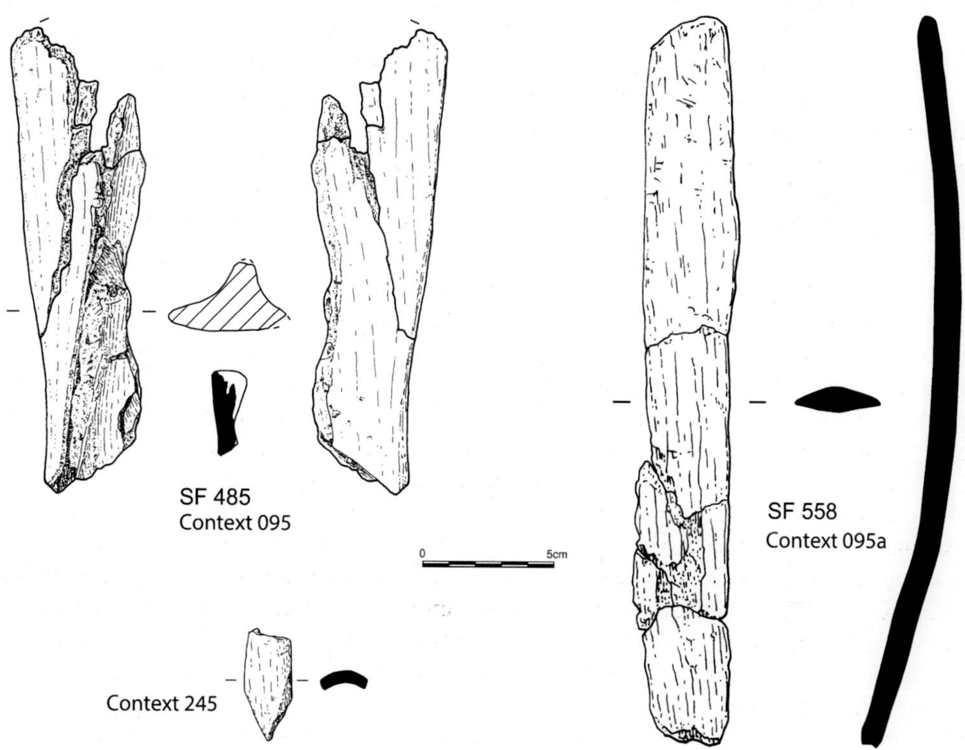

Figure 5.80. Bone artefacts from West Amesbury

SF 558 context 095a. A cattle rib (270mm long). Its poor state of preservation prevents identification of wear patterning but its context in association with a hammerstone and flint cores suggests that it could have been used in pressure-flaking of flint (Figure 5.80).

Context 245. The broken-off tip of a bone point (41mm long × 18mm wide). It is blackened through partial burning, particularly towards the end of the tip which has been formed by two oblique cuts to create a point (Figure 5.80).

5.8. Faunal remains from West Amesbury

C. Minniti, U. Albarella and S. Viner-Daniels

The animal remains from the Late Neolithic features at West Amesbury derive from packing layers (137, 179 and 245) to support the standing stones, fills of pits left by the extracted stones (132 and 159) and from the fill of a hollow (123=134=141) formed in the footprint of the extracted standing stones A, C, D and I, which belonged to the bluestone circle (Table 5.15). Materials and methods of faunal analysis are described in Chapter 7. The animal bones came from the main domesticated species, but a red deer tooth (from layer 245 of Stonehole I) and fragments of red deer bone and antler (in addition to the picks) were also identified.

An upper molar from a sheep/goat was recovered from a buried soil (172) pre-dating the henge, but this specimen is probably intrusive.

The zooarchaeological assemblages from the henge ditch and Avenue ditches are particularly small, and are characterised by a predominance of domestic mammal bones (Table 5.16). Cattle are the most common taxon, while sheep/goat and pig are represented almost equally. Red deer is represented by fragments of a shed antler, a fragment of radius and an astragalus.

The presence of a tarsometatarsus fragment of domestic fowl from the tertiary fill of the Avenue ditch (578) is probably intrusive and is likely to be of medieval date.

A single cat mandible was recovered from the uppermost fill of the henge ditch (037a). It has clear cut-marks, presumably the result of the animal having been skinned. The specimen is particularly small when compared with modern domestic cat (let alone wild cat, which is generally much larger), although damage to the carnassial tooth does not allow us to assess its size precisely. The domestic cat was introduced into Britain in the Iron Age, but did not become widespread until Roman times (O'Connor 2010). However, the context in which the cat mandible was found also contained several sherds of medieval pottery, therefore making it likely that the specimen is intrusive.

5.9. Charred plant remains and wood charcoal from West Amesbury

E. Simmons

One hundred and eighteen flotation samples comprising just over 2,600 litres of soil were processed by flotation and assessed using the methods outlined in Chapter 7.

Rich assemblages of charred plant remains and small quantities of wood charcoal fragments were found to be present in the stonehole fills and in the Chalcolithic–Bronze Age sequences in the henge ditch. The crop types represented in the charred plant remains assemblage were, however, found to be the same as those present in medieval contexts from the site (reported in Volume 4) and include rye, which is more typical of the medieval period than the Neolithic and Bronze Age. Since cereal grains from the stonehole fills at Bluestonehenge were radiocarbon-dated to the first millennium AD (see Marshall *et al.*, above, and Chapter 11), it is therefore assumed that the charred plant remains and wood charcoal in these deposits are likely to be intrusive so no further analysis has been undertaken.

5.10. Bluestonehenge and Stonehenge

M. Parker Pearson and C. Richards

On current evidence, it seems most likely that the West Amesbury stoneholes once held bluestones erected in a circle of about 25 stones. They were erected either around the same time as bluestones were set within the 56 Aubrey Holes at Stonehenge (see Chapter 4; Parker Pearson *et al.* 2009) or in the half-millennium afterwards. This could have been up to and including the time-period during which Stage 2 at Stonehenge was constructed (beginning in *2740–2505 cal BC* and ending in *2470–2300 cal BC*).

It seems likely that the stones at West Amesbury were erected at a time when chisel arrowheads were current, during *c.* 3400–2600 BC. It would seem logical if they were set up around the same time as Stonehenge Stage 1 (beginning in *3080–2950 cal BC* and ending in *2865–2755 cal BC*).

The stone circle appears to have been dismantled – and the stones presumably removed from the site – just before the construction of the encircling henge ditch and bank in the period 2470–2200 cal BC, which is dated by the broken-off antler pick in the henge ditch. This date for the dismantling of the stone circle is corroborated by the antler pick, dating to 2470–2280 cal BC, left on the ramp of Stonehole A. The stone circle must therefore have been taken down around the time of Stonehenge Stage 3 (beginning *2400–2105 cal BC* and ending *2300–2105 cal BC*).

Table 5.15. Numbers of animal bones and teeth (NISP) from the fills of Stoneholes A, C, D and J (P=packing layer) at West Amesbury. CS = coarse-sieved; FS = flotation sieve. Non-countable bones are shown in brackets

Context	*132*	*137*	*159*	*179*	*123=134=146*	*245*	
Fill type	**P**	**P**	**P**	**P**	**Hollow**	**P**	**Total**
	CS	**CS**	**CS**	**CS**	**CS**	**FS>10**	
Mammal	**NISP**	**NISP**	**NISP**	**NISP**	**NISP**	**NISP**	**NISP**
Cattle					1		1
Sheep/Goat			4				4
Pig		1(+1)	(1)		1		2
Red deer	(1)		(1)	(1)		1	1
Total	0	1	4	0	2	1	8

Table 5.16. Numbers of animal bones and teeth (NISP) from the henge ditch, the Avenue ditches and other prehistoric features. Non-countable bones are denoted in brackets.
* = probably intrusive

	Chalcolithic	**Bronze Age**	**Bronze Age**		**Prehistoric**	
	Henge/Avenue ditches		*122*	*185*	*533*	*616*
	CS	**CS**	**CS**	**CS**	**CS**	**CS**
Mammal	**NISP**	**NISP**	**NISP**	**NISP**	**NISP**	**NISP**
Cattle	3	12			2	
?Cattle		2				
Sheep/Goat	1	1			4	
Pig	2	4	2			
Horse						1
Dog	1					
Red deer	(5)	1(+3)		1		
Cat		1*				
Domestic fowl	1*					
Total	8	21	2	1	6	1

The potentially close match between the basal impression within Stonehole D and the shape of Stonehenge Bluestone 68 raises the possibility (discussed further in Chapter 4) that many of the West Amesbury circle's stones still stand today within the inner bluestone horseshoe at Stonehenge (Cleal *et al.* 1995: figs 116, 128; see Figure 4.1). For example, the trapezoidal imprints in the bottoms of Stoneholes F and I are consistent with the shapes and sizes of Bluestones 63 and 61.

If the estimated 25 stones from West Amesbury were moved to Stonehenge, the total number of bluestones used at Stonehenge rises from 56 (in the Aubrey Holes, later transferred to the Q & R Holes; see Chapter 4) to around 81. This conforms closely with Pitts' (2000: 137) estimate of 79–89 bluestones in this later phase of Stonehenge (by the time of Stage 4; beginning in *2210–2030 cal BC* and ending in *2155–1920 cal BC*). It also explains where the twenty or so 'extra' bluestones might have come from, without more stone having to be brought from Preseli at this later date.

If bluestones were moved from the riverside at West Amesbury to Stonehenge in Stage 3 of Stonehenge's construction, that places the movement of these Bluestonehenge stones in the same period during which the Stonehenge Avenue's ditches were dug (*2500–2270 cal BC* (*93% probability;* see Chapters 4 and 8). Might the West Amesbury bluestones have been dragged along the very route of the Avenue? The most gentle incline on the route of the Avenue for dragging monoliths is the stretch from its riverside end to the Avenue's elbow (see Chapter 8):

- The location of the Bluestonehenge circle on its tongue of chalk bedrock is at the riverside end of a spur which leads gently uphill between two small valleys (one beside Vespasian's Camp and the other leading towards Coneybury henge), curving northwest along a gentle slope to King Barrow Ridge (see Figure 8.1).
- Here the Avenue avoids the high ground of New King Barrows to its south and, on attaining the top of the ridge, heads westwards down the gentle slope of a dry valley leading into Stonehenge Bottom.
- However, the steep slope of the Avenue where it turns (rising southwestwards along a small ridge), just 500m

from Stonehenge, interrupts this easy progress. For people moving megaliths, it would have been best avoided in favour of following gentler contours by moving westwards up the dry valley at that point before turning southwards to Stonehenge. Such a route would have avoided the small ridge beside Newall's Mound (a natural mound immediately east of the Avenue elbow; see Chapter 8) and the solstice-aligned length of the Avenue leading into Stonehenge's northeast entrance.

The West Amesbury bluestone circle provides corroborative evidence for the notion that the route of the Stonehenge Avenue marked a path for the ancestors, leading from the domain of the living at Durrington Walls via the liminal zone of the River Avon to the domain of the dead at Stonehenge itself (Parker Pearson and Ramilisonina 1998a). Although traces of activity in the form of worked lithics are dense at the riverside end of the Avenue, the rarity of scrapers from the excavations and the paucity of Neolithic ceramics and animal bones indicate that this was more of a specialised workplace and/or ritual locale. Indeed, the paucity of recovered material contemporary with the erection of the bluestones at Bluestonehenge is consistent with Stonehenge in particular (with its 11 sherds of Grooved Ware; Cleal *et al.* 1995: 350) and stone circles in general (Richards 2013: 2–7).

What then was the purpose of the West Amesbury bluestone circle and why was it eventually dismantled? The collapsed topsoil within the stoneholes contained large quantities of charcoal, indicating that fire was an important part of activities within or around the ring. Since the absence of domestic debris indicates that these were not linked to cooking or feasting, it seems most likely that fire served to unite people around its warmth and/or to purify, perhaps together with use of the river's water as a purification agent.

The act of bringing together bluestones and sarsens within Stonehenge's Stage 3 (between *2400–2220 cal BC* and *2300–2100 cal BC*) also takes on a new light. As intimated in the discussion in Chapter 4, this may have occurred as part of an overall process of merging and consolidation, bringing the West Amesbury bluestone circle to Stonehenge, perhaps to form the inner circle of bluestones (later re-designed as an inner oval and ultimately an inner horseshoe) at the heart of the monument. In this event we witness not only new stone arrangements constructed at Stonehenge, but also an architecture that both elevated a single site to a material microcosm of an earlier local monumental landscape and also referenced the networks of practice that once extended to west Wales.

Chapter 6

Sarsens at Stonehenge

B. Chan, C. Richards, K. Whitaker and M. Parker Pearson

6.1. Stonehenge reworked – working the sarsens

C. Richards and M. Parker Pearson

Although the Welsh bluestones define the 'exotic' nature of Stonehenge, it is the gigantic sarsens comprising the outer ring and inner trilithons that create its spectacular scale of monumentality (Figures 6.1–6.2). These are dated in the new chronological framework to Stage 2, beginning in *2740–2505 cal BC* and ending in *2470–2300 cal BC* (see Table 11.7; Darvill *et al.* 2012; Marshall *et al.* 2012; Parker Pearson 2013). A handful of sarsens may have been erected during Stage 1 (beginning in *3080–2950 cal BC* and ending in *2865–2755 cal BC*). These are thought to have stood in Stoneholes B, C and 97 (within Stonehenge's northeast entrance; see Figure 4.4) and within Stonehenge (WA 2321 in the monument's east sector and possibly WA 3433 in the north sector; Cleal *et al.* 1995: 181–2, figs 80, 82, 97).

Figure 6.1. Stonehenge viewed from the west

Figure 6.2. Stonehenge viewed from the east

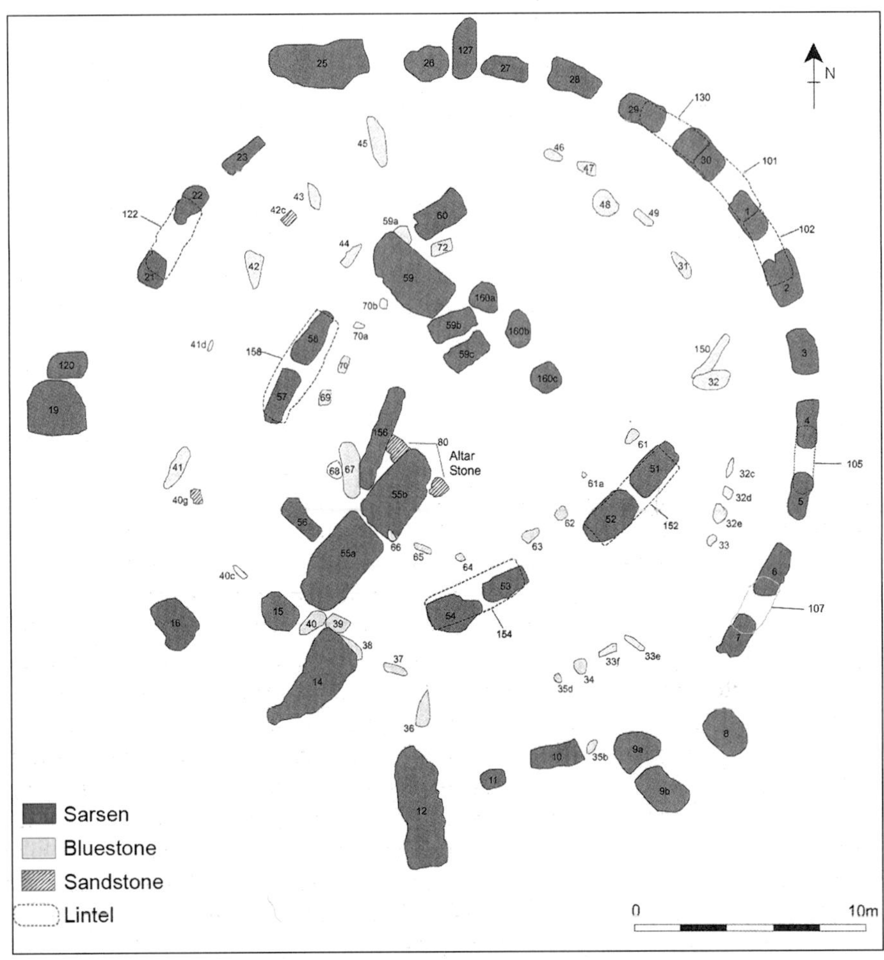

Figure 6.3. Plan of Stonehenge today, showing the sarsens in dark grey (after Richards 2017); © Julian Richards

Figure 6.4. Stonehenge viewed from the northeast

Traditionally Stonehenge's sarsens are considered to have been brought from the Marlborough Downs *c.* 20 miles (30km) to the north, though little trace remains of the large hollows that William Stukeley interpreted in the 1720s as their quarry pits (Stukeley 1869; Parker Pearson 2016b). That said, other sources for the Stonehenge sarsens have been considered on as well as beyond Salisbury Plain and a new source has now been identified in West Woods, 2 miles (3km) south of the Marlborough Downs (Nash *et al.* 2020). The arguments surrounding all these possible sources are detailed in Chapter 7.

In the architectural arrangement remaining at Stonehenge today, the bluestones are dwarfed by the remaining 52 sarsens (of an original estimated *c.* 83 stones; Figures 6.3–6.4). The estimated average weight of the sarsens comprising the outer circle is in the region of 20 tons, and the weight of the largest monolith (Stone 56) in the inner trilithon horseshoe, towering at an immense 7.30m, is *c.* 28.10 tons (Figure 6.5; Field *et al.* 2015: 129 *contra* Atkinson 1956: 24).

Despite this discrepancy in scale between the two types of stone, it is the 'exotic' bluestones that dominate both academic interest and the assemblage of waste stone recovered from all excavations within the monument. In his discussion of the 'Stonehenge layer' (the layer of stone debris at the base of the topsoil in and around the stone circle), Atkinson mentioned the lack of substantial quantities of sarsen within the confines of the monument (Atkinson 1956: 53–5). Clearly, an understanding of Stonehenge requires a deeper investigation into working practices surrounding the sarsen stones.

In his 1982 report on his excavation beside the Heel Stone, Pitts suggested that 'conventional wisdom favours the view that the sarsen megaliths were shaped at their original topographic source and that substantial debris at Stonehenge represents recent destruction' (1982: 102). This statement indicates a degree of certainty that was not exhibited by the earlier excavators of Stonehenge (*e.g.* Atkinson 1956: 117–25). The problem of where the stones were dressed appears to revolve around the apparently contradictory nature of the evidence and a series of uncritical assumptions (*cf* Montague and Gardiner 1995: 398).

Figure 6.5. Laser-scan reconstruction of the great trilithon – Stones 55, 56 and 156 (from Abbott and Anderson-Whymark 2012); © Historic England

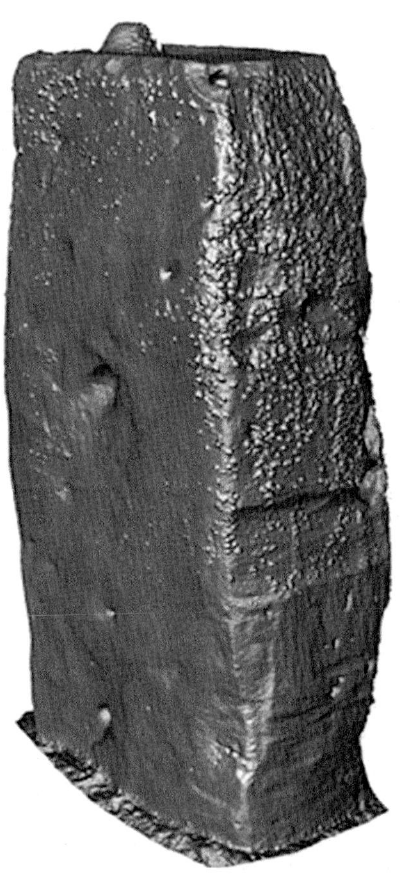

Figure 6.6. Laser scan of trilithon upright Stone 60 (from Abbott and Anderson-Whymark 2012); © Historic England

As mentioned above, with regard to the evidence obtained from the sequence of excavations at Stonehenge, there is the relative absence of sarsen debris within the 'Stonehenge layer' (Atkinson 1956: 53–5). At first sight, this would appear to indicate an off-site pattern of sarsen-working, certainly for the primary flaking, which would have entailed the use of large stone mauls. However, large mauls, both complete and broken, are present in substantial numbers within Stonehenge (Cleal *et al.* 1995: 386–7). This suggests that sarsen stone-dressing did occur at the site, the working of the large and resistant sarsen stone requiring larger hammerstones than can be expected for dressing the smaller and occasionally more easily fracturable bluestones. Moreover, the size range of the recovered mauls is consistent with their employment in all stages of stone-working, including primary stone-flaking. The laser-scan study reveals several methods of working the sarsen: the sarsen circle and trilithons are pick-dressed and the trilithons additionally have fine transverse tooling (Figure 6.6). The latter is also found on those bluestones that were dressed (Abbott and Anderson-Whymark 2012: 17–20).

Atkinson (1956: 117) does suggest that a degree of shaping would have been inherent within the sarsen-quarrying process and therefore occurred before the stones arrived at Stonehenge (see also Stone 1924: 81–2). However, 'once delivered on the site at Stonehenge the stones had to receive their final dressing, reducing them to the correct shape and section' (Atkinson 1956: 118). Atkinson (*ibid.*: 119) considered this to have occurred before the stones were erected, given the presence of tooled surfaces on the bases of the sarsen uprights below ground, and given the incorporation of stone hammers as packing stones within the stoneholes, and because it appears to be the easiest method of dressing megaliths.

Of course, the distinctive form of megalithic architecture displayed by the sarsens at Stonehenge necessarily required a degree of *in situ* dressing and modification. However, identification of the location of primary sarsen-working – basically the shaping of the stones – has proved problematic because of the nature of the 'Stonehenge layer', the interpretation of which has long been contentious (see Whitaker, below, for further discussion of the Stonehenge layer).

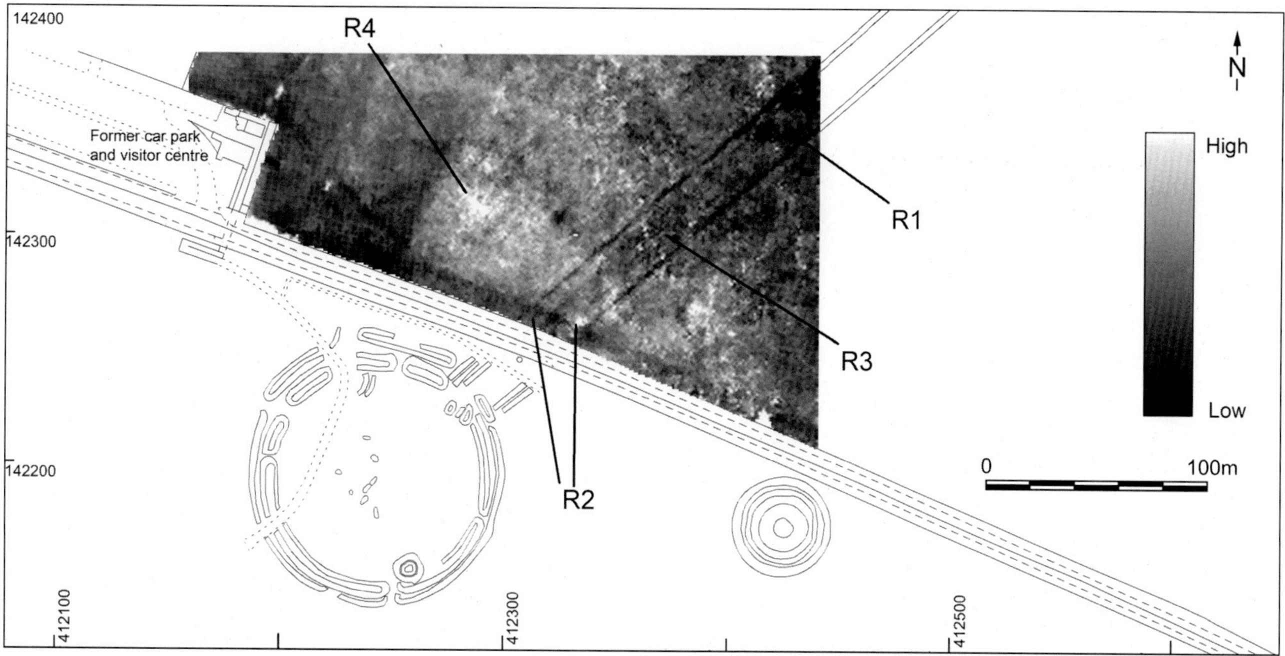

Figure 6.7. Earth resistance survey in the field north of Stonehenge; R1–R3 are features associated with the Avenue (see Chapter 8) and R4 is a high-resistance anomaly

William Hawley interpreted this layer as deriving from stone-working and construction (1925: 21–2). Conversely, Atkinson attributed it to the destruction and removal of stones (1956: 53–5). In assessing the presence of stone debris within the Stonehenge layer, Julie Gardiner notes: 'It is possible that the Sarsens were dressed on site whereas the Bluestones were not, though the distribution of sarsen fragments away from the settings does not seem to be notably different from that of the bluestone fragments, though the quantities involved may be less' (Cleal *et al.* 1995: 335).

The acceptance of sarsens having been worked within Stonehenge is based on the assumption that secondary dressing, involving pounding by mauls and hammerstones, would have created sarsen 'sand' as opposed to recognisable flakes (Atkinson 1956: 120). For instance, careful 'sampling' of different contexts, including the Stonehenge layer, during excavations by Atkinson revealed 'that [sarsen] chips represent a total volume of no more than a dozen cubic feet, a tiny fraction of the total volume of stone removed in the course of dressing. On the other hand analysis of soil from the site has shown that it contains an abnormal proportion of siliceous sand, clearly the product of dressing the stones' (*ibid.*).

The contexts of working and dressing the Stonehenge sarsen stones are clearly of particular interest not only in terms of identifying stages in the construction process, but also for understanding the spatial and temporal shifts in practice which served to define the 'rite of passage' of individual stones.

6.2. The sarsen-dressing area

B. Chan and C. Richards

For many years it has been common knowledge that examination of the molehills present within the field to the north of Stonehenge (north of the line of the old A344, the road now grassed-over) is likely to result in the recovery of sarsen fragments. Based on observations of the presence/absence of sarsen fragments in these molehills during the first four years of the SRP, the actual area producing sarsen fragments appears to run in a westerly direction from the western side of the Avenue to a point *c.* 20m east of the fence-line delineating the old visitor centre, now demolished (Figure 6.7). Far less clear is the northerly limit of the sarsen spread.

In 2007 the results of the SRP resistivity survey of this field north of the old A344 and east of the old visitor centre revealed a 'shadow-like', high-resistance anomaly (R4 in Figure 6.7) covering the area which had produced sarsen fragments in molehills. Interestingly, this 'shadow' revealed a differentiation between the eastern and western areas of the spread which coincides with a relict 1970s field boundary running north-northeast from the route of the old A344. The diffused resistivity image in the western area conforms with twentieth-century cultivation within that area, formerly a cultivated field, where the sarsen deposits have been disturbed and displaced through ploughing.

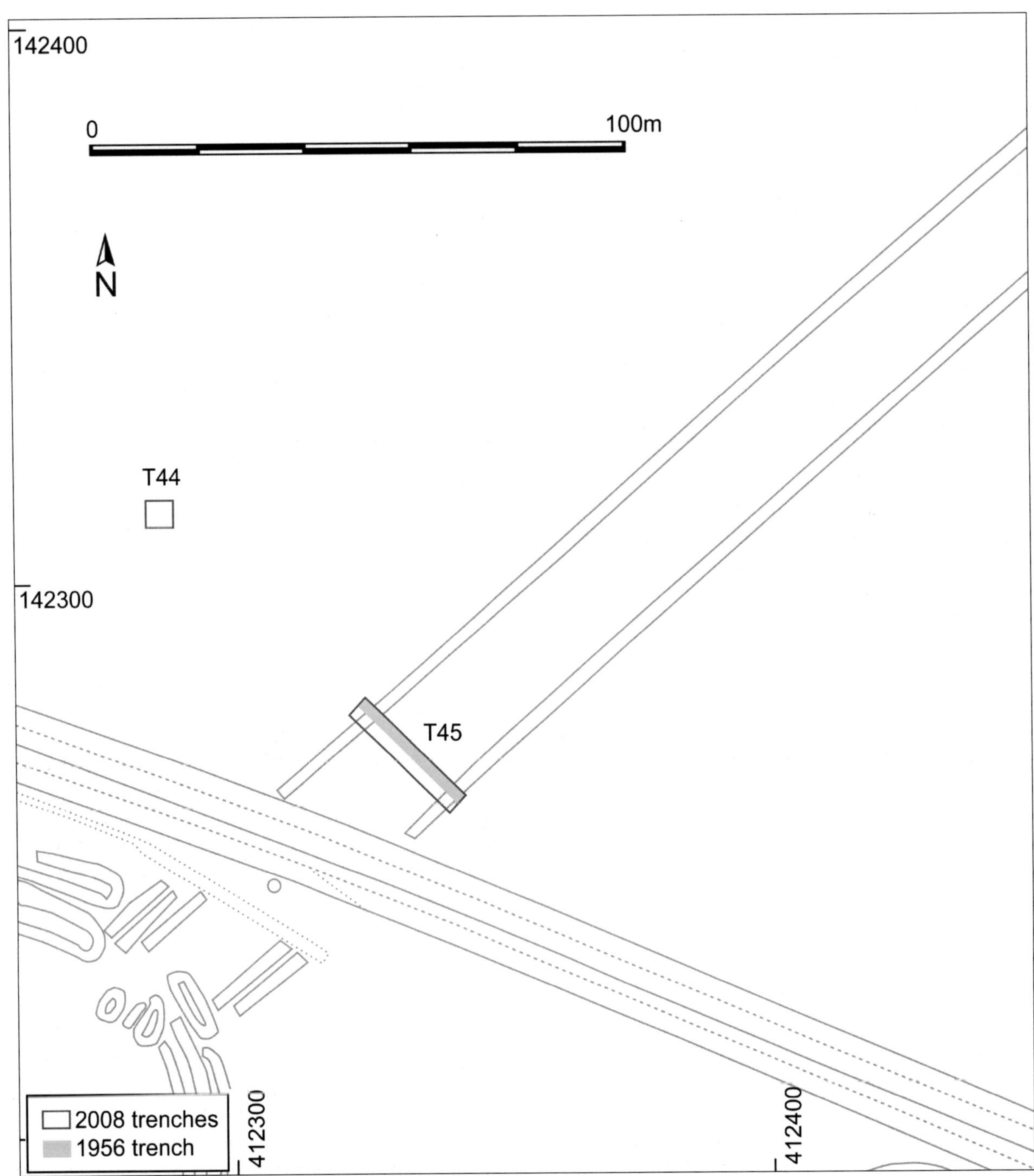

Figure 6.8. Trench 44's location in relation to Stonehenge

On the basis of these results, a small coring survey was undertaken at Easter 2008 in this area immediately north of Stonehenge, and established beyond doubt that a layer of sarsen fragments is present here beneath a sorted soil horizon. As part of the 2008 summer season of fieldwork, a 5.00m × 5.00m trench (Trench 44) was dug east of the relict field boundary (Figures 6.8–6.9). Below the turf-line an upper topsoil of completely stone-free brown loam (001) reached a depth of *c.* 0.10m. Below this a slightly more grey-brown silty loam (005) provided the matrix for a stone horizon of bluestone and sarsen debris, and worked flint (Figures 6.10). At this level, lines of flint nodules embedded in shallow periglacial grooves in the natural chalk (007) became visible (Figure 6.11). The geology of these natural features is discussed in Chapter 8,

Figure 6.9. Trench 44, viewed from the north, with Stonehenge in the background

in relation to the far more pronounced periglacial stripes in Trench 45, which was located across the Avenue.

The stone deposit was excavated in two 0.05m-thick spits, the upper within the silty loam matrix (005) and the lower (006) of similar composition and consistency but more grey in colour (Figure 6.12). The trench was excavated, and all finds recorded, on a grid system (see methodology in the lithics report, below). All excavated soil was sieved through a 10mm mesh, and layer 006 was also sieved through a 5mm mesh.

The vast majority of stone in Trench 44 was sarsen. A few flakes of different types of bluestone were distributed mainly across the western half of the trench, with several pieces of spotted dolerite in the southwest corner.

Two discrete areas of flint debitage were present in the trench and each appeared to display different characteristics. A spread radiating from the southeastern corner of the trench was of 'blade' technology and included an earlier Neolithic leaf-shaped arrowhead (see Figure 6.27). A second spread, along the west side of the trench and concentrated within its northern half, incorporated much small debitage, indicating *in situ* knapping but without any chronologically diagnostic artefacts. Given the small size of Trench 44 (its dimensions being set by English Heritage and the landowner, the National Trust, not by the excavators), it is difficult to assess the meaning or chronology of this distribution of flintwork but, judging from observations made during excavation, the southeastern and northwestern concentrations of worked flint appear to be spatially and perhaps chronologically separate entities.

In assessing the spatial and temporal integrity of this sarsen and flint deposit, the question of whether this area to the east of the relict field boundary and west of the Avenue was ever ploughed becomes relevant. The virtually stone-free, sorted topsoil (001) strongly indicates an absence of soil disturbance; nonetheless, later prehistoric or Roman cultivation cannot be dismissed. A small sherd of Roman pottery was the only obviously non-Neolithic find from layer 006. However, even if later cultivation did occur, upstanding lines of flint nodules set in the periglacial grooves have effectively restricted any post-depositional movement of lithics across them.

6.2.1. The sarsen layer

The spread of stone was not distributed evenly across the trench. Even as the upper level (005) was revealed, an irregular limit or edge to the sarsen debris, running south-southwest–north-northeast across the trench, was discernible, and a greater concentration of stone debris could be seen in the trench's central area. This distribution pattern was most clearly visible in the lower level (006) of the sarsen deposit. Overall, the distribution and density of stone debris continued throughout layers 005 and 006 to a depth of *c.* 0.15m in the centre of the trench. Little vertical sorting was apparent within the sarsen deposit, which is consistent with a single period or episode of sarsen-working.

The sarsen debris from within Trench 44 is composed of two different types: 'saccaroid' sarsen, of which the Stonehenge monoliths are made, and 'hard' or quartzite sarsen (see Howard 1982: 120–3). Saccaroid sarsen is soft, granular and easily abraded, being constituted of

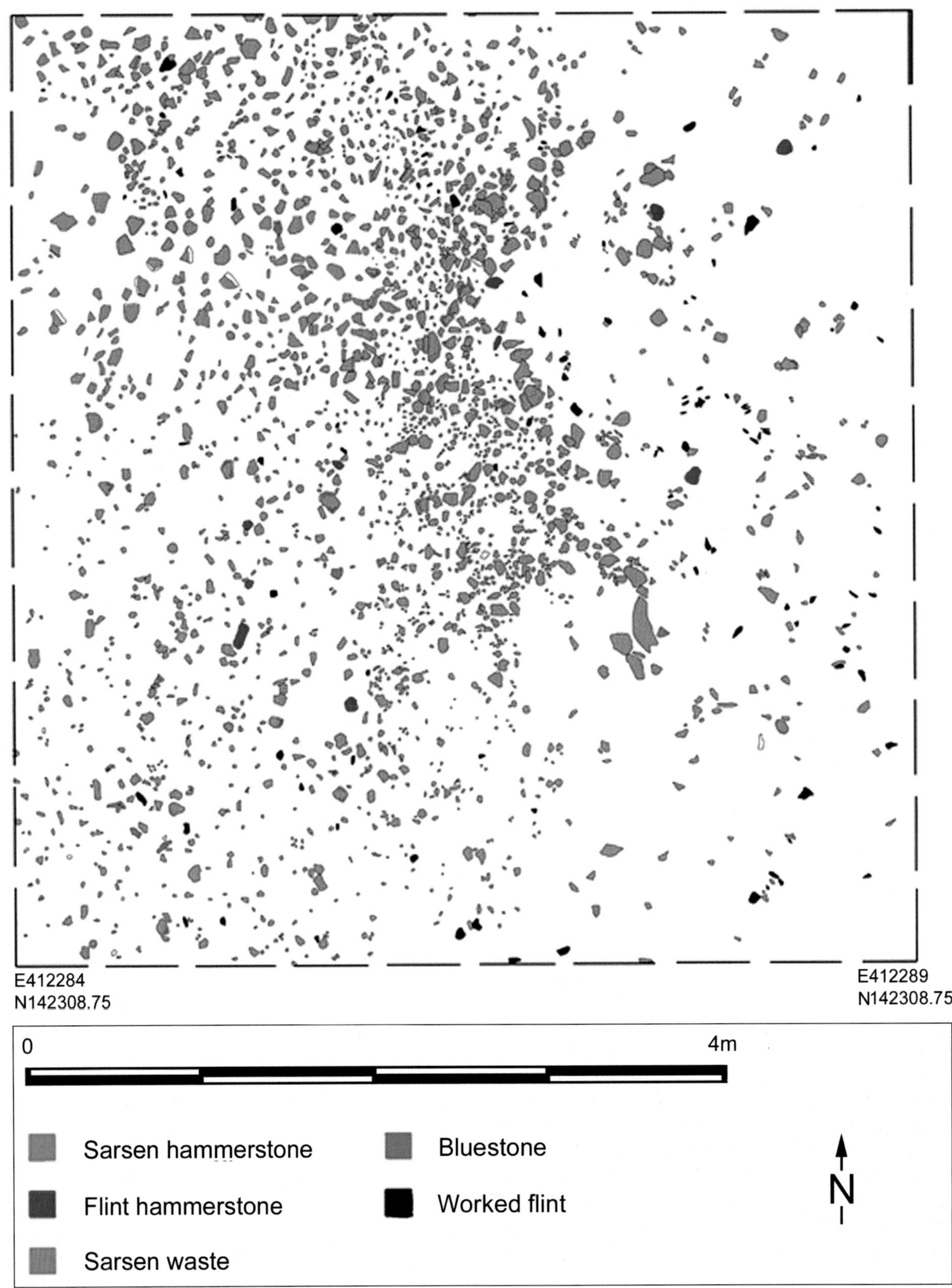

Figure 6.10. Plan of Trench 44 showing sarsen and bluestone chips, and hammerstones

Figure 6.11. Trench 44 during excavation, with east at the bottom. The periglacial stripes run diagonally

Figure 6.12 (right). Section drawing of Trench 44's baulks

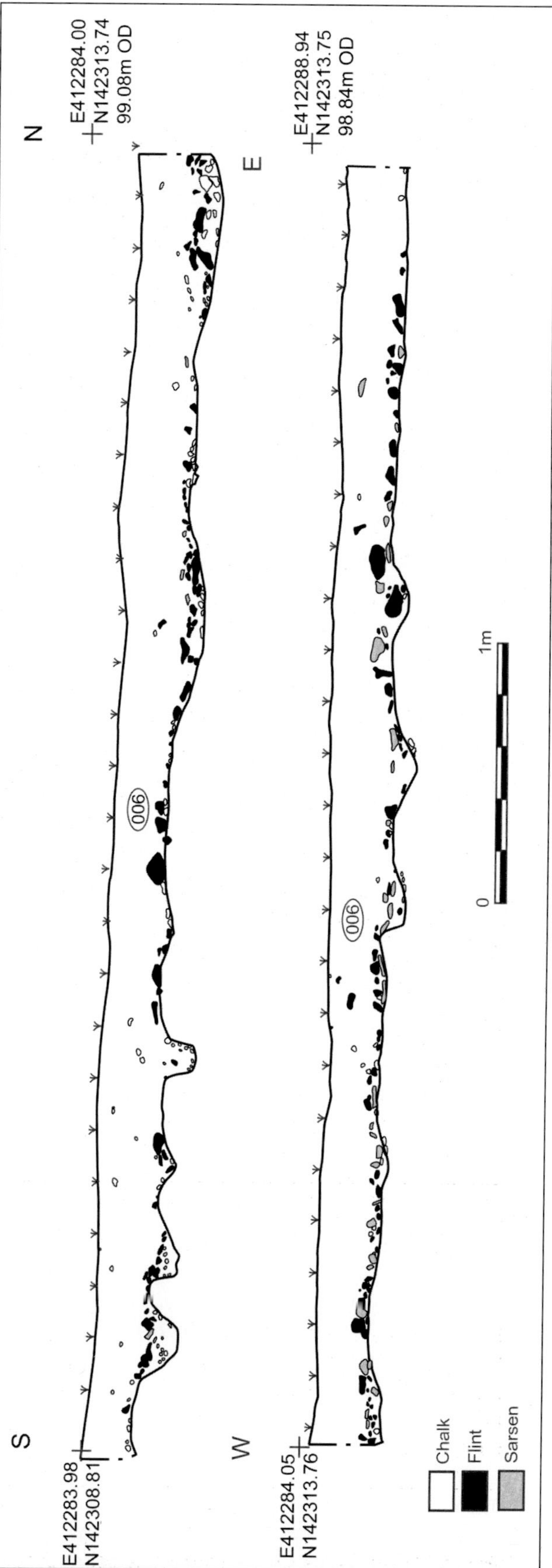

Figure 6.13. Ben Chan (left) and Hugo Anderson-Whymark re-fit sarsen fragments from Trench 44

larger grains. Quartzite sarsen is a finer-grained and much harder stone. Consequently, in the recovered assemblage, the saccaroid sarsen is grey-brown with slightly rounded, abraded edges, whereas the quartzite sarsen is fresh, unabraded and yellow-brown.

It soon became clear during excavation that all of the quartzite sarsen debris, from large flakes and lumps to smaller chips, is the remains of fractured hammerstones (Figure 6.13). Recovered in fairly similar quantities to the saccaroid material, this quartzite sarsen thus initially appeared to be over-represented, given that it is the debris from tool disintegration as opposed to waste material from working and shaping a saccaroid sarsen monolith. However, it seems likely that much of the silty 'soil' (006) is actually discoloured, saccaroid sarsen 'sand'.

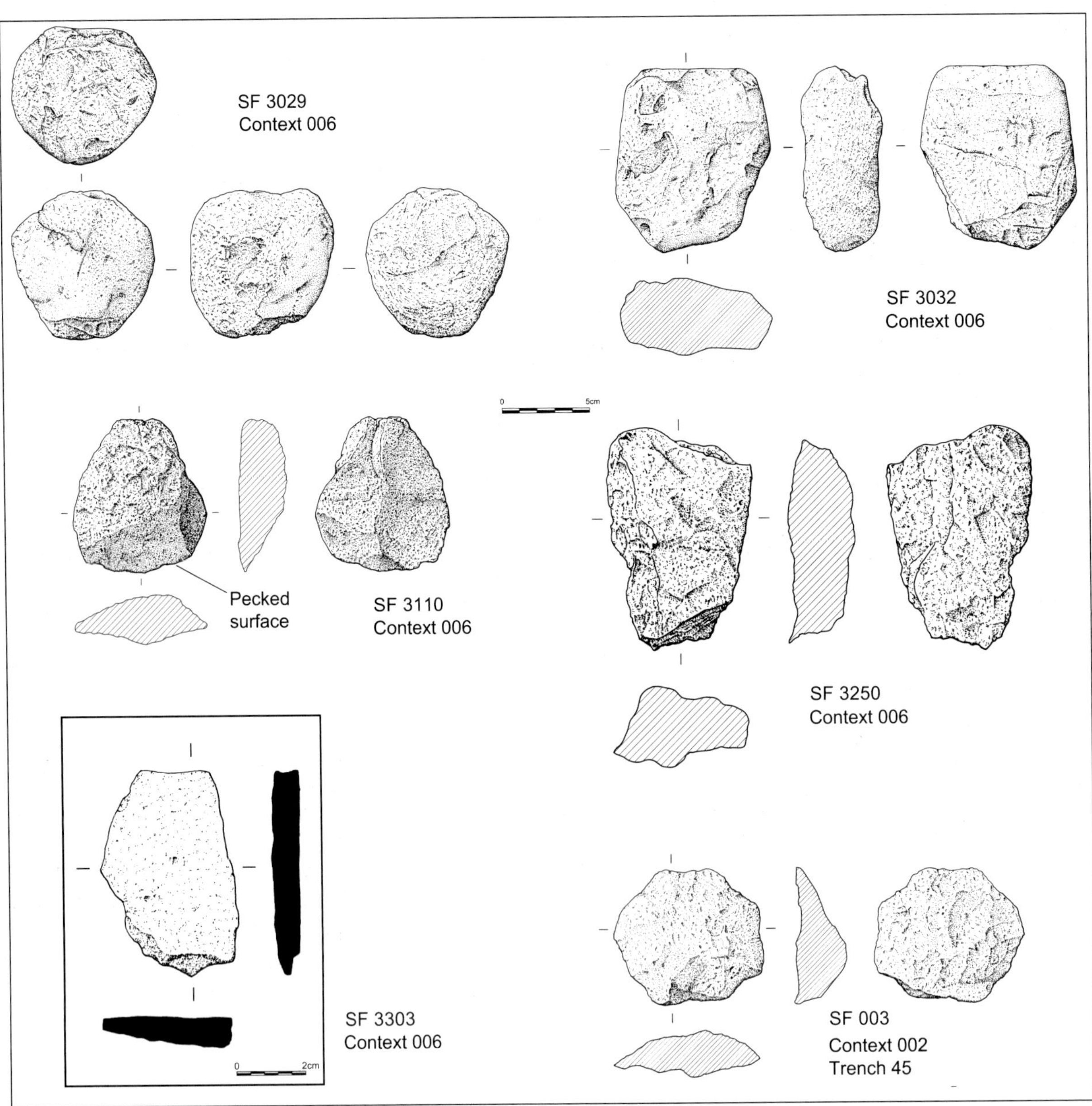

Figure 6.14. Sarsen hammerstones from Trench 44

6.2.2. Discussion

The sarsen debris within Trench 44 appears to be the working debris created during the battering and rough-shaping of a single sarsen monolith which lay south-southwest–north-northeast across the eastern part of the area exposed by the trench. Although there is no dating evidence for this stone-working activity, dressing of the sarsens is associated with Stage 2 (beginning in *2740–2505 cal BC* and ending in *2470–2300 cal BC*; see Table 11.7) so it is likely to have occurred around 2500 BC.

This clear interface in the excavated area between the area of debris and the area without debris – which would have been beneath the recumbent monolith – indicates that a single episode of working occurred at this place; had we been given permission for a larger trench (as we had initially requested), we might well have recovered the entire outline of the sarsen monolith dressed here. Nonetheless, the results of this excavation indicate a strong degree of spatial integrity for individual sarsen monoliths and their places of dressing within this working area north of Stonehenge. That these deposits may represent some form of subsequent stone destruction is rejected on the basis of the small sizes of the sarsen fragments, the spatial integrity of the working debris, and the small sizes of the hammerstones used in this area (Figure 6.14).

As well as the quartzite hammerstones, there were a few examples of flint hammerstones in Trench 44 (see Figure 6.27). Overall, the distribution of large chunks of flint and quartzite sarsen hammerstones also mirrored the south-southwest–north-northeast spread of stone debris across the trench. This pattern is, of course, to be expected given that a substantial proportion of the sarsen debris is actually composed of pieces of quartzite sarsen.

Of particular interest are the forms of quartzite sarsen hammerstones. Whilst larger examples are often referred to as 'mauls', here the term 'hammerstone' is used to designate all sizes of this stone tool (see Whitaker, below). For the sarsen hammerstones retained from excavations within Stonehenge, 'the general shape of the mauls is a flattened sphere' (Montague 1995a: 386). While examples of such sphere-shaped hammerstones are present within the Trench 44 assemblage, a greater proportion of the hammerstones are thinner, triangular-shaped objects. These appear to have suffered substantial damage along their edges and, in some cases, it is clear that the tool has fractured in half. Both pieces then continued to be used for hammering before eventually being discarded at the location of the stone-working.

While the reuse of broken hammerstones provides further evidence that the sarsen spread in Trench 44 represents *in situ* monolith-working, the thin, triangular shapes of the hammerstones require further comment. Clearly, quartzite sarsen raw material was being specially selected for hammerstones and brought to the stone-dressing area. The predominance of such thin-bladed hammerstones may indicate that they were used for careful dressing, as opposed to an initial coarse shaping of monoliths. That it was secondary dressing that occurred in this area is further confirmed by the small size of the saccaroid sarsen debris within the working area.

6.2.3. Sarsen from the sarsen-dressing area in Trench 44 and the Stonehenge Avenue in Trench 45

B. Chan

Trench 44 is described above, and the report of the excavation of Trench 45, which explored part of the Stonehenge Avenue closest to Stonehenge, is to be found in Chapter 8. To enable a meaningful comparison of the sarsen debris from both these trenches excavated in the area immediately north of Stonehenge, it is, however, necessary to report here the sarsen assemblage from the Avenue excavation (Trench 45), before the reader has encountered the report of that excavation. To separate the two sarsen assemblages would make it hard to present an overall discussion of this material. So, for the stratigraphy of Trench 45 and the worked flint from that trench, the reader should consult Chapter 8.

Large quantities of worked sarsen stone came from both trenches. Some 34,941 pieces of sarsen (282kg) were recovered from Trench 44 and 3,496 pieces (75kg) from Trench 45. These are the largest assemblages of flaked sarsen from the SRP excavations.

Other assemblages

At the Tor Stone, Bulford, the SRP excavation around a recumbent sarsen revealed the extraction pit from which it came, and the stonehole in which it was erected. Over 10kg of flaked sarsen was deposited within the extraction pit, incorporated into a flint cairn (see Chapter 7).

During the SRP excavations at Durrington Walls (reported in Volume 3), sarsen stones were found in large quantities in certain contexts, notably the fill (1192) of a shallow pit (1191) beneath the upper surface of the Durrington Walls avenue, which leads from the Avon to the east entrance through the henge bank. This pit lay close to one of three empty stoneholes and the sarsen from within the pit may be the debris from a broken-up standing stone, turned into fist-sized cobbles; these are mostly burnt, so were perhaps used as cooking stones after the sarsen standing stone was destroyed. Six of the larger sarsen blocks from pit fill 1192 are around 200mm in width, and one of these (CAT#10) has three faces that are natural weathered surfaces, indicating that it derives from a large sarsen block at least 180mm wide (but probably no wider than 250–300mm wide).

Some 86 pieces of sarsen (70.9kg) came from pit fill 1192, and a further 5,669 pieces (77.8kg) were recovered from other contexts during the SRP excavations at Durrington Walls in 2004–2007. The vast majority of these latter pieces are small chunks and cobbles, many not humanly modified other than being burnt. A similar assemblage of 151 mostly burnt sarsen stones (12.2kg), many of them even more heavily burnt than those at Durrington Walls, were recovered from the Bronze Age settlement and field system associated with the Stonehenge palisade to the west of Stonehenge, excavated by the SRP in 2008 (reported in Volume 4).

Smaller assemblages of sarsen stone were recovered from the SRP excavations at Woodhenge and the Stonehenge Avenue's elbow (reported in Volume 3 and in Chapter 8 of this volume). The Woodhenge assemblage consists of mostly small flakes (many of them burnt) and small chunks and unworked lumps (also mostly burnt). The Avenue elbow finds consist mainly of small unworked lumps, with very few chunks or flakes.

Sarsen and bluestone debris in Trench 44 and Trench 45

This section details the assemblage of worked stone from Trenches 44 and 45. There is also an assemblage of worked stone, including bluestone, from the backfill

Raw material	Frequency	Percent	Weight (g)	Percent
Quartzite sarsen	21888	62.6	174535	60.9
Saccaroid sarsen	13053	37.3	107646	37.6
Flint	15	<0.1	3269	1.1
Spotted dolerite	9	<0.1	563	0.2
Unspotted dolerite	1	<0.1	2	<0.1
Rhyolite	7	<0.1	418	0.1
Gabbro	1	<0.1	1.5	<0.1
Total	34974	100.0	286435	100.0

Table 6.1. The frequency and weight of different raw materials from Trench 44 (including flint hammerstones)

of a trench excavated by Atkinson in 1956 into the Stonehenge Avenue. The SRP's Trench 45 (Figure 6.8) reopened part of Atkinson's 1956 trench, and recovered material from this backfill which had come originally from stratified contexts. The bluestone from Atkinson's backfill represents an important addition to the corpus of Stonehenge bluestone and is reported in the petrography report in Volume 2. However, the precise contextual origin of the backfill assemblage is unknown and hence this redeposited material is not included in the following analysis.

The worked sarsen and bluestone were recorded separately from the worked flint assemblage and are reported here separately. The only exceptions to this are the flint hammerstones from Trenches 44 and 45, which are clearly associated with sarsen-working and have therefore been included within this sarsen and bluestone section.

Trench 44: the sarsen-dressing area

The excavation of Trench 44 yielded an assemblage of 34,974 pieces of worked stone (excluding the worked flint), weighing 286.4kg (Table 6.1). The soil profile of Trench 44 was effectively a worm-sorted topsoil straight on top of chalk bedrock. Within this profile, as described above, a largely artificial context boundary was imposed between the upper topsoil (005) and the lower part (006) of this worm-sorted topsoil. Nearly 90% of the worked stone by weight, and 80% by frequency, came from context 006.

Collection and recording methodology

The assemblage was recorded at the level of its lowest applicable excavation unit, which was either a context, or more commonly, a sample square within a context. Sample squares for the upper soil profile (005) were 1m × 1m, whilst those for the lower soil profile (006) were 0.50m × 0.50m. As described above, all the deposits were sieved through 10mm mesh, with layer 006 also being sieved through a 5mm mesh.

The material from each unit was sorted first into raw material and then into a series of artefact categories, with the resultant sub-assemblages being counted and weighed. The material was sorted into the following artefact categories:

1. Fragment of ground/pecked object
2. Hammerstone
3. Waste flake (<10mm)
4. Waste flake (10–50mm)
5. Waste flake (>50mm)
6. Waste fragment (<10mm)
7. Waste fragment (10–50mm)
8. Waste fragment (>50mm)

'Waste flakes' describes objects with identifiable flake attributes. 'Waste fragments' represents waste material that does not have identifiable flake attributes.

The assemblage

The assemblage is dominated by sarsen, which makes up 98.5% of the worked stone in the trench by weight and 99.9% by frequency (Table 6.1). The remaining artefacts are of various types of bluestone, except for a single piece of gabbro and 15 flint hammerstones. Within the sarsen debris, quartzite sarsen is the more common material.

The assemblage consists mainly of debitage in the form of waste flakes and waste fragments (Table 6.2). In general, waste flakes are outnumbered significantly by waste fragments, with this pattern being particularly marked within the assemblage of saccaroid sarsen when compared to quartzite sarsen.

Apart from the obvious explanation – that the stone-working in the area produced more quartzite than saccaroid sarsen flakes – there are two other factors that are likely to have affected the representation of flakes:

- In comparison to saccaroid sarsen, quartzite sarsen has a smaller grain size and tends to fracture sub-conchoidally, rendering its flake attributes easier to recognise. In contrast, when a saccaroid sarsen flake is struck, small fissures are often created on the ventral surface, emanating out from the point of impact, but a bulb of percussion is not formed and the ventral surface remains relatively flat. Therefore, in many cases the recognition of saccaroid sarsen flakes depends on the overall morphology of the piece, rather than on any individually clear and diagnostic attributes.

- The second factor is that saccaroid sarsen is softer than quartzite sarsen and therefore is more prone to fracturing during flake removal and also during post-depositional weathering. This means that flakes

Artefact type		Raw material type			Total
		Quartzite sarsen	*Saccaroid sarsen*	*Flint*	
Fragment of ground/pecked object	Count	0	8	0	8
	% within raw material type	0%	0.1%	0%	0%
Hammerstone	Count	283	9	15	307
	% within raw material type	1.3%	0.1%	100.0%	0.9%
Waste flake (<1cm)	Count	1558	2	0	1560
	% within raw material type	7.1%	0%	0%	4.5%
Waste flake (1–5cm)	Count	2062	56	0	2118
	% within raw material type	9.4%	0.4%	0%	6.1%
Waste flake (>5cm)	Count	538	155	0	693
	% within raw material type	2.5%	1.2%	0%	2.0%
Waste fragment (<1cm)	Count	6537	5471	0	12008
	% within raw material type	29.9%	41.9%	0%	34.4%
Waste fragment (1–5cm)	Count	9319	6548	0	15867
	% within raw material type	42.6%	50.2%	0%	45.4%
Waste fragment (>5cm)	Count	1591	804	0	2395
	% within raw material type	7.3%	6.2%	0%	6.9%
Total	Count	21888	13053	15	34956
	% within raw material type	100.0%	100.0%	100.0%	100.0%

Table 6.2. The assemblage of sarsen-working debris from Trench 44

of this material are more likely to have become broken up, therefore increasing the difficulty of identifying any flake attributes.

In addition to the debitage within the assemblage, there are 307 hammerstones. Nearly all are of quartzite sarsen, with smaller numbers of saccaroid sarsen and flint (Table 6.2; Figures 6.14, 6.27). The flint hammerstones are all water-worn river cobbles, quite distinct from the chalk-derived flint that is usually found in struck lithic assemblages within the Stonehenge landscape. The quartzite sarsen hammerstones were also all made from water-worn cobbles, and it is likely that both the flint and quartzite sarsen cobbles used as hammerstones were collected from the same locations. It is possible that the flint cobbles were selected mistakenly during the collection of sarsen cobbles.

The hammerstones are most often rounded and sub-angular or sub-triangular in shape, and vary in weight from 12g to 2,155g, with an average weight of 199g. The heaviest hammerstone is clearly an outlier within the assemblage, with the next heaviest hammerstone weighing 842g. In order to control for the distorting effect of this outlier, the object is not included in the histogram of the distribution of hammerstone weights (Figure 6.15).

Since many hammerstones continued to be used after flakes and spalls had come off them during their use in percussive activities, no attempt was made during the analysis to distinguish between broken and complete hammerstones. Therefore, many of the lighter hammerstones are those that have lost substantial portions of their mass as a result of flakes being detached during use. Bearing this in mind, it is likely that, at the beginning of their use, the majority of hammerstones weighed 100g–300g. These represent hammerstones that can be held comfortably in one hand and can be used one- or two-handed.

The remaining part of the assemblage consists of eight fragments from ground or pecked saccaroid sarsen objects (Table 6.2). Identification of the original forms of these objects is in some cases hampered by their fragmentary state, with the objects effectively being chunks of sarsen with one surface showing evidence of pecking. In a few cases, the technological sequence is clearer. For example, SF 3110 is a saccaroid sarsen flake with a partly cortical and partly pecked dorsal surface (Figure 6.14). The piece reveals a clear sequence of pecking followed by flaking of the outer weathered surface, and would seem to represent a flake that has been removed from a previously peck-dressed sarsen boulder.

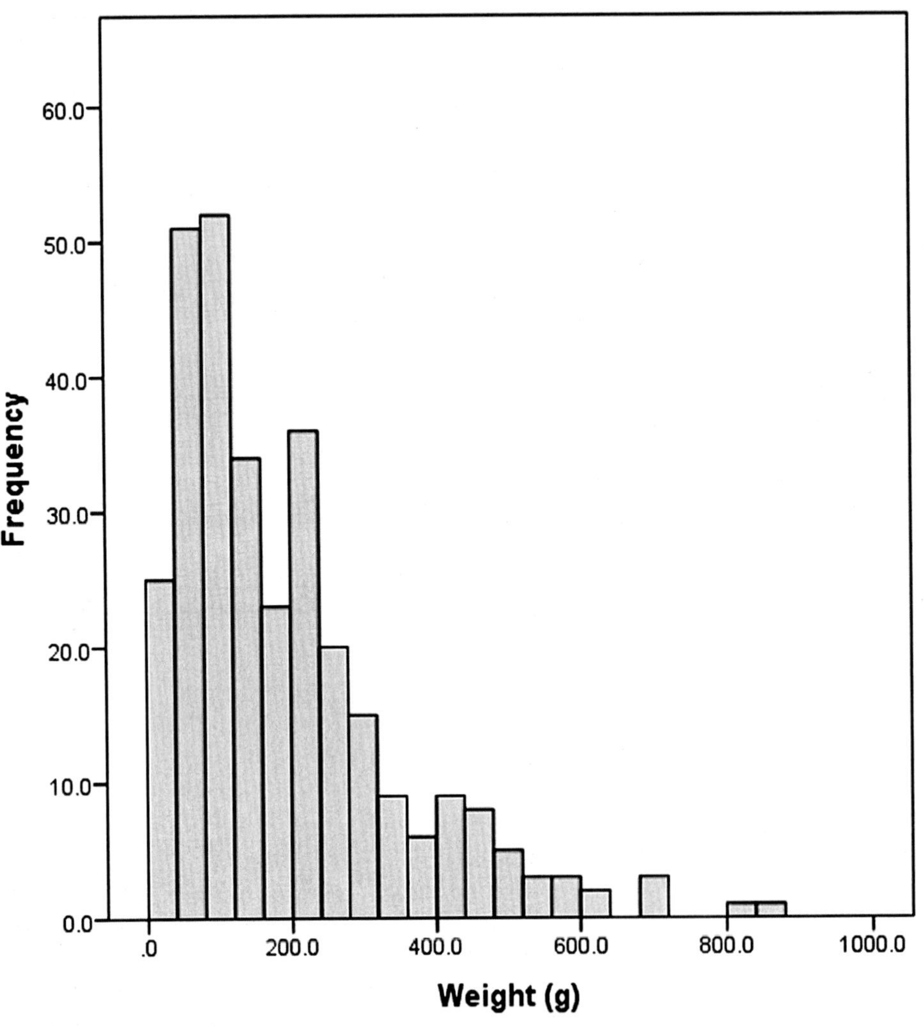

Figure 6.15. Histogram of the weights of hammerstones from Trench 44 excluding a single outlier

This is of interest as it would suggest that at least some flaking of the part-dressed megaliths followed stages of peck-dressing. This is counterintuitive in terms of the expected *chaîne opératoire* for reducing a boulder to a dressed megalith, but perhaps reflects a final dressing of a megalith during which refinements were made to its form.

The other object of interest is SF 3303, a saccaroid sarsen flake with a dorsal surface that is notably flat and smooth (Figure 6.14). Under magnification, the grain crystals appear levelled but their individual boundaries are still recognisable. This flake could be from a stone tool used for abrasive activities but, when analysed using a metallographic microscope, diagnostic polishes associated with typical grinding or abrasive contact materials were not present. As a result, it is not possible to reject the possibility that the flattening and smoothing of its surface are the result of natural weathering processes.

Spatial analysis

The spatial distribution of the sarsen-working debris within Trench 44 is both striking and unexpected. There is clear variability in the density of material across the relatively small area of the 5.00m × 5.00m trench, with the density of the combined sarsen, bluestone and flint hammerstone assemblages varying from two artefacts per 0.50m × 0.50m sample square to an incredible 2,141 artefacts per sample square. The latter 0.50m × 0.50m square, near the centre of the trench, produced 1,309 flakes and fragments of quartzite sarsen, and 827 flakes and fragments of saccaroid sarsen as well as five hammerstones.

In terms of the spatial patterning in the density of artefacts there was a clear east–west division within the trench, with a 2m-wide strip along the eastern edge of Trench 44 being relatively devoid of material, and the remaining portion of the trench having consistently high densities of debris (Figure 6.16; *cf* Figure 6.10). More specifically, the artefact spread had a dense cluster in the middle part of the trench; this has a natural fall-off in density towards the north, south and west, and came to an abrupt halt along the line of the 2m-wide low-density strip along the eastern edge of the trench. This pattern is replicated within the individual assemblages of saccaroid and quartzite sarsen (Figures 6.17–6.18).

The much smaller bluestone assemblage was spread more evenly across the area of the trench (Figure 6.19; Table 6.3). This suggests that the bluestone debris relates to a different set of activities to those represented by the sarsen assemblage, with the latter appearing to relate to a single episode of activity.

Discussion and conclusion

During initial analysis of the assemblage it was quickly realised that the assemblage is comprised of two distinct parts. The first part is the saccaroid sarsen, which is primarily debitage from the reduction of a larger block or boulder. The second part is the quartzite sarsen, all from cobbles or fragments of cobbles, most of which show signs of intense percussive wear. In essence, the assemblage consists of debris from dressing a sarsen stone, and the hammerstones used to dress it.

As soon as the initial planning of the artefact spread was completed, it was noted in the field that there was a distinct spatial patterning in the artefact scatter characterised by a 'shadow' in the artefact distribution (Figure 6.10). We can interpret this 'shadow', noticeably empty of worked stone, as being the area on which a recumbent monolith lay while it was dressed. The excavation trench exposed some (but not all) of the area beneath the recumbent monolith, and some (but not all) of the area around the monolith.

Bearing this in mind, the analysis of the data raises an obvious question. Why is the assemblage of hammerstones and their fragments (*i.e.* all the hammerstones and all the quartzite sarsen debitage) larger than the debitage from the boulder that was being worked? In answering this question, it is important to note two features:

- Even taking into account the propensity of saccaroid sarsen to fragment, and the noted difficulties in identifying flake attributes, the assemblage of saccaroid sarsen flakes is small, both in terms of the number of flakes and their individual size. The surfaces of Stonehenge's standing stones show evidence of the removal of large dressing flakes (Abbott and Anderson-Whymark 2012), but there is no evidence in the Trench 44 assemblage of large flakes of comparable size (see Figure 6.29).

- Secondly, the hammerstones within the Trench 44 assemblage, whilst numerous, are small in size when compared to the large 'mauls' found within Stonehenge (Atkinson 1956: 119). These Trench 44 hammerstones would have been incapable of removing large flakes from a sarsen boulder.

	Raw material type	Trench 44		Trench 45	
		Frequency	Percent	Frequency	Percent
Orthostat lithic types	Spotted dolerite	9	50	20	19.6
	Unspotted dolerite	1	5.6	-	-
	Rhyolite with fabric	4	22.2	28	27.5
	Rhyolite with sub-planar fabric	2	11.1	21	20.6
	Rhyolite with feldspar megacrysts	1	5.6	5	4.9
Non-orthostat lithic types	Limestone	-	-	2	2.0
	Misc. metamorphic	-	-	1	1.0
	Gabbro	1	5.6	1	1.0
	Fine-grained basic rocks	-	-	11	10.8
	Sandstone	-	-	3	2.9
	Glauconitic sandstone/ greensand	-	-	10	9.8
	Total	18	100.0	102	100.0

Table 6.3. The frequency and proportion of non-flint and non-sarsen lithic types from Trenches 44 and 45

On the basis of these two factors, it seems likely that the primary task being conducted in the area exposed within Trench 44 was the pounding and pecking of the surface of a sarsen boulder, presumably one that either did not require extensive flaking to rough it out into an acceptable monolith, or one that had already been roughly dressed into shape.

The large number of hammerstones within the relatively small area of Trench 44 suggests that working of the prone monolith was an intensive activity, probably with as many people as possible crowded around it and bashing at its surface. Alongside the 307 hammerstones within the 25sq m of the trench were 21,605 flakes and fragments of quartzite sarsen weighing over 118kg (Table 6.2). The intensity of the activity is clear when it is considered that all of this material resulted from the flaking and shattering of hammerstones as they were used to pound against a sarsen monolith. The frequent occurrence of battering and crushing extending over the flake scars of previous removals on hammerstones shows that, as hammerstones broke, people just kept on using them.

Equally, the number of useable hammerstones discarded in the area of the trench indicates that, when the dressing of the monolith was completed, the tools used to dress it were simply discarded on the spot. This level of profligacy in the use of a resource that would have had to have been collected from a riverbed (the nearest being the River Avon at least 2km away) is highly reminiscent of the character of consumption at Durrington Walls (see Volume 3) and characteristic of many of the activities of large-scale consumption taking

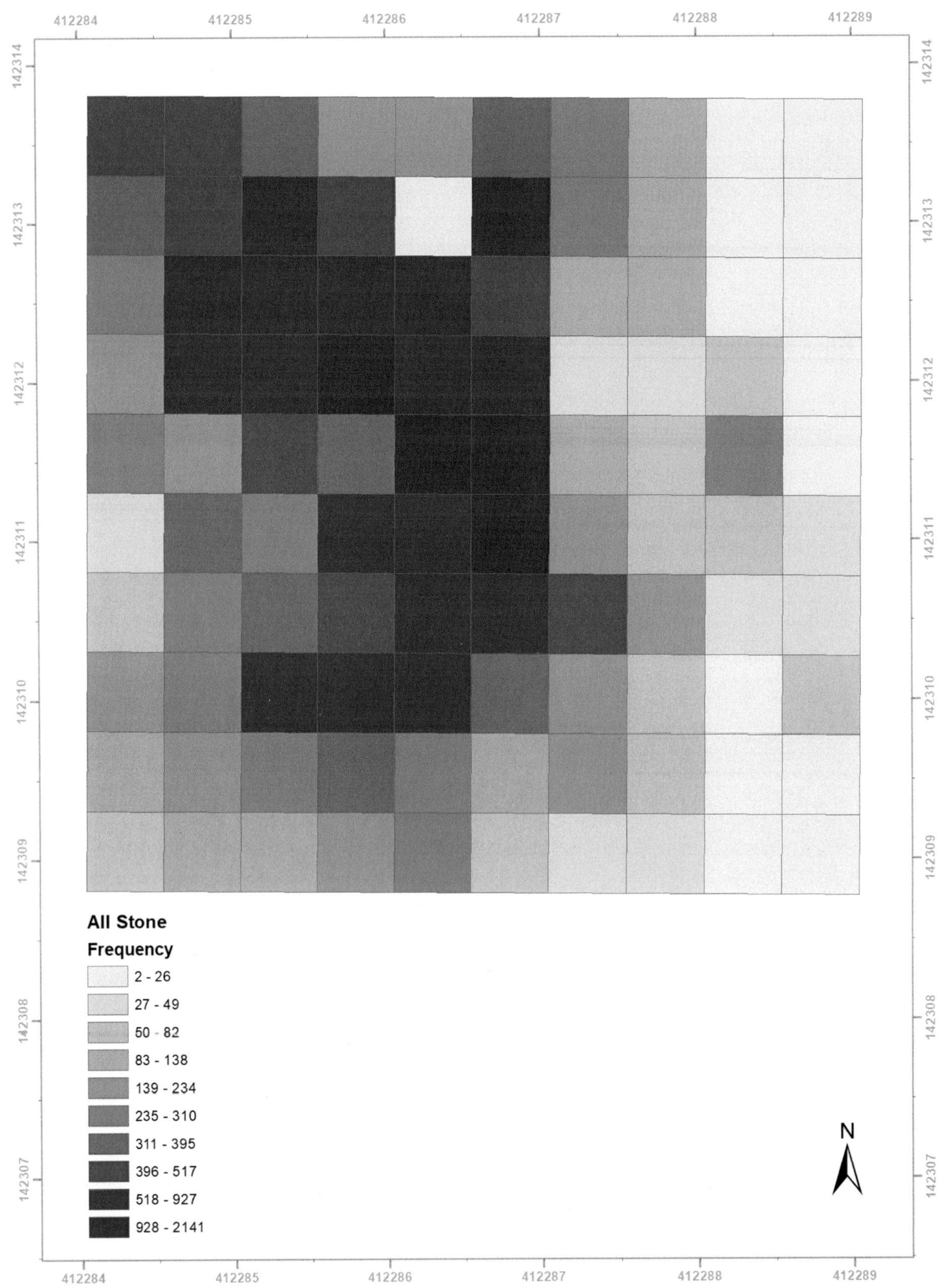

Figure 6.16. The density of all sarsen-working debris in Trench 44

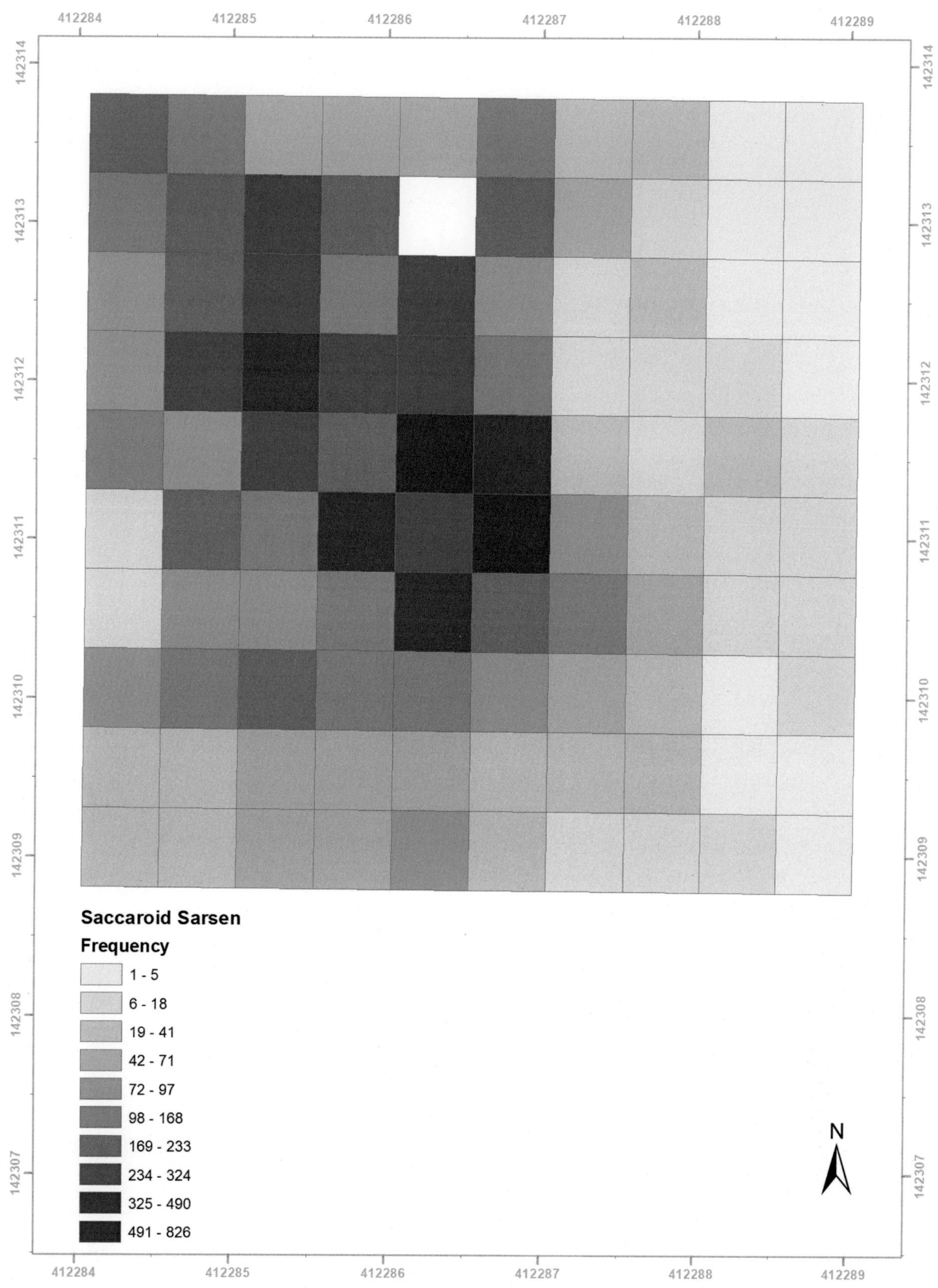

Figure 6.17. The density of saccaroid sarsen in Trench 44

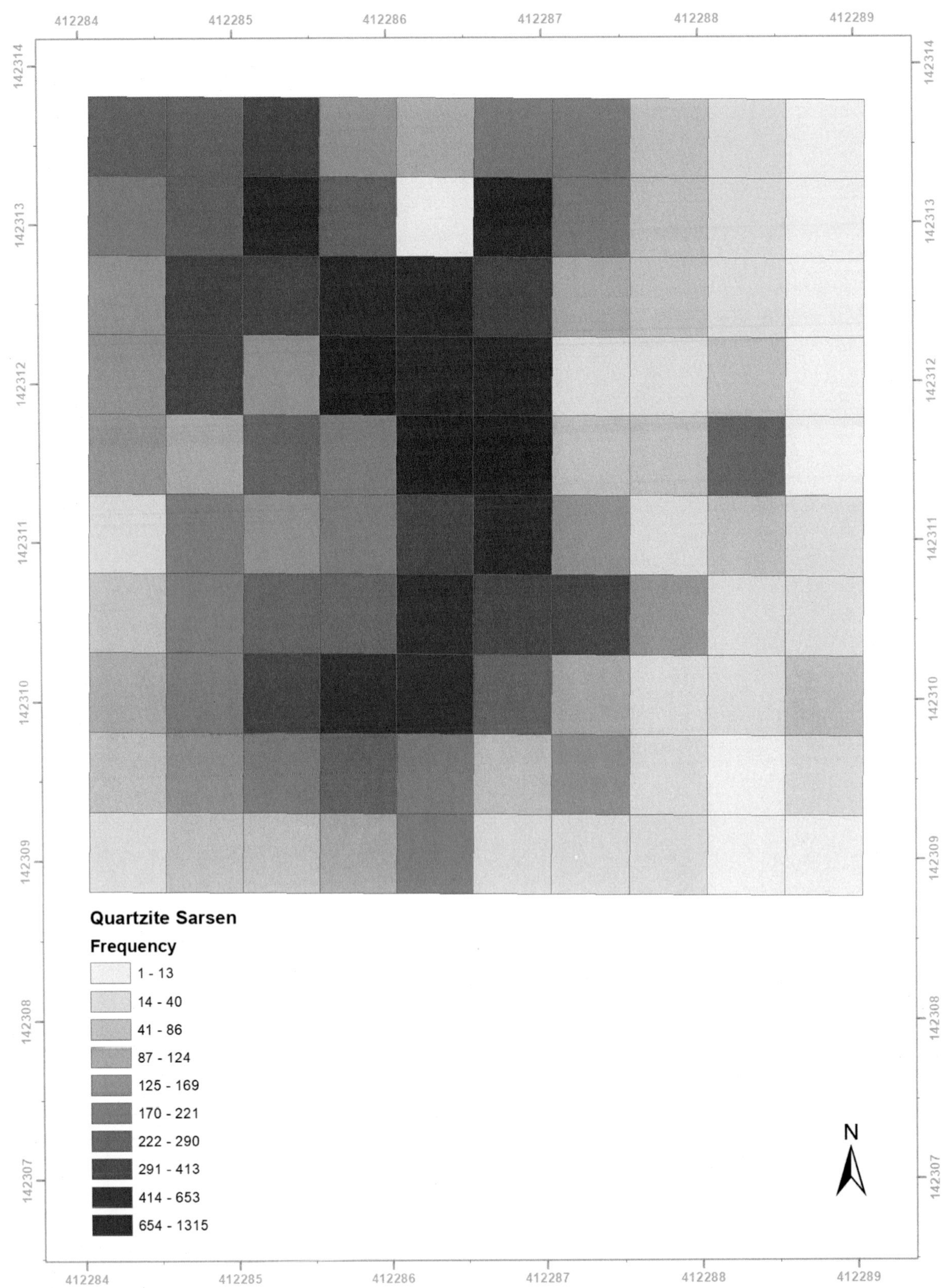

Figure 6.18. The density of quartzite sarsen in Trench 44

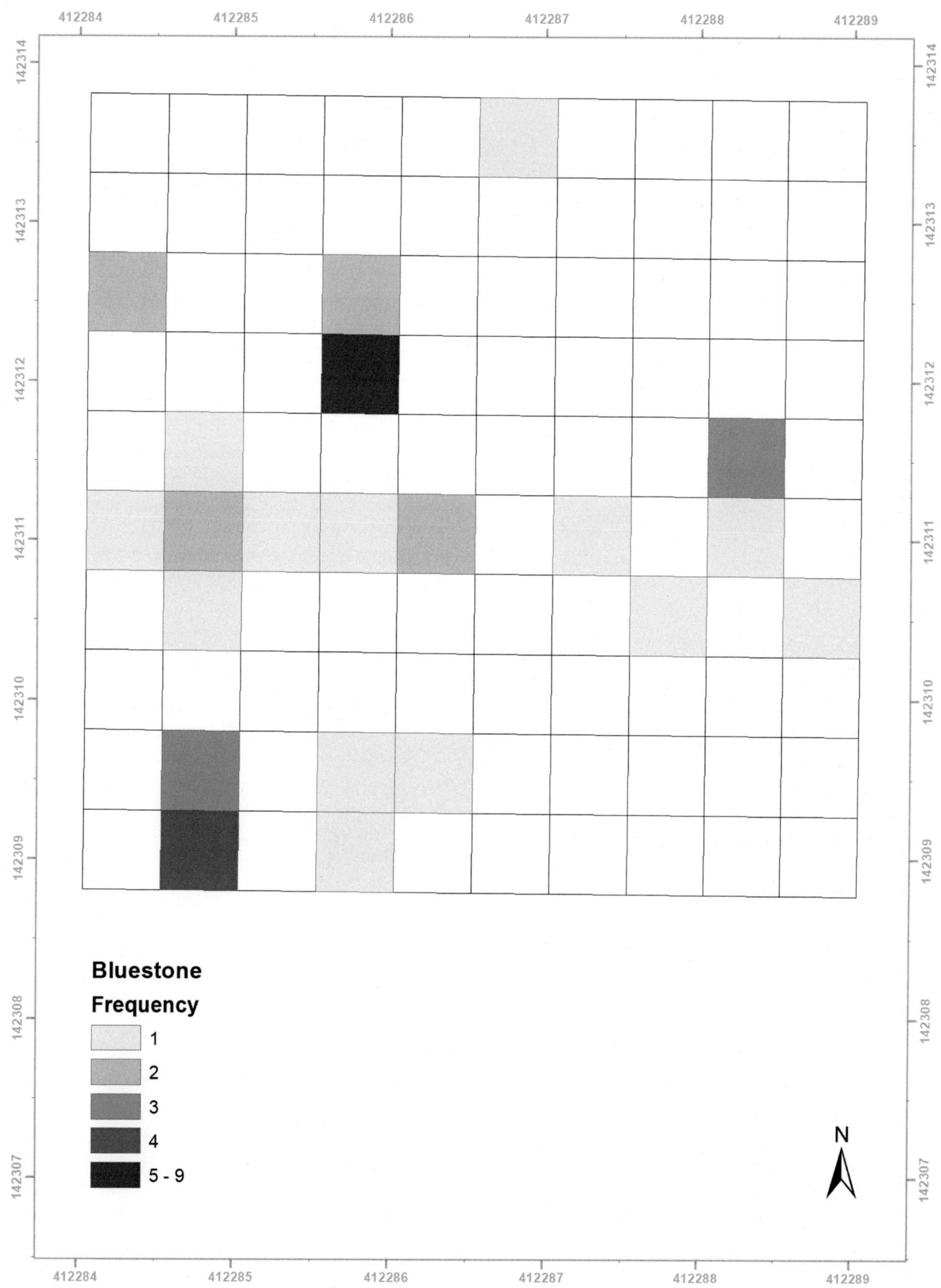

Figure 6.19. The density of bluestone chippings in Trench 44

place in the Stonehenge landscape in the mid-third millennium BC (Parker Pearson *et al.* 2011). It represents a clear choice to leave perfectly usable hammerstones strewn across the dressing floor rather than to collect them for use in dressing subsequent stones.

This perhaps reveals a desire to leave a visible reference to the scale of the work undertaken, or may equally indicate that tools used to dress a sarsen were deemed to be 'used' or polluted in some manner, rendering them inappropriate for reuse. In either case, the area exposed within Trench 44 is small in relation to the full size of a Stonehenge sarsen – only a small portion of the area covered by the recumbent monolith was excavated. Extrapolating from the number of hammerstones found in this small area of stone-dressing to the full area that would have been occupied by the entire stone and the stoneworkers, it is likely that approaching 1,000 hammerstones were required to dress this one stone and many tens of thousands would have been required to dress all the stones forming the monument.

The Trench 44 excavation has, therefore, revealed the spatial organisation of sarsen-dressing around Stonehenge and has provided an insight into the enormous network of people and resources that needed to be marshalled in order for Stonehenge to be constructed (*cf* Chan *et al.* 2016).

Raw material	Frequency	Percent	Weight (g)	Percent
Flint	4	0.1	2670	3.4
Quartzite sarsen	1449	40.9	32263	40.7
Saccaroid sarsen	2047	57.8	42458	53.5
Spotted dolerite	7	0.2	825	1.0
Rhyolite	36	1.0	1072	1.4
Total	3543	100.0	79288	100.0

Table 6.4. The frequency and weight of different raw materials from Trench 45 (including flint hammerstones)

Trench 45: the Stonehenge Avenue in front of Stonehenge

Like Trench 44, Trench 45 produced an assemblage of worked sarsen, bluestone and flint hammerstones, alongside a more conventional worked flint assemblage. As noted above, the stratigraphic report on the excavations and the report on the worked flint assemblage from Trench

Artefact type		Raw material type: *Quartzite sarsen*	*Saccaroid sarsen*	*Flint*	*Spotted dolerite*	*Rhyolite*	Total
Fragment of ground/pecked object	Count	0	1	0	0	0	1
	% within raw material type	0%	<0.1%	0%	0%	0%	<0.1%
Hammerstone	Count	53	0	4	0	0	57
	% within raw material type	3.7%	0%	100.0%	0%	0%	1.6%
Irregularly flaked object	Count	1	0	0	0	0	1
	% within raw material type	0.1%	0%	0%	0%	0%	0.0%
Waste flake (<1cm)	Count	62	2	0	0	0	64
	% within raw material type	4.3%	0.1%	0%	0%	0%	1.8%
Waste flake (1-5cm)	Count	404	99	0	0	5	508
	% within raw material type	27.9%	4.8%	0%	0%	13.9%	14.3%
Waste flake (>5cm)	Count	148	56	0	0	5	209
	% within raw material type	10.2%	2.7%	0%	0%	13.9%	5.9%
Waste fragment (<1cm)	Count	30	419	0	0	0	449
	% within raw material type	2.1%	20.5%	0%	0%	0%	12.7%
Waste fragment (1-5cm)	Count	599	1177	0	1	24	1801
	% within raw material type	41.3%	57.5%	0%	14.3%	66.7%	50.8%
Waste fragment (>5cm)	Count	152	293	0	6	2	453
	% within raw material type	10.5%	14.3%	0%	85.7%	5.6%	12.8%
Total	Count	1449	2047	4	7	36	3543
	% within raw material type	100.0%	100.0%	100.0%	100.0%	100.0%	100.0%

Table 6.5. The frequency of artefact categories by raw material type within the assemblage of sarsen-working debris and bluestone chippings from Trench 45

45 can be found in Chapter 8. This report on the sarsen and bluestone assemblage refers only to material found within newly excavated contexts, and does *not* include material retrieved from the backfill of Atkinson's 1956 trench. The bluestone assemblage is reported in detail by Ixer in Volume 2, and that report includes material from both the newly excavated contexts and the Atkinson backfill. Hence the totals for bluestone given by Ixer in Volume 2 are not the same as those used here. Excluding the worked flint assemblage, which is reported in Chapter 8, the assemblage of worked stone from Trench 45 consists of 3,543 artefacts weighing 79kg, excavated from 22 different contexts.

Collection and recording methodology

The material was recovered by dry-sieving using the standard 10mm mesh. Buried soils beneath the Avenue banks, the banks themselves and a pair of contiguous pits (055/056) were excavated using a 0.50m × 0.50m sample grid, and sieved through a 10mm mesh, with further dry-sieving of the buried soils and fill of pit 055/056 using a 5mm mesh, providing direct comparability with the recovery of material from context 006 in Trench 44. Beneath the topsoil within Trench 45, finds from all contexts newly excavated in 2008 were recorded in 1m × 1m squares within the Avenue except for the ditch fills. Prehistoric features, notably the ditch fills, the bank matrix, the buried soils and the one cut feature (pit 055/056), were extensively sampled for flotation as well as sieved. The assemblage was recorded using the same method as that used for the assemblage from Trench 44 (see above).

The assemblage

The assemblage from Trench 45 is comprised nearly entirely of sarsen, with saccaroid sarsen making up 58% of the assemblage, and quartzite sarsen making up 41% (Table 6.4). In addition, there are 43 pieces of assorted bluestone and four flint hammerstones.

As with Trench 44, the assemblage is dominated by debitage, with waste flakes making up 22% of the assemblage, and waste fragments 76% (Table 6.5). The rest of the assemblage is comprised of 57 hammerstones, a fragment of pecked saccaroid sarsen from the west bank of the Avenue (context 022), and an irregularly flaked object of quartzite sarsen from the east bank (021). The pecked object is likely a flake removed from a partially peck-dressed sarsen monolith, similar to the other examples from Trench 44.

Contextual distribution of the assemblage

The assemblage of sarsen- and bluestone-working debris was recovered from a wide range of contexts excavated within Trench 45 (Figures 6.20–6.25). However, the majority of the assemblage was retrieved from a restricted range of deposits, with 38% being derived from the fills of a pair of contiguous pits (055/056), 32% from the makeup of the banks of the Avenue (021 and 022), and 15% from the old land surface (033=053) and buried soils (038 and 043). The pits, old land surface and buried soils all pre-date the construction of the Avenue so can be assigned to Stonehenge's Stage 2 or possibly earlier. The banks of the Avenue (together with their ditches) are assigned to Stage 3 but could have been constructed initially in Stage 2.

Within these key contexts, the assemblage composition is variable in terms of the representation of different elements and raw materials (Table 6.6):

- For example, there are proportionally more waste fragments and fewer waste flakes from context 045, the upper fill of both pits (055/056), than there are from the lower fill (054) of pit 055 or from an adjacent buried soil (043, buried beneath the Avenue's eastern bank).

- Equally the upper and lower fills of the pits also have different proportions of raw material within them, with lower fill 054 having 68% quartzite sarsen and 32% saccaroid sarsen, whilst upper fill 045 has 23% quartzite sarsen and 77% saccaroid sarsen.

The fills of the pits, particularly context 045, were densely packed with sarsen, and the variability in assemblage and raw material composition confirms that the material within them is not a random sample of debitage accidentally incorporated from adjacent soil gathered up to backfill them. Rather, it seems that either the sarsen was selected and sorted for deposition or, perhaps more likely, soil from different areas, with different associated assemblage compositions, was collected to fill the pits.

Beyond the insights into the pit fills, the apparent randomness in terms of assemblage composition between contexts is hard to interpret. Sarsen-working debris was present in buried soils beneath the banks of the Avenue, which does confirm that sarsen-dressing took place prior to the Avenue's construction. Yet, on the basis of the assemblage itself, it is harder to assess whether the material incorporated into the banks of the Avenue and into the fills of its ditches (Figures 6.21–6.22) is the residue of sarsen-dressing that took place during and after the construction of the Avenue's bank and ditch, or whether it is residual debris from earlier working in this area immediately north of Stonehenge. The potential for sarsen debris to be residual within later deposits is shown by the presence of such debris within the upper fills of both of the Avenue ditches and within a number of much later wheel-ruts that scored the surface of the Avenue's interior (Figure 6.20).

Although the majority of contexts within Trench 45 contained sarsen, some did not. Sarsen was found within

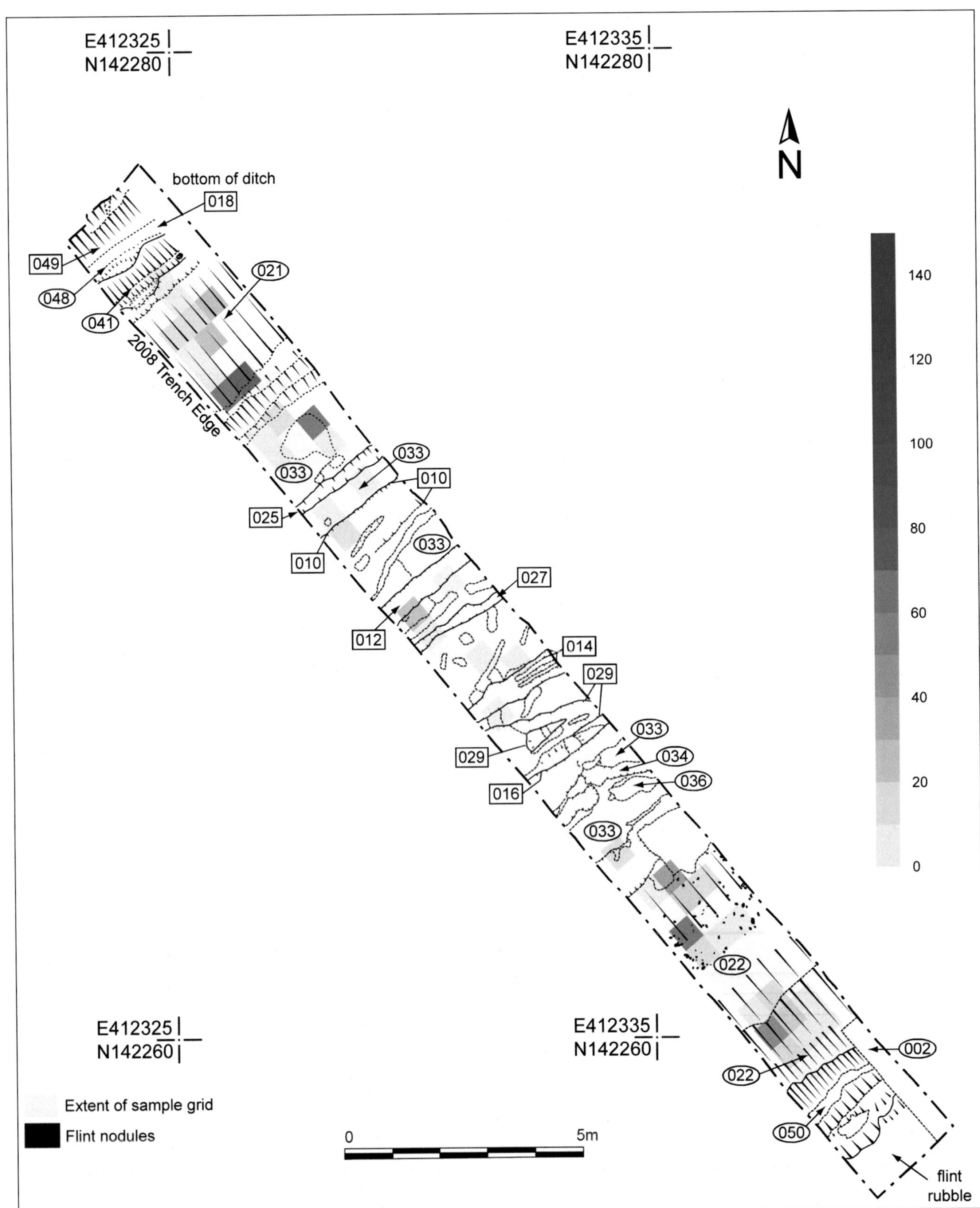

Figure 6.20. The distribution of sarsen chippings within Trench 45 (within that half not previously excavated by Atkinson)

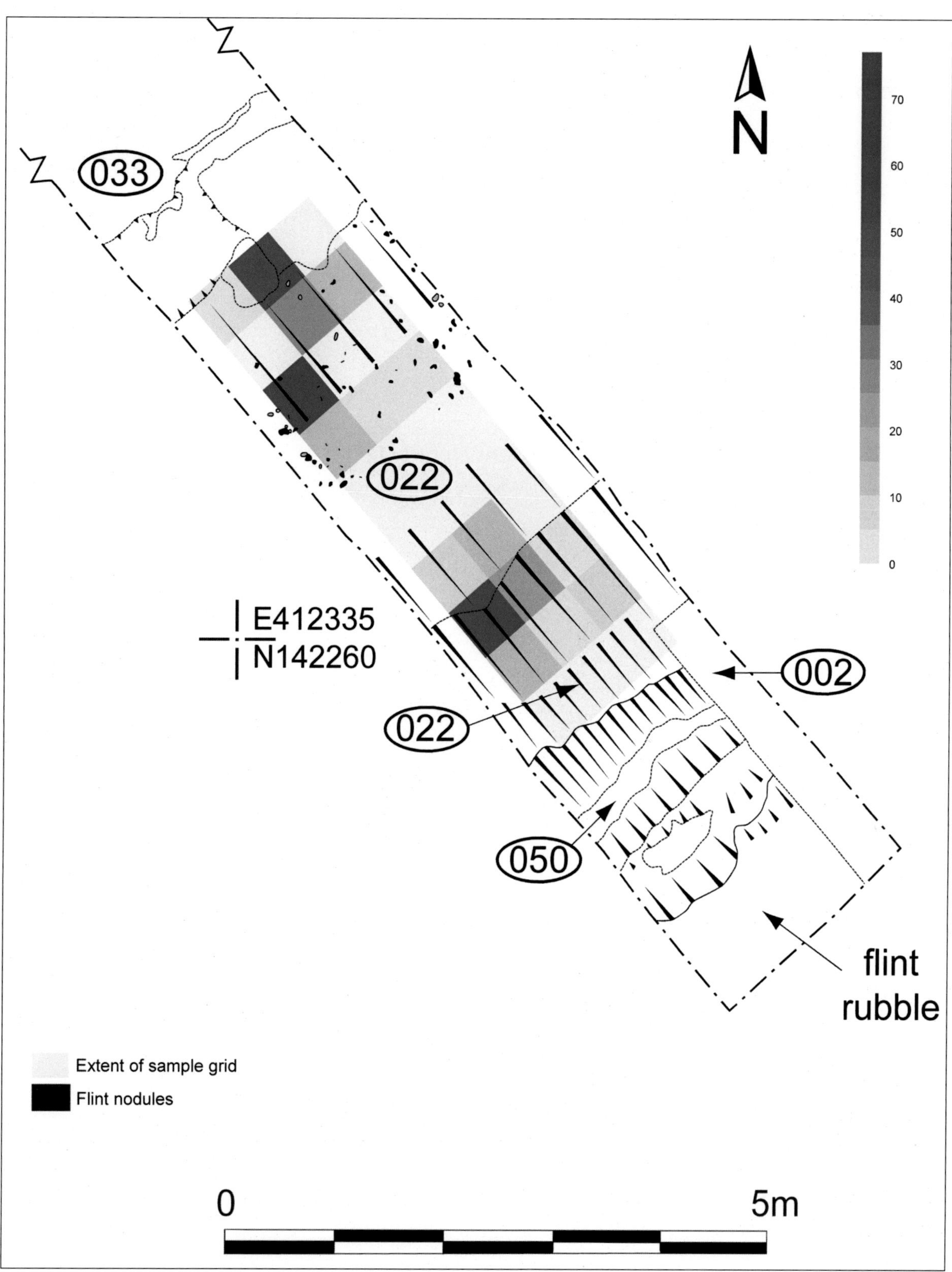

Figure 6.21. The distribution of sarsen chippings within context 022 within the east bank

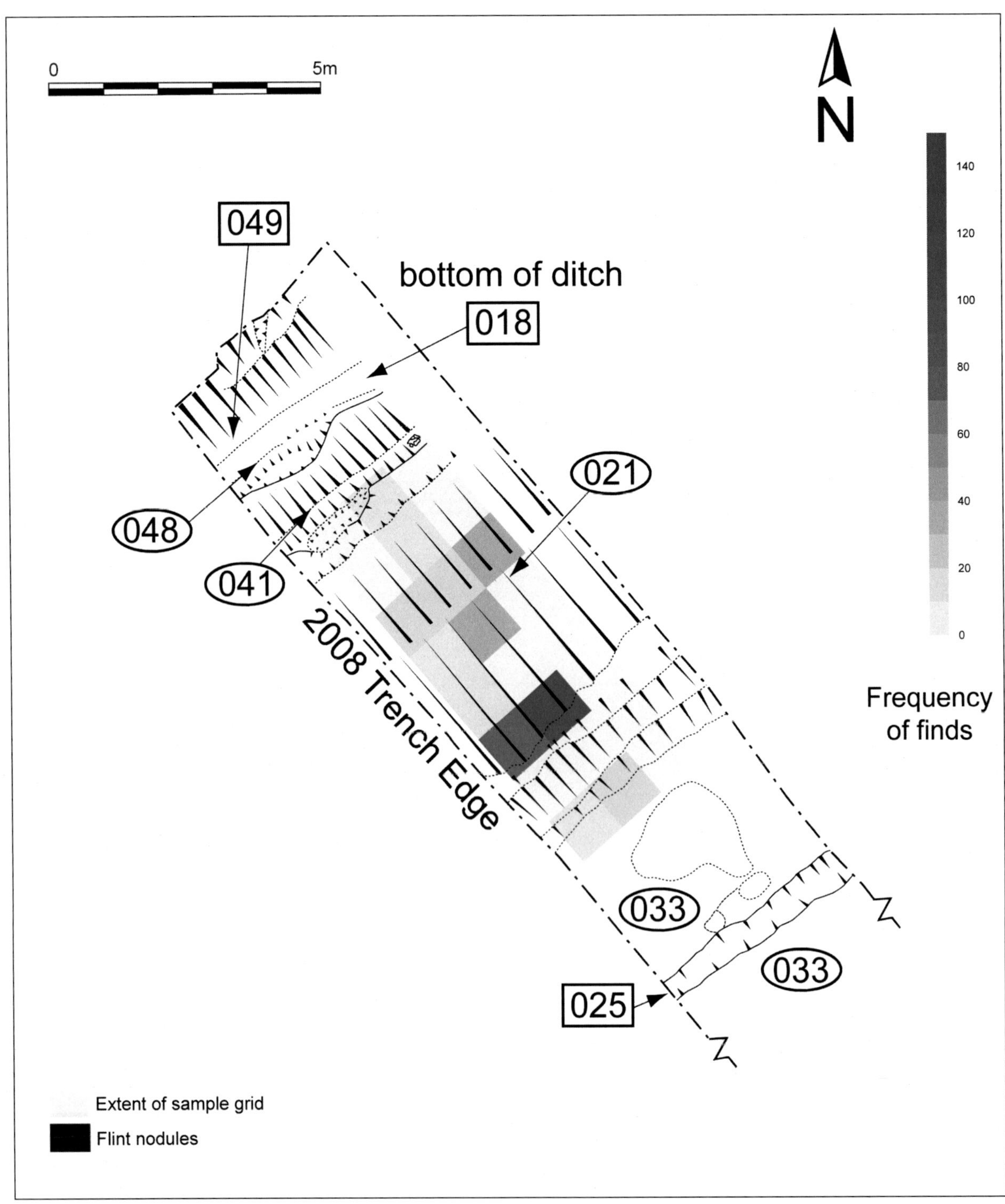

Figure 6.22. The distribution of sarsen chippings within context 021 within the west bank

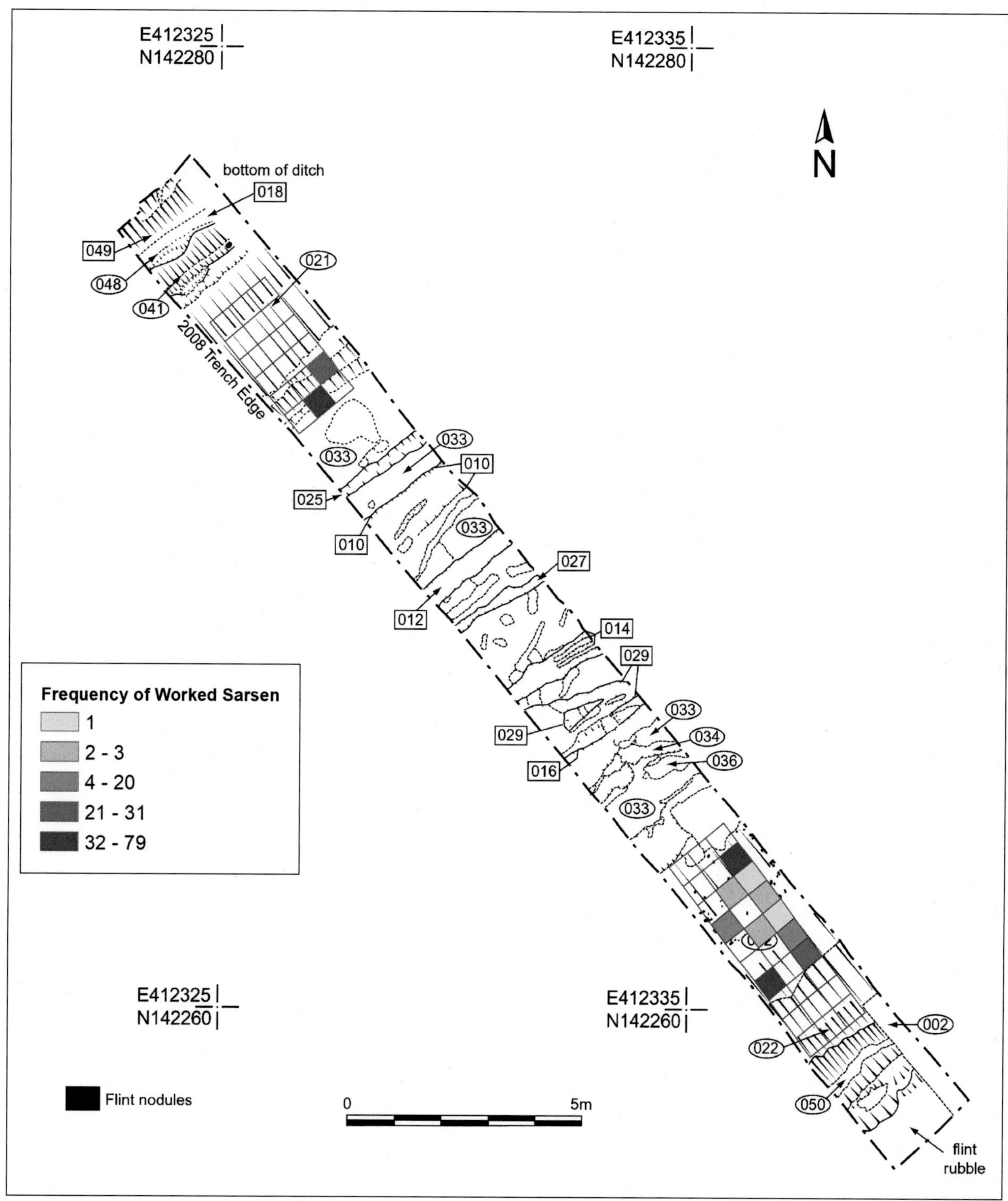

Figure 6.23. The distribution of sarsen chippings in buried soils 038 (to the northwest) and 043 (to the southeast)

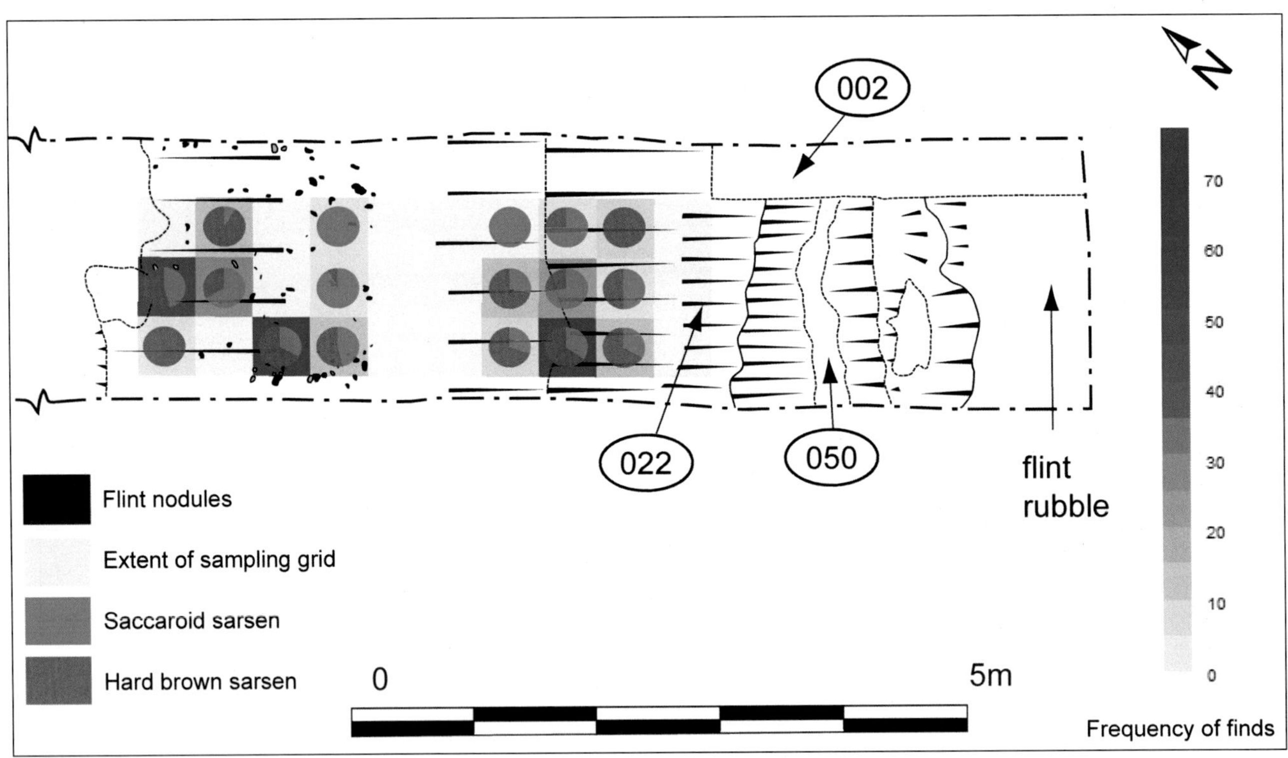

Figure 6.24. The distribution of types of sarsen chippings within the east bank

Artefact type		Context							Total
		Land surface	*Buried soils*		*Fills of pits 055 and 056*		*Avenue banks*		
		033=053	*038*	*043*	*045*	*054*	*021*	*022*	
Fragment of ground/pecked object	Count	0	0	0	0	0	0	1	1
	% within context	0%	0%	0%	0%	0%	0%	0.2%	0.0%
Hammerstone	Count	3	1	1	8	0	13	7	33
	% within context	1.9%	0.7%	0.4%	0.7%	0%	2.2%	1.2%	1.1%
Irregularly flaked object	Count	0	0	0	0	0	1	0	1
	% within context	0%	0%	0%	0%	0%	0.2%	0%	0.0%
Waste flake (<1cm)	Count	0	0	1	31	10	23	0	64
	% within context	0%	0%	5.6	2.7%	5.6%	4.0%	0%	2.1%
Waste flake (1-5cm)	Count	7	13	38	122	37	135	133	485
	% within context	4.3%	9.5%	15.8%	10.5%	20.9%	23.2%	23.7%	16.1%
Waste flake (>5cm)	Count	20	3	21	25	6	58	65	198
	% within context	12.3%	2.2%	8.8%	2.2%	3.4%	10.0%	11.6%	6.6%
Waste fragment (<1cm)	Count	1	4	14	347	41	24	5	436
	% within context	0.6%	2.9%	5.8%	29.9%	23.2%	4.1%	0.9%	14.5%
Waste fragment (1-5cm)	Count	105	100	137	504	53	268	285	1452
	% within context	64.8%	73.0%	57.1%	43.5%	29.9%	46.1%	50.8%	48.1%
Waste fragment (>5cm)	Count	26	16	29	122	30	59	65	347
	% within context	16.0%	11.7%	12.1%	10.5%	16.9%	10.2%	11.6%	11.5%
Total	Count	162	137	240	1159	177	581	561	3017
	% within context	100.0%	100.0%	100.0%	100.0%	100.0%	100.0%	100.0%	100.0%

Table 6.6. The frequency of artefact categories by context type from the main contexts in Trench 45

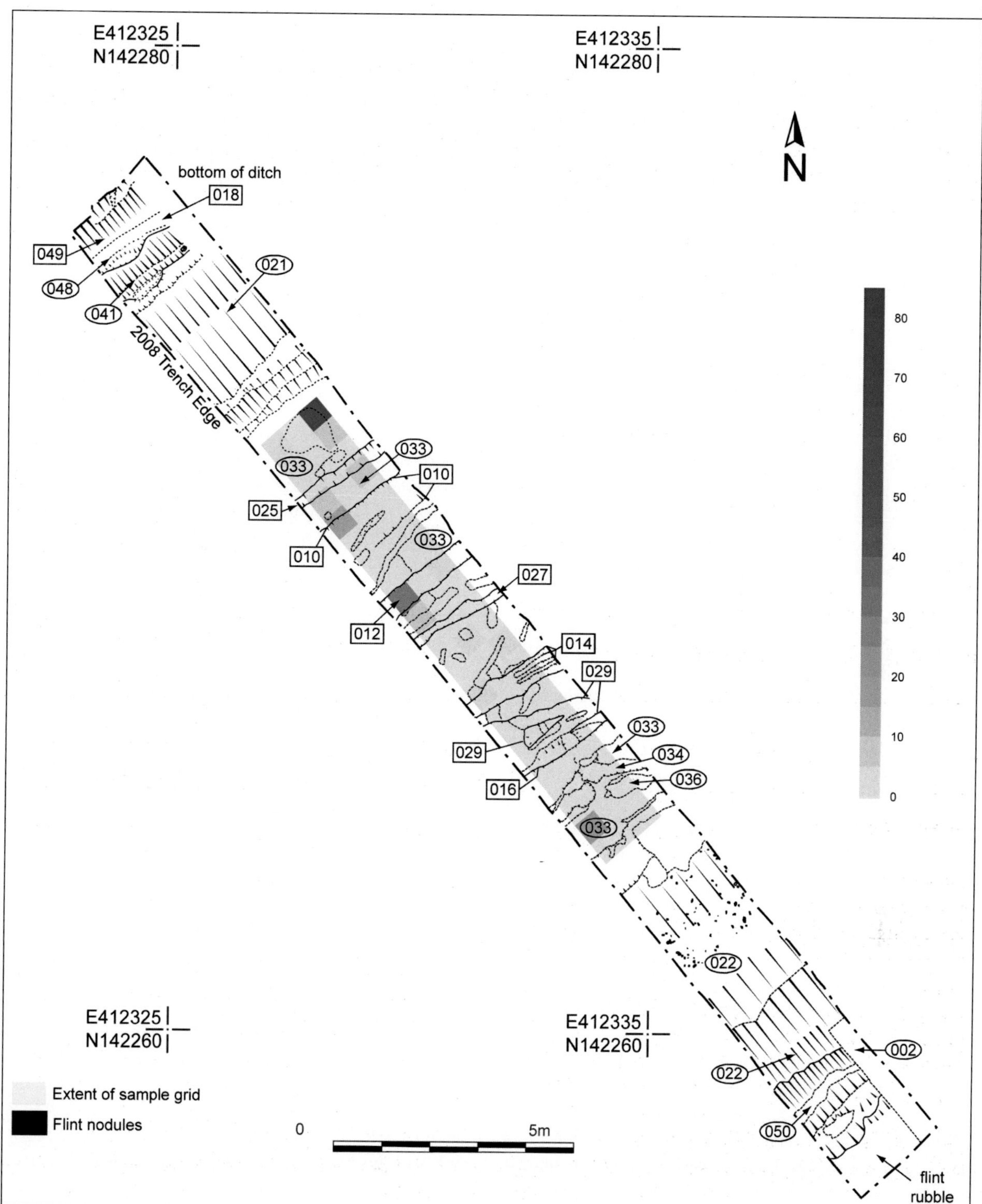

Figure 6.25. The distribution of sarsen chippings within contexts between the Avenue banks

six of the nine wheel-ruts, most of the Avenue's deposits, and the buried soils beneath its banks. Yet sarsen was entirely absent from the fills of a tree-throw (040) which was found beneath the east bank of the Avenue, and from the fills of the periglacial stripes (see Chapter 8). This provides further evidence of the periglacial origin of the 'stripes', and demonstrates that the tree-throw not only pre-dates the bank, but also the sarsen phase of Stonehenge.

It is also worth noting that the earliest contexts that produced bluestone fragments include the old land surface (053=033), a buried soil beneath the eastern bank of the Avenue (043) and the fill (045) of pits 055/056. These are, in fact, stratigraphically the earliest anthropogenic contexts within the trench. As these contexts also all contained sarsen, it is not possible to stratigraphically place the working of bluestone on the site in an earlier phase of activity (*i.e.* Stage 1) to that of sarsen-working (*i.e.* Stage 2). However, it does provide evidence that bluestones were being worked by Stage 2.

Spatial analysis

As detailed above, in the southwestern strip of Trench 45 – the newly excavated area, immediately adjacent to Atkinson's 1956 trench – a series of soil layers (see Figures 8.4, 8.6) consisting of the banks of the Avenue (021, 022), the old land surface (033=053) and buried soils (038, 043) were excavated using 0.50m × 0.50m grids. The spatial density of material revealed in detail by the grid methodology shows that sarsen was not evenly distributed along the length of the trench (Figure 6.20).

The spatial distribution of the material within different contexts has been affected by a number of factors. For example, the plot of the density of sarsen across the area of the Avenue's eastern bank (022) shows an empty area in the middle of the bank where no sarsen was found (Figure 6.21). This pattern does not, however, reflect the original distribution of the material. Rather, it is the result of the erosion of the higher middle part of the bank. Erosion was less of a factor for the western bank (021), where sarsen densities were slightly greater on the higher areas of the bank, perhaps reflecting the greater volume of soil in this part of the bank (Figure 6.22).

Land surface 033=053 is located in the centre of the Avenue, between the two banks, and represents a soil horizon where the original topsoil has been lost to erosion. The analysis of the distribution of sarsen within this context shows a low density of material evenly spread across this land surface (Figure 6.25). As a result of the loss of the topsoil from 033=053, it is difficult to assess to what extent this distribution reflects the original density of material in the area.

The same can be said for the bank deposits, as the material within them is unlikely to be *in situ*, and more likely to be material gathered up when the Avenue's ditches were dug. In this respect, the only contexts that reveal the density of sarsen on the land surface at the time of the construction of the Avenue are the buried soils 038 and 043, which were buried during the construction of the banks. The density of sarsen within these two deposits is broadly comparable with the other soil layers, but there is a clear distinction between buried soil 038 to the northwest, and 043 to the southeast (Figure 6.23). Buried soil 038 had only two sample squares that produced sarsen whereas, within 043, the material was spread sporadically across the sample grid. In both cases the distribution is highly localised, with relatively high-density sample squares being adjacent to sample squares in which no sarsen was found.

Comparing the sarsen assemblages in Trenches 44 and 45

The composition of the assemblage from Trench 45 (the Avenue) shows some variation when compared to the assemblage from Trench 44 (the sarsen-dressing area), most notably in terms of the high proportion of both hammerstones and waste flakes in comparison to waste fragments in Trench 45. Waste flakes are predominantly of quartzite sarsen and derive from spalls knocked off hammerstones during use. This is of interest because, if the hammerstones were used elsewhere and brought to the environs of Trench 45, it is unlikely that the flakes knocked off unintentionally during their use would have been brought with them. Therefore, it seems that the presence of hammerstones indicates the dressing of one or more monoliths in the vicinity of Trench 45 (on the old ground surface prior to construction of the Avenue).

The Trench 45 hammerstones themselves compare directly with Trench 44's hammerstones in terms of raw material – *i.e.* they are quartzite sarsen with a few flint cobbles – as well as size and weight (Figure 6.26). Therefore, as with Trench 44, the dressing that was conducted within the vicinity of Trench 45 is likely to have been peck-dressing rather than the flaking and roughing-out of a monolith.

If Trench 45 were the site of a sarsen-dressing event, we might expect its densities of debris to be comparable to those from Trench 44. Yet there is a massive discrepancy, with Trench 44 having a density of 1,473 artefacts per sq m and Trench 45 having a density of 91 artefacts per sq m. Trench 45's density figure is slightly lower than it should be because some of the features, such as pits 055/056, were only half-excavated (see Chapter 8), but the as yet unexcavated finds from these features would only increase the density within the trench by a relatively small amount.

Moreover, variation in assemblage composition for Trench 45 between the different pit fills and the

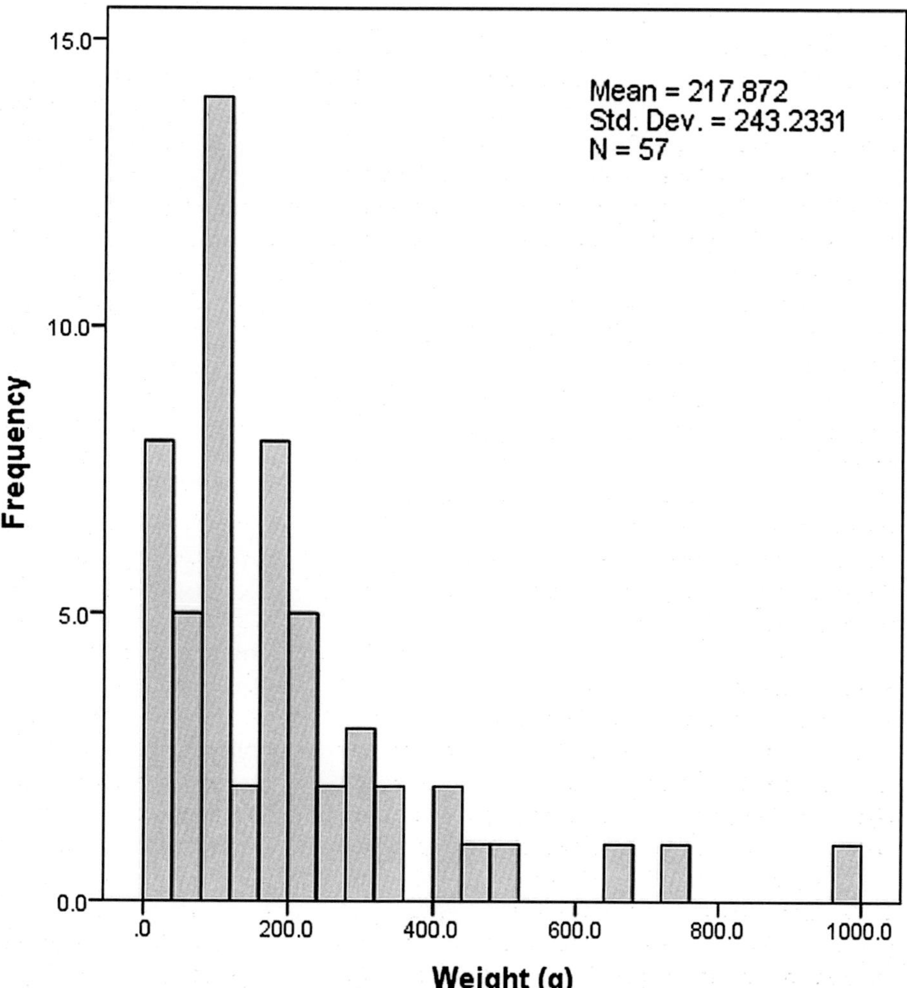

Figure 6.26. Histogram of the weights of hammerstones from Trench 45

surrounding deposits hints at differential deposition in these contexts. Either objects to be interred within the pits were selected from material to hand, or else the material in the pits was brought in from elsewhere. The localised nature of the high spots in the density of sarsen within buried soils 038 and 043 is also noteworthy (Figure 6.23), since the distribution of sarsen across a dressing area may be expected to be more continuous.

It seems likely that, whilst stone-dressing probably took place in the vicinity of Trench 45, the focus of this dressing activity was outside the area exposed by the trench rather than within it. On the basis of the higher density of material within buried soil 043 compared to buried soil 038, the focus of dressing was perhaps to the southeast of Trench 45.

It is clear that this stone-working activity occurred before the construction of the Avenue because sarsen-dressing waste is present beneath its banks. In any case, the Avenue's banks and ditches would have been an impediment to moving large monoliths in this area north of Stonehenge. Therefore, the sarsen-dressing material within the matrix of the Avenue banks and in the ditches is most probably residual.

6.2.4. Worked flint from the sarsen-dressing area in Trench 44

B. Chan

The following report details the worked flint assemblage from Trench 44, excluding the flint hammerstones which are reported above as part of the sarsen-dressing assemblage. Excluding the hammerstones, the assemblage of worked flint from Trench 44 consists of 2,040 artefacts, 32% of which came from context 005 with the remainder coming from 006.

Raw material and condition

The flint hammerstones reported above are all water-worn cobbles, which must have been retrieved from the river. The rest of the worked flint is normal chalk-derived flint typical of the Stonehenge environs. The flint has white to beige cortex, varying in thickness from 1mm–5mm and has cherty inclusions. The material is patinated but is otherwise in good condition.

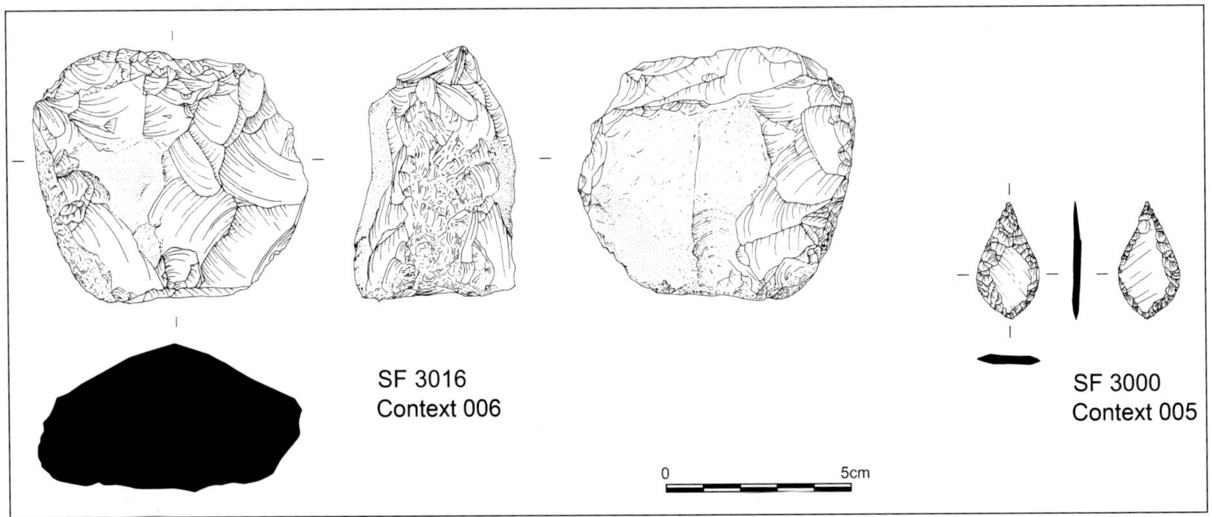

Figure 6.27. A flint hammerstone and a leaf-shaped arrowhead from Trench 44

	Artefact type	Frequency	Percent
Debitage and cores	Core on a flake	1	<0.1
	Blade	15	0.7
	Blade-like flake	12	0.6
	Bladelet	16	0.8
	Flake	1816	89.0
	Irregular waste	116	5.7
	Multi-platform flake-core	7	0.3
	Rejuvenation flake-core face/ edge	1	<0.1
	Single-platform flake-core	3	0.1
	Tested nodule/bashed lump	1	<0.1
Retouched flakes and tools	Awl	1	<0.1
	Chisel arrowhead	1	<0.1
	Edge-rounded flake	1	<0.1
	Fragmentary arrowhead	1	<0.1
	Leaf shaped arrowhead	2	0.1
	Misc. retouched flake	43	2.1
	Other scraper	2	0.1
	Scraper on a non-flake blank	1	<0.1
	Total	2040	100.0

Table 6.7. The worked flint assemblage from Trench 44

The assemblage

The assemblage of worked flint from Trench 44 consists of 89% flakes, 6% irregular waste, 0.6% cores, 2% utilised/retouch flakes, 0.3% formal tools and 2% blades, bladelets and blade-like flakes (Table 6.7).

The tools consist of an awl, an edge-rounded flake, three scrapers and four arrowheads:

- The awl is made on a triangular flake with unifacial retouch on all margins, forming two separate points, with retouch on each side of the points being on alternating faces of the tool.

- The edge-rounded flake is a broad flake with one lateral margin and the distal margin totally rounded and worn by an abrasive activity. In plan the flake has curving margins similar in shape to a scraper, but the flake has been shaped by abrasion rather than retouch. The lack of edge removals suggests that abrasion did not occur from contact with a hard material such as stone or bone. Equally, a soft material, such as plant or hide, would have been too soft to generate such extensive edge-rounding. Unfortunately, the heavy patination on the flake obscures any microscopic wear traces on its edge; however, under high-power microscopy, faint striations generated from a transverse motion can be seen on some parts of the edge, indicating that the tool was used in a scraping-type motion. The degree of edge-rounding and the morphology of the working edge have similarities with flakes that have been used to scrape a contact material of a mineral such as clay, but the overall condition of the object prohibits a definitive conclusion. Edge-ground

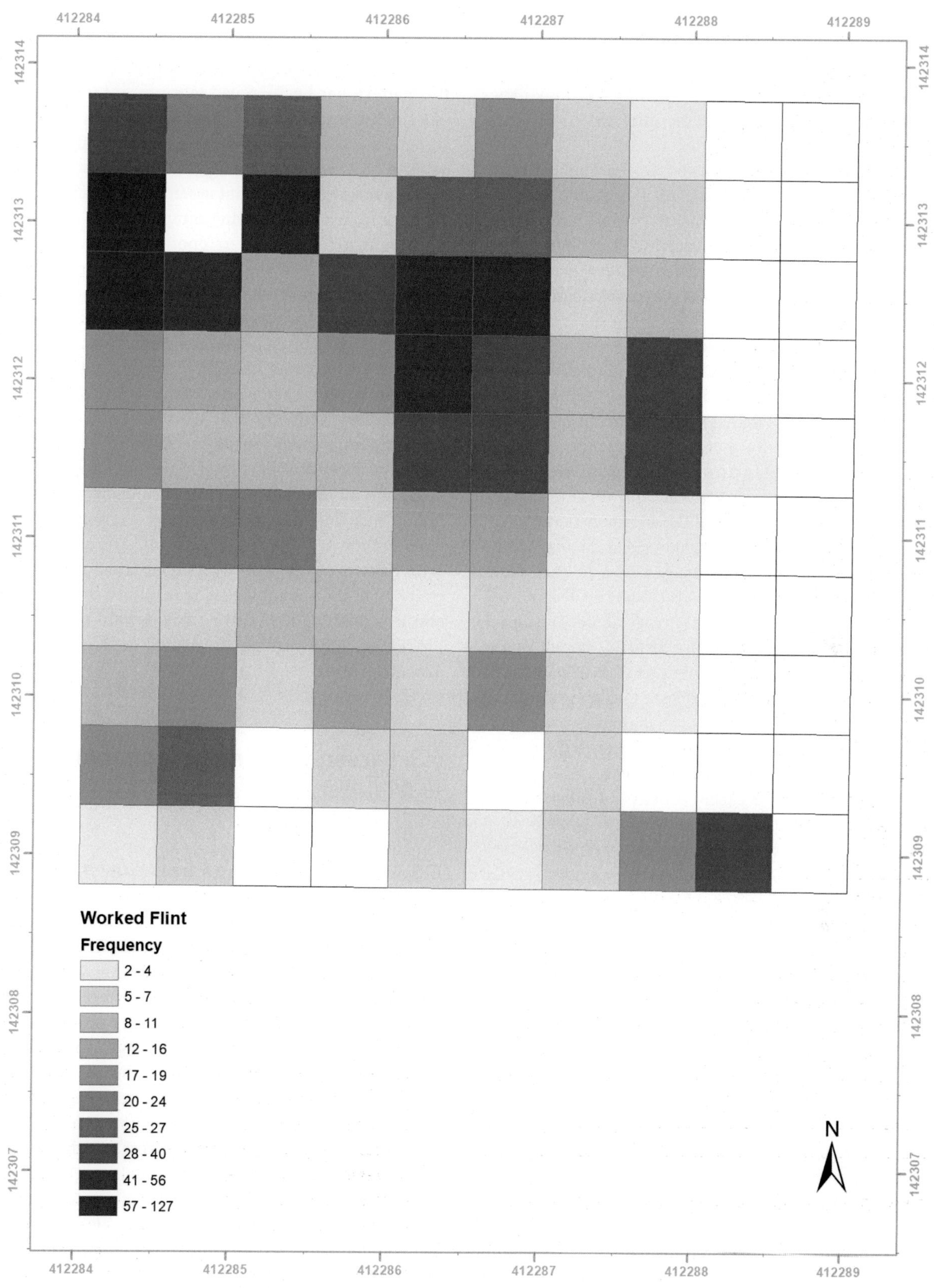

Figure 6.28. The density of worked flint in Trench 44

flakes were also found during excavations in 2008 at Stonehenge (Tim Darvill pers. comm.) and further analysis is warranted to assess whether they have similar edge-rounding and morphology.

- The four arrowheads consist of a probable chisel arrowhead, the broken tip of a probable oblique arrowhead, a poorly worked ovate leaf-shaped arrowhead found in the northwest corner of the trench, and a well-worked leaf-shaped arrowhead from the southeast corner of the trench (Figure 6.27).

Discussion and conclusion

The assemblage from Trench 44 fits broadly within the same technology as other Late Neolithic flint assemblages in the Stonehenge environs (*e.g.* Harding 1995; Chan 2010). However, the presence of Early Neolithic leaf-shaped arrowheads, one of which was found in association with a concentration of blades within the southeast corner of the trench, makes it clear that there is at least some chronological mixing within the assemblage. The blades may relate to this same early episode of activity, but this cannot be determined definitively on the basis of technology alone. The chisel arrowhead is also likely to pre-date the sarsen phase of Stonehenge (Stage 2, beginning in *2740–2505 cal BC*) and therefore, alongside the other earlier elements within the assemblage, shows that there were small-scale knapping activities in the area prior to the on-site dressing of the Stonehenge sarsen stones.

Whether or not this earlier activity indicates that this area was already of significance when the sarsens were brought here to erect Stonehenge is impossible to say, but the clustering of the blade component provides further evidence that activity was taking place in the vicinity of the site of Stonehenge prior to its construction. These artefacts also indicate the potential for the residues of small-scale activities to still survive in a relatively *in situ* state within the worm-sorted topsoil on this part of Salisbury Plain.

The large assemblage of sarsen hammerstones and sarsen-dressing waste within Trench 44 has been interpreted as resulting from an *in situ* sarsen-dressing event. This interpretation is based largely upon the spatial distribution of the material (see above), which is most convincingly explained as resulting from the presence of a recumbent monolith and the stone-dressing of its surfaces.

Despite the potential chronological mixing within the worked flint assemblage, a similar argument can be put forward for the flint. The spatial distributions of the worked flint and of the sarsen assemblage show close similarity. This is most notable with respect to the distinct fall-off in the density of both worked flint and sarsen in the 2m-wide strip along the eastern edge of Trench 44 (Figures 6.16, 6.28). For the sarsen assemblage, this pattern has been argued to represent the 'shadow' of a single monolith that lay partly within the area of the trench as it was being dressed. The distribution of the worked flint confirms this suggestion and also indicates that the majority of the flint assemblage was associated with the same stone-dressing activity.

Although flint hammerstones were used in small quantities to dress the monolith, the hammerstone nodules are water-worn and distinctive, and the shatter from them only makes up a minuscule proportion of the worked flint assemblage from Trench 44. Therefore, it must be assumed that the working of the flint, represented by the remainder of the assemblage, relates to subsidiary activities that were associated with the stone-dressing event. There are only nine identifiable tools, a very small proportion of the assemblage, and three of them – all arrowheads – are chronologically earlier than the sarsen phase of Stonehenge. Consequently, the tools do little to inform us about what sorts of flint-using activities were associated with sarsen-dressing. The vast majority of the assemblage is made up of simple flakes, and it is possible that cutting flakes were the primary product of flintworking associated with the sarsen-dressing event.

6.3. Sarsen-working at Stonehenge

K. Whitaker

6.3.1. The Stonehenge hammerstone assemblage

> 'Mauls, a more remarkable kind of hammerstone than those just enumerated...They are ponderous boulders' (Gowland 1902: 67)

Traditionally described as hammerstones and mauls, those flint, bluestone and sarsen artefacts from Stonehenge interpreted as stone-working tools were first classified by William Gowland in 1902. His typology was based on 100 artefacts that he excavated in 1901 from trenches around Stone 56 (see Figure 6.3 for stone numbering). Gowland also made the first extensive proposals for a reduction sequence for the shaped monoliths; his framework has remained largely unchallenged and unmodified (Chippindale 1994: 168).

Since 1902, newly excavated stone-working tools from Stonehenge have been categorised following Gowland on the basis of material and size. The methods and processes involved in the use of these tools have been inferred

Stage	Product/activity	Key issues
Procurement	Boulders for stone settings	Sarsen sources Bluestone sources
	Nodules and cobbles for stone-working tools Collection and transport	The morphology and processes of introduction of hammerstones
Reduction sequences	Shaped and dressed stones, waste material	Location of stone-working activities
	Stone-working tools	Hypothesised stone-working methods
Use	Erection and re-workings of stone settings	Chronological sequence of stone settings Completeness of stone settings
Discard	Final re-working of stone settings	The abandonment of Stonehenge

Table 6.8. Stages, products and key issues in the working of Stonehenge's sarsens

from observations of surface effects on the monoliths, and by using ethnographic and historical analogy (Stone 1924; Atkinson 1956). Whilst the worked nature of most of Stonehenge's monoliths is unquestionable, the technological behaviour facilitating that stone-working and embedded in the long-term planning necessary for construction of the monument is often taken for granted. The increase in quantity of the Stonehenge hammerstone assemblage, including the well-documented material from Trench 44, means that it is an appropriate time to review the hammerstone categorisations.

The assemblage investigated here includes hammerstones from Trench 44 of the SRP, excavated in 2008, as well as the historic collections from Stonehenge curated by Salisbury Museum. The key research questions guiding the analysis of the material were:

- How were the tools designed and manufactured?
- Do the tools show variability of use?
- What bearing might such variability have had on the organisation of stone-working at Stonehenge?

Accordingly, this analysis reviews the key technological issues in relation to stone-working at Stonehenge, in terms of stone procurement for the related lithologies of the monoliths and the stone-working tools, and the hypothesised reduction stages and tool use.

Terminology

Despite Gowland's distinction between different types of stone-working tools – classifying only the heaviest as 'mauls' (1902: 67) – the terms 'hammerstone' and 'maul' have since then been applied increasingly loosely, to the extent that they were used interchangeably by Cleal *et al.* (1995). For convenience, these tools are here referred to collectively as hammerstones without prejudice to interpretation of their use. The term 'stone-working' is used throughout to refer to the shaping and surface dressing of monoliths at Stonehenge. 'Monolith' is used to refer to all standing, recumbent and horizontal worked stones.

6.3.2. Previous analyses

The working practices employed during the various stages in which Stonehenge's stones were shaped are poorly understood. Apart from Hawley's briefly reported discovery of sarsen waste close to the Avenue (1923: 23), extensive evidence of *in situ* sarsen stone-working has been uncovered only in the SRP's Trench 44. The stages from stone procurement through to final re-workings of stone settings at Stonehenge (Table 6.8) are framed in terms of the stages of a *chaîne opératoire* (Sellet 1993: 106). This summarises a complex technical system that enabled the development of a long-lived monument. Whilst the concept of reduction sequences was developed as a means of categorising and ordering the techniques by which bifacial tools were made from flakable materials (Andrefsky 1998: 180), it can also be applied to the sculptural activity of removing material from a stone to achieve a specific final form (*e.g.* Van Tilburg and Pakarati 2002).

That most of the standing sarsen stones at Stonehenge are worked, in contrast to the natural forms of the standing stones in the henge at Avebury, was recognised by John Aubrey in the seventeenth century and described in some detail by William Stukeley in 1740. Stukeley commented on five characteristics:

- mortise-and-tenon joints between upright sarsen stones and lintels;
- tongue-and-groove joints between sarsen lintel stones;
- finished sarsen and bluestone surfaces;
- entasis, or tapering, of upright stones;
- positioning of the smoothest faces of sarsen stones so that they face inwards (Stukeley 1740: 16).

GOWLAND (1902); REDUCTION	Evidence and analogies	STONE (1924); REDUCTION	Evidence and analogies
Primary reduction at source • fire-setting to create a weakness along the intended fracture line • pounding with mauls to break off material (1902: 75–6)	Heavy wooden mauls used in Japan to drive in building foundations (1902: 70)	*Primary reduction at source* • splitting techniques to reduce large natural blocks (1924: 75–7)	Articulated the historical source of the sarsen fire-setting analogy; techniques to split out blocks with mauls at Hyderabad granite quarries (1924: 75–7)
Secondary reduction at Stonehenge • pounding with mauls to remove surface material in broad, parallel grooves • striking obliquely with mauls to remove ridges left between grooves (1902: 77–8) • pounding with mauls to remove surface material in narrower, shallower transverse grooves, further cutting down the surface (1902: 78)	Stones 52, 54, 55 and 59 where grooves remain (1902: 77–8)	*Secondary reduction at Stonehenge* • hammer-dressing to break off more prominent irregularities, using heavy mauls to remove large pieces and smaller tools to remove smaller pieces • surface-pounding with mauls or hammerstones to remove 'crumbled stuff' in grooves with successive heavy blows (1924: 85–6) • flint tools possibly used on bluestone, held against the surface and malleted to remove material, followed by surface-pounding and grinding (1924: 90, 98)	Techniques in the Sudan to rejuvenate querns by attrition with a pebble dropped onto the surface; and the removal of granite blocks for obelisks by hammering away gullies with mauls in Egyptian quarries. Stones 54 and 59 where grooves remain (1924: 86).
Jointing at Stonehenge • pounding with hard hammerstones to reduce ends of uprights to form tenons • grinding with water, sand and cobbles to hollow out mortises • pounding and grinding with hammerstones to shape lintel tongues and grooves (1902: 78–9)	Grinding techniques used in Japan and Egypt to make stone vessels and mortars (1902: 78)	*Jointing at Stonehenge* • hammer-dressing to reduce material around intended tenons followed by surface-pounding and grinding • pounding and grinding to hollow out mortises, create lintel tongues and grooves and seatings for lintels (1924: 95–7)	
Finishing at Stonehenge • pecking with small hammerstones, creating an 'orange peel' effect on surfaces (1902: 79)	Experimentation by a colleague using a quartzite pebble on saccaroid sarsen (1902: 79)	*Finishing at Stonehenge* • grinding with flat sarsen blocks, sand and water, to smooth surfaces (1924: 88) • pounding with hammerstones to create final tooling (1924: 94)	Experimentation by a colleague using hammerstones to pound sarsen (1924: 94). Examples of effect on Stones 55, 56, 60, 122.

Table 6.9. Stonehenge reduction sequences proposed by Gowland (1902) and Stone (1924)

The worked nature of the extant stones has been described by many observers: these features comprise the jointing, shaping and finishing effects, characterised as carpentry techniques, by which stone was treated as timber at Stonehenge (Atkinson 1956: 25–6; Burl 2006: 172–3; Cleal *et al.* 1995: 27; Abbott and Anderson-Whymark 2012). Two characteristics in particular underpin Gowland's (1902) approach to a conjectured reduction sequence by which boulders might have been shaped to achieve these forms and effects: first, the shaped rectangular cross-sections of stones and, secondly, the finely-worked jointing and smoothed surfaces, especially as exhibited by Stone 56 (visible in Figures 6.1 and 6.5).

These two observations were fundamental to Gowland's identification of the need for the stonemasons to have carried out rough shaping of the natural boulders by breaking off large pieces from the ends and sides of these commonly blocky rocks: 'In this connection it is necessary to remember that the sarsens, of which the outer circle and the trilithons consist, occur naturally in more or less flat tabular blocks; usually of much greater length than breadth, and generally ranging in thickness from about 2 to 4 feet' (Gowland 1902: 75). Gowland envisaged this roughing-out to have been achieved by means of fire and by hammering, essentially sledgehammering (*ibid.*: 75), which may be termed 'primary reduction'.

The assumption that some uneven surfaces on the ends and sides of Stonehenge's monoliths were a consequence of this roughing-out, whilst the other, flatter, natural faces required little modification, led Gowland to infer what actions were required to achieve the final forms by working down the surfaces (1902: 75, 77–8), which may be termed secondary reduction. Inference of a pounding action rests partly on the assumption that grooves observable on certain stones, such as Stones 54 and 59, represent unfinished reduction that failed to achieve fully flat, perpendicular surfaces. Well-finished surfaces, including a fine-tooled 'orange peel' effect (*ibid.*: 52, 79), and the careful jointing techniques, prompted Gowland to propose a combination of hammering, grinding and pecking (*ibid.*: 78–9) that may be termed jointing and finishing. The implication is that, as Atkinson put it, 'the dressing was carried out in several stages of increasing delicacy' (1956: 120).

Gowland's reduction sequence is essentially a rational, process-based approach (Table 6.9), elaborated by Stone (1924) and adopted by Atkinson (1956). All three authors imagined a *chaîne opératoire* that would explain observed effects in the stone settings. Yet these formulations of the conjectured reduction sequence were supported by analogies that require more critical examination. First, these authors suggested the use of fire in primary reduction, drawing on an historical precedent for saccaroid sarsen-breaking; secondly, they suggested ethnographic analogies for different types of stone-working, drawn from Japan, Egypt and India.

It is questionable whether the historical analogy of the north Wiltshire sarsen-breaking industry is useful for understanding prehistoric sarsen-working. The fire-setting technique referred to by Gowland, Stone and Atkinson is that described by Aubrey in the late seventeenth century to break sarsens around Avebury, for agricultural clearance and for obtaining building stone, a method still current in the mid-nineteenth century (Britton 1847: 44; Fowles 1980: 38). Aubrey famously described the practice as reported to him by the vicar of Avebury: 'they make a fire on that line of the stone where they would have it to crack; and after the stone is well heated, draw over a line with cold water, and immediately give it a smart knock with a smith's sledge, and it will break like the collets at the glass-house' (Aubrey quoted in Britton 1847: 44).

Atkinson (1956: 118) also refers to Stukeley's observations of the destruction of large sarsens in fire-pits, also at Avebury, by using a bonfire of straw to heat up individual sarsens before pouring water over them and removing pieces with large sledgehammers (Stukeley 1740: 15). Whilst it may be noted that, on a smaller scale, ethnographically attested methods of blank-preparation using fire have been used successfully in experiments investigating the manufacture of Neolithic jadeitite stone axes (Sheridan *et al.* 2010: 23), the aim of the historical techniques of sarsen-working was to break down boulders into pieces, whether to clear land, defy the establishment, re-organise boundaries or provide building materials to meet contemporary demands for housing and commercial development (Gillings *et al.* 2008). Total destruction of the sarsen was intended, rather than the careful removal of pieces to prepare a blank for further modification by other means.

Herbert Stone's Indian and Egyptian ethnographic analogies were drawn from nineteenth-century quarrying, where granite blocks were cut from igneous bedrock. At the Hyderabad quarries, Stone describes stone mauls being used to split large blocks away from the bedrock, before the European plug-and-feather technique was introduced (1924: 75–7). Whilst the use of mauls does pre-date the adoption of the European technology, this is nevertheless a poor relational analogy for the roughing-out of free sandstone boulders.

In contrast, for the Egyptian quarries Stone describes how stone mauls were used to pound away at the gaps around large pieces of stone intended for obelisks (1924: 86). This long-term attrition provides a more attractive analogy for inferred secondary reduction techniques involving pounding to loosen and remove rock, but the different properties of the subject rock must be borne in mind. Care must be taken in transplanting techniques for working stone types with different lithological properties.

A significant element underpinning the conjectured reduction sequences is the nature of waste stone material from Stonehenge, in particular the sarsen and bluestone chippings found throughout the 'Stonehenge layer'. This is a well-mixed deposit of prehistoric and modern material up to *c.* 0.50m deep underlying the turf, named by Hawley (1925: 21).

The relatively low proportion of sarsen waste in the Stonehenge layer (compared with bluestone) was interpreted as an indication of off-site primary reduction by Judd (1902: 115). Conversely, despite the presence of hammerstones, Atkinson saw the low proportion of sarsen as an indication that the Stonehenge layer comprised predominantly post-prehistoric, monument-destruction waste (1956: 54–5). Yet he agreed that secondary reduction and finishing activities occurred at Stonehenge, on the untested assumption that pounding out the joints and surfaces would have created quantities of sand and dust which he identified in the 'abnormal proportions of siliceous sand' in soil from the site (*ibid.*: 120). This was Stone's 'crumbled stuff' (1924: 85), created by the attrition of sarsen through sustained blows on the roughed-out boulders.

Interpretations of the Stonehenge layer have remained contentious (Cleal *et al.* 1995: 335). It has most recently been excavated by Darvill and Wainwright in 2008 (Darvill and Wainwright 2009). Lying immediately below the turf, the layer occurs both over cut features within the henge and also resting directly on the natural chalk where no features occur (Cleal *et al.* 1995: 334). It has produced stone chips, flint flakes and tools, coins ranging in date from the Roman period to the eighteenth century, clay pipe stems and a miscellany of Victorian and modern rubbish (Chippindale 1994: 168).

Demonstrable stratigraphic relationships between worked stone, the stone-working tools and waste stone excavated within the henge are rare; Stonehenge comprises well-spaced components including concentric settings with many discrete but few inter-cutting features (Cleal *et al.* 1995: 169, 329). For example, of the total of 2,173 pieces of sarsen curated from the twentieth-century excavations, only 217 (10%) can be attributed to Cleal *et al.*'s three construction phases (*ibid*: 386). Regrettably, any reliance on the Stonehenge layer to support the conjectured reduction sequences would be misplaced.

In contrast to the historical and ethnographic analogies developed by Gowland and Stone, Mike Pitts draws on Neolithic stone-knapping traditions to suggest that primary reduction of large volumes of saccaroid sarsen was achieved by flaking (2000: 215). He refers to this technique as understood in the context of knapping flint or similar materials for roughing-out stone axe-heads. He points out scars, up to 1m long, visible on the buried bases of Stones 30 and 29 (in the northeast of the sarsen circle, revealed during excavation in 1920), and he also draws on observations of the quantities of sarsen that he recovered in the 'stone floor' deposit on the north side of Stonehenge, revealed while excavating in advance of a cable trench (1982: 102).

Figure 6.29. The ventral surface of a saccaroid sarsen flake (Salisbury Museum 36/1978) from Stonehenge

Class	Type and description	Purpose
I	Axes: mostly flint, some sarsen, roughly chipped.	
II	Hammerstones or hammer-axes: flint with well-chipped, sharp curved edges.	Used for dressing softer sarsen and 'the more easily worked fissile stones' (1902: 62).
III	Hammerstones: flint, more-or-less well-rounded.	
IV	Hammerstones: hard sarsen, bluestone, more-or-less rounded, weighing 1lb to 6½lb.	Used to create fine finished surfaces on sarsen stones.
V	Mauls: hard sarsen weighing more than 36lb with two working faces on narrower sides and places in the middle where withies or hide bands could have been tied as handles.	Used to roughly break away blocks of material and to work down faces.

Table 6.10. Gowland's classification of Stonehenge stone-working tools (1902: 58–70)

Contextualising Stonehenge's unique stone-working in these archaeological terms is very valuable. Saccaroid sarsen will flake sub-conchoidally (Smith 1965; Gingell 1980; 1992; Young 1960: 400), though flaking properties may depend on the variability of silica cementation in saccaroid sarsen.

Two issues arise, however, in interpreting flaking as a key reduction technique. First, it is now virtually impossible to re-examine the bases of standing sarsens such as those exposed in 1919 and 1920. Secondly, the quality of the surviving waste assemblage from Stonehenge necessary for interpreting reduction methods is very poor. For example, in archived material from twentieth-century excavations at Stonehenge, there is one large sarsen flake, *c.* 35cm × 22cm × 4cm, with a bulb of percussion and approximately 90° platform angle (Figure 6.29) as opposed to many bags of chunks that show no flaked characteristics at all.

6.3.3. Stone-working tools

William Gowland (1902: 30) was the first to interpret worn and battered stones as hammerstones for stone-working. Before Gowland made his classification, 'batter-dashers' had been found during the Duke of Buckingham's seventeenth-century excavations at and around Stonehenge (Fowles 1980: 93), although whether these came from the henge or from barrows round about is unclear (Chippindale 1994: 47). Given a marginalia drawing by Aubrey of a club with a spiked head (Fowles 1980: 94), nor is it clear what was really meant by a 'batter-dasher'.

Gowland's typology (1902: 58–70), separating the tools into five classes (Table 6.10), is based primarily on weight followed by raw material, with the few very large tools singled out as distinct in function from the much greater number of smaller ones. Gowland divided the smallest tools, which he identified as of flint, sandstone and sarsen, into Classes I, II, and III. This division into three classes was made principally on the basis of form: Class I implements have cutting edges, Class II have one cutting edge opposite a blunt surface, and Class III are more rounded – 'much blunted and battered by use' (*ibid.*: 58–62).

Gowland maintained that these smaller tools had been used for stone-working because of the 'extremely rough usage' that they exhibit which 'could only be produced by violent contact with other stones' (1902: 62), but assumed that these tools were not tough enough to have been used on the majority of boulders used to create Stonehenge's monoliths: 'they were not suitable for shaping or dressing the harder sarsen or the diabase [bluestone] blocks, as flint is much too brittle a material for that purpose. But for dressing the softer sarsens and especially the more easily worked fissile stones, they were perfectly adapted, and were doubtless used for that purpose' (*ibid.*: 62).

As well as being bigger than Classes I–III, Gowland's Class IV and V artefacts are made of quartzite sarsen, except for one bluestone example (1902: 65–7). Of these he envisaged the smaller, weighing between 1lb (*c.* 0.45kg) and 6½lb (*c.* 3kg) as finishing tools 'undoubtedly employed... in producing the fine pitted markings which the finished surfaces of the sarsen stones present' (*ibid.*: 67). He classed the larger tools, weighing from 36lb (*c.* 16.3kg), as mauls (*ibid.*), describing working faces on their sides and 'natural inequalities' around their middles where he imagined bindings to have been secured, enabling 'two or more men' to operate them as sledges to smash away rock (*ibid.*: 70).

Gowland's typology may be questioned on a number of grounds. The assumption that flint in particular would not be an effective stone-working material on the rock types at Stonehenge remains untested in controlled conditions and the morphological typology is static, unable to acknowledge the dynamic changes in a tool that are brought about during its use (Andrefsky 1998: 29). Whilst it is reasonable to assume that massy tools would have been required to knock away large pieces of stone, as envisaged in the conjectured reduction sequence, their presence at Stonehenge rather than at presumed distant, primary-reduction locations invites closer examination.

Relationships between form, mass and use-wear have not been examined in detail. Herbert Stone, in fact, questioned some of Gowland's observations about the quartzite sarsen implements, remarking that their natural form and hardness suited them to use as hammers. He suggested that, except where altered as a result of heavy usage, their observed shapes are natural (Stone 1924: 82–3), seeing no evidence for binding or hafting to indicate more elaborate methods of use.

Gowland's analogy to illustrate the use of mauls is a poor one: the heavy wooden tool that he describes being used in Japan was actually used to drive in stones during the construction of building foundations (1902: 70) – not only was it made of a completely different material, it was also used for a very different purpose. Gowland also cites Japanese and Egyptian methods of grinding to shape stone vessels and mortars by employing a cobble with sand and water to grind out a hollow (*ibid.*: 78). This is an interesting analogue for the shaping of the mortises at Stonehenge, but he provides no detail about effects on the cobble involved.

Stone draws another interesting analogy between the Stonehenge hammerstones and a pebble used to prepare quern surfaces, the method being observed by John Robertson of the Sudan Political Service (Stone 1924: 86). Dropped repeatedly onto the surface of a slab of coarse greenstone, the 3"-diameter (7.5cm) pebble removed material from the slab – 'I then examined the pebble, and found it to be exactly like the English hammerstone in every respect' (Robertson in Passmore [1921], quoted by Stone 1924: 86). Unfortunately, neither the pebble lithology nor the wear pattern is described.

Although both Gowland and Stone innovatively brought experimentation to the tool-set analysis, their materials and methods were limited. Gowland used experimentation to examine the 'orange peel' finish observable on some sarsen settings, including the buried base of Stone 56 (1902: 52). Proposing that the smaller quartzite sarsen hammerstones were used to create this effect, his colleague Mr Stallybrass, a mason, used a quartzite pebble to peck away the surface of a piece of saccaroid sarsen (*ibid.*: 79). Whilst Mr Stallybrass was able to produce a similar effect, the specific details of the tool and technique that he used were not recorded. As weathering is likely to have affected the sarsen surfaces, interpretation of this surface 'finish' should be treated with caution.

Stone repeated the exercise with his colleague Mr Morgan, also a mason, who also used hammerstones to create the surface finish; Stone does not record many details of this task – he was interested in estimating how long surface-finishing would have taken and consequently focused on these calculations (1924: 94). This preoccupation with efficiency should be seen in the context of twentieth-century interest in explaining Stonehenge in terms of the labour required to build it and subsequent interpretations, in social evolutionary terms, of the monument's place in Late Neolithic and Early Bronze Age Britain (Atkinson 1956: 122, 138, 146–61; Renfrew 1973a; 1973b).

These early experiments were limited, poorly described and based on the assumption that the present-day surfaces of sarsen stones are as they were some 4,500 years ago when first prepared (although see Abbott and Anderson-Whymark 2012). In particular, they failed to explore the range of proposed tool uses throughout the conjectured reduction sequences, concentrating in a small way on one aspect of stone-working. This severely restricts their relevance for understanding prehistoric stone-working practices and tools.

Despite the increase in the size of the Stonehenge hammerstone assemblage throughout the twentieth century, as new material was acquired through excavation, the conjectured reduction sequence developed by Gowland in 1902 has stood untested, with the significant consequence that new evidence for saccaroid sarsen-working is difficult to interpret. A reassessment of the assemblage, significantly enlarged since Gowland's day, is thus useful to contextualize the *in situ* stone-working tools and waste found in Trench 44, exploring links between this material and the kinetics that produced the assemblage, including the impact of post-depositional formation processes.

6.3.4. Research aims and methodology

The aim of this study is to explore a range of technological attributes, to make it possible to move beyond Gowland's static typology and consider dynamic processes of hammerstone manufacture and use (Adams 2002: 3; Andrefsky 1998: 29; Willoughby 1987: 60). This analysis of the archaeological hammerstone assemblage therefore aims to investigate patterns of attributes that are assumed to relate to the life-use of the artefact, so that hypotheses about their use may later be tested through actualistic experimentation. The approach may be disadvantaged by being particularistic and restricted to the single site under examination (Willoughby 1987: 60) but the stone-working effects at Stonehenge are unique, the only other examples in the British Isles of deliberate stone-dressing (as opposed to rock art) of Neolithic monuments being

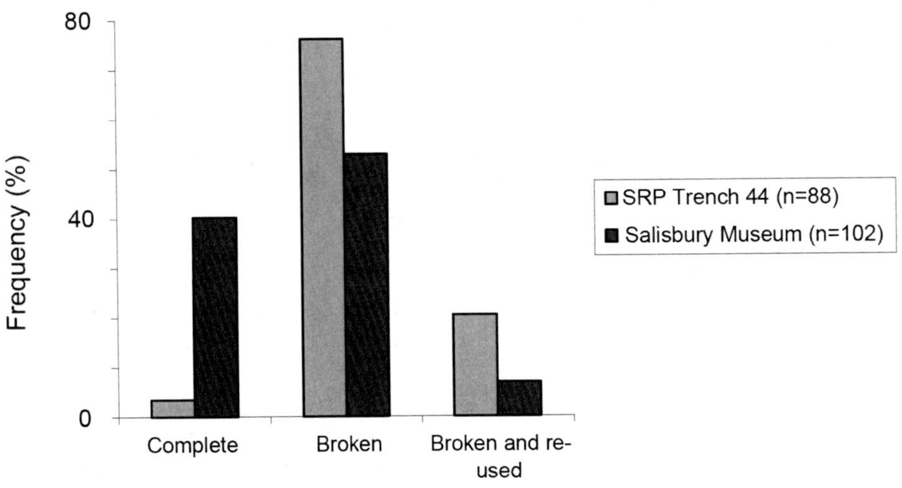

Figure 6.30. Percentages of hammerstones by completeness in Salisbury Museum and from Trench 44

limited to small surface areas of stones in the chambered tombs of Newgrange, Ireland, and Maes Howe, Orkney (Atkinson 1956: 123) and the undersides of some dolmen capstones (Cummings and Richards 2014).

Research questions

What choices may be inferred on the basis of intrinsic raw material properties? Were the tools expediently or strategically designed?

To understand the first step in manufacturing stone tools – the choice and procurement of raw materials – the quantitative and qualitative importance of each raw material and the morphology at the point of introduction to a site must be investigated (Sellet 1993: 108). These issues are assessed in terms of percentages of different lithologies present in the Stonehenge assemblage, and examined in the context of both the curatorial history of the collections and the mechanical properties of the stone.

Evidence for hafting and flaking intended to prepare the tools before use was gathered and analysed in relation to raw materials. Cortex, which can be present on both flint and sarsen, was recorded in the expectation that this would be present if unprepared nodules were brought to Stonehenge for use in the tool-set. Its presence/absence was analysed and tested for association in terms of raw material, but also in terms of tool completeness and the degree to which tools had been used (Figure 6.30); the expectation was that broken pieces and less heavily used tools would retain more cortex.

Is variability in tool form continuous?

As tools suffer attrition through use, so their form changes. In addition, broken pieces of hammerstone have varied forms. Exploring form is problematic for artefacts which have proved difficult to describe. Throughout the Stonehenge archives, the wide range of descriptive phrases used includes 'discoidal/sub-spherical', 'sub-spherical/sub-triangular', 'ovoid/sub-spherical', 'flattened sub-ovate', and 'sub-square' (Salisbury Museum, *Stonehenge Twentieth-Century Excavations*, File 51).

This subjective assessment of form that does not make use of clearly defined categories is not adequate for examining possible relationships between morphological variables and other attributes. To assess the extent to which hammerstone form is discrete or falls on a continuum, and to enable form to be examined in relation to other attributes, a consistent and replicable way of recording morphological variability was required.

Sedimentary geology's 'form factor' methodology (Blott and Pye 2008) has been adopted here to describe tool forms. There are strong morphological similarities between the hammerstones and the particles, pebbles and cobbles for which this descriptive technique was created: 'form factor' methodology is also used to understand morphological changes that these clasts undergo (Tucker 1991: 16). Length (L), width (I) and thickness (S) measurements are used to define tri-dimensional forms. Form is then described in terms of deviation from equancy, where the most equant form has equal L, I and S dimensions. Increasingly flat or elongated forms are therefore identified through their I/L and S/I ratios. The ratio data generated can be divided into equal classes which are given verbal descriptive terms that are consistent and replicable (Blott and Pye 2008: 46–9).

In addition, a single measure of form was calculated using Sneed and Folk's maximum projection sphericity (MPS) index (Blott and Pye 2008: 37). Also a geological methodology, this measure provides ratio data from 0 to 1 where 1 is a fully equant object. Different equancy

Assemblage	*N*
Salisbury Museum, Stonehenge twentieth-century excavations archive	308
Stonehenge Riverside Project (SRP), Trench 44 finds listing	266
Stonehenge Riverside Project, other 2008 season contexts	81
British Museum, online catalogue (www.britishmuseum.org.uk/collections)	5
Total	660

Table 6.11. Identifiable hammerstones and fragments from Stonehenge

indices have advantages and disadvantages, principally in the weight they give to the different second-order indices derived from L, I and S. The MPS index was selected as 'perhaps providing the best overall compromise' when evaluated against other available indices of form by Blott and Pye (*ibid.*: 42).

The expectation was that the stone-working tools would be highly equant whilst broken pieces would be less equant, so the frequency of equancy class intervals using the MPS measure for complete tools, broken pieces and broken and reused tools could be plotted and their variability calculated. The equancy of complete, broken, and broken and reused tools by raw material could then be compared by plotting the data in Zingg diagrams (Blott and Pye 2008: 42), a further expectation being that variability in form development may, to some extent, be attributable to raw material properties.

What types of macroscopic use-wear are visible and where is this located? Are there relationships between use-wear patterns and other tool attributes?

The types and locations of use-wear were recorded and compared, in the expectation that similar patterns could indicate tool use in activities from the same reduction stage. The data were compared between complete hammerstones and broken and reused pieces, and between tools made of different raw materials, in the expectation that different patterns of use would be apparent. To examine Gowland's maul classification (1902), the weight distribution of complete tools, and differences between use-wear patterns across the distribution, were analysed.

Is there a relationship between the amount of wear and tool form?

The extent to which tool form at the point of discard is dependent on how heavily the tool was used was examined by comparing form with degree of use, for both complete and broken and reused tools. The concept of roundedness is important for this question. The roundedness of tool surfaces varies and is interesting because it is independent of form (Willoughby 1987: 93): tools may be rounded without being very spherical.

Hammering tools that are more equant in form may be expected also to be more heavily used and more rounded through that use; more angular tools, which are nevertheless highly equant in form, can be expected to be less well-used and therefore more revealing of the significance of raw material and tool design prior to use. Broken pieces may be expected to be more angular because of their broken edges.

How were tools discarded? Were they reused? Is there patterning between context and tool attributes?

Whilst Cleal *et al.* (1995) looked at both complete and broken pieces of hammerstones from twentieth-century excavations at Stonehenge, possible reuse of the sarsen tools was only touched on in terms of use-wear. Unquantified numbers of implements were observed to have smoothed, ground areas on their surfaces as well as battering (*ibid.*: 387) and unspecified numbers of bluestone hammerstones were interpreted as reused pieces from larger ground or pecked objects (*ibid.*: 382).

Although five categories of primary and secondary tool use are identified by Adams (2002: 22), a less complicated system with fewer interpretative difficulties can be constructed with just three categories: percentages of *complete* pieces, of *broken* pieces, and of *broken and reused* implements could be calculated for and compared between the archived and Trench 44 assemblages. These data were also incorporated into various assessments indicated above as attributes were contrasted between, for example, complete tools and broken pieces.

The contexts in which hammerstones were deposited within Stonehenge were also examined. Problems with phasing and provenance, especially the high proportion of material from secondary contexts, raise considerable interpretative difficulties. Objects from phased features formed the focus of this exercise.

Sampling strategy

The hammerstones in the dataset are artefacts whose provenance is demonstrably from Stonehenge. The total number of curated hammerstones from Stonehenge available for this analysis, including both complete and broken pieces, was 660 (Table 6.11). The assemblages that provided the material studied in this analysis are those of Salisbury Museum and Trench 44 ($N = 574$). The museum's assemblage derives from the twentieth-century excavations at Stonehenge and therefore includes artefacts from a variety of contexts principally within the monument. Note that further hammerstones identified in the Trench 44 assemblage during post-excavation were not available for this study (see Table 6.2).

A sample comprising one-third of each of the two assemblages was selected. Bearing in mind that Gowland (1902) suggested that raw material was a significant

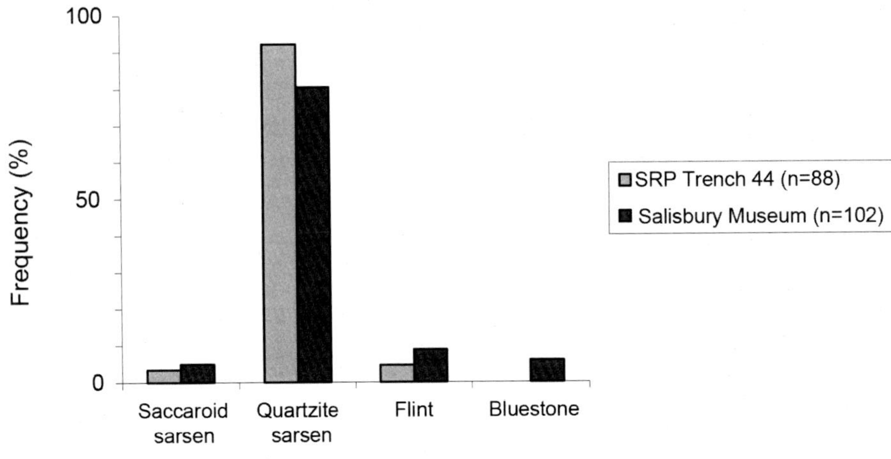

Figure 6.31. Comparison of hammerstone assemblages by raw materials

Raw material	Salisbury Museum		SRP Trench 44	
	n	% of sample	*n*	% of sample
Saccaroid sarsen	5	4.9	3	3.4
Quartzite sarsen	82	80.4	81	92
Bluestone	6	5.9	0	0
Flint	9	8.8	4	4.5
Total	102	100%	88	100%

Table 6.12 A proportionate random stratified sample of 190 hammerstones, forming 33% of the Salisbury Museum and Trench 44 assemblages

variable in relation to use, a proportionate stratified random sampling strategy was adopted to ensure that hammerstones of all stone types were represented in the sample. The sample comprises 190 artefacts (Figure 6.31; Table 6.12). 'Dataset' is used throughout to refer to the source assemblage of 574 artefacts; 'study sample' refers to the subset of 190 artefacts.

The assumption was made that all hammerstones, regardless of material, were part of the stone-working tool-set. This assumption may be questionable:

- First, eight hammerstones are from contexts allocated to Stage 1 (beginning in *3080–2950 cal BC* and ending in *2865–2755 cal BC*; see Table 11.7; formerly Cleal *et al.*'s Phases 1 and 2; Cleal *et al.* 1995: 369, 389). Stonehenge at that time is envisaged as an earth and timber monument with a circle of undressed bluestones (Hawley 1921: 36; Parker Pearson *et al.* 2015: 73). These hammerstones could therefore relate to stone-working associated with the bluestone circle, set within the Aubrey Holes, dating to the 30th century cal BC (see Chapter 4).
- Secondly, even though a stone circle was present at Stonehenge from Stage 1, some of the hammerstones at Stonehenge could have been used for activities other than working the monoliths. Nor is there any need for the bluestones of this first stone circle to have been worked with stone tools in Stage 1; the bluestones need not have been dressed with stone tools until Stage 2 (Hawley 1921: 36).
- Thirdly, flint-flaking may have occurred on site during Stage 1 and Stage 2, although the extremely poor curation levels of waste flakes make assessment of the assemblage very difficult (Cleal *et al.* 1995: 368). Some 114 worked flint flakes are curated from Stage 2 contexts at Stonehenge (*ibid.*: table 31), contemporary with the major sarsen-working period. The Stonehenge Environs Project concluded that, in the absence of imported sarsen hammerstones in its 752.5ha field-walked area, Neolithic and Bronze Age hard-hammer flint-flaking had been effected using flint hammerstones (Richards 1990: 215). However, 'hammerstone' was not used by that project as a category for sorting lithic material (*ibid.*: table 5) and this tool type was not reported on by the SEP.

Measurement and recording protocols

Specific protocols were developed to improve the consistency and replicability of recording:

Length (L), width (I), thickness (S)

The artefacts are irregular polygons, difficult to measure with any consistency. For the purposes of this study, length, width and thickness were defined as the maximum, intermediate and smallest perpendicular dimensions, not necessarily intersecting at a common point (Blott and Pye 2008: 32). A pebble-box was used to make these measurements, significantly improving accuracy levels because it locates perpendicular measurements without repositioning of objects between each observation (Bunte and Abt 2001: 28).

Weight (mass)

The intention was to take weights from archived data, thus avoiding replicating one of the few consistently recorded pieces of hammerstone information. Discrepancies between recorded and actual weights, however, were observed in the Salisbury Museum assemblage, so the entire study sample was re-weighed (Figure 6.32). The weight distribution of the museum sample was compared to that of the Trench 44 sample as part of the collection assessment, investigating the possibility that curatorial selection in the museum assemblage might have favoured larger items.

Raw material

Identification of raw material was taken from archived data. This was checked by visual inspection with the naked eye and a hand-lens of x4 magnification (Figure 6.31).

Form factor descriptors and equancy

Form, in terms of a single measure of how equant an implement is, was defined by the MPS (maximum projection sphericity) index, $\Psi P = \sqrt[3]{S^2/LI}$. Form factor descriptors, ratios and equancy are described above.

Roundedness

Roundedness refers to the relative angularity of the object rather than the extent to which it approaches circularity or sphericity (Blott and Pye 2008: 48). It was measured with reference to a standard geological Roundedness Index visual comparator.

Cortex

Both flint and sarsen may be corticated but igneous bluestones are not. Measuring or estimating the percentage area of cortex on an irregular polygon is problematic (see also *Use-wear type and degree*, below) and was not attempted. The presence or absence of cortex was recorded.

Flake scars and hafting

An indicator of strategic design, flake scars are left by the preparation of a tool blank, and use-wear may be expected to occur over them. The presence of flake scars was recorded, and features such as grooves to take straps were looked for.

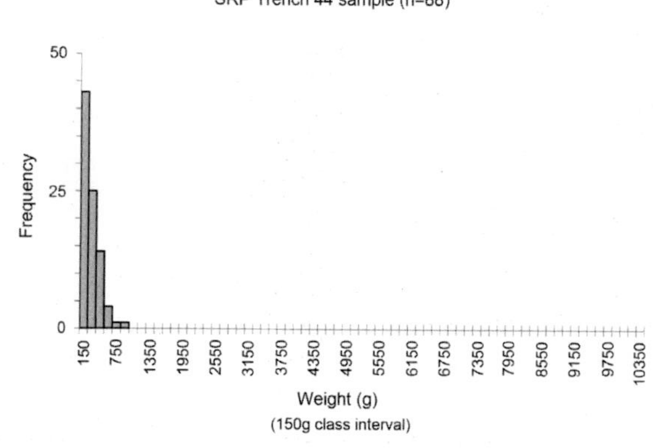

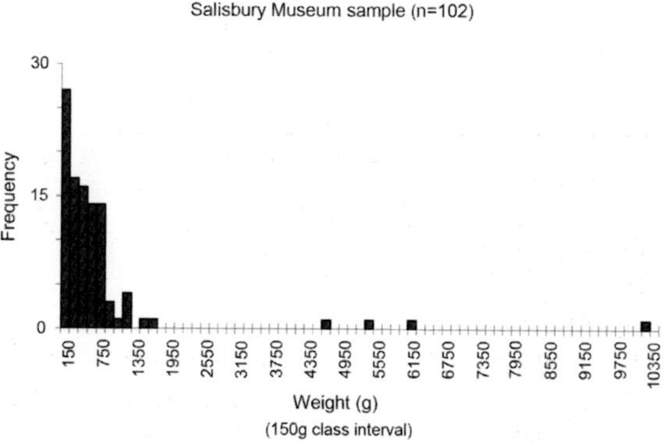

Figure 6.32. Weight profile of hammerstones from Trench 44 and Salisbury Museum samples

Use-wear location

Defining the location of use-wear on irregular, curved polygons is problematic. Adams' system is inappropriate because it requires the number of used surfaces to be recorded (2002: 25). Seven categories were defined for this assessment:

- the 'ends' of a tool (two categories) were defined by dimension L;
- circumference was selected for wear around the L–I plane (but this does not imply that this wear is continuous all the way around the tool);
- ridges were defined as the high points at the edges of scars;
- faces were defined as areas in-between ridges or, where there are no scars, on a curved or flattened surface beyond the circumference;
- wear that is 'all over' the tool occurs all around the tool, but does not necessarily imply 100% coverage;
- the final category is no use-wear.

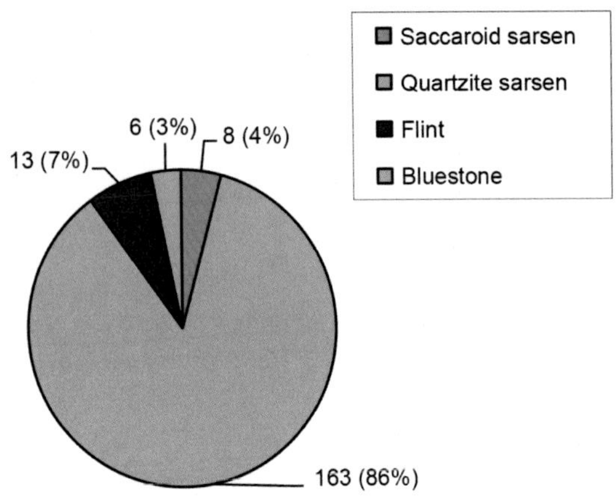

Figure 6.33. Raw materials of hammerstones in the sample

Use-wear type and degree

Adams identifies various types of use-wear for percussion tools, defined in terms of shallow or deep, uniform or irregular features with variably well-defined margins (2002: 90, 161), whilst her definition for mauls includes 'use-wear damage consistent with blunt force trauma' (*ibid.*: 161). These are difficult to measure and quantify. For the purposes of this study seven categories of macroscopic use-wear were defined. For these categories, the terminology used is:

- 'battering' indicates areas of fractured and crushed surfaces;
- 'spalls' are the small scars of chips and flakes broken off during use;
- 'grinding' indicates smoothed patches of rubbed-down surface.

How well-used the tools are is indicative of the stage they reached at the point of discard. Adams (*ibid.*: 25) identifies six categories from unused to worn-out, yet distinguishing between these six on irregular, curving, or angular surfaces is difficult. After some experimentation with different techniques, a simple visual comparator was developed with four categories; unused, partially-used, well-used, and heavily-used.

Completeness

Complete hammerstones are entire except for their surface damage. Broken pieces of hammerstones are fragments displaying use-wear on a surface, with clean fractures where detached from the parent tool. Broken and reused hammerstones have damage caused by use passing over previously cleanly fractured surfaces. This last category is problematic, because a piece of broken hammerstone picked up and used again is, in effect, a complete hammerstone. Nevertheless, the distinction was drawn to give the opportunity of identifying recycling (Adams 2002: 22).

6.3.5. Raw materials

The processes by which sarsen and bluestone were introduced to Stonehenge were influenced by these materials' availability in the surrounding area, and have been the subject of much debate. Enquiry into the availability of flint has been limited, perhaps because flint is taken for granted as a commonly available, local material.

Sarsen

Sarsen is part of the family of silcrete sandstones, formed through surface or near-surface silicification of deposits, probably by groundwater or pan-lacustrine cementation (Summerfield and Goudie 1980: 71; Tucker 1991: 56; Nash and McLaren 2007; Ullyott *et al.* 2004). The properties of sarsen, specifically its hardness, have been remarked upon since at least the sixteenth century. John Rastell's *The Pastyme of People* from 1530 is the earliest known report, mentioning that iron tools are ineffectual in working sarsen because of its toughness (quoted in Chippindale 1994: 27).

Nearly 90% of the hammerstones in the dataset (and therefore 90% of the study sample) are sarsen (Figure 6.33), predominantly quartzite sarsen. The qualitative importance of the especially dense and durable quartzite sarsen, suited for use as a stone-working tool on other lithologies (Pitts 1996: 319), contrasts with the granular saccaroid sarsen. Grains may be rubbed with the fingers from a freshly fractured saccaroid sarsen surface (Howard in Pitts 1982: 121). Under these circumstances, the 4% of tools made from saccaroid sarsen may represent expediently used pieces of stone recovered during the stone-working process. Qualitative examination with a hand-lens suggests that these tools are better-cemented examples of the saccaroid sarsen type.

Bluestone

Only 3% (n = 17) of the 574 implements in the overall dataset are of bluestone, all of the harder materials of dolerite or rhyolite (Cleal *et al.* 1995: 382). No bluestone hammerstones were excavated from Trench 44, although bluestone fragments were recovered from the stone horizon.

Rather than any of these bluestone artefacts being transported as ready-made tools from west Wales, it is more likely that they were fashioned from damaged or modified bluestone monoliths already in place at

WA object number	WA context number	Context description and phase
85	1615	Upper fill of Y Hole 2 with Romano-British material, post-monument destruction
89	1208	Aubrey Hole 17, turf and topsoil, un-phased
100	1367	South Barrow, turf and topsoil, un-phased
102	1451	Humus and Stonehenge Layer over causeway, turf and topsoil, un-phased
105	1383	Over the henge ditch, turf and topsoil, un-phased
112	3661	Stones 6/7, Stonehenge Layer, un-phased
113	1451	Humus and Stonehenge Layer over causeway, turf and topsoil, un-phased
140	1164	Aubrey Hole 4, turf and topsoil, un-phased
141	1187	Aubrey Hole 11, secondary fill, Bluestone Layer, Stage 2+
149	1234	Aubrey Hole 24, turf and topsoil, un-phased
168	3253	North Barrow ditch, Stage 2+
182	3111	Over the henge bank
225	3015	Z Hole 16, turf and topsoil, un-phased
226	3015	Z Hole 16, turf and topsoil, un-phased
286	2593	Over the henge ditch, turf and topsoil, un-phased
293	9318	Avenue Bend Trench, Avenue Ditch re-cut, Stage 4+
540	3813	no information

Table 6.13 Context and phase information for all bluestone hammerstones (after Cleal *et al.* 1995: 381, 572–4, tables 34, 66; and archive File 51/Bluestone)

Stonehenge. Cleal *et al.* note that 'some are reused fragments detached from larger ground and/or pecked objects' (1995: 382). They further suggest that previously shaped bluestones removed from the bluestone oval (Stage 4; see Chapter 4 for an overview of the structural changes at Stonehenge in each Stage) were broken up for the production of a variety of implements including hammerstones, totalling some 64 objects (*ibid.*: 331, 383).

Only two of the 17 bluestone hammerstones from Stonehenge in the dataset have been interpreted as pieces of stone detached from dressed parent rock (artefacts WA85 and WA149; Salisbury Museum, *Stonehenge Twentieth-Century Excavations* archive, File 51). Unfortunately, only three bluestone hammerstones (WA141, WA168 and WA293) were excavated from contexts created during the prehistoric life of the monument, all of them late in the sequence (Table 6.13).

Flint

Flint makes up only 7% of the dataset, and therefore 7% of the study sample. Nevertheless, flint has an important property in relation to the task of reducing other stone types to form an intended shape – it is very hard (7 on Mohs' scale; Barber *et al.* 1999: 22). Examples of flint

Flint types	Flint sources
Tabular flint	Variable quality, mined close to Durrington (Booth and Stone 1952); out-crops at Coneybury Hill and Rox Hill (Richards 1990: 215).
Nodular flint	Seams and scattered nodules throughout the Upper Chalk (Geddes 2003: 53) and surface deposits weathered-out from these Late Cretaceous levels (Richards 1990: 215).
Flint pebbles (hilltops)	Small rounded pebbles in small areas of un-eroded Tertiary deposits (Geddes 2003: 59–60; Green 1997b: 5; Tilley *et al* 2007: 189) such as on Beacon Hill Ridge and Sidbury Hill.
Flint pebbles (valleys)	Pebbles in Quaternary plateau gravels found at levels up to 100m above present valley deposits and in gravels on valley sides above present-day valley floors of the Kennet, Wylye and Avon rivers (Geddes 2003: 66–7), and angular Pleistocene gravel flints in the streambeds (Richards 1990: 140, 215; Tilley *et al.* 2007: 198).
Flint pebbles (hilltops)	Patchy deposits of Quaternary clay-with-flints including round-ed pebbles on top of higher areas of chalk (Geddes 2003: 69).

Table 6.14 Flint sources in the Stonehenge area as defined by Tilley *et al.* (2007)

hammerstones displaying battered surfaces resulting from impacts, which might have included use as hammers for flaking or rejuvenating grinding surfaces, were recognised by Evans (1897: 248–50) and flint's successful reduction of stone through pecking and hammering was clearly valued in the production of stone axes throughout the Neolithic (Andy Young pers. comm.).

Whilst most of the flint examined in detail here appears to derive from nodules, two artefacts (SR3212b and SR3187b; Salisbury Museum) are possibly from broken rounded pebbles of Tertiary or Quaternary deposits and there is a third (SR3134b) that is possibly from gravel flint (Table 6.14). The nodules may have been selected from eroded-out contexts such as river cliffs. The pebbles were perhaps gathered from Tertiary Reading Beds deposits on Sidbury Hill (13km northeast of Stonehenge) or Beacon Hill (7km east of Stonehenge; see Chapter 2). They could have been brought to both Stonehenge and Woodhenge (Tilley *et al.* 2007: 198) from these summit locations, which may have served as symbolic visual foci for Stonehenge (Exon *et al.* 2000; Tilley *et al.* 2007; see Chapter 2).

On the whole, the Stonehenge Environs Project concluded that flint procurement and use around Stonehenge were strongly topographically based and heavily reliant on the predominance of eroded-out nodules. In terms of the apparently localised patterns identified by Richards (1990), it is possible that much of the material for this small group of tools was closely sourced. Yet some of the raw materials for the flint hammerstones could have been procured in the Durrington flint mines, northeast of Durrington Walls 3km northeast of Stonehenge (Booth and Stone 1952), or from the foot of river cliffs within the Avon valley north of Amesbury, two locations not significantly distant from Stonehenge (Table 6.14).

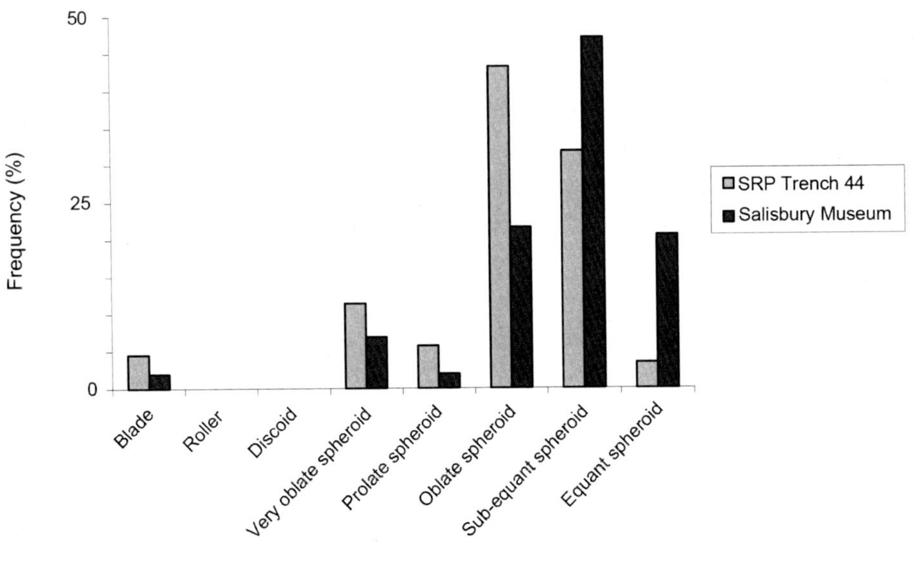

Figure 6.34. Forms of sarsen implements in the study sample

Overview

All the materials used for the hammerstones in the study sample were hard and tough, reflecting the stoneworkers' sophisticated knowledge of the different working properties of both the tools and the stone to be worked on (Pitts 1996: 319). The presence of cortex on more than 50% of items in the study sample indicates that stone for the tool-set was being brought to Stonehenge without significant preparation at collection sites. The low numerical importance of saccaroid sarsen and bluestone hammerstones could suggest expedient use of material broken from boulders undergoing preparation as stone monoliths. Yet harder, more durable pieces were mainly selected for this treatment, alongside the prolific quartzite sarsen nodules.

6.3.6. Expedient and strategic design

Following procurement, the stone appears to have undergone very little modification to meet the desired function of the tools. Only six items (3%) in the study sample (*n* = 190) have scars left by flaking. Of these, the majority (*n* = 5) are flint, the most easily flaked of the raw materials in the assemblage. All five are highly equant forms, with MPS values above 0.6 except for SR3134b, a flatter piece bifacially flaked on one edge which then underwent battering, similar to the only flaked quartzite sarsen implement (SR3132b).

Nevertheless, eight flint items had not been prepared in this way. One of these (SR3187b) is a broken piece of flint pebble with no signs of use and its identification as a hammerstone must be questioned. Seven flint items in the study sample bear evidence of use-wear and are highly equant, with MPS values above 0.6.

Cortex does not seem to have been specially removed because all bar one of the flint items have their cortex remaining, suggesting that the effect of flaking was primarily to alter the nodules' shape. Less cortex would be expected from higher levels of tool preparation. Bearing in mind that bluestone does not have cortex, nevertheless more than 50% of items in the study sample have cortex remaining:

- Some 62% of items with cortex remaining are broken hammerstone pieces (*n* = 63), as may be expected when outer material from an irregular nodule breaks off.
- These fragments with cortex make up 52% of the total of broken fragments.
- Of the complete tools, 52% (*n* = 23) still have some cortex present and 64% of tools made on broken and reused pieces of stone still retain cortex (*n* = 16).

The attrition that the tools underwent bears on the amount of cortex present. Whilst none of the most heavily used items in the study sample have surviving cortex, 98 (52%) well- or partially used hammerstones do. There is a very weak negative association between cortication and degree of use (Kendall's tau-c = -0.067) and no statistically significant evidence of a relationship between implement completeness and presence/absence of cortex (χ^2 = 1.23, df = 2).

The nature of the unmodified nodules of principally quartzitic sarsen has more influence on cortex survival than any design considerations. No items in the study sample bear evidence of hafting (*contra* Gowland 1902; *pro* Stone 1924), confirming the essentially informal and expedient nature of these tools.

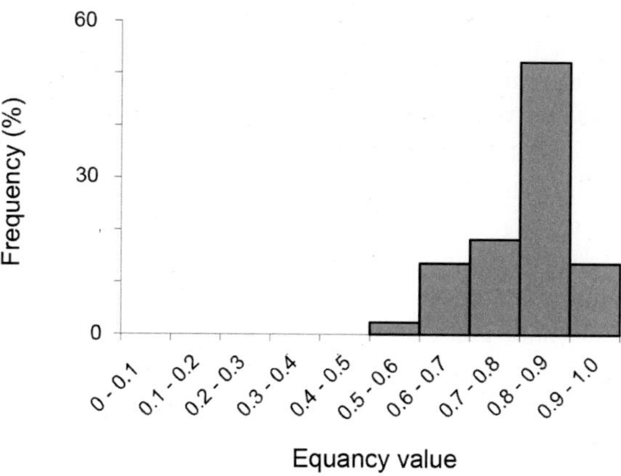

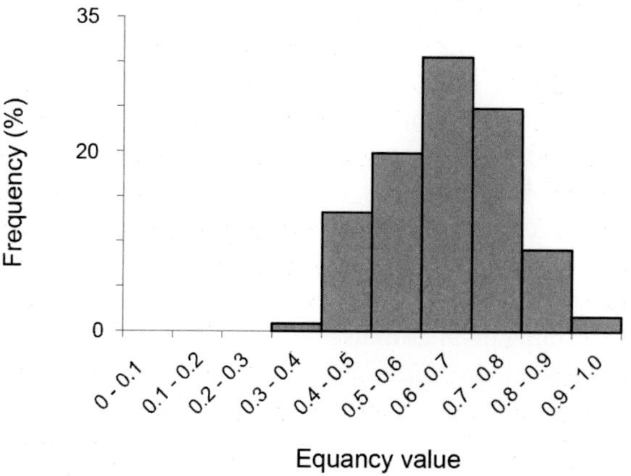

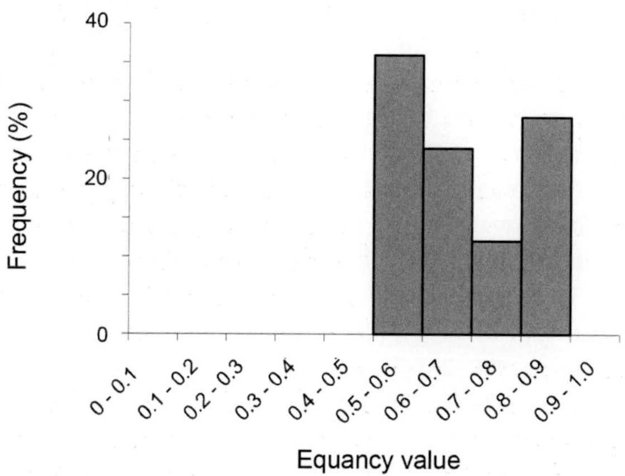

Figure 6.35. Equancy values of complete, broken, and broken and re-used hammerstones

6.3.7. Tool form, use-wear and context

Tool form

In both assemblages (Salisbury Museum collection and finds from Trench 44), items tend to be more equant; that is, their L, I and S dimensions are similar. It should be noted that the descriptors 'prolate spheroid' and 'oblate spheroid' are equally non-equant; oblate spheroids are more flattened whilst prolate spheroids are more elongated. The likely differential retention of artefacts by earlier excavators and museum curators, as mentioned above, may have had an impact on the higher numbers of more 'attractive' hammerstones of equant and sub-equant form in the Salisbury Museum assemblage (Figure 6.34).

Complete hammerstones have high equancy values and broken pieces of hammerstone tend to be less equant (Figure 6.35). The L, I and S dimensions for broken hammerstone pieces remain similar enough for many fragments to be 'chunkier', accounting for the higher values in the range, rather than thinner and longer flake-like or blade-like pieces which would produce much lower values.

The distribution for broken and reused hammerstones shows that, although the majority of these items are quite equant, this category of implement has the lowest modal equancy of 0.5–0.6 (Figure 6.35). The expectation that complete hammerstones tend to be more equant is justified. Their population mean equancy value is 0.816 ±0.026 (95% confidence; n = 44, SD = 0.087). Whilst the mean equancy value for the population of broken pieces is lower (0.644 ±0.023; 95% confidence), the standard deviation in the study sample (n = 121) of 0.123 expresses their wider range of forms. Given that quartzite sarsen dominates the assemblage, this may be indicative of the way that it breaks. The quartzite sarsen matrix is finer-grained than saccaroid sarsen, but the nodules are commonly full of silicified roots and root voids, making their breakage patterns less predictable. Chunky and therefore more equant pieces are as likely to be removed during use as thinner pieces.

The mean equancy value of the population of broken and reused pieces of hammerstone (0.677 ±0.009; 95% confidence; n = 25, SD = 0.024) is closer to the broken, discarded pieces. To some extent, these implements still reflect the broken form of the pieces prior to reuse. This is perhaps easier to visualise by referring to the Sneed and Folk diagrams (Figure 6.36).

The expectation that form might vary according to raw material is not supported. Pieces of quartzite sarsen fall into all of the categories of form present in the assemblage whilst the other materials are spread across the prolate, oblate, sub-equant and equant spheroid categories. This is confirmed by looking at the

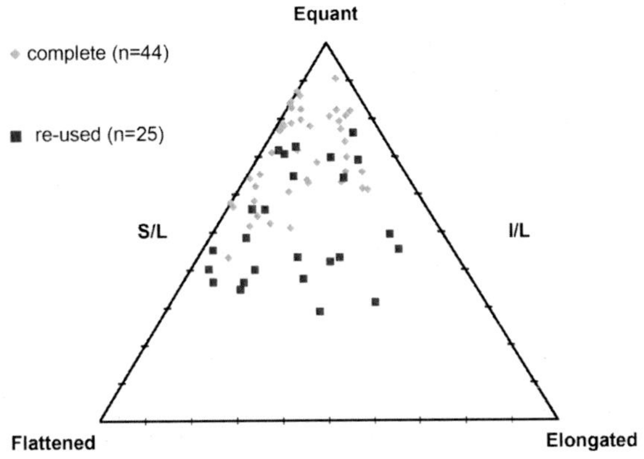

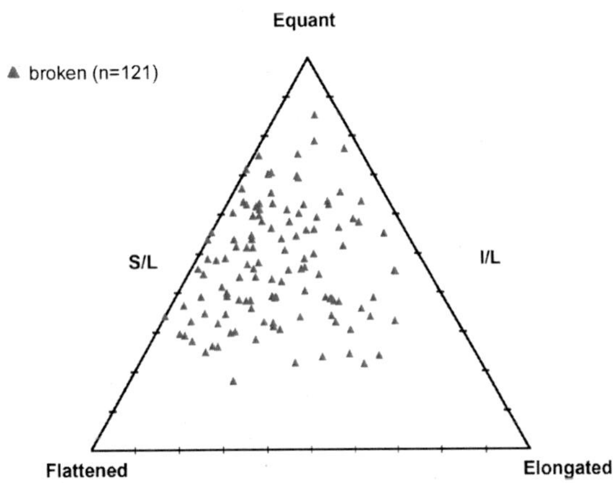

Figure 6.36. Equancy distributions for complete and reused hammerstones (top) and broken hammerstones (bottom)

distributions of complete hammerstones, broken pieces and broken and reused pieces in terms of form and raw material. Complete implements have similarly equant forms regardless of the material they are composed of. Whilst the broken pieces show more variability in form, as discussed above, the different raw materials are scattered throughout this distribution. Of the broken and reused items in the study sample, only one is not quartzite sarsen, giving inconclusive information for this category.

Raw material is an influence on form inasmuch as the nature of the nodule or broken piece is preserved. As defined here, the form attribute alone does not suggest segregated tool classes within the general categories of complete tools or broken and reused tools. There is a continuum from the most equant, complete tools to slightly less equant, reused pieces, with the range in form of broken fragments indicative of the irregular breakage brought about by use.

Use-wear

The majority of pieces examined show the effects of battering (Figure 6.37), with crushed, fractured surfaces and the scars of small spalls on areas used to strike the stone being worked. These types of use-wear are those created by fatigue mechanics in which cracks and fractures are induced by percussive kinetics (Adams 2002: 30, 151).

Fourteen items do not have any signs of use. Of these, the majority are quartzite sarsen, one is flint and one saccaroid sarsen. The broken piece of flint pebble (SR3187b) has been mentioned above. The allocation of a small piece of saccaroid sarsen (WA359; 33g) by Cleal *et al.* to the hammerstone assemblage may be a recording error; on returning to the archive data, it is not clear from the comments whether this was thought to be a piece of a whetstone reused as a hammerstone and latterly broken, or is a piece of a whetstone misclassified in the listings (Salisbury Museum, *Stonehenge Twentieth-Century Excavations* archive, File 51).

The 12 pieces of quartzite sarsen in the study sample that show no use – all broken pieces of nodule – were presumably interpreted by their excavators as having broken from hammerstones during use, but their shapes and surfaces do not indicate why they were originally classified as 'hammerstones', unless quartzite sarsen was automatically equated with the tool type. It may be noted that Hawley reported quantities of unmodified quartzite sarsen from his 1920 excavation season, describing them as unused hammerstones (1922: 37).

The main difference in macroscopic use-wear between the two assemblages is the absence of grinding on tools from Trench 44. Just over 20% of the Salisbury Museum material in the study sample exhibits grinding, including instances where battering fractures have been almost ground out. Within the small excavated area of Trench 44, activities appear to have been limited to percussion, whilst the museum assemblage indicates the additional activity of grinding. It may be rash to extrapolate from this that grinding was undertaken only within the monument as a finishing activity; the limited area of Trench 44 and other excavations north of Stonehenge may not provide a representative sample of this exterior zone. For example, Hawley uncovered a large dump of sarsen chips and sarsen sand between the Heel Stone and the southern Avenue ditch which he interpreted as resulting from dressing a large stone (Hawley 1925: 23; Cleal *et al.* 1995: 280, fig. 156).

Some 40% (n = 76) of the artefacts in the study sample show use-wear on their circumference (Figure 6.38). It should be noted that this category does not imply that use was continuous around the whole circumference, but it is more than use only at the polar ends. This suggests that the tools were being turned during use to present new striking

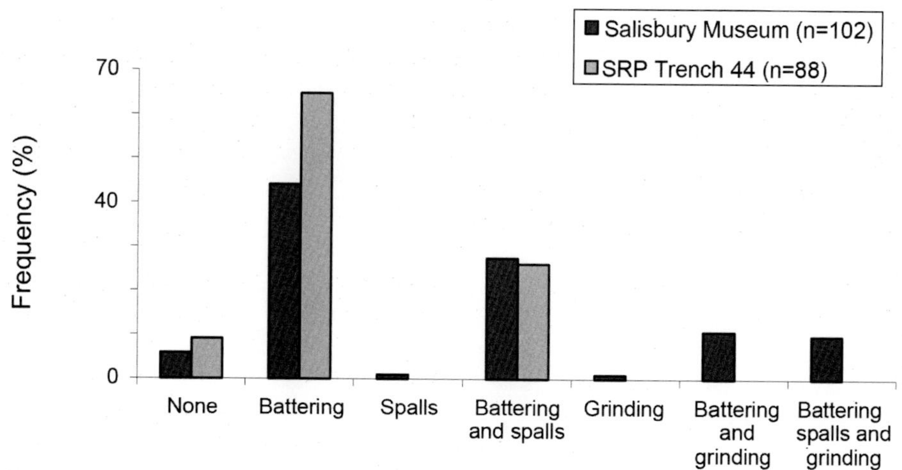

Figure 6.37. Types of hammerstone use-wear by sample group

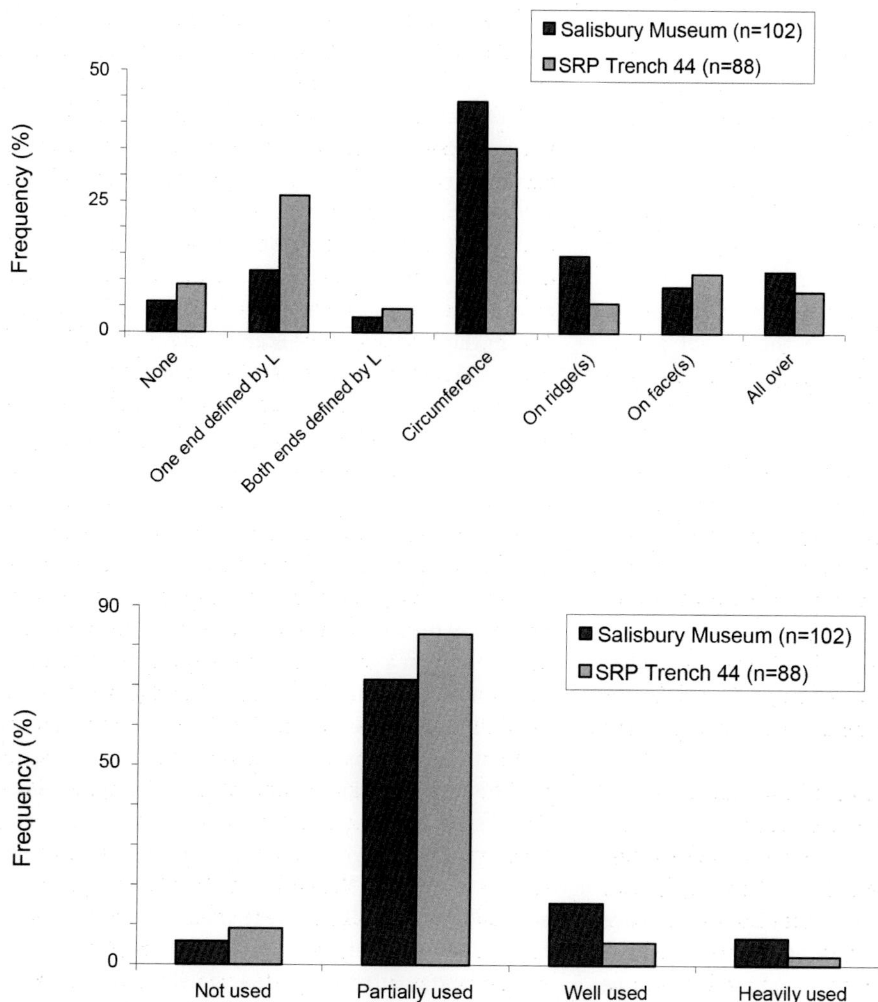

Figure 6.38. Location (top) and degree (bottom) of hammerstone use-wear in the two sample groups

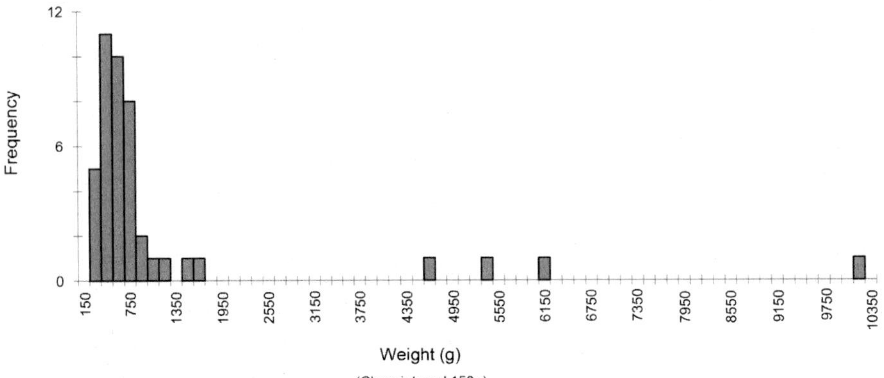

Figure 6.39. Complete hammerstones by weight

surfaces. The relatively higher instance of use-wear on one end of items from Trench 44 may be indicative of the higher number of broken pieces of hammerstones in that assemblage; the end carrying wear may have come away from the parent nodule. Few items in the study sample can be classed as well-used or heavily used.

The high level of partial use recorded in the study sample (83% in Trench 44 and 72% in the Salisbury Museum assemblage) is accounted for by the high number of discarded broken pieces that have only a little damage, and suggests that considerable breakage happened relatively early in the life of a hammerstone.

Comparison of the type and location of use-wear on complete hammerstones shows the modal group to be battered and with spalls located around the circumference (*n* = 9; 20%), followed by battering around the circumference (*n* = 6; 14%). Whilst tool circumference is the most common focus of damage (*n* = 22; 50%), the next most likely type of damage is for a complete hammerstone to have been used all over (*n* = 10; 23%). Some saccaroid and quartzite sarsen complete hammerstones that did not break during percussion were selected for grinding (*n* = 15; 34%).

The modal type of use-wear on broken and reused hammerstones is also battering, again with spalls around the circumference (*n* = 10; 40%) followed by battering around the circumference (*n* = 4; 16%). None of the broken and reused pieces were used for grinding. This may be because these tend to have more flattened forms (oblate and very oblate spheroids) and weigh less, making them less suitable for the sustained pressure required for grinding, although the ranges of size and form are such that some could have been used as grinders. Only 6% of the broken hammerstone fragments (*n* = 7) show evidence of grinding, as might be expected since the hammerstones from which the fragments derive would have been less likely to break during rubbing as opposed to percussive action.

The expectation that tools of different lithology would exhibit clearly distinct use-wear patterns is not borne out by the study sample. Saccaroid sarsen pieces (*n* = 8) are battered and spalled variously around their surfaces with one example of grinding, whilst the six bluestone pieces in the study sample are battered around their ends and circumferences. These small groups are similar to the much larger quartzite sarsen group, with percussion damage predominantly around circumferences (*n* = 58; 36%) and at one end (*n* = 28; 17%).

The 13 flint pieces in the study sample are slightly different. Whilst the modal group is battered, with spalls around the circumference (*n* = 4; 31%), five pieces have use on the ridges of flake scars (38%). This suggests that edges created through true conchoidal fractures were used for their cutting or picking effect. Use-wear attributes on the macroscopic level do not suggest characteristically different functions, other than the difference between percussion and grinding techniques.

Use-wear and weight

The overall weight profiles of the two assemblages are similar yet the numbers of items weighing more than 0.5kg in the museum assemblage stand out (Figure 6.32; see also Figure 6.15). A Kolmogorov–Smirnov test indicates that, at the 1% level, the two assemblages are from different populations in terms of weight (D = 34.36; n_a = 102; n_b = 88).

The high standard deviation for the museum sample reflects its 28 items weighing over 600g. Whilst, at the 95% confidence level, the mean weight of the Trench 44 sample is 201.31g ±32.14, the mean weight of the museum sample is 643.62g ±255.11. It should be noted that the heaviest hammerstone in the museum is, in fact, the artefact catalogued as WA483, weighing just over 29kg, with another 25 hammerstones in the archive listings recorded at over 1kg. One very large outlier (2.155kg) was found in Trench 44 but is not part of this study.

The recovery of more hammerstones since Gowland's excavation in 1901 has blurred his distinction between Class IV artefacts weighing from 1lb to 6½lb (*c.* 0.45kg to 3kg) and Class V artefacts weighing more than 36lb (*c.* 16.3kg; Gowland 1902: 65–70). The weights of nine hammerstones listed in the archive fall between Gowland's two classes.

One complication encountered when examining Gowland's identification of weight as a diagnostic characteristic of tools used in the earliest reduction stages is that, whilst he placed eight implements in his Class V (1902: 70), only three such artefacts weighing more than 16.3kg are listed in the hammerstone archive that was drawn up in the 1990s. These are WA481 (16.3kg), WA478 (17kg) and WA483 (29.2kg). None of these three seem to have been excavated by Gowland, as they have references in the Salisbury Museum archive indicating that they came from trenches dug by Hawley. The eight implements recorded by Gowland as Class V (weighing more than 36lb) are therefore not in the Salisbury Museum collection.

The heaviest hammerstones in the study sample are all complete tools. As it was not possible to re-create Gowland's dataset, the approach taken here is to look at use-wear patterns by weight of the complete tools, defining those in the top quartile weighing more than 736g as heavy hammerstones (Figure 6.39).

In general terms, the 44 complete hammerstones have been shown to be consistently highly equant, sub-rounded tools showing battering and spalls from use around their circumferences. Ten (23%) were used all over and 15 (34%) were used for grinding. The majority are quartzite sarsen (77%) with eight of flint (18%) and two of saccaroid sarsen (5%).

Comparison of use-wear types across the quartiles of this distribution show that the lighter 75% of complete hammerstones (n = 33) all show the effects of percussion kinetics. Only eight were additionally used for grinding (24% of the lighter hammerstones). Of the heaviest hammerstones (those in the top quartile, n = 11), proportionally more were used with grinding actions as well as percussion (n = 7; 64%). Only four in the top quartile do not have ground surfaces (36%). The proportion of 'light' tools that were used for grinding is significantly different (at the 2% level; TS = -2.404, df = ∞) to the higher proportion of 'heavy' tools that were used for grinding. The greater likelihood that a complete hammerstone with grinding use-wear will be heavy (P[weight top quartile/grinding] = .467, P[weight top quartile] = .25) is borne out by the presence of such use-wear on the three largest hammerstones now remaining in the museum collection (WA483, WA481 and WA478). These were not included in the study sample, but grinding on their surfaces is recorded in the archive.

Use-wear and form

Tools with the most equant form were expected to be the most rounded, shaped by use as the nodules underwent attrition. However, there is a weak statistical association between roundedness and form for the complete hammerstones (Kendall's tau-b = 0.266). Whilst these tools are highly equant, the majority are sub-angular or sub-rounded (n = 27; 61% of the sample of 44 complete hammerstones) with only 11 of the complete tools being rounded or well-rounded (25%). The six (14%) very angular or angular tools in the sample of complete hammerstones (Atk204a, WA1099_1, WA323, WA372, Atk169e and WA3813_1, all from the museum collection) are made on flint or quartzite sarsen nodules; their degree of roundedness is low because they are only partially used tools, with their angular edges remaining.

In fact, 23 (52%) complete hammerstones in the study sample are highly equant after only partial use. Only four of the six heavily used complete tools (67% of the heavily used category) have the most equant forms. These characteristics imply that the form of these complete tools has more to do with their raw material, with nodules selected for their already high equancy values before use. The small number of heavily used complete tools (n = 6; 14% of the complete tools) may indicate the extent to which the kinetics of use are not favourable to tool survival.

As expected, the broken hammerstone fragments have low roundedness values, the majority being very angular or angular (n = 77; 64%). None are rounded or well-rounded. However, there remains a weak association between roundedness and form for these broken pieces (Kendall's tau-c = 0.281). The broken hammerstone pieces have forms that are related to the way that they broke off hammerstones, being more equant not through continual surface attrition but because chunkier fragments became detached during percussion.

The expectation that hammerstones made of reused broken pieces would be more rounded than broken fragments was borne out, but not because of higher levels of use. At the 5% level, there is a significant difference (TS = -2.19, df = ∞) between the lower proportion of very angular and angular reused tools (n = 10; 40% of the reused implements) than of broken pieces (n = 77; 64% of the broken implements), showing that broken and reused hammerstones are commonly more rounded than merely broken pieces. There is a stronger association between roundedness and form for the reused tools than for either the complete tools or the broken pieces (tau-b = 0.511).

However, most of the broken and then reused pieces were used only partially (n = 24; 96%). These 24 are spread quite evenly across the observed equancy values, suggesting that the amount of use does not determine the form of the reused tools. This implies, instead, that more equant broken pieces of hammerstone were sought out

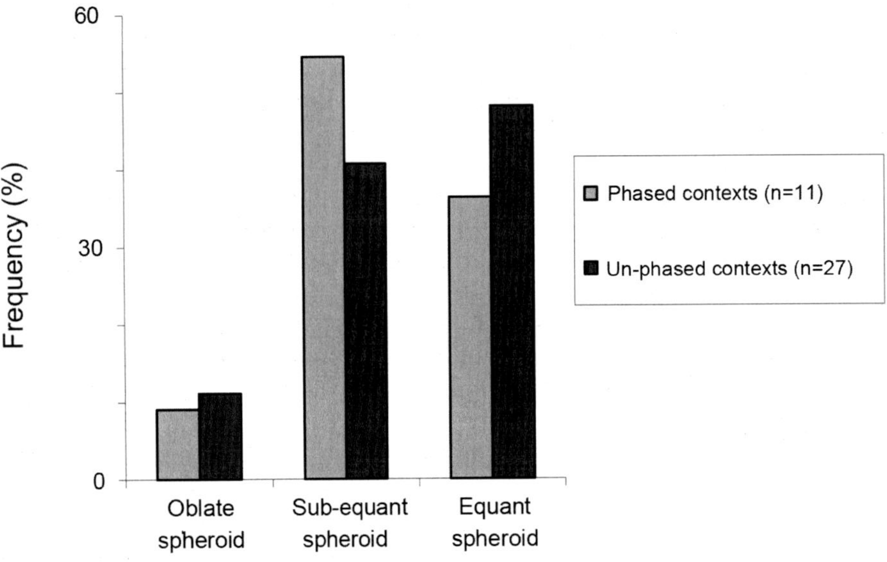

Figure 6.40. Complete hammerstone shapes by context

for reuse. The tendency to middling roundedness values for these tools may be because the pieces chosen for reuse were less irregular than either raw nodules or rejected broken pieces.

Context

Of the 102 items in the study sample from the Salisbury Museum collection, only 28 (27%) are from phased contexts, presenting some difficulty for examining the deposition of tools. The phased contexts are fills of negative features and positive banks. The un-phased contexts include layers in the monument between its component parts, above the natural chalk; these are not in cuts and include the Stonehenge layer, topsoil and turf. Nevertheless, some useful observations may be made.

In general terms, there seems to be little difference between hammerstones deposited in the cut features and those that became incorporated into un-phased layers across the monument. Only the proportion of broken and reused hammerstones is significantly lower in un-phased contexts (at the 10% level [TS = 1.8, df = ∞]) than the proportion in phased contexts. There is no statistical difference between the proportions of complete hammerstones (TS = -0.036) and broken pieces (TS = -0.833) excavated from features as opposed to those coming from layers spread across the site.

This is, to some extent, unexpected because the impression from the literature is that complete hammerstones should be expected from deposits where they have been used as packing stones (Gowland 1902; Hawley 1922). Complete tools from un-phased contexts in the study sample fall within the weight range of, and have similar forms to, those from phased contexts (Figure 6.40), yet were recovered from layers including the turf and topsoil rather than from around the bases of standing stones.

Looking in more detail at these 28 items in the sample from phased contexts, some of the interpretative issues wrestled with by Cleal *et al.* (1995) become apparent. Only three of the study sample items are recorded as coming from contexts pre-dating the worked sarsen settings of Stage 2 (beginning in *2740–2505 cal BC* and ending in *2470–2300 cal BC*):

- A broken piece of quartzite sarsen hammerstone with a partially battered face (WA184) was excavated by Atkinson from trench C44 cutting the henge bank (Cleal *et al.* 1995: 94). This 126g piece of sarsen is similar to the rest of the broken items in the sample. Regrettably the henge bank here was disturbed by later postholes cut through the bank (*ibid.*: 107), bringing the phasing of WA184 into question.

- The phasing of WA479 is similarly problematic. This 10.2kg complete hammerstone was excavated by Hawley from one of his trenches into the southern arc of the Stage 1 enclosure ditch. This well-used, heavy, sub-equant spheroid with battering, spalls and grinding all over is, however, not assigned to this phase in Cleal *et al.*'s published table of phased hammerstones (1995: 389) and this omission is not explained. Perhaps it is because the hammerstone cannot with certainty be placed in the ditch's lower fills.

- The third hammerstone (WA179) was excavated from one of the postholes allocated by Cleal *et al.* to their Phase 2, a period of possible timber settings within the henge pre-dating the sarsen settings (1995: 116–65), assigned to Stage 1 in the new phasing (Darvill *et al.* 2012; Parker Pearson 2012: 30, 107–8, 309). A sub-equant spheroid weighing 541g, this well-rounded complete hammerstone has been well used percussively around its circumference and clearly falls within the continuum of the stone-working tools, as does WA479. As the nature of the posthole fill in what is a highly disturbed area of the site (Cleal *et al.* 1995: 148) was not recorded by the excavator, it is impossible to say whether WA179 should be placed with any certainty in Stage 1.

These ambiguities make it very difficult to interpret the uses of the tool-set and the way the tools were deposited during the earliest phase of activity at Stonehenge. Despite their similarities to the rest of the assemblage, the uncertainty surrounding the contexts of these earliest hammerstones does not permit us to make inferences about stone-working activity at the site during Stage 1.

Of the 25 items in the study sample from Stage 2 and later contexts, a number do not appear to be from primary contexts:

- WA421 and WA192 are both likely to have been re-deposited in the fill of a feature cut behind trilithon 57/58;
- WA223 was re-deposited in the fill of Z Hole 16, situated immediately southwest of Stone 16;
- a broken piece of bluestone hammerstone (WA168) and other finds from the North Barrow ditch (Cleal *et al.* 1995: figs 13, 164) are thought to be fortuitous, with no evidence to suggest deliberate deposition (*ibid.*: 280).

Twenty-one hammerstones in the sample have a stronger case for having come from primary deposits. These were all excavated by Hawley (1922) from around Stone 2 and the items in the sample comprise eight complete hammerstones, nine broken pieces and four broken and reused pieces.

Comparing Hawley's published account of trench C2 around Stones 29, 30, 1 and 2 (1922: 38–45) with archived information about the individual finds indicates that, whilst some of the hammerstones came from the stonehole, others were excavated from layers around Stone 2, possibly outside of the actual cut. Their relationships cannot now be reconstructed, partly because there is no detailed plan or section drawing (Cleal *et al.* 1995: 190) and partly because the majority of these 58 items are not now identified by unique reference numbers. Thus it is effectively impossible to identify individual hammerstones from around Stone 2 in relation to their location in the trench. In the face of these uncertainties, the contrasting of characteristics of items selected for intentional deposition in a negative feature – the stonehole itself – with the characteristics of items deposited elsewhere is impracticable.

The overall impression of the contexts of deposition is of hammerstones in varying states scattered across the confused surface of the henge, with some material, including pieces of broken tools, incorporated in the fills of negative features as packing – such as those hammerstones excavated by Gowland from Stonehole 55 (1902: 53) – and as backfill. Other material remained on the surface, re-deposited over time and incorporated into the layers that now lie above the natural chalk, including the Stonehenge layer. Many of these tools and tool fragments might have been used within the monument and then left, just as the tools within the SRP Trench 44 to the north of the monument were discarded where they had been used.

This impression forms a stark contrast to nearby Durrington Walls, where the only non-flint stone from the 1966–1968 excavations comprised 55lb 5oz (*c.* 25kg) of unworked sarsen stone used as post-packing and to form a platform surface, and one greenstone axe fragment (Wainwright with Longworth 1971: 183). The sarsen assemblage from the SRP excavations (2004–2008) supports this picture, with a large quantity of sarsen blocks, chunks and cobbles from a pit fill (1192) below the surface of the Durrington Walls avenue, and from elsewhere around the site (see Chan, above).

These dramatically different distributions and forms of sarsen chime with the contrasts drawn between the contemporary timber and stone constructions in the Stonehenge landscape (Whittle 1997: 149; Parker Pearson *et al.* 2006: 233; 2007: 636). The stone-working tools and their waste were left at the place where, it is proposed, bluestone and sarsen settings materialised the concept of the ancestral dead, the domain of the ancestors (Parker Pearson and Ramilisonina 1998a; Parker Pearson *et al.* 2006), whilst very little stone was deposited at Durrington Walls, where timber settings dominated the henge interior, the proposed domain of the living.

6.3.8. Conclusions

This investigation has identified a continuum of tool use as opposed to distinct patterns of use-wear and form interpretable in terms of different function. The results of the study derive from an essentially inferential procedure and it would be valuable to validate the results by experiment (Sellet 1993: 110). A number of conclusions can be put forward at this stage.

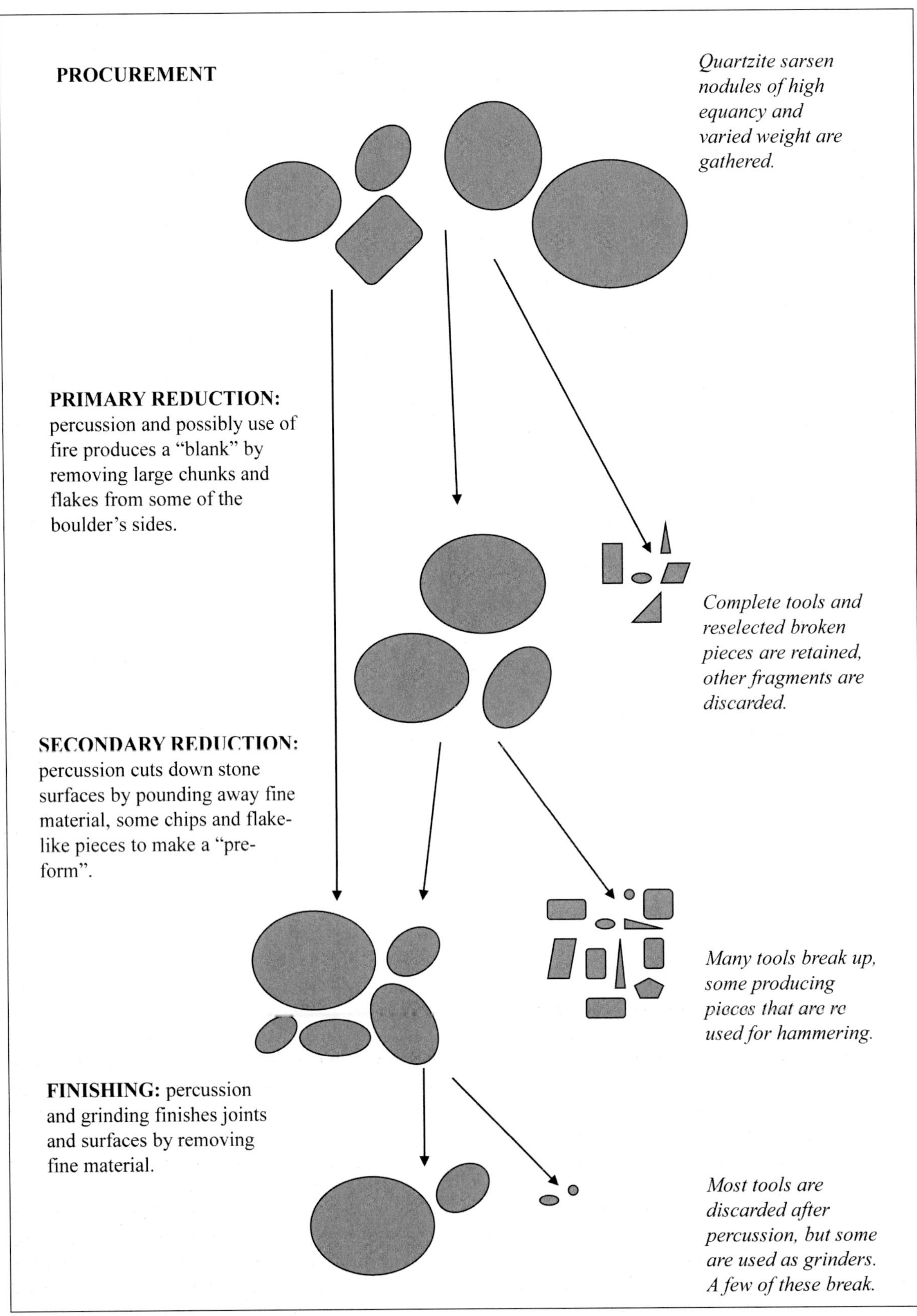

Figure 6.41. Model of hammerstone life histories

The tool-set

Selection factors influencing which tools have been chosen for museum curation, and the relatively small size of the area opened up for Trench 44, raise problems about what constitutes a representative sample of tools left at Stonehenge. Nevertheless, both percussion and grinding techniques are represented in the tools and tool fragments from within Stonehenge, whilst in the saccaroid sarsen-working area sampled within Trench 44, only percussive techniques were used. The hammerstones are informal tools made of hard, tough stones that were rarely prepared in advance of use (*pro* Stone 1924), with no evidence of hafting and only a few examples of flaking to manipulate the shape of some of the flint nodules.

The highly equant form developed by the complete hammerstones is rooted in the relatively high equancy of the nodules that were initially selected, followed by percussion mostly around their circumferences. Complete tools are more likely to be amongst the objects retained by their excavators; Hawley, for example, regularly comments on them favourably as opposed to the 'tedious recurrence of chips and other things' (Hawley 1921: 24). The relatively small number of heavily used complete tools in the assemblage implies high breakage levels rather than curatorial de-selection.

Broken pieces include the flattest forms, but chunky pieces with low levels of damage commonly broke off the irregular quartzite sarsen nodules. Whilst the tools made on reused pieces of stone have slightly flatter shapes, like the complete hammerstones their higher equancy values derive from the selection of more equant forms for reuse and the rejection of waste that was too flat or too small.

The forms of these tools do not vary with raw material, nor are there different, distinctive patterns of macroscopic use-wear on tools of the different stone types. Damage has been caused predominantly by percussion around the circumference areas of the tools, although there is evidence that the cutting properties of flint flake-scar ridges were exploited. The quartzite sarsen that dominates the assemblage shows a continuum of use. Differently-sized tools did not necessarily have a single use, with heavy tools preferred for grinding after being used for percussion, and some smaller battered pieces also used as grinders. The hammerstones from Trench 44 – commonly slightly flatter, lighter tools made on reused pieces of broken quartzite sarsen – were not selected for use as grinders.

Hammerstone life-histories

A modification of the Gowland/Stone interpretation of hammerstone function and role in reduction is laid out in Figure 6.41, focusing on quartzite sarsen as the dominant material in the assemblage.

- Theoretically, an implement could be used in primary reduction to accomplish any necessary roughing-out of a boulder.
- If it did not break during the primary reduction process, it continued to be used to remove increasingly small debris, and either broke (in some cases providing suitable fragments also to be used for percussion) or survived.
- The surviving implement was then either discarded or selected to grind down broad surfaces or to finish joints, depending on its size.

Saccaroid sarsen and bluestone pieces might have been incorporated into the tool-set during primary reduction or during secondary reduction, making use of sufficiently hard and equant debris removed from the boulder being worked. Flint nodules provided cutting edges probably used to pick away material during the later stages of stone-dressing. However, unprepared, multi-purpose quartzite sarsen nodules provided the bulk of the tool-set.

Kinetics

Comparative examples may provide analogies for stone-working at Stonehenge, focusing on the use of stone tools in monumental, sculptural work more akin to the working of Neolithic megaliths than to, for example, stone-axe manufacture or historical sarsen-breaking techniques.

The ethnohistorically attested quarrying and carving of the Rapa Nui *moai* has to be dismissed as a useful analogy, principally because the ethnographic data on methods and techniques are poor and do not distinguish between different stages or processes (Van Tilburg and Pakarati 2002). In addition, the lithological qualities of the quarried volcanic tuff and basalt tools are significantly different from sarsen.

Inca techniques of stone selection and working to supply building stone for massive walled structures are more promising as a comparison. Stone blocks of varied lithologies were selected from rock-falls or pried from fragmented rock faces (Protzen 2000: 212), a process more similar to the use of the sarsen boulders than to bedrock quarrying. Shaping and fine work were accomplished using river cobbles ranging in size from 'egg' to 'football', with a few much bigger (Protzen 1992: 212), similar to the range of Stonehenge hammerstones.

Inca stone-working techniques and tools were described by Garcilaso de la Vega (born in Cusco in 1539, shortly after the Spanish conquest), who recorded information provided to him by his Inca relatives, including the wearing-down of large walling blocks with stone tools (de la Vega 1609: 53, 296). Nevertheless, the specific actions of the hammering and grinding kinetics are not described in detail.

Generic actions, therefore, are defined for these independent variables, following Keeley's assertion that purposeful rather than mechanical actions are required in actualistic use-wear experiments (1980: 15):

- striking – direct percussion at the boulder edges to break away chunks or flake-like pieces of subject stone, creating faces with angles close to 90°;
- pounding – direct percussion on boulder faces to remove grains of subject stone, creating a surface that may be further finished by grinding.

An extended resource base

With bluestones brought over 140 miles (220km) from Wales (see Chapter 4) and sarsen, flint and other 'local' stones probably selected from sources within an area extending some 15 miles (25km) from Stonehenge to West Woods (see *Sarsen stones and the making of Stonehenge*, below), the monument's lithological compass demonstrates 'a pattern of social organisation and resource use' stretching across a vast area (Green 1997a: 260). Stone procurement was complex and far-ranging, and included Chilmark ragstone from the Vale of Wardour, to the southwest, and Upper Greensand stone from north Wiltshire. Both stone types were used as packing stones in stoneholes. Approximately one-third of the 36 packing blocks in Stonehole 1, most of the 58 packing blocks in Stonehole 30, and over half of the 47 in Stonehole 29 were of these materials (Hawley 1925: 38–44), sourced 20km or more from Stonehenge.

This pattern of extended resource use may have a history going back before the Neolithic. Mesolithic people would have experienced sarsens in the landscape whilst moving across the Downs and along the watercourses. The human relationship with these and other encountered stones would have imbued places and raw materials with histories (Field 2005; 2010). Chris Scarre (2004) has suggested that these histories and significances were incorporated into and displayed in structures, themes identified by him as common to megalithic architecture. At monuments such as the West Kennet long barrow (Piggott 1962), Avebury henge and its avenues (Gillings *et al.* 2008), the Devil's Den in Clatford Bottom (Parker Pearson 2012: 208–9) and Stonehenge itself, boulders metamorphosed into cultural objects (Field 2005: 94).

The importance of 'the much needed integration of Stonehenge into a coherent model of a functioning society' (Pitts 1982: 124) becomes even more significant if it is suggested that, as well as travelling off Salisbury Plain and away from the habitation sites of the period (which appear to have been along the Avon valley; Darvill 2006: 153), to collect stone, people travelled to the area bringing stone with them. That large numbers of people were involved in the building of Stonehenge has been suggested both on practical grounds (Atkinson 1956: 115, 122) and in terms of wider significance, with perhaps thousands of people from an extensive area participating in the construction and use of the monuments in the Stonehenge complex (Parker Pearson *et al.* 2006: 233–4, 237).

Sarsen-working at Stonehenge

Distinguishing between primary and secondary reduction techniques as envisaged in the conjectured Stonehenge *chaîne opératoire*, and interpreting the location and organisation of these activities, is frustrated by the ambiguities inherent in the stone waste from the monument interior. The evidence for *in situ* sarsen-working just outside the henge in Trench 44 adds to Hawley's reported but ill-recorded possible stone-working site close to the Avenue (1923: 23).

The extent to which Stonehenge in the mid-third millennium BC might have looked like a builders' yard (Burl 2006: 173; Parker Pearson and Ramilisonina 1998a: 319; Parker Pearson *et al.* 2006: 235) draws our attention to the episodes of stone-working. Extended chronologies for stone use at Stonehenge have led Bayliss *et al.* (2007b: 44) to envisage a social setting in which this work continued 'within a more widely shared agreement through the moral community about the necessity and desirability of the massive undertaking'. This study has explored the relationship between worked stone and stone-working tools to better understand the technological system enmeshed with the cultural imperatives and social relationships driving the work.

6.4. Sarsen stones and the making of Stonehenge

C. Richards and M. Parker Pearson with K. Whitaker

Although the origins and transportation of the bluestones at Stonehenge have tended to dominate discussions of the building of the monument, the most extraordinary display of labour enabled the extraction, dragging, dressing and erection of each sarsen. Atkinson (1956: 115–16) conservatively estimated that 1,500 people would have been necessary to drag one of the large sarsens from north Wiltshire to Stonehenge. Aubrey Burl's estimate (2006: 170) halves this number and, most recently, Harris (2019) has reassessed the estimates of time and labour to conclude that Atkinson's figures are possibly slight over-estimates.

Even with some reduction from Atkinson's estimates, it remains an extraordinarily large group of people labouring over a substantial length of time. The numbers of people required to labour on each individual stone add up to an overall expenditure of time, and of practical and material resources, that is truly astonishing. Furthermore, the spectacle of so many people working together in such

Figure 6.42. A large sarsen boulder among the Grey Wethers on the Marlborough Downs, being inspected by Dave Field (standing) and Andrew Fleming

a tremendous undertaking would have attracted many more bystanders, so it is clearly warranted to conceive of the process of monument-building as performative and risk-laden (Jones 2012; Richards 2013).

Recently there have been calls for greater theorisation of the moving of megaliths (Gillings and Pollard 2016: 553). It is undoubtedly true that, in the past, investigations of megalith transportation have been grounded in a discourse of 'engineering studies', in which practicality, efficiency and principles of least effort (*e.g.* Atkinson 1961; Richards and Whitby 1997) appear quite reasonable research parameters (see Richards 2013: 5–7). Paradoxically, Richard Atkinson clearly appreciated the astonishing materiality of Stonehenge (1956: 2–3), and understood the transportation of the sarsens as a form of 'sacred work'. For instance, despite early antiquarians' suggestion of a sarsen source further to the east (see below), he muses on the possibility of the journey of Stonehenge's sarsens actually beginning at Avebury, where each stone would 'be dragged through its already ancient circles so that the bearers could receive from the presiding arch-priest that spiritual benison and encouragement of which their forthcoming physical exertions were soon to leave them so sorely in need' (*ibid.*: 113).

Although deemed important, the social practices of construction, particularly those surrounding the journey of each sarsen stone, have not received the attention they deserve. This may partly be due to a perceived paucity of evidence. Atkinson laments 'the virtual absence of surviving specimens of tools and equipment made from perishable organic materials, and particularly from timber. Moreover, it is obvious that some engineering operations, such as the movement of heavy stones, will leave few traces for the archaeologist to identify and interpret' (1961: 292).

There are a number of ethnographic accounts that inform us of the extraordinary and layered nature of megalithic construction, including stone-dragging (*e.g.* Hoskins 1986; Adams 2007; Petrie 2012; Harris 2019). Some of the themes emanating from such studies have influenced recent narratives of stone circle construction (*e.g.* Richards 2013: 27). Equally, an emphasis on the performative character of monument construction (*e.g.* Jones 2012: 168–9) and the multi-faceted nature of intrinsic risk (Richards *et al.* 2013: 119–23), has served to define the act of building as both a generative and social process.

The deployment of sarsens in the construction of Stonehenge demands more nuanced perspectives (see Gillings and Pollard 2016: 553), however, not just because of the exceptional magnitude of the sarsen stones and the probable length of their journey, but also because they stand apart from other monoliths comprising stone circles in terms of the sequence of their material transformation and modification (for recent analysis of stone-dressing of the Stonehenge megaliths, see Abbot and Anderson-Whymark 2012; Field *et al.* 2015).

The source of most of Stonehenge's sarsens has recently been identified as West Woods, in north Wiltshire, 2 miles south of the Marlborough Downs, south of the River Kennet (Nash *et al.* 2020). A north Wiltshire origin for Stonehenge's sarsens has long been considered highly likely (for recent discussions see Chapter 7; Field *et al.* 2015; Parker Pearson 2016b; Gillings and Pollard 2016). This, of course, is not a new idea, as the earliest published suggestion that Stonehenge's saccaroid sarsens originated some 30km away on the Marlborough Downs to the north was made in 1580 (Lambarde quoted in Chippindale 1994: 37). John Aubrey, who was familiar with Stonehenge and

Figure 6.43. William Stukeley's drawing of the Broadstones at Clatford in 1723

Salisbury Plain from his youth (Fowles 1982: 17), also subscribed to this view when he recorded that Stonehenge's stones were Grey Wethers[7] and came from a pit no more than 14 miles away (Britton 1847: 44; Fowles 1982: 36; Scurr 2016: 105); this could even be the newly identified source at West Woods, only 15 miles from Stonehenge.

Stukeley specifically noted that 'from the Grey Wethers all [Stonehenge's sarsen stones] seem to be fetcht for the holes yet appear whence such were drawn' (from his commonplace book, cited by an anonymous editor in 1869: 342). Indeed, large slabs still lie on the surface of this western part of the Downs (Figure 6.42) whereas those in West Woods have been heavily affected by early modern quarrying. Stukeley reckoned that the sarsens were dragged off the high ground, some of them being collected together at Clatford on the north bank of the River Kennet (Parker Pearson 2016b). Here he recorded a group of 12 recumbent sarsens, previously noted by Aubrey as having been 'rudely hewn', and surmised that such shaped stones were originally destined for Stonehenge (Figure 6.43). These stones have not survived, having been broken up probably within a century after Stukeley sketched them in 1723.

The north Wiltshire source for the Stonehenge sarsens, now confirmed by geological analysis (Nash *et al.* forthcoming), has been suggested partly because of the current and historical distribution of sarsens in the landscape and also because of their intimate relationship and association with Avebury and other north Wiltshire sarsen monuments. Hence, J.F.S. Stone envisaged the 'transport of colossal blocks of sarsen weighing up to 50 tons apiece from the hallowed district 18 miles to the north' (1958: 94). The attribution of a special or 'sacred' quality to the sarsen spread flowing off the Marlborough Downs in rivers of stone continues today: 'the abundance of sarsen stone both afforded the region a special, rather other-worldly, character – contributing to an unfolding sense of the landscape's cosmic and mythological power – and made possible the creation of its many megalithic monuments' (Gillings and Pollard 2016: 540).

Of course, in a prehistoric context, it is easy to envisage what must have seemed the anomalous presence of extensive spreads of stones of all shapes and sizes lying on the soft chalk bedrock, seemingly 'flowing' off the high ground, inviting a range of interpretative supernatural and mythical accounts. As noted above, the proximity of sarsen stones to Avebury, combined with their presence in its monumental architecture, prompted Atkinson to suggest that the Stonehenge sarsens actually began their journey by passing through those 'ancient circles' (1956: 113).

7 A 'grey wether' is a recumbent stone that looks like a sheep from a distance (a wether being a castrated ram).

The difficulties of locating stones of sufficient magnitude (see Ashbee 1998) were thought to have entailed the use of a range of sources. Atkinson declared that 'it is out of the question that all of them [sarsens] lay ready to hand in a single valley' (1956: 113). Yet it seems that all but two of Stonehenge's sarsens were sourced at West Woods, 15 miles (25km) to the north. From here a broad trail must have been carved through the Wessex landscape, creating a spatial biography of the stones, a biography punctuated by the temporary camps of those labouring to move such enormous entities. Material remains of massive episodes of food consumption and camping involving hundreds of people may survive as observable traces at a number of places along the route of the stones between West Woods and Stonehenge.

Equally, the journey as a *rite de passage* not only necessarily transformed the stone but also those who laboured to drag its immense weight (Richards 2009; 2013: 7–9). Nor should the agency of the stone itself be underestimated, not least as it moved on its sledge in full flight, up and down slopes and hills, exerting a menacing presence to those who both attempted to compel and attempted to quell the movement of its massive bulk. How many people were injured or perished in the face of this terrible efficacy?

So, each sarsen stone arrived at Stonehenge after a long journey involving a phenomenal input of labour and consumption of material resources. Unusually for the creation of third millennium BC stone circles, the passage of the stone was as yet incomplete. To be part of Stonehenge was to be subsumed within a single architecture, wherein each stone required a degree of modification, a regime of flaking, pounding and smoothing. Judging from the deposits and debris in Trench 44, each stone maintained its identity through spatial integrity, each being dressed in a discrete and exclusive location. Pounded and flaked, the appearance of the stone gradually altered. Morphological difference between the many stones changed to similarity, enabling a conjunction and connectivity with other sarsens.

When finally erected and incorporated within the sarsen circle, each stone diminished as a single entity as it fused with other sarsens to create a single architecture. In this act, a degree of transcendence and final transformation was achieved. As a fulfilment of this process, the sarsen component of Stonehenge not only embodies the labour of thousands of people over many years – as well as a complexity of architecture that wraps around and embraces a handful of bluestones (see Richards 2013: 18–23) – but it also condenses and consumes within its monumentality the stories and biographies of dozens of massive stones and toiling people, creating the greatest manifestation of all Neolithic technologies of enchantment (*cf* Gell 1998).

Chapter 7

Sarsens in the Stonehenge landscape

C. Richards*

7.1. Sarsens in the landscape

C. Richards, M. Parker Pearson and K. Whitaker

As noted in the previous chapter, despite the Stonehenge sarsens' enormity and dominant architectural presence in the monument in comparison to the bluestones, far less interest has been expressed in the qualities of the sarsens (but see Howard 1982; new geochemical research is underway, led by David Nash; Nash *et al.* forthcoming). When the Stonehenge sarsens are discussed, the debate tends to be restricted to the practicalities of their transportation (*e.g.* Richards and Whitby 1997), and questions of origins. Surprisingly, given the high profile of Stonehenge, this discourse is extremely limited and does not extend the investigation of 'origins' to include more subtle 'biographical' narratives of extraction, transportation and relocation (but see Field *et al.* 2015), such as those concerning the Avebury sarsens and more distant stone circles (*e.g.* Gillings and Pollard 1999; 2016; Richards 2013).

In this chapter we attempt to redress the balance by presenting the results of the investigation of sarsens in the locality of Stonehenge and Durrington Walls undertaken by the SRP in 2005–2007. Detailing the transformations undergone during the early third millennium BC by the Tor Stone (east of Durrington Walls) and the Cuckoo Stone (west of Woodhenge) reveals the practices surrounding the extraction and relocation of sarsen stones, and charts chronologically the 'monumentalisation' of this extraordinary landscape. This chapter concludes with a review of the Heel Stone and the origins of Stonehenge itself (see also *The Avenue's construction and purpose* in Chapter 8).

Questions concerning the significance of sarsens in the south Wiltshire landscape during the Neolithic period, as noted above, have tended to be subsumed within debates concerning the origin of the Stonehenge sarsens. Two contrasting views concerning the source of the Stonehenge sarsens – whether local or distant – have been offered (see E.H. Stone 1924: 68–74; J.F.S. Stone 1953: 14). As discussed in the previous chapter, because of the remnant distribution of sarsen stones observable today (Figure 7.1), notably the concentration on the Marlborough Downs, it continued to be generally accepted that the Stonehenge sarsens were derived from north Wiltshire (e.g. Atkinson 1956: 110–11; Parker Pearson 2016; see Figure 6.42), recently confirmed by the matching of all but two of the 52 sarsens at Stonehenge with a likely source in West Woods, 2 miles south of the Downs (Nash *et al.* 2020). There have, however, been dissenting voices concerning the north Wiltshire source. For example, Judd suggested that the Stonehenge sarsens had been gathered 'probably at no great distance from the spot where the structure stands'

*** With contributions by:**
U. Albarella, C. Bronk Ramsey, B. Chan, G. Cook, G. Davies, I. Hajdas, P.D. Marshall, C.Minniti, D. Mitcham, S. Palstra, M. Parker Pearson, E. Simmons, C. Steele, S. Viner-Daniels, K. Welham and K. Whitaker

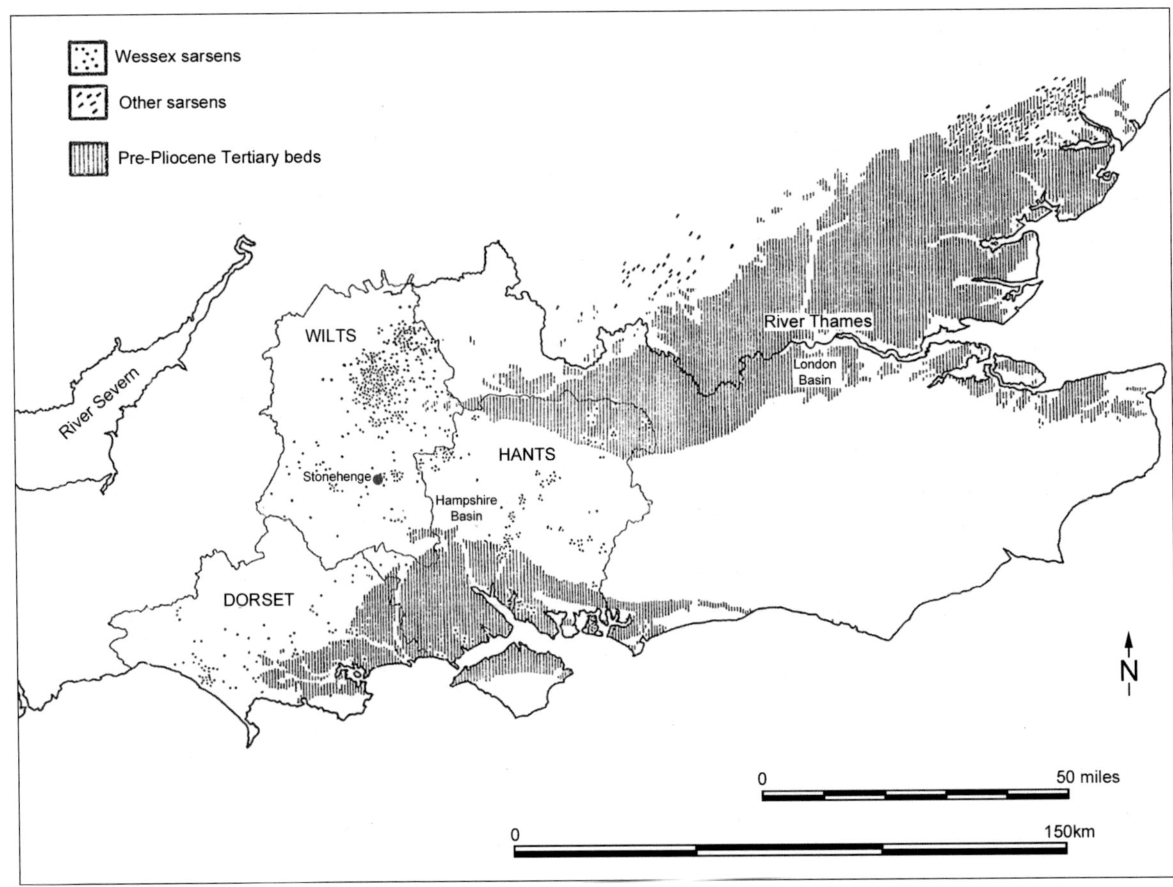

Figure 7.1. Distribution map of sarsens in southern Britain (from Bowen and Smith 1977); © Society of Antiquaries

(1902: 115), a view accepted by Thomas (1923) and E.H. Stone (1924). The Society of Antiquaries' *Evolution of the Landscape* project (Bowen and Smith 1977) recorded only eight single sarsen boulders and a pair of stones (RCHME 1977) now surviving within 5km of Stonehenge; this contrasts greatly with the spreads remaining in north Wiltshire and southwest Dorset (Figure 7.1; Bowen and Smith 1977: 189, 192, fig. 2; Field 2005).

Despite predations dating from the medieval period to the present (Bowen and Smith 1977; Carrington 1857; Clifton-Taylor 1972; de Luc 1811; Field 2005; Hoare 1819; King 1968; Smith 1884), there is impressive survival of natural sarsens in north Wiltshire (Figure 7.2).

Furthermore, in north Wiltshire, from the Early Neolithic period onwards, there appears to be a clear history of quarrying, dragging and erecting sarsens. As suggested for Brittany (Scarre 2011), the erection of individual monoliths may, in fact, have constituted an initial phase of monumentality early in the Neolithic of this part of Wessex (Field 2005: 89). For instance, an individual standing monolith was sealed beneath Arn Hill long barrow, at the western end of Salisbury Plain (McOmish *et al.* 2002: 29). It has also been suggested that empty pits beneath certain north Wiltshire long barrows may be sockets of earlier, removed standing stones (*ibid.*). Excavations around the sarsen polissoir on Lockeridge Down by Fowler (2000: 66–8) located a possible socket, thought to have been left by a fallen or felled standing stone (Pollard and Reynolds 2002: 72). Judging from this evidence, the general absence of single standing stones throughout Wessex, and the Stonehenge landscape in particular, may well be due to a combination of geology (see below), their subsequent transformation and appropriation in later constructions, and a lack of archaeological research.

The small number of sarsens close to Stonehenge and the lack of sarsen building material used in its neighbouring settlements (in contrast to the north Wiltshire villages such as Avebury, West Overton, and Lockeridge, where much sarsen was used in building) suggest that there never was a sizable number of sarsen boulders on Salisbury Plain. This is possibly because of the variability of the silicification and erosional processes in Tertiary deposits across the Hampshire and London basins and the areas on the edge of the basins, such as north Wiltshire (Figure 7.1; Green 1997a: 261). One reason why the distribution of sarsens in this region may appear thin has been suggested by McOmish

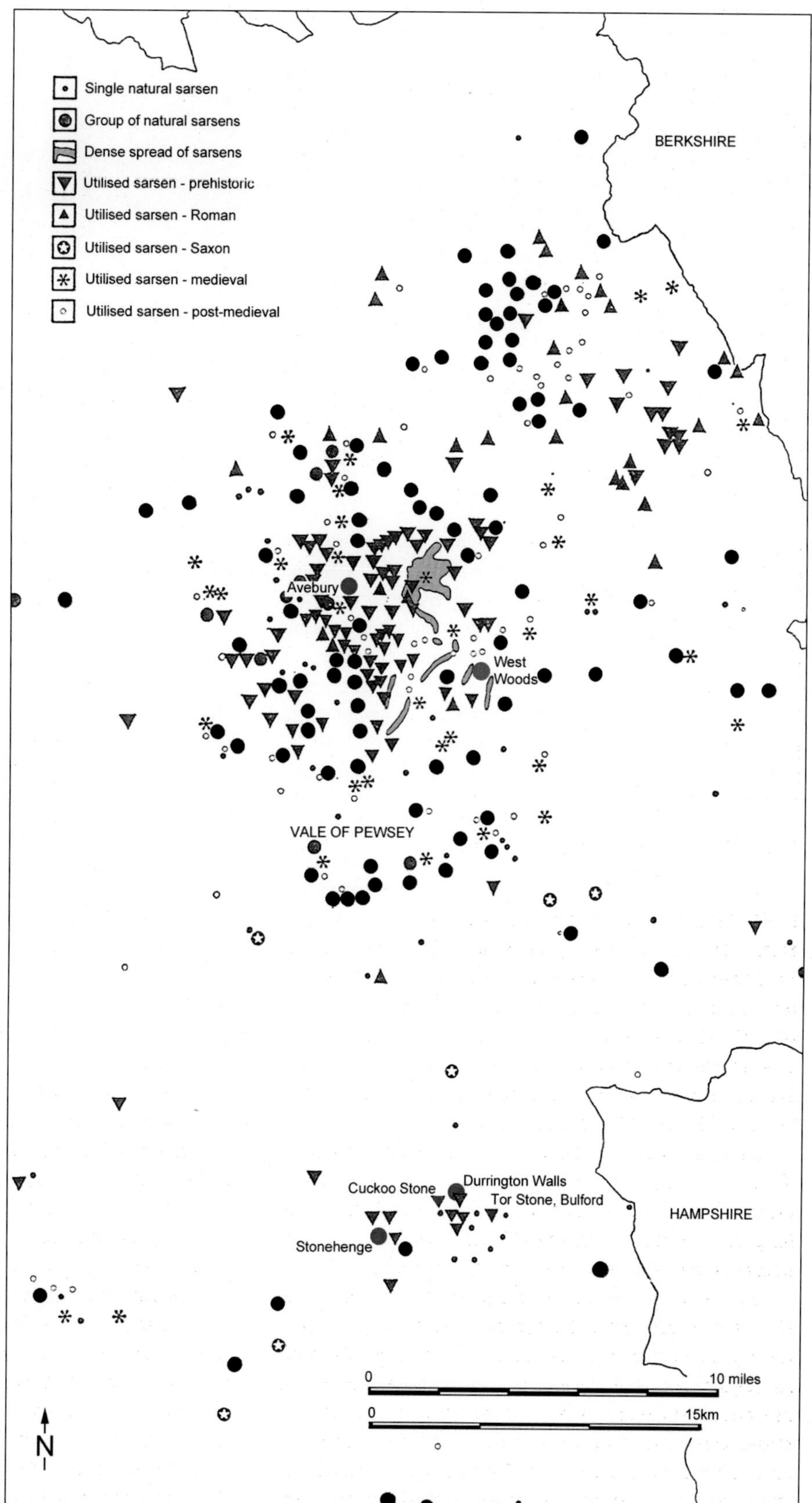

Figure 7.2. Distribution map of sarsens around Stonehenge and Avebury in Wiltshire (from Bowen and Smith 1977); showing the location of West Woods, likely to be the source of most of Stonehenge's sarsens; © Society of Antiquaries

Figure 7.3. Josh Pollard stands beside the Cuckoo Stone before excavation, viewed from the east

et al. (2002: 152): any substantial boulders cleared during the development of Salisbury Plain's 'Celtic' field systems would be obscured by lynchets. However, in comparison with north Wiltshire, the scarcity of extremely large sarsen stones in field boundaries, hedgerows and buildings in close proximity to Stonehenge (David Field pers. comm.) argues against their ever having been numerous or large enough to provide stones for the monument.

Nevertheless, there are small sarsen clusters and single stones such as the Cuckoo Stone and the Tor Stone, Bulford, 2.6km and 5.2km from Stonehenge respectively. That there might have been many more such monoliths within this area is a distinct possibility. For example, during the excavation of the Tor Stone in 2005, another substantial sarsen, previously unrecorded, was revealed after a bank and its hedgerow near Netheravon were damaged fortuitously by a military vehicle. An examination of this stone revealed it to be the broken section of a large 'monolith'-shaped stone. The large-scale OS map for this area (OS 1:10,560 1961 sheet SU14SE) marks a number of sarsen boundary stones (map symbol 'BS'), and it seems quite likely that they too are or were derived from larger broken stones.

To conclude, we can say with a certain degree of confidence that whilst there was a higher concentration of large sarsen stones in south Wiltshire, and in close proximity to Stonehenge, before the twentieth century, there is no evidence to suggest that these were of sufficient size to have been the source for the megalithic architecture of Stonehenge. Indeed, Ashbee (1998) and Darvill (2005: 114) have posited the possibility of the Stonehenge sarsens deriving from as far away as east Kent, on the basis of the difficulty in procuring sarsen blocks of sufficient size from a single source such as the Marlborough Downs. In making this suggestion, they were repeating a similar proposal voiced over 150 years ago by the Revd Edward Duke (Stone 1924: 69–70). As noted above, the question of the sarsen sources may now be largely settled by the results of current research led by David Nash (Nash *et al.* forthcoming).

Although the sarsen stones in the immediate environs of Stonehenge may not have been of sufficient magnitude to contribute to the construction of Stonehenge, and a number have certainly been destroyed or cleared, there remain two notable examples: the Tor Stone and Cuckoo Stone. Today, both stones lie recumbent in cultivated fields, and the opportunity to investigate the status and biographies of each stone was considered an important element of the SRP, with the hope that such fieldwork would provide a better understanding of sarsens in the Stonehenge landscape.

7.2. The Cuckoo Stone

C. Richards

This recumbent sarsen stone (2.1m × 1.8m × 0.90m) lies 2.6km northeast of Stonehenge at SU 1465 4334. It is in many ways a neglected element of Stonehenge's monumental landscape (Figure 7.3). It lies west of Woodhenge and southwest of Durrington Walls (see Figure 9.4). It is absent from the majority of plans of monuments in the Stonehenge area (*e.g.* Richards 1990: plan 3). It was, however, targeted as an area of geophysical interest by David and Payne (1997: 108), but only with regard to searching for related structures. While only mentioned once in the entire text of the 2005 Stonehenge research framework, that report does state that the 'definition and investigation of this site is highly desirable' (Darvill 2005: 56). This neglect may, in part, be a product of the mistaken belief that the Cuckoo Stone has at some time in the past been removed from its original position (Darvill 1997: 184).

The Cuckoo Stone continues the east–west axis of the Greater Cursus, lying 960m beyond its east end (see also Burl 1987: 43) but it should be considered as an important monument in its own right. In the SRP research design, unravelling the biography of this stone was judged essential for obtaining a broad understanding of the role and nature of sarsen stones in the Stonehenge area. A number of specific questions were addressed by the SRP:

1. Was the Cuckoo Stone ever erected as a standing stone?
2. If so, was the Cuckoo Stone moved in recent times (as suggested by Darvill 1997: 184)?
3. If erected as a standing stone, was the origin of the sarsen in the locality or close proximity?
4. Did the Cuckoo Stone provide a context for Neolithic activities (as suggested by Burl 2006: 92–3)?
5. Did the stone continue to be a focus of attention in later prehistory?

Investigations consisted of a three-stage programme of fieldwork in August–September 2007. Geophysical surveys were followed by ploughsoil sampling, in advance of the excavation of SRP Trench 23, measuring 25m (north–south) × 20m (east–west), around the recumbent stone (Figure 7.4).

7.2.1. Geophysical surveys

K. Welham and C. Steele

Geophysical surveys were conducted in 2007 with the aim of identifying the stonehole and any associated features at the site of the Cuckoo Stone. Earth resistance survey was completed using a Geoscan RM15-D earth resistance meter in the 0.50m twin electrode configuration. Readings were taken over a 30m × 30m grid at 1m intervals along traverses spaced 1m apart. Magnetometer survey was undertaken using a Geoscan Research FM256 fluxgate gradiometer over 10m × 10m grids with readings taken at 0.50m intervals along traverses spaced 1m apart, at a resolution of 0.1nT.

Around the Cuckoo Stone (Figure 7.5), the background resistance is varied and disturbed, which makes interpretation of anomalies difficult. The survey area also contains a large amount of small ferrous litter such as cartridge cases, which interfered with the magnetometer data (Figure 7.6). Large anomalies (R1/M1) near the eastern edge of the survey area were shown on excavation to have been created by a modern disturbance (context 102) filled with stones and metal that cuts into a possible Roman structure. A number of further pits detected by the geophysical survey were found on excavation to be Roman in date: pit 107 (R3/M2), pit 119 (R4/M3), pit 117 (R6/M4), pit 133 (R2) and pit 106 (R5). The strong magnetic response of M4 was due to this Roman grave pit containing iron hobnails. The excavation of these Roman features, and the finds recovered from these contexts, are reported in Volume 4.

The geophysical survey at the Cuckoo Stone detected neither the stonehole in which the monolith was erected, nor the pit from which it was extracted in prehistory (see *Excavation*, below). This may be due to the extent of modern disturbance at this site. Similarly, neither of the other two Neolithic pits (see below) nor the presence of three Early Bronze Age Collared Urn cremation burials (reported in Volume 3) were detected at this stage.

7.2.2. Lithics from the ploughsoil around the Cuckoo Stone

D. Mitcham

In advance of the excavation of Trench 23, the ploughsoil at the Cuckoo Stone, 0.28m–0.32m deep across the site, was sampled at 5% across the area of 25m × 20m around the stone, with the exception of a 3m-wide cordon around the stone itself. The topsoil from a total of 20 1m-square test pits was sieved by hand through the standard 10mm mesh, and produced 441 pieces of worked flint. The raw material is predominantly chalk-derived flint from the local area, with heavy white patination.

The ploughsoil assemblage contains no formal tools or chronologically distinctive pieces, and is entirely debitage (Table 7.1). No retouched or utilised pieces are present, and there is a significant proportion (20.4%) of miscellaneous waste. One flake was struck on brown gravel flint. The cores are both single-platform flake-cores, with a number of bashed lumps/tested nodules. The character of their working is *ad hoc*, and typical of later prehistoric flint-working. Finally, a small number of burnt unworked pieces, and a couple of burnt worked pieces were noted.

The ploughsoil assemblage in this location represents a different form of activity to the stratified archaeological deposits beneath (see Chan, below). The lack of anything which can be broadly dated to the Neolithic in the ploughsoil would suggest the possible avoidance of the Cuckoo Stone after it was erected. This supports the idea that the Neolithic pit assemblages on the site (see below) were discrete deposits of tools used in erecting the sarsen, rather than material swept off a contemporary surface into a pit. The lack of anything diagnostically Neolithic in the ploughsoil here is especially noteworthy given the site's close proximity (*c.* 300m) to Durrington Walls and to the area south of Woodhenge, both locations with much evidence of Late Neolithic activity (see Volume 3).

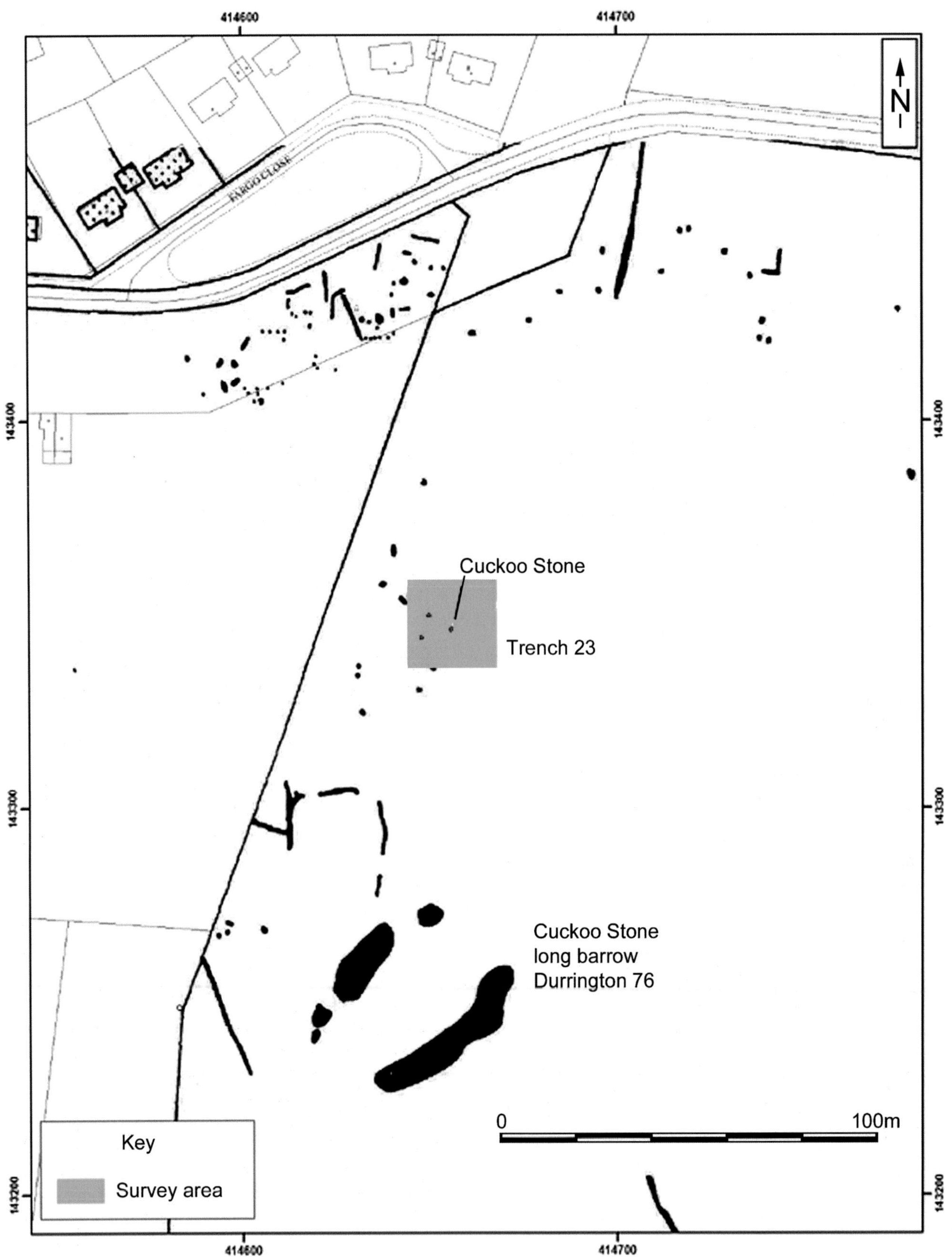

Figure 7.4. Map showing the location of the Cuckoo Stone

Artefact type	Frequency	Percent
Chip	26	5.9
Flake	317	71.9
Irregular waste	90	20.4
Single-platform flake-core	2	0.5
Tested nodule/bashed lump	6	1.4
Total	441	100.0

Table 7.1. The lithic assemblage composition from the Cuckoo Stone test pits

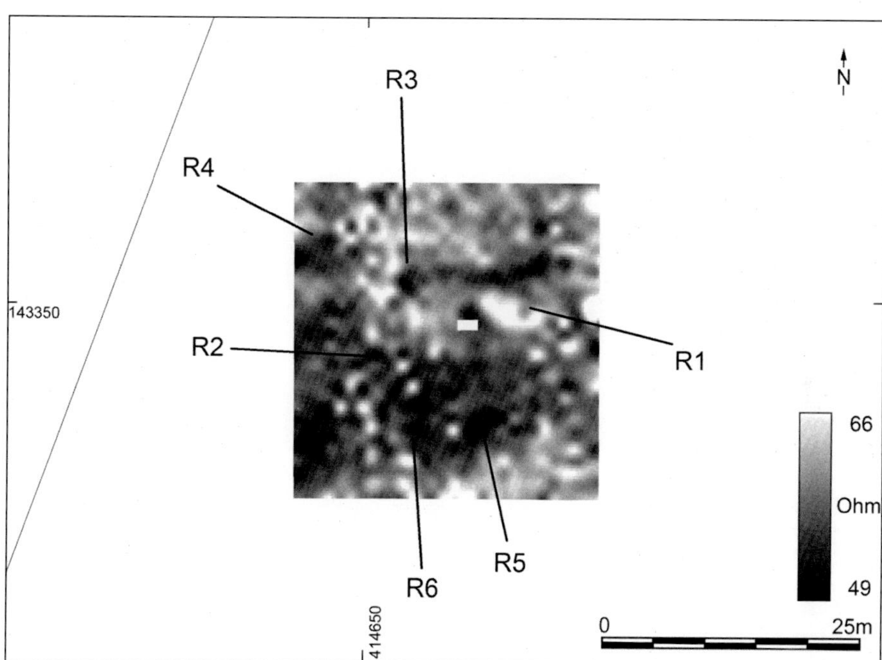

Figure 7.5. Earth resistance survey around the Cuckoo Stone

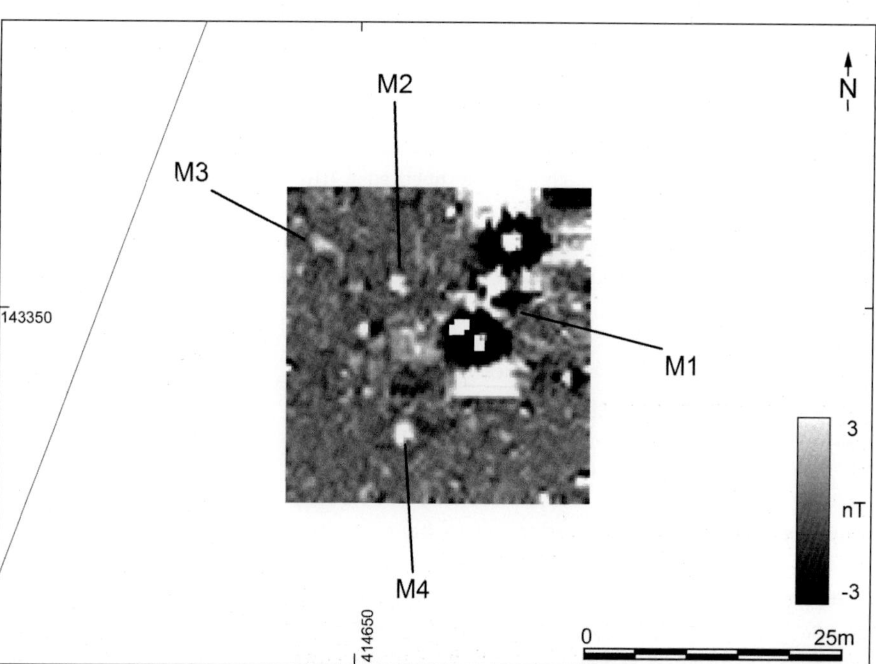

Figure 7.6. Magnetometry survey around the Cuckoo Stone

Figure 7.7. Trench 23, viewed from the southeast; the Cuckoo Stone is to the right

7.2.3. Excavation around the Cuckoo Stone

After the test-pit sampling of the ploughsoil, the entirety of Trench 23 was stripped by machine, with the exception of a 3m-wide cordon around the Cuckoo Stone itself, which was excavated entirely by hand. A metal detector survey conducted by Lee Smeaton revealed a concentration of Late Roman coins and metal objects in features around the Cuckoo Stone, particularly to the northeast (the Roman finds being reported in Volume 4).

Once the trench was cleaned, a large area of modern disturbance was immediately visible directly east of the Cuckoo Stone, where two metal earthing cables projected from an area of loosely packed flint nodules (102), which had clearly been laid in recent times to create a stable surface. It is likely that two large hoards of Late Roman coins recovered by a metal detectorist from the area of the Cuckoo Stone in 1993 came from within or close to this disturbed area (Algar 1997; Moorhead 2001). This appeared to be the only modern disturbance in the trench, apart from a series of plough grooves scarring the chalk bedrock (Figure 7.7).

A large number and range of archaeological features were clearly visible within the trench once the surface had been cleaned (Figure 7.8). All features were excavated by hand, with fills sieved through a 10mm mesh. Environmental samples of fills were taken for flotation to retrieve carbonised plant remains as well as artefactual material <10mm. The features in Trench 23 divide into the following constituents:

- the stone hollow to the west of the Cuckoo Stone, in which it once lay;
- the stone socket in which the Cuckoo Stone once stood;
- two Neolithic pits;
- three Early Bronze Age cremation burials within Collared Urns;
- a Roman building of square shape represented by a spread of loam flanked by lines of circular postholes (visible in Figures 7.7–7.8 in the southwestern quadrant of the trench);
- a possible second Roman structure (but very damaged and truncated; feature 102 northeast of the Cuckoo Stone);
- a number of large Roman pits (context numbers listed above);
- a shallow lynchet running east–west across the trench, north of the Roman building.

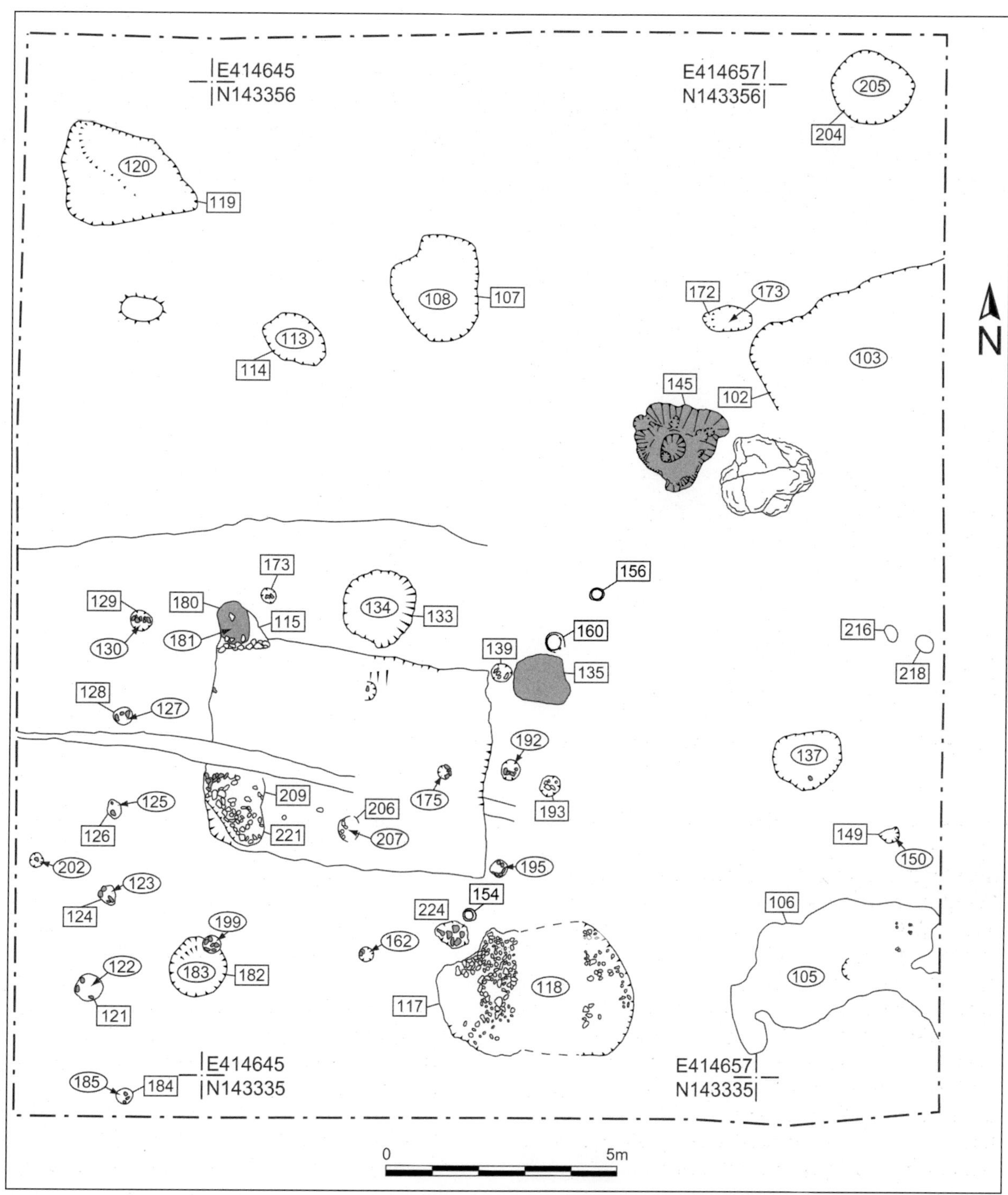

Figure 7.8. Plan of Trench 23 around the Cuckoo Stone, showing the two Neolithic pits 135 and 180

These features run chronologically from the Neolithic to the Roman period. The Early Bronze Age and Roman remains are reported in Volume 4.

The Cuckoo Stone's hole

In their natural state, sarsens effectively sit on the chalk surface (Bowen and Smith 1977; Green 1997), and become slightly embedded in the bedrock through processes of erosion and weathering caused by rain continually draining off the stones' outer surfaces onto

Figure 7.9. The Cuckoo Stone during excavation, viewed from the west

Figure 7.10. The Cuckoo Stone during excavation, viewed from the north

the soft chalk. In Trench 23 an irregular-shaped cut (145), measuring *c.* 1.64m × 1.66m, was revealed about 0.25m west of the recumbent Cuckoo Stone, and was recognised during excavation as the natural hollow or 'scoop' in the chalk bedrock in which the sarsen boulder had originally lain prone (Figures 7.8–7.10).

This scoop or hollow (145) was filled with light grey-brown, silty loam (146), which was very loose and had clearly been disturbed by rabbit burrows. As excavation of this feature commenced, the southern edge of the scoop was found to drop steeply whilst, on the northern side, a more gradual sloping profile was evident. This slope ran gently downwards to a depth of *c.* 0.23m, at which point it dropped vertically. This vertical face clearly represented a secondary cut (148) through shallow stone hollow (145); it appeared to correspond with the steeper, southern edge of the hollow.

On the northern and northeastern sides of scoop 145, where the shallow profile of this stone hollow survived, the loose upper fill (146) gave way to a compact chalky wash (147) which lay directly on the natural chalk bedrock on the gently sloping northern edge of the hollow (Figure 7.11, top). Apart from the chalky wash (147), the general fill (146) remained homogeneous as the deeper cut (148) within the hollow was excavated. Flint nodules (171) were spread both vertically and horizontally within the fill (146) although they tended to cluster towards the centre of pit 148 (Figure 7.11, top and left).

At a depth of *c.* 0.44m the silty-loam fill (146) gave way to a thin layer (*c.* 0.01m–0.04m thick) of crushed chalk spread across the bottom of pit 148 (Figure 7.11, middle). Centrally placed at the base was a small circular feature (227), 0.25m in diameter with a depth of 0.10m (Figures 7.11–7.13). Although the fill of this small feature was of crushed chalk, similar to that covering the base of the large pit (148), it contained additional organic matter.

Pit 148, cut into the natural hollow (145) in which the Cuckoo Stone once lay, is interpreted as being the socket in which the Cuckoo Stone was erected; at the base of the socket was a small posthole (227).

Unlike the stoneholes at Bluestonehenge (see Chapter 5), the stone socket here shows little sign of deliberate removal of the standing stone, other than the stone hollow's gentle north slope indicating the likely direction in which it was removed and reintroduced into this hole. Nor is there any indication of when it was removed from its socket. Today the stone lies to the east of the socket, indicating that it must have been moved to this spot by human agency though whether it was initially pulled over or fell naturally is unknown. The former is more likely given its squat form.

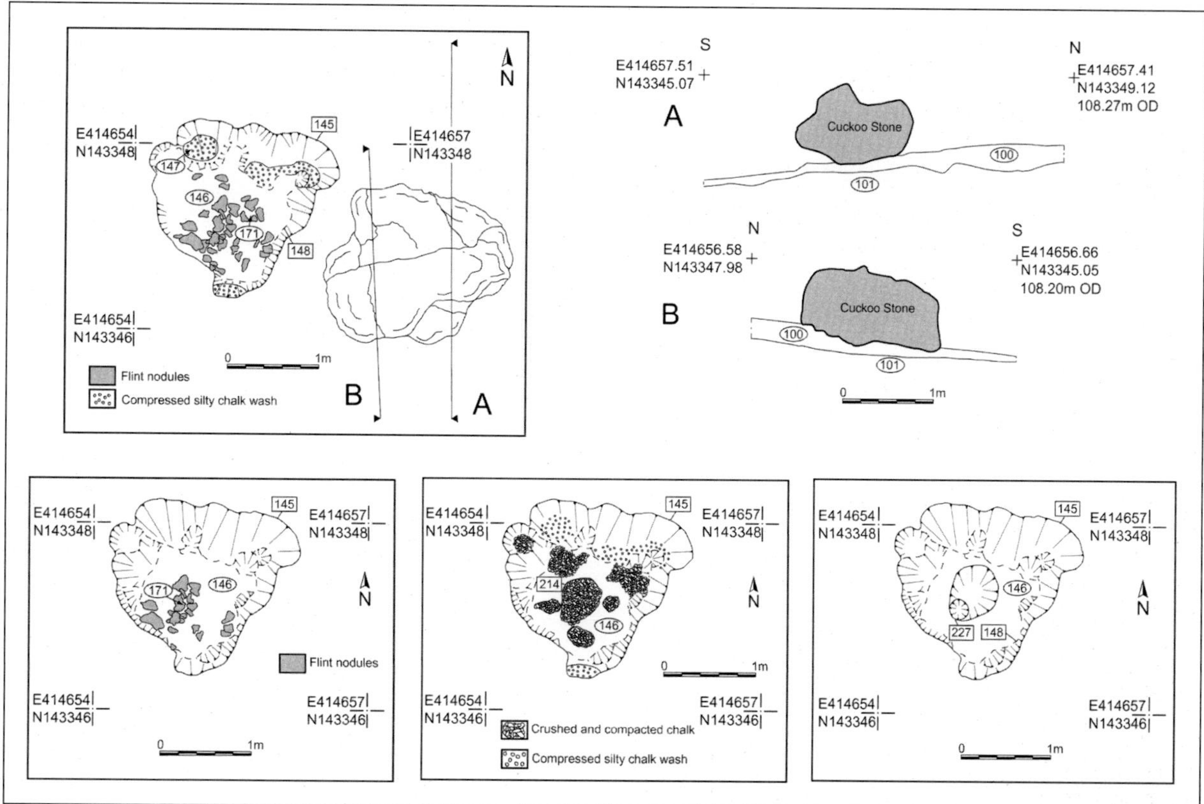

Figure 7.11 (above). Plans of the different layers within pit 145 and cross-sections through the Cuckoo Stone

Figure 7.12 (right). The Cuckoo Stone and pit 145, with west at the top of the picture

The Late Neolithic pits

Pit 135 was a fairly shallow, slightly elongated pit measuring 1.04m (north–south) × 1.17m (east–west) and 0.16m deep, situated *c.* 4m to the southwest of the Cuckoo Stone's stone hollow (Figures 7.8, 7.14). The fill (136) was a fairly compact, homogeneous silty loam, covering an antler pick (SF 265) and a cattle scapula (SF 269), together with a complete roe deer antler (SF 281), a number of worked flints (SF 271, SF 276, SF 279) including a chisel (SF 260) and a scraper (SF 261), animal bones (SF 262–SF 264, SF 266, SF 268, SF 272–SF 274, SF 277–SF 278, SF 280) and a piece of sarsen (SF 270).

The antler pick (SF 265) and scapula shovel (SF 269) in pit 135 would normally be interpreted as digging equipment. The pit's shallowness and irregular shape show little concern for morphology and more for the rapid creation of a receptacle for deposition (Figure 7.15). Consequently, a good case can be made for the blunt and battered antler pick (see Figure 7.22) and the scapula tool as having been employed in digging the stone socket for the Cuckoo Stone, afterwards being rapidly deposited nearby. The depositional sequence is consistent with this material having been placed on the base of the pit and quickly covered over in a single event. In short, the purpose of this pit may have been to facilitate the burial of a set of material objects. The cattle scapula produced a radiocarbon date of 2910–2870 cal BC at 95% confidence (OxA-18940; 4253±28 BP).

A second pit (180) was discovered during investigation of the northwest corner of a Roman timber building, the foundations of which had truncated the pit's south side (Figures 7.8, 7.16). This pit was situated *c.* 9m west-southwest of the Cuckoo Stone socket and was of oval, steep-sided form, measuring *c.* 0.64m (north–south) × 0.76m (east–west) and 0.58m deep (Figure 7.17). The fill

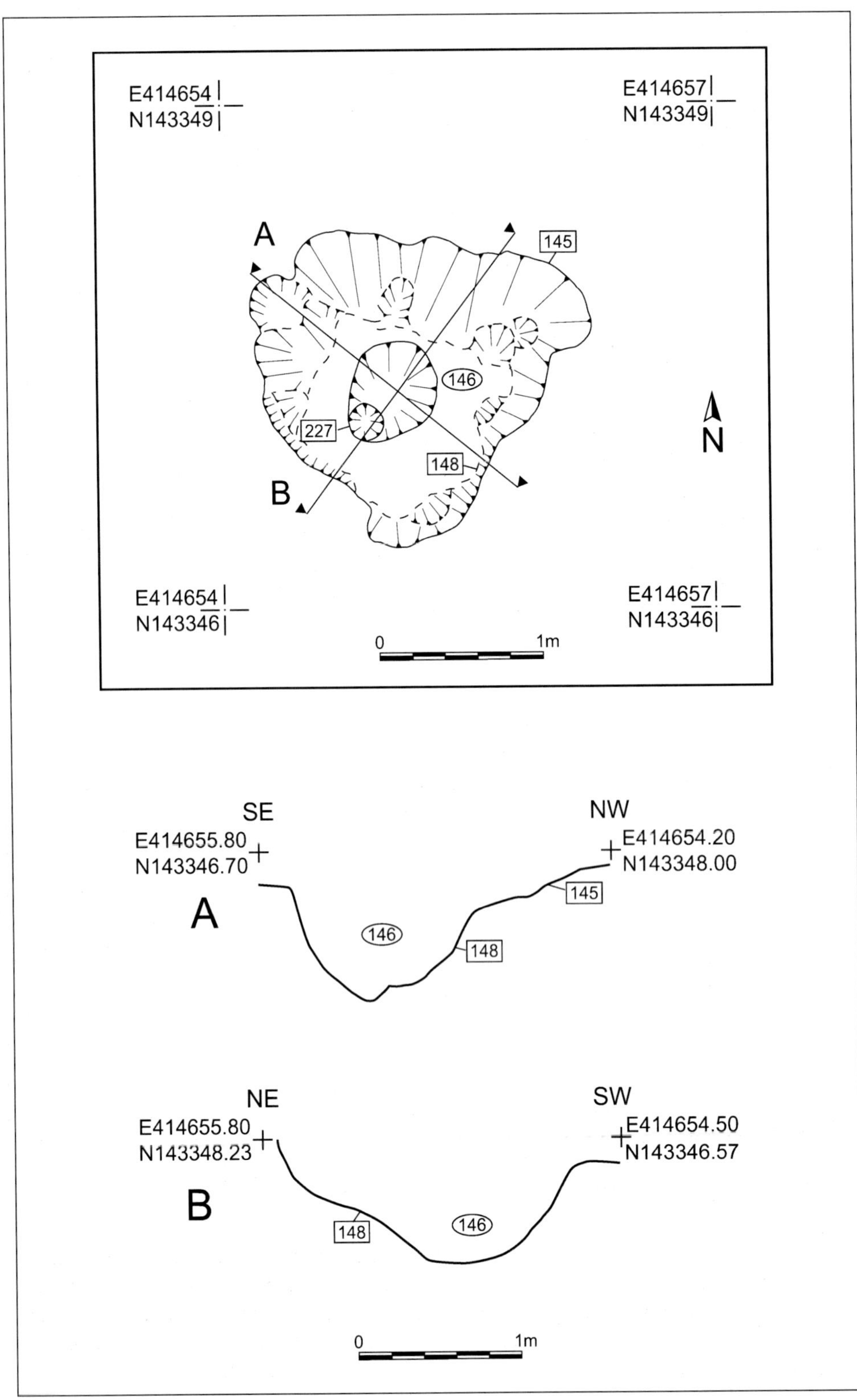

Figure 7.13. Profiles of pit 145

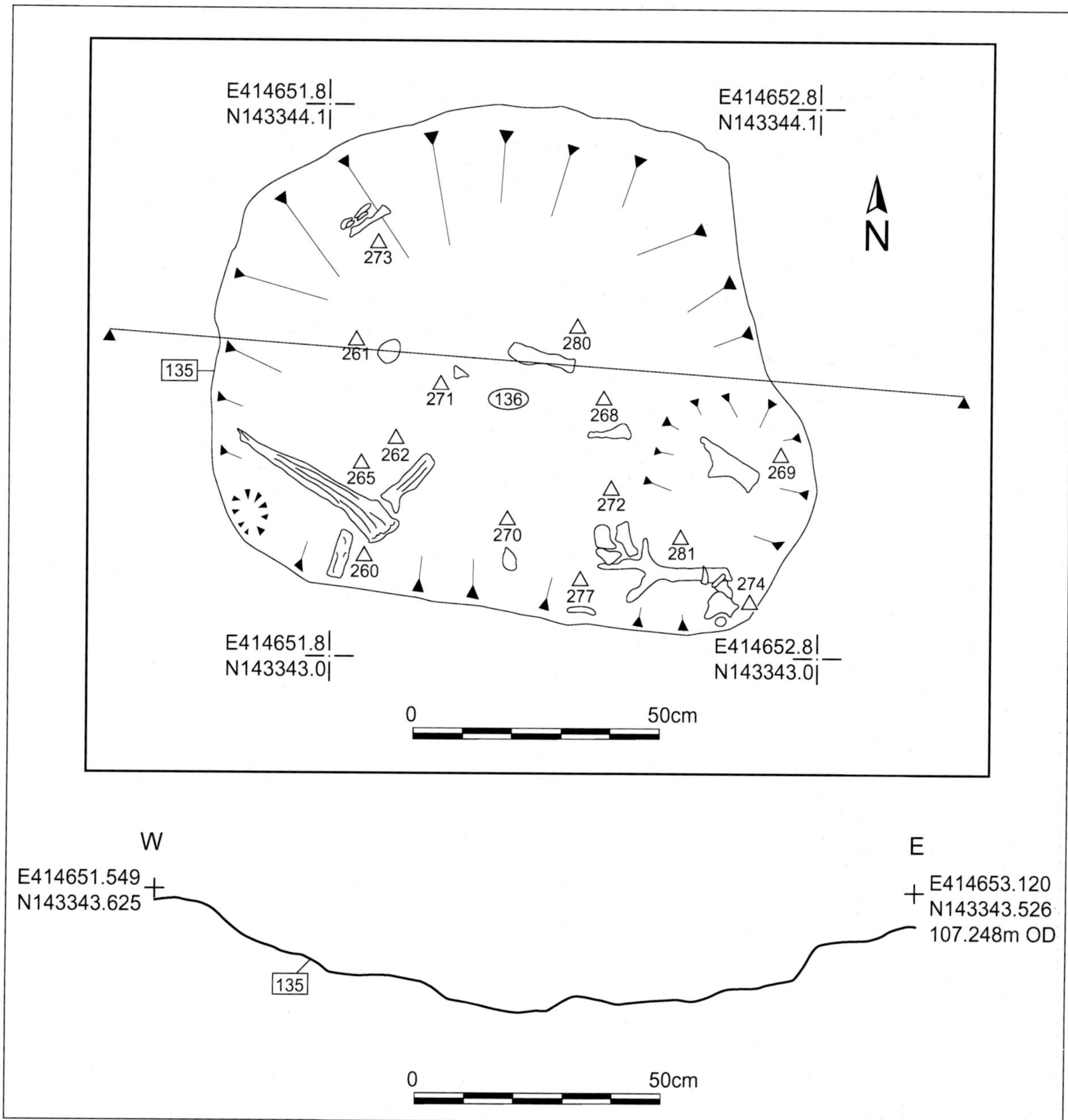

Figure 7.14. Plan and profile of pit 135 near the Cuckoo Stone

(181) was again homogeneous, being fairly compact, brown silty loam. The pit contained large amounts of worked flint (>100 pieces) and animal bone, including a small piece of roe deer antler (SF 355). A number of animal bones were wedged against the side of the pit. A radiocarbon date of 2940–2750 cal BC at 95% confidence (SUERC-46473; 4231±27 BP) was obtained on an articulating red deer bone from fill 181.

Pit 180 was more regular in appearance than pit 135 and therefore a qualitative distinction can be made between them. The large amount of animal bone within pit 180 may well represent the remains of a substantial act of consumption (although a horse bone in this deposit was found to date to the Roman period [see Marshall *et al.*, below], indicating that at least one of the animal bones was intrusive within this layer).

7.2.4. Discussion

The similarity between the shape of the Cuckoo Stone and the plan and contours of the adjacent cut feature (145) was noticed when the first plans of both were drawn

Figure 7.15. Pit 135, viewed from the south

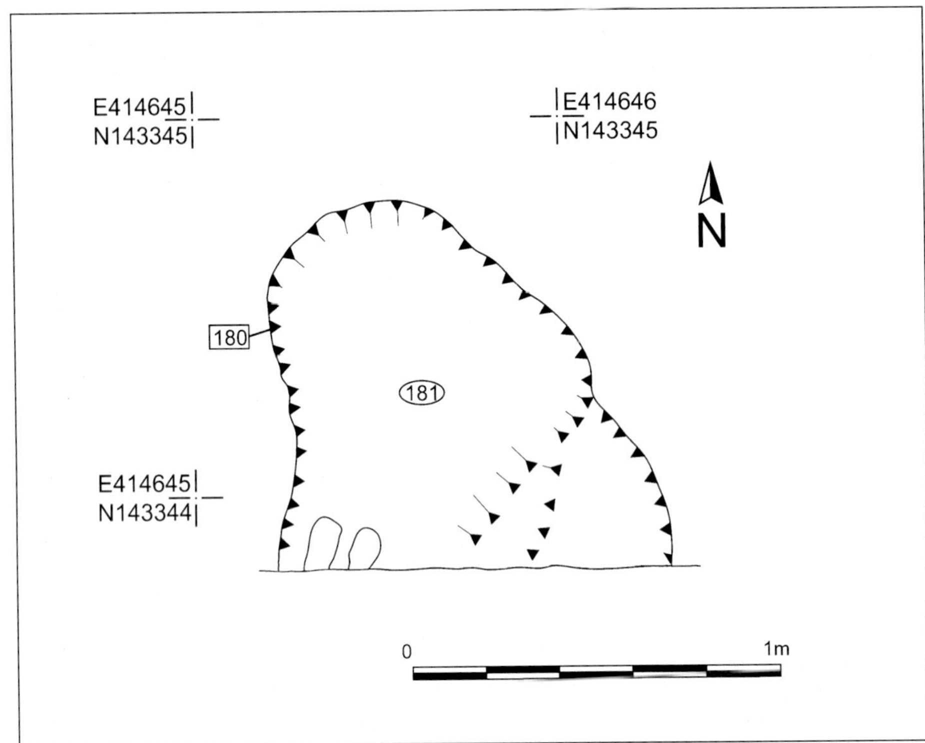

Figure 7.16. Plan of pit 180

up (see Figures 7.8, 7.11). At this point, it was realised that the scoop (145) is a stone hollow, representing the original, prone position of the Cuckoo Stone. Apart from the similarity in shape between both stone and scoop, this interpretation is supported by the results of experimental work undertaken on natural sarsens on the Marlborough Downs in 1975 (Bowen and Smith 1977). Here two sarsens (Stones I and II) were excavated in order to determine 'if the bedrock was in any way affected by their presence' (*ibid.*: 193). The experimental excavation of Stone II produced the following conclusions:

- It lay in a depression in the chalk, filled with a little clay;
- Had it been moved, it would have left an irregular, shallow depression in the chalk that would presumably have attracted an earthy fill (Bowen and Smith 1977: 195).

The presence of a natural sarsen over 2m in length within the environs of Stonehenge is of considerable interest (although we found no evidence that it was ever 5.50m long, as suggested by Burl [2006: 92]). The prehistoric biography of the Cuckoo Stone can be reconstructed in six stages from the evidence of excavation:

1. A sarsen of relatively small size, cemented from Tertiary sands over two million years ago, lay fully visible within a shallow hollow (145) in the chalk bedrock.
2. The sarsen was removed from its original position and a post (posthole 227) was erected centrally in the stone hollow
3. The post was either removed or decayed *in situ*; a stone socket (148) was dug through the stone hollow (145), and the Cuckoo Stone was erected, most likely around 2900 cal BC near the beginning of the Late Neolithic.
4. The tools possibly employed in digging the socket – an antler pick and cattle scapula – were buried within a shallow pit (135), *c.* 4m to the southwest around 2900 cal BC.
5. Around the same time, *c.* 2900 cal BC, a second pit (180) was dug further to the southwest of the Cuckoo Stone, and a mass of animal bones and antler, and over 100 worked flints were deposited within it.
6. Early in the second millennium BC, the erect Cuckoo Stone attracted three cremation deposits, within urns, placed to the southwest of the monolith.

The project's research questions (see above) were addressed successfully by the excavation, and discussion of the wider significance of our findings appears in the conclusion to this chapter.

Figure 7.17. Julia Best excavating pit 180, viewed from the north

7.2.5. The Cuckoo Stone: radiocarbon dating

P.D. Marshall, C. Bronk Ramsey and G. Cook

Seven samples were submitted for radiocarbon analysis from the trench excavated at the Cuckoo Stone. Of these, only two produced a Neolithic date. As part of a later and separate project investigating down-profile movement of small samples, four carbonised cereal grains, two each from pit fills 136 and 181, were radiocarbon-dated and were found to date to the two millennia AD, indicating that they are contaminants intrusive to these Neolithic layers (see below).

A cattle scapula from the fill (136) of pit 135 was submitted to the Oxford Radiocarbon Accelerator Unit (ORAU) (Table 7.2) and processed as described in Chapter 3. Single-entity (Ashmore 1999) fragments of cremated human bone from the three cremations, including two samples from urn 2 (context 156) and two animal bone samples (a red deer tarsal and a horse scapula) from pit 180 were dated at the Scottish Universities Environmental Research Centre (SUERC). The cremated bone samples were pre-treated following the method outlined in Lanting *et al.* (2001) and the animal bones using a modified Longin method (Longin 1971). The pre-treated samples were converted to carbon dioxide in pre-cleaned sealed quartz tubes (Vandeputte *et al.* 1996), graphitised as described by Slota *et al.* (1987), and measured by AMS (Xu *et al.* 2004; Freeman *et al.* 2010).

Radiocarbon results

The radiocarbon results are given in Table 7.2, and are quoted in accordance with the international standard known as the Trondheim convention (Stuiver and Kra 1986). They are conventional radiocarbon ages (Stuiver and Polach 1977).

Radiocarbon calibration

The calibrations of the results, relating the radiocarbon measurements directly to calendar dates (Table 7.2 and Figure 7.18) have been calculated as described in Chapter 3. The ranges in Table 7.2 have been calculated according to the maximum intercept method (Stuiver and Reimer 1986) and those in Figure 7.18 are derived from the probability method (Stuiver and Reimer 1993).

Lab number	Sample ID	Material and context	Radiocarbon age (BP)	δ13C (‰)	δ15N (‰)	C:N	Calibrated date range (95% confidence)
SUERC-32193	160 Urn 1	Cremated human bone from Collared Urn 160 (fill [161] excavated in Bristol lab) from pit 158 aligned with the Cuckoo Stone and pit 160	3490±30	-25.1			1900–1690 cal BC
SUERC-32194	156 Urn 2	Cremated human bone from Collared Urn 156 (fill [157] excavated in Bristol lab) from pit 109, 1.7m from the Cuckoo Stone	3080±30	-17.1			1430–1260 cal BC
SUERC-43223	156 Urn 2	As SUERC-32194	3536±28	-21.4			1950–1760 cal BC
SUERC-32195	154 Urn 3	Cremated human bone from Collared Urn 154 (fill [143] excavated in Bristol lab) from pit 144, 8.5m from the Cuckoo Stone	3440±30	-24.2			1880–1680 cal BC
OxA-18940	136 SF 274	Animal bone. *Bos taurus* scapula, from the fill (136) of a small pit (135) containing animal bones, lithics and an antler pick. This pit is close to the Cuckoo Stone and is thought to have been dug and filled when the Cuckoo Stone hole was dug and the stone erected.	4253±28	-21.3			2910–2870 cal BC
SUERC-32295	181	Animal bone. Horse scapula from the fill (181) of pit 180.	1880±30				cal AD 60–230
SUERC-46473	181 <4537>	Animal bone. *Cervus elaphus* (articulated tarsals) from the fill (181) of pit 180. This pit was *c*. 9m west of the Cuckoo Stone and contained large amounts of worked flint (>100 pieces) and animal bone, including a small piece of antler.	4231±27	-23.5	4.2	3.3	2940–2750 cal BC

Table 7.2. Radiocarbon results for animal bone and cremated human bone from the Cuckoo Stone

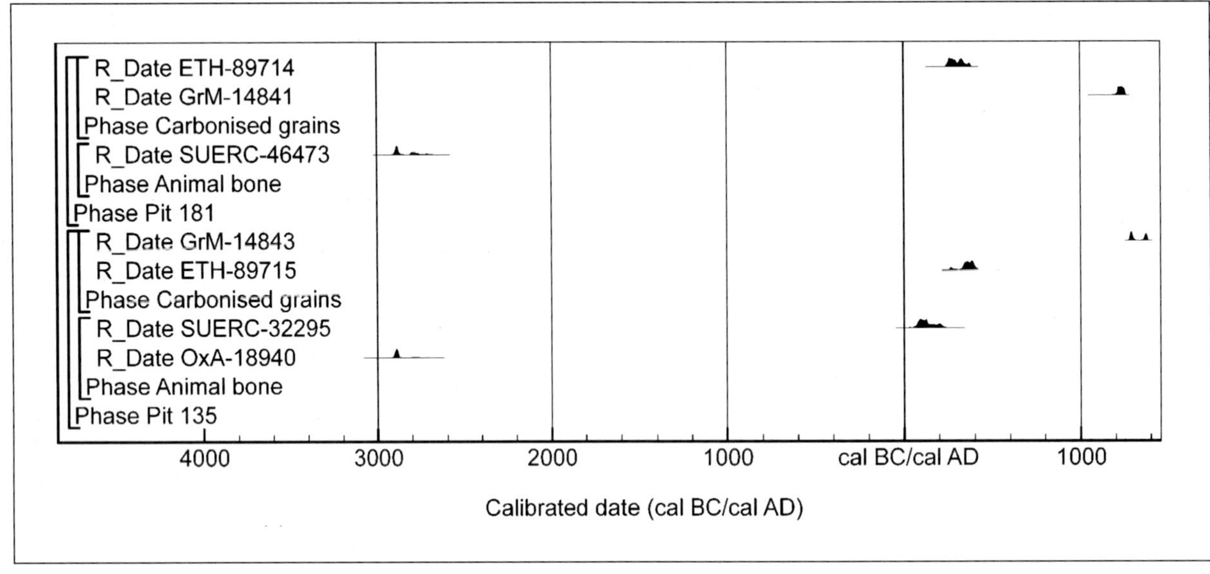

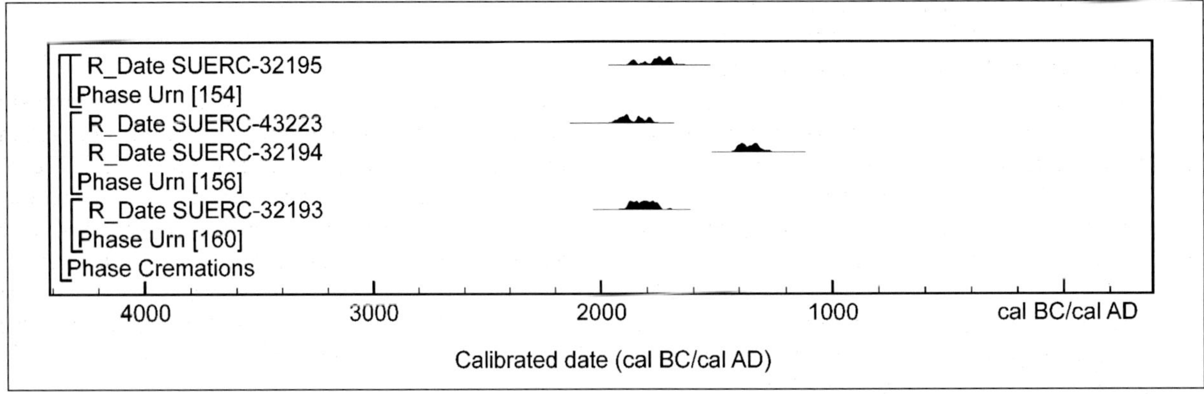

Figure 7.18. Probability distributions of radiocarbon dates from the Cuckoo Stone from Late Neolithic contexts (top) and from Early Bronze Age cremations (bottom)

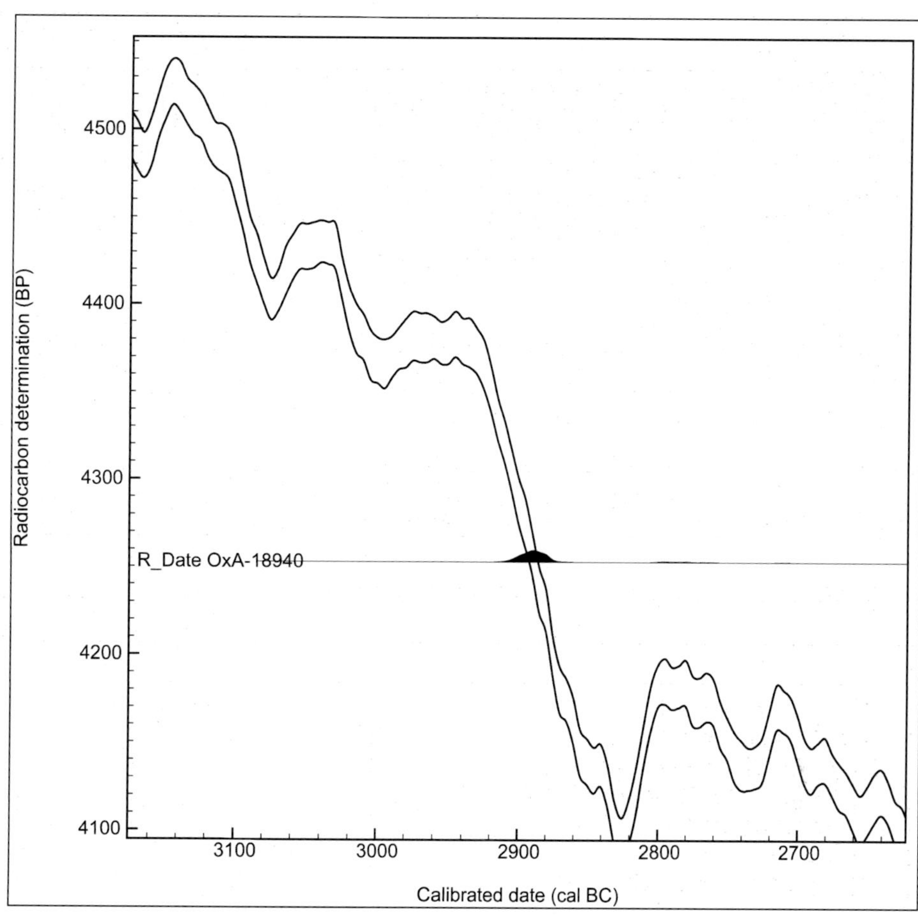

Figure 7.19. Probability distribution for OxA-18940 (pit 135) plotted on the radiocarbon calibration curve

Interpretation

The Late Neolithic pits

The cattle scapula tool within pit 135 provides a calibrated date of 2910–2870 cal BC (95% confidence; OxA-18940; 4253±28 BP; Figures 7.18–7.19). An articulating red deer tarsal from amongst the animal bones deposited within pit 180 provides a calibrated date of 2940–2750 cal BC (95% confidence; SUERC-46473; 4231±27 BP; Figure 7.18) and this deposit of animal bone may well represent the remains of a substantial 'single event' act of consumption.

The two measurements from the Neolithic pits 135 and 180 are statistically consistent (T'=0.3; T' (5%)=3.8; ν=1; Ward and Wilson 1978) and could therefore be of the same date.

The deposition of the scapula and a worn antler pick – standard components of a Neolithic toolkit used for excavation – in a shallow and irregular pit near the Cuckoo Stone suggests that they may have been employed in digging its stone socket and were then quickly deposited nearby afterwards. The date of the scapula may therefore give a date for the erection of the Cuckoo Stone.

Cremation burials

Given the unexpected late date from urn 2 (context 156) of 1430–1260 cal BC (SUERC-32194) a second sample was submitted (SUERC-43223). This determination and those from the other two urns (SUERC-32193 – urn 1 and SUERC-32195 – urn 3) are statistically consistent (T'=5.5; T' (5%)=6.0; ν=2) and could therefore be of the same actual age. These three cremations therefore all took place in the eighteenth or nineteenth centuries cal BC.

Later activity

The three cremation burials in Collared Urns were confirmed by radiocarbon dating as being deposited in the Early Bronze Age, in the eighteenth or nineteenth centuries cal BC. A horse scapula from the fill of pit 180, which was truncated by a Roman building, dates to AD 60–230 (95% confidence), during the Roman period. These are reported in full in Volume 4. The dates of the Collared Urn cremations and the horse bone are included in Table 7.2 and Figure 7.18.

Lab number	Sample ID	Material and context	Radiocarbon age (BP)	δ13C (‰) AMS	δ13C (‰) IRMS	Calibrated date range (95% confidence)
ETH-89715	102	Carbonised *Hordeum* sp. indet. grain (single) from the fill (136) of pit 135	1681±23	-23.0		cal AD 260–415
GrM-14843	102	Carbonised cf. *Triticum* sp. (free-threshing wheat) grain (single) from the fill (136) of pit 135	670±20		-23.0±0.15	cal AD 1275–1390
ETH-89714	114	Carbonised *Hordeum* sp. indet. grain (single) from the fill (180) of pit 181	1732±22	-21.5		cal AD 240–390
GrM-14841	115	Carbonised cf. *Triticum* sp. (free-threshing wheat) grain (single) from the fill (180) of pit 181	810±20		-23.0±0.15	cal AD 1205–1270

Table 7.3. Radiocarbon results for carbonised *Hordeum* sp. grains from Late Neolithic contexts 136 and 181 at the Cuckoo Stone

Artefact type	Pit 135	Hollow 145			Pit 180	Total
	136	Mixed	146	147	181	
Awl	0	0	0	0	1	1
Blade	1	0	0	0	8	9
Blade-like flake	2	1	0	0	5	8
Bladelet	2	0	1	0	8	11
Chisel	1	0	0	0	0	1
Core on a flake	0	0	0	0	1	1
Disc scraper	0	0	0	0	1	1
End-and-side scraper	1	0	0	0	3	4
End scraper	0	0	0	0	4	4
Flake	29	149	131	2	102	413
Hammerstone	0	0	1	0	0	1
Irregular waste	0	9	15	0	4	28
Misc. retouched flake	0	0	3	0	0	3
Multi-platform flake-core	0	0	1	0	2	3
Notch	0	1	1	0	0	2
Other knife	0	0	0	0	3	3
Other scraper	0	0	0	0	3	3
Petit tranchet arrowhead	1	0	0	0	0	1
Serrated flake	0	0	0	0	2	2
Single-platform blade-core	0	0	0	0	1	1
Single-platform flake-core	0	0	0	0	3	3
Tested nodule/bashed lump	0	0	1	0	0	1
Utilised/edge-damaged flake/blade	0	2	1	0	2	5
Total	37	162	155	2	153	509

Table 7.4. The worked flint assemblage from Neolithic contexts at the Cuckoo Stone

Intrusive cereal grains within the Late Neolithic pits

P. Marshall, I. Hajdas and S.W.L. Palstra

Radiocarbon measurements were obtained on four single carbonised grains from two pits adjacent to the recumbent standing Cuckoo Stone (Table 7.3). All are conventional radiocarbon ages (Stuiver and Polach 1977).

At ETH Zurich, the samples were pre-treated using the acid-base-acid (ABA) protocol outlined in Hadjas (2008) with the acid- and alkali-insoluble fraction selected for dating. All samples were combusted in an elemental analyser and graphitised using the fully automated system described by Wacker *et al.* (2010a). Graphite targets were dated using a 200kV MICADAS AMS as described by Wacker *et al.* (2010b), with data reduction undertaken using BATS (Wacker *et al.* 2010c).

At the University of Groningen, samples were pre-treated using the acid-base-acid (ABA) protocol described in Mook and Streurman (1983). After conversion to CO_2 the samples were reduced with H_2 in the presence of Fe and graphitised (Aerts-Bijma *et al.* 1997; 2001) and dated using using a 200kV MICADAS AMS (Wacker *et al.* 2010b), with data reduction undertaken using BATS (Wacker *et al.* 2010c).

Internal quality assurance procedures and international inter-comparisons (Scott *et al.* 2010a; 2010b) indicate no laboratory offsets and validate the measurement precision quoted. Calibration of the radiocarbon ages (Table 7.3) has been undertaken using the maximum intercept method (Stuiver and Reimer 1986), the program OxCal v4.3 (Bronk Ramsey 1995; 1998; 2001; 2009a; 2009b; 2017), and the IntCal13 dataset for terrestrial samples from the northern hemisphere (Reimer *et al.* 2013.).

The cereal grains are clearly intrusive (Figure 7.18) in their contexts and are not contemporary with the Late Neolithic artefacts placed in these two pits.

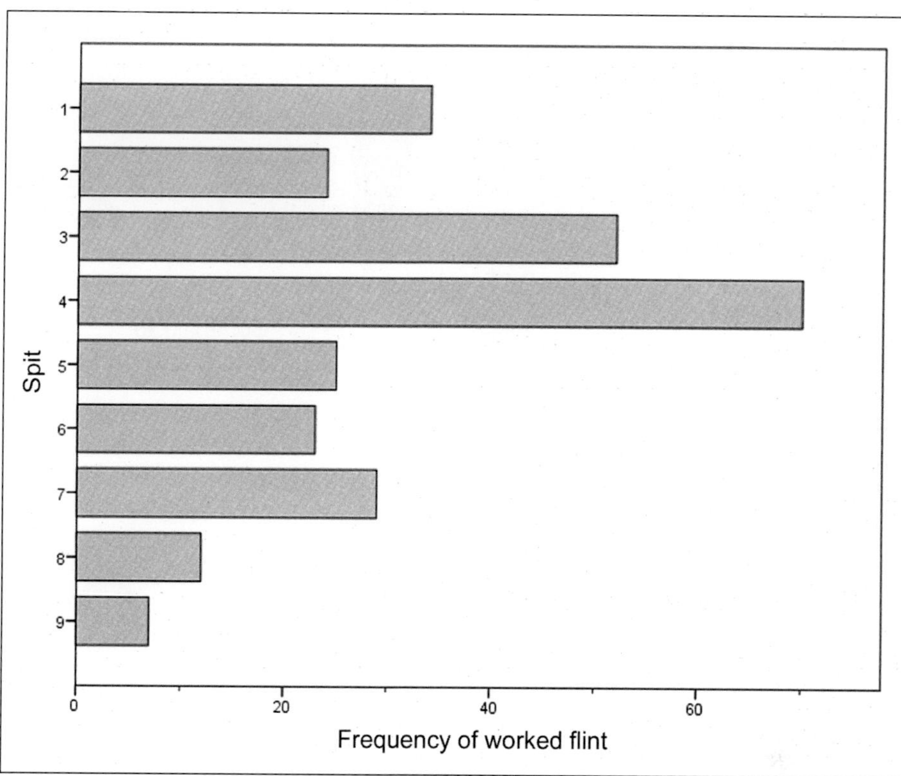

Figure 7.20. The frequency of worked flint by spit from the Cuckoo Stone hollow 145

7.2.6. Sarsen from around the Cuckoo Stone

B. Chan and C. Richards

A single sarsen stone flake (273g) was found within the stone hollow, in fill 146. Another sarsen stone flake (1.447kg) was found 10m to the south of the stone hollow, in the fill (118) of a Roman pit (117). The remaining 11 pieces (265g) of sarsen stone from the excavation are small chunks and unworked lumps, mostly burnt. Only two of these came from Neolithic pit fills (contexts 136 [16g] and 181 [90g]). The Cuckoo Stone itself reveals no indications of having been dressed or shaped, thus the two large sarsen flakes may well derive from other sarsen boulders.

7.2.7. Worked flint dating to the Neolithic from stratified contexts around the Cuckoo Stone

B. Chan

As explained in earlier chapters, the analysis and reporting of the worked flint is divided for each site by chronology, so material retrieved from post-Neolithic contexts, such as Roman features, around the Cuckoo Stone is reported in Volume 4. The assemblage of worked flint from all excavated contexts around the Cuckoo Stone consists of a total of 758 artefacts, and the Neolithic material in this report consists of 509 artefacts, derived from fills 146 and 147 of the Cuckoo Stone hollow and stone socket (features 145 and 148), the fill (181) of pit 180 and the fill (136) of pit 135 (Table 7.4).

Raw material and condition

The raw material within the assemblage is a nodular chalk-derived flint, which occurs naturally in the environs of the site and there is no indication of the use of any imported flint or chert. The flint is generally of good quality, with few inclusions, and with cortex varying in thickness from 1mm–5mm and in colour from white to off-white and yellowish. The majority of the material has a blue/grey patina and is in good/fresh condition. The main exception to this is the material from fill 146 of the stone hollow, which is of mixed condition with some of the material having abraded edges characteristic of flint from the ploughsoil. The material from pits 135 and 181 is in good condition, suggesting that it was deposited soon after its production or perhaps re-deposited from another protective context such as a pit or midden.

Contextual distribution

The assemblage from Neolithic contexts came from just three features, with nearly 63% of the worked flint derived from the Cuckoo Stone hollow (145), 30% from pit 180 and 7% from pit 135 (Table 7.4). Despite the fact that the majority of the assemblage came from the Cuckoo Stone

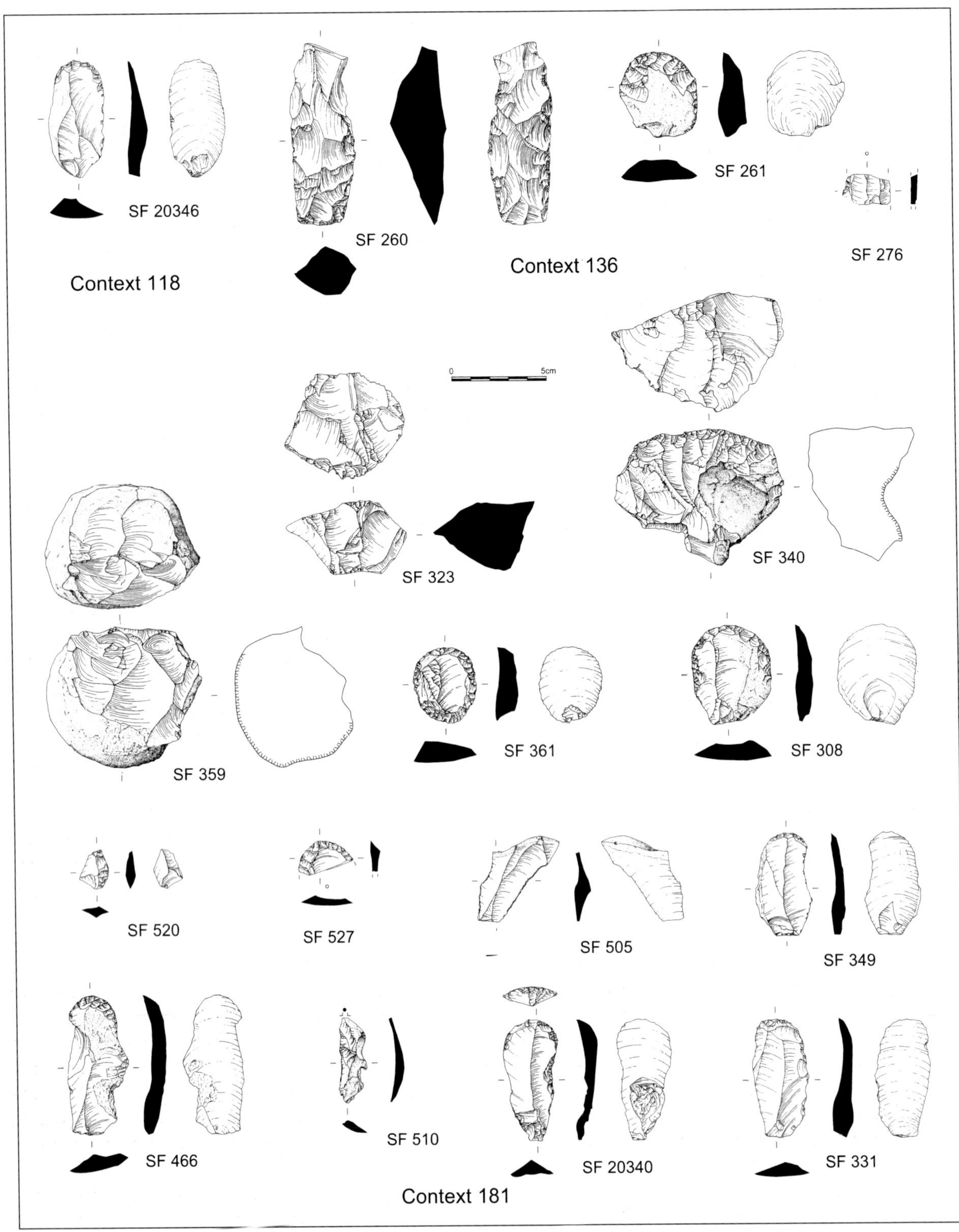

Figure 7.21. Lithics from contexts 181 (pit 180), 136 (pit 135) and 118 (Roman pit 117)

hollow, the material derived from the Neolithic pits (135 and 180) is of greater significance, for reasons which will be discussed below. The only notable find that is probably Neolithic but which was found in a later context is an end-scraper (SF 20346 from the fill [118] of a Roman feature, which also produced a large sarsen flake [see above]).

Cuckoo Stone hollow 145

The fills of the Cuckoo Stone hollow produced 319 pieces of worked flint. The assemblage is dominated by debitage, with the only retouched pieces being three miscellaneous retouched flakes and two notched flakes. The debitage consists of 282 flakes, one blade-like flake, one bladelet, a multi-platform flake core and a tested nodule. Given the size of the assemblage, the low proportion of tools and the lack of common types such as scrapers is notable. The fills also produced three fragments of unworked burnt flint.

The fills of 145 were excavated in a series of 5cm spits, and the plot of the frequency of flint per spit indicates that the majority of the material came from the middle part of the fills (from spits 3 and 4; Figure 7.20). The sides of the hollow tapered towards its base on one side so the smaller amount of material in the bottom spits may reflect the smaller volume of soil removed from those spits. In either case, it is clear that the flint assemblage was incorporated into the fills of the pit gradually as the pit infilled.

Pit 135

Fill 136 of pit 135 contained 37 pieces of worked flint (Table 7.4). The assemblage comprises just under 80% flakes, 14% blades, bladelets and blade-like flakes, a squat end-and-side scraper (SF 261; Figure 7.21) made on a cortical flake, a petit tranchet (PT) arrowhead (SF 68) and a chisel (SF 260). The arrowhead was found next to the medial section of a broken blade. This section is of similar size and shape to the arrowhead, and it is likely that it represents a blank for the production of another arrowhead of similar form. A further snapped blade (SF 276; Figure 7.21) of similar width may also represent the production of blanks for arrowhead production. The pit also contained four fragments of unworked burnt flint.

The most unusual artefact within the material from the pit is a bifacially worked tool, which can perhaps be best described as a chisel (SF 260; Figure 7.21) but also has similarities with the butt-end of a flaked axe. The object has been formed by careful bifacial flaking, which has been used to both thin the tool towards a point (in cross-section) and to create a straight cutting edge and two diverging lateral margins. Its shape is irregular in longitudinal cross-section, reflecting an inability or lack of desire to thin the object symmetrically or to create a butt as well-shaped as its cutting edge. This gives the impression of a semi-finished object, or perhaps one that broke during manufacture. This possibility, however, is countered by the fact that it is worked bifacially across all surfaces, including those where a break would have occurred if the object had broken unintentionally during manufacture. Indeed, the working across all surfaces suggests that the artefact was finished. Therefore, it seems likely that its unusual butt-end reflects rough shaping for hafting. Overall, the tool has a relatively thin cutting edge and is most likely to have been a hafted woodworking tool.

Pit 180

The fill (181) of pit 180 held an assemblage of 153 pieces of worked stone. Roughly 67% of the assemblage comprises flakes, and just under 14% are blades, bladelets or blade-like flakes (Table 7.4). In addition, the deposit contained four end-scrapers, three end-and-side scrapers, one disc-scraper, one miscellaneous scraper, two fragments of scrapers of unknown type, an awl, two serrated flakes, three miscellaneous knives and seven cores of different types (Figure 7.21). The most notable aspect of the assemblage is its high proportion of formal tools, which make up 11% of the assemblage. This is even more notable given the complete lack of miscellaneous retouched flakes, which often outnumber formal tools. Two of the flakes from the pit were burnt and there were two additional fragments of unworked burnt flint.

Within the scraper assemblage there is an emphasis on the selection of elongate flakes as blanks, with three of the end-scrapers (SF 349, SF 466, SF 20340) and one of the end-and-side scrapers (SF 331) being made on elongate flakes. Alongside the elongate scrapers are two well-worked circular scrapers, one of which is retouched around its entire circumference (SF 361) and one which is worked around *c.* 60% of its circumference (SF 308). The broken scrapers (SF 520 and SF 527) are represented by fragments of their scraping edge. The thickness of the fragments (4mm–5mm), particularly in combination with the small size of fragment SF 520, suggests that the scrapers may have been broken intentionally. The elongate scrapers were made on blanks taken from cores with prepared flaking surfaces where dorsal ridges have been used to aid the removal of longer flakes.

Both serrated flakes (SF 505 and SF 510) are made on elongate secondary flakes of blade proportions and have finely worked denticulations along one lateral margin. The denticulations were worked exclusively from the ventral surfaces of flakes and there is no macroscopically visible edge-gloss on their serrated edges.

The cores within the assemblage include four single-platform cores, two multi-platform cores and a core on a broken flake. In general, the standard of core-working is mixed and, in several cases, quite poor. For example, SF 359 represents an attempt to produce a single-platform core from a weathered spherical nodule, which was also used as a hammerstone. The attempt failed to produce a productive platform and flaking surface, a factor influenced to a great extent by the unsuitably rounded shape of the nodule.

Cores SF 323 and SF 340 indicate more controlled attempts at reduction. Both have single platforms and are worked in similar style, with SF 340 containing a few scars of blade proportions and also exhibiting some basic platform maintenance in the form of trimming to strengthen the platform edge. Despite this, neither of these cores can be said to be worked to a high standard, and regular flaws in the body of the flint suggest that the knappers were content to use partly weathered material of mixed quality. At a general level, the cores reflect the flakes and blades in the assemblage in that they exhibit occasional removals of blade proportions, but with broader flakes predominating. Certainly, there does not appear to have been a consistent emphasis on the careful and controlled removal of blades.

The assemblage contains elements of the full reduction sequence, including primary flakes produced during core trimming/preparation, secondary and tertiary flakes, cores and tools. The analysis suggested that there is little potential for refitting. The presence of scraper fragments, for which the remaining parts of the scrapers are absent, further suggests that the assemblage is incomplete. In addition, the assemblage has a notably high proportion of formal tools. Taken together, these factors suggest that there has been some degree of selectivity involved prior to the deposition of the material into the pit. The presence of 16 chips alongside the rest of the assemblage indicates that the material does also include knapping waste as well as utilisable flakes, blades and tools.

Technology and chronology

In terms of the chronology of the assemblage, the most clearly diagnostic artefact is the PT arrowhead, which should date to the Middle Neolithic or the earlier part of the Late Neolithic. Beyond that, there are a series of elements that are normally thought to have some chronological sensitivity but, as will be seen, this can be misleading. These elements are namely:

- a high proportion of blades;
- end-scrapers made on elongate flake or blade blanks;
- serrated flakes.

Although none of these artefact types are individually diagnostic, when found together they would normally be taken as indicative of an Early Neolithic date. The issue is that both pits at the Cuckoo Stone have radiocarbon determinations suggesting that they were dug around or after 2900 cal BC, soon after the beginning of the Late Neolithic.

The material from the pits is generally in good condition and therefore it seems unlikely that it was curated for centuries before being deposited. Instead, it is necessary to look critically at the chronological sensitivity of the tool types and techno-typologies in question. PT arrowheads, normally dated to the Middle to Late Neolithic, are dated to the Early Neolithic at Broome Heath, Norfolk, where two transverse arrowheads were found in pits associated with plain carinated bowls, with a flint assemblage characterised by a high proportion of blades, end-scrapers, leaf-shaped arrowheads and laurel leaves (Wainwright *et al.* 1972: 57).

Similarly, serrated flakes, which are often present in Early Neolithic assemblages, such as those from Hurst Fen, Suffolk (Clark *et al.* 1960), Kilverstone, Norfolk (Garrow *et al.* 2006) and Hemp Knoll, Wilts. (Robertson-Mackay 1980), are also present in a number of Late Neolithic assemblages. These include a number of Grooved Ware pits in the Stonehenge landscape such as at Ratfyn (Stone 1935), the Woodlands pit group (Stone 1949; Stone and Young 1948) and in pits within the Durrington 67 and Durrington 70 monuments (see Volume 3). Disc-scrapers such as that found within pit 180 are often associated with Late Neolithic assemblages, but also occur in Early Neolithic contexts at sites such as Hurst Fen (Clark *et al.* 1960: 217), Broome Heath (Wainwright *et al.* 1972) and Hambledon Hill, Dorset (Saville 2008: 690).

Therefore, it can be seen that a number of artefact types that are often taken as being chronologically sensitive may occur most commonly within assemblages of a particular period, but actually have a broader currency. A significant factor in this respect is the lack of well-stratified, well-dated assemblages spanning the boundaries of key chronological and technological transitions. One such boundary is the transition between the Middle and Late Neolithic and, as such, the date of the Cuckoo Stone pits and their assemblages is particularly significant: well-dated pit assemblages from the turn of the third millennium BC are effectively absent within the Stonehenge environs. Therefore, it is noteworthy that the Cuckoo Stone pits indicate that blade technologies persisted in one form or another into the beginning of the Late Neolithic. Given the technology within this period, it is probable that the desired product was not the blades themselves, but blade-type blanks for tools such as the PT arrowhead from pit 136 and the scrapers and serrated flakes from pit 180.

Having established that blade technologies were still being practised at the beginning of the Late Neolithic, it should be noted that the proportion of blades within the Cuckoo Stone pits is actually comparable to the Early Neolithic contexts at Woodhenge (see the Woodhenge lithics report in Chapter 3). In order to better understand the similarities and differences between these two assemblages, a level-2 metrical and technological analysis was conducted on a sample of material from pit 180 from the Cuckoo Stone, and from buried soil 051 and tree-throw fill 053 from Woodhenge. This analysis is summarised here; the detailed report appears in Volume 2.

In many respects the two assemblages have a lot in common. The proportion of blades is very similar, as is the proportion of cortex remaining on flakes and blades. Both assemblages include primary, secondary and tertiary flakes and therefore it is clear that they represent the products of an extended *chaîne opératoire* from nodule-trimming to productive core-working. Compared to the Cuckoo Stone material, the assemblage from Woodhenge shows a slight preference for the maintenance of platforms through trimming and faceting. Although this difference is only slight, it is an indication of the overall degree of control exerted over flake and blade removal. This is further suggested by Woodhenge having a higher proportion of flakes and blades with feather terminations, whereas the Cuckoo Stone assemblage has greater incidences of hinged and plunging terminations. The result of this is that the Early Neolithic Woodhenge assemblage contains more elongate products, represented by a slightly higher mean length:breadth ratio.

Taken as individual attributes, the differences between the two assemblages are not that great but, in combination, they tell a tale of a chronological shift in technology that is most apparent in the overall quality of the blades produced. The blades from Woodhenge are generally better formed, have more refined butts, and are more likely to have parallel sides with dorsal ridges perpendicular to their butts. Whilst the flintwork at the Cuckoo Stone was also produced with the general aim of producing elongate products, it was achieved with less core control, less development of the flaking surface, and less precise placement of blows on the platform.

One potential reason for this may be that core-reduction at the Cuckoo Stone was aimed at setting up cores for the removal of a few elongate and parallel-sided blanks for the production of tools such as scrapers and PTD arrowheads. In contrast, core reduction at Woodhenge was geared towards the production of blades and, potentially, blade-cores. The former would only have required enough core control to set up a few blank removals, whereas the latter would have required a core that more consistently produced blades of predictable shape. In either case, the important point is that, despite gross similarities in the proportion of blades within the two assemblages, there are detectable differences in the character of core-working between the two periods.

Discussion

Whereas the material from the pits appears to represent short episodes of activity, the artefacts from the fill of the Cuckoo Stone hollow probably derived from activity occurring over a longer period of time. This is because its different fills may date to the original extraction and erection of the stone, or to the stone's eventual collapse, or to later disturbances caused by animal burrowing. The mixed nature of this assemblage is corroborated by the abraded condition of some of the material and by the distribution of worked flint within the excavated spits, which suggests that the assemblage was incorporated over time as the hollow filled up and was subjected to later disturbance.

In this respect, there is also no sign that the material within the hollow was selected and deposited intentionally. Rather, the material was probably introduced unintentionally, over an extended period of time. Therefore, the stone hollow's assemblage perhaps reflects the general activity that took place in the immediate area around the Cuckoo Stone, rather than any specific event. This is backed up by the assemblage's similarities with the ploughsoil assemblage from the test-pitting of the area prior to full excavation (see Mitcham, above).

Whereas the assemblage from the Cuckoo Stone hollow seems to reflect the random incorporation of material, the assemblages from the pits have a clear structure to them. The use of the term 'structure' in this instance does not refer to a structure in the order or positioning of objects interred in the pits, but to a process of selection that has led to assemblages with atypical composition. The principal question is whether that reflects a structuring of the selection of material to be deposited into the pits, or reflects the practice of a task-specific activity, the residues of which ended up in the pits.

A related question, therefore, is whether the material from the pits derived from activities that took place around the Cuckoo Stone, or was brought in from elsewhere. In this respect, it should be noted that the material from the ploughsoil test pits spread across the trench produced an assemblage that lacks both tools and blades. The ploughsoil assemblage therefore has much in common with the fill of the stone hollow, but is very different to the pit assemblages. Therefore, if the pit assemblages derived from activities that took place in their vicinity, those activities were clearly highly localised and did not produce a larger assemblage of artefacts to later become incorporated into the ploughsoil.

The significance of the digging and filling of pits in the Neolithic has been widely discussed, with a consensus that the practice was intimately connected with the creation of memory, the marking of locales and the events that took places within them, and the mediation of momentous and potentially dangerous events such as the closing of a settlement (Edmonds 1999; Pollard 1999: 89; Thomas 1999: 64–74; Garrow *et al.* 2005; Garrow 2006: 8–12). In the current case, the pits in question are clearly not rubbish pits by any normal definition of the term and it is thought that they were dug next to the Cuckoo Stone at the time that the stone was taken from its hollow and erected as a standing stone.

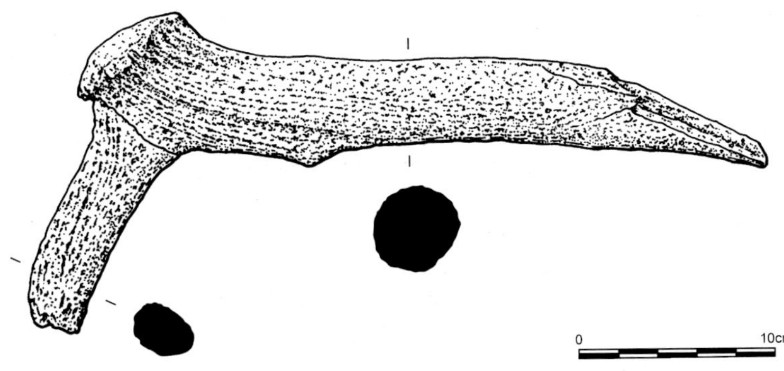

Figure 7.22. An antler pick (SF 265) from layer 136 in pit 135

Skeletal element	Zone/part
Loose teeth	> half
Mandible/maxilla	with at least one tooth present
Cranium	zygomatic
Atlas	> half
Axis	> half
Scapula	glenoid articulation
Humerus	proximal end > half distal end > half
Radius	proximal end > half distal end > half
Ulna	proximal end > half
Carpal 2–3	> half
Pelvis	ischial part of the acetabulum
Tibia	proximal end > half distal end > half
Femur	proximal end > half distal end > half
Astragalus	lateral half
Calcaneum	sustentaculum
Scafocuboid	> half
Metatarsal	proximal end > half distal end > half
Metacarpal	proximal end > half distal end > half
Phalanges 1, 2 and 3	proximal end > half

Table 7.5. Skeletal elements and zones recorded – mammals

Skeletal element	Zone/part
Scapula	articular end
Coracoid	proximal end
Humerus	distal end
Ulna	proximal end
Carpometacarpus	proximal end
Femur	distal end
Tibiotarsus	distal end
Tarsometatarsus	distal end

Table 7.6. Skeletal elements and zones recorded – birds

Given the ancestral forces that were connected with sarsens in the Neolithic, it seems likely that the erection of a sarsen was a process that required careful mediation and that the excavation and filling of the two pits were involved in this. If this is accepted, two clear possibilities concerning the contents of the pits remain:

- The first possibility is that the worked flint within the pits was involved in the process of erecting the stone – *e.g.* woodworking tools needed to prepare levers and props, or plant-processing tools used for making and repairing ropes and twine – and that the association of these objects with these tasks made them inappropriate for use elsewhere, requiring their immediate burial at the site. Similar suggestions have been made for the antler pick and cattle scapula buried in pit 135 (see above) and there is no reason that the flint objects should be thought of differently.

- The second possibility is that the mediation of whatever forces were disturbed by the erection of the sarsen required the burial of material from elsewhere, such as midden material from a settlement site.

These possibilities will be discussed in more detail in the synthesis discussion of all the lithic assemblages within Volume 2.

Conclusions

The worked flint from the Neolithic contexts at the Cuckoo Stone comes from two pits and the Cuckoo Stone hollow itself. It is believed that the three are connected, with the two pits being excavated and filled as part of the rites of removing the stone from its natural hollow and erecting it as a standing stone. The fills of the pits do not appear to have contained the residues of any persistent or widespread activity such as those that would have been connected with a settlement in the vicinity of the stone. Rather, the objects interred within them were either brought in from outside the area or were involved in the process of erecting the stone. In either case, there is a degree of selectivity involved in the interring of

Mammal	Pit 180 CS NISP	Pit 180 FS >10 NISP	Pit 135 CS NISP	Pit 135 FS >10 NISP	Pit 145 CS NISP
Cattle	2		2 (+2)		
?Cattle	1				
Sheep/goat	(1)		1 (+1)		3
?Sheep/goat	(1)				
Pig	25 (+6)	5 (+2)	2	(1)	(1)
Pig?	(1)				
Horse	1				
Red deer	26 (+6)		(2)		
Roe deer	(1)				
Rodents			1		
Total	55	5	6	0	3

Table 7.7. Numbers of animal bones and teeth (NISP) from the Neolithic features at the Cuckoo Stone. Non-countable bones are denoted in brackets. CS = from hand collection and dry sieving (>10mm fraction), FS>10 = from flotation (>10mm fraction)

material within the pits that appears to have been guided by what is perhaps best termed 'appropriateness', in this case the appropriateness of certain actions in relation to a momentous and potentially dangerous event.

7.2.8. Antler artefacts from the Cuckoo Stone

G. Davies

Three pieces of antler were recovered from Neolithic pits 135 and 180 beside the Cuckoo Stone. One of these (SF 265) was an antler pick, made from the antler of a red deer.

SF 281 context 136. A complete roe deer antler with fused skull fragments attached. The base, pedicle and beam are well-preserved but the three tines are more eroded with root etching. The three tips are all blunt but there is no evidence of working and the antler is complete. The antler is 260mm long (310mm with attached skull). The burr circumference is 162mm.

SF 265 context 136. An antler pick (38.5cm long) made from a shed red deer antler (Figure 7.22). The brow tine forms the point of the pick; this is shortened, with a blunt and battered end, but has no wear scratches. The bez tine is missing, but it appears that this did not grow; only a small bud-like projection exists where the bez tine should be. This appears to be a developmental condition and not the result of antler-working. The beam is long and straight but the surviving remains do not extend as far as the trez tine.

SF 355 context 181. A piece of roe deer antler comprising two tines from the crown of the antler. Both tines are small and in poor condition. The poor condition of the fragment precludes any identification of working or wear on the surface of the antler.

7.2.9. Faunal remains from Neolithic contexts around the Cuckoo Stone

C. Minniti, U. Albarella and S. Viner-Daniels

This report discusses the animal remains from stratified deposits that can be securely attributed to the Neolithic period from contexts around the Cuckoo Stone. Smaller assemblages of Neolithic date from Woodhenge and West Amesbury, subjected to the same methods of analysis, are reported in Chapters 3 and 5. The large assemblage from Durrington Walls (including the Southern Circle) has been studied separately and will be dealt with in the third volume of this series.

Material and methods

At all sites excavated by the SRP, all of the archaeological deposits were excavated by hand, and were then dry-sieved through a 10mm mesh. Samples from some contexts and features were processed by flotation, and sieved through meshes of 10mm, 5mm and 2mm; animal bone was retrieved from the residues. Bones that were collected by hand or through dry-sieving are described as 'coarse-sieved' (CS) in this report; the material from flotation residues is termed 'fine-sieved' (FS). Material from all collection types is discussed together because the evidence gathered from flotation samples is too limited to provide information about any biases possibly affecting the dry-sieved assemblage. No recordable material was identified in the <10mm fraction.

The mammal bones were recorded following a modified version of the method described in Davis (1992) and Albarella and Davis (1994). The 'diagnostic zones' that have always been recorded ('countable') are listed in Table 7.5 (for mammals) and Table 7.6 (for birds).

Horncores and antlers with a complete transverse section and 'non-countable' elements, such as proximal ends of the four main long bones and others of particular interest, were recorded and used in the ageing analysis, but not included in the taxonomic and body part counts. The presence of large (cattle/horse-size), medium (sheep/pig-size) and small (cat-size or smaller) vertebrae and ribs was recorded, but these have not been included in the countable totals.

The sheep/goat distinction was attempted on the following elements using the criteria described in Boessneck (1969), Kratochvil (1969), Payne (1985), and Halstead and Collins (2002): horncores (non-countable), deciduous lower third premolar (dP_3), deciduous

Skeletal element	Red deer		Pig		Equid	Cattle	Sheep/goat
	NISP	*MNI*	*NISP*	*MNI*	*NISP*	*NISP*	*NISP*
Antler							
Upper deciduous + perm. premolars			5	1		1	
Upper deciduous + perm. incisors			1	1			
Upper deciduous + perm. canines			2	1			
Upper M1/2	1	1	2	1			
Upper M3	1	1					
Lower deciduous + perm. incisors			1	1			
Lower deciduous + perm. canines			3	2			
Lower deciduous + perm. premolars			5	1			
Lower M1/2			5	2			
Cranium			(1)				
Scapula	1	1	1	1	1	1	
Humerus							(1)
Radius	1	1					
Ulna	1	1					
Metacarpal	2(+1)	1	1	1		1	
Pelvis	1(+1)	1	2(+1)	1			
Femur	1(+1)	1	(4)				
Patella	(1)						
Tibia	3	2					(1)
Astragalus	2	1	1	1			
Calcaneum	1	1	2	1			
Tarsal	2	1	1	1			
Metatarsal	2(+2)	1					
Metapodial			(1)				
Phalanx 1	5	1	4(+2)	1			
Phalanx 2	1	1	1	1			
Phalanx 3	2	1	1	1			

Table 7.8. Body parts of the mammals by number of identified specimens (NISP) and minimum number of individuals (MNI) from pit 180 at the Cuckoo Stone. Non-countable bones are shown in brackets. Unfused epiphyses are not counted. For red deer the MNI was calculated by dividing the number of phalanges by eight, all other elements by two. For pig the MNI was calculated by dividing the number of phalanges by eight, deciduous and permanent incisors and premolars by six, first and second molars by four and all other elements by two

lower fourth premolar (dP_4), permanent lower molars (when more than one tooth is present), distal humerus, proximal radius, distal metacarpal, distal tibia, astragalus, calcaneum and distal metatarsal.

The number of identified specimens (NISP) was calculated for all taxa and the minimum number of individuals (MNI) was calculated for the most common taxa (cattle, pig and red deer).

Wear stages were recorded following Grant (1982) for mandibular cattle and pig teeth, and Payne (1973; 1987) for sheep/goats. In addition, a system recently designed by Wright *et al.* (2014) was used to record wear on pig

Mammal	Butchered	Burnt
	n	*n*
Pig		2
Red deer	9	12 (8 in mid-shaft)

Table 7.9. Numbers of burnt and butchered postcranial bones from pit 180 at the Cuckoo Stone. Only countable bones have been included

upper teeth and, in addition to Grant's system, on pig lower teeth. In all cases wear was recorded on both deciduous and permanent fourth premolars, and on permanent molars, whether they were found in jaws or in isolation. Tooth measurements and wear stages were only recorded when sufficient enamel was preserved.

Measurements of fused, fusing and unfused bones were taken following the criteria described in Albarella and Davis (1994), Albarella and Payne (2005), Davis (1992), von den Driesch (1976), and Payne and Bull (1988). For all foetal and neonatal bones the greatest length of the diaphysis and the smallest width of the shaft were taken.

Results

Faunal remains were retrieved from the fills of pits 135 and 180, and from the upper fill (146) of stone hollow 145 (Table 7.7). The assemblage is very small, with the majority of the faunal remains deriving from pit 180.

Pit 180

This pit is radiocarbon-dated to the Late Neolithic on articulated tarsal bones of red deer (see *Radiocarbon dating*, above). It is possible that most of the pit content, including the animal bones, was deposited as part of a single depositional event. However, the presence of a horse scapula radiocarbon-dated to the Roman period indicates that at least some of the material is intrusive. That said, the stratigraphic evidence and the occurrence of bones in articulation suggest that most of the deposit was undisturbed and is likely to be Late Neolithic.

Most of the animal bones are in an excellent state of preservation. Canid gnawing marks were noted only on the intrusive horse scapula, suggesting that most of the bone material was rapidly buried after disposal. Pig and red deer are the best represented species, but a few bones and teeth of cattle, sheep/goat and horse, as well as a fragment of roe deer antler (SF 355), were also found (Table 7.7). Assuming that most of the material is Late Neolithic, the scarcity of sheep/goat is consistent with what is known for the period, but the small number of cattle bones is more unusual; the horse is patently intrusive into a Late Neolithic assemblage. Given the small sample size, general conclusions about Neolithic animal exploitation should be avoided in favour of focusing specifically on the pit and its surroundings.

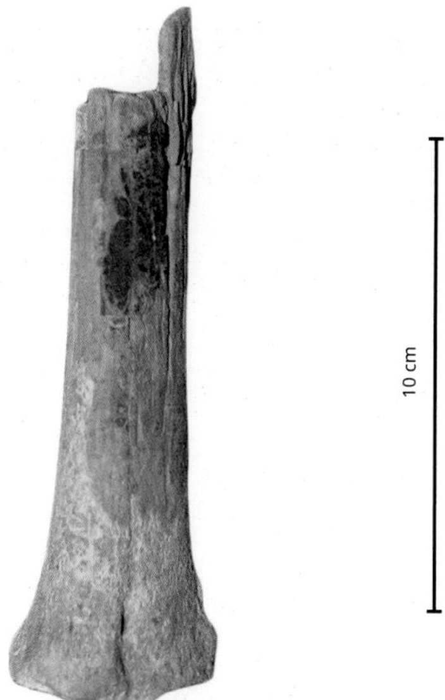

Figure 7.23. Red deer metacarpal burnt and chopped mid-shaft, from pit 180 at the Cuckoo Stone

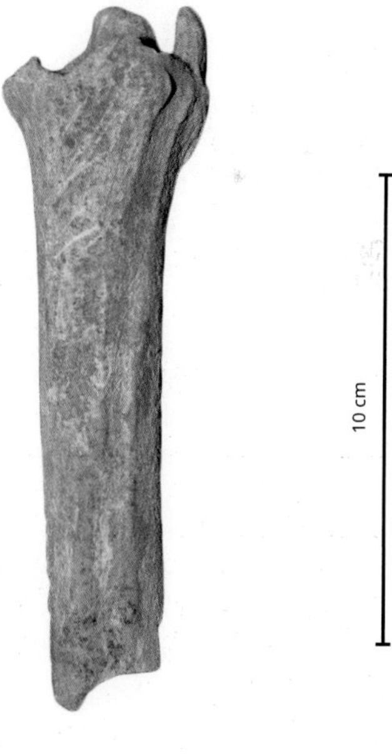

Figure 7.24. Red deer tibia burnt and chopped mid-shaft, from pit 180 at the Cuckoo Stone

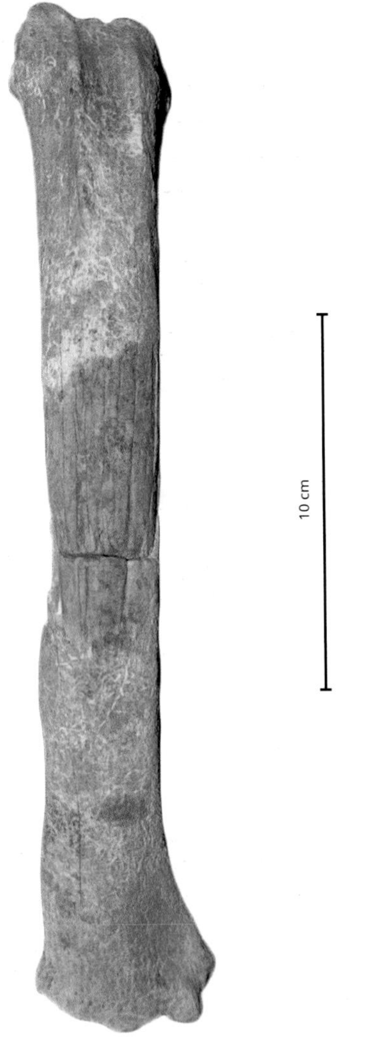

Figure 7.25. Red deer radius burnt and chopped mid-shaft, from pit 180 at the Cuckoo Stone

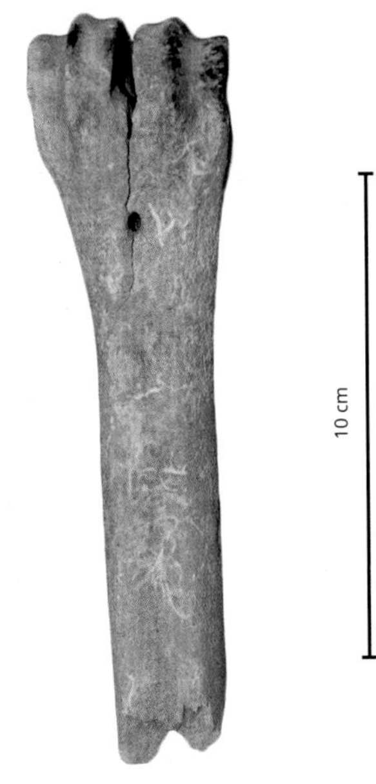

Figure 7.26. Red deer metatarsal with burn marks on distal condyles, from pit 180 at the Cuckoo Stone

Red deer remains form a large part of the assemblage. The minimum number of individuals (MNI) count indicates that at least two adult animals are represented (Table 7.8). Apart from two upper teeth, all the red deer remains are postcranial bones, perhaps suggesting that some heads might have been removed off-site. The absence of antler within the assemblage may indicate that only females or young animals are present (this is discussed further below). Two red deer tarsal bones (an astragalus and a scafocuboid, submitted for radiocarbon-dating) were found in articulation, thus indicating primary deposition of these remains.

The red deer bones are mostly burnt (Table 7.9). Eight long bones exhibit a pattern of burning that has been observed on other sites of the period: long bones (in this case a radius, a femur, metapodials and tibiae) have areas of burning, chopping and breakage on the midshaft (Figures 7.23–7.24). Pieces of a radius that is burnt and broken in half across the midshaft, were refitted in the lab (Figure 7.25). This pattern of damage is suggestive of marrow extraction, and is well known from prehistoric sites (Binford 1981), though it is found in later periods too (Maltby 1987; Albarella 1999). A similar pattern of burning and butchery has already been observed on cattle bones from Late Neolithic contexts at Durrington Walls (Albarella and Serjeantson 2002).

Two other red deer specimens – an astragalus and a distal metatarsal (Figure 7.26) – show patterns of burning which affect less than half of the astragalus and the metatarsal condyles. At Durrington Walls a similar pattern of burning was noted on pig bones from Late Neolithic contexts (Albarella and Serjeantson 2002) and is likely to be linked to the roasting techniques employed to cook joints of meat. The astragalus–metatarsal joint on the hind limb was exposed to fire, with the result that those parts (which hold only a small amount of flesh) became burnt.

Although we were confident, on the basis of stratigraphy and bone preservation, that most of the red deer specimens from pit 180 are Late Neolithic, we decided to check whether a biometric distinction between Neolithic and Roman deer could be undertaken. Red deer measurements from the Cuckoo Stone contexts are few, but can be optimised by employing a log ratio

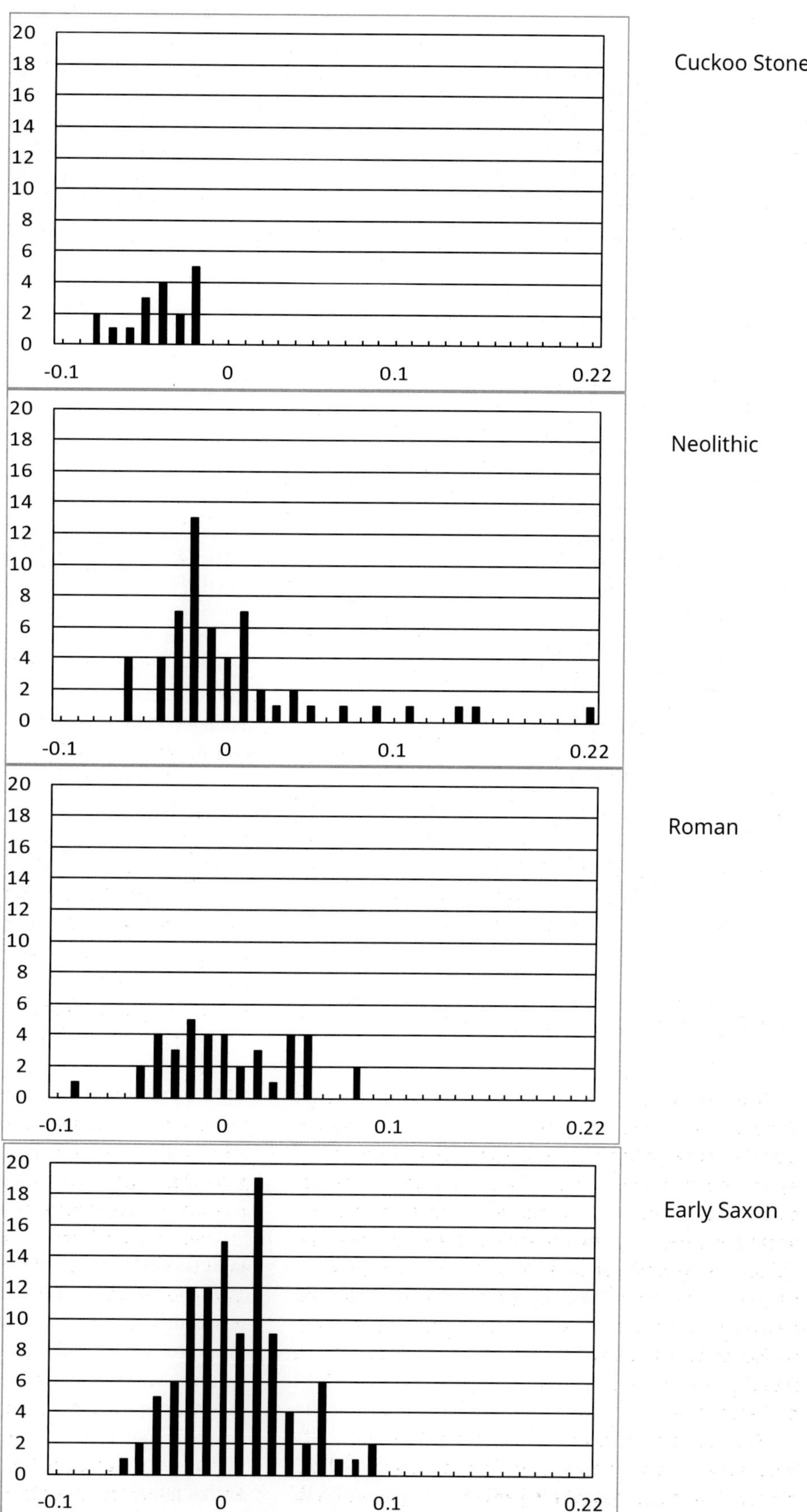

Figure 7.27. Comparative red deer log ratio diagrams for post-cranial measurements. The standard is from the mean of each post-cranial measurement from the Mesolithic assemblage of Star Carr, Yorkshire (Legge and Rowley-Conwy 1988)

Skeletal element	Unfused	Fused
Femur (proximal)	3	
Calcaneum	1	
Phalanx 1	4	
Phalanx 2		1

Table 7.10. Frequencies of unfused and fused bones of pig from pit 180 at the Cuckoo Stone

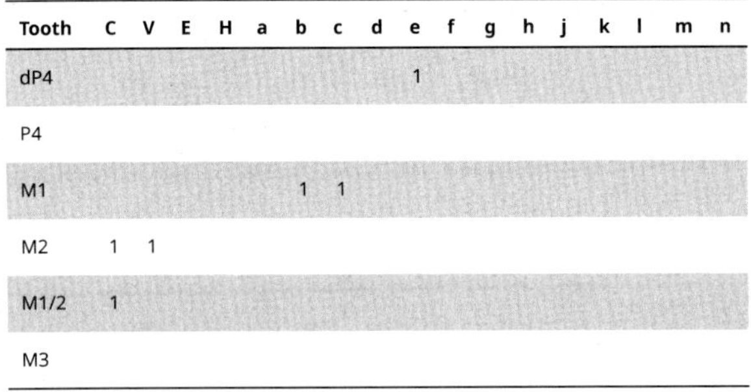

Tooth	C	V	E	H	a	b	c	d	e	f	g	h	j	k	l	m	n
dP4									1								
P4																	
M1						1	1										
M2	1	1															
M1/2	1																
M3																	

Table 7.11. Pig tooth wear stages of individual teeth from pit 180 at the Cuckoo Stone

technique (*sensu* Simpson *et al.* 1960). For comparison, data have been included from:

- Early Neolithic Lambourn long barrow, Runnymede Bridge (both Berks.) and Hambledon Hill (Wilts.) (after Howard 2007);
- Late Neolithic Durrington Walls (see Volume 3);
- Roman Fullerton (Hants.), Chedworth (Glos.) (Hammon 2002; 2008), Winchester (Hants.; Maltby 2010), Elms Farm (Essex; Johnstone and Albarella 2002) and Shakenoak Farm (Oxon.; Cram 1973);
- Early Saxon Wroxeter (Salop.; Hammon 2011).

The Cuckoo Stone specimens fall mainly within the Neolithic range (Figure 7.27), although at its smaller end. Red deer are sexually dimorphic so it is possible that the sample represents mostly smaller female animals, an interpretation that is reinforced by the absence of antler within the assemblage. The Cuckoo Stone red deer are significantly smaller than those from Roman and Early Saxon sites.

Pig post-cranial bones and teeth are equally well represented in pit 180 (Table 7.8). According to the MNI count, at least two animals are represented. Except for a single second phalanx, all pig postcranial bones are unfused, suggesting that the pigs were slaughtered before about two years of age (Table 7.10). This is supported by the wear stages of isolated teeth (Table 7.11) which include

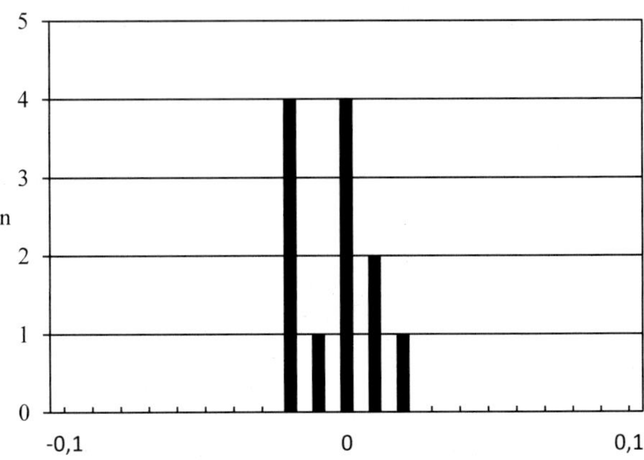

Figure 7.28. Pig log ratio diagram for teeth measurements from pit 180 at the Cuckoo Stone. The standard is the mean of the sample from Late Neolithic Durrington Walls (Albarella and Payne 2005)

deciduous teeth, permanent molars at early wear stages, and molars that are unworn. This points to the presence of immature and juvenile pigs at the site.

The pigs are of a size comparable with those from Late Neolithic Durrington Walls (Figure 7.28; data from Albarella and Payne 2005). Since these Late Neolithic pigs are regarded as fully domestic, it follows that the Cuckoo Stone pigs are also likely to have been domestic.

Pit 135

This Late Neolithic pit (135) produced six countable animal remains, from cattle, pig, sheep/goat and rodent (Table 7.7). There are also two fragments of deer antler (see Davies, above), one of which, from a roe deer, retains the pedicle and must therefore have been removed from the head of a dead animal (SF 281). The other antler (SF 265) has been shed and could therefore have been collected without an animal having been killed.

Stone hollow 145

Pit 145 (the hole in which the Cuckoo Stone originally lay, and was then erected) is likely to be contemporary with pit 135, although its upper fill is likely to be later in date. This upper fill contained just three countable bones from sheep/goats.

Discussion

The Late Neolithic assemblage from pit 180 has a higher proportion of pigs than cattle, which fits the pattern observed at Late Neolithic Durrington Walls. This is the reverse of the pattern found at several Neolithic sites in southern and central England where cattle are more frequent than pigs (Serjeantson 1998; 2011). Although a Roman horse scapula indicates later intrusion into the top of this pit, most of the Late Neolithic pit deposit was left untouched by this disturbance.

Feature number	135	135	180	180	180	180
Context number	**136**	**136**	**181**	**181**	**181**	**181**
Sample number	**100**	**102**	**111**	**113**	**114**	**115**
Feature type	*Pit*	*Pit*	*Pit*	*Pit*	*Pit*	*Pit*
Phase	*Late Neolithic*	*Late Neolithic*	*Late Neolithic*	*Late Neolithic*	*Late Neolithic*	*Late Neolithic*
Total volume of soil processed (litres)	25	57	17.5	6	4	22
Cereals and other economic plants						
Hordeum sp. (barley)						
indeterminate grain (hulled)					1	1
indeterminate grain		3			2	1
cf Hordeum sp.						
grain				1		
cf Triticum sp. (free-threshing wheat)						
grain		2				2
rachis node	1					
Triticum sp. (glume wheat)						
glume base			1			
Triticum sp. indet. (indeterminate wheat)						
grain	1	3				1
Cerealia indet.						
grain		2			1	
Non-seed charred plant material						
<2mm herbaceous plant root/stem	9	28	2		4	1
cf tuber/rhizome indet.		3				
>1mm parenchyma fragment (undifferentiated plant storage tissue)		1	2			
vitrified material	1					
Wild/weed plant seeds						
Papaver cf *rhoeas* (common poppy)	1					
Rumex crispus/conglomeratus/ obtusifolius (curled/clustered/ broad-leaved dock)			1		1	
>2mm Poaceae spp (large-seeded grass family)		1	1			

Table 7.12. Charred plant remains from pits 135 and 180 at the Cuckoo Stone

The high frequency of red deer in the assemblage, along with the particular pattern of burning and breaking observed on many of the bones, and the distribution of body parts (*i.e.* the near-absence of antler and cranial bone), suggests that the bones of this species could derive from a single event of meat and marrow consumption. According to MNI calculations, this episode would have included large portions of at least two individuals, perhaps both females. Red deer were hunted in the Neolithic of Britain, but, in general, their remains are found relatively infrequently at Neolithic sites (Serjeantson 1996).

From the biometrical data it is difficult to characterise the red deer specimens. The animals deposited beside the Cuckoo Stone were at the smaller extreme of the Neolithic and Roman red deer size range. Previous studies have shown that red deer in Britain from Mesolithic and Neolithic sites are similar in size, although the Neolithic specimens tend to be slightly smaller. Subsequently there is a tendency towards decreasing size up to the Iron Age (Noddle 1982; Howard 2007) and an increase in size during the Roman period, although significant regional variation may be expected (Noddle 1982).

7.2.10. Charred plant remains from around the Cuckoo Stone

E. Simmons

Fourteen flotation samples, comprising just over 130 litres of soil, were processed by flotation and assessed using the methods outlined in Chapter 3.

The majority of the sampled contexts were found to contain either no charred material, or charred material that is considered likely to be intrusive and therefore of low research potential. Small quantities of charred cereal grain, cereal chaff and wild or weed plant seeds were found to be present in the fill (136) of pit 135 and the fill (181) of pit 180. However, some if not all of the charred plant remains recovered from these pit fills are intrusive (see Marshall *et al.*, above).

Species represented

Eleven cereal grains and one glume wheat glume base were present in the four samples from pit fill 181 (Table 7.12). Eleven cereal grains and one probable free-threshing wheat rachis node were present in the two samples from pit fill 136. Preservation of the cereal grains is poor, with all of the grains exhibiting some form of puffing or distortion and many grains lacking epidermis. The species represented are barley (*Hordeum* sp.), probable free-threshing wheat (*Triticum* sp.) and glume wheat (*Triticum* sp.). Two of the barley grains from pit fill 181 are identifiable as hulled barley. Two cereal grains from pit fill 181 and two cereal grains from pit fill 136 were identified as probable free-threshing wheat. The single probable free-threshing wheat rachis node fragment recovered from pit fill 136, and the single glume base of glume wheat recovered from pit fill 181, are too poorly preserved for further identification to be possible.

A small number of charred seeds from wild or weed plant species are also present (Table 7.12). Two seeds identified as docks (*Rumex crispus/conglomeratus/obtusifolius)* are present in the assemblage from pit fill 181, along with one large (>2mm in length) grass seed (Poaceae). One seed of probable common poppy (*Papaver* cf *rhoeas*) and one large grass seed are present in the material from pit fill 136.

Other charred plant remains present in both pit fill assemblages include parenchyma fragments (undifferentiated plant storage tissue), small (<2mm in diameter) unidentified herbaceous plant root/stem material, unidentified tuber/rhizome fragments and indeterminate vitrified material.

Discussion

The cereal grains are likely to have been charred accidentally during parching or food preparation. The cereal chaff may represent waste from crop-processing or, given the small quantity of material present, may equally represent residual chaff which was associated with cleaned grain. The association of charred wild plant seeds with cereal grains and chaff suggests that they are likely to represent weed seeds harvested along with arable crops and charred as waste during crop-processing. It is also possible, however, that the wild plant seeds represent charred vegetation from other sources such as kindling, or vegetation from the local area that became charred incidentally and incorporated into the pit fills.

Common poppy (*Papaver rhoeas*) is widespread in modern-day plant communities on the chalk and is especially present on cultivated and waste ground (Grose 1979: 105). Of the three potential species of dock represented, curled dock (*Rumex crispus*) and broad-leaved dock (*Rumex obtusifolius*) are common in present-day plant communities on cultivated ground as well as on waste ground and in grassy places. Clustered dock (*Rumex conglomeratus*) is common in damp fields and marshes as well as near ponds, rivers and lakes (*ibid.*: 487).

Hulled barley is a typical crop type of the Neolithic in southern Britain. Emmer wheat is the most frequently recovered wheat type from Neolithic sites, although it was not possible to identify whether the glume base of glume wheat in pit fill 181 was of emmer wheat, because of its poor preservation. Free-threshing wheat is a less frequently recovered wheat type in charred plant assemblages from Neolithic sites but has been recorded as a minor component of such assemblages (Helbaek 1953; Moffett *et al.* 1989; Campbell and Straker 2003; Jones and Rowley-Conwy 2007).

Where radiocarbon dating of cereal grains from early prehistoric assemblages has been carried out, however, the dates indicate that such grains are frequently intrusive (Stevens and Fuller 2012; Pelling *et al.* 2015). In particular, free-threshing wheat grains in prehistoric contexts should generally be regarded as likely to be intrusive (Pelling *et al.* 2015: 88). For example, cereal grains present in Late Neolithic contexts from Durrington Walls (reported in Volume 3), which were radiocarbon-dated (Pelling *et al.* 2015), were found to be intrusive, highlighting the issue of contamination in assemblages of charred plant remains, particularly in samples from chalk soils (Atkinson 1957).

Although the cereal grain from these Cuckoo Stone pits was known to be probably intrusive, four radiocarbon dates were obtained on *Hordeum* sp. grains, two each from pit 180 and pit 135. The dates fall in the first two millennia AD, revealing that these grains are intrusive within these Late Neolithic fills (see Marshall *et al.*, above).

It has been noted that charred cereal grains of Late Neolithic date are extremely sparse in archaeobotanical assemblages from the Stonehenge and Avebury areas (Pelling and Campbell 2013: 37; Campbell 2013: 176). Barley grain, probable emmer wheat grain and free-threshing

Site	Woodhenge	Cuckoo Stone	Cuckoo Stone
Context number	**51**	**136**	**181**
Sample number	**11, 12, 14, 16, 17**	**102**	**115**
Feature type	*Buried soil*	*Pit*	*Pit*
Phase	*Early Neolithic*	*Late Neolithic*	*Late Neolithic*
Taxon (number of fragments)			
Taxus baccata L. (yew)	13		
Prunus cf *spinosa* (blackthorn)	1		
Prunus sp. (cherries blackthorn)	2		
Pomoideae (hawthorn/wild apple/wild pear/whitebeams)	7		2
Rhamnus cathartica L. (buckthorn)	1		
Ulmus sp. (elm)		4	1
Quercus sp. (oak)	9	8	12
Alnus glutinosa (L.) Gaertn. (alder)	1		
Corylus avellana L. (hazel)	33	32	32
Indeterminate		6	3
Ligneous structure observations (number of fragments)			
Strong ring curvature	3	2	2
Intermediate ring curvature	1	1	4
Weak ring curvature		1	
Tyloses in vessel cavities			1
Fungal hyphae in vessel cavities		4	8
Vitrification	11	8	9

Table 7.13. Wood charcoal by species from pits 135 and 180 at the Cuckoo Stone, compared with Woodhenge

wheat grain are present in low-density assemblages of charred plant remains recovered from the West Kennet palisade enclosures in the Avebury area, although again it must be noted that some of this material may be intrusive from later activity (Fairbairn 1997: 137). Cereal pollen is, however, present in a pollen profile from the floodplain of the river Avon, at a date probably contemporary with the Cuckoo Stone pits (see Chapter 9).

7.2.11. Wood charcoal from around the Cuckoo Stone

E. Simmons

The 14 flotation samples, comprising just over 130 litres of soil, produced moderate assemblages of 50 wood charcoal fragments >2mm in size in cross-section, from the fill (136) of pit 135 and the fill (181) of pit 180. The wood charcoal assemblages from the fills of both pits were therefore selected for full identification, using the methods outlined in Chapter 3. Although bone and antler from both pit fills were radiocarbon-dated to the earlier Late Neolithic (see *Radiocarbon dating*, above), there is a possibility, as with the charred plant remains assemblage, that at least some of the wood charcoal fragments may be intrusive.

Species represented

The taxa present in the charcoal assemblages and observations of the ligneous structure of the charcoal fragments are recorded in Table 7.13, alongside data from Early Neolithic contexts at Woodhenge. Taxa present in the charcoal assemblage from both pit fill 136 and pit fill 181 are hazel (*Corylus avellana*), oak (*Quercus* sp.) and elm (*Ulmus* sp.). Charcoal of hawthorn/apple/pear/whitebeam (Pomoideae) is also present in pit fill 181.

It is often not possible to identify charcoal beyond a certain taxonomic level given the similarities between related genera. Pomoideae is a large sub-family of the Rosaceae (rose family), containing many species that cannot be differentiated using morphological characteristics, although the native woody plant species most likely represented would be *Pyrus communis*

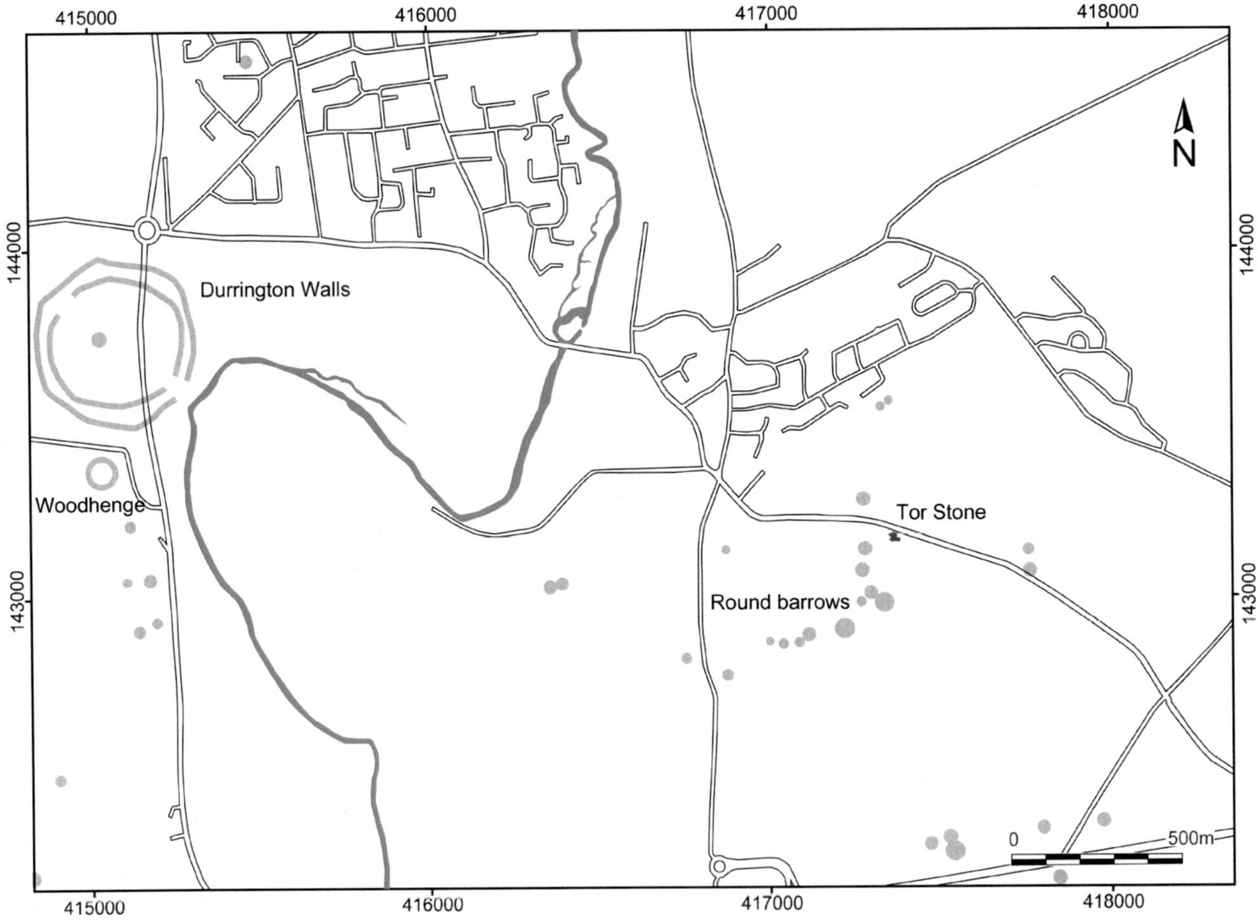

Figure 7.29. Map showing the location of the Tor Stone, Bulford

L. (wild pear), *Malus sylvestris* (L.) Mill. (crab apple), *Sorbus domestica* L. (service tree), *Sorbus aucuparia* L. (rowan), *Sorbus aria* (L.) Crantz (common whitebeam), *Crataegus monogyna* Jacq. (hawthorn) or *Crataegus laevigata* (Poir.) DC. (Midland hawthorn).

Oak charcoal cannot be identified to species using morphological characteristics so either *Quercus petraea* (Matt.) Leibl. (sessile oak) or *Quercus robur* L. (pendunculate oak) is represented. The species of oak most likely to be present is *Quercus robur* L., which is generally dominant on the heavy basic soils of southern and eastern England (Godwin 1975: 279) and is the dominant oak species in present-day woodland communities in Wiltshire (Grose 1979: 504). Elm charcoal also cannot be identified to species. The three species of elm probably native to the British Isles are *Ulmus glabra* Huds. (wych elm), *Ulmus procera* Salisb. (English elm) or *Ulmus minor* ssp. *minor* Mill. (small-leaved elm; Godwin 1975: 244).

The size of the wood charcoal fragments was generally too small for a reliable assessment to be made of growth-ring curvature. It was, however, possible to determine growth-ring curvatures on four of the hazel charcoal fragments from pit fill 136, of which one has weak curvature, one has intermediate curvature and two have strong curvature. It was also possible to determine growth-ring curvature on six of the charcoal fragments from pit fill 181, of which one hazel and one indeterminate fragment have strong curvature, and one hazel, two oak and one Pomoideae fragment have intermediate curvature. Thick-walled tyloses are present in the vessel cavities of one of the elm charcoal fragments. Fungal hyphae are present in the vessel cavities of four of the charcoal fragments from pit fill 136 and eight of the charcoal fragments from pit fill 181.

Preservation of the wood charcoal fragments was relatively good, with only eight fragments in pit fill 136 and nine fragments in pit fill 181 exhibiting some form of vitrification.

Discussion

A relatively low diversity of taxa is represented in the charcoal assemblage from pit fills 136 and 181, possibly indicating the preferential selection of certain taxa for use as fuel. This low diversity of taxa may, however, also be related to the relatively small sample size. Note, however, that the greater diversity of taxa in the Early Neolithic assemblage from Woodhenge was produced from a smaller quantity of soil.

It was not generally possible to determine the diameter of the wood used, given the small size of the majority of the charcoal fragments, although weak, intermediate and strong ring curvatures were noted as present, suggesting the use of a mix of small and larger diameter wood. Tyloses, indicating the use of mature heartwood, were observed in the vessel cavities of one of the elm charcoal fragments. The use of at least some dead or rotting wood is suggested by the presence of fungal hyphae in the vessel cavities of a small number of the wood charcoal fragments.

The composition of the charcoal assemblage is likely to have been influenced by a number of taphonomic factors, including anthropogenic wood-collection strategies, combustion factors, and depositional and post-depositional processes (Théry-Parisot *et al.* 2010). It is unlikely, therefore, that the dominance of a particular taxon within the charcoal assemblage directly reflects a dominance of that taxon in the surrounding environment. It is also likely that woodland and the uses of wood had ceremonial and symbolic associations (Austin 2000: 64), especially here adjacent to the Durrington Walls complex of Late Neolithic timber monuments (Wainwright with Longworth 1971; Parker Pearson 2012: 70–108).

Hazel is the most abundant taxon present in the charcoal assemblages from both pit fills. The use and properties of hazel wood, and of oak – the next most abundant taxon – are discussed in the wood charcoal report in Chapter 3. Elm is a somewhat poor fuel wood, apart from where heartwood has been well-seasoned (Webster 1919: 45; Porter 1990: 93). Elm is, however, a very durable wood, resistant to splitting, and is therefore a useful structural timber (Rackham 2003: 267). Taxa potentially represented by Pomoideae, such as hawthorn, apple and pear, are also good fuel woods, producing good heat and burning slowly (Webster 1919: 45; Porter 1990: 93).

Hazel is a common underwood shrub in open woodland but can also grow to canopy height (Rackham 2003: 203). Oak and elm are mixed deciduous woodland trees although elm was in decline across Britain from around 3800 BC (Rackham 2003: 104). The presence of elm charcoal in the pit fills indicates that elm was still a component of the local woodlands at the time of deposition within the pits, although the low proportion of elm may suggest that it was a minor component of woodland at this time.

Hawthorn, wild apple, wild pear and most of the members of the whitebeam genus, which are potentially represented by Pomoideae, are all underwood shrubs or trees of open woodland (*ibid.*: 349). Hawthorn and whitebeam are also characteristic components of chalk scrub, which colonises open grassland on chalk soils in areas where grazing pressure is reduced (Tansley 1968: 127–8; Rodwell 1991: 338–9; Vera 2000: 343–4). Hazel can also be present in chalk scrub, but is less common than other shrubs, and saplings of trees such as oak and elm can also be present (Tansley 1968: 127; Rodwell 1991: 334).

Figure 7.30. The Tor Stone, Bulford, looking east towards Beacon Hill

The charcoal assemblage composition of pit fills 136 and 181 is therefore consistent with open woodland, woodland clearings and woodland fringes as well as with chalk scrub colonising areas of open grassland. Palaeo-environmental evidence from the Stonehenge and Durrington Walls environs indicates that the environment near the Cuckoo Stone pits during the Late Neolithic was generally open grazed grassland, although with a woodland presence in the wider landscape (French *et al.* 2012; see Chapter 9). Pollen data from the palaeo-channel of the River Avon adjacent to Durrington Walls provides evidence for Late Neolithic woodland of oak, hazel and some lime, along with a marked increase in alder. Elm pollen begins to decline at a point which is probably contemporary with the Cuckoo Stone pits (*ibid.*; see Chapter 9).

The absence of lime and alder from the charcoal assemblage demonstrates that charcoal assemblage composition is only a partial indication of available woodland. Alder is, however, a poor fuel wood unless previously converted to charcoal (Rackham 2003: 305–6) and lime can be under-represented in charcoal assemblages as a result of the susceptibility of lime charcoal to fragmentation.

Oak, hazel and Pomoideae charcoal are present in Late Neolithic charcoal assemblages from King Barrow Ridge and Coneybury henge, along with a range of underwood or scrub taxa (Gale 1990: 253). Oak, hazel and Pomoideae are also predominant taxa in the rich

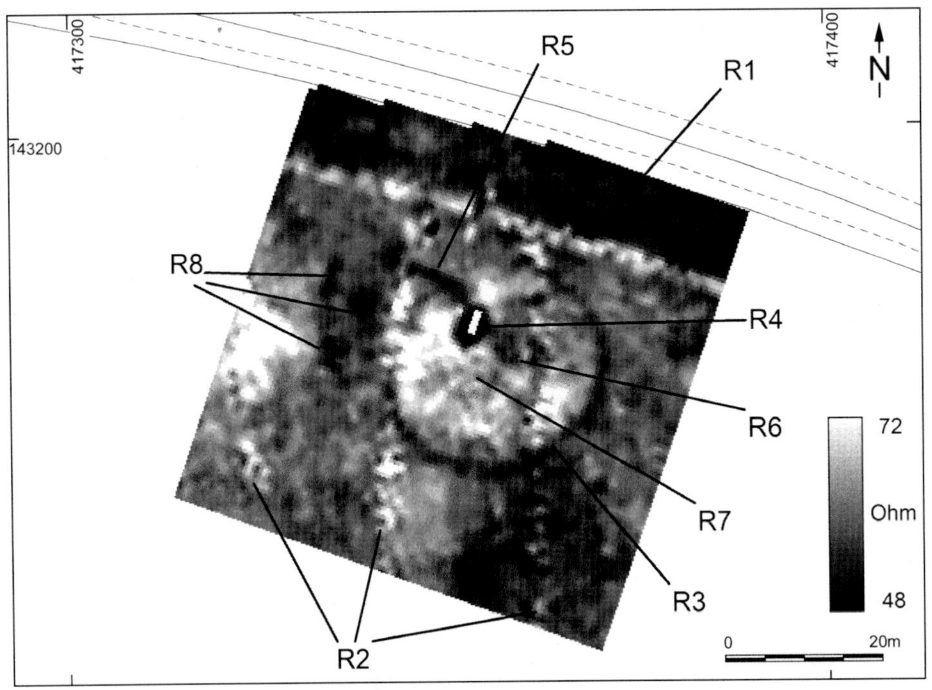

Figure 7.31. Earth resistance survey around the Tor Stone, Bulford

charcoal assemblage from Durrington Walls (reported in Volume 3). Although elm is present in earlier Neolithic deposits from the Stonehenge region (Gale 1990: 253), it is generally not present in Late Neolithic charcoal assemblages. Note, however, that elm is the only taxon present in these Late Neolithic contexts which is absent from Early Neolithic Woodhenge.

7.3. The Tor Stone, Bulford

C. Richards

Viewed from the great henge monument of Durrington Walls, the eastern horizon is formed by a linear stretch of conjoined hills, the highest being Beacon Hill (see Chapter 2). Together these hills create a lengthy northeast–southwest-orientated 'ridgeway', which eventually swings around to the west and begins a gradual descent towards the River Avon. This represents the sole elevated route of access into the Stonehenge complex, with other routes being low-lying along river valleys. Indeed, the ridge overlooks two river valleys, the River Avon and Nine Mile River (see Figure 2.1). As the ridge descends to the south and west, it slowly levels out and broadens; it is in this position (SU 17364 43180) that the Tor Stone lies recumbent in a field to the southeast of Bulford village (Figure 7.29). This sarsen stone is of a tapering shape ideal for a standing monolith (Figure 7.30).

Early in 2005, this substantial sarsen was brought to our attention by Mr Clive Atkins. In September 2005, as part of the SRP investigations into landscape and sarsen stones, the Bulford sarsen, or Tor Stone as it has become known (in memory of Chris Tilley's dog Tor), was examined and its immediate environs excavated. The stone lies approximately 25m inside the fence-line to its north, aligned north–south with its pointed end to the south, and measures *c.* 2.80m long × 1.50m wide × 0.50m thick. Given its elongated shape, the stone was immediately recognised as a possible fallen monolith. Consultation of transcribed cropmarks for the field revealed the stone as lying within a ring ditch of *c.* 25m diameter.

That this recumbent sarsen had remained uninvestigated is remarkable, given its close proximity to Stonehenge. This is clearly a consequence of the River Avon providing a physical and conceptual demarcation of the 'Stonehenge landscape', with its magnified archaeological importance. In lying beyond this boundary, the Tor Stone, had, amazingly, not only remained unrecognised for its archaeological significance but also its presence may not have been recorded. It may be 'the stone on the Bulford Road to Beacon Hill' recorded in Hawley's diary for 12/2/1920, that he noted formed a straight line with a stone in the river at Bulford and a stone on the Down west of Larkhill.

The Tor Stone has had a chequered history and is fortunate to have survived intact. For example, several years ago, the farmer, Mr Hann, attempted to move and bury the stone in a rubble pit at the northwest corner of the field. Fortunately, this act was halted by a representative of the local council. The stone was subsequently dragged back to its place of origin. Mr Hann told us that the stone had actually been replaced

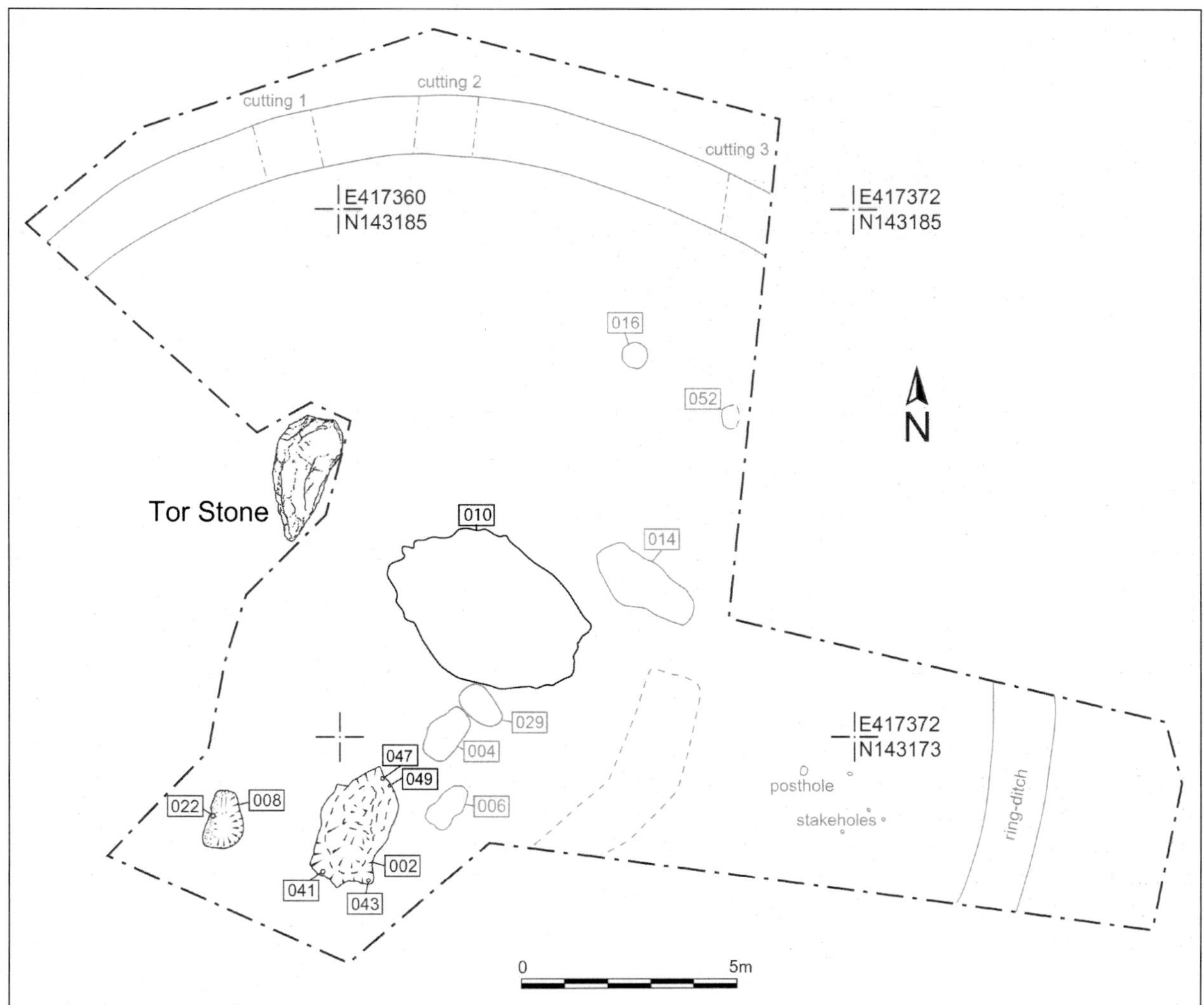

Figure 7.32. Plan of Trench 10 at the Tor Stone, Bulford. Neolithic features are in black

with some accuracy to within a couple of yards of its original position. Another local inhabitant recalled an earlier instance of the stone being dragged the few yards to the edge of the field, but this too was noticed and the sarsen was subsequently replaced. It now lies 6m north of the pit in which it originally stood and is swivelled 180° from its likely recumbent position before the recent episodes of interference (see below).

The presence of this stone just 5.2km from Stonehenge is truly remarkable, and it was decided to undertake excavations around the stone to:

1. determine if the Tor Stone was originally a standing monolith and, if so, locate its socket and position;
2. investigate any deposits associated with the monolith;
3. establish the relationship between the ring ditch and monolith;
4. determine if the ring ditch was continuous, or was broken by an entrance.

7.3.1. Geophysical survey

K. Welham and C. Steele

Geophysical survey at the Tor Stone, Bulford was undertaken in 2005. The survey was conducted with the aim of identifying a stonehole where the stone once stood and any associated features. Earth resistance survey was completed using a Geoscan RM15-D earth resistance meter in the 0.50m twin electrode configuration. Readings were taken over 20m × 20m grids at 1m intervals along traverses spaced 1m apart.

The data from the Tor Stone (Figure 7.31) show that the surrounding area has been moderately disturbed by agricultural activity, as can be seen by the response of the hedge boundary (R1) in the north of the survey area, and three parallel linear features (R2) crossing the survey area from north to south. The ring ditch (R3) was detected and appears to have an entrance or causeway in the north of the circuit. However, when excavated, the ditch was

Figure 7.33. Trench 10 at Bulford, viewed from the west

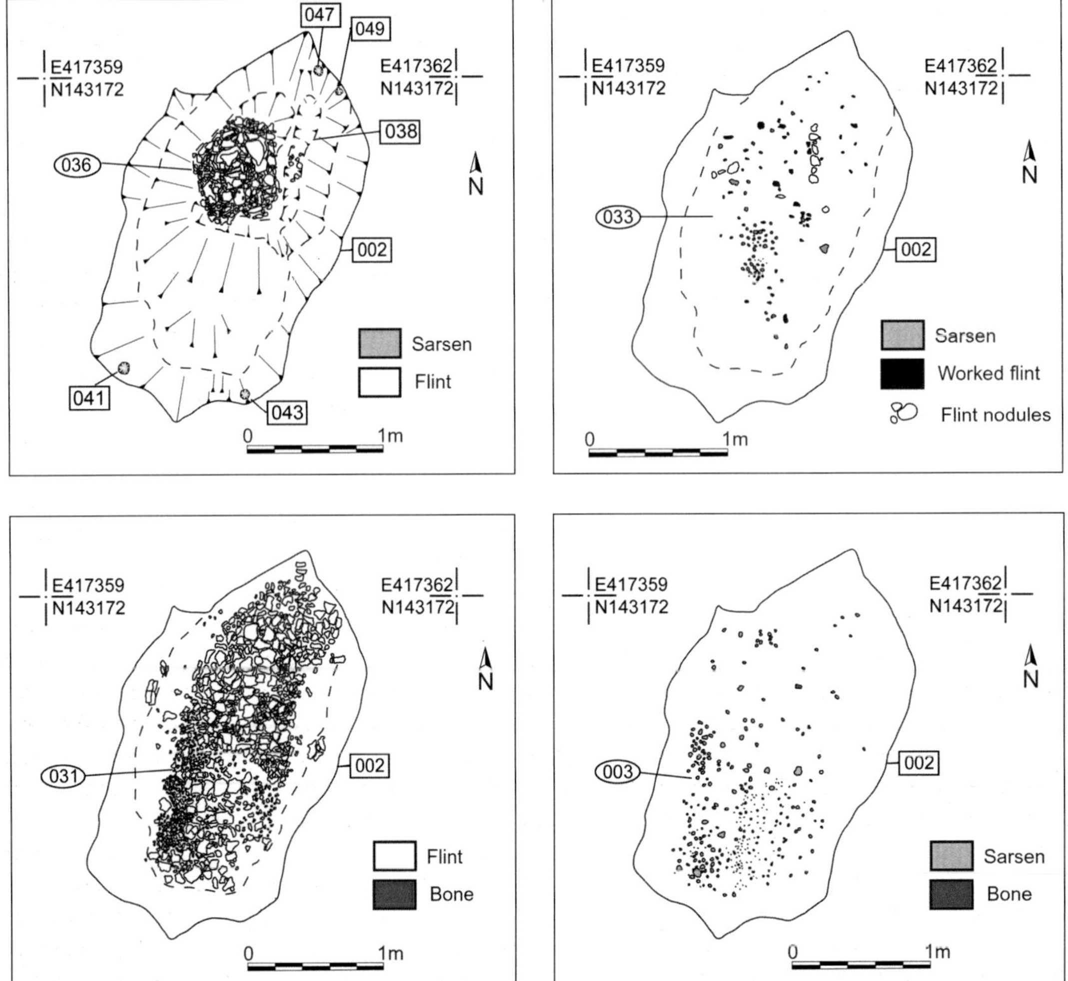

Figure 7.34. Plans of different layers within extraction pit 002 at Bulford; in stratigraphic order left to right and top to bottom (earliest at top left)

Figure 7.35. Extraction pit 002, containing its fill of broken flint, viewed from the east

Figure 7.36. Extraction pit 002, after excavation, viewed from the south

shown to form a complete circle. The current position of the Tor Stone is shown in these data (R4) and it is possible that a high-resistance anomaly (R5) to the northwest of it is the rubble pit related to the recent movement and short-term relocation of the stone. Several responses likely to be indicative of pits (R6–R8) are also present in these data. Anomalies R6 and R7 were excavated; R6 was found on excavation to be a shallow pit likely to have been the base of the hollow in which the sarsen originally lay and from which it was extracted in prehistory, whilst R7 was shown to be the stonehole in which the Tor Stone once stood.

7.3.2. Excavation around the Tor Stone, Bulford

An irregular L-shaped trench (SRP Trench 10), up to *c.* 25m east–west by *c.* 20m north–south, was dug around the east side of the recumbent stone, no longer in its original position but moved a short distance north from that location by the farmer. The excavation revealed around a dozen features within the ring ditch (Figures 7.32–7.33).

The features considered to be associated with the sarsen monolith and its erection consist of a hollow (002) in which this sarsen is thought to have originally lain, a socket (008) within which the stone is thought to have stood when erected, and a large pit (010) which may also be an early prehistoric feature. All three features are thought to have been used and filled in the Neolithic, prior to the use of this location for cremation burials underneath the centre of a round barrow (indicated by the ring ditch) in the Early Bronze Age. These burials consist of a cremation grave (004) containing two Early Bronze Age Food Vessels and multiple grave goods, and a second Early Bronze Age cremation grave (029) which cuts it. Other features are undated (pits 006, 014, 016 and 052). All these later features, including the ring ditch, are reported in Volume 4.

The stone hollow (002)

An irregular sloping scoop or hollow (002), measuring *c.* 3.00m × 1.70m, was located in the southern part of the trench (Figures 7.33–7.36). It was up to 0.15m deep, cutting into the surface of the chalk bedrock (Figure 7.36). As with the Cuckoo Stone, this hollow shares the same shape and contours as the sarsen monolith (ascertained by making a cast of the pit and comparing it with the stone itself; Figure 7.37). As described earlier, in its natural state a sarsen boulder becomes slightly embedded in the chalk bedrock on which it lies, as a result of erosion and weathering (see *Excavation around the Cuckoo Stone,* above; Bowen and Smith 1977; Green 1997). In Trench 10, the shape of the hollow was slightly larger than that of the stone, indicating that the sarsen was loosened by digging around its perimeter and then extracted by levering and hauling it out of the ground. The chalk surface at the base of the hollow was found to be smooth. Together with the ramp on the south side of the hollow, this is interpreted as the result of friction created by dragging the stone out of the ground in a southerly direction.

Pairs of stakeholes (047, 049; 041, 043) were found on the northern and southern edges of the extraction hollow (002). Each contained a similar fill of grey-brown silty loam (048, 050; 042, 044). This arrangement is interpreted as the result of driving four posts of *c.* 0.06m–0.10m diameter into the ground at each end of the stone. Whether these posts actually facilitated the hauling and levering of the stone or relate to a prior activity is difficult to know. The posts certainly do not relate to subsequent activities as they were sealed by later deposits within the hollow.

A small linear feature (038; 0.90m × 0.22m and 0.05m deep) cut into the bottom of the hollow (002) within its northeast quadrant (Figure 7.34). It was filled with light brown silt and chalk lumps (039). Aligned north-northeast–south-southwest between stake-holes 047 and 043, this narrow linear slot may have been caused by dragging the stone out of its hollow

Figure 7.37. A foam cast within extraction pit 002, with the Tor Stone in the background, viewed from the south

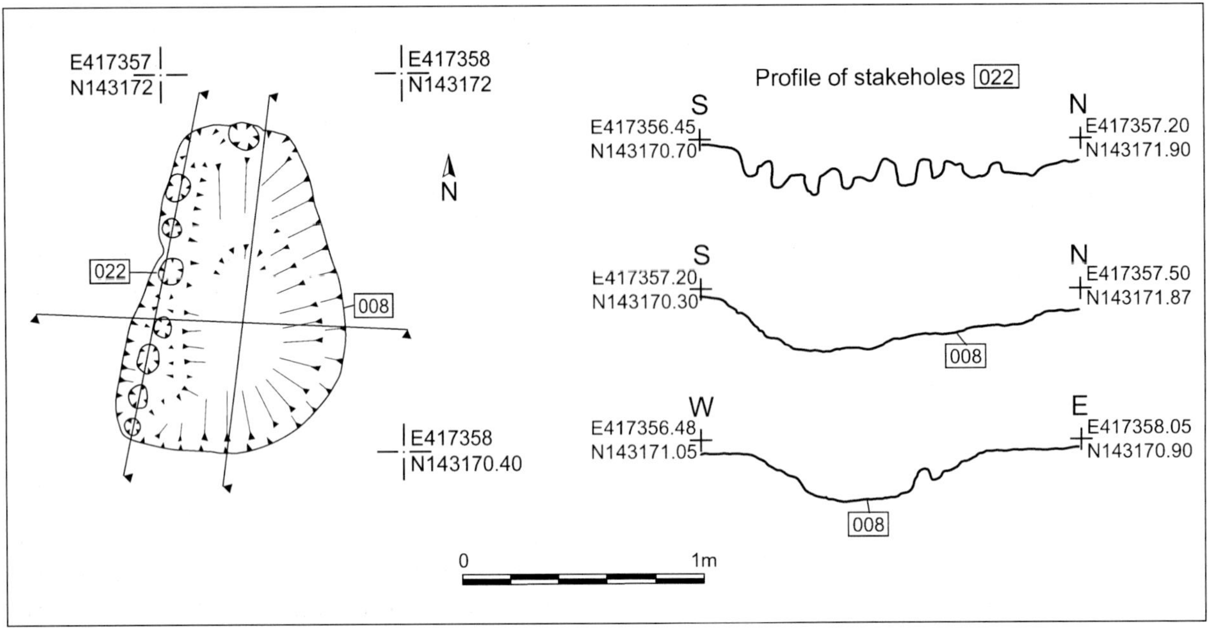

Figure 7.38. Plan and section drawings of stone socket 008 at Bulford

The hollow (002) was filled with knapped flint, unworked broken flint nodules and sarsen flakes (Figure 7.35). When excavated these deposits appeared as a mass of flint with sarsen flakes (031 and 036), within an orange-brown silt matrix (003, 033 and 035) which continued down to a very thin and partial silt (034 and 040) forming a basal deposit. Given the level of sub-surface compaction and erosion of the chalk surface, it seems probable that the flint and sarsen deposits (031 and 036) are the remains of a raised flint cairn. The presence of two patches of micro-debitage in the southern area of the flint fill conjures up an image of two people knapping flint on either side of the hollow.

This sequence of fills within the hollow suggests that, as well as erecting the monolith, attention was also directed by the megalith-builders towards the empty quarry hollow (002), perhaps to commemorate and mark the place whence the stone derived. As with the Cuckoo Stone, the circumstances or period in which the Tor Stone was toppled, or fell, cannot be elucidated.

Figure 7.39. Stone socket 008 at Bulford, viewed from the east

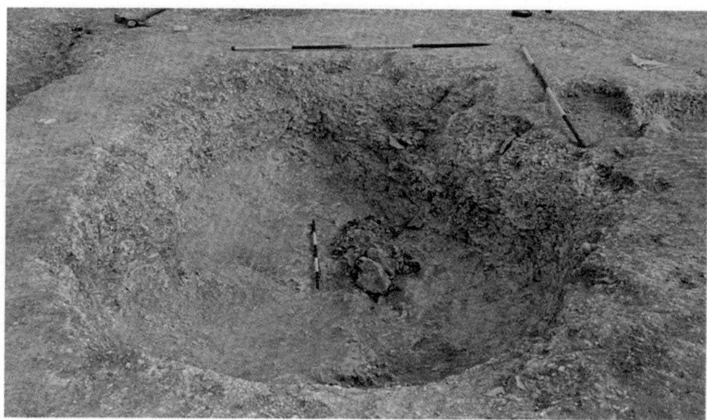

Figure 7.40. The large pit (010) at Bulford with a ridge of redeposited, compact chalk (037) running along its base, viewed from the west

Stone socket (008)

Some 3m west of the hollow (002) lies a second pit (008). This pit is triangular or D-form in plan, measuring *c.* 1.35m × 0.90m and 0.20m deep (Figures 7.33, 7.38–7.39). With the loss of up to 0.25m of the chalk bedrock since prehistory, we can estimate that the pit was dug originally to a depth of about 0.50m below the old land surface. Compressed chalk rubble and silt (021) lay at the base of the pit where a rough impression of the base of the Tor Stone was visible in an off-centre position (Figure 7.39). The remaining brown-orange silty loam fill (009) of the socket was a deposit that accumulated after removal of the standing stone.

A line of eight stakeholes (022) was present along the western edge of the socket (Figures 7.38–7.39). These were filled with a homogeneous stone-free, mid-brown silty loam (023). The stakes effectively lined the rear of the stone socket and may be interpreted as anti-friction devices allowing the stone to slide smoothly down the flat, western face of the socket. Such a use of wooden stakes is a feature of examined stone sockets at Avebury (Gillings and Pollard 2008).

Pit 010

This was a large rectangular pit with rounded corners, measuring 4.10m × 3.16m and 0.80m deep (Figures 7.33, 7.40). It occupied a central position adjacent to the Early Bronze Age burial pits (004 and 029) and, given its size, great expectation surrounded its excavation. It was almost totally filled with uniform, compact light brown-orange silty loam (011), which gave way to a partial and thin light brown basal silt (027). During the excavation, a few worked flints and sarsen flakes were recovered from its fills but not in any great number. A ridge of compact chalk (037) ran east–west across the base of the pit, with a substantial flint nodule being embedded in its western extent. A small shelf or platform had been cut into the southeastern wall of the pit. Upon this shelf lay a pile of sarsen flakes; unexpectedly, a piece of iron was discovered stratified beneath the flakes.

When fully excavated, it was clear that the large pit had originally been dug as three separate pits: two interlinking in the north and an elongated pit to the south. Just what the purpose of this pit was is unknown. The presence of iron indicates later disturbance but the flint assemblage, including a fabricator and two large hammerstones (see Chan, below), is consistent with a prehistoric date.

Discussion

As with the Cuckoo Stone, the erection of the Tor Stone as a standing stone adjacent to its naturally occurring position has implications for discussions concerning the significance of the locations of monoliths in the Neolithic landscape.

The marking of the extraction pit with a flint cairn – commemorating the removal of a large and anomalous sarsen – is of particular significance as it is also a practice employed to mark and cover pits, postholes and human burials in the fourth and third millennia BC. Examples of the latter can be found beneath the long barrow at Fussell's Lodge, Wilts. (Ashbee 1966: 8, plate 7a). Within the Southern Circle at Durrington Walls, the position of a timber upright (posthole 32) was marked by a flint cairn (Wainwright with Longworth 1971: 35). Similarly, at nearby Woodlands, pit 1 was capped with a flint cairn (Stone and Young 1948). In these three examples close to Bulford, we see a convergence of practice in the coverage and commemoration of quite different contexts and features. Yet all have one aspect in common, each was marking a specific event involving removal or placement *in the earth*.

However, there is a specificity in this practice because only certain features were singled out for this treatment – a single posthole in the Southern Circle, for instance, or a single pit among the Woodlands group. Perhaps attention

	Artefact type		Feature number 002	008	010	Total
Debitage and cores	Blade	Count	4	0	1	5
		% within feature group	0.1%	0%	1.7%	0.1%
	Blade-like flake	Count	1	0	0	1
		% within feature group	<0.1%	0%	0%	<0.1%
	Bladelet	Count	4	0	0	4
		% within feature group	0.1%	0%	0%	0.1%
	Core on a flake	Count	1	0	0	1
		% within feature group	<0.1%	0%	0%	<0.1%
	Crested blade	Count	1	0	0	1
		% within feature group	<0.1%	0%	0%	<0.1%
	Flake	Count	4410	1	50	4461
		% within feature group	92.5%	100.0%	83.3%	92.4%
	Irregular waste	Count	307	0	0	307
		% within feature group	6.4%	0%	0%	6.4%
	Keeled non-discoidal flake-core	Count	1	0	0	1
		% within feature group	<0.1%	0%	0%	<0.1%
	Levallois/other discoidal flake-core	Count	1	0	0	1
		% within feature group	<0.1%	0%	0%	<0.1%
	Multi-platform flake-core	Count	4	0	0	4
		% within feature group	0.1%	0%	0%	0.1%
	Other blade-core	Count	8	0	0	8
		% within feature group	0.2%	0%	0%	0.2%
	Single-platform flake-core	Count	3	0	0	3
		% within feature group	0.1%	0%	0%	0.1%
	Tested nodule/bashed lump	Count	4	0	0	4
		% within feature group	0.1%	0%	0%	0.1%
	Unclassifiable/fragmentary core	Count	3	0	1	4
		% within feature group	0.1%	0%	1.7%	0.1%
Retouched flakes and tools	Denticulate	Count	1	0	0	1
		% within feature group	<0.1%	0%	0%	<0.1%
	Fabricator	Count	0	0	1	1
		% within feature group	0%	0%	1.7%	<0.1%
	Hammerstone	Count	4	0	2	6
		% within feature group	0.1%	0%	3.3%	0.1%
	Misc. retouched flake	Count	4	0	1	5
		% within feature group	0.1%	0%	1.7%	0.1%
	Utilised/edge-damaged flake/blade	Count	4	0	4	8
		% within feature group	0.1%	0%	6.7%	0.2%
	Total	Count	4765	1	60	4826
		% within feature group	100.0%	100.0%	100.0%	100.0%

Table 7.14. The worked flint assemblage from Neolithic contexts at the Tor Stone by feature group

should be redirected to the practice of flint-knapping itself, in terms of the time spent by a person working stone over an open feature. There is a certain intimacy involved in this act: in the case of the stone hollow of the Tor Stone, knapping flakes were carefully spread across the open pit. The excavation of the hollow at the Tor Stone site reveals indications of separation between layers of flint flakes (*e.g.* layer 033). Consequently, the formation of the flint cairn comprised a series of events involving a return to a particular place and the knapping and deposition of flint. Such repeated actions suggest acts of commemoration and an intimate link between Neolithic people and the place where the Tor Stone lay *before* it was erected.

A large quantity of sarsen debris was found in the stone hollow or extraction pit for the Tor Stone, incorporated with the knapped and naturally broken flint (see below; Figure 7.35). Yet the Tor Stone exhibits no evidence of having been dressed (although it is a little damaged following the repeated attempts at removal). Hence, it is necessary to question the presence of sarsen flakes as a component of the flint cairn in the extraction pit. If these were not derived from the Tor Stone, we need to look further afield. There is only one place in the vicinity that was littered with sarsen flakes and that is Stonehenge. If the flakes were indeed derived from Stonehenge, this act provides insight into notions of materiality, sanctity and remembrance (discussed further below).

7.3.3. Sarsen from around the Tor Stone, Bulford

B. Chan and C. Richards

Of the 3,929 pieces (10.788kg) of sarsen from Trench 10, the vast majority come from contexts 003, 031 and 033, with smaller quantities in contexts 034, 035, 036 and 040; all of these are layers within the stone hollow or extraction pit (002). A large sarsen flake (SF 188; 790g) was found in layer 011 of pit 010 but otherwise the sarsen assemblage consists of small flakes and chunks.

7.3.4. Worked flint from Neolithic contexts around the Tor Stone, Bulford

B. Chan

The Tor Stone excavations yielded an assemblage of 4,883 pieces of worked flint, of which 4,826 came from stone hollow 002, with a much smaller amount of material coming from stonehole 008 and large pit 010 (Table 7.14). The pit is of uncertain chronology but is thought to be prehistoric in date. The remainder of the assemblage, from contexts that are dated securely to the Bronze Age, is reported in Volume 4.

Raw material and condition

The assemblage is all of nodular chalk-derived flint, much of which is in the form of weathered nodules with thermal flaws. The material is patinated but is otherwise in good condition. Alongside the worked flint, much of the mass of the flint cairn in stone hollow 002 was made up of unworked, thermally fractured nodules. This material was not quantified but was noted both in the field and during the subsequent analysis to make up about half of the flint from the cairn. Although this material is unworked in techno-typological terms (*i.e.* it comprises only thermally fractured surfaces and lacks diagnostic features of percussion and conchoidal fracturing), it is possible that the nodules were reduced by percussion but were so thermally flawed that they simply fractured along existing thermal fractures that lay within the nodules.

Contextual distribution

The assemblage from likely Neolithic contexts is overwhelmingly derived from stone hollow 002, with only a single flake found within stonehole 008, and a slightly larger assemblage from pit 010 (Table 7.14). Although the date of pit 010 is uncertain, its assemblage has some similarities with that from stone hollow 002 as will be highlighted below.

Stone hollow 002

The assemblage from stone hollow 002 was derived from contexts 003, 031, 033, 034, 035, 036, 039 and 040, and comprises 4,765 pieces of worked flint (Table 7.15). This total includes 26 pieces of flint from fill 039 which technically was the fill of a small linear cut within the stone hollow. The rest of the deposits represent the makeup of a cairn, which consisted of a mass of flint and sarsen within a silt matrix. We suggest that at least some of the flint was knapped directly onto the cairn (see above).

As a whole, the assemblage from the stone hollow is dominated by flakes, which make up 93% of the assemblage. These flakes are generally broad and squat, with many being small and of limited potential for either trimming nodules or forming blanks for tools.

Alongside the flakes, there is a relatively high proportion of irregular waste and a relatively low proportion of cores in comparison to other sites in the Stonehenge landscape. The cores include tested nodules, a keeled core, a discoidal core, and single- and multi-platform flake-cores. The cores are generally poorly worked and unsystematic in terms of their reduction and therefore in keeping with the flake assemblage. Alongside the cores there are four flint hammerstones from within the cairn, with the two from context 031 being unusually large, with heavy

	Artefact type		Context number 003	031	033	034	035	036	039	040	Total
Debitage and cores	Blade	Count	3	1	0	0	0	0	0	0	4
		% within context no.	0.1%	0.1%	0%	0%	0%	0%	0%	0%	0.1%
	Blade-like flake	Count	1	0	0	0	0	0	0	0	1
		% within context no.	<0.1%	0%	0%	0%	0%	0%	0%	0%	<0.1%
	Bladelet	Count	4	0	0	0	0	0	0	0	4
		% within context no.	0.2%	0%	0%	0%	0%	0%	0%	0%	0.1%
	Core on a flake	Count	1	0	0	0	0	0	0	0	1
		% within context no.	<0.1%	0%	0%	0%	0%	0%	0%	0%	<0.1%
	Crested blade	Count	1	0	0	0	0	0	0	0	1
		% within context no.	<0.1%	0%	0%	0%	0%	0%	0%	0%	<0.1%
	Flake	Count	2402	607	684	188	27	309	23	170	4410
		% within context no.	94.0%	88.6%	92.8%	93.1%	81.8%	89.6%	88.5%	93.9%	92.5%
	Irregular waste	Count	132	73	48	12	6	22	3	11	307
		% within context no.	5.2%	10.7%	6.5%	5.9%	18.2%	6.4%	11.5%	6.1%	6.4%
	Keeled non-discoidal flake-core	Count	0	0	1	0	0	0	0	0	1
		% within context no.	0%	0%	0.1%	0%	0%	0%	0%	0%	<0.1%
	Levallois/other discoidal flake-core	Count	0	0	0	0	0	1	0	0	1
		% within context no.	0%	0%	0%	0%	0%	0.3%	0%	0%	<0.1%
	Multi-platform flake-core	Count	2	0	0	0	0	2	0	0	4
		% within context no.	0.1%	0%	0%	0%	0%	0.6%	0%	0%	0.1%
	Other blade-core	Count	2	0	2	0	0	4	0	0	8
		% within context no.	0.1%	0%	0.3%	0%	0%	1.2%	0%	0%	0.2%
	Single-platform flake-core	Count	0	0	1	0	0	2	0	0	3
		% within context no.	0%	0%	0.1%	0%	0%	0.6%	0%	0%	0.1%
	Tested nodule/bashed lump	Count	4	0	0	0	0	0	0	0	4
		% within context no.	0.2%	0%	0%	0%	0%	0%	0%	0%	0.1%
	Unclassifiable/fragmentary core	Count	0	0	0	1	0	2	0	0	3
		% within context no.	0%	0%	0%	0.5%	0%	0.6%	0%	0%	0.1%
Retouched flakes and tools	Denticulate	Count	0	0	1	0	0	0	0	0	1
		% within context no.	0%	0%	0.1%	0%	0%	0%	0%	0%	<0.1%
	Hammerstone	Count	0	2	0	0	0	2	0	0	4
		% within context no.	0%	0.3%	0%	0%	0%	0.6%	0%	0%	0.1%
	Misc. retouched flake	Count	1	2	0	1	0	0	0	0	4
		% within context no.	<0.1%	0.3%	0%	0.5%	0%	0%	0%	0%	0.1%
	Utilised/edge-damaged flake/blade	Count	3	0	0	0	0	1	0	0	4
		% within context no.	0.1%	0%	0%	0%	0%	0.3%	0%	0%	0.1%
Total		Count	2556	685	737	202	33	345	26	181	4765
		% within context no.	100.0%	100.0%	100.0%	100.0%	100.0%	100.0%	100.0%	100.0%	100.0%

Table 7.15. The worked flint assemblage from stone hollow 002 at the Tor Stone by context number

percussive wear indicating extensive use. These latter hammerstones are large enough that they were likely used for quartering nodules, rather than for the production of utilisable flakes.

The assemblage from the stone hollow that has been detailed thus far is uniform in the sense that it mostly relates to the rapid and unsystematic reduction of nodules into a mass of flint. This is in keeping with the idea that the assemblage represents the reduction of nodules for the sole purpose of producing material with which to construct a cairn. What is therefore surprising is that, in addition to this material, the assemblage also contains half of a broken tool which is either a notched flake, or more probably a crude denticulate.

More remarkable are the small proportion of blades, the presence of a probable crested blade and, most notably, eight blade-cores. Whilst these cores do not exhibit signs of highly structured blade-working, they did all produce blades and therefore required a level of core control beyond what would be expected from the expedient production of debitage for the construction of a cairn. The deliberate character of the blade-working is further suggested by the presence of the crested blade. The preparation of crested blades to initiate blade removals is a technique which is very rarely attested in the Neolithic assemblages of the Stonehenge landscape. Also remarkable is that the blade-cores are almost equal in number to the blade products themselves.

The last component of the assemblage from the stone hollow is represented by a small assemblage of retouched flakes and utilised/edge-damaged flakes. By themselves, they are relatively unremarkable but they provide further evidence that the flint cairn was not made up entirely of material knapped solely for the purpose of constructing the cairn itself.

Pit 010

Compared to the assemblage from stone hollow 002, the assemblage from pit 010 is small, particularly when it is borne in mind that the pit was both markedly longer and wider than the stone hollow. The pit contained 60 pieces of worked flint, mostly comprising flakes, in addition to a core, four utilised/edge-damaged flakes, a retouched flake, a blade, a fabricator and two hammerstones (Table 7.14). The fabricator is well-made, with bifacial retouch down both lateral margins, and was evidently used, in that it had a worn and rounded tip.

Despite the large difference in terms of the size of the assemblages from the pit and the stone hollow, they are linked in that they both contain large hammerstones. Weighing in at over 900g, the hammerstone from pit 010 is even larger than those from stone hollow 002 but is similarly worn, with heavy percussive wear over its surface. Perhaps equally remarkable is the core from pit 010, which weighs 7.8kg and is, in reality, a large nodule that has had several quartering flakes removed from it. The core and the hammerstone both indicate the primary quartering of nodules to produce cores for further working.

Discussion and conclusions

The pit, stone hollow and stonehole at the Tor Stone produced a sizeable assemblage of worked flint. The stonehole produced only a single flake and, accordingly, it is hard to ascribe much archaeological significance to it. The assemblages from the other two features are therefore of more interest. By far the larger assemblage came from the stone hollow, which, as described above, has a dual character. On the one hand, the majority of it appears to represent the knapping of flint just for the purpose of generating material with which to build up the cairn. On the other hand, there is an unusual number of blade-cores amongst the assemblage and hence more considered flintworking is also represented.

The purpose of the cairn was clearly to mark the hollow from which the Tor Stone had been removed. What is also clear is that the flint and sarsen that made up the cairn were brought to the hollow, rather than originally excavated from within it. We know this is the case for the sarsen assemblage because the Tor Stone itself was not dressed (see above). Equally, the sides of the hollow could not have produced enough flint nodules to fill it. The presence of almost as many blade-cores as there are blade products also makes it clear that material was either brought from further afield to be placed within the cairn or, perhaps more likely, the knapping that produced the cairn also created useable products that were taken away for use elsewhere.

In terms of the source of the flint that made up the cairn, it is worth considering the possibility that pit 010 was actually a quarry pit dug to retrieve the flint needed to make the cairn. The problem of dating the pit means that it is impossible to be certain of this. However, if the iron found in pit 010 was indeed intrusive, then this pit could have been linked to flint provision:

- As suggested above, the assemblage from pit 010 contains a hammerstone similar to those found within stone hollow 002, and the large core with quartering flakes may possibly have been used to produce material that could be flaked onto the cairn.
- Furthermore, the flint in the cairn consisted largely of thermally flawed nodules, of the type that could be found within a shallow pit relatively near to the surface.
- Lastly, the pit was dug as a series of pits that were joined together into a single large feature. The digging-out of the pit left a chalk ridge down its centre, in which was embedded a large nodule. The sequential nature of the excavation of the pit may indicate that it was enlarged in a piecemeal fashion until enough flint had been extracted to make up the cairn within the stone hollow.

Regardless of the contemporaneity of pit 010 and stone hollow 002, it is clear that, as with the Cuckoo Stone, the lifting of a naturally recumbent sarsen and its erection as a standing stone was a momentous event that required marking in some manner. Whilst the significant differences between the assemblages associated with the two stones point to varied and contingent responses to outwardly similar events, it is notable that in both cases flint played a central role in the observances that were required.

7.3.5. Charred plant remains and wood charcoal from around the Tor Stone, Bulford

E. Simmons

Forty-seven flotation samples, comprising over 500 litres of soil, were processed by flotation and assessed using the methods outlined in Chapter 3.

The silt matrix (003, 033 and 035) of the mass of flint and sarsen flakes (031 and 036) in stone hollow 002 produced four indeterminate barley grains (*Hordeum* sp. indet.), an indeterminate barley rachis node, three tentatively identified free-threshing wheat grains (*Triticum* sp.), nine indeterminate wheat grains (*Triticum* sp. indet.) and seven indeterminate cereal grains. A seed of common mallow (*Malva sylvestris*), a plant commonly associated with waste and rough ground, two vetch/wild pea seeds (*Vicia/Lathyrus* spp) and a large grass seed (>2mm, Poaceae) were also noted as present.

The presence of free-threshing wheat indicates that there is a high probability that at least some of the assemblage is intrusive material from later activity at the site (see the discussion of charred plant remains from the Cuckoo Stone pits, above). As no direct dating evidence was available for the fills of the stone hollow, no further analysis of the charred plant remains assemblage was undertaken. Wood charcoal fragments are occasionally present in the samples, but no wood charcoal analysis was undertaken given the small quantities of fragments >2mm in size in cross-section.

7.4. Local sarsen stones and the origins of Stonehenge

C. Richards

In the introduction to this chapter, the possible presence of substantial sarsen stones in the Stonehenge landscape was discussed. Whilst they are not of the magnitude of the Stonehenge sarsens, the occurrence of the 2.80m-long Tor Stone and the 2m-long Cuckoo Stone within the environs of Stonehenge is of considerable interest. The presence of further large sarsens in its environs in the fourth–third millennia cal BC is highly likely, on the basis both of recent discoveries and the historic use of substantial blocks of sarsen as boundary markers (see also Burl 2006: 92–3). The implications of this possible presence of large sarsens will be returned to below; however, here suffice it to consider the practices surrounding the extraction and erection of the Cuckoo Stone and Tor Stone.

Initially it is important to keep in mind the great ontological import of the extraction and raising of a large stone from a recumbent position that it had occupied for millennia. Whilst we may accept the former presence of other substantial sarsens in the Stonehenge landscape, their numbers are unlikely to have been particularly high. Consequently, these sarsen stones would have been highly anomalous, well-known and woven into cosmogonic schemes.

Their physical appearance may have varied according to the geological process of their exposure on the chalk bedrock. For example, the exploration of two recumbent sarsens on the Marlborough Downs by Bowen and Smith (1977: 193–5) revealed two variant natural processes at work:

- The first stone (I) lay on the surface of the chalk, with an outline of dissolved bedrock around its perimeter.
- The second sarsen (II) was actually embedded in the chalk, lying in a natural hollow that mirrored its shape.

Apart from the differences that would be encountered when extracting such stones (a level surface as opposed to a hollow), this difference in the natural positioning of sarsen boulders may well have affected the visibility of a stone in the landscape, with the former type being more prominent than the latter. Excavation of the Cuckoo Stone and Tor Stone has demonstrated that they both lay in hollows in the chalk bedrock.

The investigations of the Cuckoo Stone and Tor Stone revealed a degree of divergence in both the treatment of the stone and the material practices surrounding extraction and erection. Taking the Tor Stone first, the sequence of events appears to have been fairly straightforward. A recumbent sarsen, *c.* 2.80m long × 1.50m wide and thus weighing *c.* 4 tonnes, was excavated from the slight depression in which it was embedded. Because it lay in a shallow hollow, its extraction through leverage and dragging must have been relatively easy. The Tor Stone was subsequently erected a mere 3m away from this stone hollow.

Rather than backfilling the empty hollow with soil and turf, people gathered together flint nodules and brought them to the site. While some nodules were deposited complete into the hollow, many were knapped *in situ*, as evidenced by two patches of micro-debitage present in the southern area of the flint fill. Sarsen flakes were also brought to the site and placed with the flint, originally forming a raised flint and sarsen cairn. Over the next four or five millennia, this cairn became truncated as a result of sub-surface compaction, erosion of the chalk surface and cultivation.

In the inscribing practice of raising a megalith, we are witnessing acts of both reciprocity and commemoration (*cf* Gillings and Pollard 2016: 551). First, the reciprocal acts of taking something (the stone) and returning something (the deposition of the flint and sarsen cairn) are enhanced through the agency involved in flint-knapping and transporting sarsen

Figure 7.41. The Heel Stone at Stonehenge, viewed from the south when excavations were taking place in 2013 along the route of the decommissioned A344 road

flakes. Second, the filling and marking of the extraction pit, commemorating with a flint cairn the removal of a large and anomalous sarsen stone, is of particular interest as it is also a practice reserved to mark and cover pits and postholes more generally in the locality. As detailed above, a single post at Durrington Walls was marked by a flint cairn and at nearby Woodlands, a pit was capped with a flint cairn. In these examples we see a convergence of practice in the sealing and commemoration of quite different contexts and features. Yet all have one aspect in common: each marks a specific event involving removal, absence and closure.

A further point to consider is the incorporation of sarsen with the knapped and naturally broken flint. The Tor Stone shows no evidence of having been dressed. Hence, it is necessary to question the presence of sarsen flakes as a component of the flint cairn. These were not derived from the Tor Stone, and, as mentioned above, the nearest source of sarsen flakes would have been Stonehenge.

If sarsen was brought to the Tor Stone from Stonehenge, this indicates a perceived connectivity of particular things, substances and places. Something was being given back for something removed. Yet what was returned is qualitatively different: the pile of knapped flint forming the majority of the deposit is such that it would allow the place of extraction to be visually prominent. The place was memorialised through both imagery (we noticed that, when wet, the flint deposit glistened in the early morning sunshine) and through practice, *e.g.* acts of knapping and the procuring of sarsen flakes from Stonehenge. Nor should it be forgotten that this commemorative treatment of the stone hollow occurred even though it was situated only a few metres away from the erect Tor Stone.

The transformation of the Cuckoo Stone from a recumbent sarsen to a standing stone followed a slightly different sequence of events. As with the Tor Stone, the Cuckoo Stone, a sarsen weighing *c.* 6.5 tonnes, lay as a fully visible landscape feature, and was similarly set within a shallow hollow in the chalk surface. The sarsen was removed from its original position, dragged aside and a post was inserted centrally in the empty hollow (the basal cut [227] of this posthole being found at the base of the stone socket). The post was either subsequently removed or decayed *in situ* and a stone socket was dug through the hollow, and the Cuckoo Stone was erected.

The tools employed in digging the socket – an antler pick and a cattle scapula shovel – appear to have been deliberately buried within a shallow pit, *c.* 4m to the southwest. Around the same time, a small feasting event occurred; animal bones and over 100 worked flints were deposited in a second pit positioned to the southwest of the Cuckoo Stone. Once erect, both the Tor Stone and Cuckoo Stone would come to attract cremation deposits many centuries later (see Volume 4).

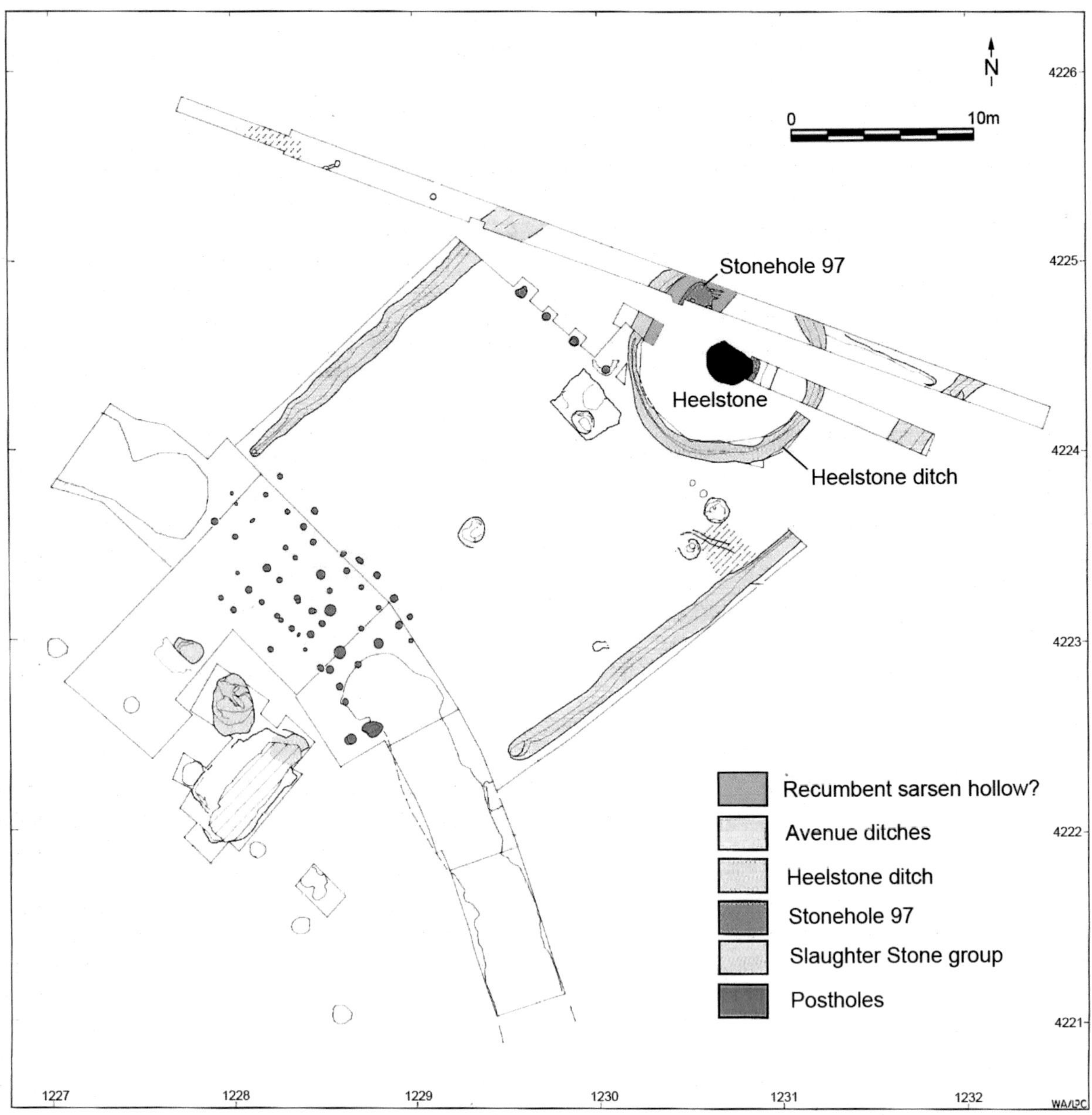

Figure 7.42. Plan of features excavated between Stonehenge's northeast entrance and the Heel Stone by Hawley (1922–1923), Atkinson *et al.* (1953 and 1956) and Pitts (1979–1980). It shows the location of the suspected recumbent sarsen hollow northwest of the Heel Stone (from Cleal *et al.* 1995: fig. 156); © Historic England

The significant difference between the erection of the Tor Stone and the erection of the Cuckoo Stone is the relationship between the stone, the place of erection and its source. In the case of the former, erection occurred a few metres away from the extraction hollow, which was commemorated by creating a flint cairn. The Cuckoo Stone, however, was eventually erected in its original location – the hollow in which it had lain recumbent – but not until a small post had been erected in the base of the hollow, a post which was then either extracted or allowed to decay. It is this sequence, presenting a clear archaeological signature, that provides the basis for a re-evaluation of another undressed sarsen in the locality, the massive Heel Stone at Stonehenge (Figure 7.41).

The standing stone known as the Heel Stone (Stone 96) is a well-known component of Stonehenge (see Figure 8.9). It is a large, undressed sarsen standing 4.88m above ground and estimated to weigh over 35 tonnes. Yet its morphology and location have not received a great deal of critical evaluation, apart from very specific discourses concerned with solar alignment and monument orientation (*e.g.* Newham 1972: 5; Burl 1976: 305). Curiously, it is the only sarsen outside the main Stonehenge enclosure ditch and, as if to compensate, it possesses an encircling ditch of its own (see Figures 4.6–4.10). If the Stonehenge ditch is considered to be a vital element of the monument, serving to wrap and contain the megalithic architecture, and demarcate qualitatively different spaces, it must be wondered why the Heel Stone was not positioned within its confines.

Moreover, in direct contrast to the other sarsens at Stonehenge, which have all been modified and dressed (with the probable exception of one of the Station Stones [Stone 91]; Abbott and Anderson-Whymark 2012: 24), why is the Heel Stone in its natural, amorphous state? Burl (2006: 96) provides one solution in suggesting that the Heel Stone preceded Stonehenge as an early standing stone. This is an interesting idea but it is suggested here that the biography of the Heel Stone involves a more complex narrative.

In 1979, Mike Pitts conducted a rescue excavation adjacent to the Heel Stone along the verge of the grassed-over A344. Although the excavation trench was narrow, an unexpected discovery was made when an unknown stone socket (Stonehole 97) was exposed (see Figure 4.4). Initially, it was considered to have held a missing stone that was paired with the Heel Stone (Pitts 1982: 83–6). Later it was wondered whether the stonehole once held the Heel Stone itself, with the massive sarsen having simply been moved to its current location at a later date (Cleal *et al.* 1995: 274).

Whilst a definite interpretation of the archaeological features constituting the stone socket was presented by Pitts (1982: 82–6), the evidence is far from straightforward. For instance, the impression of the posited Stone 97 was clearly identified, but only when the fill of a much larger, elongated hollow had been removed (*ibid.*: figs 5, 7). The exact dimensions of this larger hollow were difficult to establish because it ran out of the narrow trench on either side. However, Pitts (*ibid.*: 82) argued convincingly that it was at least 5m in length, because another portion of it had been uncovered in a trench previously excavated by Atkinson, Piggott and Stone in 1956, who had misidentified it as part of the Heel Stone ramp (Atkinson 1979: 203; Cleal *et al.* 1995, fig. 157). The impression of the absent Stone 97 was observed at the base of the hollow, where remnants of *in situ* and displaced packing materials were present. Interestingly, at the base of the stone socket, preceding the erection of the stone, were two small holes interpreted as possible postholes (Pitts 1982: 87).

In the light of the results obtained from the excavation of the Cuckoo Stone, a reassessment of the Heel Stone is possible. Drawing on evidence from Stone II on Overton Down (Bowen and Smith 1977: 193–5), and on discussions with Mike Pitts, the rather confusing features and deposits encountered beside the Heel Stone in 1979 were reassessed (see also Pitts 2008: 15). Since neither end of the elongated pit or hollow in which Stone 97 was erected was discovered by either Pitts or Atkinson in their separate trenches, we can safely assume that it measures well over 5m in length. A lateral dimension of the irregular hollow can only be estimated at *c.* 1.75m, since its western edge was obliterated by the cutting of the later Heel Stone ditch. In having a depth of a metre or less, the hollow was also relatively shallow.

This long, shallow, irregular hollow has been interpreted as a natural depression in the chalk which once contained a large recumbent sarsen (Figure 7.42). A comparison of the dimensions of the hollow and the Heel Stone reveals a degree of correspondence, providing a possibility that it was actually this large stone, and not another unknown and hypothetical stone, which once rested here as a natural recumbent sarsen: 'Stone 97' and the Heel Stone could be argued to be the same stone. Given the magnitude of the Heel Stone, it could easily have constituted the largest natural sarsen in the locality.

The subsequent treatment of this large sarsen is suggested to mirror that of the Cuckoo Stone. Initially it could have been dug out and dragged from its natural recumbent position, leaving a substantial extraction hollow (Pitts 1982: fig. 5). Pitts discovered three parallel grooves, running towards the edge of the hollow, which he interpreted as 'casts left by the decay of wooden rods, possibly used to manipulate the stone during erection or removal' (*ibid.*: 87, fig. 7). These features could be considered to relate to cuts made in the chalk to enable timbers to be employed in levering and manipulating the *c.* 35 tonne stone from its resting place.

Subsequently, at least one timber post was erected in the stone hollow, either decaying *in situ* or later being removed, echoing the timber post dug into the Cuckoo Stone's hollow before the stone was erected. Finally, the massive sarsen was erected in a vertical position, and packed around with chalk rubble. At a later date, 'Stone 97' was removed from this position and relocated as the Heel Stone *c.* 4m to the east.

This interpretation can, however, be called into question by recent portable X-ray fluorescence (PXRF) analysis of the chemistry of Stonehenge's sarsens which reveals that the bulk of Stonehenge's sarsen stones, including the Heel Stone, share a similar chemistry, suggesting that they are from a similar location (David Nash pers. comm.) which is more likely to be West Woods than the Marlborough Downs or Salisbury Plain. Thus the geological evidence may refute the hypothesis that the Heel Stone derives from the immediate vicinity of Stonehenge.

For Burl (2006: 96), it was the erection of the Heel Stone as an early standing stone which directly influenced the positioning of Stonehenge itself. However, as we shall see in the following chapter, there were other extraordinary features that also contributed to the choice of location for

Stonehenge. It is possible that the Heel Stone once stood further to the west. Furthermore, if the Heel Stone was brought here in Stage 1 and erected in Stonehole 97, the magnitude of this immense natural sarsen may well have always overshadowed other sarsen stones in the locality, including both the Tor Stone and Cuckoo Stone.

In conclusion, the extraction of the recumbent Cuckoo Stone and Tor Stone from their resting places and erecting them in a vertical position would have had immense ontological implications (see also Chapter 6). These events would not only have constituted a *rite of passage* for the stone – and for those undertaking the labour (see Richards 2013: 143–7) – but also visually altered the builders' world. In this way, the erection of stones cannot have been purely to increase their visual impact (although this would undoubtedly be the case), but would have altered their ontological status: parallels between the human posture and vertical stones cannot have been missed or ignored. Certainly, in the context of this special landscape, the raising of the Cuckoo Stone and possibly the Tor Stone (although this is undated) was part of a process of lithicisation that would reach its zenith by the mid-third millennium cal BC with the spectacular display of megalithic architecture and material vibrancy that is Stonehenge.

Chapter 8

The Stonehenge Avenue

M. Parker Pearson, R. Pullen, D. Robinson and A. Teather*

8.1. Research background and objectives

M. Parker Pearson

The Stonehenge Avenue was first recorded by John Aubrey and William Stukeley, in the seventeenth and eighteenth centuries. It runs between the northeast entrance of Stonehenge and the River Avon. Taking Stonehenge as the nominal starting point of the Avenue, its first 500m downhill from Stonehenge are aligned on the midsummer solstice sunrise. Thereafter the Avenue turns eastwards at its 'elbow', crosses the dry valley of Stonehenge Bottom and runs uphill onto King Barrow ridge before following the gentlest gradient downhill southeastwards towards the river (Figure 8.1).

The Avenue consists of two parallel ditches, each about 1.50m wide and 0.80m deep, spaced about 21m apart and running for 2.8km. Prior to the SRP investigations, the location of the Avenue's eastern terminal was unknown. That it actually terminated at West Amesbury henge and Bluestonehenge beside the river was only demonstrated in 2009 (see Chapter 5).

Unlike the Greater Cursus, the Stonehenge Avenue has an open end (where it meets the northeast entrance of Stonehenge). Its banks were on the inside of the ditches, on the evidence of where they survive, where their 'bank shadow' (raised areas of protected chalk under a subsequently eroded bank) survives, and where tip lines in the ditches indicate the position of the bank (Cleal *et al.* 1995: 304–7). Only in one excavated trench was there evidence that the Avenue might have also had an external bank; this is Cutting 83, excavated in 1968 along the northern edge of the now-defunct A344 (Cleal *et al.* 1995: 315–17, fig. 180).

Before the work of the SRP, at least 15 trenches had been excavated across different sections of the Avenue since the time of William Hawley in the 1920s, four of them within 50m of the Avenue's terminal at Stonehenge (Cleal *et al.* 1995: plan 3). Finds from the ditch fills have been relatively few and consist mostly of worked flints, animal bones and antler picks. Although radiocarbon dates were obtained previously from samples of antler and bone, it was only during the re-dating programme of the 1990s that the chronology of the Avenue's use and construction could be established with any confidence (Cleal *et al.* 1995: 533–4). Based on three dates from ditch fills close to Stonehenge and a fourth east of the elbow, the early fills of the ditches accumulated in the second half of the third millennium BC. Thus the Avenue's construction most likely dates to the Chalcolithic period and probably occurred within Stonehenge's Stage 3, or even Stage 2.

Evidence for re-cutting of the ditches has been recorded at three locations along the length of the Avenue, towards both its east and west ends (Cleal *et al.* 1995: 307). This introduces difficulties in establishing construction dates since it can be difficult to identify re-

*** With contributions by:**
M. Allen, O. Bayer, C. Bronk Ramsey, B. Chan, G. Cook, C.A.I. French, N. Linford, P.D. Marshall, D. Mitcham, A. Payne, C. Ruggles, E. Simmons, C. Steele and K. Welham

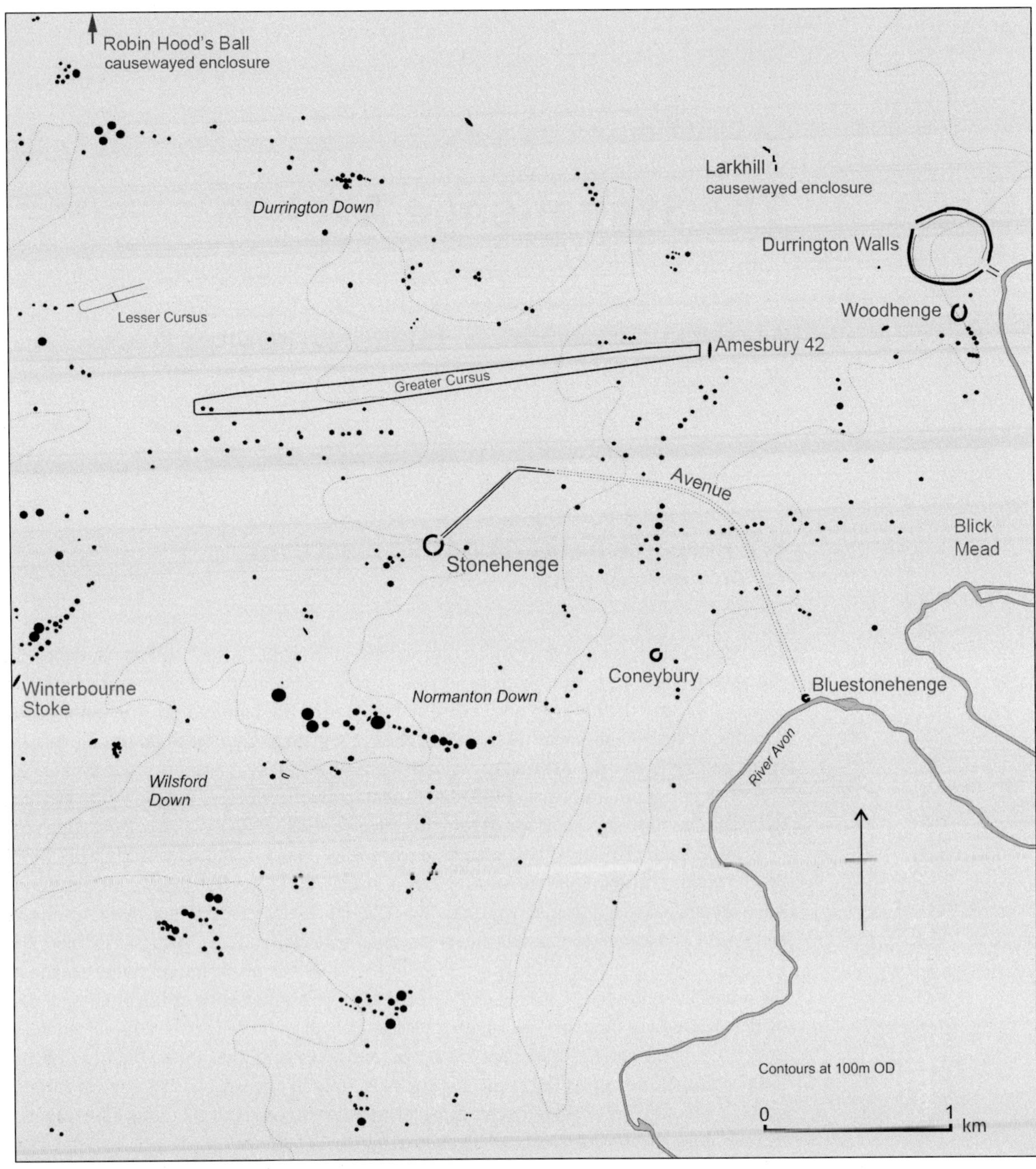

Figure 8.1. The Stonehenge prehistoric landscape, showing the route of the Stonehenge Avenue

cutting of ditches when fill has been removed cleanly from a rock-cut feature such as the Avenue ditches. The problem is compounded by the limited abilities and imprecise records of some of the early excavators, and by the limited lengths of ditch excavated at any one time. Although the earliest date for the Avenue's construction of 2580–2280 cal BC at 95% confidence (OxA-4884; 3935±50 BP; Table 8.1) comes from an antler pick on the bottom of the ditch (in the terminal of the northern ditch at the entrance to Stonehenge), it was excavated in 1923 by William Hawley whose sparse records provide no way of knowing whether it lay within primary fill or within the bottom of a re-cut.

One of the main reasons for re-excavating Richard Atkinson's trenches across the Avenue, one of them *c.* 50m from Stonehenge (Trench 45) and the others at the Avenue elbow, was to enhance the records he had made. In particular, Trench 45 was excavated to investigate the linear gullies that he recorded in his trench (Cutting 48 [C48]). These gullies were potentially on the same solstitial orientation – southwest–northeast – as the Avenue, raising questions about whether they were humanly created or were natural. Mike Allen had pronounced them to be periglacial features, on the basis of Atkinson's 1956 section drawing and photograph (Cleal *et al.* 1995: 311) but we wanted to know more about them and their relationship to the Avenue.

The gullies in C48, re-excavated in 2008, are indeed periglacial features and take the form of fissures or gullies filled with fine silt produced from soliflucted chalk formed under the tundra conditions of a previous Ice Age (see Allen and French, below). They are sometimes referred to as 'stripes' and are frost-heave cryoturbation features. On the Wiltshire chalk, these cryoturbation structures are found on slopes of less than 5° (Williams 1973: 26–7). Those recorded within Atkinson's trench (C48) are unusually wide and deep, probably as the result of periglacial channelling of water between two parallel chalk ridges of natural origin.

The eastern end of the Avenue, at the River Avon, is described in Chapter 5 but other features associated with the Avenue are also discussed in this chapter:

- The Stonehenge end of the Avenue;
- the Avenue bend or elbow;
- a natural knoll known as Newall's Mound, at the Avenue bend;
- the Gate Ditch, a linear feature close to and north of the Avenue bend, thought to date to the Bronze Age (previously excavated by Atkinson);
- the Oblique Ditch, a linear feature cutting the Avenue at the bend, thought to be of no great antiquity (previously excavated by Atkinson);
- a postulated northern 'branch' of the Avenue running from its elbow towards the eastern end of the Greater Cursus (identified as an avenue by Stukeley but later dismissed);
- the possible rows of standing stones that Stukeley thought sat upon the Avenue banks (see the chapter's conclusion for details).

8.1.1. Geophysical surveys

K. Welham, C. Steele, N. Linford and A. Payne

Geophysical surveys of the Stonehenge Avenue were undertaken between 2007 and 2009. Earth resistance survey covered the area between the A344 (now decommissioned and grassed-over) and the Avenue bend and magnetometry survey extended from the road to 60m southwest of the bend (Figures 8.2–8.3). These surveys were carried out in order to explore:

- the possibility that the Avenue was constructed in two phases;
- the nature of the Gate Ditch;
- any features in the interior of the Avenue, between its banks.

Earth resistance survey was carried out using Geoscan RM15-D earth resistance meters in the 0.50m twin electrode configuration. Readings were taken at 1m intervals along north–south traverses spaced 1m apart over 20m grids. Magnetometer survey was undertaken with Bartington Grad601 fluxgate gradiometers. Readings were recorded at 0.25m intervals along north–south traverses spaced 1m apart using the 200 nTm^{-1} range setting of the magnetometer over 30m grids. The data were affected by modern disturbance, differential land use, and both modern and relict field boundaries. The earth resistance data were greatly affected by changes to the underlying geology in this area: a band of Icknield soils can be seen on the plot as an amorphous area of high resistance crossing the northeast of the survey (Figure 8.2). This change in geology caused a reversal in the geophysical response for some features as a result of changes in soil moisture.

The ditches of the Avenue are clearly visible in both datasets (R1/M1) and it can be seen that the magnetic response of the ditches increases towards the Avenue bend (Figure 8.3). This has been identified in other magnetic surveys of the monument (Cleal *et al.* 1995; David and Payne 1997; Darvill *et al.* 2013; Gaffney *et al.* 2012) and suggests better survival of *in situ* deposits further from Stonehenge. In the earth resistance data, the response of the Avenue ditches at the bend is somewhat confused and intermittent due to the underlying geology, although the ditches have been shown in other magnetometry surveys to be complete.

In the magnetometry data there is an area of disturbance (M2) north of the former A344 that represents one of Richard Atkinson's 1956 excavation trenches across the Avenue (trench C48; Cleal *et al.* 1995: 309–11, plan 3). The banks of the Avenue may have been detected here (R2) but are most noticeable to the north of Atkinson's trench (M3). Within the bounds of the Avenue are a number of parallel linear features (R3/M4), with a particularly strong response in the magnetometry data near to the Avenue bend. These were shown during excavation to be indicative of cart-ruts.

There is a general northeast–southwest linear trend in both datasets across the entirety of the survey area, which represents the presence of periglacial stripes. These were revealed during the excavation of Trench 45 (see below), and were also identified in Trench 44 (the stone-dressing area), to the west of the Avenue (see Chapter 6); such linear features, probably also periglacial stripes, are also present in other surveys of the area. Whilst they are commonly found on chalklands, only within the Avenue do they appear to be unusually wide and deep (see Allen and French, below).

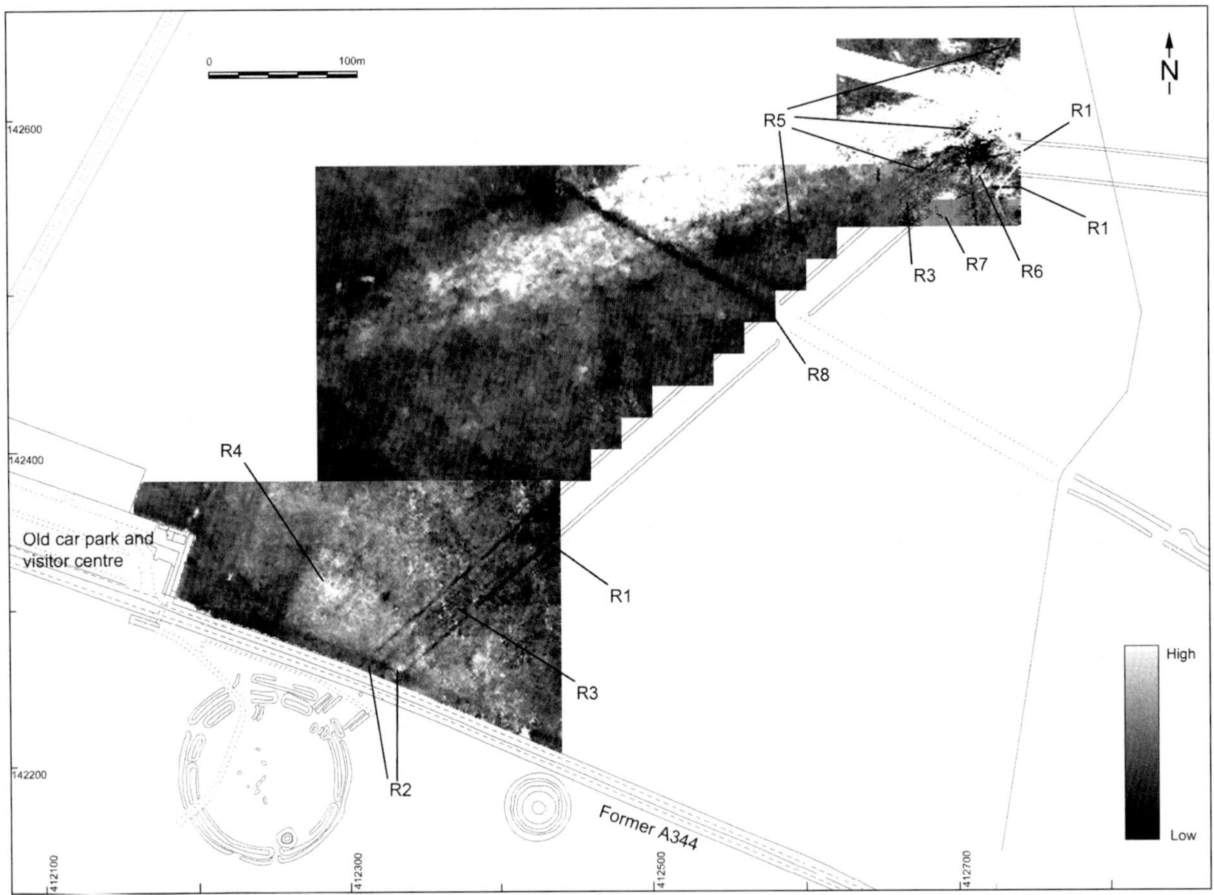

Figure 8.2. Earth resistance survey of the Avenue

Extending west from the centre of the Avenue, adjacent to the old A344, is a weak high resistance anomaly (R4) covering an area of approximately 75m × 60m. This was revealed during excavation of Trench 44 to represent a large spread of sarsen flakes (see Chapter 6).

The Gate Ditch (R5/M5) appears most clearly in the magnetometry data, and its southern terminal and possible entrance gap can be seen. The Gate Ditch is more ephemeral in the earth resistance data, although it can be seen near the Avenue bend. The Oblique Ditch (R6) and the natural knoll of Newall's Mound (R7) were also detected in the earth resistance data. A feature already known from historical records to be an eighteenth-century road (R8/M6) that crosses the Avenue was also detected.

8.2. The Stonehenge Avenue at Stonehenge (Trench 45)

M. Parker Pearson and R. Pullen

In 2008, one of Richard Atkinson's trenches (C48; Cleal *et al.* 1995: 309–11, plan 3) was re-excavated as SRP Trench 45, close to the Heel Stone and north of the A344 road (shown in Figure 8.55). Atkinson's trench cut northwest–southeast across the Stonehenge Avenue, to take in both outer ditches and their banks. Trench 45 was located to re-open the area excavated by Atkinson and to extend 2m southwestwards beyond the edge of Atkinson's trench (see Figure 6.8). The 2008 excavations investigated the Avenue's ditches and banks as well as various features within the Avenue, including two areas of buried land surface.

The assemblage of sarsen recovered from Trench 45 is reported in Chapter 6, alongside the sarsen from the stone-dressing area in adjacent Trench 44. Other material from Trench 45 appears in this chapter.

8.2.1. Research aims and objectives

The Avenue sequence

The Avenue's sequence was divided by Cleal *et al.* (1995) into Phases 3a, 3b and 3c, broadly contemporary with Stage 2 of construction within the centre of Stonehenge (Stage 2 in the new phasing being equivalent to Phase 3 in the old phasing; see Chapters 4–5 for the dates of the Stages). Although Cleal *et al.* (1995: 319) considered that the Avenue was constructed

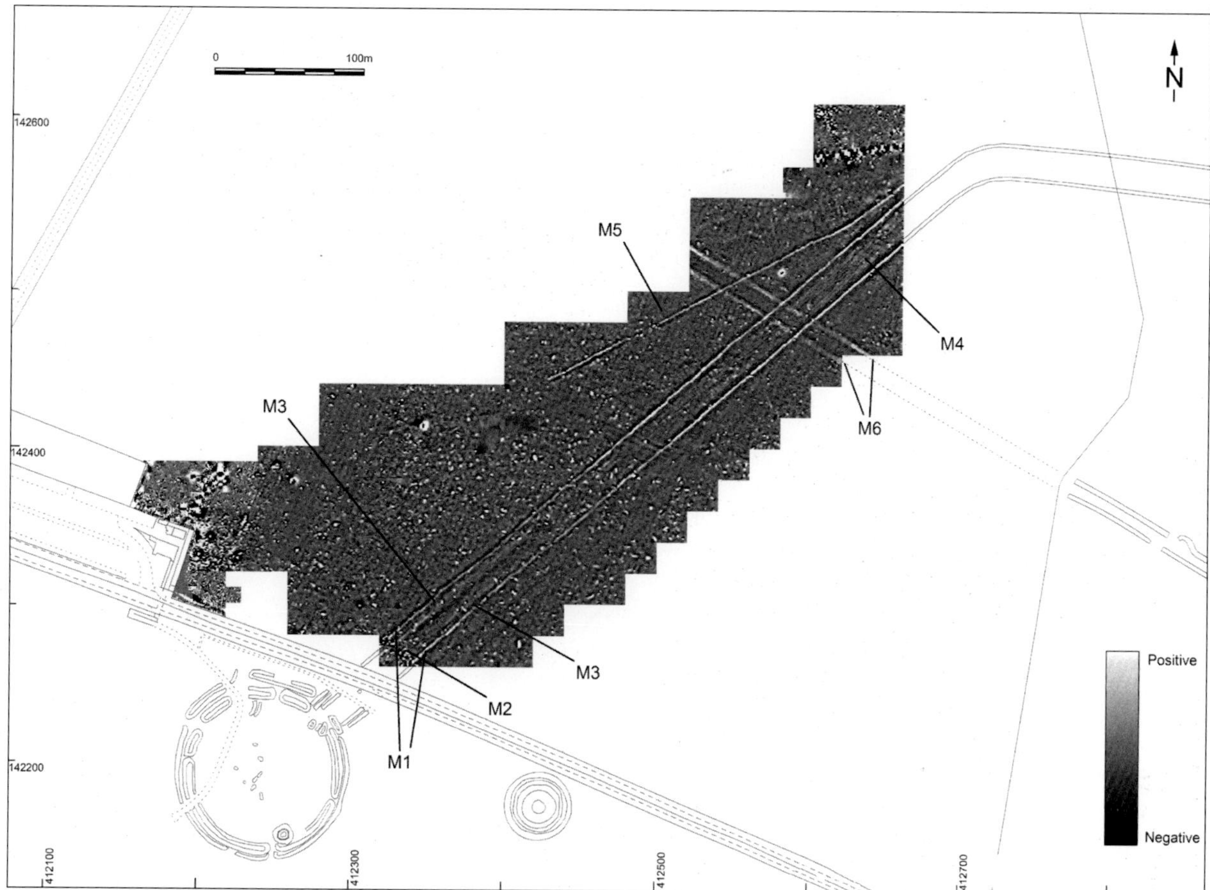

Figure 8.3. Magnetometry survey of the Avenue

as a single build, Darvill (2005: 48) suggested that it was built in two stages, with the section from the elbow to the riverside being added later. A more recent review suggested that the Avenue ditch was re-cut more thoroughly and extensively than previously thought, with the Avenue bank and ditch being first constructed around the time that the sarsens were erected at Stonehenge, *i.e.* Stage 2 (Parker Pearson *et al.* 2007). A research aim of the 2008 excavations by the SRP was to clarify the construction sequence of the banks and ditches and obtain new radiocarbon dates.

The 'periglacial stripes' within the Stonehenge Avenue

In 1956, Richard Atkinson excavated a 2m-wide × 26m-long trench (C48) across the Stonehenge Avenue, about 33m northeast of the Heel Stone (Cleal *et al.* 1995: 309–11). He recorded seven parallel features within the Avenue, running northeast–southwest, the outer ones of which were sealed beneath the Avenue's banks. These features were up to 0.50m deep and appear to have run on the same alignment as the Avenue, on its solstitial axis. On the basis of Atkinson's photograph and advised by Mike Allen, Rebecca Montague later interpreted these linear features cut into the chalk bedrock as periglacial stripes (Cleal *et al.* 1995: 312, fig. 178).

Geophysical surveys along this length of the Avenue in 1988, 1990, 2007 and 2008 picked out up to seven parallel linear anomalies contained within the space between the Avenue's parallel ditches, running along the 500m length of the Avenue from outside Stonehenge to its bend or elbow (*e.g.* Payne in Cleal *et al.* 1995: fig. 265). The 2007 and 2008 resistivity and magnetometry surveys demonstrated that these anomalies lie both within the Avenue and outside it, especially to its south (Figures 8.2–8.3). At the elbow they appear to stop together, in a straight line perpendicular to their long axis. The aim of the 2008 excavations was to verify whether the enigmatic features in trench C48 were humanly formed or natural, and to ascertain whether the linear anomalies near the elbow were the same features as those visible in Atkinson's excavation.

The relationship between the stone-dressing area and the Stonehenge Avenue

The results of earth resistance survey in 2008 indicated that there is a large spread of sarsen flakes immediately west of the start of the Stonehenge Avenue and north of the A344. This is visible on the earth resistance plot as an area of high resistance measuring approximately 75m east–west × 60m north–south (see Chapter 6).

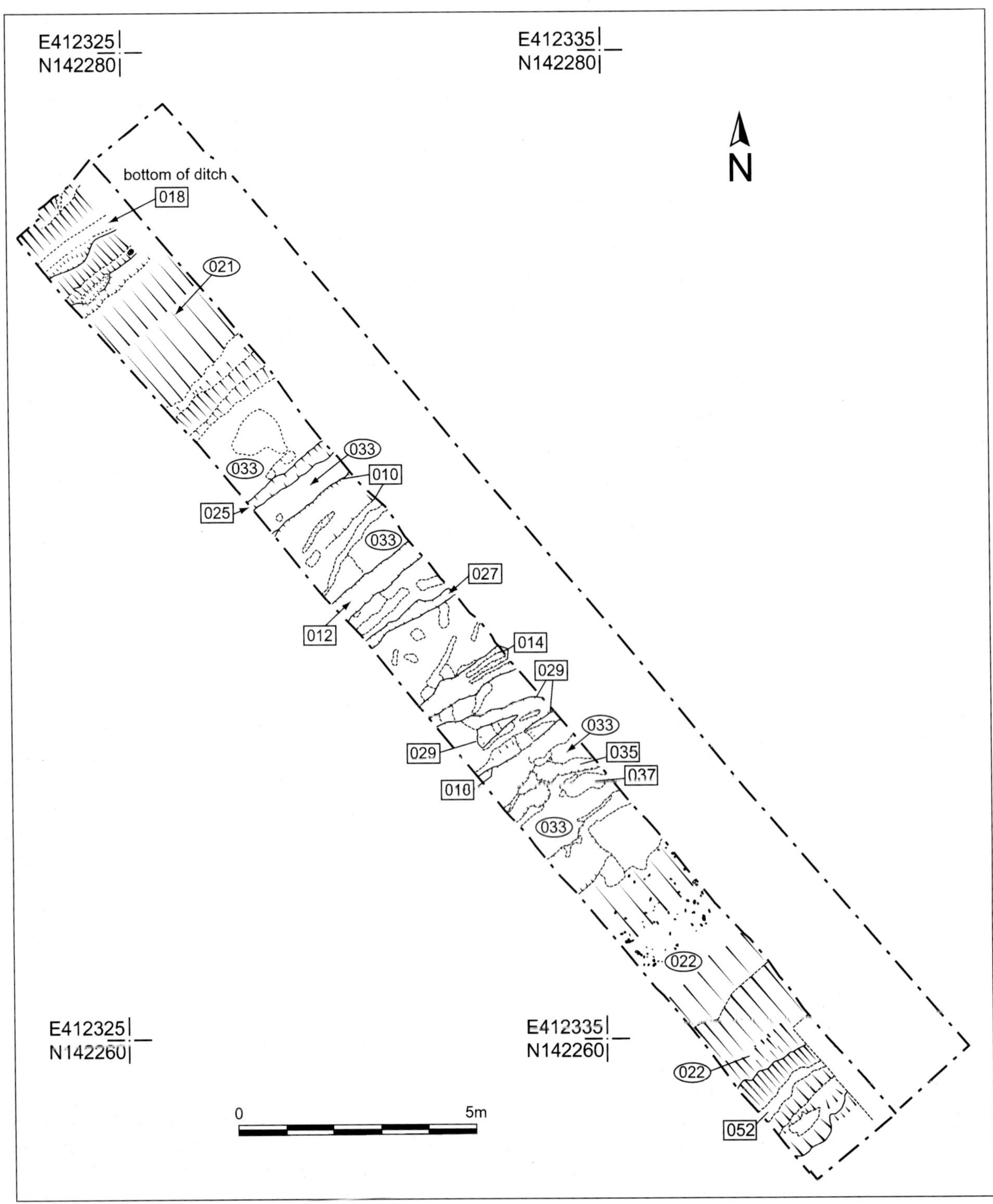

Figure 8.4. Plan of Trench 45 across the Stonehenge Avenue, showing the wheel-ruts within the trench's southwestern half; none survived within Atkinson's trench (the northeastern half)

This area extends to within the western part of the Stonehenge Avenue, east of the Avenue's western ditch. If remnants of this sarsen scatter could be detected beneath the Avenue bank, the stratigraphic relationship of the sarsen-dressing to the construction of the Avenue would be established.

The Avenue's flint surface

In 1923 William Hawley noted that the Avenue had a flint surface leading from the Heel Stone as far as the sarsen circle of Stonehenge (Hawley's diary entries for 24/5/23, 30/5/23 and 27/6/23). No such surface was recognised by Atkinson or other excavators along the Avenue. Excavations at the Stonehenge end of the Avenue in 2008 would establish whether this flint surface did or did not continue north of the Heel Stone.

Further research questions

The SRP proposed two further research questions for investigation: whether there was a pre-solstitial line of stoneholes (including Stoneholes B, C and 97) running northeastwards out of the entrance of Stonehenge (see Figure 7.42); and whether the Avenue banks were lined with stoneholes, as Stukeley and Gale concluded in 1719 (see Figure 8.52). However, the restrictions imposed by the National Trust and English Heritage on trench size prevented these questions from being addressed.

8.2.2. The excavation

At the location of SRP Trench 45, the Avenue is 23.50m wide, measured from the outer edges of each ditch. The trench was positioned to run northwest–southeast, extending from outside the western bank and ditch, crossing the interior of the Avenue, and terminating beyond the eastern bank and ditch.

Richard Atkinson's 1956 trench C48 was re-opened by hand and its width was doubled by extending 2m towards the southwest, again dug by hand, creating a trench 4m wide in total and 26m long (Figures 8.4–8.14). This provided an appropriately large area of periglacial stripes to be examined to determine their precise character. After removal of backfill and of turf and topsoil across the entire trench, a half-metre wide baulk was left between Atkinson's trench and the new extension, visible in Figures 8.7 and 8.9. This left untouched an area of the Avenue banks, so that the banks could be reconstructed to their current height when backfilling the excavation trench. Thus the area excavated in Trench 45 was effectively 1.50m wide and 26m long.

Atkinson's trench (SRP context 023) was at least 1m south of the location in which it was mapped and was also skewed on a slightly different axis to its published plan. As a result, the area initially de-turfed in 2008 did not fully correspond with that of the 1956 trench. The alignment of Trench 45 was adjusted, but the initial de-turfing created a slightly butterfly-shaped trench plan; the de-turfed area outside Atkinson's trench in the northeast was left unexcavated (see Figure 8.9).

All topsoil (001 and 002) and 1956 backfill (003) was sieved through a 10mm mesh. There were many pieces of worked flint, sarsen and bluestone in Atkinson's backfill (003), as well as a single sherd of Beaker pottery. Given that the re-opened area of trench C58 had been fully excavated in 1956, as expected no prehistoric deposits or features were encountered in this area of Trench 45 in 2008, and only one natural feature had not been fully excavated by Atkinson's team (tree-throw hole 040; see below). Removal of the topsoil and backfill from this strip of the 2008 trench therefore revealed immediately the periglacial stripes cutting into the bedrock. In contrast, the southwestern extension to the trench contained many cut features in its upper levels, in particular a series of cart-ruts, which were planned and excavated before being removed (Figure 8.4).

Thus, the plan of the entire trench after surface cleaning and removal of backfill (Figure 8.5) highlights the periglacial stripes in the Atkinson area, but shows the *wheel-ruts* (at a much higher stratigraphic level) in the southwestern extension. The reader should bear in mind that the cart-ruts are *not* equivalent to, or related to, the periglacial stripes and should refer to the sections (particularly Figure 8.12) and the stratigraphic matrix (Figure 8.21) to see the stratigraphic relationship of the cart-ruts to the periglacial stripes that lay beneath them.

The newly excavated area of Trench 45 (the extension to the southwest) was excavated in 1m × 1m squares to recover distributions of sarsen, flint and bluestone debris (Figure 8.6 and see Figures 6.20–6.25). Prehistoric features – notably the ditch fills, the bank matrix, buried soils beneath the banks and the one cut feature (pit 055/056) – were extensively sampled for flotation as well as sieved through a 10mm mesh. The buried soils beneath the banks and the fills of the cut feature were additionally sieved through a 5mm mesh, to ensure compatibility of finds retrieval with the stone-dressing surface (006) in Trench 44 (see Chapter 6). The fills of those features identified as wheel-ruts were sieved through a 10mm mesh.

Natural landforms and features

Periglacial stripes

The linear features excavated by Atkinson all turned out to be periglacial stripes, consisting of deep and wide fissures in the chalk bedrock (059), which were filled with clean, beige-coloured silt (058) covered by orange-brown loam (057). These were generally over 0.40m wide and 0.45m deep (Figures 8.5–8.9, 8.11–8.12), contrasting with the much smaller periglacial stripes running diagonally across Trench 44 (less than 0.20m wide and 0.10m deep), less than 50m to the northwest (see Chapter 6 and Figure 6.9).

The periglacial stripes identified within Atkinson's 1956 trench (C48) continued into the 2008 extension of

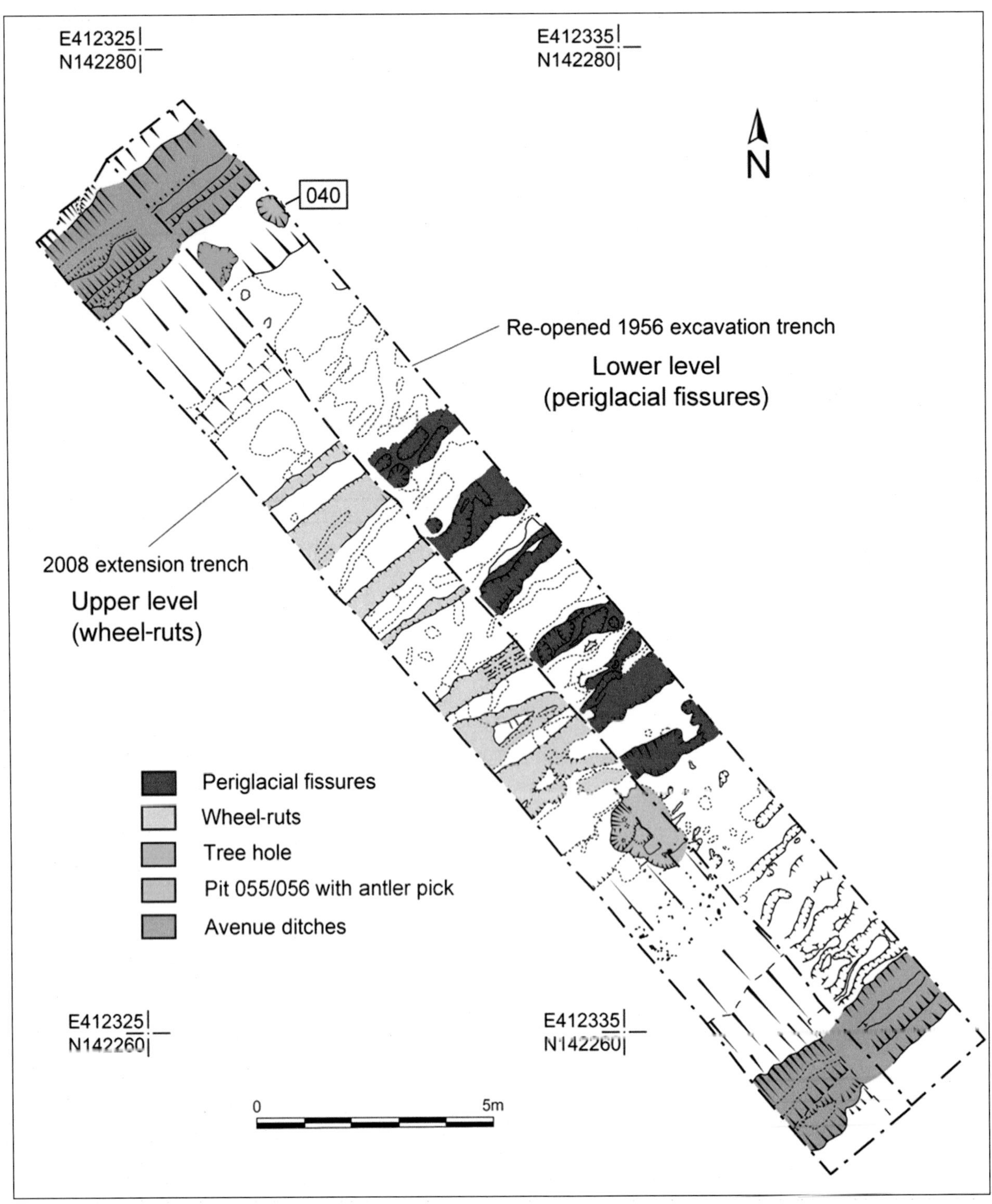

Figure 8.5. Interpretive plan of Trench 45 showing the wheel-ruts within the trench's southwestern half, and the periglacial fissures at a deeper level in the bottom of Atkinson's trench (the northeastern half)

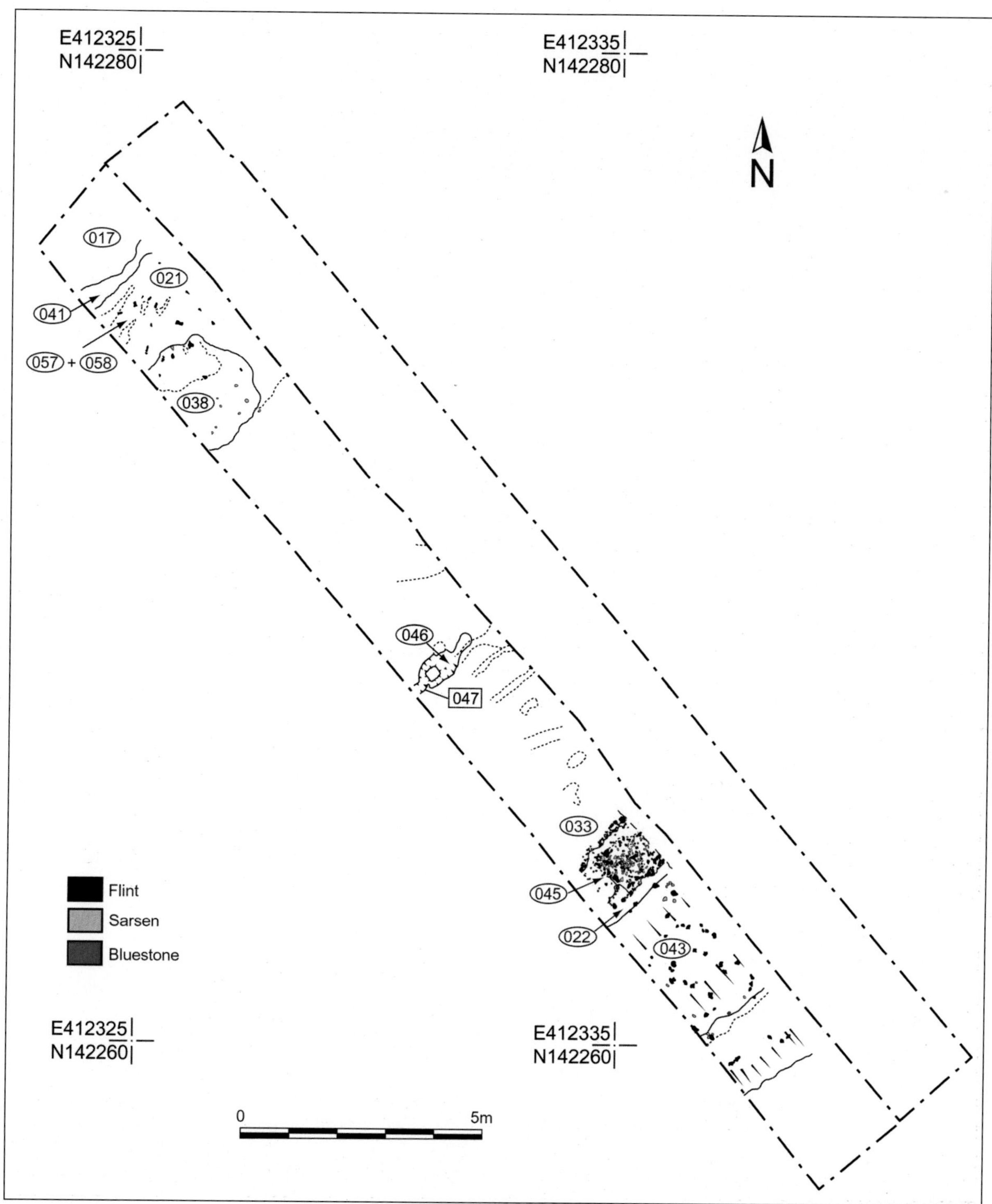

Figure 8.6. Plan of sarsen and flint debris and one of the bluestone fragments beneath the banks of the Avenue and their surroundings

Figure 8.7. Periglacial fissures within the centre of Trench 45; southwest is at the top of the photo

Trench 45. Their surfaces were recorded stratigraphically below the archaeological deposits (Figures 8.8, 8.11–8.12) but their fills were, in the main, left unexcavated. The same context numbering was used for these periglacial features throughout Trench 45 in both Atkinson's re-opened trench and in the SRP's extension of it. The periglacial fissures in the SRP extension continued their northeast–southwest direction, and were of similar dimensions as seen in Atkinson's trench. For the geomorphology of periglacial stripes, see Allen and French, below.

Chalk ridges

The uneven surface of the chalk – raised beneath the Avenue banks and lower in the area in between (Figure 8.13) – was initially thought to be the result of differential weathering, in which the chalk surface beneath the banks had been protected to a greater degree than outside them. However, it became clear that the raised chalk surfaces are far wider than the areas protected by bank material. These are natural, parallel ridges in the chalk, 5m wide. They are much wider than the human-made banks which were constructed on top of them, following the same alignment as these natural features, although those banks have been spread well beyond their original dimensions (likely to have been no more than 3m wide, given the relatively small size of the ditches from which their fill originated).

The significance of the natural chalk ridges, visible as earthworks in prehistory, and of the periglacial stripes, visible as parchmarks in dry conditions, is discussed fully in *The route of the Stonehenge Avenue*, below.

Tree-throw holes

Among the natural features dug out by Atkinson, a small tree hole (no context number) cut through the ancient land surface (033=053) within his south section beneath the western bank of the Avenue. He missed a larger tree-throw hole (040), 0.50m deep and up to 1.40m across, beneath the western edge of the same bank (021) against the north section (Figure 8.5); it was filled with grey-brown silt (044) beneath a yellow-brown silt (039), both sampled for mollusca and soil micromorphology (Figure 8.11). The only other natural disturbance within Trench 45 was an animal burrow (047 filled with 046) in the middle of the Avenue; this is undated and may well be relatively recent (Figure 8.6).

Linear hollows

Two linear hollows, 7m apart and running parallel northeast–southwest, were visible in the bedrock within Trench 45, on the inside edges of the two chalk ridges. One lies immediately west of pit 055/056 (see below) and the other is the large periglacial fissure immediately east of the western chalk ridge. They are below the depth of the Avenue's wheel-ruts and they coincide with two lines of periglacial fissures in Trench 45.

Outside Trench 45, 6m–9m south of the Avenue's southern ditch, a northeast–southwest aligned linear hollow runs parallel with the Avenue (marked in green in Figure 8.54, south of the chalk ridges marked in blue). It is also visible on the magnetometry plot, as is a second linear feature, running for the same length and almost parallel *c.* 10m to its southeast (Figure 8.3). Although not excavated, these can be interpreted as periglacial fissures.

Pre-Avenue activity

Above the ancient land surface (033=053), two areas of preserved buried soils survive, one (038) beneath the western bank of the Avenue (also known as the northern bank) and the other (043) beneath the eastern bank (also known as the southern bank) (Figures 8.6, 8.10–8.12). The two patches of buried soil were composed of a light yellow-brown silt with inclusions of very small chalk lumps and broken flint. The buried soils were 0.05m–0.13m thick and contained few inclusions other than small flakes of sarsen and occasional bluestone (Figure 8.15). To maximise recovery of these flakes and any other micro-debris, the buried soil was excavated and floated in 0.50m × 0.50m squares (see Figure 6.23).

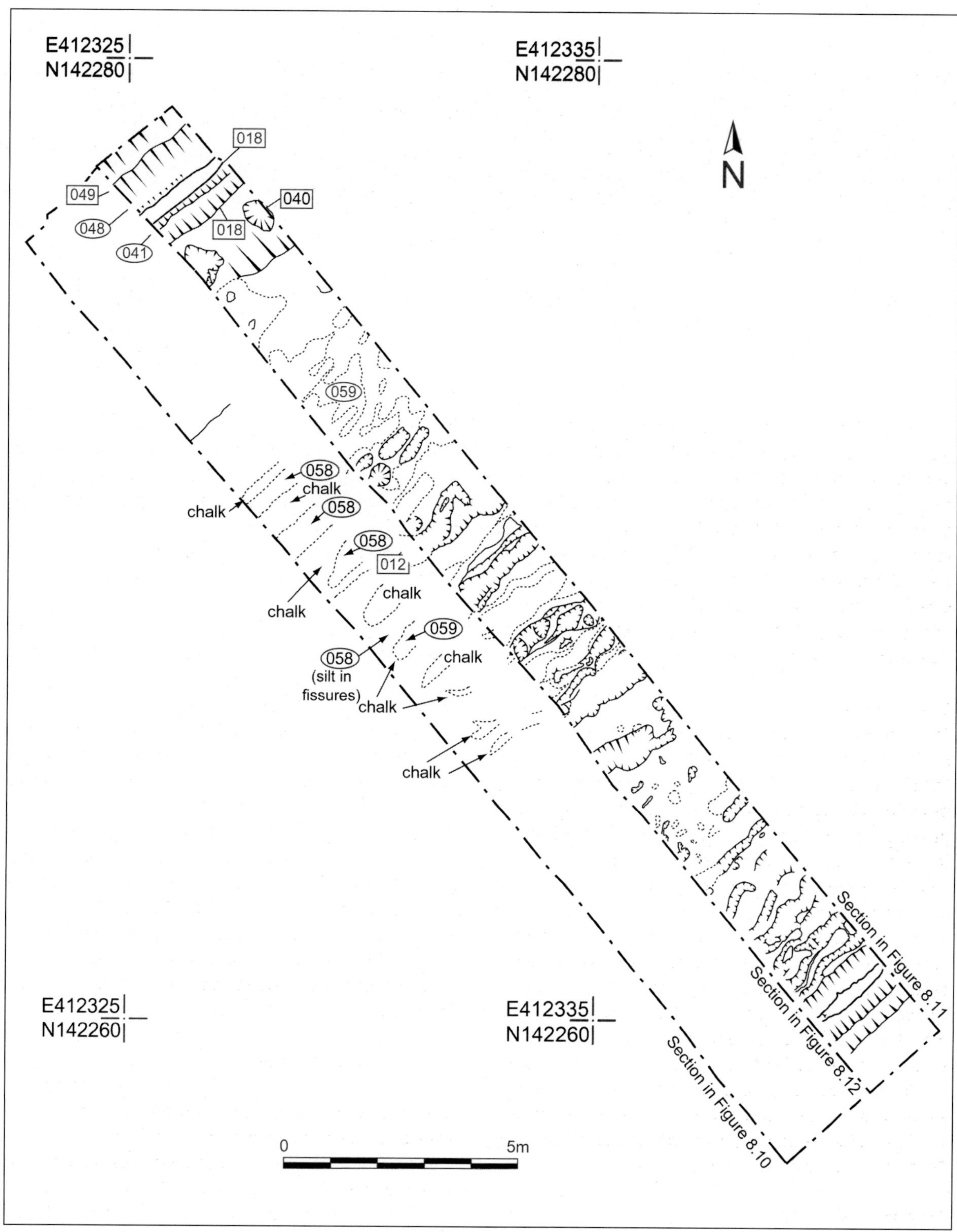

Figure 8.8. Plan of periglacial fissures within Trench 45, including those recorded in 2008 (as well as those already excavated by Atkinson)

Figure 8.9. Trench 45, viewed from the northeast

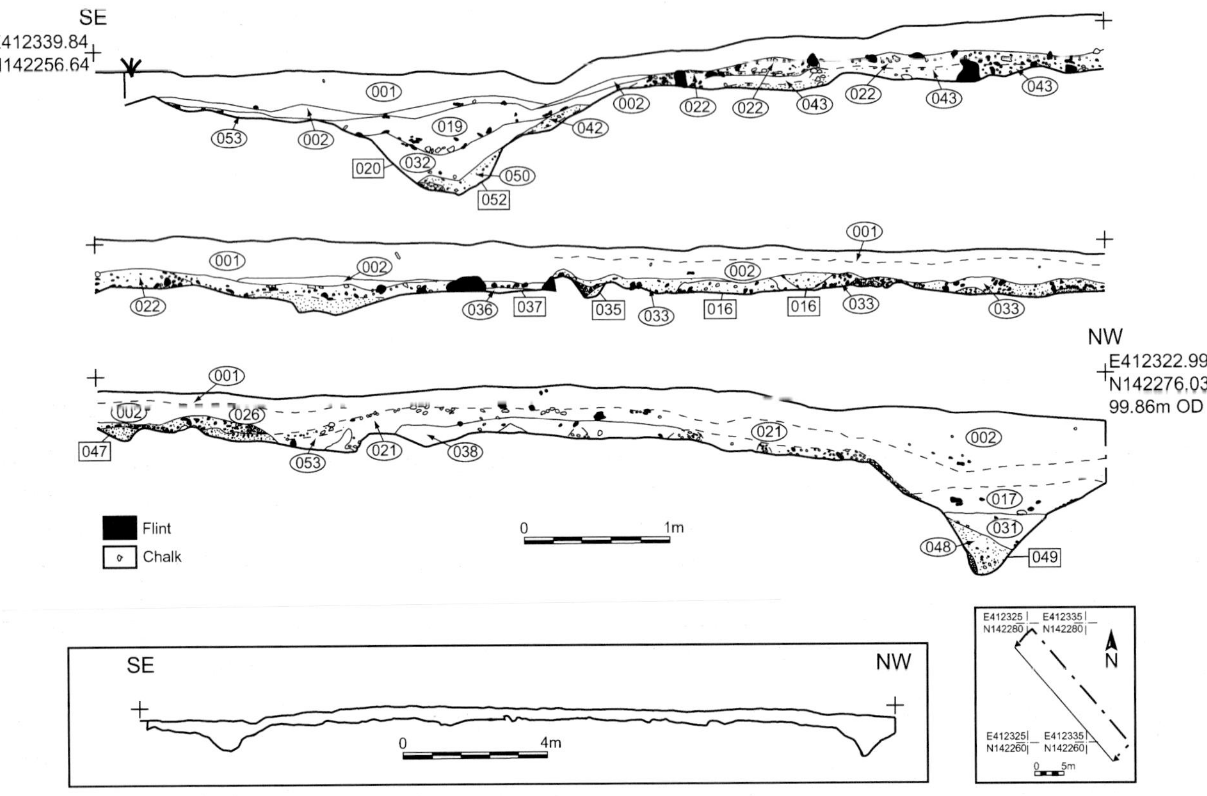

Figure 8.10. Section drawing of the northeast-facing section in Trench 45

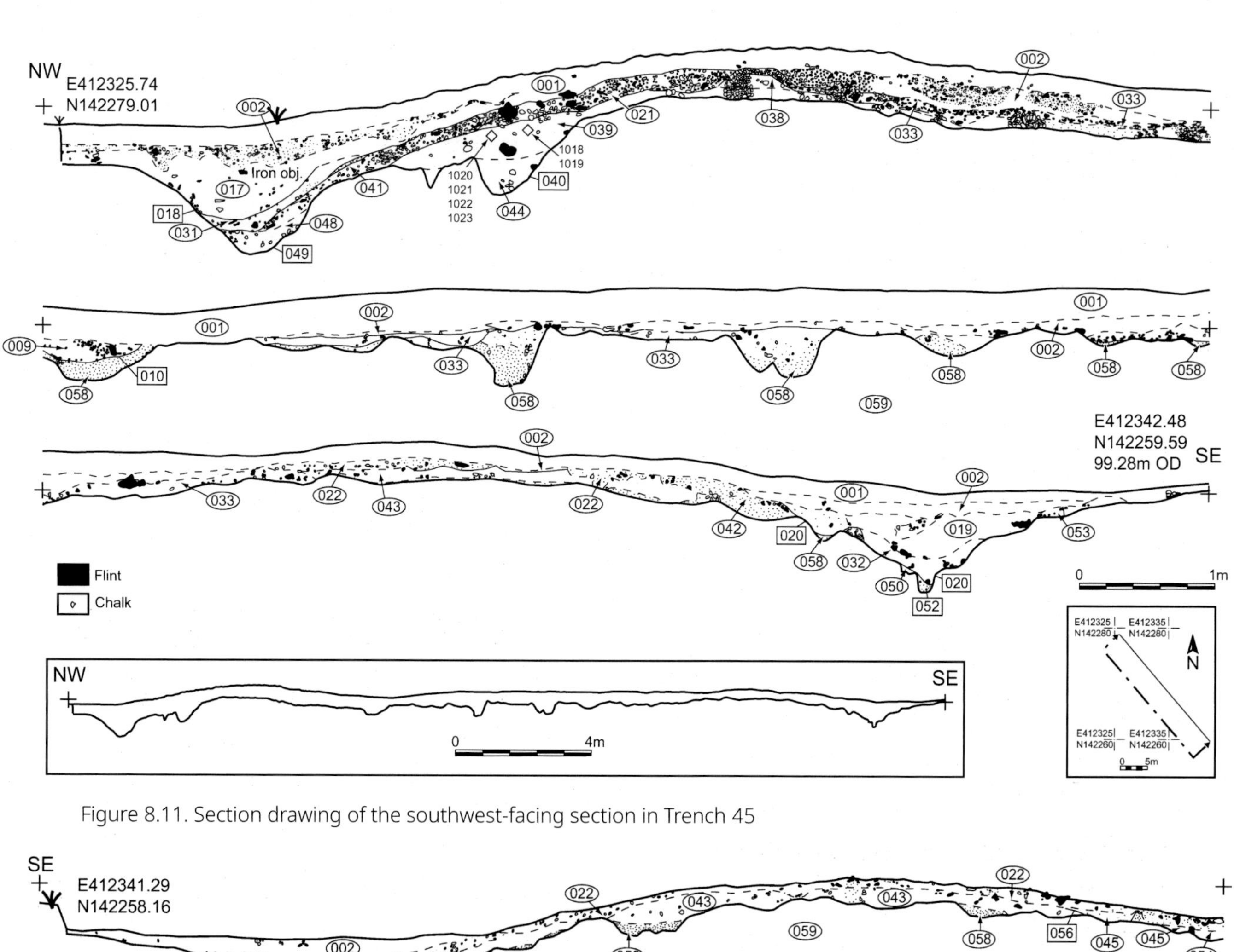

Figure 8.11. Section drawing of the southwest-facing section in Trench 45

Figure 8.12. Central baulk section of Trench 45, northeast-facing, with topsoil removed

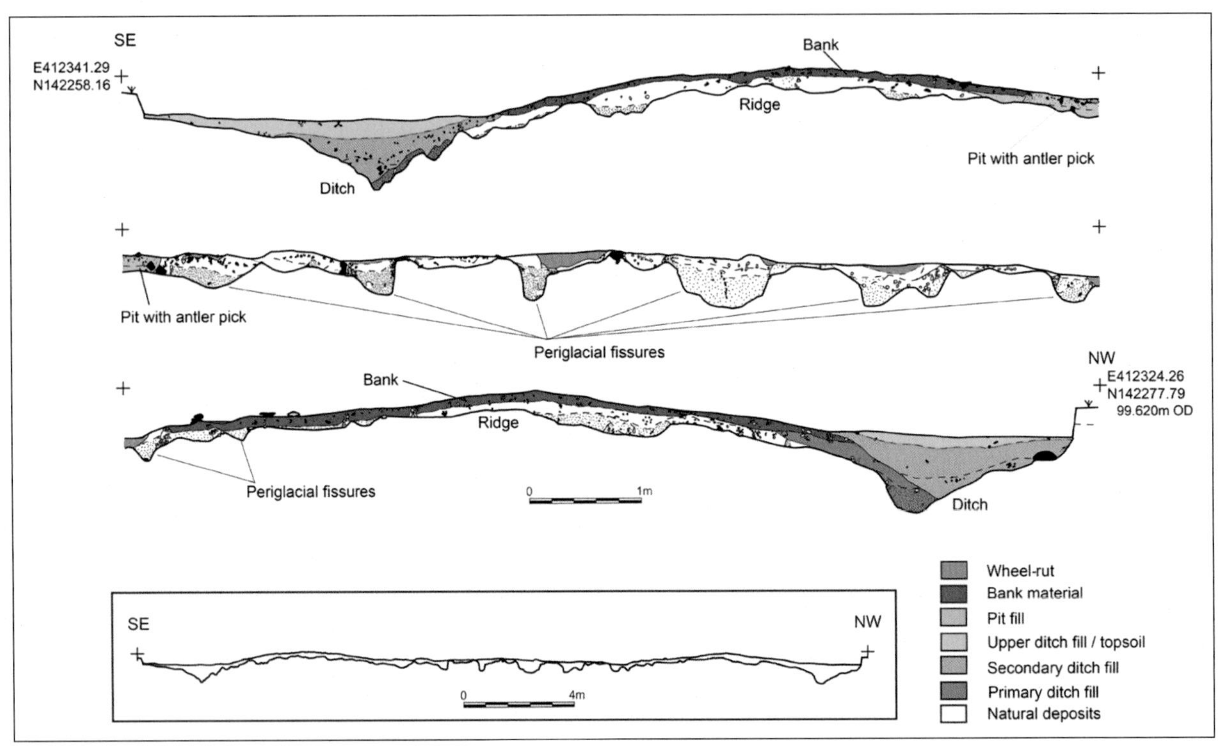

Figure 8.13. Central baulk section of Trench 45, northeast-facing, with interpretation

Figure 8.14. Trench 45, viewed from the northeast, showing periglacial fissures

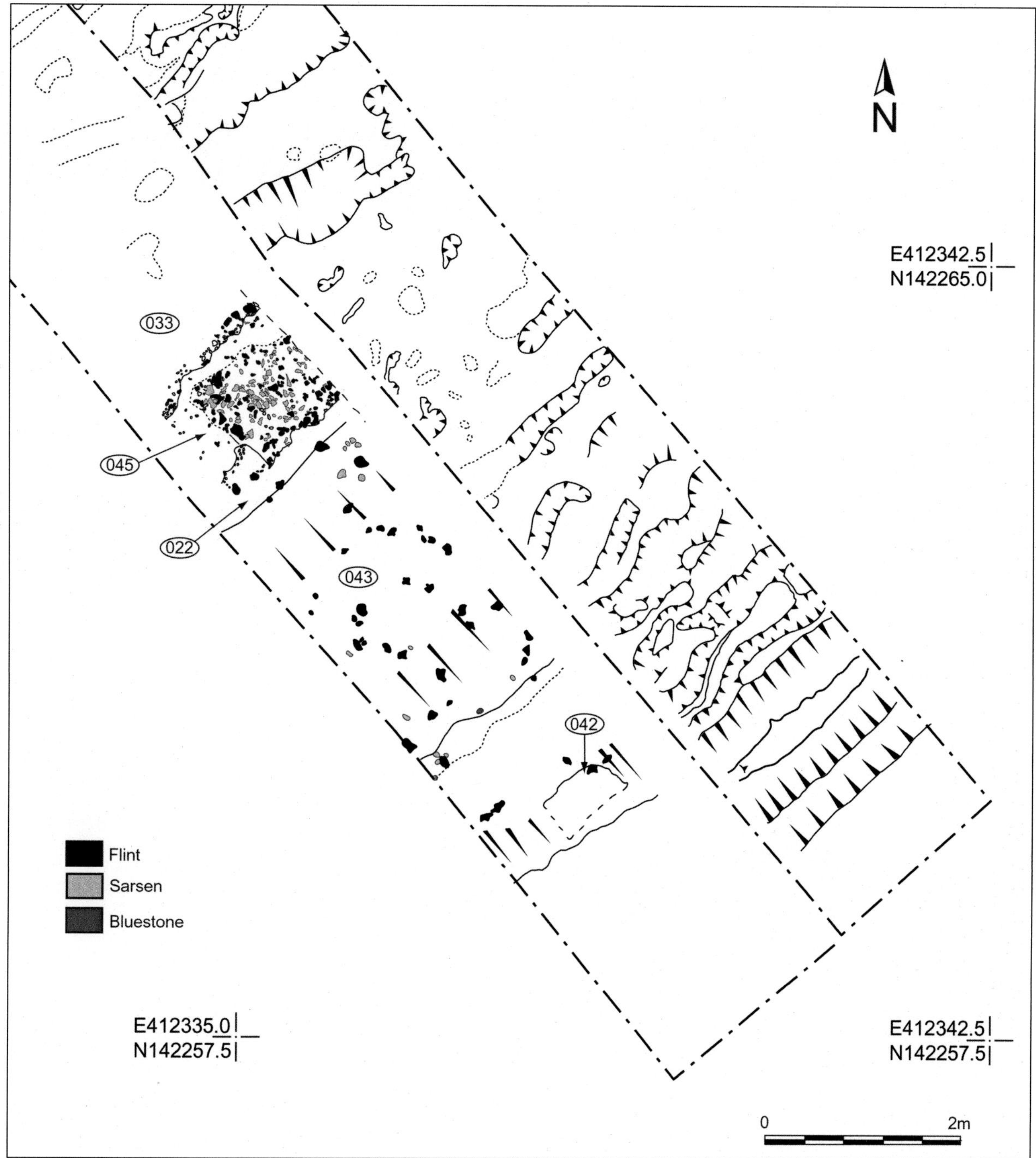

Figure 8.15. Plan of the southeast end of Trench 45, showing the distribution of sarsen chippings and one of the bluestone fragments

The presence of sarsen chips within the buried soil beneath the Avenue banks is particularly significant. The earth resistance survey demonstrated an area of high resistance, extending 65m north of the A344 and as far west as the interior of the Avenue, which appears to be an extensive sarsen-dressing area (see Chapter 6). Whilst a large number of sarsen and bluestone fragments were found on the surface of the subsoil within the Avenue, on top of its banks, within the banks, and within the ditch fills, the presence of sarsen flakes in the buried soil beneath the banks indicates that dressing of the sarsens was being carried out prior to the Avenue's construction.

The most reliable date for construction of the Avenue comes from an antler pick recovered from the bottom

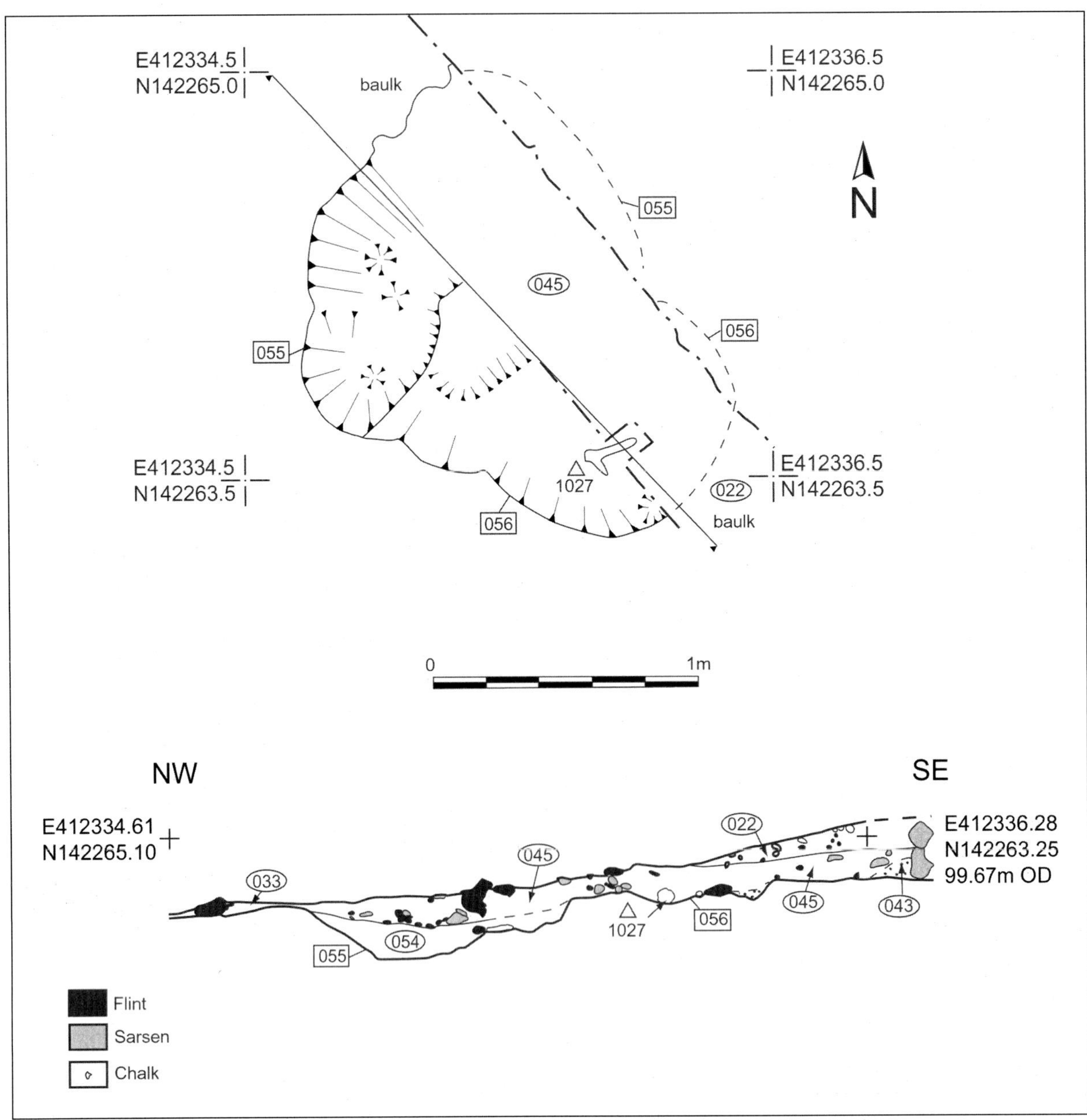

Figure 8.16. Plan of pit 055/056 that contained the antler pick

of the Stonehenge terminal of the western (or northern) ditch by William Hawley in 1923 (Cleal *et al.* 1995: 327), at 2580–2280 cal BC (95% confidence [OxA-4884; 3935±50 BP]).

Paired pits 055 and 056 with an antler pick

A pair of shallow pits (055 and 056) lay within the eastern part of the interior of the Avenue, partly beneath the baulk preserved between the 2008 trench and the re-opened area of the 1956 trench (Figures 8.5, 8.12, 8.16). They were probably dug as a single feature in which 055 was the deeper part and 056 formed a shallow shelf to the east of this larger pit. The northeastern edges of these pits had lain within the 1956 trench and were destroyed without record by Atkinson; it is highly likely that their shallow upper fill (045) went unrecognised at the time.

Collectively, pit 055/056 measured 1.70m east–west and *c.* 1.40m north–south. Pit 055 was 1.20m east–west, *c.* 1.40m north–south and up to 0.23m deep, while pit 056 was *c.* 0.80m east–west, *c.* 0.90m north–south and up to 0.14m deep. A 0.13m-thick layer of stone-free brown loam (054) filled the deeper part of pit 055, while both pits were filled with 0.10m–0.14m-deep brown loam containing sarsen and bluestone chips as well as small chalk lumps and broken flint (045; Figures 8.5, 8.12, 8.16).

Figure 8.17. Pit 055/056 with its antler pick (visible above the scale), viewed from the southwest

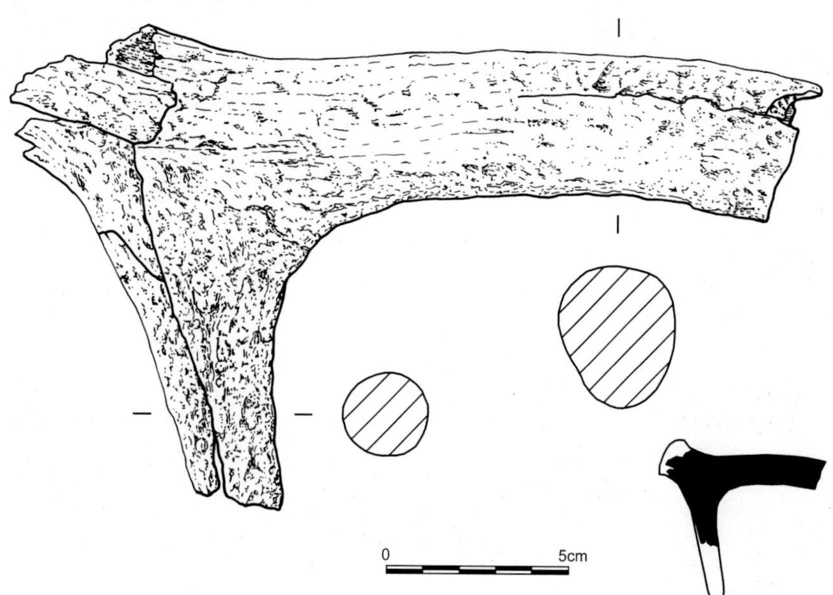

Figure 8.18. The antler pick (SF 1027) from the fill of pit 055/056 within Trench 45

The quantities of sarsen chips in fill 045 were unusually dense (Figure 8.15). This upper layer was excavated in 0.50m × 0.50m squares and was sieved through a 5mm mesh as well as sampled for flotation. Only the southwestern half of the pair of pits was dug out, leaving half of the pit preserved for the future within the 0.50m-wide baulk running between the 1956 and 2008 trenches.

A small red deer antler pick (SF 1027) lay on the base of pit 056 within fill 045 (Figures 8.16–8.17). The pick (216mm long) has been fashioned by removal of the burr and brow tine, making the more sharply angled bez tine the point of the pick (Figure 8.18). This is unusual because most antler picks have the brow tine as their point, with the bez tine removed (Serjeantson and Gardiner 1995). This pick also has an unusually short handle. Its tip is broken off; the pick's poor condition prevents any identification of marks from working or wear. Three separate samples from the antler pick were submitted for radiocarbon-dating (SUERC-23205, OxA-20011 and OxA-20350). The weighted mean of the dates is *2310–2200 cal BC* (Table 8.1).

The stratigraphic context of deposition of this tool, on completion of the digging-out of the pit and prior to its backfilling, is unclear:

- Deposition of the antler pick appears to pre-date the construction of the Avenue's bank and ditch, since pit fill 045 lay beneath bank fill (022) of the Avenue.
- However, layer 022 appeared to be composed of both the primary bank of the Avenue and also a later, more widely spread deposit of bank fill added when the Avenue ditch was re-cut (*i.e.* after re-cut 020, see below), and which is stratified above the top of pit fill

Figure 8.19. The western Avenue ditch, viewed from the southwest; cut 018 is the re-cut into the fill (048) of the original ditch cut (049)

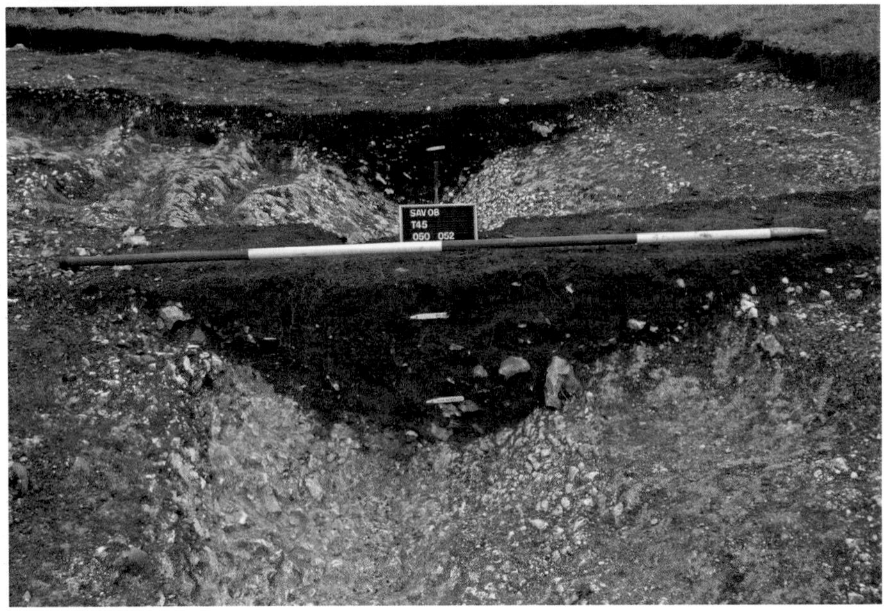

Figure 8.20. The eastern Avenue ditch, viewed from the southwest

> 045. This later bank material (forming the top of 022) showed up as a darker, more organic layer of chalk lumps to the west of and overlying the clean chalk lumps (at the base of 022) that are presumably upcast from the initial digging-out of the Avenue's ditch.

The modelling of all available radiocarbon dates for the Avenue suggests that the second scenario is more likely to be true, that the pit post-dates the initial digging of the Avenue ditch and pre-dates the re-cut of the ditch (see Marshall *et al.*, below)

The purpose of this pair of pits (055 and 056) is not entirely clear. The large amounts of sarsen debris in layer 045 (see the sarsen report in Chapter 6) led to expectations that this might be a stonehole for a standing stone. However, the lack of compression of the soft periglacial sediments and eroded chalk protuberances at the base of pits 055 and 056 indicates that no stone ever stood here. The uneven bottoms of the pits indicate that softer periglacial sediments (057 and 058) had been removed to greater depth than the harder chalk protuberances (059). It is possible that the pits were an exploratory investigation into the nature of the below-ground deposits to find out what was responsible for the parchmark-striping effects of the large and deep periglacial fissures, running between the two parallel natural chalk ridges, that would have been visible in prehistory on the surface (see above). Sacrifice of an antler pick might be considered an over-generous response to the digging of such a shallow, irregular and unprepossessing pair of holes.

The Avenue's banks and ditches

The Avenue is 23.50m wide at this point, from the outer edges of each ditch. Excavation revealed that the ditches flanking the Avenue here are 1.50m wide and 0.80m deep (eastern ditch 052) and 1.60m wide and 0.90m deep (western ditch 049). The profile of the western ditch is V-shaped whilst the eastern ditch has a slightly more rounded profile with a small V-shaped gully at its base (Figures 8.10–8.12, 8.19–8.20; note that all the deposits and fills shown in Figure 8.12 were seen *only* in section in 2008: the section drawing shows the northeast-facing section of Atkinson's re-opened trench and all deposits within that trench had been removed in 1956).

The banks (western bank 021; eastern bank 022) are about 0.10m thick and 4m (021) – 4.30m wide (022). The bank fills are composed of small chalk lumps and broken flint set within matrices of mid-grey/yellow silt (021) and dark grey-brown silt (022). As noted in the discussion of pits 055/056 (above) and in discussion of the ditch re-cutting (below) the banks may have been formed by more than one episode of deposition, the first from initial digging of the ditches and a second from re-cutting of the ditches. The bank layers are too thin to clearly distinguish such separate episodes other than noting a very thin upper deposit of dirty chalk that may be upcast from the re-cutting of the ditches (see below).

Excavation revealed that the primary fills of the ditches were largely removed by the re-cuts (fill 048 in the western ditch removed by re-cut 018 and fill 050 in the eastern ditch by re-cut 020; Figures 8.8, 8.10–8.12, 8.21; see below). The western ditch's primary fill (048) consisted of a creamy, compacted, light buff matrix with chalk lumps 0.01m–0.05m in size. The eastern ditch's primary fill (050) consisted of a compacted, buff matrix with chalk lumps 0.01m–0.05m in size. Both primary fills were sampled for flotation.

Bank material has slipped on top of both primary fills in the ditches. A mid-yellow/brown silt (041) lay on the western ditch's inner edge over ditch fill 048, and there was a light yellow-brown silt (042) within the eastern ditch's inner edge, observed during excavation to lie over ditch fill 050.

Between the Avenue banks, no evidence was found for a 'road surface' of broken flint, as proposed by Hawley. Although the uneven, corrugated ground surface of the Avenue was strewn with flint nodules and generally small pieces of shattered and broken flint, none of this appeared to have derived from anything other than natural weathering of the tops of the periglacial features.

Re-cutting of the Avenue's ditches

Both Avenue ditches were re-cut (Figures 8.5, 8.10–8.13). The western ditch was re-cut by a shallower ditch (018) with a V-shaped profile, filled with a largely stone-free, dark yellow-brown silt (031 below 017). Its lower component (031) was distinguished from its upper one (017) by a lens of larger, sorted flint fragments and a small knapping cluster (030), which was about 0.05m deep and 0.15m wide, within the centre of the ditch.

The eastern ditch was re-cut by a shallower ditch (020) with a V-shaped profile, filled with a largely stone-free, dark yellow-brown silt (032 below 019). Its lower component (032) was distinguished from its upper one (019) by a lens of larger flint fragments.

Both ditch re-cuts post-date the original bank construction (composed of 021 and the bottom of 022) and their dug-out fills have left little trace on the top of the bank, either because they have subsequently been largely removed by weathering and erosion and/or because the upcast material was spread very thinly (perhaps even outside the Avenue banks). The upcast fills may be visible as a very thin layer of dirty chalk lumps less than 0.03m thick.

The dark yellow-brown silts filling the re-cut ditches are unusual in containing very little chalk. They are similar to the loess-like fill of the final re-cut within the Greater Cursus' southern ditch, excavated in 2007 (see Chapter 3). Tentatively, their formation can be ascribed to a process of in-filling with windblown soils exposed by disturbance of grass cover during a large-scale phase of cultivation, perhaps during the Early Bronze Age.

Wheel-ruts

Nine cartwheel-ruts were identified in the upper deposits within the 2008 extension to Atkinson's excavated area. All are shown in plan in Figures 8.4 and 8.5 and in section in Figures 8.10–8.12. The cart-ruts were not present in the area of the Atkinson trench, since all the deposits at this stratigraphic level were removed in 1956.

Rut 025 (filled by 024) cut the western bank of the Avenue and was 0.28m wide and 0.10m deep (below the base of the turfline). Further east, rut 010 (filled by 009) was 0.33m wide and 0.15m deep. To its east, rut 012 (filled by 011) was 0.45m–0.55m wide and 0.08m–0.18m deep. To its east, rut 027 (filled by 026) was 0.30m wide and 0.08m deep. To its east, rut 014 (filled by 013) was 0.35m–0.40m wide and 0.10m–0.12m deep. These five ruts were aligned broadly along the Avenue, heading from Stonehenge towards the ruts identified at the Avenue bend in Trench 48 (see below), and beyond to those within the 'northern extension of the Avenue' in Trench 56 (see below) and within the Greater Cursus at Trench 40 (see Chapter 3), heading towards Larkhill.

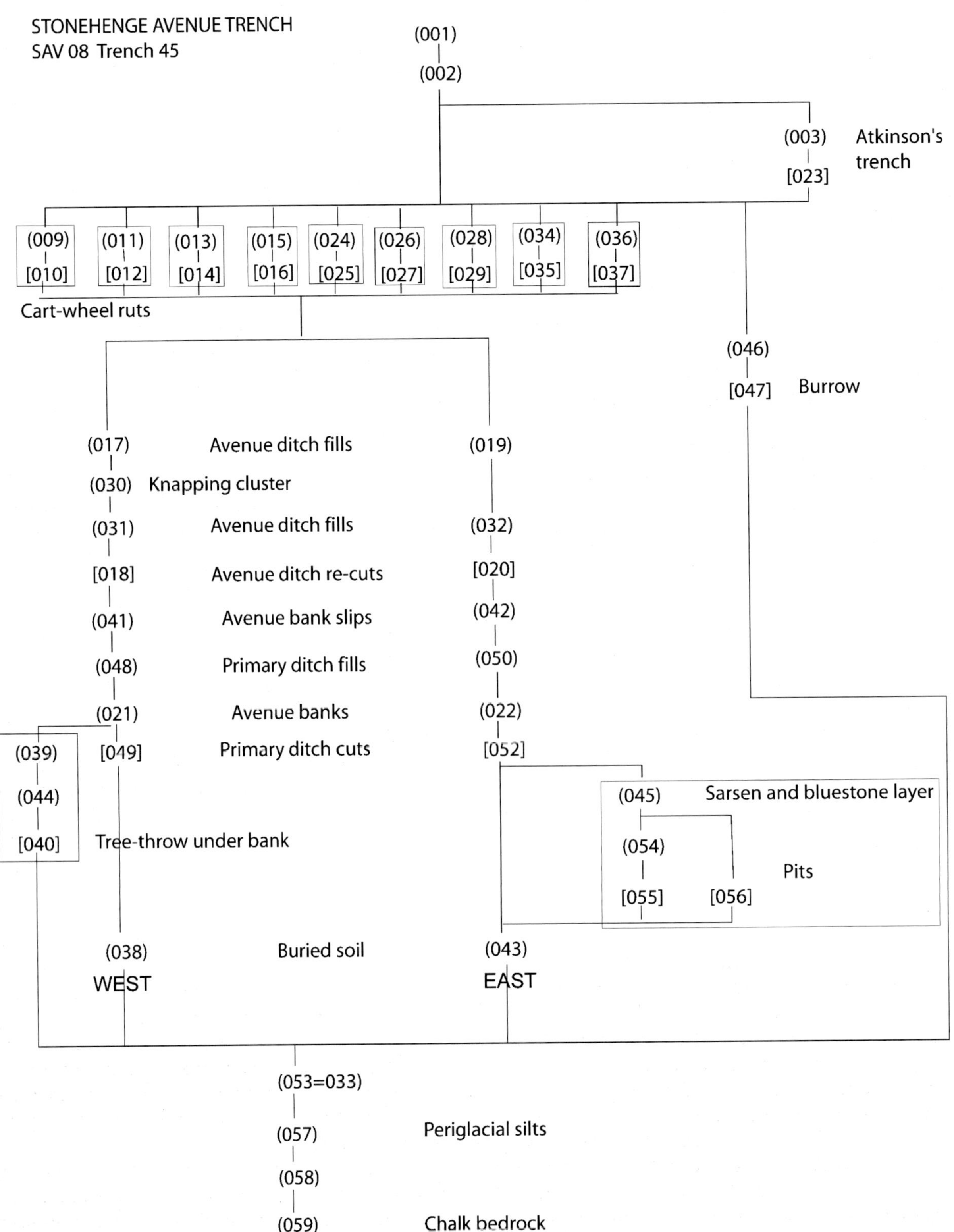

Figure 8.21. Stratigraphic matrix for Trench 45

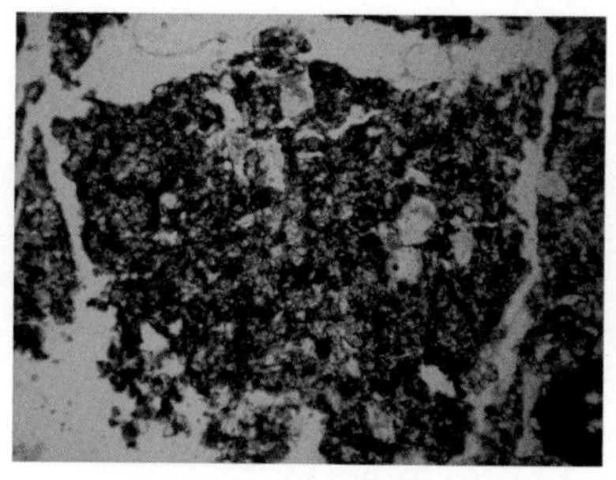
a

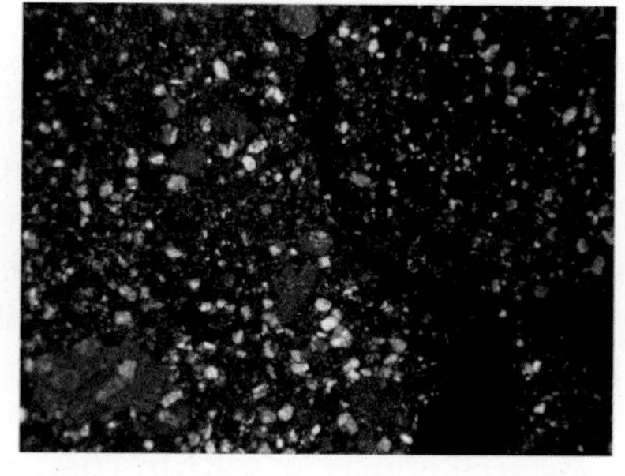
b

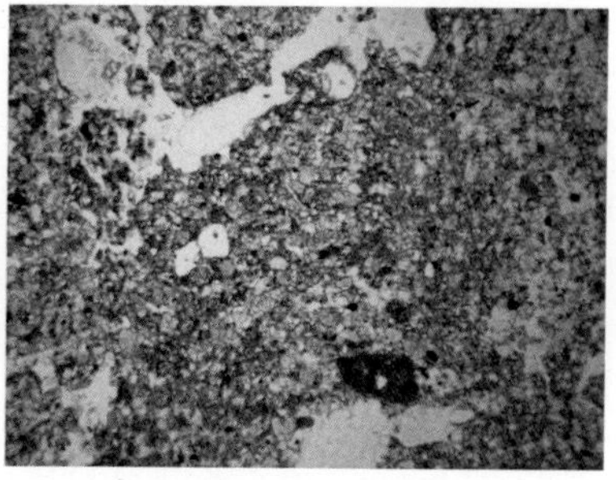
c

Figure 8.22. Photomicrographs of: a) organic, fine sandy (clay) loam fabric of the buried soil beneath the western Avenue bank in Trench 45, profile 50/1 (frame width = 4.5mm; plane-polarised light); b) micritic fine sandy (clay) loam fabric in the tree-throw hole beneath the western Avenue bank in Trench 45, profile 52/1 (frame width = 4.5mm; cross-polarised light); c) the mixture of micritic and non-micritic fine sandy loam fabric with micro-charcoal in Trench 45, profile 52/1 (frame width = 4.5mm; plane-polarised light)

The remaining four ruts in Trench 45 lay further to the east and were aligned eastwards, so as to cross the eastern (southern) bank and ditch of the Avenue, heading for Amesbury. The most westerly was rut 029 (filled by 028), 0.45m–0.55m wide and 0.08m–0.18m deep. To its east, rut 016 (filled by 015) was 0.50m–0.80m wide and 0.06m–0.08m deep. To its east, rut 035 (filled by 034) was 0.20m wide and 0.04m deep. To its east, rut 037 (filled by 036) was 0.30m wide and 0.02m–0.08m deep, merging with rut 035 at the edge of Atkinson's trench. The only dating evidence within these wheel-ruts was a small sherd of glazed medieval pottery.

8.2.3. Soil micromorphology of soils within the Stonehenge Avenue (Trench 45)

C.A.I. French

This trench revealed a thin (*c.* 10cm–20cm), humic silt topsoil over weathered chalk natural which contained a large number of deep periglacial stripe features (Figures 8.7–8.8; see Allen and French 2008) situated between the two bank-and-ditch features of the Stonehenge Avenue. Beneath the eroded remnants of both banks there was a thin buried soil surviving, and this was sampled in two locations, from beneath context 021 (the western bank; Profile 50; sample 1016) and context 022 (the eastern bank; Profile 51; sample 1017), on the south side of Atkinson's trench. In addition, a third soil profile (Profile 52) was observed beneath chalk rubble slip on the outer edge of the western bank preserved in association with a tree-throw hole (040).

The buried soil profile is a dark brown (humic), silt loam (or Ah horizon) with about 35% small chalk fragments, overlying a thin B horizon of pale yellowish-brown calcitic silt, all developed on the weathered chalk substrate. The soil profile (50) beneath the western Avenue bank is much better preserved than the soil profile (51) beneath the eastern Avenue bank. The tree-throw hole (in Profile 52) contained a much thicker Ah horizon-like deposit. This soil is probably a poorly developed brown earth soil associated with grassland.

Unfortunately, Trenches 48, 57 and 58, cutting through the Avenue banks downslope at the Avenue elbow (see below), did not appear to have any substantial preservation of an *in situ* buried soil.

Profile 50

The soil beneath the chalk rubble bank material of the western bank of the Stonehenge Avenue is approximately 19cm thick and is composed of a golden-brown to greyish-brown, small aggregated, micritic, fine sandy clay loam developed on weathered chalk (Figure 8.22a). Down-profile, the clay component decreases slightly (from 30% to 20%), the fine ped structure becomes smaller, blocky and defined by fine vertical channels, and the micritic calcium carbonate content increases slightly (from 30% to 40%). The clay component is a poorly oriented, impure or dusty clay within the groundmass, with up to one-third affected by amorphous sesquioxide impregnation. There is no organic Ah or turf horizon evident either along the entire profile or in this bank-buried soil section in this part of the profile.

This soil exhibits some stability and pedogenesis in terms of soil structure and a clay component well-incorporated in the groundmass, but it also displays the calcitic, small blocky features (Avery 1980; Limbrey 1975). This suggests that this soil was once a decalcified brown earth which had more or less transformed into a rendzina prior to burial by the Avenue bank; the radiocarbon dating of the construction of the Avenue (see below) suggests a date in the early third millennium BC. In particular, the substantial amount of very fine sand-size and coarse silt material (*c.* 30%–40%) may also suggest that there is a substantial loessic component to this soil, as postulated by Catt (1978). The upper one-third of this horizon, equating to the turf horizon of this rendzina soil, is missing, and was most probably truncated during the construction of the Avenue bank.

Profile 51

The soil beneath the chalk rubble bank material of the eastern bank of the Stonehenge Avenue is much more poorly preserved. It is approximately 9cm–10cm thick and is composed of a greyish-brown, small aggregated to pellety, micritic, fine sandy clay loam developed on weathered chalk. It is very similar in terms of composition to the lowermost part of Profile 50 discussed above, and appears to represent the lower one-third or A/C horizon of a rendzina soil.

Profile 52

This soil-like deposit from a possible tree-throw located on the eastern edge of the western ditch of the Avenue is a mixture of chalk fragments, pellety organic matter or turf fragments and a yellowish-brown micritic sandy (clay) loam (Figure 8.22b–c). There is a minor component of organic material, some amorphous iron impregnation of the channels, some illuvial dusty clay coating sand grains and in the groundmass, and common micritic calcium carbonate. To all intents, this deposit is a like a disturbed rendzina soil, just as one would expect for the fill of a tree-throw hole.

8.2.4. Geology, geomorphology and buried soils

M. Allen and C.A.I. French

This section discusses the presence and significance of periglacial stripes at the southern end of the Avenue (Trench 45) in comparison to those within the adjacent sarsen stone-working area (Trench 44).

Periglacial stripes (not to be confused with periglacial stone 'stripes and polygons' or patterned ground; French 1976: 184) are frost-heave cryoturbation features primarily created by *in situ* freeze-thaw alteration of the chalk combined with ice and 'glacio'-fluvial removal of loose chalk material. Cryoturbation structures have been described on the chalk of Wiltshire by Evans (1968: 14): on slopes the 'general result is … of parallel gullies orientated in a downhill direction', usually slightly diagonally across the slope. They are often filled with silty calcareous deposits including an admixture of material derived from weathered or soliflucted chalk and reworked aeolian silt deposits (loess).

These features commonly have the form of semi-irregular 'stripes' with steep but sloping sides and narrow bottoms, and they are often slightly asymmetrical. It is common for them to be about 0.08m–0.15m wide and 0.08m deep or less, with deeper elements being 0.15m deep. Spacing is variable and has been commonly observed to be at about 0.60m–0.75m to 3.50m intervals.

Previously identified periglacial features within the Stonehenge Avenue

Although periglaciation and periglacial features have been recognised geomorphologically for many years (*e.g.* Te Punga 1957), they were only recognised on the chalk within an archaeological context in 1968 and 1969 by John Evans (Evans 1968; 1972). They were also recorded in archaeological excavations in Sussex in the 1970s (Drewett 1978), by which time they were commonly recognised by archaeologists. Excavation of the Stonehenge Avenue by Atkinson in 1956 (trench C48; Montague 1995b: 311, fig. 178) revealed 'parallel sub-linear features' which Montague (advised by Allen) interpreted as 'almost certainly periglacial features'. Similar features were recorded on the north side of Stonehenge by Pitts (1982) and noted by Evans in his excavations with Atkinson near the Avenue's elbow (Evans 1984; see *The Stonehenge Avenue bend*, below).

Those recorded inside the Avenue in Atkinson's excavation (C48; Cleal *et al.* 1995: fig. 178) are, however, extraordinarily large and deep, being *c.* 0.40m–0.70m across and typically 0.50m deep (*ibid.*: 309, fig. 178). In contrast, typical widths on chalkland are 0.08m–0.15m and typical depths about 0.08m–0.12m. The orientation of these features within the Avenue was not recorded in plan by Atkinson, but from the excavation photograph Montague (1995b: 311) describes them as 'aligned approximately north-west to south-east'.

Periglacial features within Trench 45 on the Stonehenge Avenue

The periglacial stripes in Trench 45 were closely spaced, parallel, sub-linear features typically 0.40m–0.50m across and 0.45m deep (measured from the top of the chalk bedrock as revealed after all overlying deposits had been stripped away), containing a cemented, very pale brown (10YR 7/4) calcareous marl with common, very small chalk pieces (recorded as context number 058 in 2008), and overlain by a brown (7.5YR 4/4) silty clay loam with some small, rare medium-sized chalk pieces (context 057). The presence of this typical upper fill indicates a lack of severe truncation. Although Trench 45 did not extend sufficiently beyond the Avenue ditches to test the occurrence of features of this magnitude outside the Avenue, at least two more are visible in the magnetometer plot on the south side of the southern Avenue ditch (see Figure 8.3).

Periglacial features within Trench 44 to the west of the Stonehenge Avenue

Periglacial stripes, albeit much smaller, were also present in Trench 44 beneath the sarsen stone scatter (see Chapter 6 and Figure 6.11). Morphologically the features in Trench 44 (recorded as context 007), although well pronounced, are more typical of common periglacial stripes as recorded elsewhere on the chalklands of southern England. They were *c.* 0.15m across and 0.10m deep (from the top of the chalk bedrock). Although clearly periglacial stripes, they were filled with stone-free humic 'A horizon' material with many fine, fleshy roots despite being sealed beneath the sarsen stone scatter. The humic rendzina profile here is only 0.18m–0.28m deep, with a deeply developed, worm-sorted horizon under long-term grassland. Worm-working and biotic activity (fine rooting) has acted to re-work all the periglacial material into the A horizon which now fills the features. However, relict patches of typical periglacial silty calcareous fills were present locally on the sides and in the base of a number of the features, confirming that these are periglacial cryoturbation features or stripes.

Conclusion

The presence of extraordinarily large and closely spaced periglacial stripes within the Avenue is possibly explained by the presence of parallel natural ridges of chalk bedrock on either side of the concentration of stripes, and a natural dishing of the area between the chalk ridges. This would have concentrated water and thus freeze-thaw action between these two parallel ridges, thereby accentuating periglacial cryoturbation processes, and enlarging the periglacial stripes. The archaeological coincidence and significance of these features between low ridges is potentially very important.

The most significant result of excavating Trench 45 was the discovery that the Stonehenge Avenue was built upon a pair of parallel natural ridges either side of a series of unusually large and deep periglacial stripes, all coincidentally aligned on the midsummer sunrise/midwinter sunset solstitial axis. This unusual natural feature was embellished by the cutting of parallel ditches along the outer edges of the two ridges, and enhancing these ridges by piling bank material from these ditches on top of them. This manipulation of a natural feature may partly explain why Stonehenge was located where it is.

8.2.5. Discussion

M. Parker Pearson

The aim of excavating Trench 45 was to establish the sequence of the Avenue's construction and confirm that the linear gullies running within the Avenue were indeed periglacial fissures. Distributions of sarsen and bluestone chips on the buried land surface underneath the Avenue's banks confirmed that the Avenue was constructed after Stage 2 of Stonehenge was constructed. An antler pick in a pit beneath the Avenue's bank fill (probably the fill deposited after the Avenue ditches were re-cut) also provided a radiocarbon date.

Perhaps the most significant finding was that the Avenue ditches follow the line of a pair of parallel natural chalk ridges within which the parallel periglacial fissures run. This remarkable coincidence of a geological landform on a solstitial axis has to be considered as a feature which was meaningful to people of the third millennium cal BC – so much so that they embellished and accentuated it by heightening the ridges with artificial banks flanked by ditches.

The discovery that the Avenue follows the general direction of this series of natural striations adds a new dimension to the interpretation of its solstitial alignment. For a full discussion, see the concluding sections of this chapter.

8.3. The Stonehenge Avenue bend (Trenches 46, 48, 57 and 58)

D. Robinson and O. Bayer

8.3.1. Research background

The Avenue elbow or bend is the point 500m from Stonehenge where the Avenue bends sharply from its solstice orientation and heads eastwards from the reticulated coombe system known as Stonehenge Bottom uphill towards King Barrow Ridge (Figure 8.1). A group of natural and artificial features all meet in this general area:

- The linear feature known as the Gate Ditch runs close to and parallel with the Avenue's northwest side for a short stretch here (R5/M5 on Figures 8.2–8.3; Figures 8.23, 8.25).
- The linear feature known as the Oblique Ditch runs northeast–southwest and cuts the northern or western ditch of the Avenue (R6 on Figure 8.2).
- Stonehenge Bottom runs north–south through this area (see Figure 2.1), and there is a curiously straight depression (the 'possible northern branch' of the Avenue) running 5° to the east of the Avenue's solstitial line from Stonehenge Bottom to beneath the eastern end of the Greater Cursus.
- In addition, a natural knoll named by Atkinson in 1953 as Newall's Mound (from R.S. Newall's suggestion that it served as a sighting point from Stonehenge; Evans 1984: 22–4; Cleal *et al.* 1995: 292) lies close to the southern (eastern) ditch of the Avenue in this area.

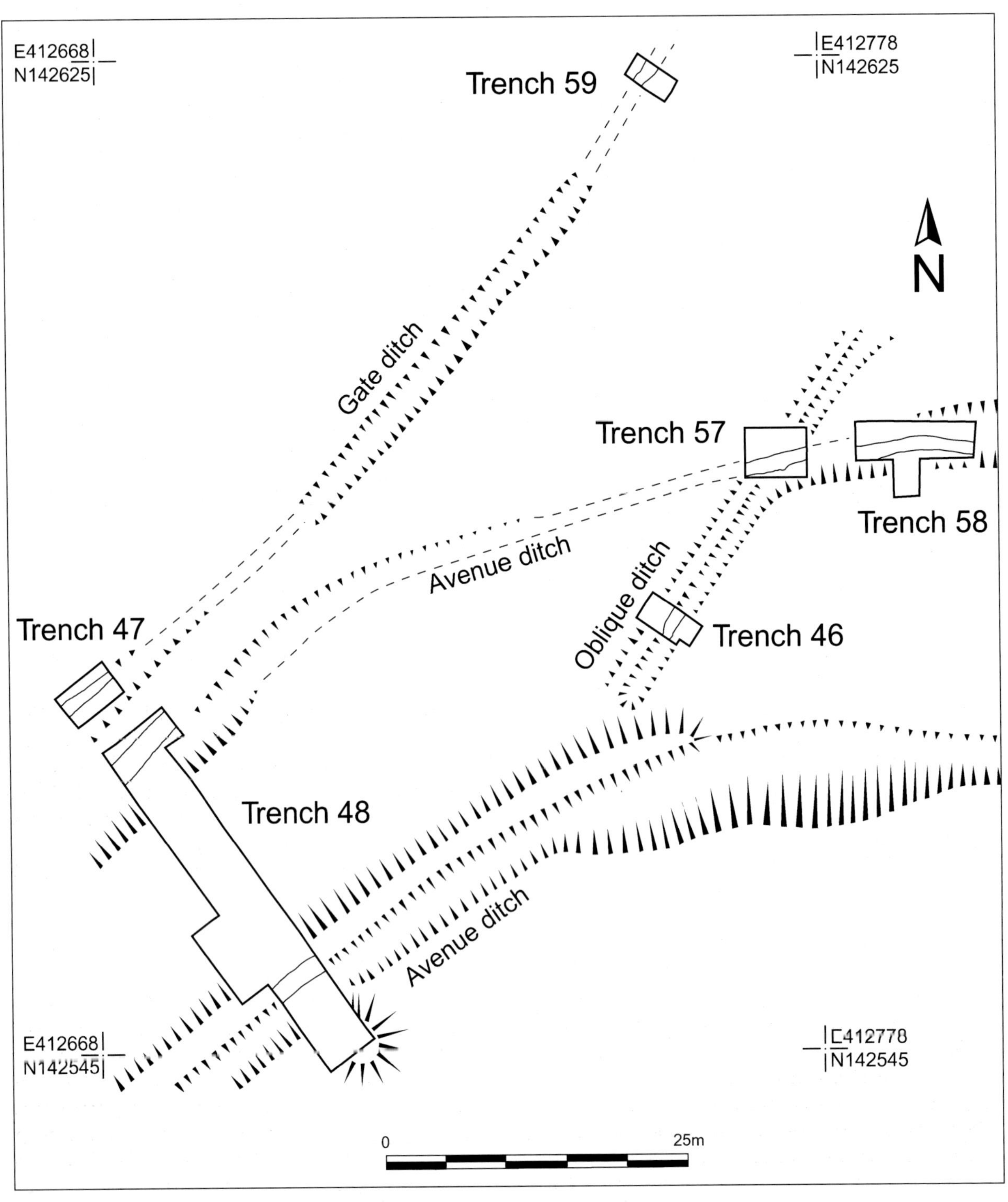

Figure 8.23. Locations of trenches excavated on the Avenue bend in 2008, re-opening those previously dug by Atkinson (after Cleal *et al*. 1995: plan 4); © Historic England

Figure 8.24. View of the Avenue bend trenches, looking to the southwest

Eight excavations, all by Richard Atkinson, took place within this location. All were small interventions to investigate ditch fills and relationships between them. Only those involving John Evans were adequately recorded and written up. In 1953 Atkinson dug small trenches into:

- the Gate Ditch (C37, C being 'cutting');
- the Oblique Ditch (C38);
- the northern ditch of the Avenue (C39);
- the southern ditch of the Avenue adjacent to Newall's Mound (C40);
- the junction of the northern Avenue ditch and the Oblique Ditch (C95).

In 1978, Atkinson and Evans returned to C40 and re-opened it (C62). They also continued its line across the Avenue with two further trenches (C96 across the northern Avenue ditch and C97 across the Gate Ditch). John Evans published his report on these latter trenches in 1984 and the results of all the excavations – as far as they could be gleaned – were summarised by Cleal *et al.* (1995: 301). However, Atkinson's interventions remained frustratingly undocumented in any real sense and an important research aim of the SRP in 2008 was to locate and reopen Atkinson's 'cuttings', in order to record the (previously exposed) sections through the features and deposits he excavated in this part of the Avenue.

The elbow or bend in the Avenue

There has been some uncertainty as to whether the Avenue was constructed in a single build or whether it was constructed in two stages. One hypothesis has been that a first stage involved the construction of the straight stretch between Stonehenge itself and the elbow, on the solstice axis. A later stage, it is hypothesised, saw the addition of the eastward-leading stretch from the elbow to King Barrow Ridge and hence to the River Avon (Atkinson 1979: 214). The change of direction in the Avenue is indeed suggestive of sequencing in the ditch and bank construction. English Heritage's magnetometer survey plot (Figure 8.25; Payne in Cleal *et al.* 1995: fig. 265) shows a marked change in the alignment and density of the anomaly produced by both Avenue ditches where they depart from the straight line of the solstitial axis. This certainly appeared to hint at the ditches having been dug as two separate episodes of construction.

Richard Atkinson's 1953 trench (C40) was positioned directly on this potential junction within the southern Avenue ditch. The SRP research aim was to reopen and extend that trench (for which no archive survives other than one section drawing and a few photographs; Cleal *et al.* 1995: fig. 175), with the objectives of recording Atkinson's sections and discovering if there is any evidence here of two phases of construction. Additionally, Atkinson and Evans' 1978 trench across the northern ditch (C96) lies just to the south of the putative junction, so the intact stratigraphy within the ditch here could be examined by excavating the area encompassing C40 and C96 to see if one phase of the Avenue butted up against an earlier one.

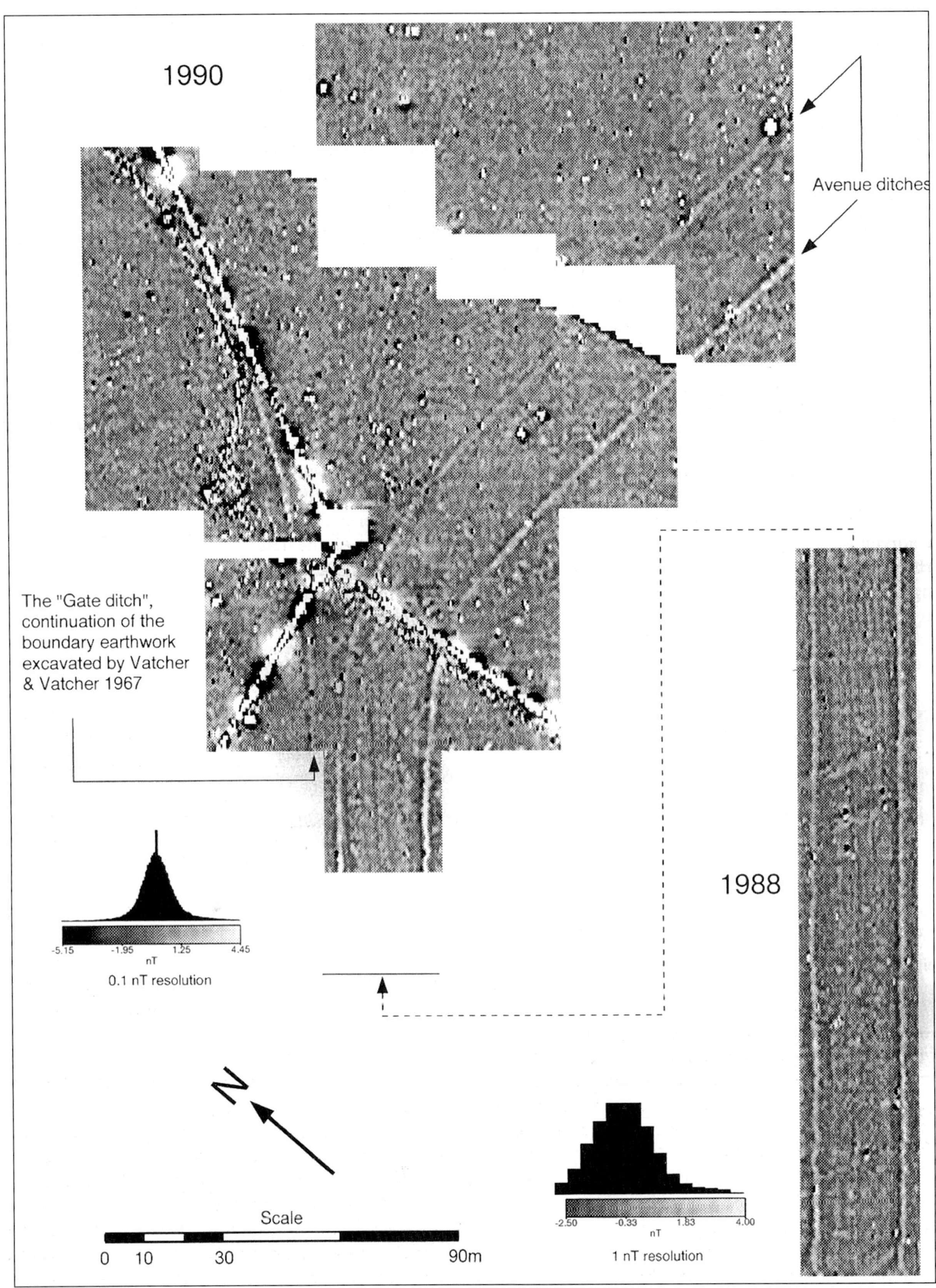

Figure 8.25. Magnetometry survey of the Avenue bend carried out in 1988 and 1990 (from David and Payne 1997); © British Academy

The parallel linear anomalies within the Avenue

Magnetometer surveys in 1988 and 1990 (Figure 8.25; Payne in Cleal *et al.* 1995: fig. 265), as well as an earth resistance survey in 2007 by SRP (Figure 8.2; see above), showed an unusual set of up to nine parallel anomalies running within and along the 500m length of the Avenue from outside Stonehenge to the elbow. Our research objective was to determine whether these were continuations of the periglacial stripes observed in Trench 45 or were wheel-ruts of more recent origin.

Internal features within the Avenue at its elbow

One objective of the SRP excavations in 2008 was to determine whether any cultural features or deposits lay within this part of the Avenue. Geophysical anomalies at the bend include several oval-shaped low-resistance features; according to Cleal *et al.* (1995: 312), 'these features cannot be fully described and interpreted until they have been excavated.'

The Avenue banks protecting buried soils at the elbow

Evans and Atkinson's archaeological investigations apparently revealed a 'bank shadow' on the inner sides of the ditches (the sides along which the banks once stood; Cleal *et al.* 1995: 302, figs 175–176). Bank shadows are shown (*ibid.*) as extending approximately 2m–4m from the ditches towards the Avenue interior, and are discussed briefly: 'In some areas a raised area of chalk rubble mixed with quantities of soil and stones was excavated but was not considered to be undisturbed bank material *sensu stricto*' (*ibid.*: 304), *i.e.* the lines of the banks are discernible although the banks survive merely as 'shadows'. A research objective was to determine whether any remnant patches of bank might have 'potential of undisturbed buried soils' (*ibid.*).

The Gate Ditch

The Gate Ditch is a 660m-long ditch running broadly southwest–northeast, parallel with the Avenue for a short distance, from just northwest of Stonehenge to north of the Avenue's elbow (Cleal *et al.* 1995: 292). Its line is continued to the southwest, after a gap of 360m (Figure 8.3; *ibid.*: fig. 71), by the Palisade Ditch which runs southwest for a further 600m. These two lengths of ditches appear to be part of the same feature (*ibid.*: 292), a land boundary that forms the western side of a large sub-rectangular enclosure or precinct around Stonehenge and the Early Bronze Age round barrows on Normanton Down (Pollard *et al.* 2017: fig. 9). Whereas the area outside this precinct developed extensive Bronze Age field systems, the land within it did not (*ibid.*: fig. 8).

Re-excavation of Atkinson and Evans' trench (C97) into the Gate Ditch was intended to gather further environmental and dating evidence from this suspected Bronze Age feature (reported on in Volume 4), notably to establish whether it was part of a large-scale boundary associated with the Stonehenge Palisade Ditch (Pollard *et al.* 2017; see Volume 4). SRP Trenches 47 and 59 into the Gate Ditch, which appears to date to the Early Bronze Age, are reported on in Volume 4. However, the few lithic finds from these two trenches are included in this volume (see Chan, below) amongst the larger Avenue bend assemblage.

Excavation methods

All six trenches (Trenches 46, 47, 48, 57, 58, 59) located at the Avenue bend were dug by hand in 2008 (Figures 8.23–8.24). After hand-excavation of the ploughsoil (001), all excavated fills (including previous excavators' backfills) were sieved through a 10mm mesh.

8.3.2. Trench 46: the Oblique Ditch

A 2.50m × 5m trench was hand-excavated across the linear feature known as the 'Oblique Ditch' at the point where it is cut by Atkinson's 1953 cutting 38 (Figures 8.26–8.27). The aim was to locate Atkinson's cutting (C38) and re-open it where it cut the Oblique Ditch so as to record the ditch's section. This had not been drawn or recorded when it was dug in 1953. The area opened as Trench 46 had to be sufficiently large to locate the relevant part of Atkinson's trench (C38) but most of it was excavated only to a depth just below the turf; only the area of C38 was fully excavated.

A 1m × 4m portion of the backfill of cutting 38 (context 094) was removed to reveal both the previously exposed sections across the Oblique Ditch. This allowed for a re-examination of this ditch (119) and a linear feature (126/129) which runs parallel to, and immediately to the southeast of it. Note that all the ditch fills recorded in 2008 were seen only in section, *not* in plan, having been removed by Atkinson from this re-exposed area of the Oblique Ditch. No further areas of ditch fill were removed by the SRP.

The Oblique Ditch

The Oblique Ditch (119) was exposed in section by the removal of the backfill of cutting 38 (fill 094). At this point the ditch is aligned approximately northeast–southwest, *c.* 1.60m wide and up to 0.50m deep, cutting through a layer of periglacial deposit (120) into the solid chalk bedrock. The ditch has a gentle concave, bowl-shaped profile and is filled by a thin primary deposit of silty loam (layer 121/132), overlain by a secondary deposit of silty clay (123/131), overlain by modern topsoil (001; Figure 8.28). A possible bank shadow was noticed on the northwest side of the Oblique Ditch. A chalk bead (SF chalk catalogue C23) of likely Early Bronze Age date was found in the section in layer 121 (see Teather, below).

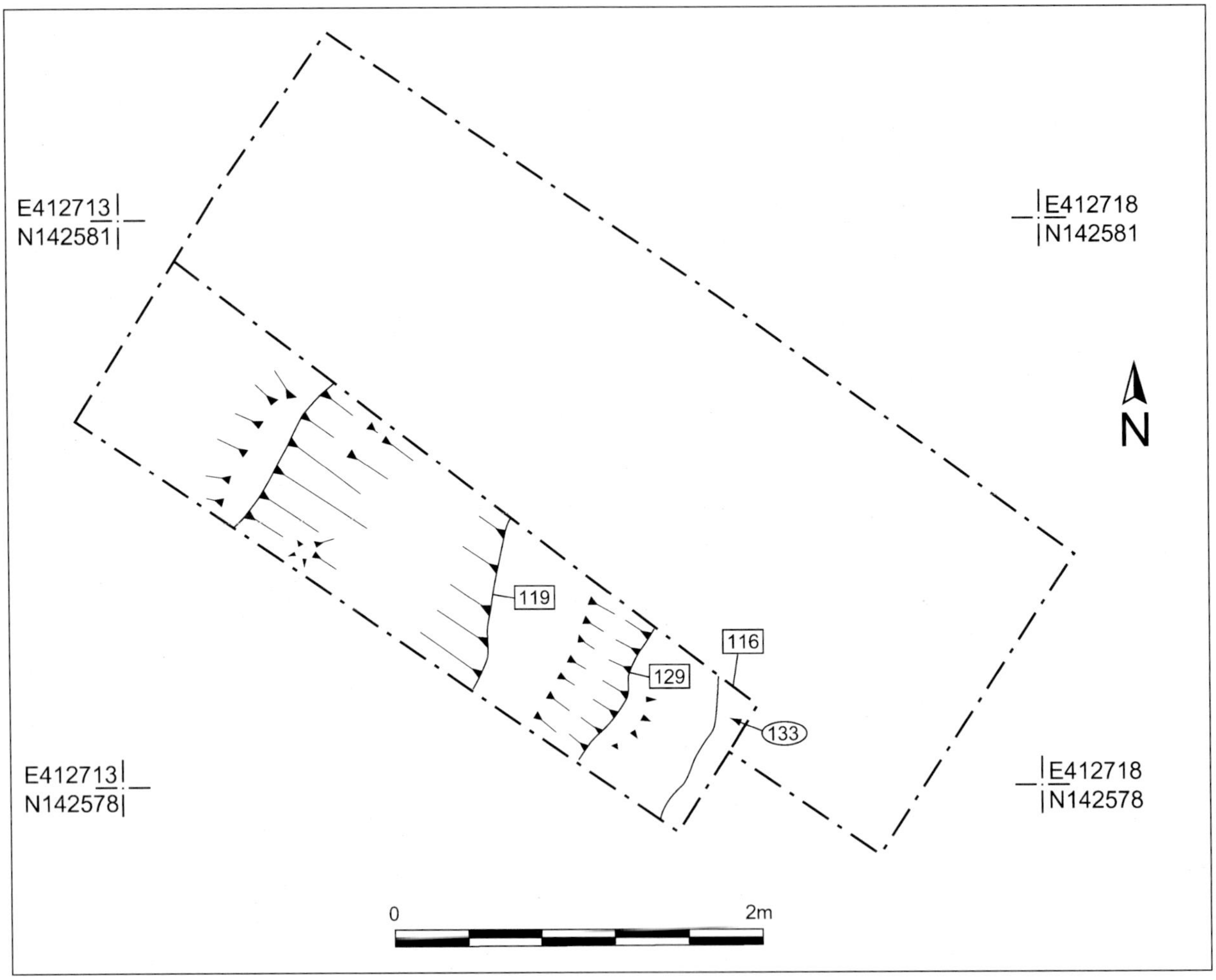

E412713
N142581

E412718
N142581

N

119

116

129

133

E412713
N142578

E412718
N142578

0

2m

Figure 8.26. Plan of Trench 46 across the Oblique Ditch

Figure 8.27. Trench 46, viewed from the southeast

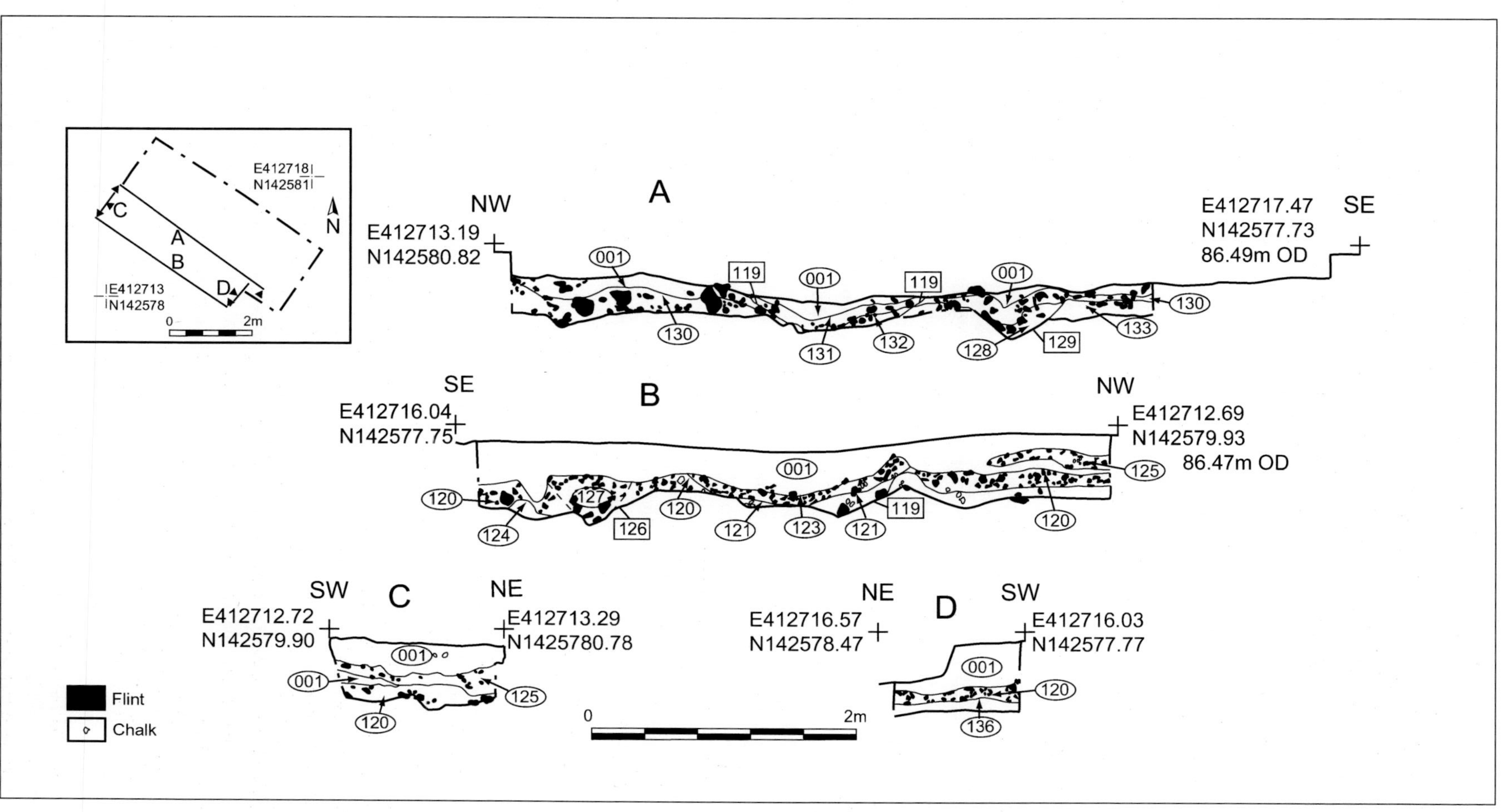

Figure 8.28. Section drawings from Trench 46

Linear feature 126/129

A linear feature (126/129), *c.* 0.50m wide by 0.27m deep, runs parallel with the Oblique Ditch, approximately 0.50m to its southeast. Feature 126/129 is sub-triangular in profile, cut through a periglacial deposit (133) into chalk bedrock, with flattish, slightly concave sides (at about 30°) and a narrow, rounded base. In the northeastern section drawing of cutting 38, this feature has a primary fill of firm clay (128) overlain by looser clay-silt (130). In the southwestern section, cut 126/129 has a single fill of silty loam (127). The relationship between the Oblique Ditch and feature 126/129 is uncertain. The latter is possibly a wheel-rut similar to those seen in Trenches 47, 48 and 58 (see below).

What is the Oblique Ditch?

The orientation of the Oblique Ditch and the fact that it cuts through the northern Avenue ditch suggest that it is related to the historic use of the Avenue as a trackway. It may thus not be of any great antiquity. However, the discovery in the section in its primary fill (121) of a chalk bead, possibly dating to the Early Bronze Age (see below), suggests that it could be a prehistoric feature.

8.3.3. Trench 48: on the Avenue bend

A 5m × 32m trench was dug by hand across the Avenue to encompass Atkinson's cutting 40 (1953) and Atkinson and Evans' cuttings 62 and 96 (both 1978) (Figures 8.29–8.31). The Avenue here is 24.5m across, from the outer edges of its parallel ditches. This trench had two extensions:

- at its northwestern end, a 5m × 3m box extended northeastwards from cutting 96 along the length of the northern Avenue ditch, to establish whether the ditch changed shape or orientation at this point;
- a 3m × 7m extension within the interior of the Avenue on its southeast side, against the Avenue's southern bank, investigated the possible survival of any remnant bank material, and buried soil beneath it, within the 'bank shadow', as well as investigating an oval geophysical anomaly within this area.

Newall's Mound and periglacial deposits

Removal of Atkinson and Evans' backfill from cutting 40/62 (fill 009 in cut 166) exposed their previous section through Newall's Mound and a large, irregularly-shaped periglacial hollow (105). Our excavations confirmed previous interpretations that Newall's Mound (*c.* 20m in diameter and *c.* 0.30m high) is indeed natural. It is comprised of layers of clay and silty clay (103, 104 and 115) with naturally shattered flints and occasional cobble-sized pieces of sarsen (Figure 8.32). This material is a glacial wash deposited during the Pleistocene, transported over frozen ground by glacial melt-waters from the north during high-energy thaw events. Coming down the drainage basin of Stonehenge Bottom, this periglacial clay-with-flints was deposited in Stonehenge Bottom and along at least a portion of the tongue of chalk that forms the ridgeline occupied by the Avenue from Stonehenge to the bend.

Newall's Mound survives as a positive feature above the surface of the chalk. Its irregular profile of layers within the clay and flint fill of the hollow can be explained as resulting from bioturbation by tree roots (Figure 8.33). Thus it may have survived in this upstanding form due to the presence of one or more large trees on top of it, the tree-roots having provided a defence against erosion in the post-glacial period. This point in the Avenue might therefore have been marked not simply by Newall's Mound but additionally by one or more large trees on top of it.

Underneath the ploughsoil (001), a flint and chalk layer within a light brown, silty clay with occasional sarsen lumps (016) covered much of Trench 48's surface and is the same material as that which comprises Newall's Mound. Layer 016 was removed in 1m squares down to solid chalk, sieved through 10mm mesh, and the scarcity of artefacts or ecofacts within it confirms that is was largely undisturbed by human activity. These 1m squares included a 2m × 5m area within the interior of the Avenue, all within the southeastern trench extension, and a line of squares along the northwestern end of the trench. Only occasional worked lithics were found in the squares and no humanly created features were found sealed under this layer. What were found under layer 016, however, were small periglacial stripes, oriented at an oblique angle across the Avenue, running broadly north–south (marked with dashed lines on Figure 8.30). These periglacial stripes are not the long, wide linear anomalies distinguishable within Trench 45.

Wheel-ruts

The most numerous artificial features found in Trench 48 were 15 linear strips, filled with dark brown silty clay, and cut into layer 016 (029, 031 *etc.* in Figures 8.29, 8.36). They varied in dimensions between 0.15m and 0.41m wide × 0.06m–0.11m deep.

Several observations can be made concerning these features. Firstly, their spacing indicates that they are ruts made by cart-wheels. Some of them cut through the northern Avenue ditch (see below), showing that they post-date it. Secondly, they do not run over Newall's Mound, suggesting that it remained high enough in historical times to serve as an obstacle to movement. Nor do they run along the contours of the steep natural slope outside (north of) the northern Avenue ditch, presumably because this would

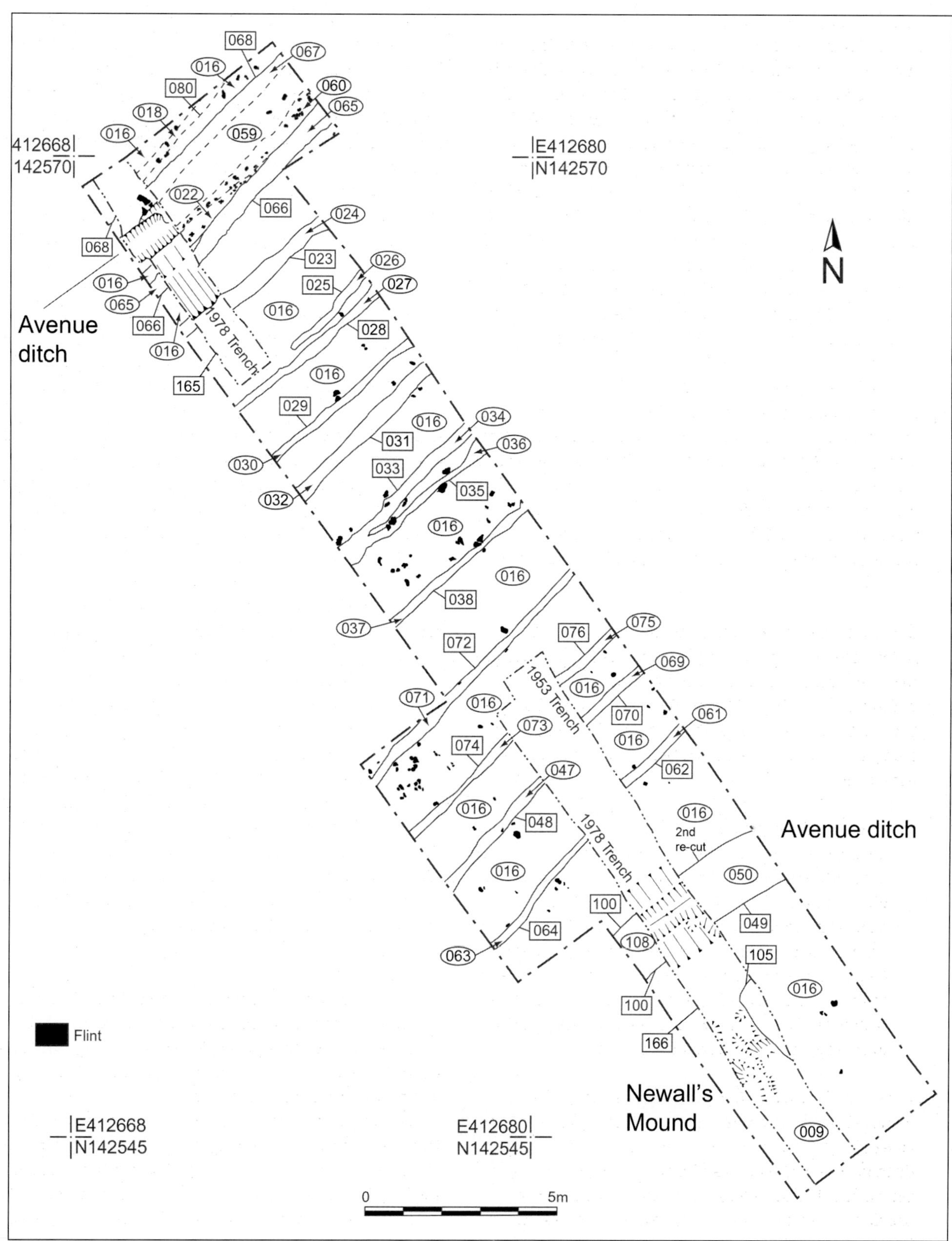

Figure 8.29. Plan of upper features in Trench 48 on the Avenue bend

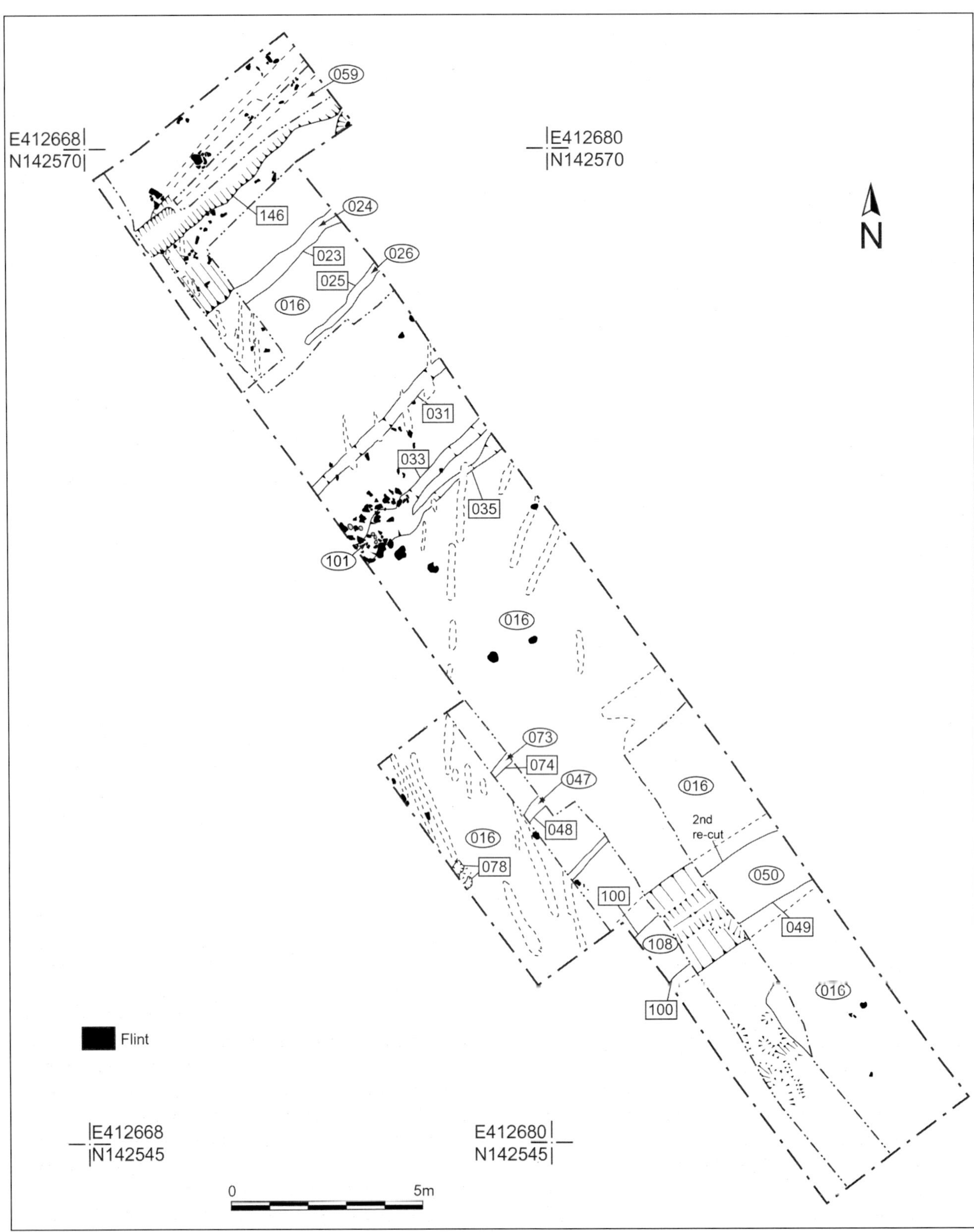

Figure 8.30. Plan of lower features in Trench 48 on the Avenue bend

Figure 8.31. Trenches 47 and 48, viewed from the west

have destabilised the carts. Thirdly, these ruts penetrate into periglacial layer 016, some of them being deep enough to have scarred the chalk bedrock underneath. Therefore, these linear wheel-ruts (and not the periglacial stripes, which are on a slightly different orientation here at the Avenue bend; Figure 8.30) are the anomalies that run the length of the Avenue north of the eighteenth-century road, as seen in the geophysical plots (*e.g.* Figure 8.3). Fourthly, we may conclude that during historical times the Avenue provided a routeway along the chalk spur leading to and from Stonehenge.

Other features within the Avenue

Two further features penetrating into 016 proved to be natural or associated with wheel-ruts (Figure 8.30). The first (078), beside the trench edge of the southeastern extension, was a collection of small, irregularly-shaped hollows (0.33m wide × 0.13m deep) filled with dark brown silty clay (077). This was most likely a tree-throw hole. The second, found in the middle of the Avenue and partially within the southern trench section, was a mid-brown patch of silty clay (101) in a slight depression (0.70m wide × 0.08m deep) cut along its edges by two merging wheel-ruts (033 and 035) of similar fill (one of which [034] contained three crumbs of Roman pottery; Figures 8.30, 8.36). A few sarsen lumps were found in the shallow depression (101) along with natural flint nodules embedded in the chalk. It appears that this feature is the result of wear associated with the wheel-ruts. Therefore, no features contemporary with the Avenue (other than its ditches) were found in the Avenue bend area.

The southern Avenue Ditch

The removal of backfill (009) from cutting 40/62, which measured 15m × 2m (SRP cut 166), exposed Atkinson and Evans' sections within that cutting. Evans took a snail column in 1978 from this cutting, and its location was seen in 2008 in the northeast-facing section. Importantly, the deposits and cut features visible in both the long sections of the re-opened cutting 40/62 indicate that the Avenue's southern (or eastern) ditch was re-cut here to the extent that, except for some of the primary fills, almost all of its original fills were removed, (probably) in prehistory (Figures 8.34–8.36; the deposits shown in the section drawings of the reopened cutting were seen *only* in section in 2008, not in plan).

The original cut of the Avenue's southern ditch (100; up to 0.64m deep) was filled with primary silts comprised of degraded chalk (097, 099 and 110) interspersed with narrow lenses of silty clays (098, 111, 112, 113 and 114). This indicates that the original ditch was left to silt up before any re-cutting occurred. However, the ditch was subsequently

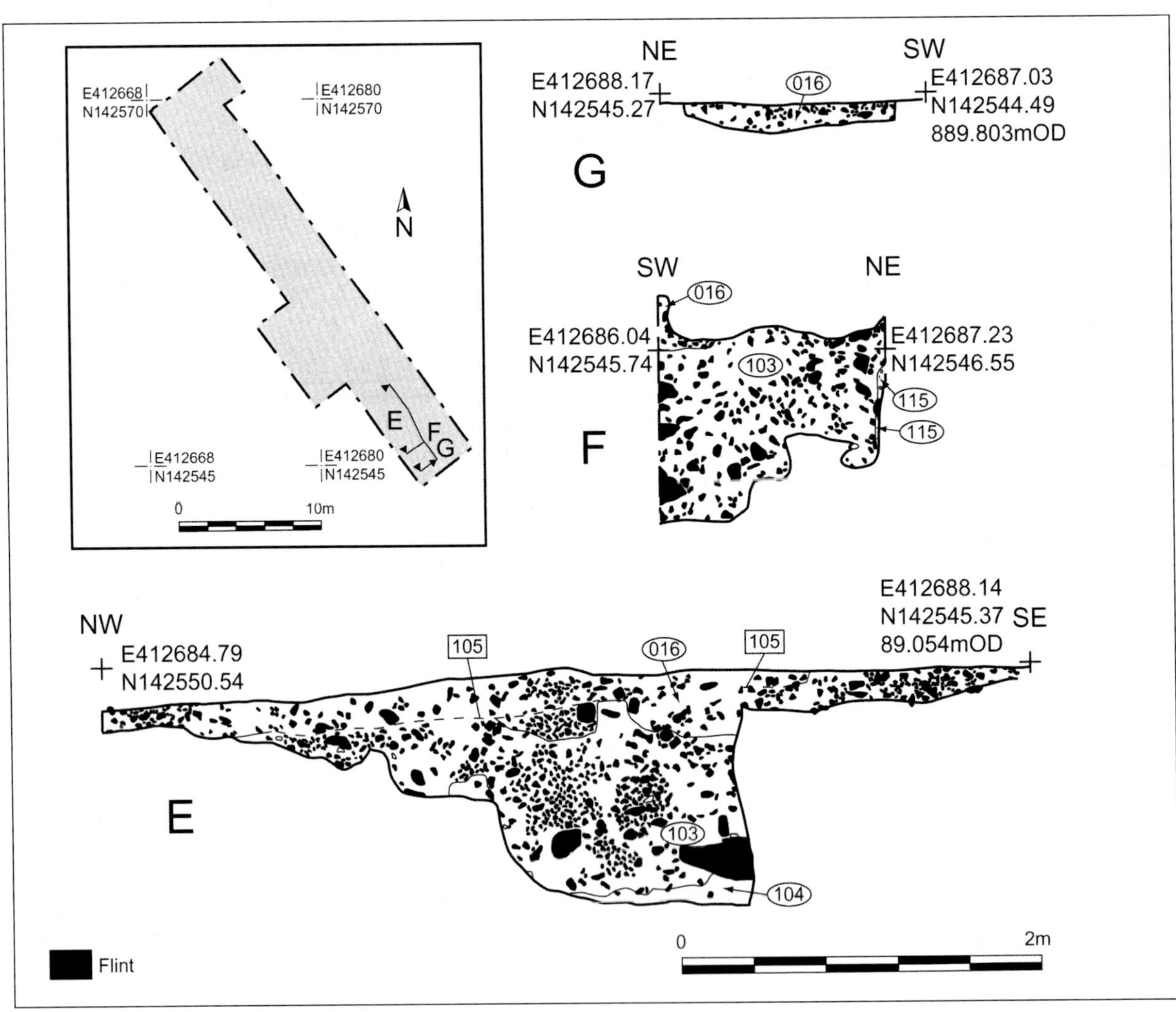

Figure 8.32. Section drawings in the southeast end of Trench 48 including the periglacial hollow

re-cut by cut 049 (0.76m deep) which scoured out most of the original ditch fill (Figures 8.29, 8.34–8.35). The cut was fairly steep-sided, with a rounded base. This was filled by 095 (in the southwest-facing section) and 109 (in the northeast-facing section). A second re-cut (Figures 8.34, 8.35) was filled by 096, a dark-brown clay silt with small to medium-sized flints indicating tip-lines. This implies that the fills of the re-cuts were the result of weathering rather than intentional backfill. That no stable lenses were seen at the base of the re-cuts implies that this weathering of the ditch fill must have occurred quite rapidly. The upper fill (050 and 108) was topsoil that had slumped into the top of the ditch.

The southern Avenue's bank shadow

No buried soils were found upon removal of topsoil (001) across the inner side of the southern (or eastern) Avenue ditch, under the bank shadow. In fact, this area was truncated by a wheel-rut (064 filled by 063, and 062 filled by 061), indicating that any bank surviving at the time that the wheel-ruts were made would have been so ephemeral as to pose no obstacle whatsoever. This implies that the bank, if it had ever been substantial, had been eroded almost flat by the historical period.

The northern Avenue ditch

Removing Atkinson and Evans' backfill (008) from cutting 96 (SRP cut 165; 6.50m × 1.50m), exposed their sections through the northern (or western) Avenue ditch and bank shadow (Figure 8.34 A & B). The location from where Evans removed his snail-sampling column was seen in the northeast-facing section. Unlike the southern Avenue ditch, no evidence of re-cutting of the ditch was visible in either section. The cut of the ditch (012; 0.92m wide × 0.33m deep) here was fairly steep-sided with a rounded, narrow, and irregular base. The

Figure 8.33. The periglacial hollow in Trench 48, viewed from the south

very thin primary fill (021) was a light brown silty clay with eroded chalk, covered by clay-silt upper fills (020 and 017), all the result of natural weathering and silting rather than intentional backfill.

To investigate whether the Avenue ditch was comprised of two phases, a 4.60m longitudinal section removed the interior (southeastern) portion of the ditch fill between Atkinson and Evans' cut and the northwest edge of the 2008 trench (section C in Figure 8.34). Half of the ditch fill was left *in situ* for future investigation. No evidence of re-cutting was observable. The ditch cut (146, the same as 012) indicates a shallow (only *c.* 0.22m deep), irregular shape that continues on a straight course (Figure 8.30). The ditch sides and bases were somewhat segmented, indicating that the ditch was dug out in segments that were then conjoined. The fills indicate natural weathering and infilling of the ditch. Along with 021, the rest of the primary fill (135) along the ditch's length was a mid-brown silty clay lens running along the base of the cut (146), followed by pale yellowish-brown compact chalk with silty clay (134, the same as 021) running in incomplete lengths across the entire section. This, in turn, was covered by a dark brown silty clay with chalk inclusions and pea gravel (060, the same as 020) and then the upper fill (059, the same as 017) a dark brown silty clay with occasional flint and chalk.

The northern Avenue's bank shadow

As with the southern Avenue bank shadow, no buried soils were found beneath the bank shadow area on the inner side of the northern Avenue ditch. After removal of Atkinson and Evans' backfill (008) from cutting 96 (cut 165), the bank shadow (022) did show in section on the slope immediately inside the edge of the ditch, but again was truncated by a wheel-rut (066 filled with 065). Another rut was present at the top of the slope on the north side of the Avenue (023 filled with 024), reiterating the fact that the bank was not substantial at this location in the historical period.

8.3.4. Trench 57: the Oblique Ditch and Avenue

A 4m × 5m trench was hand-excavated at the point of intersection of the Oblique Ditch and the northern Avenue ditch in the area of Atkinson's 1953 cutting 95 (Figures 8.23, 8.37– 8.38). As no section drawings from Atkinson's excavation of C95 survive, a primary objective of the 2008 re-excavation was to expose, clean and record these sections. Cutting 95 consisted of two diagonally opposed quadrants of the junction of the Oblique Ditch with the northern Avenue ditch (Cleal *et al.* 1995: plan 4 zone E).

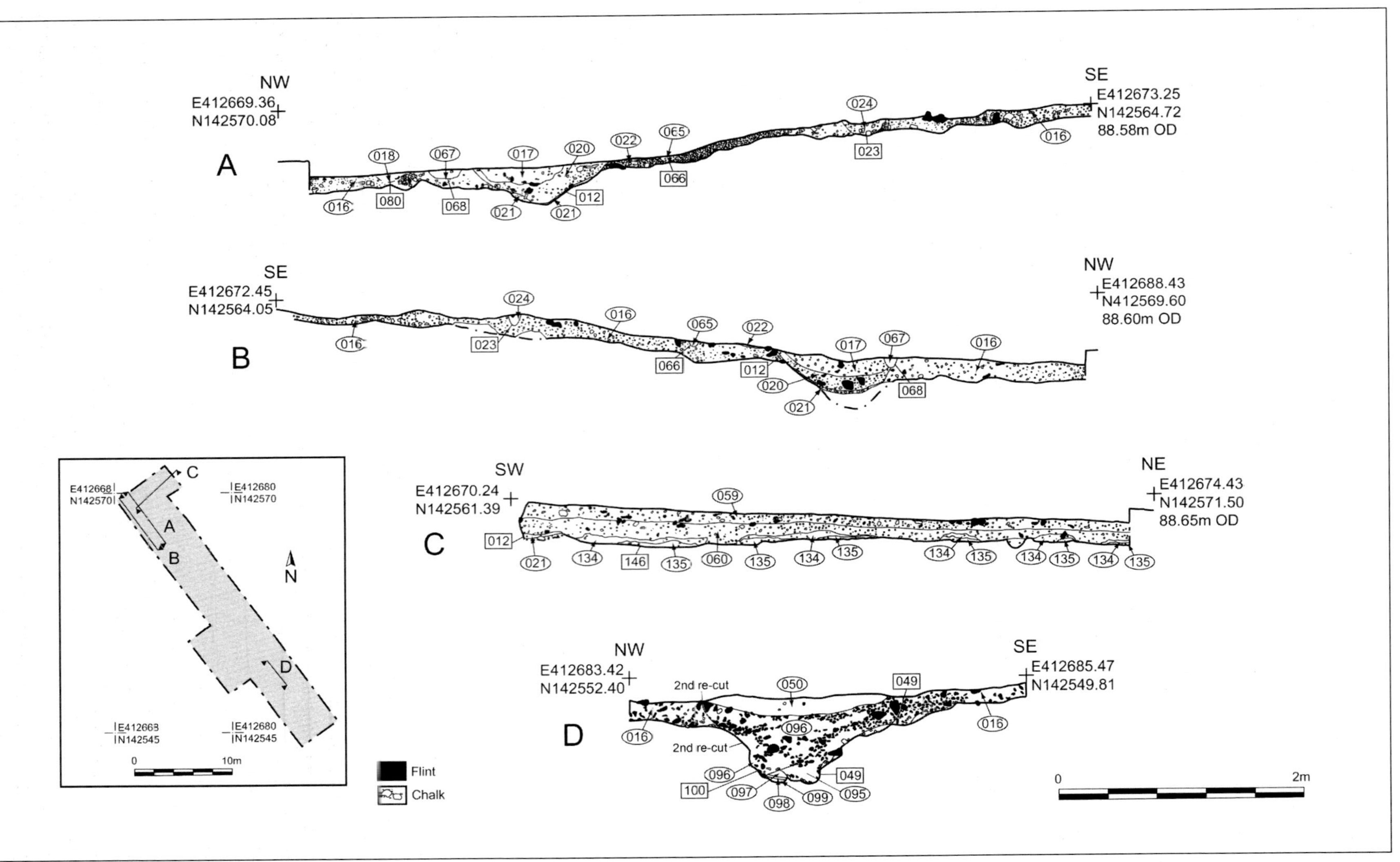

Figure 8.34. Section drawings from Trench 48

Figure 8.35. The southern/eastern Avenue ditch showing its two re-cuts viewed from the southwest

The Avenue ditch

A *c.* 3m length of the base of the northern Avenue ditch (149) was exposed by the removal of the backfill of cutting 95 (SRP cut 118 filled by 117).

Ditch 149 cuts through a chalk- and flint-rich, silty loam layer of weathered bedrock into the underlying solid chalk bedrock. The ditch is slightly irregular in plan, measuring 1.10m–1.20m wide, and up to 0.57m deep, with a concave, bowl-shaped profile (Figure 8.39); there are a number of pronounced undulations in its base, possibly left by the removal of *in situ* flint nodules. The ditch was filled by a sequence of silty clay deposits, differentiated by the frequency of flint inclusions (150/156 is the primary deposit, 151/157 the secondary and 152 the tertiary deposit).

The tertiary fill (152) of the Avenue ditch is stratigraphically equivalent to layer 159 (dark brown humic loam) which lay under the turf and topsoil (001) throughout most of the trench but over the fill (154/158) of the Oblique Ditch. Against the southern edge of the trench, layer 159 lay on top of a deposit of large and medium-sized flint nodules in a brown silt matrix (162). Layer 162, interpreted as a dump of flint nodules, was deposited after the Oblique Ditch was cut and filled.

Trench 57 was too limited in extent to expose any traces of a bank on the southern upslope side of the Avenue ditch.

The Oblique Ditch

In Trench 57, the Oblique Ditch (153) cuts through the line of the northern Avenue ditch at an angle of approximately 50°. Over 2.50m of the base of the Oblique Ditch was exposed by removal of Atkinson's backfill (117). In this exposure, the Oblique Ditch measures 0.55m wide by 0.53m deep, with a shallow concave profile. It cuts through a chalk- and flint-rich, silty loam layer, thought to be weathered bedrock, into the underlying solid chalk bedrock. It also cuts through the secondary fill (151/157) of the northern Avenue ditch. It contained a single fill (154/158) of compact silt with frequent flint fragments. This fill was stratigraphically earlier than layers 162, 159 and 001.

As noted for Trench 46, above, the fact that the Oblique Ditch cuts through the northern Avenue ditch suggests that it is related to the historic use of the Avenue as a trackway.

8.3.5. Trench 58: the Avenue east of the bend

A T-shaped trench (10m × 3m east–west, with a perpendicular extension 2.20m × 3m on its southern edge) was hand-excavated on the line of the northern Avenue ditch in the area of Atkinson's 1953 cutting 39 (Figure 8.40). Cutting 39 is located just to the north of the

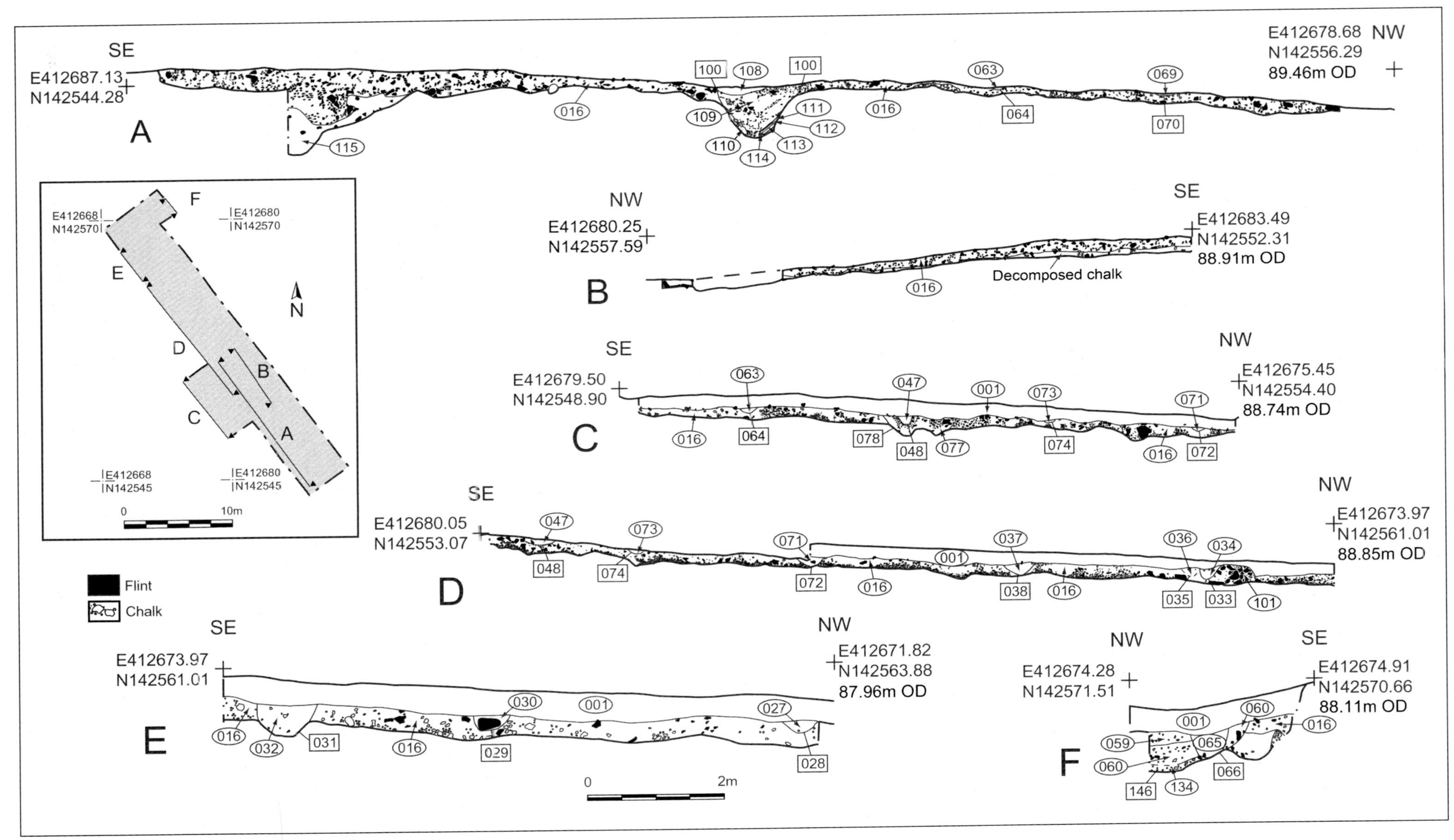

Figure 8.36. Section drawings from Trench 48

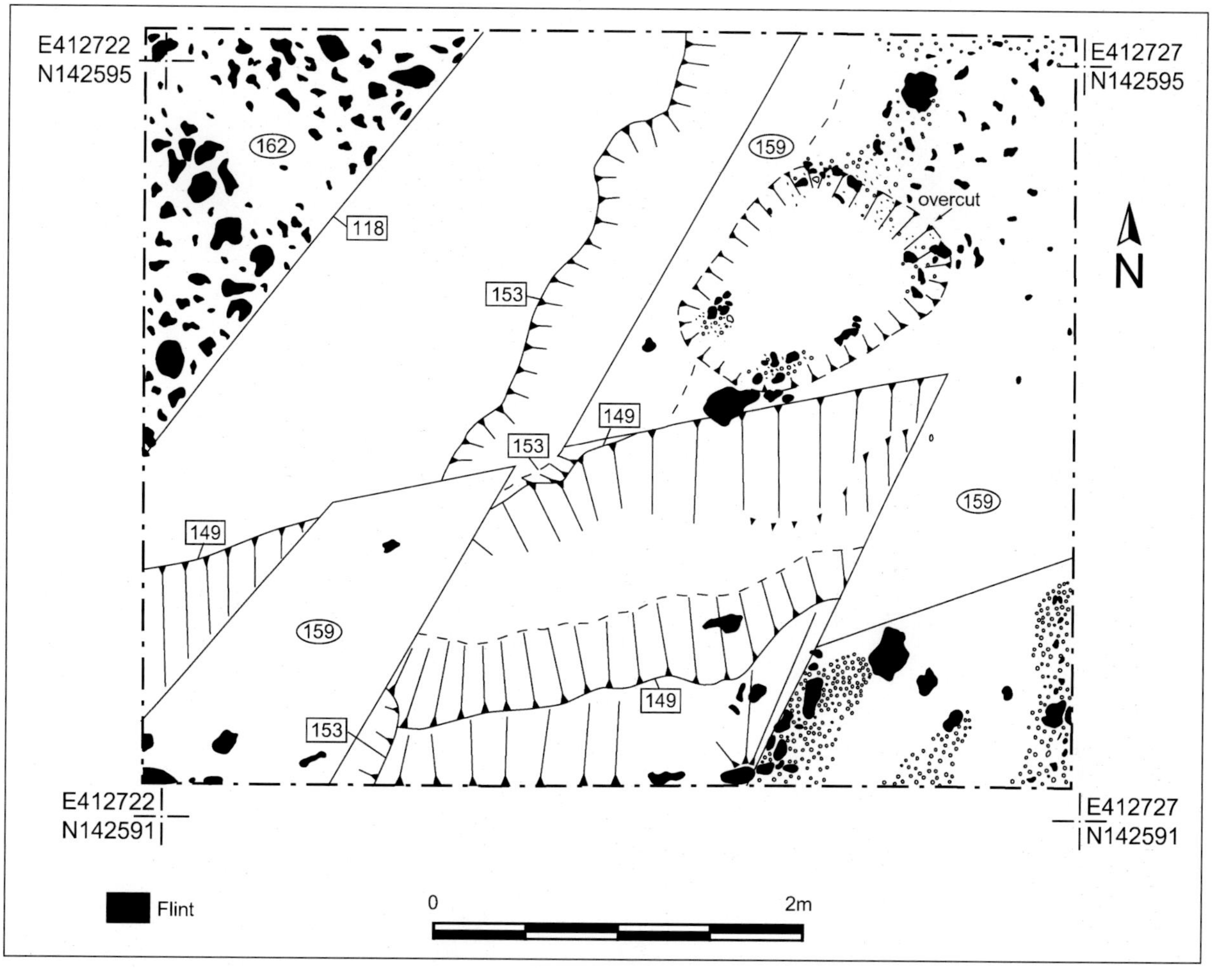

Figure 8.37. Plan of Trench 57 showing the northern Avenue ditch and the Oblique Ditch

Figure 8.38. Trench 57, viewed from the west

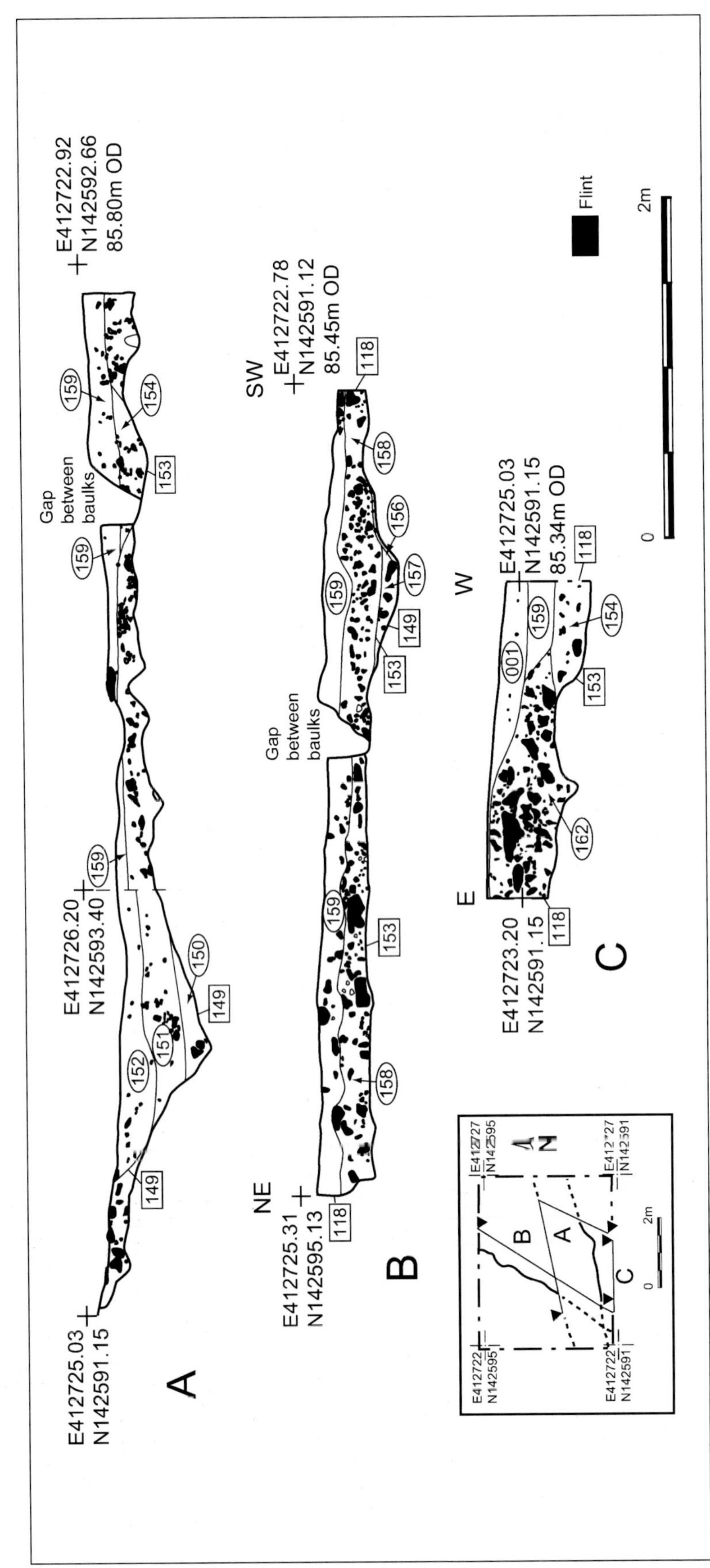

Figure 8.39. Section drawings from Trench 57

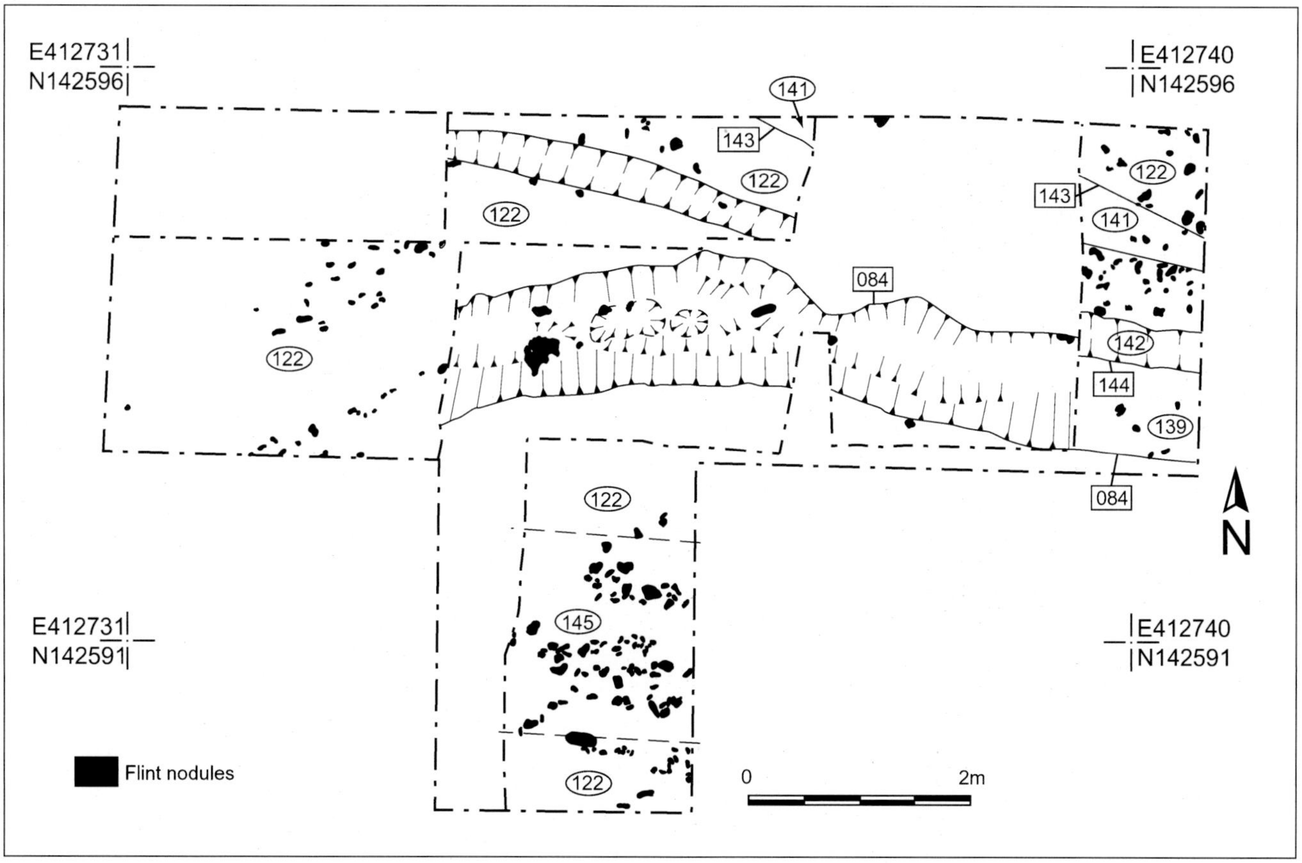

Figure 8.40. Plan of Trench 58 showing the northern Avenue ditch

Figure 8.41. Trench 58, viewed from the east

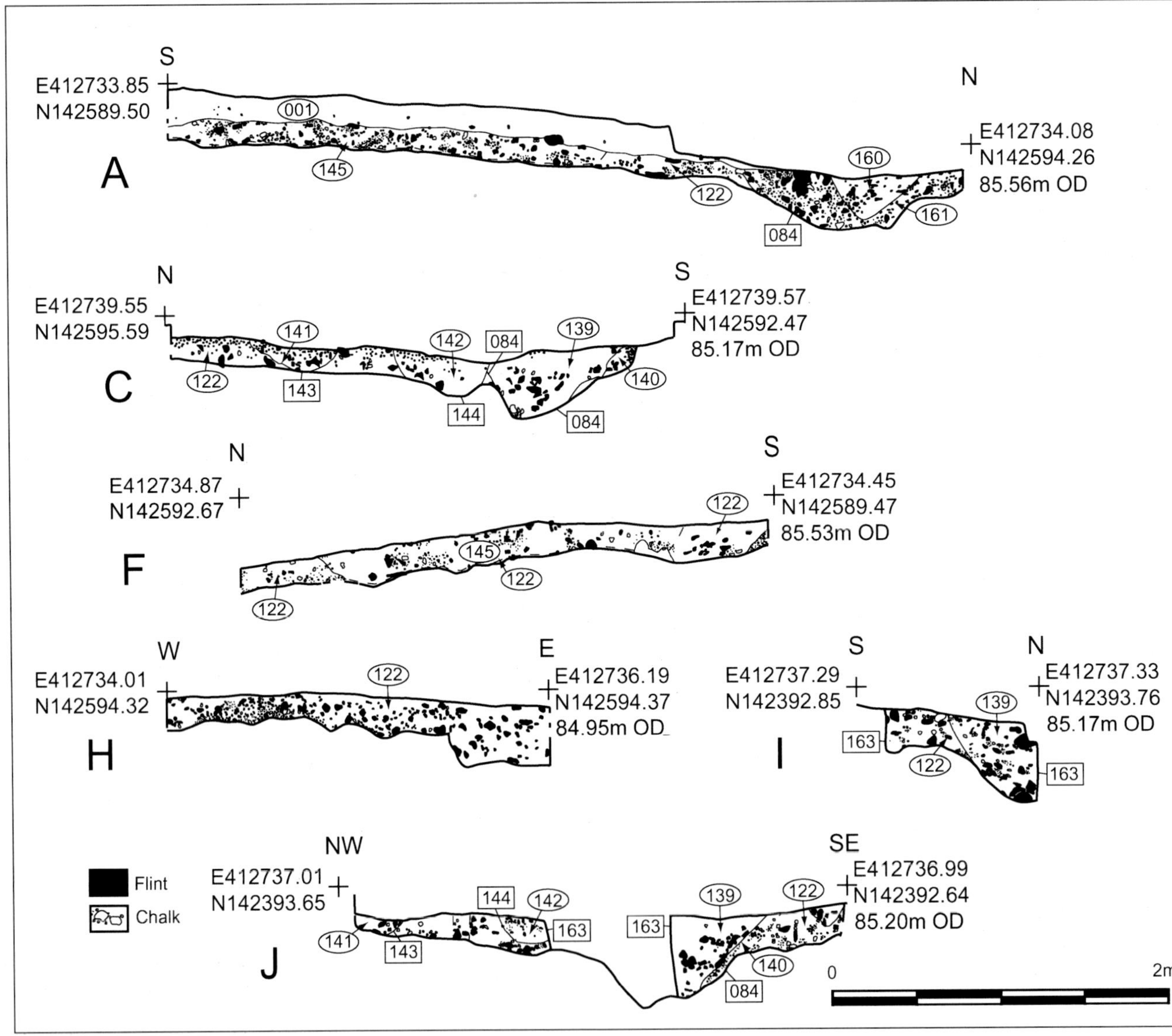

Figure 8.42. (continued on opposite page) Section drawings from Trench 58

Avenue bend, where the Avenue turns to the east before crossing the dry valley of Stonehenge Bottom.

Cutting 39 consisted of a series of opposed quadrants, running for approximately 0.50m along the line of the northern Avenue ditch (Figure 8.41; Cleal *et al.* 1995: plan 4 zone E). An elongated extension trench ran south from the central quadrant across the line of the northern Avenue bank. During the re-excavation of C39 in 2008, the backfill (006) from the 1953 excavation was removed, except for the western portion of Atkinson's southern extension trench. As for the other SRP trenches near the Avenue bend, a primary objective was to record the previously exposed sections within Atkinson's cutting, and the unexcavated fills were seen in section, not in plan.

The northern Avenue ditch

Following the removal of backfill (006) from Atkinson's trench (SRP cut 163), a 5.60m length of the base of the northern Avenue ditch (cut 084) was exposed. Ditch 084 cuts through layer 122, a chalk- and flint-rich, silty loam thought to be weathered bedrock, into the underlying solid chalk bedrock. The ditch (084), 0.90m–1.10m wide and up to 0.45m deep, has a concave, bowl-shaped profile (Figure 8.42). The ditch is slightly irregular in plan with a number of pronounced undulations along its base, possibly left by the removal of *in situ* flint nodules. A thin primary deposit of chalk-rich silt (140) lay on the southern side of ditch 084, presumably washed in from up the slope to the south, perhaps from the Avenue's northern bank (145). The majority of ditch 084 was filled with a series of friable silty clays containing varying amounts of chalk and flint fragments (fills 139, 160 and 161). No re-cuts were noticed during excavation but the uneven bottom of ditch 084 and the steep-sided interface between fills 161 and 160 could be evidence of one or even two episodes of re-cutting (Figure 8.42A).

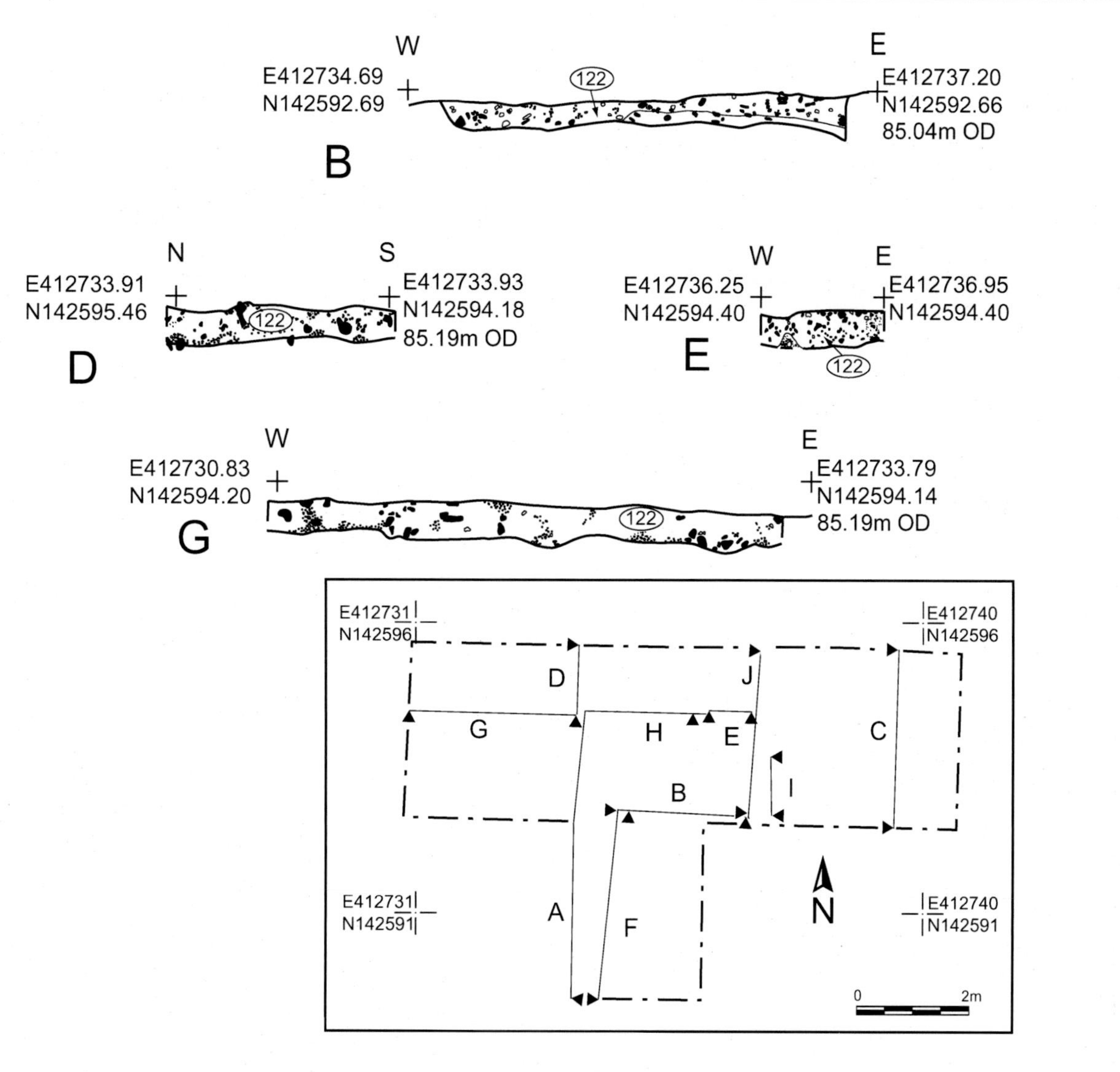

The northern Avenue bank

A 0.17m-thick and 2.60m-wide linear deposit of silty loam with frequent large flint inclusions (145) runs parallel with, upslope and immediately to the south of, the northern Avenue ditch. This layer overlies the weathered natural layer 122 and is thought to be the remains of the northern Avenue's bank, its 'shadow'.

Wheel-ruts

Two linear features (143 and 144) ran approximately parallel to, and overlying the unexcavated portions of the northern edge of the Avenue's upper ditch fill (139). Only feature 144 was excavated. It measured 0.30m–0.40m wide and 0.15m–0.20m deep and had a rounded, concave profile. These features may be wheel-ruts similar to those seen in Trenches 46 and 48 (see above) and Trench 56 (see below).

8.3.6. Conclusion

Excavations at the Avenue's elbow achieved various objectives:

1. The aim of 'salvaging' and recording Atkinson's sections was fully realised in all trenches, allowing evaluation of ditch morphologies.
2. No evidence was found to support the hypothesis for two phases of Avenue construction, consisting of an earliest phase from Stonehenge as far as the Avenue bend and a later addition from the Avenue bend towards the River Avon. Instead, the evidence is best interpreted as a single build for the Avenue along its entire length from Stonehenge to the river, with stretches of its southern and possibly also its northern ditches being re-cut on at least one occasion. This evidence for a single build along its entire length is supported by the discovery of a Late

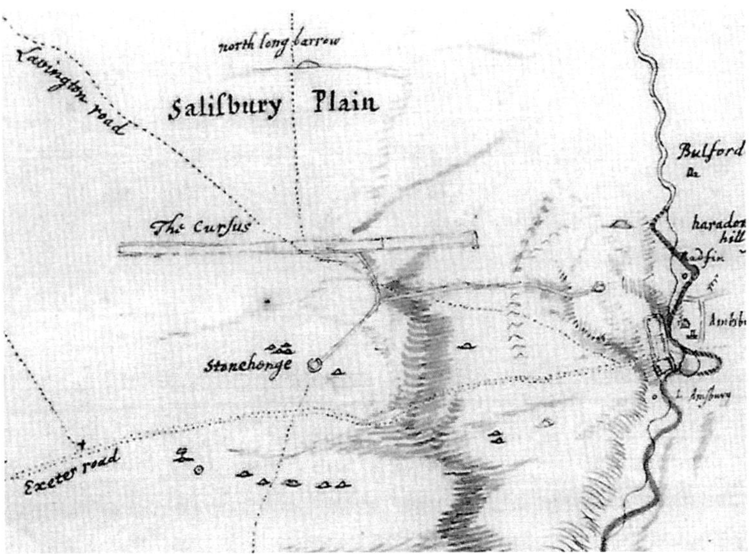

Figure 8.43. Stukeley's sketch plan from his 1721–1724 manuscript, showing the 'northern extension' of the Avenue; note that he was unaware of the path of the eastern end of the Avenue which was already obscured by ploughing

Neolithic oblique arrowhead in fresh condition in the northern Avenue ditch at West Amesbury (see Chapter 5).

3. The geophysical linear stripes within the Avenue's elbow were shown to be neither periglacial nor pre-Avenue features but instead are wheel-ruts most likely of medieval (or possibly Roman) date.
4. No other anthropogenic features were found within the Avenue nor did the bank shadow preserve any bank fills or buried soils.

Perhaps the most significant finding from the Avenue bend excavations is the observation that the construction of the Avenue was carefully laid out in relation to subtleties of topography and geology. This is seen most clearly in the example of the northern Avenue ditch which carefully follows the lower contour of the natural ridge of chalk as it heads along its solstitial axis from Stonehenge to Stonehenge Bottom. The diminutive nature of the ditch was compensated in this way, since the slightly higher ground would have accentuated the bank that can be presumed to have existed in parallel to the ditch. The bend of the Avenue curves along the contour as it drops into Stonehenge Bottom. This demonstrates that those who laid out the Avenue paid close attention to the local topography and the lie of the land. What is curious, however, is that the history of each ditch appears to have been quite different. The southern Avenue ditch was re-cut at least twice at the bend while the northern ditch appears to have been left largely unaltered except perhaps beyond the bend in Trench 58.

Finally, what happened to the Avenue's banks? Why is so little of the material of them left? They do not seem to have eroded away due to vehicle activity (as shown by the wheel-ruts) because tip lines were generally not evident in the ditch fills. It may be that the banks were never particularly substantial, in which case it is possible that not all the chalk dug out of the ditches was used to form the banks.

8.4. The Stonehenge Avenue's 'northern branch' (Trench 56)

M. Parker Pearson and A. Teather

William Stukeley was the first to suggest that there might be a northern branch of the Avenue (1740: 150), leading from its elbow (or bend) to the eastern end of the Cursus (Figure 8.43). He described this as a 'western' branch of the Avenue (Burl and Mortimer 2005: 92–3, note 109), but this hypothetical branch is more commonly called the 'northern branch' or 'northern extension'. Stukeley's idea was reiterated by Colt Hoare, Petrie, and, initially, O.G.S. Crawford but was finally dismissed in print in 1979 (RCHME 1979: 13), when Desmond Bonney described the Oblique Ditch as a later earthwork and the 'feature' running towards the Greater Cursus as a natural watercourse (the latter had already been recognised as such by Crawford in 1923).

This dry watercourse is a striking landscape feature. It is almost entirely straight and runs for 700m down the centre of a small valley from the southern ditch of the Cursus to Stonehenge Bottom (see Figure 2.3 for the coombe system of Stonehenge Bottom). It is also just 4° off the Avenue's alignment with Stonehenge, so that anyone walking south along it has an excellent view along the Avenue towards the monument (which is very slightly to the left of one's gaze directly ahead). In phenomenological terms it is a remarkable feature which might well have seemed a significant and constructed element of the landscape at the time of Stonehenge and perhaps even earlier.

Aerial photographs of the watercourse show it as a soilmark or cropmark, a diffuse feature up to 30m wide, separating in places into a pair of sub-parallel marks. Today its contours have been softened by weathering and cultivation, and there is a thin blanket of colluvium apparent at its junction with Stonehenge Bottom. It is interesting to speculate on how it would have looked in prehistoric times, as a sharper and more dramatic feature which possibly formed an important processional route towards Stonehenge prior to the construction of the Avenue (or at least that part of the Avenue's length from the elbow to the river).

Since this feature had never been thoroughly investigated, two research questions were formulated to determine whether this natural feature had played a significant role in this landscape.

1. Why does the watercourse sometimes described as the 'northern branch of the Avenue' run so straight, and has it been humanly modified at any time in the past?
2. What are the parallel 'stripes' (identified by geophysics) which run at a slightly different angle to the line of the dry valley?

8.4.1. The excavation

A 2m-wide and 35m-long trench was dug by hand across the dry watercourse, close to the line of an earlier auger transect by Mike Allen (Figures 8.44–8.45). After removal of the turf, the ploughsoil (001; 0.17m–0.32m deep) was excavated by hand in 1m × 1m squares, and sieved through a 10mm mesh. Beneath the ploughsoil in the centre of the trench, an 18.2m-long deposit of colluvium (002) covered a variety of artificial and natural features which were all excavated.

Natural features

A number of periglacial features had formed in the chalk bedrock (collectively 014; the fills are labelled on Figure 8.44). These were filled with orange-brown silt containing flint nodules, broken flint and chalk lumps. Nine of them were linear features:

- one of them ran northwest–southeast at the southeastern end of the trench (filled by 003);
- three ran northeast–southwest towards the southeastern end of the trench (filled by 005, 006 and 007),
- three ran northeast–southwest in the centre and northwestern part of the trench (025, 030 and 027);
- two ran northwest–southeast towards the northwestern end of the trench (008 and 013).

The remaining eight natural features were partial (extending into the section) or irregular in shape (004, 021, 022, 023, 024, 026, 028 and 029). The largest of these was a 1.89m-long and 0.63m-deep void in the southwest-facing section, filled by a layer of olive-brown silt (026) on top of a pale grey basal deposit (031; Figure 8.44). This may have been a tree-throw hole, as may some of the other irregular features, but none had the distinctive half-moon plan of tree-throw holes.

Wheel-ruts

Five wheel-ruts were identified within Trench 56, all of them oriented northeast–southwest, perpendicular to the axis of the trench. Four of them (015 filled by 009 [0.34m wide × 0.12m deep], 016 filled by 010 [0.18m wide × 0.12m deep], 017 filled by 011 [0.29m wide × 0.05m deep], and 018 filled by 012 [0.12m wide × 0.02m deep]) were located towards the northwestern end of the trench, beneath the ploughsoil (001) and cut into the valley-side chalk bedrock; some of these wheel-ruts are identifiable in the magnetometer survey as a bunched group of linear anomalies. The fifth (032 filled by 019 [0.14m wide × 0.04m deep]) was buried beneath colluvium (002) within the central part of the trench and is detectable as a minor linear anomaly on the magnetometer plot.

All of the wheel-ruts were filled by orange-brown silt, except for 032, the fill (019) of which was a light brown clay. There was no dateable material in any of the ruts.

The wheel-ruts probably form part of the same routeway as those detected further southwest at the Stonehenge end of the Avenue (Trench 45), at the Avenue bend (Trenches 46 and 48) and to the northeast within the Greater Cursus (Trench 40). These may be joined together to indicate a route used by wheeled vehicles from Stonehenge northeastwards along the Avenue, crossing Stonehenge Bottom and then climbing up the gentle incline of the 'northern branch' valley, crossing the Cursus and heading for Larkhill. The visible earthworks formed by the ruts, prior to their subsequently being ploughed flat, may well have been the cause of Stukeley and Colt Hoare's speculation about a northern extension of the Avenue.

Without dateable material from the ruts themselves, the date of this routeway's use is uncertain but it is unlikely to have been before the Roman period. Indeed, the evidence for substantial activity within Stonehenge during the Roman period (Darvill and Wainwright 2009) could be linked to the initial use of this cart track, perhaps to carry broken sarsens and bluestones away from Stonehenge, to be used elsewhere as building materials.

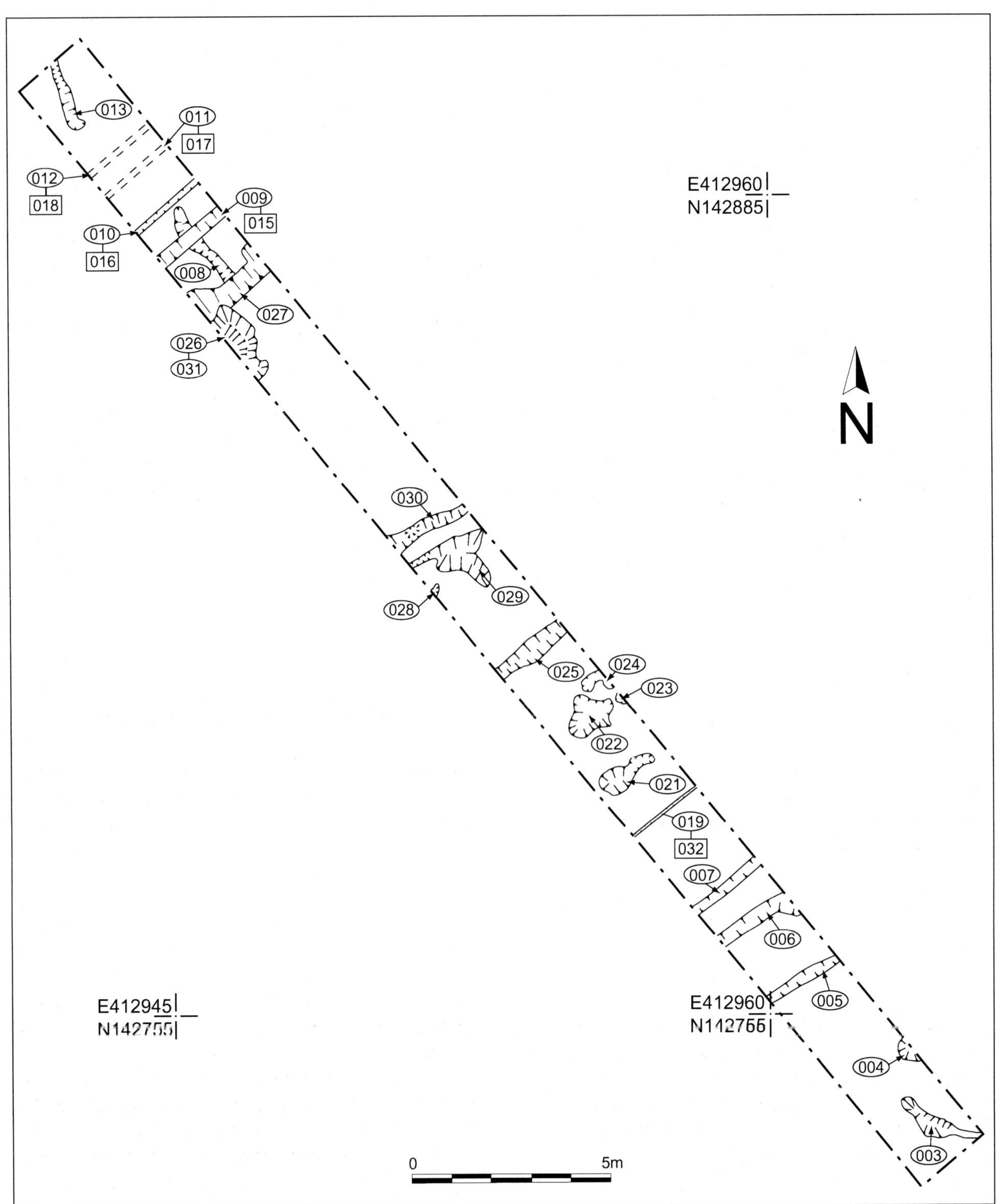

Figure 8.44. Plan of Trench 56 across the 'northern Avenue extension'

Figure 8.45. Trench 56, viewed from the northeast, looking towards the Avenue bend excavations and Stonehenge

The colluvial layer (002)

This was a thin layer, 0.10m deep and 18.2m wide, across the lowest part of the valley floor. It contained a few burnt flints and some worked flints. Only one wheel-rut (032) was identified beneath this deposit. Since the use of wheeled vehicles is likely to date to the Roman period or later, it is probable that this colluvium formed during the last 2,000 years.

The ploughsoil (001)

This is a thin, stone-free, silty calcareous grey rendzina, mostly 0.17m–0.22m deep but increasing to 0.32m in the centre of the valley. Three small sherds (two of them probably Iron Age) were found in the ploughsoil, together with a small assemblage of worked flint and some burnt flints.

8.4.2. Conclusion

The minor tributary dry valley of Stonehenge Bottom contains little colluvium. The notable absence of hillwash, especially within Stonehenge Bottom, has puzzled several authors (Bell 1986; Richards 1990: 210–11; Allen in Cleal *et al.* 1995: 332). Julian Richards has suggested that the absence of hillwash is a result of scouring of the coombe by winterbournes. Alternatively, there may have been only limited cultivation disturbance of the soil in the area, with the catchment of Stonehenge Bottom largely under long-term grassland and pasture (Allen 1995a & b; 1997).

The shallowness of colluvium in this valley does not reflect an absence of colluvium in the wider Stonehenge landscape. Bell recorded hillwash at a number of locations in the immediate area (Richards 1990: 210–11; Allen 1994: 271, fig. 56), and shallow colluvial deposits have been recorded south of King Barrow Ridge (Allen 1997).

The only cultural features excavated within Trench 56 were five wheel-ruts, most likely dating to the Roman period or later. Possible Iron Age sherds in the ploughsoil above the thin layer of colluvium suggest that it may have formed in the first millennium BC but the presence of a cart-rut sealed beneath the colluvial layer hints at a rather later date for the hillwash.

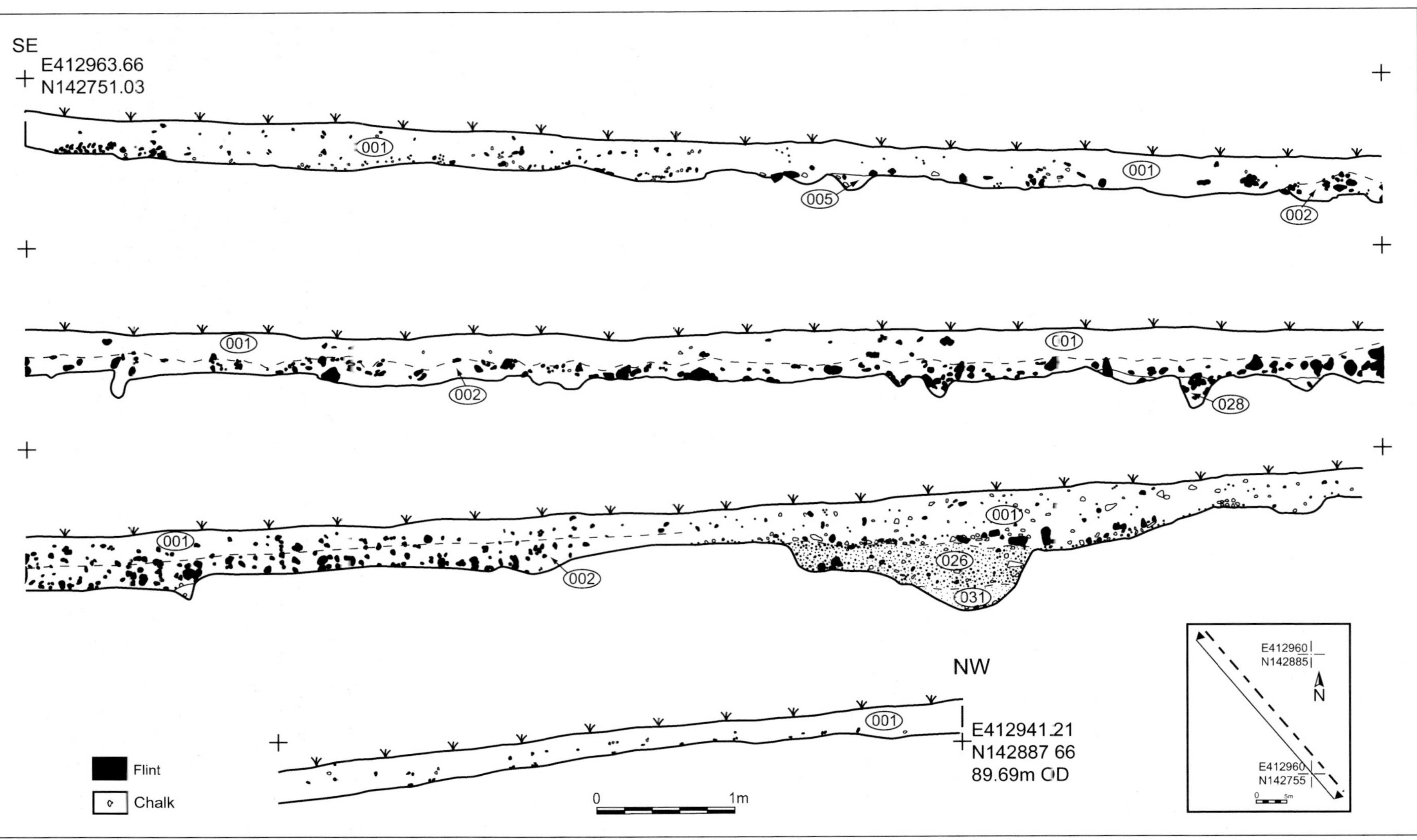

Figure 8.46. Long section within Trench 56

Lab number	Sample ID	Material and context	Radiocarbon age (BP)	$\delta^{13}C$ (‰)	Calibrated date range (95% confidence)	Posterior density estimate (95% probability)
OxA-20011	SAV 045 (1027)	Antler, *Cervus elaphus*, from the base of pit 056 within the fill (045)	3868±28	-23.1		
OxA-20350	SAV 045 (1027)	As OxA-20011	3836±29	-23.5		
SUERC-23205	SAV 045 (1027)	As OxA-20011	3770±30	-23.3		
Weighted mean (T'=5.8; T' (5%)=6.0; v=2; Ward and Wilson 1978)			3827±17		2345–2200 cal BC	*2310–2200 cal BC*
BM-1164	Sample 1	Antler, *Cervus elaphus*, from Northern Ditch, Stonehenge terminal (C6), 0.50m above ditch bottom	3678±68	-23.7	2290–1880 cal BC	*2285–1960 cal BC*
HAR-2013	9718	Antler pick from Southern Ditch, north side of A344 (C83), fill near bottom	3720±70	-23.6	2340–1920 cal BC	*2400–2210 cal BC*
OxA-4884	1912	Antler pick from Northern Ditch, Stonehenge terminal (C6), on bottom	3935±50	-20.4	2580–2280 cal BC	*2500–2270 (93%)* or *2255–2230 (2%) cal BC*
OxA-4905	9716	Animal bone from Southern Ditch 0.9km from Avon terminal (C86), on bottom	3865±40	-22.1	2470–2200 cal BC	*2450–2200 cal BC*
I-3216		Ox scapula from Northern Ditch near Avon terminal + ox scapula & antler tine from the Southern Ditch (C86)	2750±100		1200–770 cal BC	-
BM-1079	Sample 2 (Salisbury Museum ref no 4765)	Antler, *Cervus elaphus*, from Northern Ditch near Avon terminal (C87)	3020±180	-24.8	1690–810 cal BC	-

Table 8.1. Radiocarbon results from the Stonehenge Avenue

8.5. Scientific and artefactual analyses

8.5.1. Radiocarbon dating of the Stonehenge Avenue

P.D. Marshall, C. Bronk Ramsey and G. Cook

Previous dating

Six radiocarbon dates have previously been obtained from samples excavated at various locations along the Avenue (Table 8.1): one from AERE Harwell (HAR-2013), two from the British Museum (BM-1079 and BM-1164), two from the Oxford Radiocarbon Accelerator Unit (ORAU; OxA-4884 and OxA-4905), and one from Teledyne Isotopes (I-3216; Allen and Bayliss 1995). Two of these measurements were rejected by Allen and Bayliss (1995: 518–19), I-3216 on the grounds that it contains bones from different trenches, and BM-1079 because of potential contamination by humic acids. We have chosen to follow Allen and Bayliss (1995) and also exclude these two measurements from the analysis outlined below.

New dating

Replicate samples from a small red deer antler pick (SF 1027) laid on the base of a pit (fill 045 of pit 056; Trench 45) were dated at ORAU and the Scottish Universities Environmental Research Centre (SUERC) in 2009.

Radiocarbon analysis

The samples were processed and calibrated as described in Chapter 3. The ORAU sample was measured twice (OxA-20011 and OxA-20350), the second result forming part of internal laboratory quality assurance procedures. The calibrations of these results, which relate the radiocarbon measurements directly to the calendrical time scale, are given in Table 8.1 and in Figure 8.47. The calibrated date ranges quoted in italics are *posterior density estimates* derived from mathematical modelling of archaeological problems (see below). The ranges in plain type in Table 8.1 have been calculated according to the maximum intercept method (Stuiver and Reimer 1986). All other ranges are derived from the probability method (Stuiver and Reimer 1993).

Methodological approach

A Bayesian approach has been adopted for the interpretation of the chronology from the Avenue (see Chapter 3 for a description of this method). In the case of the Avenue, it is the chronology of the ditches and banks that is under consideration, not the dates of individual samples. The dates of this activity can be estimated not only using the scientific dating information from the radiocarbon measurements, but also by using the stratigraphic relationships between samples. The algorithm used in the models described below can be derived from the structures shown in Figures 8.47 and 8.48.

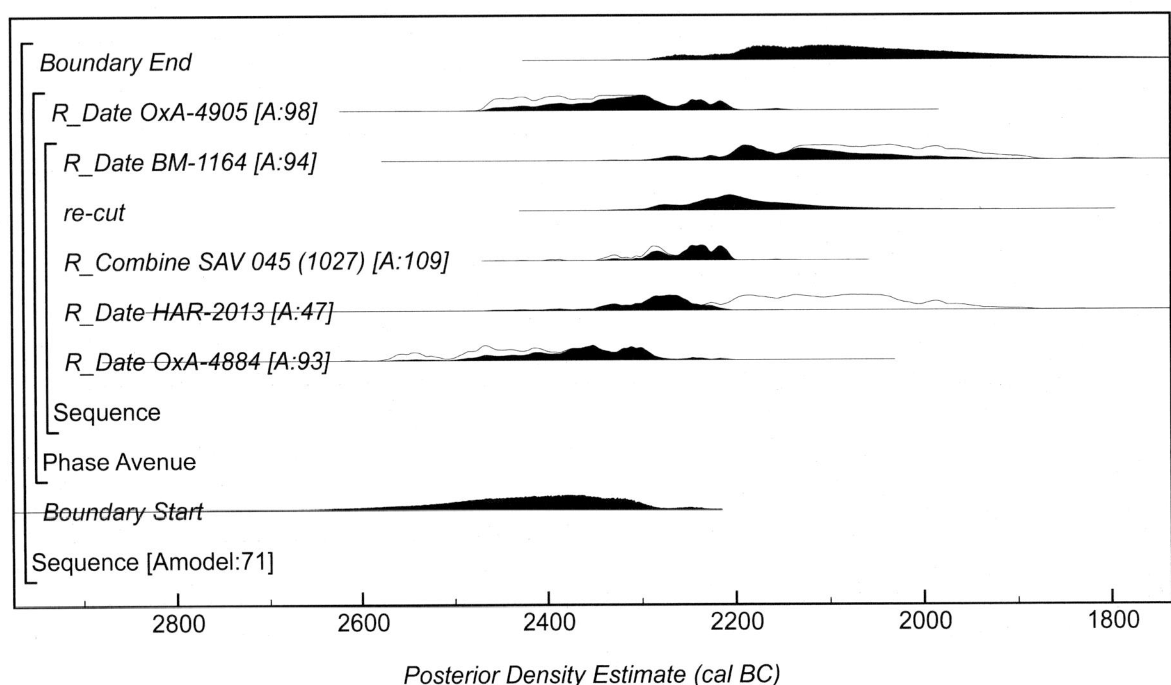

Figure 8.47. Probability distribution of dates from the Stonehenge Avenue (model 1). Each distribution represents the relative probability that an event occurs at a particular time. For each radiocarbon date, two distributions have been plotted: one in outline which is the result of simple radiocarbon calibration, and a solid one based on the chronological model used. The other distributions correspond to aspects of the model. For example, the distribution '*re_cut*' is the estimate for when the re-cutting of the Avenue ditch took place. The large square brackets down the left-hand side of the diagram and the OxCal keywords define the overall model exactly

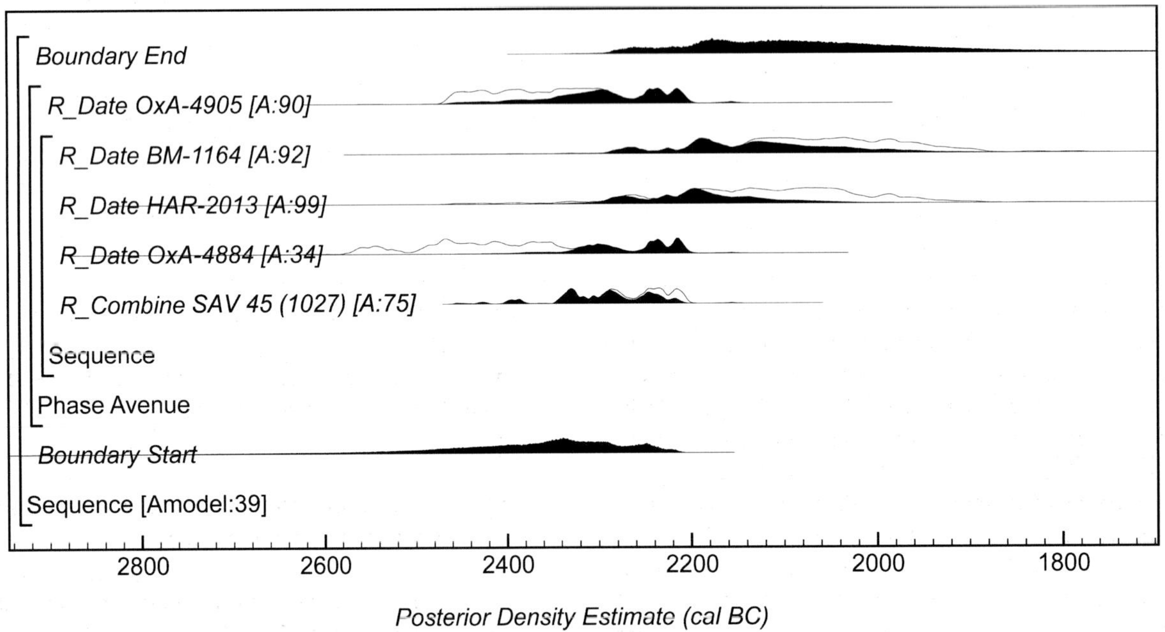

Figure 8.48. Probability distribution of dates from the Stonehenge Avenue (model 2)

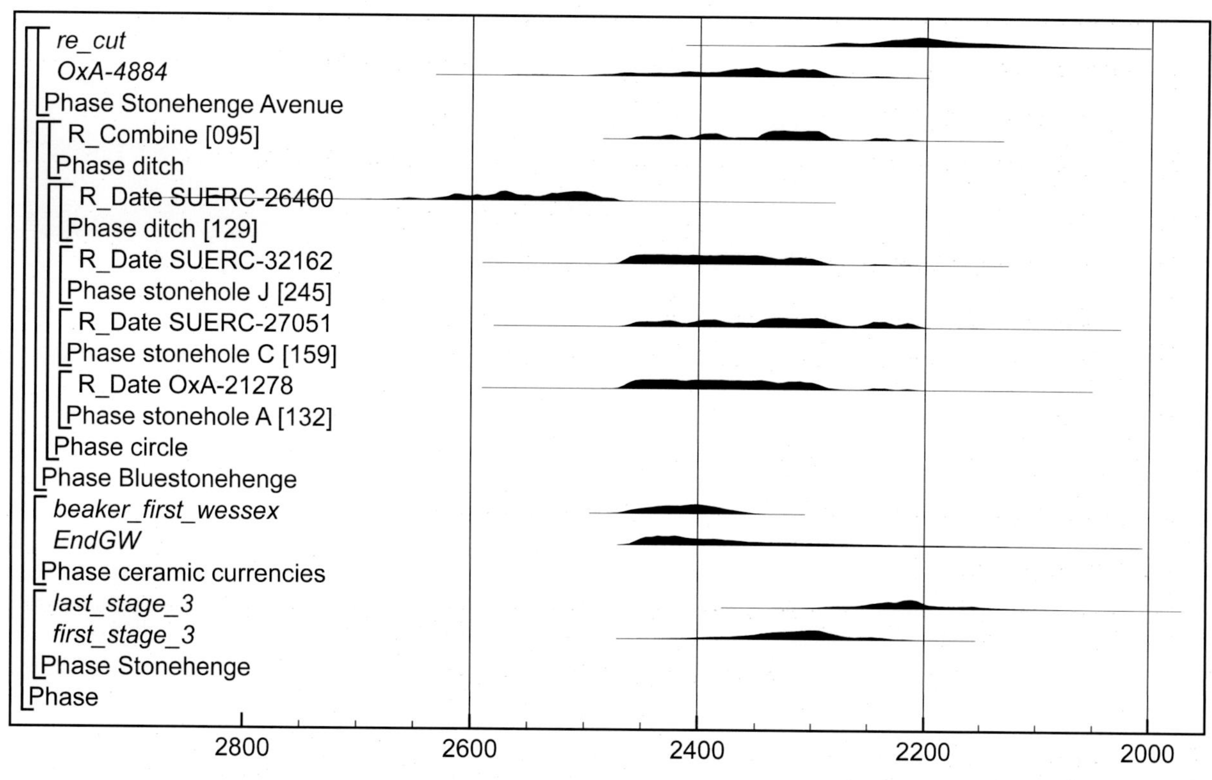

Figure 8.49. Probability distributions of dates from the Stonehenge Avenue (a) and from Bluestonehenge (b) with selected parameters for the Stonehenge Avenue, the introduction of Beakers into Wessex (Parker Pearson *et al.* 2019: fig. 2.2), the end of Grooved Ware (Barclay and Marshall 2011) and the beginning and end of Stage 3 at Stonehenge (Darvill *et al.* 2012: fig. 2)

Samples and sequence

The three measurements on antler pick SF 1027 (OxA-20011, OxA-20350, and SUERC-23205) are statistically consistent (T'=5.8; T' (5%)=6.0; ν=2; Ward and Wilson 1978), and a weighted mean has therefore been taken before calibration (SF 1027: 3827±17 BP).

The stratigraphic relationship between the pit containing the antler pick and the Avenue's eastern (southern) ditch and bank is not entirely straightforward. Whilst the top of the pit is covered by bank material, this may derive not from the ditch's initial construction but from its later re-cutting. The grubbiness of the chalk forming that part of the interior bank spread over the top of the pit argues against this particular bank fill being constructed from rock-fresh chalk. Thus it may have been deposited well after the ditch's initial digging-out. Further evidence for re-cutting of the ditch was found 20m south of Trench 45 (in C83; Cleal *et al.* 1995: 307) as well as in Trench 45 itself; thus the majority of fills of the ditches can be assumed to have accumulated after the re-cutting event. Models based on two different archaeological interpretations of the relationship between the Avenue banks and pit 056, containing the antler pick (SF 1027), were constructed, reflecting the ambiguities of the archaeological sequence.

In Model 1 (Figure 8.47), pit 056 is interpreted as post-dating the initial Avenue ditches but pre-dating the re-cutting of the ditches, so the sequence is as follows:

- Initial ditch cutting = OxA-4884
- Below/within junction of primary ditch fill and re-cut = HAR-2013
- Under bank material deriving from the re-cut = SF 1027
- About 0.50m above the ditch bottom (presumably in re-cut) = BM-1164

In Model 2 (Figure 8.48), pit 056 is interpreted as pre-dating both the initial ditch and the re-cutting:

- Under primary bank material deriving from the cutting of the initial ditch = SF 1027
- Initial ditch cutting = OxA-4884
- Below/within junction of primary ditch fill and re-cut = HAR-2013
- About 0.50m above the ditch bottom (presumably in re-cut) = BM-1164

Model 1 shows good overall agreement between the radiocarbon dates and stratigraphy (Amodel = 71%; Figure 8.47), while Model 2 shows poor agreement (Amodel = 39%; Figure 8.48). An overall agreement index of 60% is recommended as the threshold for showing consistency between the prior information and the radiocarbon results (Bayliss *et al.* 2007a; Bronk Ramsey 1995). The implications are therefore that the archaeological sequence in Model 1 is more likely to be true, with the antler pick (SF 1027), and therefore the digging of pit 056, post-dating the initial Avenue ditch but pre-dating the re-cutting.

The antler (OxA-4884) recovered by Hawley in 1923 from the bottom of the Stonehenge terminal of the northern ditch (Cleal *et al.* 1995: 327) provides the best estimate for the date of construction of the Avenue of *2500–2270 cal BC (93% probability*; Figure 8.47) and probably *2420–2285 cal BC* (*68% probability*). Model 1 also provides an estimate for the re-cutting of the ditches, of *2250–2135 cal BC* (*67% probability; re-cut;* Figure 8.47). This model (Figures 8.47 and 8.49) can be compared with the sequence for Stonehenge itself (see Chapter 11).

8.5.2. Worked flint from the Avenue at Stonehenge (Trench 45)

B. Chan

The assemblage from Trench 45 consists of 608 artefacts and includes blades, flakes, cores, irregular waste and two miscellaneous retouched flakes (Table 8.2). It is notable that it contains no formal tools. The majority of the assemblage came from the topsoil and Atkinson's backfill (36%), followed by the ditches (32%) and banks (15%) of the Stonehenge Avenue. The other significant concentrations were an assemblage of 25 artefacts retrieved from a knapping cluster (030) in the top of the primary fill of the western/northern ditch, and 27 artefacts from the upper fill (045) of pits 055 and 056. Neither of these assemblages is any different to the overall assemblage from the trench.

Only 25% of the assemblage comes from contexts of secure Neolithic–Chalcolithic date, with the majority of it coming from the topsoil and the upper fills of the Avenue ditches. There is little difference between the material from contexts of different phases, suggesting that the worked flint within later contexts is mostly residual, and this may also be the case for the material within the banks of the Avenue and the fills of its ditches.

Discussion and conclusion

The assemblage from Trench 45 is relatively small, and is mostly residual within later contexts. The composition of the assemblage is most notable for its lack of formal tools, and the presence of only two miscellaneous retouched flakes. This is a significant difference to the assemblage

Artefact type	Frequency	Percent
Blade	12	2.0
Bladelet	1	0.2
Flake	546	89.8
Irregular waste	35	5.8
Misc. retouched flake	2	0.3
Multi-platform flake-core	4	0.7
Single-platform flake-core	6	1.0
Tested nodule/bashed lump	2	0.3
Total	608	100.0

Table 8.2. The worked flint assemblage from Trench 45

from Trench 44, located 50m to the northwest (see Chapter 6). It also confirms a pattern found across the Stonehenge landscape, in which the assemblages from the mounds, banks and ditches of Neolithic monuments such as the Greater Cursus and Amesbury 42 long barrow (see Chapter 3), as well as the Stonehenge Avenue, are relatively devoid of tools, a pattern that contrasts significantly with assemblages from large and dense concentrations of flintwork that are presumably related to settlement and occupation, such as Durrington Walls (see Volume 2), as well as to non-settlement contexts such as the Cuckoo Stone pits (see Chapter 7). The significance of this pattern will be discussed in the synthetic overview in Volume 2.

8.5.3. Worked flint from the Avenue bend and the Avenue's 'northern branch'

B. Chan

The combined assemblage from the excavation of the Stonehenge Avenue bend and Gate Ditch (Trenches 46, 47, 48, 57, 58 and 59) and the Avenue's putative 'northern branch' (Trench 56) consists of 2,941 artefacts. The artefacts are all struck flint, except for two flint hammerstones. The material was retrieved from seven different excavation trenches, with most of it coming from Trenches 48 and 58 (Table 8.3). Much of the assemblage was residual within later deposits, and the only prehistoric features that contained worked flint were the northern Avenue ditch, the southern Avenue ditch and the Gate Ditch (Trenches 47 and 59, for which the stratigraphy is reported in Volume 4 since it appears to date to the Early Bronze Age).

Raw material and condition

The assemblage consists entirely of chalk-derived flint typical of the local area. The flint has dark grey varying to light grey cherty inclusions and a beige chalky cortex, which varies in thickness from 2mm–10mm. All of the flint is patinated to varying degrees. The flint from

Trench number	Frequency	Percent
46	26	0.9
47	167	5.7
48	1516	51.5
56	234	8.0
57	199	6.8
58	677	23.0
59	122	4.1
Total	2941	100.0

Table 8.3. The worked flint assemblage from the Avenue bend, the Gate Ditch and the 'northern branch'

Trenches 46, 47, 56, 57, 58 and 59 is heavily patinated, with most material being light grey to white in colour. The flint from Trench 48 is noticeably less patinated than that from the other trenches, with a significant proportion being dark grey and blue-grey in colour. The lower degree of patination of the Trench 48 material is most likely due to the presence of the deposits of glacial wash which cover the trench and make up Newall's Mound (see above). In general, the flint of the entire assemblage is in fair condition but abraded edges are common. This reflects the fact that much of the assemblage was residual within later deposits and has been subjected to some movement by the plough.

Assemblage composition, technology and chronology

The distinguishing feature of the assemblage is the complete lack of formal tools (Table 8.4). The assemblage also has a low proportion of cores and retouched flakes and a high proportion of flakes. Blades, bladelets and blade-like flakes make up a minor proportion of the assemblage, significantly less than encountered within assemblages from Early Neolithic sites in the area. There are two hammerstones in the assemblage, one of which has been very heavily used until it has become almost spherical and one with very light percussive wear. The significant numbers of utilised/edge-damaged flakes are largely plough-damaged.

There are no diagnostic tools within the assemblage, but the debitage mainly represents the products of a broad-flake technology, exercised with no care taken over core control or platform maintenance. Flakes are generally broad with thick butts. This type of flake-working is only broadly diagnostic, but most likely dates to the Late Neolithic–Bronze Age. Alongside the production of flakes, there is a minor element of blade-working in the assemblage. The majority of these blades were removed with limited core control and may possibly be Early Neolithic. Four of the blades are well-worked and show

	Artefact type	Frequency	Percent
Debitage and cores	Blade	28	1.0
	Blade-like flake	4	0.1
	Bladelet	1	<0.1
	Core on a flake	2	0.1
	Flake	2749	93.5
	Irregular waste	23	0.8
	Keeled non-discoidal flake-core	1	<0.1
	Multi-platform flake-core	9	0.3
	Single-platform flake-core	4	0.1
	Tested nodule/bashed lump	3	0.1
Retouched flakes and tools	Hammerstone	2	0.1
	Misc. retouched flake	7	0.2
	Utilised/edge-damaged flake/blade	108	3.7
	Total	2941	100.0

Table 8.4. The worked flint assemblage by artefact type from the Avenue bend, the Gate Ditch and the 'northern branch'

evidence of butt-preparation in the form of trimming or faceting; these blades may be Early Neolithic or later Mesolithic in date.

The spatial and contextual distribution of the assemblage

Over 55% of the assemblage came from the re-excavated backfill of Atkinson's and Atkinson and Evans' trenches (Cleal *et al.* 1995: 301). A further 30% of the assemblage came from demonstrably later deposits, such as the topsoil and the fills of wheel-ruts. With a further 8% of the material being intrusive in glacial wash or residual within colluvium, only 7% of the assemblage came from prehistoric features.

The material from prehistoric features consists of 99 artefacts from the fills of the northern Avenue ditch (012=146), 11 artefacts from the fill of the re-cut (049) of the southern Avenue ditch, seven artefacts from the soil shadow of the Avenue bank and 65 artefacts from fills of the Gate Ditch (015).

Only two flint chips were found within the primary fills of either of the Avenue ditches, with the remainder of the assemblage coming from secondary and especially tertiary ditch fills. These deposits will have accumulated over a long period of time and the material within them is likely to be mixed chronologically, with much of it potentially being residual material washed into the ditch. The assemblage from the ditch fills is exactly the same as that from the later deposits and consists of over 90% flakes alongside a few blades and edge-damaged flakes. There is no clear evidence for the intentional deposition of artefacts within any of the ditch fills. It is therefore likely that most of the material is effectively residual and represents material from the wider artefact scatter in the area of the excavations that has unintentionally been incorporated into later deposits.

Discussion and conclusion

The excavation of the putative northern branch of the Stonehenge Avenue revealed no prehistoric features and nearly all of the material in the assemblage came from the topsoil and colluvium (see Mitcham, below), with a single flake being found within the fill of a wheel-rut. From the excavations of the Stonehenge Avenue bend only a minuscule proportion of the assemblage can confidently be linked to the period of construction and initial use of the Stonehenge Avenue.

Whilst the excavated volume of primary ditch fills was relatively small, these deposits did not seem to be associated with the deposition of worked flint. Given the size of the assemblage from later contexts, there was clearly some degree of lithic-working activity and/ or worked flint deposition in the wider area around the Avenue bend. Whilst this activity may broadly be dated to the later Neolithic–Bronze Age, the exact timing and nature of it is unclear.

The recognition of a scatter of worked flint across the area of the Avenue bend is of some significance as the trenches were located in an area that was not covered by fieldwalking during the Stonehenge Environs Project (Richards 1990). In the light of the technology of the assemblage, this confirms the general pattern of widespread surface flint material dating to the Late Neolithic–Bronze Age covering much of the Stonehenge landscape.

8.5.4. Lithics from the ploughsoil of the 'northern extension'

D. Mitcham

As part of the SRP investigations into the natural feature known as the northern branch of the Avenue, Trench 56's topsoil was excavated in 70 1m × 1m squares. This produced an assemblage of 741 pieces of worked flint. The raw material consists of local chalkland flint, often with a heavy white patina, the same as described elsewhere for most of the SRP sites.

Tools

The assemblage contains only two tools, a barbed-and-tanged arrowhead of Chalcolithic–Early Bronze Age date and an end-scraper. The arrowhead is broken and appears to be unfinished. It is, therefore, possible that this piece was discarded close to its place of manufacture, if the break occurred during that process. The end-scraper is heavily patinated and damaged; it is not particularly diagnostic and can only be ascribed a general, later prehistoric date.

Debitage

The material recorded is predominantly debitage, with 703 flakes accounting for 94.9% of the assemblage. It is very similar in character to ploughsoil assemblages throughout the Stonehenge landscape, and is not diagnostic, other than being of later prehistoric date. Some of the material is quite heavily patinated and damaged.

A single thinning flake is difficult to ascribe much significance to. Four miscellaneous retouched flakes were recorded but are not diagnostic on their own. The final point to make about the debitage is that the flaking technology is almost exclusively flake-based, with only four blades present, accounting for just 0.5% of the assemblage.

Cores

Only two complete flake cores were recovered, one a single-platform core and the other a multiple-platform example.

Discussion

To conclude, it is worth noting that the northern Avenue extension excavation did not produce any lithic material to suggest Mesolithic or Early Neolithic activity. The character of the material is consistent with activity during the Early Bronze Age, whilst some of the activity could date to the Middle Bronze Age, given the lack of diagnostic tool forms.

8.5.5. A chalk artefact from the Oblique Ditch (Trench 46)

A. Teather

A rectangular, pendant-style chalk bead (SF chalk catalogue C23), recently broken, was excavated from the primary fill (121) of the Oblique Ditch at the bend in the Stonehenge Avenue (Trench 46). The bead is 23mm long, 14.5mm wide and 11mm in depth, with squared sides and a largely unfinished rear face (Figure 8.50). Its perforation (6.2mm long) is oblique, exhibiting a spall on the finished front (where it is 3.5mm wide). The perforation is 3.4mm wide on the reverse.

This bead is a particularly well-made piece that is slightly different in form to those found at Durrington Walls (reported in Volume 3), being larger and more angular. There are few parallels although the closest in artefact form suggest a date later than the Neolithic. A rectangular pumice pendant, 18mm in length and associated with shale beads, was excavated in the Neolithic tomb of Taversoe Tuick on Rousay, Orkney

(Clarke *et al.* 1985: 237). A second pumice pendant, broken across the perforation and slightly longer at 38mm, was found associated with the burial of a single individual inside Unival Neolithic chambered tomb in South Uist, Outer Hebrides (Henshall 1972: 533).

While these finds from inside the Neolithic tombs of Taversoe Tuick and Unival are not radiocarbon-dated, their artefactual associations suggest their deposition in the Early Bronze Age, perhaps *c.* 2200–1800 BC. Although the Oblique Ditch is otherwise undated, it is later than the Chalcolithic-period ditch fills of the Stonehenge Avenue since it cuts the Avenue's northern ditch. This would be consistent with an Early Bronze Age date for both the bead and the Oblique Ditch.

Figure 8.50. A chalk bead (SF C23) from the primary fill of the Oblique Ditch

8.5.6. Charred plant remains and wood charcoal from the Stonehenge Avenue

E. Simmons

Thirty-five flotation samples comprising just under 700 litres of soil were processed by flotation and assessed using the methods outlined in Chapter 3.

No charred plant remains were found to be present in the sampled contexts. Wood charcoal fragments were occasionally present, but no wood charcoal analysis was undertaken given the small quantities of fragments >2mm in size.

8.6. The orientation of the Stonehenge Avenue and its implications

C. Ruggles

It has long been recognised that the straight section of the Stonehenge Avenue from the elbow up to Stonehenge itself, being closely aligned with the axis of the sarsen monument, is at least approximately solstitially aligned. Various attempts had been made prior to 2007 to establish the Avenue's orientation as precisely as possible from features visible on the surface, including theodolite surveys ranging from Lockyer's (1909: 65–6), who obtained a mean true azimuth (in the northeast direction) of 49.6°±0.1° (actually 49.65° near the terminal and 49.55° near the elbow) through to Atkinson's (1978), who obtained 49.9°±0.05° (actually 49.87° for the northwestern ditch end-to-end and 49.94° for the southeastern bank). Cleal *et al.*'s plan at 1:5000 scale (1995: plan 3), geo-referenced to the National Grid, shows the positions of excavations both at the terminal and the elbow, and the line of the Avenue extrapolated between them. The grid azimuth obtained from this plan is 49.3°±0.1°, corresponding to a true azimuth of 49.4°±0.1° and therefore closer to Lockyer's estimate than Atkinson's.

On 27 August 2008, a survey was undertaken in order to determine the orientation of the Avenue ditches and to reassess their astronomical potential while excavations were in progress close to the elbow (Trench 48) and at the top of the Avenue, on the north side of the old A344 road (Trench 45). The Avenue ditches were clearly visible in both of these trenches, as were a number of the natural striations between them. A survey station was set up just off the line of the northwestern ditch, 7m north of the excavated segment close to the elbow in Trench 48. From here, points in the trench at the top of the hill (Trench 45) could also be sighted directly.

A critical feature of archaeoastronomical surveys is the need to determine with sufficient precision the direction of true north (or equivalently, the 'plate-bearing minus azimuth' correction, PB–Az) (Ruggles 1999: 168–9), which is normally done by astronomical means. For daytime surveys the typical method is to take a series of 12 sun-azimuth observations, which minimises most types of error, but a prerequisite is a clear view of the sun. In the case of the survey in question, only a single sun-azimuth reading was obtained, raising the possibility of gross error, but sightings of four datum points on the site survey grid set up by the SRP team provided a consistency check.

The orientations obtained for the straight lines joining the excavated segments were 49.92°±0.005° for the northwestern ditch and 49.915°±0.01° for the southeastern ditch. Thus we adopt 49.92° as the mean orientation. We note in passing that Atkinson's 1978 estimate was close to this figure.

The horizon to the northeast, as viewed along the Avenue from its terminal at Stonehenge, is obscured by trees, but its altitude in the absence of vegetation has been calculated by many authors, and a figure of +0.6°±0.05° is generally agreed (see Ruggles 2006 for references). This yields a declination (Ruggles 1999: 18–19) of +24.0°±0.1°, corresponding to the centre of the sun rising at the summer solstice in around 2500 cal BC, as is well known.

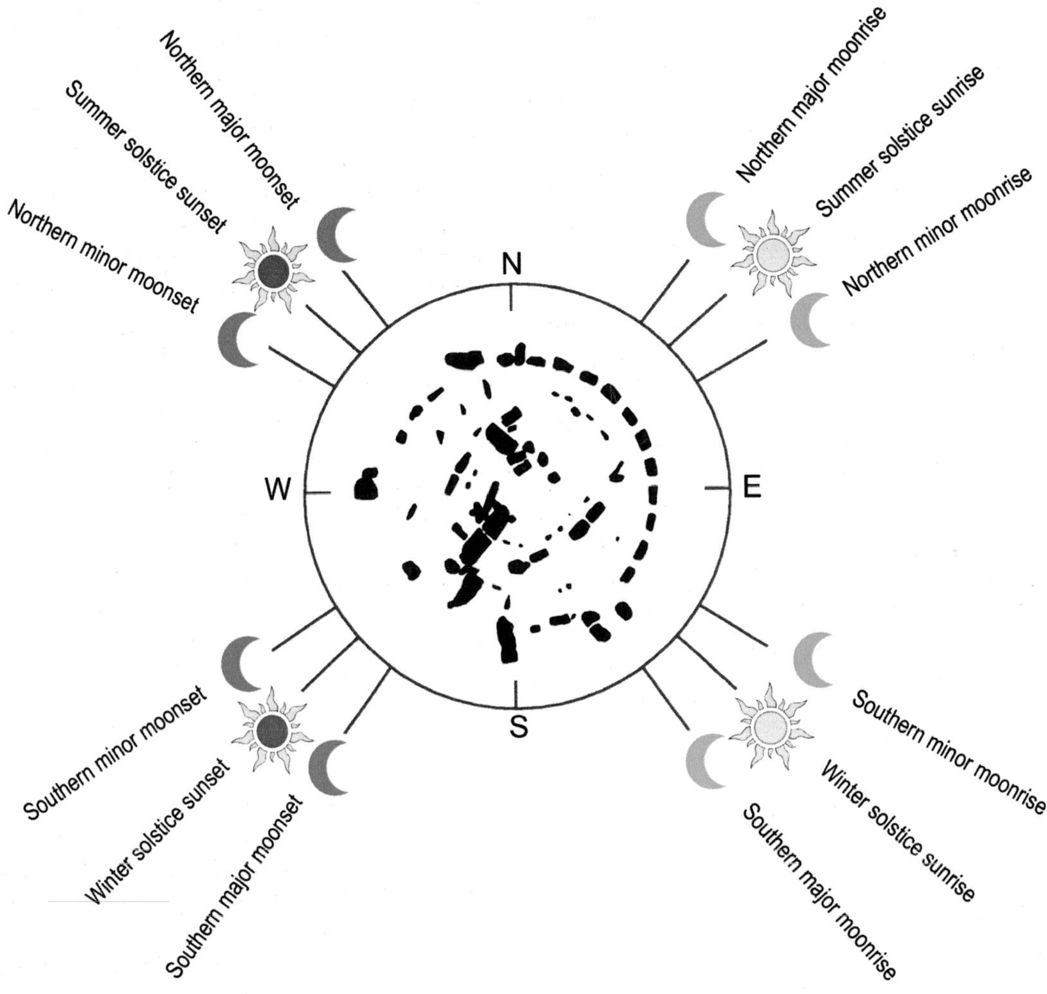

Figure 8.51. Directions of solstice sunrises and sunsets and of major moonrises and moonsets at Stonehenge

In the opposite direction, however, the horizon altitude that defines the astronomical alignment from the bottom of the slope from Stonehenge that extends downhill to the Avenue elbow is not that of the more distant skyline seen from Stonehenge itself but the local skyline, formed by points further upslope from Stonehenge. Initially, this altitude is about +2°. By ~20m southwards from the elbow, it has dropped to *c.* +1.5° and the sarsen monument first makes its dramatic appearance (Cleal *et al.* 1995: 40). By ~200m south of the elbow, the altitude has dropped to +0.5° and the landscape beyond Stonehenge starts to become visible (see Ruggles 2006: table 4).

The corresponding declination for altitudes of +2°, +1.5°, +1° and +0.5° is –22.5°, –22.9°, –23.4° and –23.9° respectively. Comparing these values with the declination of the setting winter solstice sun around 2500 cal BC (centre –24.0°, upper limb –23.75°), it is clear that only in the upper part of this segment of the Avenue (towards Stonehenge) would the setting winter solstice sun have been seen to set in line with the Avenue ahead; seen from lower down (away from Stonehenge), the solstitial sun would have set further to the left. As has been noted elsewhere (Ruggles 2006: 11), at the point where the sarsen monument first appears in view when walking towards it from the elbow, the setting midwinter sun would, in fact, have been seen to sink down just to its left, its upper limb just making contact with the bottom left corner of the visible monument as the sun finally disappeared. From points further uphill towards Stonehenge, the solstice sun would have been seen to set into the monument (Figure 8.51).

The discovery that the Avenue ditches follow the general direction of a series of natural striations adds a new dimension to the interpretation of the solstitial alignment of the Avenue. It could perhaps be argued that, if these formed a natural approach to the monument and were in fact a key factor in defining its axial orientation, then the solstitial alignment of the monument could be fortuitous. But to argue in this way would be to follow an ethnocentric perspective in which the approximate solstitial orientation of the natural striations is dismissed as a coincidence of nature. If, on the other hand, the striations were visible in the landscape in prehistory and were seen to be aligned upon the setting winter solstice sun, then this would surely have been a powerful affirmation of cosmic harmony (*cf* Ruggles 2007: 318 for another example) and could well have singled out the site of the future Stonehenge as a place of particular sacred or cosmic significance (Allen *et al.* 2016).

In this context, what should we make of the fact that only the uphill stretch of the Avenue, nearer Stonehenge, is accurately solstitially aligned in the southwest direction? The direction of the constructed Avenue does not necessarily follow exactly the direction of the striations, which are, in any case, more variable.

Be this as it may, an approximate solstitial alignment may well have been enough for people to make the connection between the landscape and the sun, and to mark out the site of the future Stonehenge as a place of particular sacred or cosmic significance. This visible connection was enhanced and elaborated in the construction both of the stone monument itself and of the formal approach to it.

8.7. The Avenue's construction and purpose

M. Parker Pearson

8.7.1. The date of the Stonehenge Avenue

The Stonehenge Avenue appears to have been built after the erection of Stonehenge's sarsen trilithons and circle in Stage 2 (which ended in *2470–2300 cal BC* [*95% probability*]; see Table 11.7 and the Appendix in Chapter 1). The date of construction of the Avenue can be established on the grounds of both its radiocarbon-dating (*2500–2270 cal BC*; *93% probability*; see Marshall *et al.*, above) and its stratigraphy. In the latter case, the deposition of quantities of sarsen debris in the buried soil beneath the Avenue banks (as recorded in Trench 45) coincides with the interpretation of an area of high resistance as further sarsen debris forming a fan-shaped concentration around the northeast entrance to Stonehenge's ditched enclosure (see Chapter 6). These observations of sarsen debris suggest the likelihood that sarsens were dressed across a wide area north of Stonehenge's entrance, spreading across the zone where the Avenue was later constructed. Thus the Avenue was not constructed to drag the sarsens to Stonehenge.

The SRP excavations at the riverside at West Amesbury indicate that, at its eastern end, the Avenue was constructed to within 80m or so of the River Avon, terminating beside a small henge close to the river's edge (see Chapter 5). Whilst this henge surrounded an earlier feature – a stone circle known as 'Bluestonehenge', dismantled in 2470–2280 cal BC during the Chalcolithic – its date of 2460–2210 cal BC is near contemporary with the Avenue's construction at its western end. Although the primary fills of the riverside end of the Stonehenge Avenue's ditches are not radiocarbon-dated (since no suitable material was present in the fills), the presence of the small West Amesbury henge at its riverside terminal suggests that the Avenue, or at least its route down to the river, was also in place at this time. This is supported by the discovery of a Late Neolithic oblique arrowhead in mint condition in one of the Avenue's ditches at the riverside (see Chapter 5).

The SRP excavations at the Avenue elbow in 2008 were designed, in part, to establish whether the Avenue was built in two stages; an apparent kink revealed by geophysical survey at the elbow (see Figure 8.25) was thought to have possibly been caused by a mismatch between two constructional stages, one along the solstice axis and the other a possibly separate extension leading eastwards to King Barrow Ridge. However, the SRP excavations revealed that this 'kink' does not exist below ground in the Avenue's alignment or construction. Of course, that does not mean that the Avenue was necessarily built in one go, as a single entity, since there could have been a break in construction at any point beyond the elbow, after the Avenue turned towards the river. However, in the light of the West Amesbury henge's date, consistent with that of the Avenue's construction at its western end, it seems most likely that the Avenue was constructed as a single build.

Thereafter, the Avenue's ditches were cleaned out by a series of re-cuts along its length. Radiocarbon dates for antler picks and animal bones from these re-cuts at varying distances along the Avenue (Montague 1995b: 319–27; see Marshall *et al.*, above) indicate that most or all re-cutting occurred in the Early Bronze Age during *2250–2135 cal BC* (*67% probability*). Thus, the Avenue was deemed sufficiently important for its course and appearance to be reinstated over a period of many years in the latter part of the third millennium BC.

8.7.2. Did the Stonehenge Avenue originally include two parallel stone rows?

As mentioned at the beginning of this chapter, the area permitted for excavation by English Heritage and the National Trust at the Stonehenge end of the Avenue was not large enough to allow the project to fully address the question of whether two parallel rows of standing stones

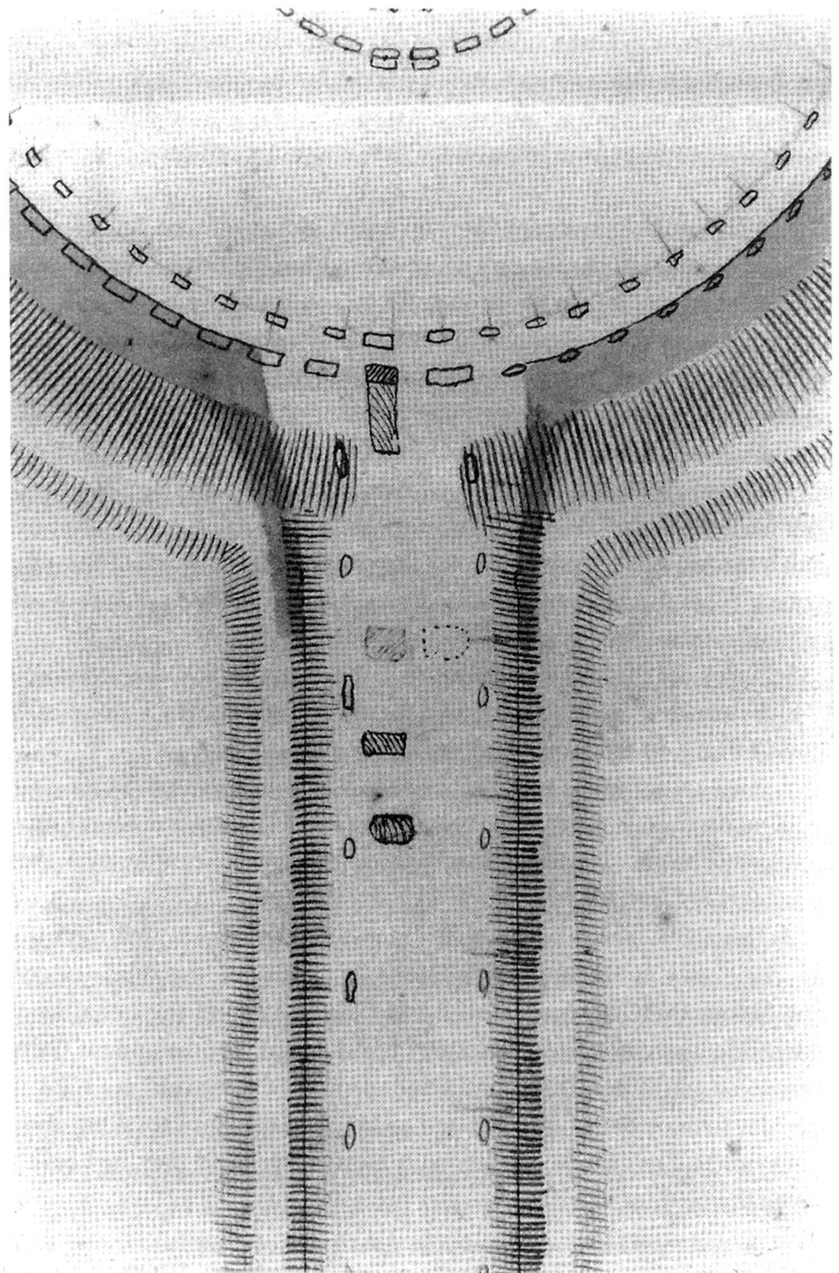

Figure 8.52. Stukeley and Gale's 1719 plan of depressions that they interpreted as stoneholes lining the Stonehenge Avenue (from Burl 2006: fig. 28)

had run along the insides of the Avenue's banks, as proposed by William Stukeley and Roger Gale, 300 years ago.

In his 1722–1724 manuscript 'The History of the Temples of the Antient Celts', Stukeley wrote:

> 'It may be reckoned bold to assert an Avenue at Stonehenge when there is not one Stone left but I did not invent it, having been able to measure the very intervals of almost every Stone, from the manifest hollows left in their stations and probably they were taken away when Christianity first prevaild here... I am thro'ly convincd of my self: I don't wonder so much at the 99 that are gone as at the poor one [the Heel Stone] remaining' (cited in Burl and Mortimer 2005: 16).

Stukeley even drew a plan of the locations of those stoneholes nearest Stonehenge's northeast entrance (Figure 8.52).

Yet none of this was mentioned in Stukeley's publication on Stonehenge in 1740, leading his colleague Roger Gale to write to him:

'I think you have omitted a remarkable particular, which is that the avenue up to the chief entrance was formerly planted with great stones, opposite to each other, on the side banks of it, for I well remember we observed the holes where they had been fixt, when you and I surveyed the place' (letter of 20 May 1740, cited in Burl and Mortimer 2005: 16).

Both Rodney Castleden (1993: 131–2) and Aubrey Burl (Burl and Mortimer 2005: 16–17, note 80; Burl 2006: fig. 28) have supported the earlier statement by Stukeley – the manuscript allusion to stoneholes – which echoes the two stone-lined avenues of West Kennet and Beckhampton at Avebury that Stukeley recorded (Gillings *et al.* 2008). Yet no such lines of regularly spaced pits have been identified by geophysics nor were any such features located in appropriate positions within Hawley's or our trenches beyond the northeast entrance to Stonehenge.

In addition, the evidence from Trench 44 (see Chapter 6) and Trench 45 (see above) that this part of the Avenue has not been ploughed makes it likely that the contours of the ground visible in Stukeley's day would not be dramatically different from today (see Field *et al.* 2012). Trench 45, across the Avenue banks, was restricted to a width of just 4m, so it is just possible that it was simply too narrow to have coincided with any widely-spaced stoneholes. Whilst the SRP was thus unable to entirely resolve this puzzle, the evidence as far as it goes would suggest that these stoneholes never existed.

It seems probable that Stukeley himself may have changed his mind to reject the idea, even without the benefits of geophysics or twentieth-century excavation. In his unpublished manuscript of 1721–1724, he deleted several sections referring to the stoneholes (the words in square brackets in the following quotation were crossed out by Stukeley himself in his manuscript):

'When Mr Roger Gale & I measured it more than once [there is not one stone left therof, yet a curious eye without difficulty will discern a mark of the holes whence they were taken tho' the ground] is so much trod upon, & moreover the course of a horse race traverses it about the middle. This magnificent Walk or Entry is made by two [rows of stones containing fifty on a side so that in the whole they completed the number that makes but one side of those at Abury, yet therein it cannot be denyd that this proportion fully answers the more contracted extent of the whole work]..." (cited in Burl and Mortimer 2005: 78).

Whilst some uncertainty remains about the possibility of parallel stone rows along Stonehenge's Avenue, the balance of evidence indicates that Stukeley was correct in this apparent rejection of his own theory.

8.7.3. The route of the Stonehenge Avenue

Since the date range of the Avenue's construction also coincides with that for the dismantling of Bluestonehenge (see Chapter 5), it is possible that its purpose was to mark the line along which the 25 or so bluestones from the stone circle beside the River Avon were dragged towards Stonehenge, perhaps to be installed as a circle of similar diameter and spacings within the monument's centre in Stage 3 (beginning in *2400–2220 cal BC* and ending in *2300–2100 cal BC*; formerly Phase 3iii [Cleal *et al.* 1995]). In this respect, it is interesting that the Avenue's path from West Amesbury to the elbow takes the easiest route in terms of the shallowest incline afforded by the terrain. Thus the Avenue may have been constructed as a monumentalisation of a pre-existing route from the river to Stonehenge, its banks and ditches serving the same purpose as the henge earthworks at West Amesbury, of marking or commemorating an already significant space.

It may be that an alternative and earlier route from West Amesbury's riverside to Stonehenge led, as the crow flies, directly between the two, regardless of the terrain. Along this alternative route, the walker climbs a steep valley side onto the relatively level summit where an area of Middle Neolithic pits (West Amesbury Farm; Pitts 2017) and Late Neolithic Coneybury henge (Richards 1990) are located, approximately halfway between Bluestonehenge and Stonehenge (see Figure 8.1). There is then a steep descent and rise towards Stonehenge's southern entrance (see Figure 4.4).

This steeper, more direct route between Bluestonehenge and Stonehenge might have had an earlier period of use, during the Middle Neolithic and the early part of the Late Neolithic. The Neolithic pits at West Amesbury Farm, containing Peterborough Ware pottery, are dated to the 34th–31st centuries BC (Pitts 2017) whilst the potential timber monument within Coneybury henge is associated with an animal bone radiocarbon-dated to before 2900 BC (Richards 1990: 123–58).

Returning to the route of the Avenue, its initial stretch of 210m from Stonehenge to the point where the two natural chalk ridges appear to end (marked in blue in Figure 8.54) may have been perceived as a natural avenue for some time before the Avenue's construction. The two Avenue ditches follow alongside these natural chalk ridges leading from the entrance of Stonehenge, past the Heel Stone and for a further 190m northeast along the midsummer solstice sunrise axis (Figure 8.54). Although these natural ridges (and presumably the wide and deep periglacial fissures running inside and parallel with them) terminate just over a third of the way along the 500m-long straight stretch, the Avenue does not turn away from this solstice axis until it reaches a small natural prominence (Newall's Mound), located on the inner side of the eastern Avenue ditch. As Atkinson and Evans established (Evans

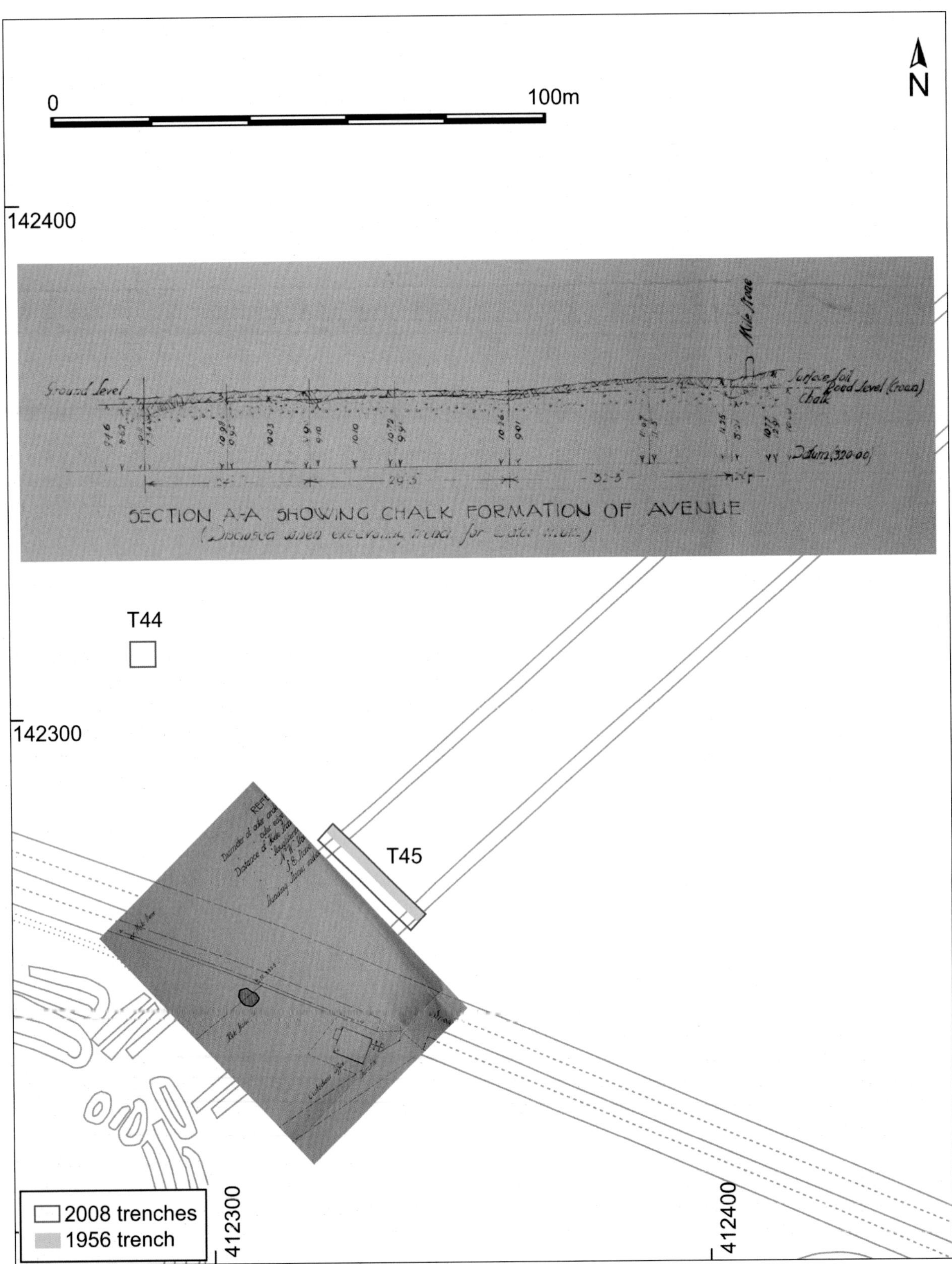

Figure 8.53. The section drawing across the Avenue within the 1919 trench alongside the A344 road (with thanks to Marlyn Barber)

1984), this mound is not only on the midsummer solstice sunrise axis from Stonehenge but is also an entirely natural feature formed of a deposit of clay-with-flints.

However, previous researchers failed to realise that, like the natural chalk ridges and the wide and deep periglacial fissures within them, this natural mound may have been incorporated into the Stonehenge builders' cultural construction of their world (*cf* Bradley 2000). As Allen and French point out (see above), this clay-formed feature could not have survived as an upstanding mound into the Holocene unless its soft matrix were held in place by a prehistoric tree or stand of trees, as indicated by the evidence for tree-root bioturbation.

8.7.4. Natural features associated with the Stonehenge Avenue

Within Trench 45, immediately north of the Heel Stone and Stonehenge's northeast entrance, the Avenue is located on top of two parallel ridges of geological origin which run for *c.* 150m northeast from this trench. These two chalk ridges can be seen closer to Stonehenge in William Hawley's photographs of his 1923 excavations in front of the entrance to Stonehenge (Hawley 1925: plate X; Cleal *et al.* 1995: fig. 182 lower left, fig. 184). Distinct rises in the chalk, although the Avenue banks were entirely missing, were also noted by Pitts in his roadside trench along the south side of the A344 (Pitts 1982: 94, plate 10a, fig. 15; Cleal *et al.* 1995: 318). They were not recognised in the Vatchers' 1968 trench along the north side of the A344 (Cleal *et al.* 1995: fig. 180). Instead, chalk 'banks' up to 20cm high were recorded here (*ibid.*: 315) though the western (northern) Avenue 'bank' was apparently cut by the Avenue ditch (*ibid.*: 316). It is likely that these 'banks' in the Vatchers' records are actually raised chalk 'eminences' (Pitts 1982: 94) – the two ridges recognised in all the other trenches excavated across this part of the Avenue.

In addition, a hitherto unpublished section drawing, from a water-main trench excavated in May 1919, of the chalk bedrock along the south side of the A344 (kindly provided by Martyn Barber) illustrates the raised bedrock of these two ridges ('Section A-A showing chalk formation of Avenue [disclosed when excavating trench for water main]'; Figure 8.53):

- On the right of the drawing (west), the western/northern Avenue ditch runs beside a significant ridge of chalk bedrock some 30 feet (9.10m) wide and up to 20" (0.51m) high.
- This terminates on its east side in a shallow, V-shaped hollow, the other side of which is a more level stretch of bedrock 29 feet (8.80m) wide.
- This ends on its east side in a second shallow hollow, from which the bedrock rises on its east side, forming the second ridge 24 feet (7.30m) wide and 9" (0.23m) high, terminating at the eastern/southern Avenue ditch.

Just how far the unusually large periglacial fissures between the parallel ridges run towards Stonehenge from Trench 45 was partly ascertained in 2013 during Wessex Archaeology's excavation beneath the old A344 (Allen *et al.* 2016: 997–8). The periglacial fissures were seen to continue as far as the 1919 trench, to within a few metres of the Heel Stone, being recorded during excavation in aerial photographs taken by Adam Stanford (Figure 8.55) and in ground-level photographs taken by Tim Daw (pers. comm.).

The 500m-long stretch of Avenue from Stonehenge to its elbow and Newall's Mound may have a profound significance for Stonehenge's solstitial alignment and also for understanding the reason why Stonehenge is located where it is. Newall's Mound appears to have formed a natural hump up to 20m in diameter and 0.30m high at the Avenue's elbow (Field *et al.* 2012: 21–2). Survey within the centre of Stonehenge has identified the remains of a chalk mound, up to 15m in diameter and 0.25m high, southeast of Trilithon 53/54 (see Figure 8.54; Field and Pearson 2010: 7, fig. 7). The raised height of chalk bedrock in Darvill and Wainwright's adjacent trench, dug in 2008 (Darvill and Wainwright 2009), indicates that this mound too most likely has a natural origin (Field and Pearson 2010: 61–2). Thus the two mounds, some 500m apart, provide an alignment on the midwinter solstice sunset–midsummer solstice sunrise.

In the 580m between the two apparently natural mounds run the two parallel chalk ridges, for 210m. They appear to start at the terminus of the Avenue ditches at Stonehenge's northeast entrance, visible in Hawley's excavation photograph (Hawley 1925: plate X; Cleal *et al.* 1995: fig. 184), about 50m northeast of Field *et al.*'s chalk mound. As described above, the ridges appear to terminate where the prominence of the Avenue banks' earthworks declines, about 150m northeast of Trench 45 (Field *et al.* 2012). If this diminution of the Avenue banks indicates the petering-out of the natural chalk ridges on which they lie, it provides a total length of about 210m for the ridges, nearly halfway to the Avenue elbow (Figure 8.54).

Until Allen and French identified these raised areas of chalk bedrock as natural ridges, between which a series of unusually deep and wide periglacial fissures had formed, my initial interpretation in the field of the ridges was that they had formed as a result of differential weathering of the bedrock's surface, leaving the bedrock standing higher where it has been protected beneath the Avenue's banks. Yet there are sound reasons why this explanation is unsatisfactory.

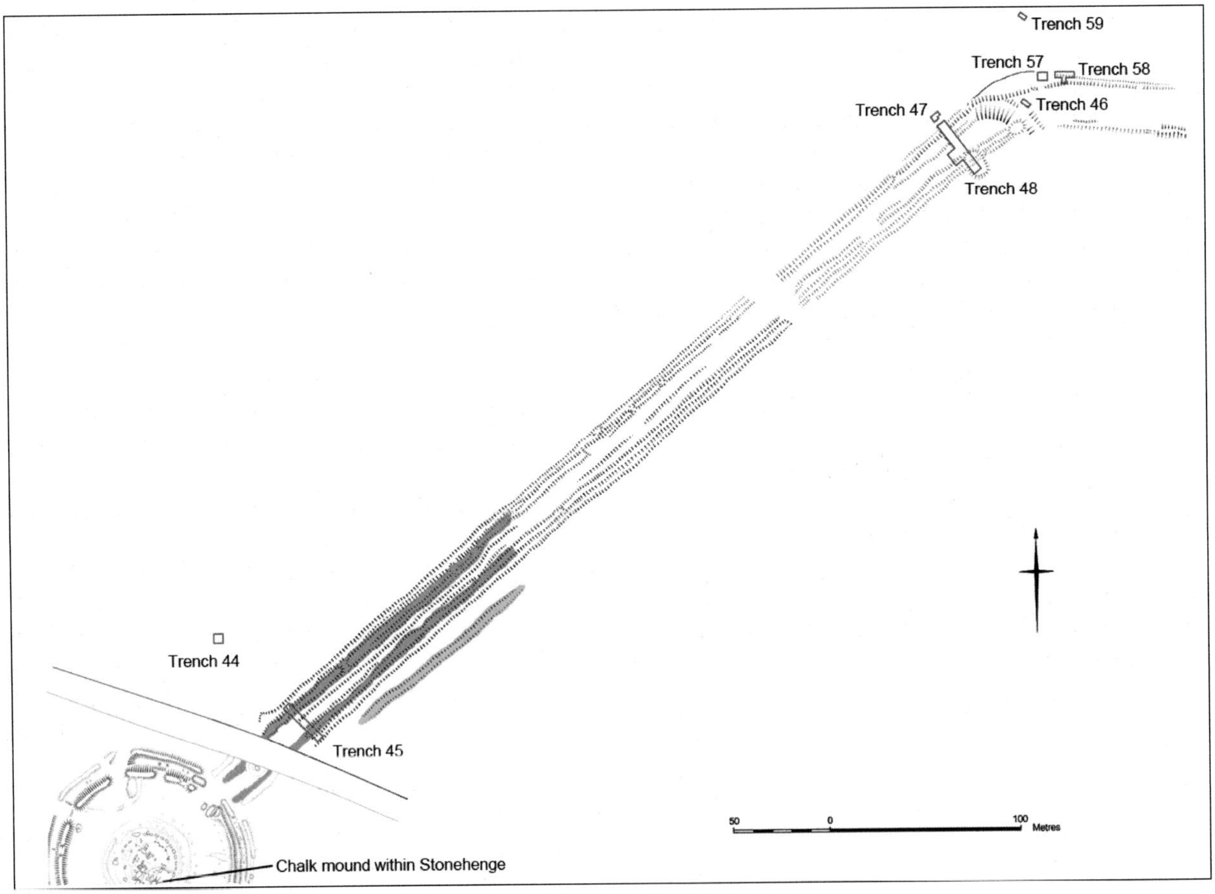

Trench 59
Trench 57
Trench 58
Trench 47
Trench 46
Trench 48
Trench 44
Trench 45
50 0 100 Metres
Chalk mound within Stonehenge

Figure 8.54. Interpretive earthwork plan of the Avenue between Stonehenge and the bend (after Field *et al.* 2012: figs 10 and 12; © Historic England). The Avenue's earthworks are shaded blue where they overlie the natural chalk ridges; the linear hollow is shaded green

Figure 8.55. Excavations in 2013 by Wessex Archaeology of the Avenue beneath the removed A344 road, viewed from the northeast

Firstly, the chalk ridges are not found in those sections dug across the Avenue at the Avenue bend, 450m northeast of Trench 45 (see above; Cleal *et al.* 1995: figs 176–7) even though the Avenue ditches revealed in the trenches dug around the Avenue bend are little different in size than in Trench 45. Since the ditches are the same size in both areas, it seems unlikely that the banks would have been much smaller at the Avenue bend, and thus less protective of the underlying chalk bedrock.

Secondly, comparison with other Neolithic bank profiles shows that the chalk ridges are disproportionately large to have resulted from differential weathering of bank-protected bedrock. Our excavations of the Greater Cursus ditch, a much larger ditch with a likely more substantial bank, failed to reveal any significant stretches of raised bedrock beneath the line of the bank (see Chapter 3). It is only under the bank of Stonehenge's circular enclosure (see Figure 4.4) that there is evidence of a similar degree of elevation of the top of the bedrock (Cleal *et al.* 1995: fig. 48 [trench C42]). Here the protected surface of chalk bedrock is up to 0.50m higher than the surrounding chalk surface, similar to the maximum height of the Avenue ridges. Yet the 4m-wide and 1.50m-deep Stonehenge ditch would have produced three times as much spoil for the bank as each of the Avenue's ditches.

We can conclude that the unusual height of preserved bedrock beneath this 210m-long section of the Avenue's banks is out of proportion to the relatively small size of the banks – and thus the area possibly protected from weathering – on top of these two low ridges. This raises a number of possibilities, all of which seem unlikely. The Avenue's banks could have been augmented by spoil derived from sources other than the Avenue ditches alone, at least for this 210m length, but there is no evidence for excess sediments from any such augmented banks having eroded off their sides.

The possibility that the chalk ridges were made by people must be considered, but is easily dismissed. Since the presence of the chalk ridges is assumed to be responsible for the formation of the unusually deep and wide periglacial fissures running between them (see Allen and French, above), the ridges would have to have been formed at least by the end of the last glaciation. For the ridges to have been created by human agency, they would have to have been constructed in the Devensian period, before *c.* 27,000 years ago, a scenario which seems inherently unlikely.

The deep and wide periglacial fissures running parallel within the depression between the two ridges, although clearly visible in Trench 45, cannot be traced on geophysical survey plots since any signal produced by the periglacial stripes (within the vicinity of Trench 45) is merged with and indistinguishable from wheel-ruts (of likely medieval date) running for over 500m from the area of Trench 45 along the Avenue to its elbow and beyond, towards the Cursus's east end. It should be borne in mind that wheel-ruts within the Avenue are most likely responsible in large part or entirely for these geophysical linear anomalies (see also Darvill *et al.* 2013: 83–4).

Certainly by the point where they reach the Avenue elbow, these geophysical anomalies on the same orientation as the Avenue cannot be periglacial fissures since the excavation of Trench 48 has shown that the orientation of fissures at the Avenue's elbow is no longer parallel with the Avenue's banks and ditches at that point (whereas the wheel-ruts are; see Figures 8.29–8.30). The suggestion that the chalk ridges were created by accelerated erosion of the area within the Avenue's interior caused by its being used as a cart track (Darvill *et al.* 2013: 83) is not borne out by the height of the wheel-ruts well above bedrock within Trench 45; the wheel-ruts cannot have been responsible for altering the contours of the bedrock (see Figure 8.13). Furthermore, the area between the Avenue's banks is no lower than the ground surface outside the Avenue's ditches: there is no evidence that wheeled carts created an eroded 'hollow way' within the Avenue's interior.

Another natural feature runs parallel with the two ridges on their east side. This is a 4m-wide linear hollow, 0.10m deep, offset 6m–9m east of the eastern Avenue ditch; it runs northeastwards almost from the north side of the former A344 for 120m. Although this linear hollow (marked in green in Figure 8.54) could be described as resulting from wear from traffic or as a possible slight ditch (Field *et al.* 2012: 20), neither explanation is convincing:

- The ditches of the Avenue show up as both magnetic and earth resistance anomalies, but this hollow is not visible as an earth resistance anomaly, indicating that it is not a ditch.
- Were the hollow the result of wear from traffic, it is headed in the wrong direction, towards the ditch and bank of Stonehenge's circular enclosure, which would have effectively barred the route.

Thus it is difficult to explain this as a humanly created feature. The same can be said for another magnetic anomaly of about the same length, presumably another linear hollow (though not visible on the surface as an earthwork), running broadly parallel with it, about 9m to its south (see Figure 8.3).

Two similar linear hollows, 7m apart, were recorded in Trench 45 and in the 1919 water-main trench, inside the Avenue's banks and ditches and running parallel against the interior edges of the two ridges. Whilst both linear hollows inside the Avenue could arguably have been caused by traffic wear since they head towards the entrance of Stonehenge's enclosure, their positioning on top of wide, deep periglacial fissures in Trench 45 suggests that a natural origin is more likely.

Overall, the effect of these various ridges and hollows is to create a corrugated area of land surface 210m long (northeast–southwest) and up to 45m wide, formed of five corrugations of varying heights (the westernmost one being the highest and steepest) approximately 6m–9m apart. Ground-penetrating radar survey by Dick van der Roest and Glyn Hobson of GT Frontline in 2009 revealed that these corrugations are not the result of varying sub-surface geology since they do not exhibit the shelving produced by dipping strata of varying hardness. Thus an origin through geomorphological processes appears more likely.

Yet exactly how the geomorphological features were formed remains something of a mystery. They would appear to have been sculpted by erosional forces removing large swathes of chalk bedrock on each side of them along this part of the valley slope. This must have occurred in the periglacial conditions of the last Ice Age, when freeze-thaw processes led to the creation of wide and deep fissures running parallel to the ridges and caused channelling of water between ridges.

8.7.5. The cultural significance of natural features associated with the Avenue

Whatever the precise formation processes behind the chalk ridges, their cultural significance cannot be denied. They would have been clearly visible natural features marking the sun's solstice axis in the land. Prehistoric people dug out the Avenue's ditches along their sides, on that solstitial alignment. We may posit a similar set of circumstances at Durrington Walls, where the midsummer solstice sunset-aligned avenue leading up the coombe from the River Avon is bedded on a natural surface of broken flints leading up the coombe bottom (see Volume 3; Parker Pearson *et al.* 2007).

Such an alignment where the earth and heavens meet might well have been considered an *axis mundi*, where universe and people had their origins. *Axes mundi* are known from antiquity (such as Delphi in Greece) and the concept of a sacred 'centre' on which the world depends is common to many cultures worldwide (Eliade 1961). The location of Stonehenge (on an otherwise unremarkable slope rather than on a summit or prominence) may thus be explained by Neolithic people's cultural appropriation of these natural features, in conjunction with the presence in the landscape of a naturally situated massive recumbent sarsen, to form a powerful supernatural nexus of heaven and earth. This may well explain why Stonehenge was not located in more 'obvious' locations, such as on the crest of Normanton Down, or closer to the two cursuses, or nearer the river.

It is possible that these natural chalk ridges were first appreciated by hunter-gatherers of the Early Mesolithic, who dug four pits and erected pine posts in three of the pits[8] in the ninth–eighth/seventh millennia BC, in the area to the northwest of Stonehenge which was for many years buried under a car park and visitor centre (Limbrey in Vatcher and Vatcher 1973; Allen in Cleal *et al.* 1995: 43–7; shown in Figure 8.2). The three pits used as postholes (A, B and C) form an approximately straight line from a fourth, undated hole, interpreted as a tree hole; all four features are aligned approximately on Beacon Hill to the east. A fifth feature (pit 9580) lay 100m to the east, slightly south of the west–east axis of the other pits; it is thought to have been dug as a post-pit but redesigned as a broad, shallow pit, with the post either being removed or never inserted (Allen in Cleal *et al.* 1995: 45).

Five charcoal samples from pit 9580 and two of the post-pits provide dates from the ninth–seventh millennia BC (Marshall *et al.* 2012: table 1). Since it is uncertain whether the charcoal samples used for the radiocarbon-dating derived from heartwood or sapwood, it is difficult to know whether they reliably date the construction of the post-pits. If the charcoal did indeed come from burnt sapwood, then the posts were not all erected at the same time; the post in post-pit A would probably have rotted away before a post was erected in post-pit B (and potentially in pit 9580).

Excavation within the centre of Stonehenge in 2008 yielded further evidence of Mesolithic activity here, an unstratified fragment of wood charcoal dating to 7330–7060 cal BC (OxA-18655; Darvill and Wainwright 2009; Marshall *et al.* 2012: table 2). Although not associated with a pit or other Mesolithic feature, it indicates the possibility of relatively widespread activity at this time over a wide area of Stonehenge's vicinity and possibly the existence of one or more significant Mesolithic features where Stonehenge later stood. Further possible evidence of Late Mesolithic activity on the future site of Stonehenge is provided by a longbone fragment from a cattle-sized mammal dating to 4350–3970 cal BC (95% confidence; OxA-4902; 5350±80 BP; Marshall *et al.* 2012: table 2) from the packing of Stone 27 in the sarsen circle (Cleal *et al.* 1995: 189–90, 441, 522–3).

Traces of Mesolithic activity have also been found in excavations around Stonehenge in recent years. There are Mesolithic flints in the ploughsoil assemblages from SRP Trenches 53 and 54 in the Palisade field 500m west of Stonehenge (a primarily Bronze Age site, so reported in Volume 4). Mesolithic activity was, however, much more dense along the valley of the Avon and its tributary dry valleys; for example, a small assemblage of Mesolithic flintwork (and a Late Upper Palaeolithic crested blade) was

8 Pollard (2017) has suggested that, whilst these pits had sacred significance, they never held posts.

recovered from the buried soil beneath West Amesbury henge's eroded bank (see Chapter 5).

By far the most impressive Mesolithic assemblage is from beside a cut-off palaeo-channel at Blick Mead, east of the Iron Age hillfort of Vespasian's Camp (see Figure 9.4; Jacques and Phillips 2014 ; Jacques *et al.* 2018). Some 40,000 worked flints and over 300 animal bones have so far been recovered from a limited area here; these probably relate to a much larger occupation area extending along up to 300m of the valley side (David Jacques pers. comm.). Nineteen radiocarbon determinations on animal bones and teeth from Blick Mead provide the longest span of dates for any persistent place within the British Mesolithic.

This string of dates from east of Vespasian's Camp raises an intriguing prospect. Until recently, the lack of any dating of materials from Stonehenge or its vicinity between the early seventh and late fifth millennia BC inhibited any thoughts of long-term continuity between the Early Mesolithic and the Neolithic. Consequently, the occurrence at Stonehenge of two phenomena – the Mesolithic post-pits in the former carpark area and the utilisation by later prehistoric people of the solstitial axis as embodied within natural features – could only be explained as the re-discovery and re-appropriation by Neolithic people of Early Mesolithic people's formerly sacred places. However, these recently obtained radiocarbon dates from Blick Mead raise the possibility that the Stonehenge area had a long-lived significance, originating well before the construction of Stonehenge Stage 1.

It is tempting to think of the former Stonehenge car park's three post-pits and 'tree hole' as no more than Mesolithic 'pointers' or signposts eastwards towards the head of the valley where a dense and long-occupied gathering site was located. Yet there are several reasons why the posts may have represented more than this. Firstly, the posts were located within a dry valley (a tributary of Stonehenge Bottom): if they had been designed to be seen from a distance, a better location would have been upslope, to the south and east. Furthermore, the presence of dated Mesolithic material from pit 9580 and from inside Stonehenge suggests a greater significance for these posts and their location away from the river and the likely settlement areas, perhaps associated with a sacred domain above and beside the valley-side gathering places. It is possible that Mesolithic people recognised the remarkable alignment of landscape features on the solstitial axis; this place would thus constitute an *axis mundi* that was returned to time and again throughout the Mesolithic and into the Neolithic. Eventually the locale would be monumentalised in stone, perhaps to enhance and memorialise this gathering-place for the unification of Britain's Neolithic farmers from across southern Britain.

Chapter 9

The River Avon, Stonehenge and Durrington Walls

M. Parker Pearson, C. Richards, C.A.I. French, M. Allen, R. Scaife, C. Tilley and W. Bennett

9.1. Rivers and monumental architecture in the third millennium BC

M. Parker Pearson and C. Richards

The River Avon begins as a convergence of two small rivers – the eastern and western Avon. On the northern side of the western Avon, the river encircles one side of the large henge at Marden (Wainwright *et al.* 1971), and then immediately passes a second, smaller henge at Wilsford. The eastern and western branches of the Avon converge at Upavon and the river then meanders south, passing the massive henge monument at Durrington Walls on its west bank. That the River Avon has a clear relationship with *two* of the largest henge monuments in Wessex before it reaches the Stonehenge Avenue is not insignificant yet is rarely commented upon. Apart from creating a degree of unity for two of the most spectacular displays of monumentality in Late Neolithic Britain, the River Avon provides a passage, via the Stonehenge Avenue, to Stonehenge.

This amalgam of divergent sites and activities, stretching across a broad sweep of the third-millennium BC landscape of Wiltshire, is a consequence of an architecture of incorporation, fusing the river with constructed monumentality. Indeed, a main research objective of the first fieldwork element of the Stonehenge Riverside Project was to explore the relationship between Durrington Walls and the adjacent river. In this investigation we were successful, with the discovery of a short, 180m-long avenue linking the two (Parker Pearson *et al.* 2007: 631–3; see Volume 3).

More generally, one of the principal characteristics which define the Middle–Late Neolithic period in Britain and Ireland is the extraordinary and lavish mobilisation of labour, manifested by the building of large monuments such as passage graves, henge monuments, and timber and stone circles. In many areas we see the agglomeration of monuments, a constructional process that has been described as creating ceremonial complexes (*e.g.* Noble and Brophy 2015; Thomas 2015) or ritual landscapes (*e.g.* Gale 2012: 161). The development of such complexes often appears 'organic', with the location of later sites being predetermined by the presence of earlier monuments.

Throughout Britain and Ireland, many monumental complexes developed in close proximity to rivers, such as the Brú na Bóinne, Ireland (Cooney 2000: 153–8), the Milfield basin, Northumberland (Harding 1981), Thornborough, Yorkshire (Harding

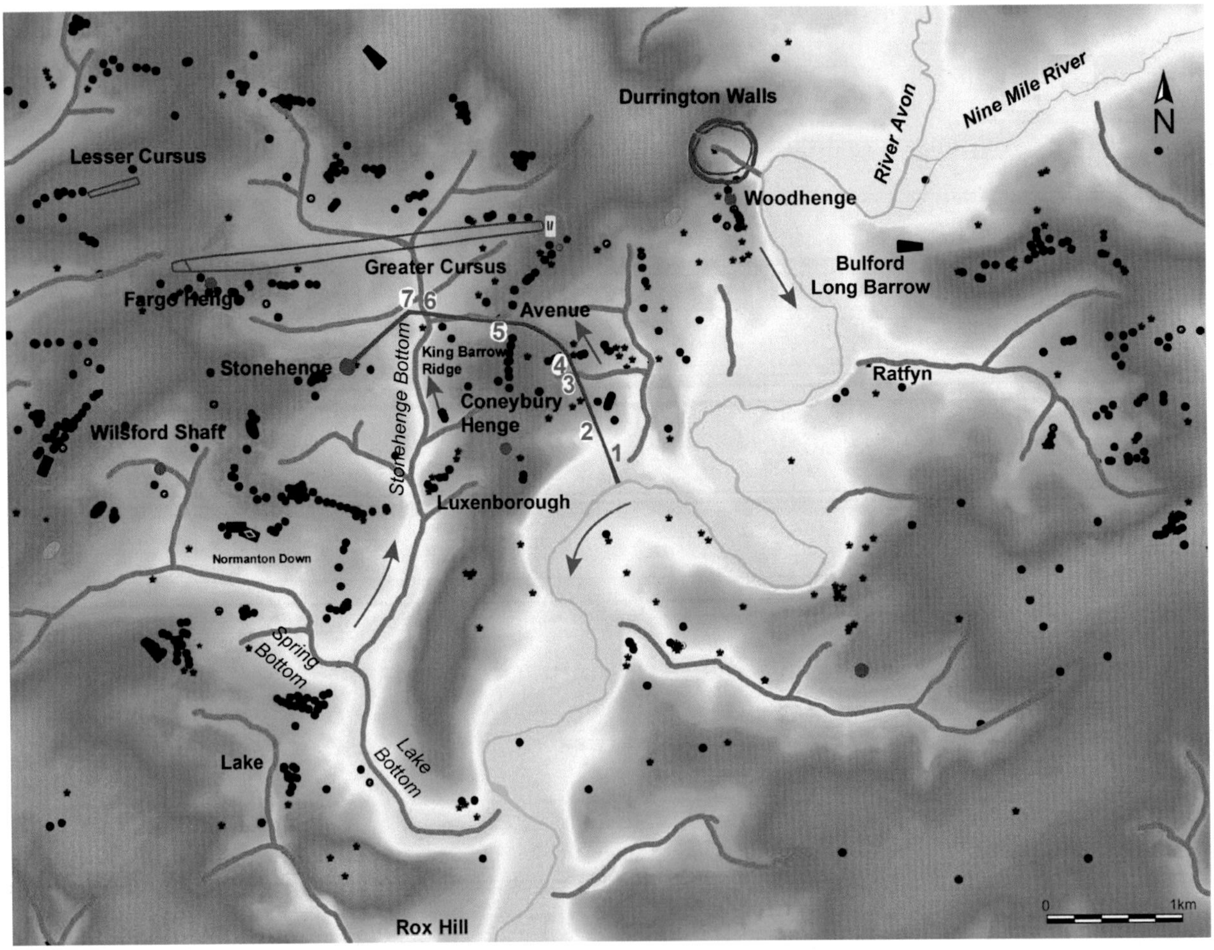

Figure 9.1. Map of the river and land journeys to Stonehenge from the Avon

Figure 9.2. The canoe trip down the Avon, commencing at Durrington Walls; Chris Tilley sits in the stern with Wayne Bennett in front of him while Colin Richards paddles

2013), Forteviot, Perthshire (Noble and Brophy 2015) and Dorchester-on-Thames, Oxfordshire (Atkinson *et al.* 1951; Whittle *et al.* 1992).

However, the relationship between late fourth–early third millennium BC 'ceremonial complexes' and rivers is neither straightforward nor consistent. For example, many of the complexes, including Stonehenge, developed around precursor cursus monuments. Whilst rivers and cursus monuments are clearly related (see Brophy 1999; 2000; 2015), there is no consistency in either the orientation of these linear monuments or the direction of river-flow. Equally, the distance and connectivity between cursus monuments and rivers is highly variable.

This variability is also evident in complexes without cursuses. For example, at Brú na Bóinne, the River Boyne wraps around and almost 'embraces' the large collection of passage graves, henge monuments, timber and stone circles. Indeed, these monuments appear to be contained within the large loop of the river rather than being directly connected to it. A very different relationship is evident at Thornborough (Harding 2013), where an alignment of henge monuments runs parallel to the River Ure. Here, the shared orientation of their opposed entrances seems to reference the direction of the flowing river. The single- and double-entrance henge monuments in the Milfield basin (Harding 1981) differ yet again in being situated on elevated gravel terraces overlooking the Rivers Till and Glen, with only some entrances aligned on the direction of water flow.

A more direct association and integration of monuments and river is evident in the Stonehenge complex (Figure 9.1). Here the River Avon appears to act as a direct and directional conduit linking Durrington Walls (and associated monuments) with the Stonehenge Avenue and Stonehenge itself. In other words the narrative of the Stonehenge monumental landscape is a story which, to a large degree, is predicated on the River Avon, and the logic of monument location is linked to the direction of flow of the river. In this we begin to appreciate the potency of natural features in the creation of Late Neolithic monumental architecture, at both an intra- and inter-site level, and the efficacy of the river as a conduit between qualitatively different domains.

Because of the centrality of the River Avon in providing cohesion to the monumental Stonehenge landscape, a key research objective of the SRP was to examine the scheme proposed by Parker Pearson and Ramilisonina (1998a; 1998b), that Durrington Walls was the domain of the living, and Stonehenge the domain of the ancestors, with the Avon forming a fundamental link between the two (see Chapter 1). The SRP explored the multifaceted nature of the river from two completely different analytical standpoints:

- This chapter firstly presents the results of geoarchaeological investigations, undertaken to determine the position and environment of the River Avon during the third millennium BC.

- Second, a phenomenological account is provided of travelling downstream from Durrington Walls to where the Stonehenge Avenue meets the River Avon at West Amesbury (Figure 9.2), and then along the Stonehenge Avenue to Stonehenge. This journey also explored the route from the Avon to Stonehenge northwards across the coombes and grassland. This captures the physical character and experience of this extraordinary journey by water and land, and the significance of the routes along these natural and cultural features.

9.2. The Avon palaeo-channel

C.A.I. French and M. Allen

In the 2005–2006 field seasons, geoarchaeological research within the SRP focused on an augering survey on the eastern side of the modern River Avon, between Bulford and the A303 about 1.50km downstream. A series of seven hand-augered transects were made (Figure 9.3: Transects G, H, J, K, M, N and P), with auger holes normally spaced at 20m intervals.

9.2.1. The River Avon augering survey

Three palaeo-channels were identified in the present-day floodplain. The earliest (and main) prehistoric channel is just about visible on the modern ground surface and on a 1947 aerial photograph (RAF/CPE/UK/2006/frame 3208; NMR, Swindon). It is located *c.* 200m to the east of the Undercliff, or about 35m east of the eastern entrance of Durrington Walls, at the intersection of Transects A and B (Figure 9.3: borehole 15; Figure 9.4). This former channel revealed itself to be gently meandering, primarily either to the east and northeast of the present river or more or less on the current alignment of the river. It is about 1.50m–2m in depth and *c.* 50m–60m in width, situated within a broad braid plain under deposits (<0.50m–1.15m) of redeposited calcitic hillwash and alluvial materials. Palynological assessment by Rob Scaife suggests that this was the main prehistoric channel, and this significant profile was analysed for pollen and radiocarbon assay (see Scaife, below).

A second palaeo-channel was visible in Transect B in the vicinity of borehole 8 (Figures 9.3–9.4), and comprised a *c.* 1.20m depth of humified reed peat. This was sampled for palynological assessment and dating, and could be of later prehistoric and historic age. In terms of deposit type sequence, it appears to be contemporary with the latter/upper part of the first palaeo-channel.

Most significantly, the present river at the Undercliff must be in the same position as the main prehistoric channel because no other channel deposits were evident in the floodplain to the southeast except for a shallow

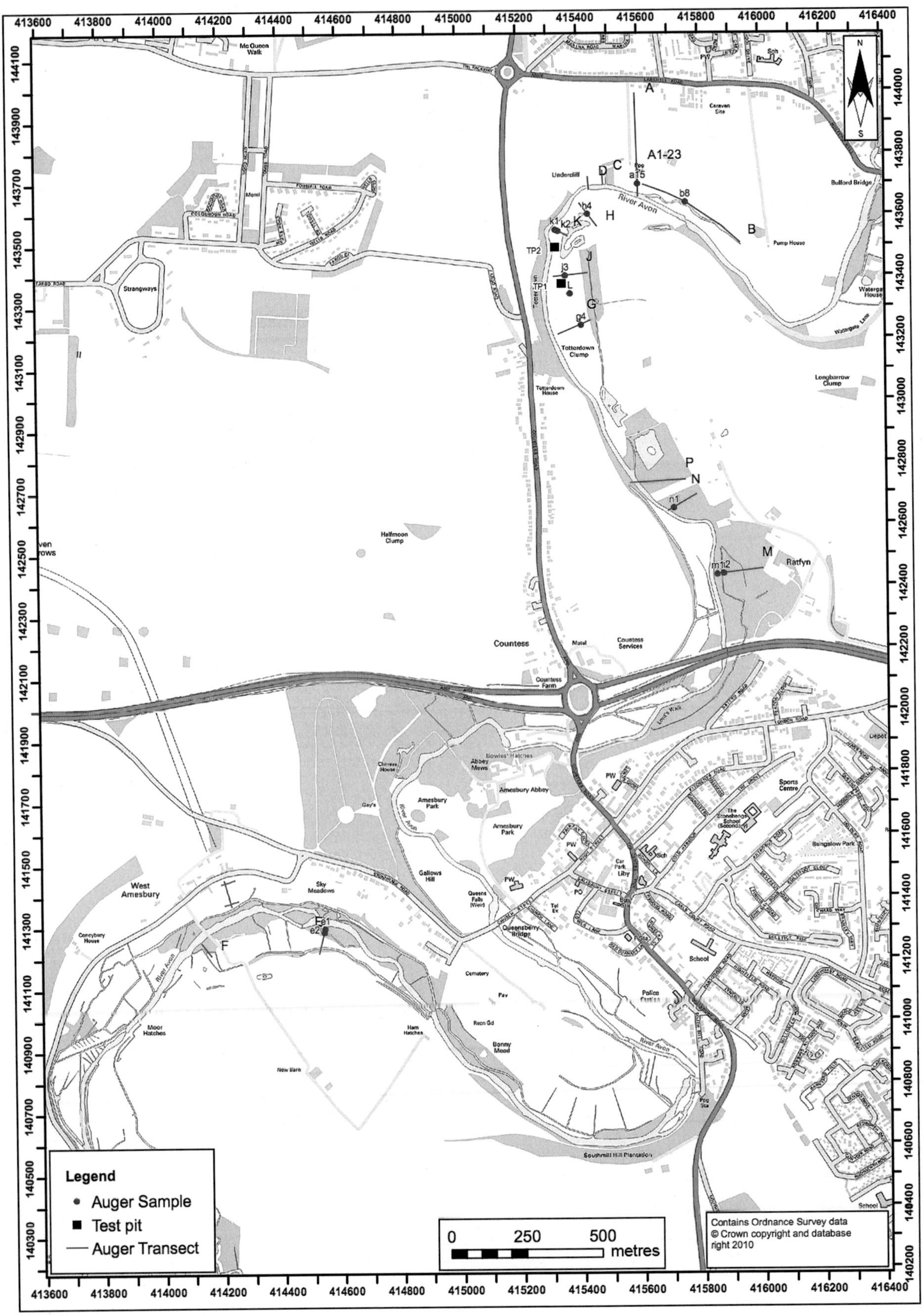

Figure 9.3. Map of locations of augering transects along the Avon valley from Durrington Walls to the Stonehenge Avenue

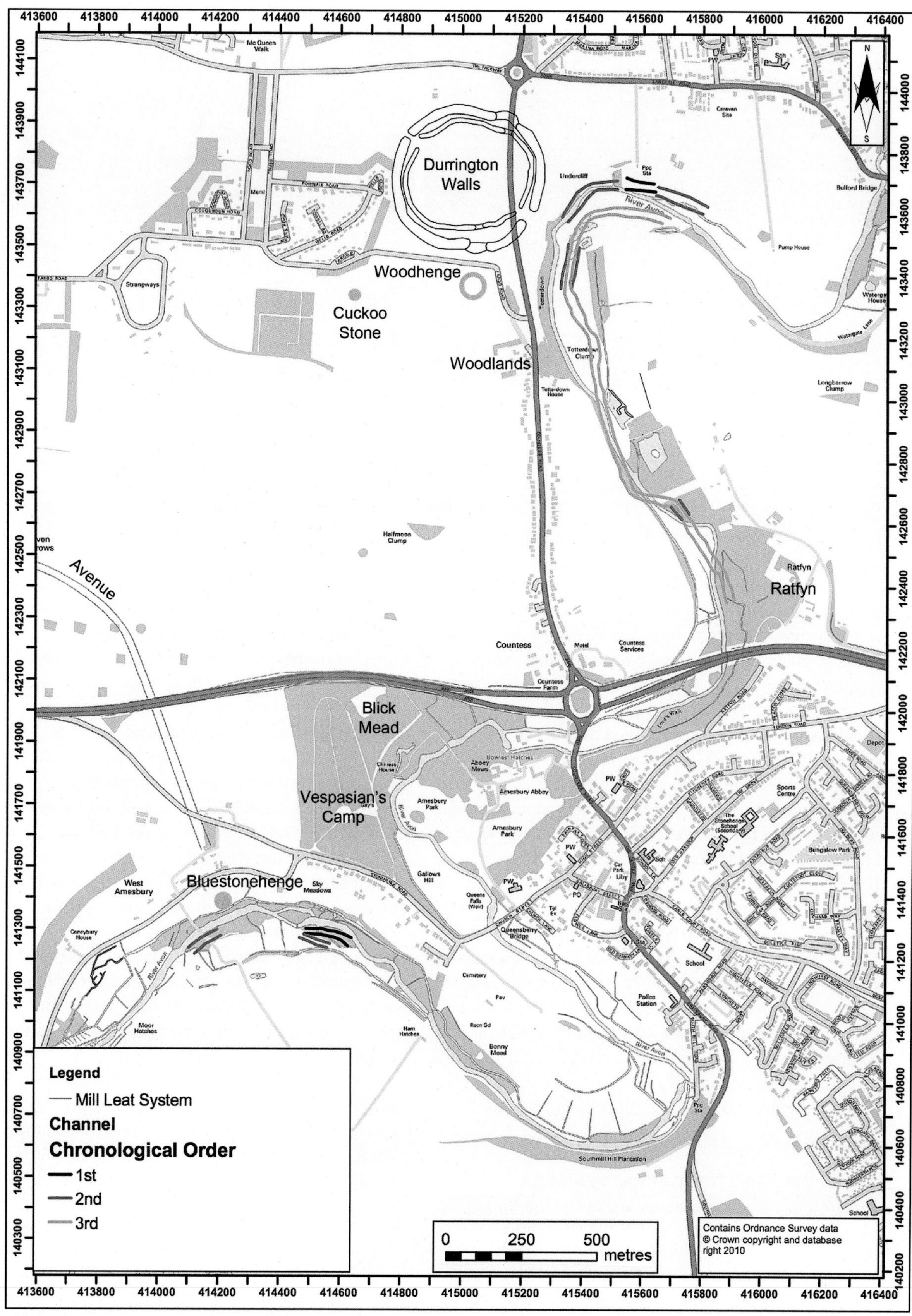

Figure 9.4. Conjectural map of the main channels identified along the Avon valley

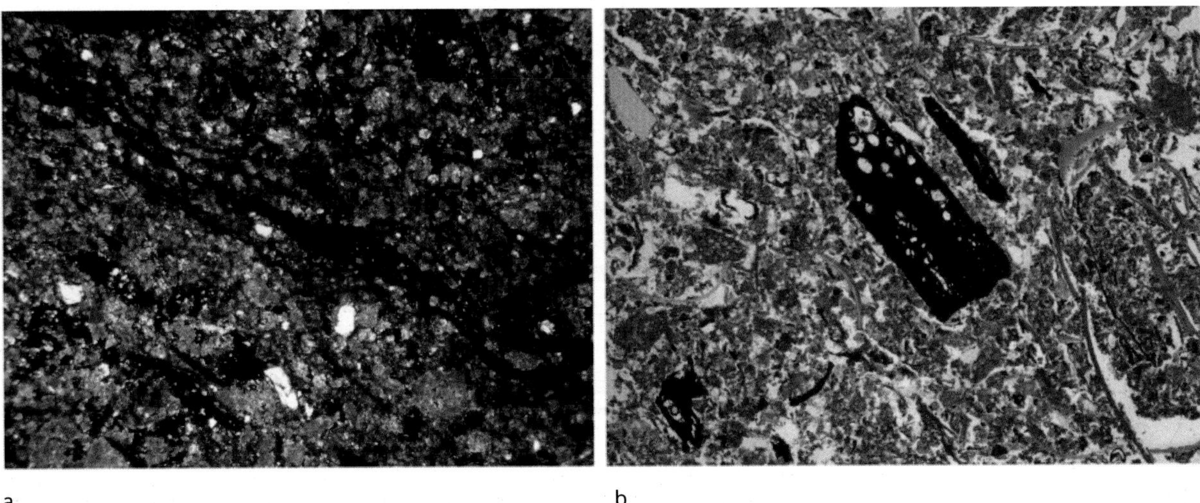

Figure 9.5. Photomicrographs of a) finely horizontally bedded micritic calcium carbonate with abundant iron- and clay-replaced plant tissue at the base of Test Pit 2, Avon valley (frame width = 4.5mm; cross-polarised light); b) wood charcoal and plant tissue fragments in the micritic sediment at the base of Test Pit 2, Avon valley (frame width = 2cm; plane-polarised light)

(<0.85m) and hillwash-infilled precursor channel to the present river. This much later (or third) palaeo-channel is consistently located along the eastern edge of the present river course. This palaeo-channel sequence was characterised by a colluvially-derived, calcareous silt with an organic silt loam or alluvial deposit above, sometimes with thin lenses of reed peat. Its course runs just south of Transect B and was observed in Transects C and D, and then crosses over the current river to the southeast to run parallel to the present river channel where it was observed in Transect N (Figure 9.4). This channel is probably the latest, historic-period channel, no more than a few hundred years old, active prior to the creation of the current river course.

There is a similarly infilled channel on the southeasternmost edge of the modern floodplain, marked by a copse along the 70m contour line (east of Transects G and J), which is associated with a ditched channel for the nineteenth-century mill upstream and a series of embanked 'lazy beds'. A number of recently established fish-ponds and a sewage works occupy much of the remainder of the present floodplain zone.

9.2.2. Palaeo-channel excavations

In addition to the hand-auger survey of the floodplain of the River Avon outside and to the east of the eastern entrance to Durrington Walls and the river cliff, two test pits were excavated by machine. Test Pit 1 was located in the centre of the palaeo-channel about 200m to the south of the river cliff, and a second trench (TP 2) was located on the western edge of the palaeo-channel to the east and just downstream of where the Durrington Walls avenue, discovered by the SRP excavations in 2005, meets the river cliff (Figure 9.3). Both test pits were necessary to examine the depositionary sequence, to collect samples for palynological and molluscan analysis, and to obtain dating material (*i.e.* wood, charcoal, peat and cultural material).

Test Pit 1 (2m × 3m × *c.* 1.50m deep) revealed a 1.50m-deep sequence of: 30cm–40cm of modern meadow turf, above hillwash-derived alluvial deposits over a depth of *c.* 80cm–90cm, and a basal reed peat (*c.* 30cm–40cm thick) containing well-preserved reed cases and wood fragments, some of which appear to have been slightly charred, but which contained no artefacts other than two struck flint flakes. This sequence was developed on a channel-bed deposit of fine gravel and coarse sand. A full profile sequence was sampled for pollen analysis and associated radiometric dating (but not analysed further since the results were likely to duplicate those obtained from Boreholes 8 and 15).

Test Pit 2 (2m × 2m × *c.* 1.50m deep) revealed a different sequence over a depth of 1.35m. This comprised about 50cm of made-ground (0–50cm; comprised of chalk rubble and silt loam soil, probably derived from dredging of the river and the excavation of the adjacent fish ponds), overlying *c.* 20cm of a dark brown, silt loam alluvium (50cm–70cm), *c.* 30cm of greyish-brown, calcareous silt loam colluvium (70cm–102cm), and *c.* 20cm of dark brown, silty clay loam (102cm–124cm), all developed on *c.* 10cm of pale grey coarse sand (124cm–135cm) overlying flint gravel, chalk fragments and coarse sand riverbed deposits (135cm+). The basal coarse sand deposit may well be derived from nearby greensand geological deposits. Interestingly, greensand was used as a temper in Grooved Ware pottery (Ros Cleal and Mike Allen pers. comm.; Cleal 1994; see Volume 3), and this would be a possible localised source for this material. The silty clay loam deposit at *c.* 100cm–120cm may be an incipient soil and old land surface formed in alluvial material, and was consequently sampled for micromorphological analysis.

Two molluscan samples and a beetle sample were taken from the southern trench, but failed to provide further information as a result of poor preservation. Charcoal and carbonised plant remains were also recovered during processing of the snail samples. The paucity of artefacts from the northern test pit was disappointing but this was almost 30m from the 'drop zone' at the end of the Durrington Walls avenue; the optimum location for such deposits is buried directly beneath the present riverbed and thus inaccessible because of SSSI restrictions.

These two sequences and the auger survey results of 2006 would suggest that there was an earlier prehistoric river channel that was both much deeper and wider than the modern river, by a factor of about 3:1. Initially, water flow in the river channel was sufficiently fast to not allow any build-up in the channel bed until a slight change of course, westwards, to essentially the route of the modern river course. This change of course cut off parts of the former channel and allowed the formation of the first organic peat deposits under conditions of standing water and reed growth. The aggradation of more inorganic deposits derived from soil erosion from the associated downland slopes. Obviously, determining the timing of these events is crucial to the interpretation of landscape and land-use change on the associated prehistoric archaeological sites.

9.2.3. Soil micromorphology

The basal deposits of the floodplain sequence in Test Pit 2 were composed of finely horizontally bedded micritic calcium carbonate with abundant iron- and clay-replaced plant tissue (Figure 9.5a), with a few wood charcoal fragments (Figure 9.5b), all accumulated on a substrate of first greensand and then chalk and flint pebbles. This suggests that the deposit accumulated in very shallow and often drying water conditions, possibly at the outer edge of the channel, with a standing vegetation that was regularly flattened and mixed by water flow. Interestingly, there was a reasonable quantity of included fine charcoal fragments present, presumably derived from human activities immediately upstream and perhaps even from the adjacent Durrington Walls henge.

9.3. Palynology of the Avon palaeo-channel

R. Scaife

Until relatively recently, there have been few pollen data which pertain specifically to the past vegetation and environment of the chalklands, a fact noted by Turner (1970: 98–9): 'It is rather unfortunate that the South-East chalk land, so long regarded on archaeological grounds as an area densely settled by Neolithic man, should be so poor in plant-preserving deposits'.

Prior to this statement, pollen data from adjacent to the chalk of southeast England comprised only those from work by Godwin (1962) at Wingham and Frogholt in Kent, discussing Holocene peat of late prehistoric age, and work by Lambert (1964) on a Late-Devensian (Allerød) soil at Brook, Kent.

Whilst this situation remains largely unchanged, it has to some extent been redressed by a number of pollen studies undertaken specifically to study the enigmatic palaeoecology of this archaeologically important zone. Information on local chalkland habitats has previously relied largely on the analyses of mollusca as proxies for vegetation environment and change (Bell 1983; Allen and Scaife 2007). Initial attempts at pollen analysis within the chalkland zone were undertaken by Thorley (1971a and b; 1981), Scaife (1980) and Waton (1982). All of these studies, however, relate to sediments on lithologies in close proximity to the downlands of Sussex, the Isle of Wight, Hampshire and Dorset. Increasing knowledge of pollen transport and taphonomy now indicates that, whilst there are representations of the floras of the chalklands more broadly, the bulk of the pollen, in fact, comes from on or in very close proximity to the sites sampled.

Durrington Walls has provided pollen data from a late prehistoric palaeosol underlying hillwash/ colluvium (Evans 1971c; Dimbleby and Evans 1974). More recently, peat deposits and alluvial sediments were located on the nearby River Avon floodplain (Cleal *et al.* 2004; see French and Allen, above). Pollen is variably preserved since the site has remained wet. Data show the development of early Holocene vegetation woodland with pine and hazel dominance and subsequently (after a hiatus spanning the middle Holocene) woodland clearance and expansion of open grassland habitats during the Neolithic and Bronze Age (Scaife 2004). Detailed stratigraphical survey within the Avon floodplain (see above) has demonstrated the extent of the peat sequence. As a result, two cores from different locations were taken and their results are presented here.

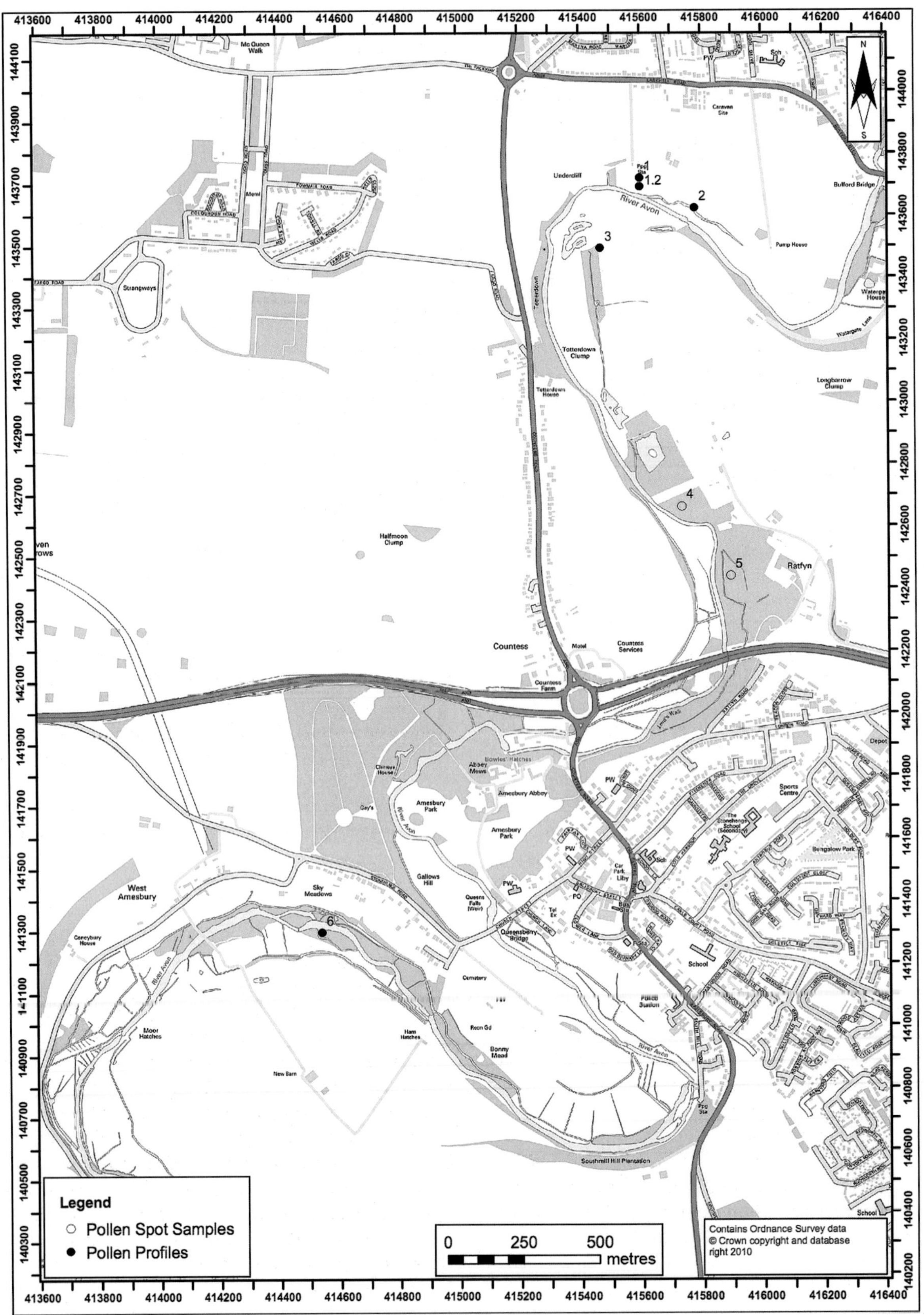

Figure 9.6. Map of locations of pollen sampling along the Avon valley from Durrington Walls to the Stonehenge Avenue

Sum =	% total dry land pollen (tdlp)
Marsh/aquatic =	% tdlp + sum of marsh/aquatics
Spores =	% tdlp + sum of spores

Table 9.1. Calculation of pollen percentages

9.3.1. The pollen data

Of the two radiocarbon-dated pollen sequences presented here, the first (borehole 8; Figure 9.6: location 2) is of later prehistoric and historic age, with a radiocarbon date of 1020–840 cal BC at 95.4% confidence (SUERC-32211/GU-22774; 2790±30 BP) for the base of the accumulation. The second (borehole 15: location 1.2) provides a deeper and longer temporal profile through the main prehistoric river channel, dating back to the early Holocene at 7080–6820 cal BC at 95.4% confidence (GU-22778; 8045±30 BP) and is similar to the first analysis of Cleal *et al.* (2004; location 1) which had a basal age of 8280–7300 cal BC at 95.4% probability (GU-3239; 8640±200 BP). A number of hiatuses may be present but this second profile (borehole 15) similarly extends into the historic period, with an uppermost radiocarbon date of cal AD 1210–1290 (GU-22779; 770±30 BP).

Typically for such a calcareous environment with alkaline flushes, pollen is very variably preserved, being absent and extremely sparse in many of the samples. This applies especially to the lower part of borehole 15, that is, especially in the early and middle Holocene levels. The upper and more recent (historic) period has better preservation.

Pollen was extracted and concentrated using standard techniques (Moore and Webb 1978; Moore *et al.* 1991) although a double (Erdtman) acetolysis was found to be beneficial. Because of the variable preservation of the pollen, sums were variable, with up to 700 grains plus spores per level identified and counted. Pollen diagrams (Figures 9.7–9.8) have been constructed and plotted using Tilia and Tilia Graph. Percentages in Figure 9.7 have been calculated as in Table 9.1.

Taxonomy in general follows that of Moore and Webb (1978), modified according to Bennett *et al.* (1994) for pollen types and Stace (1992) for plant descriptions. These procedures were carried out in the Palaeoecology Laboratory of the School of Geography, University of Southampton. Local pollen assemblage zones (l.p.a.z.) have been recognised which define the principal, inherent changes in the pollen assemblages seen in the profiles. From these, vegetation community and environmental inferences can be drawn.

The characteristics of the profiles and the local pollen assemblage zonation of the two profiles are given in Tables 9.2 and 9.3.

9.3.2. Borehole 15

This profile is the temporally longer and more useful of the two pollen profiles. Radiocarbon dates from between 7080–6820 cal BC (GU-22778; 8045±30 BP) and 790–510 cal BC (GU-22775; 2490±30 BP) have been obtained. Intermediate dates have also been obtained which provide ages for phases of environmental change, including the longevity of a substantial hiatus in the sediment accumulation.

Radiocarbon-dating of this profile and the earlier analysis of a nearby site (Cleal *et al.* 2004; Scaife 2004) show that humic sediment started to accrue during the early Holocene (Flandrian 1a; Pre-Boreal) from *c.* 9,000 BP. As such, the vegetation shows the typical, early Holocene, seral development of woodland which occurred after the close of the Devensian cold stage at 10,000 BP as taxa migrated from their glacial refugia consequent upon temperature amelioration. This was a phase of highly dynamic vegetation, with the asynchronous arrival and colonisation of the principal woodland taxa by the end of the early Holocene (Godwin 1975; Birks 1989). Vegetation development was controlled by factors including location of refugia from which trees migrated, reproductive factors, competitive ability and soil development. Archaeologically this corresponds with the Early Mesolithic. Although there are general and recognised patterns of tree colonisation throughout the country, local variations can be perceived in the arrival and importance of the dominant species (see below).

Borehole 15 has a basal age of *c.* 9,000 BP. Initially, pine was important along with incoming hazel while some pioneer birch remained. Small numbers of lime (*Tilia*) and alder (*Alnus*) pollen grains, recognised as degraded and stained more darkly, are likely to have derived from earlier, reworked (interglacial) sediments. These species of trees became of substantial importance only later, especially during the middle Holocene (Flandrian II; Atlantic). The values of pine and hazel suggest that the local environment was not wholly dominated by these trees but that they probably occurred as stands of woodland or scattered trees.

Herb communities were also important, with both on-site grass-sedge fen and drier, possible short-turf grassland as indicated by rock rose (*Helianthemum*), salad burnet (*Sanguisorba minor*), ribwort plantain (*Plantago lanceolata*) and possibly *Plantago media*, although the latter pollen taxon may also include *Plantago major*. Both of the former are also diagnostic of calcareous habitats. Occasional juniper (*Juniperus*) also attests to remaining open woodland or scrub. These plants appear to be elements of the open, Late-Devensian vegetation which remained prior to early Holocene woodland colonisation.

Local pollen assemblage zone 2 is delimited by the arrival of oak (*Quercus*) and elm (*Ulmus*) as the next phase of seral woodland succession. Willow (*Salix*) colonised the valley bottom. Hazel (*Corylus*), although present in the

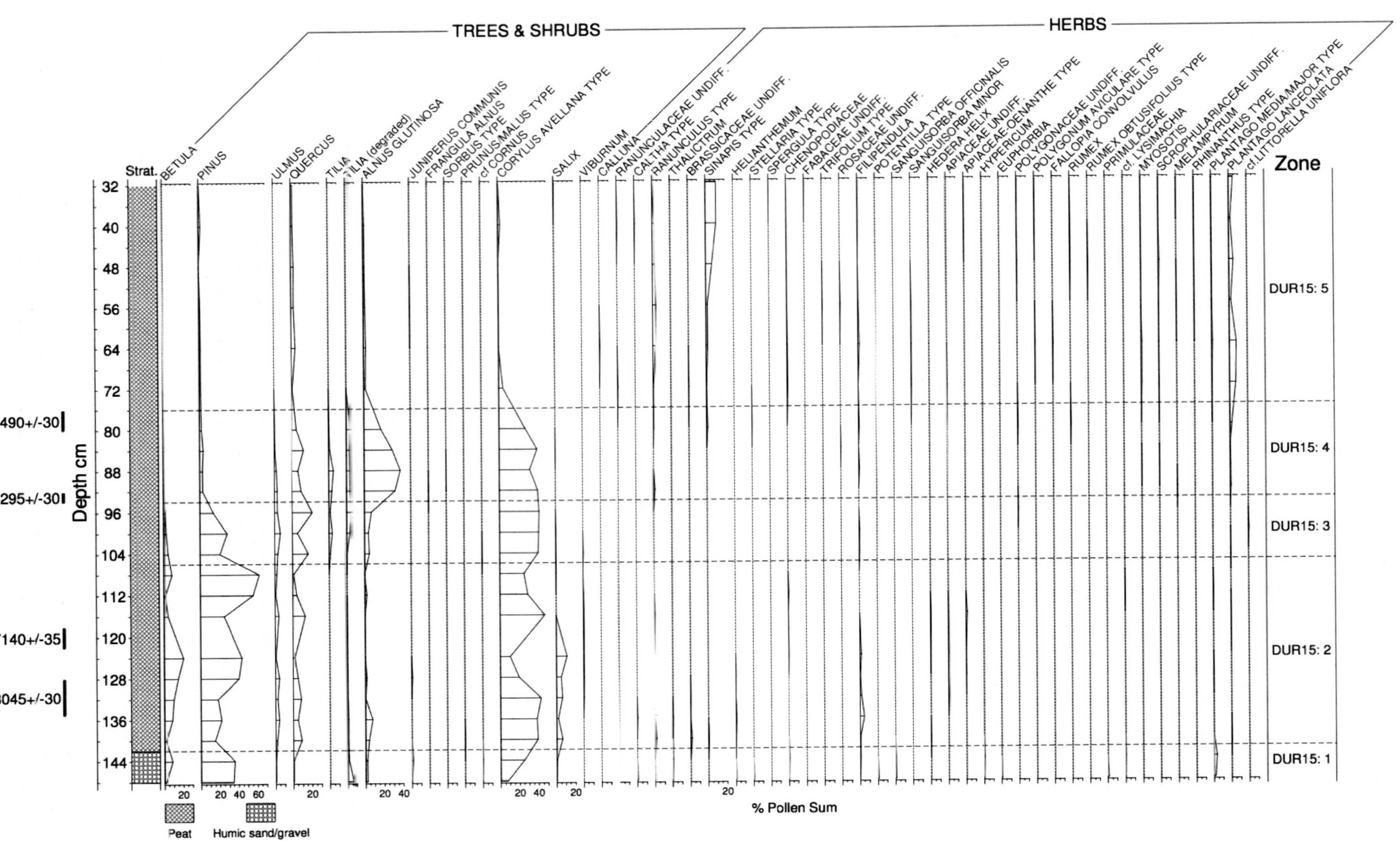

Figure 9.7. Pollen diagram from Borehole 15 (ɔart 1)

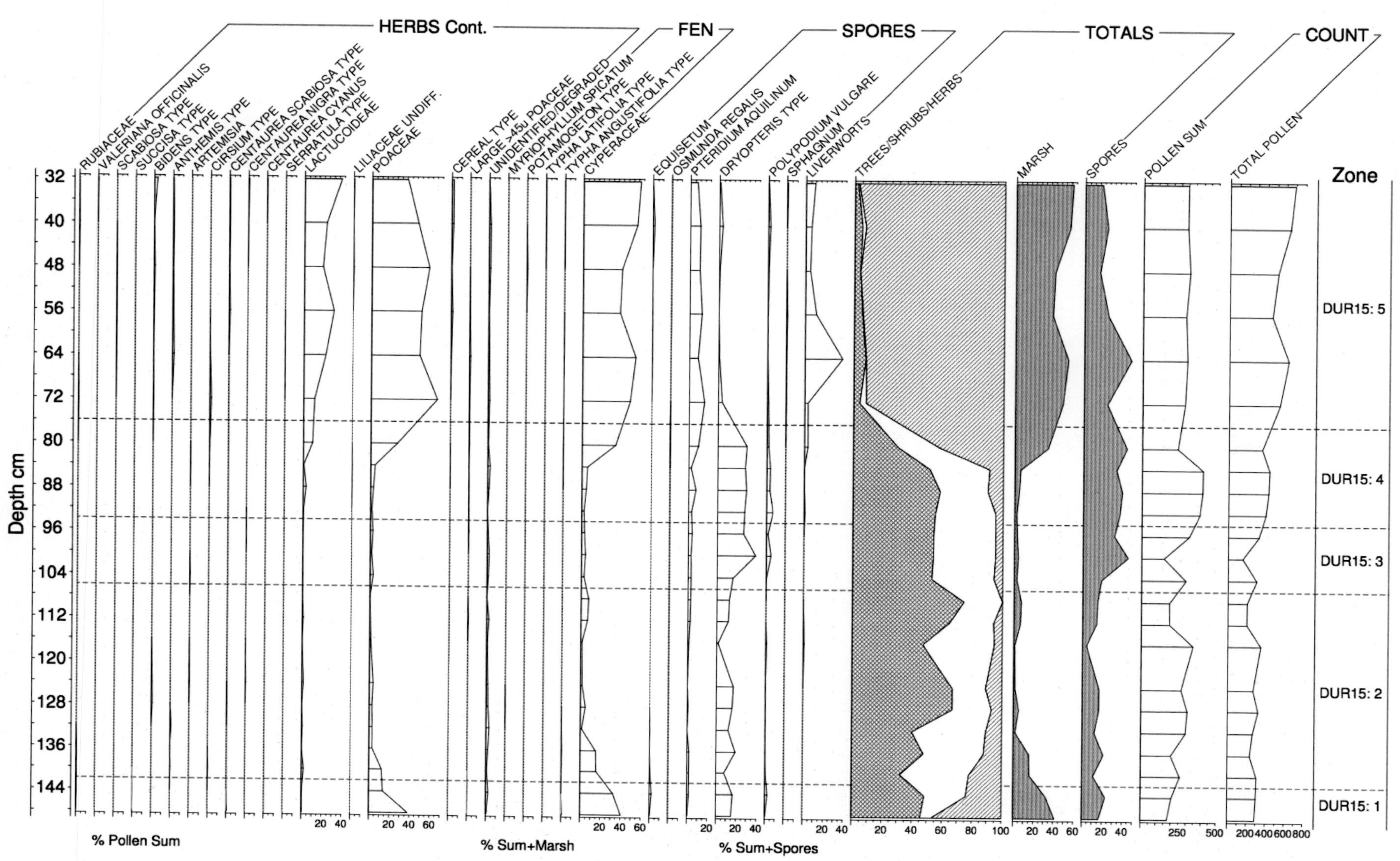

Figure 9.8. Pollen diagram from Borehole 15 (part 2)

Zone	Description
Borehole 15: 5 0.76m–0.32m *Plantago lanceolata*-Lactucoideae-Poaceae-Cyperaceae	There is a marked reduction of trees and expansion of herbs at the base of this zone after a possible hiatus. There remain only traces of *Pinus* (long distance?), *Quercus, Alnus* and *Corylus avellana* type. *Juniperus* at 0.56m is of note. Herbs, in contrast, are dominant with Poaceae (initial peak to 65%), with Lactucoideae increasing to 35% in the upper sample. *Plantago lanceolata* (to 10%) and cereal type (2%–3%) are also of note in this zone. *Sinapis* type increases in the upper half of the zone (10%). Marsh/fen taxa are well represented with Cyperaceae dominant (55% sum + marsh) with sporadic *Potamogeton* type, *Typha latifolia* and *Typha angustifolia/Sparganium* type. Numbers of spores of *Dryopteris* type decline markedly while *Pteridium* becomes most important (15%–16%). *Sphagnum* is present consistently but in small numbers. Liverworts (unknown sp.) peak to 40% (sum + spores).
Borehole 15: 4 0.94m–0.76m *Tilia-Alnus-Corylus avellana* type	*Alnus* (39%) and *Corylus avellana* type (49%) are dominant and showing some decline. Pollen is absent at *c.* 0.76m in a possible sub-aerial phase. *Pinus* and *Ulmus* are present in only small numbers (to 5%). *Tilia* (as an under-represented taxon) remains relatively important. Herbs start to become more important across the upper zone boundary with Poaceae increasing (30%) and Cyperaceae at 35%. Other herbs include *Plantago lanceolata* from the top of the zone with increasing Lactucoideae and the first cereal pollen grain at 0.84m. Spores of *Dryopteris* type remain dominant (25% sum + spores) with *Polypodium* (2%–3%), increasing numbers of *Pteridium* (to 15%) and *Osmunda regalis* at the top of the zone. Liverworts become important from this zone (sp.?).
Borehole 15: 3 1.06m–0.94m *Quercus-Tilia-Corylus avellana* type	Delimited by incoming of *Tilia* (to 10%) including both well-preserved and degraded pollen. *Betula* and *Pinus* decline, the latter from high values to low levels at the top of this zone. *Quercus* remains important (to 20%) with *Corylus avellana* type (to 45%). *Alnus* values start to increase from sporadic occurrences in the preceding zone to 10%. There are few herbs with Poaceae and Cyperaceae in low numbers (to *c.* 5%). Spores of *Dryopteris* type peak to 40% (sum + spores) with some increase in *Polypodium*.
Borehole 15: 2 1.42m–1.06m *Pinus-Betula-Quercus-Ulmus-Corylus avellana* type	This zone is characterised by dominance of trees with declining herb percentages. *Betula* increases to a peak at 1.24m (28%) and *Pinus* to its greatest value (68%) at 1.08m. *Ulmus* (5%) and *Quercus* are incoming. Sporadic occurrences of badly degraded *Tilia* (secondary?) remain. A minor peak of *Alnus*, also degraded, occurs at the base of the zone. *Corylus avellana* type, after its increase in zone 1, attains its highest values (50% at 1.16m). Other trees/shrubs include occasional *Juniperus* and *Viburnum* and autochthonous *Salix* (19%), the latter important at the base of the zone (sub-zone). There is, however, a reduction in mid-zone. Herbs remain important but in less diversity and smaller numbers after decline of Poaceae and Cyperaceae of zone 1 (to 5% and fluctuating 10% respectively). These include taxa of wetland/floodplain (*Filipendula*, Apiaceae spp). Spore totals remain similar to zone 1 with *Dryopteris* type most important and small numbers of *Pteridium* and *Polypodium*.
Borehole 15: 1 1.48m–1.42m Pinus	*Pinus* (35%) is dominant in this basal zone with increasing values of *Corylus avellana* type (6% to 24%). There are small numbers of *Betula*. Degraded *Tilia* and *Alnus*. Shrubs include *Juniperus* and possibly *Cornus*. Herbs are important with Poaceae (declining from 33% to 15%) and Cyperaceae (declining from 40% to 35%). Along with the latter fen taxon, *Typha angustifolia* type is present. Spores include monolete forms, *Dryopteris* type and sparse *Polypodium*, with *Pteridium aquilinum* and *Equisetum*.

Table 9.2. Pollen zonation of Borehole 15

preceding zone, became important and, along with pine, formed the Boreal pine-hazel described by Godwin (1956; 1975a), possibly with hazel forming a shrub layer in pine woodland. A radiocarbon date of 8045±30 BP (GU-22778) confirms a Boreal age (Flandrian Ib). The arrival of oak and elm is significant as these, along with lime (*Tilia*) in many regions, out-competed birch and pine to become the dominant woodland elements during the Boreal period and certainly by the middle Holocene (Atlantic). This change was asynchronous, with dates varying across Britain. Here, however, pine maintained its dominance throughout the Boreal period and into the middle Holocene.

The question of whether pine remained an important woodland component after the Boreal period has been debated and, until recently, has been postulated only for certain areas of southern Britain. This is based on charcoal and pollen evidence although the latter remains enigmatic in view of the propensity for pine pollen to be transported by wind over great distances. Whilst native pine woodland is found today in Scotland, Godwin (1976) first postulated its post-Boreal occurrence on the sandy soils of the East Anglian Breckland. Haskins (1978), Cameron and Scaife (1988) and Scaife (1994; 2007) in Dorset and Scaife (1980) on the Isle of Wight have similarly provided tentative evidence for the continuity of pine in the landscape of southern England even through to the sub-Boreal period (Neolithic and Bronze Age). Pine charcoal has also been recovered from archaeological sites from similarly late Holocene phases (Allen and Scaife 2007: 21). Wimborne Minster, Dorset, provides the most comparable evidence, with similarly high pollen percentages dated to the middle Holocene (Scaife 1994; 2007). These data now show conclusively that, in addition to the importance of pine in the middle Holocene in Scotland (native to the present day), there were localised stands growing on edaphically suitable regions of southern England. These were probably not only on the sandy Tertiary lithologies, but also on the shallow calcareous soils, gravels and river terraces of the Avon.

Sediments are compacted in this profile, and it is clear that a lengthy Holocene time-span is represented in this *c.* 1.50m sequence. The middle Holocene (Flandrian II; the Atlantic period) is bracketed within the upper half of l.p.a.z. 2 and within l.p.a.z. 3, with dates of 6070–5920 cal BC at 95.4% confidence (GU-22777; 7140±35 BP) at 1.20m and 3020–2870 cal BC at 95.4% confidence (GU-22776; 4295±30 BP), the latter being of Late Neolithic age. Whilst pine, discussed above, was present but declining in importance by the latter date, oak, elm and especially hazel retained their coverage while lime and alder became more significant.

The low values of lime are a further indication that the character of woodland adjacent to this site differs from most areas of southern and eastern England (though see the charcoal report in Chapter 7). Throughout most of this region, pollen values of lime are much higher, suggesting that it was dominant or at least co-dominant with other woodland elements (Moore 1977; Greig 1982; Scaife 1980; 2000; 2003). Although lime is generally poorly represented in pollen assemblages (Andersen 1970; 1973), being entomophilous and flowering when other trees are in full leaf in summer, pollen numbers should be much

Borehole 8: 2 0.48m–0.76m Poaceae-Cyperaceae-Lactucoideae	This zone is defined by a reduction of the trees and shrubs noted in zone 1 and an expansion of herbs. The latter remain dominated by Poaceae (60–65%). Lactucoideae become increasingly important with highest values at the top of the profile (to 53%). Although there are very few trees, *Picea* is present (a single grain). Spores remain dominated by *Pteridium aquilinum*.
Borehole 8: 1 0.76m–1.28m *Quercus-Corylus avellana* type-Poaceae-Cyperaceae	There is more tree and shrub pollen than in the subsequent zone. *Quercus* (18%) and *Corylus avellana* type (16%) are most important with smaller numbers of *Fagus sylvatica*, *Alnus* and sporadic occurrences of *Betula*, *Pinus*, *Ulmus* and *Fraxinus excelsior*. Herbs are, however, dominant with Poaceae attaining high values (65%). In addition, there is a diverse range of herb taxa which includes cereal type (to 6%), *Plantago lanceolata* (peak to 18% at 1.12m; a possible sub-zone), *Sinapis* type, *Ranunculus* type, and Lactucoideae. Marsh taxa are important with dominant Cyperaceae (to *c*.50% sum + marsh). Spores comprise largely *Pteridium aquilinum*.

Table 9.3. Pollen zonation of Borehole 8

greater in this profile, given the topography of the nearby chalk escarpment and its suitable soils. Although some lime is present, it is possible that the inertia of the existing woodland (pine, hazel, and oak) may have restricted its expansion within this local area. It is also possible that interfluve soils may have been unsuited because of the presence of acid *mor* from the pine community. As with all pollen data, the taphonomy of the pollen is always open to debate and discussion. Pollen here derives from on-site vegetation and, at least during the woodland phases, from a relatively small region around the site. This would undoubtedly have included the adjacent chalk interfluves, whilst fluvial transport along the River Avon, together with pollen reworking and overbank deposition, may also have played a role.

From 0.94m, (l.p.a.z. 3/4 division), radiocarbon-dated to 3020–2870 cal BC at 95.4% confidence (GU-22776; 4295±30 BP), there are changes in the character of woodland and on-site vegetation. Pine pollen remains in the profile but with markedly smaller values, suggesting that it may only have been present in small quantities – if at all – in proximity to the site. There are also apparent reductions in birch and elm. Lime and hazel remain at their preceding levels. The most diagnostic feature is the increase in alder (*Alnus*) to relatively high values, and it is probable that it had become established in greater numbers along the banks of the Avon and on its floodplain. Pollen numbers are probably not great enough to propose a dominant floodplain alder carr growing on the sample site.

Of significance at 0.84m, just prior to the boundary between pollen zones DUR15: 4 and DUR15: 5 at 0.82m, is the first occurrence of cereal pollen in this profile. The radiocarbon date of 3020–2870 cal BC (4295±30 BP; GU-22776) at 0.92m suggests that this pollen assemblage zone spans the period of the adjacent Durrington Walls and thus provides an environmental context for the henge in the middle of the third millennium BC. With the decline of elm, the occurrence of cereal pollen and the start of a continuous record of ribwort plantain (*Plantago lanceolata*), it is tempting to attribute these events to the period of the Neolithic elm decline (Smith 1970; Girling 1988). This has been variously dated within the region at between *c*. 3500 BC and 2800 BC (Scaife 1988). Certainly, there is evidence of increased human impact, with arable and possibly pastoral activities in the local environment. This may have been contemporaneous with the Cuckoo Stone pits (see Chapter 7) and just before the first settlement structures at Durrington Walls (see Volume 3).

The period of Durrington Walls' occupation can be seen to have been one of remaining oak and hazel woodland with lime growing on better drained soils, and with alder fringing the river and along areas of its floodplain. Initially, some probably localised woodland clearance was carried out. There is no real indication as to whether these clearances were ephemeral, landnam-type events consisting of short cycles of clearance, cultivation and subsequent woodland regeneration.

At 0.80m in borehole 15's profile, there is a significant change from a locally wooded landscape to one devoid of trees. Whilst the lower part of l.p.a.z. 4 has been dated to the beginning of the Late Neolithic, a date of 790–510 cal BC at 95.4% probability (GU-22775; 2490±30 BP) was obtained in the upper part of l.p.a.z. 4 and at the base of l.p.a.z. 5. Although thin bands of sediment can represent long time-spans through oxidation and compaction of the peat, the major change in both pollen and sediment character suggests a hiatus in the profile. This uppermost zone (l.p.a.z. 5) represents the upper floodplain sediments which are found across the greater part of the valley, and correlates with borehole 8 (see below).

The vegetation was now open, with only relatively low representation of tree and shrub pollen (largely oak and hazel). The floodplain habitat had changed from alder to a probably wetter grass-sedge fen community. The surrounding drier soils of the interfluves were predominantly grassland/pasture habitats but with some evidence for cereal cropping. It can be noted that cereal pollen is usually less well-represented in pollen assemblages than the pollen of grassland species, and may thus have been more important than attested in the pollen diagram. This habitat remained little changed throughout the remaining upper part of the pollen diagram.

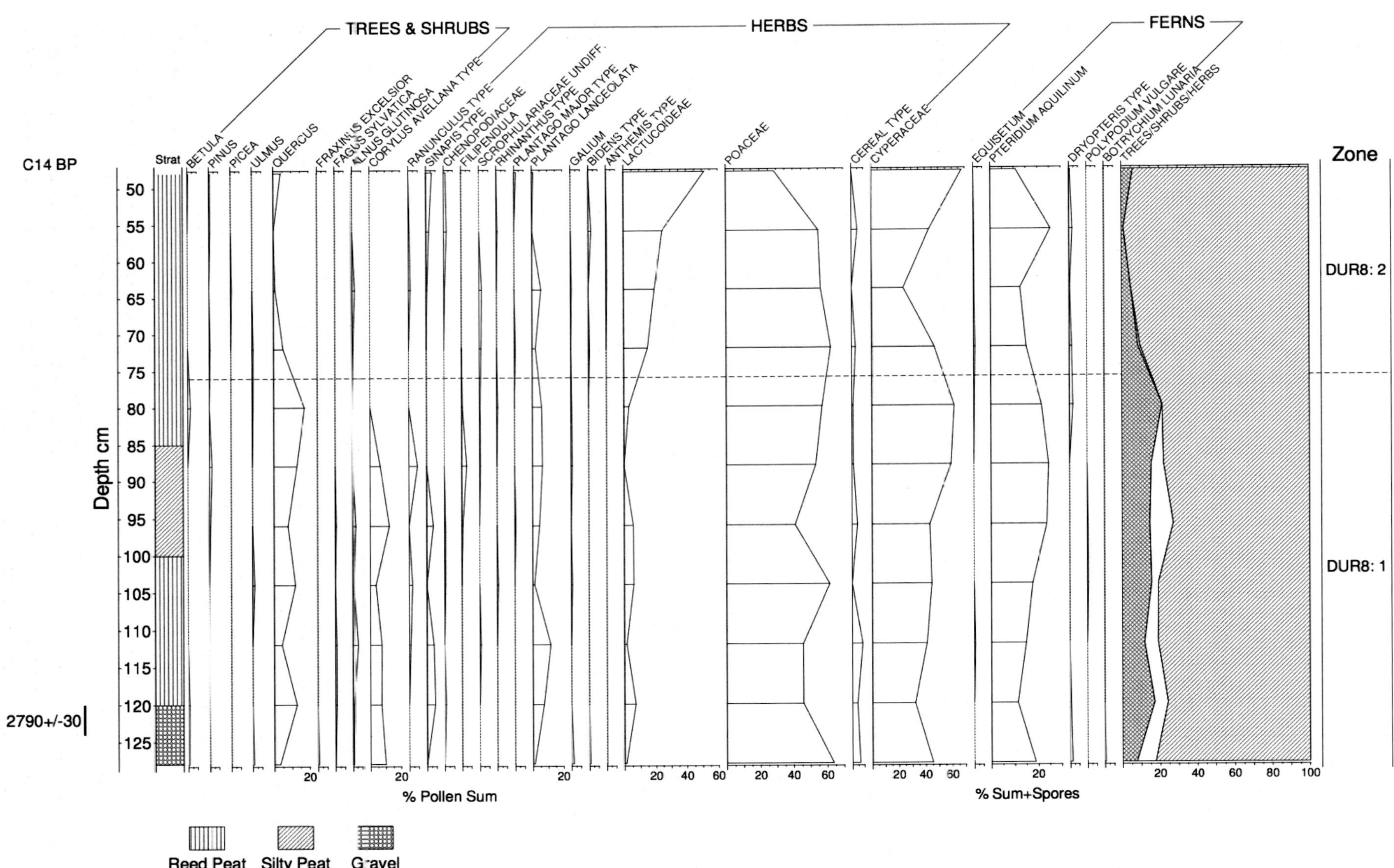

Figure 9.9. Pollen diagram from Borehole 8

9.3.3. Borehole 8

This stratigraphically and temporally shorter sequence provides information on the more recent vegetation and environment. A radiocarbon measurement of 1020–840 cal BC at 95.4% confidence (SUERC-32211/GU-22774; 2790±30 BP) at 1.24m–1.20m, near the base of this peat and alluvial sediment profile, takes this sequence back to the Late Bronze Age and, as such, it is comparable with the upper local pollen assemblage zone (l.p.a.z. 5) of borehole 15. Two local pollen assemblage zones have been recognised in borehole 8 and are characterised in Table 9.3.

Palynologically, there are close similarities between the sequence in borehole 8 and the sequence in the upper part of borehole 15, and clearly their sediments accumulated after the major phases of prehistoric woodland clearance. These clearance phases were, successively, the Neolithic elm decline, subsequent Early Bronze Age clearance for agriculture, and the Middle Bronze Age lime decline.

The dominance of herb pollen, with few trees and shrubs, indicates a locally open environment. Where trees and shrubs do exist, oak (*Quercus*) and hazel (*Corylus*) remain the typical woodland elements of the very late prehistoric and historic periods. It is probable that these pollen, being anemophilous, come from more regional sources. Beech (*Fagus sylvatica*) is present in small numbers in l.p.a.z. 1. Given its poor pollen dispersion and resulting strong under-representation in pollen assemblages, the occurrence of beech here suggests that it may have been present locally, and it is highly probable that it was growing on the downland scarp. The notable absence of lime (*Tilia*), present in the earlier phases of borehole 15, also reveals that the final clearance had occurred of what would have been dominant local woodland.

In this profile, as in the highest zone of borehole 15 (borehole 15: 5), herbs are dominant. Grasses and other taxa associated with grassland (*e.g.* ribwort plantain) appear most important and suggest that pasture was locally important. However, cereal pollen is also present, especially in the lower part of the profile (l.p.a.z. borehole 8: 1), in sufficient quantity to suggest that arable cultivation was practised in relative proximity. This would have been on the drier interfluve soils adjacent to the floodplain.

Throughout the profile, sedges (Cyperaceae) are an important component of the pollen assemblages. There is little alder pollen and, along with grasses, a grass-sedge fen is indicated as the on-site floodplain vegetation habitat. Other fen taxa and taxa of wet/damp ground are also sparse, with occasional tall herbs including marsh marigold, greater burnet, meadowsweet, and marsh valerian. Standing or slow-flowing water is shown by the presence of cysts of algal *Pediastrum* and probably water pondweed (*Potamogeton*). The expansion of dandelion types (Lactucoideae) in the upper part of the profile (l.p.a.z. borehole 8: 2) may correspond with declining woodland (the reductions in oak and hazel pollen). However, their enhanced numbers are more probably due to the effects of differential preservation of this robust pollen in the upper sediment levels, causing its over-representation. This is typical of sediments subjected to a fluctuating water table, thereby introducing oxidising conditions.

Although undated, with soil formation taking place in the upper sediments, there are indications of an expansion of pine pollen, a useful palynological marker (Long *et al.* 1999). If present in these upper levels, this would indicate a date of *c.* AD 1700 when pine (and also other exotics such as spruce and fir) were introduced into parks, gardens and subsequently forestry plantations after John Evelyn's publication of *Sylva, a Discourse of Forest Trees* (1664). As at West Amesbury (Scaife 2006), the presence of spruce (*Picea*) in the uppermost levels is also attributed to planting in parks and gardens in recent centuries.

9.3.4. Patterns of vegetation change

Pollen data from the chalklands are rare as a result of the alkalinity of the ground water and especially the passage of oxygenated ground (spring) water through the peat. Other pertinent factors also include the relative paucity of peat-forming sites compared with upland Britain, the contrasting rainfall deficit and, in many cases, the past cutting of peat for fuel, a factor not widely recognised for southern Britain.

Thus, the data obtained from Durrington add to the small but growing corpus of information which is now available from this palaeoecologically interesting zone. It is fortunate that here and at the adjacent site of Amesbury (Scaife 2004), pollen has been preserved back to the early Holocene which, coupled with radiocarbon-dating and sedimentological analysis, provides an insight into the early Holocene (Flandrian I) development of woodland after the close of the last (Devensian) cold stage, the middle Holocene (Flandrian II) stability and subsequent prehistoric and historic human impact on the established woodland.

The overall vegetational history of this locale of the Avon floodplain and adjacent chalk escarpment has now been established from a number of studies. These include the two borehole/core studies presented here, along with previous examinations of the floodplain (Scaife 2004; 2005; 2006; 2007; locations 1, 3–6 in Figure 9.6). From Durrington Walls, Dimbleby obtained pollen from a soil/turf providing data to compare with Evans' molluscan analysis (Evans 1971c). These results can be compared with more regional pollen studies from Avebury (Dimbleby 1965), Cranborne Chase (French *et al.* 2003; 2007), Winchester (Waton 1982) and the Isle of Wight (Scaife 1980), all of which pertain to the changing habitats of the chalk downland of central southern England.

The early Holocene

The sites of earlier analysis of the palaeo-channel (Scaife 2004) and of borehole 15 are in close proximity, and both provide data on the early Holocene. A peat located in a basal depression at Durrington pumping station (location 1 in Figure 9.6) provided a radiocarbon date of 8640±200 BP (GU-3239; Cleal *et al.* 2004). This earlier analysis also established the importance of pine woodland at the site as one of the seral elements in the establishment of woodland after the close of the Late-Devensian stadial. Neither profile shows the initial dominance of juniper, followed by birch, as the initial Holocene pioneers immediately after the close of the Devensian cold stage. This is due to the basal sediments in the profile from borehole 15 starting to accrue from the early Boreal rather than the pre-Boreal (*i.e.* at *c.* 9,500 BP or later). Such vegetation is likely to have existed, colonising the areas of open herbaceous vegetation of the Late-Devensian Younger Dryas. However, it is clear that some of these more heliophilous elements remained and that pine woodland spread. After the subsequent arrival of oak and elm, these failed to become wholly dominant, as is usually seen in pollen diagrams from southern England.

As at Cranborne Chase (French *et al.* 2000; 2003; 2007; French and Lewis 2005; Scaife 2003; 2005; 2007) and the Caburn, Sussex (Waller and Hamilton 1998; 2000), more heliophilous taxa remained. These included birch and juniper (possibly scrub) and also herbs such as ribwort plantain (*Plantago lanceolata*), rock rose (*Helianthemum*), salad burnet (*Sanguisorba minor*) and others. The latter are especially diagnostic of short-turf, calcareous grassland. This suggests that areas of more open vegetation existed on the chalk well into the early Holocene along with areas of birch and juniper scrub. More typical woodland of pine and hazel, with expanding oak and elm, are, however, also in evidence, whilst pine woodlands were clearly expanding and subsequently became dominant in many areas.

The middle Holocene: Atlantic Flandrian II

Oak, elm and lime now became established after their arrival into the region. Similarly, lime (*Tilia*, probably *Tilia cordata*), was the last of the forest dominants to arrive, immediately prior to the separation of Britain from mainland Europe. It is now accepted that lime became dominant or at least co-dominant on suitable soils across southern and eastern England during this period (Moore 1977; Scaife 1980; 1987; 2000; 2003; Greig 1982) and it is seen throughout this region. This importance was maintained until its demise during the later prehistoric period.

This dominance of lime appears not to have been the case at Durrington Walls (Evans 1971c) where, although lime is present, the importance (or even dominance) of pine continued. This is atypical of most of the southern region, where lime became dominant. Moreover, the Durrington Walls picture is mirrored at Wimborne Minster (Scaife 1994: 2007), where a similar, radiocarbon-dated peat has also been examined. It is this chalkland region which was, perhaps, responsible for the consistent but small values of middle Holocene pine pollen recovered from sites across southern England.

The late Holocene: late prehistoric and historic periods

The Late Neolithic radiocarbon date of 3020–2870 cal BC at 95.4% confidence (GU-22776; 4295±30 BP) for l.p.a.z. 4 at *c.* 0.92m in borehole 15 is associated with a stratigraphic change from peat to silty peat. It is possible that the change from peat to silty peat might also represent a hiatus in sediment accumulation. It is likely that the increased minerogenic component occurred in response to increased human activity, with resulting soil erosion and sediment run-off from the adjacent interfluves. This would correspond with the date of the Cuckoo Stone pits (see Chapter 7) but is later than the Early/Middle Neolithic activity in 3500–3100 cal BC on the old ground surface prior to the Late Neolithic settlement and henge at Durrington Walls (Wainwright with Longworth 1971: 14). This also corresponds with the date of Stonehenge Stage 1 (Darvill *et al.* 2012; Marshall *et al.* 2012; see Table 11.5)

During the time-period relating to this zone of borehole 15, alder became established on the floodplain. Pine, of previous importance, may have remained in small numbers (although regional and/or long-distance sources are not ruled out) whilst oak, lime and hazel were important. There is less elm pollen than in the middle Holocene, probably as a result of the widely documented Neolithic elm decline (*e.g.* Smith 1970; Scaife 1988; Girling 1988). The first cereal record is in the upper part of this zone. Cereal and wild grasses started to increase after *c.* 2300 BC, during the Chalcolithic or at the start of the Early Bronze Age. Thus, it appears that woodland remained important during most of the Neolithic. Pollen influx into this alder-dominated floodplain would have been more restricted than in the preceding, more open fen and, as such, although woodland clearly remained, there is a strong likelihood that human activity took place within a mosaic of woodland and open or cleared ground.

Analyses of the mollusca by Evans and soil pollen by Dimbleby at Durrington Walls similarly showed a reduction of trees and a change to open landscape during the Late Neolithic (Evans 1971c). The pollen provided evidence of a shaded habitat of hazel with some birch, pine, oak, lime and elm, of similar character to that provided by borehole 15. Subsequently, there was a reduction in these trees, especially hazel, and an expansion of fern spores (largely bracken), suggesting opening-up of the landscape. Dimbleby, however, questioned whether this phase of openness was correct because his pollen data were at variance with the molluscan analysis of Evans; he surmised that this phase of openness might have belonged to a later stage of ecological development.

Although Evans (1971c) demonstrated evidence for a woodland environment from the mollusca, he showed that there was some clearance, probably for cultivation, during the Middle Neolithic and that, by the Late Neolithic, when Durrington Walls was occupied, the local environment at least was treeless and comprised short-turf grassland. This is, therefore, commensurate with the record obtained from borehole 15, except that, in the longer pollen record, it appears that the importance of hazel noted by Dimbleby continued well into later prehistory and possibly into the early historic period. This might be attributed to remaining growth on the lower valley slopes or even on drier areas of the Avon floodplain.

After a substantial stratigraphic hiatus (separating zones 4 and 5 in borehole 15), prior to *c.* 800–500 BC, the pollen data from the Durrington sites and further downstream come from the veneer of floodplain alluvium and humic/organic deposits which occur along the Avon floodplain. Pollen data from all of these Avon valley sites show that a significant phase(s) of woodland clearance had taken place to create agricultural land. The data here show a predominantly grassland flora, suggesting a largely pastoral environment as might be expected on the chalk, with creation of downland. However, small numbers of cereal pollen attest to at least the use of – and probable local growth of – cereals.

It is likely that woodland clearance may have been responsible for increasing wetness in the valley, and for the further onset of sediment accumulation. This would have been caused by increased surface run-off and a higher water table through a reduction in evapotranspiration rates and increased surface sediment supply/run-off as woodland was removed for agriculture. This also accords with the archaeology of Durrington Walls and its vicinity (French *et al.* 2012; see Volume 3). Radiocarbon-dating shows that this woodland clearance occurred in this area around Durrington Walls in 1020–840 cal BC (SUERC-32211/GU-22774; 2790±30 BP, the base of borehole 8) during the Late Bronze Age. This habitat remained almost unchanged through to the present except for draining of the floodplain for rough pasture, which also initiated pedogenesis of the upper floodplain sediment. Hence, there is an absence of pollen in the upper 0.30m–0.50m of soil/sediment.

9.3.5. Conclusion

These two pollen profiles obtained from the River Avon floodplain, in close proximity to Durrington Walls, have produced a vegetational and environmental history spanning the greater part of the Holocene, although there are some hiatuses. With so few such pollen data from calcareous environments, this study (along with earlier analysis of the Avon floodplain) provides an insight into the differing periods of Holocene vegetation change, and the causes of sediment deposition in the valley. These appear to have been climatically controlled both at the Devensian–Holocene boundary and at the Boreal/Atlantic transition, with increased wetness and peat accumulation and increased minerogenic sedimentation resulting from human activity on the interfluves.

The pollen profiles obtained from this site demonstrate that certain areas of southern England – on the higher chalklands – may have remained a more open environment than other areas of heavily wooded seral vegetation which have been frequently demonstrated. Here, there is evidence that areas of calcareous grassland and scrub (possibly some juniper and hazel) remained, most probably on the adjacent downland. Furthermore, this site – along with Wimborne Minster downstream – shows that pine, once it had migrated into the region, maintained importance into the middle Holocene (Flandrian II; Atlantic). This differs from the majority of sites in southern England which show that pine was out-competed by oak, elm and lime by the end of the early Holocene, lime especially becoming the dominant woodland taxon of the middle Holocene.

Of specific interest is the elucidation of the environment associated with Neolithic activity at Durrington Walls. This period of activity has been difficult to define in the pollen record because of the compacted nature of the peat. However, all indications are that the near landscape remained at least partially wooded with oak, elm, lime and hazel (the latter being especially important, possibly as open scrub) during the Early and Middle Neolithic, while alder became increasingly important on the river's floodplain. However, from the Middle to the Late Neolithic, there are indications that the landscape became more open as grassland (probably for pasture) and, tentatively, for cereal cultivation.

After a cessation of sediment accretion, it appears that at *c.* 500 BC there was an increase in wetness in the valley which re-invigorated peat deposition and sediment alluviation on the floodplain. This may be attributed to increased human activity on the interfluves during the Late Bronze Age and Early Iron Age. Expansion of agriculture is seen, with increased pollen from arable and pastoral sources. This event caused a veneer of alluvial sediments to accumulate along the length of the River Avon's floodplain, in the process covering the meandering palaeo-channel fills which have provided the longer pollen records. The overall character of the environment became one of open agricultural land, with few trees on the adjacent downland, and grass-sedge fen and rough pasture on the river floodplain. This remained throughout the historic period, with the only apparent change being towards increasing dryness of the floodplain, possibly through drainage and the extension of floodplain pasture.

9.4. Along the River Avon

C. Tilley and W. Bennett

The River Avon is the major permanent watercourse in the study area, and its significance is crucial for an understanding of prehistoric settlement in the region in general and the location of monuments and their interrelationships in particular. The Avon links the Stonehenge landscape with other important archaeological landscapes – to the north, the Vale of Pewsey and the Marlborough Downs, and to the south, Christchurch harbour and the sea – thus constituting a major channel of communication. It has long been suggested as one potential route by which the bluestones were moved to Stonehenge from southwest Wales (Atkinson 1956: 57, 103–4).

Within the study area (Durrington Walls to Lake Bottom; Figure 9.1), the Avon forms a comparatively wide valley for much of its course, meandering along the valley floor from north to south. Numerous coombes or dry valleys connect with it, to both the east and the west. A short distance (500m) to the south of its confluence with the Nine Mile River (a winterbourne and one of the few other 'living' rivers in the area) the Avon makes a dramatic series of huge meanders in the Durrington/Amesbury area before straightening again further to the south. Here steep river cliffs are prominent at various points on either side of the river. These continue along the southern course of the Avon to Salisbury and beyond (Figure 9.1).

To the north of Durrington, steep river cliffs only occur near to Netheravon and Figheldean. These are both lower and less dramatic than those to the south of Durrington. For the most part, the river valley here is rather broad and gentle, lacking any dramatic scarps or edges. There are no Neolithic monuments of any kind directly associated with these northern reaches of the river with the exception of the Wilsford henge and, notably, Marden henge (Leary *et al.* 2010), a considerable distance away to the north, past which the western Avon loops, directly to both the west and the south of the monument. By contrast, Early Bronze Age barrows and barrow cemeteries are quite numerous although most do not appear to be directly related to the course of the river, the major cemeteries being located up to 1km or more away (but nevertheless on the upper valley slopes or bluffs associated with the river). Bronze Age barrow groups occur along the tops of the river cliffs at Netheravon and Figheldean and, further away, along spurs separated by coombe systems on the eastern side of the river.

At precisely the point where the first huge meanders and the steep river cliffs begin to the south of the modern settlement of Durrington (Figure 9.4), a whole series of Neolithic and Chalcolithic ceremonial monuments are directly connected or linked in various ways with the river: the Durrington Walls henge and Woodhenge, the Coneybury henge and the Avenue linking Stonehenge to the river (Figure 9.1). In addition, a large long barrow (Bulford; Figure 9.1) is associated with the river almost opposite the eastern entrance to Durrington Walls. Neolithic pits occur above the river cliffs at Woodlands and Ratfyn. Early Bronze Age barrows directly associated with the river's course are far fewer: a few to the south of Woodhenge, the Ratfyn barrow standing on the river cliff there, and a few barrows located within Vespasian's Camp, on Coneybury Hill, and at Lake at the southern end of, or entrance to, Stonehenge Bottom.

There are four factors that make the course of the Avon, south of Durrington, appear special. All these features lend an added significance to the Avon here and to the manner in which it is linked with the major ceremonial monuments:

1. The huge meandering river loops. Meanders of comparable size and complexity, bounding tongues of land up to 1.50km long and 250m–500m wide, simply do not occur to the north or south. Similar but less pronounced loops only reappear south of Downton, along the eastern edge of Cranborne Chase about 20km away.

2. The appearance of high river cliffs along the river banks at regular intervals. The Durrington area marks a point of transition between two different types of valley system along the Avon: gentle and sloping to the north and punctuated by heights to the south.

3. Associated with these meanders and river cliffs are wide flood plains and marshy areas (which are seasonally inundated with water), stranded 'dry' river cliffs (along the bottom of which the river once ran before changing its course) and oxbow lakes, most notably today in the floodplain east of the river opposite Durrington Walls.

4. A change also occurs in the relationship between the coombes (dry valleys) and the manner in which they are linked up with the river's course. To the north of Durrington, their directionality is consistently northeast–southwest. To the south of Durrington, those coombes along the Avon's western side run for the most part north–south or northwest–southeast. This is, in effect, a reversal of the previous main axis in relation to the river, while those coombes to the east of the river maintain the northeast–southwest axis or run more in an east–west direction.

Route	SLD	RD	CT	EFT
Durrington Walls - Avenue terminal	2.2km	6.5km	1hr 46	3hr 53
Durrington Walls - Lake	4.7km	10.0km	2hr 45	5hr 30

Key	
SLD	straight line (map) distance
RD	river distance
CT	canoeing time* (*Time spent negotiating contemporary obstacles such as weirs, sluices and low bridges deducted from these figures.)
EFT	estimated floating time (without paddling, in a heavily over-loaded canoe with a weight of *c.* 500kg. Time measured from Durrington Walls to Queens Falls Weir, Amesbury)

Table 9.4. Canoeing distances and travelling times along the course of the Avon from Durrington Walls to the riverside terminal of the Stonehenge Avenue and to Lake (the entrance to Stonehenge Bottom)

9.4.1. The Avon valley: from Durrington Walls to Lake Bottom

An initial research hypothesis for the SRP was the possible existence of a ceremonial passage from Durrington Walls to Stonehenge along the River Avon and then following the line of the Avenue (see Chapter 1). An alternative, and possibly older, passage between the two monuments might have followed the course of the Avon and then the dry valley of Stonehenge Bottom. Fieldwork involved following the course of the Avon by canoe to explore the experiential effects of these two passages through the landscape (Figure 9.2). Distances and canoeing times are given in Table 9.4.

On leaving Durrington Walls along its avenue leading southeast towards the river, the ground drops away steeply at a 3m-high river cliff, obscuring view of the site. The river's course at this point directly below Durrington Walls is unlikely to have changed much since prehistory, although it was wider and deeper (see French and Allen, above). Later on, when the henge was built, the entrance to Durrington Walls would probably have been visible from the river with the formerly massive banks of the henge standing to their original height.

Moving downriver from the Durrington Walls riverside, the river cliff to the right (the west bank) gradually steepens, blocking all view of the wider landscape, and then drops away. To the left there is an extensive, flat floodplain and, in places, views here are quite extensive. For about 500m the long barrow opposite Durrington (Bulford; Figure 2.1: no. 4) is visible, between 750m and 1km away from the river. After the first river cliff to the right ends, the land slopes far more gently upwards and away, and one can see as far as 200m in this direction up towards the Woodlands pits (Stone and Young 1948). After this slope, the land is completely flat on either side. In the past this must have been a substantial area of marsh and probably a seasonal lake.

After twenty minutes of canoeing, the next river cliff at Ratfyn comes into view ahead, on the east bank. The river then bends and passes to the left, below it for about 750m. The presence of charcoal-filled pits here (and at Woodlands; Stone 1935; 1949; Stone and Young 1948) suggests the possibility of fires being lit along the top of the cliffs on both the east and west banks of the river, to mark auspicious occasions and the ceremonial passage being undertaken along the river beneath them. To the right, the land is flat and marshy. Today, trees block all views of the wider landscape in this direction but, in the third millennium BC, this valley may have been largely cleared of trees or gently wooded (see Scaife, above, and Cleal *et al.* 2004). Without this dense tree cover, one would have been able to look up a gentle slope westwards towards the Woodlands pits but Woodhenge would have remained out of sight at the top of the ridge to the north. The Ratfyn cliff then ends and the land is flat on either side of the river.

After a further 14 minutes paddling, another steep river cliff emerges to the right, and one passes below it for a couple of minutes. This recedes from view and the land is now completely flat on either side of the river. After a further five minutes, another river cliff (Southern Hill) comes into view ahead and one proceeds towards and then passes beneath it on the left, with a broad marshy area to the right. This river cliff ends and is replaced by gently sloping land, up across which there are views for a few hundred metres. Straight ahead, Coneybury Hill comes into view.

A coombe then comes into view to the right, the first encountered since leaving Durrington Walls, and then, just beyond it, the site of Bluestonehenge and the riverside end of the Stonehenge Avenue (see Chapter 5) become visible. The land in this area in front of the coombe is very low-lying and, in the past, may have been an extensive, seasonally flooded marsh, periodically widening the river's course. The henge and the riverside end of the Avenue, however, sit on a raised chalk spur rising above the low ground.

The river then bends to pass beneath the river cliff below Coneybury Hill, about 300m distant from an ancient river cliff to the right that limits the view in this direction. The river then bends again to pass beneath a short river cliff of the Coneybury ridge to the right. Immediately after this, the Amesbury Down river cliff appears straight ahead and the river curves round to flow beneath it to the left for about 500m, before passing through flats on either side where another river cliff at Lake comes into view straight ahead.

At the point at which the river bends to flow beneath the river cliff at Lake to the right, the southern scarp edge of Lake Bottom (the entrance to Stonehenge Bottom) is visible straight ahead, about 800m away, together with a strategically placed large Early Bronze Age barrow. Finally the river meanders into the basin of Lake Bottom, an area that probably constituted a lake in the past, with the valley of Stonehenge Bottom leading off to the right.

On this entire journey the only monuments visible are Durrington Walls and the nearby long barrow (no. 4) at the beginning, Bluestonehenge stone circle and latterly the banks of West Amesbury henge enclosing it, the banks of the Stonehenge Avenue, and the large Early Bronze Age barrow at the entrance to Lake Bottom. One passes seven river cliffs in a right/left/right succession, four to the right and three to the left, varying between a few hundred metres and 750m in length and up to 30m high. Two coombes run down and meet the river, both to the right. The first is next to the riverside end of, or entrance to, the Stonehenge Avenue, the second is the beginning of Stonehenge Bottom. These mark two very different alternative turning-points from the river inland to Stonehenge.

As can be seen in Table 9.4, the huge meanders of the Avon along this stretch of the river cause the river passage to be roughly three times longer than a straight-line walking distance, and the time taken to paddle down it is quite considerable. The river loops not only considerably extend the journey time but also have a disorientating effect. Without the aid of a map, one soon loses all sense of direction and any awareness of whether one is heading north, south, east or west. The river loops dislocate both in space and in time. The important point to be made here is that such a cumulative disorientating effect is exactly what would be expected if this river journey was intended as a rite of passage or a transition between different social states. A short distance becomes a very long one, and all sense of direction rapidly becomes lost. The key aids to orientation along the journey are the river cliffs. Otherwise very little of the landscape is visible from the water because of the trees, reeds and vegetation growing along the banks.

The river cliffs are encountered in a regular sequence, alternating between one side and another along the course of the river as one passes beneath them but, at various points, when seen from upstream, they appear to be straight ahead. The walking distance from one river cliff to another on the same bank is short; from the Ratfyn cliffs to those at Southmill is just over 1km. If one imagines people standing on these river cliffs looking down on those passing in canoes below, it would be possible for the same people to move and reappear on another cliff long before the canoes passed below. From a riverine perspective one might encounter the same faces one had already passed a long time before!

It is also worth pointing out how the disorientating effects of the meanders are enhanced by this succession of river cliffs, and how the cliffs vary when seen from the river, to the left, the right, or straight ahead (and behind) when seen at a distance. These cliffs occur to the east, west and south but never to the north of the river flow. Other features provide great variety and surprises along the river route. The river cliffs create a differentiated river where it passes beneath them – dark and enclosed on one side, light and open on the other. Here the river is shallow on one side and deep on the other.

Today the river runs fast, gurgles, and is very shallow, only ankle-deep in places. In other parts it is considerably deeper, up to 2m, and the flow is more sluggish and silent. This would have been the case even without the modern weirs and sluices. Deep-water pools would have formed along its course at some points and shallow shelves at others. Being a chalk stream, it is exceptionally bright and crystal-clear, exposing its chalk and flint bottom. The symbolic bones of the land were thus visible below the water, except where banks were undercut and covered the riverbed with oozing mud. A wide range of aquatic plants, fish and fowl add infinite variety to passage along it.

9.4.2. Walking the Avenue: from the Avon to Stonehenge

A lake along the river course, or a seasonally flooded and marshy area, may originally have constituted the original terrain (now water meadows) on either side of Bluestonehenge at the entrance to the Avenue.

The Avenue runs uphill away from the Avon, adjacent to a coombe about 200m to the east. This coombe is rather broad, with gentle slopes on each side. Rather than connecting with, and following the line of the coombe to the north, the Avenue immediately slights the topography, diverges and runs diagonally up a slope to the north-northwest. From the beginning of the Avenue, one probable (destroyed) Early Neolithic long barrow and three associated Early Bronze Age round barrows would have been visible upslope to the northeast. To the southwest the Early Bronze Age Coneybury King Barrow is skylined. The skyline ahead, looking up the Avenue, is reduced to about 100m.

After about 250m, having passed the probable long barrow to the right, a pair of round barrows, one on either side of the Avenue, come into sight (Figure 9.1: point 1). Passing these barrows, the Beacon Hill Ridge becomes visible for the first time to the east and the King Barrows come into view to the northwest. The Avenue continues its gradual ascent up and across the hill slope (Figure 9.1: point 2).

From just to the north of the present A303, about 750m up the Avenue (Figure 9.1: point 3), the coombe to the east can be seen bifurcating and swinging around to the west. From this point, Woodhenge becomes visible, with Sidbury Hill beyond, and a much greater extent of Beacon Hill Ridge is revealed. The Coneybury King Barrow is prominent along this entire stretch of the Avenue.

The Avenue continues to run diagonally up the slope to the summit of the ridge and crosses over the top of a coombe arm as it fades out and becomes indistinct. Ahead and sited on the very top of the ridge, six Early Bronze Age round barrows, three to the west and three (all now destroyed) to the east of the course of the Avenue, once dominated the skyline. The Avenue passes through these barrows which previously formed a façade on either side of it, skylined as one walks along the course of the Avenue from the south (Figure 9.1: point 4).

Passing across the top of the coombe and up the slope towards these barrows, the King Barrows to the left (west) appear particularly impressive as does Beacon Hill Ridge to the right (east). Just before the 'façade' of six round barrows is reached, some of the Old King Barrows come into view on the skyline's near-horizon to the north.

Passing through the barrow 'façade', another shallow coombe arm becomes visible to the north, running east to west. At the point at which the ridge-top begins to dip down to this coombe, the Avenue veers away to the west, to climb to the top of the King Barrow Ridge, traversing the very head of the coombe across the slope. The Early Neolithic causewayed enclosure of Robin Hood's Ball comes into view to the northwest (see Figure 2.1).

The Avenue crosses the King Barrow Ridge on slightly sloping ground to the north, with higher ground to the south (Figure 9.1: point 5). The King Barrows (New and Old) themselves do not form a symmetrical 'portal' through which the earthwork runs and, like other Early Bronze Age round barrows, were not constructed at the same time as the Avenue. From the top of the ridge, a vast panorama opens up, in which Stonehenge is visually dominant as one looks ahead. To the west, the Greater Cursus and its associated barrows and western terminal are prominent, as is the Winterbourne Stoke Crossroads long barrow and round barrows (see Figure 2.1: no. 17). The Fargo plantation 'henge' (Stone 1938) would also have been visible. To the southwest, the Normanton Down and the Lake barrow groups are prominent. To the northwest, Robin Hood's Ball is on the horizon. A locally important round barrow is visible down-slope to the right (north) of the Avenue. To the east, Woodhenge is visible and Beacon Hill Ridge is prominent beyond.

The Avenue crosses the slope, dropping down towards Stonehenge Bottom, avoiding the line of a shallow coombe to the south. The land rising up to the south of this coombe gradually blocks all views in this direction and the view also becomes progressively more restricted to the west. As one moves down towards Stonehenge Bottom, the Cursus barrows become skylined and more and more visually dominant.

At the point at which the Avenue crosses Stonehenge Bottom (Figure 9.1: point 6), the coombe is very wide and poorly defined, forming an irregular basin that narrows and becomes well-defined once more to the north and the south. Here there is a possible small round barrow in the coombe bottom itself to the left (south), just before the kink in the Avenue – here Stonehenge disappears from view.

Stonehenge comes into view again (Figure 9.1: point 7) as one goes up a gentle slope, with the easternmost Cursus round barrow skylined and visually dominant ahead. The Avenue then swings round again at its 'elbow' or bend (see Chapter 8), rather awkwardly just below the lip of the bluff and almost as an afterthought. From here it runs straight up towards Stonehenge, which becomes ever more impressive ahead. The change in direction aligns the Avenue on the midsummer sunrise. Just before Stonehenge is reached, the Normanton Down barrow group comes into view beyond.

9.4.3. Walking Stonehenge Bottom: from Lake to the Greater Cursus

Stonehenge Bottom is both the longest and topographically (in terms of its depth and width) the most significant coombe or dry valley in the study area. From Lake on the River Avon to just west of Durrington Walls, it runs for about 8km. Another feature that makes it especially significant is that it is one of very few coombes running approximately north–south through the landscape. In this respect it resembles the River Avon and the other seasonal or winterbourne rivers (the Till and the Bourne) more than the other coombes. Although a dry valley today for almost all the year, after periods of exceptionally heavy rain it floods and still forms a temporary living watercourse from south of the A303 to the Avon (information from the farmer at Springbottom Farm).

The place-name 'Lake' implies that, in the past, the Avon may have formed a flooded area or lake at this point. At Lake, the coombe is wide, with a flat bottom up to 100m wide. The coombe is steep-sided to the left (south) and rises much more gently to the right (north). Looking ahead, a ridge (Rox Hill) appears to block the passage and terminate the coombe system. At the entry to the coombe, there is a prominent round barrow near to the top of the slope to the left, skylined from the coombe bottom. Opposite it and halfway up the gentle slopes to the right, a further three to four round barrows (now destroyed) were once visible. Walking along the coombe, which at first runs east–west, the most prominent landmark is Rox Hill. This would have made a perfect location for skylined barrows but they are absent.

After 800m the coombe bends around to the right and runs northwest; suddenly a new vista is presented. Directly ahead, a large round barrow in the Lake Down barrow cemetery is visible. This almost immediately disappears as one continues to walk up the coombe. The coombe changes character, becoming a shallow V-shape in profile, its left-hand side becoming shallower and broader and its bottom more constricted. The coombe meanders to the left and the right, and views along it are restricted to 500m or less. The coombe sides restrict the visual field to the left and right, with the long vista ahead funnelling one's perspective.

Another round barrow comes into view (part of the Lake group) and is skylined to the left. Below it, close to the very bottom of the coombe, there are two small round barrows to the left which lie just above the margins of the seasonal water flow along the coombe bottom. Beyond these barrows, the coombe swings around to the right and broadens out again, with a flat bottom about 100m wide.

At Springbottom Farm the coombe bifurcates for the first time, with one branch, to the left, cutting west across the landscape between the Normanton Down and Lake barrow groups. The main branch, to the right, continues to the north. At this point there is uncertainty about which way to continue. The coombe now changes character again, to become a broad V-shaped valley with a flat bottom about 15m wide. Views to either side are restricted up to the coombe lips and no monuments are visible. After about 800m, the coombe sides become shallower and broaden out, and a distinctive bottom is lost.

Around this point a large round barrow (now destroyed) was visible straight ahead along the line of the coombe to the north, at the end of a ridge at Luxenborough. From the coombe, this ridge-end to the southwest of Coneybury Hill appears to be a rounded knoll. Just to the south of this 'knoll' the coombe bifurcates again, with a northeastern branch cutting into Coneybury Hill just to the southeast of Coneybury henge. Passing to the left of the ridge-end, the view to the right is severely restricted by a steep scarp slope.

The main coombe line continues to the north and divides again, with a shallow arm running up to the south of Stonehenge. Looking up this side branch, the long barrow to the southwest of Stonehenge (see Figure 2.1: no. 23) and the 'midwinter sunset' round barrow are skylined on the horizon at the end of the coombe branch. As one continues northwards, the coombe soon bifurcates again, this time to the right, but no monuments are visible. The left (western side) of the coombe is a gentle slope while the right (eastern) side remains much steeper and well-defined, resembling a river cliff.

As one walks north along the coombe bottom, the large round barrow immediately to the east of Stonehenge comes into view and, immediately afterwards, Stonehenge itself appears dramatically on the skyline, and in close proximity – it is only about 700m distant to the northwest. Stonehenge then falls out of view just to the south of the A303 but the round barrow to the east of it is still visually dominant. This barrow does not appear at all dramatic from Stonehenge itself but, from the coombe, it is most impressive. It is as if its sudden visual presence announces that of Stonehenge itself.

To the north of the A303, both Stonehenge and the round barrow to its east fall out of sight. The line of the Avenue crossing the coombe is visible ahead. This next section of the coombe remains strongly defined to the right (east) but only weakly defined to the left (west). After *c.* 250m, the round barrow to the east of Stonehenge comes into view again and, shortly afterwards, so does Stonehenge itself.

The coombe base widens out and is ill-defined on either side as an irregular bowl where the Avenue crosses it. Stonehenge falls out of sight again. A round barrow is skylined on the side of the coombe to the right, just to the south of the line of the Avenue. As one crosses the line of the Avenue, some of the King Barrows come into view. The tips of the Stonehenge trilithons return into view about 50m beyond and, after a further 100m, the whole of Stonehenge is fully visible again. Looking ahead, Stonehenge Bottom appears to end by the line of the Greater Cursus.

The coombe now narrows again, with well-defined edges both to the left and the right, and a broad, flat bottom. Stonehenge disappears again and then reappears at the centre of the point at which the Greater Cursus meets the coombe (see Chapter 2). The coombe then bifurcates again to the left and right before gradually fading away. Passing around to the right, the northern bank of the Cursus and the round barrows running alongside it are at first skylined and then lost from view, and barrow groups to the north and northeast become visible.

9.4.4. Conclusion

Travelling along the River Avon through the centre of the Stonehenge landscape is a disorientating experience – disorientating in terms of space (one rapidly begins to lose sense of where one is and in what direction one is travelling) and disorientating in terms of time (it takes a very long time to travel what is only a short distance as the crow flies). Such an effect would make this river route an ideal component of rites of passage linking Durrington Walls and Stonehenge via their avenues.

If the river route served to disorientate, we might conceive of subsequent passage along the Stonehenge Avenue, with its broad sweeps and vistas, especially from the top of King Barrow Ridge, as a process of re-orientation and integration in relation to a sense of place. Along the river, virtually no monuments are visible. As one moves up the Avenue, more and more come into view, culminating with the panorama of what might seem almost the entire world from the King Barrow Ridge top. On the way, one passes through barrow 'portals' announcing what is to come. These Early Bronze Age round barrows claim one's attention as a series of portals, culminating in King Barrow Ridge; it is hard to disentangle today the experiencing of the Avenue when it was built, from the subsequent experiencing of the Avenue during the Bronze Age. That said, all of these round barrows re-worked and re-emphasised the original route to Stonehenge.

Travelling along the coombes also has a disorientating effect, not only because views to either side are restricted, but also because of the manner in which the coombes wend and wind their way through the landscape, with numerous side branches and 'dead' ends. It is also a comforting experience moving through these sheltered valleys. Walking Stonehenge Bottom, one can pass through a landscape littered with monuments and hardly see or encounter a single one until one has almost reached Stonehenge. The drama of seeing the stones from such a short distance away for the first time is utterly different from the long-drawn-out approach to that monument following the course of the Stonehenge Avenue.

On a concluding note it is interesting to remark on the utterly different character of the Greater and Lesser Cursuses, as processional ways across the landscape, in comparison to the Avenue. Those linear monuments are imposed on the landscape in a highly artificial manner (see Chapter 2). By contrast, the Avenue twists, turns and curves. In this respect, it resembles a coombe except, of course, that coombes do not cross ridge-tops. This may be its symbolic significance: an artificial coombe inscribed across the Stonehenge landscape.

9.5. The River Avon: a journey from life to death?

M. Parker Pearson and C. Richards

Tilley and Bennett's reflections on the course and character of the River Avon, and their narrative of the journey between Durrington Walls and Stonehenge, provide an awareness of the transformatory qualities of the passage of the river in conjunction with the 'confined' and controlled passage of the Stonehenge Avenue. By taking the path of the river through its meandering valley and the route of the Avenue around to the north of Stonehenge, a process of concealment and revelation would have been achieved through a landscape that was already very open, at least on the higher ground.

In the scheme first proposed by Parker Pearson and Ramilisonina – that Durrington Walls was the domain of living, and Stonehenge the domain of the ancestors – the exact role of the River Avon was not specified, apart from the observation that the different realms represented by Durrington Walls and Stonehenge were 'both linked by the flow of the River Avon' (1998a: 316). If Durrington Walls and associated monuments were a place for the living, accommodating ritual practices associated with passage and transition, and Stonehenge a place of the ancestors, what was the actual role of the river and in what social practices was it incorporated? For example, did people – living or deceased – physically travel downriver to achieve a transformed state, or was the river a metaphoric route for a more intangible passage?

From the very beginning of the Neolithic period in Britain (and, indeed, before), river systems provided the main thoroughfares through a heavily wooded landscape (Cummings 2017: 112). So not only did river valleys act as routes and pathways, but the ever-flowing waters of the rivers were a dynamic materiality, always moving, always flowing to another place. There is steadily increasing evidence that these unique characteristics were exploited in the ritual transformation from life to death. Not only have Neolithic–Chalcolithic human skeletal remains been recovered from a number of major rivers in Britain (see Bradley and Gordon 1988; Evans *et al.* 1993: 147; Garton *et al.* 1996; 1997; Harding and Healy 2007: 227; Knüsel and Carr 1995; Lamdin-Whymark 2008: 191–7; Schulting and Bradley 2013: table 6; Turner *et al.* 2002), but they have also yielded a range of objects which frequently accompany Neolithic burials in other contexts (Richards 1996). Given this evidence, we concur with Garton *et al.* who, after assessing Late Neolithic skeletal material recovered from a palaeo-channel of the River Trent, suggest that such evidence 'may help us understand what happened to the majority of the population at this time [early–mid-third millennium BC] when they died' (1996: 11).

If a number of major British rivers provided conduits for the journey from life to death through the deposition of human remains into their flowing waters, was the River Avon also a receptacle for the dead? If so, the river already possessed a role in Neolithic mortuary practices long before the massive henge monuments of Marden and Durrington Walls were erected along its bank. At this earlier time, the flow of major rivers running through the land to empty in the ocean may have provided a pathway for the deceased to return to a distant homeland or travel to a different realm. Under such circumstances, the apparent aversion to the consumption of marine fish in the Neolithic (Richards and Hedges 1999b; Cramp *et al.* 2014) could be understandable as a taboo (see Thomas 2013).

Either way, rivers in the third millennium BC were intimately associated, through traditional practice, with displacement, transition and transformation. Consequently, as discussed in this chapter's introduction, flowing water and the path of the river could be utilised in conjunction with monumentality to achieve a range of different 'architectural' configurations and effects. In this vein, the River Avon may or may not have received skeletal remains of the dead during the third millennium BC. But there can be little question that it served as a direct conduit between different places, monuments and realms.

Chapter 10

The people of Stonehenge

C. Willis*

Human skeletal remains have long been recovered from Stonehenge, but any interpretation of mortuary practices and burial rites is hindered by the lack of attention given to human remains during early archaeological excavations, by archaic forms of record-keeping and reporting, and by the loss of many of the excavated human bones. During the twentieth century alone, archaeologists excavated, among other areas within Stonehenge, 34 of the 56 Aubrey Holes (see Chapter 4), with William Hawley and Robert Newall opening 32 of them between 1920 and 1924 (AH1–AH30, AH55 and AH56), producing *c.* 35 cremation deposits (see Figure 4.4). Their excavations also produced three articulated human skeletons, a further 18 or more cremation deposits, and hundreds of disarticulated human bones (McKinley 1995: 451–6, tables 57–[58]).

In 1950, Atkinson, Piggott and Stone excavated AH31 and AH32, the latter yielding one or more cremation deposits. They also recovered dozens of disarticulated cremated and unburnt human remains from their trenches through the Ditch and Bank (the ditch and inner bank that encircle the sarsens, constructed in *2995–2900 cal BC*; 95% probability; see Chapter 11). In 1978, Atkinson and Evans re-excavated and extended one of Atkinson's old trenches (C42, extended as C61) and recovered a Beaker-period inhumation burial (known as the Stonehenge Archer; Evans 1984) from the Ditch, just west of the northeast entrance. Further archaeological excavations have revealed disarticulated, cremated and unburnt human bones in various locations, such as a human tarsal recovered near the Heel Stone in a context containing a medieval sherd (Pitts 1982: 90) and a human tooth from immediately below the turf beside Stone 10 (Darvill and Wainwright 2009; see Table 11.6).

Overall, excavations of almost half of Stonehenge's interior between 1919 and 2008 have yielded approximately 60 cremation burials, multiple disarticulated cremated bone fragments, four complete human skeletons, and over 40 fragments of unburnt human bones (McKinley 1995: 453–5; Pitts 2000: 116; Parker Pearson *et al.* 2009: 23; Willis *et al.* 2016). All of the cremated bones excavated from the Aubrey Holes (except 150g of bone from AH32 and 1.5g from AH24), and the 18 cremation deposits from the Ditch fill and Bank were reburied in Aubrey Hole 7 (AH7) in 1935 by Robert Newall and William Young. In 2008, these previously disturbed cremated human remains were re-excavated as part of the SRP (Figures 10.5–10.8). The research aims and objectives, and the excavation of AH7, are reported in Chapter 4.

One of the aims was to identify different individuals within AH7's mixed assemblage and obtain radiocarbon dates from each of these. These samples were further analysed for strontium isotope ratios in a ground-breaking project that revealed patterns of lifetime mobility consistent with migration to Stonehenge from west Wales where the bluestones originate (Snoeck *et al.* 2018). These results are discussed further in Volume 2.

*** With a contribution by:**
T. Waldron

The report on the radiocarbon-dating of cremated bones from AH7, and of other human bones from Stonehenge, appears in Chapter 11, as part of the full report on all the radiocarbon dates from Stonehenge. The earliest of the AH7 individuals is dated to 3340–2940 cal BC and the latest to 2865–2585 cal BC (both at 95% confidence), with the sequence of dates subject to several statistical models (see Chapter 11). The Aubrey Hole burials thus date to the Late Neolithic (3000–2500 BC) as do most other human remains at Stonehenge, although some date to the Chalcolithic (2500–2200 BC) and later (Parker Pearson *et al.* 2009; see Chapter 11).

10.1. Review of previously excavated human material

Despite best intentions, most of the cremated and unburnt human bones from Stonehenge were either reinterred in AH7 or have been lost or badly damaged since they were excavated; some were destroyed by bombing during the Second World War.

William Hawley's excavation diaries from the 1920s suggest that his workmen excavated around 35 cremation deposits from the Aubrey Holes (Table 10.1), with a further 17 from the Ditch and one from beneath the Bank (Figure 10.1; Table 10.2). In a few instances, Hawley mentioned that he believed there to be more than one individual within each context; however, since Hawley had very little experience in identifying skeletal elements (especially cremated fragments), his counts cannot be relied upon for accurately determining the number of people buried at Stonehenge.

The cremated remains were retained by Hawley's assistant Robert Newall until 1935, when he made arrangements with W.E.V. Young (curator of the Alexander Keiller Museum, Avebury) to re-inter the remains within Aubrey Hole 7 (see Figure 4.15). On Monday, 28 January 1935, Young recorded the following in his diary:

> 'This morning I re-excavated Aubrey Hole No 7 – one of the holes previously excavated by Colonel Hawley, F.S.A. – after removing a border of about one foot of the turf which surrounds the chalk-covered patch that marks the hole. I cut the turf in four "unequal" portions, and so was able, eventually to replace it in exactly the same position again ... I had cleaned out the hole, exposing its original undisturbed chalk around the side and bottom once again and had everything ready, when Mr Newall arrived with the bones at half-past two. There were four sand bags full. These were placed at the bottom of the Aubrey Hole, together with a stout leaden plate which bore an inscription, recording at length all the circumstances which led to their being deposited here, and the date. The hole was then filled in immediately while Mr Newall was present, and after I had re-laid the turf bordering, and put a layer of fresh, white chalk inside, there were hardly any indications to shew that it had ever been touched!!' (Young 1935).

Peter Berridge, Richard Atkinson's research assistant during the 1970s, compiled a list of all recorded instances of human bones from both Hawley's and Atkinson's excavations (Tables 10.2–10.3). This list includes human bones recorded as being recovered from the Ditch and the interior areas of Stonehenge but no longer available for study (McKinley 1995: table 57).

The cremation deposit excavated by Atkinson and Piggott from the Ditch in 1950, along with the small amount of cremated bone kept from AH32 and some unburnt bone, were analysed by Jacqueline McKinley in the 1990s (Table 10.3). The main ditch cremation deposit (54/821 from C42) contained the remains of a young female adult, around 25 years of age. Also within the deposit was a probable sub-adult, an additional cremated adult, an unburnt ankle bone of an adult, and a toe bone from a young to mature adult (18–45 years old; McKinley 1995: 458). Various adult and possible sub-adult bones were identified among the unburnt bones, though an MNI could not be determined given the disarticulated nature of the bones and the loss of material from the dataset (McKinley 1995: 456).

Hawley excavated three inhumation graves at Stonehenge in the 1920s (Figure 10.1). He sent two of the skeletons to Sir Arthur Keith of the Royal College of Surgeons in London. It was believed that both of those skeletons were destroyed when the RCS building was bombed in 1941. However, Mike Pitts later discovered that the skeleton excavated in 1923 had survived the bombing and had been transferred to the Natural History Museum in London.

The first skeleton, excavated in March 1922, was recovered from the Ditch just south of the northeast entrance, 0.56m below ground level. Hawley noted that many of the skeletal elements were missing (such as the mandible, maxilla, hand and foot bones, one hip bone and all the limb bones except a femur and humerus; Hawley 1922: 60). The estimated height of the individual is 1.70m (based on Hawley's measurement of the humeral length). The skeleton was considered by Hawley to be a relatively modern interment so the bones were discarded at the time of excavation (Hawley 1922: 59).

Table 10.1 (opposite). Hawley's description of the cremated bone excavated from the Aubrey Holes (after Cleal *et al.* 1995: 99–101, plus amendments by the author from Hawley's diaries). BGL 'below ground level'

Aubrey Hole	Date excavated	Cremation	MNI	Charcoal	Hawley's notes
1	29/04/1920	1 x fragment	-	A little	Cremated bone fragment recovered 27" BGL
2	13/04/1920	Yes	1	-	Very few bones of a cremation: scattered from just under the turf to 25" BGL
3	06/04/1920	Yes	1	-	Cremated bones on the edge of the Hole, just under the turf to 20" BGL. Unburnt deer pelvis over cremation. Hawley determined it was an adult cremation.
4	03/03/1920	Yes	2	21" to 26" BGL	Cremation on the edge to the chalk walls to the middle of the hole to 24" BGL. Hawley mentions that one of the cremations is that of a young adult. Unclear if there were discrete deposits for the two individuals.
5	31/03/1920	Yes	2?	-	Scattered cremation from 10" to 27" BGL. There might have been two cremations: an unfused epiphysis of a femoral head and an unfused proximal epiphysis of a tibia, and a fused femur; may be female. [Author's note: this could be either from one older juvenile of 14-18 years, whose bones are starting to fuse, or from two individuals of two different age ranges, *e.g.* one child and one adult].
6	30/03/1920	Yes	1	A little at 18" BGL	Cart track disturbed the cremation deposit in the upper layers. Mixed with a little wood ash 18" to 30" BGL.
7	05/03/1920	Yes	1	A little on the bottom in the centre of AH7	A scattered cremation below the turf in the top rubble and continued on the southeast side of the hole down to the bottom (36" BGL). Cremation: young adult? Evidence of squatting due to extension of articular face of astragalus.
8	27/03/1920	Yes	1	27" BGL	Small adult cremation scattered amongst the wood ash
9	25/03/1920	Yes	1	24" to 31" BGL	Scattered cremation at 10" to 31" BGL, diffused amongst the charcoal
10	24/03/1920	Yes	1	-	Cremation from 21" to 24", covering the whole bottom of the Hole
11	24/03/1920	Yes	1	-	Cremation diffuses throughout the Hole, from just below the turf to the bottom (36" deep). Hawley mentions that this cremation is an adult.
12	23/03/1920	Yes	4	Ash in cup-shaped recess cut into chalk rubble	Probably four cremations: one was 12" BGL and above the chalk in the earthy chalky rubble, while the others were from 17" BGL and continued to the bottom of the Hole (35" deep). The last cremation was in a cup-shaped recess 15" diameter, mixed in with wood ash. One adult cremation. Two bone pins found with the cremations.
13	22/03/1920	Yes	1	-	Very small cremation at 29" BGL
14	22/07/1920	Yes	1	-	Adult cremation 19" to 30" BGL with regular upright sides
15	19/03/1920	Yes	1	-	Definitely a child cremation, 18" to 34" BGL (bottom of the Hole)
16	18/03/1920	Yes	1	More ash than in any other Hole	Large, young male cremation, 19" to 27" BGL (bottom of the Hole) and diffused amongst the wood ash
17	11/08/1920	Yes	2	-	Adult female cremation in the Hole and in a small cup-shaped depression at the inside edge of the Hole. A few bones from another cremation.
18	10/07/1922	Yes	1	-	Cremation 13" to 31" BGL
19	08/08/1921	No	0	Some burnt wood 8" BGL	No sign of burnt bones; probably the oxygen of the air changed these into grey powder (Author's note: the introduction of oxygen to cremated bones will not render them into powder).
20	19/02/1920	Yes	1	-	Scattered cremation
21	09/03/1920	Yes	1	Nearly on bottom (3′ 4" deep)	Small cremation 15" to 30" BGL, maybe a young individual. Cremation was not found within the wood ash.
22	10/03/1920	Uncertain	1?	-	In one part of the diary, Hawley writes there is 'no evidence of cremation', yet in another account, he says 'scattered bones of cremation were found'.
23	10/03/1920	Uncertain	1?	-	In one part of the diary, Hawley writes there is 'no evidence of cremation', yet in another account, he says 'a scanty cremation'.
24	11/03/1920	Yes	1?	Large quantity oak 24" to 3′ 1" BGL	A large adult male cremation, diffused amongst a large quantity of wood ash 24" to 37" BGL (bottom of the Hole). Inner edge of the Hole sloped and contained a small saucer-shaped depression (15" in diameter and 5" deep) containing a few cremated bones.
25	12/03/1920	No	0	-	None
26	19/02/1920	No	0	-	None
27	12/07/1921	No	0	-	None
28	12/07/1921	Yes	1	Black patch of burnt wood 33" BGL	14 pieces of calcined human bone above 33" BGL [Author's note: this is probably referring to cremated bone with calcium carbonate over the bone surface].
29	July-Oct 1921	Yes	1	Sooty matter at bottom of the Hole	A few cremated bones in a bowl-shaped recess on the southwest edge at 18" BGL. Many pieces of cremated bone distributed in isolated pieces in the soil filling the hole.
30	06/08/1924	No	0	A lot of black ash on west side	None
31	1950	No	0	-	[Excavated by Atkinson]
32	1950	Yes	1	Burnt earth and charcoal	[*In situ* cremation excavated by Atkinson]
?46	?19th cent	-	0	-	-
55	20/11/1922	No	0	Good deal of black wood ash	None
56	12/05/1920	No	0	-	None

Area	Date excavated	Burial type	Context number	Original cat. no	Berridge number	Hawley's and Berridge's notes
C1 Stonehole 6	05/02/1920	I	1050–1055	-	HB1	Fragments 'perhaps human cranium'
C2	29/06/1920	I?	1074	-	HB5	One human tooth, associated with '22 sherds of BA pottery. Could be part of...cremation'
C2 Posthole close to Stone 2	09/03/1920	I	2787	-	HB25	Two fragments of human cranium
C5 Stonehole 2	05/11/1922	I	1475	-	HB28	A few bones of a child
C7 Near AH11	21/09/1923	C	1830	-	HC42	Small cremation, immediately below turf
C7	25/09/1923	C	2010	-	HC43	Small cremation...on or near rampart
C7		C	1774	-	HC41	Small patch of cremated bone close to surface of rampart slope
C9		C	1678	-	HB18	Most of skeleton of an adult in shallow grave between YH9 and 10, but below Stonehenge Layer
C10	17/05/1924	C	2010	-	HC45	'An occasional fragment of cremated human bone but no sign of an actual cremation'
C10	26/06/1924	C	2125	-	HC80	'6 or 8 pieces of calcined bones...could perhaps be human cremation though could just be burnt animal bone'
C10	16/05/1924	C	2007	-	HC44	'Vein' of cremated bone 'about 1 inch or possibily 1½ inches thick...and the width of the patch was 10 inches'. Immediately below turf with lump of sarsen and a number of large natural flints very close and above, ?possibly a cairn (McKinley 1995: 454)
C10		C	2013	-	HC46/47	Two small patches of cremated bones
C10	26/05/1924	C	2014	-	HC48	Small amount of cremated bone associated with polished macehead in 'small depression of cist scraped 2 inches deep in the solid chalk which only partly held the remains...the protruding mass was covered with 3 inches of rubble'.
C10	21/05/1924	C	2020/22		HC49–52	'Four cremated interments. Two side by side...one mass joining the other...other two very insignificant'. In slight hollow depressions 'but bones were mostly on top of these'. The other two were 0.60m apart.
C10	27/05/1924	C	2042	-	HC53	In small, shallow recess in rubble. Bones mostly 'in the sod of turf above the place'.
C12 North of Stone 59	25/08/1926	I	2724	-	HB25	The bones were 'in a disordered mass and had evidently been thrown there without ceremony'. No details. Context was very disturbed with material from Bronze Age to modern dates mixed with the bones.
C18 Ditch		C	1269	-	HC34	Cremation in bowl-shaped hollow, stag pelvis above it
C22 Ditch		I	1399	-	HB8	In poor condition and much missing, including most of the limb bones. In grave cut.
C24 Ditch		I	1431	-	HB11/12	Small vertebra and other small bones including ribs and 2 femurs
C25	12/10/1922	C	1557	-	HC39	Small group of cremated bone in a 'small bowl-shaped recess rather larger than a finger bowl' cut into Ditch
C25		C	1552	-	HC37/8	Mass of cremated bone (including teeth) but no ash
C25		C	1284	-	HC36	Thoroughly calcined to whiteness, including a few teeth
C26		C	3903	-	HC56	Entire cremation but 'head has been mostly consumed'
C26	17/07/1924	C	2465	-	HC54/55	Two small patches of cremated human bone 'without cist' in humus
C28		C	2542	-	HC59	Very white and clean with hardly a sign of burnt ash, inserted into Ditch
C28		C	2538	-	HC65	Few bones, very blackened. Scoop cut into Ditch
C28		C	2580	-	HC61/62	Complete cremation, but Hawley states there was also an infant because 'parts of the skull are thinner than parts of, probably, another'. Cut into Counterscarp
C28		C	2601	-	HC64	Very small group. Scoop cut into Ditch
C28	17–19/06/1925	C	2819	-	HC60	Complete cremation. Cut into Counterscarp
C28	23/07/1925	C	2817	-	HC63	In 'cyst...cut in the solid chalk of the counterscarp from above and fortunately...near the edge of the ditch'
C29 Ditch		I	2663	-	HB22	Skull fragment
C31	05/03/1920	I	1307	-	HB2	'Remains of 2 ulna bones of a child and 2 phalanges of a hand' found while removing wire fence, ?near Aubrey Hole 7
C41 Ditch		I	3893	S54.68	-	Finger or toe bones
C42		I		S54/912.2		'Phalange' over Ditch
C42 Ditch		I	3898	S54/822	-	Ulna
C42 Ditch		I	3899	S54/818	-	Ulna or tibia
C52		I	3866	S58/6	-	'Finger or toe' bones. Note on record card says 'not human'
C56		I	3509	S64.51	-	'8 finger or toe bones, 3 skull fragments + 1 misc'. Note on record card says 'not human'
C81 Palisade Ditch		I	9827	PUP57	-	Skull fragment
?HB11/12		I	1430/1	-	HB13	A few bones including skull and jaw, with ox skull and jaw
?		C	1563	-	HC40	Handful of bone
?HC56		C	3905	-	HC57/58	Associated with skewer pin, in contiguous cists

Table 10.2. Description of the human bone excavated from the Ditch and interior areas of Stonehenge but no longer available for study, from Hawley's diary and from Berridge's notes (after McKinley 1995: 453–5, table 57). Comments in quotation marks are taken directly from Hawley's diary. Burial type: C = cremation; I = unburnt bone (inhumation)

Context number	Berridge number	Original cat. no.	Burial type	Crem. weight	Skeletal element	Age	Sex	Notes
3008	?HC78/9	S50/?	C	150.7g	-	Adult	-	AH32
1560	HB14	-	I	-	Cranial vault	-	Possible female	C25: Ditch fill. [Author's note: this entry does *not* show up in Berridge's list (his Table 6.6)]
3893	-	54/13	C	6.4g	-	-	-	C41: Ditch fill
3893	-	54/15	C	1.9g	-	-	-	C41: Ditch fill. ?Human.
3893	-	54/30	I	-	Cranial vault	-	-	C41: Ditch fill
3893	-	54/32	C	1.9g	-	-	-	C41: Ditch fill
3893	-	54/33	C	2.5g	-	-	-	C41: Ditch fill
3893	-	54/35	C	7.7g	-	-	-	C41: Ditch fill
3893	-	54/36	C	4.7g	-	-	-	C41: Ditch fill
3893	-	54/40	C	3.9g	-	-	-	C41: Ditch fill
3893	-	54/41	C	5.8g	-	-	-	C41: Ditch fill
3893	-	54/43	C	11.1g	-	-	-	C41: Ditch fill
3893	-	54/44	C	8.0g	-	Young to mature adult	-	C41: Ditch fill
3893	-	54/45	C	12.6g	-	-	-	C41: Ditch fill. ?Bird.
3893	-	54/52	C	2.6g	-	-	-	C41: Ditch fill
3893	-	54/53	C	1.5g	-	-	-	C41: Ditch fill
3893	-	54/54	C	2.6g	-	-	-	C41: Ditch fill
3893	-	54/55	C	0.4g	-	-	-	C41: Ditch fill
3893	-	54/59	C	0.8g	-	-	-	C41: Ditch fill
3893	-	54/66	C	0.9g	-	-	-	C41: Ditch fill
3893	-	54/69	C	1.2g	-	-	-	C41: Ditch fill
3893	-	54/73	C	0.5g	-	-	-	C41: Ditch fill. ?Human or ?faunal.
3893	-	54/74	C	0.4g	-	-	-	C41: Ditch fill
3893	-	54/75	I	-	Long bone	-	-	C41: Ditch fill. ?Human.
3898	-	54/820	C	0.8g	-	Adult	-	C41: Ditch fill
3898	-	54/821	C	1546.6g	-	Young to mature adult	Female	C42: Ditch fill
3898	-	54/841	C	4.4g	-	-	-	C42: Ditch fill
3898	-	54/843	I	-	Cuboid	Adult	-	C42: Ditch fill
3898	-	54/848	I	-	Phalanx	Young to mature adult	-	C42: Ditch fill
1885	-	-	I	-	Rib	-	-	C8: Posthole [Hawley only mentions animal bone from this context, presumably the radiocarbon-dated pig rib – see Chapter 11]
2559	HB26	-	I	-	Tooth	Juvenile to young adult	-	C10: over Ditch
1562	HB15	-	I	-	Cranial vault	-	-	C25: Ditch fill
1260	HB3	-	I	-	Tibia	Adult	-	C18: Ditch fill
1282	HB27	-	I	-	Cranial vault	Adult	Possible male	C19: Ditch fill
1291	HB6	-	I	-	Fibula	Adult	-	C20: Ditch fill
2589	HB20	-	I	-	Cranial vault	Mature to older adult	-	C28: Ditch fill
3899	-	54/801	-	-	-	-	-	C42: upper Ditch fill. Fossil.
3899	-	54/802	-	-	-	-	-	C42: upper Ditch fill. Animal.
3899	-	54/803	C	1.8g	-	-	-	
3899	-	54/804	I	-	Rib	-	-	C42: upper Ditch fill. ?Human.
3899	-	54/805	C	0.4g	-	-	-	C42: upper Ditch fill
3899	-	54/812	C	1.1g	-	-	-	C42: upper Ditch fill
3899	-	54/813	C	1.8g	-	-	-	C42: upper Ditch fill
3899	-	54/816	C	5.6g	-	-	-	C42: upper Ditch fill
1236	HC28	-	C	1.5g	-	Mature to older adult	Possible female	AH24
3253	-	56/89	I	-	?Talus	-	-	C50: South Barrow ditch

Table 10.3 (continued overleaf). Summary of all human bones from Atkinson and Piggott's excavations, as analysed by Jacqueline McKinley (after McKinley 1995: table 59[58])

Context number	Berridge number	Original cat. no.	Burial type	Crem. weight	Skeletal element	Age	Sex	Notes
1401	HB9/10	-	I	-	Skull, upper limb	Young to mature adult	-	C22: feature cut into Ditch
9490	-	PUP69	I	-	Skull, axial, upper limb, lower limb	Young adult	Male	C81: Palisade Ditch, grave cut
1944	HB30	-	I	-	Tooth	Infant	-	ZH13
2886	HB29	-	I	-	Skull	Juvenile to adult	-	C29: Ditch fill
1280	HC35		C	10.8g	-	-	-	C19: over Ditch
1290	HB6		I	-	Tibia	Adult	-	C19: over Ditch
1384	?HB7		I	-	Ulna, frag upper limb	Adult	-	C21
1815	HB29		I	-	Tooth	Young adult	-	C7
2674		S56/21	I	-	Tooth	Juvenile to young adult	-	C12
3543		64/35	I	-	Tooth	-	-	C58: Stonehole 27
3892		54/21	C	0.5g	-	-	-	C41: Ditch fill
1628	HB17		I	-	-	-	-	YH6. Animal.
2597	HB21		I	-	Skull	Young to mature adult	-	C26: top of Ditch
3852	HB16		I	-	Teeth	Adult	-	YH4
3891		54/106.1	C	0.7g	-	-	-	C41: Ditch upper fill
3891		54/109.6	I	-	Tarsals	-	-	C42: topsoil
3896		54/902.2	I	-	Cranial vault	-	-	C42: topsoil
3896		54/909.2	I	-	Metatarsal	Adult	-	C42: topsoil
3896		54/909.2	C	1.2g	-	-	-	C42: topsoil
3896		54/909.6	I	-	-	-	-	C42: topsoil; faunal?
3896		54/907.5	C	1.5g	-	-	-	C42: topsoil
3896		54/909.6	C	0.5g	-	-	-	C42: topsoil
3897		54/910.17	C	3.3g	-	-	-	C42: Ditch upper fill
3897		54/913.8	C	4.1g	-	-	-	C42: topsoil
3813	-	-	I	-	Skull, axial, upper limb	Mature to old adult × 2	-	unstratified

The second skeleton (Royal College of Surgeons reference: 4.10.4) was found in 1923 in a 0.66m-deep grave southeast of the stones, just outside the sarsen circle next to Y Hole 9 (Figures 10.1–10.2; Hawley 1923: 259; Pitts 2000: 302; Pitts *et al.* 2002: 131). This was the skeleton of a mature adult male, decapitated prior to burial in cal AD 660–880 (see Table 11.1; Pitts *et al.* 2007).

The third skeleton, undated and presumably destroyed in 1941, consisted of a mass of disturbed bones in a pit, 2.40m long and 0.75m deep, inside the sarsen circle, excavated in 1926 (Hawley 1926: 12; Pitts 2000: 302; Pitts *et al.* 2002: 131). Assessment of this skeleton by Arthur Keith at the Royal College of Surgeons revealed it to be a male, approximately 1.70m tall, with a damaged skull. Also included in the burial were several cattle and sheep bones and an adult female mandible (Pitts 2000: 302).

In 1935, Frank Stevens (then curator of what is now Salisbury Museum) sent a different collection of human bones recovered 'from the bottom of the Ditch' to Dr A.J.E. Cave at the Royal College of Surgeons. As Mike Pitts relates (2000: 116–18), these bones were 'insufficiently packed and were badly broken in transit'. All that remains of this collection is an inventory listing the basic skeletal elements, such as 'an indeterminate piece of a thick cranial vault' (*ibid.*: 117).

Also in 1935, Manchester Museum received a collection of animal bones recovered from the Ditch at Stonehenge. Among them, Wilfrid Jackson found human bones mixed in with the sheep and cattle bones from the humus (upper) and silt (lower) layers (Kennard and Jackson 1935: 434; Pitts 2000: 118).

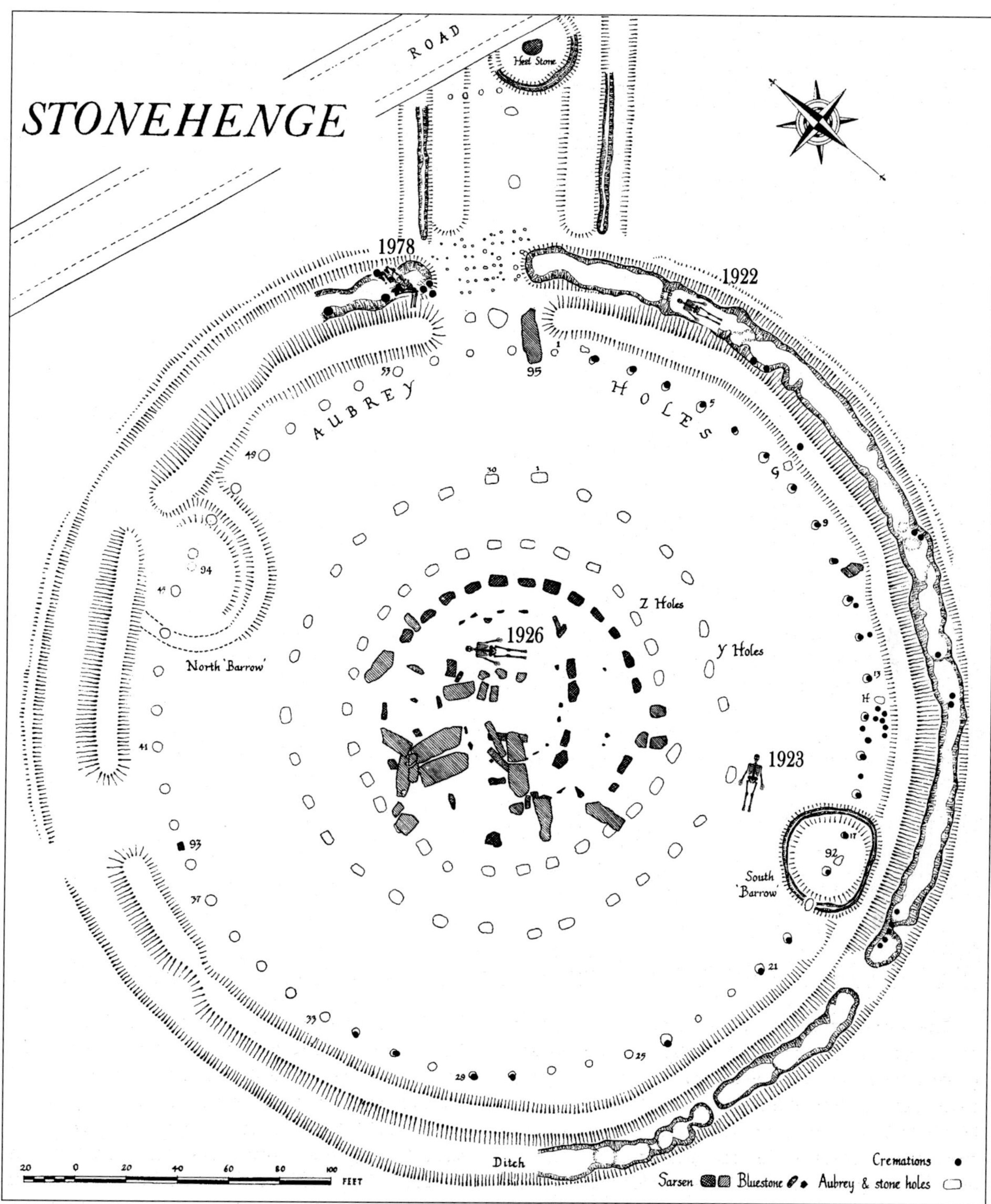

Figure 10.1. Locations of human bone found at Stonehenge, including the cremated remains from in and around the Aubrey Holes, the Ditch, and the Bank. The locations of the four known articulated skeletons recovered in 1922, 1923, 1926 and 1978 are also shown. Note that the orientation of the 1922 burial is not known (after Newall 1956: 139); © Antiquity

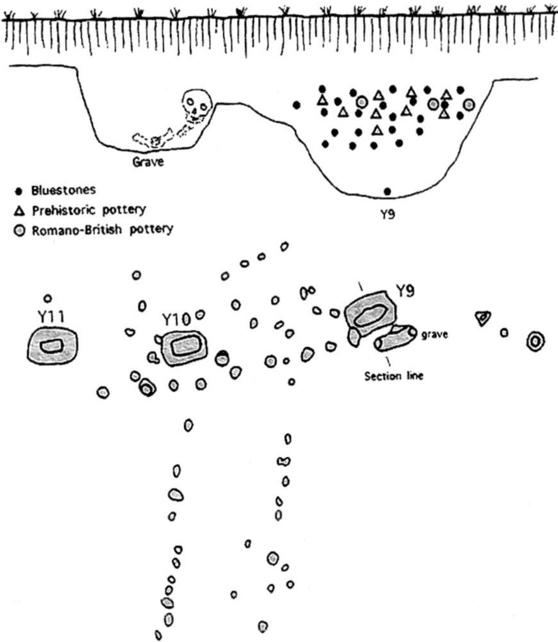

Figure 10.2. A section drawn by Newall and a plan drawn by the Office of Works of the grave excavated by Hawley in 1923 (after Cleal *et al*. 1995: fig. 152); © Historic England

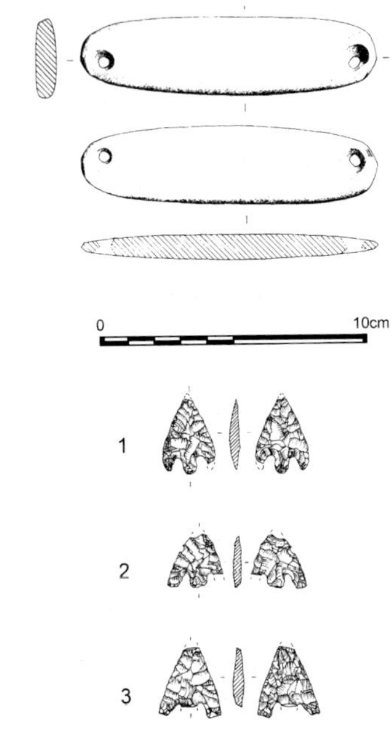

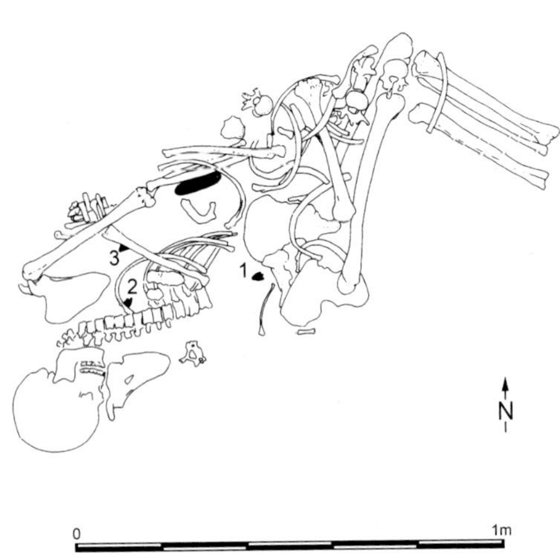

Figure 10.3. The Beaker-period burial from the Stonehenge Ditch, found in 1978 by Atkinson and Evans. The sketch plan illustrates the skeleton (also known as the 'Stonehenge Archer'), with his associated arrowheads and bracer (after Evans 1984: 14); © Wiltshire Archaeological & Natural History Society

In 1978, Atkinson and Evans' excavation of a trench in the Ditch on the north side of Stonehenge uncovered an undisturbed adult male skeleton, now known as the Stonehenge Archer, dating to 2400–2140 cal BC (Figures 10.1, 10.3–10.4; see Table 11.1; Evans 1984; Pitts 2000: 111–13). Three barbed-and-tanged arrowheads within the articulated skeleton and impact injuries to the ribs and sternum caused by arrowheads indicate how he died. Interestingly, the foot bones were missing from the skeleton at the time of excavation but were subsequently located at Cardiff University in the early 1980s (Pitts 2000: 120–1): an earlier, adjacent trench excavated by Atkinson and Piggott in 1950 had truncated the skeleton and these small bones had been retrieved, albeit unknowingly, during that excavation.

At the time that Newall reburied Hawley's assemblage of cremated bones in AH7, archaeologists and scientists alike believed that cremated human bones provided very little osteological information. For example, Professor C.M. Fürst, Chief Inspector of Antiquities in Stockholm, stated in 1930:

> 'I would straight away place on record my considered opinion, based on experience, that cremated remains of human bones in burial urns are almost always devoid of any anthropological interest, especially in cases of such in a mass cemetery. From an anthropological point of view, therefore, these bones are of no scientific value, and I consider that nothing is lost if they are neither submitted to nor preserved in the Museums' (Fürst 1930).

Pitts (2000: 121) has estimated that the total number of people buried at Stonehenge in prehistory is 240,

Figure 10.4. The Stonehenge Archer; this is the only photographic documentation of an inhumed burial at Stonehenge (from Evans 1984: 14); © WANHS

based on his assumption that many of the cremation deposits would have contained the remains of two or three individuals. However, if each cremation burial consisted of the remains of only one individual, then a more conservative estimate would be 150 people (Parker Pearson *et al.* 2009: 23). The cremated remains reburied in AH7 came from the Aubrey Holes, the Ditch and the Bank, and it is estimated that these remains belong to 52–58 individuals. It is, therefore, fortunate that Hawley (and latterly Newall) did not simply destroy most of the cremated remains from Stonehenge: this is a sizeable assemblage. Of these estimated 52–58 people whose remains were retrieved from AH7 in 2008, only 26 unique individuals have been identified from the intermixed assemblage of cremated bone fragments. Chapter 4 describes the lack of contextual separation of the assemblage within the Aubrey Hole, and the impossibility of distinguishing discrete, identifiable cremation burials in the redeposited material.

10.2. The cremated bone assemblage from Aubrey Hole 7

Osteological analysis was carried out on the mixed cremated bone assemblage recovered from AH7 in order to reconstruct the demographic structure of the population of Stonehenge, to investigate the proportions of biological sex, age at death, health and, wherever possible, to better understand cremation rites and mortuary rituals performed for the deceased. Of the estimated 52–58 deposits/burials of cremated human remains placed within AH7 in 1935 (McKinley 1995: 451; Parker Pearson *et al.* 2009: 23), 26 have been identified

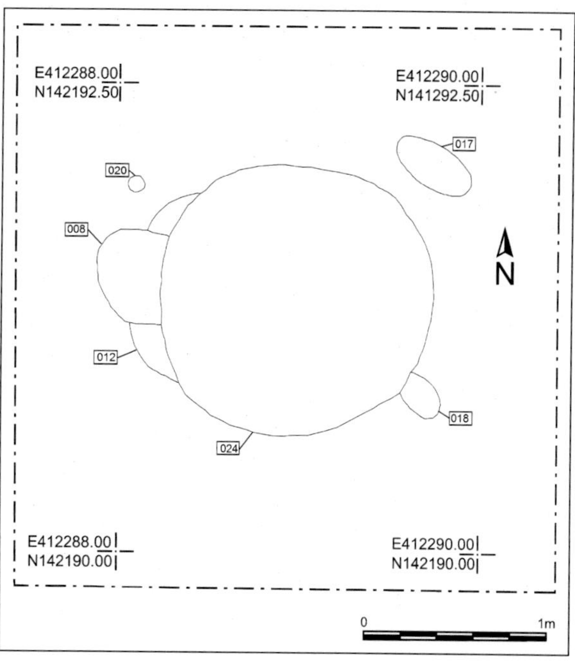

Figure 10.5. Plan of Aubrey Hole 7 after removal of the turf (024 is Hawley's cut; 020 is a stakehole; 017 and 018 are features; and 008 is a primary cremation burial pit)

by this analysis as unique individuals: 21 adults and five sub-adults. The SRP excavation also recovered an undisturbed cremation burial of a mature adult female, missed by both Hawley in 1920 and Newall in 1935. This burial, in a small, circular pit adjacent to AH7 (fill 007 in pit 008; Figure 10.5), contributes further to our understanding of the cremation deposits excavated by Hawley and by Atkinson within Stonehenge.

Methodology of recording

The cremated human remains from both AH7 and the undisturbed cremation deposit were assessed according to English Heritage guidelines (Mays *et al.* 2002) and the recommendations published by the British Association for Biological Anthropology and Osteoarchaeology and the Chartered Institute for Archaeologists (Brickley and McKinley 2004). Consultation with Jacqueline McKinley, osteological consultant to the SRP, was also undertaken throughout the analysis.

The material excavated from each of the AH7 grid squares (see Chapter 4 for excavation methods) was sieved using a series of Endecott's Laboratory Test Sieves with certified 10mm, 5mm, and 2mm apertures, in addition to a base sieve to catch material smaller than 2mm. The 10mm and 5mm fractions were then sorted in the laboratory to separate the human material from any non-human material such as animal bone, chalk, other stone and pyre debris. The weights of all the sieved fractions were recorded in grams

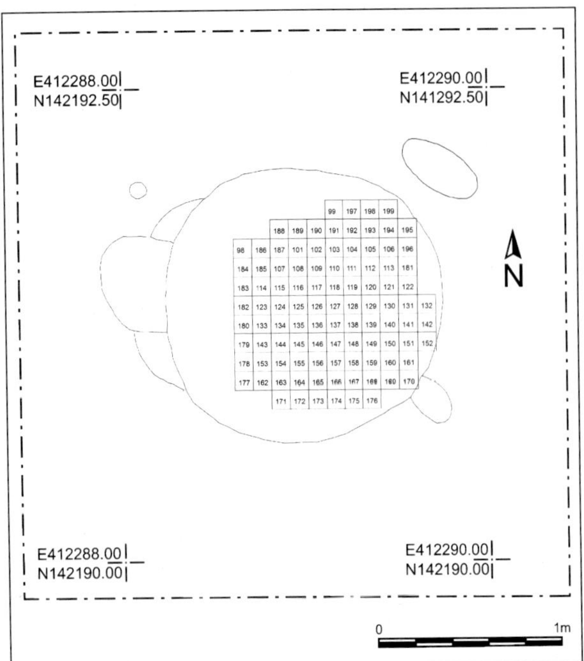

Figure 10.6. Plan of the labelled grid squares of the upper spit (Spit 1) within Aubrey Hole 7

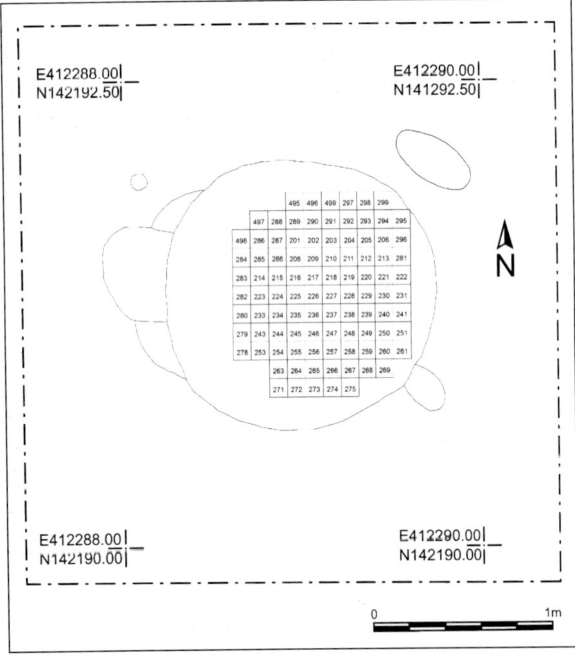

Figure 10.7. Plan of the middle spit (Spit 2) showing all the labelled squares

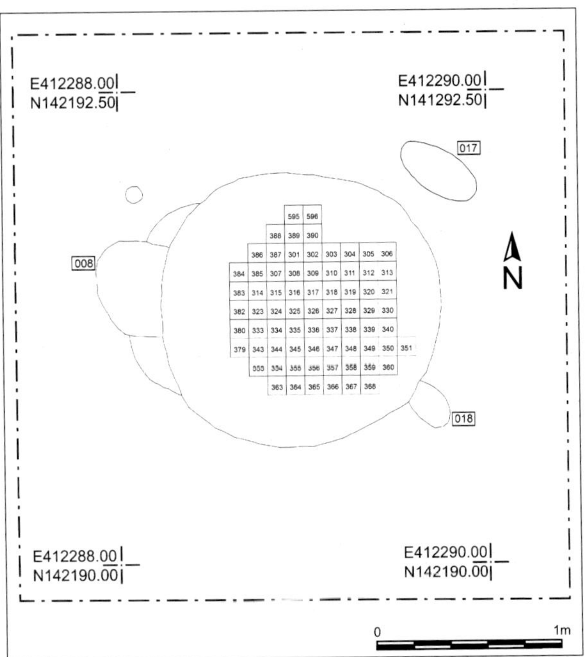

Figure 10.8. Plan of the bottom spit (Spit 3) showing all the labelled squares

(g) to two decimal places, but only the 10mm and 5mm sieve fractions from each grid square were recorded as being the total weight for that grid square.[8] This is due to the presence of irrelevant material (*e.g.* tiny pieces of chalk) in the unsorted 2mm and base sieve fractions which, if included in the total weight, would skew the overall results. Weights were recorded using a Fisher Scientific SG-602 digital balance.

The cremated remains were then cleaned to remove excess sediment and air-dried prior to osteological analysis.

Methodology of analysis

Within each grid square context, the cremated bone fragments were separated into identifiable skeletal elements and a maximum measurement of the longest bone from each of the 10mm and 5mm sieve fractions was taken, using digital Sylvan S_Cal Pro callipers (IP67). Other attributes such as preservation and the colour of the bones were also recorded.

Analysis of the cremated skeletal elements enabled recording of, wherever possible, the minimum number of

8 During osteological analysis, it was noted that seven bags of cremated remains were labelled with duplicate numbers. They were analysed separately (as *e.g.* 163a and 163b) and it is assumed that they come from the 'missing' grid squares from Spit 1 (numbers 109, 118, 123, 125, 132, 152 and 170; see Figure 10.6) which were found not to have any bags of cremated bones associated with them. At present, there is no feasible way of knowing which duplicated bag of cremated bones belongs to which empty grid number. Fortunately, these duplicated numbers do not affect any of the osteological results.

Figure 10.9. Examples of calcium carbonate adhering to radial fragments from adjacent grid squares 282 and 223

individuals (MNI), age at death, biological sex, and health. Information on pyre technology and the efficiency of the cremation process were also recorded, in order to gain an understanding of the technology and ritual aspects of prehistoric cremation rites. Photographs were taken prior to the cremated remains being returned to the appropriate context bag. The combination of these main steps meant that data recording occurred without requiring repeated handling of the cremated remains.

Burials of cremated human remains within archaeological contexts often incorporate less than 50% of the bone left over after a cremation (McKinley 2000: 408; McKinley and Bond 2001: 284). Of this, approximately 30%–50% of the bones may be identifiable to specific skeletal elements. The shortage of identifiable bones, together with the degree of bone fragmentation, has a major impact on the quantity and quality of information retrieved through osteological analysis of cremated remains. Indeed, analysis becomes increasingly more difficult as bone fragment size decreases. As such, demographic information from the mixed assemblage from AH7 is based solely on recorded data and measurements in addition to expected averages from other sites within prehistoric Britain.

Weight

The entire assemblage was sieved, sorted and weighed as described above. A total weight of 45.28566kg was recovered from AH7; of which 38,038.85g is comprised of adult bones and 169.72g of sub-adult bones. The remainder of the assemblage is so fragmented that the bone cannot be identified as either adult or sub-adult. For cremated remains from modern crematoria, an average weight of 1,625.9g is expected (McKinley 1993: 285) whereas cremated human remains from archaeological contexts in Britain have an average weight of 800g per adult individual (McKinley 1994). An archaeologically recovered cremation burial consists of those bone fragments that, having survived the burning of body, were then collected (in antiquity) from the pyre site and redeposited, often elsewhere, sometimes immediately and sometimes after a long period of curation.

Holck (1986) and Lange *et al.* (1987) have suggested that cremated bone weights of more than 2,141g–2,500g may be indicative of the presence of multiple individuals buried together but this has been disputed by Wahl (1982: 25) and by McKinley and Bond (2001), who have recorded undisturbed single adult burials weighing up to 3.0kg. Conversely, double cremation burials consisting of less than 2.0kg of bone fragments are not uncommon, while burials comprising an adult and a sub-adult together can yield a much lower weight of cremated bone (McKinley and Bond 2001: 285). These vast ranges of published weights for cremation burials consisting of multiple individuals are directly related to the varying quantities of cremated bone recovered from the pyre sites and subsequently deposited elsewhere.

If McKinley's archaeological average is applied to the mixed assemblage from Aubrey Hole 7, then 45.28566kg (total weight of AH7) divided by 800g (average archaeological adult weight) gives an MNI of 57. Although this number is purely speculative, it accords relatively well with the estimated 52–58 cremation deposits that Hawley excavated.

Hawley noted a single instance in which he came across a cremation burial in the Ditch where 'the bones were a good deal cemented together by liquid calcium carbonate which had percolated through them from the chalk covering them' (1926: 154). Since this observation was made towards the end of his excavations at Stonehenge, it raised the possibility that this was a singular instance (or at least a rare one) where a specific burial could be re-assembled on the basis of its calcium carbonate cementation, distinguishing it from the mixed mass of bone fragments in AH7.

However, during analysis calcium carbonate was found on many of the bone fragments from AH7 (Figure 10.9), within many grid squares from all spit layers, on adult and sub-adult bones, on bones exhibiting different weathering conditions, as well as on the undisturbed cremation deposit (fill 007 of pit 008). This dashes any hopes of identifying the cemented bones from this particular burial, described by Hawley as that

Sieve fraction	Maximum length	Skeletal element	Overall fraction average
10mm	121.43mm	Humerus (grid sq 309)	61.60mm
5mm	68.30mm	Fibula (grid sq 390)	33.95mm

Table 10.4. Maximum bone fragment size from AH7 from the 10mm and 5mm sieve fractions, and the overall calculated maximum bone size average

Figure 10.10. Inefficient cremation whereby the bones temporarily reached a high temperature, but the fire was not successful in burning away all the organic material (rib fragments from grid square 229)

Figure 10.11. Seven different colour examples of femoral fragments, all from grid square 254, resulting from differences in pyre temperatures

of an adult and possibly a child, since this condition is clearly widespread throughout the assemblage. It should also be noted that the additional weight of the calcium carbonate on the bones slightly skews the overall weight results of AH7 as it is not possible to remove the calcium carbonate without damaging the bone underneath.

Maximum fragment size

As described above, the maximum bone fragment size from both the 10mm and 5mm sieve fractions was recorded in millimetres (mm) to two decimal places for material from each of the separate grid squares from AH7 and for the undisturbed deposit of context 007 (the cremation burial adjacent to AH7, described in Chapter 4). An overall fragment size average for each 10mm and 5mm sieve fraction was then calculated.

Cremated human bone fragments from archaeological sites in Britain have an average maximum length of 45.2mm, with the largest measuring 134mm (McKinley 1994: 341). Urned cremated remains have a higher degree of protection following deposition and therefore produce larger fragment sizes, while un-urned and disturbed cremated remains have much smaller fragment sizes. Additionally, bone fragmentation is a natural result of the cremation process, the pyre technology, and the mortuary rituals. Thus, measurements of maximum fragment size should be considered as post-depositional sizes rather than indicating bone size at the time of deposition since the cremated fragments are affected both by the manner of burial and by any post-depositional disturbances (*ibid.*: 339).

The maximum bone lengths from AH7 are above the expected average, as is the average for the entire assemblage (Table 10.4). This is despite the assemblage having been originally excavated in 1920–1924 and then redeposited in 1935, actions which would have further fragmented the bones. These above-average measurements may therefore be indicative of the cremated remains having been protected within organic baskets, bags or boxes at the time of their initial deposition at Stonehenge. It may also further indicate a lack of interference during the cremation process, *e.g.* limited movement of the hot, brittle bones on the pyre, and/or minimal tending of the pyre during the later stages of the cremation. Since continued probing for skeletal bones while hot results in increased bone fragmentation (McKinley 1994: 340), these cremated bones may have been left to cool completely, prior to being collected from the extinguished pyre.

Colour and efficiency of cremation

The efficiency of cremation on an open pyre is dependent on the availability of oxygen, the time required to cremate, the weather, the quantity and quality of the wood, and the maximum pyre temperatures (McKinley 2000: 407; Walker *et al.* 2008). Any variations in these factors will influence the outcome of the cremation process and, in turn, its efficiency in cremating a corpse.

Since heat cannot be circulated or retained on an open pyre, the highest temperatures are found at the centre of the pyre, with lower temperatures on its peripheries. The colour of the cremated bone is often

Table 10.5. Changes in bone colour due to rises in pyre temperature (after Shipman *et al.* 1984)

Stage	Temperature	Colour
1	20°C to 285°C	Pale yellow, brown
2	285°C to 525°C	Reddish-brown, dark grey-brown, neutral grey, reddish-yellow
3	525°C to 645°C	Neutral black, medium blue, some reddish-yellow
4	645°C to 940°C	Neutral white, light blue-grey, medium grey
5	940+ °C	Neutral white, light grey

Figure 10.12. Unburnt human femur fragment (grid square 121)

used as an indicator of the maximum temperatures reached by the pyre during the cremation process (Shipman *et al.* 1984; Holden *et al.* 1995a and b). Fully oxidised bone – that is, bone that has been fully burnt on the pyre – will become buff-white in colour, while colours of blue, grey, brown, and black indicate varying degrees of oxidisation (Table 10.5).

In recent years, it has been argued that bone colouration is not a reliable method for determining pyre temperatures (*e.g.* Thompson 2004). Instead, Fourier transform infrared spectroscopy (FTIR) and X-ray diffraction have been used to measure the crystallinity index. FTIR can be used to establish the intensity of burning, and thus whether remains were cremated differently to each other. Results from FTIR analysis can be compared with contemporary samples and other remains, to distinguish between burned and unburned material (Thompson *et al.* 2011; 2013: 416; see also Snoeck *et al.* 2018).

Despite misgivings about the unreliability of colouration for assessing pyre temperature, colour was recorded for the cremated remains from AH7, from the 10mm and 5mm sieve fractions from each grid square, in the hope that it would offer at least a coarse guide to varying pyre conditions. The majority of bones exhibit varying shades of light grey and white, and are considered to have been efficiently cremated, having reached a temperature high enough to effectively burn away all the organic material within the matrix of the bone. This means that pyres were allowed to burn for a long time at a high temperature.

Approximately an eighth (*c.* 12%) of the assemblage contains bones that are various shades of grey and white on the cortex (outside) of the bone but black inside, signifying that the organic component was not completely burned away. These bones probably reached a high temperature (as seen by the white cortex), but then fell into the ashes at the bottom of the pyre before the organic material (black) could become completely cremated (Figure 10.10).

A wide range of colours was noted within the material from each grid square, signifying not only the various temperatures reached by the bones, but also, perhaps, mixing of bones of many different individuals. In grid square 254, for example, seven different colours were noted on seven separate femoral fragments (Figure 10.11). Although a range of colours may be expected on a single cremated skeleton, it is unusual for there to be so many variations on one bone. Thus, the variety of colours exhibited within this grid square probably reflects the presence of multiple individuals (which is to be expected from a commingled assemblage). It is nevertheless interesting because it illustrates varying degrees of efficiency in the cremation process for these putatively different individuals.

A very small number of unburnt human bone fragments was recovered among the cremated material (Figure 10.12). These bones could have been added either accidently or deliberately to the cremation deposits in prehistory, or added by Hawley or Newall to the assemblage of cremated bones before or during their re-interment in 1935. The unburnt bones are heavily weathered.

Completeness and preservation

As noted above, the majority of prehistoric deposits in Britain containing cremated human bones do not generally constitute the remains of an entire individual. There has been a suggestion that perhaps the status of the deceased could be reflected in the time and care that it took to collect bones for burial; consistently high proportions of bone recovery have been noted for primary burials under Early Bronze Age round barrows (McKinley 2000: 415). While this cannot necessarily be

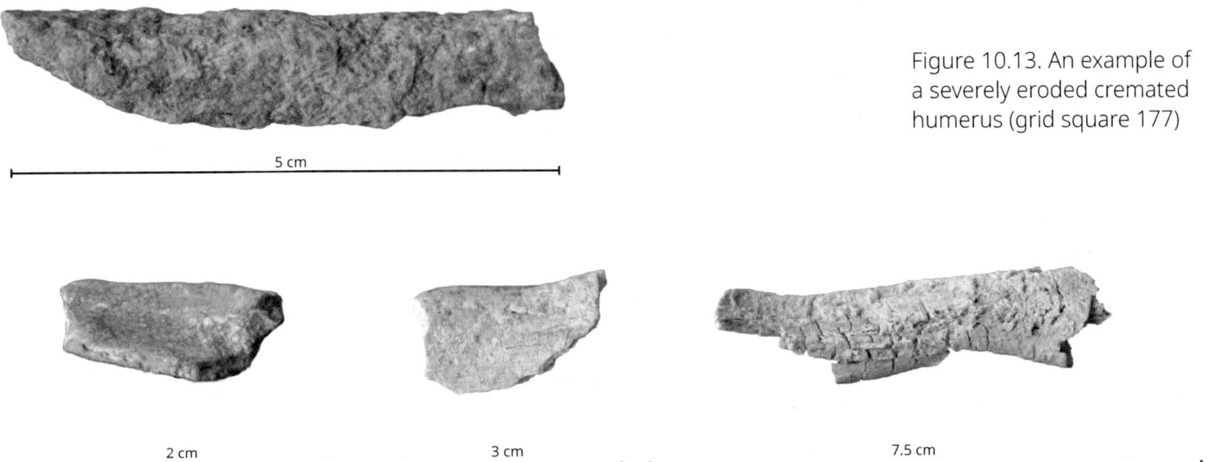

Figure 10.13. An example of a severely eroded cremated humerus (grid square 177)

Figure 10.14. Examples of different staining on bones (from left: grid squares 006 [no. 3, bag 14, 5mm–10mm], 314, and 357)

assumed to be the case for the Late Neolithic burials of Stonehenge, there does appear to be a high level of recovery and representation for at least some of the individuals whose remains ended up in AH7.

Small bones such as hyoids and distal phalanges, which are typically lost amongst the charcoal and ashes of the pyre, were recovered from AH7 though not in any significant quantity. A distribution of the major skeletal elements by weight reveals an attention to bone recovery in antiquity for a few individuals, but not for everyone buried at Stonehenge (Table 10.6). There is very little evidence of clavicles, sacra, carpals and tarsals, especially when considering that this assemblage derives from around 52–58 individuals. This could be due to the degree of fragmentation inhibiting recognition of a particular skeletal element during analysis, or to smaller bones having been missed during collection from the pyre.

Archaeological deposits of cremated remains generally consist of a random selection of skeletal elements, usually with skull fragments predominating, indicative of their preferential survival and subsequent retrieval from the pyre (McKinley 2000: 415). However, due to the mixed nature of the AH7 assemblage, conclusions cannot be drawn concerning any evidence for deliberate exclusion of specific skeletal elements at the time of burial.

The cremated remains are mostly preserved in excellent condition, with only a few exhibiting slight surface erosion from roots; they have been graded between 0–1 overall (Brickley and McKinley 2004). In addition, it was noted that there are quite a few fragments of bone that are heavily weathered; these have been graded as 5 (Figure 10.13). A small minority of bones, mostly consisting of trabecular bone (spongy bone), are very brittle and friable[9].

Small patches of red, orange, pink, and blue staining were also noted on some of the cremated bones, indicative of metallic elements within minerals leaching out of the soil (Figure 10.14).

Pyre technology

Carbonised wood fragments were recorded in 72 grid squares from AH7 and these fragments have been separated from the cremated bones. The presence of small carbonised wood fragments could suggest that bones were scooped up *en masse* from the pyre sites. Alternatively, the carbonised wood remains may have little or no relation to the cremated bone assemblage, potentially deriving from mixing of contexts during and after Hawley's archaeological excavations in the 1920s.

Hawley summarised his findings about the Stonehenge cremation burials in his interim report of 1926, noting differences between those buried in the Ditch and those buried in the Aubrey Holes (Table 10.1). Of the former he states: 'A peculiarity about the interments was that in the greater number of cases there was hardly any burnt wood ash present, showing that the bones had been carefully taken out of the mass of the fire after it had cooled' (1926: 157–8). In contrast, 'There was far more wood ash with the burials in the Aubrey holes, which in most cases (but not in all) seemed to contain all the bones, but in every case they had apparently been brought from a distant place for interment' (1926: 158). Thus it is very possible

9 These bones have subsequently been wrapped in bubble wrap and placed inside small plastic boxes for added protection during storage.

Skeletal element	Total weight	Adult	Foetal	Infant	Young child	Older child	Juvenile	Sub-adult
Cranium	7346.17	7346.17						
Mandible	188.87	181.29		0.15				7.43
Maxilla	63.65	62.42			0.65	0.58		
Teeth	41.34	40.84				0.11		0.39
Humerus	3617.91	3598.85		0.99	9.75	8.32		
Ulna	878.21	878.05		0.16				
Radius	1239.39	1237.57			0.53	0.55		0.74
Carpals	18.40	18.40						
Scapula	742.23	741.68	0.19		0.36			
Clavicle	122.04	114.49			3.02	3.4	0.54	0.59
Ribs	1072.72	1070.59		0.72		1.08		0.33
Hyoid	1.03	1.03						
Manubrium	7.32	6.17						1.15
Cervical	81.88	81.88						
Thoracic	252.85	252.85						
Lumbar	219.12	219.12						
Sacrum	68.36	64.52			1.2			2.64
Coccyx	0.87	0.87						
Misc Verts	605.23	605.02			0.21			
Pelvis	762.21	756.77			1.32			4.12
Femur	9201.40	9130.91		2.36	10.62	3.34	42.24	11.93
Tibia	1472.86	1450.98			5.29	7.16	8.4	1.03
Fibula	802.06	802.06						
Tarsals	52.77	52.77						
MC/MT	137.67	136.40			0.39	0.13		0.75
Phalanx	83.44	83.44						
Patella	81.72	77.86			2.05		1.81	
Total	29161.72	29013.00	0.31	4.43	35.39	30.42	43.93	45.24

Table 10.6. Weight distribution in grams (g) of the major skeletal elements recovered from AH7. Unidentifiable bone fragments (*e.g.* small long bone and trabecular fragments) have not been included in this table

that many of the carbonised wood fragments recovered from amongst the cremated bone fragments in AH7 derive from cremation deposits that were originally deposited in Aubrey Holes.

Minimum number of individuals (MNI)

The MNI is usually derived by counting the most frequently represented skeletal element. Within AH7 the most commonly duplicated bone fragment is the right petrous portion, which contains the internal auditory meatus (IAM). A total of 24 right IAMs were recovered; therefore a minimum number of 24 unique individuals can be identified. It is difficult to distinguish differences between adult and juvenile petrous bones (Baker *et al.* 2005: 37), and thus these 24 right IAMs could derive from adults, sub-adults or indeed a mixture of age ranges (see *Age at death* for further discussion).

Occipital bones, easily identifiable by their external and/or internal occipital protuberances, are the second most commonly duplicated bone fragments. A total of 21 adult occipital bones were recovered and, in addition, five sub-adults were counted from other skeletal elements (Table 10.7). Therefore an MNI of 26 individuals has been identified within the AH7 assemblage. The MNI can also be derived by counting any obvious age-related differences in bone growth, development and degeneration.

Category	Broad age range	MNI	Age-diagnostic skeletal elements
Foetus – neonate	Conception to 1 month after birth	1	Scapula
Infant	1 month to 1 year	1	Mandible, humerus, ulna, ribs, femur
Young child	1 to 5 years	1	Maxilla, humerus, radius, scapula, clavicle, sacrum, pelvis, femur, tibia, patella, metacarpals/metatarsals
Older child	5 to 12 years	1	Maxilla, teeth, humerus, radius, clavicle, ribs, femur, tibia, metacarpals/metatarsals
Juvenile	12 to 18 years	1	Clavicle, femur, tibia, patella

Table 10.7. Tabulation of the sub-adults by age category, listing the bones from which age determination is made for each of the categories. Since there is no duplication of bones within a category, it is assumed that there is only one individual from each age range

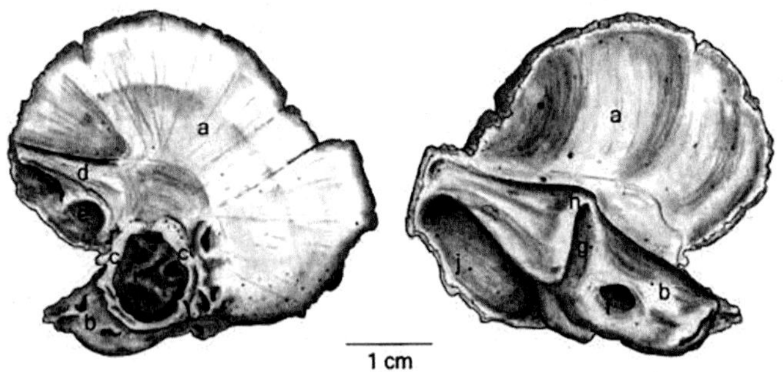

Figure 10.15. The temporal bone of an infant (left=external; right=internal); (b) is the petrous portion and (f) is the internal auditory meatus (from Baker *et al.* 2005: 37); © Texas A&M University Press

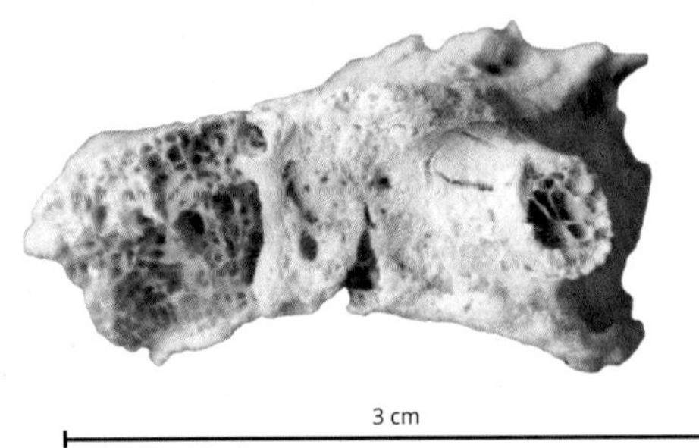

Figure 10.16. An example of osteophytosis of a cervical vertebra from grid square 347 which may indicate degenerative joint disease (DJD) in an older adult

Age at death

Cremated human remains can usually be placed into broad age categories (such as foetus, infant, young child, older child, juvenile, young adult, mature adult and old adult). In rare instances, a more precise age estimation may be achieved through the recovery of skeletal material with age-diagnostic morphological features such as developing permanent teeth (Smith 1984; Moorrees *et al.* 1963; Ubelaker 1978), auricular surface changes (Lovejoy *et al.* 1985), cranial suture closure (Meindl and Lovejoy 1985), epiphyseal union (Schwartz 2007), pubic symphysis changes (Suchey and Brooks 1990) and the length of sub-adult long bones (Scheuer and Black 2000).

Estimating age at death on a commingled assemblage of approximately 52–58 individuals (for which an MNI of only 26 has been established) is complicated not only by the variations in sub-adult skeletal growth and development, and by the fragmented nature of the bones, but also by the rates of bone shrinkage resulting from the cremation process. This suggests that unique bones that appear, from their measurements, to belong within the same age category could potentially come from the same individual or, just as likely, from multiple individuals if bone shrinkage has occurred. Thus, while all age-diagnostic bones were recorded, only the frequencies with which they appear can be extrapolated from the data.

The most commonly found skeletal element from AH7 is the petrous portion from the temporal bone, which houses the internal components of the ear. The petrous temporal bone, located on each side of the cranium is a complex-shaped bone which is easily recognisable and easily assigned to left and right sides (Figure 10.15). The petrous portion of the temporal bone changes very little during childhood growth and into adulthood: new-born babies have fully functioning hearing upon birth (as opposed to some of their other senses, such as eyesight, which require continued development after birth; Baker *et al.* 2005: 37). Since the shape of the petrous portion changes relatively little, it is almost impossible to determine age at death from this bone and thus the 24 right internal auditory meatii (IAMs) recovered from the mixed assemblage could be from individuals of any age. They cannot, therefore, be used to determine age at death for the AH7 assemblage.

Category	Broad age range	MNI	Age-diagnostic skeletal elements
Young adult	18 to 35 years	3	Pubis and auricular surfaces
Mature adult	35 to 50 years	4	Auricular surfaces
Older adult	50+ years	1	Degenerative joint disease (DJD) in the spine, severe dental wear to tooth roots

Table 10.8. Ageing descriptions for adult bone fragments

The second most commonly found skeletal element from the commingled assemblage is the occipital bone, a large bone located at the back and lower part of the cranium. The occipital bone is easily identifiable due to its thick ridges and protuberances, and can be used to determine whether the individual was an adult or sub-adult at the time of death. The occipital bone has a simple structure in that the diploë (spongy bone of the cranium) is sandwiched between compact bone to produce an external and internal occipital protuberance. A human skeleton only contains one of these occipital protuberances, thus the recovery of multiple occipital bones with this feature indicates multiple individuals. There are 21 unique adult occipital bone fragments recovered from AH7 but no unique occipital bones from sub-adults. Therefore it was also important to identify juvenile age-diagnostic features on the skeletal fragments in order to determine the number of individuals from each of the sub-adult age categories.

From the age-diagnostic features of the cremated remains, five unique sub-adults are identified (Table 10.7). As there is no duplication of skeletal elements in any of the age categories, an assumption is made that only one individual is represented within each category. Analysis of the sub-adults did take shrinkage into consideration to determine broad age range but, given the fragmented nature of the bones, it is difficult to make any more precise determinations of age at death (McKinley 1997: 131).

In addition to the growth and development characteristics recorded on the bones of children, varying broad ages of adults were also identified (Table 10.8). Within the mixed assemblage, two pubic symphyses (grid squares 164 and 258) and nine unique auricular surfaces (grid squares 263, 273, 291, 303, 334, 344, 345, 354 and 382/323) from both the left and right sides of the hip bones were recovered. The symphyseal face of the pubic bones revealed billowing, comprising ridges and furrows across the surfaces, and is scored at phase 1 (15 to 24 years: young adult age range) according to the Suchey-Brooks method (1990). The auricular surfaces of the ilia revealed varying degrees of degenerative changes and have been scored within a range of categories starting from 25 years (phase 2: young adult) through to 49 years (phase 6: mature adult; Lovejoy *et al.* 1985).

Evidence for older adults (over 50 years) is observed in the pathological conditions affecting individuals suffering from activity-related degenerative problems indicative of advanced years (see *Pathology* for further discussion). At least one individual was afflicted with degenerative joint disease (DJD) in that one sacral, five cervical, six thoracic and three lumbar vertebrae within the AH7 assemblage exhibit osteophytosis along the margins of the vertebral body (Figure 10.16). It is more than probable that these afflicted bones belong to more than one individual; however, without any duplicating skeletal elements, it is not possible at present to determine the exact number of individuals suffering from DJD. Further evidence for older adults is provided by the remainder of a tooth root that shows severe wear. During any cremation process, tooth enamel usually shatters, so it is rare to be able to assess occlusal attrition. However, this tooth stub (from grid square 292) shows wear which surpassed the dental enamel and continued down to the tooth root (Figure 10.17).

Based on the osteological analysis, 81% (*n*=21) of the 26 individuals from AH7 are adults. This high proportion of adult individuals does not follow expected mortality curves for the Neolithic period (Figure 10.18). Three possible scenarios need to be explored:

- Firstly, the low representation of sub-adults may be a result of bone loss either during the cremation process or through post-depositional factors such as natural disturbances or soil quality.
- Secondly, the low representation may be a result of human influence, either through biased collection of bones from the pyre or through biased archaeological retrieval.
- Thirdly, the low ratio of sub-adults to adults may be the result of conscious decisions not to bury many children at Stonehenge, a site potentially reserved for the preferential burial of a select group of people.

Archaeological human bones, whether adult or sub-adult, go through heat-induced chemical changes during the cremation process which endows them with greater mechanical strength. This hardness allows for a high degree of cremated-bone preservation within soils, both neutral and acidic, in which unburnt bone may not be preserved (Mays 2010: 209). Additionally, natural post-

Figure 10.17. Severe wear on a tooth from grid square 292, likely to derive from an older adult

depositional disturbances (such as repeated freezing and thawing, mammal tunnelling, or flooding) will only displace or fragment cremated bones and not obliterate them from the archaeological record. The relative rarity of sub-adult bones at Stonehenge, in comparison to the bones of adults, is thus unlikely to result from post-depositional differences in survival or preservation.

Upon completion of the cremation, the cooled cremated bones would have been collected from the remnants of the pyre prior to being buried at Stonehenge. The presence of small bones (*e.g.* phalanges which tend to fall down into the base of the pyre, and teeth which normally fall out of the mouth during the cremation process) in the assemblage from AH7 indicates a level of care in bone recovery from the funerary pyres. It is therefore highly unlikely that intentionally biased cremated bone collection was occurring during the Neolithic period and, even if the odd human bone was kept as a *memento mori*, this would not explain the rarity of sub-adult bones in AH7.

Neither does loss of sub-adult bones during archaeological excavation provide an adequate explanation. While Hawley himself admits in his diary to discarding the odd cremated bone, to have created this anomalous ratio of adult to sub-adult, he would have to have discarded many *hundreds* of sub-adult bones in a systematic and conscious manner, an idea which is clearly not plausible.

The third scenario is, therefore, the most likely: Stonehenge was a cemetery for a consciously selected group of people who were buried separately to the rest of the population. This separation would have given the deceased individuals social prestige intrinsically linked to an important monument. Stonehenge would have been seen as a powerful symbol in the Neolithic period, a testament to a wide community's commemoration of the chosen dead.

Sex

Some measurements specifically developed for studies of cremated remains (*e.g.* van Vark 1975; Gejvall 1981) have limited interpretational use for AH7 given the commingled and fragmented nature of the assemblage, and the incomplete recovery from the pyre sites in antiquity of all the bones required to ascertain sex osteologically. The determination of biological sex relies on recovering sexually diagnostic features from cremated bone fragments. In archaeological deposits, cremated pelvic bones are either not usually recovered or are often too small to allow for confident sexing (McKinley 2000: 411). Skull bones, regardless of fragment size, can aid in determining sex but must be confidently assignable to separate individuals. Diagnostic features from pelvic bone fragments (*e.g.* sciatic notches, pubic symphyses and auricular surfaces) and from skull fragments (*e.g.* mastoid processes, frontal bones, mandibular fragments and eye orbits) have been recovered from AH7 but could not be confidently sexed to any specific individuals.

Twenty-one unique adult occipital bones have been identified from AH7 and are the second most commonly recovered skeletal element. As described above, this bone is easily identifiable due to its thick ridges and bony protuberances. The occipital protuberance is a morphological characteristic used to determine sex: a large and thick external protuberance is considered to be a male trait (Figures 10.19–10.20), while a small, less-ridged protuberance is female (Feremback *et al.* 1980). Of the 21 unique adult occipital bones recovered from AH7, nine have been identified as male, five are female and seven are of indeterminable sex.

As described above, the most commonly recovered bone from AH7 is the easily recognisable petrous temporal bone, located on each side of the cranium (Figure 10.15). Forensic and archaeological advances in analysing non-cremated petrous bones have produced reliable techniques for determining sex by measuring the lateral angle of the canal (Lynnerup *et al.* 2006; Norén *et al.* 2005; Graw *et al.* 2004; Wahl and Graw 2001) with an 83.2% correct adult sex classification (Norén *et al.* 2005).

This bone is one of the densest structures of the human skeleton and, because of its extreme mechanical strength, it is not thought to suffer from the same heat-related changes during a cremation as other skeletal bones (Graw *et al.* 2004: 113; Lynnerup *et al.* 2006: 118). However, further research is required to examine the effects on the lateral angles of the petrous bone of rapid dehydration of the bone tissue at high temperatures, since all other skeletal elements in the human body are affected by high temperatures, causing warping and shrinking during the cremation process. There are currently no studies which look at this rapid loss of moisture in the petrous bone and consequently there *may* be some changes to the lateral angle by warping and shrinkage (Masotti *et al.* 2013: 1042). Additionally, no studies have examined the rates of shrinkage or warping comparing temperatures achieved in modern crematoria (850°–1200°C for 120 minutes) and those achieved on prehistoric pyres (800°–1000°C for up to 8 hours). Furthermore, a preliminary study has recently suggested that the advancement of age may affect the

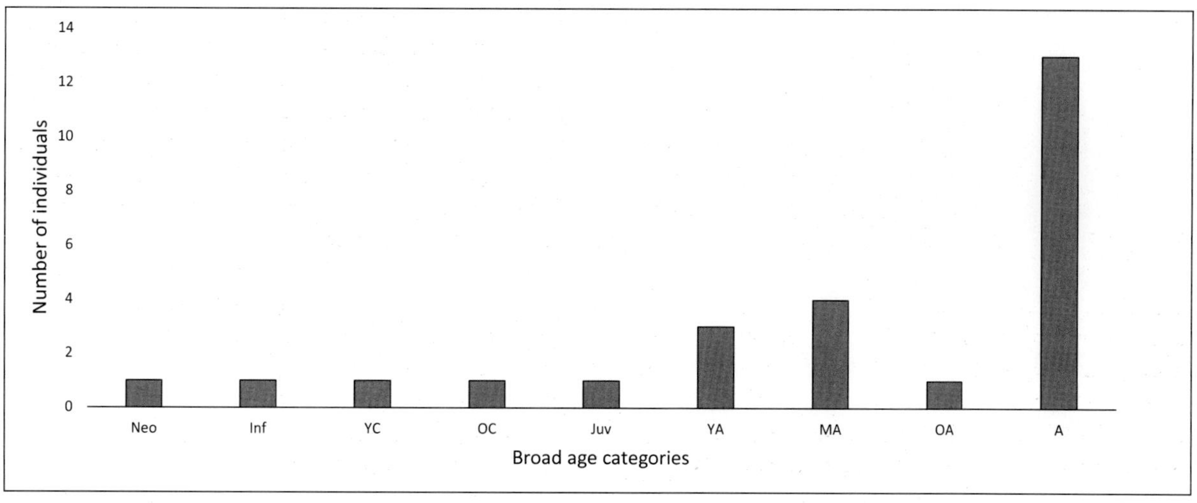

Figure 10.18. Age distribution of the cremated human remains from Aubrey Hole 7 (*n*=26). The high proportions of adult and sub-adult individuals do not follow expected mortality curves

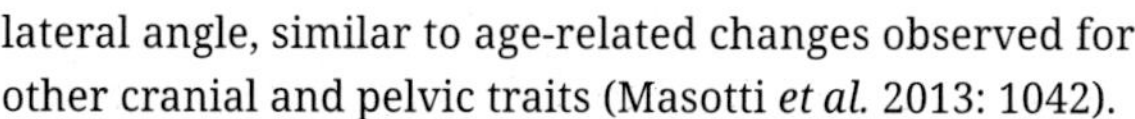

Figure 10.19. Examples of complete external occipital protuberances (EOP): a left fragment from grid square 307 and a right fragment from grid square 390a

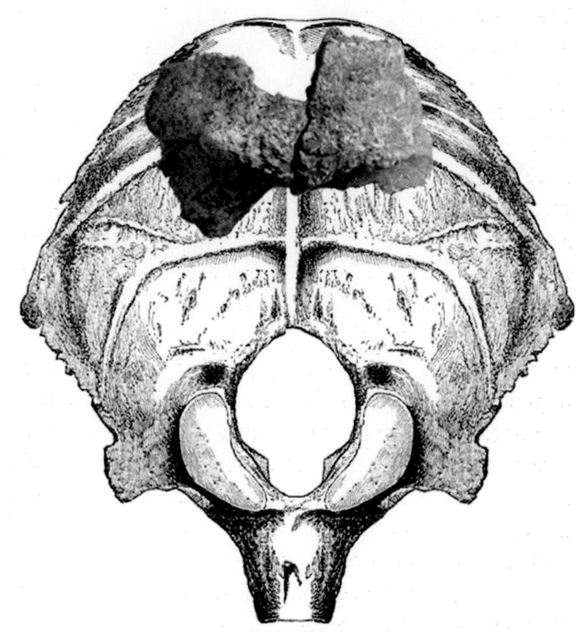

Figure 10.20. The external occipital protuberance (EOP) superimposed onto an occipital bone drawing (from Gray's *Anatomy*) to depict the location of the bone fragment. This example is of a probable male adult

lateral angle, similar to age-related changes observed for other cranial and pelvic traits (Masotti *et al.* 2013: 1042).

Since the reliability of accurately determining sex osteologically relies on using complete skeletons, in particular the skull and pelvic bones, this becomes problematic when bone fragments are used (Graw *et al.* 2004: 113), particularly so for a commingled cremated assemblage such as that from AH7. CT scanning of the petrous bones (rather than casting moulds of the canals) was used in order to increase the accuracy of the sexing results by enabling the examination of canals prior to measurement. All CT scans of the lateral angles from AH7 petrous bones show non-warped canals.

The petrous bones were scanned at the Royal Hallamshire Hospital, Sheffield, using a GE Lightspeed VCT CT scanner. Each fragment was placed on a foam rest and positioned so that the internal auditory meatus was aligned to the axial-scan plane. The bone fragments were scanned using a 0.625mm slice-thickness and reconstructed on a bone algorithm. The use of the bone algorithm created a sharp and highly enhanced image that allowed the post-processed image to be manipulated for taking accurate measurements (Figure 10.21).

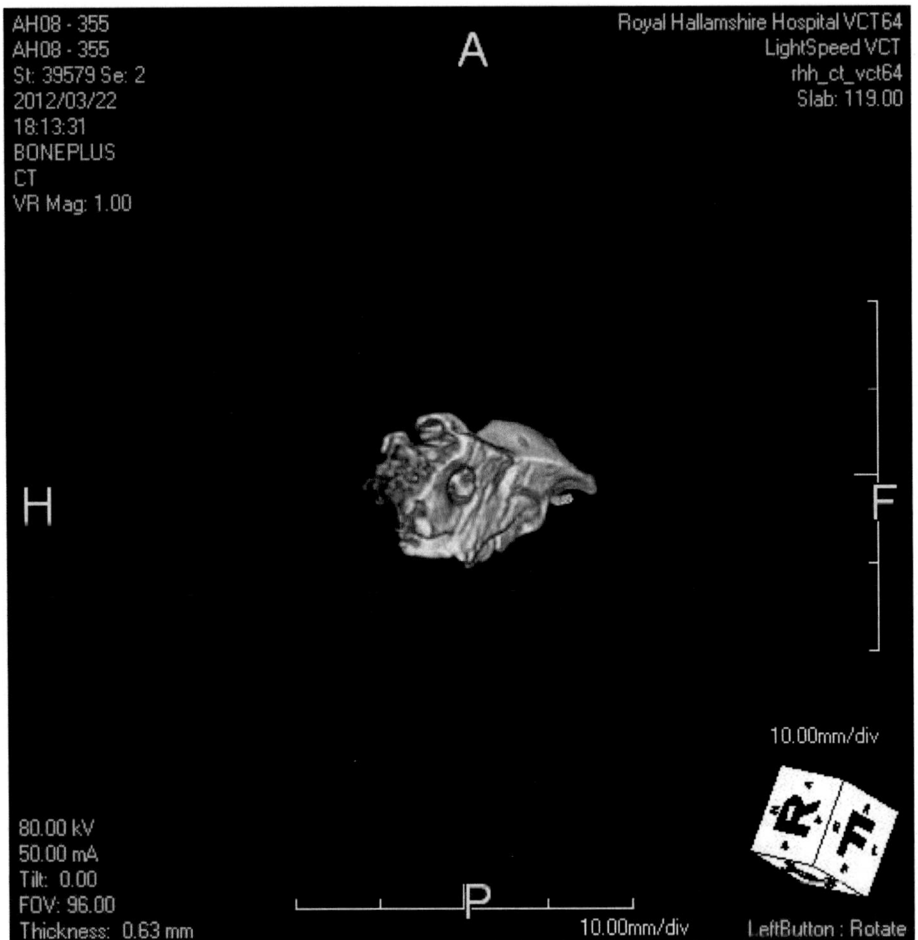

Figure 10.21. An example of a reconstructed petrous bone from a computerised tomography (CT) scan on an algorithm for recording bone (grid square 355)

The axial image was then reconstructed in the coronal plane and 1mm coronal images were produced. The way in which the petrous bones were initially aligned for scanning means that each coronal image equates to an axial slice through the fragment. This allows for the images to be used to measure the lateral angle of the internal auditory meatus for the purpose of this study (Figure 10.22).

The results from measuring the lateral angles of the IAMs reveal nine males, 14 females and three of unknown sex (Figure 10.23). Both adults and sub-adults may be represented in this group of sexed individuals.

The combined results from determining sex on the occipital bones and the lateral angles of the IAMs show that males and females are almost equally represented at Stonehenge (Figure 10.24). Whilst the very low number of sub-adult bones in the assemblage indicates the deliberate exclusion of children and teenagers from burial at Stonehenge, it seems that Neolithic people did not differentiate between the sexes when it came to burying adults there. Indeed, there is a slightly higher number of women (*n*=14, IAMs) compared with men (*n*=9), which may have implications regarding some women's higher social status.

Pathology

Pathological conditions are recorded from AH7; however, the figures are considered to be raw counts since the assemblage is mixed, fragmented, and incomplete. As a consequence, it is difficult to determine the percentage of 'healthy' individuals and 'unhealthy' individuals; therefore, only the observable pathological conditions will be discussed. Burials at Stonehenge stretch from the beginning of the Late Neolithic (3000–2500 BC) to the Chalcolithic (2500–2200 BC; see Chapter 11). Consequently, skeletal elements can inform us of changes in lifestyle patterns relating to diet, health, subsistence and other aspects of these people's lives (Roberts and Cox 2003: 74). The AH7 assemblage is chronologically later than the majority of Roberts and Cox's (2003) British Neolithic sample and earlier than most of their Bronze Age sample but their discussion of changes between these periods can be drawn upon here.

The most common condition recorded on the adult bone fragments is that of degenerative changes to the spinal column. Many vertebral bodies exhibit mild to moderate osteophytosis (new bone growth) around the margins of the vertebral bodies (Figure 10.25),

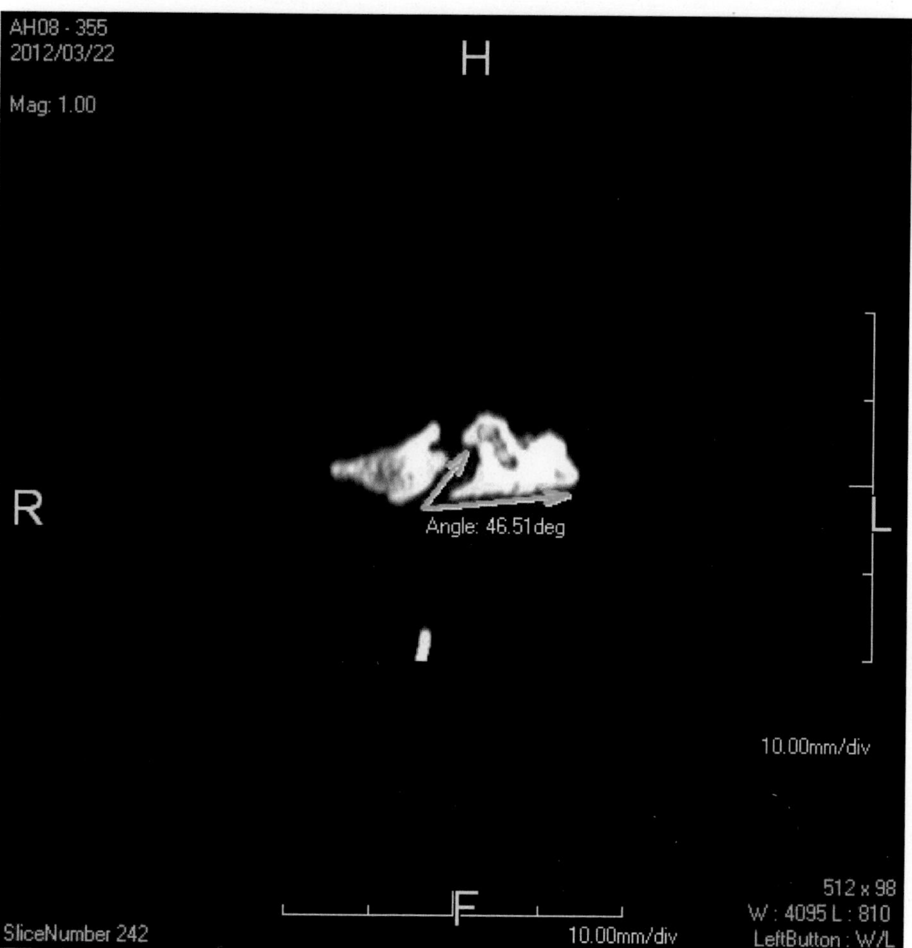

Figure 10.22. An example of an axial slice through the petrous bone (grid square 355) to measure the lateral angle of the internal auditory meatus

and Schmorl's nodes (indentations) on their surfaces (Figure 10.26). These changes are often the result of degeneration of the intervertebral disks caused by advanced age or occupation, among other factors such as genetic disposition and high-caloric diets, and may be considered to be osteoarthritis (Roberts and Cox 2003: 32). Also noted were degenerative changes to the neck of a femur and along the intercondylar ridge of a distal femur, again linked to osteoarthritis affecting the synovial joints.

Osteoarthritis has been linked to occupation, developing over a long period of time, which is why it is typically found in mature and older adults (*e.g.* Lovell 1994; Walker and Hollimon 1989; Waldron and Cox 1989). However, other factors such as genetic, nutritional and metabolic patterns as well as trauma may also affect the structural integrity of the joints; therefore occupation is not considered solely to be a direct indicator of osteoarthritis (Molnar *et al.* 2011: 286). In Roberts and Cox's study, spinal joint disease affected 1.8% of individuals in the Neolithic and rose to 6.9% during the Bronze Age, while spinal osteoarthritis increased from 7.0% to 10.7%. The occurrence of Schmorl's nodes rose from 1.3% to 4.8% and approximately 10.2% of Neolithic individuals had osteoarthritis, rising to 16.8% in the Bronze Age (Roberts and Cox 2003: 78). These figures, while useful in understanding population health and disease in prehistoric Britain, reflect the health of *non-cremated* skeletons rather than cremated ones. Thus caution is advised as the patterns among cremated individuals may raise or, indeed, lower these values for these populations.

Degenerative changes in the spinal columns from AH7 may be the result of activity-related strain, especially when considering the numerous large musculoskeletal stress markers (MSMs) noted on femoral and humeral long bone fragments. MSMs are a result of the habitual activities performed throughout an individual's lifetime, which cause varying degrees of stress on the skeleton and are correlated with age (Hawkey and Merbs 2005; Molnar *et al.* 2011: 285). Though the fragmented and commingled nature of the AH7 assemblage prevents any conclusions based on the number of individuals with osteoarthritis or MSMs, it is clear that many individuals buried at Stonehenge had frequently engaged in repetitive activities over a long period of time, which resulted in robust MSMs (Figure 10.27) and in degenerative changes to their spinal columns and synovial joints.

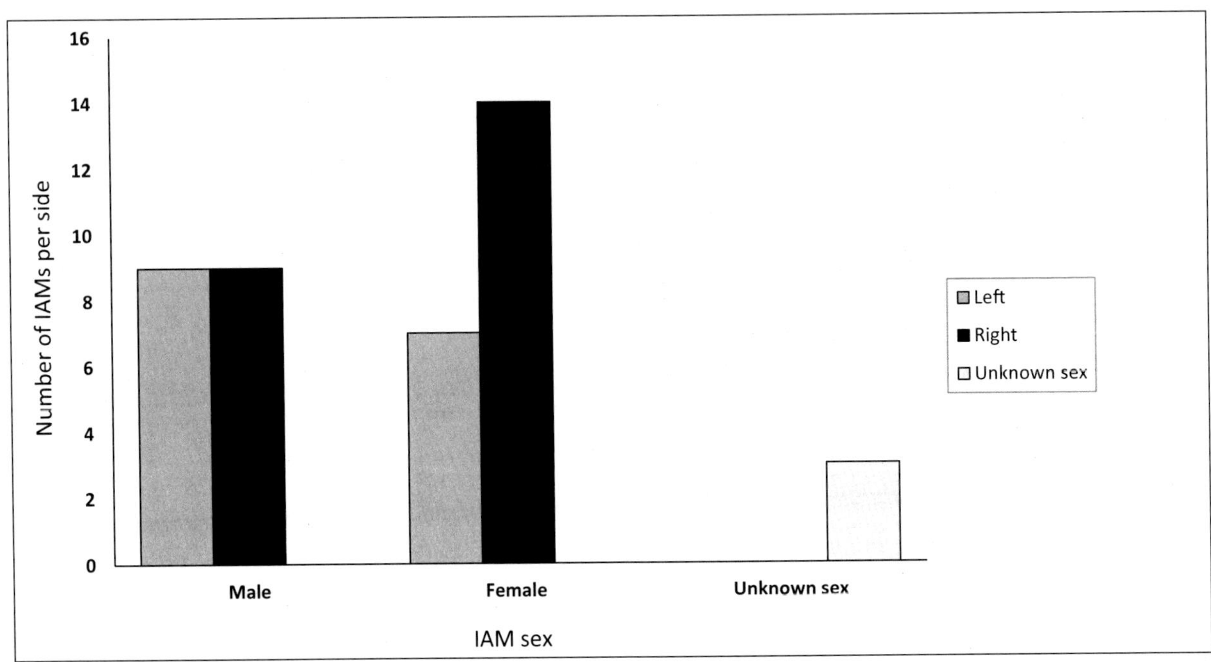

Figure 10.23. Results of sexing by measuring the lateral angles of the internal auditory canal of the petrous bones from Aubrey Hole 7. These results potentially derive from both adult and sub-adult individuals

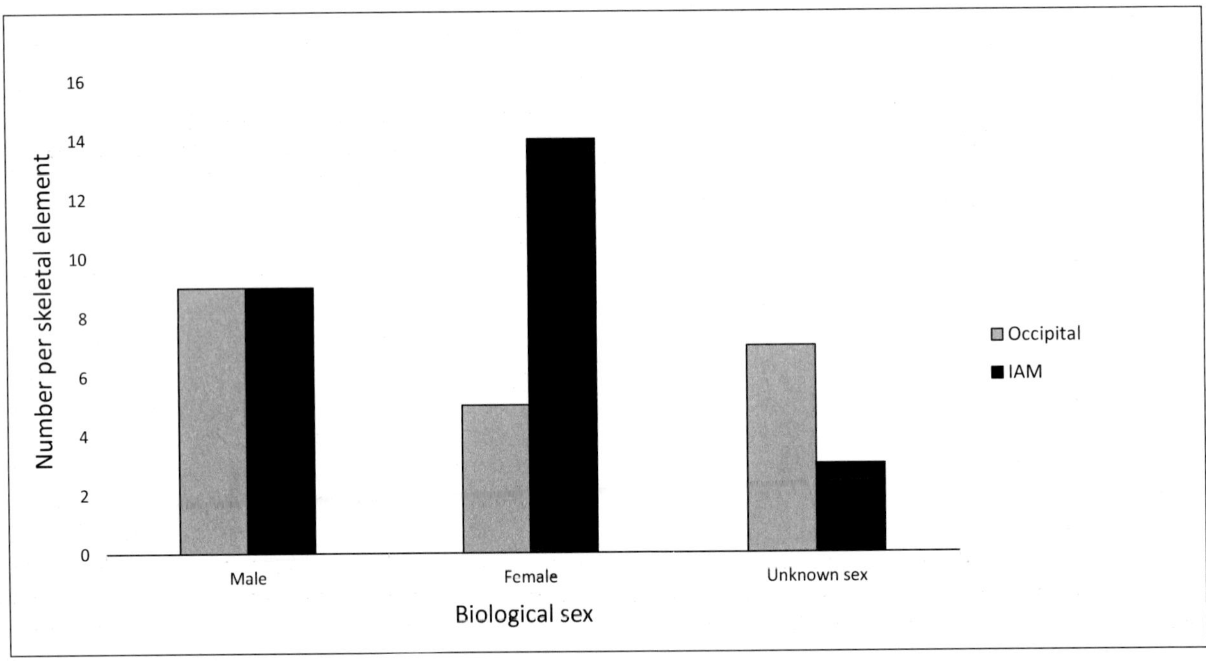

Figure 10.24. Combined results of sexing of the occipital bones (grey) and of sex-related variation in the lateral angle (black)

Periostitis, a non-specific inflammation resulting from infection or trauma, is observed on the periosteum (a layer of connective tissue that surrounds the bone). It is usually localised rather than affecting the entire bone, and appears as tiny porous plates of bone adhering to the surface of regular bone. Within the AH7 assemblage, periostitis is noted on single fragments of clavicle, fibula, radius (Figure 10.28), and tibia (Figure 10.29).

Severe occlusal wear was noted on a molar from grid square 292 (see Figure 10.17). Usually, the enamel of erupted teeth shatters during the cremation process, leaving only the tooth roots; occlusal wear is usually lost (McKinley

Figure 10.25. An example of mild osteophytosis around the superior and inferior margins of a thoracic vertebra (grid square 240)

Figure 10.26. An example of Schmorl's nodes on the surface of a lumbar body (grid square 241)

Figure 10.27. A large musculoskeletal stress marker from the deltoid muscle on the humerus (grid square 145)

Figure 10.28. Periostitis on a radial fragment (grid square 338)

Figure 10.29. Periostitis on a tibia fragment (grid square 337)

2000: 410). However, the wear on this molar exceeded the enamel, as it is worn down to the tooth root. Wear such as this can be found in older adults, or can be attributed to some sort of activity affecting the back teeth. Instances of other probable occlusal wear were noted on a small number of teeth; however, since most of the enamel has been either burnt or broken off (either from the cremation process or subsequent burial and re-burial), positive determinations could not be made with confidence.

Aneurysm of the popliteal artery

T. Waldron

One of the specimens recovered from the assemblage is the distal fifth of a left femur which shows the presence of a defect in the popliteal fossa on the back of the bone (Figures 10.30–10.31). The defect is oval in shape, with its long axis orientated in the long axis of the bone. It measures 25.5mm in length, and 21.8mm in breadth and is approximately 10mm in depth. The edges of the lesion are smooth, with no evidence of remodelling, and its walls are smooth. The most likely explanation for the defect is that it results from the pulsatile pressure from an aneurysm of the popliteal artery.

The popliteal artery is the continuation of the femoral artery as it passes through the popliteal fossa. It divides at the lower border of the popliteus muscle into the anterior and posterior tibial arteries and thus is the major supplier of blood to the lower leg. It is the most common site for an aneurysm of any of the peripheral arteries, is often bilateral and may occur with aneurysms elsewhere, most notably of the aorta. Popliteal artery aneurysms are relatively uncommon but become more prevalent with increasing age, occurring in about 1% of men aged between 65 and 80; they are rare in women. They are usually found in association with arteriosclerotic change but may be a complication of some connective tissue disorders (Hall *et al.* 2013). They were particularly common in the eighteenth and nineteenth centuries when they seem to have been an occupational hazard of horsemen, coachmen, and young men who had physically demanding jobs (Suy 2006).

It is interesting that smaller aneurysms (less than 20mm in diameter) seem to produce more symptoms than larger ones (Ascher *et al.* 2003). The most common effect is to reduce blood supply to the leg, resulting in pain on exercise (claudication) or, in more severe cases,

Figure 10.30. Posterior view of a distal femur showing a popliteal aneurysm

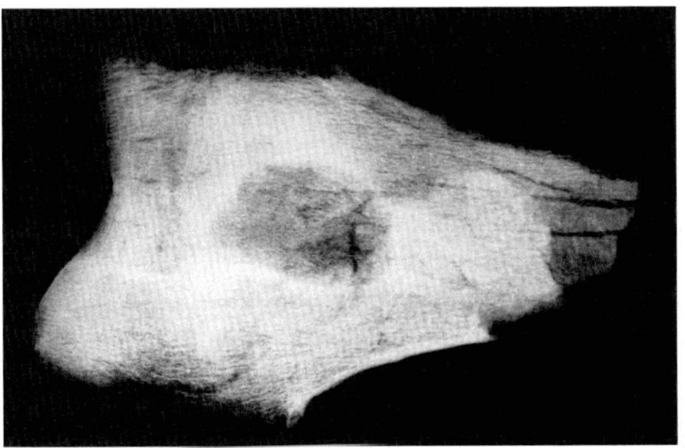

Figure 10.31. X-ray image of the popliteal aneurysm

Figure 10.32. Aubrey Hole 7 after excavation with the adjacent primary cremation deposit (007) showing as a dark circular patch (highlighted by the red circle)

Figure 10.33. The primary cremation deposit (007) in half-section, showing the northern half of the fill

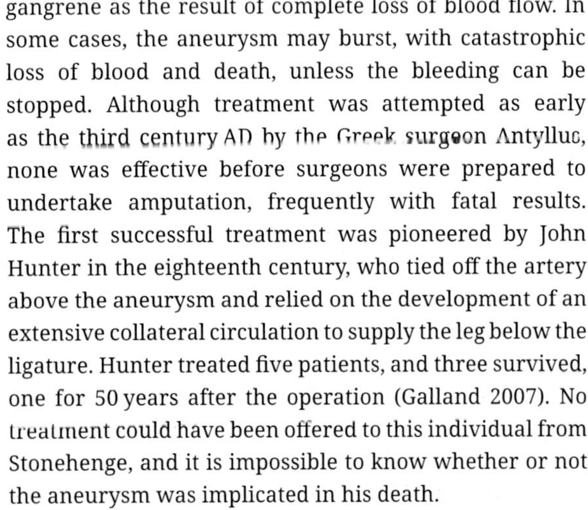

gangrene as the result of complete loss of blood flow. In some cases, the aneurysm may burst, with catastrophic loss of blood and death, unless the bleeding can be stopped. Although treatment was attempted as early as the third century AD by the Greek surgeon Antyllus, none was effective before surgeons were prepared to undertake amputation, frequently with fatal results. The first successful treatment was pioneered by John Hunter in the eighteenth century, who tied off the artery above the aneurysm and relied on the development of an extensive collateral circulation to supply the leg below the ligature. Hunter treated five patients, and three survived, one for 50 years after the operation (Galland 2007). No treatment could have been offered to this individual from Stonehenge, and it is impossible to know whether or not the aneurysm was implicated in his death.

Evidence of aneurysms may be seen on occasion in skeletal remains, most commonly those occurring on the vertebral artery, or sometimes on the descending aorta, in both cases resulting in pressure defects in vertebrae adjacent to the lesion (Waldron and Antoine 2002). This is the first palaeopathological case of an aneurysm of the popliteal artery.

10.3. A primary cremation deposit adjacent to Aubrey Hole 7

An undisturbed primary cremation deposit (007) was recovered from a small, bowl-shaped pit (008) adjacent to AH7 (Figures 10.32–10.33; see Chapter 4 and Figure 10.5). This deposit was missed in 1920 by Hawley during his initial excavation of Aubrey Hole 7 and then again in 1935 by Newall and Young when the cremated bones were re-interred. An important find in its own right, this cremation deposit is the first to be excavated at Stonehenge using modern archaeological methods.

Maximum fragment size

The longest bone fragment from the 10mm sieve fraction (Table 10.9) is above the expected average of 45.2mm from other archaeological sites in Britain, and the maximum length even from the 5mm fraction is close to that average (McKinley 1994: 341). As with the other bone fragments from AH7, this suggests that the bones were protected within an organic bag or container at the time of burial. This supports the observation made during the SRP excavation that the cremated bones formed a circular deposit, about 0.30m in diameter, resulting from burial within a circular organic container (see Chapter 4).

Weight

The total weight of the undisturbed cremation deposit (007) is 1,101.47g from the 10mm and 5mm sieve fractions (1,173.08g total weight including the 2mm and base sieve fractions). The weight is above the expected average of 800g for one adult individual, though still within the expected range of <3kg (McKinley 1993).

Colour

The colour of the bones ranges between various shades of grey and white, signifying that the deposit was efficiently cremated (Figure 10.34). A few fragments have yellow-brown colouration, probably as a result of staining from the surrounding soil. Only a few fragments are grey with dark grey organic material left in the cortex.

Completeness and preservation

While a higher than expected weight was recorded for these adult female remains (1,101.47g; see *Sex*, below), the weight distribution of the major skeletal elements suggests a low level of bone collection from the pyre (Table 10.10). There is a distinct lack of vertebral bodies, carpals, metacarpals, tarsals and metatarsals (as also seen overall in the AH7 assemblage), and only a small proportion of mandibular and maxillary bones, pelvis, and phalanges were present in the deposit.

The distribution of the cremated remains can also be considered in another way (Table 10.11). The distribution indicates a high level of recovery in antiquity of skeletal fragments except for axial fragments, which show a very low level of collection. This indicates that, while the deposit appears to contain a random selection of skeletal elements, the majority of the spinal column was not included in the deposition.

In terms of preservation, the bones from this undisturbed cremation deposit remain in very good overall condition, with only a few exhibiting slight surface erosion by roots. This merits a grade of 0–1 (after Brickley and McKinley 2004).

Sieve fraction	Maximum length	Skeletal element
10mm	88.80mm	Humerus
5mm	40.30mm	Humerus

Table 10.9. Maximum bone fragment size from the undisturbed cremation deposit (007) from pit 008 adjacent to AH7

Figure 10.34. Typical colouration of the cremated bones from 007

Pyre technology

No carbonised wood fragments were recovered from this deposit, thus there is no trace of any pyre materials. This may suggest that the inclusion of carbonised pyre remains was not acceptable and that the deposit was carefully sorted to remove any such pieces prior to transport and burial. This adds weight to the possibility, suggested above, that the carbonised wood fragments found in AH7 were accidental and/or subsequent inclusions. The apparent care taken to exclude charcoal from 007 contrasts quite sharply with the low level of bone recovery for this burial, suggesting that only a portion of a cremated individual was acceptable for burial. This matches Hawley's observations concerning those cremation burials (albeit in the Ditch), where he concluded that wood ash was carefully removed. However, it contrasts with his observations about cremation deposits in the Aubrey Holes which included far more wood ash (Hawley 1926: 157–8).

Minimum number of individuals

Analysis of the cremated human remains from this undisturbed context reveals no evidence of any skeletal duplication or of any different age-related bone features that might suggest the presence of additional individuals within the deposit.

Skeletal element	Total weight (g)
Cranium	284.38
Mandible	8.57
Maxilla	4.35
Teeth	1.6
Humerus	74.93
Ulna	18.46
Radius	25.34
Carpals	0
Scapula	4.24
Clavicle	2.57
Ribs	18.68
Hyoid	0
Manubrium	0
Cervical	4.34
Thoracic	0
Lumbar	0
Sacrum	0
Coccyx	0
Misc. vertebrae	25.1
Pelvis	1.04
Femur	157.29
Tibia	12.56
Fibula	9.46
Tarsals	0
MC/MT	0
Phalanx	1.57
Patella	0
Total	654.48g

Table 10.10. Weight distribution of the major skeletal elements recovered from the undisturbed cremation deposit (007). Unidentifiable bone fragments (*e.g.* small long bone and trabecular fragments) have not been included in this table

Age at death

This individual was a mature adult, 35–50 years old at the time of death. Age determination is based on the degenerative joint changes to the upper neck, which typically appear later in adulthood as a result of activity-related stress on the bones. Also recorded were fused long bone fragments (Schwartz 2007) and permanent teeth with evidence of heavy wear (Smith 1984; Moorrees *et al.* 1963; Ubelaker 1978).

Sex

Biological sex was determined by analysis of a small mastoid process (Ferembach *et al.* 1980), indistinct canine eminences (Schwartz 2007), and gracile long bones

Skeletal area	Weight (g)	Distribution
Skull	298.90	45.7%
Axial	48.12	7.3%
Upper limb	126.33	19.3%
Lower limb	181.13	27.7%

Table 10.11. Weight distribution of cremation deposit 007, based on the four major areas of the skeleton

which can all be considered female characteristics. One occipital bone fragment is quite robust and has a large musculoskeletal stress marker (MSM) on it. Although such a robust MSM is usually considered a male feature (especially if it were found in isolation), this is probably a result of activity-related stress, which is also supported by the degenerative changes in the cervical vertebrae. This individual would have had enlarged neck muscles where they were attached to the back of the cranium, and may have taken part in repetitive activities eventually leading to osteoarthritis of the neck. Determining sex from additional morphological characteristics on the bones was not possible given their fragmentary condition

Pathology

Degenerative changes to the neck are exhibited by slight compression and moderate osteophytosis around the margins of a cervical vertebra (Figure 10.35), and also by degenerative changes on the surfaces for attachment of the alar ligaments on the second cervical vertebra (Figure 10.36). Since this deposit does not contain any thoracic or lumbar vertebrae, it is unknown to what extent the degenerative changes occurred further down the spinal column; however, the one other cervical vertebra in this deposit did not show any osteophytes around its margins. Therefore, it is assumed that degenerative changes were localised around the upper neck area of this individual.

This individual also exhibited interesting dental conditions. A possible abscess in the alveolar bone was noted between the upper right first and second incisors (Figure 10.37). Dental abscesses are relatively rare among Neolithic skeletons, being recorded in only 1.8% of cases (*n*=14/772) by Roberts and Cox (2003: 68). Attributed to complications of dental caries, heavy attrition and periodontal disease, dental abscesses usually develop at the apex of the tooth root, where pus builds up inside the alveolar bone. A hole then opens up to drain the pus and it is this hole that is visible on the maxillary bone of 007. The cremation process (and perhaps the subsequent burial) has eradicated some of these features, rendering it difficult to diagnose it confidently and definitively as an abscess.

Heavy wear on the right upper first and second incisors (I^1 and I^2) and moderate wear on the right upper third molar (M^3) were also recorded for this individual. Occlusal wear occurs as a consequence of chewing foods, wearing down tooth surfaces. The higher parts of the teeth become abraded to form flat surfaces and, over time, the tooth enamel and even the entire tooth crown may be worn down (Hillson 2002: 250; Schwartz 2007: 187).

Ante-mortem tooth loss (AMTL) of the left mandibular M_1 and M_2 and alveolar resorption of the tooth sockets are recorded for this individual. AMTL is relatively low in the Neolithic with 4.4% (n=8/181) of Roberts and Cox's dataset exhibiting tooth loss (Roberts and Cox 2003: 68). It can be caused by variations in the consistency of an individual's diet, by nutritional deficiency diseases, by trauma, or by removal for cultural or ritual reasons (Lukacs 2007: 158). Taking into consideration that this individual exhibits other dental conditions, it is probable that dietary factors were a contributory cause to her poor dental health, rather than trauma or deliberate removal.

Dietary factors can cause severe occlusal wear, which can result in pulp exposure, dental abscesses and, ultimately, tooth loss (Lukacs and Pal 1993). Additionally, foods high in carbohydrates may further cause the development of carious lesions which, in turn, produce pulp exposure, abscesses and, finally, AMTL (Lukacs 1992). Accumulations of calculus may also result in periodontal disease and alveolar resorption, eventually leading to AMTL (Lukacs 2007: 158). Although there is no evidence of calculus on the teeth, its presence cannot be totally discounted as any calculus is likely to have burned away during the cremation process. Since this individual already exhibits occlusal wear on three teeth, a likely dental abscess, AMTL of at least two teeth, and alveolar resorption of tooth roots, then dietary factors and/or poor oral hygiene were probably the direct causes of her overall dental condition.

Calcium carbonate

Calcium carbonate was observed on a variety of cremated bone fragments from this undisturbed deposit. This suggests that the one deposit noted by Hawley (1926: 154) where the bones were cemented together with calcium carbonate was not an isolated occurrence, but was present amongst multiple deposits of human bone at Stonehenge.

Faunal remains

A non-cremated animal tooth was noted as being recovered from this undisturbed cremation deposit. However, it cannot now be located in the excavation archive.

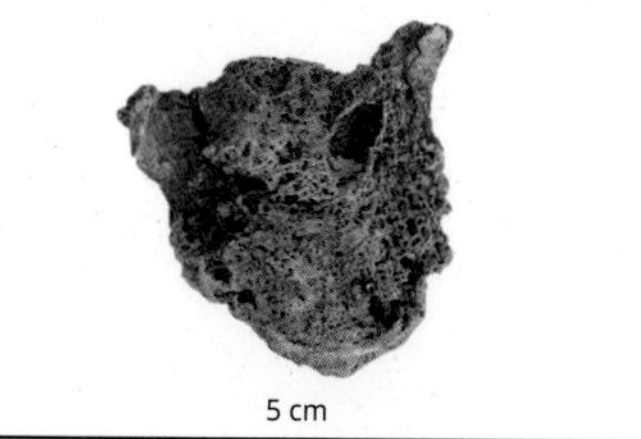

Figure 10.35. Degenerative joint changes to a cervical vertebra from 007

Figure 10.36. Lateral view of the dens of the second cervical vertebra from 007; the surfaces for the alar ligaments show bony degenerative changes

Figure 10.37. A possible abscess in a maxillary bone from 007

Chapter 11

Radiocarbon dating of Stonehenge

P.D. Marshall, C. Bronk Ramsey, G. Cook and M. Parker Pearson

11.1. Research background

Bayesian modelling of the radiocarbon dates from Stonehenge by Allen and Bayliss (1995) – as part of the publication of the twentieth-century excavations (Cleal *et al.* 1995) – provided the first robust chronology for the site. Minor revisions to that original chronological model were subsequently published (Bayliss *et al.* 1997; Bronk Ramsey and Bayliss 2000). The results of more recent investigations (Parker Pearson *et al.* 2007; 2009; Darvill and Wainwright 2009) led to revised phasing of the construction and use of Stonehenge, and the new chronological framework – a five-stage sequence – was published in 2012 (Darvill *et al.* 2012; Marshall *et al.* 2012).

This chapter focuses on the dating of Stonehenge itself and its associated human remains, but one of the overall research objectives of the Stonehenge Riverside Project was to clarify the chronology of other monuments in the Stonehenge landscape. Radiocarbon dates from the SRP excavations at the Greater Cursus, Woodhenge, West Amesbury (Bluestonehenge), the Cuckoo Stone, the Stonehenge Avenue and the palaeochannels of the River Avon are reported in earlier chapters in this volume; see the Table of Contents for the relevant table and figure numbers. Radiocarbon dates from the SRP excavations at Durrington Walls appear in Volume 3.

11.2. The chronology of Stonehenge's stages of construction

The first stage of activity and the initial construction of the monument comprised the digging of a segmented circular ditch (with an internal bank and counterscarp, and entrances to the northeast and south), the digging-out and use of the Aubrey Holes, and the interment of cremation burials (Marshall *et al.* 2012; Cleal *et al.*1995).

Stage 2 saw the erection of the sarsen circle and trilithons, with the bluestones arranged within them in the Q and R Holes. Stages 3 to 4 involved the dismantling and rearrangement of the Welsh bluestones, as well as the construction of the Avenue, and Stage 5 the excavation of the Y and Z Holes. A longer account of the chronology of construction and other activity can be found in Chapter 4, and full details of the Stages are published in Parker Pearson (2012), Darvill *et al.* (2012) and Marshall *et al.* (2012). Discussion of the chronological model for the five Stages can be found at the end of this chapter (see Table 11.7 for the dating of the Stages).

Lab number	Material and context	Radiocarbon age (BP)	δ^{13}C (‰)	δ^{15}N (‰)	C:N	Calibrated date range (95% confidence)	Reference
OxA-4886	Human bone, right femur. Burial cut into secondary ditch fill, (4028), [C61.1]. The 'Stonehenge Archer'.	3960±60	-21.2				Allen & Bayliss 1995
OxA-5044	As OxA-4886	3785±70	-20.7				Allen & Bayliss 1995
OxA-5045	As OxA-4886	3825±60	-20.6				Allen & Bayliss 1995
OxA-5046	As OxA-4886	3775±55	-20.6				Allen & Bayliss 1995
BM-1582	As OxA-4886	3715±70	-21.8				Burleigh *et al.* 1982
Beaker-age burial	Weighted mean (T'=8.7, T'(5%)=9.5, ν=1; Ward and Wilson 1978)	3819±28				2400–2140 cal BC	
OxA-13193	Human bone. Skeleton 4.10.4 from grave inside the stone circle on the central axis, close to Y Hole 9	1258±34	-19.5	8.6	3.3	cal AD 660–880	Pitts *et al.* 2007

Table 11.1. Radiocarbon results from Stonehenge burials prior to the start of the Stonehenge Riverside Project

11.3. Human remains from Stonehenge: existing and new radiocarbon determinations

Prior to the programme of radiocarbon dating undertaken on human remains as part of the SRP, only two inhumations from Stonehenge had been dated (Table 11.1; Figure 11.1). One of these is the Stonehenge Archer, buried in the top of the secondary fills of the main Ditch close to the western terminal of its northeast entrance (Evans 1984). The five determinations (BM-1582, OxA-4886 and OxA-5044–46) from this burial are statistically consistent (T'=8.7, T'(5%)=9.5, ν=1; Ward and Wilson 1978) and so a weighted mean (3819±28 BP) provides the best estimate for its date.

A skeleton excavated by Hawley inside the stone circle in 1923 (Royal College of Surgeons 4.10.4) was rediscovered in 1999 (Pitts *et al.* 2002; 2007). Two new samples were dated from Skeleton 4.10.4 but these measurements (OxA-9921 and 9931; Pitts *et al.* 2002) were withdrawn following the discovery of a contamination problem in the ultrafiltration protocol used for the processing of bone at Oxford in 2002 (Bronk Ramsey *et al.* 2000): this error resulted in some bone samples giving ages which were about 100–300 radiocarbon years (BP) too old (Bronk Ramsey *et al.* 2004a). The two withdrawn dates were replaced by a new determination (OxA-13193; 1258±34 BP; Pitts *et al.* 2007). OxA-13193 is statistically consistent (T'=0.6, T'(5%)=3.6, ν=1; Ward and Wilson 1978) with an all-but-undocumented result from leg bone shafts of the same skeleton obtained from AERE Harwell in 1976 (1190±80 BP; Pitts 2000: 318; Pitts *et al.* 2002: 134).

As part of the SRP, new radiocarbon determinations (presented in full below) were obtained from cremated human remains excavated from the Ditch and the Aubrey Holes, and from five unburnt fragments of human bone and two teeth from the ditch fills, a stone setting and a possible posthole. In addition, a single human tooth excavated as part of the SPACES project (Darvill and Wainwright 2009) has also been dated (see *Stone settings*, below).

11.4. Animal bone and antler from Stonehenge: existing and new radiocarbon determinations

All available radiocarbon dates obtained from antler and animal bone fragments were employed to create the model for Stonehenge's Stages 1–5 published in Marshall *et al.* (2012: tables 1–3) and Darvill *et al.* (2012). The details of each sample are not repeated here; the reader should refer to those publications and Cleal *et al.* (1995) for information on location, date of excavation, *etc.* for each dated sample shown in the figures in this chapter. Details of the methodology used for chronological modelling of the radiocarbon dates follows that outlined below in the report on the Aubrey Hole cremated remains.

Since publication of the model in 2012, a new radiocarbon date on animal bone has been obtained from curated material, in the collections of Salisbury Museum, from Hawley's 1923 excavations. A fragment of pig rib was available from Cutting 8, between Stones 8 and 9 (Cleal *et al.* 1995: 541, figs 69, 274). This sample, from the fill (1885) of a posthole (1884), provides the only non-human radiocarbon determination obtained by the SRP as part of the investigation of Stonehenge itself. This sample (Table 11.2) was dated instead of the supposed human rib from this context (McKinley 1995: table 59 [58]; see Table 10.3), which could not be located in the archives (Parker Pearson *et al.* 2009: 29). The result (OxA-V-2232-51; 3977±31 BP) provides a *terminus post quem* for the infilling of the posthole, as the single fragment of pig bone could be residual (see Figure 11.7).

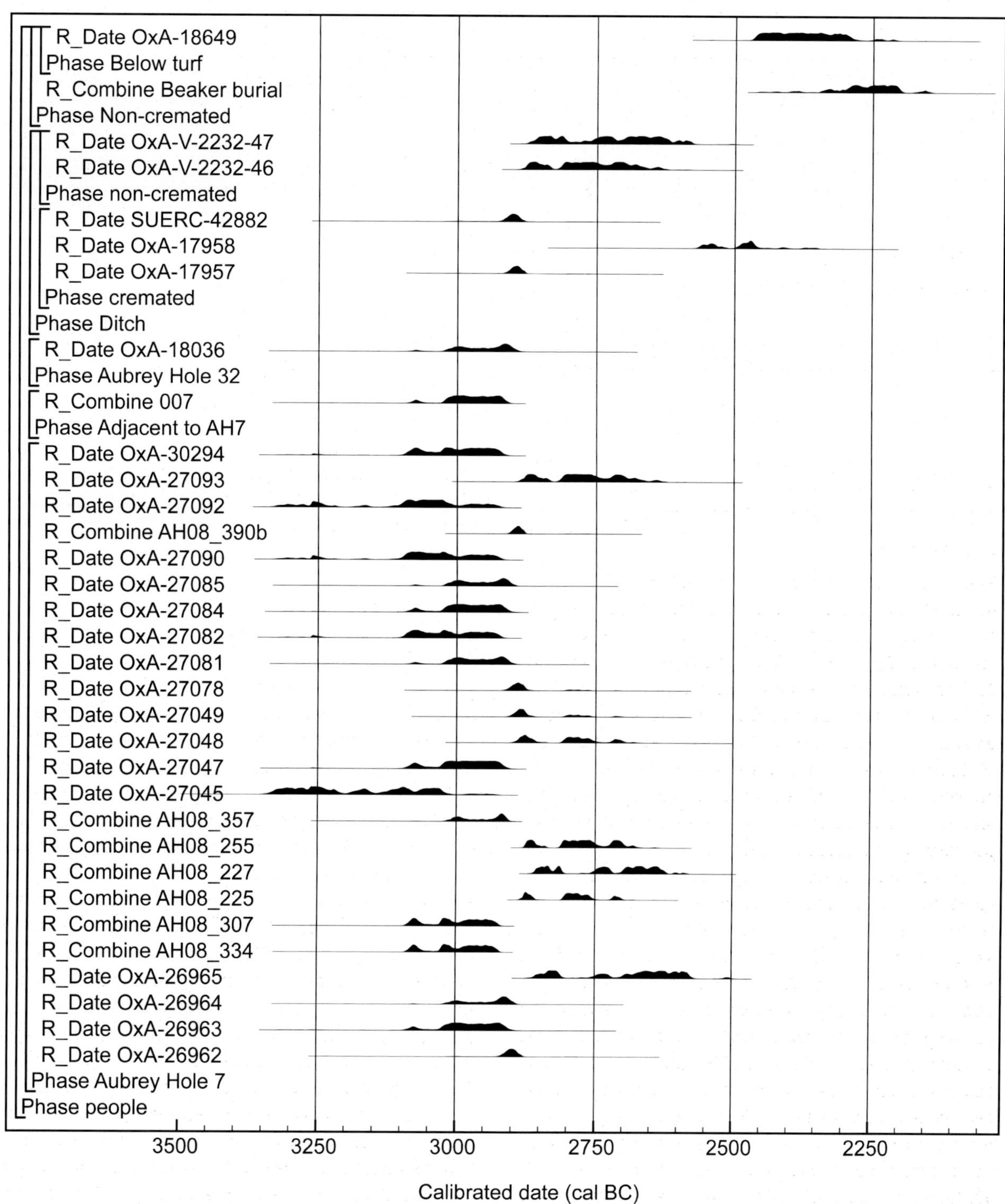

Figure 11.1. Probability distributions of third millennium cal BC human dates from Stonehenge. The distributions are the result of simple radiocarbon calibration (Stuiver and Reimer 1993)

Lab number	Material and context	Radiocarbon age (BP)	$\delta^{13}C$ (‰)	$\delta^{13}C$ (‰) diet	$\delta^{15}N$ (‰)	C:N	Calibrated date range (95% confidence)
OxA-V-2232-51	Pig rib fragment. Posthole 1884 filled by (1885), between Stones 8 and 9, C8	3977±31	−20.5	−20.5	6.4	3.3	2580–2460 cal BC

Table 11.2. Radiocarbon result for posthole 1884

Lab number	Material and context	Radiocarbon age (BP)	$\delta^{13}C$ (‰)	$\delta^{13}C$ (‰) diet	$\delta^{15}N$ (‰)	C:N	Calibrated date range (95% confidence)
OxA-V-2232-46	Human skull. Context 1560, Ditch fill, C25. 1 of 4 fragments	4169±31	−21.8	−21.8	9.9	3.4	2890–2620 cal BC
OxA-V-2232-47	Human skull, older mature adult or older adult. Context 2589, Ditch fill, C28	4127±31	−21.9	−21.9	10.4	3.4	2880–2570 cal BC
OxA-V-2232-34	Human tooth dentine from root of lower 2nd premolar. Context 3543, Stonehole 27 upper fill, C58	1181±25	−18.6	−19.1	9.3	3.2	cal AD 770–950
OxA-V-2232-35	Human tooth dentine from root of upper left 1st premolar. Context 1815, eastern area, C7	1236±25	−19.3	−19.5	11	3.2	cal AD 680–890
OxA-V-2232-48	Human skull. Context 1282, Ditch fill, C19. 1 of 2 conjoining fragments	1646±27	−20.3	−20.2	10.9	3.3	cal AD 340–530
OxA-V-2232-49	Human skull. Context 3896, Ditch fill, C42	2379±28	−20.3	−20.5	8.9	3.3	520–390 cal BC
OxA-V-2232-50	Human adult ulna. Context 1384, Ditch fill, C21	3436±30	−20.5	−20.8	10.5	3.3	1880–1680 cal BC

Table 11.3. Non-cremated human bone radiocarbon results

11.5. The radiocarbon determinations and chronological modelling: the Ditch

As noted above, all available radiocarbon dates obtained from antler, animal bone and human bone fragments from the Ditch were used to create the model published in Marshall *et al.* (2012). Details of the antler and animal bone samples are published elsewhere (Allen and Bayliss 1995; Bayliss *et al.* 1997; Bronk Ramsey and Bayliss 2000; Marshall *et al.* 2012), and only information on the human bone fragments dated by the SRP on archival material is presented here.

In total, eight samples of human bone were dated from the fills of the Ditch by the SRP, three from cremated and five from unburnt human bone fragments. The five unburnt fragments (and two teeth from other contexts; see *Stone settings*, below) were selected 'to establish whether any of them were contemporary with Stonehenge's three principal stages of use within the third millennium cal BC' (Parker Pearson *et al.* 2009: 27).

Unburnt human remains

The unburnt human bones and teeth (Table 11.3) were combusted and dated at the Oxford Radiocarbon Accelerator Unit (ORAU) on ultrafiltered collagen samples prepared at the Max Planck Institute for Evolutionary Anthropology, Leipzig, following the methods described by Richards and Hedges (1999) and Brown *et al.* (1988). These measurements also include the number of the AMS wheel (*e.g.* 2232) that the sample was measured in and its position within it (*e.g.* 46; Brock *et al.* 2010).

The unburnt human bone samples from the ditch fills that produced dates within the third millennium BC (Table 11.3) are:

- OxA-V-2232-46, one of four fragments from the same parietal found in the upper filling of the Ditch (C25) excavated by Hawley in 1922 (Cleal *et al.* 1995: 125–6).
- OxA-V-2232-47, a single fragment of human skull from the fill of the Ditch in C28 (eastern section) excavated in 1925.

The remaining three unburnt fragments produced significantly later dates and are interpreted as being intrusive or from the very top of the ditch fills. The dates of these fragments are therefore excluded from the model of the Ditch chronology:

- OxA-V-2232-48, one of two conjoining skull fragments from the secondary ditch fill (C19) excavated in 1920–1921, is significantly later than the Beaker-age burial (the Stonehenge Archer) that provides a *terminus ante quem* for the secondary infilling of the Ditch, and the sample must therefore be intrusive.
- OxA-2232-49, a single fragment of skull from the 'topsoil' (McKinley 1995: table 59 [58]) of the ditch fill in Cutting 42, produced a date in the first millennium cal BC.
- OxA-2232-50, a single adult ulna from ditch fill (1384, C21), cannot be assigned securely to this ditch fill because the entries for this area of the ditch in Hawley's diary are missing (Cleal *et al.* 1995: 84). It produced a date in the second millennium cal BC.

Lab number	Sample ID	Material and context	Radiocarbon age (BP)	δ13C (‰)	Calibrated date range (95% confidence)
Aubrey Hole 7					
OxA-26962	110	Cremated human occipital bone, probable adult, ?female	4281±31	-22.0	2920–2870 cal BC
OxA-26963	173	Cremated human occipital bone, probable adult	4358±34	-23.5	3090–2890 cal BC
OxA-26964	221	Cremated human occipital bone, probable adult	4325±31	-24.3	3020–2890 cal BC
OxA-26965	223	Cremated human occipital bone, adult, ?male	4101±30	-22.6	2870–2500 cal BC
OxA-26966	227	Cremated human occipital bone, probable adult, ?female	4168±29	-23.7	
SUERC-42892	227	As OxA-26966	4107±19	-19.7	
		Weighted mean (T'=3.1; v=1; T'(5%)=3.8; Ward and Wilson 1978)	4125±16		2865–2585 cal BC
OxA-27045	246	Cremated human occipital bone, adult	4456±36	-21.5	3340–2940 cal BC
OxA-27046	255	Cremated human occipital bone, probable adult	4195±31	-18.5	
SUERC-42893	255	As OxA-27046	4164±19	-20.8	
		Weighted mean (T'=0.7; v=1; T'(5%)=3.8; Ward and Wilson 1978)	4173±17		2880–2675 cal BC
OxA-27047	280	Cremated human occipital bone, adult male	4377±31	-21.8	3100–2900 cal BC
OxA-27048	281	Cremated human occipital bone, adult, ?male	4210±31	-22.4	2900–2690 cal BC
OxA-27049	288	Cremated human occipital bone, adult, ?male	4237±30	-22.5	2910–2750 cal BC
OxA-27077	307	Cremated human occipital bone, adult male	4418±31	-24.9	
SUERC-42885	307A	As OxA-27077	4385±20	-24.4	
		Weighted mean (T'=0.8; v=1; T'(5%)=3.8; Ward and Wilson 1978)	4395±17		3095–2920 cal BC
OxA-27078	330	Cremated human occipital bone, adult,	4255±33	-24.2	2920–2790 cal BC
OxA-27079	334	Cremated human occipital bone, probable adult, ?female	4391±30	-22.8	
SUERC-42883	334	As OxA-27079	4394±18	-22.3	
		Weighted mean (T'=0.0; v=1; T'(5%)=3.8; Ward and Wilson 1978)	4393±16		3090–2920 cal BC
OxA-27080	357	Cremated human occipital bone, adult male	4325±32	-22.5	
SUERC-42895	357	As OxA-27080	4350±19	-22.6	
		Weighted mean (T'=0.5; v=1; T'(5%)=3.8; Ward and Wilson 1978)	4344±17		3020–2900 cal BC
OxA-27081	366	Cremated human occipital bone, probable adult, ?female	4348±30	-23.0	3090–2890 cal BC
OxA-27082	389	Cremated human occipital bone, probable adult, ?female	4404±26	-19.9	3270–2910 cal BC
OxA-27083	390b	Cremated human occipital bone, adult	4261±30	-19.8	
OxA-27091	390b	As OxA-27083	4255±30	-20.6	
		Weighted mean (T'=0.0; v=1; T'(5%)=3.8; Ward and Wilson 1978)	4258±22		2910–2875 cal BC
OxA-27084	596	Cremated human occipital bone, adult male	4364±31	-20.3	3090–2900 cal BC
OxA-27085	211	Cremated human proximal left diaphyseal humerus, child, 5–12 years	4340±30	-23.3	3080–2890 cal BC
OxA-27089	225	Cremated human occipital bone, adult male	4132±31	-20.9	
SUERC-42886	225A	As OxA-27089	4219±20	-21.6	
		Weighted mean (T'=5.5; v=1; T'(5%)=3.8; Ward and Wilson 1978)	4194±17		2890–2695 cal BC
OxA-27090	336	Cremated human occipital bone, probable adult	4413±32	-23.5	3310–2910 cal BC
OxA-27092	344	Cremated human right diaphyseal humerus, child, 1–5 years	4426±33	-23.6	3330–2920 cal BC
OxA-27093	382+323	Cremated human proximal left femoral diaphysis, juvenile, 12–18 years	4180±34	-23.4	2890–2630 cal BC
OxA-30294	289	Cremated human occipital bone, adult male	4392±30		3100–2910 cal BC
Cremation deposit adjacent to AH7					
OxA-27086	007	Cremated human bone, femoral shaft fragment	4317±33	-21.5	
SUERC-30410	007	As OxA-27086	4420±35		
		Weighted mean (T'=4.6; v=1; T'(5%)=3.8; Ward and Wilson 1978)	4366±25		3090–2900 cal BC
Aubrey Hole 32					
OxA-18036		Cremated human longbone fragment	4332±35		3080–2890 cal BC
Ditch fills					
OxA-17957		Cremated human bone, humerus, young/mature adult [3898], C42, 54/841	4271±29		2920–2870 cal BC
SUERC-42882		Cremated human bone, [3898], C42, 54/821	4289±20	-20.4	2920–2880 cal BC
OxA-17958		Cremated human bone, radius, young/mature adult, [3893], C41, 54/36	3961±29		2570–2360 cal BC

Table 11.4. Cremated human bone radiocarbon results

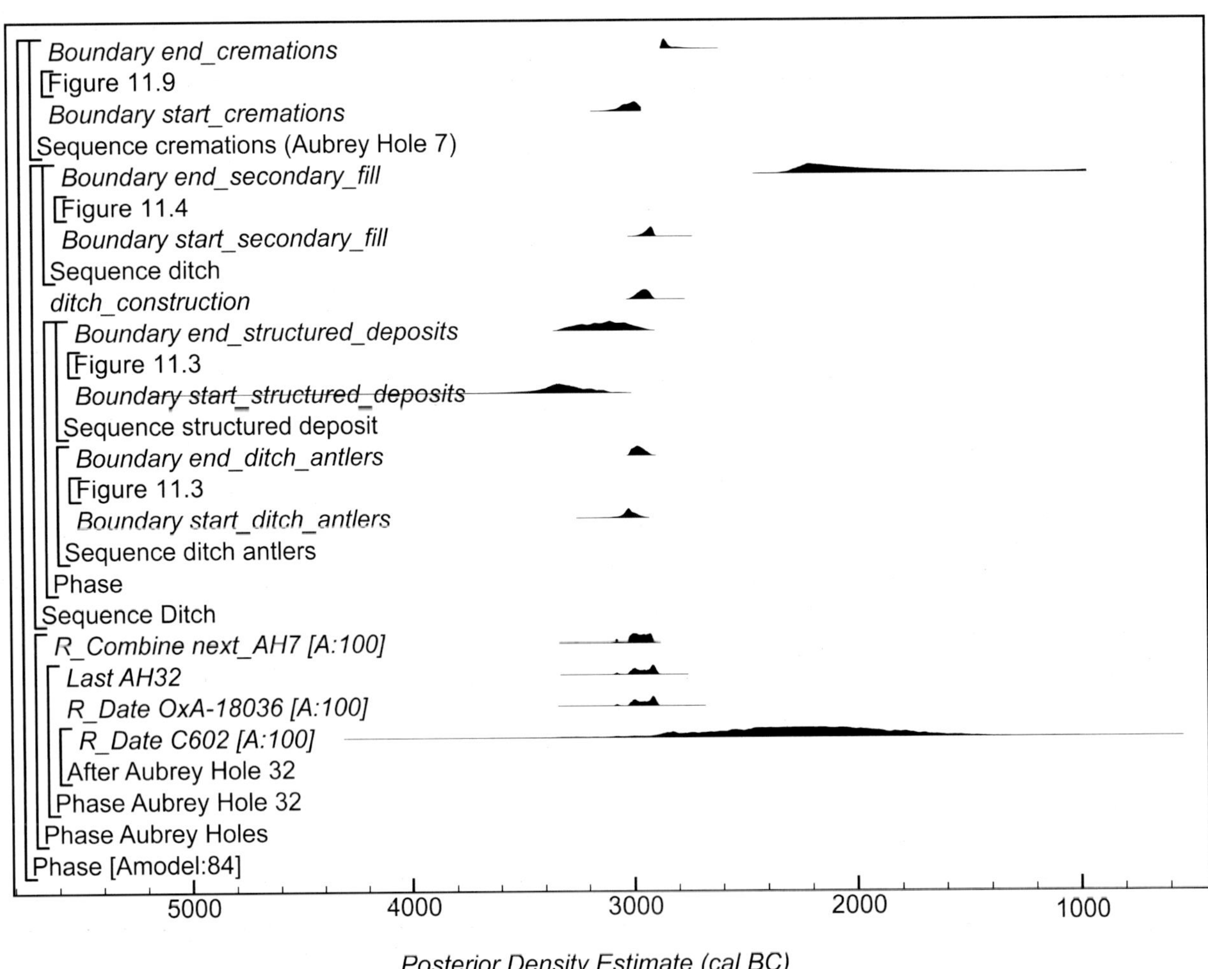

Figure 11.2. Overall structure for the chronology of the Ditch and Aubrey Holes. The component sections of this model are shown in Figures 11.3–11.4 and 11.9. The large square brackets down the left-hand side of the figure, along with the OxCal keywords define the overall model exactly

Cremated human remains

The three cremated human bone fragments from ditch fills are OxA-17958, OxA-17957 and SUERC-42882 (Table 11.4). Since the 1995 radiocarbon-dating programme for Stonehenge (Cleal *et al.* 1995; Bronk Ramsey and Bayliss 2000), the ability to date cremated bone has advanced (Lanting and Brindley 1998, Lanting *et al.* 2001; Van Strydonck *et al.* 2005), allowing, for the first time, the direct dating of human cremated remains found at Stonehenge. Laboratory methods for the analysis of cremated bone, and the methods used to model the results, are described in the report on the Aubrey Hole cremations, below.

- OxA-17958: Atkinson recovered 78.9g of cremated human bone from Cutting 41 near the west terminal of the Ditch at the northeast entrance (context 3893; McKinley 1995: table 59 [58]). This cremated material was collected from the upper ditch silt, ditch fill, and upper ditch fill, suggesting that the burial had been disturbed. Given the uncertainty about the exact location of the sample (54/36), the determination (OxA-17958) only provides an accurate date for the cremation of the individual. This date therefore appears in Figure 11.1 but does not contribute to the chronological model for the construction and filling of the Ditch (Figure 11.2). Furthermore, it is a statistical outlier and should be treated with caution in the chronological models of the burials in Figures 11.9–11.11 (see *Chronological modelling of burials at Stonehenge*, below).
- OxA-17957 and SUERC-42882: Cutting 42, west of the Stonehenge Ditch's northeast entrance, was excavated by Atkinson in 1954 and contained the cremation burial (54/821; Atkinson's catalogue

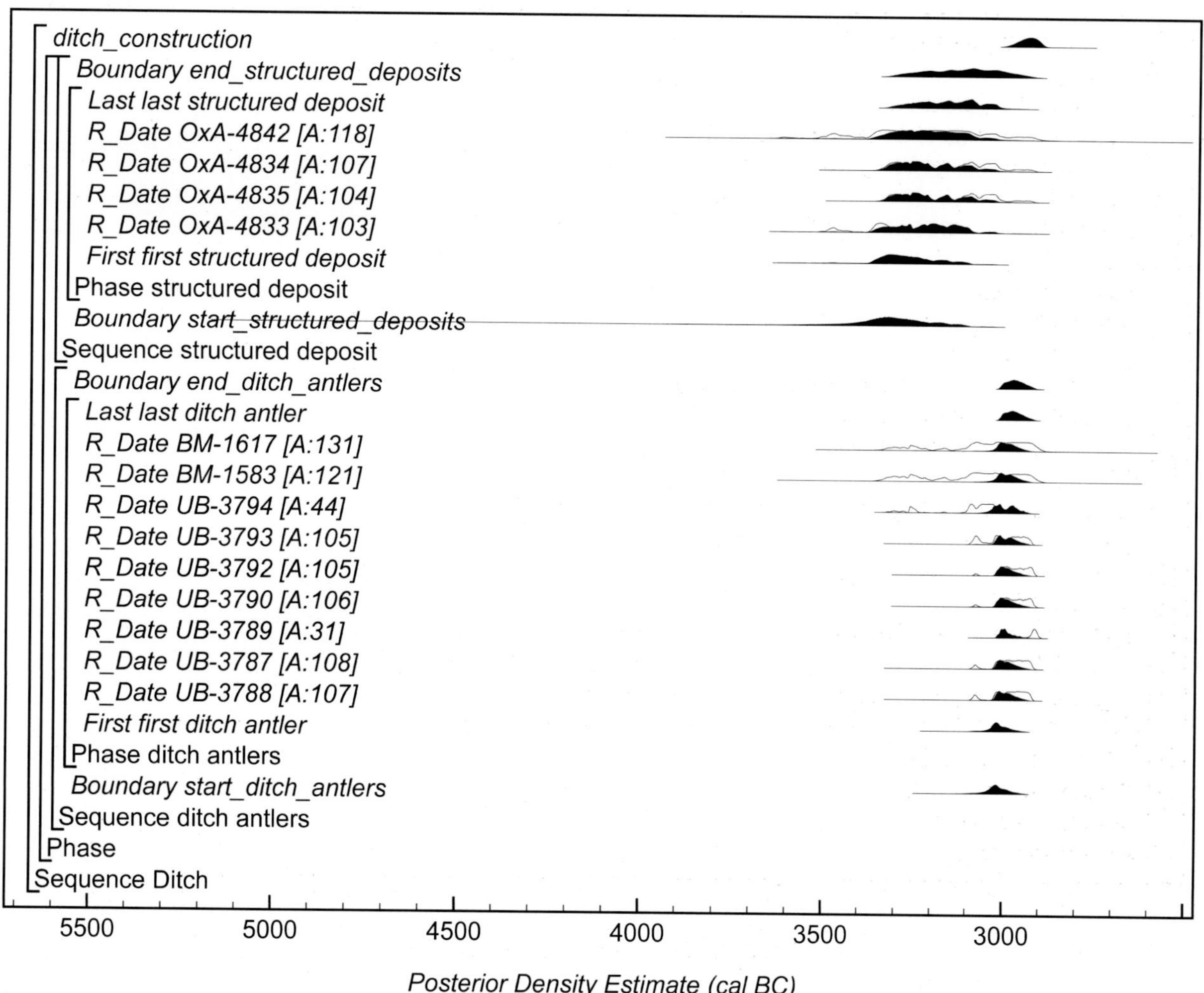

Figure 11.3. Probability distributions of dates from the Ditch – antlers and structured deposits. Each distribution represents the relative probability that an event occurs at a particular time. For each of the radiocarbon dates two distributions have been plotted, one in outline, which is the result of simple calibration, and a solid one, which is based on the chronological model used. Figures in brackets after the laboratory numbers are the individual indices of agreement which provide an indication of the consistency of the radiocarbon dates with the prior information included in the model (Bronk Ramsey 1995). The large square brackets down the left-hand side along with the OxCal keywords define the model exactly

number) of a young adult female (context 3898; McKinley 1995: 458). The large amount of bone (1,546.6g) that had been collected for burial after the cremation of the body represents a minimum of 45% of the expected bone weight and possibly most of the recoverable bone (McKinley 1993; 1995: 458). Two other small amounts of cremated bone from context 3898 (54/820, 54/841) and some fragments of unburnt human bone (54/843 and 54/848) were scattered in the ditch fills and might have derived from the same cremation – there is no osteological evidence to suggest that they did not (Jacqueline McKinley pers. comm.).

The bone fragment 54/841 was dated in 2007 (OxA-17957; Parker Pearson *et al.* 2009: 26) and was used in the model published in Marshall *et al.* (2012). However, it does not derive from the single discrete deposit (54/821), but from a fragment found separately in the fill. A bone fragment from the *in situ* cremation 54/821 was subsequently dated in 2012 (SUERC-42882). Thus, in order to not bias the chronological modelling, we have chosen to exclude the date (OxA-17957) on the loose bone fragment from the analysis below.

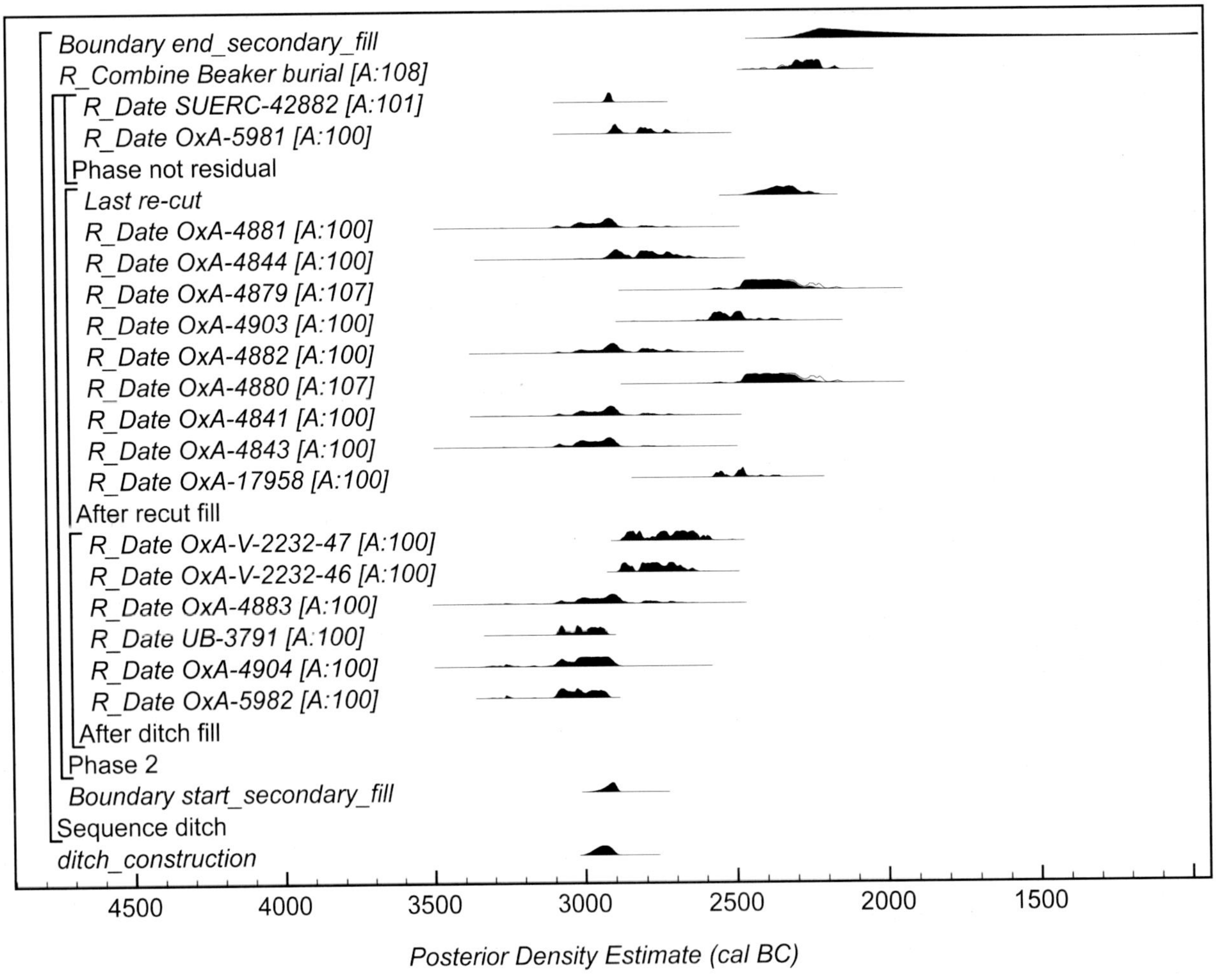

Boundary end_secondary_fill
R_Combine Beaker burial [A:108]
R_Date SUERC-42882 [A:101]
R_Date OxA-5981 [A:100]
Phase not residual
Last re-cut
R_Date OxA-4881 [A:100]
R_Date OxA-4844 [A:100]
R_Date OxA-4879 [A:107]
R_Date OxA-4903 [A:100]
R_Date OxA-4882 [A:100]
R_Date OxA-4880 [A:107]
R_Date OxA-4841 [A:100]
R_Date OxA-4843 [A:100]
R_Date OxA-17958 [A:100]
After recut fill
R_Date OxA-V-2232-47 [A:100]
R_Date OxA-V-2232-46 [A:100]
R_Date OxA-4883 [A:100]
R_Date UB-3791 [A:100]
R_Date OxA-4904 [A:100]
R_Date OxA-5982 [A:100]
After ditch fill
Phase 2
Boundary start_secondary_fill
Sequence ditch
ditch_construction
4500
4000
3500
3000
2500
2000
1500
Posterior Density Estimate (cal BC)

Figure 11.4. Probability distributions of dates from the Ditch fill and Beaker-age burial. The format is identical to Figure 11.3

Interval
0
50
100
150
200
250
300
Interval (yrs)

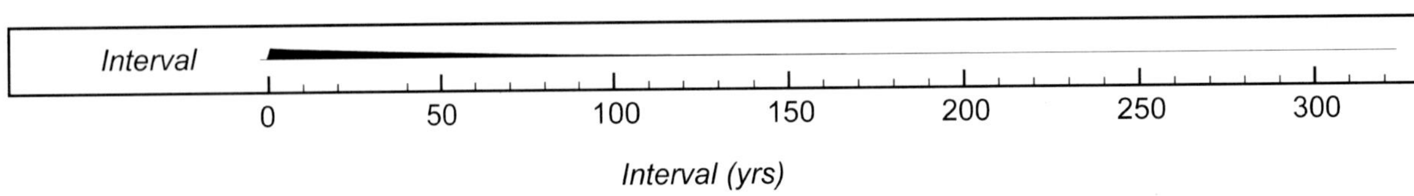

Figure 11.5. Estimated difference between the date of the latest structured deposit (*end_structured_deposits*; Figure 11.3) and the date when construction of the Ditch was completed (*ditch_construction*; Figure 11.2)

Difference
0
100
200
300
400
Interval (yrs)

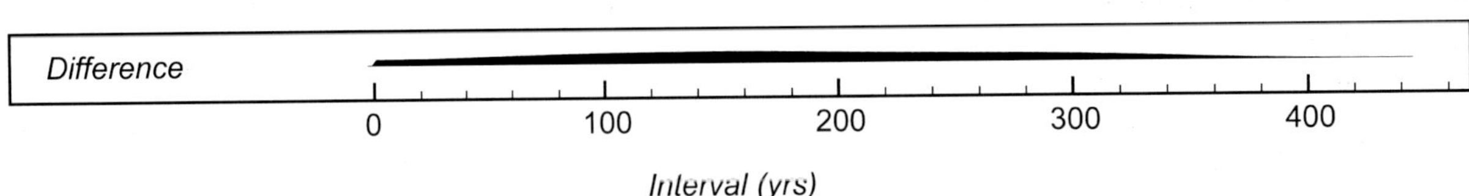

Figure 11.6. Probability distribution showing the number of calendar years over which antlers used for construction of the Ditch were collected. This distribution is derived from the model shown in Figure 11.2

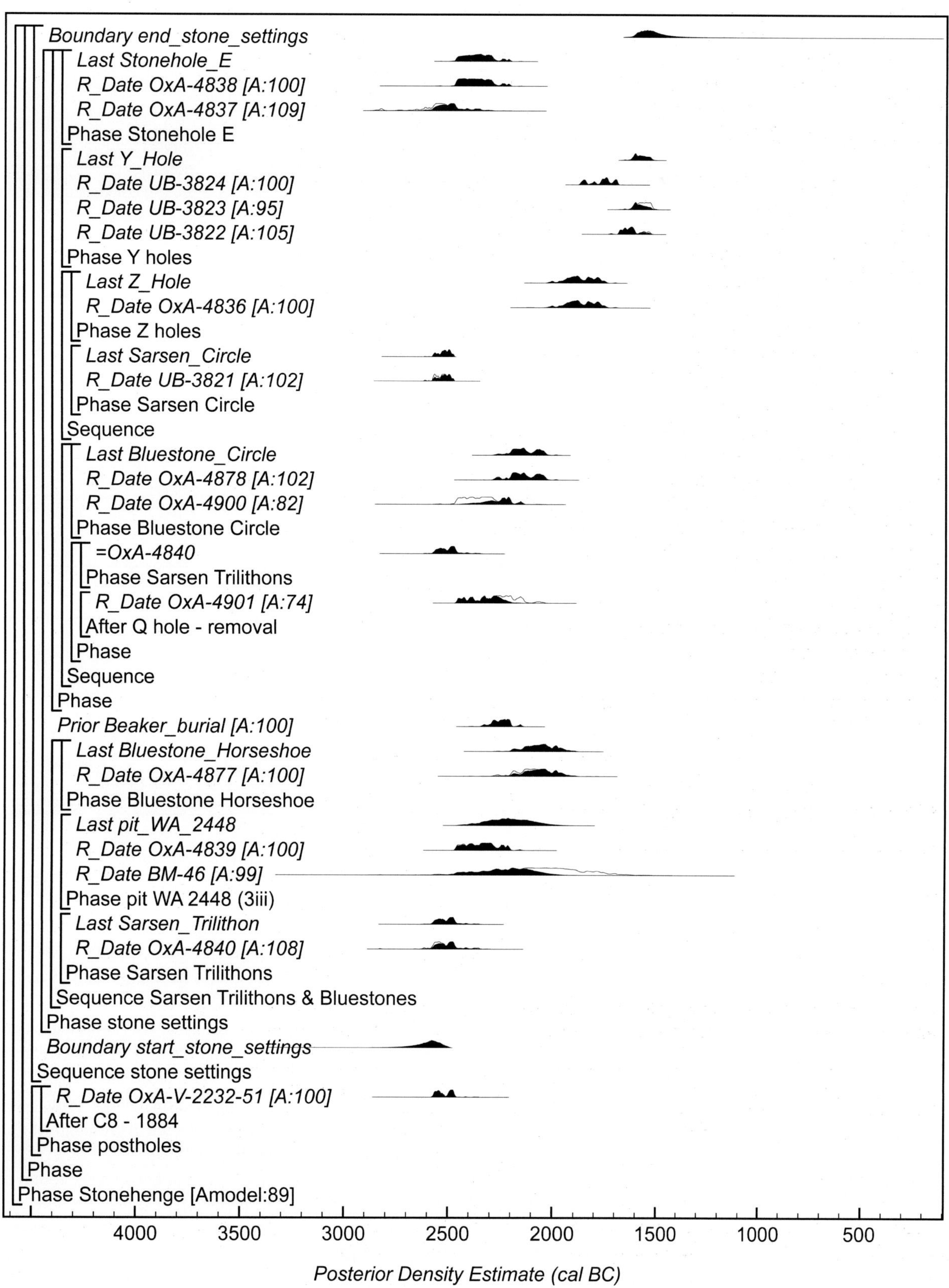

Figure 11.7. Probability distributions of dates from the stone settings. The format is identical to Figure 11.1

Parameter	95% probability (cal BC)	68% probability (cal BC)
Sarsen Circle	*2580–2475*	*2570–2560 (5%)* or *2540–2485 (63%)*
Sarsen Trilithons	*2585–2400 (93%)* or *2380–2350 (2%)*	*2565–2465*
Stonehole E	*2470–2275 (89%)* or *2255–2205 (6%)*	*2435–2295*
Bluestone Circle	*2275–2025*	*2205–2125 (46%)* or *2090–2045 (22%)*
Bluestone Horseshoe	*2205–1920*	*2140–2010 (59%)* or *2000–1920 (9%)*
Z Holes	*2015–1745*	*1945–1870 (39%)* or *1845–1775 (29%)*
Y Holes	*1635–1520*	*1620–1550*

Table 11.5. Highest posterior density intervals for the construction of the stone settings (see Figure 11.7)

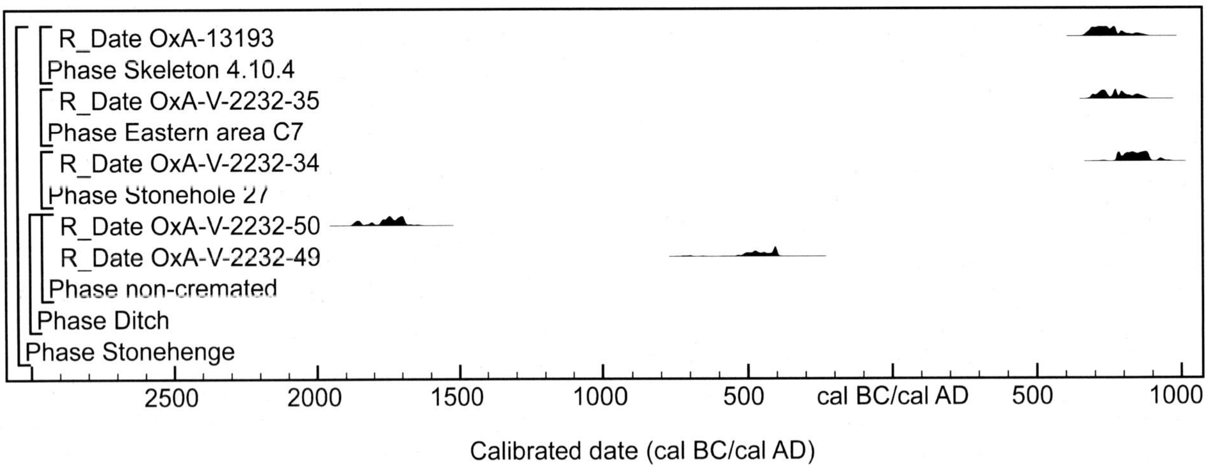

Figure 11.8. Probability distributions of second millennium cal BC and later human dates from Stonehenge. The distributions are the result of simple radiocarbon calibration (Stuiver and Reimer 1993)

Lab number	Material and context	Radiocarbon age (BP)	δ¹³C (‰)	Calibrated date range (95% confidence)	Reference
OxA-18649	Human tooth (M2) from immediately below the turf [STH08 1 16]	3883±31	-20.8	2470–2210 cal BC	Darvill & Wainwright 2009

Table 11.6. Radiocarbon result for a human tooth recovered during the SPACES excavation at Stonehenge

The Ditch chronology

A minor change to the model for the Ditch published in 2012 has therefore now been made, and the revised model is shown in Figure 11.4. OxA-17957, the cremated human bone fragment (54/841) from the ditch fill, can now be excluded from the model, and replaced with the date from the *in situ* deposit (SUERC-42882). SUERC-42882 therefore replaces OxA-17957 in the revised model for the Ditch chronology, and provides a constraint for the digging of the Ditch. It is worth noting that the two measurements are statistically consistent (T'=0.3; ν=1; T'(5%)=3.8) and could therefore be of the same actual age, meaning that they could both derive from the same cremation. Both dates are included in the probability distribution of third-millennium burials (Figure 11.1).

The model for the Ditch chronology (Figures 11.2–11.4) shows good agreement between the radiocarbon dates for all the dated samples from the Ditch and prior information of their stratigraphic position (Amodel: 84). This produces an estimate for the digging of the Ditch of *2995–2900 cal BC* (*95% probability*; *ditch_construction*; Figure 11.2) and probably *2970–2915 cal BC* (*68% probability*).

The antlers found within the Ditch are presumed to have been used for the digging of the Ditch. They were collected over a period of *1–120 years* (*95% probability*; Figure 11.6) and probably *1–55 years* (*68% probability*), which can probably be considered as an indication of the length of time that it might have taken to dig the Ditch.

A number of deposits of animal bones were found on the base of the Ditch terminals either side of the southern entrance. The radiocarbon dating reveals that these were structured deposits of curated material, since they date to between *3650–3090 cal BC* (*95% probability*; *start_structured_deposits*; Figure 11.3) or *3405–3165 cal BC* (*68% probability*) and *3305–2950 cal BC* (*95% probability*; *end_structured_deposits*; Figure 11.3) or *3235–3000 cal BC*

(*68% probability*). We can therefore estimate that the latest of these deposits was already *5–345 years* old (*95% probability*) or *55–270 years* old (*68% probability*) when it was placed on the base of the Ditch (Figure 11.5).

11.6. The radiocarbon determinations and chronological modelling: the stone settings

The results of the radiocarbon dating programme published in Cleal *et al.* (1995) acknowledged the very limited number of samples available for dating from the phases of activity associated with the stone settings, their possible timber precursors, and the Avenue. Since 1995, small-scale excavations of the Avenue (see Chapter 8) and the interior of Stonehenge (Darvill and Wainwright 2009) have taken place with the aim of addressing this issue.

However, the number of reliable radiocarbon measurements available for modelling the third millennium cal BC chronology of Stonehenge's interior and its Avenue is still only 22 and of these, seven are from the Avenue! The radiocarbon dates from the Avenue, and its chronology, are presented in Chapter 8.

The existing dates available for Stonehenge itself were used in the construction of the chronological model and the revised Stages published in 2012 (Darvill *et al.* 2012; Marshall *et al.* 2012) and the reader should refer to those and other publications (Cleal *et al.* 1995; Bayliss *et al.* 1997; Bronk Ramsey and Bayliss 2000) for details of the contexts within previous excavations that produced dated samples, and information on the radiocarbon dates themselves. A description of the various stone settings and their sequence of construction can be found in Chapter 4 and the appendix to Chapter 1.

The chronological model for the stone settings, and earlier postholes, is shown in Figure 11.7 which is derived from the revised sequence outlined by Darvill *et al.* (2012). This model shows good overall agreement (Amodel: 89). Estimates for the dates of construction of the stone settings are shown in Table 11.5.

New dating since publication of the revised chronological Stages in 2012 of three unburnt human teeth from Stonehenge makes little contribution to our understanding of the monument's chronology. Two unburnt human teeth curated at Salisbury Museum were submitted for dating by the SRP. Samples from the two teeth were taken from dentine in their roots. One was a lower left second premolar (OxA-2232-34) from the upper fill (WA 3543; Stonehenge layer) of Stonehole 27, excavated by Atkinson in 1964 (Cleal *et al.* 1995: 188–91). The other was an upper left first premolar (OxA-V-2232-35) recovered by Hawley in 1923 from a possible posthole (1815) in Cutting 7 in the eastern area (McKinley 1995: table 59 [58]). Both teeth produced dates in the first millennium cal AD (Table 11.3; Figure 11.8) and do not contribute to the chronological model for the construction and use of Stonehenge.

In addition, a single human tooth (OxA-18649), excavated within the stone circle in 2008 as part of the SPACES project (Darvill and Wainwright 2009), has also been dated (Table 11.6; Figure 11.1). This sample from immediately below the turf (context 1), although prehistoric in date, may not actually originate from Stonehenge as the turf was imported and put down some 20–25 years ago, possibly incorporating topsoil from beyond the monument (Darvill and Wainwright 2009: 7).

11.7. The radiocarbon determinations and chronological modelling: the cremated human remains from the Aubrey Holes

A description of the Aubrey Holes, and of the SRP excavation of Aubrey Hole 7, can be found in Chapter 4. Osteological analysis of the cremated human remains recovered from Aubrey Hole 7 (AH7), from the pit adjacent to it, and from Aubrey Hole 32 (AH32) appears in Chapter 10,

Laboratory methods

Samples of calcined and non-calcined human bone and teeth from Stonehenge were submitted for radiocarbon-dating to the Scottish Universities Environmental Research Centre (SUERC) and ORAU. Both laboratories maintain a continual programme of quality assurance procedures, as described in Chapter 3.

The initial samples submitted formed a joint radiocarbon-dating programme by the SRP and Beaker People Project (Parker Pearson *et al.* 2016), started in 2007 to determine when Stonehenge was used as a burial space (Parker Pearson *et al.* 2009: 24). The samples of cremated bone dated in 2008, 2012 and 2014 from the excavation of AH7 and an associated cremation (burial 007) form part of the investigation into what is considered to be the largest cemetery yet known from this period.

The samples dated at SUERC were processed using the protocol for dating cremated bone as described in Chapter 7. Samples of cremated human bone dated at ORAU were also pre-treated as described in Chapter 7, before being combusted, graphitised and dated by AMS as described by Brock *et al.* (2010), Dee and Bronk Ramsey (2000) and Bronk Ramsey *et al.* (2004b). The samples with laboratory codes OxA-27089–27093 were all measured as small graphite targets.

Radiocarbon results

The results are conventional radiocarbon ages (Stuiver and Polach 1997) and are listed in Table 11.4. These ages have been calculated using the fractionation correction provided by the $\delta^{13}C$ values measured on the dated material in the AMS. These values include both the natural isotopic composition of the sample and fractionation that occurs during laboratory processing. They are not reported. The $\delta^{13}C$ values reported in Table 11.4 are those measured on sub-samples of the combusted CO_2 by conventional mass spectrometry.

In the case of cremated bone, the meaning of these values is currently unclear, as the natural isotopic ratio of the original bone has been fractionated during both the ancient cremation process and by the selective acid digestion of the bone used during pre-treatment. They are reported, however, in the hope that their meaning will become clear in the future.

The calibrated date ranges for the samples have been calculated using the maximum intercept method (Stuiver and Reimer 1986), and are quoted with end points rounded outwards to ten years, or five years if the error is <25 years. The probability distributions of the calibrated dates, calculated using the probability method (Stuiver and Reimer 1993), are shown in Figure 11.1. They have been calculated using OxCal v4.1.7 (Bronk Ramsey 2009a) and the internationally-agreed atmospheric calibration dataset for the northern hemisphere, IntCal09 (Reimer *et al.* 2009).

In situ cremations from the Aubrey Holes

At present only a single sample (OxA-18036) from an *in situ* cremation burial within an Aubrey Hole has been dated (AH32, excavated by Atkinson and curated in Salisbury Museum; Atkinson *et al.* 1952; Parker Pearson *et al.* 2009: 26). The importance of this sample is due to the fact that it is 'possibly from a primary context' (Walker 1995a: 101), a view reinforced by the reinterpretation of the Aubrey Holes as stoneholes (Parker Pearson *et al.* 2009: 32). In other cases, cremation deposits were interpreted by Hawley as inserted after the standing stones in these holes had been erected and even after they had been withdrawn (Walker 1995b: 152; Willis *et al.* 2016: 352). Thus the cremation deposit in this Aubrey Hole seems to have been the exception to the normal practice, apparently contemporary with erection of the standing stone, with cremated bones mixed into the chalk rubble packing around its base.

The 150.7g of cremated bone recovered from context 3008 (AH32) probably represents only part of the whole cremation burial (maximum 15% of expected body weight; McKinley 1993; 1995: 458). A few scattered fragments of cremated bone from the 'disturbed main fill' were recovered (Atkinson *et al.* 1952) but this material does not survive and therefore it is not possible to determine whether it formed part of the same burial (McKinley 1995: 458).

Re-excavation of Aubrey Hole 7 in 2008 revealed a bowl-shaped pit (008) immediately adjacent to the cut of the Aubrey Hole itself, containing an undisturbed cremation burial (007; weight 1,101.47g). Unfortunately, pit 008's relationship with AH7 could not be established because of truncation by previous excavations, although it is likely that the cremation is later than the Aubrey Hole which may have acted as a focus for its deposition (see Chapter 4 for the excavation report).

Two measurements on calcined femoral shaft fragments from the cremation deposit (007) in pit 008 (SUERC-30410, 4420±35 BP; and OxA-27086, 4317±33 BP) are statistically consistent at 99% confidence ($T'=4.6$; $\nu=1$; $T'(1\%)=6.6$), and a weighted mean (4366±25 BP) has been taken as the best estimate of the date of the cremation.

The measurements on the dated *in situ* cremation burials, from AH32 (OxA-18036; 4332±35 BP) and pit 008 adjacent to AH7 (weighted mean 007: 4366±25 BP), are statistically consistent ($T'=0.6$; $\nu=1$; $T'(5\%)=3.8$; Ward and Wilson 1978) and could therefore be of the same actual age. Given that only two independent events associated with the Aubrey Holes have been dated, we have not modelled this phase of activity. Figure 11.2 therefore shows the chronological relationship between the digging of the Ditch (see above) and the dated cremations from AH32 and the pit adjacent to AH7.

The cremated human remains recovered from Aubrey Hole 7

For a full account of the circumstances of the burial of cremated remains in AH7 in 1935, and their retrieval in 2008 by the SRP, see Chapter 4. For the detailed osteological analysis of these remains, see Chapter 10.

During excavation and analysis, it proved impossible to separate out the 52–58 separate cremation deposits that are likely to have filled the four sandbags (long since decayed) that Hawley's assistant, Robert Newall, deposited in AH7 in 1935. Examination of all the bone fragments recovered from AH7 in 2008 revealed that an MNI of 21 adults and five sub-adults could be identified from the adult occipital bones and sub-adult skeletal elements.

A total of 24 right internal auditory meatii (IAM) of the petrous bones were identified (with the left IAMs numbering 15) but it is difficult to distinguish differences between adult and juvenile petrous bones (Baker *et al.* 2005: 37), and thus these 24 right IAMs could derive from adults, sub-adults or indeed a mixture of age ranges.

Although right IAMs therefore provide the largest total MNI, it was decided that another element, the occipital bone of the skull (with almost as high an MNI of 21 adults) provided the best element for sampling for radiocarbon dating, for several reasons:

1. The occipital bones (see Figures 10.19–10.20) were firmly identifiable as belonging to adults.
2. The IAM's complex structure has the potential for yielding future insights with new techniques (see Figures 10.15, 10.21–10.22), so full preservation is the best course of action for this bone.
3. The occipital bone has a simple structure and thus has low potential for future analysis; it can also be easily CT-scanned to make duplicate copies.
4. The relatively large size of the occipital fragments, and the proportion and high density of their compact bone (as opposed to trabecular/diploë bone) makes these bone fragments more appropriate for radiocarbon-dating without destroying the entire fragment or removing diagnostic features.
5. The morphological characteristics of the occipital bone can be used to determine biological sex, thereby providing an important extra dimension for investigating the dated individuals.

Estimation of sub-adult MNI in the assemblage was produced by counting the number of duplicated skeletal elements in each of the broad age categories: infant, young child and juvenile. An MNI of five sub-adults was identified but only three were selected for sampling for radiocarbon-dating. For example, the age category of 'infant' is represented by a single bone fragment that would be entirely destroyed in the dating process and may, in any case, be too small a sample to obtain a radiocarbon date.

Samples from six of the individuals from AH7 dated at ORAU were also dated at SUERC as part of a further quality assurance programme, given the importance of the assemblage (Table 11.4). In addition, a single sample (390) was dated twice at ORAU as part of the laboratory's normal internal quality assurance protocols.

Five of the six replicate measurements are statistically consistent (Table 11.4) with only the measurements on sample 225 (OxA-27089 and SUERC-42886) being statistically inconsistent at 95% confidence (T'=5.5; ν=1; T'(5%)=3.8). However, these measurements on sample 225 are statistically consistent at 99% confidence (T'=5.5; ν=1; T'(1%)=6.6) and thus weighted means of all the replicate results have been taken as providing the best estimate of the dates of cremation of these individuals.

11.8. Chronological modelling of burials at Stonehenge

The radiocarbon dates from cremated and non-cremated human remains clearly fall into a coherent group concentrated in the first half of the third millennium cal BC (Figure 11.1), excluding the Beaker-period burial and the tooth (OxA-18649; this might have been brought to the site recently). The measurements are not, however, statistically consistent (T'=1343.4; T'(5%)=27; ν= 39.9; Ward and Wilson 1978), and so they certainly represent more than one episode of activity.

Simple visual inspection of the calibrated radiocarbon dates does not allow us to assess the date of Late Neolithic funerary activity at Stonehenge accurately, since the calibration process does not allow for the fact that these radiocarbon dates are related by spatial association (but not by stratigraphic association) – they all come from the same site. Bayesian statistical modelling is required to account for this dependence (Buck *et al.* 1992; Bronk Ramsey 2009a; Bayliss *et al.* 2007a), which we have undertaken using OxCal v.4.1.7 (Bronk Ramsey 1995; 1998; 2001; 2009a). The date ranges from these models are given *in italics* to distinguish them from simple, calibrated radiocarbon dates.

The model shown in Figure 11.9 interprets the burials as representing a continuous period of activity (Buck *et al.* 1992). This model has poor agreement (Amodel: 55; Bronk Ramsey 1995: 429), with one sample (OxA-17958) considerably later than the main group of early third millennium cal BC burials.

The two main approaches for dealing with outliers in radiocarbon dating are to eliminate them manually from the analysis or to use a more objective statistical approach (Bronk Ramsey 2009b; Christen 1994). We have used the first and excluded OxA-17958 from the model shown in Figure 11.10 (see *The Ditch*, above). This model has good agreement (Amodel: 89) and estimates that burial activity started in *3070–2945 cal BC (95% probability: Start;* Figure 11.10) and probably *3030–2965 cal BC (68% probability)* and ended in *2860–2755 cal BC (95% probability: End;* Figure 11.10) and probably *2860–2820 cal BC (68% probability)*.

There are, though, no archaeological grounds for the exclusion of OxA-17958 given that this cremated human bone can be assumed to be part of a cremation burial, however partial. Hawley noted that cremation burials in the Ditch were indeed very partial (in contrast to those from the Aubrey Holes). In addition, they were found predominantly in its upper fills and are therefore likely to be late in the chronology of the Ditch (Hawley 1928: 157). As a consequence of their incompleteness, cremation burials from the Ditch are thus likely to be under-represented by (or even absent among) recovered occipitals from the AH7 assemblage.

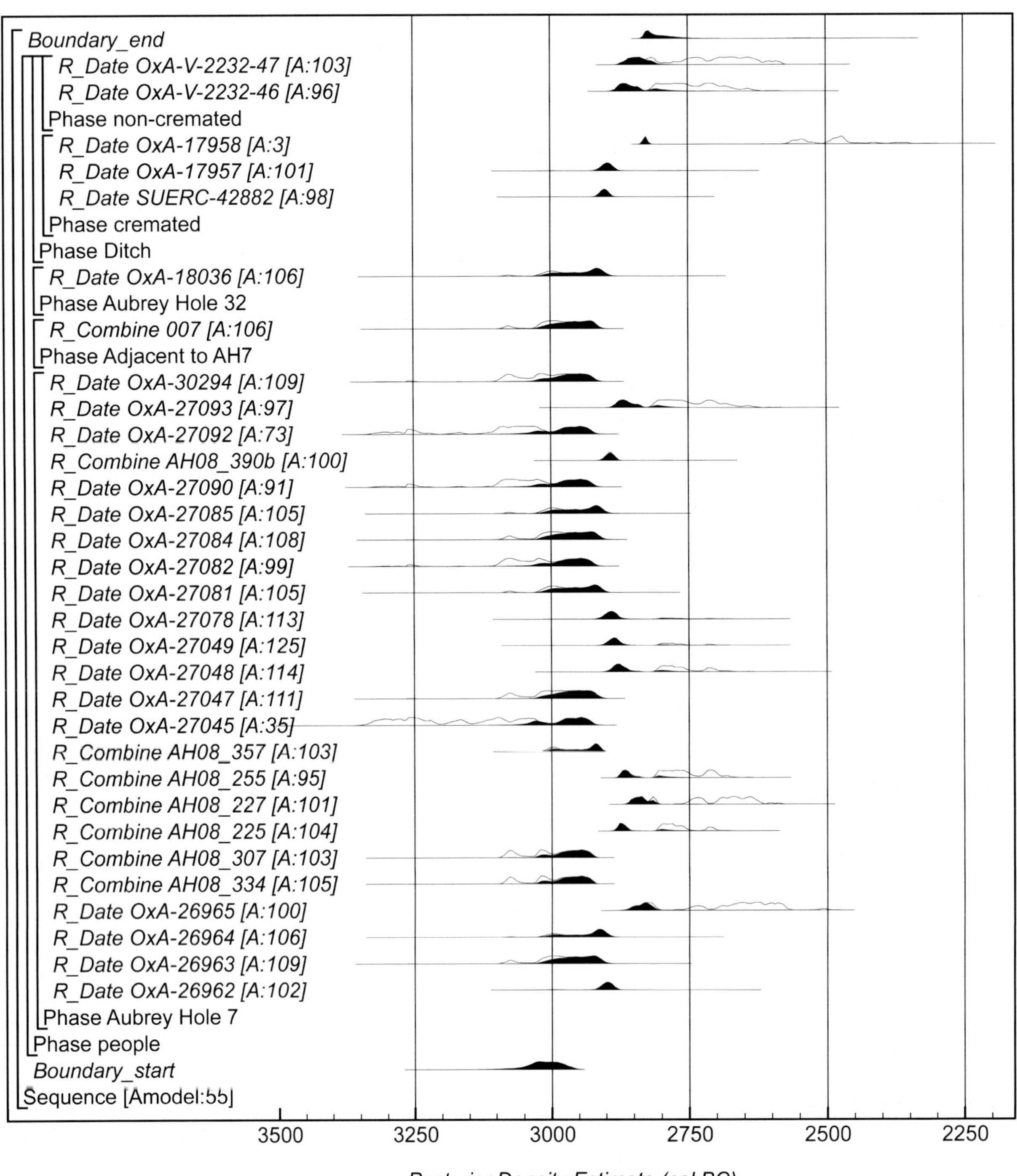

Figure 11.9. Probability distributions of dates from Stonehenge third millennium cal BC burials (uniform model). Each distribution represents the relative probability that an event occurs at a particular time. For each radiocarbon date, two distributions have been plotted: one in outline which is the result of simple radiocarbon calibration, and a solid one based on the chronological model used. The other distributions correspond to aspects of the model. For example, the distribution '*Boundary_start*' is the estimate for when burial activity started. The large square brackets down the left-hand side of the diagram and the OxCal keywords define the overall model exactly

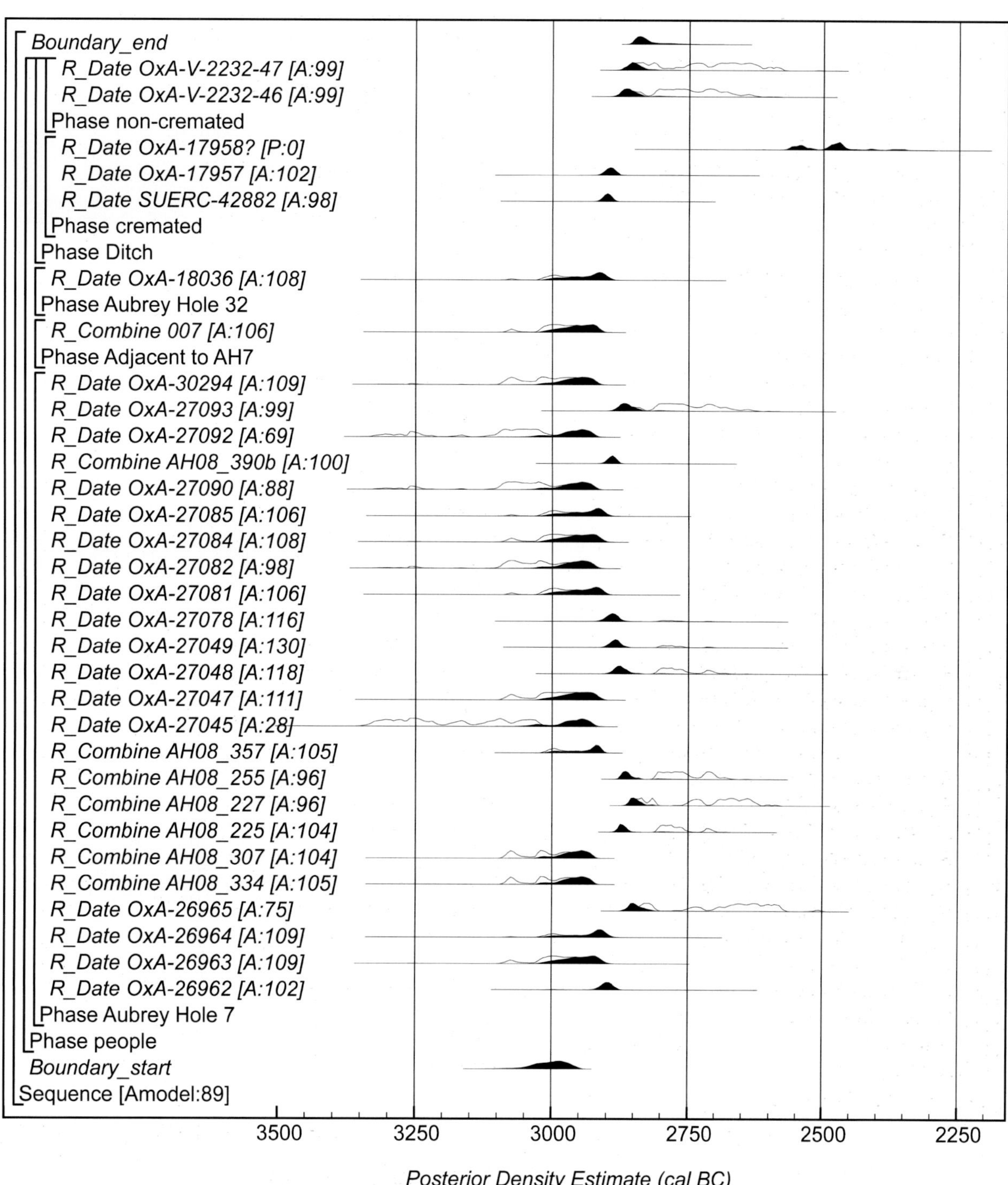

Figure 11.10. Probability distributions of dates from Stonehenge third millennium cal BC burials (OxA-17958 is excluded); the format is identical to Figure 11.9

Trapezoidal models for phases of activity (Lee and Bronk Ramsey 2013) are useful for situations where we expect activity to follow the pattern of a gradual increase, then a period of constant activity, and finally a gradual decrease, unlike the assumptions of a uniform model (Buck *et al.* 1992) that posits a constant phase of activity. The model shown in Figure 11.11 utilises the trapezoid model of Karlsberg (2006) as implemented in OxCal v4.2 (Lee and Bronk Ramsey 2013).

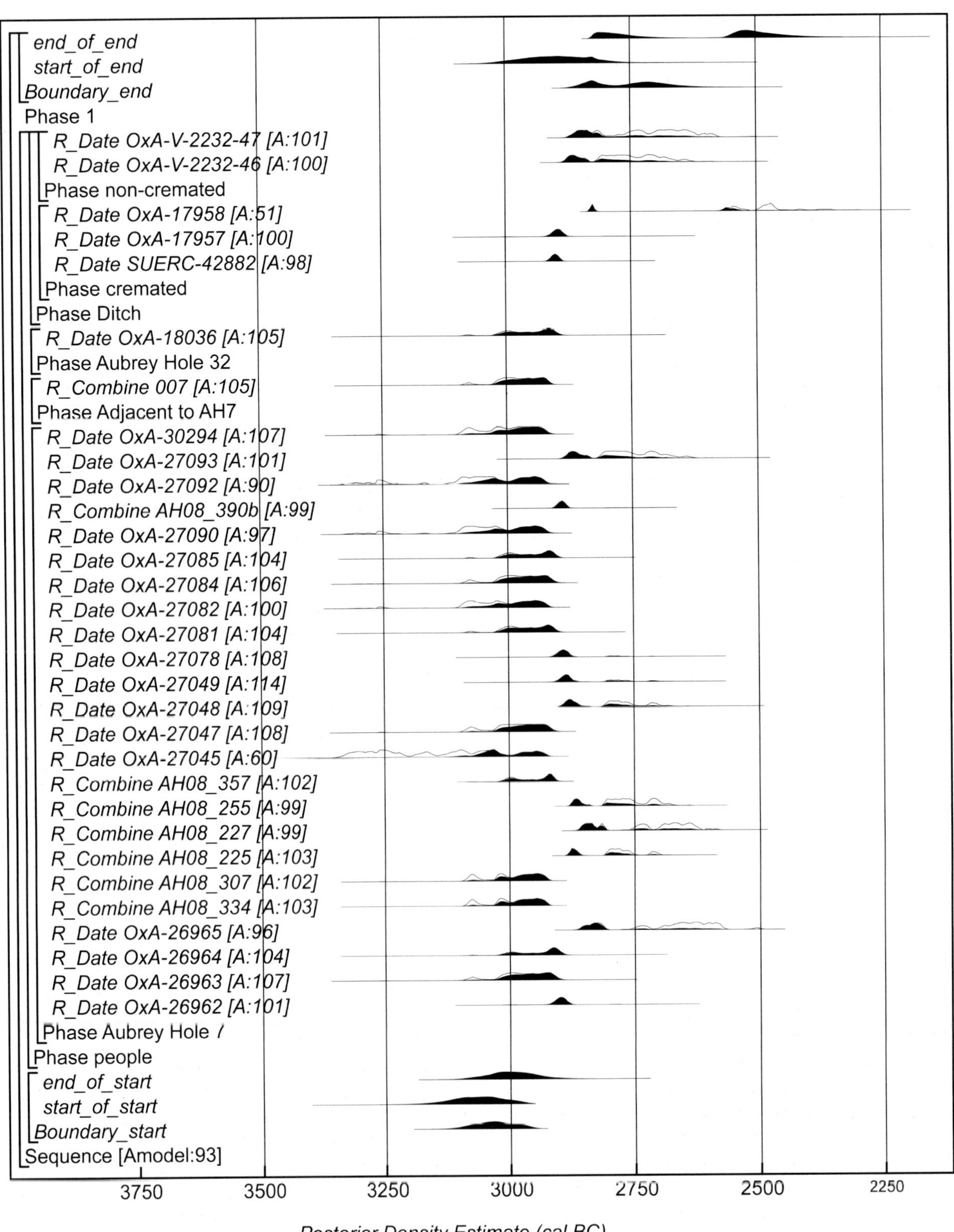

Figure 11.11. Probability distributions of dates from Stonehenge third millennium cal BC burials (trapezium model); the format is identical to Figure 11.9

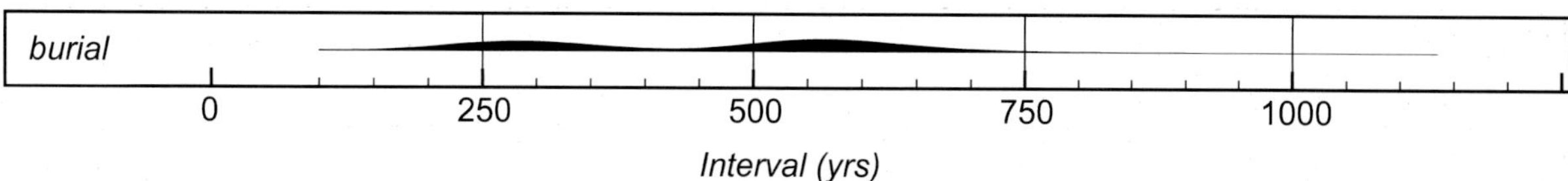

Figure 11.12. Probability distribution showing the number of calendar years during which burial took place at Stonehenge (the distribution is derived from the model shown in Figure 11.11)

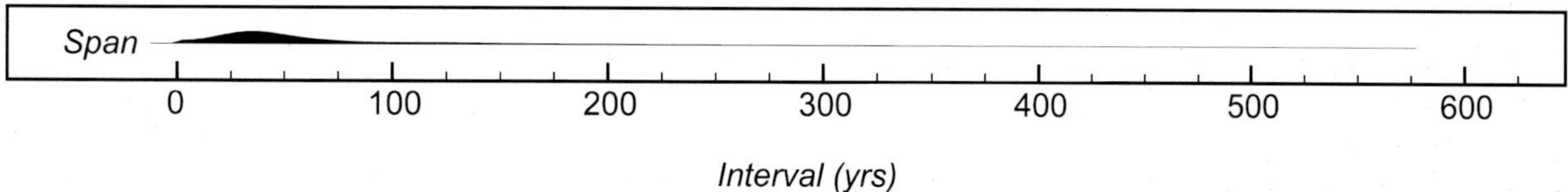

Figure 11.13. Probability distribution showing the number of calendar years during which cremation burial took place at Forteviot

This model (Figure 11.11) has good overall agreement (Amodel: 93) and provides an estimate for the first burial of *3180–2965 cal BC (95% probability: start_of_start;* Figure 11.11) or *3075–2985 cal BC (68% probability).* This model estimates that the last cremation burial took place in *2830–2685* cal BC *(40% probability: end_of_end;* Figure 11.11) or *2565–2380 cal BC (55% probability)* and probably *2825–2760 cal BC (28% probability)* or *2550–2465 cal BC (40% probability).* The model estimates that cremation burial took place for *170–715 years (95% probability;* Figure 11.12) and probably *225–345 years (26% probability)* or *485–650 years (26% probability).*

A trapezoid prior model more accurately reflects the uncertainties in processes such as the use of a cremation cemetery. In the uniform model, there is an abrupt increase from no use to maximum use while the trapezoid model allows for a gradual increase followed by a period of constant deposition, followed by a gradual decline. The parameters from the uniform phase of activity model (Figure 11.10) give more precise estimates than those of the trapezoid parameters. This is because the parameters from this model estimate the onset and end of significant cremation activity, whereas those from the trapezoid model (Figure 11.11) represent the very first and last use.

Hence, even though the estimated start and end dates in Figure 11.10 (a uniform phase of activity) give more precise temporal constraints for the use of Stonehenge as a cemetery, the trapezoid phase model (Figure 11.11) is still preferred. This is because we do not have the archaeological information to show that there was an abrupt change *a priori*. We believe that the trapezoid model better reflects the nature of the archaeological data contributing to the model's prior information.

11.9. Discussion

Cremation burials

There are very few human remains in Britain dated to the early and mid-third millennium cal BC, a period when the rite of inhumation burial seems, by and large, not to have been practised (rare exceptions are documented in Healy 2012). Instead, cremation burials probably of this date are known from a small number of sites. Stonehenge is the largest known cemetery from this period, with small cemeteries excavated at Dorchester-on-Thames (Atkinson *et al.* 1951) and Forteviot (Noble and Brophy 2011; Noble *et al.* 2017). Cremation burials that may also date to this period, or slightly earlier, have been found at Barford, Warks. (Oswald 1969), Duggleby Howe, North Yorks. (Mortimer 1905); Llandegai, Gwynedd (Houlder 1968; Lynch and Musson 2004) and West Stow, Suffolk (West 1990).

Within the Stonehenge World Heritage Site, a small penannular enclosure south of Winterbourne Stoke Crossroads contained deposits of cremated bone (Arup Atkins 2017b: 19–21). A sample from the largest of these cremation deposits provided a date of 2890–2620 cal BC (95% confidence; SUERC-70556; 4167±33 BP). Single cremation burials of slightly later date are known from Durrington MoD HQ (2590–2460 cal BC (95% confidence; SUERC-49176; 4000±34 BP); Thompson and Powell 2018: 17–18) and Woodhenge, where a cremation burial dating to 2580–2460 cal BC (95% confidence; OxA-19047; 3997±30 BP) was excavated from within posthole C14 (Cunnington 1929: 29; to be reported on in Volume 3). An undated cremation deposit from Coneybury henge may also belong to this period on the basis of its stratigraphic position within the henge ditch (Richards 1990: 158).

With relatively few cremation burials independently dated from this period, the Stonehenge assemblage is the most important in Britain, regardless of the significance of the site itself. The radiocarbon-dating programme has

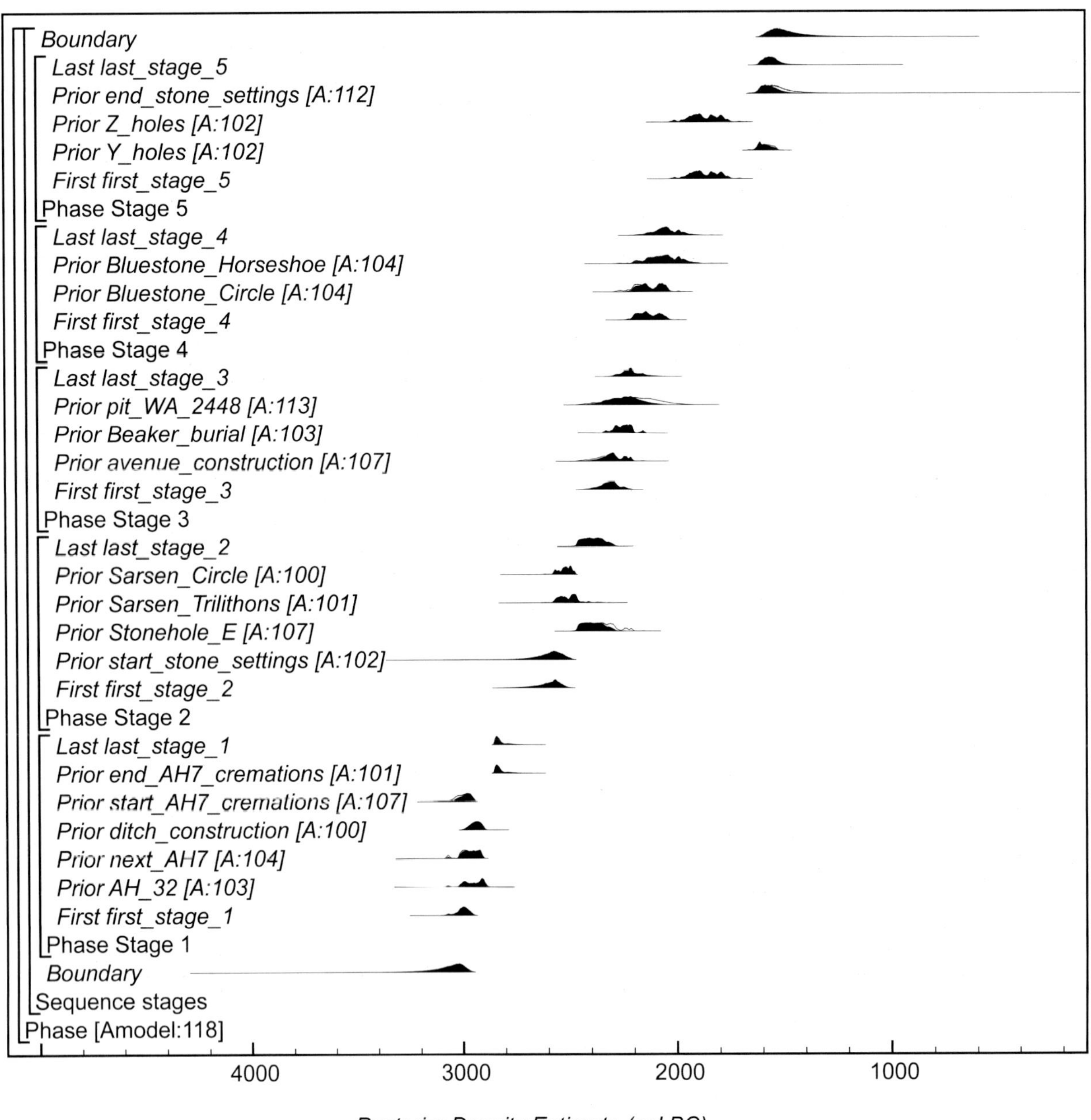

Figure 11.14. Chronological model for the five stages. The probability distributions for the major archaeological events at Stonehenge have been taken from the models shown in Figures 11.2–11.4 and 11.7 and are shown in outline. Other distributions are based on the chronological model defined here, and shown in black

revealed that use of the site as a cremation cemetery was long-lived, lasting many centuries. This is in clear contrast to the albeit much smaller cremation cemetery at Forteviot, for example, where the dated cremation activity is estimated to have lasted between *5–75 years* (*68% probability*; Figure 11.13).

The five Stages of construction at Stonehenge

Using the revised sequence outlined by Darvill *et al.* (2012), the estimates for the main constructional phases of the monument have been incorporated into a model (Figure 11.14) as standardised likelihoods to provide an indication of the chronology of Stonehenge through its five main stages. The model shows good overall agreement (Amodel: 118). The estimates for the start

Parameter	95% probability (cal BC)	68% probability (cal BC)
first_stage_1	3080–2950	3025–2970
last_stage_1	2865–2755	2860–2820
first_stage_2	2740–2505	2630–2530
last_stage_2	2470–2300	2450–2340
first_stage_3	2400–2220	2350–2270
last_stage_3	2300–2100	2260–2150
first_stage_4	2210–2030	2195–2115 (51%) or 2090–2060 (17%)
last_stage_4	2155–1920	2100–1975
first_stage_5	2010–1745 (1%) or 1980–1745 (94%)	1940–1870 (38%) or 1845–1770 (30%)
last_stage_5	1620–1465	1600–1525

Table 11.7. Highest posterior density intervals for the beginnings and endings of the five stages of construction (see Figure 11.15)

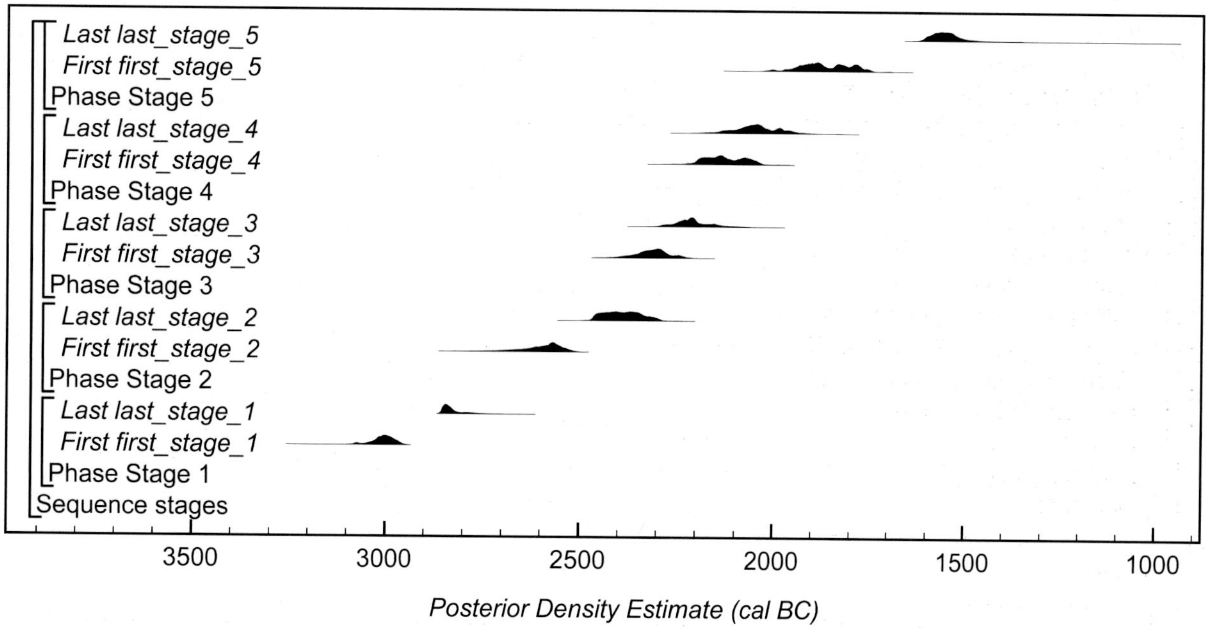

Figure 11.15. Beginnings and endings for the five stages. The distributions are derived from the model shown in Figure 11.14

and end date of each of the five stages are derived from the first and last dated events in each stage (Table 11.7; Figure 11.15).

Figure 11.16 and Table 11.8 show the span of the five stages, while Figure 11.17 and Table 11.9 set out the estimated intervals between the five stages. The most notable feature is the estimated length of time between the end of Stage 1 (Ditch, Bank, Aubrey Holes and cremations) and the start of Stage 2 (the sarsen stone settings).

It may be that some of the pits, postholes and stakeholes within the earthwork enclosure date to this period of apparent inactivity, especially as many of these cut features stratigraphically pre-date the sarsen stone settings. At present the only actually dating evidence for these is a *terminus post quem* of 2580–2460 cal BC (95% confidence) provided by OxA-V-2232-51 for posthole 1884 in Cutting 8 (see *Animal bone and antler*, above).

Undoubtedly the most important results for understanding the chronology of Stonehenge derive from the dating of cremated bone from Aubrey Holes 7 and 32 and from burial 007 in pit 008 on the edge of Aubrey Hole 7. The dating of the *in situ* cremated bones from AH32 and burial 007 has, for the first time, allowed such features to be independently dated; the dating of the AH7 assemblage does not date the Aubrey Holes (since Hawley's assemblage also contains remains originally deposited in the Ditch and Bank). Before the advent of radiocarbon-dating of cremated bone (Lanting *et al.* 2001), the Aubrey Holes had simply

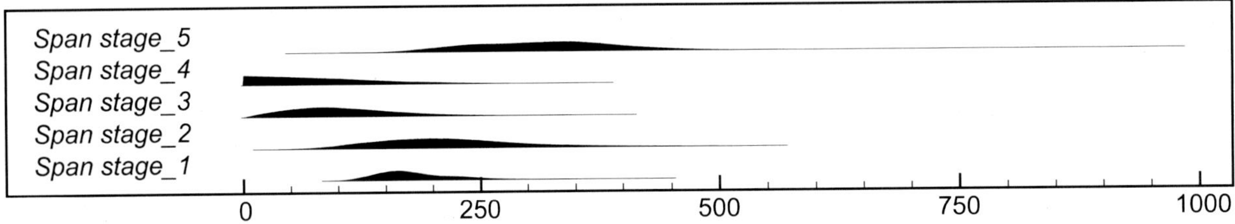

Figure 11.16. Probability distribution showing the number of calendar years which the five stages lasted. The distributions are derived from the model shown in Figure 11.14

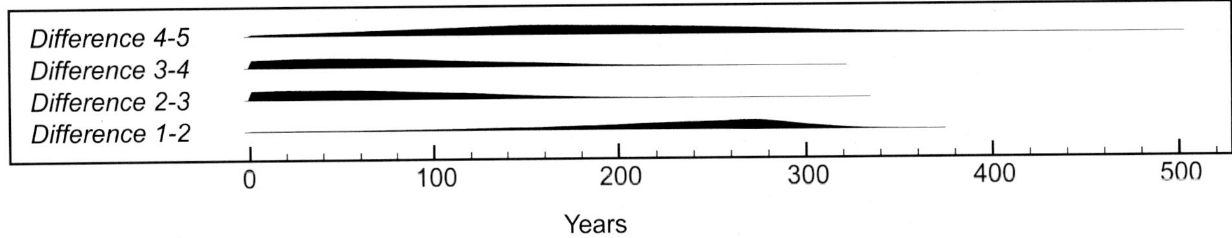

Figure 11.17. Probability distribution showing the number of calendar years between the start and end of stages. The distributions are derived from the model shown in Figure 11.14

Parameter	95% probability (years)	68% probability (years)
Stage 1	105–270	125–210
Stage 2	75–375	120–270
Stage 3	5–215	35–145
Stage 4	1–205	1–110
Stage 5	165–465	225–390

Table 11.8. Highest posterior density spans of the five stages of construction (see Figure 11.16)

Parameter	95% probability (years)	68% probability (years)
Stage 1–2	75–335	185–305
Stage 2–3	1–170	1–100
Stage 3–4	1–185	1–105
Stage 4–5	10–335	90–270

Table 11.9. Highest posterior density intervals between the five stages of construction

been assigned to the first phase of activity at Stonehenge on the basis that their accurate layout could not have been achieved with the sarsen circle and trilithons (Stage 2) in place (Walker 1995: 96). The Aubrey Holes can now be placed firmly in Stage 1 of the Stonehenge sequence.

At present the chronological models for the sarsen stone settings (along with alternative readings – see Marshall *et al.* 2012) are all based on the belief that the major settings were the product of single (relatively quick) unitary episodes of activity rather than the result of longer and more piecemeal episodes of construction (Bayliss *et al.* 1997: 46). Given the limited number of samples available, such an assumption remains the only realistic way of modelling the chronology.

Previous sensitivity analyses (Marshall *et al.* 2012) have demonstrated that the key component of the models that determines differences between the models of Stonehenge's chronology is the relationship between the sarsen circle and the trilithons. The choice of a preferred model is, therefore, at present a simple matter of archaeological interpretation, and the model could be refined were further excavation to provide more samples associated with the major constructional events (for example, the erection of the sarsen circle). The model we have presented here is our preference for the chronology of the monument because it incorporates the most reliable reading of the stratigraphy of the monument's interior (Darvill and Wainwright 2009; Darvill *et al.* 2012; Parker Pearson *et al.* 2007; 2009).

Bibliography

Abbott, M. and Anderson-Whymark, H. with Aspden, D., Badcock, A., Davies, T., Felter, M., Ixer, R., Parker Pearson, M. and Richards, C. 2012. *Stonehenge laser scan: archaeological analysis*. Research Report 32-2012. Swindon: English Heritage.

Adams, J.L. 2002. *Ground Stone Analysis*. Tucson: Center for Desert Archaeology.

Adams, R.L. 2007. *The megalithic tradition of West Sumba, Indonesia: an ethnoarchaeological investigation of megalith construction*. Unpublished PhD thesis, Department of Archaeology, Simon Fraser University.

Aerts-Bijma, A.T., Meijer, H.A.J. and van der Plicht, J. 1997. AMS sample handling in Groningen. *Nuclear Instruments and Methods in Physics Research Section B: Beam Interactions with Materials and Atoms* 123: 221–5.

Aerts-Bijma, A.T., van der Plicht, J. and Meijer, H.A.J. 2001. Automatic AMS sample combustion and CO2 collection. *Radiocarbon* 43: 293–8.

Albarella, U. 1999. 'The mystery of husbandry': medieval animals and the problem of integrating historical and archaeological evidence. *Antiquity* 73: 867–75.

Albarella, U. and Davis, S.J.M. 1994. *The Saxon and medieval animal bones excavated 1985–1989 from West Cotton, Northamptonshire*. Ancient Monuments Laboratory Report 17/94. London: English Heritage.

Albarella, U. and Payne, S. 2005. Neolithic pigs from Durrington Walls, Wiltshire, England: a biometrical database. *Journal of Archaeological Science* 32: 589–99.

Albarella, U. and Serjeantson, D. 2002. A passion for pork: meat consumption at the British Late Neolithic site of Durrington Walls. In P. Miracle and N. Milner (eds) *Consuming Passions and Patterns of Consumption*. Cambridge: McDonald Institute. 33–49.

Alexander, J., Ozanne, P.C. and Ozanne, A. 1960. A report on the investigation of a round barrow at Arreton Down, Isle of Wight. *Proceedings of the Prehistoric Society* 26: 263–302.

Algar, D. 1997. Durrington, Wiltshire. In R. Bland and J. Orna-Ornstein (eds) *Coin Hoards from Roman Britain 10*. London: British Museum Press. 296–338.

Allen, M.J. 1994. *The land-use history of the southern English chalklands with an evaluation of the Beaker period using environmental data: colluvial deposits and cultural indicators*. Unpublished PhD thesis, University of Southampton.

Allen, M.J. 1995a. Before Stonehenge: Mesolithic human activity in a wildwood landscape. In R.M.J. Cleal, K.E. Walker and R. Montague, *Stonehenge in its Landscape: twentieth-century excavations*. London: English Heritage. 470–3.

Allen M.J. 1995b. Before Stonehenge. In R.M.J. Cleal, K.E. Walker and R. Montague, *Stonehenge in its Landscape: twentieth-century excavations*. London: English Heritage. 41–63.

Allen, M.J. 1997a. Environment and land use: the economic development of the communities who built Stonehenge (an economy to support the stones). In B.W. Cunliffe and C. Renfrew (eds) *Science and Stonehenge*. Oxford: Oxford University Press. 115–44.

Allen, M.J. 1997b. Land-use history: land molluscan evidence. In R.J.C. Smith, F. Healy, M.J. Allen, E.L. Morris, I. Barnes and P.J. Woodward, *Excavations along the Route of the Dorchester By-Pass, Dorset, 1986-8*. Salisbury: Wessex Archaeology. 166–83.

Allen, M.J. 1997c. Landscape, land-use and farming. In R.J.C. Smith, F. Healy, M.J. Allen, E.L. Morris, I. Barnes and P.J. Woodward, *Excavations along the Route of the Dorchester By-Pass, Dorset, 1986-8*. Salisbury: Wessex Archaeology. 277–83.

Allen, M.J. 2002. The chalkland landscape of Cranborne Chase: a prehistoric human ecology. *Landscapes* 3: 55–69.

Allen, M.J. 2017a. The southern English chalklands: molluscan evidence for the nature of the post-glacial woodland cover. In M.J. Allen (ed.) *Molluscs in Archaeology: methods, approaches and applications*. Oxford: Oxbow. 144–64.

Allen, M.J. 2017b. The geoarchaeology of context: sampling for land snails (on archaeological sites and colluvium). In M.J. Allen (ed.) *Molluscs in Archaeology: methods, approaches and applications*. Oxford: Oxbow. 30–47.

Allen, M.J. and Bayliss, A. 1995. Appendix 2. The radiocarbon dating programme. In R.M.J. Cleal, K.E. Walker and R. Montague, *Stonehenge in its Landscape: twentieth-century excavations*. London: English Heritage. 511–35.

Allen, M.J. and Gardiner, J. 2002. A sense of time: cultural markers in the Mesolithic of southern England. In B. David and M. Wilson (eds) *Inscribed Landscapes: marking and making places*. Honolulu: University of Hawai'i Press. 139–53.

Allen, M.J. and Gardiner, J. 2009. If you go down to the woods today: a re-evaluation of the chalkland postglacial woodland: implications for prehistoric communities. In M.J. Allen, N. Sharples and T. O'Connor (eds) *Land and People: papers in memory of John G. Evans*. Oxford: Oxbow. 49–66.

Allen M.J. and Scaife, R.G. 2007. A new downland prehistory: long term environmental change on the southern English chalklands. In A. Fleming and R. Hingley (eds) *Prehistoric and Roman Landscapes: landscape history after Hoskins*. Macclesfield: Windgather Press. 16–31.

Allen, M.J., Chan, B., Cleal, R.M.J., French, C., Marshall, P., Pollard, J., Pullen, R., Richards, C., Ruggles, C., Robinson, D., Rylatt, J., Thomas, J., Welham, K. and Parker Pearson, M. 2016. Stonehenge's Avenue and Bluestonehenge. *Antiquity* 90: 991–1008.

Allen, M.J., Entwistle, R. and Richards, J. 1990. Molluscan studies. In J. Richards, *The Stonehenge Environs Project*. London: English Heritage. 253–8.

Anderberg, A.L. 1994. *Atlas of Seeds and Small Fruits of Northwest-European Plant Species (Sweden, Norway, Denmark, East Fennoscandia and Iceland) with Morphological Descriptions. Part 4, Resedaceae–Umbelliferae*. Stockholm: Swedish Museum of Natural History.

Andersen, S.T. 1970. *The Relative Pollen Productivity and Pollen Representation of North European Trees, and Correction Factors for Tree Pollen Spectra*. Danmarks Geologiske Undersøgelse (Ser. II) 96. Copenhagen: C.A. Reitzel.

Andersen, S.T. 1973. The differential pollen productivity of trees and its significance for the interpretation of a pollen diagram from a forested region. In H.J.B Birks and R.G. West (eds) *Quaternary Plant Ecology*. Oxford: Blackwell. 109–15.

Andrefsky, W. 1998. *Lithics: macroscopic approaches to analysis*. Cambridge: Cambridge University Press.

Aronson, M. 2010. *If Stones Could Speak: unlocking the secrets of Stonehenge*. Washington DC: National Geographic.

Arup Atkins Joint Venture. 2017a. *A303 Amesbury to Berwick Down: geophysical survey report stage 1 final*. Salisbury: Arup Atkins and Wessex Archaeology.

Arup Atkins Joint Venture. 2017b. *A303 Amesbury to Berwick Down: archaeological trial trench evaluation*. Salisbury: Arup Atkins and Wessex Archaeology.

Ascher, E., Markevich, N., Schutzer, R.W., Kallakuri, S., Jacob, T. and Hingorani, A.P. 2003. Small popliteal artery aneurysms: are they clinically significant? *Journal of Vascular Surgery* 37: 755–60.

Ashbee, P. 1966. Fussell's Lodge long barrow excavations, 1957. *Archaeologia* 100: 1–80.

Ashbee, P. 1970. *The Earthen Long Barrow in Britain*. London: Dent.

Ashbee, P. 1998. Stonehenge: its possible non-completion, slighting and dilapidation. *Wiltshire Archaeological and Natural History Magazine* 91: 139–43.

Ashbee, P., Bell, M. and Proudfoot, E. 1989. *Wilsford Shaft: excavations 1960–62*. London: English Heritage.

Ashbee, P., Smith, I.F. and Evans, J.G. 1979. Excavation of three long barrows near Avebury, Wiltshire. *Proceedings of the Prehistoric Society* 45: 207–300.

Ashmore, P.J. 1999. Radiocarbon dating: avoiding errors by avoiding mixed samples. *Antiquity* 73: 124–30.

Ashmore, W. and Knapp, A.B. 1999. Archaeological landscapes: constructed, conceptualised, ideational. In W. Ashmore and A.B. Knapp (eds) *Archaeologies of Landscape: contemporary perspectives*. Oxford: Blackwell. 1–30.

Atkinson, R.J.C. 1951. The excavations at Dorchester, Oxfordshire, 1946–51. *Archaeological Newsletter* 44: 56–9.

Atkinson, R.J.C. 1956. *Stonehenge*. London: Hamish Hamilton.

Atkinson, R.J.C. 1957. Worms and weathering. *Antiquity* 31: 219–33.

Atkinson, R.J.C. 1961. Neolithic engineering. *Antiquity* 35: 292–9.

Atkinson, R.J.C. 1979. *Stonehenge*. 3rd edition. Harmondsworth: Penguin.

Atkinson, R.J.C., Piggott, C.M. and Sandars, N. 1951. *Excavations at Dorchester, Oxon*. Oxford: Ashmolean Museum.

Atkinson, R.J.C., Piggott, S. and Stone, J.F.S. 1952. The excavation of two additional holes at Stonehenge, and new evidence for the date of the monument. *Antiquaries Journal* 32: 14–20.

Austin, P. 2000. The emperor's new garden: woodland, trees and people in the Neolithic of southern Britain. In A.S. Fairbairn (ed.) *Plants in Neolithic Britain and Beyond*. Neolithic Studies Group Seminar Papers 5. Oxford: Oxbow. 63–78.

Avery, B.W. 1980. *Soil Classification for England and Wales*. Soil Survey Technical Monograph 14. Harpenden: Lawes Agricultural Trust.

Baker, B.J., Dupras, T.L. and Tocheri, M.W. 2005. *Osteology of Infants and Children*. College Station TX: Texas A&M University Press.

Balfour-Brown, F.L. 1964. Charcoal. In N. Thomas, The Neolithic causewayed camp at Robin Hood's Ball, Shrewton. *Wiltshire Archaeological and Natural History Magazine* 59: 1–27.

Ballin, T.B. 2011. The Levallois-like approach of Late Neolithic Britain. In A. Saville (ed.) *Flint and Stone in the Neolithic Period*. Oxford: Oxbow. 37–61.

Barber, M., Field, D. and Topping, P. 1999. *The Neolithic Flint Mines of England*. Swindon: English Heritage and RCHME.

Barclay, A.J. 2011. The pottery [Boscombe Bowmen]. In A.P. Fitzpatrick, *The Amesbury Archer and the Boscombe Bowmen: Bell Beaker burials at Boscombe Down, Amesbury, Wiltshire*. Salisbury: Wessex Archaeology. 36–54.

Barclay, A.J. 2014. Re-dating the Coneybury Anomaly and its implications for understanding the earliest Neolithic pottery from southern England. *Past* 77: 11–13.

Barclay, A.J. and Bayliss, A. 1999. Cursus monuments and the radiocarbon problem. In A.J. Barclay and J. Harding (eds) *Pathways and Ceremonies: the cursus monuments of Britain and Ireland*. Oxford: Oxbow. 11–29.

Barclay, A.J. and Halpin, C. 1998. *Excavations at Barrow Hills, Radley, Oxfordshire. Volume 1, The Neolithic and Bronze Age monument complex*. Thames Valley Landscapes monograph 11. Oxford: Oxford Archaeological Unit.

Barclay, A.J. and Marshall, P. with Higham, T. 2011. Chronology and the radiocarbon dating programme. In A.P. Fitzpatrick, *The Amesbury Archer and the Boscombe Bowmen: Bell Beaker burials at Boscombe Down, Amesbury, Wiltshire*. Salisbury: Wessex Archaeology. 167–84.

Barrett, J.C. 1994. *Fragments from Antiquity: an archaeology of social life in Britain, 2900–1200 BC*. Oxford: Blackwell.

Barrett, J.C., Bradley, R. and Green, M. 1991. *Landscape, Monuments and Society: the prehistory of Cranborne Chase*. Cambridge: Cambridge University Press.

Barton, N. and Bergman, C. 1992. The finds: debitage and cores. In R.N.E. Barton (ed.) *Hengistbury Head, Dorset. Volume 2, The Late Upper Palaeolithic and Early Mesolithic sites*. Oxford: Oxford University Committee for Archaeology. 96–108.

Batchelor, D. 1997. Mapping the Stonehenge World Heritage Site. In B.W. Cunliffe and C. Renfrew (eds) *Science and Stonehenge*. Oxford: Oxford University Press. 61–72.

Bayer, O. and Griffiths, D. 2016. *A pilot study for integrated landscape survey on the Salisbury Plain Training Area: geophysical and photogrammetric surveys of Robin Hood's Ball causewayed enclosure*. Oxford: Oxford University Department for Continuing Education. https://www.conted.ox.ac.uk/mnt/attachments/rhb2016_web.pdf

Bayliss, A., Bronk Ramsey, C. and McCormac, F.G. 1997. Dating Stonehenge. In B.W. Cunliffe and C. Renfrew (eds) *Science and Stonehenge*. Oxford: Oxford University Press. 39–59.

Bayliss, A., Bronk Ramsey, C., van der Plicht, J. and Whittle, A. 2007a. Bradshaw and Bayes: towards a timetable for the Neolithic. *Cambridge Journal of Archaeology* 17 (supplement): 1–28.

Bayliss, A., Healy, F., Whittle, A. and Cooney, G. 2011. Neolithic narratives: British and Irish enclosures in their timescapes. In A.W.R. Whittle, F. Healy, and A. Bayliss, *Gathering Time: dating the Early Neolithic enclosures of southern Britain and Ireland*. Oxford: Oxbow. 682–847.

Bayliss, A., Hedges, R., Otlet, R., Switsur, R. and Walker, J. 2012. *Radiocarbon Dates from Samples Funded by English Heritage between 1981 and 1988*. Swindon: English Heritage.

Bayliss, A., McAvoy, F. and Whittle, A.W.R. 2007b. The world recreated: redating Silbury Hill in its monumental landscape. *Antiquity* 81: 26–53.

Bell, M. 1983. Valley sediments as evidence of prehistoric land-use: a study based on dry valleys in south east England. *Proceeding of the Prehistoric Society* 49: 119–50.

Bell, M. 1986. Archaeological evidence for the date, cause and extent of soil erosion on the chalk. *Journal of the South East Soils Discussion Group* 3: 72–83.

Bell, M. and Walker M.J.C. 2005. *Late Quaternary Environmental Change: physical and human perspectives*. 2nd edition. Harlow: Pearson Prentice Hall.

Bell, M., Fowler, P.J. and Hillson, S. 1996. *The Experimental Earthwork Project 1960–1992*. York: CBA Research Report 100.

Bender, B. 1998. *Stonehenge: making space*. London: Berg.

Bennett, K.D., Whittington, G. and Edwards, K.J. 1994. Recent plant nomenclatural changes and pollen morphology in the British Isles. *Quaternary Newsletter* 73: 1–6.

Berggren, G. 1981. *Atlas of Seeds and Small Fruits of Northwest-European Plant Species (Sweden, Norway, Denmark, East Fennoscandia and Iceland) with Morphological Descriptions. Part 3, Salicaceae–Crucifera*. Stockholm: Swedish Museum of Natural History.

Bevins, R.E, Ixer, R.A. and Pearce, N.G. 2013. Carn Goedog is the likely major source of Stonehenge doleritic bluestones: evidence based on compatible element geochemistry and principal components analysis. *Journal of Archaeological Science* 42: 179–93.

Bewley, R., Crutchley, S.P. and Shell, C.A. 2005. New light on an ancient landscape: lidar survey in the Stonehenge World Heritage Site. *Antiquity* 79: 636–47.

Binford, L.R. 1981. *Bones: ancient men and modern myths*. London: Academic Press.

Birks, H.J.B. 1989. Holocene isochrone maps and patterns of tree spreading in the British Isles. *Journal of Biogeography* 16: 503–40.

Blott, S.J. and Pye, K. 2008. Particle shape: a review and new methods of characterization and classification. *Sedimentology* 55: 31–63.

Boardman, S. and Jones, G. 1990. Experiments on the effects of charring on cereal plant components. *Journal of Archaeological Science* 17: 1–11.

Boessneck, J. 1969. Osteological difference between sheep (*Ovis aries* Linne) and goat (*Capra hircus* Linne). In D. Brothwell and E. Higgs (eds) *Science in Archaeology*. London: Thames & Hudson. 331–58.

Booth, A.St.J. and Stone, J.F.S. 1952. A trial flint-mine at Durrington, Wiltshire. *Wiltshire Archaeological and Natural History Magazine* 54: 381–8.

Bowden, M. 2011. *Stonehenge World Heritage Site Landscape Project: earthworks at Lake and West Amesbury*. Research Report 92-2011. Swindon: English Heritage.

Bowden, M., Soutar, S., Field, D. and Barber, M. 2015. *The Stonehenge Landscape: analysing the Stonehenge World Heritage Site*. Swindon: Historic England.

Bowen, H.C. and Smith, I.F. 1977. Sarsen stones in Wessex: the Society's first investigations in the Evolution of the Landscape Project. *Antiquaries Journal* 57: 185–96.

Bowman S. 1990. *Radiocarbon Dating*. London: British Museum Press.

Bradley, R. 1993. *Altering the Earth: the origins of monuments in Britain and continental Europe*. Edinburgh: Society of Antiquaries of Scotland.

Bradley, R. 1998. *The Significance of Monuments*. London: Routledge.

Bradley, R. 2000. *An Archaeology of Natural Places*. London: Routledge.

Bradley, R. 2002. *The Past in Prehistoric Societies*. London: Routledge.

Bradley, R. and Chambers, R. 1988. A new study of the cursus complex at Dorchester-on-Thames. *Oxford Journal of Archaeology* 7: 271–89.

Bradley, R. and Gordon, K. 1988 Human skulls from the River Thames, their dating and significance. *Antiquity* 62: 503–9.

Brickley, M. and McKinley, J.I. (eds) 2004. *Guidelines to the Standards for Recording Human Remains*. Technical Paper 7. Southampton and Reading: BABAO and IFA.

Britton, J. (ed.) 1847. *The Natural History of Wiltshire, by John Aubrey FRS (written between 1656 and 1691)*. London: Wiltshire Topographical Society.

Brock, F., Higham, T., Ditchfield, P. and Bronk Ramsey, C. 2010. Current pretreatment methods for AMS radiocarbon dating at the Oxford Radiocarbon Accelerator Unit (ORAU). *Radiocarbon* 52: 103–12.

Bronk Ramsey, C. 1995. Radiocarbon calibration and analysis of stratigraphy: the OxCal program. *Radiocarbon* 37: 425–30.

Bronk Ramsey, C. 1998. Probability and dating. *Radiocarbon* 40: 461–74.

Bronk Ramsey, C. 2001. Development of the radiocarbon calibration program OxCal. *Radiocarbon* 43: 355–63.

Bronk Ramsey, C. 2009a. Bayesian analysis of radiocarbon dates. *Radiocarbon* 51: 337–60.

Bronk Ramsey, C. 2009b. Dealing with outliers and offsets in radiocarbon dating. *Radiocarbon* 51: 1023–45.

Bronk Ramsey, C. and Bayliss, A. 2000. Dating Stonehenge. In K. Lockyear, T.J.T. Sly and V. Mihăilescu-Bîrliba (eds) *CAA 96: computer applications and quantitative methods in archaeology*. Oxford: BAR (International Series) 845. 29–39.

Bronk Ramsey, C., Ditchfield, P. and Humm, M. 2004b. Using a gas ion source for radiocarbon AMS and GC-AMS. *Radiocarbon* 46: 25–32.

Bronk Ramsey, C., Higham, T.F.G., Bowles, A. and Hedges, R.E.M. 2004a. Improvements to the pretreatment of bone at Oxford. *Radiocarbon* 46: 155–63.

Bronk Ramsey, C., Pettitt, P.B., Hedges, R.E.M., Hodgins, G.W.L. and Owen, D.C. 2000. Radiocarbon dates from the Oxford AMS system: Archaeometry datelist 30. *Archaeometry* 42: 459–79.

Brophy, K. 1999. Seeing the cursus as a symbolic river. *British Archaeology* 44: 6–7.

Brophy, K. 2000. Water coincidence? Cursus monuments and rivers. In A. Ritchie (ed.) *Neolithic Orkney in its European Context*. Oxford: Oxbow. 59–70.

Brophy, K. 2015. *Reading between the Lines: the Neolithic cursus monuments of Scotland*. London: Routledge.

Brothwell, D. and Pollard, M. (eds) 2001. *Handbook of Archaeological Sciences*. London.

Brown, N. 1997. A landscape of two halves: the Neolithic of the Chelmer valley/Blackwater estuary, Essex. In P. Topping (ed.) *Neolithic Landscapes*. Neolithic Studies Group Seminar Papers 2. Oxford: Oxbow. 87–98.

Brown, T.A., Nelson, D.E. and Southon, J.R. 1988. Improved collagen extraction by modified Longin method. *Radiocarbon* 30: 171–7.

Buck, C.E., Cavanagh, W.G. and Litton, C.D. 1996. *Bayesian Approach to Interpreting Archaeological Data*. Chichester: Wiley-Blackwell.

Buck, C.E., Litton, C.D. and Smith, A.F.M. 1992. Calibration of radiocarbon results pertaining to related archaeological events. *Journal of Archaeological Science* 19: 497–512.

Budd, P., Chenery, C., Montgomery, J. and Evans, J. 2003. You are what you ate: isotopic analysis in the reconstruction of prehistoric residency. In M. Parker Pearson (ed.) *Food, Culture and Identity in the Neolithic and Early Bronze Age*. Oxford: BAR (International Series) 1117. 69–78.

Bullock, P. and Murphy, C.P. 1979. Evolution of a paleo-argillic brown earth (paleudalf) from Oxfordshire, England. *Geoderma* 22: 225–52.

Bullock, P., Fedoroff, N., Jongerius, A., Stoops, G. and Tursina, T. 1985. *Handbook for Soil Thin Section Description.* Wolverhampton: Waine Research Publications.

Bunte, K. and Abt, S.R. 2001. *Sampling surface and sub-surface particle-size distributions in wadable gravel- and cobble-bed streams for analysis in sediment transport, hydraulics, and stream-bed monitoring.* General Technical Report RMRS-GTR-74. Fort Collins CO: US Department of Agriculture, Forest Service, Rocky Mountain Research Station.

Burl, A.W. 1987. *The Stonehenge People.* London: Dent.

Burl, A.W. 2000. *The Stone Circles of Britain, Ireland and Brittany.* New Haven CT: Yale University Press.

Burl, A.W. 2006. *Stonehenge: a new history of the world's greatest stone circle.* London: Constable.

Burl, A.W. and Mortimer, N. (eds) 2005. *Stukeley's Stonehenge: an unpublished manuscript, 1721–1724.* New Haven CT: Yale University Press.

Butler, C. 2005 *Prehistoric Flintwork.* Stroud: Tempus.

Campbell, G. 2013. Evidence for Neolithic cereal cultivation in the Avebury region. In J. Leary, D. Field and G. Campbell (eds) *Silbury Hill: the largest prehistoric mound in Europe.* Swindon: English Heritage. 176–9.

Cappers, R.T.J., Bekker, R.M. and Jans, J.E.A. 2006. *Digital Seed Atlas of the Netherlands.* Eelde: Barkhuis Publishing.

Carrington, F.A. 1857. The old market house and great fire of Marlborough. *Wiltshire Archaeological and Natural History Magazine* 3: 106–14.

Carruthers, D. 1990. Carbonised plant remains. In J. Richards, *The Stonehenge Environs Project.* London: English Heritage. 250–2.

Carter, S.P. 1990. The stratification and taphonomy of shells in calcareous soils: implications for land snail analysis in archaeology. *Journal of Archaeological Science* 17: 495–507.

Carton, J., Pollard, J. and Zakrzewski, S. 2016. An Early Neolithic mortuary deposit from the Woodford G2 long barrow. *Wiltshire Archaeological and Natural History Magazine* 109: 79–90.

Cartwright, C. 1993. Wood charcoal. In A. Whittle, A.J. Rouse and J.G. Evans (eds) A Neolithic downland monument in its environment: excavations at the Easton Down long barrow, Bishops Cannings, north Wiltshire. *Proceedings of the Prehistoric Society* 59: 221–2.

Cartwright, C. 1999. The charcoal assemblages. In A. Whittle, J. Pollard and C. Grigson, *The Harmony of Symbols: the Windmill Hill causewayed enclosure.* Oxford: Oxbow. 157–61.

Castleden, R. 1993. *The Making of Stonehenge.* London: Routledge.

Catt, J.A. 1978. The contribution of loess to soils in southern England. In S. Limbrey and J.G. Evans (eds) *The Effect of Man on the Landscape: the lowland zone.* London: Council for British Archaeology. 12–20.

Chamberlain, A.T. 1994. *Human Remains.* London: British Museum Press.

Chan, B. 2010. Durrington Walls then and now: the description, interpretation and meaning of a monstrous assemblage. *Lithics* 31: 44–54.

Chan, B. 2011. Stonehenge, looking from the inside out: a comparative analysis of landscape surveys in southern Britain. In A. Saville (ed.) *Flint and Stone in the Neolithic Period.* Neolithic Studies Group Seminar Papers 11. Oxford: Oxbow. 116–38.

Chan, B., Viner, S., Parker Pearson, M., Albarella, U. and Ixer, R. 2016. Resourcing Stonehenge: patterns of human, animal and goods mobility in the Late Neolithic. In J. Leary and T. Kador (eds) *Moving On in Neolithic Studies: understanding mobile lives.* Oxford: Oxbow. 28–44.

Chippindale, C. 1994. *Stonehenge Complete.* Revised edition. London: Thames & Hudson.

Christen, J.A. 1994. Summarizing a set of radiocarbon determinations: a robust approach. *Applied Statistics* 43: 489–512.

Christie, P.M. 1963. The Stonehenge Cursus. *Wiltshire Archaeological and Natural History Magazine* 58: 370–82.

Clark, J.G.D., Higgs, E.S. and Longworth, I.H. 1960. Excavations at the Neolithic site at Hurst Fen, Mildenhall, Suffolk. *Proceedings of the Prehistoric Society* 26: 202–45.

Clarke, D.L. 1970. *Beaker Pottery of Great Britain and Ireland.* Cambridge: Cambridge University Press.

Clarke, D.V., Cowie, T.G. and Foxon, A. 1985. *Symbols of Power at the Time of Stonehenge.* Edinburgh: HMSO.

Cleal, R.M.J. 1990a. The prehistoric pottery [Coneybury Anomaly]. In J. Richards, *The Stonehenge Environs Project.* London: English Heritage. 45–57.

Cleal, R.M.J. 1990b. The prehistoric pottery [An early Neolithic pit on the King Barrow Ridge]. In J. Richards, *The Stonehenge Environs Project.* London: English Heritage. 65–6.

Cleal, R.M.J. 1994. The pottery. In R.M.J. Cleal and M.J. Allen, Investigations of tree-damaged barrows on King Barrow Ridge and Luxenborough Plantation, Amesbury. *Wiltshire Archaeological and Natural History Magazine* 87: 62–72.

Cleal, R.M.J. 1995a. Earlier prehistoric pottery. In R.M.J. Cleal, K.E. Walker and R. Montague, *Stonehenge in its Landscape: twentieth-century excavations.* London: English Heritage. 349–67.

Cleal, R.M.J. 1995b. Pottery fabrics in Wessex in the fourth to second millennia BC. In I. Kinnes and G. Varndell (eds) *Unbaked Urns of Rudely Shape: essays on British and Irish pottery for Ian Longworth.* Oxford. Oxbow. 185–94.

Cleal, R.M.J. 2011. The pottery [Amesbury Archer]. In A.P. Fitzpatrick, *The Amesbury Archer and the Boscombe Bowmen: Bell Beaker burials at Boscombe Down, Amesbury, Wiltshire.* Salisbury: Wessex Archaeology. 140–54.

Cleal, R.M.J. with Raymond, F. 1990. The prehistoric pottery. In J. Richards, *The Stonehenge Environs Project.* London: English Heritage. 233–46.

Cleal, R.M.J., Allen, M.J. and Newman, C. 2004. An archaeological and environmental study of the Neolithic and later prehistoric landscape of the Avon valley and Durrington Walls environs. *Wiltshire Archaeological and Natural History Magazine* 97: 218–48.

Cleal, R.M.J., Walker, K.E. and Montague, R. 1995. *Stonehenge in its Landscape: twentieth-century excavations.* London: English Heritage.

Clifton-Taylor, A. 1972. *The Pattern of English Building.* London: Faber and Faber.

Colt Hoare, R. 1812. *The Ancient History of Wiltshire. Volume 1.* London: William Millar.

Colt Hoare, R. 1819 [1975]. *The Ancient History of Wiltshire.* Wakefield: EP Publishing Ltd.

Cooney, G. 2000. *Landscapes of Neolithic Ireland.* London: Routledge.

Cornwall, I. and Hodges, H. 1964. Thin sections of British Neolithic pottery: Windmill Hill – a test site. *Bulletin of the Institute of Archaeology* 4: 29–33.

Cox, P. 1988. Excavation and survey on Furzey island, Poole harbour, Dorset, 1985. *Proceedings of the Dorset Natural History and Archaeological Society* 110: 65–72.

Craig, O., Mulville, J., Parker Pearson, M., Sokol, R., Gelsthorpe, K., Stacey, R. and Collins, M. 2000. Detecting milk proteins in ancient pots. *Nature* 408: 312.

Cram, C.L. 1973. *Excavations at Shakenoak Farm near Wilcote, Oxfordshire. Part 4, Site C.* Oxford: privately published. 145–64.

Cramp, L.J.E., Jones, J., Sheridan, A., Smyth, J., Whelton, H., Mulville, J., Sharples, N. and Evershed, R.P. 2014. Immediate replacement of fishing with dairying by the earliest farmers of the northeast Atlantic archipelagos. *Proceedings of the Royal Society B: Biological Sciences* 281 (1780). www.jstor.org/stable/43600379.

Cummings, V. and Richards, C. 2014. The essence of the dolmen: the architecture of megalithic construction. *Préhistoires Méditerranéennes* 5. http://pm.revues.org/944.

Cunliffe, B.W. and Renfrew, C. (eds) 1997. *Science and Stonehenge.* Oxford: Oxford University Press.

Cunnington, M.E. 1914. List of the long barrows of Wiltshire. *Wiltshire Archaeological and Natural History Magazine* 38: 379–414.

Cunnington, M.E. 1929. *Woodhenge.* Devizes: George Simpson.

Darvill, T.C. 1997. Ever increasing circles: the sacred geographies of Stonehenge and its landscape. In B.W. Cunliffe and C. Renfrew (eds) *Science and Stonehenge.* Oxford: Oxford University Press. 167–202.

Darvill, T.C. 2005. *Stonehenge World Heritage Site: an archaeological research framework.* London and Bournemouth: English Heritage and Bournemouth University.

Darvill, T.C. 2006. *Stonehenge: the biography of a landscape.* Stroud: Tempus.

Darvill, T.C. and Wainwright, G.J. 2009. Stonehenge excavations 2008. *Antiquaries Journal* 89: 1–19.

Darvill, T.C., Lüth, F., Rassmann, K., Fischer, A. and Winkelmann, K. 2013. Stonehenge, Wiltshire, UK: high resolution geophysical surveys in the surrounding landscape, 2011. *European Journal of Archaeology* 16: 63–93.

Darvill, T.C., Marshall, P., Parker Pearson, M. and Wainwright, G.J. 2012. Stonehenge remodeled. *Antiquity* 86: 1021–40.

David, A. and Payne, A. 1997. Geophysical surveys within the Stonehenge landscape: a review of past endeavour and future potential. In B.W. Cunliffe and C. Renfrew (eds) *Science and Stonehenge.* Oxford: Oxford University Press. 73–113.

Davis, S.J.M. 1992. *A rapid method for recording information about mammal bones from archaeological sites.* Ancient Monuments Laboratory Report 19/92. London: English Heritage.

de la Vega, G. 1609 [trans. 1688]. *The Royal Commentaries of Peru.* London: Miles Flesher for Christopher Wilkinson.

de Luc, J.A. 1811. *Geological Travels. Volume III, Travels in England.* London: F.C. and J. Rivington.

Dee, M. and Bronk Ramsey, C. 2000. Refinement of graphite target production at ORAU. *Nuclear Instruments and Methods in Physics Research B* 172: 449–53.

Delorme, M. 1985. *Curious Wiltshire.* Bradford-on-Avon: Ex Libris Press.

Dimbleby, G.W. 1965a. Charcoal. In G. Connah, Excavations at Knap Hill, Alton Priors, 1961. *Wiltshire Archaeological and Natural History Magazine* 60: 1–23.

Dimbleby, G.W. 1965b. The buried soil under outer bank V and pollen analysis. In I.F. Smith, *Windmill Hill and Avebury.* Oxford: Oxford University Press. 34–8.

Dimbleby, G.W. 1966. Appendix III, Plant remains. In P. Ashbee, The Fussell's Lodge long barrow excavations 1957. *Archaeologia* 100: 63–73.

Dimbleby, G.W. 1979. Pollen analysis. In P. Ashbee, I.F. Smith and J.G. Evans, Excavation of three long barrows near Avebury, Wiltshire. *Proceedings of the Prehistoric Society* 45: 207–300.

Dimbleby, G.W. and Evans, J.G. 1974. Pollen and land snail analysis of calcareous soils. *Journal of Archaeological Science* 1: 117–33.

Drew, C.D. and Piggott, S. 1936. The excavation of long barrow 163a on Thickthorn Down, Dorset. *Proceedings of the Prehistoric Society* 2: 77–96.

Drewett, P. 1975. The excavation of an oval burial mound of the third millennium BC at Alfriston, East Sussex, 1974. *Proceedings of the Prehistoric Society* 41: 119–52.

Drewett, P. 1978. The Neolithic. In P. Drewett (ed.) *The Archaeology of Sussex to AD 1500*. London: Council for British Archaeology. 23–9.

Dudd, S.N., Evershed, R.P. and Gibson, A.M. 1999. Evidence for varying patterns of exploitation of animal products in different prehistoric pottery traditions based on lipids preserved in surface and absorbed residues. *Journal of Archaeological Science* 26: 1473–82.

Edmonds, M. 1995. *Stone Tools and Society: working stone in Neolithic and Bronze Age Britain.* London: Batsford.

Edmonds, M. 1999. *Ancestral Geographies of the Neolithic: landscapes, monuments and memory*. London: Routledge.

Edmonds, M. and Richards, C. (eds) 1998. *Understanding the Neolithic of North-Western Europe.* Glasgow: Cruithne Press.

English Heritage 2000. *Stonehenge World Heritage Site: management plan.* London: English Heritage.

Entwistle, R. 1990. Land mollusca [W58, Amesbury 42 long barrow]. In J. Richards, *The Stonehenge Environs Project.* London: English Heritage. 105–9.

Evans, C., Pollard, J. and Knight, M. 1999. Life in woods: tree-throws, 'settlement' and forest cognition. *Oxford Journal of Archaeology* 18: 241–54.

Evans, J. 1897. *The Ancient Stone Implements, Weapons and Ornaments of Great Britain.* London: Longman, Green and Company.

Evans, J.G. 1968. Periglacial deposits on the chalk of Wiltshire. *Wiltshire Archaeological and Natural History Magazine* 63: 12–29.

Evans, J.G. 1971a. Habitat change on the calcareous soils of Britain: the impact of Neolithic man. In D.D.A. Simpson (ed.) *Economy and Settlement in Neolithic and Early Bronze Age Britain and Europe.* Leicester: Leicester University Press. 27–73.

Evans, J.G. 1971b. Notes on the environment of early farming communities in Britain. In D.D.A. Simpson (ed.) *Economy and Settlement in Neolithic and Early Bronze Age Britain and Europe.* Leicester: Leicester University Press. 11–26.

Evans, J.G. 1971c. Durrington Walls: the pre-henge environment. In G.J. Wainwright with I.H. Longworth, *Durrington Walls: excavations 1966–68*. London: Society of Antiquaries. 329–37.

Evans, J.G. 1972. *Land Snails in Archaeology.* London: Seminar Press.

Evans, J.G. 1975. *The Environment of Early Man in the British Isles*. London: Paul Elek.

Evans, J.G. 1984. Stonehenge: the environment in the Late Neolithic and Early Bronze Age and a Beaker-Age burial. *Wiltshire Archaeological and Natural History Magazine* 78: 7–30.

Evans, J.G. and Jones, H. 1979. Woodhenge. In G. J. Wainwright (ed.) *Mount Pleasant, Dorset: excavations 1970–1971*. London: Society of Antiquaries. 190–213.

Evans, J.G., Limbrey, S., Máté, I. and Mount, R. 1993. An environmental history of the upper Kennet valley, Wiltshire, for the last 10,000 years. *Proceedings of the Prehistoric Society* 59: 139–95.

Evelyn, J. 1664. *Sylva, or a Discourse of Forest Trees, and the propagation of timber in his majesties dominions.* London: Royal Society.

Evens, E.D., Grinsell, L.V., Piggott, S. and Wallis, F.S. 1962. Fourth report of the sub-committee on the petrological identification of stone axes. *Proceedings of the Prehistoric Society* 28: 209–66.

Exon, S., Gaffney, V., Woodward, A. and Yorston, R. 2000. *Stonehenge Landscapes.* Oxford: Archaeopress.

Fairbairn, A.S. 1997. Charred plant remains. In A. Whittle (ed.) *Sacred Mound, Holy Rings: Silbury Hill and the West Kennet palisade enclosures: a later Neolithic complex in north Wiltshire.* Oxford: Oxbow. 134–8.

Fairbairn, A.S. 1999. Charred plant remains. In A. Whittle, J. Pollard and C. Grigson (eds) *The Harmony of Symbols: the Windmill Hill causewayed enclosure.* Oxford: Oxbow. 139–56.

Fairbairn, A.S. 2000. On the spread of crops across Neolithic Britain, with special reference to southern England. In A.S. Fairbairn (ed.) *Plants in Neolithic Britain and Beyond.* Neolithic Studies Group Seminar Papers 5. Oxford: Oxbow. 106–21.

Farrer, P. 1917. Excavations in 'The Cursus', July 1917. Unpublished manuscript.

Fedoroff, N. 1968. Génèse et morphologie des sols à horizon B textural en France atlantique. *Science du Sols* 1: 29–65.

Ferembach, D., Schwidetzky, I. and Stloukal, M. 1980. Recommendations for age and sex diagnoses of skeletons. *Journal of Human Evolution* 9: 517–49.

Field, D. 2005. Some observations on perception, consolidation and change in a land of stones. In G. Brown, D. Field and D. McOmish (eds) *The Avebury Landscape.* Oxford: Oxbow. 87–94.

Field, D. 2006. *Earthen Long Barrows.* Stroud: Tempus.

Field, D. 2008. *Use of Land in Central Southern England during the Neolithic and Early Bronze Age.* Oxford: BAR (British Series) 458.

Field, D. 2010. Pen Pits, New Grange and progress in the archaeology of extraction. In M. Brewer-LaPorta, A. Burke and D. Field (eds) *Ancient Mines and Quarries: a trans-Atlantic perspective.* Oxford: Oxbow. 162–72.

Field, D. and Pearson, T. 2010. *Stonehenge World Heritage Site Landscape Project: Stonehenge, Amesbury, Wiltshire archaeological survey report.* Research Report 109-2010. Swindon: English Heritage.

Field, D., Anderson-Whymark, H., Linford, N., Barber, M., Bowden, M., Linford, P. and Topping, P. 2015. Analytical surveys of Stonehenge and its environs, 2009–2013. Part 2 – the stones. *Proceedings of the Prehistoric Society* 81: 125–48.

Field, D., Bowden, M. and Soutar, S. 2012. *Stonehenge World Heritage Site Landscape Project: the Avenue and Stonehenge Bottom archaeological survey report.* Research Report 31-2012. Swindon: English Heritage.

Field, D., Linford, N., Barber, M., Anderson-Whymark, H., Bowden, M., Topping, P. and Linford, P. 2014. Analytical surveys of Stonehenge and its immediate environs, 2009–2013. Part 1 – the landscape and earthworks. *Proceedings of the Prehistoric Society* 80: 1–32.

Fisher, P.F. 1982. A review of lessivage and Neolithic cultivation in southern England. *Journal of Archaeological Science* 9: 299–304.

Fitzpatrick, A. 2004. A sacred circle on Boscombe Down. *Current Archaeology* 195: 106–7.

Flinders Petrie, W.M. 1880. *Stonehenge: plans, description, and theories.* London: Edward Stanford.

Fowler, P.J. 2000. *Landscape Plotted and Pieced: landscape history and local archaeology in Fyfield and Overton, Wiltshire.* London: Society of Antiquaries.

Fowles, J. and Legg, R. (eds) 1980–2. *Monumenta Britannica or A Miscellany of British Antiquities by Mr John Aubrey...compiled mainly between the years 1665 and 1693.* Parts 1–3. Two volumes. Milborne Port: Dorset Publishing Company.

Freeman, S.P.H.T., Cook, G.T., Dougans, A.B., Naysmith, P., Wicken, K.M. and Xu, S. 2010. Improved SSAMS performance. *Nuclear Instruments and Methods in Physics Research B* 268: 715–17.

French, C. 2003. *Geoarchaeology in Action: studies in soil micromorphology and landscape evolution.* London: Routledge.

French, C. 2008. The palaeosols at Durrington Walls. Unpublished report for the Stonehenge Riverside Project.

French, C., Allen, M.J. and Scaife, R.G. 2000. Palaeoenvironmental and archaeological investigations on Wyke Down and in the upper Allen valley, Cranbourne Chase, Dorset, England: interim summary report for 1998–9. *Proceedings of the Dorset Natural History and Archaeological Society* 122: 53–71.

French, C., Lewis, H., Allen, M.J., Green, M., Scaife, R.G. and Gardiner, J. 2007. *Prehistoric Landscape Development and Human Impact in the Upper Allen Valley, Cranborne Chase, Dorset.* Cambridge: McDonald Institute.

French, C., Lewis, H., Allen, M.J., Scaife, R.G. and Green, M. 2003. Archaeological and palaeo-environmental investigations of the upper Allen valley, Cranborne Chase, Dorset (1998–2000): a new model of earlier Holocene landscape development. *Proceedings of the Prehistoric Society* 69: 201–34.

French, C., Lewis, H., Scaife, R. and Allen, M.J. 2005. New perspectives on Holocene landscape development in the southern English chalklands: the upper Allen valley, Cranborne Chase, Dorset. *Geoarchaeology* 20: 109–34.

French, C., Scaife, R. and Allen, M.J. with Parker Pearson M., Pollard, J., Richards, C., Thomas, J. and Welham, K. 2012. Durrington Walls to West Amesbury by way of Stonehenge: a major transformation of the Holocene landscape. *Antiquaries Journal* 92: 1–36.

French, H.M. 1976. *The Periglacial Environment.* London: Longman.

Froom, R. and Cook, J. 2005. *Late Glacial Long Blade Sites in the Kennet Valley: excavations and fieldwork at Avington VI, Wawcott XII and Crown Acres.* London: British Museum.

Fürst, C.M. 1930. *Zur Anthropologie der prähistorischen Griechen in Argolis: nebst Beschreibung einiger älteren Schädel aus historischer Zeit.* Lunds Universitets Årsskrift NF 26 (8). Lund: C.W.K. Gleerup.

Gaffney, C., Gaffney, V., Neubauer, W., Baldwin, E., Chapman, H., Garwood, P., Moulden, H., Sparrow, T., Bates, R., Löcker, K., Hinterleitner, A., Trinks, I., Nau, E., Zitz, T., Floery, S., Verhoeven, G. and Doneus, M. 2012. The Stonehenge Hidden Landscapes Project. *Archaeological Prospection* 19: 147–55.

Gaffney, V., Baldwin, E., Bates, M., Bates, C.R., Gaffney, C., Hamilton, D., Kinnaird, T., Neubauer, W., Yorston, R., Allaby, R., Chapman, H., Garwood, P., Löcker, K., Hinterleitner, A., Sparrow, T., Trinks, I. and Wallner, M. 2020. A massive, Late Neolithic pit structure associated with Durrington Walls henge. Internet Archaeology 55. https://doi.org/10.11141/ia.55.4

Gale, J. 2012. Late Neolithic henge monuments as foci for evolving funerary landscapes. Knowlton henge complex and the barrow cemeteries of the Allen valley, Dorset, UK – a case study. *eTopoi: Journal for Ancient Studies* 3: 161–7.

Gale, R. 1990. Charcoals. In J. Richards, *The Stonehenge Environs Project.* London: English Heritage. 252–3.

Galland, B.B. 2007. Popliteal aneurysms: from John Hunter to the 21st century. *Annals of the Royal College of Surgeons of England* 89: 466–71.

Garrow, D., Beadsmoore, E. and Knight, M. 2005. Pit clusters and the temporality of occupation: an earlier Neolithic site at Kilverstone, Thetford, Norfolk. *Proceedings of the Prehistoric Society* 71: 139–57.

Garrow, D., Lucy, S. and Gibson, D. 2006. *Excavations at Kilverstone, Norfolk: an episodic landscape history*. Cambridge: East Anglian Archaeology 13.

Garton, D., Howard, A. and Pearce, M. 1996. Neolithic riverside ritual? Excavations at Langford Lowlands, Nottinghamshire. In R.J.A. Wilson (ed.) *From River Trent to Raqqa*. Nottingham: Department of Archaeology, University of Nottingham. 9–11.

Garton, D., Howard, A. and Pearce, M. 1997. Archaeological investigations at Langford quarry, Nottinghamshire, 1995–6. *Tarmac Papers* 1: 29–40.

Geddes, I. 2003. *Hidden Depths: Wiltshire's geology and landscapes*. Bradford-on-Avon: Ex Libris Press.

Gejvall, N.G. 1981. Determination of burnt bones from prehistoric graves. *OSSA Letters* 2: 1–13.

Gell, A. 1998. *Art and Agency: an anthropological theory*. Oxford: Clarendon.

Gibson, A.M. 2010a. Dating Balbirnie: recent radiocarbon dates from the stone circle and cairn at Balbirnie, Fife, and a review of its place in the overall Balfarg/ Balbirnie site sequence. *Proceedings of the Society of Antiquaries of Scotland* 140: 51–77.

Gibson, A.M. 2010b. New dates for Sarn-y-bryn-caled, Powys, Wales. *Proceedings of the Prehistoric Society* 76: 351–6.

Gibson, A.M. and Bayliss, A. 2009. Recent research at Duggleby Howe, North Yorkshire. *Archaeological Journal* 166: 39–78.

Gibson, A.M., Allen, M.J., Bradley, P., Carruthers, W., Challinor, D., French, C., Hamilton, D., Mainland, I., McCarthy, M., Ogden, A., Scaife, R., Sheridan, A. and Walmsley, C. 2011. Report on the excavation at the Duggleby Howe causewayed enclosure, North Yorkshire, May–July 2009. *Archaeological Journal* 168: 1–63.

Gillings, M. and Pollard, J. 2004. *Avebury*. London: Duckworth.

Gillings, M. and Pollard, J. 2016. Making megaliths: shifting and unstable stones in the Neolithic of the Avebury landscape. *Cambridge Archaeological Journal* 26: 537–59.

Gillings, M., Pollard, J., Wheatley, D. and Peterson, R. 2008. *Landscape of the Megaliths: excavation and fieldwork on the Avebury monuments 1997–2003*. Oxford: Oxbow.

Gingell, C.J. 1988. Twelve Wiltshire round barrows: excavations in 1959 and 1961 by F. de M. and H.L. Vatcher. *Wiltshire Archaeological and Natural History Magazine* 82: 18–96.

Girling, M.A. 1988. The bark beetle *Scolytus scolytus* (Fabricius) and the possible role of elm disease in the early Neolithic. In M. Jones (ed.) *Archaeology and the Flora of the British Isles*. Oxford: Oxford University Committee for Archaeology. 34–8.

Godwin, H. 1956. *The History of the British Flora*. Cambridge: Cambridge University Press.

Godwin, H. 1962. Vegetational history of the Kentish chalk downs as seen at Wingham and Frogholt. *Veröffentlichungen des Geobotanischen Institutes der Eidg. Techn. Hochschule, Stiftung Rubel, in Zurich* 37: 83–99.

Godwin, H. 1975. *The History of the British Flora*. 2nd edition. Cambridge: Cambridge University Press.

Goldberg, P. and Macphail, R.I. 2006. *Practical and Theoretical Geoarchaeology*. Oxford: Blackwell Publishing.

Gowland, W. 1902. Recent excavations at Stonehenge. *Archaeologia* 58: 37–105.

Grant, A. 1982. The use of tooth wear as a guide to the age of domestic ungulates. In B. Wilson, C. Grigson and S. Payne (eds) *Ageing and Sexing Animal Bones from Archaeological Sites*. Oxford: BAR (British Series) 109. 91–108.

Graw, M., Wahl, J. and Ahlbrecht, M. 2004. Course of the *meatus acusticus internus* as criterion for sex differentiation. *Forensic Science International* 147: 113–17.

Green, C.P. 1997a. The provenance of rocks used in the construction of Stonehenge. In B.W. Cunliffe and C. Renfrew (eds) *Science and Stonehenge*. Oxford: Oxford University Press. 257–70.

Green, C.P. 1997b. Stonehenge: geology and prehistory. *Proceedings of the Geologists Association* 108: 1–10.

Green, H.S. 1980. *The Flint Arrowheads of the British Isles*. Oxford: BAR (British Series) 75 i & ii.

Green, M. 2000. *A Landscape Revealed: 10,000 years on a chalkland farm*. Stroud: Tempus.

Greenwell, W. 1877. *British Barrows: a record of the examination of sepulchral mounds in various parts of England*. Oxford: Clarendon.

Greig, J.R.A. 1982. Past and present lime woods of Europe. In M. Bell and S. Limbrey (eds) *Archaeological Aspects of Woodland Ecology*. Oxford: BAR (International Series) 146. 23–55.

Grose, D. 1979. *The Flora of Wiltshire*. Wakefield: EP Publishing Ltd.

Hall, H.A., Minc, S. and Babrowski, T. 2013. Peripheral artery aneurysm. *Surgical Clinics of North America* 93: 911–23.

Halstead, P.J. and Collins, P. 2002. Sorting the sheep from the goats: morphological distinctions between the mandibles and mandibular teeth of adult *Ovis* and *Capra*. *Journal of Archaeological Science* 29: 545–53.

Hammon, A. 2002. *Chedworth Roman villa: garden courtyard and lower courtyard excavations: report on the vertebrate remains*. Unpublished report, University of Sheffield.

Hammon, A. 2008. The animal bones. In B.W. Cunliffe and C. Poole (eds) *The Danebury Environs Roman Programme: a Wessex landscape during the Roman era. Volume 2, Part 3*. Oxford: English Heritage and Oxford University School of Archaeology Monograph 71. 150–61.

Hammon, A. 2011. Understanding the Romano-British–early medieval transition: a zooarchaeological perspective from Wroxeter (Viroconium Cornoviorum). *Britannia* 42: 275–305. https://doi.org/10.1017/S0068113X11000055

Harding, A.F. 1981. Excavations in the prehistoric ritual complex near Milfield, Northumberland. *Proceedings of the Prehistoric Society* 47: 87–135.

Harding, J. 2013. *Cult, Religion and Pilgrimage: archaeological investigations at the Neolithic and Bronze Age monument complex of Thornborough, North Yorkshire.* York: Council for British Archaeology Report 174.

Harding, J. and Healy, F. 2007. *The Raunds Area Project: a Neolithic and Bronze Age landscape in Northamptonshire.* Swindon: English Heritage.

Harding, P. 1990. The analysis of a sealed knapping deposit from the phase 1 ditch. In J. Richards, *The Stonehenge Environs Project.* London: English Heritage. 99–104.

Harding, P. 1995. Flint. In R.M.J. Cleal, K.E. Walker, and R. Montague, *Stonehenge in its Landscape: twentieth-century excavations.* London: English Heritage. 368–75.

Harding, P. and Gingell, C. 1986. The excavation of two long barrows by F. de M. and H.F.W.L. Vatcher. *Wiltshire Archaeological and Natural History Magazine* 80: 7–22.

Harris, B. 2019. *Landscapes of labour: a quantitative study of earth- and stone-moving in prehistoric northern Wessex.* Unpublished PhD thesis, University College London.

Haskins, L.E. 1978. *The vegetational history of south-east Dorset.* Unpublished PhD thesis, University of Southampton.

Hather, J. 2000. *The Identification of the North European Woods: a guide for archaeologists and conservators.* London: Archetype.

Hawkey, D.E. and Merbs, C.F. 2005. Activity-induced musculoskeletal stress markers (MSM) and subsistence strategy changes among ancient Hudson Bay Eskimos. *International Journal of Osteoarchaeology* 5: 324–38.

Hawley, W. 1921. The excavations at Stonehenge. *Antiquaries Journal* 1: 19–39.

Hawley, W. 1922. Second report on the excavations at Stonehenge. *Antiquaries Journal* 2: 36–51.

Hawley, W. 1923. Third report on the excavations at Stonehenge. *Antiquaries Journal* 3: 13–20.

Hawley, W. 1924. Fourth report on the excavations at Stonehenge. *Antiquaries Journal* 4: 30–9.

Hawley, W. 1925. Report of the excavations at Stonehenge during the season of 1923. *Antiquaries Journal* 5: 21–50.

Hawley, W. 1926. Report on the excavations at Stonehenge during the season of 1924. *Antiquaries Journal* 6: 1–25.

Hawley, W. 1928. Report on the excavations at Stonehenge during 1925 and 1926. *Antiquaries Journal* 8: 149–76.

Healy, F. 2012. Chronology, corpses, ceramics, copper and lithics. In M.J. Allen, J. Gardiner and A Sheridan (eds) *Is There a British Chalcolithic? People, place and polity in the later 3rd millennium BC.* Oxford: Oxbow. 144–63.

Healy, F., Bayliss, A., Whittle, A., Allen, M.J., Mercer, R., Rawlings, M., Sharples, N. and Thomas, N. 2011. South Wessex. In A.W.R. Whittle, F. Healy, and A. Bayliss, *Gathering Time: dating the Early Neolithic enclosures of southern Britain and Ireland.* Oxford: Oxbow. 110–206.

Hedges, J. and Buckley, D. 1981. *Springfield and the Cursus Problem.* Chelmsford: Essex County Council.

Henshall, A.S. 1972. *The Chambered Tombs of Scotland. Volume 2.* Edinburgh: Edinburgh University Press.

Higgs, E. 1959. The excavation of a Late Mesolithic site at Downton, near Salisbury, Wilts. *Proceedings of the Prehistoric Society* 25: 209–323.

Hillam, J., Morgan, R. and Tyers, I. 1987. Sapwood estimates and the dating of short ring sequences. In R.G.W. Ward (ed.) *Applications of Tree-Ring Studies: current research in dendrochronology and related areas.* Oxford: BAR (International Series) 333. 165–85.

Hillman, G.C., Mason, S., de Moulins, D. and Nesbitt, M. 1995. Identification of the archaeological remains of wheat: the 1992 London workshop. *Circaea* 12: 195–210.

Hillson, S. 2002. *Dental Anthropology.* 3rd edition. Cambridge: Cambridge University Press.

Hodder, I. 1999. *The Archaeological Process: an introduction.* Oxford: Blackwell.

Holck, P. 1986. *Cremated Bones: a medical-anthropological study of an archaeological material on cremation burials.* Antropologiske Skrifter 1. Oslo: University of Oslo.

Holden, J.L., Phakey, P.P. and Clement, J.G. 1995a. Scanning electron microscope observations of incinerated human femoral bone: a case study. *Forensic Science International* 74: 17–28.

Holden, J.L., Phakey, P.P. and Clement, J.G. 1995b. Scanning electron microscope observations of heat-treated human bone. *Forensic Science International* 74: 29–45.

Hopson, P.M., Farrant, A.R., Newell, A.J., Marks, R.J., Booth, K.A., Bateson, L.B., Woods, M.A., Wilkinson, I.P., Brayson, J. and Evans, D.J. 2007. *Geology of the Salisbury District – a brief explanation of the geological map. Sheet Explanation of the British Geological Survey 1:50,000 Sheet 298 Salisbury (England and Wales).* Nottingham: British Geological Survey.

Hoskins, J. 1986. So my name shall live: stone-dragging and grave-building in Kodi, West Sumba. *Bijdragen tot de Taal-, Land- en Volkenkunde* 142: 31–51.

Houlder, C. 1968. The henge monuments at Llandegai. *Antiquity* 42: 216–31.

Howard, H. 1982. A petrological study of the rock specimens from excavations at Stonehenge, 1979–1980. In M. Pitts, On the road to Stonehenge: report on investigations beside the A344 in 1968, 1979 and 1980. *Proceedings of the Prehistoric Society* 48: 104–26.

Howard, S. 2007. *A biometrical analysis of red and roe deer from Mesolithic and Neolithic sites in Britain.* Unpublished MSc dissertation, University of Sheffield.

Ixer, R.A. and Bevins, R.E. 2011. Craig Rhos-y-felin, Pont Saeson is the dominant source of the Stonehenge rhyolitic 'debitage'. *Archaeology in Wales* 50: 21–31.

Ixer, R.A. and Bevins, R.E. 2016. Volcanic group A debitage: its description and distribution within the Stonehenge landscape. *Wiltshire Archaeological and Natural History Magazine* 109: 1–14.

Ixer, R.A. and Turner, P. 2006. A detailed re-examination of the petrology of the Altar Stone and other non-sarsen sandstones from Stonehenge as a guide to their provenance. *Wiltshire Archaeological and Natural History Magazine* 99: 1–9.

Ixer, R.A., Bevins, R.E. and Gize, A.P. 2015. 'Volcanics with sub-planar texture' in the Stonehenge landscape. *Wiltshire Archaeological and Natural History Magazine* 108: 1–14.

Ixer, R.A., Turner, P., Molyneux, S. and Bevins, R. 2017. The petrography, geological age and distribution of the Lower Palaeozoic Sandstone debitage from the Stonehenge landscape. *Wiltshire Archaeological Magazine and Natural History Magazine* 110: 1–16.

Jacobi, R.M. 2004. The Late Upper Palaeolithic lithic collection from Gough's Cave, Cheddar, Somerset and human use of the cave. *Proceedings of the Prehistoric Society* 70: 1–92.

Jacomet, S. 2006. *Identification of Cereal Remains from Archaeological Sites.* 2nd edition. Basel: IPAS Basal University.

Jacques, D. and Phillips, T. 2014. Mesolithic settlement near Stonehenge: excavations at Blick Mead, Vespasian's Camp, Amesbury. *Wiltshire Archaeological and Natural History Magazine* 10: 7–27.

Jacques, D., Phillips, T. and Clarke, M. 2010. A reassessment of the importance of Vespasian's Camp in the Stonehenge landscape. *Past* 66: 14–16.

Jacques, D., Phillips, T. and Lyons, T. 2012. Vespasian's Camp: cradle of Stonehenge? *Current Archaeology* 271: 28–33.

Jacques, D., Phillips, T. and Lyons, T. 2018. *Blick Mead: exploring the 'first place' in the Stonehenge landscape.* Oxford: Peter Lang.

Johnston, R. 1999. An empty path? Processions, memories and the Dorset cursus. In A.J. Barclay and J. Harding (eds) *Pathways and Ceremonies: the cursus monuments of Britain and Ireland.* Oxford: Oxbow. 39–48.

Johnstone, C. and Albarella, U. 2002. *The Late Iron Age and Romano-British mammal and bird bone assemblage from Elms Farm, Heybridge, Essex (site code: HYEF93-95).* Report 45/2002. Portsmouth: English Heritage Centre for Archaeology.

Jones, G. 1990. The application of present-day cereal processing studies to charred archaeobotanical remains. *Circaea* 6: 91–6.

Jones, G. 2000. Evaluating the importance of cultivation and collecting in Neolithic Britain. In A.S. Fairbairn (ed.) *Plants in Neolithic Britain and Beyond.* Neolithic Studies Group Seminar Papers 5. Oxford: Oxbow. 78–84.

Jones, M.K. 1980. Carbonised cereals from Grooved Ware contexts. *Proceedings of the Prehistoric Society* 46: 61–3.

Jones, M.K. 2001. *The Molecule Hunt: how archaeologists are bringing the past back to life.* London: Penguin.

Judd, J.W. 1902. Note on the nature of and origin of the rock-fragments found in the excavations made at Stonehenge by Mr Gowland in 1901. In W. Gowland, Recent excavations at Stonehenge. *Archaeologia* 58: 106–18.

Juel Jensen, H. 1994. *Flint Tools and Plant Working: hidden traces of Stone Age technology.* Aarhus: Aarhus University Press.

Jukes Brown, A. 1905. *The Geology of the Country South and East of Devizes.* London: HMSO.

Karlsberg, A.J. 2006. *Flexible Bayesian methods for archaeological dating.* Unpublished PhD thesis, University of Sheffield.

Keeley, L.H. 1980. *Experimental Determination of Stone Tool Use.* Chicago: University of Chicago Press.

Kellaway, G.A. 1971. Glaciation and the stones of Stonehenge. *Nature* 232: 30–5.

Kennard, A., and Jackson, W.J. 1935. Reports on 1. The non-marine mollusca, and 2. The animal remains from the Stonehenge excavations of 1920–6. *Antiquaries Journal* 15: 432–40.

Kerney, M.P. 1999. *Atlas of the Land and Freshwater Molluscs of Britain and Ireland.* Colchester: Harley Books.

Kerney, M.P., Brown, E.H. and Chandler, T.J. 1964. The late-glacial and post-glacial history of the chalk escarpment near Brook, Kent. *Philosophical Transactions of the Royal Society of London B* 248: 135–204.

King, N.E. 1968. The Kennet Valley sarsen industry. *Wiltshire Archaeological and Natural History Magazine* 63: 83–93.

Kinnes, I. 1992. *Non-megalithic Long Barrows and Allied Structures in the British Neolithic.* London: British Museum.

Knüsel, C. and Carr, G.C. 1995. On the significance of the crania from the River Thames and its tributaries. *Antiquity* 69: 162–9.

Kratochvil, Z. 1969. Species criteria on the distal section of the tibia in *Ovis ammon* F. *aries* L. and *Capra aegagrus* F. *hircus* L. *Acta Veterinaria* 30: 483–90.

Lamdin-Whymark, H. 2008. *The Residue of Ritualised Action: Neolithic deposition practices in the middle Thames valley.* Oxford: BAR (British Series) 466.

Lange, M., Schutkowski, H., Hummel, S. and Herrmann, B. 1987. *A Bibliography on Cremations (PACT).* Rixensart: Hackens.

Lanting, J.N. and Brindley, A.L. 1998. Dating cremated bone: the dawn of a new era. *Journal of Irish Archaeology* 10: 1–8.

Lanting, J.N., Aerts-Bijma, A.T. and van der Plicht, J. 2001. Dating of cremated bone. *Radiocarbon* 43: 249–54.

Larsson, M. and Parker Pearson, M. (eds) 2007. *From Stonehenge to the Baltic: cultural diversity in the third millennium BC.* Oxford: BAR (International Series) 1692.

Leach, S. 2015. *Going Underground: an anthropological and taphonomic study of human skeletal remains from caves and rock shelters in Yorkshire.* Two volumes. Leeds: Yorkshire Archaeological Society.

Leary, J., Field, D. and Russell, M. 2010. Marvels at Marden henge. *Past* 66: 13–14.

Lee, S. and Bronk Ramsey, C. 2013. Development and application of the trapezoidal model for archaeological chronologies. *Radiocarbon* 54: 107–22.

Leivers, M. and Powell, A.B. 2016. *A Research Framework for the Stonehenge, Avebury and Associated Sites World Heritage Site.* Three volumes. Old Sarum: Wessex Archaeology.

Lewis, J.S.C. with Rackham, J. 2011. *Three Ways Wharf, Uxbridge: a Lateglacial and Early Holocene hunter-gatherer site in the Colne valley.* London: Museum of London.

Lidén, K. 1995. Megaliths, agriculture, and social complexity: a diet study of two Swedish megalith populations. *Journal of Anthropological Archaeology* 14: 404–17.

Limbrey, S. 1975. *Soil Science and Archaeology.* London: Academic Press.

Lockyer, N. 1909. *Stonehenge and other British Stone Monuments Astronomically Considered.* 2nd edition. London: Macmillan.

Long, A.J., Scaife, R.G. and Edwards, R.J. 1999. Pine pollen in intertidal sediments from Poole harbour, UK: implications for Late-Holocene sediment accretion rates and sea-level rise. *Quaternary International* 55: 3–16.

Longin, R. 1971. New method of collagen extraction for radiocarbon dating. *Nature* 230: 241–2.

Longworth, I.H. 1971. The Neolithic pottery. In G.J. Wainwright with I.H. Longworth, *Durrington Walls: excavations 1966–1968.* London: Society of Antiquaries. 48–155.

Longworth, I.H. 1979. The Neolithic and Bronze Age pottery [Woodhenge]. In G.J. Wainwright, *Mount Pleasant, Dorset: excavations 1970–1971.* London: Society of Antiquaries. 91.

Loveday, R. 2006. *Inscribed Across the Landscape: the cursus enigma.* Stroud: Tempus.

Lovejoy, C.O., Meindl, R.S., Pryzbeck, T.R. and Mensforth, R.P. 1985. Chronological metamorphosis of the auricular surface of the ilium: a new method for the determination of adult skeletal age at death. *American Journal of Physical Anthropology* 68: 15–28.

Lovell, N.C. 1994. Spinal arthritis and physical stress at Bronze Age Harappa. *American Journal of Physical Anthropology* 93: 149–64.

Lucas, G. 2001. *Critical Approaches to Fieldwork: contemporary and historical archaeological practice.* London: Routledge.

Lukacs, J.R. 1992. Dental paleopathology and agricultural intensification in South Asia: new evidence from Bronze Age Harappa. *American Journal of Physical Anthropology* 87: 133–50.

Lukacs, J.R. 2007. Dental trauma and antemortem tooth loss in prehistoric Canary Islanders: prevalence and contributing factors. *International Journal of Osteoarchaeology* 17: 157–73.

Lukacs, J.R. and Pal, J.N. 1993. Mesolithic subsistence in north India: inferences from dental attributes. *Current Anthropology* 34: 745–65.

Lynch, F. and Musson, C. 2004. A prehistoric and early medieval complex at Llandegai, near Bangor, north Wales. *Archaeologia Cambrensis* 150: 17–142.

Lynnerup, N., Schulz, M., Madelung, A. and Graw, M. 2006. Diameter of the human internal acoustic meatus and sex determination. *International Journal of Osteoarchaeology* 16: 118–23.

Macphail, R.I. and Crowther, J. 2008. A303, Stonehenge: soil micromorphology, chemistry, particle size and magnetic susceptibility. Unpublished report, Wessex Archaeology.

Maltby, M. 1987. *The animal bones from the excavations at Owslebury, Hants: an Iron Age and early Romano-British settlement.* Ancient Monuments Laboratory Report 6/87. London: English Heritage.

Maltby, M. 2010. *Feeding a Roman Town: environmental evidence from excavations in Winchester, 1972–1985.* Winchester: Winchester Museums.

Margueire, D. and Hunot, J.V. 2007. Charcoal analysis and dendrology: data from archaeological sites in north-western France. *Journal of Archaeological Science* 34: 1417–33.

Marshall, P., Darvill, T.C., Parker Pearson, M. and Wainwright, G.J. 2012. *Stonehenge, Amesbury, Wiltshire: chronological modelling. Scientific dating report.* Research Report 1-2012. Swindon: English Heritage.

Marshall, S. 2016. *Exploring Avebury: the essential guide.* Stroud: History Press.

Masotti, S., Succi-Leonelli, E. and Gualdi-Russo, E. 2013. Cremated human remains: is measurement of the lateral angle of the meatus acusticus internus a reliable method for sex determination? *International Journal of Legal Medicine* 127: 1039–44.

Mays, S. 1998. *The Archaeology of Human Bones.* London: Routledge.

Mays, S. 2010. *The Archaeology of Human Bones.* 2nd edition. London: Routledge.

Mays, S., Brickley, M. and Dodwell, N. 2002. *Human bones from archaeological sites: guidelines for producing assessment documents and analytical reports*. Swindon: English Heritage.

Mays, S., Roberts, D., Marshall, P., Pike, A.W.G., van Heekeren, V., Bronk Ramsey, C., Dunbar, E., Reimer, P., Linscott, B., Radini, A., Lowe, A., Dowle, A., Speller, C., Vallender, J. and Bedford, J. 2018. Lives before and after Stonehenge: an osteobiographical study of four prehistoric burials recently excavated from the Stonehenge World Heritage Site. *Journal of Archaeological Science Reports* 20: 692–710.

McKinley, J.I. 1993. Bone fragment size and weights of bone from modern British cremations and its implications for the interpretation of archaeological cremations. *International Journal of Osteoarchaeology* 3: 283–7.

McKinley, J.I. 1994. Bone fragment size in British cremation burials and its implications for pyre technology and ritual. *Journal of Archaeological Science* 21: 339–42.

McKinley, J.I. 1995. Human bone. In R.M.J. Cleal, K.E. Walker and R. Montague, *Stonehenge in its Landscape: twentieth-century excavations*. London: English Heritage. 451–61.

McKinley, J.I. 1997. Bronze Age 'barrows' and funerary rites and rituals of cremation. *Proceedings of the Prehistoric Society* 63: 129–45.

McKinley, J.I. 2000. The analysis of cremated bone. In M. Cox and S. Mays (eds) *Human Osteology in Archaeology and Forensic Science*. London: Greenwich Medical Media. 403–22.

McKinley, J.I. and Bond, J.M. 2001. Cremated bone. In D.R. Brothwell and A.M. Pollard (eds) *Handbook of Archaeological Sciences*. Chichester: Wiley. 281–92.

McOmish, D., Field, D. and Brown, G. 2002. *The Field Archaeology of the Salisbury Plain Training Area*. Swindon: English Heritage.

McParland, L.C., Collinson, M.E., Scott, A.C., Campbell, G. and Veal, R. 2010. Is vitrification in charcoal a result of high temperature burning of wood? *Journal of Archaeological Science* 37: 2679–87.

Meindl, R.S. and Lovejoy, C.O. 1985. Ectocranial suture closure: a revised method for the determination of skeletal age at death based on the lateral-anterior sutures. *American Journal of Physical Anthropology* 68: 57–66.

Mercer, R. 1999. The origins of warfare in the British Isles. In J. Carman and A. Harding (eds) *Ancient Warfare: archaeological perspectives*. Stroud: Sutton. 143–56.

Molnar, P., Ahlstrom, T.P. and Leden, I. 2011. Osteoarthritis and activity: an analysis of the relationship between eburnation, musculoskeletal stress markers (MSM) and age in two Neolithic hunter-gatherer populations from Gotland, Sweden. *International Journal of Osteoarchaeology* 21: 283–91.

Montague, R. 1995a. Stone. In R.M.J. Cleal, K.E. Walker and R. Montague, *Stonehenge in its Landscape: twentieth-century excavations*. London: English Heritage. 375–90.

Montague, R. 1995b. Construction and use of the Avenue. In R.M.J. Cleal, K.E. Walker and R. Montague, *Stonehenge in its Landscape: twentieth-century excavations*. London: English Heritage. 291–327.

Montague, R. and Gardiner, J. 1995. Other stone. In R.M.J. Cleal, K.E. Walker and R. Montague, *Stonehenge in its Landscape: twentieth-century excavations*. London: English Heritage. 390–9.

Mook, W.G. 1986. Business meeting: recommendations/resolutions adopted by the twelfth international radiocarbon conference. *Radiocarbon* 28: 799.

Moore, P.D. 1977. Ancient distribution of lime trees in Britain. *Nature* 268: 13–14.

Moore, P.D. and Webb, J.A. 1978. *An Illustrated Guide to Pollen Analysis*. London: Hodder and Stoughton.

Moore, P.D., Webb, J.A. and Collinson, M.E. 1991. *Pollen Analysis*. 2nd edition. Oxford: Blackwell Scientific.

Moorhead, T.S.N. 2001. *Roman coin finds from Wiltshire*. Unpublished MPhil dissertation, University College London.

Moorrees, C.F.A., Fanning, E.A. and Hunt, E.E. jr. 1963. Formation and resorption of three deciduous teeth in children. *American Journal of Physical Anthropology* 21: 205–13.

Morgan, C.L. 1887. The stones of Stanton Drew: their source and origin. *Proceedings of the Somerset Archaeological and Natural History Society* 33: 37–50.

Mortimer, J.R. 1905. *Fifty Years' Researches in British and Saxon Burial Mounds of East Yorkshire*. London: A. Brown & Sons.

Muhkerjee, A., Gibson, A.M. and Evershed, R.P. 2008. Trends in pig product processing at British Neolithic Grooved Ware sites traced through organic residues in potsherds. *Journal of Archaeological Science* 35: 2059–73.

Murphy, C.P. 1986. *Thin Section Preparation of Soils and Sediments*. Berkhamsted: AB Academic.

Nash, D.J. and McLaren, S.J. 2007. *Geochemical Sediments and Landscapes*. Oxford: Blackwell.

Nash, D.J., Ciborowski, T.J.R., Ullyot, J.S., Parker Pearson, M., Darvill, T., Maniatis, G., Greaney, S. and Whitaker, K. 2020. Origins of the sarsen megaliths at Stonehenge. *Science Advances* 6: eabc0133.

Needham, S. 2005. Transforming Beaker culture in north-west Europe: processes of fusion and fission. *Proceedings of the Prehistoric Society* 71: 171–217.

Newall, R.S. 1929. Stonehenge. *Antiquity* 3: 75–88.

Newall, R.S. 1956. Stonehenge: a review. *Antiquity* 30: 137–41.

Newcomer, M.H. 1971. Some quantitative experiments in hand axe manufacture. *World Archaeology* 3: 85–94.

Noble, G. and Brophy, K. 2015. Ritual and remembrance at a prehistoric ceremonial complex in central Scotland: excavations at Forteviot, Perth and Kinross. *Antiquity* 85: 787–804.

Noble, G. and Brophy, K. with Hamilton, D., Leach, S. and Sheridan, A. 2017. Cremation practices and the creation of monument complexes: the Neolithic cremation cemetery at Forteviot, Strathearn, Perth and Kinross, Scotland, and its comparanda. *Proceedings of the Prehistoric Society* 83: 213–45.

Noddle, B. 1982. The size of red deer in Britain – past and present, with some reference to fallow deer. In C. Grigson, M. Bell and S. Limbrey (eds) *Archaeological Aspects of Woodland Ecology*. Oxford: BAR (International Series) 146. 315–33.

Norén, A., Lynnerup, N., Czarnetzki, A. and Graw, M. 2005. Lateral angle: a method for sexing using the petrous bone. *American Journal of Physical Anthropology* 128: 318–23.

Oswald, A. 1969. Excavations at Barford, Warwickshire. *Transactions of the Birmingham and Warwickshire Archaeological Society* 83: 3–54.

Parker Pearson, M. 2000. Ancestors, bones and stones in Neolithic and Early Bronze Age Britain and Ireland. In A. Ritchie (ed.) *Neolithic Orkney in its European Context*. Cambridge: McDonald Institute. 203–14.

Parker Pearson, M. 2002. Placing the physical and incorporeal dead: Stonehenge and changing concepts of ancestral space in Neolithic Britain. In H. Silverman and D.B. Small (eds) *The Place and Space of Death*. AP3A No. 11. Arlington VA: American Anthropological Association. 145–60.

Parker Pearson, M. 2007. The Stonehenge Riverside Project: excavations at the east entrance of Durrington Walls. In M. Larsson and M. Parker Pearson (eds) *From Stonehenge to the Baltic: cultural diversity in the third millennium BC*. Oxford: BAR (International Series) 1692. 125–44.

Parker Pearson, M. 2012. *Stonehenge: exploring the greatest Stone Age mystery*. London: Simon & Schuster.

Parker Pearson, M. 2016a. From corpse to skeleton: dealing with the dead in prehistory. *Bulletins et Mémoires de la Société d'Anthropologie de Paris* 28: 4–16.

Parker Pearson, M. 2016b. The sarsen stones of Stonehenge. *Proceedings of the Geologists' Association* 127: 363–9.

Parker Pearson, M. and Ramilisonina. 1998a. Stonehenge for the ancestors: the stones pass on the message. *Antiquity* 72: 308–26.

Parker Pearson, M. and Ramilisonina. 1998b. Stonehenge for the ancestors: part two. *Antiquity* 72: 855–6.

Parker Pearson, M. and Thorpe, I.J. (eds) 2005. *Warfare, Violence and Slavery in Prehistory: proceedings of a Prehistoric Society conference at Sheffield University*. Oxford: BAR (International Series) S1374.

Parker Pearson, M., Bevins, R., Ixer, R., Pollard, J., Richards, C., Welham, K., Chan, B., Edinborough, K., Hamilton, D., Macphail, R., Schlee, D., Simmons, E. and Smith, M. 2015. Craig Rhos-y-felin: a Welsh bluestone megalith quarry for Stonehenge. *Antiquity* 89: 1331–52.

Parker Pearson, M., Chamberlain, A., Jay, M., Marshall, P., Pollard, J., Richards, C., Thomas, J., Tilley, C. and Welham, K. 2009. Who was buried at Stonehenge? *Antiquity* 83: 23–39.

Parker Pearson, M., Chamberlain, A., Jay, M., Richards, M., Evans, J. and Sheridan, A. (eds) 2018. *The Beaker People: isotopes, mobility and diet in prehistoric Britain*. Oxford: Oxbow.

Parker Pearson, M., Chamberlain, A., Jay, M., Richards, M., Sheridan, A., Curtis, N., Evans, J., Gibson, A.M., Hutchison, M., Mahoney, P., Marshall, P., Montgomery, J., Needham, S., Pellegrini, M., Wilkin, N. and Thomas, S. 2016. Beaker people in Britain: migration, mobility and diet. *Antiquity* 90: 620–37.

Parker Pearson, M., Cleal, R., Marshall, P., Needham, S., Pollard, J., Richards, C., Ruggles, C., Sheridan, A., Thomas, J., Tilley, C., Welham, K., Chamberlain, A., Chenery, C., Evans, J., Knüsel, C., Linford, N., Martin, L., Montgomery, J., Payne, A. and Richards, M. 2007. The age of Stonehenge. *Antiquity* 81: 617–39.

Parker Pearson, M., Pollard, J., Richards, C., Thomas, J., Tilley, C. and Welham, K. 2006. Stonehenge, its river and its landscape: unravelling the mysteries of a prehistoric sacred place. *Archäologischer Anzeiger* 2006/1: 237–58.

Parker Pearson, M. with Pollard, J., Richards, C., Thomas, J. and Welham, K. 2015. *Stonehenge: making sense of a prehistoric mystery*. York: Council for British Archaeology.

Parker Pearson, M., Pollard, J., Richards, C., Thomas, J., Welham, K., Albarella, U., Chan, B., Marshall, P. and Viner, S. 2011. Feeding Stonehenge: feasting in Late Neolithic Britain. In G. Aranda Jiménez, S. Montón-Subías and M. Sánchez Romero (eds) *Guess Who's Coming to Dinner: commensality rituals in the prehistoric societies of Europe and the Near East*. Oxford: Oxbow. 73–90.

Parker Pearson, M., Pollard, J., Richards, C. and Welham, K. 2017. The origins of Stonehenge: on the track of the bluestones. *Archaeology International* 20: 54–9.

Parker Pearson, M., Pollard, J., Richards, C., Welham, K., Casswell, C., French, C., Shaw, D., Simmons, E., Stanford, A., Bevins, R.E. and Ixer, R.A. 2019. Megalithic quarries for Stonehenge's bluestones. *Antiquity* 93: 45–62.

Parker Pearson, M., Richards, C., Allen, M., Payne, A. and Welham, K. 2004. The Stonehenge Riverside Project: research design and initial results. *Journal of Nordic Archaeological Science* 14: 45–60.

Passmore, A.D. 1921. Hammerstones. *Proceedings of the Prehistoric Society* 3: 444–7.

Payne, A. 2006 *Stonehenge Riverside Project, West Amesbury and Greater Cursus, Wiltshire: report on geophysical surveys, July 2006*. Research Report 41-2007. Swindon: English Heritage.

Payne, S. 1973. Kill-off patterns in sheep and goats: the mandibles from Asvan Kale. *Anatolian Studies* 23: 281–303.

Payne, S. 1985. Morphological distinctions between the mandibular teeth of young sheep, *Ovis*, and goats, *Capra*. *Journal of Archaeological Science* 12: 139–47.

Payne, S. 1987. Reference codes for the wear state in the mandibular cheek teeth of sheep and goats. *Journal of Archaeological Science* 14: 609–14.

Payne, S. and Bull, G. 1988. Components of variation in measurements of pig bones and teeth, and the use of measurements to distinguish wild from domestic pig remains. *ArchaeoZoologia* 2: 27–66.

Peacock, D.P.S. 1969. Neolithic pottery production in Cornwall. *Antiquity* 43: 145–9.

Pearson, G.W. 1986. Precise calendrical dating of known growth-period samples using a 'curve fitting' technique. *Radiocarbon* 28: 292–9.

Pearson, T. and Field, D. 2011. *Stonehenge WHS Landscape Project: Stonehenge Cursus, Amesbury, Wiltshire: archaeological survey report*. Research Report 103-2011. Swindon: English Heritage.

Pelling, R. and Campbell, G. 2013. The plant resources. In M. Canti, G. Campbell and S. Greaney (eds) *Stonehenge World Heritage Site synthesis: prehistoric landscape, environment and economy*. Research Report 45-2013. Swindon: English Heritage. 37–60.

Pelling, R., Campbell, G., Carruthers, W., Hunter, K. and Marshall, P. 2015. Exploring contamination (intrusion and residuality) in the archaeobotanical record: case studies from central and southern England. *Vegetation History and Archaeobotany* 24: 85–99.

Petrie, J. 2012. *Living stone: materiality and monumentality in West Sumba, Indonesia*. Unpublished PhD thesis, University of Manchester.

Piggott, S. 1948a. The excavations at Cairnpapple Hill, West Lothian, 1947–8. *Proceedings of the Society of Antiquaries of Scotland* 82: 68–123.

Piggott, S. 1948b. Destroyed megaliths in north Wiltshire. *Wiltshire Archaeological and Natural History Magazine* 52: 390–2.

Piggott, S. 1962. *The West Kennet Long Barrow: excavations 1955–56*. London: HMSO.

Pitts, M.W. 1982. On the road to Stonehenge: report on investigations beside the A344 in 1968, 1979 and 1980. *Proceedings of the Prehistoric Society* 48: 75–132.

Pitts, M.W. 1996. The stone axe in Neolithic Britain. *Proceedings of the Prehistoric Society* 61: 311–71.

Pitts, M.W. 2000. *Hengeworld*. London: Century.

Pitts, M.W. 2001. Excavating the Sanctuary: new investigations on Overton Hill, Avebury. *Wiltshire Archaeological and Natural History Magazine* 94: 1–23.

Pitts, M.W. 2017. Stonehenge finds tell of divided society. *British Archaeology* 153: 6–7.

Pitts, M.W., Bayliss, A., McKinley, J., Boylston, A., Budd, P., Evans, J., Chenery, C., Reynolds, A. and Semple S. 2002. An Anglo-Saxon decapitation and burial at Stonehenge. *Wiltshire Archaeological and Natural History Magazine* 95: 131–46.

Pitts, M.W., Hamilton, D. and Reynolds, A. 2007. A revised date for the early medieval execution at Stonehenge. *Wiltshire Archaeological and Natural History Magazine* 100: 202–3.

Pollard, J. 1995a. Inscribing space: formal deposition at the later Neolithic monument of Woodhenge, Wiltshire. *Proceedings of the Prehistoric Society* 61: 137–56.

Pollard, J. 1995b. The Durrington 68 timber circle: a forgotten Late Neolithic monument. *Wiltshire Archaeological and Natural History Magazine* 88: 122–5.

Pollard, J. 1999. 'These places have their moments': thoughts on settlement practices in the British Neolithic. In J. Brück and M. Goodman (eds) *Making Places in the Prehistoric World: themes in settlement archaeology*. London: UCL Press. 76–93.

Pollard, J. 2017. Substantial and significant pits in the Mesolithic of Britain and adjacent regions. *Hunter-Gatherer Research* 3: 165–84.

Pollard, J. and Reynolds, A. 2002. *Avebury: the biography of a landscape*. Stroud: Tempus.

Pollard, J. and Robinson, D. 2007. A return to Woodhenge: the results and implications of the 2006 excavations. In M. Larsson and M. Parker Pearson (eds) *From Stonehenge to the Baltic: cultural diversity in the third millennium BC*. Oxford: BAR (International Series) 1692. 159–68.

Pollard, J. and Ruggles, C. 2001. Shifting perceptions: spatial order, cosmology, and patterns of deposition at Stonehenge. *Cambridge Archaeological Journal* 11: 69–90.

Pollard, J., Garwood, P., Parker Pearson, M., Richards, C., Thomas, J. and Welham, K. 2017. Remembered and imagined belongings: Stonehenge in the age of first metals. In P. Bickle, V. Cummings, D. Hofmann and J. Pollard (eds) *The Neolithic of Europe: essays in honour of Alasdair Whittle*. Oxford: Oxbow. 279–97.

Porter, V. 1990. *Small Woods and Hedgerows*. London: Penguin.

Powell, A.B., Barclay, A.J., Mepham, L. and Stevens, C.J. 2015. *Imperial College Sports Ground and RMC Land, Harlington: the development of prehistoric and later communities in the Colne valley and on the Heathrow terraces*. Old Sarum: Wessex Archaeology.

Protzen, J.-P. 2000. Inca architecture. In L.L. Minelli (ed.) *The Inca World: the development of pre-Columbian Peru AD1000–1534*. Norman: University of Oklahoma Press. 193–217.

Pryor, F. 2001. *Seahenge: new discoveries in prehistoric Britain*. London: HarperCollins.

Pryor, F. 2003. *Britain BC: life in Britain and Ireland before the Romans*. London: HarperCollins.

Rackham, O. 2003. *Ancient Woodland: its history, vegetation and uses in England*. Dalbeattie: Castlepoint Press.

RCHME 1977. Evolution of the Landscape. Sarsens: shortened list. Unpublished report, Salisbury.

RCHME 1979. *Stonehenge and its Environs*. Edinburgh: Edinburgh University Press.

Reimer, P.J., Baillie, M.G.L., Bard, E., Bayliss, A., Beck, J.W., Blackwell, P.G., Bronk Ramsey, C., Buck, C.E., Burr, G.S., Edwards, R.L., Friedrich, M., Grootes, P.M., Guilderson, T.P., Hajdas, I., Heaton, T.J., Hogg, A.G., Hughen, K.A., Kaiser, K.F., Kromer, B., McCormac, G., Manning, S., Reimer, R.W., Remmele, S., Richards, D.A., Southon, J.R., Talamo, S., Taylor, F.W., Turney, C.S.M., van der Plicht, J. and Weyhenmeyer, C.E. 2009. IntCal09 and Marine09 radiocarbon age calibration curves, 0–50,000 years cal BP. *Radiocarbon* 51: 1111–50.

Reimer, P.J., Bard, E., Bayliss, A., Beck, J.W., Blackwell, P.G., Bronk Ramsey, C., Buck, C.E., Cheng, H., Edwards, R.L., Friedrich, M., Grootes, P.M., Guilderson, T.P., Haflidason, H., Hajdas, I., Hatté, C., Heaton, T.J., Hoffmann, D.L., Hogg, A.G., Hughen, K.A., Kaiser, K.F., Kromer, B., Manning, S.W., Niu, M., Reimer, R.W., Richards, D.A., Scott, E.M., Southon, J.R., Staff, R.A., Turney, C.S.M. and van der Plicht, J. 2013. IntCal13 and Marine13 radiocarbon age calibration curves 0–50,000 years cal BP. *Radiocarbon* 55: 1869–87.

Renfrew, C. 1973a. Monuments, mobilization and social organization in Neolithic Wessex. In C. Renfrew (ed.) *The Explanation of Culture Change: models in prehistory*. London: Duckworth. 539–58.

Renfrew, C. 1973b. *Before Civilization*. London: Jonathan Cape.

Richards, C. 1996. Henges and water: towards an elemental understanding of monumentality and landscape in Late Neolithic Britain. *Journal of Material Culture Studies* 1: 313–36.

Richards, C. (ed.) 2013. *Building the Great Stone Circles of the North*. Oxford: Windgather Press.

Richards, C. and Thomas, J. 1984. Ritual activity and structured deposition in later Neolithic Wessex. In R. Bradley and J. Gardiner (eds) *Neolithic Studies: a review of some current research*. Oxford: BAR (British Series) 133. 189–218.

Richards, C., Brown, J., Jones, S., Hall, A. and Muir, T. 2013. Monumental risk: megalithic quarrying at Staneyhill and Vestra Fiold, Mainland, Orkney. In C. Richards (ed.) *Building the Great Stone Circles of the North*. Oxford: Windgather Press. 119–48.

Richards, J. 1990. *The Stonehenge Environs Project*. London: English Heritage.

Richards, J. 1991. *Stonehenge*. London: English Heritage and Batsford.

Richards, J. 2017. *Stonehenge: the story so far*. Swindon: Historic England.

Richards, J. and Whitby, M. 1997. The engineering of Stonehenge. In B.W. Cunliffe and C. Renfrew (eds) *Science and Stonehenge*. Oxford: Oxford University Press. 231–56.

Richards, M. and Hedges, R.E.M. 1999a. Stable isotope evidence for similarities in the types of marine foods used by Late Mesolithic humans at sites along the Atlantic coast of Europe. *Journal of Archaeological Science* 26: 717–22.

Richards, M. and Hedges, R.E.M. 1999b. A Neolithic revolution? New evidence of diet in the British Neolithic. *Antiquity* 73: 891–7.

Roberts, C. and Cox, M. 2003. *Health and Disease in Britain: from prehistory to the present day*. Stroud: Sutton.

Roberts, D., Valdez-Tullett, A., Marshall, P., Last, J., Oswald, A., Barclay, A., Bishop, B., Dunbar, E., Forward, A., Law, M., Linford, N., Linford, P., López-Dóriga, I., Manning, A., Payne, A., Pelling, R., Powell, A.B., Reimer, P., Russell, M., Small, F., Soutar, S., Vallender, J., Winter, E. and Worley, F. 2018. Recent investigations at two long barrows and reflections on their context in the Stonehenge World Heritage Site and environs. *Internet Archaeology* 47. https://doi.org/10.11141/ia.47.7

Robertson-Mackay, M.E. 1980. A 'head and hooves' burial beneath a round barrow, with other Neolithic and Bronze Age sites, on Hemp Knoll, near Avebury, Wiltshire. *Proceedings of the Prehistoric Society* 46: 123–76.

Robinson, M. 2000. Further considerations of Neolithic charred cereals, fruits and nuts. In A.S. Fairbairn (ed.) *Plants in Neolithic Britain and Beyond*. Neolithic Studies Group Seminar Papers 5. Oxford: Oxbow Books. 84–90.

Rodwell, J.S. 1991. *British Plant Communities. Volume 1, Woodlands and scrub*. Cambridge: Cambridge University Press.

Rodwell, J.S. 1992. *British Plant Communities. Volume 3, Grasslands and montane communities*. Cambridge: Cambridge University Press.

Roskams, S. 2000. *Excavation*. Cambridge: Cambridge University Press.

Ruggles, C. 1997. Astronomy and Stonehenge. In B.W. Cunliffe and C. Renfrew (eds) *Science and Stonehenge*. Oxford: Oxford University Press. 203–29.

Ruggles, C. 1999. *Astronomy in Prehistoric Britain and Ireland*. New Haven: Yale University Press.

Ruggles, C. 2006. Interpreting solstitial alignments in Late Neolithic Wessex. *Archaeoastronomy* 20: 1–27.

Ruggles, C. 2007. Cosmology, calendar, and temple orientations in ancient Hawai'i. In C. Ruggles and G. Urton (eds) *Skywatching in the Ancient World: new perspectives in cultural astronomy*. Boulder: University Press of Colorado. 287–329.

Saville, A. 1980. Five flint assemblages from excavated sites in Wiltshire. *Wiltshire Archaeological and Natural History Magazine* 72: 1–27.

Saville, A. 2008. The flint and chert artefacts. In R. Mercer and F. Healy, *Hambledon Hill, Dorset, England: excavation and survey of a Neolithic monument complex and its surrounding landscape*. Swindon: English Heritage. 640–743.

Scaife, R.G. 1980. *Late Devensian and Flandrian palaeoecological studies in the Isle of Wight*. Unpublished PhD thesis, University of London.

Scaife, R.G. 1988. The elm decline in the pollen record of south east England and its relationship to early agriculture. In M. Jones (ed.) *Archaeology and the Flora of the British Isles*. Oxford: Oxford University Committee for Archaeology. 21–33.

Scaife, R.G. 1994. Pollen analysis of the River Allen floodplain, Wimborne town centre, Dorset. Unpublished report for Southern Archaeological Services.

Scaife, R.G. 1995. Boreal and Sub-Boreal chalk landscape: pollen evidence. In R.M.J. Cleal, K.E. Walker and R. Montague, *Stonehenge in its Landscape: twentieth-century excavations*. London: English Heritage. 51–5.

Scaife, R.G. 2000. Holocene vegetation development in London. In J. Sidell, K. Wilkinson, R.G. Scaife and N. Cameron (eds) *The Holocene Evolution of the London Thames: archaeological excavations (1991–1998) for the London Underground Limited, Jubilee Line extension project*. London: Museum of London. 111–17.

Scaife, R.G. 2003. The palaeoecological background. In C. Pope, L. Snow and D. Allen (eds) *The Isle of Wight Flora*. Wimborne: Dovecote Press. 19–31.

Scaife, R.G. 2006. Preliminary pollen analysis of floodplain sediments of the River Avon at Amesbury: potential for establishing the vegetation history of the Stonehenge region. Unpublished report for SRP.

Scaife, R.G. 2007. Palynological analysis. In C. French, H. Lewis, M.J. Allen, M. Green, R.G. Scaife and J. Gardiner (eds) *Prehistoric Landscape Development and Human Impact in the Upper Allen Valley, Cranborne Chase, Dorset*. Cambridge: McDonald Institute. 43–64.

Scarre, C. 2004. Displaying the stones: the materiality of 'megalithic' monuments. In E. DeMarrais, C. Gosden and C. Renfrew (eds) *Rethinking Materiality: the engagement of mind with the material world*. Cambridge: McDonald Institute. 141–52.

Scarre, C. 2011. *Landscapes of Neolithic Brittany*. Oxford: Oxford University Press.

Scheuer, L. and Black, S. 2000. *Developmental Juvenile Osteology*. San Diego: Academic Press.

Schulting, R. 2012. Skeletal evidence for interpersonal violence: beyond mortuary monuments in southern Britain. In R. Schulting and L. Fibiger (eds) *Sticks, Stones, and Broken Bones: Neolithic violence in a European perspective*. Oxford: Oxford University Press. 223–48.

Schulting, R. and Bradley, R. 2013. 'Of human remains and weapons in the neighbourhood of London': new radiocarbon dates on Thames 'river skulls' exhibiting injuries. *Archaeological Journal* 170: 30–77.

Schulting, R. and Wysocki, M. 2005. 'In this chambered tumulus were found cleft skulls…': an assessment of the evidence for cranial trauma in the British Neolithic. *Proceedings of the Prehistoric Society* 71: 107–38.

Schwartz, J.H. 2007. *Skeleton Keys: an introduction to human skeletal morphology, development, and analysis*. 2nd edition. Oxford: Oxford University Press.

Schweingruber, F.H. 1990. *Microscopic Wood Anatomy*. Birmensdorf: Swiss Federal Institute for Forest, Snow and Landscape Research.

Scott, E.M. 2003. The third international radiocarbon intercomparison (TIRI) and the fourth international radiocarbon intercomparison (FIRI) 1990–2002: results, analyses, and conclusions. *Radiocarbon* 45: 135–408.

Scott, E.M., Cook, G. and Naysmith, P. 2010a. A report on phase 2 of the fifth international radiocarbon intercomparison (VIRI). *Radiocarbon* 52: 846–58.

Scott, E.M., Cook, G. and Naysmith, P. 2010b. The fifth international radiocarbon intercomparison (VIRI): an assessment of laboratory performance in stage 3. *Radiocarbon* 53: 859–65.

Scourse, J.D. 1997. Transport of the Stonehenge bluestones: testing the glacial hypothesis. In B.W. Cunliffe and C. Renfrew (eds) *Science and Stonehenge*. Oxford: Oxford University Press. 271–314.

Scurr, R. 2016. *John Aubrey: my own life*. London: Vintage.

Sellet, F. 1993. Chaîne opératoire: the concept and its applications. *Lithic Technology* 18: 106–12.

Serjeantson, D. 1996. The animal bones. In S. Needham and T. Spence (eds) *Refuse and Disposal at Area 16 East, Runnymede*. London: British Museum. 194–223.

Serjeantson, D. 1998. Review of environmental archaeology in southern Britain: Neolithic and Early Bronze Age (4000–1500 BC). The development of agriculture and animal husbandry: the animal bones. Unpublished report for Ancient Monuments Laboratory, English Heritage.

Serjeantson, D. 2011. *Review of animal remains from the Neolithic and Early Bronze Age of southern Britain (4000 BC–1500 BC)*. Research Report 29-2011. Swindon: English Heritage.

Serjeantson, D. and Gardiner, J. 1995. Antler implements and ox scapulae shovels. In R.M.J. Cleal, K.E. Walker and R. Montague, *Stonehenge in its Landscape: twentieth-century excavations*. London: English Heritage. 414–30.

Sheldon, J. 1979. Charcoal. In P. Ashbee, I.F. Smith and J.G. Evans, Excavation of three long barrows near Avebury, Wiltshire. *Proceedings of the Prehistoric Society* 45: 207–300.

Sheridan, A. 2007. From Picardie to Pickering and Pencraig Hill? New information on the 'Carinated Bowl Neolithic' in northern Britain. *Proceedings of the British Academy* 144: 441–92.

Sheridan, A., Field, D., Pailler, Y., Petrequin, P., Errera, M. and Cassen, S. 2010. The Breamore jadeitite axehead and other Neolithic axeheads of Alpine rock from central southern England. *Wiltshire Archaeological and Natural History Magazine* 103: 16–34.

Shipman, P., Giraud, F. and Schoeninger, M. 1984. Burnt bones and teeth: an experimental study of color, morphology, crystal structure and shrinkage. *Journal of Archaeological Science* 11: 307–25.

Simpson, G.G., Roe, A. and Lewontin, R.C. 1960. *Quantitative Zoology*. New York: Harcourt Brace.

Slota, P.J. jr., Jull, A.J.T., Linick, T.W. and Toolin, L.J. 1987. Preparation of small samples for ^{14}C accelerator targets by catalytic reduction of CO. *Radiocarbon* 29: 303–6.

Smith, A.C. 1884. *Guide to the British and Roman Antiquities of the North Wiltshire Downs*. Marlborough: Marlborough College Natural History Society.

Smith, A.G. 1970. The influence of Mesolithic and Neolithic man on British vegetation: a discussion. In D. Walker and R.G. West (eds) *Studies in the Vegetational History of the British Isles*. Cambridge: Cambridge University Press. 81–96.

Smith, B.H. 1984. Patterns of molar wear in hunter-gatherers and agriculturalists. *American Journal of Physical Anthropologists* 63: 39–56.

Smith, G. 1973. Excavation of the Stonehenge Avenue at West Amesbury, Wiltshire. *Wiltshire Archaeological and Natural History Magazine* 68: 42–56.

Smith, H., Marshall, P. and Parker Pearson, M. 2001. Reconstructing house activity areas. In U. Albarella (ed.) *Environmental Archaeology: meaning and purpose*. London: Kluwer. 249–70.

Smith, I.F. 1965. *Windmill Hill and Avebury: excavations by Alexander Keiller 1925–1939*. Oxford: Clarendon Press.

Smith, R.W. 1984. The ecology of Neolithic farming systems as exemplified by the Avebury region of Wiltshire. *Proceedings of the Prehistoric Society* 50: 99–120.

Smyth, J. 2014. *Settlement in the Irish Neolithic: new discoveries on the edge of Europe*. Oxford: Oxbow.

Snoeck, C., Pouncett, J., Claeys, P., Goderis, S., Mattielli, N., Parker Pearson, M., Willis, C., Zazzo, A., Lee-Thorp, J. and Schulting, R. 2018. Strontium isotope analyses on cremated human remains from Stonehenge support links with west Wales. *Scientific Reports* (2018) 8: 10790.

Stace, C. 1991. *New Flora of the British Isles*. Cambridge: Cambridge University Press.

Stace, C. 2005. *New Flora of the British Isles*. 2nd edition. Cambridge: Cambridge University Press.

Stenhouse, M.J. and Baxter, M.S. 1983. 14C dating reproducibility: evidence from routine dating of archaeological samples. *PACT* 8: 147–61.

Stevens, C.J. 2007. Reconsidering the evidence: towards an understanding of the social contexts of subsistence production in Neolithic Britain. In S. Colledge and J. Conolly (eds) *The Origins and Spread of Domestic Plants in Southwest Asia and Europe*. London: UCL Institute of Archaeology Publications. 375–89.

Stevens, C.J. and Fuller, D.Q. 2012. Did Neolithic farming fail? The case for a Bronze Age agricultural revolution in the British Isles. *Antiquity* 86: 707–22.

Stone, E.H. 1924. *The Stones of Stonehenge*. London: Robert Scott.

Stone, J.F.S. 1935. Some discoveries at Ratfyn, Amesbury, and their bearing on the date of Woodhenge. *Wiltshire Archaeological and Natural History Magazine* 47: 55–67.

Stone, J.F.S. 1938. An Early Bronze Age grave in Fargo plantation near Stonehenge. *Wiltshire Archaeological and Natural History Magazine* 48: 357–70.

Stone, J.F.S. 1947. The Stonehenge cursus and its affinities. *Archaeological Journal* 104: 7–9.

Stone, J.F.S. 1949. Some Grooved Ware pottery from the Woodhenge area. *Proceedings of the Prehistoric Society* 15: 122–7.

Stone, J.F.S. 1953. *Stonehenge: in light of modern research*. Salisbury: P. Jay & Son.

Stone, J.F.S. and Young, W. 1948. Two pits of Grooved Ware date near Woodhenge. *Wiltshire Archaeological and Natural History Magazine* 52: 287–306.

Stonehenge Hidden Landscapes Project. 2012. Interim geophysical survey report: field season 2 (2011–2012). Unpublished report for the National Trust and English Heritage.

Stoops, G. 2003. *Guidelines for Analysis and Description of Soil and Regolith Thin Sections*. Madison WI: Soil Science Society of America.

Stuijts, I. 2006. Charcoal sampling sites and procedures: practical themes from Ireland. In A. Dufraisse (ed.) *Charcoal Analysis: new analytical tools and methods for archaeology*. Oxford: BAR (International Series) 1483. 25–33.

Stuiver, M. and Kra, R.S. 1986. Editorial comment. *Radiocarbon* 28 (2B): ii.

Stuiver, M. and Polach, H.A. 1977. Reporting of ^{14}C data. *Radiocarbon* 19: 355–63.

Stuiver, M. and Reimer, P.J. 1986. A computer program for radiocarbon age calculation. *Radiocarbon* 28: 1022–30.

Stuiver, M. and Reimer, P.J. 1993. Extended ^{14}C data base and revised CALIB 3.0 ^{14}C age calibration program. *Radiocarbon* 35: 215–30.

Stukeley, W. 1722–24. *The History of the Temples of the Antient Celts, I, II.* Oxford: Bodleian Library MS Eng. Misc. c. 323.

Stukeley, W. 1740. *Stonehenge: a temple restor'd to the British druids and Abury, a temple of the British druids.* London: Innys and Manby.

Stukeley, W. 1869. Extracts from a common-place book of Dr Stukeley. *Wiltshire Archaeological and Natural History Magazine* 11: 341–4.

Suchey, J. and Brooks, S. 1990. Skeletal age determination based on the *os pubis*: a comparison of the Acsádi-Nemeskéri and Suchey-Brooks methods. *Human Evolution* 5: 227–38.

Summerfield, M.A. and Goudie, A.S. 1980. The sarsens of southern England: their palaeoenvironmental interpretation with reference to other silcretes. In D.K.C. Jones (ed.) *The Shaping of Southern England.* London: Academic Press. 71–100.

Suy, R. 2006. The varying morphology and aetiology of arterial aneurysms: a historical review. *Acta Angiologia* 12: 1–6.

Taylor, R.E. and Aitken, M.J. 1997. *Chronometric Dating in Archaeology*. New York: Plenum Press.

Te Punga, M.T. 1957. Periglaciation in southern England. *Tijdschrift van het Koninklijk Nederlandsch Aardrijkskundig Genootschap* 64: 401–12.

Teather, A.M. 2016. *Mining and Materiality: Neolithic chalk artefacts and their depositional contexts in southern Britain.* Oxford: Archaeopress.

Teather, A.M. 2017. More than 'other stone' – new methods to analyse prehistoric chalk artefacts. In R. Shaffrey (ed.) *Written in Stone: function, form, and provenancing of a range of prehistoric stone objects.* Southampton: Highfield Press. 303–21.

Tegel, W., Elburg, R., Hakelberg, D., Stäuble, H. and Büntgen, U. 2012. Early Neolithic water wells reveal the world's oldest wood architecture. *PLoS ONE* 7(12): e51374. https://doi.org/10.1371/journal.pone.0051374

Théry-Parisot, I., Chabal, L. and Chrzavzez, J. 2010. Anthracology and taphonomy, from wood gathering to charcoal analysis: a review of the taphonomic processes modifying charcoal assemblages, in archaeological contexts. *Palaeogeography, Palaeoclimatology, Palaeoecology* 291: 142–53.

Thomas, H.H. 1923. The source of the stones of Stonehenge. *Antiquaries Journal* 3: 239–60.

Thomas, J.S. 1999. *Understanding the Neolithic.* London: Routledge.

Thomas, J.S. 2006. On the origins and development of cursus monuments in Britain. *Proceedings of the Prehistoric Society 72*: 229–41.

Thomas, J.S. 2007. The internal features at Durrington Walls: investigations in the Southern Circle and Western Enclosures 2005–2006. In M. Larsson and M. Parker Pearson (eds) *From Stonehenge to the Baltic: cultural diversity in the third millennium BC.* Oxford: BAR (International Series) 1692. 145–57.

Thomas, J.S. 2013. *The Birth of Neolithic Britain: an interpretive account.* Oxford: Oxford University Press.

Thomas, J.S. 2015. *A Neolithic Ceremonial Complex in Galloway: excavations at Dunragit and Doughduil 1999–2002.* Oxford: Oxbow.

Thomas, J.S., Parker Pearson, M., Pollard, J., Richards, C., Tilley, C. and Welham, K. 2009. The date of the Stonehenge Cursus. *Antiquity* 83: 40–53.

Thomas, N. 1964. The Neolithic causewayed camp at Robin Hood's Ball, Shrewton. *Wiltshire Archaeological and Natural History Magazine* 59: 1–27.

Thompson, S. and Powell, A.B. 2018. *Along Prehistoric Lines: Neolithic, Iron Age and Romano-British activity at the former MoD headquarters, Durrington, Wiltshire.* Salisbury: Wessex Archaeology.

Thompson, S., Leivers, M. and Barclay, A. 2017. The Larkhill causewayed enclosure: rethinking the Early Neolithic Stonehenge landscape. *Current Archaeology* 326: 30–4.

Thompson, T.J.U. 2004. Recent advances in the study of burned bone and their implications for forensic anthropology. *Forensic Science International* 146 suppl.: S203–5.

Thompson, T.J.U., Islam, M. and Bonniere, M. 2013. A new statistical approach for determining the crystallinity of heat-altered bone mineral from FTIR spectra. *Journal of Archaeological Science* 40: 416–22.

Thompson, T.J.U., Islam, M., Piduru, K. and Marcel, A. 2011. An investigation into the internal and external variables acting on crystallinity index using Fourier transform infrared spectroscopy on unaltered and burned bone. *Palaeogeography, Palaeoclimatology, Palaeoecology* 299: 168–74.

Thorley, A. 1971a. *An investigation into the history of native tree species in south east England using the pollen analysis technique.* Unpublished PhD thesis, King's College, University of London.

Thorley, A. 1971b. Vegetational history of the Vale of Brooks. *Institute of British Geographers Conference Proceedings* 5: 47–50.

Thorley, A. 1981. Pollen analytical evidence relating to the vegetational history of the Chalk. *Journal of Biogeography* 8: 93–106.

Thorpe, R.S., Williams-Thorpe, O., Jenkins, D.G. and Watson, J.S. with contributions by Ixer, R.A. and Thomas, R.G. 1991. The geological sources and transport of the bluestones of Stonehenge, Wiltshire, UK. *Proceedings of the Prehistoric Society* 57: 103–57.

Thurnam, J. 1869. On ancient British barrows, especially those of Wiltshire and the adjoining counties. Part I, Long barrows. *Archaeologia* 42: 161–244.

Tilley, C. 1994. *A Phenomenology of Landscape: places, paths and monuments.* London: Berg.

Tilley, C., Richards, C., Bennett, W. and Field, D. 2007. Stonehenge – its landscape and its architecture: a reanalysis. In M. Larsson and M. Parker Pearson (eds) *From Stonehenge to the Baltic: cultural diversity in the third millennium BC*. Oxford: BAR (International Series) 1692. 183–204.

Tolan-Smith, C. 2008. Mesolithic Britain. In G. Bailey and P. Spikins (eds) *Mesolithic Europe*. Cambridge: Cambridge University Press. 132–57.

Tucker, M.E. 1991. *Sedimentary Geology*. Oxford: Blackwell Scientific.

Turner, A., Gonzalez, S. and Ohman, J.C. 2002. Prehistoric human and ungulate remains from Preston docks, Lancashire, UK: problems of river finds. *Journal of Archaeological Science* 29: 423–33.

Turner, J. 1970. Post-Neolithic disturbances of British vegetation. In D. Walker and R.G. West (eds) *Studies in the Vegetational History of the British Isles*. Cambridge: Cambridge University Press. 97–116.

Ubelaker, D.H. 1978. *Human Skeletal Remains: excavation, analysis, interpretation*. Chicago: Aldine Publishing.

Ullyott, J.S. and Nash, D.J. 2006. Micromorphology and geochemistry of groundwater silcretes in the eastern South Downs, UK. *Sedimentology* 53: 387–412.

Ullyott, J.S., Nash, D.J., Whiteman, C.A. and Mortimore, R.N. 2004. Distribution, petrology and mode of development of silcretes (sarsens and puddingstones) on the eastern South Downs, UK. *Earth Surface Processes and Landforms* 29: 1509–39.

Van Strydonck, M., Boudin, M., Hoefens, M. and de Mulder, G. 2005. 14C-dating of cremated bones – why does it work? *Lunula* 13: 3–10.

Van Tilburg, J.A. and Pakarati, A. 2002. The Rapa Nui carver's perspective: notes and observations on the experimental replication of monolithic sculpture (*moai*). In A. Herle (ed.) *Changing Themes in the Study of Pacific Art*. Honolulu: University of Hawaii Press. 280–90.

van Vark, G.N. 1975. Human cremated skeletal material by multivariate statistics: method II. *OSSA* 2: 47–68.

Vandeputte, K., Moens, L. and Dams, R. 1996. Improved sealed-tube combustion of organic samples to CO_2 for stable isotopic analysis, radiocarbon dating and percent carbon determinations. *Analytical Letters* 29: 2761–74.

Vatcher, F. de M. 1961. The excavation of a long mortuary enclosure on Normanton Down, Wiltshire. *Proceedings of the Prehistoric Society* 27: 160–73.

Vatcher, L. and Vatcher, F. de M. 1973. Excavation of three post-holes in the Stonehenge car park. *Wiltshire Archaeological and Natural History Magazine* 68: 57–63.

Vera, F.W.M. 1997. *Metaforen voor de wildernis: eik, hazelaar, rund en paard.* Unpublished PhD thesis, Landbouwuniversiteit te Wageningen.

von den Driesch, A. 1976. *A Guide to the Measurement of Animal Bones from Archaeological Sites*. Cambridge MA: Peabody Museum of Archaeology and Ethnology, Harvard University.

Wacker, L., Bonani, G., Friedrich, M., Hajdas, I., Kromer, B., Němec, M., Ruff, M., Suter, M., Synal, H.A. and Vockenhuber, C. 2010a. MICADAS: routine and high-precision radiocarbon dating. *Radiocarbon* 52: 252–62.

Wacker, L., Christl, M. and Synal, H.A. 2010c. Bats: a new tool for AMS data reduction. *Nuclear Instruments and Methods in Physics Research Section B: Beam Interactions with Materials and Atoms* 268: 976–9.

Wacker, L., Němec, M. and Bourquin, J. 2010b. A revolutionary graphitisation system: fully automated, compact and simple. *Nuclear Instruments and Methods in Physics Research Section B: Beam Interactions with Materials and Atoms* 268: 931–4.

Wahl, J. 1982. Leichenbranduntersuchungen: ein Überblick über die Bearbeitungs- und Aussagemöglichkeiten von Brandgrabern. *Prähistorische Zeitschrift* 57: 1–125.

Wahl, J. and Graw, M. 2001. Metric sex differentiation of the *pars petrosa ossis temporalis*. *International Journal of Legal Medicine* 114: 215–23.

Wainwright, G.J. 1971. The excavation of prehistoric and Romano-British settlements near Durrington Walls, Wiltshire, 1970. *Wiltshire Archaeological and Natural History Magazine* 66: 76–128.

Wainwright, G.J. 1973. The excavation of prehistoric and Romano-British settlements at Eaton Heath, Norwich. *Archaeological Journal* 130: 1–43.

Wainwright, G.J. 1997. Future directions for the study of Stonehenge and its landscape. In B. Cunliffe and C. Renfrew (eds) *Science and Stonehenge*. Oxford: Oxford University Press. 335–41.

Wainwright, G.J. with Longworth, I.H. 1971. *Durrington Walls: excavations 1966–1968*. London: Society of Antiquaries.

Wainwright, G.J., Dimbleby, G.W., Evans, A. and Evans, J.G. 1972. The excavation of a Neolithic settlement on Broome Heath, Ditchingham, Norfolk, England. *Proceedings of the Prehistoric Society* 38: 1–97.

Wainwright, G.J., Evans, J.G. and Longworth, I.H. 1971. The excavation of a Late Neolithic enclosure at Marden, Wiltshire. *Antiquaries Journal* 51: 177–239.

Waldron, T. and Antoine, D. 2002. Tortuosity or aneurysm? The palaeopathology of some abnormalities of the vertebral artery. *International Journal of Osteoarchaeology* 12: 79–88.

Waldron, T. and Cox, M. 1989. Occupational arthropathy: evidence from the past. *Journal of Industrial Medicine* 46: 420–2.

Walker, K.E. 1995a. Cut and primary fill of the Aubrey Holes. In R.M.J. Cleal, K.E. Walker and R. Montague, *Stonehenge in its Landscape: twentieth-century excavations*. London: English Heritage. 94–107.

Walker, K.E. 1995b. Secondary use of the Aubrey Holes. In R.M.J. Cleal, K.E. Walker and R. Montague, *Stone-*

henge in its Landscape: twentieth-century excavations. London: English Heritage. 152–5.

Walker, P. and Hollimon, S. 1989. Changes in osteoarthritis associated with the development of a maritime economy among southern Californian Indians. *International Journal of Anthropology* 4: 171–83.

Walker, P.L., Miller, K.W. and Richman, R. 2008. Time, temperature, and oxygen availability: an experimental study of the effects of environmental conditions on the color and organic content of cremated bones. In C.S. Schmidt (ed.) *Analysis of Burned Human Remains*. New York: Elsevier Press. 129–36.

Waller, M.P. and Hamilton, S.D. 1998. The vegetational history of the South Downs: Mount Caburn. In J.B. Murton, C. Whiteman, M.R. Bates, D.R. Bridgeland, A.J. Long, M.B. Roberts and M.P. Waller (eds) *The Quaternary of Kent and Sussex*. London: Quaternary Research Association. 115–20.

Waller, M.P. and Hamilton, S.D. 2000. Vegetation history of the English chalklands: a mid-Holocene pollen sequence from the Caburn, East Sussex. *Journal of Quaternary Science* 15: 253–72.

Ward, G.K. and Wilson, S.R. 1978. Procedures for comparing and combining radiocarbon age-determinations – critique. *Archaeometry* 20: 19–31.

Waton, P.V. 1982. Man's impact on the chalklands: some new pollen evidence. In M. Bell and S. Limbrey (eds) *Archaeological Aspects of Woodland Ecology*. Oxford: BAR (International Series) 146. 75–91.

Webster, A.D. 1919. *Firewoods: their production and fuel values*. London: Fisher Unwin.

Wessex Archaeology. 2009. *Airman's Corner, Winterbourne Stoke, Wiltshire: detailed gradiometry survey*. Salisbury: Wessex Archaeology Report 71420.02. http://unidoc.wiltshire.gov.uk/UniDoc/Document/File/Uy8yMDA5LzE1MjcsOTM0NTI=

West, I. 2011. *Erratics and Sarsen Stones of the Wessex Coast and adjacent land areas*. http://www.southampton.ac.uk/~imw/Sarsens-Erratics.htm

West, S.E. 1990. *West Stow: the prehistoric and Romano-British occupation*. Bury St Edmunds: East Anglian Archaeology 48.

Whittle, A.W.R. 1977. *The Earlier Neolithic in Southern England and its Continental Background*. Oxford: BAR (International Series) 35.

Whittle, A.W.R. 1996. *Europe in the Neolithic: the creation of new worlds*. Cambridge: Cambridge University Press.

Whittle, A.W.R. 1997. Remembered and imagined belongings: Stonehenge in its traditions and structures of meaning. In B.W. Cunliffe and C. Renfrew (eds) *Science and Stonehenge*. Oxford: Oxford University Press. 145–66.

Whittle, A.W.R. 1998. People and the diverse past: two comments on 'Stonehenge for the ancestors'. *Antiquity* 72: 852–54.

Whittle, A.W.R., Atkinson, R.J.C., Chambers, R. and Thomas, N. 1992. Excavations in the Neolithic and Bronze Age complex at Dorchester-on-Thames, Oxfordshire, 1947–1952 and 1981. *Proceedings of the Prehistoric Society* 58: 143–201.

Whittle, A.W.R., Barclay, A., Bayliss, A., McFadyen, L., Schulting, R. and Wysocki, M. 2007. Building for the dead: events, processes and changing worldviews from the thirty-eighth to the thirty-fourth centuries cal. BC in southern Britain. *Cambridge Archaeological Journal* 17 (suppl.): 123–47.

Whittle, A.W.R., Healy, F.H. and Bayliss, A. 2011. *Gathering Time: dating the Early Neolithic enclosures of southern Britain and Ireland*. Oxford: Oxbow.

Whittle A.W.R., Rouse A.J. and Evans J.G. 1993. A Neolithic downland monument in its environment: excavations at the Easton Down long barrow, Bishops Cannings, north Wiltshire. *Proceedings of the Prehistoric Society* 59: 197–239.

Williams, R.B.G. 1973. Frost and the works of man. *Antiquity* 47: 19–31.

Williams-Thorpe, O., Green, C.P. and Scourse, J.D. 1997. The Stonehenge bluestones: discussion. In B.W. Cunliffe and C. Renfrew (eds) *Science and Stonehenge*. Oxford: Oxford University Press. 315–18.

Williams-Thorpe, O., Jones, M.C., Potts, P.J. and Webb, P.C. 2006. Preseli dolerite bluestones: axe-heads, Stonehenge monoliths, and outcrop sources. *Oxford Journal of Archaeology* 25: 29–46.

Willis, C. 2020. *Stonehenge and Middle to Late Neolithic burial practices in mainland Britain, 3400–2400 BC*. Unpublished PhD thesis, University College London.

Willis, C., Marshall, P., McKinley, J.I., Pitts, M., Pollard, J., Richards, C., Richards, J., Thomas, J., Waldron, T., Welham, K. and Parker Pearson, M. 2016. The dead of Stonehenge. *Antiquity* 90: 337–56.

Willoughby, P.R. 1987. *Spheroids and Battered Stones in the African Early and Middle Stone Age*. Oxford: BAR (International Series) 321.

Wright, E., Viner-Daniels, S., Parker Pearson, M. and Albarella, U. 2014. Age and season of pig slaughter at Late Neolithic Durrington Walls (Wiltshire, UK) as detected through a new system for recording tooth wear. *Journal of Archaeological Science* 52: 497–514.

Xu, S., Anderson, R., Bryant, C., Cook, G.T., Dougans, A., Freeman, F., Naysmith, P., Schnabel, C. and Scott, E.M. 2004. Capabilities of the new SUERC 5MV AMS facility for ^{14}C dating. *Radiocarbon* 46: 59–64.

Young, W.E.V. 1935. *Leaves from My Journal VII*. Manuscript diary, Library of the Wiltshire Archaeological and Natural History Society (Devizes).

Young, W.E.V. 1960. Sarsen implements of Palaeolithic form from Winterbourne Monkton. *Wiltshire Archaeological and Natural History Magazine* 57: 400.

List of Figures

Chapter 4

Chapter 5

Chapter 6

Chapter 7

Chapter 8

Chapter 9

Chapter 10

Chapter 11

List of Tables

Chapter 10

Chapter 11

Contributors

Umberto Albarella, Department of Archaeology, University of Sheffield, Sheffield

Mike Allen, Allen Environmental Archaeology, Codford, Warminster

Olaf Bayer, Historic England, The Engine House, Swindon

Wayne Bennett, c/o Chris Tilley, Department of Anthropology, University College London, London

Christopher Bronk Ramsey, ORAU, Research Laboratory for Archaeology, University of Oxford

Chris Casswell, DigVentures Ltd., London

Andrew Chamberlain, Department of Earth and Environmental Sciences, University of Manchester, Manchester

Ben Chan, Department of Archaeology, University of Southampton, Southampton

Rosamund Cleal, Avebury Museum, National Trust, Avebury

Gordon Cook, SUERC, Rankine Avenue, East Kilbride, Glasgow

Glyn Davies, ArcHeritage, Sheffield

Irene de Luis, archaeological illustrator, Sheffield, Irene@irenedeluis.plus.com

Mark Dover, c/o Kate Welham, Department of Archaeology and Anthropology, Bournemouth University, Bournemouth

David Field, independent consultant, davidjfield1950@gmail.com

Charles French, Department of Archaeology, University of Cambridge, Cambridge

Irka Hajdas, Department of Earth Sciences, ETH Zürich, Zürich

Ian Heath, Enrichment Through Archaeology, <enrichmentthrougharchaeology.com>

Rob Ixer, Institute of Archaeology, University College London, London

Neil Linford, Historic England, Fort Cumberland, Eastney, Portsmouth

Peter Marshall, Chronologies, 25 Onslow Road, Sheffield

Louise Martin, Historic England, Fort Cumberland, Eastney, Portsmouth

Claudia Minniti, Università del Salento, Lecce

Douglas Mitcham, Yorkshire Dales National Park Authority, Yoredale, Bainbridge

Bob Nunn, c/o Mike Parker Pearson, Institute of Archaeology, University College London, London

Sanne Palstra, Faculty of Science and Engineering, University of Groningen, Groningen

Mike Parker Pearson, Institute of Archaeology, University College London, London

Andy Payne, Historic England, Fort Cumberland, Eastney, Portsmouth

Paul Pettitt, Department of Archaeology, Durham University, Durham

Mike Pitts, Digging Deeper <mikepitts.wordpress.com>

Joshua Pollard, Department of Archaeology, University of Southampton, Southampton

Rebecca Pullen, Historic England, 37 Tanner Row, York

Colin Richards, Archaeology Institute, University of the Highlands and Islands, Orkney

Julian Richards, Archaemedia, Julian@archaemedia.co.uk

David Robinson, School of Forensic and Applied Sciences, University of Central Lancashire, Preston

Clive Ruggles, Department of Archaeology, University of Leicester, Leicester

Jim Rylatt, Past Participate, jim@pastparticipate.co.uk
Rob Scaife, Department of Archaeology, University of Southampton, Southampton
Ellen Simmons, Department of Archaeology, University of Sheffield, Sheffield
Adam Stanford, Aerial-Cam Ltd., aerial-cam.co.uk
Charlene Steele, c/o Kate Welham, Department of Archaeology and Anthropology, Bournemouth University, Bournemouth
James Sugrue, Barton Willmore, London
Anne Teather, Past Participate, anne@pastparticipate.co.uk
Julian Thomas, Department of Classics, Ancient History and Archaeology, University of Manchester, Manchester
Chris Tilley, Department of Anthropology, University College London, London
Sarah Viner-Daniels, c/o Department of Archaeology, University of Sheffield, Sheffield
Tony Waldron, Institute of Archaeology, University College London, London
Kate Welham, Department of Archaeology and Anthropology, Bournemouth University, Bournemouth
Katy Whitaker, Historic England, The Engine House, Swindon
Christie Willis, independent consultant, arkybones@yahoo.co.uk

Index

Numbers in *italic* denote pages with figures. Numbers in **bold** denote pages with tables. Places are in Wiltshire unless stated otherwise.

Printed by Printforce, United Kingdom